# MEDICINES

# MEDICINES

## The Comprehensive Guide

PARRAGON

Copyright © 1991 by The Book Creation Company

This edition published in 1993
by Parragon Book Service, Bristol.

Printed and bound in Great Britain by BPCC Paperbacks Ltd.

# Contents

# PREFACE

This dictionary is a comprehensive guide to the range of medicines
that are available in the United Kingdom today. This revised
second edition contains all the many new drugs (both generic and
proprietary) that have been developed and marketed since
publication of the first edition in 1988 along with those that
remain on the market. It is not intended to be a guide to the
prescription or administration of drugs; a qualified practitioner
should always be consulted before any medicine is taken.

**How to use this book**

The book is divided into sections. It begins with an introduction to
medicinal drugs in general, with chapters covering the prescribing
of drugs, the drug industry and the misuse of drugs. These are
followed by a chart listing some common disorders and the drugs
used to treat them.

The main A-Z section of the book contains entries that describe
the medicinal drugs available. The drugs are listed under their
generic and proprietary names. There are also articles covering
the major drug types (indicated by *), other substances, such as
vitamins and minerals, which can also be administered
therapeutically, and various preparations, such as 'cough sweets'
and 'sun creams', that contain drugs. The A-Z is thoroughly cross-
referenced. Cross-references are indicated by SMALL CAPITALS.
Many of the articles detail the possible side-effects (indicated by
▲) and list warnings (indicated by ●) to be borne in mind when
administering a particular drug.

Drugs are usually named in one of two ways. The **generic name**
(without an initial capital letter) is the official chemical name, and
should describe the active constituent regardless of the source of
the drug. The **proprietary name** (with an initial capital letter) is

a brand name, a preparation of a drug, or mixture of drugs, that represents a particular formulation from a particular manufacturer.

Doctors are generally encouraged to prescribe drugs using the generic name, because it is simpler and often cheaper. Established drugs may be available as a standard preparation; for instance *paracetamol B.P.* has to be formulated as laid down in the British Pharmacopoeia. This ensures that it will dissolve within a certain time and will contain a precise amount of the active chemical. More or less the same preparation is available under a number of different proprietary names, and they are generally more expensive. However, when a new drug is first introduced it is usually protected by a patent granted to a single manufacturer or distributor, and the proprietary and generic preparation will be identical. Although the method of description will differ, the packaging will generally show both names, but with prominence given to the proprietary name. When the patent expires, and if the drug is still believed to be of value, then several manufacturers may market the same generic drug under their own brand names (often with small differences of formulation, such as sustained-release tablets), alongside versions marketed under the generic name.

These arrangements with two or more names for the same drug are, of course, complicated. A number of authoritative listings of drugs have evolved, each with its particular use, particularly in respect of official or authoritative accounts of dosage, side-effects, indications and contra-indications according to disease state, interactions with other drugs, and other technical matters. This book is not a substitute for these professional guides, but represents a synopsis of some of their contents (more details may be found in the publications listed below).

Established preparations are described in the British Pharmacopoeia and Martindale's Extra Pharmacopoeia. The British National Formulary (BNF) is an impartial guide prepared jointly by the British Medical Association and the Royal Pharmaceutical Society of Great Britain. It is revised twice yearly, and distributed free to hospital doctors. The Monthly Index of Medical Specialities (MIMS) is a listing of proprietary drugs distributed mainly to General Practitioners. The ABPI Handbook (Association of the British Pharmaceutical Industry) is a compendium of detailed data sheets on proprietary preparations. A critique of selected current drugs is given fortnightly in Drugs and Therapeutics Bulletin (Consumers Association) and there are selected articles on the side-effects of drugs in Adverse Drug Reactions Bulletin (Meditext).

Even this number of publications has difficulty in keeping the prescriber of drugs up to date, and there are advantages in using computer database equivalents in hospitals and general practice. A further problem in keeping pace with developments is in promptly warning prescribers about newly reported adverse effects of drugs, which are monitored by 'yellow forms' sent in by doctors to the Committee on Safety of Medicines (or now Medicines Control Agency). This, along with the substantial number of changes made to compile this edition of *Medicines, The Comprehensive Guide*, indicates from year to year the marked and unceasing rate of change that occurs in the drug industry and medical research.

# INTRODUCTION

This dictionary is concerned with the wide range of medicines available in Britain that are used in the prevention, diagnosis and treatment of disease. Although vitamins are included in this definition, there is less emphasis in the main part of the book on dietary supplements in general, or on 'social' drugs (such as alcohol, caffeine, nicotine, and so on), except where they are of direct medical relevance. There is, additionally, coverage of some related medical items such as sun creams.

The book may be of interest and use to various groups of people, especially medical and paramedical workers at the training stage of their careers. These might include nurses, pharmacists, doctors and students of biomedical subjects such as pharmacology. However, it will also be of undoubted interest and use to non-specialists with a general or personal interest in medicines.

The dictionary is cross-referenced in a way that allows identification of the main active components of medicines under their generic names (the approved chemical name, such as paracetamol) or under the proprietary name (the trade name of that particular formulation, such as Panadol). There is also cross-referencing that relates a drug to a major pharmacological class of drugs.

Although this book is in no sense a medical dictionary, it should make it possible, starting from an interest in a certain type of drug, to obtain some idea of the purpose behind its use in disease, and also some of the difficulties (such as side-effects) that might be encountered.

To provide the reader with some background in this area, the following account describes the roles of both prescription and 'over-the-counter' drugs, and in particular points to the benefits, risks and complexities of drug action that make these risks difficult to calculate.

## Drug safety

The safety of the chemicals we refer to as 'medicines' or 'drugs' is an issue that needs to be confronted whenever they are prescribed or used, and here this dictionary should prove helpful. No drug is 'safe' in the sense that it can never harm any individual, and this applies equally to those chemicals not always thought of as drugs (for instance vitamins, food additives or nicotine). The dose may be critical; vitamins are important for good health but, if taken in excess, the same chemicals can cause toxic effects. Unfortunately, this has often been shown to occur. Pharmacology (the study of how drugs work) and toxicology (the study of the adverse effects of chemicals) have always been closely related. The comment on early 19th-century practice – 'patients may have died, but they died cured' – is still relevant today. In the 20th century dramatic improvements in the remedies for a host of common, or not so common, complaints have been made, although treatments available at the present time for AIDS and cancer tend to exemplify the 19th-century dilemma.

## Prescription of drugs

In spite of advances resulting from the outstanding success of medicinal chemists and pharmacologists in producing new drugs for both humans and animals, there is still some uncertainty as to how we are to use them wisely and responsibly. Clearly the medical profession, whether in general or hospital practice, must shoulder this task and the training of doctors in this area is of steadily increasing complexity. This dictionary indicates medicines that are available in Britain only on medical prescription; these require unambiguous instructions and advice from physicians and pharmacists as to their proper use. These instructions may include the size and frequency of dose, possible interactions with other drugs, and likely side-effects.

However desirable clear instructions may be in an ideal world, in practice difficulties may arise for various reasons, and here the dictionary may help people to take a co-operative and responsible part in their own treatment. In the case of side-effects or contra-indications, the patient needs to know of the possibility of adverse reactions in advance so that the doctor can be informed if these occur, and intervene or offer alternative treatment.

## Non-prescription or 'over-the-counter' drugs

Many potentially dangerous drugs can be obtained on prescription only, but some of those more commonly available are neither easy to use correctly nor entirely free from side-effects. The risks inherent in self-medication are happily minimized in Britain, where well-trained pharmacists (present for most of the time in chemists' shops) are qualified to give advice when approached with clear queries.

It is common knowledge that the nation's medicine cabinets, bedside drawers and kitchen shelves overflow with part-used or outdated prescriptions, and invitingly-named proprietary medicines acquired for complaints of which perhaps little recollection remains. The temptation to indulge in self-medication is often greatest at just those times when professional help is unavailable. Moreover, in an age of mass travel, sufferers may find themselves in a country where proprietary drugs, including, for example, antibiotics or steroids, are available 'over-the-counter'. Often, they have only the generic name to guide them in their purchase. In these circumstances this dictionary may prove invaluable. Other readers will be helped in choosing a sensible collection of basic medicines for their everyday needs.

### Why do drugs have side-effects?

Side-effects may be of two basic kinds. First, some may be inherent in the way a drug acts pharmacologically and these may prove very difficult or impossible to circumvent. The side-effect of drowsiness and sedation, for example, is so common with the antihistamines used in the treatment of hay fever that it is accepted by most sufferers as inevitable; with more recent preparations of these drugs, however, this inconvenience is minimized by chemical alterations that restrict the drug's access to the brain. Similarly, conventional 'sleeping pills' naturally tend to reduce alertness in the morning, and shorter-acting benzodiazepine drugs of this class are now available. In cases like these, co-operation between patient and physician may result in finding a more individually acceptable preparation.

Other side-effects may be less predictable and are often referred to as 'idiosyncratic' (e.g. when there is a true allergic response by the body's immune system). These adverse reactions can present a very real risk and are difficult to predict other than by asking the patient about any previous reactions to particular classes of drugs, for example, antibiotics. However, this depends on the patient being able to recall drug names and classes over long periods of time. Even a little knowledge of this sort is very desirable.

## Why is there variability in drug response?

Drug therapy would be very much simplified if we were all exactly alike, but the very differences that make us the individuals we are also cause changes in sensitivities and responses to chemicals, including drugs. With an obvious difference such as body size, it follows that it would be unrealistic to expect a normal recommended dose to be as effective in a large man as it would be in a small woman of half the weight. Similarly, a drug dose may be less well absorbed when taken after a meal than it would be on an empty stomach.

It is less obvious why some drugs have different, even opposite, effects in young children, and among people of different cultural groups or sexes. We are, however, products of our environment and our genes, and we are becoming increasingly aware that it is the genes in particular that may effect our metabolism and hence our sensitivity to drugs. Because our genetic make-up varies with family, race and sex, it may soon become possible to make an informed guess as to the outcome of a given therapy when a patient's full family history is known.

Problems inherent in treating the very young or elderly, pregnant women and other special cases, are so great that it is almost certainly better to take no medication unless advised by a physician. In view of all these complicating factors, no doses have been recommended in this dictionary.

## What are drug interactions?

Uncertainties in predicting the outcome of treatment by a single drug become considerably more complicated when two or more drugs are taken at the same time, because interactions between them are quite likely. Thus, for example, a 'social' drug such as alcohol may markedly aggravate the eroding effect of aspirin on the stomach lining, or enhance the sedative effect of antihistamine or other depressant drugs. In this way, two commonly available chemicals, each with an acceptable risk factor, may become potentially dangerous in unorthodox combination. Some of these risks may be avoided by sufficient knowledge about certain products. But conversely, ignorance of the composition of medicines may lead to accidental overdose. An example may be seen in the uses of cold cures: many of these contain a full dose of paracetamol and, if taken together with headache treatment also containing paracetamol, would cause some overdosage.

### What is drug dependence or addiction?

Drug dependence is a term that describes the overall situation in which, after using a drug continuously, the individual suffers in some way if the treatment is suddenly stopped. The body has become tolerant to the drug and an increased dosage may then be required over a period of time to elicit the same effect. Withdrawal symptoms may be seen; these are commonly the reverse of the expected effect of the drug (for example, anxiety following the use of a tranquillizer, or a rise in blood pressure when the treatment to lower it is stopped). These symptoms, whether psychological or physical in manifestation, are the principal reason why a treatment is only gradually withdrawn or replaced by another. It has been recognized only recently that some quite common medicines (for example, tranquillizers of the benzodiazepine class) produce marked habituation over an extended period of time.

It is generally known that some 'social' drugs (chemicals taken non-medically or illicitly) cause habituation or addiction. Examples such as heroin and, of course, alcohol come readily to mind. That these problems exist also with prescription drugs is disturbing, and further highlights the need for useful dialogue between patient and doctor.

### The versatile aspirin tablet

It should be clear from the points raised already that ingestion of any chemical has its risks. To some extent these risks are dose-related, and this can be illustrated by the use of aspirin at different dose levels for different purposes.

At doses much lower than are commonly used at present, aspirin may, in the future, become standard continuous therapy as a prophylactic, to prevent disease and prolong life. Clinical trials still in progress suggest it may, in middle life, give some protection from arterial thrombotic disease, with a consequent lower risk of clot formation in the blood vessels of the heart and brain. This would, in turn, reduce the risk of heart attacks and strokes.

At perhaps four to eight times this dose the standard aspirin tablet (300 mg), for use against minor aches and pains and fevers, does its job quite effectively, although many people find the accompanying dyspepsia (a stomach pain like indigestion) a problem. There is commonly also a variable but usually small blood loss from minor haemorrhages in the intestine. These normally pass unnoticed, except when some anaemia results after long-term use. Some patients suffer asthma-like symptoms, the origin of which may not be fully recognized; aspirin commonly produces an allergic response in those who are susceptible. Rarely, an individual may even die from an idiosyncratic adverse response to perhaps a single aspirin tablet.

At even higher dosages, the sufferer from rheumatoid arthritis may find that the beneficial effects of aspirin on joint pain and movement often outweigh the gastrointestinal upsets and other adverse effects of the drug.

### Is paracetamol better than aspirin?

Given these worrying aspects of aspirin's action it is disturbing to learn how many tons of it have been consumed annually, and to discover that perhaps one person in three has taken a preparation containing salicylates on any given day. For this reason, paracetamol has been actively promoted as an alternative medication. But paracetamol has only weak anti-inflammatory action and is not so effective against pain resulting from tissue injury (although it is an effective antipyretic in the treatment of fevers).

Moreover, drugs of this class are frequently used for attempted suicide, or 'parasuicide' ('mock' suicide, used as a cry for help). Aspirin in overdose is commonly used in suicide attempts. It is most disturbing that paracetamol overdose, unless treated very promptly, results in death some days later from irreversible liver failure, whereas aspirin overdose is easier to deal with.

### Are the benefits of drug therapy worth the risks involved?

The answer to this question must be 'yes', but with reservations. This brief account of some of the problems associated with drug therapy is intended to help the reader to understand why no drug should be taken casually or carelessly. However, there are enormous benefits to be gained from the considerable range of drugs available when a medical condition warrants their use. Examples of drugs – many quite recently developed – that may be used to alleviate suffering and prolong life are known to all, yet there are always new steps to be taken and much is still little understood. At all stages the contribution that this dictionary may make towards effective communication between patient, physician and pharmacist can only be of value.

# PRESCRIBING DRUGS

The prescribing of a drug or other medication by a family doctor can be a difficult decision in the face of what are sometimes conflicting pressures. These pressures take on relative strengths according to the circumstances. Some of them might be as follows:

Pressure from the patient/client to be given at least some sort of prescription, and not to leave the surgery 'empty-handed', without a tangible outcome of the consultation.

Pressure from the pharmaceutical industry to recognize the patient as a clinical 'problem' requiring treatment (for example, sleeplessness requiring sleeping tablets), rather than as a more complex whole-person problem.

Pressure to maintain rational prescribing considerations, attempting to match the clinical problem with an appropriate therapeutic pharmacological response.

Pressure from budgetary considerations. Although the drug industry gives more emphasis in its advertising to cost details, new and expensive drugs are still heavily advertised. However, NHS reforms, in particular, the introduction of a prescribing budget is forcing GPs into balancing the practice economy against therapeutic potential rather than seeking a performance-linked reward for sensible generic prescribing.

The Department of Health circulates doctors with information about prescribing costs, and GP's drug prescribing computer software packages include cost as well as increasingly comprehensive generic indexing.

There are subtle variations on these themes, and there are also subconscious or subliminal pressures on doctors when they are prescribing. The final act of prescribing may therefore be entirely rational or in some cases somewhat irrational. The doctor's intentions may be open and shared by the patient, or concealed as in the prescription of a placebo. Prescribing may therefore be done as a result of client demand, mutual understanding or even the doctor's desperation.

Good prescribing demands a therapeutic intention, and doctors must therefore bear certain factors in mind. For instance, a prescribed drug should be effective, cheap where possible, as free as possible from side-effects, and easily administered. Other considerations are lack of toxicity in overdose, and length of effective shelf-life or efficacy after opening. It is to be hoped that these considerations are increasingly taken into account during the development of new drugs, but nevertheless the strong influence of advertising and fashion often seems to override progress in these areas.

## A doctor's choice

A family doctor has a bewildering array of drugs to choose from. He or she receives a barrage of advertising from the drug industry, a sort of 'peer review' from medical colleagues, professional guidance from organizations such as Which? (Drug and Therapeutics Bulletin), as well as insistent but variable suggestions from a relatively well-informed lay public.

The doctor also has reference books produced by the drug industry and by the state as guides to prescribing. These invaluable manuals, such as the Monthly Index of Medical Specialities (MIMS) and the British National Formulary (BNF), indicate conditions, drugs, treatment regimes, dosages, contra-indications, side-effects, and so on, as well as the cost of drugs. It is one of a doctor's responsibilities to assimilate as much of this information a possible.

Drugs are called by their chemical names, by agreed and approved generic names (as in the British Pharmacopoeia – BP) and by commercial, trade or proprietary names. Such a system is necessary to enable the doctor and pharmacist to be absolutely sure that they are prescribing the correct preparation.

There is very sensible pressure on doctors to prescribe generically, but this is of course countered energetically by drug company advertising.

Hospitals generally construct their own prescribing formulary and tend to stick to generic prescribing. This is much less the case in general practice, although some family doctors have adopted formularies or constructed their own. If all doctors were to prescribe generically there would be a considerable saving to the

National Health Service budget; computer software prescribing packages with generic or prescribing indexing makes this much easier.

## How drugs are prescribed

Prescribing by doctors within the British National Health Service is done using a prescription pad or Form FP10 (increasingly more frequently done by computer), on which the doctor writes the name of the drug, dosage information and total to be dispensed. This is taken by the patient to a pharmacist (commonly called a chemist in Britain) who dispenses the drug according to the prescription. Prescribed drugs are free for children and the elderly, as well as for full-time students, people on low incomes and those with exemption certificates (such as pregnant and lactating women). Doctors may also prescribe drugs privately, and in such cases the patient then pays the chemist at the retail price. Some doctors do their own dispensing.

Many medicines are taken without being prescribed by doctors because the patients know or are advised by friends, relatives, pharmacists or the media to take drugs such as simple analgesics (for example aspirin or paracetamol), antihistamines for conditions such as hay fever, or mixtures to treat coughs, diarrhoea or indigestion. The doctors' help is sought only when the patient is not confident about the problem or does not know of a cheap and readily available effective remedy. About 99 per cent of all homes contain some medication, and about one-third of this is self-prescribed and bought at a chemist's shop.

## Drugs and disease

A doctor meets a vast array of conditions, some of which require very powerful or potentially dangerous drugs needing skilled management – for example, in the treatment of heart failure or cancer. At other times prescribing may be very simple, such as choosing an antifungal cream to treat athlete's foot. It is through the study of pharmacology (the science of the action of drugs) and therapeutics (the use of drugs clinically), together with competence in diagnosis, that the doctor is able to match a patient's clinical condition with a particular treatment.

The drugs chosen should be as 'friendly' to the patient as possible. For example, doctors tend to select systemic drugs that are easily taken by mouth and which reliably produce effective treatment levels in the body with a minimum of side-effects. The doctor needs to know whether the drug should be taken with, before or after food, if it interacts with alcohol, or if it is made inactive by certain foods (as some antibiotics are by milk). The doctor should be aware, if a woman is pregnant, whether the drug would harm the unborn baby. The doctor also needs to know whether a patient is taking any other form of medication – for example, a traveller taking prophylactic antimalarial tablets or a woman taking the oral contraceptive pill – because there could be serious pharmacological interactions between these and other prescribed drugs.

Retail pharmacists in Britain are now required to use a microcomputer when printing their labels for bottles or packets of drugs. Information stored on the computer relates to side-effects, drug interactions, and so on, and is a valuable safety precaution.

Some compromises clearly have to be made. For example, eye drops and certain lotions have a very short life after opening, as has glyceryl trinitrate (commonly used to treat angina), which is ineffective after about a month.

The balance between therapeutic effect and dangerous or unwanted side-effects is a constant consideration. It is widely known, for example, that steroids can control such serious disorders as asthma, rheumatoid arthritis and polymyalgia, but the prolonged systemic use of steroids is hazardous and has serious disadvantages. Similarly anti-cancer treatment, which aims at killing cancer cells, constantly falls just short of killing the patient too, and doctors have to monitor the patient's overall condition carefully and be prepared to stop the drugs or adjust the dose as the patient's condition dictates.

Many drugs are prescribed for short episodes, such as antibiotics for tonsillitis or a course of anti-inflammatory drugs for the muscular condition known as 'frozen shoulder'. Others may have to be taken on a permanent basis, as in the treatment of hypertension, thyroid disease, epilepsy, diabetes or gout. Patients on long-term medication require carefully planned repeat prescribing, with a built-in review according to the particular properties of the drug concerned. For example, depressed or manic patients taking the fairly frequently prescribed lithium carbonate need regular blood tests to check thyroid function and the therapeutic level of the drug.

## Prescribing in general practice

Two-thirds of general practice prescribing is for repeat prescriptions; 95 per cent of such requests are immediately granted without discussion, and 55 per cent of patients over 75 years of age are on regular repeat prescriptions.

Certain drugs, such as powerful painkillers and some hypnotics, cause 'tolerance', which means that they become progressively less effective in a given dose, and therefore have to be given in increasingly large amounts. This is a comparable situation to drug addiction or alcoholism, and can be a serious prescribing problem.

A common difficulty in general practice concerns the patients' compliance. Many patients receive a doctors' prescription but never take the medicine, although the doctor believes they are doing so according to instructions. Similarly, patients may take only a small amount of a particular course – typically stopping as soon as the symptoms improve or seem to disappear, even though the disease itself has not been cured. Very commonly tablets are muddled up in the wrong bottles, and this can lead, for example, to patients taking sleeping pills believing they are their early morning diuretic tablets.

These problems may sound unlikely, but they are in fact very common. A doctor's home visit – particularly to an elderly or confused patient – often reveals horrifying inconsistencies between what the doctor believes the patient is taking and what is actually happening.

Because of the high cost of prescriptions, many patients do not collect all the items on their prescription but only the ones that *they* consider the most important. Furthermore, some studies have shown that young men commonly fail to present their prescriptions to a chemist, because their primary intention in visiting the doctor is to collect a medical certificate to justify absence from work and to claim sick pay.

Clearly these sorts of problems apply to general practice rather than to hospital medicine. Administering drugs through intravenous drips and injections is normally only appropriate where nursing staff are available.

Thus prescribing drugs in general practice requires, for safety, another dimension which ensures patient's compliance – that is, *explanation*. It is imperative for a doctor to give the patient a chance to understand the purpose for which the drug is being given, and to explain which possible side-effects may be expected and how to deal with them, as well as to give reasons why a course of a particular duration is required.

Doctors prescribe for infants, children, adults and the elderly. Many paediatric preparations are liquid and are administered by the child's parents, but it is also a good idea for a doctor to be aware of the taste of children's medicines. Tablets for the elderly should be easy to swallow and supplied in containers that can be opened by weak or arthritic hands. Pharmacists are particularly helpful in this last respect.

General practice prescribing is a co-operative exercise between the patient/client, doctor and pharmacist. Good communications between all three leads to a successful outcome. The doctor often requires the pharmacist to 'back up' and explain the prescription, however, and studies show that pharmacists spend more time explaining drug treatments to patients than doctors do. Similarly, a patient's first request for help may be to a pharmacist, who may suggest that a doctor's advice or prescription is needed.

The doctor and pharmacist thus work together, with the pharmacist sometimes providing a safety net for errors arising out of a doctor's haste or inexperience. Naturally if a patient already has a clear idea of the medical condition and prescribing rationale, a successful outcome is much more likely to be assured.

# THE DRUG INDUSTRY

The pharmaceutical industry, or drug industry as it is commonly called, is one of the most buoyant and expanding areas of commerce of the 20th century. This is because it fills an essential need and yet still has many tasks to fulfil. There are several aspects of the industry which should be distinguished.

First, there is research and development (R & D). This is the activity that, in the long run, produces new medicines, and for this reason will be discussed at greatest length here. It is a highly labour-intensive and expanding field, involving chemical, biological and clinical investigations, and has tended to concentrate in Western countries, where there are scientists and doctors with the necessary specialist skills. As in many industrial endeavours, the United States is the major participant, but Britain also plays an active role in this area. More than half of Britain's several thousand research pharmacologists are employed in the industry, with the remainder in university and research institutions. This mix seems quite fertile for the growth of new ideas and the development of new drugs. Other countries with a major involvement include West Germany, France, Switzerland and Italy – all countries with successful chemical industries.

Second, there is toxicological evaluation of the proposed drug, in which studies are carried out according to guidelines set up (in Britain) by the Committee on Safety of Medicines (renamed Medicines Control Agency). Experiments are performed by qualified toxicologists trained to identify and predict possible toxic actions that a chemical might have in human patients. These studies are both time-consuming (commonly taking several years to complete) and very costly, but are nevertheless essential before use of the chemical in people can be considered.

Third, there are pre- and post-marketing clinical trials. These are essential for the all-important confirmation that a drug is effective in humans and for the equally important licensing of drugs. Licensing takes place in countries with statutory bodies entrusted with the job of ensuring new drugs are at least as effective as existing remedies and that they are as safe as possible. These bodies usually also monitor adverse reactions after a drug has been licensed.

Fourth, there is manufacturing and formulation, in which active ingredients (pure drugs) are frequently imported from a parent or manufacturing company located elsewhere, and then incorporated into the often quite complex formulations that are the responsibility of the pharmaceutical chemists. These represent the actual 'medicines' (for example, tablets, syrups, ointments or ampoules) that are used in practice.

Fifth, there is marketing, which is targeted throughout the world and differs little from marketing of other products except that, in Britain for example, the target group (doctors) is neither the final consumer nor the person who is necessarily financially liable. There is also a critical distinction between proprietary (trade name) and generic (active drug) products which is tied into local licensing and legal arrangements in much the same way as the use of trade marks.

Of course, this 20th-century industrial approach to drug development is by no means the only one. Many of the drugs in use today in the West are of plant or natural origin, and have been listed, often as impure extracts, in our pharmacopoeias for many centuries. In the East, especially in China, such listings cover thousands of remedies and often date back to several centuries BC.

### Relationship of industrial activities to academic research

In the past, and probably in the future, the development of new drugs has often been the result of a judicious mix of academic and applied research, in such a way that the various stages leading up to the development of a successful drug are difficult to disentangle. For instance, although many people have a general idea about the story of the discovery and development of insulin or penicillin, or the structure of DNA, to those involved the events were not particularly simple (as dramatized accounts have illustrated). Perhaps the truth is that it is often impossible to tell accurately where ideas come from. On the other hand, manpower and effort are generally directed towards a certain useful application.

Given these uncertainties, it seems wise for a country to create an environment where there is proper training of scientists at undergraduate and postgraduate levels, adequate research funds for fundamental academic ('blue skies') research, and a firm industrial base for the exploitation of resultant ideas. Sadly in Britain, direct or indirect government funding for most aspects of scientific research is falling behind in real terms at a time when such research is growing in cost due to improvements in technology. The result is, of necessity, a growing emphasis in academic research on short term (and therefore less costly) projects which are consequently less likely to result in fundamental breakthroughs. This paucity of funding has to be balanced increasingly by charity-sponsored research, for instance by the Wellcome Trust for general medical research, directed towards a named disease (such as cancer, diabetes or asthma), or by industry itself funding longer-term projects in co-operation with universities or within its own structure. Just how effective this piecemeal approach will be remains to be seen.

## How does industry find a new drug?

There is no simple answer to this question, but the following account deals with the main avenues of exploration.

Natural products have been used since the beginnings of civilization. The main search for these has been directed towards their use in medical remedies or as agents to modify the state of mind. On this latter use it is certainly difficult to find today a hallucinogenic or euphoric plant drug that has not already been tried. Poppy heads have been found in the earliest sites of civilization, and there seems no race that does not know how to produce alcohol. Because man was a 'pharmacologist before he was a farmer' (as one eminent pharmacologist put it), it is not surprising that we have a rich storehouse of products to draw on.

'Natural' does not necessarily mean 'safe', however, in spite of the views of many herbalists old and new. In fact, during the earlier part of this century, much effort in pharmacology was devoted to developing reliable biological tests that allowed potentially lethal natural substances to be used as therapeutic agents at lower dosage. For many such natural substances, the margin between the useful therapeutic dose and the lethal dose is terrifyingly small. Such agents include digitalis, an extract of foxglove leaves used for heart failure (cardiac glycosides); extract of bovine pancreas used to control blood glucose in severe diabetes (insulin); and many plant alkaloids such as atropine (from deadly nightshade) and strychnine (from nux vomica), which have been almost as popular with poisoners as with doctors!

Nevertheless, substances of this sort, to which we must certainly add opium, have proved the starting point for the development of new medicines. These agents have been purified to the stage of knowing the exact chemical composition of the active constituents, followed by systematic modifications of their chemical structure and testing of the resultant compounds. In spite of the spectacular advances, progress has sometimes been slow. It was, for instance, only quite recently that from among the many thousands of morphine-like compounds (from opium) that have been tested, scientists have discovered possible powerful pain-relieving analgesics that are not so addictive and do not have, to such a degree, other serious side-effects (such as depression of respiration and stimulation of vomiting).

Serendipity is a word popular with experimental scientists – meaning the happy art of making useful discoveries by accident; pharmacology in particular has benefited from this process, and it should always be considered whether some unexpected action of a drug may be usefully harnessed. In fact, many drugs we use today, such as penicillin, have uses deriving from essentially chance observations. This awareness that drug actions are often not predictable has also led to the formal process known as random screening.

In random biological screening, new compounds are investigated in a series of biological tests designed to identify certain actions that might be useful therapeutically. Only very few compounds are thought worthy enough to be passed on to more complicated tests, and eventually to tests on humans. Such screening is very wasteful from many points of view, but has certainly yielded many useful drugs. Particularly when the 'screens' are chosen on a sound basis.

Rational drug design is now becoming a practical method of advance. Not only is it likely to be much less wasteful and chancy than some of the approaches already outlined, but it offers hope of discovering drugs of a genuinely new type to treat hitherto untreatable diseases. If we have a sound understanding of the workings of the body and how it goes wrong in disease, then in principle a suitable type of drug can be designed in the pharmacologist's mind. Then, with the determined help of the medicinal chemist, this can be translated into a drug for testing first in animals and later in human patients.

One man (Sir James Black) has the distinction of doing this particular trick twice, to originate two of the most widely prescribed classes of drugs in history, for which he has recently been awarded a Nobel Prize. First, working with colleagues at ICI Pharmaceuticals in the early 1960s, he recognized the importance of the observation that a small change in the chemical structure of a compound similar to adrenaline produced a drug that, in contrast to adrenaline, reduced the heart rate and blood pressure. Today, these so-called beta-blockers are used daily in millions of patients with high blood pressure, angina or abnormal heart rhythms.

Not content with this triumph, Black, working with colleagues at Smith, Kline & French Laboratories (UK), again exploited some earlier academic findings that suggested that the local hormone histamine acted in the stomach to cause gastric acid secretion by a different mechanism to its action elsewhere, such as causing hay fever (for which antihistamines were already available). After a prolonged and exhaustive search, a different type of antihistamine which was active in the stomach (called an $H_2$ antagonist) was finally developed by making chemical modifications to the histamine molecule itself. Today this type of drug is the only really effective treatment for peptic ulcers, and the newest member of this class, ranitidine (Zantac), is the most prescribed proprietary drug in the world. It should be pointed out, though, that such advances are not accomplished every day, and the examples given also had elements of all the other approaches described.

'Me-too' drugs is the derogatory term for agents developed, often with little extra initiative, out of the fundamental and costly advances of others. The costs of an original investigative programme are huge (perhaps some tens of millions of pounds) and the success rate so low (perhaps one chemical in 100,000 proves to be of real value and sufficiently low in toxicity), that the 'me-too approach' is much favoured, particularly by small companies and unsuccessful competitors. The method is to seek chemically similar compounds with similar pharmacological activity, but which do not have effective patent cover, and to promote them actively as alternatives to the parent compound, often in some novel combination with another drug also of value in that application. This approach is understandable on commercial grounds, but does result in many alternative remedies of very similar properties, and this tends to confuse effective therapy and lead to a disinclination by the authorities to license such drugs.

## Drugs testing and marketing

When a compound with a promising drug action has been found, there follows an extensive programme of testing to explore and define the new drug's pharmacological actions, often using animals in order to predict what is likely to happen in humans. By law in most countries, the potential drug must then undergo what is described as toxicity testing (in Britain according to regulations laid down by the Committee on Safety of Medicines, now MCA). Although the usefulness of some of the tests is open to debate, the necessity for toxicological evaluation is unquestionable before exposure of the compound to the public is even considered. Nowadays testing involves extensive studies to evaluate the mutagenic and likely carcinogenic properties of a compound, and studies involving several generations of animals to examine possible effects on the foetus. This is imperative if disasters such as that caused by thalidomide are to be avoided in the future.

The clinical pharmacologist can then proceed with testing in humans, termed clinical trials. Initially, healthy male volunteers are exposed to the drug under carefully controlled conditions, with groups taking either the substance being tested or a 'dummy' compound (placebo). Once the pharmacologist is satisfied that the drug is safe and has no undesirable or unexpected side-effects, testing is begun using real patients, again under very controlled conditions. For certain drugs that are known to be toxic, but offer hope for treatment of incurable conditions such as cancer, testing is carried out in patients only. This is mainly because of ethical reasons not only with regard to endangering healthy volunteers, but also with regard to patients who may benefit from taking such drugs when no alternative treatment is effective.

If the final phase of the clinical trial is successful, the drug may be granted a product licence, and the drug is then allowed to be marketed for general use. The clinical trial has not, however, ended – and in a sense it never does because doctors have to file reports on adverse reactions to any drug, and particularly to new ones.

## The rate of change

It will be clear from the points already made that drug design and marketing is a very dynamic area. In the three years since the first edition of *Medicines, The Comprehensive Guide* about 300 new preparations have been introduced, and a similar number of older medicines withdrawn. Although this rate of turnover is a sign of evolution, it does present problems in the prescribing habits of doctors. By no means all of the recently introduced drugs represent a breakthrough in terms of agents with entirely new types of action. Nevertheless many doctors will be prescribing drugs of types not even thought of when they were training.

Some of these relatively new classes of drug are worth noting. Obviously there is a desperate and urgent need for drugs that are of some value in the treatment of AIDS, and listed in this new edition are the first of such drugs. In the treatment of hypertension and heart problems there has been much research, and this has been rewarded with several new approaches. *Calcium-channel blockers* (CALCIUM ANTAGONISTS in this book), though recently introduced have rapidly gained an established place in treating cardiovascular and other disease states. Also in this area ACE INHIBITORS and PHOSPHODIESTERASE INHIBITORS show some promise.

However, advances that make noticeable differences to the patient do not necessarily reflect dramatic developments of new classes of drugs, and here minimization of side-effects is a prime objective. For instance, as all sufferers from hay fever know, the classic ANTIHISTAMINES (that date back to 1937) are so prone to causing drowsiness that it may be impractical or unwise to drive a car or do skilled work while taking them. This book lists a number of antihistamines that are, to a degree, improved in this respect. This selectivity was achieved by designing compounds that do not cross the blood-brain barrier, and so are restricted in their potential actions on the brain.

In other instances improvements have been made in the safety-margin of drugs, to the extent that there is a lifting of restriction from prescription-only to over-the-counter availability. In the case of the generic drug IBUPROFEN, which is of value in conditions from a simple headache to rheumatoid arthritis, it is encouraging that although this class of drug (NSAID) is notorious for its side-effects, this particular example is regarded as sufficiently safe to licence for non-prescription use as a mild analgesic. Interestingly, the generic drug has, even from the same manufacturers, quite different proprietary names when intended for prescription, for instance BRUFEN, as compared to NUROFEN over-the-counter (along with a dozen names from other manufacturers). In other countries the proprietary names are different again, though the generic name remains constant. The naming of drug preparations is influenced by the same marketing considerations as for any other kind of commodity.

In relation to adverse reactions to medical treatments in general and to the side-effects of drugs in particular, it is likely that it will always be the case that some drugs are used to treat the side-effects rather than the disease itself. An important advance in this type of action is provided by the very recent introduction of the ANTINAUSEANT drug ONDANSETRON (ZOFRAN; Glaxo). One of the most distressing aspects of radiation therapy or chemotherapy for cancer, is the extreme nausea and vomiting that is so commonly caused, and it is here that this new type of drug (with a novel mechanism of action) is providing much needed relief.

## The future

Although academic research in productive concert with the drug industry has has a number of triumphs, there is still much to do. In general, progress in treating viral infections is slow, and is likely to remain so because these organisms can change their forms readily. Other diseases are not yet sufficiently well understood to allow any confident prediction of successful, rational solutions, such as Alzheimer's disease and other diseases of the central nervous system. However, there are signs that drugs may indeed be developed that will help memory and other cognitive processes, and so-called 'smart drugs' may well appear in future editions of this book.

# THE MISUSE OF DRUGS

The major personal problems associated with the misuse of mood-altering, or psychoactive, drugs relate to health. But using drugs – particularly if they are illegal – can bring with it all kinds of other difficulties; damaged personal relationships and job prospects, as well as legal problems, either through the possession of illegal substances or from a need to commit crimes to pay for them.

Most of the drugs discussed here are controlled in Britain under the Misuse of Drugs Act, which aims to prevent the non-medical use of certain drugs. Some of them, such as cannabis and LSD, have no currently recognized medical uses. Others, like amphetamines and heroin, still have restricted medical use, but are deemed to be drugs that can cause the wider social problem of dependency and are thus more strictly controlled than most of the drugs available to doctors for prescribing.

Some drugs are banned and others (like alcohol and tobacco) are not. Historically this has more to do with the expediencies of politics, economics and international diplomacy than with public health. Legality or otherwise often bears little relation to the potential for physical or psychological damage inherent in a particular drug. However, this article has less to say about familiar legal drugs – such as alcohol, caffeine and tobacco – than about those that are 'controlled'.

## Definitions
Several terms can be employed to describe the non-medical use of drugs: drug dependence, drug addiction, drug abuse, recreational drug use, and so on. Some of these terms have unhelpfully pejorative connotations – 'drug addict', for example, conjures up images of somebody who will do anything for a fix – and for many people the very fact that a drug is illegal makes its use, however

moderate, 'abuse'. For the sake of simplicity, all references to drug dependence, chronic drug use, and so on denote circumstances in which drug abuse has become the dominant feature of an individual's life, to the detriment of relationships, work and health.

Significant medical terms include tolerance, withdrawal and dependence. Tolerance occurs when the body becomes tolerant to the effects of a drug, so that increasingly higher doses are needed to achieve the same effect. Withdrawal is the reaction of the body to the sudden absence of a drug to which it has adapted. Symptoms of withdrawal can range from the headaches some people experience if they miss their morning cup of coffee to the influenza-like effects of heroin withdrawal and the possibly fatal convulsions or seizures that can accompany the sudden cessation of alcohol or barbiturates. Physical dependence occurs when somebody continues to take drugs in order to avoid the physical discomforts of withdrawal. A person can suffer withdrawal symptoms and be physically dependent on a drug without any lasting desire to carry on taking it. For example, this can happen when somebody who has been given morphine in hospital for chronic pain over a period of time is suddenly taken off the drug before going home.

## Drug misuse – the risks

Drug effects are strongly influenced by the amount taken, how much has been taken before, what the user wants and expects to happen, the surroundings in which it is taken, and the reactions of other people. All these influences are themselves tied up with social and cultural attitudes to, and beliefs about drugs, as well as more general social conditions. Even the same person may react differently at different times. So it is usually misleading to make simple cause-and-effect statements such as 'drug X always causes condition Y'.

Many people who use drugs come to no harm and may feel they have benefited from the effects of drugs in improving their social, intellectual or physical performance or helping them to relax. And they may well be right. But there are very serious risks, and some of the most significant aspects of the risks of drug taking relate to all or most drugs, whether they are illegal or not.

Taking a drug carries with it the risks specific to that drug or drug type. What follows is a guide to the general dangers of taking *any* drug.

## Too much

In the short-term, taking too much of a drug at once risks
accidents, because the person may be out of control, may suffocate
(by choking on vomit if he or she is unconscious) or may even
overdose. The greatest potential for overdosing exists with drugs
such as alcohol, barbiturates or heroin, because they depress the
nervous system and in sufficient quantity can cause, for example,
respiratory collapse. Overdosing is also a risk when drugs are used
together or within a short time of each other. This 'doubling up'
can cause a fatal overdose that might not have occurred if only
one of the drugs had been used. Alcohol, for instance, is often
implicated in what may initially be regarded as a heroin or
tranquillizer overdose.

Over a longer time period, too much drug use can have multiple
adverse effects on somebody's life. There can be problems with
relationships with family and friends, finding or keeping a job, and
keeping healthy – partly because the normal desire for food is
diminished. Spare money is diverted into buying drugs and energy
is used in finding the money for drugs (which may lead to crime).

## Wrong time, wrong place

Even in moderate doses, most of the drugs described here (except
stimulants such as amphetamines and cocaine) impair bodily
control, reaction time and attention span. This means that no
matter how people feel, they will become a danger to themselves
and others. Low doses of stimulants can enhance performance –
which is the main reason why people take them – but performance
rapidly deteriorates as the dose is increased.

## No two people are the same

Drugs affect different people in different ways – much depends on
individual physical and psychological make-up, as the following
examples show. A person with a latent mental condition can suffer
long-term damage through taking LSD just once. Any drug that
increases heart-rate by even a small degree, such as cannabis,
can be painful for somebody suffering from angina. One person
might still be standing after ten pints of lager, whereas another is
on the floor after only two glasses of wine. The lighter your body
weight, the greater will be the effects of drugs and so the risks are
greater for a small person than for somebody who is heavier.

## Injecting

For various reasons, injecting is the most dangerous way of taking a drug. Users who share their injecting equipment put themselves in a higher-risk category for contracting HIV, because blood is one of the ways in which the virus is transmitted. Where needles, syringes and so on are being shared, injecting into the muscle or just under the skin is just as dangerous as injecting into a vein. Furthermore, AIDS is not the only disease associated with injecting. In fact, users are more at risk from contracting hepatitis, which is also a life-threatening, blood-borne disease.

With an injection, all the drug is taken at once. As a result, an overdose is more likely than if the drug is smoked or sniffed, when it is taken a little at a time it allows the user to stop if he or she wants to.

Some users try to inject drugs such as barbiturates, tranquillizers and painkillers, which are not meant to be injected because they are in pill form and do not dissolve properly when crushed. The filler used to make up the tablets can be highly irritant to the skin tissues. Similarly, illicit drugs in powder form, such as heroin, amphetamine and cocaine, are often adulterated with other materials that do not dissolve for injecting. In all these cases, users may suffer from abscesses, abnormal swelling of the limbs or serious inflammation of the veins. Abscesses can also occur through using unsterilized or dirty equipment for injecting.

## What is it?

Drugs offered on the illicit market are not always what they are claimed to be, and a wide range of impurities or contaminants can get into drugs sold on the street. This may result from the unsterile environment of illegal drug manufacture, or because drugs are mixed (or 'cut') with a number of substances to increase their weight and therefore the seller's profit. A sample of street heroin, for example, could contain any combination of talc, glucose powder, flour, chalk dust or another drug substance such as barbiturate powder. An added danger is that even if users know what they are getting, they cannot tell how strong it is in relation to what they are used to taking. An unusually pure sample could easily cause an overdose.

DRUGS THAT DEPRESS THE NERVOUS SYSTEM

## Alcohol

The most commonly available and misused depressant drug is

alcohol. It is the drug most often used to enhance the effects of other depressants and, when taken with barbiturates, tranquillizers or heroin, can precipitate an overdose that might not otherwise have happened. And as with barbiturates, sudden withdrawal from alcohol can be fatal.

## Barbiturates

These are the best-known of the drugs classified as hypnosedatives – that is, drugs which calm people down (sedatives) and in higher doses act as sleeping pills (hypnotics).

Short-acting barbiturates used as sleeping pills are the ones most often taken for their intoxicating effects. They include Tuinal, Seconal and Nembutal, and there is little doubt that they are the most inherently dangerous of the drugs misused in Britain. Partly because of these dangers, their only recommended medical use is for the treatment of severe intractable insomnia.

Barbiturates come in the form of tablets, ampoules, suppositories, solutions or commonly as coloured capsules. They are usually taken by mouth; misusers also generally take them by mouth, occasionally with alcohol, but they may also prepare the powders for injection.

Barbiturates depress the central nervous system in the same way alcohol does. They produce similar effects lasting from three to six hours, depending on dose. A small dose usually makes people feel relaxed, as if they have had one or two drinks, and it is possible for the user to control the effects to some extent. With larger doses this becomes difficult, and the sedative effects take over.

Somebody trying to keep awake after a moderate to large dose (several pills) is often clumsy, with poor control of speech and body movements, which can result in accidental injury. Somebody in this state can be extremely happy, very miserable or just confused.

Large doses can produce unconsciousness and eventually respiratory failure and death. Death from overdose is an ever-present danger because the fatal amount is very near the normal dose. These effects and dangers are worse if alcohol has also been taken.

Tolerance and dependence are likely to develop with barbiturates. The dependence has a strong physical (as well as psychological) basis. So after high doses the withdrawal effects can include irritability, nervousness, sleeplessness, faintness and sickness, twitching and delirium. If convulsions occur, there may also be lasting brain damage. Sudden withdrawal from high doses of barbiturates can kill.

Heavy users are also vulnerable to bronchitis and pneumonia (because the cough reflex is depressed), hypothermia (because the drug blocks normal responses to cold) and repeated accidental overdose. Most of these risks are increased if the drug is injected. Injecting barbiturates is possibly the most dangerous form of drug abuse.

## Benzodiazepine tranquillizers

Benzodiazepines are the most commonly prescribed minor tranquillizers (for daytime anxiety relief) and hypnotics (to promote sleep). They include products such as Valium, Librium and Ativan. Because of a relative absence of undesirable side-effects (such as drowsiness and poor co-ordination) and their relative safety in overdose, the benzodiazepines have come to replace barbiturates as prescribed sedatives and sleeping pills.

Most benzodiazepine treatments involve long-term repeat prescriptions, and up to half of these are issued without the doctor seeing the patient. Twice as many women as men use these drugs.

Prescribed or stolen benzodiazepines are available on the illicit market. They are often taken to help users through periods when their main choice of drug is unavailable, or to augment the effects of other depressant-type drugs, such as alcohol or opiates, and to offset the effect of amphetamine sulphate. One benzodiazepine, temazepam, became a street drug of choice because its liquid formulation allowed users to inject the drug. Even though the formulation has been changed, the practice of injecting the drug continues.

Benzodiazepines depress mental activity and alertness, but do not generally make people as drowsy or clumsy as the barbiturates. But they do affect driving and similar skills. Like alcohol, tranquillizers can sometimes release aggression by lowering inhibitions. Any benzodiazepine in a high enough dose can cause sleep. These effects usually last three to six hours. Many more benzodiazepines than barbiturates have to be taken to give a lethal dose. Like the other effects described, this could happen at a lower dosage level if alcohol has been taken.

On their own, benzodiazepines rarely produce the feeling of happiness that comes with barbiturates or alcohol. After up to two weeks' continuous use, benzodiazepines may become ineffective as

sleeping pills, and after four months ineffective against anxiety.
Dependence is probably mainly psychological. The 'pills' are
relied upon to help cope with pressure or problems, and there may
be severe anxiety and panic if the drug is temporarily unavailable.

Sometimes severe withdrawal symptoms occur if tolerance
effects or stressful life events have led the user to increase the
dose. Generally mild withdrawal symptoms can occur in a
substantial minority of patients after a few years' treatment with
normal therapeutic doses, and in the majority after six to eight
years. Withdrawal effects after suddenly stopping benzodiazepines
often take several days to appear and then last for two to three
weeks or longer. They can include insomnia, anxiety, perceptual
hypersensitivity, tremor, irritability, nausea and vomiting, and
after unusually high doses may include convulsions and mental
confusion. These are not life-threatening, and not as common as
with the barbiturates, but can be extremely distressing.
Withdrawal symptoms seem particularly noticeable with shorter-
acting benzodiazepines such as lorazepam and temazepam.

DRUGS THAT REDUCE PAIN

## Opiates

These are a group of drugs derived from the opium poppy, which
have generally similar effects, notably analgesia. As well as being
prescribed as painkillers, opiates have medical uses as cough
suppressants and anti-diarrhoea agents. Opium is the dried 'milk'
of the opium poppy. It contains morphine and codeine, both
effective painkillers, and from morphine it is not difficult to
produce heroin, which is more than twice as potent as morphine.

When misused, opiates can be smoked, swallowed or dissolved in
water and injected. Heroin is rarely swallowed (because this is
relatively ineffective), but it can be smoked or sniffed liked
cocaine. When smoked, heroin powder is heated and the fumes
inhaled, commonly through a small tube – a practice known as
'chasing the dragon'. Some opiate mixtures are effectively
rendered non-injectable by the substance used to dilute or dissolve
the powder. This is the case with methadone mixture, which is one
reason why it is frequently prescribed to opiate addicts.

Other opiates include pethidine (often used as a painkiller in
childbirth), dipipanone (Diconal), dihydrocodeine (DF 118) and
buprenorphine (Temgesic). Illicit users often crush tablets such as
Diconal or Temgesic for injecting. They are not meant for this

purpose and using them in this way may cause abscesses, blood clots, gangrene or inflammation of a vein.

In Britain, illicit heroin is usually around 20 to 30 per cent pure, adulterated with anything from glucose powder and chalk dust to barbiturate powder.

Pure opiates in moderate doses produce a range of mild effects in addition to killing pain. Like sedatives they depress brain activity, including reflexes such as coughing, breathing and heart-rate. They also widen blood vessels (giving a feeling of warmth) and cause constipation by reducing bowel activity.

Even with doses high enough to create feeling of great happiness, there is little interference with sensation, muscle co-ordination or intellect, although at higher doses lethargy takes over. Overdose results in unconsciousness and coma, and (very rarely) death from respiratory failure. Overdose is more likely if other depressant drugs such as alcohol or barbiturates are used at the same time.

Opiates cause a relaxed detachment from pain, desires and anxiety. They make people feel drowsy, warm and content, and relieve stress and discomfort. In people who have developed physical dependence and tolerance to opiates, however, pleasure is replaced by the relief of getting the drugs. They need it just to stay 'normal'.

Along with or instead of these reactions, a first-time user often feels sick and vomits, especially after injecting. Sniffing heroin gives a slower and weaker effect than injection. When heroin is smoked, its effects can be expected to come on as quickly as after injection, but to be less strong.

Overdoses can occur when people take what was their usual dose after coming off drugs for a time and tolerance has faded. After several weeks on high doses, sudden withdrawal causes discomfort similar to influenza. The effects start eight to twenty-four hours after the last dose of heroin and include aches, tremor, sweating and chills, sneezing and yawning, and muscular spasms. They gradually fade in seven to ten days, but a feeling of weakness and loss of well-being may last for several months. Physical dependence is not as important as the strong psychological dependence developed by some long-term users. Dependence of any kind is not inevitable, however.

Damage to the body is common among opiate users, although not usually from the drugs themselves. Damage is caused by repeated injections, often with dirty needles, and by the substances mixed with the drugs. Also apathy and reduced appetite can contribute to disease because of poor diet, self-neglect and living conditions associated with bad housing. As tolerance dependence develops, money problems exacerbate self-neglect and a poor quality of life.

## DRUGS THAT STIMULATE THE NERVOUS SYSTEM

### Amphetamines

These drugs were commonly prescribed in pill form during World War II to combat physical fatigue, and in the 1950s and 1960s they were used as anti-depressants and slimming pills. Most amphetamines available on the streets today is in the form of illicitly produced amphetamine sulphate powder. Mainly it is sniffed, but increasingly in some parts of Britain it is injected.

Amphetamine sulphate has a purity of only about 15 per cent or less and is heavily adulterated. Because it is of such low purity, heavy users can consume several grams a day.

Amphetamines arouse and activate the user in much the same way as the body's natural adrenaline. Breathing and heart-rate speed up, the pupils widen and appetite decreases. The user feels more energetic, confident and cheerful. Because of these effects, there is a risk of psychological dependence. As the body's energy lessens, the main feelings may become anxiety, irritability and restlessness. High doses (especially if repeated over several days) can produce delirium, panic, hallucinations and feelings of persecution.

The effects of a single dose last about three to four hours, and leave the user feeling tired. The body may need a couple of days to recover fully. To maintain the desired effects, regular users have to take increasing doses, often many times the prescribed medical dose. When they eventually stop, they are likely to feel depressed, dull and very hungry, because amphetamines merely postpone tiredness and hunger, and do not satisfy the body's need for rest and food. Heavy use also carries the risk of damaged blood vessels and heart failure, especially among people with already high blood pressure or heart-rate, or among people (such as athletes) who take strenuous exercise while using the drug.

Regular uses of high doses may develop delusions, hallucinations and feelings of persecution. Sometimes these develop into mental disorder from which it can take several months to recover. High doses also weaken the user because of lack of sleep and food, and lower resistance to disease. All of these factors can have serious effects on health.

Ecstasy is a hallucinogenic amphetamine, although at low doses the effects are similar to LSD. Regular or high dose use can have similar effects to those described above for heavy amphetamine use.

## Caffeine

This is the most commonly used stimulant drug, found in small quantities in coffee, tea, chocolate and cola drinks. Consumption of 500 to 600 mg of caffeine a day (around 8 cups of instant coffee or tea) can cause anxiety and restlessness. At 15 cups a day, effects such as light flashes and ringing in the ears may be experienced, together with insomnia, faster heart-rate and breathing, muscle tremor and nausea, vomiting and diarrhoea. Regular drinkers often feel tired and irritable if they miss their usual morning coffee; psychological dependence can develop to such an extent that people find it hard to stop drinking coffee even for medical reasons – such as high blood pressure or anxiety.

## Cocaine

Cocaine is a white powder, derived from the leaves of the South American coca shrub, with powerful stimulant properties similar to amphetamine. It is occasionally injected, sometimes mixed with heroin, but more commonly a small amount is sniffed through a tube and absorbed into the blood supply via the nasal membranes. Cocaine can also be smoked through a process known as 'freebasing', in which the cocaine base is 'freed' from the acid hydrochloride. The drug known as 'Crack' is simply freebased cocaine produced by a simpler method.

Cocaine is harder to obtain and more expensive than amphetamine sulphate powder, but people already involved in drug taking circles can currently obtain 60 to 70 per cent pure cocaine for about six or seven times the price of a gram of amphetamine. In fact, it is even more expensive compared to amphetamine than the price difference suggests, because an average "dose" of amphetamine sulphate can last hours, whereas a line of cocaine normally lasts for only about 20 to 30 minutes, and freebase or crack for much less than that. The typical 'weekend' user might sniff gram or so over the weekend; regular users with sufficient resources might consume one to two grams a day. Crack is becoming increasingly available in some inner city areas.

Like amphetamines, cocaine causes excitement and mental exhilaration, producing feelings of well-being, reduced hunger, indifference to pain and tiredness, and great physical strength and mental capacity. Sometimes these effects are replaced by anxiety or panic, however. When sniffed, the mental effects peak after about 15 to 30 minutes and then are reduced. To maintain the effect the drug may have to be taken more frequently.

Large doses or a number of quickly repeated doses over a period of hours can give the person feelings of anxiety, agitation and persecution, and can produce hallucinations. These effects generally fade as the drug disappears from the body. The after-effects of cocaine include tiredness and depression. High doses can cause death from respiratory failure or heart attack, but this is a rare occurrence.

Users are often tempted to step up the dose because of the feelings of physical and mental well-being produced by cocaine. Users who stop taking the drug feel tired, sleepy and depressed, which reinforces the temptation to repeat the dose. With regular use, increasingly unpleasant effects develop and these generally persuade people to stop using it for a while. Happiness is replaced by an uncomfortable state of restlessness, excitability, sickness, sleeplessness and weight loss. With continued use this may change into a persecuted state of mind. Regular users may seem nervous, excitable and suspicious. Confused exhaustion caused by lack of sleep is also common. All these effects generally clear up once the use is stopped. Repeated sniffing damages the nasal membranes and may damage the structure separating the nostrils.

## Tobacco

More people are regular users of tobacco than of any other drug, and some drug users have reported that it was harder to give up cigarettes than heroin. Even so, nicotine is the cause of many chronic health conditions, including coronary heart disease and lung cancer. More people in Britain die from tobacco-related diseases than from the effects of all the other drugs put together, including alcohol – at least 100,000 every year.

### DRUGS THAT ALTER PERCEPTION

## Cannabis

Cannabis – also called hash, pot or grass – does not fit easily into any drug group. In low doses, it can be a sedative: in high doses, a hallucinogenic. It is by far the most widely used illegal drug in Britain – several million people have tried it at least once. It is most commonly smoked, often mixed with tobacco, but it can also be swallowed, usually mixed with food.

The results of taking cannabis (by smoking a "joint") depend largely on the expectations, motivations and mood of the user, the amount used, and the situation. Most people do not experience much at first, and "learn" which effects to look out for. The most common, and also most sought-after, effects are talkativeness, cheerfulness, relaxation and greater appreciation of sound and colour. Cannabis reduces people's ability to do complicated tasks and can affect short-term memory. Because people cannot concentrate as well, it is dangerous to drive or work machinery after taking cannabis.

With higher doses, vision may be distorted. Inexperienced people using high doses, and others using the drug when anxious or depressed, may find their unpleasant feelings strengthened. Sometimes they experience short-term panic. There is virtually no danger of a fatal overdose. The effects generally start a few minutes after smoking. They may last up to one hour with low doses, and for several hours with high ones. Normally there is no hangover.

There is no proof that cannabis use over a long time causes lasting damage to physical or mental health. This may be because the kinds of study needed to detect slow-to-develop and uncommon results have not been done. However, like tobacco smoke, frequently inhaled cannabis probably causes bronchitis and other breathing disorders, and may cause lung cancer.

People who use cannabis are more likely to try other drugs. Likewise people who smoke tobacco or drink are more likely to try cannabis. In neither case is there any evidence that using one drug actually causes people to use another. Cannabis does not seem to produce physical dependence, although regular users can come to feel a psychological need for the drug's effects.

As with other calming drugs, people who often get "high" on cannabis may appear apathetic, dull and neglect their appearance, but there is no evidence that cannabis destroys people's motivation to work. But, while intoxicated, users do less well on tasks requiring concentration. The effects of cannabis may cause special risks for people with existing respiratory or heart disorders. Heavy use by people with disturbed personalities can bring on a temporary mental disorder.

## LSD and other psychedelics

In Britain, the main psychedelic drugs are LSD and hallucinogenic 'magic' mushrooms. Lysergic acid diethylamide – LSD – is a white powder, but the minute amounts sufficient for a 'trip' are generally mixed with other substances and formed into tablets or capsules to be taken by mouth. In solution, the drug may also be taken absorbed on paper, gelatine sheets or sugar cubes. The strength of the preparations is uncertain, and often substances offered as LSD contain no LSD at all. Nevertheless three or four "tabs" of LSD would induce a full-blown hallucinogenic experience.

A trip begins about 30 minutes or an hour after taking LSD. It peaks after two to six hours and fades after about 12 hours, depending on the dose. It usually goes through several stages. Experiences are hard to describe, partly because they vary, and partly because they can be very different from our normal ways of seeing the world. Effects depend on the user's mood and situation, as well as the dose. They often include an awareness of strong colours and distortion of vision and hearing. But true hallucinations – believing something is there when it is not – are rare. Reactions may include heightened self-awareness and mystical or ecstatic experiences. A feeling of being outside one's body is commonly reported. Brief but vivid re-experiences of a part of a previous trip ("flashbacks") have also been described, especially after frequent use. These can leave the person feeling disorientated, and can be distressing, but are only rarely dangerous.

Unpleasant reactions ('bad trips') may include depression, dizziness, disorientation and sometimes panic. These are more likely if the user is unstable, anxious or depressed, or in hostile or unfamiliar surroundings. Deaths because of suicide or hallucinations, although much publicized, are rare.

LSD is not always used as an aid to insight. Smaller doses may be taken in a more casual, recreational fashion, but because such tiny amounts are sufficient to induce quite marked effects it can be difficult to control fully the amount used. There is no proof of physical damage from repeated use of LSD: the main hazards are psychological. Acute anxiety or brief mental disorders may occur, but can usually be dealt with by reassurance from a friend. Prolonged serious disorders are also rare; they are most likely in people with already existing mental problems.

It is difficult to combine a trip with a task requiring

concentration. The ability to drive, for instance, is seriously reduced. People who do drive while under the influence of the drug could endanger themselves and others. There is no physical dependence. Frequent use is discouraged by the fact that, for several days after taking LSD, further doses are less effective.

## Magic mushrooms

The main varieties of hallucinogenic mushrooms found in Britain are Fly Agaric (Amanita muscaria) and Liberty Cap.

Magic mushrooms have very similar effects to LSD. The biggest danger lies in picking the wrong mushrooms, which may turn out to be highly poisonous rather than 'mind blowing'. Magic mushrooms are usually eaten, either alone or with food.

# CHART OF COMMON DISORDERS

This chart provides rapid access to the alphabetical listing of drugs and drug types in terms of various common disorders and the types of drug often used to treat them. However, it is not a guide to treatment. In all cases of illness, a professional medical practitioner should be consulted before any drug is taken. (Words in SMALL CAPITALS appear as headings in the alphabetical listing.)

| COMMON DISORDERS | DRUG TYPE COMMONLY USED |
| --- | --- |
| **Aches, mild pain**<br>Headache, period pains, joint and muscle ache, toothache, and other mild local pain | ANALGESICS |

It is very important that a medical practitioner is consulted about any ache or pain that persists or grows worse.

| | |
| --- | --- |
| **Allergies**<br>General | ANTIHISTAMINES |
| Small skin reactions, such as rashes and insect bites | ANTIHISTAMINES; and other various proprietary ANTI-INFLAMMATORY preparations |
| Itching | Various soothing lotions and creams |
| **Babies' problems**<br>Teething | ANALGESICS; various topical preparations containing analgesic or local ANAESTHETIC agents |

| | |
|---|---|
| Fungal infections (such as thrush) | ANTIFUNGALS |
| Nappy rash | Various soothing creams and lotions |
| Diarrhoea, vomiting | In infants these should not treated with drugs. Dilute glucose solutions with mineral additives are sometimes used to replace lost fluids and minerals |

### Cold, cough, fever, sore throat

| | |
|---|---|
| Headache, fever, aching muscles | ANALGESICS |
| Sore throat | Various medicated throat lozenges and syrups |
| Nasal congestion | DECONGESTANTS |
| Cough | ANTITUSSIVES; EXPECTORANTS |

Medicated inhalations and various proprietary mixtures are also available.

### Gastrointestinal problems

| | |
|---|---|
| Acid or irritated stomach, hiatus hernia, mild ulcer symptoms | ANTACIDS |
| Nausea, travel sickness | ANTI-EMETICS |
| Diarrhoea | ANTIDIARRHOEALS |
| Constipation | LAXATIVES |
| Haemorrhoids (piles) | Various antihaemorrhoid creams and suppositories |

### Skin problems  (see also allergies)

| | |
|---|---|
| Burns, cuts and grazes | ANTISEPTICS |
| Fungal infection (such as athlete's foot) | ANTIFUNGALS |
| Boils | ANTISEPTICS |

| | |
|---|---|
| Head and body lice | Various lotions or shampoos are available |
| Acne | ANTISEPTICS; KERATOLYTICS |
| Dandruff | Various medicated shampoos |
| Dermatitis | ANTIHISTAMINES; hormonal preparations |

# THE HOME MEDICINE CABINET

A typical home medicine cabinet contains a number of over-the-counter preparations used to treat common disorders, such as those in the chart above; it also has a number of other items that may be useful in first aid. It is recommended that anyone preparing a complete home medicine cabinet should consult his or her family doctor for advice about specific products that may suit their needs, but a basic home first aid kit might contain the following:

antiseptic cream or lotion
analgesics
mild saline eyewash
travel sickness tablets
antihistamines
soothing lotions
antacids
cough and cold remedies
mild laxatives

smelling salts
bandages (wide and narrow)
adhesive plasters
absorbent gauze dressings
tissues for cleansing
cotton wool
safety pins
scissors

## Warnings
- All medicines should be kept well out of the reach of children.
- Prescribed drugs should not be kept in a first aid cabinet in case they are used by someone to whom they were not prescribed.
- Courses of drugs prescribed by a doctor should always be completed, so usually there will not be any drugs left over. If there are, however, when the course is finished they should be disposed of by flushing them down the toilet, so that there is no risk of them being found and used incorrectly – for example by children thinking they are sweets.

● Never use drugs that have been prescribed to another person.
● Most drugs have a limited lifespan; this is usually marked on the container. Do not use drugs after their expiry date.

**AAA Spray** (*Armour*) is a proprietary, non-prescription, ANTISEPTIC mouth and throat spray, used to treat a sore throat, irritation caused by post-nasal drip, or minor infections. Apart from its antiseptic constituent, AAA Spray also contains a very small proportion of the local ANAESTHETIC BENZOCAINE.

**Abicol** (*Boots*) is a proprietary ANTIHYPERTENSIVE drug, available only on prescription, used to treat high blood pressure (hypertension) and to slow the heart rate. Produced in the form of tablets, Abicol's active constituents are the RAUWOLFIA ALKALOID reserpine and the DIURETIC bendrofluazide. It is not recommended for administration to children.
▲/● side-effects/warning: *see* BENDROFLUAZIDE; RESERPINE.

**Abidec** (*Parke, Davis*) is a proprietary non-prescription MULTIVITAMIN compound that is not available from the National Health Service. Produced in the form of capsules and drops, Abidec contains RETINOL (vitamin A), several forms of vitamin B (THIAMINE, RIBOFLAVINE, PYRIDOXINE and NICOTINAMIDE), ASCORBIC ACID (vitamin C) and ERGOCALCIFEROL (vitamin D).

**Accupro** (*Parke-Davis*) is a proprietary form of the ANTIHYPERTENSIVE drug quinapril used to treat high blood pressure (hypertension), and in combination with a DIURETIC or CARDIAC GLYCOSIDE in congestive heart failure. It is available only on prescription in the form of tablets (in three strengths).
▲/● side-effects/warning: *see* QUINAPRIL.

**acebutolol** is a BETA-BLOCKER, a drug used in the treatment of angina (heart pain) and cardiac

arrhythmias (heartbeat irregularities). It is also used to treat high blood pressure (*see* ANTIHYPERTENSIVE) usually in conjunction with a THIAZIDE DIURETIC. Acebutolol is also used to decrease the heart rate and to control other symptoms that occur in hyperthyroidism. Administration is oral in the form of capsules, or in the case of emergency treatment of cardiac arrhythmias it may be given by slow intravenous injection.
▲ side-effects: the most common are nausea, vomiting, diarrhoea, fatigue and dizziness, although slow heartbeat, hypotension (low blood pressure) and cold toes and fingers may also occur.
● warning: acebutolol should not be given to patients with asthma or bronchospasm, excessive acidity in the metabolism, partial heart block or slowness of the heartbeat. It should be administered with great care to patients with heart failure (failure of the heart to contract effectively). *Related articles:* SECADREX; SECTRAL.

**Acepril** (*Duncan, Flockhart*) is a proprietary ANTIHYPERTENSIVE drug, available only on prescription, used to treat high blood pressure and cardiac failure, particularly when THIAZIDES or BETA-BLOCKERS have failed or are not tolerated. Produced in the form of tablets (in three strengths), Acepril is a preparation of the powerful enzyme inhibitor captopril.
▲/● side-effects/warning: *see* CAPTOPRIL.

**acetazolamide** is a mildly DIURETIC drug used to treat pressure in the eyeball (glaucoma) by reducing the formation of the aqueous humour. Secondary uses include the

**A**

treatment of grand mal and focal epilepsy, the accumulation of fluid in the tissues (oedema), and premenstrual tension. Administration is oral in the form of tablets or capsules, or by injection or infusion; some forms are not recommended for children. Sodium and/or potassium supplements may be required during treatment.

▲ side-effects: there may be drowsiness, numbness and tingling of the hands and feet, flushes and headache, thirst, and frequency of urination.

✹ warning: acetazolamide should not be administered to patients with sodium or potassium deficiency, or with malfunction of the adrenal glands, and should be administered with caution to patients who are pregnant or lactating, diabetic, or who have gout. Monitoring of the blood count and of electrolyte levels is essential. *Related article:* DIAMOX.

**acetohexamide** is a drug used to treat (adult-onset) diabetes mellitus, one of the SULPHONYLUREAS which work by augmenting insulin secretion (as opposed to compensating for its absence). Administration is oral in the form of tablets.

▲ side-effects: there may be some sensitivity reaction (such as a rash).

✹ warning: acetohexamide should not be administered to patients who suffer from liver or kidney disease, from endocrine disorders or from stress; who are pregnant or lactating. *Related article:* DIMELOR

**Acetoxyl** (*Stiefel*) is a proprietary, non-prescription, topical preparation for the treatment of acne. Produced in the form of a gel (in two strengths – 2.5% and 5%), its active constituent is

benzoyl peroxide, which has both KERATOLYTIC and ANTIMICROBIAL properties.

▲ / ✹ side-effects/warning: *see* BENZOYL PEROXIDE.

**acetylcholine chloride** is a PARASYMPATHOMIMETIC drug that, in very mild solution and in combination with a mild solution of MANNITOL, is used to irrigate the eye during eye surgery. By itself it has the effect of rapidly contracting the pupil (miosis). Acetylcholine is the natural neurotransmitter released from cholinergic nerves (*see* ANTICHOLINERGIC).

**acetylcysteine** is a MUCOLYTIC drug, used to reduce the viscosity of sputum and thus facilitate expectoration (the coughing up of sputum) in patients with disorders of the upper respiratory tract, such as asthma and bronchitis. It may also be used to treat abdominal complications associated with cystic fibrosis; to increase lachrymation (the production of tears); or as an antidote to overdosage of PARACETAMOL. Administration is oral in the form of a solution of dissolved granules, as eye-drops, by injection or infusion, or by nebulisation through a face-mask or mouthpiece.

▲ side-effects: there may be nausea and vomiting, and stomatis (inflammation of the mouth).

✹ warning: acetylcysteine should be administered with caution to patients who are elderly or those with severe respiratory insufficiency. *Related articles:* FABROL; ILUBE; PARVOLEX.

**Achromycin** (*Lederle*) is a proprietary form of the broad-spectrum ANTIBIOTIC tetracycline hydrochloride, available only on prescription. Used to treat many types of microbial infections both systemically and on the skin and in the ears and eyes (notably trachoma). Achromycin is produced in many forms: as tablets (in two types), as a syrup, as an ointment (in two strengths), as an ophthalmic oil suspension (for use as drops), and powdered in vials for reconstitution and injection. Some forms are not recommended for children or pregnant women.

▲/✿ side-effects/warning: *see*
TETRACYCLINE.

**Achromycin V** (*Lederle*) is a form of the proprietary, tetracycline ANTIBIOTIC Achromycin that also contains a buffer – a substance that does not change its acid-alkali balance (pH) if it is diluted. Produced in the form of capsules and as a syrup, it is not recommended for children or pregnant women.

▲/✿ side-effects/warning: *see*
TETRACYCLINE.

**Acidol-Pepsin** (*Sterling Research*) is a proprietary non-prescription compound used to make up a deficiency of hydrochloric acid and other digestive juices in the stomach. Produced in the form of tablets, Acidol-Pepsin contains betaine hydrochloride and the gastric enzyme pepsin.

▲/✿ side-effects/warning: *see*
BETAINE HYDROCHLORIDE.

**Aci-Jel** (*Ortho-Cilag*) is a proprietary, non-prescription, ANTISEPTIC preparation used to treat non-specific vaginal infections and to restore acidity to the vagina. Aci-jel is produced in the form of a jelly (supplied with a special applicator), and its active constituent is acetic acid, which has antibacterial properties.

▲ side-effects: there may be local irritation and/or inflammation.

**Aclacin** (*Lundbeck*) is a proprietary antibiotic CYTOTOXIC. It is therefore used to treat certain

leukaemias. Available only on prescription, it is produced in the form of powder for reconstitution as a medium for fast-running infusion. Its active constituent is aclarubicin hydrochloride.

▲/✿ side-effects/warning: *see*
ACLARUBICIN
HYDROCHLORIDE.

**aclarubicin hydrochloride** is a powerful CYTOTOXIC drug that is also an antibiotic, used especially to treat acute non-lymphocytic leukaemia in patients who have not responded to, or who have relapsed from, other chemotherapy. It is a recently introduced agent with properties similar to doxorubicin. Administration is by fast-running infusion.

▲ side-effects: there may be nausea and vomiting, hair loss and reduction in the blood-forming capacity of the bone-marrow are all fairly common side-effects.

✿ warning: aclarubicin hydrochloride should be administered with caution to patients with heart disease, who are elderly, or who are receiving radiotherapy in the cardiac region. Heart monitoring is essential throughout treatment: high doses tend to cause eventual heart dysfunction. Leakage of the drug from the site of infusion into the tissues may cause tissue damage.
*Related articles:* ACLACIN;
DOXORUBICIN HYDROCHLORIDE.

**Acnegel** (*Kirby-Warrick*) is a proprietary, non-prescription, topical preparation for the treatment of acne. Produced in the form of a gel (in two strengths – 5% and 10% – the latter under the trade name Acnegel Forte), its active constituent is benzoyl peroxide, which has both KERATOLYTIC and ANTIMICROBIAL properties.

▲/● side-effects/warning: *see*
BENZOYL PEROXIDE.

**Acnidazil** (*Janssen*) is a
proprietary, non-prescription,
topical preparation for the
treatment of acne. Produced in
the form of a cream, its active
constituents are benzoyl peroxide,
which has both KERATOLYTIC and
ANTIBACTERIAL properties, and
the ANTIFUNGAL agent miconazole
nitrate.
▲/● side-effects/warning: *see*
BENZOYL PEROXIDE;
MICONAZOLE.

**acrivastine** is an ANTIHISTAMINE
drug used primarily to treat
allergic symptoms such as hay
fever and skin rashes.
Administration is oral in the form
of capsules.
▲ side-effects: sedation is
relatively slight for an
antihistamine, though there
may be headaches.
● warning: acrivastine should
not be administered to patients
who are pregnant, and should
be administered with caution
to those with epilepsy,
glaucoma, liver disease or
enlargement of the prostate
gland.
*Related article:* SEMPREX.

**acrosoxacin** is an ANTIBIOTIC
agent of the quinolone family
used to treat the sexually-
transmitted disease gonorrhoea in
patients who are allergic to
penicillin, or whose strain of
gonorrhoea is resistant to
penicillin-type antibiotics.
Administration is oral in the form
of capsules. It is not recommended
for children.
▲ side-effects: there may be
dizziness, drowsiness and
headache, to a degree that
concentration or intricacy of
movement or thought are
impaired; there may also be
gastrointestinal disturbances.

● warning: acrosoxacin should be
administered with caution to
epileptics, or patients who have
impaired kidney or liver
function, or who are pregnant
or breast-feeding.
*Related article:* ERADACIN.

**Actal** (*WinPharm*) is a proprietary,
non-prescription, compound
ANTACID, which is also available
from the National Health Service.
It is used to treat acid stomach
and indigestion, and produced in
the form of tablets for chewing
and as a suspension. Actal's active
constituent is ALEXITOL SODIUM.

**Acthar Gel** (*Armour*) is a
proprietary preparation of
adrenocorticotrophic HORMONE
(ACTH, or corticotrophin),
available only on prescription.
The hormone controls the
secretions of corticosteroids by
the adrenal glands. In the form of
injections of the hormone in a
hydrolysed gelatin base, Acthar
Gel replaces hormonal deficiency
and treats rheumatic diseases,
skin and nerve disorders,
asthma and hay fever, and
gastrointestinal disturbances. It
may also be administered to test
adrenal function.

**ACTH/CMC** (*Ferring*) is a
proprietary preparation of
adrenocorticotrophic HORMONE
(ACTH, or corticotrophin),
available only on prescription.
The hormone controls the
secretions of corticosteroids by
the adrenal glands. In the form of
injections of the hormone in a
carmellose base, ACTH/CMC
replaces hormonal deficiency and
treats rheumatic diseases, skin
and nerve disorders, asthma and
hay fever, and gastrointestinal
disturbances. It may also be
administered to test adrenal
function.

**Actidil** (*Wellcome*) is a proprietary,
non-prescription ANTIHISTAMINE
drug used to treat various allergic

conditions, particularly conditions of the nose (allergic rhinitis) and skin (urticaria). It may also be used to assist sedation or as a premedication before surgery. Produced in the form of tablets and as a syrup for dilution (the syrup once dilute retains potency for 14 days), Actidil is a preparation of triprolidine hydrochloride.

▲ / ✿ side-effects/warning: *see* TRIPROLIDINE.

**Actifed** (*Wellcome*) is a proprietary, non-prescription, compound nasal and respiratory DECONGESTANT, which is not available from the National Health Service. Produced in the form of tablets and as a syrup for dilution (the syrup once dilute retains potency for 14 days), Actifed contains the SYMPATHO-MIMETIC VASOCONSTRICTOR ephedrine and the ANTIHISTAMINE triprolidine.

▲ / ✿ side-effects/warning: *see* EPHEDRINE; TRIPROLIDINE.

**Actifed Compound Linctus** (*Wellcome*) is a proprietary, non-prescription, compound cough preparation, which is not available from the National Health Service. Produced in the form of an elixir for dilution (the elixir once dilute retains potency for 14 days), the Compound Linctus contains the SYMPATHOMIMETIC VASO-CONSTRICTOR ephedrine, the ANTIHISTAMINE triprolidine, and the NARCOTIC ANTITUSSIVE dextromethorphan.

▲ / ✿ side-effects/warning: *see* DEXTROMETHORPHAN; EPHEDRINE; TRIPROLIDINE.

**Actifed Expectorant** (*Wellcome*) is a proprietary, non-prescription, compound EXPECTORANT, which is not available from the National Health Service. Produced in the form of an elixir for dilution (the

elixir once dilute retains potency for 14 days), the preparation contains the VASOCONSTRICTOR ephedrine, the ANTIHISTAMINE triprolidine, and the expectorant guaiphenesin.

▲ / ✿ side-effects/warning: *see* EPHEDRINE; TRIPROLIDINE.

**Actilase** (*Boehringer Ingelheim*) is a proprietary FIBRINOLYTIC, available only on prescription, used primarily to treat thrombosis and embolism. Produced in the form of powder for reconstitution as a medium for injection, Actilase is a preparation of the drug alteplase.

▲ / ✿ side-effects/warning: *see* ALTEPLASE.

**Actinac** (*Roussel*) is a proprietary lotion, to be made up from powder and a diluent solvent, representing a topical treatment for acne. Available only on prescription, Actinac's active constituents include the broad-spectrum ANTIBIOTIC CHLORAMPHENICOL and the STEROID HYDROCORTISONE.

**actinomycin D** is an ANTIBIOTIC drug that is also CYTOTOXIC, and therefore used to treat cancer (particularly cancer of the kidney, the womb or the testes). In addition it has immuno-suppressive properties and may be used in combination with other similar drugs during transplant surgery to prevent tissue rejection. Dosage is critical to each individual patient. Administration is by injection of a bolus of the drug into a vein.

▲ side-effects: hair loss is common, even to total baldness; there may be inflammation of the mucous lining of the mouth (stomatitis), nausea and vomiting. There may also be increased sensitivity to radiotherapy.

✦ warning: suppression of the bone-marrow's function of producing red blood cells is inevitable, and regular blood counts are essential.
*Related article:* COSMEGEN LYOVAC.

**Actraphane** (*Novo*) is a proprietary, intermediate-duration combination of mixed INSULINS (isophane insulin 70%, neutral insulin 30%) used to treat patients with diabetes mellitus.

**Actrapid** (*Novo*) is a proprietary, quick-acting preparation of neutral INSULIN, used to treat patients with diabetes mellitus.

**Acupan** (*Carnegie*) is a proprietary, non-narcotic ANALGESIC, available only on prescription, used to treat severe pain (such as that following surgery, or in cancer or toothache). Produced in the form of tablets and in ampoules for injection, Acupan is a preparation of nefopam hydrochloride.
▲/✦ side-effects/warning: *see* NEFOPAM.

**AC Vax** (A + C) (*SK&F*) is a VACCINE, now called meningococcal polysaccharide vaccine, prepared from Neisseria meningitidis (meningococcus) groups A and C. It is designed to give protection against the organism meningococcus, which can cause serious infection including meningitis. It may be indicated for travellers intending to go 'rough' to parts of the world where the risk of meningococcal infection is much higher than in the United Kingdom, e.g. parts of India and Saudi Arabia and much of Africa. It is recommended for adults and children aged over 2 months by deep subcutaneous or intramuscular injection.

▲/✦ side-effects/warning: *see* MENINGOCOCCAL POLYSACCHARIDE VACCINE.

**acyclovir** is an ANTIVIRAL agent used specifically to treat infection by herpes viruses (such as shingles, chickenpox, cold sores including genital sores, and herpes infections of the eye). It works by inhibiting the action of two virally coded enzymes in cells used by the virus to replicate itself. To be effective, however, treatment of an infection must begin early. It may be valuable in immunocompromised patients. The drug may also be used prophylactically to prevent individuals at risk from contracting a herpes disease. Administration is oral, topical or by infusion.
▲ side-effects: applied topically, there may be a temporary burning or stinging sensation; some patients experience a localized drying of the skin. Taken orally, acyclovir may give rise to gastrointestinal disturbance and various blood cell deficiencies; there may also be fatigue and a rash.
✦ warning: acyclovir should be administered with caution to patients who are pregnant or who have impaired kidney function. To be effective, treatment of an infection must begin as early as possible. Adequate fluid intake must be maintained.
*Related article:* ZOVIRAX.

**Adalat** (*Bayer*) is a proprietary CALCIUM-ANTAGONIST VASODILATOR, available only on prescription, used to treat angina pectoris, coldness and numbness of the fingers (Raynaud's phenomenon) and (under the trade name Adalat Retard) high blood pressure (hypertension). Produced in the form of capsules, as sustained-release tablets, and as an injection. The active constituent in both preparations is nifedipine. None of the preparations is recommended for children.

▲/ⓕ side-effects/warning: see NIFEDIPINE.

**Adcortyl** (*Squibb*) is a proprietary form of the ANTI-INFLAMMATORY glucocorticoid (CORTICOSTEROID) drug triamcinolone acetonide, available only on prescription. Produced in the form of ointment or cream, Adcortyl is used to treat skin infections (such as dermatitis), psoriasis, insect bites and sunburn. A version is available that includes the ANTIBIOTIC NEOMYCIN and the ANTIMICROBIAL agent gramicidin, known as Adcortyl with Graneodin. In ORABASE paste, Adcortyl is used to treat oral and dental inflammations. Produced as injections, Adcortyl is used in two different ways in order to achieve either of two distinct purposes: intradermal injection relieves some scaly skin diseases (such as lichen planus); injection directly into a joint relieves pain, swelling and stiffness (such as with rheumatoid arthritis, bursitis and tenosynovitis).

▲/ⓕ side-effects/warning: see TRIAMCINOLONE ACETONIDE.

**Addamel** (*KabiVitrum*) contains additional electrolytes and trace elements for use in association with Vamin (proprietary) infusion fluids, for the intravenous nutrition of a patient in whom feeding via the alimentary tract is not possible.

**Addiphos** (*KabiVitrum*) contains additional phosphate for use in association with Vamin (proprietary) infusion fluids, for the intravenous nutrition of a patient in whom feeding via the alimentary tract is not possible.

**Adifax** (*Servier*) is an APPETITE SUPPRESSANT, and is a proprietary form of dexfenfluramine hydrochloride, used to treat obesity, available only on prescription. The preparation is available in the form of capsules.

▲/ⓕ side-effects/warning: see FENFLURAMINE HYDROCHLORIDE.
*Related article:* PONDERAX.

**Adizem-60** (*Napp*) is a proprietary form of diltiazem hydrochloride, the VASODILATOR, which is a CALCIUM-ANTAGONIST drug used in the prevention and treatment of angina pectoris (heart pain), especially in cases where beta-blockers are not tolerated or have been ineffective. Administration is oral in the form of coated tablets.

▲/ⓕ side-effects/warning: see DILTIAZEM HYDROCHLORIDE.

**Adizem-SR** (*Napp*) is a proprietary form of diltiazem hydrochloride, the VASODILATOR, which is a CALCIUM-ANTAGONIST drug used in the prevention and treatment of angina pectoris (heart pain), especially in cases where beta-blockers are not tolerated or have been ineffective. Administration is oral in the form of sustained-release tablets.
Not suitable for the elderly or those with kidney impairment.

▲/ⓕ side-effects/warning: see DILTIAZEM HYDROCHLORIDE.

**adrenaline** is a hormone (a catecholamine) produced and secreted (along with smaller amounts of the closely related substance noradrenaline) by the central core (medulla) of the adrenal glands into the bloodstream. Together with adrenaline (which acts as a NEUROTRANSMITTER, transmitting neural impulses from nerves to other nerves, muscles or glands) it mediates responses of the body to stimulation of the sympathetic nervous system – which is primarily concerned with reactions to stress. In the face of stress, or the need for exertion, the body uses adrenaline (and noradrenaline) to cause constriction of the small blood vessels (vasoconstriction, so increasing blood pressure), increased blood flow through the heart while the heart rate is raised, increased rate and depth of respiration, and relaxation of the muscles of the intestinal walls and bronchioles. And it is to effect one or more of these responses that adrenaline, as a SYMPATHOMIMETIC, may be administered therapeutically. In an emergency, for example, adrenaline may be injected to restart the heart, or to treat for anaphylactic shock. Because adrenaline relaxes bronchial muscles it is used to relieve bronchial spasm in acute attacks of bronchial asthma, in which case it is injected subcutaneously. Intramuscular injections are given for control of prolonged asthma attacks. In addition, adrenaline administered simultaneously with a local ANAESTHETIC considerably lengthens the duration of effect of the anaesthetic. More commonly, adrenaline is administered in solution in eye-drops to treat glaucoma. Administration is by injection or inhalation; one proprietary solution is in the form of a cream.

▲ side-effects: there is an increase in heart rate; there may also be headache, anxiety, and coldness in the fingertips and toes. High dosage may lead to tremor and the accumulation of fluid in the lungs. Adrenaline in eye-drops may cause redness of the eye.

● warning: adrenaline should be administered with caution to patients who suffer from insufficient blood supply to the heart, from high blood pressure (hypertension), from diabetes, or from overactivity of the thyroid gland (hyperthyroidism), or who are already taking drugs that affect the heart or mood. *Related articles:* BROVON; EPIFRIN; EPPY; GANDA; ISOPTO EPINAL; MARCAIN; MIN-I-JET ADRENALINE; RYBARVIN; SIMPLENE; XYLOCAINE; XYLOTOX.

**Adriamycin** (*Farmitalia Carlo Erba*) is a proprietary ANTIBIOTIC drug that is also CYTOTOXIC, and therefore used to treat cancer (particularly leukaemia, lymphoma and certain solid tumours). Available only on prescription, it is produced in the form of powder for reconstitution as a medium for fast-running infusion (generally at three-week intervals). Its active constituent is doxorubicin hydrochloride.
▲/● side-effects/warning: *see* DOXORUBICIN HYDROCHLORIDE.

**adsorbed diphtheria and tetanus vaccine** is diphtheria and tetanus VACCINE adsorbed on to a mineral carrier. *see* DIPHTHERIA AND TETANUS VACCINE.

**adsorbed diphtheria, tetanus and pertussis vaccine** is diphtheria, pertussis (whooping cough) and tetanus (DPT) VACCINE adsorbed on to a mineral carrier. *see* DIPHTHERIA, PERTUSSIS AND TETANUS (DPT) VACCINE.

**adsorbed tetanus vaccine** is tetanus VACCINE adsorbed on to a mineral carrier. *see* TETANUS VACCINE.

**Aerolin Autohaler** (*Riker*) is a proprietary form of the selective BETA-RECEPTOR STIMULANT salbutamol (as sulphate), used as a BRONCHODILATOR in patients with asthma and other breathing problems. Available only on prescription, Aerolin Autohaler appears as an breath-actuated metered aerosol inhalant. Patients should not exceed the prescribed or stated dose, and should follow the manufacturer's directions closely.

▲/✪ side-effects/warning: *see* SALBUTAMOL.

**Aerolin 400** (*Riker*) is a proprietary form of the selective BETA-RECEPTOR STIMULANT salbutamol (as sulphate), used as a BRONCHODILATOR in patients with asthma and other breathing problems. Available only on prescription, Aerolin 400 appears as a metered aerosol inhalant. Patients should not exceed the prescribed or stated dose, and should follow the manufacturer's directions closely.

▲/✪ side-effects/warning: *see* SALBUTAMOL.

**Aerosporin** (*Calmic*) is a proprietary form of the ANTIBIOTIC drug polymyxin B sulphate, available only on prescription, which is active against gram-negative bacteria. It is produced in the form of powder for reconstitution as a medium for injections.

▲/✪ side-effects/warning: *see* POLYMYXIN B SULPHATE.

**Afrazine** (*Kirby-Warrick*) is a proprietary non-prescription preparation of the nasal DECONGESTANT oxymetazoline hydrochloride, a SYMPATHO-MIMETIC, which is not available from the National Health Service. It is produced in the form of nose-drops (in two strengths) and as a nasal spray.

▲/✪ side-effects/warning: *see* OXYMETAZOLINE.

**Agarol** (*Warner-Lambert*) is a proprietary, non-prescription, compound LAXATIVE, which is not

available from the National Health Service. Produced in the form of a liquid (mixture) for dilution (the mixture once dilute retains potency for 28 days), Agarol contains the seaweed extract gel agar, together with PHENOLPHTHALEIN and liquid paraffin.

▲ side-effects: laxative effects may continue for several days; there may be dysfunction of the kidneys, leading possibly to discoloration of the urine. A mild skin rash may appear.

**Aglutella Azeta** (*G F Dietary Supplies*) is a proprietary (non-prescription) brand of gluten-free cream-filled wafers, which are also low in protein, sodium and potassium. They are intended for consumption by patients with gluten sensitivity (as with coeliac disease), amino-acid abnormalities (such as phenylketonuria), or kidney or liver failure.

**Aglutella Gentili** (*G F Dietary Supplies*) is a proprietary (non-prescription) brand of gluten-, sucrose- and lactose-free pasta – spaghetti, spaghetti rings, macaroni, macaroni spirals, and tagliatelle – intended for consumption by patients with gluten sensitivity (as with coeliac disease), amino-acid abnormalities (such as phenylketonuria), or kidney or liver failure.

**Akineton** (*Abbott*) is a proprietary preparation of the ANTI-CHOLINERGIC drug biperiden, available only on prescription, used to relieve some of the symptoms of parkinsonism (*see* ANTIPARKINSONISM), specifically tremor of the hands, overall rigidity of posture, and the tendency to produce an excess of saliva. It is thought to work by compensating for the lack of dopamine in the brain, which is the major cause of such parkinsonian symptoms, and is produced in the form of tablets and in ampoules for injection.

▲/✿ side-effects/warning: see BIPERIDEN.

**Albay** (*Dome/Hollister-Stier*) is either of two preparations – of bee venom and of wasp venom – for use in diagnosing and desensitizing patients who are allergic to them. Available only on prescription, solutions of one or the other venom are administered as injections in increasingly less dilute form so that treatment is progressive.

✿ warning: injections should be administered under close medical supervision and in locations where emergency facilities for full cardio-respiratory resuscitation are immediately available. Albay preparations should not be given to patients who are pregnant, or who suffer from asthma.

**Albucid** (*Nicholas*) is a proprietary ANTIBIOTIC of the SULPHONAMIDE family. Available only on prescription, it is used to treat eye infections. Produced in the form of eye-drops and (under the trade name Albucid Ointment) as an ointment (in either a water-miscible base or an oily base), Albucid's active constituent is the sulphonamide sulphacetamide sodium.

▲/✿ side-effects/warning: see SULPHACETAMIDE.

**Albumaid** (*Scientific Hospital Supplies*) is the brand name of a series of proprietary foods for special diets, as required mostly in hospitals and clinics. They are produced as powders for reconstitution. Albumaid Complete contains protein, amino

acids, vitamins, minerals and trace elements, and has no carbohydrate or fat. Albumaid XP contains protein, carbohydrate, vitamins, minerals, and amino acids, but less than 0.01%, phenylalanine and no fat. Albumaid XP Concentrate contains protein, vitamins, minerals, trace elements, and amino acids, but less than 0.025% phenylalanine and no carbohydrate or fat. Other Albumaid preparations generally follow the pattern of Albumaid XP, but instead of a minimum content of phenylalanine contain minimum quantities of (respectively) the amino acids cystine, histidine, methionine or tyrosine.

**albumin** is a protein, one of the major constituents of blood. When the level is low (hypoproteinaemia), as after burns or surgery, this may be corrected by administration of HUMAN ALBUMIN SOLUTION by intravenous infusion.
*Related article:* HUMAN ALBUMIN SOLUTION.

**Albuminar** (*Armour*) is a proprietary form of HUMAN ALBUMIN SOLUTION used to treat low blood protein (hypoproteinaemia) especially after burns and surgery. The preparation, which is available only on prescription, is available in vials for intravenous infusion, both in isotonic and concentrated forms; called Albuminar-5, Albuminar-20, and Albuminar-25.
▲/✿ side-effects/warning: see HUMAN ALBUMIN SOLUTION.

**albumin solution** is a non-proprietary preparation of albumin, used to correct low blood protein. See HUMAN ALBUMIN SOLUTION.

**Albumin solution** (*SNBTS*) is a proprietary form of HUMAN

ALBUMIN SOLUTION used to treat low blood protein (hypoproteinaemia) especially after burns and surgery. The preparation, which is available only on prescription, is available in vials for intravenous infusion, in the concentrated form only.

▲/● side-effects/warning: see HUMAN ALBUMIN SOLUTION.

**alclometasone dipropionate** is a CORTICOSTEROID drug used for topical application to treat inflammatory skin disorders in which the cause of inflammation is deemed not to be infection – in particular to treat eczema. Administration is as a cream or an ointment. Dosage should be the minimum to achieve the required response.

▲ side-effects: side-effects are rare, but may include skin sensitivity and hair growth.

● warning: as with all corticosteroids, alclometasone dipropionate treats the symptoms and does not treat any underlying disorder. An undetected infection may thus become worse although its symptoms may be suppressed by the drug.

*Related article:* MODRASONE.

**Alcobon** (*Roche*) is a proprietary ANTIFUNGAL drug available only on prescription, used to treat systemic infections by yeasts (such as candidiasis, or thrush). Produced for hospital use only in the form of tablets and in infusion flasks, Alcobon is a preparation of flucytosine.

▲/● side-effects/warning: see FLUCYTOSINE.

**Alcoderm** (*Alcon*) is a proprietary non-prescription skin emollient (softener and soother), used to treat dry or itchy skin. Produced in the form of a cream and a lotion, Alcoderm's major constituents are liquid paraffin and a moisturizer.

**alcohol** is the name of a class of compounds derived from hydrocarbons. For medical purposes, a strong solution of ethyl alcohol can be used as an ANTISEPTIC (particularly to prepare skin before injection) or as a preservative.

**Alcopar** (*Wellcome*) is a proprietary non-prescription ANTHELMINTIC drug, used to treat infections by roundworms, specifically by hookworms. Produced in the form of granules in sachets for solution in water, Alcopar is a preparation of bephenium hydroxynaphthoate.

▲ side-effects: see BEPHENIUM.

**alcuronium chloride** is a SKELETAL MUSCLE RELAXANT, of the type known as competitive or non-depolarizing. It is used during surgical operations to achieve long-duration paralysis. Administration is by injection, but only after the patient has been rendered unconscious – the muscle spasm it causes might be painful to a conscious patient. *Related article:* ALLOFERIN.

**Aldactide 50** (*Gold Cross*) is a proprietary, potassium-sparing DIURETIC drug, available only on prescription, used to treat congestive heart failure and high blood pressure (see ANTIHYPERTENSIVE). Produced in the form of tablets, Aldactide 50 is a compound of the weak, but catalytic, diuretic spironolactone together with the THIAZIDE hydroflumethiazide. A half-strength version of the compound is also available (under the trade name Aldactide 25).

▲/● side-effects/warning: see HYDROFLUMETHIAZIDE; SPIRONOLACTONE.

**Aldactone** (*Searle*) is a proprietary, potassium-sparing DIURETIC drug, available only on prescription, used to treat congestive heart failure, high blood pressure (see ANTIHYPERTENSIVE), cirrhosis of the liver, and the accumulation of fluids within the tissues (oedema). Produced in the form of tablets, Aldactone is a preparation of the comparatively weak diuretic spironolactone.

▲/❋ side-effects/warning: see SPIRONOLACTONE.

**Aldomet** (*Merck, Sharp & Dohme*) is a proprietary form of the powerful drug methyldopa, which is thought to act on the central nervous system (the brain). Available only on prescription, Aldomet is used – usually in combination with a DIURETIC drug – to treat moderate to very high blood pressure (see ANTIHYPERTENSIVE). It is produced in the form of tablets (in three strengths) and in ampoules for injection (as methyldopate hydrochloride).

▲/❋ side-effects/warning: see METHYLDOPA.

**Alembicol D** (*Alembic*) is a proprietary preparation of fatty acids derived from coconut oil, used as a dietary supplement in patients who suffer from impaired absorption of fats. In the form of a liquid, it is available either without prescription or on prescription, at the discretion of the doctor.

**Aleudrin** (*Lewis*) is a proprietary, BETA-RECEPTOR STIMULANT BRONCHODILATOR, available only on prescription, used to treat asthma and bronchitis. Produced in the form of tablets and as a solution for spraying, Aleudrin is a preparation of the SYMPATHO-MIMETIC isoprenaline sulphate.

▲/❋ side-effects/warning: see ISOPRENALINE.

**Alexan** (*Pfizer*) is a proprietary preparation of the CYTOTOXIC

drug cytarabine used to treat cancer, particularly acute forms of leukaemia. Available only on prescription, it is produced in ampoules for injection.

▲/❋ side-effects/warning: see CYTARABINE.

**Alexan 100** (*Pfizer*) is a proprietary preparation of the CYTOTOXIC drug cytarabine used to treat cancer, particularly acute forms of leukaemia. Available only on prescription, it is produced in ampoules for intravenous infusion, and is five times as strong as ALEXAN.

▲/❋ side-effects/warning: see CYTARABINE.

**alexitol sodium** is a non-proprietary (non-prescription) ANTACID, used to treat indigestion and acid stomach. It is produced in the form of tablets, and is not recommended for children.

**alfacalcidol** is a synthesized form of CALCIFEROL (VITAMIN D), used to make up body deficiencies, particularly in the treatment of types of hypoparathyroidism and rickets. Calcium levels in the body should be regularly monitored during treatment. Administration is oral in the form of capsules or drops.

❋ warning: overdosage may cause kidney damage. Although an increased amount of vitamin D is necessary during pregnancy, high body levels while lactating may cause corresponding high blood levels of calcium in the breast-fed infant.
*Related article:* ONE-ALPHA.

**alfentanil** is a narcotic ANALGESIC, used for short surgical operations, for outpatient surgery, or in combination to enhance the effect of general ANAESTHETICS (particularly barbiturate) drugs.

Administration is by intravenous infusion, and may be continuous during prolonged surgical procedures. Its proprietary form is on the controlled drugs list.

▲ side-effects: there may be respiratory depression (severely shallow breathing), worsened by nausea and vomiting; the heart rate may slow and blood pressure fall.

✿ warning: respiration may become depressed during and following treatment; the use of alfentanil to assist with childbirth may lead to respiratory depression in the newborn. Alfentanil should therefore be administered with caution to patients who already suffer from respiratory disorders. Dosage should be reduced for the elderly and for patients who suffer from chronic liver disease.
*Related article:* RAPIFEN.

**Algesal** (*Duphar*) is a proprietary, non-prescription COUNTER-IRRITANT preparation, which, in the form of a cream applied to the skin, produces an irritation of sensory nerve endings that offsets the pain of underlying muscle or joint ailments. It is not recommended for children aged under 6 years.

✿ warning: Algesal should not be used on inflamed or broken skin, or on mucous membranes.

**Algicon** (*Rorer*) is a proprietary, non-prescription ANTACID compound, which has an additional suppressant effect on the muscles controlling the flow of food along the alimentary canal, so discouraging any reflux backwards. Produced in the form of tablets and as a suspension, Algicon contains ALUMINIUM HYDROXIDE and several magnesium and potassium salts. It is not recommended for children.

✿ warning: Algicon should not be administered to patients with kidney failure, or who are very weak. Diabetics should be wary of taking it because it contains sucrose.

**Algipan** (*Wyeth*) is a proprietary, non-prescription COUNTER-IRRITANT compound, which, in the form of a cream or a spray applied to the skin, produces an irritation of sensory nerve endings that offsets the pain of underlying muscle or joint ailments. The spray also has a chilling effect.

✿ warning: Algipan should not be used on inflamed or broken skin, or on mucous membranes.

**Algitec** (*Smith, Kline & French*) is a proprietary preparation of the drug cimetidine, combined with alginate. Available only on prescription it is used to treat gastro-oesophageal reflux disease. Algitec is produced in the form of chewable tablets (called Chewtab) and as a suspension.

▲/✿ side-effects/warning: *see* CIMETIDINE.

**Alimix** (*Cilag*) is a stomach and intestine MOTILITY STIMULANT. It is a proprietary form of cisapride, available only on prescription in the form of tablets which are taken 15-30 minutes before meals.

▲/✿ side-effects/warning: *see* CISAPRIDE.

**Alka-Donna** (*Carlton*) is a proprietary, non-prescription, ANTI-CHOLINERGIC compound, which is not available from the National Health Service. It is used to treat muscle spasm of the intestinal walls, and the resulting gastrointestinal discomfort. Produced as a suspension, Alka-Donna's active constituents are belladonna alkaloids, aluminium hydroxide and magnesium trisilicate.

▲/◉ side-effects/warning: *see*
ALUMINIUM HYDROXIDE;
BELLADONNA; MAGNESIUM
TRISILICATE.

**Alka-Donna-P** (*Carlton*) is a form
of the proprietary ANTI-
CHOLINERGIC compound
ALKA-DONNA, which is not
available from the National
Health Service, and is on the
cotrolled drugs list because it
additionally contains the
BARBITURATE phenobarbitone.
▲/◉ side-effects/warning: *see*
PHENOBARBITONE.

**Alkeran** (*Wellcome*) is a
proprietary CYTOTOXIC drug,
available only on prescription,
used to treat multiple myeloma,
breast cancer and cancer of the
ovary. Produced in the form of
tablets (in two strengths) and
(under the trade name Alkeran
Injection) as powder for
reconstitution with a solvent for
injection, Alkeran is a
preparation of melphalan.
▲/◉ side-effects/warning: *see*
MELPHALAN.

**Allbee with C** (*Robins*) is a
proprietary, non-prescription
MULTIVITAMIN preparation that is
not available from the National
Health Service. Used to treat
vitamin deficiencies and produced
in the form of capsules, Allbee
with C – as its name indicates –
consists of several forms of
vitamin B (THIAMINE,
RIBOFLAVINE, PYRIDOXINE,
NICOTINAMIDE and PANTOTHENIC
ACID) together with ASCORBIC
ACID (vitamin C).

**Allegron** (*Dista*) is a proprietary
ANTIDEPRESSANT, available only
on prescription, used to treat
depressive illness. It is also used
for children to stop bed-wetting at
night. Produced in the form of
tablets (in two strengths),
Allegron is a preparation of the
TRICYCLIC drug nortriptyline
hydrochloride.

▲/◉ side-effects/warning: *see*
NORTRIPTYLINE.

**Aller-eze** is a proprietary, non-
prescription ANTIHISTAMINE, in
which the active constituent is
clemastine hydrogen fumarate.
▲/◉ side-effects/warning: *see*
CLEMASTINE.

**Alloferin** (*Roche*) is a proprietary
SKELETAL MUSCLE RELAXANT,
available only on prescription, of
the type known as competitive or
non-depolarizing. It is used
during surgical operations, but
only after the patient has been
rendered unconscious. Produced
in ampoules for injection,
Alloferin is a preparation of
alcuronium chloride.
▲/◉ side-effects/warning: *see*
ALCURONIUM CHLORIDE.

**allopurinol** is a XANTHINE-
OXIDASE INHIBITOR, a drug used to
combat an excess of uric acid in
the blood, and thus to try to
prevent gout. Once begun –
provided that there are no acute
gout attacks – treatment should
be continued indefinitely.
Administration is oral in the form
of tablets, but before beginning
treatment an inflammatory
analgesic should be administered
for about 4 weeks.
▲ side-effects: there may be
gastrointestinal disturbances.
Rarely, there may be headache,
dizziness and high blood
pressure (hypertension), hair
loss, and/or problems with the
sense of taste.
◉ warning: if an acute gout
attack or a rash with high
temperature occurs, treatment
should cease at once, and
continue only after the attack
has subsided. Allopurinol
should be administered with
caution to patients who suffer
from liver or kidney disease.
*Related articles:* ALORAL;
ALULINE; CAPLENAL; COSURIC;
HAMARIN; ZYLORIC.

**allyloestrenol** is a PROGESTOGEN, an analogue of the natural female sex HORMONE progesterone, responsible for the changing state of the lining of the womb preparatory to, or during, pregnancy. It is used to treat recurrent miscarriage or failure of a blastocyst to implant following conception; it may also be used to treat premenstrual tension. Administration is oral in the form of tablets.

▲ side-effects: there may be skin disorders (such as acne), accumulation of fluid in the tissues (oedema) and associated weight gain, breast tenderness, and/or gastrointestinal disturbances.

✿ warning: allyloestrenol should not be administered to patients with undiagnosed vaginal bleeding, incomplete abortion, or any form of thrombosis; and should be administered with caution to patients who are diabetic, who suffer from high blood pressure (hypertension), from heart, liver or kidney disease, or who are lactating.
*Related article:* GESTANIN.

**almasilate suspension** is a non-proprietary, non-prescription ANTACID preparation that has an additional suppressant effect on the muscles controlling the flow of food along the alimentary canal, so discouraging any reflux backwards. It is used to treat the symptoms of peptic ulcer or acidity in the stomach. Produced in the form of a liquid, almasilate suspension is not recommended for children.

**Almazine** (*Steinhard*) is a proprietary ANXIOLYTIC, used as a tranquillizer especially in relieving attacks of phobia. Produced in the form of tablets (in two strengths), Almazine is a preparation of the BENZO-DIAZEPINE lorazepam.

▲ / ✿ side-effects/warning: *see* LORAZEPAM.

**Almevax** (*Wellcome*) is a proprietary VACCINE against German measles (rubella) in the form of a solution containing live but attenuated viruses of the Wistar RA27/3 strain. Available only on prescription, and administered in the form of injection, it is intended specifically for the immunization of non-pregnant women.

**Almodan** (*Berk*) is a proprietary ANTIBIOTIC, available only on prescription, used to treat systemic bacterial infections and infections of the upper respiratory tract, of the ear, nose and throat, and of the urogenital tracts; it is sometimes used also to treat typhoid fever. Produced in the form of a powder (as sodium salt) in vials for reconstitution in a medium for injection, Almodan is a preparation of the broad-spectrum PENICILLIN amoxycillin.
▲ / ✿ side-effects/warning: *see* AMOXYCILLIN.

**Alophen** is a powerful proprietary, non-prescription, compound LAXATIVE containing several strong, natural ingredients. Produced in the form of pills, Alophen contains essence of aloes, belladonna extract, phenolphthalein and ipecacuanha – all effective in their own right.

▲ side-effects: laxative effects may continue for several days; there may be dysfunction of the kidneys, leading possibly to discoloration of the urine. A mild skin rash may appear.

**Aloral** (*Lagap*) is a proprietary form of the XANTHINE-OXIDASE INHIBITOR allopurinol, used to treat high levels of uric acid in the bloodstream (which may otherwise cause gout). Available only on prescription, Aloral is produced in the form of tablets (in two strengths).

▲/● side-effects/warning: *see*
ALLOPURINOL.

**aloxiprin** is a non-narcotic
ANALGESIC. It is a form of ASPIRIN
that additionally contains a buffer
(a substance that does not change
its acid-alkali balance) that
counters acidity. This means that
aspirin's detrimental effect on the
lining of the stomach is
considerably reduced.
▲/● side-effects/warning: *see*
ASPIRIN.
*Related article:* PALAPRIN
FORTE.

**alpha-blockers (alpha-**
**adrenoceptor antagonists)** are
drugs that inhibit the action of the
HORMONE ADRENALINE, released
from the adrenal gland, the
NEUROTRANSMITTER
NORADRENALINE, which is released
from sympathetic nerves, and
related substances (known as the
catecholamines) at sites in the
body where the recognition site
for these substances is known as
an alpha adrenoceptor. The main
effect of alpha-blockers is to lower
the blood pressure and they are
therefore used to treat some types
of hypertension. They are also
used to treat poor circulation in
the extremities of the body and to
treat an excess of catecholamines
in the body. Examples include
PHENTOLAMINE and PRAZOSIN.

**Alphaderm** (*Norwich Eaton*) is a
proprietary cream preparation
containing urea (10%) with the
corticosteroid hydrocortisone
(1%) dispersed in a slightly oily
base. Available only on
prescription, the cream is used as
a topical application for the
treatment of ichthyosis (dry and
horny epidermis) and other mild
inflammations of the skin.
▲/● side-effects/warning: *see*
HYDROCORTISONE.

**Alpha Keri** (*Bristol-Myers*) is a
proprietary, non-prescription skin
emollient (softener and soother)

for use in the bath. Containing
mineral and lanolin oils, it can
also be massaged into the skin to
treat dry or itchy areas.

**alpha tocopheryl acetate** is a
form of VITAMIN E (tocopherol),
used to treat deficiency and
generally as a vitamin
supplement. Administration is
oral in the form of tablets for
chewing, capsules and in
suspension, or as a paraffin-based
ointment.
*Related articles:* EPHYNAL; VITA-E.

**Alphosyl** (*Stafford-Miller*) is a
proprietary, non-prescription
preparation used to treat eczema
and psoriasis. Produced in the
form of a water-based cream, as a
lotion, and shampoo. Alphosyl's
major active constituent is COAL
TAR extract.

**Alphosyl HC** (*Stafford-Miller*) is a
proprietary COAL TAR and
CORTICOSTEROID preparation,
available only on prescription,
used to treat psoriasis. Produced
in the form of a water-based
cream, Alphosyl HC's steroid
constituent is hydrocortisone.
▲/● side-effects/warning: *see*
HYDROCORTISONE.

**alprazolam** is an ANXIOLYTIC drug,
one of the BENZODIAZEPINES used
to treat anxiety in either the short
or the long term. Administration
is oral in the form of tablets. It is
not recommended for children.
▲ side-effects: there may be
drowsiness, dizziness,
headache, dry mouth and
shallow breathing;
hypersensitive reactions may
occur.
● warning: alprazolam may
reduce a patient's
concentration and intricacy of
movement or thought; it may
also enhance the effects of
alcohol consumption.
Prolonged use or abrupt

withdrawal should be avoided. It should be administered with caution to patients who suffer from respiratory difficulties, glaucoma, or kidney or liver disorders; who are in the last stages of pregnancy; or who are elderly or debilitated.
*Related article:* XANAX.

**alprostadil** is PROSTAGLANDIN E1, used to maintain babies born with the congenital heart defect ductus arteriosus, while emergency preparations are made for corrective surgery and intensive care. Administration is by infusion in dilute solution.
▲ side-effects: in addition to the symptoms of the congenital defect, administration of the drug may cause breathing difficulties and low blood pressure.
✿ warning: monitoring of arterial pressure is essential; a close watch must also be kept for haemorrhage, hypotension and slow or fast heart rate, high temperature and flushing. Prolonged use may cause bone deformity and damage to the pulmonary artery.
*Related article:* PROSTIN VR.

**Alrheumat** (*Bayer*) is a proprietary, non-steroid, ANTI-INFLAMMATORY, non-narcotic ANALGESIC drug, available only on prescription. It is used to relieve pain – particularly arthritic and rheumatic pain – and to treat other musculo-skeletal disorders. Its active constituent is ketoprofen, and it is produced in the form of capsules and anal suppositories. Not recommended for children, Alrheumat should be administered with care to patients with a peptic ulcer, gastrointestinal haemorrhage or asthma, or who are pregnant or lactating.

▲ / ✿ side-effects/warning: *see* KETOPROFEN.

**Altacaps** (*Roussel*) is a proprietary, non-prescription ANTACID preparation, which is not available from the National Health Service, used to soothe heartburn, infection of the oesophagus, hiatus hernia and peptic ulcer. Produced in the form of a suspension within gelatin capsules, Altacaps contain the antacid-deflatulent HYDRO-TALCITE together with the antifoaming agent DIMETHICONE. It is not recommended for children.

**Altacite** (*Roussel*) is a proprietary, non-prescription ANTACID, which is not available from the National Health Service. Produced in the form of tablets for chewing and as a sugar-free suspension, Altacite's active constituent is HYDRO-TALCITE, a readily dissociated compound that also has deflatulent properties.

**Altacite Plus** (*Roussel*) is a proprietary, non-prescription ANTACID preparation used to soothe acid stomach, indigestion, flatulence and peptic ulcer. Produced in the form of a suspension, Altacite Plus contains the antacid-deflatulent HYDROTALCITE together with the antifoaming agent DIMETHICONE, and is not recommended for children aged under 8 years. A version of Altacite Plus is produced in the form of tablets, but it is not available from the National Health Service.

**alteplase** is a FIBRINOLYTIC DRUG. It is used to break up blood clots, and is therefore particularly useful in treating many types of thrombosis and embolisms, especially myocardial infarction. It is produced in the form of powder for reconstitution as a medium for injection.

▲ side-effects: nausea, vomiting, and bleeding, particularly from site of injection. Allergic reactions have been reported.

❦ warning: should not be administered to patients with blood disorders involving defective coagulation; who are liable to bleed (for example, by menstruation, peptic ulceration or because of recent trauma or surgery); those with hypertension, acute pancreatitis, liver disease, or who are pregnant. It should be not be administered to those showing allergic reaction to steptokinase or anistreplase, or who have been treated recently with these.

*Related article:* ACTILASE.

**Alu-cap** (*Riker*) is a proprietary, non-prescription ANTACID preparation used to soothe an acid stomach. It is produced in the form of capsules containing aluminium hydroxide, and is not recommended for children.

▲ / ❦ side-effects/warning: see ALUMINIUM HYDROXIDE.

**Aludrox** (*Wyeth*) is a proprietary, non-prescription ANTACID preparation used to soothe acid stomach, indigestion and peptic ulcer. It is produced in the form of a gel containing aluminium hydroxide, and is not recommended for children aged under 2 years. Versions of Aludrox available only on prescription are produced in the form of tablets under the trade name Aludrox Tablets; and as a gel or a suspension (incorporating AMBUTONIUM BROMIDE and MAGNESIUM salts) under the trade name Aludrox SA. Aludrox SA suspension is not recommended for children.

▲ / ❦ side-effects/warning: see ALUMINIUM HYDROXIDE.

**Aluhyde** (*Sinclair*) is a proprietary, non-prescription

ANTACID compound, which is not available from the National Health Service. It is used to treat acidity of the stomach resulting from spasm of the muscular stomach wall. Produced in the form of tablets containing aluminium hydroxide, MAGNESIUM TRISILICATE and an ANTICHOLINERGIC extract of belladonna, Aluhyde is not recommended for children.

▲ / ❦ side-effects/warning: see ALUMINIUM HYDROXIDE; BELLADONNA.

**Aluline** (*Steinhard*) is a proprietary form of the XANTHINE-OXIDASE INHIBITOR allopurinol, used to treat high levels of uric acid in the bloodstream (which may otherwise cause gout). Available only on prescription, Aluline is produced in the form of tablets (in two strengths).

▲ / ❦ side-effects/warning: see ALLOPURINOL.

**alum** is used therapeutically as an astringent, particularly to treat mouth pain and in mouth-washes.

❦ warning: treatment with alum may in fact cause tissue damage and actually defer healing.

**aluminium acetate** is an astringent DISINFECTANT, used primarily to clean sites of infection and inflammation, particularly in the case of weeping or suppurating wounds or sores, eczema, and infections of the outer ear. Administration is in the form of a lotion (containing aluminium acetate in dilute solution) or as drops.

**aluminium chloride** is a powerful antiperspirant. Administration is topical in the form of a lotion or aerosol comprising a 20% solution. It also acts as an astringent.

▲ side-effects: there may be skin irritation (which may require

treatment with a cortico-
steroid).
◆ warning: Keep away from the
eyes; do not shave armpit
within 12 hours of application
there.
*Related articles:* ANHYDROL
FORTE; DRICLOR.

**aluminium glycinate** is an
ANTACID, which, because it is
relatively insoluble in water, is
long-acting when retained in the
stomach.

**aluminium hydroxide** is an
ANTACID, which, because it is
relatively insoluble in water, is
long-acting when retained in the
stomach. Used to treat digestive
problems from acid stomach to
peptic ulcers or oesophageal
reflux. Administration is oral in
the form of tablets for chewing or
sucking, as a gel, or in a
compound liquid mixture. Some
proprietary preparations are not
recommended for children.
*Related articles:* ALGICON; ALKA-
DONNA; ALU-CAP; ALUDROX;
ALUHYDE; ANDURSIL; ASILONE;
DIJEX; DIOVOL; GASTROCOTE;
GASTRON; GAVISCON; GELUSIL;
KOLANTICON; MAALOX; MUCAINE;
MUCOGEL; POLYCROL;
PYROGASTRONE; SILOXYL; SIMECO;
TOPAL; UNIGEST.

**Alunex** (*Steinhard*) is a
proprietary, non-prescription
ANTIHISTAMINE, used to treat
allergic conditions such as hay
fever and urticaria. Produced in
the form of tablets, Alunex is a
preparation of chlorpheniramine
maleate. It may cause drowsiness.
▲/◆ side-effects/warning: *see*
CHLORPHENIRAMINE.

**Alupent** (*Boehringer Ingelheim*) is
a proprietary compound
BRONCHODILATOR, available only
on prescription, which works as a
selective SMOOTH MUSCLE
RELAXANT. Administered orally in

the form of tablets, as an aerosol
spray (under the trade name
Alupent Aerosol) or as a sugar-
free syrup (under the trade name
Alupent Syrup) to treat
bronchospasm, it thus relieves the
effects of asthma, emphysema and
chronic bronchitis. In every form
of Alupent, the active constituent
is the BETA-RECEPTOR STIMULANT
orciprenaline sulphate.
▲/◆ side-effects/warning: *see*
ORCIPRENALINE.

**Alupram** (*Steinhard*) is a
proprietary ANXIOLYTIC and
SKELETAL MUSCLE RELAXANT,
available only on prescription.
Produced for both purposes in the
form of tablets (in three
strengths), Alupram is a
preparation of the
BENZODIAZEPINE diazepam.
▲/◆ side-effects/warning: *see*
DIAZEPAM.

**Aluzine** (*Steinhard*) is a
proprietary DIURETIC drug,
available only on prescription,
used to treat the accumulation of
fluids in the tissues (oedema),
particularly caused by kidney
failure. Produced in the form of
tablets (in three strengths),
Aluzine is a preparation of
frusemide.
▲/◆ side-effects/warning: *see*
FRUSEMIDE.

**alverine citrate** is an
ANTISPASMODIC drug used to treat
muscle spasm in both the
gastrointestinal tract (leading to
abdominal pain and constipation)
and the uterus or vagina (leading
to menstrual discomfort).
Administration is oral in the form
of capsules and soluble granules.
It is not recommended for
children.
◆ warning: alverine citrate
should not be administered to
patients who suffer from
paralytic ileus.
*Related articles:* NORMACOL;
SPASMONAL.

**amantadine hydrochloride** is an ANTIVIRAL agent used to prevent infection with the influenza A2 virus (but not other types of influenza virus) and in the treatment of shingles. Administration is oral in the form of capsules or as a dilute syrup.

▲ side-effects: there is commonly restlessness and inability to concentrate; there may also be dizziness and insomnia, gastrointestinal disturbances, swelling resulting from fluid retention in the tissues, and skin discoloration. A regular blood count is advisable.

✹ warning: amantadine should not be administered to patients who suffer from gastric ulcers or from epilepsy. It should be administered with caution to patients who suffer from heart, liver or kidney disease, psychosis, or long-term eczema; who are pregnant or lactating; who are in a state of confusion; or who are elderly. Withdrawal of treatment must be gradual.
*Related article:* MANTADINE.

**Ambaxin** (*Upjohn*) is a proprietary ANTIBIOTIC, available only on prescription, used to treat systemic bacterial infections and infections of the upper respiratory tract, the ear, nose and throat, and the urogenital tracts. Produced in the form of tablets, Ambaxin is a preparation of the broad-spectrum penicillin bacampicillin.

▲/✹ side-effects/warning: *see* BACAMPICILLIN.

**ambutonium bromide** is an ANTISPASMODIC drug used to assist in treating a peptic ulcer. Mildly ANTICHOLINERGIC too, it is administered orally in the form of a dilute suspension containing other antispasmodics.

▲ side-effects: there may be thirst and a constantly dry mouth, visual disturbances with sensitivity to light,

✹ warning: ambutonium bromide, like all anticholinergics, inhibits the secretions of the stomach, thus slowing the process of digestion, leading possibly to constipation. It should be administered with caution to patients who suffer from retention of urine, heart disease, or muscular disorders of the intestines, pressure within the eyeballs (glaucoma), an oscillating or irregular heartbeat, and/or difficulty in urinating.
*Related article:* ALUDROX.

**amethocaine hydrochloride** is a local ANAESTHETIC used in creams and in solution for topical application or instillation into the bladder, and in eye-drops for ophthalmic treatment. It is absorbed rapidly from mucous membrane surfaces.

▲ side-effects: rarely, there are hypersensitive reactions.

✹ warning: topical administration may cause initial stinging. It should be given with caution to patients with epilepsy, impaired cardiac conduction or respiratory damage, or with liver damage.
*Related article:* MINIMS AMETHOCAINE HYDROCHLORIDE; NOXYFLEX.

**Amfipen** (*Brocades*) is a proprietary ANTIBIOTIC, available only on prescription, used to treat systemic bacterial infections and infections of the upper respiratory tract, the ear, nose and throat, and the urogenital tracts. Produced in the form of capsules (in two strengths), as a powder for reconstitution, as a syrup (in two strengths, under the trade name Amfipen Syrup), and in vials for injection (in two strengths, under the name Amfipen Injection), Amfipen is a preparation of the broad-spectrum penicillin ampicillin.

▲/✱ side-effects/warning: see
AMPICILLIN.

**amikacin** is an ANTIBIOTIC drug
(of the aminoglycoside family),
used to treat several serious
bacterial infections, particularly
those due to gram-negative
organisms that prove to be
resistant to the more generally
used aminoglycosides GENTAMICIN
and TOBRAMYCIN. Administration
is by intramuscular or intravenous injection or infusion.
▲ side-effects: extended and/or
high dosage may cause
irreversible deafness;
temporary kidney malfunction
may occur.
✱ warning: amikacin should not
be administered to patients
who are pregnant (because the
drug can cross the placenta),
and should be administered
with caution to patients with
impaired function of the
kidney. Careful monitoring for
toxicity is advisable during
treatment.

**Amikin** (*Bristol-Myers*) is a
proprietary preparation of the
aminoglycoside ANTIBIOTIC
amikacin, available only on
prescription, used to treat several
serious bacterial infections,
particularly those that prove to
be resistant to the more generally
used aminoglycoside GENTAMICIN.
Amikin is produced in vials for
injection or infusion (as amikacin
sulphate) in two strengths.
▲/✱ side-effects/warning: see
AMIKACIN.

**Amilco** (*Norton*) is a proprietary,
potassium-sparing DIURETIC drug,
available only on prescription,
used to treat oedema associated
with congestive heart failure,
high blood pressure (see
ANTIHYPERTENSIVE) and cirrhosis
of the liver. Produced in the form
of tablets, it represents a
compound of the weak but

catalytic diuretic AMILORIDE
hydrochloride together with the
THIAZIDE hydrochlorothiazide.
▲/✱ side-effects/warning: see
HYDROCHLOROTHIAZIDE.

**amiloride** is a mild DIURETIC drug
that causes the retention of
potassium (it is potassium-
sparing) and is thus commonly
used in combination with other
diuretics – such as the THIAZIDES –
which normally cause a loss of
potassium from the body. It is
then used particularly to treat the
accumulation of fluids in the
tissues (oedema).
▲ side-effects: there may be skin
rashes. Some patients become
confused.
✱ warning: amiloride should not
be administered to patients
who have high blood potassium
levels or who are taking
potassium supplements; it
should be administered with
caution to patients who suffer
from cirrhosis of the liver or
impaired kidney function, are
diabetic, or are pregnant.
*Related articles:* AMILCO;
FRUMIL; KALTEN; MIDAMOR;
MODURET 25; MODURETIC;
NAVISPARE; NORMETIC.

**Aminex** (*Cow & Gate*) is a brand of
non-prescription, lactose- and
sucrose-free biscuits intended for
consumption by patients suffering
from lactose or sucrose
intolerance, amino-acid
abnormalities (such as
phenylketonuria), kidney failure,
or cirrhosis of the liver. Mostly
carbohydrate, the biscuits
contain a small proportion of fat,
and less than 1% of protein.

**aminobenzoic acid** is an unusual
drug, sometimes classed as one of
the VITAMIN B complex, that helps
to protect the skin from
ultraviolet radiation. For this
reason, aminobenzoic acid is a
constituent in many suntan

lotions, but also in some barrier preparations to ward off the effects of repeated radiotherapy. Administration is topical, in the form of creams and lotions.

⊛ warning: protection is temporary, and creams and lotions must be reapplied every so often. Some patients are in any case more sensitive to ultraviolet radiation than others.
*Related articles:* COPPERTONE SUPERSHADE 15; DELIAL 10; PIZ BUIN; ROC TOTAL SUNBLOCK; SPECTRABAN.

**Aminofusin L600** (*Merck*) is a proprietary form of nutrition for intravenous infusion into patients who are unable to take in food via the alimentary canal. Available only on prescription, it contains amino acids, the sugar-substitute sorbitol, vitamins and electrolytes.

**Aminofusin L1000** (*Merck*) is the same as AMINOFUSIN L600 with the addition of ethanol (ethyl alcohol).

**Aminofusin L Forte** (*Merck*) is much like AMINOFUSIN L600 but contains more amino acids, vitamins and electrolytes, but no sorbitol.

**aminoglutethimide** is a drug used to treat advanced breast cancer in women who have passed the menopause or had both ovaries removed. It may also be used to palliate the effects of advanced cancer of the prostate gland in men. Administration is oral in the form of tablets.

▲ side-effects: commonly there is drowsiness; there may even be a rash resembling measles.

⊛ warning: simultaneous corticosteroid treatment is essential to replace hormones absent. Despite initial symptoms of toxicity, dosage

must be progressively increased over 2 to 4 weeks.
*Related article:* ORIMETEN.

**Aminogran** (*Allen & Hanburys*) is a proprietary, non-prescription form of nutritional supplement for patients with amino-acid abnormalities (such as phenylketonuria). It comprises a food supplement containing all essential amino acids except for phenylalanine. There is in addition a mineral mixture – intended to be combined with the food supplement, or for use with independent synthetic diets – containing all necessary minerals.

**aminophylline** is a BRONCHODILATOR used mostly in sustained-release forms of administration, generally to treat moderate but chronic asthma over periods of around 12 hours at a time. It can alternatively be used to treat cardiac, pulmonary or renal oedema, and angina pectoris. Administration is usually oral in the form of tablets, but it may be by injection. It is not recommended for children.

▲ side-effects: there may be nausea and gastrointestinal disturbances, an increase or irregularity in the heartbeat, and/or insomnia.

⊛ warning: treatment at first should be gradually progressive in the quantity administered. Aminophylline should be administered with caution to patients who suffer from heart or liver disease, or from peptic ulcer; or who are pregnant or lactating.
*Related articles:* PECRAM; PHYLLOCONTIN CONTINUS; THEODROX.

**Aminoplasmal** (*Braun*) is a proprietary form of nutrition for intravenous infusion into patients who are unable to take in food via the alimentary canal. Available only on prescription, it contains amino acids and electrolytes. Various strengths are produced, differentiated by suffixes to the trade name: Ped, L5 and L10.

**Aminoplex 12** (*Geistlich*) is a proprietary form of nutrition for intravenous infusion into patients who are unable to take in food via the alimentary canal. Available only on prescription, it contains amino acids, malic acid and electrolytes. Another version, Aminoplex 5, additionally contains the sugar-substitute sorbitol and ethanol (ethyl alcohol); a third version, Aminoplex 14, additionally contains vitamins.

**amiodarone** is a potentially toxic drug used to treat severe irregularity of the heartbeat, especially in cases where for one reason or another alternative drugs cannot be used. It is also used in the treatment of angina pectoris. Administration is oral in the form of tablets, or by injection.
▲ side-effects: deposits on the cornea of the eyes and associated sensitivity to light are inevitable, but reversible on withdrawal of treatment. There may be other neurological effects.
✪ warning: amiodarone should not be administered to patients who suffer from very slow heartbeat, thyroid dysfunction, or shock; or who are pregnant or lactating. Dosage in each individual case should be the minimum to achieve the desired results. There should be regular testing of thyroid, liver and pulmonary function.
*Related article:* CORDARONE X.

**amitriptyline** is an ANTI-DEPRESSANT drug that also has sedative properties. The sedation may be a benefit to agitated or

violent patients, or to those who care for them. In contrast to the treatment of depressive illness, however, the drug may be used to prevent bed-wetting at night in youngsters. Administration is oral in the form of tablets, capsules or a dilute mixture. It is not recommended for young children.
▲ side-effects: common effects include loss of intricacy in movement or thought, dry mouth and blurred vision; there may also be difficulty in urinating, sweating and irregular heartbeat, behavioural disturbances, a rash, a state of confusion, and/or a loss of libido. Rarely, there are also blood deficiencies.
✪ warning: amitriptyline should not be administered to patients who suffer from heart disease or psychosis; it should be administered with caution to patients who suffer from diabetes, epilepsy, liver or thyroid disease, glaucoma or urinary retention; or who are pregnant or lactating. Withdrawal of treatment must be gradual.
*Related articles:* DOMICAL; ELAVIL; LENTIZOL; TRYPTIZOL.

**amlodipine** is a CALCIUM ANTAGONIST drug, used as an ANTIHYPERTENSIVE to treat raised blood pressure (hypertension) and to prevent angina (heart pain). It is available in the form of tablets.
▲ side-effects: these include flushing, dizziness, headache, palpitations, elevated heart rate, oedema, and fatigue.
✪ warning: the dose should be reduced when treating patients with impaired liver or kidney function, and avoided in pregnancy or in cases with some types of heart defect.
*Related article:* ISTIN.

**ammonia and ipecacuanha** is a non-proprietary formulation intended as an EXPECTORANT to promote the expulsion of excess bronchial secretions. It is not available as a mixture from the National Health Service. In effect, the mixture is a dilute solution of two potential EMETICS.

**ammonium chloride** is an EMETIC that in dilute solution may be used instead as a constituent of expectorant mixtures (sometimes in combination with opiates as cough suppressants). But it is more often for its acidifying properties that ammonium chloride is used: either to rectify the body's acid/alkali balance in a patient who is dehydrated, or for the therapeutic acidification of the urine.
*Related articles:* BENILYN EXPECTORANT; HISTALIX.

**amodiaquine** is an ANTIMALARIAL drug used as one of the major weapons against tertian malaria; it is sometimes also used to treat leprosy or rheumatoid arthritis. Administration is oral in the form of tablets.
▲ side-effects: there may be nausea, vomiting and headache; some patients enter a state of lethargy. Blood disorders may occur. Prolonged treatment may lead to deposits on the cornea of the eyes and a greyish discoloration of the skin, fingernails and palate.
● warning: amodiaquine should be administered with caution to patients who suffer from impaired liver or kidney function, porphyria, or psoriasis. Regular ophthalmic examination is recommended.

*amoebicidal* drugs treat infection by the microscopic protozoan organisms known as amoebae, which cause such

disorders as amoebic dysentery and hepatic amoebiasis. Best-known and most-used is metronidazole, both for acute intestinal forms of infection (amoebic dysentery) and amoebic abscesses of the liver. An alternative amoebicidal drug for this treatment is tinidazole. In cases in which amoebic cysts are being passed on defecation, but there are no further symptoms in the patient, the drug of choice is diloxanide furoate.
▲/● side-effects/warning: *see* DILOXANIDE FUROATE; METRONIDAZOLE; TINIDAZOLE.
*Related articles:* AVLOCLOR; FLAGYL; FLAGYL S; FURAMIDE; METROLYL; NIDAZOL; ZADSTAT.

**amoxapine** is a TRICYCLIC ANTIDEPRESSANT drug used to treat depressive illness.
▲ side-effects: common effects include loss of intricacy of thought or in movement (tardive dyskinesia), dry mouth and blurred vision; there may also be difficulty in urinating, sweating and irregular heartbeat, behavioural disturbances, rashes, a state of confusion, menstrual irregularities, breast enlargement, and change in libido. Rarely, there are also blood deficiencies.
● warning: amoxapine should not be administered to patients who suffer from heart disease or psychosis; it should be administered with caution to patients who suffer from diabetes, epilepsy, liver or thyroid disease, glaucoma or urinary retention; or who are pregnant or lactating. Withdrawal of treatment must be gradual.
*Related article:* ASENDIS.

**Amoxil** (*Bencard*) is a proprietary ANTIBIOTIC, available only on prescription, used to treat systemic bacterial infections and infections of the upper respiratory tract, of the ear, nose and throat, and of the urogenital tracts; it is sometimes used also to treat typhoid fever. Produced in the form of capsules (in two strengths), as sugar-free, soluble (dispersible) tablets, as a syrup for dilution (in two strengths; the potency of the syrup once diluted is retained for 14 days), as a suspension for children, in the form of powder in sachets, as a sugar-free powder in sachets, and as a powder in vials for reconstitution as a medium for injection. Amoxil is a preparation of the broad-spectrum PENICILLIN amoxycillin.

▲/● side-effects/warning: *see* AMOXYCILLIN.

**amoxycillin** is a broad-spectrum penicillin-type ANTIBIOTIC, closely related to AMPICILLIN. Readily absorbed orally, it is used to treat many infections, especially infections of the urogenital tracts, the upper respiratory tract, or the middle ear. It is also sometimes used to treat typhoid fever or to prevent infection following dental surgery. Administration is oral in the form of capsules or liquids, or by injection.

▲ side-effects: there may be sensitivity reactions such as rashes, high temperature and joint pain. Allergic patients may suffer anaphylactic shock. The most common side-effect, however, is diarrhoea.

● warning: amoxycillin should not be administered to patients who are known to be allergic to penicillin-type antibiotics; it should be administered with caution to those with impaired kidney function.
*Related articles:* ALMODAN; AMOXIL; AUGMENTIN.

**amphotericin** is a broad-spectrum ANTIFUNGAL agent used particularly to treat infection by fungal organisms. It can be given by infusion, and is extremely important in the treatment of systemic fungal infections and is active against almost all fungi and yeasts. However, it is a toxic drug and side-effects are common. Administration is oral in the form of tablets, lozenges or liquids, or by infusion.

▲ side-effects: treatment by infusion may cause nausea, vomiting, severe weight loss and ringing in the ears (tinnitus); some patients experience a marked reduction in blood potassium. Prolonged or high dosage may cause kidney damage.

● warning: amphotericin should not be administered to patients who are already undergoing drug treatment that may affect kidney function. During treatment by infusion, tests on kidney function are essential; the site of injection must be changed frequently.
*Related articles:* FUNGILIN; FUNGIZONE.

**ampicillin** is a broad-spectrum, penicillin-type ANTIBIOTIC, orally absorbed – although absorption is reduced by the presence of food in the stomach or intestines – and used to treat many infections and especially infections of the urogenital tracts, of the upper respiratory tract, or of the middle ear. However, many bacteria have over the past two decades become resistant to ampicillin. Administration is oral in the form of capsules or liquids, or by injection.

▲ side-effects: there may be sensitivity reactions such as rashes (invariably in patients suffering from glandular fever), high temperature and joint pain. Allergic patients may

**A**

suffer anaphylactic shock. The most common side-effect, however, is diarrhoea.

✚ warning: ampicillin should not be administered to patients who are known to be allergic to penicillin-type antibiotics; in case anaphylactic shock ensues it should be administered with caution to those with impaired kidney function.

*Related articles:* AMPICLOX; AMPIFEN; BRITCIN; DICAPEN; FLU-AMP; MAGNAPEN; PENBRITIN; VIDOPEN.

**Ampiclox** (*Beecham*) is a proprietary ANTIBIOTIC, available only on prescription, used to treat systemic bacterial infections and infections of the upper respiratory tract, of the ear, nose and throat, and of the urogenital tracts. Produced in vials for injection, Ampiclox is a compound preparation of the broad-spectrum penicillinase-sensitive ampicillin and the penicillinase-resistant cloxacillin.

▲/✚ side-effects/warning: *see* AMPICILLIN; CLOXACILLIN.

**amsacrine** is a synthetic ANTICANCER agent, which has the effect of halting the production of new, potentially cancerous cells. It is used specifically in the treatment of acute leukaemia in adults. Administration is by infusion.

▲ side-effects: nausea and vomiting, with hair loss, is common. The drug is a skin irritant. Rarely, patients have suffered convulsions.

✚ warning: amsacrine should be administered with caution to patients with heart disease, liver or kidney damage, or who are pregnant or elderly. Blood monitoring, particularly in relation to potassium levels, is essential. The capacity of the bone-marrow to produce blood

cells is depressed.
*Related article:* AMSIDINE.

**Amsidine** (*Parke-Davis*) is a proprietary ANTICANCER drug, available only on prescription, used to treat certain forms of leukaemia. It works by preventing the production of new, potentially cancerous cells. Produced in the form of a concentrate for intravenous infusion, generally for hospital use only, Amsidine is a preparation of amsacrine.

▲/✚ side-effects/warning: *see* AMSACRINE.

**amylobarbitone** is a BARBITURATE, used only when absolutely necessary as a HYPNOTIC to treat severe and intractable insomnia. Administration is oral in the form of tablets and capsules, or (as amylobarbitone sodium) by injection. Proprietary forms are all on the controlled drugs list.

▲ side-effects: concentration and the speed of movement and thought are affected. There may be drowsiness, dizziness and shallow breathing, with headache. Some patients experience hypersensitivity reactions. (The drug enhances the effects of alcohol consumption.)

✚ warning: amylobarbitone should not be administered to patients whose insomnia is caused by pain, who have porphyria, who are pregnant or lactating, who are elderly or debilitated, or who have a history of drug (including alcohol) abuse. It should be administered with caution to those with kidney, liver or lung disease. Use of the drug should be avoided as far as possible. Repeated doses are cumulative in effect, and may lead to real sedation; abrupt withdrawal of treatment, on the other hand,

may cause serious withdrawal symptoms. Tolerance and dependence (addiction) occur readily.
*Related articles:* AMYTAL; SODIUM AMYTAL; TUINAL.

**Amytal** (*Lilly*) is a proprietary HYPNOTIC drug, a BARBITURATE, and on the controlled drugs list; it is used to treat persistent and intractable insomnia. A dangerous and potentially addictive drug, it is produced in the form of tablets (in five strengths) and is a preparation of amylobarbitone. It is not recommended for children.
▲/✚ side-effects/warning: *see* AMYLOBARBITONE.

**Anacal** (*Panpharma*) is a proprietary compound CORTICOSTEROID preparation, available only on prescription, used in topical application to treat inflammation of the colon and rectum, haemorrhoids and related conditions. Produced in the form of rectal ointment and as anal suppositories, Anacal is a preparation that includes the steroid prednisolone and the antiseptic hexachlorophane. It is not recommended for children aged under 7 years.
▲/✚ side-effects/warning: *see* HEXACHLOROPHANE; PREDNISOLONE.

**Anadin** (*Whitehall Laboratories*) is a proprietory, non-prescription compound, non-narcotic ANALGESIC produced in the form of tablets and as capsules. Anadin is a preparation of aspirin, caffeine and quinine sulphate.
▲/✚ side-effects/warning: *see* ASPIRIN; CAFFEINE; QUININE.

**Anadin Extra** (*Whitehall Laboratories*) is a proprietory, non-prescription compound, non-narcotic ANALGESIC produced in the form of tablets and as

capsules. Anadin is a preparation of aspirin, caffeine and paracetamol.
▲/✚ side-effects/warning: *see* ASPIRIN; CAFFEINE; PARACETOMOL.

\***anaesthetic** is a drug that reduces sensation; such drugs affect either a specific local area – a local anaesthetic – or the whole body with loss of conciousness – a general anaesthetic.
　The drug used to induce general anaesthesia is generally different from the drug or drugs used to continue it. Frequently used drugs for the induction of anaesthesia include THIOPENTONE SODIUM and ETOMIDATE. For the continuation of anaesthesia, common drugs include oxygen-nitrous oxide mixtures and HALOTHANE. Prior to induction, a patient is usually given a premedication, a drug to calm the nerves and to promote diuresis (passing of water), an hour or so before an operation is due. Such premedications include OPIATES and BENZODIAZEPINES. Other drugs in addition to general anaesthetics are used during surgery; for most internal surgery a SKELETAL MUSCLE RELAXANT, or perhaps a narcotic ANALGESIC, is also required.
　Local anaesthetics are injected or absorbed in the area of the body where they are intended to take effect; they work by temporarily impairing the functioning of local nerves. Frequently used local anaesthetics include LIGNOCAINE, which is often used in dental surgery. One form of local anaesthesia, known as epidural anaesthesia, is produced by injection of anaesthetic into the membranes surrounding the spinal cord, which causes numbness from the abdomen down. Epidurals are used mainly during childbirth. Common

epidural anaesthetics are
LIGNOCAINE and BUPIVACAINE
HYDROCHLORIDE.

**Anaflex** (*Geistlich*) is a
proprietary, non-prescription
ANTIMICROBIAL preparation,
applied topically to treat minor
skin infections. Produced in the
form of a water-miscible cream.
Anaflex is a preparation of the
drug POLYNOXYLIN.

**Anafranil** (*Geigy*) is a proprietary
ANTIDEPRESSANT, available only
on prescription, used to relieve
the symptoms of depressive illness
and as an additional treatment in
phobic and obsessional states. It
is also used to treat attacks of
muscular weakness that occur in
narcolepsy. Produced in the form
of capsules (in three strengths), as
sustained-release tablets (under
the name Afranil SR), as a syrup
(the potency of the dilute syrup
lasts for 7 days), and in ampoules
for injection, Anafranil is a
preparation of the tricyclic
antidepressant clomipramine
hydrochloride. None of these
preparations is recommended for
children.

▲/● side-effects/warning: *see*
CLOMIPRAMINE
HYDROCHLORIDE.

*__analgesic__ is a drug that relieves
pain. Because pain is a subjective
experience that can arise from
many causes, there are many
ways that drugs can be used to
relieve it. However, the term
analgesic is best restricted to two
main classes of drug.
First, NARCOTIC analgesics are
drugs such as MORPHINE, which
have powerful actions on the
central nervous system and alter
the perception of pain. Because of
the numerous possible side-
effects, the most important of
which is drug dependence
(habituation), this class is usually
used under medical supervision,

and normally the drugs are only
available on prescription. Other
notable side-effects commonly
include depression of respiration,
nausea and sometimes
hypotension, constipation,
inhibition of coughing, and
constriction of the pupils. Other
members of this class include
HEROIN, PENTAZOCINE,
METHADONE, PETHIDINE and
CODEINE, in descending order
of potency with respect to
their ability to deal with severe
pain.
Second, non-narcotic
analgesics are drugs such as
ASPIRIN, which have no serious
tendency to produce dependence,
but are by no means free of side-
effects. This class is referred to by
many names, including weak
analgesics and, in medical circles,
NSAIDs (non-steroidal anti-
inflammatory drugs). The latter
term refers to the valuable ANTI-
INFLAMMATORY action of some
members of the class (a property
shared with the CORTICO-
STEROIDS). This class of drug is
used for a variety of purposes,
ranging from mild aches and
pains (at normal dosage) to the
treatment of rheumatoid arthritis
(at higher dosage). PARACETAMOL
does not have strong anti-
inflammatory actions, but, as with
other drugs in this class, has the
valuable ability to lower raised
body temperature (ANTIPYRETIC
action). In spite of these
important actions and uses, all
members of the class have side-
effects of concern, which for
aspirin-like drugs include
gastrointestinal upsets ranging
from dyspepsia to serious
haemorrhage. Other examples of
drugs of this class include
IBUPROFEN and INDOMETHACIN.
Often drugs in this class are used
in combination with each other
(e.g. paracetamol and codeine) or
with drugs of other classes (e.g.
caffeine).

28

Apart from these two main classes, there are other drugs that are sometimes referred to as analgesics because of their ability to relieve pain (e.g. local anaesthetics in the USA). To achieve the degree of pain relief necessary for major surgical operations general ANAESTHETICS are used, but often in conjunction with narcotic analgesics.

**Anapolon 50** (*Syntex*) is a proprietary form of the anabolic STEROID oxymetholone, available only on prescription, used to build up the body following major surgery or long-term debilitating disease, or to treat osteoporosis (brittle bones). Sometimes administered also to treat sex-hormone-linked cancers, it is additionally used in the treatment of certain forms of anaemia, although how it works in this respect – and even whether it works – remains the subject of some debate: variations in patient response are wide. It is produced in the form of tablets.

▲/● side-effects/warning: *see* OXYMETHOLONE.

**ancrod** is an effective ANTICOAGULANT derived from an enzyme that is a constituent of the venom of the Malaysian pit-viper. It works by breaking down the protein fibrinogen, which is necessary for the formation of blood clots. The effects may be experienced for between 12 and 24 hours (and in some cases an antidote may have to be administered too – although that may also cause sensitivity problems). Its therapeutic use is in the treatment of deep-vein thrombosis (blood clots), especially the sort that occur following surgery, and it is occasionally used to prevent thrombosis. Administration is by injection.

▲ side-effects: the major side-effects are bleeding and sensitivity/allergic reactions. Brittle bones and hair loss may result from prolonged use.

● warning: ancrod should not be administered to patients who are pregnant; it should be administered with extreme caution to those with haemophilia or other bleeding disorders (such as ulcers), high blood pressure (hypertension), severe liver disease, or who have had recent surgery (especially of the eye or nervous system). The antidote should be on hand in case of emergency, preferably with fresh (frozen) plasma as back-up. Initial infusion must be administered slowly, and during treatment there must be constant blood monitoring. *Related article:* ARVIN.

**Andrews** (*Sterling Health*) is a proprietary, non-prescription ANTACID, produced in the form of a powder. By dissolving various amounts in water, the solution may also be used as a laxative or simply a refreshing drink. Andrews contains sodium bicarbonate and magnesium sulphate.

▲/● side-effects/warning: *see* MAGNESIUM SULPHATE; SODIUM BICARBONATE.

**Androcur** (*Schering*) is a proprietary hormonal drug that acts as a male sex HORMONE antagonist. Available only on prescription, it is used to treat severe hypersexuality and sexual deviation in men. Produced in the form of tablets, Androcur is a preparation of the anti-androgen cyproterone acetate.

▲/● side-effects/warning: *see* CYPROTERONE ACETATE.

**androgens** are male sex HORMONES that stimulate the development of male sex organs and male secondary sexual characteristics. In men they are produced primarily by the testes in the form of testosterone and androsterone. However in both men and women, androgens are also produced by the adrenal glands, and in women small quantities are also secreted by the ovaries. An excessive amount in women causes masculinization. There are also synthetic androgens. Therapeutically, androgens are administered to make up hormonal deficiency, and may also be used to treat sex-hormone-linked cancers, such as breast cancer in women.

▲ side-effects: there is salt and water retention, with increased bone growth. In women there is masculinization.

◆ warning: androgens should not be administered to patients who suffer from male-sex-hormone-linked cancers, such as cancer of the prostate gland, or who are pregnant.
*see* TESTOSTERONE.

**Andursil** (*Geigy*) is a proprietary non-prescription compound ANTACID, which is not available from the National Health Service. Used to treat severe indigestion, heartburn, gastric and peptic ulcers, and hiatus hernia, it is produced in the form of a sugar-free suspension representing a preparation of ALUMINIUM HYDROXIDE, MAGNESIUM HYDROXIDE, MAGNESIUM CARBONATE and the antifoaming agent DIMETHICONE. Tablets containing the same constituents but without magnesium hydroxide are also available. Neither of these preparations is recommended for children.

**Anectine** (*Calmic*) is a proprietary MUSCLE RELAXANT, available only on prescription, which has an effect for only 5 minutes. It is used to relax muscles during surgical anaesthesia and this facilitates some surgical procedures (e.g. inserting a ventilator into the windpipe). Produced in ampoules for injection, Anectine is a preparation of suxamethonium chloride.
▲/◆ side-effects/warning: *see* SUXAMETHONIUM CHLORIDE.

**Anethaine** (*Evans*) is a proprietary, non-prescription local ANAESTHETIC, used to treat painful skin conditions and itching. Produced in the form of a water-miscible cream for topical application, Anethaine is a preparation of amethocaine hydrochloride.
▲/◆ side-effects/warning: *see* AMETHOCAINE.

**Aneurone** (*Philip Harris*) is a proprietary mixture prescribed principally to stimulate the appetite. Available on prescription only to private patients, it is a syrup preparation of STRYCHNINE hydrochloride, THIAMINE hydrochloride (vitamin $B_1$), CAFFEINE, compound GENTIAN infusion and SODIUM ACID PHOSPHATE for dilution (the potency of the syrup once diluted is retained for 14 days).

**Anexate** (*Roche*) is a BENZODIAZEPINE antagonist used to reverse the central sedative effects of benzodiazepines in anaesthesia, intensive care and diagnostic procedures. Administration is by slow intravenous infusion.
▲/◆ side-effects/warning: *see* FLUMAZENIL.

**Angettes 75** (*Bristol-Myers*) is a proprietary preparation of the ANTI-INFLAMMATORY, non-narcotic ANALGESIC drug ASPIRIN, used here to reduce blood platelet adhesion, and thus formation of blood clots (thrombi). It is particularly indicated after problems relating to blocked blood vessels, such as myocardial infarction. Angettes is available without prescription, in the form of tablets.

▲/✛ side-effects/warning: *see* ASPIRIN.

**Angilol** (*DDSA Pharmaceuticals*) is a proprietary ANTI-HYPERTENSIVE BETA-BLOCKER, available only on prescription, used not only to treat high blood pressure (hypertension), but also to relieve angina pectoris (heart pain) and to slow and/or regularize the heartbeat in order to prevent a recurrent heart attack. The drug may also be used to treat an excess of thyroid hormones in the bloodstream (thyrotoxicosis) or to try to prevent migraine attacks. Produced in the form of tablets (in four strengths), Angilol is a preparation of the beta-blocker propranolol hydrochloride.

▲/✛ side-effects/warning: *see* PROPRANOLOL.

**Anhydrol Forte** (*Dermal*) is a proprietary, medicated antiperspirant, available only on prescription, used to treat abnormally heavy sweating (hyperhydrosis) of the armpits, hands and feet. Produced in a roll-on bottle, Anhydrol Forte is a 20% solution of aluminium chloride hexahydrate. The solution is inflammable so care should be taken when it is used.

▲/✛ side-effects/warning: *see* ALUMINIUM CHLORIDE.

**Anodesyn** (*Crookes Products*) is a proprietary, non-prescription OINTMENT used to soothe and treat haemorrhoids and anal itching. Also available in the form of anal suppositories, Anodesyn is a compound preparation that includes the SYMPATHOMIMETIC ephedrine hydrochloride and the local

ANAESTHETIC lignocaine hydrochloride. Prolonged use should be avoided.

▲/✛ side-effects/warning: *see* EPHEDRINE HYDROCHLORIDE; LIGNOCAINE.

**Anquil** (*Janssen*) is a proprietary ANTIPSYCHOTIC drug, available only on prescription, used to treat psychosis (especially schizophrenia) and as a major TRANQUILLIZER in patients undergoing behavioural disturbance. It is used to treat deviant and antisocial sexual behaviour, and it may also be used in the short term to treat severe anxiety (especially in the case of terminal disease) or to treat an intractable hiccup. Produced in the form of tablets, Anquil is a preparation of the powerful drug benperidol. It is not recommended for children.

▲/✛ side-effects/warning: *see* BENPERIDOL.

**Antabuse** (*CP Pharmaceuticals*) is a proprietary preparation of the drug disulfiram, available only on prescription. It is used as an adjunct in the treatment of alcoholism because, in combination with the consumption of even small quantities of alcohol, it gives rise to unpleasant reactions – such as flushing, headache, palpitations, nausea and vomiting. Produced in the form of tablets, Antabuse is not recommended for children.

▲/✛ side-effects/warning: *see* DISULFIRAM.

**\*antacid** is a drug that effectively neutralizes the hydrochloric acid that the stomach produces as a means of digestion. Much of indigestion is caused by an excessive quantity of acids in the stomach (particularly after alcohol consumption), and simple indigestion can be complicated by the effects of stomach acids on peptic ulcers or hernias. Antacids thus reduce acidity, but may themselves cause flatulence or diarrhoea as side-effects. Antacids may also impair the absorption of other drugs. Most-used and best-known antacids include ALUMINIUM HYDROXIDE, SODIUM BICARBONATE, MAGNESIUM HYDROXIDE and CALCIUM CARBONATE.

**antazoline** is an ANTIHISTAMINE used to treat topical allergic conditions. It is thus used in combination with other drugs to treat allergic skin irritations, stings and bites, and in combination with other antihistamines to relieve the symptoms of allergic conjunctivitis. Administration is in the form of a cream or as eye-drops. *Related articles:* OTRIVINE-ANTISTIN; R.B.C.; VASOCON A.

**Antepar** (*Wellcome*) is a proprietary, non-prescription ANTHELMINTIC drug used to treat infestation by threadworms or roundworms. A laxative administered simultaneously is often expedient. Produced in the form of tablets and as an elixir for dilution (the potency of the elixir once diluted is retained for 14 days), Antepar is a preparation of piperazine hydrate.
▲/✿ side-effects/warning: *see* PIPERAZINE.

**Antepsin** (*Ayerst*) is a proprietary drug used to promote the healing of peptic ulcers in the stomach and duodenum. Available only on prescription, it is thought to work by forming a protective coating over an ulcer under which the ulcer is then able to heal. It is also used in the treatment of acid stomach. Produced in the form of tablets, and as a suspension, Antepsin is a preparation of the aluminium sucrose sulphate sucralfate.

▲/✿ side-effects/warning: *see* SUCRALFATE.

\***anthelmintic drugs** are used to treat infections by parasitic organisms of the helminth (worm) family. The threadworm, the roundworm and the tapeworm are the most common helminths responsible for infection in the UK. In warmer underdeveloped countries illness caused by helminths, e.g. hookworms (anaemia and debilitation), schistosomes (bilharzia) and filaria (elephantiasis and onchocerciasis) is a major health problem. Most worms infest the intestines; diagnosis often corresponds to evidence of their presence as shown in the faeces. Drugs can then be administered, and the worms are killed or anaesthetized and excreted in the normal way. Complications arise if the worms migrate within the body, in which case in order to make the environment in the body untenable for the worms, the treatment becomes severely unpleasant for the patient. In the case of threadworms, medication should be combined with hygienic measures (e.g. short finger-nails) and the whole family should be treated. Among the most useful and best-known anthelmintics are PIPERAZINE, MEBENDAZOLE, PRAZIQUANTEL, DIETHYLCARBAMAZINE and THIABENDAZOLE.

**Anthisan** (*May & Baker*) is a proprietary, non-prescription ANTIHISTAMINE, used to treat allergic conditions (such as hay fever) and symptoms of itching and rashes. Produced in the form of tablets and as a cream, Anthisan is a preparation of mepyramine maleate.
▲/✿ side-effects/warning: *see* MEPYRAMINE.

**Anthranol** (*Stiefel*) is a proprietary antipsoriatic,

available only on prescription, used to treat serious, non-infective skin inflammation, in particular psoriasis. Produced in the form of an ointment (in three strengths), Anthranol is a preparation of the powerful drug dithranol with salicylic acid.

▲/⊕ side-effects/warning: see DITHRANOL; SALICYLIC ACID.

**anthrax vaccine** is generally required only by patients who are exposed to anthrax-infected hides and acarcasses, or who handle imported bonemeal, fishmeal and feedstuffs. Available only on prescription, this inactivated bacterial vaccine consists of a suspension administered by injection in three doses over 9 weeks followed by another shot after 6 months; thereafter there may be an annual booster if necessary.

**\*anti-allergic** drugs relieve the symptoms of allergic sensitivity to specific substances. These substances may be endogenous (in the patients body), or they may be exogenous (present in the environment). Because allergic reactions generally cause the internal release of histamine, the most effective drugs for the purpose are the ANTIHISTAMINES. However, some allergic reactions include inflammatory symptoms, and in such cases the CORTICOSTEROIDS may afford useful relief. How certain corticosteroids may relieve asthmatic symptoms is not fully understood, but the effect may be due to the reduction of inflammatory responses in the lining of the airways. There are many other types of drugs that also treat the symptoms of asthma, including the SYMPATHOMIMETICS and the ANTICHOLINERGIC or xanthine BRONCHODILATORS. In allergic emergencies – anaphylactic shock

– blood pressure is severely lowered and initial treatment is generally an injection of ADRENALINE (which may have to be repeated), followed by intravenous infusion of an antihistamine (such as CHLORPHENIRAMINE). SODIUM CROMOGLYCATE is an anti-allergic drug that prevents the release of histamine from cells, unlike antihistamines which antagonize histamine.

**\*anti-androgens** are a class of drugs that are HORMONE ANTAGONIST, usually acting to prevent the action of the hormone at its receptors by competing for that site, though sometimes acting to prevent release of the hormones. Examples include: AMINOGLUTETHIMIDE; FLUTAMIDE.

**\*antiarrhythmic** drugs strengthen and regularize a heartbeat that has become unsteady and is not showing its usual patter of activity. But because there are many ways in which the heartbeat can falter – atrial tachycardia, ventricular tachycardia, atrial flutter or fibrillation, and the severe heartbeat irregularity that may follow a heart attack (myocardial infarction), for example – there is a variety of drugs available, each for a fairly specific use. Best-known and most used antiarrhythmic drugs include DIGOXIN (a CARDIAC GLYCOSIDE), VERAPAMIL (a CALCIUM ANTAGONIST) and LIGNOCAINE (a local ANAESTHETIC, especially used for ventricular arrhythmia); also extremely effective are the BETA-BLOCKERS (which also treat high blood pressure and angina pectoris).

**\*anti-asthmatic** drugs relieve the symptoms of bronchial asthma or prevent recurrent attacks. The symptoms of asthma include spasm of the muscles in the bronchial passages and breathing difficulties, so some anti-asthmatic drugs are BRONCHODILATORS and some are also SMOOTH MUSCLE RELAXANTS. The SYMPATHOMIMETICS are drugs in common use, notable examples being SALBUTAMOL and TERBUTALINE. In an emergency situation, CORTICOSTEROIDS may also be required to limit inflammatory responses in the mucous membranes of the air passages, and are being increasingly used by inhalation in the prevention of asthmatic attacks. But there are many other types of drugs used in the treatment of asthma. In the prevention of asthmatic attacks, regular dosage of SODIUM CROMOGLYCATE is the preferred therapy, although some patients use KETOTIFEN instead. ANTIHISTAMINES may also be used, although they are perhaps more useful in treating other allergic symptoms (such as hay fever or rashes).

see ANTI-ALLERGIC.

*antibacterial drugs have a selectively toxic action on bacteria. They can be used both topically, i.e. on the skin or the eye, to treat infections of superficial tissues or systemically, carried by the blood following absorbtion or injection, to the site of the infection. As bacteria are the largest and most diverse group of pathogenic micro-organisms, antibacterials form the major constituent group of ANTIBIOTICS.

*antibiotics are, strictly speaking, natural products secreted by micro-organisms into their environment where they inhibit the growth of competing micro-organisms of different species. But in common usage, and in this book, the term is applied to any

drug – natural or synthetic – that has a selectively toxic action on bacteria or similar non-nucleated, single-celled micro-organisms (including chlamydia, rickettsia and mycoplasma); such drugs have no effect on viruses. Most synthetic antibiotics are modelled on natural substances. When administered by an appropriate route, such as orally, by injection or by infusion, antibiotics kill infective bacteria (bactericidal action) or inhibit their growth (bacteriostatic action). The selectively toxic action on invading bacteria exploits differences between bacteria and their human host cells. Major target sites are the bacterial cell wall located outside the cell membrane (human cells have only a cell membrane), and the bacterial ribosome (the protein-synthesizing organelle within its cell), which is different in bacteria and in human cells. Antibiotics of the PENICILLIN and CEPHALOSPORIN families (collectively known as beta-lactam antibiotics) attack the bacterial cell wall, whereas aminoglycoside and TETRA-CYCLINE antibiotics attack the bacterial ribosomes. Viruses, which lack both cell walls and ribosomes, are therefore resistant to these and other similar antibiotics.

Because there is such a diversity of disease-causing (pathogenic) bacteria, it is not surprising that specific infections are best treated using specific antibiotics developed to combat them. But unfortunately, with the continuing widespread use of antibiotics, certain strains of common bacteria have developed resistance to antibiotics that were formerly effective against them. This is now a major problem. Another problem is the occurance of "superinfections", in which the use of a broad-spectrum antibiotic disturbs the normal, harmless bacterial population in the body as well as the pathogenic ones. In mild cases this may allow, for example, an existing but latent oral or vaginal thrush infection to become worse, or mild diarrhoea to develop. In rare cases the superinfection that develops is more serious than the disorder for which the antibiotic was administered.

*anticancer drugs are mostly CYTOTOXIC: they work by interfering one way or another with cell replication or production, so preventing the growth of new tissue. Inevitably, this means that normal cell production is also affected and thus there may be some severe side-effects. They are generally administered in combination in a series of treatments known collectively as chemotherapy. But there are other forms of anticancer therapy. In cases where the growth of a tumour is linked to the presence of a sex hormone (as with some cases of breast cancer or cancer of the prostate gland), treatment with sex hormones opposite to the patient's own sex can be extremely beneficial, although side-effects may be psychologically stressful. The CORTICOSTEROIDS PREDNISONE and PREDNISOLONE are also used as anticancer drugs in the treatment of the lymphatic cancer Hodgkin's disease and other forms of lymphoma, and may be helpful additionally in halting the progress of hormone-linked breast cancer.

*anticholinergic drugs inhibit the action, release or production of the substance acetylcholine (a NEUROTRANSMITTER), which plays an important part in the nervous system, and tends to relax smooth muscle, to reduce the secretion of saliva, digestive juices and sweat, and to dilate the pupil of the eye. They may thus be used as ANTISPASMODICS, in the treatment of parkinsonian symptoms or of peptic ulcers, and in ophthalmic examinations. However, use of such drugs is commonly accompanied by side-effects, including dry mouth, dry skin, blurred vision, an increased heart rate, constipation and difficulty in urinating. ATROPINE is an example of an anticholinergic drug.

*anticoagulants are agents that prevent the clotting of blood and disolve blood clots that have formed. The blood's own natural anticoagulant is HEPARIN, probably still the most effective anticoagulant known. Synthetic anticoagulants (such as WARFARIN, NICOUMALONE and PHENINDIONE) take longer to act and work by affecting clotting factors within the blood; they are thus less capable than heparin of breaking up clots that have already formed. Therapeutically, anticoagulants are used to prevent the formation of, and to treat blood clots in, conditions such as thrombosis and embolism, especially following surgery. They are also used to prevent blood clots in patients fitted with a heart pacemaker or with arteriosclerosis.

*anticonvulsant drugs prevent the onset of epileptic seizures or reduce their severity if they do occur. The best-known and most-used anticonvulsant is SODIUM VALPROATE, which is used to treat all forms of epilepsy; others include those used solely to treat grand mal forms of epilepsy (such as CARBEMAZEPINE and PHENYTOIN) and those used solely to treat petit mal forms (such as ETHOSUXIMIDE). In every case, dosage must be adjusted to the requirements of each individual patient.

**\*antidepressants** are drugs that relieve the symptoms of depressive illness. There are two main groups of drugs used for the purpose. One is the group nominally called tricyclic antidepressants, which include AMITRYPTILINE, IMIPRAMINE and DOXEPIN, and are effective in alleviating a number of associated symptoms – although they have anticholinergic side-effects. The other group consists of the monoamine-oxidase inhibitors (MAOIs), including for example ISOCARBOXAZID, TRANYLCYPROMINE and PHENELZINE, which are now used less commonly because they have severe side-effects. A third type of antidepressant consists of the amino acid TRYPTOPHAN. Caution must be taken in prescribing antidepressant drugs.

**\*antidiarrhoeal** drugs prevent the onset of diarrhoea or assist in treating it if the symptom is already present. Yet the main medical treatment while diarrhoea lasts is always the replacement of fluids and minerals. Because there is a perceived need on the part of the general public, however, antidiarrhoeals are generally available, without prescription. Many are adsorbent mixtures that bind faecal material into solid masses; such mixtures include those containing KAOLIN, CHALK or METHYLCELLULOSE – preparations which may also be useful in controlling faecal consistency for patients who have undergone colostomy or ileostomy. Other antidiarrhoeals work by reducing the movement of the intestines (peristalsis) and this slows down the movement of faecal material: OPIATES such as CODEINE PHOSPHATE and MORPHINE are efficient at this. Diarrhoea caused by inflammatory disorders may be relieved by treatment with CORTICOSTEROIDS.

**\*anti-emetic**, or antinauseant, drugs prevent vomiting, and are therefore used primarily to prevent travel sickness, to relieve vertigo experienced by patients with infection of the organs of balance in the ears, or to alleviate nausea in patients undergoing chemotherapy for cancer. No specific type of drugs is used for the purpose, although most of the ANTIHISTAMINES are effective. HYOSCINE is also useful, as in many cases are the PHENOTHIAZINE derivatives (such as CHLORPROMAZINE and PROCHLORPERAZINE). In all cases, treatment causes drowsiness and reduces concentration, and enhances the effects of alcohol consumption. Anti-emetic drugs should not be administered to treat vomiting in pregnancy: most can cause harm to a foetus.

**\*anti-epileptic** drugs are more usually described as anticonvulsant drugs (even though mild forms of epilepsy may not cause convulsions).
*see* ANTICONVULSANT.

**\*antifungal** drugs are used to treat infections caused by fungal micro-organisms; they may be naturally or synthetically produced. Usually fungal infections are not a major problem in healthy, well-nourished individuals. However, superficial, localized infections such as thrush, caused by Candida albicans, and athlete's foot or ringworm, caused by fungi of the dermatophyte group, are common. Severe infections occur most frequently where the host's immunity is low, for example following immunosuppression for transplant surgery. Under such conditions fungi that are not normally pathogenic can exploit the situation and generate a life-threatening infection. Unfortunately the most potent antifungal drugs also tend to be highly toxic, and therefore severe systemic fungal infections remain a considerable danger. NYSTATIN and IMIDAZOLES such as CLOTRIMAZOLE are used for local treatment, with GRISEOFULVIN as an alternative. AMPHOTERICIN and FLUCYTOSINE are reserved for systemic fungal infections. The most common form of fungal infection in childhood is thrush. It usually occurs in the mouth and in the nappy area of infants. The treatment most often used involves topical nystatin or MICONAZOLE.

**\*antihistamines** are drugs that inhibit the effects in the body of histamine. Such a release occurs naturally as the result of a patient's coming into contact with a substance to which he or she is allergically sensitive, and the resultant symptoms if not more serious may be those of hay fever, urticaria, itching (pruritus) or even asthma. Many antihistamines also have ANTI-EMETIC properties, and are thus used to prevent travel sickness, vertigo, or the effects of chemotherapy in the treatment of cancer. Side-effects following administration commonly include drowsiness (and a small number of antihistamines are used as sedatives), dizziness, blurred vision, gastrointestinal disturbances and a lack of muscular co-ordination.

Conventionally, only the earlier discovered drugs that act on histamine's $H_1$ receptors are referred to by the general name 'antihistamines'. Somewhat confusingly, however, the recently discovered drugs used in

the treatment of peptic ulcers (e.g. CIMETIDINE, RANITIDINE) are also antihistamines, but act on another class of receptor ($H_2$) that is involved in gastric secretion. *see* ASTEMIZOLE; AZATADINE MALEATE; BROMPHENIRAMINE MALEATE; CINNARIZINE; CLEMASTINE; CYCLIZINE; CYPROHEPTADINE HYDROCHLORIDE; DIMENHYDRINATE; DIMETHINDENE MALEATE; DIPHENHYDRAMINE HYDROCHLORIDE; HYDROXYZINE HYDROCHLORIDE; MEBHYDROLIN; MEPYRAMINE MALEATE; MEQUITAZINE; OXATOMIDE; PHENINDAMINE TARTRATE; PHENIRAMINE MALEATE; PROMETHAZINE HYDROCHLORIDE; TERFENADINE; TRIMEPRAZINE TARTRATE; TRIPROLIDINE HYDROCHLORIDE.

**\*antihypertensive** drugs reduce high blood pressure (hypertension – a group of diseases of different origins) and so reduce a patient's risk of heart attacks, kidney failure or a stroke; many also treat angina pectoris (heart pain). There are several large groups of drugs used for the purpose, each with a specific mode of action, but before any drugs are administered a check should be made on the patient's diet and lifestyle to see if therapy without drugs can be advised. All DIURETIC drugs act as antihypertensives, and often a mild diuretic may be all that is required. If further treatment is necessary, any of the BETA-BLOCKERS may be used, with or without simultaneous administration of a diuretic. Other treatments include the use of a VASODILATOR (such as NIFEDIPINE or HYDRALAZINE). Some antihypertensive drugs act directly on the brain centre responsible for monitoring blood pressure: these include the RAUWOLFIA ALKALOIDS. Other antihypertensives inhibit the factors in the body that respond to stress, so preventing the release of hormones such as adrenaline and noradrenaline: these include DEBRISOQUINE. All require frequent and regular monitoring.

**\*anti-inflammatory** drugs are those used to reduce inflammation (the body's defensive reaction when tissue is injured). The way they work depends on the type of drug (e.g. CORTICOSTEROID or NSAID), but may involve actions such as the reduction of blood flow to the inflamed area, or an inhibitory effect on the chemicals released in the tissue that cause the inflammation.

**\*antimalarial** drugs are used to treat or prevent malaria. The disease is caused by infection of the red blood cells with a small organism called a protozoon (of the genus Plasmodium), which is carried by the Anopheles mosquito. Infection occurs as a result of the female mosquito's bite. The class of drug most frequently used to treat or prevent infection by the malaria protozoon are the quinidines, of which CHLOROQUINE is the standard. However, in some parts of the world, some forms of the protozoon that causes malaria are resistant to chloroquine; in such cases, the traditional remedy for malaria, QUININE, is used. Quinine may also be used in patients who cannot tolerate chloroquine. The prevention of malaria by drugs cannot be guaranteed. However, administration of chloroquine, PROGUANIL or PYRIMETHAMINE before, and for a period after, travelling to a tropical place, is thought to provide reasonable protection.

**\*antimicrobials** are drugs used to treat infections caused by microbes. These include the major

classes of pathogenic micro-organisms covered in this book – viruses, mycoplasma, rickettsia, chlamydia, protozoa, bacteria and fungi (but not helminths – worms). Antimicrobial is therefore a wide term embracing ANTIBACTERIALS, ANTIBIOTICS, ANTIPROTOZOALS, ANTIVIRALS and ANTIFUNGALS. A drug that combines both the properties of an antibacterial and an antifungal could be more concisely termed an antimicrobial. However, in this text more specific terms are used where possible.

**\*antinauseants** are usually described as anti-emetics, although theoretically they remedy nausea (the sensation that makes people feel as if they are about to vomit) rather than prevent vomiting. The term is used occasionally to make this distinction.
*see* ANTI-EMETIC.

**\*antiparkinsonism** drugs are used to treat parkinsonism, which is the symptoms of a number of disorders of the central nervous system, including muscle tremor and rigidity (extrapyramidal symptoms), especially in the limbs, and results from an imbalance of the actions of the neurotransmitters acetylcholine and dopamine. In classic Parkinson's disease this is due to the degeneration of dopamine-containing nerves; however, parkinsonian extrapyramidal side-effects may be caused by treatment with several types of drugs, especially ANTIPSYCHOTICS (e.g. HALOPERIDOL). Treatment of parkinsonism may be by ANTICHOLINERGIC drugs (e.g. BENZHEXOL), or by drugs that increase dopamine release (e.g. LEVODOPA). The former class is more useful for controlling fine tremor - including that induced by drugs – and the latter class for overcoming difficulty in commencing movement and slowness brought about by degenerative disease. Over-compensation is common and a good balance difficult to achieve.

**\*antiperspirants** are substances that help to prevent sweating. Medically they are needed only in cases of severe hyperhydrosis – when some disorder of the sweat glands causes constant and streaming perspiration. In such cases, aluminium chloride in mild solution is an effective treatment. Dusting powders may also be useful to dry the skin. But in all other cases there should be no need for antiperspirants, and indeed they may be harmful in preventing the body's normal means of cooling from functioning adequately.
▲/✚ side-effects/warning: *see* ALUMINIUM CHLORIDE.

**\*antiprotozoal** drugs are used to treat or prevent infections caused by micro-organisms called protozoa. Of these the most important, in terms of illness and death, are the protozoa of the genus Plasmodium, which cause malaria. Other major protozoal diseases found in tropical countries include trypano-somiasis, leishmaniasis and amoebic dysentery. Protozoal infections more familiar in this country include toxoplasmosis, trichomoniasis and giardiasis. A common form of pneumonia is caused in immunosuppressed patients (including those suffering from AIDS) by the protozoon Pneumocytis carinii.
*see* ANTIMALARIAL DRUGS.

**\*antipsychotic**, or neuroleptic, drugs calm and soothe patients without impairing consciousness. They are used mainly to treat psychologically disturbed patients, particularly those who manifest the complex behavioural patterns of schizophrenia, but in the short-term they may also be used to treat severe anxiety. Affecting mood, they may also worsen or help to alleviate depression. Antipsychotics exert their effect by acting in the brain. They exhibit many side-effects, including abnormal face and body movements, and restlessness; these may resemble the symptoms of the condition being treated. The use of other drugs may be required to control these side-effects. Antipsychotic drugs include HALOPERIDOL, FLUPENTHIXOL DECANOATE and the PHENOTHIAZINE derivatives, especially CHLORPROMAZINE and THIORIDAZINE; SULPIRIDE demands careful adjustment of dosage depending on effect; BENPERIDOL is used mostly to control antisocial sexual behaviour or hyperactivity. Those antipsychotics with markedly depressant side-effects are known as major TRANQUILLIZERS.

**\*antipyretic** drugs reduce high body temperature. Best-known and most-used antipyretic drugs include the ANALGESICS ASPIRIN, PARACETAMOL, MEFENAMIC ACID and PHENYLBUTAZONE.

**\*antirheumatic** drugs are used to relieve the pain and the inflammation of rheumatism and arthritis, and sometimes of other musculo-skeletal disorders. The primary form of treatment is with non-steroidal ANTI-INFLAMMATORY (NSAID) non-narcotic ANALGESICS such as ASPIRIN, SODIUM SALICYLATE, the aspirin-paracetamol ester BENORYLATE, INDOMETHACIN, FENOPROFEN, IBUPROFEN and PHENYLBUTAZONE. CORTICOSTEROIDS may also be used for their notable anti-inflammatory properties. Suitable steroids include PREDNISOLONE and TRIAMCINOLONE. Finally, there are some drugs that seem to halt the progressive advance of rheumatism; some have unpleasant side-effects, others may take up to 6 months to have any effect. They include gold (in the form of SODIUM AUROTHIOMALATE) and PENICILLAMINE, and some drugs otherwise mostly used as IMMUNOSUPPRESSANTS.

\*antiseptics are agents that destroy micro-organisms, or inhibit their activity to a level such that they are less or no longer harmful to health. Antiseptics may be applied to the skin, burns or wounds to prevent infections and to limit the spread of pathogenic micro-organisms. The term is often used synonymously with DISINFECTANT.

\*antiserum is a general term used to describe certain preparations of blood serum rich in particular antibodies. Antiserums are used to provide (passive) immunity to diseases, or to provide some measure of treatment if the disease has already been contracted. The general term used to describe part of the disease-causing entity recognized by the immune system is 'antigen'. If an antigen is injected into an animal, the animal produces antibodies in response to the antigen. An antiserum is a sample of blood serum containing these antibodies. Most antiserums are prepared from blood of antigen-treated horses, and when the purified antiserums are used to immunize humans they often cause hypersensitivity reactions. For this reason use of such preparations is now very rare, and they have to a large extent been replaced by preparations of human antibodies.

\*antispasmodic, or spasmolytic, drugs relieve spasm (rigidity) in

smooth muscle (muscle that is not under voluntary control, such as the muscles in the upper respiratory tract and those of the intestinal walls), and form part of the group of drugs known collectively as SMOOTH MUSCLE RELAXANTS. They are therefore most used as BRONCHODILATORS or to relieve abdominal pain due to intestinal colic; however, they may also be used to stimulate the heart in the treatment of angina pectoris (heart pain). Best-known antispasmodics include the BELLADONNA alkaloids, PIPERIDOLATE HYDROCHLORIDE and OPIATES such as PAPAVERINE. Many of them give rise to ANTICHOLINERGIC side-effects.

Antistin-Privine (*Ciba*) is a proprietary non-prescription compound solution for use in treating allergic nasal conditions such as hay fever. Not available from the National Health Service, and produced in the form of nose-drops and a nasal spray, it is a combination of the ANTIHISTAMINE antazoline sulphate and the SYMPATHOMIMETIC naphazoline.
*see* ANTAZOLINE.

\*antitubercular (or antituberculous) drugs are used in combination to treat tuberculosis. The initial phase of treatment usually employs three drugs (ordinarily ISONIAZID, RIFAMPICIN and PYRAZINAMIDE with STREPTOMYCIN or ETHAMBUTOL as possible alternatives) in order to tackle the disease as efficiently as possible, while reducing the risk of encountering bacterial resistance. If the first line of treatment is successful, after about 2 months treatment usually continues with only two of the initial three drugs (one of which is generally isoniazid).

If the first line of treatment was not successful, for example because the patient suffered intolerable side-effects or because the disease was resistant to drugs, then other drugs (e.g. CAPREO-MYCIN and CYCLOSERINE) are used to treat the patient. The duration of treatment depends on the combination of drugs used.

**\*antitussives** are drugs that assist in the treatment of coughs. Sometimes the term antitussive is used to describe only those drugs that suppress coughing rather than drugs used to treat the cause of coughing. Cough suppressants include OPIATES such as DEXTRO-METHORPHAN, NOSCAPINE, METHADONE and CODEINE. They tend to cause constipation as a side-effect and so should not be used for prolonged periods. Other antitussive preparations are EXPECTORANTS and demulcents. Expectorants are drugs used to decrease the viscosity of mucus or to increase the secretion of liquid mucus in dry, irritant, unproductive coughs, the idea being that air passages will become lubricated, thereby making the cough more productive. Expectorants include AMMONIUM CHLORIDE and IPECACUANHA. These expectorants are included in many proprietary compound cough medicines. Demulcents also help to reduce the viscosity of mucus and relieve dry, unproductive coughs. All of these drugs are used to soothe coughs rather than treat the underlying cause of the cough, such as an infection.

**\*antivenin** is an antidote to the poison in a snake-bite, a scorpion's sting, or a bite from any other poisonous creature (such as a spider). Normally, it is an ANTISERUM, and is injected into the bloodstream for immediate relief. Identification of the poisonous creature is important so that the right antidote can be selected.

**\*antiviral**, drugs are relatively few in number and their effectiveness is often restricted to preventive or disease-limitation treatment. This is perhaps not surprising as viruses reproduce by taking over the biochemical machinery of the host cells and perverting it to their own needs. Therefore, it is extremely difficult to design a drug that can differentiate between attacking a vital viral mechanism and the host cell itself. However, some antiviral drugs can be lifesavers, especially in immuno-compromised individuals. Infections due to the herpes viruses (e.g., cold sores, genital herpes and chicken pox) may be prevented or contained by early treatment with ACYCLOVIR. Serious cytomegaloviral infections may also be contained by treatment with ganciclovir. Severe respiratory infections in children are treated with ribavirin. As more of the molecular biology of the virus-host interactions becomes known, more selective antivirals are possible.

**Antoin** (*Cox*) is a proprietary, non-prescription compound ANALGESIC, which is not available from the National Health Service. Used to relieve mild to moderate pain anywhere in the body, and produced in the form of soluble (dispersible) tablets, Antoin is a preparation of aspirin with the OPIATE codeine phosphate and the mild stimulant caffeine citrate. It is not recommended for children.
▲/✿ side-effects/warning: see ASPIRIN; CAFFEINE; CODEINE PHOSPHATE.

**Antraderm** (*Brocades*) is a proprietary form of the powerful drug dithranol, available on prescription, used to treat serious, non-infective skin inflammations, particularly psoriasis. It is produced in the form of a wax stick for topical application. In three strengths, the strongest under the trade name Antraderm Forte, the weakest under the name Antraderm Mild, it is available only on prescription, except for Antraderm Mild.

▲/✿ side-effects/warning: *see* DITHRANOL.

**Anturan** (*Geigy*) is a proprietary preparation of the drug sulphinpyrazone, available only on prescription, used to treat and prevent gout, and especially recurrent attacks of arthritic gout. It works by reducing blood levels of uric acid by increasing its excretion in the urine. It is produced in the form of tablets (in two strengths). The effectiveness of Anturan in children has not been established.

▲/✿ side-effects/warning: *see* SULPHINPYRAZONE.

**Anugesic-HC** (*Parke-Davis*) is a proprietary CORTICOSTEROID preparation, available only on prescription, used to treat haemorrhoids and itching, swelling and inflammation in the anal region. Produced in the form of a cream (for application with a rectal nozzle), and as anal suppositories, it is a preparation that includes the steroid hydrocortisone acetate, the antiparasitic benzyl benzoate, and the local anaesthetic pramoxine hydrochloride, together with mild astringents and antiseptics. It is not recommended for children.

▲/✿ side-effects/warning: *see* BENZYL BENZOATE; HYDROCORTISONE.

**Anusol** (*Warner*) is a proprietary, non-prescription, soothing preparation used to treat haemorrhoids and itching, and discomfort in the anal region. Produced in the form of a cream

(for application with a rectal nozzle), as an ointment (for similar application), and as anal suppositories, it is a preparation of the mild astringent ZINC OXIDE with other astringents and an antiseptic. It is not recommended for children.

**Anusol-HC** (*Warner*) is a proprietary CORTICOSTEROID preparation, used to treat haemorrhoids and inflammation in the anal region. Produced in the form of an ointment (for application with a rectal nozzle) and as anal suppositories, it is a preparation of the corticosteroid hydrocortisone acetate, the antiparasitic benzyl benzoate, and the mild astringent ZINC OXIDE, with other astringents and antiseptics. It is not recommended for children.

▲/✿ side-effects/warning: *see* BENZYL BENZOATE; HYDROCORTISONE.

**\*anxiolytic** drugs relieve medically diagnosed anxiety states and should be prescribed only for patients whose anxiety in the face of stress is actually hindering the prospect of its resolution. Treatment should be at the lowest dosage effective, and must not be prolonged: psychological dependence (if not physical addiction) readily occurs and may make withdrawal difficult. Best-known and most-used anxiolytic drugs are the BENZODIAZEPINES, such as DIAZEPAM, CHLORDIAZEPOXIDE, LORAZEPAM and CLOBAZAM; others include MEPROBAMATE and some of the ANTIPSYCHOTIC drugs used in low dosage. The benzodiazepines are sometimes used in the relief of withdrawal symptoms caused by addiction to other drugs (such as alcohol). Drugs of this class may also be referred to as minor TRANQUILLIZERS.

Apisate (*Wyeth*) is a proprietary APPETITE SUPPRESSANT, which is on the controlled drugs list. Produced in the form of sustained-release tablets, Apisate is a preparation of the amphetamine-related drug diethylpropion hydrochloride together with a vitamin supplement of THIAMINE (vitamin B₁), RIBOFLAVINE (vitamin B₂), PYRIDOXINE (vitamin B₆), and the B vitamin derivative NICOTINAMIDE. Treatment must be in the short term and under strict medical supervision; the drug is not recommended for children.
▲/✚ side-effects/warning: see DIETHYLPROPION HYDROCHLORIDE.

APP (*Consolidated*) is a proprietary compound ANTISPASMODIC drug, available on prescription only to private patients. It is used in the treatment of gastrointestinal muscle spasm, travel sickness, peptic ulcers or other gastrointestinal disturbances. Produced in the form of tablets and as a powder, APP is a preparation of the OPIATE papaverine, together with the ANTICHOLINERGIC homatropine methylbromide, and the ANTACIDS aluminium hydroxide, calcium carbonate, magnesium carbonate and magnesium trisilicate. It is not recommended for children.
▲/✚ side-effects/warning: see CALCIUM CARBONATE; MAGNESIUM CARBONATE; PAPAVERINE.

*appetite suppressants are intended to assist in the medical treatment of obesity – in which the primary therapy has to be in the form of diet. They work either by acting on the brain or by bulking out the food eaten so that the body feels it has actually taken more than it has. Appetite suppressants that act on the brain include DIETHYLPROPION

HYDROCHLORIDE, FENFLURAMINE HYDROCHLORIDE and PHENTERMINE; bulking agents include STERCULIA and METHYLCELLULOSE. Treatment should be in the short-term only: psychological dependence readily occurs.

Apresoline (*Ciba*) is a proprietary VASODILATOR, available only on prescription, used to treat moderate to severe high blood pressure (hypertension). It can also be used to treat heart failure. It is a useful adjunct to diuretic and beta-blocker therapy. Produced in the form of tablets (in two strengths) and as a powder for reconstitution as a medium for injection, Apresoline is a preparation of hydralazine hydrochloride.
▲/✚ side-effects/warning: see HYDRALAZINE.

Aprinox (*Boots*) is a proprietary DIURETIC, available only on prescription, used to treat high blood pressure (see ANTI-HYPERTENSIVE) and the accumulation of fluid within the tissues (oedema). Produced in the form of tablets (in two strengths), Aprinox is a preparation of the THIAZIDE bendrofluazide.
▲/✚ side-effects/warning: see BENDROFLUAZIDE.

Aproten (*Ultrapharm*) is a proprietary, non-prescription brand of gluten-free, low-protein food preparations, for the use of patients with phenylketonuria and similar amino acid abnormalities, kidney or liver failure, cirrhosis of the liver, coeliac disease, or gluten sensitivity. It is produced in the form of various types of pasta, as biscuits, as crispbread and as flour.

aprotinin is a drug that has the effect of inhibiting certain digestive enzymes secreted by the pancreas. It is thus primarily used to assist in the treatment of pancreatitis, particularly after surgery on or around the pancreas. As well as affecting the digestive enzymes it is thought to affect enzymes involved in forming blood clots. It is thus also thought to have ANTICOAGULANT properties and may also be used to prevent thrombosis following surgery elsewhere in the body.

▲ side-effects: some patients experience serious sensitivity reactions (that may require emergency treatment).
*Related article:* TRASYLOL.

**Apsifen** (*Approved Prescription Services*) is a proprietary, non-narcotic ANALGESIC, available only on prescription, used to relieve pain, particularly the pain of rheumatic disease and other musculo-skeletal disorders. It is produced in the form of tablets, which can be film- or sugar-coated; the film-coated are available in 3 strengths and the sugar-coated in 2 strengths. Apsifen is a preparation of the ANTI-INFLAMMATORY drug ibuprofen.

▲/ ✪ side-effects/warning: *see* IBUPROFEN.

**Apsin V.K.** (*Approved Prescription Services*) is a proprietary ANTIBIOTIC, available only on prescription, used to treat bacterial infections of the skin and of the ear, nose and throat. It is similar to the original penicillin, penicillin G, though less active, but it does have the advantage of being orally absorbed. However, its absorbtion is too irregular for it to be recommended for treating severe infections. Produced in the form of tablets and as a syrup (in two strengths) for dilution (the potency of the syrup once dilute is retained for 7 days if stored at a temperature below 15 degrees

centigrade), Apsin V.K. is a preparation of the PENICILLIN phenoxymethylpenicillin (penicillin V).

▲/ ✪ side-effects/warning: *see* PHENOXYMETHYLPENICILLIN.

**Apsolol** (*Approved Prescription Services*) is a proprietary ANTIHYPERTENSIVE drug, available only on prescription, used not only to treat high blood pressure (hypertension), but also to relieve angina pectoris (heart pain) and to slow and/or regularize the heartbeat in order to prevent a recurrent heart attack or to relieve anxiety. The drug may also be used to treat the effects of an excess of thyroid hormones in the bloodstream (thyrotoxicosis) or to try to prevent migraine attacks. Produced in the form of tablets (in four strengths), Apsolol is a preparation of the BETA-BLOCKER propranolol hydrochloride.

▲/ ✪ side-effects/warning: *see* PROPRANOLOL.

**Apsolox** (*Approved Prescription Services*) is a proprietary ANTIHYPERTENSIVE drug, available only on prescription, used not only to treat high blood pressure (hypertension), but also to relieve angina pectoris (heart pain) and to slow and/or regularize the heartbeat in order to prevent a recurrent heart attack. The drug may also be used to treat the effects of an excess of thyroid hormones in the bloodstream (thyrotoxicosis). Produced in the form of tablets (in four strengths), Apsolox is a preparation of the BETA-BLOCKER oxprenolol hydrochloride.

▲/ ✪ side-effects/warning: *see* OXPRENOLOL.

**Aquadrate** (*Norwich Eaton*) is a proprietary, non-prescription preparation, used to treat conditions in which the skin becomes scaly and hardens in layers. It is used to treat certain eczemas and chronic dry skin conditions. Produced in the form of a cream, Aquadrate is a preparation of the natural DIURETIC urea.

**Aquadry** (*Thackraycare*) is a proprietary, non-prescription medical adhesive (with a brush) used in the maintenance of a stoma (a surgically produced outlet in the skin surface following the surgical curtailment of the intestines).

**aqueous iodine solution** is a non-proprietary solution of iodine and potassium iodide in water (and is known also as Lugol's solution). It is used as an iodine supplement for patients suffering from an excess of thyroid HORMONES in the bloodstream (thyrotoxicosis), especially prior to thyroid surgery.
▲/ ✿ side-effects/warning: *see* IODINE.

**arachis oil** is peanut oil, used primarily as an emollient in treating crusts on skin surfaces in such conditions as psoriasis, cradle cap, dandruff and eczema (often in combination with calamine). It is also a constituent in many anal suppositories.

**Aradolene** (*Rorer*) is a proprietary, non-prescription COUNTER-IRRITANT cream, which, applied topically, causes irritation. This irritation in turn offsets the pain of underlying muscle and joint ailments. It is thus used to treat rheumatic pains, and is a preparation of diethylamine salicylate together with natural oils.

**Aramine** (*Merck, Sharp & Dohme*) is a proprietary SYMPATHOMIMETIC VASOCONSTRICTOR, available only on prescription, most often used

to raise blood pressure in a patient under general anaesthesia or in conditions of severe shock. It is a preparation of metaraminol in ampoules for injection or infusion.
▲/ ✿ side-effects/warning: *see* METARAMINOL.

**Aredia** (*Ciba*) is a proprietary form of the drug disodium pamidronate, which is used to treat tumour-induced abnormal calcium metabolism resulting in raised blood levels. It is available, on prescription, in a form for slow intravenous infusion.
▲/ ✿ side-effects/warning: *see* DISODIUM PAMIDRONATE.

**Arelix** (*Hoechst*) is a proprietary DIURETIC, available only on prescription, used to treat mild to moderate high blood pressure (*see* ANTIHYPERTENSIVE). Produced in the form of sustained-release capsules, Arelix is a preparation of piretanide. There has been insufficient experience of the use of this drug in children and therefore dosage recommendations for children have not been made.
▲/ ✿ side-effects/warning: *see* PIRETANIDE.

**Arfonad** (*Roche*) is a proprietary preparation of the ganglion blocker drug trimetaphan camsylate, available only on prescription, used to reduce blood pressure to a low level (hypotension) during surgery. It is produced in ampoules for injection; it may also be administered by intravenous infusion.
▲/ ✿ side-effects/warning: *see* TRIMETAPHAN CAMSYLATE.

**Arilvax** (*Wellcome*) is a proprietary form of VACCINE against yellow fever. It consists of a suspension containing live but weakened viruses, which are

cultured in chick embryos.
Available only on prescription, it
is produced in vials with a diluent.
It is not recommended for children
under the age of 9 months.

⚕ warning: *see* YELLOW FEVER
VACCINE.

**Arobon** (*Nestlé*) is a proprietary,
non-prescription preparation used
to treat diarrhoea. Produced in
the form of a sugar-free powder (to
be taken orally in liquid), Arobon
is a preparation of the adsorbent
substance CERATONIA in a mixture
of starch and cocoa.

**Arpicolin** (*RP Drugs*) is a
proprietary preparation of the
ANTICHOLINERGIC drug
procyclidine hydrochloride,
available only on prescription,
used in the treatment of
parkinsonism and to control
tremors induced by drugs (*see*
ANTIPARKINSONISM). Produced in
the form of a syrup (in two
strengths), Arpicolin is not
recommended for children.

▲/ ⚕ side-effects/warning: *see*
PROCYCLIDINE.

**Arpimycin** (*RP Drugs*) is a
proprietary ANTIBIOTIC, available
only on prescription, used both to
treat many forms of infection
(particularly pneumonia and
legionnaires' disease) and to
prevent others (particularly
sinusitis, diphtheria and
whooping cough); it is also used as
an alternative to penicillin-type
antibiotics in patients who are
allergic or whose infections are
resistant to penicillins. Produced
in the form of a mixture (in three
strengths) for dilution (the
potency of the syrup once diluted
is retained for 7 days), Arpimycin
is a preparation of the macrolide
antibiotic erythromycin.

▲/ ⚕ side-effects/warning: *see*
ERYTHROMYCIN.

**Arret** (*Janssen*) is a proprietary
ANTIDIARRHOEAL drug, which
works by reducing the speed at

which material travels along the
intestines. Produced in the form
of capsules and as a syrup (for
adults), Arret is a preparation of
the OPIATE loperamide
hydrochloride. It is not
recommended for children aged
under 4 years.

▲/ ⚕ side-effects/warning: *see*
LOPERAMIDE.

**Artane** (*Lederle*) is a proprietary
preparation of the ANTI-
CHOLINERGIC drug benzhexol
hydrochloride, available only on
prescription, used in the
treatment of parkinsonism and to
control tremors and involuntary
movement. Produced in the form
of tablets (in two strengths), and
as a powder (for oral use). Artane
is not recommended for children.

▲/ ⚕ side-effects/warning: *see*
BENZHEXOL HYDROCHLORIDE.

**Arthmol** (*Knoll*) is a proprietary
form of the ANTIARRHYTHMIC drug
propafenone hydrochloride used
to prevent and treat irregularities
of heart beat (arrhythmias), and is
available only on prescription in
the form of tablets in two
strengths.

▲/ ⚕ side-effects/warning: *see*
PROPAFENONE
HYDROCHLORIDE.

**Artracin** (*DDSA
Pharmaceuticals*) is a proprietary,
non-steroidal, ANTI-
INFLAMMATORY non-narcotic
ANALGESIC, available only on
prescription, used to treat the
pain of rheumatic and other
musculo-skeletal disorders
(including gout). Produced in the
form of capsules (in two
strengths), Artracin is a
preparation of indomethacin. It is
not recommended for children.

▲/ ⚕ side-effects/warning: *see*
INDOMETHACIN.

**Arvin** (*Armour*) is a proprietary
preparation of the ANTI-

COAGULANT ancrod, available only on prescription (and generally only for hospital use), used to treat or prevent thrombosis (blood clots). Administration is by injection. Arvin Antidote is also available for emergencies.

▲ / ✚ side-effects/warning: see ANCROD.

**Asacol** (*Smith Kline & French*) is a proprietary form of the drug mesalazine, used to treat patients who suffer from ulcerative colitis but who are unable to tolerate the more commonly used drug sulphasalazine. Available only on prescription, Asacol is produced in the form of resin-coated tablets and suppositories.

▲ / ✚ side-effects/warning: see MESALAZINE.

**Ascabiol** (*May & Baker*) is a proprietary, non-prescription preparation of BENZYL BENZOATE in suspension, used to treat infestation of the skin of the trunk and limbs by itch-mites (scabies) or sometimes to treat infestation by lice. A skin irritant, it is not suitable for use on the head, face and neck; for children it should be in diluted form (or another preparation should be used).

▲ side-effects: there is commonly skin irritation; there may also be a temporary burning sensation. Sensitivity may cause a rash.

✚ warning: keep Ascabiol away from the eyes, and avoid taking it by the mouth.

**Ascalix** (*Wallace*) is a proprietary, non-prescription ANTHELMINTIC drug used to treat infestation by threadworms or roundworms. Produced in the form of syrup (in bottles and in sachets), Ascalix is a preparation of piperazine hydrate.

▲ / ✚ side-effects/warning: see PIPERAZINE.

**ascorbic acid** is the chemical name of the water-soluble VITAMIN C. Essential in the diet, the vitamin is instrumental in the development and maintenance of cells and tissues. Deficiency leads to scurvy and to certain other disorders associated particularly with the elderly. Good food sources are green vegetables and citrus fruits. Vitamin C supplements are rarely necessary; when they are, it is only in small quantities. Administration is oral in the form of tablets, or by injection.

✚ warning: ascorbic acid in food is lost by over-cooking or through the action of ultraviolet light.
*Related article:* REDOXON.

**Asendis** (*Lederle*) is a proprietary form of the TRICYCLIC ANTI-DEPRESSANT drug amoxapine, used to treat depressive illness. Available, only on prescription, in the form of tablets in three strengths.

▲ / ✚ side-effects/warning: see AMOXAPINE.

**Aserbine** (*Bencard*) is a proprietary, non-prescription cream containing three acids (malic, benzoic and salicylic) and other additives, used to cleanse and remove hard, dry, dead skin from ulcers, burns and bedsores so that natural healing can take place. The same preparation is also available in the form of a solution.

✚ warning: contact with the eyes should be avoided, and Aserbine should only be applied externally.

**Asilone** (*Berk*) is a proprietary, non-prescription ANTACID compound, which is not available from the National Health Service. It is used to treat acid stomach, flatulence, heartburn and gastritis, and to soothe peptic

ulcers. It is produced in the form
of tablets. Asilone is a
combination of the antacids
ALUMINIUM HYDROXIDE and
MAGNESIUM oxide ('magnesia')
together with the antifoaming
agent DIMETHICONE.

**Asmaven** (*Approved Prescription
Services*) is a proprietary form of
the BETA-RECEPTOR STIMULANT,
BRONCHODILATOR salbutamol,
available only on prescription. It
is able to relax the muscles of the
breathing airways and is thus
used in the treatment of asthma
and bronchitis. Asmaven is
sometimes used in the
management of premature labour.
It is produced in the form of
tablets (in two strengths) and as a
solute inhalant. Using the
inhalant, patients should not
exceed the prescribed dose and
should be careful to follow the
manufacturer's directions.
▲/● side-effects/warning: see
SALBUTAMOL.

**Aspav** (*Cox*) is a proprietary
compound ANALGESIC, available
only on prescription, used to
relieve pain, especially pain
following surgery or caused by
inoperable cancer. Produced in
the form of dissolvable tablets,
Aspav is a combination of aspirin
and the OPIATE papaveretum. It is
not recommended for children.
▲/● side-effects/warning: see
ASPIRIN; PAPAVERETUM.

**Aspellin** (*Rorer*) is a proprietary,
non-prescription LINIMENT,
which, when applied to the skin,
produces an irritation that in
turn counteracts rheumatic pain
or pains in muscles and joints or
tendons. It may also soothe
chilblains. Also available in the
form of a spray, Aspellin's active
constituents include ASPIRIN,
menthol and camphor.
● warning: Aspellin should not
be used on inflamed or broken
skin, or on mucous membranes.

**aspirin**, or acetylsalicylic acid, is a
well-known and widely used non-
narcotic ANALGESIC, which also
has ANTI-INFLAMMATORY
properties and is useful in
reducing high body temperature
(ANTIPYRETIC). As an analgesic it
relieves mild to moderate pain,
particularly headache, toothache,
menstrual pain and the aches of
rheumatic disease. Its
temperature-reducing capacity
helps in the treatment of the
common cold, fevers or influenza.
Aspirin is also used as an
ANTICOAGULANT. In tablet form,
aspirin may irritate the stomach
lining and many forms of soluble
aspirin, in trying to avoid this
drawback, include chalk. Other
proprietary forms combine aspirin
with such drugs as codeine or
paracetamol. Administration is
oral or, rarely, by injection. It is
advised that aspirin should not be
administered to children aged
under 12 years, unless specially
indicated. Some people are
allergic to aspirin.
▲ side-effects: gastric irritation
with or without haemorrhage
is common, although such
effects may be neutralized to
some extent by taking the drug
after food. Aspirin may
enhance the effect of some
hypoglycaemic and
anticoagulant drugs.
● warning: irritation of the
stomach lining may, in
susceptible patients, cause
nausea, vomiting, pain and
bleeding (which may lead to
anaemia if prolonged).
Overdosage may cause ringing
in the ears (tinnitus), dizziness,
nausea, vomiting, headache,
hyperventilation, and
sometimes a state of confusion
or delirium followed by coma.
Aspirin may also dispose a
patient to bronchospasm,
which in asthmatic patients
may prove problematic.
Repeated overdosage may

result in kidney damage.
*Related articles:* ANGETTES;
ANTOIN; ASPAV; ASPELLIN;
CAPRIN; CLARADIN; CODIS;
DOLOXENE COMPOUND;
EQUAGESIC; HYPON; LABOPRIN;
MIGRAVESS; MYOLGIN; NU-
SEALS ASPIRIN; PALAPRIN
FORTE; PLATET; ROBAXISAL
FORTE; SOLPRIN; TRANCOPRIN;
VEGANIN.

**astemizole** is a relatively new
ANTIHISTAMINE used to treat the
symptoms of allergic disorders. It
joins a new class of drugs, which
have little sedative effect.
Administration is oral in the form
of tablets.
▲ side-effects: side-effects are
comparatively uncommon, but
there may be headache. There
may also be sufficient
drowsiness to counter-indicate
driving or operating
machinery.
✿ warning: astemizole should be
administered with caution to
patients with epilepsy,
glaucoma, liver disease or
enlargement of the prostate
gland, in pregnancy, or to the
elderly.
*Related articles:* HISMANAL;
POLLON-EZE.

**A.T. 10** (*Sterling Research*) is a
proprietary, non-prescription
preparation of CALCIFEROL
(vitamin D) in the form of its
analogue dihydrotachysterol.
Used to increase the absorption
and improve the use of calcium in
the body, A.T. 10 is produced as a
solution in a dropper bottle;
administration is oral only.
✿ warning: *see*
DIHYDROTACHYSTEROL.

**Atarax** (*Pfizer*) is a proprietary
ANTIHISTAMINE, available only on
prescription. It is used to treat
emotional disturbances and
anxiety (*see* ANXIOLYTIC), which
may manifest as physical

symptoms. It is also used to treat
physical conditions caused by
allergy (such as itching and mild
rashes). Atarax may also be used
as a SEDATIVE (e.g. before or after
surgery), and as an ANTI-EMETIC.
Produced in the form of tablets (in
two strengths) and as a syrup
(under the trade name Atarax
Syrup), Atarax is a preparation of
hydroxyzine hydrochloride.
▲ / ✿ side-effects/warning: *see*
HYDROXYZINE
HYDROCHLORIDE.

**atenolol** is a BETA-BLOCKER drug
that is capable of reducing the
heart rate and the heart's force of
contraction. It is used to treat
high blood pressure (*see*
ANTIHYPERTENSIVE), angina,
changes in heart rhythm and
heart attacks. It is not
recommended for children.
▲ side-effects: the heartbeat may
slow more than intended; there
may be some gastrointestinal
or respiratory disturbance, and
tiredness of muscles. Fingers
and toes may turn cold. Rarely,
there are rashes.
✿ warning: atenolol should be
administered with caution to
those who are pregnant or
lactating, to patients
undergoing anaesthesia, and to
those with asthma. The dose of
atenolol should be reduced in
the event of kidney failure.
Special attention should be
paid to signs of heart failure;
atenolol should be
administered with caution to
patients who may be
susceptible to heart failure. As
with other beta-blockers,
treatment with atenolol should
not be discontinued abruptly.
*Related article:* BETA-ADALAT;
TENIFEN; TENORMIN.

**Atensine** (*Berk*) is a proprietary
ANXIOLYTIC, available on
prescription only to private
patients, used both as an

**A**

anxiolytic or minor
TRANQUILLIZER (to treat states of
anxiety, insomnia and nervous
tension) and to relieve muscle
spasm and cerebral palsy. It may
also be used as a premedication
for dental operations. Produced in
the form of tablets (in three
strengths), Atensine is a
preparation of the
BENZODIAZEPINE diazepam.
▲/✿ side-effects/warning: see
DIAZEPAM.

**Ativan** (*Wyeth*) is a proprietary
ANXIOLYTIC, available only on
prescription, used as an
anxiolytic or minor
TRANQUILLIZER (to treat anxiety,
phobias, and as a HYPNOTIC in
insomnia), as a sedative or
premedication before surgery, and
– as an emergency treatment – to
control status epilepticus (in
which epileptic fits succeed each
other so closely that the patient
does not recover consciousness
and is gradually deprived of
oxygen). Produced in the form of
tablets (in two strengths) and in
ampoules for injection, Ativan
represents a preparation of the
BENZODIAZEPINE lorazepam.
▲/✿ side-effects/warning: see
LORAZEPAM.

**Atkinson and Barkers** (*Strenol*)
is a proprietary, non-prescription
preparation of infant's gripe
mixture. It contains the ANTACIDS
sodium bicarbonate and
magnesium carbonate.
▲/✿ side-effects/warning: see
SODIUM BICARBONATE;
MAGNESIUM CARBONATE.

**Atlas Dermalex** is a proprietary,
non-prescription ANTIBACTERIAL
in the form of a water-miscible
cream, used primarily to prevent
bedsores and to moisturize dry
skin. Active constituents include
TRICLOSAN.

**Atmocol** (*Thackray*) is a
proprietary, non-prescription
aerosol deodorant, used to

freshen and sanitize a stoma (an
outlet from the intestines to the
surface of the skin).

**atracurium besylate** is a
SKELETAL MUSCLE RELAXANT, the
effects of which can be reversed
by other drugs. Administration is
by injection, usually under
general anaesthetic during
surgery – effects on the muscles of
a conscious patient may be
painful.
▲ side-effects: rarely, atracurium
may cause transient
hypotension (lowered blood
pressure).
✿ warning: patients treated with
atracurium besylate must have
their respiration controlled
and monitored until the drug's
effects have worn off or been
antagonized. The effect of
repeated dosage, unlike that of
most competitive muscle
relaxants, is not cumulative.
Some patients may be sensitive
to this drug, and its safety
during pregnancy or caesarean
section is not known.
*Related article:* TRACRIUM.

**Atromid-S** (*ICI*) is a proprietary
form of the drug clofibrate,
available only on prescription,
used to treat high levels of
cholesterol or other lipids (fats) in
the blood. Atromid-S is produced
as gelatin capsules, and is not
recommended for children.
▲/✿ side-effects/warning: see
CLOFIBRATE.

**atropine** is a powerful
ANTICHOLINERGIC drug obtained
from plants including belladonna
(deadly nightshade). It is able to
depress certain functions of the
autonomic nervous system, and is
a useful ANTISPASMODIC. In
combination with morphine it
may be used as a premedication to
relax the muscles prior to
surgery. It is also used to dilate
the pupil of the eye for

ophthalmic surgery (although this requires care in order not to trigger off latent glaucoma). Atropine is able to decrease gastric acid secretion and is therefore sometimes used to treat peptic ulcers. Administration is oral, as eye-drops, or by injection.

▲ side-effects: there is commonly dry mouth and thirst; there may also be visual disturbances, and constipation.

✦ warning: atropine should not be administered to patients with enlargement of the prostate gland.

**atropine methonitrate** is a less toxic salt of the ANTICHOLINERGIC ATROPINE, used as an ANTISPASMODIC, particularly in the treatment of pyloric stenosis (obstruction of the stomach exit) when surgery is not possible. It is also used as a BRONCHODILATOR in the treatment of asthma and whooping cough in children. Administration is oral in the form of a solution, or by means of an inhaler. In general, however, the use of the drug is not recommended.

▲ side-effects: there is commonly dry mouth and thirst; there may also be visual disturbances (including sensitivity to light), flushing, irregular heartbeat, dry skin, rashes, difficulty in urinating and constipation. Rarely, there may be high temperature accompanied by delirium.

✦ warning: atropine methonitrate should not be administered to patients with glaucoma; it should be administered with caution to those with heart problems and rapid heart rate, ulcerative colitis, urinary retention or enlargement of the prostate gland; who are elderly; or who are lactating. Some people may be allergic to this drug.

**atropine sulphate** is used as a secondary drug in the treatment of gastrointestinal disorders that involve muscle spasm of the intestinal wall, and for dilating the pupil for ophthalmic investigations. Administration is oral in the form of tablets, by injection or as eye-drops.

▲ side-effects: there is commonly dry mouth and thirst; there may also be visual disturbances, flushing, irregular heartbeat, sensitivity to light and constipation. Rarely, there may be high temperature accompanied by delirium or hallucinations.

✦ warning: atropine sulphate should not be administered to patients who suffer from glaucoma; it should be administered with caution to those who suffer from heart problems and rapid heart rate, ulcerative colitis, urinary retention or enlargement of the prostate gland; who are elderly; or who are pregnant or lactating.
*Related article:* ISOPTO.

**Atrovent** (*Boehringer Ingelheim*) is a proprietary preparation of the ANTICHOLINERGIC, BRONCHODILATOR ipratropium bromide, available only on prescription, used to treat chronic bronchitis and other disorders of the upper respiratory tract. It is produced in the form of an aerosol spray (in two strengths, the stronger under the name Atrovent Forte) and as a solution for use in a nebulizer. Using either method, patients should not exceed the prescribed dose and should be careful to follow the manufacturer's directions; treatment should be initiated under hospital supervision.

▲/✦ side-effects/warning: *see* IPRATROPIUM.

**Audax** (*Napp*) is a proprietary, non-prescription, non-narcotic

ANALGESIC in the form of ear-drops, used to soothe pain associated with infection of the outer or middle ear. Its active constituent is choline salicylate.
✚ warning: see CHOLINE SALICYLATE.

**Audicort** (*Lederle*) is a proprietary, anti-inflammatory ANTI-BACTERIAL and ANTIFUNGAL, available only on prescription, used in the treatment of bacterial and/or fungal infections of the outer ear. It contains the CORTICOSTEROID triamcinolone acetonide, the local anaesthetic benzocaine, the ANTIBIOTIC neomycin, and the ANTIFUNGAL drug undecenoic acid.
▲/✚ side-effects/warning: see NEOMYCIN.

**Augmentin** (*Beecham*) is a proprietary preparation of the penicillin-like ANTIBIOTIC amoxycillin together with an enhancing agent, clavulanic acid. This inhibits enzymes produced by some bacteria (penicillinases), which break down amoxycillin so making it ineffective. Thus the combination is active against many infections which would normally be resistant to amoxycillin alone. It extends the range and efficiency of amoxycillin as an antibiotic. It is used primarily to treat infections of the skin, ear, nose and throat, and urinary tract, and is produced in a number of forms: as tablets, as a solution (under the name Augmentin Dispersible), in milder versions as a powder for solution (under the names Augmentin Paediatric and Augmentin Junior), and in vials for injections or infusion (under the trade name Augmentin Intravenous).
▲/✚ side-effects/warning: see AMOXYCILLIN.

**Aureocort** (*Lederle*) is a proprietary ANTIBIOTIC preparation for topical

application, available only on prescription, used to treat inflammations of the skin where infection is also present. Produced as a water-miscible cream, an anhydrous ointment, and an aerosol spray, Aureocort contains the CORTICOSTEROID triamcinolone acetonide and the TETRACYCLINE antibiotic chlortetracycline hydrochloride.
▲/✚ side-effects/warning: see CHLORTETRACYCLINE.

**Aureomycin** (*Lederle*) is a proprietary, broad-spectrum ANTIBIOTIC, available only on prescription, used to treat a wide range of bacterial infections. It is produced in the form of capsules (in which form it is not recommended for women who are pregnant or for children under 12 years), as a cream and as an ointment. In every form it is a preparation of the TETRACYCLINE chlortetracycline hydrochloride.
▲/✚ side-effects/warning: see CHLORTETRACYCLINE.

**Aveeno Regular** (*Dendron*) is a proprietary, non-prescription bath additive for soothing and softening the skin, and to relieve itching in conditions such as prickly heat and eczema. Produced in the form of powder in sachets, it is a preparation of oat protein.

**Aveeno Oilated** (*Dendron*) is a proprietary, non-prescription bath additive for soothing and softening the skin, and to relieve itching in conditions such as prickly heat and eczema. Produced in the form of powder in sachets, it is a preparation of oat protein and liquid paraffin.

**Aventyl** (*Lilly*) is a proprietary ANTIDEPRESSANT drug, available only on prescription, used to treat depressive illness – but also used to treat nocturnal bedwetting in children (although not recommended for children aged under 6 years or for treatment periods of longer than three months). Produced in the form of capsules (in two strengths), Aventyl represents a preparation of nortriptyline hydrochloride.

▲/● side-effects/warning: see NORTRIPTYLINE.

**Avloclor** (*ICI*) is a proprietary ANTIMALARIAL drug, available only on prescription, used primarily to prevent or treat certain forms of malaria, but also used as an AMOEBICIDAL drug to treat amoebic hepatitis, and to treat rheumatoid arthritis. Produced in the form of tablets, Avloclor is a preparation of chloroquine phosphate. In children under 12 years of age, Avloclor is used only to prevent or to suppress malaria.

▲/● side-effects/warning: see CHLOROQUINE.

**Avomine** (*May & Baker*) is a proprietary, non-prescription ANTINAUSEANT drug used to treat symptoms of nausea, vomiting and/or vertigo caused by certain diseases, motion sickness, or some forms of drug therapy. Produced in the form of tablets, Avomine is a preparation of promethazine theoclate.

▲/● side-effects/warning: see PROMETHAZINE THEOCLATE.

**Azactam** (*Squibb*) is a proprietary ANTIBIOTIC, available only on prescription, used to treat severe infections caused by gram-negative bacteria, including gonorrhoea and infections of the urinary tract. Produced in the form of powder for reconstitution as a medium for injection or infusion, Azactam is a preparation of aztreonam.

▲/● side-effects/warning: see AZTREONAM.

**Azamune** (*Penn*) is a proprietary IMMUNOSUPPRESSANT drug, available only on prescription, used to reduce the possibility of tissue rejection in patients who undergo donor skin grafts or organ transplants. It may also be used to treat other conditions where the more usual corticosteroid therapies have failed. Produced in the form of tablets, Azamune is a preparation of the CYTOTOXIC drug azathioprine.

▲/● side-effects/warning: see AZATHIOPRINE.

**azapropazone** is a non-steroidal ANTI-INFLAMMATORY non-narcotic ANALGESIC, used primarily to treat rheumatic and arthritic complaints, gout, and musculo-skeletal pain. Administration is oral in the form of capsules and tablets. It is not recommended for children.

▲ side-effects: there is commonly a rash; there may also be a sensitivity to light. Sometimes there is accumulation of fluid within the tissues (oedema) and consequent weight gain. There may be gastrointestinal upsets.

● warning: azapropazone should not be administered to patients with peptic ulcer or impairment of kidney function, or who are taking sulphonamides; it should be administered with caution to those with impaired liver function or with allergic disorders, who are elderly, or who are pregnant. It should not be given to patients who are taking phenytoin, drugs that lower the blood sugar level, or anticoagulants. *Related article:* RHEUMOX.

**azatadine maleate** is an ANTIHISTAMINE drug, used primarily to treat allergic symptoms such as hay fever and urticaria, and those arising from insect bites and stings. Administration is oral in the form of tablets, or as a syrup. Its proprietary form is not recommended for children aged under 12 months.

▲ side-effects: sedation may affect patients' capacity for speed of thought and movement; there may be nausea, headaches and/or weight gain, dry mouth, gastrointestinal disturbances and visual problems.

✿ warning: patients taking azatadine maleate should avoid alcohol. It should be administered with caution to patients who are pregnant, or with glaucoma, urinary retention, intestinal obstruction, enlargement of the prostate gland, peptic ulcer, epilepsy or liver disease.
*Related articles:* CONGESTEZE; OPTIMINE.

**azathioprine** is a powerful IMMUNOSUPPRESSANT drug used mostly to reduce the possibility of tissue rejection in patients who undergo donor grafts or transplants. It may also be used to treat autoimmune diseases, some collagen disorders, and other conditions where the more usual steroid therapies have failed. Administration is oral in the form of tablets, or by injection.

▲ side-effects: there may be suppression of the bone-marrow's function, rashes and liver damage.

✿ warning: as with all CYTOTOXIC drugs, patients receiving azathioprine are prone to infections. Constant checking of blood counts is essential to monitor and adjust dosage for any bone-marrow toxicity.
*Related articles:* AZAMUNE; IMURAN.

**azlocillin** is a penicillin-type ANTIBIOTIC used primarily to treat infections by a type of gram-

negative bacteria called Pseudomonas, and particularly in serious infections of the urinary tract and respiratory tract, and for septicaemia. Administration is by injection or infusion.

▲ side-effects: there may be some allergic reactions – such as a rash – and high temperature; some patients experience pain in the joints. Diarrhoea may occur.

✿ warning: azlocillin should not be administered to patients who are known to be allergic to penicillins; it should be administered with caution to those who have impaired kidney function, or who are pregnant.
*Related article:* SECUROPEN.

**aztreonam** is an ANTIBIOTIC used to treat severe infections caused by gram-negative bacteria. Administration is by injection or infusion. A relatively recent addition to the pharmacopoeia of the beta lactam type (which includes the penicillins), aztreonam is thought to arouse fewer sensitivity reactions than are caused by many other antibiotics of the beta lactam type.

▲ side-effects: there may be diarrhoea and vomiting; skin rashes may occur, with pain or inflammation at the site of injection or infusion. Rarely, there may be reduction in the number of white cells in the blood, causing bleeding and lowered resistance to infection.

✿ warning: aztreonam should not be administered to patients who are pregnant; it should be administered with caution to those who are known to be sensitive to penicillin or cephalosporin, who have impaired kidney or liver function, or who are lactating.
*Related article:* AZACTAM.

**bacampicillin hydrochloride** is a broad-spectrum, penicillin-type ANTIBIOTIC, a derivative of AMPICILLIN, which is converted to ampicillin in the bloodstream. Used to treat many infections, especially those of the urogenital areas, upper respiratory tract and middle ear, it is administered orally in the form of tablets.

▲ side-effects: there may be sensitivity reactions, ranging from a minor rash to urticaria, high temperature and joint pain, or even to anaphylactic shock. The most common side-effect, however, is simply diarrhoea.

● warning: bacampicillin hydrochloride should not be administered to patients who are known to be allergic to penicillin-type antibiotics; it should be administered with caution to those with impaired kidney function.
*Related article:* AMBAXIN.

**bacitracin** is an ANTIBIOTIC drug, a polypeptide, usually used in the form of bacitracin zinc, for the treatment of infections of the skin. It is usually combined with other antibiotics in the form of an ointment or powder for topical application.
*Related articles:* CICATRIN; POLYBACTRIN; POLYFAX; TRIBIOTIC; TRI-CITATRIN.

**baclofen** is a drug used as a SKELETAL MUSCLE RELAXANT that relaxes muscles which are in spasm, especially muscles in the limbs, and particularly when caused by injury or disease in the central nervous system. Although it is chemically unrelated to any other ANTISPASMODIC drug, it has similar clinical uses to certain of the benzodiazepine group of drugs. Administration is oral in the form of tablets or a dilute sugar-free liquid.

▲ side-effects: there may be drowsiness and fatigue, weakness and low blood pressure (hypotension); elderly or debilitated patients may enter a state of confusion. Nausea and vomiting may occur.

● warning: baclofen should be administered with caution to patients with impaired cerebrovascular system, epilepsy, or psychiatric conditions, or who are elderly. Initial dosage should be gradually increased (to avoid sedation); withdrawal of treatment should be equally gradual.
*Related article:* LIORESAL.

**Bacticlens** (*Smith & Nephew*) is a proprietary, non-prescription DISINFECTANT, used to treat minor wounds and burns on the skin. Produced in the form of a solution in sachets, Bacticlens is a preparation of chlorhexidine gluconate.

▲/● side-effects/warning: *see* CHLORHEXIDINE.

**Bactigras** (*Smith & Nephew*) is a proprietary, non-prescription dressing in the form of gauze impregnated with chlorhexidine acetate. It is used to treat wounds and ulcers.

▲/● side-effects/warning: *see* CHLORHEXIDINE.

**Bactrian** (*Loveridge*) is a proprietary, non-prescription ANTISEPTIC cream used in the treatment of minor burns and abrasions. It contains the antiseptic CETRIMIDE in very dilute solution.

**Bactrim** (*Roche*) is a proprietary ANTIBACTERIAL available only on prescription, used to treat bacterial infections, especially infections of the urinary tract, sinusitis and bronchitis, and infections of bones and joints. Produced in the form of tablets (in three strengths), as soluble (dispersible) tablets, as a suspension for dilution (the potency of the suspension once dilute is retained for 14 days), as a sugar-free syrup for dilution (the potency of the syrup once dilute is retained for 14 days), and in ampoules for intravenous infusion (following dilution). Bactrim is a compound preparation, co-trimoxazole, which is five parts of a SULPHONAMIDE, sulphamethazole, to one part of TRIMETHOPRIM.

▲/ ✿ side-effects/warning: *see* CO-TRIMOXAZOLE.

**Bactroban** (*Beecham*) is a proprietary ANTIBIOTIC, available only on prescription, used in topical applications to treat bacterial infections of the skin. Produced in the form of a water-miscible ointment, Bactroban is a preparation of MUPIROCIN in dilute solution.

✿ warning: the ointment may sting on application.

**Bactroban nasal** (*Beecham*) is a proprietary ANTIBIOTIC available only on prescription, used to treat staphylococcal infections in and around the nostrils. Produced in the form of an ointment for topical application, Bactroban nasal is a preparation of the antibiotic drug mupirocin.

▲/ ✿ side-effects/warning: *see* MUPIROCIN.

**Balanced Salt Solution** (*Alcon; Cooper Vision Optics*) is a proprietary, non-prescription sterile solution, used as an eye-wash. It is a preparation of SODIUM CHLORIDE, SODIUM CITRATE, sodium acetate, MAGNESIUM CHLORIDE and POTASSIUM CHLORIDE.

**Balmosa** (*Pharmax*) is a proprietary, non-prescription COUNTER-IRRITANT cream which,

applied topically, causes an irritation of the sensory nerve endings that has the effect of beneficially offsetting the pain of underlying muscle and joint ailments. It is thus used to treat rheumatic pains, lumbago and sciatica. It is a preparation that contains methyl salicylate, camphor, menthol and capsicum resin.

**Balneum** (*Merck*) is a proprietary, non-prescription skin emollient (softener and soother) for use in the bath; it is a preparation of soya oil in a fragrant solution. It is also produced in the form of Balneum with Tar, to treat psoriasis and eczema.

**Balspray** (*Bullen*) is a proprietary skin cleanser and protective spray used to sanitize a stoma (an outlet in the skin surface representing the surgical curtailment of the intestines). A powder for the same purpose is produced under the same name.

**Baltar** (*Merck*) is a proprietary, non-prescription, medicated fragrant shampoo used to treat dandruff and psoriasis: its active constituent is coal tar

▲/ ✿ side-effects/warning: *see* COAL TAR.

**bamethan sulphate** is a VASODILATOR used to improve blood circulation in the forearms and hands, and calves and feet, during exercise. Administration is oral in the form of tablets.

▲ side-effects: there may be an increase in the heart rate, and flushing. Low blood pressure may cause dizziness on the patient's rising from a sitting or lying position.

✿ warning: bamethan sulphate should not be administered to patients who have recently suffered a heart attack; it should be administered with caution to those with angina pectoris. The drug cannot treat the symptoms of poor peripheral circulation that occur while the body is at rest.

**Banocide** (*Wellcome*) is a proprietary preparation of the drug diethylcarbamazine, used to treat infestations by filarial worm-parasites (such as those that cause elephantiasis, lymphangitis, loiasis and onchocerciasis). It may also be used to treat certain stages of toxocaral infections. Side-effects are inevitable, and may be severe (but should be treated with other drugs); close monitoring is essential throughout treatment, but particularly at first. Several courses of treatment may be necessary. It is produced in the form of tablets.
▲/◆ side-effects/warning: *see* DIETHYLCARBAMAZINE.

**Baratol** (*Wyeth*) is a proprietary ANTIHYPERTENSIVE drug, available only on prescription, and often used in combination with other antihypertensives. Produced in the form of tablets (in two strengths), Baratol is a preparation of (the ALPHA-BLOCKER) indoramin hydrochloride.
▲/◆ side-effects/warning: *see* INDORAMIN.

**barbiturates** are a group of drugs derived from barbituric acid, with a wide range of essentially depressent actions. They are used mostly as SEDATIVES and ANAESTHETICS. They work by direct action on the brain, depressing specific centres, and may be slow- or fast-acting; all are extremely effective. However, all also quite rapidly produce tolerance and then both psychological and physical dependence, and for that reason are used as sparingly as possible.

Moreover, prolonged use even in small dosage can have serious toxic side-effects, potentially leading to death. Best-known and most used barbiturates include the minor tranquillizers amylobarbitone and pentobarbitone, the sedative and anticonvulsant phenobarbitone, and the anaesthetic thiopentone. Administration is oral in the form of tablets, or by injection.
▲ side-effects: there is drowsiness and dizziness within a hangover effect; there may be shallow breathing and headache. Some patients experience sensitivity reactions that may be serious.
◆ warning: barbiturates should be avoided wherever possible. They should not in any case be administered to patients who suffer from insomnia caused by pain or from porphyria, who are pregnant or lactating, who are elderly, debilitated or very young, or who have a history of drug or alcohol abuse (barbiturates greatly enhance the effects of alcohol). Barbiturates should be administered with caution to those with kidney or liver disease, or impaired lung function. Prolonged use should be avoided, as should abrupt withdrawal of treatment (which might lead to withdrawal symptoms). Tolerance develops when barbiturates are taken repeatedly, an increasingly larger dose being necessary to produce the same effect; continued use leads to psychological and physical dependence.
*see* AMYLOBARBITONE; BUTOBARBITONE; CYCLOBARBITONE CALCIUM; METHYLPHENOBARBITONE; PHENOBARBITONE;

57

QUINALBARBITONE SODIUM;
THIOPENTONE SODIUM.

**Barquinol HC** (*Fisons*) is a proprietary, non-prescription corticosteroid cream used to treat mild inflammations of the skin. Apart from its anti-inflammatory properties it also has some ANTIBACTERIAL and ANTIFUNGAL activity because in addition to the steroid hydrocortisone acetate it also contains the iodine-based antiseptic clioquinol.
▲/✚ side-effects/warning: *see* CLIOQUINOL.

**Baxan** (*Bristol-Myers*) is a proprietary ANTIBIOTIC, available only on prescription, used to treat many infections, especially those of the skin and soft tissues, the respiratory and urinary tracts, and the middle ear. Produced in the form of capsules, and as a suspension (in three strengths) for dilution, Baxan is a preparation of the CEPHALOSPORIN cefadroxil monohydrate.
▲/✚ side-effects/warning: *see* CEFADROXIL.

**Baycaron** (*Bayer*) is a proprietary DIURETIC, available only on prescription, used to treat fluid retention in the tissues (oedema) and high blood pressure (*see* ANTIHYPERTENSIVE); it may thus also be used to treat some of the symptoms of premenstrual syndrome. Simultaneous administration of a POTASSIUM supplement is often advised. Produced in the form of tablets, Baycaron is a preparation of the THIAZIDE-like drug mefruside, and is not recommended for children.
▲/✚ side-effects/warning: *see* MEFRUSIDE.

**Bayolin** (*Bayer*) is a proprietary, non-prescription COUNTER-IRRITANT cream, which, when applied topically, causes an irritation of the sensory nerve endings that offsets the pain of underlying muscle and joint ailments. It is used particularly to treat rheumatic pain, and contains a derivative of the anticoagulant HEPARIN together with glycol salicylate and benzyl nicotinate.

**Baypen** (*Bayer*) is a proprietary, broad-spectrum, penicillin-type ANTIBIOTIC, used to treat many infections and to prevent others following abdominal and/or uterine surgery. Produced in the form of powder in vials for reconstitution as a medium for injection or infusion, Baypen is a preparation of mezlocillin.
▲/✚ side-effects/warning: *see* MEZLOCILLIN.

**BC 500** (*Ayerst*) is a proprietary, non-prescription multivitamin supplement, which is not available from the National Health Service. It is used to treat deficiency of vitamins B and C, particularly in conditions such as convalescence from debilitating illness or chronic alcoholism, and contains THIAMINE (vitamin $B_1$), RIBOFLAVINE (vitamin $B_2$), PYRIDOXINE (vitamin $B_6$), NICOTINAMIDE (of the B complex), PANTOTHENIC ACID (of the B complex), and ASCORBIC ACID (vitamin C).

**BC 500 with Iron** (*Ayerst*) is a preparation of the proprietary, non-prescription multivitamin supplement BC 500, which also includes IRON in the form of ferrous fumarate. It is used especially to treat deficiencies of vitamins B and C, and of iron (as for example may occur during pregnancy).
▲/✚ side-effects/warning: *see* FERROUS FUMARATE.

**BCG vaccine** (*bacillus Calmette-Guérin* vaccine) is a strain of the tuberculosis bacillus that no longer causes the disease in humans but does cause the formation in the body of the specific antibodies, and so can be used as the base for an ANTITUBERCULAR vaccine. It is administered intradermally.

**beclamide** is an ANTICONVULSANT drug for various epileptic disorders (including grand mal and psychomotor epilepsies) and in the management of some behavioural disorders in non-epileptic patients. Administration is oral in the form of tablets.
▲ side-effects: there may be gastrointestinal disturbance and impaired kidney function, leading to weight loss; a rash may appear. Some patients experience dizziness. The white blood cell count may be reduced.
✦ warning: beclamide is used as a secondary form of therapy: previous antiepileptic drug treatment should be continued in parallel for a month as treatment with beclamide is gradually introduced.
*Related article:* NYDRANE.

**Becloforte** (*Allen & Hanburys*) is a proprietary preparation of the CORTICOSTEROID drug beclomethasone dipropionate, available only on prescription, used to treat the symptoms of asthma, chronic bronchitis and emphysema. Produced in an aerosol for inhalation, one form (Becloforte VM) comes with a volumatic, it is not recommended for children.
▲/✦ side-effects/warning: *see* BECLOMETHASONE DIPROPIONATE.

**beclomethasone dipropionate** is a CORTICOSTEROID used primarily to treat the symptoms of asthma, chronic bronchitis and emphysema. It is thought to work by reducing inflammation in the

mucous lining of the bronchial passages, and stemming allergic reactions. For many patients the best results are achieved if a BRONCHODILATOR such as salbutamol is inhaled about 10 minutes before administration. (One proprietary preparation combines the two.) The drug is also used in the form of a cream or an ointment for topical application to treat serious non-infective inflammations on the skin, or as a nasal spray to treat conditions such as hay fever. For bronchial treatment, however, it is produced mostly in aerosols for inhalation, although it is available also as powder for insufflation or as a suspension for nebulization.
▲ side-effects: some patients undergoing bronchial treatment experience hoarseness; large doses increase a risk of fungal infection. The nasal spray may cause initial sneezing.
✦ warning: as with all corticosteroids, beclomethasone treats the symptoms and has no effect on any underlying infection: such an infection, if remaining undetected, may reach potentially serious proportions while its symptoms are masked by the corticosteroid. In any case, prolonged use should be avoided because of side-effects. Prolonged high doses may give adrenal suppression.
*Related articles:* BECLOFORTE; BECOTIDE; VENTIDE.

**Becodisks** (*Allen and Hanburys*) is a proprietary preparation of the CORTICO-STEROID drug beclomethasone dipropionate, available only on prescription, used to treat the symptoms of asthma, chronic bronchitis and emphysema. It is produced as a powder for inhalation in discs containing 8

**B**

blisters for use with a Diskhaler device.

▲/❋ side-effects/warning: *see* BECLOMETHASONE DIPROPIONATE.

**Beconase** (*Allen & Hanburys*) is a proprietary nasal spray, available only on prescription, used to treat conditions such as hay fever. Produced in both an aerosol and a nasal applicator, Beconase is a preparation of the CORTICOSTEROID beclomethasone dipropionate.

▲/❋ side-effects/warning: *see* BECLOMETHASONE DIPROPIONATE.

**Becosym** is a proprietary, non-prescription VITAMIN B supplement, which is not available from the National Health Service. Produced in the form of tablets (in two strengths, the stronger under the trade name Becosym Forte), and as a syrup for dilution (the potency of the syrup once dilute is retained for 14 days), Becosym contains several forms of vitamin B, including THIAMINE, RIBOFLAVINE and PYRIDOXINE.

**Becotide** (*Allen & Hanburys*) is a proprietary preparation of the CORTICOSTEROID drug beclomethasone dipropionate, available only on prescription, used to treat the symptoms of asthma, chronic bronchitis and emphysema. It is produced in an aerosol for inhalation (in two strengths, the stronger under the name Becotide 100), in inhalation cartridges (using the name Rotacaps), and as a suspension for nebulization.

▲/❋ side-effects/warning: *see* BECLOMETHASONE DIPROPIONATE.

**Bedranol** (*Lagap*) is a proprietary ANTIHYPERTENSIVE drug of the BETA-BLOCKER class, available

only on prescription, used to treat high blood pressure (hypertension), and also to relieve angina pectoris and to slow and/or regularize the heartbeat in order to prevent a recurrent heart attack. The drug may also be used to treat the effect of an excess of thyroid hormones in the bloodstream (thyrotoxicosis) or to prevent migraine attacks. Produced in the form of tablets (in four strengths), Bedranol is a preparation of the beta-blocker propranolol hydrochloride.

▲/❋ side-effects/warning: *see* PROPRANOLOL.

**Bedranol S.R.** (*Lagap*) is a proprietary BETA-BLOCKER, available only on prescription, used to treat angina pectoris (heart pain), myocardial infarction, heart arrhythmias, high blood pressure (hypertension) and anxiety; to try to prevent migraine attacks; and to assist in the treatment of excess thyroid hormones in the blood (thyrotoxicosis). Produced in the form of sustained-release capsules Bedranol S.R. is a preparation of propranolol hydrochloride. In the treatment of most of the disorders listed above, it is not recommended for children.

▲/❋ side-effects/warning: *see* PROPRANOLOL.

**Beecham's Powders** (*Beecham Health Care*) is a proprietary, non-prescription cold relief preparation. It contains paracetamol, caffeine and ascorbic acid.

▲/❋ side-effects/warning: *see* ASCORBIC ACID, CAFFEINE, PARACETAMOL.

**belladonna** is the name of both a solanaceous plant (deadly nightshade) and of the alkaloids produced from it and related plants, from which in turn the drugs ATROPINE (hyoscyamine) and HYOSCINE are extracted. Both of those pure drugs have several uses, but the plant alkaloids too are used therapeutically – mostly (in compounds with aluminium or magnesium salts) to assist in the treatment of gastrointestinal disorders caused by smooth muscle spasm in the intestine, because the alkaloids have antispasmodic properties.

▲ side-effects: there is commonly dry mouth and thirst; there may also be visual disturbances, flushing, irregular heartbeat and constipation.

✿ warning: belladonna alkaloids should not be administered to patients with enlargement of the prostate gland or with glaucoma; they should be administered with caution to those with heart problems and rapid heart rate, ulcerative colitis, or urinary retention; who are elderly; or who are lactating.

*Related articles:* ALKA-DONNA; ALKA-DONNA-P; ALUHYDE; BELLOCARB; CARBELLON; NEUTRADONNA.

**Bellocarb** (*Sinclair*) is a proprietary, non-prescription ANTICHOLINERGIC compound, which is not available from the National Health Service. It is used to treat muscle spasm of the intestine, and other gastro-intestinal upsets including stomach acidity. Produced in the form of tablets, Bellocarb's active constituents are belladonna extract, magnesium trisilicate, and magnesium carbonate.

▲/✿ side-effects/warning: *see* BELLADONNA; MAGNESIUM CARBONATE; MAGNESIUM TRISILICATE.

**Benadon** (*Roche*) is a proprietary, non-prescription VITAMIN B supplement, which is not available from the National Health Service. Used to treat vitamin deficiency and associated symptoms, Benadon is a preparation of vitamin B₆: PYRIDOXINE hydrochloride. It is produced in the form of tablets (in two strengths).

**Benadryl** (*Parke-Davis*) is a proprietary, non-prescription ANTIHISTAMINE used to treat the symptoms of (allergy-based) conditions such as hay fever and urticaria. It also has ANTINAUSEANT properties and is used to treat or prevent travel sickness, vertigo and infections of the inner or middle ear. Produced in the form of capsules, Benadryl is a preparation of the somewhat sedative antihistamine diphenhydramine hydrochloride. It is not recommended for children.

▲/✿ side-effects/warning: *see* DIPHENHYDRAMINE HYDROCHLORIDE.

**Bendogen** (*Lagap*) is a proprietary ANTIHYPERTENSIVE drug, available only on prescription, used to treat moderate to severe high blood pressure (hypertension), especially when other forms of treatment have failed. Administered in combination with a DIURETIC or a BETA-BLOCKER, Bendogen works by inhibiting the release in the body of the neurotransmitter NORADRENALINE. It represents a preparation of bethanidine sulphate, and is produced in the form of tablets (in two strengths).

▲/✿ side-effects/warning: *see* BETHANIDINE SULPHATE.

**bendrofluazide** is a THIAZIDE DIURETIC that may be used to treat hypertension, either alone or in conjunction with other ANTIHYPERTENSIVE agents, because it has a slight lowering effect on blood pressure. Like the

B

other thiazides, bendrofluazide is used in the treatment of oedema associated with congestive heart failure and renal and hepatic disorders. Blood potassium levels should be monitored in patients taking thiazide diuretics because they may deplete body reserves of potassium. However, potassium supplements or potassium-sparing diuretics should be added only when appropriate (hyper-calcaemia is particularly hazardous in the elderly). Administration is oral in the form of tablets.

▲ side-effects: there may be tiredness and skin rashes, thirst, nausea, dizziness. In men, temporary impotence may occur.

◆ warning: bendrofluazide should not be administered to patients with kidney failure or urinary retention, or who are lactating. It should be administered with caution to those who are pregnant. It may aggravate conditions of diabetes or gout. *Related articles:* APRINOX; BERKOZIDE; CENTYL; NEO-NACLEX; URIZIDE.

**Benemid** (*Merck, Sharp & Dohme*) is a proprietary preparation of the compound drug probenecid, which, because it reduces blood levels of uric acid by promoting its excretion in the urine, is used primarily to treat gout. Available only on prescription, it is produced in the form of tablets, and is not recommended for children.

▲/◆ side-effects/warning: *see* PROBENECID.

**Benerva** (*Roche*) is a proprietary non-prescription VITAMIN B supplement, which is not available from the National Health Service. Used to treat vitamin deficiency and associated symptoms, Benerva is a preparation of vitamin $B_1$.

THIAMINE hydrochloride. It is produced in the form of tablets (in six strengths) and (available only on prescription) in ampoules for injection (in two strengths).

**Benerva Compound** (*Roche*) is a proprietary, non-prescription VITAMIN B supplement, which is not available from the National Health Service. Used to treat vitamin deficiency and associated symptoms, Benerva Compound is a preparation of various forms of vitamin B; it is produced in the form of tablets.

**benethamine penicillin** is a penicillin-type ANTIBIOTIC that is used, along with other penicillins, to treat and prevent infections caused by sensitive gram-positive organisms such as streptococci. It is a very soluble salt of BENZYLPENICILLIN (penicillin G), which is slowly released from the injection site to give low plasma levels over a long period of time. Administration is by deep intramuscular injection.

▲ side-effects: there may be sensitivity reactions ranging from a minor rash to urticaria and joint pains, and (occasionally) to high temperature or anaphylactic shock.

◆ warning: benethamine penicillin should not be administered to patients who are known to be allergic to penicillins; it should be administered with caution to those who suffer from impaired kidney function. *Related articles:* CAPITOL; TRIPLOPEN.

**Bengué's Balsam** (*Bengué*) is a proprietary, non-prescription COUNTER-IRRITANT ointment, which, when applied topically, causes an irritation of the sensory nerve endings that offsets the pain of underlying muscle and joint ailments. It is thus used to treat rheumatic pains, and contains methyl salicylate and menthol in a lanolin base.

♣ warning: Lanolin causes sensitivity reactions in some patients.

**Bengué's Balsam SG** (*Bengué*) is a proprietary, non-prescription COUNTER-IRRITANT cream, which, when applied topically, causes an irritation of the sensory nerve endings that offsets the pain of underlying muscle and joint ailments. It is thus used to treat rheumatic pains, and contains methyl salicylate and menthol in a vanishing-cream base.

**Benoral** (*Sterling Research*) is a proprietary, non-prescription non-narcotic ANALGESIC used to treat mild to moderate pain, especially the pain of rheumatic disease and other musculo-skeletal disorders. Produced in the form of tablets, as a powder in sachets for solution, and as a sugar-free suspension for dilution (the potency of the suspension once dilute is retained for 14 days), Benoral is a preparation of an ester derived from both ASPIRIN and PARACETAMOL called benorylate.

▲ / ♣ side-effects/warning: see BENORYLATE.

**benorylate** is a non-narcotic ANALGESIC, with both anti-inflammatory and antipyretic actions, which is chemically derived from both ASPIRIN and PARACETAMOL, and is used particularly to treat the pain of rheumatic disease and other musculo-skeletal disorders, and to lower a high temperature. The paracetamol constituent is released more slowly into the bloodstream than the aspirin. Administration is oral in the form of tablets, a solution or a dilute suspension.

▲ side-effects: gastrointestinal disturbance is fairly common, but there may also be nausea

and bleeding. Some patients experience hearing disturbances and vertigo. A few proceed to hypersensitivity reactions, blood disorders, or a state of confusion. Prolonged use or overdosage may cause liver damage.

♣ warning: benorylate should not be administered to patients intolerant of aspirin, with peptic ulcers, who are already taking aspirin or paracetamol in some other form, or who are aged under 12 years. It should be administered with caution to those with allergic conditions, who have impaired kidney or liver function, who suffer from alcoholism, or from dehydration; who are elderly; who are pregnant or lactating; or who are already taking anticoagulant drugs.
*Related article:* BENORAL.

**benoxinate** is an alternative name for the local ANAESTHETIC oxybuprocaine, used in eye-drops.
*see* OXYBUPROCAINE.

**Benoxyl** (*Stiefel*) is a proprietary preparation of the drug benzoyl peroxide, which, when applied topically in the form of a cream or an ointment, removes hardened or dead skin (it is KERATOLYTIC) while simultaneously treating bacterial infection. It is most used in the treatment of acne. In its standard form (under the name Benoxyl 5) it is produced as both a cream and an ointment, and in a version that additionally contains sulphur (under the name Benoxyl 5 with Sulphur). There is also a stronger version of the standard (produced under the trade name Benoxyl 10) that appears as a lotion, and a corresponding cream that includes sulphur (produced under the name Benoxyl 10 with Sulphur). Finally, there is a preparation that is stronger still (produced under the name

Benoxyl 20); it too is marketed as a lotion, and removes hard and dead skin from the edges of skin ulcers and lesions.

▲/✿ side-effects/warning: *see* BENZOYL PEROXIDE.

**benperidol** is a powerful ANTIPSYCHOTIC drug, used to treat and tranquillize psychotics, especially suitable for treating antisocial and deviant forms of sexual behaviour. Administration is oral in the form of tablets. It is not recommended for children.

▲ side-effects: sedation and extrapyramidal symptoms are likely to occur. There may also be restlessness, insomnia and nightmares; rashes and jaundice may appear; and there may be dry mouth, gastrointestinal disturbance, difficulties in urinating, and blurred vision. Muscles in the neck and back, and sometimes the arms, may undergo spasms. Rarely, there is weight loss and impaired kidney function.

✿ warning: benperidol should not be administered to patients who have a reduction in the bone-marrow's capacity to produce blood cells, or certain types of glaucoma. It should be administered only with caution to those with heart or vascular disease, kidney or liver disease, parkinsonism, or depression; or who are pregnant or lactating. *Related article:* ANQUIL.

**benserazide** is an enzyme inhibitor that is administered therapeutically in combination with the powerful drug levodopa to treat parkinsonism, but not the parkinsonian symptoms induced by drugs (*see* ANTIPARKINSONISM) The benserazide prevents too rapid a breakdown in the body of the levodopa (into dopamine), allowing more levodopa to reach the brain to make up the deficiency (of dopamine) that is

the major cause of parkinsonian symptoms. Administration of the combination is oral in the form of capsules.

▲/✿ side-effects/warning: complex mode of action makes side-effects and interactions with many other drugs likely, so great care should be taken in its use. Also *see* LEVODOPA. *Related article:* MADOPAR.

**Bentex** (*Steinhard*) is a proprietary preparation of the drug benzhexol hydrochloride, available only on prescription, used to relieve some of the symptoms of parkinsonism (*see* ANTIPARKINSONISM), specifically overall rigidity of posture, and the tendency to produce an excess of saliva. (The drug also has the capacity to treat these conditions in some cases where they are produced by drugs.) It is thought to work by compensating indirectly for the lack of dopamine in the brain that is the major cause of such parkinsonian symptoms. Bentex is produced in the form of tablets (in two strengths), to be taken before or after food. Counselling of patients is advised.

▲/✿ side-effects/warning: *see* BENZHEXOL HYDROCHLORIDE

**bentonite** is an absorbent powder administered therapeutically in emergencies to absorb corrosive substances like paraquat (the toxic horticultural preparation) in cases of accidental poisoning, and to reduce further absorption by the body. The entire alimentary canal has then to be evacuated, bathed, cleaned and soothed.

**Benylin Expectorant** (*Parke-Davis*) is a proprietary, non-prescription EXPECTORANT, which is not available from the National Health Service. Intended to promote the coughing up of bronchial secretions that might otherwise clog the air passages, it contains the expectorant AMMONIUM CHLORIDE, the ANTIHISTAMINE diphenhydramine hydrochloride, sodium citrate, and menthol. It is produced in the form of a syrup for dilution (the potency of the syrup once dilute is retained for 14 days), and is not recommended for children aged under 12 months. A version without ammonium chloride is also available (under the name Benylin Paediatric); and there is a version that additionally includes the ANALGESIC codeine phosphate (under the name Benylin with Codeine).

▲/❁ side-effects/warning: *see* CODEINE PHOSPHATE; DIPHENHYDRAMINE HYDROCHLORIDE; SODIUM CITRATE.

**Benzagel** (*Bioglan*) is a proprietary preparation of the drug benzoyl peroxide, which when applied topically in the form of a gel removes hardened or dead skin (it is KERATOLYTIC) while simultaneously treating bacterial infection. It is most used in the treatment of acne, and is produced in two strengths (under the names Benzagel 5 and Benzagel 10, the figures representing the percentage of solute).

▲/❁ side-effects/warning: *see* BENZOYL PEROXIDE.

**benzalkonium chloride** is an astringent ANTISEPTIC that also has some KERATOLYTIC properties and may be used in topical application to remove hard, dead skin from around wounds or ulcers, or to dissolve warts. It is also used on minor abrasions and burns, and (in the form of lozenges to be sucked) on mouth ulcers or gum disease, simply as a disinfectant. For other than oral

purposes, administration is topical in the form of a cream or, combined with bromine, as a paint.

❁ warning: in topical application, keep benzalkonium chloride off normal skin.
*Related articles:* CAPITOL; DRAPOLENE.

**benzathine penicillin** is a penicillin-type ANTIBIOTIC that is used to treat many bacterial infections. In high dosage, given intramuscularly, it is used especially to treat syphilis (although PROCAINE PENICILLIN appears more effective in this) or to prevent patients at risk from contracting rheumatic fever. Administration is oral in the form of a suspension or drops, or by injection.

▲ side-effects: there may be sensitivity reactions ranging from a minor rash to urticaria and joint pains, and (occasionally) to high temperature or anaphylactic shock.
❁ warning: benzathine penicillin should not be administered to patients who are known to be allergic to penicillins; it should be administered with caution to those with impaired kidney function.
*Related article:* PENIDURAL.

**benzhexol hydrochloride** is an ANTICHOLINERGIC agent employed in the treatment of some types of parkinsonism (*see* ANTI-PARKINSONISM). It increases mobility and decreases rigidity, but it has only a limited effect on tremors. The tendency to produce an excess of saliva is also reduced by benzhexol. (The drug also has the capacity to treat these conditions in some cases where they are produced by drugs.) It is thought to work by compensating for the lack of dopamine in the brain, which is the major cause of such parkinsonian symptoms by reducing the cholinergic excess. Administration which may be in parallel with the administration of other drugs used for the relief of parkinsonism - is oral in the form of tablets or sustained-release capsules, or as a dilute syrup.

▲ side-effects: there may be dry mouth, dizziness and blurred vision, and/or gastrointestinal disturbances. Some patients experience sensitivity reactions and anxiety. Rarely, and in susceptible patients, there may be confusion, agitation and psychological disturbance (at which point treatment must be withdrawn).

● warning: benzhexol hydrochloride should not be administered to patients who have not only tremor but distinct involuntary movements; it should be administered with caution to those with impaired kidney or liver function, cardiovascular disease, glaucoma, or urinary retention. Withdrawal of treatment must be gradual.

*Related articles:* ARTANE; BENTEX; BROFLEX.

**benzocaine** is a mild local ANAESTHETIC used in topical application for the relief of pain in the skin surface or mucous membranes, particularly in or around the mouth and throat, or (in combination with other drugs) in the ears. Administration is in various forms: as a cream, as anal suppositories, as an ointment, and as ear-drops.

● warning: prolonged use should be avoided; some patients experience sensitivity reactions.

*Related articles:* AUDICORT; DEQUACAINE; MEDILAVE; SOLARCAINE.

**benzodiazepines** are a large group of drugs that have a marked effect upon the central nervous system. The effect varies with different members of the group, however, and some are used primarily as SEDATIVES or HYPNOTICS, whereas others are used more as ANXIOLYTICS, MUSCLE RELAXANTS or ANTICONVULSANTS. Those that are used as hypnotics have virtually replaced the barbiturates, for the benzodiazepines are just as effective but are much safer in the event of an overdose, although some caution is necessary in treating patients who suffer from respiratory depression. There are now antagonists for reversing the effects of benzodiazepines (for instance at the end of operations): *see* FLUMAZENIL. It is now realized that dependence may result from continued usage, and that also there may be a paradoxical increase in hostility and aggresion in those on longer-term treatment. Best-known and most-used benzodiazepines include diazepam (used particularly to control the convulsions of epilepsy or drug poisoning), nitrazepam (a widely used hypnotic), lorazepam (an anxiolytic) and loprazolam (a tranquillizer used to treat insomnia).

▲/● side-effects/warning: *see* ALPRAZOLAM; BROMAZEPAM; CHLORDIAZEPOXIDE; CLONAZEPAM; DIAZEPAM; FLUNITRAZEPAM; FLURAZEPAM; KETAZOLAM; LOPRAZOLAM; LORAZEPAM; LORMETAZEPAM; MEDAZEPAM; OXAZEPAM; TEMAZEPAM.

**benzoic acid ointment** is a non-proprietary ANTIFUNGAL compound formulation (known also as Whitfield's ointment) used most commonly to treat patches of the fungal infection ringworm. It contains the active substances benzoic acid and salicylic acid in an emulsifying ointment base.

**benzoin tincture** is a non-proprietary compound formulation of balsamic resins used both as a base from which vapours may be inhaled (when added to boiling water) in order to clear the nose, and as a disinfectant in the treatment of bedsores or in the sanitary care of a stoma (an outlet in the skin surface that represents the surgical curtailment of the intestines).

**benzoyl peroxide** is a KERATOLYTIC agent used in combination with other drugs or with sulphur in the treatment of skin conditions such as acne, or skin infections such as athlete's foot (which is a fungal infection). Administration is topical in the form of a cream, lotion or gel.

▲ side-effects: some patients experience skin irritation.

✦ warning: benzoyl peroxide should not be used to treat the skin disease of the facial blood vessels rosacea. Topical application must avoid the eyes, mouth, and mucous membranes. (The drug may bleach fabrics.)

*Related articles:* ACETOXYL; ACNEGEL; ACNIDAZIL; BENOXYL; BENZAGEL; NERICUR; PANOXYL; QUINODERM; QUINOPED.

**benztropine mesylate** is an ANTICHOLINERGIC agent employed in the treatment of some types of parkinsonism (*see* ANTI-PARKINSONISM). It increases mobility and decreases rigidity, but it has only a limited effect on tremors. The tendency to produce an excess of saliva is also reduced. (The drug also has the capacity to treat these conditions, in some cases, where they are produced by drugs.) It is thought to work by compensating for the lack of

dopamine in the brain, which is the major cause of such parkinsonian symptoms, and because it additionally has some sedative properties it is sometimes used in preference to the similar drug benzhexol hydrochloride. Administration – which may be in parallel with the administration of levodopa – is oral in the form of tablets, or by injection.

▲ side-effects: there may be drowsiness, dry mouth, dizziness and blurred vision, and/or gastrointestinal disturbances. Some patients experience sensitivity reactions.

✦ warning: benztropine mesylate should not be administered to patients who suffer not merely from tremor but from distinct involuntary movements; it should be administered with caution to those with impaired kidney or liver function, cardiovascular disease, glaucoma, or urinary retention. Withdrawal of treatment must be gradual.

*Related article:* COGENTIN.

**benzydamine hydrochloride** has ANALGESIC, local ANAESTHETIC and ANTI-INFLAMMATORY actions. It is used in topical application as a cream to relieve muscle or joint pain, or as a liquid mouthwash or spray to relieve the pain of mouth ulcers and other sores or inflammations in the mouth and throat. Some patients prefer to use the liquid in dilute form.

▲ side-effects: some patients experience a stinging sensation or numbness on initial application.

✦ warning: benzydamine is not recommended for continual use over more than 7 days. As a spray it is not suitable for children aged under 6 years; as

a mouthwash it is not suitable
for those aged under 13 years.
*Related article:* DIFFLAM.

**benzyl benzoate** is a transparent
liquid with an aromatic smell,
used to treat infestation of the
skin of the trunk and limbs by
itch-mites (scabies) or by lice
(pediculosis). A skin irritant, it
is not suitable for use on the head,
face and neck, and treatment of
children should be in diluted form
(or by another preparation
altogether). Administration is in
the form of a from-the-neck-down
application two days
consecutively, without washing
in the interval.
*Related article:* ASCABIOL.

**benzylpenicillin** is the chemical
name for the first of the
penicillins to be isolated and used
as an ANTIBIOTIC. An alternative
name is penicillin G. Despite the
many hundreds of antibiotics
introduced since, it still remains
the drug of choice in treating
many severe infections including
those caused by sensitive strains
of meningococcus (meningitis,
septicaemia), pneumococcus
(pneumonia, meningitis) and
streptococcus (bacterial sore
throat, scarlet fever, septicaemia).
In its long-acting forms, PROCAINE
PENICILLIN and BENZATHINE
PENICILLIN, it has an important
role in treating gonorrhea and
syphilis. Since benzylpenicillin is
inactivated by digestive acids in
the stomach it has to be injected.
Its rapid excretion by the kidney
also means frequent
administration is necessary,
unless long-acting preparations
are used.
▲ side-effects: there may be
sensitivity reactions ranging
from a minor rash to urticaria
and joint pains, and
(occasionally) to high
temperature or anaphylactic
shock.

◆ warning: benzylpenicillin
should not be administered to
patients known to be allergic
to penicillins; it should be
administered with caution to
those with impaired kidney
function.
*Related article:* CRYSTAPEN.

**bephenium** is an ANTHELMINTIC
drug used specifically to treat
infestation of the small intestine
by hookworms, which draw blood
from the point of their attachment
to the intestinal wall and may
thus cause iron-deficiency
anaemia. Administration is oral
in the form of a solution.
▲ side-effects: there may be
occasional nausea and
vomiting; some patients
experience diarrhoea,
headache and vertigo.
*Related article:* ALCOPAR.

**Berkatens** (*Berk*) is a proprietary
CALCIUM ANTAGONIST drug,
available only on prescription,
used to treat high blood pressure
(*see* ANTIHYPERTENSIVE),
heartbeat irregularities (*see* ANTI-
ARRHYTHMIC), and angina pectoris
(heart pain). It works primarily by
decreasing the excitability of the
cells. Produced in the form of
tablets (in four strengths),
Berkatens is a preparation of
verapamil hydrochloride.
▲/◆ side-effects/warning: *see*
VERAPAMIL HYDROCHLORIDE.

**Berkmycen** (*Berk*) is a
proprietary ANTIBIOTIC, available
only on prescription, used to treat
infections of the soft tissues and
respiratory tract. Produced in the
form of tablets, Berkmycen is a
preparation of the TETRACYCLINE
oxytetracycline dihydrate. It
should not be used for children
aged under 2 years.
▲/◆ side-effects/warning: *see*
OXYTETRACYCLINE.

**Berkolol** (*Berk*) is a proprietary
BETA-BLOCKER, available only on

prescription, used to treat high
blood pressure (*see* ANTI-
HYPERTENSIVE), usually in
combination with a DIURETIC, to
relieve angina pectoris (heart
pain) and to slow and/or
regularize the heartbeat in order
to prevent a recurrent heart
attack. The drug may also be
used to treat symptoms of
hyperthroidism or to reduce
frequency of migraine attacks.
Produced in the form of tablets (in
four strengths), Berkolol is a
preparation of the BETA-BLOCKER
propranolol hydrochloride.
▲/ ● side-effects/warning: *see*
PROPRANOLOL.

**Berkozide** (*Berk*) is a proprietary
DIURETIC, available only on
prescription, used to treat high
blood pressure (*see* ANTI-
HYPERTENSIVE) and an
accumulation of fluid within the
tissues (oedema). Produced in the
form of tablets (in two strengths),
Berkozide is a preparation of the
THIAZIDE bendrofluazide. It is not
recommended for children.
▲/ ● side-effects/warning: *see*
BENDROFLUAZIDE.

**Berotec** (*Boehringer Ingelheim*) is
a proprietary BRONCHODILATOR,
available only on prescription,
used to treat conditions such as
asthma and chronic bronchitis.
Produced in the form of an
aerosol inhalant (with metered
inhalation) and a solution for
nebulization. Berotec is a
preparation of fenoterol
hydrobromide. Inhalation of the
nebulized solution is not
recommended for children aged
under 6 years.
▲/ ● side-effects/warning: *see*
FENOTEROL.

**Beta-Adalat** (*Bayer*) is a
proprietary preparations of the
CALCIUM ANTAGONIST nifedipine
together with the BETA-BLOCKER
atenolol. Available only on

prescription, it is used to treat
angina pectoris (heart pain), and
high blood pressure
(hypertension) in patients where
either drug alone has be
inadequate. It is produced in the
form of capsules.
▲/ ● side-effects/warning: *see*
NIFEDIPINE; ATENOLOL.

**\*beta-blockers** (beta-adrenoceptor
blockers) are drugs that inhibit
the action of the hormonal and
neurotransmitter substances
ADRENALINE and NORADRENALINE
(and the other catecholamines) in
the body. These catecholamines
are involved in bodily response to
stress: among other actions they
speed the heart and constrict
some blood vessels, so increasing
blood pressure, suppress digestion
and generally prepare the body
for emergency action. In patients
with heart conditions, with
diseases of the blood vessels or
with high blood pressure
(hypertension), stresses that
release catecholamines may
quickly lead to angina pectoris
(heart pain) and an inability of
the heart to pump blood
sufficiently. Beta-blockers are
administered so that the receptor
sites that would normally react to
the presence of the
catecholamines remain
comparatively inactivated. Beta-
blockers are thus used in the
treatment of cardiac arrhythmias
(heartbeat irregularities) and as
ANTIHYPERTENSIVES. However,
some of them have additional
effects on catecholamine-sensitive
receptor sites elsewhere in the
body, particularly in the
bronchial passages, and care must
thus be taken in prescribing for
patients with disorders of the
respiratory tract, because their
use may induce asthma attacks.
These drugs are also used to treat
the symptoms of over-active
thyroid glands (hyperthyroidism).
Best-known and most used beta-

blockers include propranolol, sotalol, oxprenolol and acebutolol.

▲/ ❋ side-effects/warning: see ACEBUTOLOL; ATENOLOL; BETAXOLOL HYDROCHLORIDE; LABETALOL HYDROCHLORIDE; METOPROLOL; NADOLOL; OXPRENOLOL; PENBUTOLOL SULPHATE; PINDOLOL; PRACTOLOL; PROPRANOLOL; SOTALOL HYDROCHLORIDE; TIMOLOL MALEATE.

**Beta-Cardone** (*Duncan, Flockhart*) is a proprietary BETA-BLOCKER, available only on prescription, used to treat high blood pressure (see ANTI-HYPERTENSIVE), heartbeat irregularities and angina pectoris (heart pain), and to prevent secondary heart attacks. Produced in the form of tablets (in three strengths), Beta-Cardone is a preparation of sotalol hydrochloride. It is not recommended for children.

▲/ ❋ side-effects/warning: see SOTALOL HYDROCHLORIDE.

**Betadine** (*Napp*) is a proprietary, non-prescription group of preparations of the ANTISEPTIC povidone-iodine, produced in the form of pessaries, a gel and a solution (all together a vaginal cleansing kit) for the treatment of bacterial infections in the vagina and cervix. A more dilute solution may also be used as a mouthwash and gargle for inflammations in the mouth and throat. For the treatment of skin infections it is produced in solutions of differing concentrations as an antiseptic paint, an alcoholic lotion, a scalp and skin cleanser, a shampoo, a skin cleanser solution, and a surgical scrub; it is also produced as a dry powder for insufflation. In the form of a water-miscible ointment it is used to dress leg ulcers.

▲/ ❋ side-effects/warning: see POVIDONE-IODINE.

**Betagen** (*Allergan*) is a proprietary form of the BETA-BLOCKER levobunolol hydro-chloride, used to treat glaucoma. It is thought to work by slowing the rate of production of the aqueous humour in the eyeball, but it may be absorbed and have systemic effects as well. Available only on prescription, it is used in the form of eye-drops.

▲/ ❋ side-effects/warning: see LEVOBUNOLOL HYDROCHLORIDE.

**betahistine hydrochloride** is an ANTINAUSEANT drug used specifically to treat the vertigo and nausea associated with Ménière's disease (which also causes constant noises in the ears), although as a VASODILATOR it is also used to treat other disorders and infections of the middle and inner ears. Administration is oral in the form of tablets.

▲ side-effects: sometimes the drug, while helping to relieve vertigo, actually causes nausea; some patients experience a headache; rarely, there may be a rash.

❋ warning: betahistine hydrochloride should not be administered to patients who suffer from disorders that cause abnormal secretion from the adrenal glands (phaeochro-mocytoma); it should be administered with caution to those who suffer from asthma or peptic ulcer.
*Related article:* SERC.

**betaine hydrochloride** is an unusual drug used to increase gastric acids in patients whose stomach secretions have for one reason or another been reduced. Administration is oral in the form of a solution made from crushed tablets dissolved in water, taken through a straw after meals. The tablets also contain the stomach enzyme pepsin. The drug is not recommended for children.

▲ side-effects: high dosage may naturally result in acid stomach and the associated symptoms.

✿ warning: the solution should be taken through a straw (or a glass tube) in order to protect the teeth.
*Related article:* ACIDOL-PEPSIN.

**Betaloc** (*Astra*) is a proprietary preparation of the BETA-BLOCKER metoprolol tartrate, available only on prescription, used to control and regulate the heart rate and to treat high blood pressure (*see* ANTIHYPERTENSIVE), angina pectoris (heart pain), or in the treatment of hyperthyroidism; it is additionally used in the prevention of migraine attacks. Produced in a standard form of tablets (in two strengths) and in ampoules for injection, a stronger form is also available (under the trade name Betaloc-SA) as sustained-release tablets ('Durules'). None of these is recommended for children.

▲/ ✿ side-effects/warning: *see* METOPROLOL TARTRATE.

**betamethasone** is a synthetic CORTICOSTEROID, used for its ANTI-INFLAMMATORY effect to treat many kinds of inflammation, and especially those caused by allergic disorders. Unlike most corticosteroids, it does not cause salt or fluid retention in the body, and is thus particularly useful in treating conditions such as cerebral oedema (fluid retention in the brain). Administration is oral in the form of tablets, or by injection.

▲ side-effects: systemic treatment of susceptible patients may engender a euphoria – or a state of confusion or depression.

Rarely, there is peptic ulcer.

✿ warning: betamethasone should be administered with great caution to patients with infectious diseases, chronic renal failure, and uraemia; it should be administered with caution to the elderly (in whom overdosage can cause osteoporosis, 'brittle bones'). In children, administration of betamethasone may lead to stunting of growth. As with all corticosteroids, betamethasone treats only inflammatory symptoms; an undetected and potentially serious infection may have its effects masked by the drug until it is well established.
*Related articles:* BETNELAN; BETNESOL.

**betamethasone dipropionate** is a synthetic CORTICOSTEROID used in topical application to treat severe, non-infective skin inflammations (such as eczema), particularly in cases where less powerful steroids have failed. Administration is in the form of a cream or ointment, or as a lotion for the scalp.

▲ side-effects: as with all corticosteroids, betamethasone dipropionate treats only the external symptoms; an undetected and potentially serious infection may have its effects masked by the drug until it has become well established. There may be local thinning of the skin, with increased hair growth. Younger patients, especially girls, may experience a local outbreak of acne.

✿ warning: betamethasone dipropionate should not be administered to patients with the skin blood vessel disorder rosacea, or from any form of internal ulcer. Absorption through the skin where dosage is high may result in a

**B**

reduction of the secretion of natural corticosteroids by the adrenal glands, with consequent symptoms.
*Related articles:* DIPROSALIC; DIPROSONE.

**betamethasone sodium phosphate** is a synthetic CORTICOSTEROID used in topical application to treat both mild, local forms of inflammation (particularly of the eyes, ears or nose, and occasionally also to assist in the treatment of more severe non-infective skin inflammations, such as eczema. Administration is in the form of drops (for eye, ear or nose), and as an ointment.
▲ side-effects: as with all corticosteroids, betamethasone sodium phosphate treats only the external symptoms; an undetected and potentially serious infection may have its effects masked by the drug until it has become well established. There may be local thinning of the skin, with increased hair growth. Younger patients, especially girls, may experience a local outbreak of acne.
✺ warning: betamethasone sodium phosphate should not be administered to patients with the skin blood vessel disorder rosacea. Prolonged use may lead to absorption through the skin which in turn may result in a reduction of the secretion of natural corticosteroids by the adrenal glands.
*Related articles:* BETNESOL; VISTA-METHASONE.

**betamethasone valerate** is a synthetic CORTICOSTEROID used in topical application to treat severe, non-infective skin inflammations such as eczema, particularly in cases where less powerful steroids have failed.

Administration is in the form of a cream or ointment, or as a lotion. It is also sometimes used for its properties as a BRONCHODILATOR in the treatment of asthma.
▲ side-effects: as with all corticosteroids, betamethasone valerate treats only the external symptoms; an undetected and potentially serious infection may have its effects masked by the drug until it has become well established. There may be local thinning of the skin, with increased hair growth. Younger patients, especially girls, may experience a local outbreak of acne.
✺ warning: betamethasone valerate should not be administered to patients who suffer from the skin blood vessel disorder rosacea, or from any form of internal ulcer. Absorption through the skin where dosage is high may result in a reduction of the secretion of natural corticosteroids by the adrenal glands, with consequent symptoms.
*Related articles:* BETNOVATE; BETNOVATE-C; BETNOVATE-N; BETNOVATE-RD; FUCIBET.

**\*beta-receptor stimulants** (beta-adrenoceptor stimulants; beta-agonists) are a class of drugs that act at sites, called beta-receptors, that 'recognise' the natural neurotransmitters or hormones of the sympathetic nervous system. Drugs that act at such sites are regarded as SYMPATHOMIMETICS. Notable actions of beta-receptor stimulants include bronchodilation, speeding and strengthening of the heart beat and inhibition of contraction of the uterus. Importantly, differences in receptors at different sites allow, for example, beta-receptor stimulant drugs that give bronchodilation in asthma sufferers without overstimulation of the heart (in this case known as beta₂-receptor stimulants). The BETA-BLOCKERS have roughly the reverse of the actions of beta-receptor stimulants.

**betaxolol hydrochloride** is a BETA-BLOCKER of fairly recent introduction used orally to treat high blood pressure (*see* ANTIHYPERTENSIVE); for this purpose administration is in the form of tablets. In dilute solution, however, the drug is also used in the form of eye-drops.
▲ side-effects: there may be some gastrointestinal or slight respiratory disturbance following oral administration. Ophthalmic treatment may result in temporarily dry eyes; some patients experience sensitivity reactions; the drug should be used in those with cardiac disease only as appropriate.
✦ warning: as an antihypertensive drug, betaxolol hydrochloride should not be administered to patients who suffer from asthmatic symptoms; it should be administered with great caution to those with impaired kidney function, or who are nearing the end of pregnancy or who are lactating. Withdrawal of treatment should be gradual. Ophthalmic betaxolol should not be administered to patients with severe sinus bradycardia cardiagenic shock or to patients with overt cardiac failure.
*Related articles:* BETOPTIC; KERLONE.

**bethanechol chloride** is a PARASYMPATHOMIMETIC drug. It is used to stimulate motility in the intestines, but perhaps its most common use is to treat urinary retention, particularly following surgery. Administration is oral in the form of tablets or by injection.
▲ side-effects: there may be sweating, blurred vision, nausea and vomiting, and a slow heart rate.
✦ warning: Bathanechol chloride should not be administered to patients who suffer from medicinal, urinary or intestinal obstruction. It should be administered with caution to those who suffer from epilepsy, parkinsonism or thyroid disorders, or who are elderly. It should not be administered during pregnancy.
*Related article:* MYOTONINE CHLORIDE.

**bethanidine sulphate** is an ANTIHYPERTENSIVE drug used to treat moderate to severe high blood pressure (hypertension), especially when other forms of treatment have failed. It works by inhibiting the release of the neurotransmitter (catecholamine) noradrenaline. Administration is oral in the form of tablets, usually with a DIURETIC (such as a THIAZIDE) or a BETA-BLOCKER.
▲ side-effects: there may be low blood pressure (hypotension), nasal congestion, and fluid retention leading to weight gain.
✦ warning: bethanidine sulphate should not be administered to patients who suffer from disease of the adrenal glands or from kidney failure; it should be administered with caution to those who are pregnant. Resultant low blood pressure, especially on rising from sitting or lying down, may cause falls in the elderly.
*Related articles:* BENDOGEN; ESBATAL.

**Betim** (*Burgess*) is a proprietary BETA-BLOCKER, available only on prescription, used to treat high blood pressure (*see* ANTI-

HYPERTENSIVE), heartbeat
irregularities and angina pectoris
(heart pain), and to prevent
secondary heart attacks and also
migraine. Produced in the form of
tablets, Betim represents a
preparation of timolol maleate. It
is not recommended for children.
▲/◕ side-effects/warning: see
TIMOLOL MALEATE.

**Betnelan** (*Glaxo*) is a proprietary
CORTICOSTEROID preparation,
available only on prescription,
used to treat inflammation
especially in rheumatic or
allergic conditions, and
particularly in severe asthma.
Produced in the form of tablets,
Betnelan is a preparation of the
glucocorticoid betamethasone. It
is not recommended for children
aged under 12 months.
▲/◕ side-effects/warning: see
BETAMETHASONE.

**Betnesol** (*Glaxo*) is a proprietary
CORTICOSTEROID preparation,
available only on prescription,
used to treat local inflammations
as well as more widespread
rheumatic or allergic conditions,
particularly severe asthma.
Produced in the form of tablets
and in ampoules for injection,
Betnesol represents a preparation
of the glucocorticoid
betamethasone. The tablets are
not recommended for children
aged under 12 months. Betnesol
ear-, eye- and nose-drops and eye
ointment are used for local
inflammations, and are an
alternative preparation of
betamethasone sodium
phosphate. A preparation is also
available that additionally
contains the antiseptic
ANTIBIOTIC neomycin sulphate; it
too is produced in the form of ear-,
eye- and nose-drops and eye
ointment (under the trade name
Betnesol-N).
▲/◕ side-effects/warning: see
BETAMETHASONE;

BETAMETHASONE SODIUM
PHOSPHATE; NEOMYCIN.

**Betnovate** (*Glaxo*) is a proprietary
group of CORTICOSTEROID
preparations, available only on
prescription, used to treat severe
non-infective skin inflammations
such as eczema, especially in
patients who are not responding
to less powerful corticosteroids.
Produced in the form of a water-
miscible cream, an ointment in an
anhydrous paraffin base, a lotion,
and a scalp application in an
alcohol base, Betnovate is a
preparation of betamethasone
valerate. A rectal ointment
(applied with an applicator) is
also available, representing a
compound preparation of
betamethasone valerate together
with the local ANAESTHETIC
lignocaine hydrochloride and the
VASOCONSTRICTOR phenylephrine
hydrochloride.
▲/◕ side-effects/warning: see
BETAMETHASONE VALERATE;
LIGNOCAINE;
PHENYLEPHRINE.

**Betnovate-C** (*Glaxo*) is a
proprietary CORTICOSTEROID,
available only on prescription,
used to treat severe non-infective
skin inflammations such as
eczema. Produced in the form of a
water-miscible cream and an
ointment in a paraffin base,
Betnovate-C is a compound
preparation of the steroid
betamethasone valerate and the
ANTIMICROBIAL clioquinol.
▲/◕ side-effects/warning: see
BETAMETHASONE VALERATE;
CLIOQUINOL.

**Betnovate-N** (*Glaxo*) is a
proprietary CORTICOSTEROID,
available only on prescription,
used to treat severe non-infective
skin inflammations such as
eczema. Produced in the form of a
water-miscible cream, and an
ointment in a paraffin base,

Betnovate-N is a compound preparation of the steroid betamethasone valerate and the ANTIBACTERIAL ANTIBIOTIC neomycin sulphate.

▲/✿ side-effects/warning: *see* BETAMETHASONE VALERATE; NEOMYCIN.

**Betnovate-RD** (*Glaxo*) is a proprietary CORTICOSTEROID, available only on prescription, used as the basis for maintenance therapy in the treatment of severe non-infective skin inflammation (such as eczema) once control has initially been achieved with BETNOVATE. Produced in the form of a water-miscible cream and as an ointment in an anhydrous paraffin base, Betnovate-RD is a preparation of betamethasone valerate.

▲/✿ side-effects/warning: *see* BETAMETHASONE VALERATE.

**Betoptic** (*Alcon*) is a proprietary BETA-BLOCKER, available only on prescription, used in the form of eye-drops to treat various forms of glaucoma. It is a preparation of betaxolol hydrochloride and is not recommended for children.

▲/✿ side-effects/warning: *see* BETAXOLOL HYDROCHLORIDE.

**bezafibrate** is used to reduce the level of fats (lipids) such as cholesterol in the bloodstream when these are raised (hyperlipidaemia). It works by inhibiting lipid synthesis. Generally, it is administered only to patients in whom a strict and regular dietary regime is not having the desired effect, although during treatment such a regime should additionally be adhered to. Administration is oral in the form of tablets.

▲ side-effects: there may be nausea and abdominal pain; rarely, there may be itching or urticaria. In men, impotence very occasionally occurs.

✿ warning: bezafibrate should not be administered to patients with severely impaired kidney or liver function, disease of the gall bladder, or associated blood disorders, or who are pregnant.
*Related article:* BEZALIP.

**Bezalip** (*MCP Pharmaceuticals*) is a proprietary preparation of the drug bezafibrate, available only on prescription, used to treat high levels of fats (lipids) such as cholesterol in the bloodstream (hyperlipidaemia). It works by inhibiting production of fat. Produced in the form of tablets (in two strengths, the stronger form under the trade name Bezalip-Mono), it is not recommended for children.

▲/✿ side-effects/warning: *see* BEZAFIBRATE.

**Bi-Aglut** (*Ultrapharm*) represents a brand of non-prescription gluten-free biscuits. Gluten-, lactose-, and milk-protein-free cracker toast is also available for the dietary needs of patients who are unable to tolerate those substances, such as in coeliac disease.

**BiCNU** (*Bristol-Myers*) is a proprietary CYTOTOXIC drug, available only on prescription, used in the treatment of leukaemia, lymphomas and some solid tumours. It works by disrupting DNA production in new-forming cells and so preventing normal cell reproduction. Produced in the form of a powder for reconstitution as a medium for injection or in vials, BiCNU is a preparation of carmustine.

▲/✿ side-effects/warning: *see* CARMUSTINE.

**Bilarcil** is a preparation of the organo-phosphorous drug METRIPHONATE, used specifically to treat infections by parasitic Schistosoma haematobium worms (which cause bilharziasis) in various organs. It is not marketed in the United Kingdom.

**BiNovum** (*Ortho-Cilag*) is an ORAL CONTRACEPTIVE available only on prescription, which combines the OESTROGEN ethinyloestradiol with the PROGESTOGEN norethisterone. It is produced in calender packs of 21 tablets which together with 7 tablet-free days represent one complete menstrual cycle.
▲/✚ side-effects/warning: *see* ETHINYLOESTRADIOL; NORETHISTERONE.

**Biogasterone** (*Winthrop*) is a proprietary gastric ulcer treatment. Available only on prescription, it protects the stomach lining from excess acid and enzymes in a way that is not well understood. Biogasterone is produced in the form of tablets and is a preparation of carbenoxolone sodium. It is not recommended for children.
▲/✚ side-effects/warning: *see* CARBENOXOLONE SODIUM.

**Biophylline** (*Delandale*) is a proprietary, non-prescription BRONCHODILATOR, used to treat asthmatic bronchospasm and chronic bronchitis. Produced in the form of sustained-release tablets (in two strengths), and as a syrup. It is a preparation of the drug theophylline.
▲/✚ side-effects/warning: *see* THEOPHYLLINE.

**Bioplex** (*Thames*) is a proprietary drug, available only on prescription, used to treat mouth ulcers. Produced in the form of granules to be dissolved in warm water for use as a mouth-wash, Bioplex is a preparation of the drug carbenoxolone sodium.
▲/✚ side-effects/warning: *see* CARBENOXOLONE SODIUM.

**Bioral** (*Winthrop*) is a proprietary, non-prescription preparation, used to treat mouth ulcers and other sores in and around the mouth. Produced in the form of a gel, Bioral is a preparation of the drug carbenoxolone sodium.
▲/✚ side-effects/warning: *see* CARBENOXOLONE SODIUM.

**Biorphen** (*Bio-Medical*) is a proprietary ANTICHOLINERGIC drug, available only on prescription, used to relieve some of the symptoms of parkinsonism, especially muscle rigidity and the tendency to produce an excess of saliva (*see* ANTIPARKINSONISM). The drug also has the capacity to treat these conditions in some cases where they are produced by drugs. It is thought to work by compensating for the lack of dopamine in the brain that is the major cause of such parkinsonian symptoms. Produced in the form of a sugar-free elixir, Biorphen represents a preparation of orphenadrine hydrochloride. Counselling of patients is advised.
▲/✚ side-effects/warning: *see* ORPHENADRINE HYDROCHLORIDE.

**biperiden** lactate is an ANTICHOLERGENIC agent employed in the treatment of some types of parkinsonism (*see* ANTIPARKINSONISM). It increases mobility and decreases rigidity, but it has only a limited effect on tremors. The tendency to produce an excess of saliva is also reduced. (The drug also has the capacity to treat these conditions in some cases where they are produced by drugs.) It is thought to work by compensating for the lack of dopamine in the brain that is the major cause of such parkinsonian symptoms, and because it additionally has some sedative properties it is sometimes used in preference to the similar drug benzhexol hydrochloride. Administration – which may be in parallel with the administration of other drugs used to relieve parkinsonism – is oral in the form of tablets, or by injection.

▲ side-effects: there may be drowsiness, dry mouth, dizziness and blurred vision, and/or gastrointestinal disturbances. Some patients experience sensitivity reactions.

● warning: biperiden should be administered only to patients with mild tremor and rigidity; it should be administered with caution to those with impaired kidney or liver function, cardiovascular disease, glaucoma, or urinary retention. Withdrawal of treatment must be gradual.
*Related article:* AKINETON.

**bisacodyl** is a stimulant LAXATIVE used not only to promote defecation and relieve constipation, but also to evacuate the colon prior to rectal examination or surgery. It probably works by stimulating the walls of the intestine. Administration is either oral in the form of tablets (full effects are achieved after 10 hours), or topical as anal suppositories (effects achieved within 1 hour). It is not recommended for children.

▲ side-effects: there may be abdominal pain, nausea,or vomiting. Suppositories sometimes cause rectal irritation.

● warning: bisacodyl should not be administered to patients with intestinal obstruction.
*Related article:* DULCOLAX.

**bismuth subgallate** is a mild astringent used as a dusting powder in some skin disorders, and as suppositories in the treatment of haemorrhoids. It has

also been administered by mouth to help control the odour and consistency of stools in patients with a colostomy or ileostomy

▲ side-effects: there may be disturbance of the gastrointestinal tract, discolouration of mucous membranes and mild jaundice.

● warning: prolonged administration by mouth should be avoided.
*Related article:* ANUSOL.

**Bisodol** (*Whitehall Laboratories*) is a proprietary, non-prescription ANTACID produced in the form of tablets and as a powder. It contains sodium bicarbonate and magnesium carbonate.

● warning: *see* MAGNESIUM CARBONATE; SODIUM BICARBONATE.

**bisoprolol fumarate** is a BETA-BLOCKER used to treat hypertension and angina pectoris (heart pain). Administration is in the form of tablets.

▲/● side-effects/warning: *see* PROPRANOLOL
*Related articles:* EMCOR; MONOCOR.

**BJ6** (*Macarthys; Thornton & Ross*) is a proprietary, non-prescription ophthalmic preparation, used to treat sore eyes caused by chronically reduced tear secretion. Produced in the form of eye-drops, BJ6 is a preparation of the water-soluble, cellulose-derivative hypromellose.

**bleomycin** is an ANTIBIOTIC that also has CYTOTOXIC properties. Unlike most ANTICANCER drugs, however, it has virtually no depressant effect on the blood-producing capacity of the bone-marrow. It is used particularly to treat cancer of the upper part of the gut and of the genital tract, and lymphomas. Sensitivity reactions are not uncommon, the symptoms of which are chills and fever a few hours after administration: these can be dealt with by the simultaneous administration of a CORTICOSTEROID (such as hydrocortisone). Bleomycin is administered by injection. The proprietary preparation of the same name is produced by Lundbeck and is available only on prescription.

▲ side-effects: there is generally nausea and vomiting (for which additional medications may be prescribed). Increased pigmentation of the skin and some hair loss is common. Some patients experience inflammation of the mucous membranes.

◈ warning: high dosage increases a risk of pulmonary fibrosis, a lung disease that is potentially very serious. Regular monitoring of lung function is essential.

**Blocadren** (*Merck, Sharp & Dohme*) is a proprietary BETA-BLOCKER, available only on prescription, used to treat high blood pressure (*see* ANTI-HYPERTENSIVE), angina pectoris (heart pain) and to prevent migraine and heart attack. Produced in the form of tablets, Blocadren represents a preparation of timolol maleate. It is not recommended for children.

▲/◈ side-effects/warning: *see* TIMOLOL MALEATE.

**Bocasan** (*Cooper*) is a proprietary, non-prescription ANTISEPTIC, used to cleanse and disinfect the mouth. Produced in the form of sealed sachets to be emptied into water to produce a mouth-wash, Bocasin is a preparation of sodium perborate.

◈ warning: *see* SODIUM PERBORATE.

**Bolvidon** (*Organon*) is a proprietary ANTIDEPRESSANT, available only on prescription,

used to treat depressive illness especially where sedation is needed. Produced in the form of tablets (in three strengths), Bolvidon is a preparation of mianserin hydrochloride. It is not recommended for children.

▲/◈ side-effects/warning: *see* MIANSERIN.

**Bonjela** (*Reckitt & Colman*) is a proprietary, non-prescription oral gel, used to treat mouth ulcers and to relieve pain during teething. Bonjela represents a preparation of choline salicylate (and is sugar-free).

◈ warning: *see* CHOLINE SALICYLATE.

**Boots Covering Cream** (*Boots*) is a proprietary, non-prescription camouflage cream, in four shades, designed for use in masking scars and other skin disfigurements. It may be obtained on prescription if the skin disfigurement is the result of surgery or is giving rise to emotional disturbance.

**botulism antitoxin** is a preparation that neutralizes the toxins produced by the botulism bacteria (rather than acting to counter the presence of the bacteria, as would a vaccine). In this way, it may be administered not only to people at risk from the disease following exposure to an infected patient, but also to the infected patient as a means of treatment. However, there are some strains of botulism in relation to which the antitoxin is not effective. Moreover, hypersensitivity reactions are common (and it is essential that an administering doctor has all relevant details of a patient's medical history, with regard especially to allergies). Administration is by injection or infusion, depending on whether it is for the purpose of prophylaxis or treatment.

**bowel cleansing solutions**
contain inorganic salts and iso-
osmotic buffer, and are used prior
to colonic surgery, colonoscopy
or barium enema to ensure the
bowel is free of solid contents.
They are available in the form of
sachets for making up in water.

▲ side-effects: nausea and
occasionally vomiting,
transient abdominal cramps,
bloated feeling, running nose,
skin irritations.

● warning: bowel cleansing
solutions are not recommended
for pregnant women, patients
with ulcerative colitis or who
are unconscious or
semiconscious. Bowel
cleansing solutions should not
be used for patients suffering
from certain gastrointestinal
conditions such as perforated
bowel or obstruction. They are
not treatments for
constipation.
*Related articles:* GOLYTELY;
KLEAN-PREP.

**Bradilan** (*Napp*) is a proprietary,
non-prescription VASODILATOR,
used to treat circulatory disorders
of the hands and feet, chilblains,
night cramps, and to limit high
blood levels of cholesterol or
triglycerides (hyperlipidaemia).
Produced in the form of tablets,
Bradilan is a preparation of the
vitamin B derivative
nicofuranose, and is not
recommended for children.

▲/● side-effects/warning: *see*
NICOFURANOSE.

**Bradosol** (*Ciba*) is a proprietary,
non-prescription DISINFECTANT,
used to treat infections in the
mouth and throat. Produced in
the form of lozenges, Bradosol is a
preparation of domiphen bromide.
It is also available with the local
ANAESTHETIC lignocaine
(Bradosol Plus).

**bran** is perhaps the best-known
natural bulking agent used to

keep people 'regular' or, if
necessary, as a LAXATIVE to treat
constipation. In either case it
works by increasing the overall
mass of faeces, so stimulating
bowel movement (although in fact
the full effect may not be
achieved for more than 36 hours).
As an excellent form of dietary
fibre, bran may be said to reduce
the risk of diverticular disease
while actively assisting digestion.

▲ side-effects: some patients
cannot tolerate bran
(particularly patients sensitive
to the compound gluten).

● warning: bran should not be
consumed if there is any
possibility of intestinal
blockage: adequate fluid intake
must be maintained to avoid
faecal impaction. Calcium and
iron absorption may be
impaired.
*Related articles:* FYBRANTA;
PROCTOFIBE.

**Brasivol** (*Stiefel*) is a proprietary,
non-prescription abrasive
preparation, used to cleanse skin
that suffers from acne. It is
produced in the form of a paste
containing particles of aluminium
oxide in three grades (fine,
medium, and coarse) within a
soap base. Treatment ordinarily
begins with the fine grade and
progresses to the medium and the
coarse in more severe cases.

**Bretylate** (*Wellcome*) is a
proprietary ANTIARRHYTHMIC
drug, available only on
prescription, used to treat
heartbeat irregularities and to
prevent a speeding up of the heart
rate. Produced in ampoules for
injection, Bretylate is a
preparation of the
ANTIHYPERTENSIVE drug
bretylium tosylate.

▲/● side-effects/warning: *see*
BRETYLIUM TOSYLATE.

**bretylium tosylate** is an
ANTIHYPERTENSIVE and

ANTIARRHYTHMIC drug used
primarily to treat heartbeat
irregularities and to prevent a
speeding up of the heart rate.
Administered usually following a
heart attack, the drug may cause
a marked fall in blood pressure;
administration is most often by
intramuscular injection.
▲ side-effects: the fall in blood
pressure on initial
administration may be
extreme; there may also be
nausea and vomiting.
✷ warning: bretylium tosylate
should not be administered to
patients who are already
taking sympathomimetic
drugs.
*Related article:* BRETYLATE.

**Brevinor** (*Syntex*) is a proprietary
ORAL CONTRACEPTIVE, available
only on prescription, which
combines the OESTROGEN
ethinyloestradiol with the
PROGESTOGEN norethisterone. It is
produced in packs of 21 tablets
which together with 7 tablet-free
days represent one complete
menstrual cycle.
▲/✷ side-effects/warning: *see*
ETHINYLOESTRADIOL;
NORETHISTERONE.

**Bricanyl** (*Astra*) is a proprietary
form of the BRONCHODILATOR
terbutaline sulphate, available
only on prescription, which acts
as a selective BETA-RECEPTOR
STIMULANT and SMOOTH MUSCLE
RELAXANT and so relieves the
bronchial spasms associated with
such conditions as asthma and
bronchitis. It is produced in the
form of tablets, as a sugar-free
syrup for dilution (the potency of
the syrup once dilute is retained
for 14 days; it is not recommended
for children aged under 3 years),
in ampoules for injection, as an
inhalant within an aerosol that
emits metered doses, in a 'spacer
inhaler' (metered inhalation
using a 'spacer tube' and a

collapsible extended mouthpiece),
as a breath-actuated, dry powder
inhaler (turbohaler), in 'respules'
(single-dose units for
nebulization; not recommended
for children weighing under 25
kg), and as a respirator solution
(for use with a nebulizer or a
ventilator). Sustained-release
tablets are also available (under
the trade name Bricanyl SA).
Associated compound
preparations are also available,
though not from the National
Health Service, under the trade
name Bricanyl Expectorant (a
sugar-free terbutaline sulphate
and guaiphenesin elixir for
dilution: the potency of the elixir
once dilute is retained for 14
days). Bricanyl injection and
tablets may also be used as a
means of slowing premature
labour.
▲/✷ side-effects/warning: *see*
TERBUTALINE.

**Brietal Sodium** (*Lilly*) is a
proprietary preparation of the
short-acting general ANAESTHETIC
methohexitone, in the form of
methohexitone sodium. It is used
mainly for the initial induction of
anaesthesia or for short, minor
operations. Available only on
prescription, Brietal Sodium is
produced in vials for intravenous
injection (in three strengths).
▲/✷ side-effects/warning: *see*
METHOHEXITONE SODIUM.

**brilliant green and crystal violet
paint** is a non-proprietary
antiseptic paint used primarily to
prepare skin for surgery. It
combines the two dyes brilliant
green and gentian violet (also
called crystal violet).
*see* GENTIAN VIOLET.

**Brinaldix K** (*Sandoz*) is a
proprietary DIURETIC, available
only on prescription, used to treat
an accumulation of fluid within
the tissues (oedema) and high
blood pressure (*see* ANTI-

HYPERTENSIVE). Produced in the form of tablets, Brinaldix K is a compound preparation of the THIAZIDE-like drug clopamide with the potassium supplement POTASSIUM CHLORIDE.

▲/✿ side-effects/warning: see CLOPAMIDE.

**Britcin** (*DDSA Pharmaceuticals*) is a proprietary ANTIBIOTIC, available only on prescription, used to treat systemic bacterial infections and infections of the upper respiratory tract, of the ear, nose and throat, and of the urogenital areas. Produced in the form of capsules (in two strengths), Britcin is a preparation of the broad-spectrum PENICILLIN ampicillin.

▲/✿ side-effects/warning: see AMPICILLIN.

**Britiazem** (*Thames*) is a proprietary form of diltiazem hydrochloride, the VASODILATOR, which is a CALCIUM-ANTAGONIST drug used in the prevention and treatment of angina pectoris (heart pain), especially in cases where beta-blockers are not tolerated or have been ineffective. Administration is oral in the form of tablets.

▲/✿ side-effects/warning: see DILTIAZEM HYDROCHLORIDE.

**Brocadopa** (*Brocades*) is a proprietary form of the immensely powerful drug levodopa, used to treat parkinsonism (see ANTIPARKINSONIAM). It is particularly good at relieving the rigidity and slowness of movement associated with the disease, although it does not always improve the tremor. Levodopa is converted inside the body to dopamine – and it is the lack of dopamine in the brain that it is thought Brocadopa compensates for. It is produced in the form of capsules (in three strengths).

▲/✿ side-effects/warning: see LEVODOPA.

**Broflex** (*Bio-Medical*) is a proprietary preparation of the drug benzhexol hydrochloride, available only on prescription, used to relieve some of the symptoms of parkinsonism specifically the overall rigidity of the posture, and the tendency to produce an excess of saliva. The drug also has the capacity to treat these conditions in some cases where they are produced by drugs (see ANTIPARKINSONISM). It is thought to work by compensating for the lack of dopamine in the brain, which is the major cause of such parkinsonism symptoms. Broflex is produced in the form of a syrup for dilution (the potency of the syrup once diluted is retained for 14 days), to be taken before or after food; counselling of patients is advised. Broflex is not recommended for children.

▲/✿ side-effects/warning: see BENZHEXOL HYDROCHLORIDE.

**Brolene** (*May & Baker*) is a proprietary, non-prescription preparation with ANTIFUNGAL and ANTIBACTERIAL properties, used to treat bacterial infections in the eyelid and conjunctiva. Produced in the form of eye-drops, Brolene is a preparation of propamidine isethionate.

**bromazepam** is an ANXIOLYTIC drug, one of the BENZODIAZEPINES used to treat anxiety in either the short or the long term. Administration is oral in the form of tablets. It is not recommended for children.

▲ side-effects: there may be drowsiness, dizziness, headache, dry mouth and shallow breathing; hypersensitivity reactions may occur.

✿ warning: bromazepam may reduce a patient's concentration and speed of

movement or thought; it may also enhance the effects of alcohol consumption. Prolonged use or abrupt withdrawal of treatment should be avoided. It should be administered with caution to patients with respiratory difficulties, glaucoma, or kidney or liver disease; who are in the last stages of pregnancy; or who are elderly or debilitated.
*Related article:* LEXOTAN.

**bromelains** is a proteolytic enzyme preparation with actions much like the digestive enzymes of the stomach, that breaks down complex molecules into their constituent amino acids for subsequent absorption. It is administered therapeutically – in the form of tablets – to relieve inflammatory swelling caused by an accumulation of fluid (oedema) in soft tissues. This it is thought to do by dissolving dead tissue, cellular debris and congealed blood for rapid transportation from the site of inflammation.
▲ side-effects: there may be nausea and vomiting; some patients break out in a rash.
● warning: bromelains should not be administered to patients who are already taking oral anticoagulants; it should be administered with caution to those who suffer from blood clotting abnormalities, or impaired liver or kidney function. (Because the drug is derived from pineapples, it should not be administered either to patients who are allergically sensitive to the fruit.)

**bromhexine hydrochloride** is a MUCOLYTIC drug that reduces the viscosity of sputum in the air passages, so making it easier to cough up phlegm. It is particularly useful in treating

conditions such as chronic bronchitis where the sputum tends to thicken and adhere to the walls of the air passages. Administration is oral in the form of tablets or a dilute elixir, or by injection.
▲ side-effects: there may be gastrointestinal irritation.
● warning: bromhexine hydrochloride should be administered with caution to patients who suffer from gastric ulcers.

**bromocriptine** is a drug used primarily to treat parkinsonism, but not the parkinsonian symptoms caused by certain drug therapies (*see* ANTIPARKINSONISM). It works by stimulating the dopamine receptors in the brain as if dopamine was present in the correct amount. In this it is slightly different from the more commonly used treatment with levodopa, which actually is converted to dopamine in the body. It is thus particularly useful in the treatment of patients who for one reason or another cannot tolerate levodopa. Occasionally, the two drugs are combined. However, bromocriptine is alternatively used to treat delayed puberty caused by hormonal insufficiency, to relieve certain menstrual disorders, or to reduce or halt lactation. Administration of bromocriptine is oral in the form of tablets and capsules.
▲ side-effects: there may be nausea, vomiting, headache, dizziness especially on rising from sitting or lying down (because of reduced blood pressure), and drowsiness. High dosage may cause hallucinations, a state of confusion, and leg cramps.
● warning: full, regular monitoring of various body systems is essential during

treatment, particularly to check on whether there is pituitary enlargement. *Related article:* PARLODEL.

**brompheniramine maleate** is an ANTIHISTAMINE, used to treat the symptoms of allergic conditions like hay fever and urticaria; it is also used, in combination with other drugs, in expectorants to loosen a dry cough. Administration is oral in the form of tablets, sustained-release tablets, and a dilute elixir.

▲ side-effects: sedation may affect patients' capacity for speed of thought and movement; there may be nausea, headaches and/or weight gain, dry mouth, gastrointestinal disturbances and visual problems.

● warning: brompheniramine maleate should not be administered to patients who are pregnant, or who suffer from glaucoma, urinary retention, intestinal obstruction, enlargement of the prostate gland, or peptic ulcer; it should be administered with caution to those who suffer from epilepsy or liver disease. *Related articles:* DIMOTANE; DIMOTANE EXPECTORANT; DIMOTANE PLUS; DIMOTANE WITH CODEINE; DIMOTAPP.

**Brompton Cocktails** are various compound ANALGESIC elixirs containing MORPHINE or its derivatives (such as DIAMORPHINE better known as heroin – and COCAINE). They were once widely used for the relief of severe pain during the final stages of terminal disease; now, however, preparations simply of one narcotic analgesic or another are preferred.

**Bronchilator** (*Sterling Research*) is a proprietary BRONCHODILATOR, available only on prescription,

used in the form of an inhalant to treat bronchial asthma and chronic bronchitis. Produced in an aerosol, Bronchilator represents a compound preparation of the two SYMPATHOMIMETIC drugs isoetharine mesylate and phenylephrine hydrochloride. It is not recommended for children.

▲ / ● side-effects/warning: *see* ISOETHARINE; PHENYLEPHRINE.

**Bronchodil** (*Keymer*) is a proprietary BRONCHODILATOR, available only on prescription, used to treat bronchospasm in asthma and chronic bronchitis. Produced in the form of tablets, as a sugar-free elixir for dilution (the potency of the elixir once dilute is retained for 14 days), and a metered-dose aerosol, Bronchodil is a preparation of the SYMPATHOMIMETIC reproterol hydrochloride. None of these products is recommended for children aged under 6 years.

▲ / ● side-effects/warning: *see* REPROTEROL HYDROCHLORIDE.

**\*bronchodilator** is any agent that relaxes the smooth muscle of the bronchial passages, so allowing more air to flow in or out. There are many conditions that cause spasm in the bronchial muscles (bronchospasm), but the most common are asthma and bronchitis. The type of drug most commonly used to treat bronchospasm is the SYMPATHOMIMETIC or BETA-RECEPTOR STIMULANT. Sympathomimetic drugs work by stimulating receptors on smooth muscle of the airways that respond to adrenal hormones and sympathetic neurotransmitters – i.e. they are in effect the opposite of beta-blockers – and are generally safe and effective though may become less effective on continued usage. Best-known and most used sympathomimetic bronchodilators include SALBUTAMOL, TERBUTALINE, ISOPRENALINE, FENOTEROL, RIMITEROL and EPHEDRINE HYDROCHLORIDE. Other forms of bronchodilator therapy include CORTICOSTEROIDS, ANTIHISTAMINES (which inhibit the allergic response that causes the symptoms of asthma) such as SODIUM CROMOGLYCATE, and such drugs as THEOPHYLLINE. Many bronchodilators are available in the form of aerosols, ventilator sprays or nebulizing mists. In high dosage, some can affect the heart rate. There may also be fine muscular tremor, headaches and nervous tension.

**bronopol** is an ANTIMICROBIAL agent used as a preservative in shampoos, cosmetics and suppositories.

**Brufen** (*Boots*) is a proprietary, non-narcotic ANALGESIC that has valuable additional anti-inflammatory properties. Available only on prescription, Brufen is used to relieve pain – particularly the pain of rheumatic disease and other musculo-skeletal disorders – and is produced in the form of tablets (in three strengths) and as a syrup for dilution (the potency of the syrup once dilute is retained for 14 days) as a preparation of ibuprofen.

▲/◆ side-effects/warning: *see* IBUPROFEN.

**Brulidine** (*May & Baker*) is a proprietary, non-prescription, antiseptic, water-miscible cream, used to treat minor burns and abrasions.

**budesonide** is a CORTICOSTEROID drug used primarily to treat the symptoms of asthma, chronic bronchitis and emphysema. It is

thought to work by reducing inflammation in the mucous lining of the bronchial passages, and reducing allergic reactions. For many patients the best results are achieved if a BRONCHO-DILATOR, such as salbutamol, is inhaled about 10 minutes before administration of butesonide. The drug is also used to treat the symptoms of nasal allergies such as hay fever. In both cases, administration is by inhaler (either from an aerosol or from a nasal spray).

▲ side-effects: some patients undergoing bronchial treatment experience hoarseness. Large doses may increase the risk of fungal infection.

◆ warning: as with all corticosteroids, budesonide treats the symptoms and has no effect on any underlying infection: such an infection, remaining undetected, may reach potentially serious proportions while its symptoms are masked by the corticosteroid. In any case, prolonged use should be avoided.
*Related articles:* PREFERID; PULMICORT; RHINOCORT.

**bufexamac** is an anti-inflammatory agent used (in dilute solution) in topical application to treat mild inflammations of the skin. It is produced in the form of a water-miscible cream.
*Related article:* PARFENAC.

**buffer** is a solution in which the concentration of hydrogen ions (pH, i.e. the acid-alkali balance) remains pretty well constant despite any further addition of alkali or acid. The body has its own buffering system, maintaining the pH in the blood and extracellular fluids, known as the bicarbonate system.

84

**bumetanide** is a quick-acting, powerful DIURETIC with relatively short duration of action, which works by inhibiting reabsorption of ions in part of the kidney known as the loop of Henle. It is used to treat fluid retention in the tissues (oedema) and high blood pressure (*see* ANTIHYPERTENSIVE), and to assist a diseased kidney by promoting the excretion of urine. Administration is oral in the form of tablets or a sugar-free liquid, or by injection.

▲ side-effects: diuretic effect corresponds to dosage; large doses may cause deafness or ringing in the ears (tinnitus). There may be a skin rash.

✿ warning: bumetanide should not be administered to patients who have suffered kidney disease or who have gout, diabetes, an enlarged prostate gland, or cirrhosis of the liver. Treatment may cause a deficiency of chloride, potassium and sodium in the body.
*Related article:* BURINEX.

**Buminate** (*Baxter*) is a proprietary form of HUMAN ALBUMIN SOLUTION used to treat low blood protein (hypoproteinaemia) especially after burns and surgery. The preparation, which is available only on prescription, is available in vials for intravenous infusion, both in isotonic and concentrated forms.

▲/✿ side-effects/warning: *see* HUMAN ALBUMIN SOLUTION.

**bupivacaine hydrochloride** is a long-acting local ANAESTHETIC related to lignocaine but is more powerful and has greater duration of action. Because of this, it is often administered by injection epidurally via the spinal membranes (particularly during labour).

▲ side-effects: there may be slow heart rate and low blood pressure (hypotension), which may in high dosage tend towards cardiac arrest. Some patients enter states of euphoria, agitation or respiratory depression.

✿ warning: bupivacaine hydrochloride should not be administered to patients who suffer from the neural disorder myasthenia gravis or from heart block, or who are suffering from an insufficient supply of blood (as in shock); it should be administered with caution to those with impaired heart or liver function, or epilepsy. Dosage should be reduced for the elderly or debilitated. Facilities for emergency cardio-respiratory resuscitation should be on hand during treatment.
*Related article:* MARCAIN.

**buprenorphine** is a narcotic ANALGESIC that is long-acting and is used to treat moderate to severe levels of pain. Its effects last much longer than morphine, with a single sublingual dose lasting up to 12 hours. Although it is thought not to be as seriously addictive as morphine, it is on the Controlled Drugs list. Since it has some opiate antagonist properties it may be dangerous to use in combination with other narcotic analgesics and can precipitate withdrawal symptoms in those habituated to, for instance, morphine or diamorphine. Its effects are not fully reversed by the usual opiate antagonist, naloxone. Administration is oral in the form of tablets placed sublingually, or by intramuscular or slow intravenous injection.

▲ side-effects: nausea, vomiting, dizziness, sweating and drowsiness are fairly common. There may be hypotension, mood changes and other side-

B

85

effects. Rarely, there may be shallow breathing.

◆ warning: buprenorphine should not be administered to patients who suffer from head injury or increased intracranial pressure; it should be administered with caution to those with impaired kidney or liver function, asthma, depressed respiration, insufficient secretion of thyroid hormones (hypothyroidism) or low blood pressure (hypotension), or who are pregnant or lactating. Dosage should be reduced for the elderly or debilitated. It may precipitate withdrawal if given with other narcotic analgesics, and naloxone may not fully reverse its effects.
*Related article:* TEMGESIC.

**Burinex** (*Leo*) is a proprietary DIURETIC drug, available only on prescription, used to treat the accumulation of fluids in the tissues (oedema) associated with congestive heart failure, and to assist a diseased kidney by promoting the excretion of urine. Produced in the form of tablets (in two strengths), as a sugar-free liquid, and in ampoules for injection, Burinex represents a preparation of bumetanide. A compound preparation of bumetanide together with the potassium supplement POTASSIUM CHLORIDE is also available (under the name Burinex K). Neither of these products is recommended for children.

▲/◆ side-effects/warning: *see* BUMETANIDE.

**Buscopan** (*Boehringer Ingelheim*) is a proprietary, ANTI-CHOLINERGIC, ANTISPASMODIC drug, available only on prescription, used to treat overactivity or spasm of the smooth muscle of the stomach or intestinal walls (causing

constipation) or of the muscles of the vagina (causing painful menstruation). Produced in the form of tablets (not recommended for children aged under 6 years) and in ampoules for injection (not recommended for children), Buscopan is a preparation of the SMOOTH MUSCLE RELAXANT hyoscine butylbromide.

▲/◆ side-effects/warning: *see* HYOSCINE.

**buserelin** acts as a GONADOTROPHIN-RELEASING HORMONE, and is used therapeutically to treat cancer of the prostate gland. Such a cancer is sex-hormone-linked, and the effect of buserelin is – after an initial, brief formation of testosterone – to halt the production of androgens in the testes. Administration (in the form of buserelin acetate) is by injection or as a nasal spray.

▲ side-effects: to all intents and purposes, use of buserelin has the effect of castration. There is weight gain with a rounding of the body and a complete lack of facial hair. There is loss of libido and may be hot flushes.

◆ warning: treatment is initially by injection; maintenance of treatment is by nasal spray. Some patients experience increased tumour growth for the first fortnight of treatment, to the extent even of compressing the spinal cord. If necessary, therapy to avoid this complication may include the simultaneous administration of an anti-androgen (such as cyproterone acetate).
*Related article:* SUPREFACT.

**busulphan** is a CYTOTOXIC drug used principally as a factor in chemotherapy to treat certain forms of leukaemia. It works by direct interference with the DNA of new-forming cells, preventing

normal cell replication.
Administration is oral in the form
of tablets.

▲ side-effects: there is commonly
nausea and vomiting; there is
often also hair loss. An
increase in skin pigmentation
may cause a change in
coloration. Rarely, there is
lung damage.

✿ warning: prolonged treatment
may cause sterility in men and
an early menopause in women.
Regular and frequent blood
counts are essential, for
irreversible bone-marrow
damage may be caused by
overdosage even by a small
amount.
*Related article:* MYLERAN.

**Butacote** (*Geigy*) is a proprietary,
ANTI-INFLAMMATORY, non-narcotic
ANALGESIC, available only on
prescription (and now generally
only in hospitals), used to treat
rheumatic disease of the type that
causes bone fusion or deformity,
especially in the backbone.
Produced in the form of tablets (in
two strengths), Butacote is a
preparation of phenylbutazone.
▲ / ✿ side-effects/warning: *see*
PHENYLBUTAZONE.

**Butazone** (*DDSA
Pharmaceuticals*) is a proprietary,
ANTI-INFLAMMATORY, non-narcotic
ANALGESIC drug, available only
on prescription in hospitals, used
to treat rheumatic disease
involving especially the
backbone. Produced in the form of
tablets (in two strengths),
Butazone represents a
preparation of phenylbutazone.
▲ / ✿ side-effects/warning: *see*
PHENYLBUTAZONE.

**butobarbitone** is a BARBITURATE
used only when absolutely
necessary as a HYPNOTIC, to treat
severe and intractable insomnia.
Administration is oral in the form
of tablets – the proprietary

preparation is on the controlled
drugs list – to be taken about half
an hour before retiring.

▲ side-effects: concentration and
the speed of movement and
thought are affected. There
may be drowsiness, dizziness
and shallow breathing, with
headache. Some patients
experience hypersensitivity
reactions. (The drug enhances
the effects of alcohol
consumption.)

✿ warning: butobarbitone should
not be administered to patients
whose insomnia is caused by
pain, who suffer from
porphyria, who are pregnant or
lactating, who are elderly or
debilitated, or who have a
history of drug (including
alcohol) abuse. It should be
administered with caution to
those who suffer from kidney,
liver or lung disease. Use of the
drug should be avoided as far
as possible. Repeated doses are
cumulative in effect, and may
lead to real sedation; abrupt
withdrawal of treatment, on
the other hand, may cause
serious withdrawal symptoms.
Tolerance and dependence
occur readily.
*Related article:* SONERYL.

**butriptyline** is an
ANTIDEPRESSANT drug that also
has some sedative properties,
used to treat depressive illness,
especially where there is some
degree also of anxiety.
Administration of butriptyline
is oral in the form of
tablets.

▲ side-effects: common effects
include a loss of intricacy in
concentration, movement and
thought, dry mouth, and
blurred vision; there may also
be difficulty in urinating,
sweating, and irregular
heartbeat, behavioural
disturbances, a rash, a state of
confusion, and/or a loss of

libido. Rarely, there are also blood deficiencies.

◆ warning: butriptyline should not be administered to patients who suffer from heart disease or psychosis; it should be administered with caution to those with diabetes, epilepsy, liver or thyroid disease, glaucoma, or urinary retention; or who are pregnant or lactating. Withdrawal of treatment must be gradual. *Related article:* EVADYNE.

**Cacit** (*Norwich Eaton*) is a proprietary MINERAL SUPPLEMENT of calcium, in the form of CALCIUM CARBONATE. It is available without prescription, in a form of effervescent tablets providing calcium citrate when dissolved in water.
▲/❋ side-effects/warning: *see* CALCIUM.

**Cafadol** (*Typharm*) is a non-prescription compound ANALGESIC, which is not available from the National Health Service. Used for mild pain, it is produced in the form of tablets. Cafadol is a compound of paracetamol and caffeine.
▲/❋ side-effects/warning: *see* CAFFEINE; PARACETAMOL.

**Cafergot** (*Sandoz*) is a proprietary ANALGESIC, available only on prescription, used to treat migraine. Produced in the form of tablets and suppositories, Cafergot is a compound of caffeine and ergotamine tartrate. Not recommended for pregnant women or nursing mothers, or those with high blood pressure or heart problems.
▲/❋ side-effects/warning: *see* CAFFEINE; ERGOTAMINE TARTRATE.

**caffeine** is a weak STIMULANT. Present in both tea and coffee, it is included in many ANALGESIC preparations, often to increase absorption. In the form of caffeine sodium benzoate, it is used as a cardiac stimulant.
▲ side-effects: excessive doses may cause headache either directly or on withdrawal.
❋ warning: caffeine should not be taken simultaneously with aspirin, or increased gastric irritation may occur.

**Calaband** (*Seton*) is a proprietary, non-prescription form of bandaging, impregnated with ZINC OXIDE, CALAMINE, glycerol and other soothing substances. (Further bandaging is required to hold it in place.)

**Caladryl** (*Warner-Lambert*) is a proprietary, non-prescription ANTIHISTAMINE, used to treat skin irritations, stings and bites, and sunburn. Produced in the form of cream or lotion, Caladryl contains CALAMINE, diphenhydramine hydrochloride and camphor in solution.
▲/❋ side-effects/warning: *see* CALAMINE; DIPHENHYDRAMINE HYDROCHLORIDE.

**calamine** is a preparation that cools and soothes itching skin. Produced in the form of a lotion, cream or ointment, it is actually a suspension of mainly zinc carbonate.

**calamine and coal tar ointment** is a preparation combining the soothing effects of CALAMINE (zinc carbonate) and the ANTISEPTIC properties of COAL TAR, which also relieves itching and softens hard skin.

**Calcichew** (*Shire*) is a proprietary MINERAL SUPPLEMENT of calcium, in the form of CALCIUM CARBONATE. It is available without prescription, in the form of chewable tablets.
▲/❋ side-effects/warning: *see* CALCIUM.

**calciferol** is the chemical name for the fat-soluble VITAMIN D. It occurs in four main forms ($D_1$ to $D_4$) which are formed in plants or in human skin by the action of sunlight. The $D_2$ form is often-referred to in medicine as ERGOCALCIFEROL. Vitamin D promotes the absorption of calcium and, to a lesser extent, phosphorus into the bones; a deficiency of vitamin D therefore results in bone deficiency disorders, e.g. rickets in children. Good food sources in normal diets include eggs, milk and cheese; fish liver oil is particularly rich as a dietary supplement. Vitamin D deficiency is commonly found in communities eating unleavened bread, in the elderly, and where disease prevents good absorption of the vitamin from foodstuffs. Therapeutic replacement of vitamin D in cases of severe deficiency requires quantities of the vitamin best provided (despite the cost) by one of the synthetic vitamin D analogues, though as with most vitamins too large doses can produce adverse effects (hypervitaminosis). Replacement forms include: ALFACALCIDOL, DIHYDROTACHYSTEROL or CALCITRIOL.

▲ side-effects: there may be nausea, vomiting, anorexia, lassitude, diarrhoea, weight loss, sweating, headache, thirst, dizziness.

❋ warning: patients receiving high doses of calciferol should have their plasma calcium concentration checked regularly. In lactating mothers who are breast-feeding and taking calcipherol-containg preparations, children may show elevated blood calcium levels.

*Related articles:* CALCIUM AND ERGOCALCIFEROL TABLETS; CHOCOVITE; ERGOCALCIFEROL.

**Calcimax** (*Wallace*) is a proprietary, non-prescription, mineral-and-vitamin compound, which is not available from the National Health Service. Produced in the form of a syrup, it contains calcium, several forms of vitamin B (THIAMINE, RIBOFLAVINE, PYRIDOXINE, CYANOCOBALAMIN, NICOTINAMIDE and pantothenol), ASCORBIC ACID (vitamin C) and CALCIFEROL (vitamin D).

**Calciparine** (*Labaz*) is a proprietary form of the ANTICOAGULANT heparin calcium, available only on prescription, used to treat various forms of thrombosis. It is produced in syringes and in ampoules for injection.

▲/❋ side-effects/warning: *see* HEPARIN.

**Calcisorb** (*Riker*) is a proprietary, non-prescription preparation used to help reduce high calcium levels in the bloodstream. It effects this by inhibiting calcium absorption from food. Produced in the form of powder for solution in water, or to sprinkle over food (here children should be supervised). Calcisorb is a preparation of sodium cellulose phosphate. It may cause diarrhoea in some users.

▲/❋ side-effects/warning: *see* SODIUM CELLULOSE PHOSPHATE.

**Calcitare** (*Armour*) is a proprietary form of the thyroid hormone calcitonin, available only on prescription, used to lower blood levels of calcium (which are significant in maintaining the replication of bone cells) and to treat certain bone diseases. Calcitare is produced in the form of powder for reconstitution in a gelatin diluent as injections.

▲/❋ side-effects/warning: *see* CALCITONIN.

**calcitonin** is a hormone produced and secreted by the thyroid gland at the base of the neck. Its function is to lower the levels of calcium and phosphate in the blood, and so together with the correspondingly opposite action of a parathyroid hormone to regulate those levels. Therapeutically introduced calcitonin obviously has the same effect, and may thus be used to treat certain bone diseases in which the levels of calcium have become too high. Because these diseases may cause such symptoms as pain or deafness, treatment with calcitonin may give great relief. Administration is ordinarily by injection.

▲ side-effects: there may be nausea, with vomiting and flushing; there may also be a tingling sensation in the hands and a peculiar taste in the mouth. Inflammation may arise at the site of injection.

✸ warning: prolonged use of calcitonin derived from animals may eventually lead to the body's producing antibodies against it, and consequent neutralization of its effect. Some patients may be sensitive to animal calcitonin.
*Related articles:* CALCITARE; MIACALCIC.

**calcitriol** is a synthesized form of CALCIFEROL (vitamin D), used to make up body deficiencies, particularly in patients who have had a kidney removed. Calcium levels in the body should be regularly monitored during treatment. Administration is oral in the form of capsules.

✸ warning: overdosage may cause kidney damage. Although an increased amount of vitamin D is necessary during pregnancy, high body levels while lactating may cause corresponding high blood levels of calcium in the breast-fed infant.
*Related article:* ROCALTROL.

**calcium** is a metallic element essential in compound form for the normal growth and development of the body, and especially (in the form of calcium phosphate) of the bones and the teeth. It is also a constituent of blood, its level regulated by the opposing actions of the hormones

CALCITONIN and parathyroid hormone (parathormone). Its uptake from food ingested is the responsibility of CALCIFEROL (vitamin D). Good food sources are all dairy products. Salts of calcium used therapeutically include the antidiarrhoeal antacid calcium carbonate, the folinic acid supplement calcium folinate, the calcium supplements calcium gluconate and calcium lactate, and the sulphonamide calcium sulphaloxate.

✸ warning: deficiency of vitamin D leads to calcium deficiency, and corresponding bone, blood and nerve disorders. Conversely, excess calcium in the body may cause the formation of stones (calculi, generally composed of calcium oxalate), particularly in the kidney or gall bladder.
*Related articles:* CALCICHEW; CALCIUM-500; CACIT; CALCIUM AND ERGOCALCIFEROL TABLETS; CALCIUM CARBONATE; CALCIUM FOLINATE; CALCIUM GLUCONATE; CALCIUM LACTATE; CALCIUM-SANDOZ; CALCIUM SULPHALOXATE; CITRICAL; OSSOPAN; SANDOCAL.

**Calcium-500** (*Macarthys*) is a proprietary MINERAL SUPPLEMENT of calcium, in the form of CALCIUM CARBONATE. It is available without prescription, in the form of tablets.
▲/✸ side-effects/warning: *see* CALCIUM.

**calcium and ergocalciferol tablets** are a non-proprietary combination of vitamin D₂ ERGOCALCIFEROL and CALCIUM used for the treatment of nutritional or absorptive deficiencies.
▲/✸ side-effects/warning: *see* CALCIFEROL; CALCIUM.
*Related article:* CHOCOVITE.

**\*calcium antagonists** (calcium channel antagonists; calcium channel blockers) are a relatively new class of drugs used as ANTIHYPERTENSIVES in the treatment of high blood pressure. They act by reducing calcium entry to the heart, which reduces the force of the heartbeat and therefore lowers blood pressure. Examples include DILTIAZEM and VERAPAMIL.

**calcium carbonate**, or chalk, is used therapeutically both as an ANTACID in the treatment of peptic ulcers, and as an ANTIDIARRHOEAL preparation (generally in combination with an astringent). Administration is oral in the form of tablets or as a powder in solution.
▲ side-effects: treatment with calcium carbonate as an antacid may cause belching (through the liberation of carbon dioxide).
✱ warning: prolonged use as an antacid can induce tolerance and eventually cause reduced acid secretion. There may also be abnormally high levels of calcium in the blood. Antacids may impair the absorption of other drugs.
*Related articles:* NULACIN; RABRO.

**calcium carbonate mixture** is an ANTACID representing a non-proprietary formulation of calcium carbonate, magnesium carbonate and sodium bicarbonate, together with tincture of cardamom and a dilute syrup.
▲ / ✱ side-effects/warning: *see* CALCIUM CARBONATE; MAGNESIUM CARBONATE; SODIUM BICARBONATE.

**calcium folinate** is the usual form in which folinic acid (a derivative of folic acid, a vitamin of the VITAMIN B complex) is administered as a supplement to patients who are susceptible to the toxic effects of certain anticancer drugs – especially METHOTREXATE or PYRIMETHAMINE – and to treat some types of anaemia.
*see* FOLINIC ACID.

**calcium gluconate** is one of several common forms in which CALCIUM is administered as a supplement to patients who suffer with calcium deficiency (through dietary insufficiency or disease) or who temporarily need more (as in pregnancy and lactation), with or without the simultaneous administration of CALCIFEROL (vitamin D). It can also be used to treat allergic conditions, such as urticaria, and to relieve the pain of chilblains. Administration is oral in the form of tablets (which may be chewed) or (in solution) by injection or infusion.
▲ side-effects: following treatment by injection or infusion there may be a slowing of the heart rate together with heartbeat irregularity. There may be irritation at the site of injection.
✱ warning: calcium gluconate should be administered with caution to patients who suffer from heart disease.
*Related article:* SANDOCAL.

**calcium lactate** is one of several common forms in which CALCIUM is administered as a supplement to patients who suffer from calcium deficiency (through dietary insufficiency or disease) or who temporarily need more (as in pregnancy and lactation), with or without the simultaneous administration of CALCIFEROL (vitamin D). Administration is oral in the form of tablets (which may be chewed) or (in solution) by injection or infusion.
▲ side-effects: following treatment by injection or infusion there may be a slowing

of the heart rate together with heartbeat irregularity. There may be irritation at the site of injection.

❋ warning: calcium lactate should be administered with caution to patients who suffer from heart disease.
*Related article:* SANDOCAL.

**Calcium Leucovorin** (*Lederle*) is a proprietary preparation of folinic acid, available only on prescription, administered as a supplement to patients who are susceptible to the toxic effects of certain anticancer drugs – especially METHOTREXATE or PYRIMETHAMINE – and used to treat various forms of anaemia. It is produced in the form of tablets, and in ampoules or as powder for reconstitution as injections.
▲/❋ side-effects/warning: *see* FOLINIC ACID.

**Calcium Resonium** (*Winthrop*) is a proprietary, non-prescription preparation used to treat high blood POTASSIUM levels, particularly in patients who suffer from fluid retention or who undergo kidney dialysis. It is produced in the form of a powdered resin, as a calcium polystyrene salt.

**Calcium-Sandoz** (*Sandoz*) is a proprietary MINERAL SUPPLEMENT of calcium as calcium glucobionate. It is available in two forms, as a syrup without prescription, and only on prescription in a form for injection.
▲/❋ side-effects/warning: *see* CALCIUM.

**calcium sulphaloxate** is a SULPHONAMIDE that has now largely been replaced by others because it is poorly absorbed. Formerly, however, it was popularly prescribed to treat infections of the intestines and to

prevent infection during surgery. It is still sometimes used to treat chronic diarrhoea. Use may lead to the appearance of rashes.

**Calfig** (*Sterling Health*) is a proprietary, non-prescription LAXATIVE. Its active constituent is extract of senna leaf.
▲/❋ side-effects/warning: *see* SENNA

**Callusolve** (*Dermal*) is a proprietary, non-prescription preparation, used to treat warts and remove hard, dead skin. Produced in the form of a solute paint, Callusolve is a preparation of the keratolytic benzalkonium chloride as a bromine adduct. Avoid normal skin.
❋ warning: *see* BENZALKONIUM CHLORIDE.

**Calmurid** (*Pharmacia*) is a proprietary, non-prescription preparation, used to treat conditions in which the skin becomes scaly and hardens in layers. Produced in the form of a water-miscible cream for dilution (the cream once dilute retains potency for 14 days), Calmurid is a combination of the DIURETIC urea and lactic acid.

**Calmurid HC** (*Pharmacia*) is a proprietary CORTICOSTEROID preparation, available only on prescription, used to treat conditions in which the skin becomes dry and hardens in layers. Produced in the form of a water-miscible cream for dilution (the cream once dilute retains potency for 14 days), Calmurid HC is a combination of the steroid hydrocortisone, the DIURETIC urea and lactic acid.
▲/❋ side-effects/warning: *see* HYDROCORTISONE.

**Calogen** (*Scientific Hospital Supplies*) is a proprietary, non-prescription dietary supplement used in the nutrition of patients with kidney disease. Produced in the form of a gluten-free emulsion, Calogen comprises ARACHIS OIL in water.

**Calonutrin** (*Geistlich*) is a proprietary, non-prescription dietary supplement used in the nutrition of patients who suffer from kidney disease, cirrhosis of the liver or amino acid abnormality (such as phenylketonuria). Produced in the form of powder, Calonutrin comprises many simple sugars (especially glucose).

**Caloreen** (*Roussel*) is a proprietary, non-prescription dietary supplement used in the nutrition of patients who suffer from kidney disease, cirrhosis of the liver or amino-acid abnormality (such as phenylketonuria). Produced in the form of powder, Caloreen comprises many simple sugars (especially glucose).

**Calpol** (*Calmic*) is a proprietary form of the non-narcotic ANALGESIC paracetamol. It is produced in the form of a suspension in two strengths: the weaker (non-prescription) is produced under the name Calpol Infant, which is also available in a sugar-free form; the stronger (not available from the National Health Service) under the name Calpol Six Plus.
▲/❋ side-effects/warning: *see* PARACETAMOL.

**Calsynar** (*Armour*) is a proprietary synthesized form of calcitonin (salcatonin), one of the two hormones that regulate blood levels of calcium in the body. Available only on prescription, Calsynar is used to treat several types of serious bone disease, including cancer, and is produced in ampoules (in two strengths) for injection.

▲/❋ side-effects/warning: *see* CALCITONIN; SALCATONIN.

**CAM** (*Rybar*) is a proprietary, non-prescription SYMPATHOMIMETIC, a BRONCHODILATOR used to treat patients suffering from asthma and other conditions involving bronchial spasm. Produced in the form of a syrup, CAM's active constituent is EPHEDRINE HYDROCHLORIDE. CAM is not recommended for children aged under 18 months.

**Camcolit** (*Norgine*) is a proprietary ANTIDEPRESSANT drug, available only on prescription, used to treat acute mania and to prevent manic-depressive bouts. Produced in the form of tablets (in two strengths), Camcolit is a preparation of lithium carbonate. It is not recommended for children.
▲/❋ side-effects/warning: *see* LITHIUM.

**Canesten** (*Bayer*) is a proprietary, non-prescription ANTIFUNGAL preparation, used to treat particularly vaginal thrush and dermatophyte infections of the skin, such as athlete's foot. Treatment is topical and should be continued for the full course to prevent recurrence. Produced in the form of vaginal tablets (pessaries), as a solution, as a spray, as a cream and as a dusting-powder, Canesten is a preparation of clotrimazole. Canesten vaginal cream, vaginal tablets (in two strengths) and a Duopak containing vaginal tablets and cream are available only on prescription.
▲/❋ side-effects/warning: *see* CLOTRIMAZOLE.

**Canesten 1** (*Bayer*) is a proprietary ANTIFUNGAL preparation, available only on prescription, used to treat vaginal infections. Produced in the form of

vaginal tablets (pessaries),
Canesten 1 – which is a stronger
version of CANESTEN – is also a
preparation of clotrimazole.
▲/❋ side-effects/warning: *see*
CLOTRIMAZOLE.

**Canesten 10% VC** (*Bayer*) is a
proprietary ANTIFUNGAL cream,
available only on prescription,
used to treat vaginal infections.
To be inserted through a special
applicator, Canesten 10% VC is a
preparation of clotrimazole.
▲/❋ side-effects/warning: *see*
CLOTRIMAZOLE.

**Canesten-HC** (*Bayer*) is a
proprietary ANTIFUNGAL
CORTICOSTEROID preparation,
available only on prescription,
used to treat fungal infections,
particularly those that cause
inflammation. Produced in the
form of a cream for topical
application, Canesten-HC consists
of a combination of clotrimazole
and hydrocortisone.
▲/❋ side-effects/warning: *see*
CLOTRIMAZOLE.

**cannabis** is one name for a drug
prepared from the Indian hemp
plant Cannabis sativa: other
names include bhang, dagga,
hashish, marijuana and pot. Its
use seems of little therapeutic
value, and its social use is illegal
although fairly widespread. (It
may be prescribed only under
licence from the Home Secretary.)
A synthetic cannabinoid,
NABILONE, is used in cancer
chemotherapy to reduce nausea
and vomiting.
▲ side-effects: smoked or
ingested, cannabis is a
psychedelic, causing
comparatively mild
hallucinations with euphoria,
heightening awareness and
particularly affecting the sense
of time. Withdrawal symptoms
are rare, but use tends to
increase tolerance.

❋ warning: prolonged use is
thought eventually to result in
brain damage, and is thought
by some to lead a user to
experiment with addictive
'hard' drugs, although it is
difficult to test this theory.

**Cantil** (*MCP Pharmaceuticals*) is a
proprietary ANTICHOLINERGIC
drug, available only on
prescription, used as a SMOOTH
MUSCLE RELAXANT to treat rigidity
(spasm) or hyperactivity of the
muscles of the colon. Produced in
the form of tablets, Cantil is a
preparation of the MUSCLE
RELAXANT mepenzolate bromide. It
is not recommended for children
aged under 6 years.
▲/❋ side-effects/warning: *see*
MEPENZOLATE BROMIDE.

**Capastat** (*Dista*) is a proprietary
ANTITUBERCULAR drug, used to
treat tuberculosis resistant to
other drugs. Produced in the form
of powder for reconstitution as
intramuscular injections,
Capastat is a preparation of the
ANTIBIOTIC capreomycin sulphate.
It is not usually recommended for
children.
▲/❋ side-effects/warning: *see*
CAPREOMYCIN.

**Capitol** (*Dermal*) is a proprietary,
non-prescription ANTIBACTERIAL
preparation, used to treat
dandruff and other scalp
conditions. Produced in the form
of a gel applied as a shampoo,
Capitol is a preparation of the
antiseptic BENZALKONIUM
CHLORIDE.

**Caplenal** (*Berk*) is a proprietary
form of the XANTHINE-OXIDASE
INHIBITOR allopurinol, used as a
long-term treatment of gout and
high levels of uric acid in the
bloodstream. It exacerbates
symptoms of gout if given during
an attack. Available only on
prescription, Caplenal is produced

in the form of tablets (in two strengths) and is not recommended for children.

▲/● side-effects/warning: *see* ALLOPURINOL.

**Capoten** (*Squibb*) is a proprietary ANTIHYPERTENSIVE drug, available only on prescription, used accordingly to treat high blood pressure (hypertension) and to slow the heart rate. Although well tolerated, the long-term effects are unknown and so it tends to be used when THIAZIDES or BETA-BLOCKERS have failed or are not tolerated. It works by inhibiting enzymes involved in producing vasoactive hormones in the blood. Produced in the form of tablets (in three strengths), Capoten is a preparation of the powerful drug captopril.

▲/● side-effects/warning: *see* CAPTOPRIL.

**capreomycin** is an ANTIBIOTIC drug used specifically in the treatment of tuberculosis that proves to be resistant to the first-line drugs, or in cases where those drugs are not tolerated. Administration is by intramuscular injection.

▲ side-effects: there may be kidney toxicity and impaired hearing with or without ringing in the ears (tinnitus) or vertigo; sometimes there are sensitivity reactions such as rashes or urticaria.

● warning: capreomycin should not be administered to patients who are pregnant, and should be administered with caution to those who have impaired function of the liver, kidney or sense of hearing (functions that should be monitored during treatment), or who are already taking other ototoxic antibiotics, or who are lactating.

*Related article:* CAPASTAT.

**Caprin** (*Sinclair*) is a proprietary, non-prescription preparation of the non-narcotic ANALGESIC aspirin, used particularly to treat headache and rheumatic conditions. Produced in the form of sustained-release tablets, Caprin is not recommended for children aged under 12 years.

▲/● side-effects/warning: *see* ASPIRIN.

**captopril** is a powerful VASODILATOR used in the treatment of high blood pressure (hypertension) particularly when THIAZIDE drugs have failed to be fully effective or are not tolerated. It may also be used to treat heart failure, although a supplementary DIURETIC is then commonly administered. Captopril works by inhibiting enzymes involved in producing vasoactive hormones in the blood thus dilating the smaller arteries. Administration of captopril is oral in the form of tablets.

▲ side-effects: there may be marked low blood pressure (hypotension); thereafter there may be a loss of the sense of taste and a dry cough; sometimes there is abdominal pain and/or a rash. In patients with impaired kidney function (or who are given a high dosage) there may be changes in the composition of the blood, and protein in the urine.

● warning: captopril should not be administered to patients who are pregnant, and administered with caution to those who are lactating. The first dose may cause very rapid reduction in blood pressure, especially if a diuretic is given simultaneously; dosage thereafter may be adjusted for optimum effect. Monitoring of kidney function, white blood cell count and urinary contents during treatment is essential.

*Related articles:* ACEPRIL; CAPOTEN.

**Carace** (*Morson*) is a proprietary form of the ANTIHYPERTENSIVE drug lisinopril used to treat high blood pressure (hypertension), and in combination with a DIURETIC or CARDIAC GLYCOSIDE in congestive heart failure. It is available only on prescription in the form of tablets (in four strengths).
▲/◆ side-effects/warning: *see* LISINOPRIL.

**carbachol** is a PARASYMPATHO-MIMETIC that is used to treat some heart and circulatory conditions, or to lower pressure in the eyeball while contracting the pupil (in the treatment of glaucoma), but perhaps its most common use is to treat urinary retention, particularly following surgery. Administration is oral in the form of tablets, by injection, or as eye-drops.
▲ side-effects: there may be sweating and blurred vision, nausea and vomiting, and a slow heart rate.
◆ warning: carbachol should not be administered to patients who suffer from urinary or intestinal blockage or haemorrhage, or who have recently had a heart attack. It should be administered with caution to those who suffer from heart disease, epilepsy, parkinsonism or thyroid disorders, or who are elderly.
*Related article:* ISOPTO.

**carbamazepine** is an ANTICONVULSANT drug used, sometimes in combination with other drugs, particularly to treat grand mal epilepsy both during seizures and on a maintenance basis. In smaller doses it is effective in reducing attacks of trigeminal neuralgia (a searing pain in paroxysms along the

trigeminal nerve in the face) or the neural disorders that may accompany diabetes mellitus, again on a maintenance basis. Surprisingly, it also has DIURETIC properties, and is sometimes alternatively used in that capacity to assist treatment for diabetes insipidus.
▲ side-effects: there may be blurring of vision and unsteadiness; high dosage may cause severe dizziness. Sometimes there are gastrointestinal disturbances; occasionally there is a rash.
◆ warning: carbamazepine should not be administered to patients who suffer from certain heart defects or porphyria, or to those using or having recently used any of the MAO inhibitor drugs; it should be administered with caution to those who suffer from impaired function of the liver or glaucoma, or who are lactating. Dosage should begin at a minimum level and be adjusted upwards for optimum effect. Blood monitoring is essential if high doses are administered.
*Related article:* TEGRETOL.

**carbaryl** is an insecticide used in the treatment of scalp or pubic lice. Administration is (in aqueous or alcohol solution) in the form of a lotion, or shampoo which is applied to wet hair, allowed to dry, and then rinsed after a specified time (usually about 12 hours). The procedure may need to be repeated after a week.
◆ warning: keep away from the eyes.
*Related articles:* CARYLDERM; CLINICIDE; DERBAC-C; SULEO-C.

**Carbellon** (*Medo*) is a proprietary, non-prescription ANTI-CHOLINERGIC compound, which is not available from the National Health Service. It is used to treat muscle spasm (rigidity) of the intestinal walls, and resulting gastrointestinal upsets. Produced in the form of tablets, Carbellon's active constituents are belladonna extract, charcoal and magnesium hydroxide.

▲/✿ side-effects/warning: *see* BELLADONNA; CHARCOAL; MAGNESIUM HYDROXIDE.

**carbenicillin** is an ANTIBIOTIC of the penicillin family. Used to treat serious infections caused by sensitive gram-negative organisms, often in combination with aminoglycoside antibiotics. Administration is by injection or infusion in the case of systemic infections, or by intramuscular injections for urinary tract infections. It has now largely been superseded by more potent agents.

▲ side-effects: there may be sensitivity reactions – serious ones in hypersensitive patients. Body temperature may rise, and there may be pains in the joints and skin rashes or urticaria; potassium and platelet levels in the blood may decline.

✿ warning: carbenicillin should not be administered to patients known to be sensitive to penicillins, and should be administered with caution to those who suffer from impaired kidney function.

*Related article:* PYOPEN.

**carbenoxolone sodium** is a compound derivative of a constituent of liquorice used as a treatment for gastric ulcers because it protects the stomach lining from excess acid and enzymes – in a way that is not well understood. Although used primarily to treat gastric or intestinal ulcers, it may also be used locally to soothe mouth ulcers. Administration is oral in the form of tablets (to be chewed

or swallowed) as capsules, as a gel, or as a compound liquid.

▲ side-effects: there may be fluid retention in the tissues (oedema); heartburn is not uncommon. Patients with high blood pressure (hypertension) or muscular weakness may find these conditions aggravated during treatment.

✿ warning: carbenoxolone sodium should be administered with caution to patients who suffer from impaired function of the liver or kidneys, heart disease, high blood pressure, or who are elderly. The drug is potassium-depleting: potassium supplements should accompany treatment (with or without THIAZIDE diuretics).

*Related articles:* BIOGASTRONE; DUOGASTRONE; PYROGASTRONE.

**carbidopa** is a drug administered in combination with levodopa to treat parkinsonism, but not the parkinsonian symptoms induced by other drugs (*see* ANTI-PARKINSONISM). It is levodopa that actually has the major effect. Carbidopa inhibits the breakdown of levodopa (to dopamine) in the body before it reaches the brain, where it carries out its function. The presence of carbidopa allows the dose of levodopa to be at a minimum, thus also minimizing potentially severe side-effects, and speeds the therapeutic response. But it is also responsible for producing involuntary movements. Administration of carbidopa and levodopa is in the form of single compound tablets.

▲/✿ side-effects/warning: *see* LEVODOPA.

*Related article:* SINEMET.

**carbimazole** prevents the production or secretion of the hormone thyroxine by the thyroid gland, so treating an excess in the blood of thyroid HORMONES and the symptoms that it causes (thyrotoxicosis). Treatment may be on a maintenance basis over a long period (dosage adjusted to optimum effect), or may be merely preliminary to surgical removal of the thyroid gland. Administration is oral in the form of tablets.

▲ side-effects: an itching rash is common, but may indicate a need for alternative treatment. There may also be nausea and headache; occasionally there is jaundice or hair loss (alopecia).

✿ warning: carbimazole should not be administered to patients with obstruction of the upper respiratory tract, and should be administered with extreme caution to patients who are pregnant or lactating.
*Related article:* NEO-MERCAZOLE.

**carbinoxamine** is a short-acting ANTIHISTAMINE that is an anti-allergic constituent in one or two cough linctuses and, because it also has mild ANTINAUSEANT properties, is also found in some proprietary preparations to prevent travel sickness.

**carbocisteine** is a MUCOLYTIC drug, used accordingly to reduce the viscosity of sputum and thus facilitate expectoration (the coughing up of sputum) in patients with disorders of the upper respiratory tract such as asthma and bronchitis. It may also be used to treat accumulations of mucus in the middle ear ('glue ear') in children. Administration is oral in the form of tablets, capsules or syrup.

▲ side-effects: side-effects are uncommon, but there may be gastrointestinal disturbance, with nausea, or a rash.

✿ warning: carbocisteine should not be administered to patients with a peptic ulcer; it should be

administered with caution to those who are pregnant.
*Related article:* MUCODYNE.

**Carbo-Cort** (*Lagap*) is a proprietary cream, available only on prescription, for topical application to conditions of chronic eczema and psoriasis and other dermatoses (skin conditions). It is a compound of the CORTICOSTEROID hydrocortisone with the cleansing agent COAL TAR.

▲/✿ side-effects/warning: see HYDROCORTISONE.

**Carbo-Dome** (*Lagap*) is a proprietary, non-prescription ANTISEPTIC used to treat non-infective skin conditions like psoriasis. Produced in the form of a water-miscible cream, Carbo-Dome's active constituent is COAL TAR.

**Carbomix** (*Penn*) is a proprietary, non-prescription adsorbent preparation, used to treat patients suffering from poisoning or a drug overdose. Produced in the form of granulated powder to be mixed with water, Carbomix's active constituent is CHARCOAL.

**carboplatin** is a CYTOTOXIC drug derived from the ANTICANCER drug cisplatin, and similarly used to treat cancer of the ovary. Side-effects of nausea and vomiting are less than those caused by cisplatin. Administration is by injection.

▲ side-effects: there may be nausea and vomiting, progressive deafness and symptoms of kidney dysfunction. The blood-forming capacity of the bone-marrow may be suppressed (and treatment should not be repeated within 4 weeks).

✿ warning: an anti-emetic may be administered simultaneously to lessen the risk of nausea and

vomiting. Monitoring of
kidney function and the sense
of hearing is advisable.
*Related article:* PARAPLATIN.

**carboprost** is a drug used in
patients unresponsive to
ERGOMETRINE and OXYTOCIN to
treat post-partum haemorrhage
due to uterine atony. It is
available in the form for deep
intramuscular injection.
▲ side-effects: there may be
nausea and vomiting, headache
and dizziness, diarrhoea,
flushing, chills and
hyperthermia. Occasionally
raised blood pressure, oedema
of the lungs and shortness of
breath. There may be pain at
the site of injection.
✿ warning: use with caution in
patients with a history of
glaucoma (raised intraocular
pressure), anaemia, jaundice,
epilepsy, asthma, abnormal
blood pressure (high or low),
and uterine scars. It should not
be used to induce labour.
*Related article:* HEMABATE.

**Cardene** (*Syntex*) is a proprietary
form of the CALCIUM ANTAGONIST
ANTIHYPERTENSIVE drug
nicardipine hydrochloride,
available only on prescription,
used to prevent or treat chronic
angina and high blood pressure
(hypertension). Produced in the
form of capsules (in two
strengths), Cardene is not
recommended for children.
▲/✿ side-effects/warning: *see*
NICARDIPINE.

**Cardiacap** (*Consolidated*) is a
proprietary, non-prescription
VASODILATOR, used in the
prevention or treatment of
angina. Produced in the form of
sustained-release capsules,
Cardiacap is a preparation of
pentaerythritol tetranitrate.
It is not recommended for
children.

▲/✿ side-effects/warning: *see*
PENTAERYTHRITOL
TETRANITRATE.

**cardiac glycosides** are a class of
drugs that have a pronounced
effect on the heart, increasing the
force of contraction of cardiac
muscle. They therefore have an
important use in the treatment of
congestive heart failure.
Examples include OUABAIN and
DIGOXIN.

**Cardura** (*Invicta*) is an
ANTIHYPERTENSIVE drug, an
ALPHA-BLOCKER, used to treat high
blood pressure (hypertension). A
proprietary form of doxazosin,
available only on prescription,
the preparation is available in
tablets in three strengths.
▲/✿ side-effects/warning: *see*
DOXAZOSIN.

**carfecillin sodium** is a penicillin-
like ANTIBIOTIC with a similar
spectrum of activity to
CARBENICILLIN. It is used
particularly to treat susceptible
gram-negative infections of the
urinary tract. Administration is
oral in the form of tablets.
▲ side-effects: there may be
sensitivity reactions – serious
ones in hypersensitive
patients. Body temperature
may rise, and there may be
pains in the joints and skin
rashes or urticaria.
✿ warning: carfecillin sodium
should not be administered to
patients known to be sensitive
to penicillin, and should be
administered with caution to
those with impaired kidney
function.

**Carisoma** (*Pharmax*) is a
proprietary SKELETAL MUSCLE
RELAXANT, available only on
prescription, used to relieve
muscle spasm by direct action on
the central nervous system.
Produced in the form of tablets (in

two strengths), Carisoma is a preparation of carisoprodol. It is not recommended for children.
▲ / ✿ side-effects/warning: *see* CARISOPRODOL.

**carisoprodol** is a SKELETAL MUSCLE RELAXANT, which works by directly affecting certain areas of the central nervous system, and is used to relieve muscle spasm in muscles used for voluntary movement. Administration is oral in the form of tablets.
▲ side-effects: there is commonly drowsiness and dizziness; there may also be dry mouth, headache, shallow breathing, low blood pressure (hypotension), general debility and gastrointestinal disturbances. Rarely, there are visual disturbances and a rash.
✿ warning: carisoprodol should not be administered to patients with porphyria, or who are lactating; it should be administered with caution to those who are epileptic. Withdrawal from treatment must be gradual. Prolonged overdosage may cause muscle atrophy.
*Related article:* CARISOMA.

**carmellose sodium** is a substance used as the basis for a paste and a powder that is spread or sprinkled over lesions in or around the mouth in order to protect them while they heal. Both paste and powder also contain soft animal and vegetable proteins.
*Related articles:* ORABASE; ORAHESIVE.

**carmustine** is a CYTOTOXIC drug that works by direct interference with DNA, thus preventing normal cell replication. It is used to treat some solid tumours and the lymphatic cancer, Hodgkin's disease. Prolonged treatment may produce considerable toxicity and associated side-effects.

Administration is by intravenous injection.
▲ side-effects: there is commonly nausea and vomiting. The blood-producing capacity of the bone-marrow is impaired (although the effect is delayed, and treatment should therefore not be repeated within 4 weeks). There may be hair loss.
✿ warning: the drug causes permanent sterility in men early in treatment, and prolonged treatment may lead to an early menopause in women; prolonged treatment has also been associated with the incidence of leukaemia following simultaneous irradiation treatment. Blood count monitoring is essential. Dosage should be the minimum still to be effective.
*Related article:* BiCNU.

**Carobel, Instant** (*Cow & Gate*) is a proprietary, non-prescription powder, used to thicken liquid and semi-liquid diets in the treatment of vomiting. Carobel is a preparation of carob seed flour.

**carteolol hydrochloride** is a BETA-BLOCKER used to treat angina pectoris (heart pain). Administration is in the form of tablets. It has properties similar to propranolol.
▲ / ✿ side-effects/warning: *see* PROPRANOLOL.
*Related article:* CARTROL.

**Cartrol** (*Sanofi*) is a proprietary form of the BETA-BLOCKER careolol hydrochloride available only on prescription, used to treat angina pectoris (heart pain). Available in the form of tablets.
▲ / ✿ side-effects/warning: *see* PROPRANOLOL.

**Carylderm** (*Napp*) is a proprietary, non-prescription drug used to treat infestations of the scalp and pubic hair by lice.

Produced in the form of a lotion and a shampoo, Carylderm is a preparation of the pediculicide carbaryl.
⬥ warning: see CARBARYL.

**cascara** is a slightly old-fashioned but powerful stimulant LAXATIVE, which acts by increasing the muscular activity of the intestinal walls. It is now used less commonly, not just because of its cumulatively detrimental side-effects but because it may take up to 8 hours to have any relieving effect on constipation. Administration is oral in the form of tablets.
▲ side-effects: the urine may be coloured red. Prolonged use of such a stimulant can eventually wear out the muscles on which it works, thus causing severe intestinal problems in terms of motility and absorption.
⬥ warning: cascara should not be taken by any patient who is breast-feeding, and is not recommended for children.

**Casilan** (*Farley*) is a proprietary, non-prescription protein dietary supplement used to treat patients who are undernourished through lack of food or poor internal absorption. Produced in the form of powder for reconstitution, Casilan contains all essential amino acids and is gluten-free and low in electrolytes.

**castor oil** is a slightly old-fashioned stimulant LAXATIVE, which probably acts by increasing the muscular activity of the intestinal walls. It is now used less commonly because of its cumulatively detrimental side-effects, although its use in hospitals and clinics before surgical examinations and procedures is still well attested. Yet it may take up to 8 hours to relieve constipation. Administration is oral.

▲ side-effects: there may be nausea and vomiting. Prolonged use of such a stimulant can eventually wear out the muscles on which it works, thus causing severe intestinal problems in terms of motility and absorption.
⬥ warning: castor oil should not be taken by any patient who is menstruating, pregnant or lactating, or who suffers from intestinal obstruction.

**Catapres** (*Boehringer Ingelheim*) is a proprietary ANTI-HYPERTENSIVE drug, available only on prescription, used to treat high blood pressure (hypertension). Produced in the form of tablets (in two strengths), capsules and ampoules for injection, Catapres is a preparation of clonidine hydrochloride. It is not recommended for children.
▲/⬥ side-effects/warning: see CLONIDINE HYDROCHLORIDE.

**Caved-S** (*Tillotts*) is a proprietary, non-prescription ANTACID, used to treat the symptoms of peptic ulcers. Produced in the form of tablets, Caved-S contains a compound form of a constituent of liquorice, ALUMINIUM HYDROXIDE gel, MAGNESIUM CARBONATE and SODIUM BICARBONATE. It is not recommended for children under the age of 10 years.

**CCNU** (*Lundbeck*) is a proprietary CYTOTOXIC drug, available only on prescription, used mainly in cancer chemotherapy. Produced in the form of capsules (in two strengths), CCNU is a preparation of lomustine.
▲/⬥ side-effects/warning: see LOMUSTINE.

**Ceanel Concentrate** (*Quinoderm*) is a proprietary, non-prescription ANTIBACTERIAL and ANTIFUNGAL preparation, used to treat psoriasis and other non-infective scalp conditions. Produced in the form of a shampoo, Ceanel Concentrate contains the antiseptic CETRIMIDE, the antifungal undecenoic acid, and the astringent ethyl alcohol.

▲/● side-effects/warning: *see* CETRIMIDE.

**Ce-Cobalin** (*Paines & Byrne*) is a proprietary, non-prescription VITAMIN preparation, which is not available from the National Health Service. Produced in the form of a syrup, Ce-Cobalin is a compound of CYANOCOBALAMIN (vitamin B$_{12}$) and ASCORBIC ACID (vitamin C).

**Cedilanid** (*Sandoz*) is a proprietary CARDIAC GLYCOSIDE heart stimulant, available only on prescription, used to treat heart failure and severe heartbeat irregularities. Produced in the form of tablets, Cedilanid is a preparation of LANATOSIDE C (which is converted on ingestion into the better-known digoxin).

▲/● side-effects/warning: *see* DIGOXIN.

**Cedocard** (*Tillotts*) represents a series of proprietary forms of the VASODILATOR isosorbide dinitrate, used to prevent and treat angina pectoris. Produced in the form of tablets (in four strengths, under the names Cedocard-5, Cedocard-10, Cedocard-20 and Cedocard-40), as sustained-release tablets (under the name Cedocard Retard) and in flasks (ampoules) for infusion (under the name Cedocard I.V.), not one of these preparations is recommended for children.

▲/● side-effects/warning: *see* ISOSORBIDE DINITRATE.

**cefaclor** is a broad-spectrum ANTIBIOTIC, one of the first generation CEPHALOSPORINS, now primarily used to treat infections of the urinary tract and the respiratory tract. Administration is oral in the form of capsules or a dilute suspension.

▲ side-effects: there may be sensitivity reactions – some of which may be serious. Sometimes there is nausea and vomiting, with diarrhoea.

● warning: cefaclor should not be administered to patients who might be sensitive to penicillins in general and cephalosporins in particular. It should be administered with caution to those with impaired kidney function. Prolonged skin reactions may occur in children.

*Related article:* DISTACLOR.

**cefadroxil** is a broad-spectrum ANTIBIOTIC, one of the first generation CEPHALOSPORINS, now primarily used to treat bacterial infections of the skin, soft tissues and the urinary tract. Administration is oral in the form of capsules or a dilute suspension.

▲ side-effects: there may be sensitivity reactions – some of which may be serious. Sometimes there is nausea and vomiting, with diarrhoea.

● warning: cefadroxil should not be administered to patients who might be sensitive to penicillins in general and cephalosporins in particular. It should be administered with caution to those who suffer from impaired kidney function.

*Related article:* BAXAN.

**Cefizox** (*Wellcome*) is a proprietary ANTIBIOTIC, available only on prescription, used to treat gonorrhoea and infections in the upper respiratory tract and urinary tract. Produced in the form of powder for reconstitution as injections, Cefizox is a preparation of the CEPHALOSPORIN ceftizoxime as a salt of sodium. It is not recommended for children aged under 3 months.

▲/ ✹ side-effects/warning: *see* CEFTIZOXIME.

**cefotaxime** is a broad-spectrum ANTIBIOTIC, one of the third generation CEPHALOSPORINS, used to treat a wide range of bacterial infections, particularly of the skin and soft tissues, the urinary tract, the meninges of the brain (meningitis) and the blood (septicaemia). It is also used to prevent infection during surgery. Administration is by intravenous or intramuscular injection.

▲ side-effects: there may be sensitivity reactions – some of which may be serious. Sometimes there is nausea and vomiting, with diarrhoea.

✹ warning: cefotaxime should not be administered to patients who might be sensitive to penicillins in general and cephalosporins in particular. It should be administered with caution to those with impaired kidney function, or who are pregnant or lactating.

*Related article:* CLAFORAN.

**cefoxitin** is a broad-spectrum ANTIBIOTIC, one of the second generation CEPHALOSPORINS, used to treat a wide range of bacterial infections, particularly gram-negative infections of the skin and soft tissues, the urinary tract, the respiratory tract, the peritoneum (peritonitis) and the blood (septicaemia). Because of its activity against mixed aerobic and anaerobic *Bacteroides fragilis* infections it is also used to prevent infection during or following gynaecological or obstetric surgery. Administration is by intravenous or intramuscular injection.

▲ side-effects: there may be sensitivity reactions – some of which may be serious.

Sometimes there is nausea and vomiting, with diarrhoea.

✹ warning: cefoxitin should not be administered to patients who might be sensitive to penicillins in general and cephalosporins in particular. It should be administered with caution to those with impaired kidney function.

*Related article:* MEFOXIN.

**cefsulodin** is a broad-spectrum ANTIBIOTIC, one of the first generation CEPHALOSPORINS, used primarily to treat pseudomonal infections and for surgical prophylaxis. Administration is by intravenous or intramuscular injection.

▲ side-effects: there may be sensitivity reactions – some of which may be serious. Sometimes there is nausea and vomiting, with diarrhoea.

✹ warning: cefsulodin should not be administered to patients who might be sensitive to penicillins in general and cephalosporins in particular. It should be administered with caution to those with impaired kidney function, or who are pregnant. Monitoring of blood counts during treatment is essential.

*Related article:* MONASPOR.

**ceftazidime** is a broad-spectrum ANTIBIOTIC, one of the third generation CEPHALOSPORINS. It is the most active of the cephalosporins against bacterial infections, particularly of the skin and soft tissues, the urinary tract, the respiratory tract, the ear, nose and throat, the bones and the joints, the gastro-intestinal tract, the meninges (meningitis) and the blood (septicaemia). It is also used to treat infection in patients whose immune systems are defective. Administration is by intravenous or intramuscular injection.

▲ side-effects: there may be sensitivity reactions – some of which may be serious. Alternatively, sometimes there is nausea and vomiting, with diarrhoea.

● warning: ceftazidime should not be administered to patients who might be sensitive to penicillins in general and cephalosporins in particular, or to patients who are already taking certain diuretic drugs. It should be administered with caution to those who suffer from impaired kidney function, or who are pregnant.
*Related article:* FORTUM.

**ceftizoxime** is a broad-spectrum ANTIBIOTIC, one of the third generation CEPHALOSPORINS, used to treat a wide range of gram-negative bacterial infections, particularly of the skin and soft tissues, the urinary tract, the genital organs, the lower respiratory tract, the meninges of the brain (meningitis) and the blood (septicaemia). It is also used to treat infection in patients whose immune systems are defective. Administration is by intravenous or intramuscular injection.

▲ side-effects: there may be sensitivity reactions – some of which may be serious. Alternatively, sometimes there is nausea and vomiting, with diarrhoea.

● warning: ceftizoxime should not be administered to patients who might be sensitive to penicillins in general and cephalosporins in particular. It should be administered with caution to those who suffer from impaired kidney function.
*Related article:* CEFIZOX.

**cefuroxime** is a broad-spectrum ANTIBIOTIC, one of the second generation CEPHALOSPORINS, used

to treat a wide range of bacterial infections, particularly gram-negative infections of the urinary tract, the respiratory tract, the genital tract, and the meninges (meningitis). It is also used to prevent infection during surgery. Administration is by intravenous or intramuscular injection.

▲ side-effects: there may be sensitivity reactions – some of which may be serious. Alternatively, sometimes there is nausea and vomiting, with diarrhoea.

● warning: cefuroxime should not be administered to patients who might be sensitive to penicillins in general and cephalosporins in particular, or to patients who are already taking certain diuretic drugs. It should be administered with caution to those who suffer from impaired kidney function, or who are pregnant.
*Related article:* ZINACEF.

**Celbenin** (*Beecham*) is a proprietary, penicillin-type ANTIBIOTIC, available only on prescription, used to treat many forms of infection but particularly those caused by penicillin-resistant bacteria. Produced in the form of powder for reconstitution as injections, Celbenin is a preparation of methicillin sodium.

▲/● side-effects/warning: *see* METHICILLIN.

**Celevac** (*Boehringer Ingelheim*) is a proprietary, non-prescription form of the type of LAXATIVE known as a bulking agent, which works by increasing the overall mass of faeces within the rectum, so stimulating bowel movement. It can thus be used to treat either constipation or diarrhoea, to control the consistency of faeces for patients with colostomy, and to reduce appetite in the medical treatment of obesity. Produced in

the form of tablets, Celevac
represents a preparation of
methylcellulose. (Celevac
granules are not available from
the National Health Service.)
▲/✪ side-effects/warning: *see*
METHYLCELLULOSE.

**Centyl** (*Burgess*) is a proprietary
DIURETIC, available only on
prescription, used – particularly
in combination with
ANTIHYPERTENSIVE drugs – to
treat an accumulation of fluid in
the tissues (oedema) and high
blood pressure (hypertension).
Produced in the form of tablets (in
two strengths), Centyl is a
preparation of bendrofluazide.
▲/✪ side-effects/warning: *see*
BENDROFLUAZIDE.

**Centyl-K** (*Burgess*) is a
proprietary DIURETIC, available
only on prescription, used to treat
an accumulation of fluid in the
tissues (oedema) and high blood
pressure (hypertension).
Produced in the form of tablets,
Centyl-K is a preparation of
bendrofluazide with a potassium
supplement for sustained release.
▲/✪ side-effects/warning: *see*
BENDROFLUAZIDE.

**cephalexin** is a broad-spectrum
ANTIBIOTIC, one of the orally
active CEPHALOSPORINS, which
may be used to treat a wide range
of bacterial infections,
particularly sensitive urinary
tract infections. Administration is
in the form of capsules, tablets
and liquids.
  ▲ side-effects: there may be
  sensitivity reactions – some of
  which may be serious.
  Sometimes there is nausea and
  vomiting, with diarrhoea.
  ✪ warning: cephalexin should
  not be administered to patients
  who might be sensitive to
  penicillins in general and
  cephalosporins in particular. It
  should be administered with

caution to those with impaired
kidney function.
  *Related articles:* CEPOREX;
  KEFLEX.

**cephalosporins** are broad-
spectrum ANTIBIOTICS that act
against both gram-positive and
gram-negative bacteria. They
bear a strong resemblance in
chemical structure to the
penicillins: both contain a beta
lactam ring, hence their
classification as beta lactam
antibiotics. The similarity in
structure extends to mechanism
of action: both inhibit the
synthesis of the bacterial cell
wall, so killing growing bacteria
(bactericidal). As a group the
cephalosporins are generally
active against streptococci,
staphylococci and a number of
gram-negative bacteria including
many coliforms. Some second
generation cephalosporins are
resistant to inactivation by
bacterial penicillinase enzymes;
this widens the range of sensitive
gram-negative organisms,
including *Haemophilus
influenzae*. Some of the latest,
third generation, cephalosporins,
such as ceftazidime, are active
against pseudomonal infections.
Many cephalosporins are actively
excreted by the kidney, therefore
reaching considerably higher
concentrations in the urine than
in the blood. For this reason they
may be used to treat infections of
the urinary tract during their
own excretion. In general
cephalosporins are rarely the
drug of first choice, but provide a
useful alternative or reserve
option for particular situations.
The currently used
cephalosporins are relatively non-
toxic, with only occasional blood
clotting problems, superinfections
and hypersensitivity reactions
(only 10% of patients allergic to
penicillin show sensitivity to
cephalosporins).

▲/✿ side-effects/warning: *see*
CEFACLOR; CEFADROXIL;
CEFOTAXIME; CEFOXITIN;
CEFSULODIN; CEFTAZIDIME;
CEFTIZOXIME; CEFUROXIME;
CEPHALEXIN; CEPHALOTHIN;
CEPHAMANDOLE;
CEPHAZOLIN; CEPHRADINE;
LATAMOXEF DISODIUM.

**cephalothin** is a broad-spectrum
ANTIBIOTIC, one of the first
CEPHALOSPORINS, which can be
used to treat a wide range of
bacterial infections, particularly
of the skin and soft tissues, the
urinary tract, upper respiratory
tract, and middle ear. It is also
used to prevent infection during
surgery. Administration is by
injection.
▲ side-effects: there may be
sensitivity reactions – some of
which may be serious.
Sometimes there is nausea and
vomiting, with diarrhoea.
✿ warning: cephalothin should
not be administered to patients
who might be sensitive to
penicillins in general and
cephalosporins in particular,
or to those with impaired
kidney functions.
*Related article:* KEFLIN.

**cephamandole** is a broad-
spectrum ANTIBIOTIC, one of the
second generation
CEPHALOSPORINS. It is less
susceptible to inactivation by
bacterial penicillinases, and for
this reason is effective against a
greater range of gram-negative
bacteria such as penicillin
resistant *Neisseria gonorrhoeae*
and *Haemophilus influenzae*.
Cephamandole is used to treat a
wide range of bacterial infections,
particularly of the skin and soft
tissues, the genito-urinary
tract, upper respiratory tract, and
middle ear. It is also used
to prevent infection during
surgery. Administration is by
injection.

▲ side-effects: there may be
sensitivity reactions – some
of which may be serious.
Sometimes there is nausea
and vomiting, with diarrhoea.
✿ warning: cephamandole should
not be administered to patients
who might be sensitive to
penicillins in general and
cephalosporins in particular. It
should be administered with
caution to those with impaired
kidney function.
*Related article:* KEFADOL.

**cephazolin** is a broad-spectrum
ANTIBIOTIC, one of the first
CEPHALOSPORINS, used to treat a
wide range of bacterial infections,
particularly of the skin and soft
tissues, urinary tract, upper
respiratory tract, and middle ear.
It is also used to prevent infection
during surgery. Administration is
by injection.
▲ side-effects: there may be
sensitivity reactions – some of
which may be serious.
Sometimes there is nausea and
vomiting, with diarrhoea.
✿ warning: cephazolin should not
be administered to patients
who might be sensitive to
penicillins in general and
cephalosporins in particular. It
should be administered with
caution to those with impaired
kidney function.
*Related article:* KEFZOL.

**cephradine** is a broad-spectrum
ANTIBIOTIC, one of the first
CEPHALOSPORINS, used to treat a
wide range of bacterial infections,
particularly streptococcal
infections of the skin and soft
tissues, the urinary tract, upper
respiratory tract, and middle ear.
It is also used to prevent infection
during surgery. Administration is
oral in the form of capsules or a
dilute syrup, or by injection.
▲ side-effects: there may be
sensitivity reactions – some of
which may be serious.

Sometimes there is nausea and vomiting, with diarrhoea.

◈ warning: cephradine should not be administered to patients who might be sensitive to penicillins in general and cephalosporins in particular. It should be administered with caution to those with impaired kidney function.
*Related article:* VELOSEF.

**Ceporex** (*Glaxo*) is a proprietary ANTIBIOTIC, available only on prescription, used to treat infections in the respiratory tract, urogenital area, soft tissues and middle ear. Produced in the form of capsules (in two strengths), as tablets (in two strengths), as drops for children, as a suspension (in two strengths), and as a syrup (in three strengths) for dilution (the potency of the syrup once diluted is retained for 7 days), Ceporex is a preparation of the CEPHALOSPORIN cephalexin.
▲/◈ side-effects/warning: *see* CEPHALEXIN.

**ceratonia** is an adsorbent substance which, when mixed with starch and cocoa in a sugar-free mixture, may be taken orally to treat diarrhoea. It works by binding together faecal material into a mass.
*Related article:* AROBON.

**Cerumol** (*Laboratories for Applied Biology*) is a proprietary, non-prescription preparation used to remove wax from the ear. Produced in the form of ear-drops, Cerumol's active constituent is the ANTIBACTERIAL/ANTIFUNGAL/astringent agent CHLORBUTOL.

**Cervagem** (*May & Baker*) is a proprietary drug of the PROSTAGLANDIN gemeprost, available only on prescription, administered by cervix as a vaginal pessary to cause dilation before induction of labour and in earlier surgical procedures.
▲/◈ side-effects/warning: *see* GEMEPROST.

**Cesamet** (*Lilly*) is a proprietary ANTI-EMETIC, available only on prescription, used to treat nausea in patients undergoing chemical therapy in the treatment of cancer. Produced in the form of capsules, Cesamet's active constituent is the synthetic drug nabilone. It is not recommended for children.
▲/◈ side-effects/warning: *see* NABILONE.

**Cetavlex** (*Care*) is a proprietary, non-prescription ANTISEPTIC, used to treat cuts and abrasions. Produced in the form of a water-based cream, Cetavlex's active constituent is CETRIMIDE.

**Cetavlon P.C.** (*Care*) is a proprietary, non-prescription DISINFECTANT, used to treat dandruff. Produced in the form of a solution to be used as a shampoo, Cetavlon P.C.'s active constituent is CETRIMIDE.

**cetirizine** is a relatively new ANTIHISTAMINE used to treat the symptoms of allergic disorders. It joins a new class of drugs, which have little sedative effect. Administration is oral in the form of tablets.
▲ side-effects: side-effects are comparatively uncommon, but there may be headache. There may also be sufficient drowsiness to counter-indicate driving or operating machinery.
◈ warning: cetirizine should be administered with caution to patients with epilepsy, glaucoma, liver or kidney disease (use lower dose), or enlargement of the prostate gland, in pregnancy, or to the elderly.
*Related article:* ZIRTEK.

**Cetriclens** (*Smith & Nephew Medical*) is a proprietary, non-prescription DISINFECTANT, used to clean skin and wounds. Produced in the form of a solution (in two strengths, the stronger under the name Cetriclens Forte), Cetriclens is a compound preparation of two antiseptics, CHLORHEXIDINE GLUCONATE and CETRIMIDE.

**cetrimide** is a detergent that has ANTISEPTIC properties; therapeutically, it is often combined with the antiseptic CHLORHEXIDINE. It is used in the form of a solution as a disinfectant for the skin and scalp, burns and wounds and in the form of a water-miscible cream as a soap substitute in the care of conditions such as acne and seborrhoea. In use, it should be kept away from the eyes and out of body cavities; some patients find it a mild skin irritant.

**cetylpyridinium chloride** in mild solution is used as a mouth-wash or gargle for oral hygiene. *Related article:* MEROCET.

**C-Film** (*Arun*) is a proprietary, non-prescription SPERMICIDAL contraceptive for use in combination with barrier methods of contraception (such as a condom). Produced in the form of a water-soluble film, C-Film is a preparation of an alcohol ester.

**chalk** may be used in a non-proprietary formulation ('chalk mixture') to assist in the treatment of diarrhoea. It works by acting as an adsorbent, binding together faecal material. Its bland taste has usually to be disguised with strongly pleasant-tasting or (especially in powdered form – 'chalk powder') highly aromatic substances, and an adequate intake of fluids has also

to be consciously maintained during treatment.

**chalk with opium mixture** is a non-proprietary formulation of spiced ('aromatic') chalk powder and MORPHINE in a sugary solution, used when taken orally to treat diarrhoea. The chalk is intended to adsorb faecal material, and the morphine to reduce motility within the colon. The mixture may cause sedation. Prolonged use may lead to dependence (addiction).

**charcoal** is an adsorbent material used medically for its adsorbency in either of two ways. Its primary use is in soaking up poisons in the stomach or small intestine – especially drug overdoses in cases when only a small quantity of the drug may be extremely toxic. Powdered, it is taken in solution, repeated as necessary. But its secondary use is as a constituent in antidiarrhoeal preparations, in which it is effective in binding together faecal material. In this use it is also effective in relieving flatulence.

\*chelating agent is any chemical compound which, when inside the body, binds to itself specific metallic ions before being excreted in the normal way. Chelating agents can thus be used to treat metal poisoning – poisoning by lead, for example. They may be incorporated in barrier creams for industrial protection.

**Chemocycline** (*Consolidated*) is a proprietary ANTIBIOTIC, available only on prescription, used to treat any of many infections. Produced in the form of tablets and as a syrup for dilution (the potency of the syrup once dilute is retained for 14 days), Chemocycline is a preparation of the TETRACYCLINE oxytetracycline.

▲/✿ side-effects/warning: see OXYTETRACYCLINE.

**Chemotrim Paed** (*RP Drugs*) is a proprietary ANTIBIOTIC, available only on prescription, used to treat infections of the respiratory, urinary and gastrointestinal tracts. Produced in the form of a suspension specifically intended for children, Chemotrim Paed is a compound combination of trimethoprim with sulphamethoxazole a compound itself known as co-trimoxazole. It is not recommended for children aged under 6 weeks.

▲/✿ side-effects/warning: see CO-TRIMOXAZOLE; SULPHAMETHOXAZOLE; TRIMETHOPRIM.

**Chendol** (*CP Pharmaceuticals*) is a proprietary preparation of chenodeoxycholic acid, available only on prescription, used to dissolve cholesterol gallstones that are radiolucent and not particularly large. Treatment is usually carried out in hospital under suitable monitoring. Produced in the form of capsules and as tablets, Chendol is not recommended for children.

▲/✿ side-effects/warning: see CHENODEOXYCHOLIC ACID.

**chenodeoxycholic acid** is an acid that has the capacity to dissolve some cholesterol gallstones in situ; the stones must not be particularly large and must be radiolucent – the drug does not affect radio-opaque calculi. It is used mainly in patients who prefer medical to surgical treatment, or for whom surgery is inadvisable. In one in four patients treated with the acid, however, gallstones recur within 12 months. Administration is oral in the form of capsules or tablets.

▲ side-effects: there is diarrhoea and itching; some patients

experience mild dysfunction of the liver.

✿ warning: chenodeoxycholic acid should not be administered to patients whose stones are large or radio-opaque or impair gall bladder function; those with chronic liver disease or inflammatory disorders of the intestines; or who are pregnant. Frequent monitoring is essential: treatment should take place in hospital.
*Related articles:* CHENDOL; CHENOFALK.

**Chenofalk** (*Thames*) is a proprietary preparation of chenodeoxycholic acid, available only on prescription, used to dissolve cholesterol gallstones that are radiolucent and not particularly large. Treatment is usually carried out in hospital under suitable monitoring. Produced in the form of capsules, Chenofalk is not recommended for children.

▲/✿ side-effects/warning: see CHENODEOXYCHOLIC ACID.

**Children's Vitamin Drops** (*Hough*) is a proprietary form of VITAMINS recommended by the Department of Health as a routine supplement to the diet of young children from 6 months to 2-5 years. Available without prescription, direct to families under the Welfare Food Scheme. The preparation contains vitamins A, C and D.

**Chiron** (*Downs*) is a proprietary, non-prescription barrier cream containing an ANTISEPTIC, used to protect and keep clean a stoma (an outlet on the skin surface following the surgical curtailment of the intestines).

**Chironair** (*Downs*) is a proprietary, non-prescription deodorant solution to be inserted

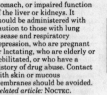

into the appliance or bag that is attached to a stoma (an outlet on the skin surface following the surgical curtailment of the intestines).

**Chloractil** (*DDSA Pharmaceuticals*) is a proprietary preparation of the powerful PHENOTHIAZINE drug chlorpromazine hydrochloride, used primarily as a major TRANQUILLIZER in patients who are undergoing behavioural disturbances, or who are psychotic (see ANTIPSYCHOTIC) particularly schizophrenia. More mundanely, it is used to treat severe anxiety, or as an anti-emetic sedative prior to surgery. Available only on prescription, Chloractil is produced in the form of tablets (in three strengths).
▲/✿ side-effects/warning: see CHLORPROMAZINE HYDROCHLORIDE.

**chloral hydrate** is a water-soluble SEDATIVE and HYPNOTIC, which is uncommonly rapid-acting. It is particularly useful in inducing sleep in children or elderly patients, although the drug must be administered in very mild solution in order to minimize gastric irritation. Administration is thus usually oral, although it can alternatively be rectal. Overdosage results in toxic effects; prolonged use may lead to dependence (addiction).
▲ side-effects: concentration and speed of thought and movement are affected. There is often drowsiness and dizziness, with dry mouth. Sensitivity reactions are also fairly common, especially in the form of rashes. Susceptible patients may experience excitement or confusion.
✿ warning: chloral hydrate should not be administered to patients with severe heart disease, inflammation of the stomach, or impaired function of the liver or kidneys. It should be administered with caution to those with lung disease and respiratory depression, who are pregnant or lactating, who are elderly or debilitated, or who have a history of drug abuse. Contact with skin or mucous membranes should be avoided.
*Related article:* NOCTEC.

**chlorambucil** is a CYTOTOXIC drug used in the treatment of cancer, particularly leukaemia, the lymphatic cancer Hodgkin's disease, and cancer of the ovaries. It works by interfering with the DNA of new cells, so preventing normal cell replication. However, the drug can also be used as an IMMUNOSUPPRESSANT in connection with rheumatoid arthritis. Administration is oral in the form of tablets.
▲ side-effects: there may be nausea and vomiting; there may also be hair loss and rashes. The capacity of the bone-marrow to produce red blood cells is markedly reduced.
✿ warning: almost all men are rendered permanently sterile early in treatment although potency is unaffected, and prolonged treatment may cause an early menopause in women. Regular and frequent blood counts are essential.
*Related article:* LEUKERAN.

**chloramphenicol** is a broad-spectrum ANTIBIOTIC with the capacity to treat many forms of infection effectively. However, the serious side-effects that accompany its systemic use demand that it is ordinarily restricted to the treatment of certain severe infections such as typhoid fever, haemophilus meningitis and some other penicillin-resistant forms of meningitis. In topical application to the eyes, ears or skin, when its serious toxicity is not encountered, the drug is useful in treating such conditions as bacterial conjunctivitis, otitis externa, or many types of skin infection. Topical administration is in the form of eye-drops, ear-drops or a cream. Systemic administration is in the form of capsules or a dilute suspension, or by injection or infusion.

▲ side-effects: idiosyncratic reactions are rare, but potentially life-threatening. Systemic treatment may cause serious damage to the bone marrow, resulting in critical blood cell deficiencies

◆ warning: chloramphenicol should not be administered to patients who are pregnant or lactating; it should be administered with caution to those with impaired liver or kidney function. In forms for topical application, it should be kept away from open wounds. Prolonged or repeated use should be avoided. Regular blood counts are essential.
*Related articles:*
CHLOROMYCETIN; KEMICETINE; MINIMS; OPULETS; SNO PHENICOL.

**Chlorasept 2000** (*Travenol*) is a proprietary DISINFECTANT, available only on prescription, used to cleanse skin and wounds. Produced in sachets of solution (in five strengths), Chlorasept 2000 is a preparation of CHLORHEXIDINE acetate.

**Chloraseptic** (*Norwich Eaton*) is a proprietary, non-prescription disinfectant, used to treat minor mouth and gum disorders, sore throats and mouth ulcers. Produced in the form of a solution for application with a spray or as a gargle, Chloraseptic is a

preparation of PHENOL. It is not recommended for children aged under 6 years.

**Chlorasol** (*Schering-Prebbles*) is a proprietary, non-prescription DISINFECTANT and cleanser, used to treat skin infections, and especially in cleansing wounds and ulcers. Produced in the form of a solution in sachets, Chlorasol is a preparation of SODIUM HYPOCHLORITE.

**chlorbutol** is an ANTIBACTERIAL and ANTIFUNGAL agent, which also has astringent and even mildly SEDATIVE properties. It is used in eye-drops and ear-drops, in powder form for topical use, as a constituent in motion sickness preparations, and as a preservative in injection solutions.
*Related article:* CERUMOL.

**chlordiazepoxide** is an ANXIOLYTIC drug, one of the BENZODIAZEPINES, used to treat anxiety in the short- or long-term, and to assist in the treatment of acute alcohol withdrawal symptoms. It may also be used as a SKELETAL MUSCLE RELAXANT. Continued use results in tolerance and may lead to dependence (addiction). Administration is oral in the form of capsules and tablets.

▲ side-effects: concentration and speed of thought and movement may be affected; the effects of alcohol consumption may also be enhanced. There may be drowsiness, dizziness, headache, dry mouth and shallow breathing; hypersensitivity reactions may occur.

◆ warning: chlordiazepoxide should be administered with caution to patients with respiratory difficulties, glaucoma, or kidney or liver impairment; who are in the last

stages of pregnancy; or who are elderly, debilitated, or have a history of drug abuse. Prolonged use or abrupt withdrawal of treatment should be avoided.
*Related articles:* LIBRIUM; TROPIUM.

**chlorhexidine** is an ANTISEPTIC that is a constituent in many DISINFECTANT preparations, for use especially prior to surgery or in obstetrics, but that is primarily used (in the form of chlorhexidine gluconate, chlorhexidine acetate or chlorhexidine hydrochloride) either as a mouth wash for oral hygiene, or as a dressing for minor skin wounds and infections; it is also used for instillation in the bladder to relieve minor infections.
▲ side-effects: some patients experience sensitivity reactions.
● warning: caution should be exercised in assessing suitable solution concentration for bladder instillation: too high a concentration may lead to the appearance of blood in the urine. Avoid contact with mucous membranes.
*Related articles:* BACTICLENS; BACTIGRAS; CETRICLENS; CHLORASEPT 2000; CORSODYL; ELUDRIL; HIBIDIL; HIBISCRUB; HIBISOL; HIBITANE; INSTILLAGEL; NASEPTIN; NYSTAFORM; ROTERSEPT; SAVLOCLENS; SAVLODIL; SAVLON HOSPITAL CONCENTRATE; TISEPT; TRAVASEPT; UNISEPT; UROTAINER.

**chlorinated lime and boric acid solution** is a non-proprietary formulation of chlorinated lime and boric acid, designed for topical application to disinfect and cleanse wounds and ulcers. It is applied as a wet dressing.

**chlorinated soda solution** is a non-proprietary formulation designed for topical application to disinfect and cleanse wounds and ulcers. Containing boric acid, chlorinated lime and sodium carbonate it is an irritant solution and surrounding tissues should be protected with a layer of petroleum jelly during treatment.

**chlormethiazole** is a HYPNOTIC drug that also has ANTICONVULSANT properties. It is useful in treating severe insomnia, epilepsy, and for quieting agitated elderly patients, and is also used under strict medical supervision in the treatment of the withdrawal symptoms of alcohol. Occasionally it is used in the operating theatre as an additional sedative anaesthetic. Administration (in the form of chlormethiazole edisylate) is oral as capsules or dilute syrup, or by injection or infusion.
▲ side-effects: there may be headache, sneezing and gastrointestinal disturbance. High dosage by intravenous infusion may cause depressed breathing and reduced heart rate, and presents a risk of thrombophlebitis.
● warning: chlormethiazole should be administered with caution to patients with restricted breathing, or impaired liver or kidney function, who are pregnant or lactating, who are elderly or debilitated, or who have a history of drug abuse. Prolonged use should be avoided; withdrawal of treatment should be gradual.
*Related article:* HEMINEVRIN.

**chlormezanone** is an ANXIOLYTIC drug that has HYPNOTIC properties and may also be used as a SKELETAL MUSCLE RELAXANT. It is

thus used to treat anxiety and
tension in the short term
(including premenstrual
syndrome), to induce sleep and to
relieve muscle spasm.
Administration is oral in the form
of tablets.

▲ side-effects: concentration and
speed of thought and
movement may be affected; the
effects of alcohol consumption
may also be enhanced. There
may be drowsiness, dizziness,
headache, dry mouth and
shallow breathing;
hypersensitivity reactions may
occur.

✿ warning: chlormezanone
should be administered with
caution to patients with
respiratory difficulties, closed
angle glaucoma, or kidney or
liver disease; who are in the
last stages of pregnancy; or
who are elderly or debilitated.
Prolonged use or abrupt
withdrawal of treatment
should be avoided.
*Related article:* TRANCOPAL.

**Chloromycetin** (*Parke-Davis*) is a
proprietary, broad-spectrum
ANTIBIOTIC, available only on
prescription, used to treat
potentially dangerous bacterial
infections, such as typhoid fever
and meningitis. Produced in the
form of capsules, as a suspension
for dilution (the potency of the
dilute suspension is retained for
14 days), as eye-ointment and eye-
drops, as a powder, and in vials
for injection, Chloromycetin is a
preparation of chloramphenicol.
▲/✿ side-effects/warning: *see*
CHLORAMPHENICOL.

**Chloromycetin Hydrocortisone**
(*Parke-Davis*) is a proprietary
ANTIBIOTIC and CORTICOSTEROID
preparation, available only on
prescription, used to treat eye
infections. Produced in the form
of an eye ointment,
Chloromycetin Hydrocortisone

contains the antibiotic
chloramphenicol and the steroid
hydrocortisone.
▲/✿ side-effects/warning: *see*
CHLORAMPHENICOL;
HYDROCORTISONE.

**chloroquine** is the major
ANTIMALARIAL drug in use,
effective against all three
*Plasmodium* species that cause
malaria, and used both to treat
and to prevent contraction of the
disease. However, it does not kill
those forms of the parasite that
migrate to the liver, and thus
cannot prevent relapses caused by
any form of *Plasmodium* that does
so. Moreover, strains of
*Plasmodium falciparum* have
recently exhibited resistance to
chloroquine in certain areas of the
world, and in those areas
alternative therapy is now
advised. Chloroquine is sometimes
also used to treat infection caused
by amoebae, or to halt the
progress of rheumatic disease.
Administration is oral in the form
of tablets or a dilute syrup, or by
injection or infusion.
▲ side-effects: there may be
nausea and vomiting, with
headache and itching;
gastrointestinal disturbance
may be severe; some patients
break out in a rash. Susceptible
patients may undergo
psychotic episodes. Prolonged
high dosage may cause ringing
in the ears (tinnitus) and
damage to the cornea and
retina of the eyes.
✿ warning: chloroquine should
not be administered to patients
with retinal disease, or who are
allergic to quinine; it should be
administered with caution to
patients with porphyria,
psoriasis, or who have impaired
kidney or liver function; who
are elderly; or who are
children. Prolonged treatment
should be punctuated by
ophthalmic checks.

*Related articles:* AVLOCLOR;
MALARIVON; NIVAQUINE.

**chlorothiazide** is a DIURETIC, one
of the THIAZIDES, used to treat
fluid retention in the tissues
(oedema), high blood pressure
(hypertension) and mild to
moderate heart failure. Because
all thiazides tend to deplete body
reserves of potassium,
chlorothiazide may be
administered in combination
either with potassium
supplements or with diuretics that
are complementarily potassium-
sparing. Administration is oral in
the form of tablets.
▲ side-effects: there may be
tiredness and a rash. In men,
temporary impotence may
occur.
✦ warning: chlorothiazide should
not be administered to patients
with kidney failure or urinary
retention, or who are lactating.
It should be administered with
caution to those who are
pregnant. It may aggravate
conditions of diabetes or gout.
*Related article:* SALURIC.

**chloroxylenol** is an ANTISEPTIC
effective in killing some bacteria
but not others, and is an
established constituent in at least
one well-known skin disinfectant.
A few patients experience mild
skin irritation that may lead to
sensitivity reactions, however.

**chlorpheniramine** is an
ANTIHISTAMINE, used to treat the
symptoms of allergic conditions
like hay fever and urticaria; it is
also sometimes used in
emergencies to treat anaphylactic
shock. Administration (as
chlorpheniramine maleate) is oral
in the form of tablets, sustained-
release tablets and a dilute syrup,
or by injection.
▲ side-effects: concentration and
speed of thought and movement
may be affected. There may be

nausea, headaches, and/or
weight gain, dry mouth,
gastrointestinal disturbances
and visual problems. Treatment
by injection may cause tissue
irritation that leads to a
temporary drop in blood
pressure.
✦ warning: chlorpheniramine
maleate should not be
administered to patients who
are pregnant, or who have
glaucoma, urinary retention,
intestinal obstruction,
enlargement of the prostate
gland, or peptic ulcer; it should
be administered with caution to
those with epilepsy or liver
disease.
*Related articles:* ALUNEX;
PIRITON.

**chlorpromazine** is an
ANTIPSYCHOTIC drug used as a
major TRANQUILLIZER for patients
suffering from schizophrenia and
other psychoses, particularly
during behavioural disturbances.
The drug may also be used in the
short term to treat severe anxiety,
to soothe patients who are dying,
as a premedication prior to
surgery, and to remedy an
intractable hiccup. It may also be
used to relieve nausea and vertigo
caused by disorders in the middle
or inner ear. Administration (as
chlorpromazine hydrochloride) is
oral in the form of tablets or an
elixir, as anal suppositories, or by
intramuscular injection.
▲ side-effects: concentration and
speed of thought and movement
are affected; the effects of
alcohol consumption are
enhanced. There may be dry
mouth and blocked nose,
constipation and difficulty in
urinating, and blurred vision;
menstrual disturbances in
women or impotence in men
may occur, with weight gain;
there may be sensitivity
reactions. Some patients feel
cold and depressed, and tend to

suffer from poor sleep patterns. Blood pressure may be low and the heartbeat irregular. Prolonged high dosage may cause opacity in the cornea and lens of the eyes, and a purple pigmentation of the skin. Treatment by intramuscular injection may be painful.

✿ warning: chlorpromazine hydrochloride should not be administered to patients with certain forms of glaucoma, whose blood-cell formation by the bone-marrow is reduced, or who are taking drugs that depress certain centres of the brain and spinal cord. It should be administered with caution to those with lung disease, cardiovascular disease, epilepsy, parkinsonism, abnormal secretion by the adrenal glands, impaired liver or kidney function, undersecretion of thyroid hormones (hypothyroidism), enlargement of the prostate gland, or any form of acute infection; who are pregnant or lactating; or who are elderly. Prolonged use requires regular checks on eye function and skin pigmentation. Withdrawal of treatment should be gradual. *Related articles:* CHLORACTIL; LARGACTIL.

**chlorpropamide** is a SULPHONYLUREA, used in the treatment of adult-onset diabetes mellitus because it promotes the production of insulin in whatever remains of the pancreas's capacity for it. Its effect lasts longer than that of most similar drugs. Unusually for a sulphonylurea, chlorpropamide can also be used to treat diabetes insipidus, although only mild cases caused by pituitary or thalamic malfunction, because it also reduces frequency of urination. Administration is oral in the form of tablets.

▲ side-effects: there may be some sensitivity reactions (such as a rash). There may also be mild gastrointestinal disturbance or headache. The consumption of alcohol may cause flushing.

✿ warning: chlorpropamide should not be administered to patients with liver or kidney disease, endocrine disorders, or who are under stress; who are pregnant or lactating; who are already taking corticosteroids or oral contraceptives, oral anticoagulants, or aspirin and other antibiotics. *Related articles:* DIABINESE; GLYMESE.

**chlorprothixene** is an ANTIPSYCHOTIC drug used as a major TRANQUILLIZER in patients suffering from schizophrenia and other psychoses, particularly during behavioural disturbances. The drug may also be used in the short term to treat severe anxiety. Administration is oral in the form of tablets. It is not suitable for children.

▲ side-effects: concentration and speed of thought and movement are affected; the effects of alcohol consumption are enhanced. There may be dry mouth and blocked nose, constipation and difficulty in urinating, and blurred vision; menstrual disturbances in women or impotence in men may occur, with weight gain; there may be sensitivity reactions. Some patients feel cold and depressed, and tend to suffer from poor sleep patterns. Blood pressure may be low and the heartbeat irregular. Prolonged high dosage may cause opacity in the cornea and lens of the eyes, and a purple pigmentation of the skin. Treatment by intramuscular injection may be painful.

✦ warning: chlorprothixene should not be administered to patients with certain forms of glaucoma, whose blood-cell formation by the bone-marrow is reduced, or who are taking drugs that depress certain centres of the brain and spinal cord. It should be administered with caution to those with lung disease, cardiovascular disease, epilepsy, parkinsonism, abnormal secretion by the adrenal glands, impaired liver or kidney function, undersecretion of thyroid hormones (hypothyroidism), enlargement of the prostate gland or any form of acute infection; who are pregnant or lactating; or who are elderly. Prolonged use requires regular checks on eye function and skin pigmentation. Withdrawal of treatment should be gradual. *Related article:* TARACTAN.

**chlortetracycline** is a broad-spectrum TETRACYCLINE ANTIBIOTIC used to treat many forms of infection caused by several types of micro-organism, conditions it is particularly used to treat include infections of the urinary tract, of the respiratory tract, in and around the eye, of the genital organs, and of the skin, including acne and impetigo. Administration (as chlortetracycline hydrochloride) is oral in the form of capsules or a solution, or topical in the form of a cream, an ointment, and an ophthalmic ointment.
▲ side-effects: there may be nausea and vomiting, with diarrhoea. Occasionally, there is sensitivity to light or some other sensitivity reaction.
✦ warning: chlortetracycline should not be administered systemically to patients who are aged under 12 years, who are pregnant, or with impaired

kidney function; it should be administered with caution to those who are lactating. The cream and the ointment may stain fabric.
*Related article:* AUREOMYCIN.

**chlorthalidone** is a DIURETIC related to the THIAZIDES, used to treat fluid retention in the tissues (oedema), high blood pressure (hypertension) and diabetes insipidus. Because all thiazides tend to deplete body reserves of potassium, chlorthalidone may be administered in combination either with potassium supplements or with diuretics that are complementarily potassium-sparing. Administration is oral in the form of tablets.
▲ side-effects: there may be tiredness and a rash. In men, temporary impotence may occur.
✦ warning: chlorthalidone should not be administered to patients with kidney failure or urinary retention, or who are lactating. It should be administered with caution to those who are pregnant. It may aggravate conditions of diabetes or gout.
*Related article:* HYGROTON.

**Chocovite** (*Torbet*) is a proprietary, non-prescription CALCIUM supplement, not available from the National Health Service. Produced in the form of tablets, Chocovite contains CALCIUM GLUCONATE and a form of CALCIFEROL (vitamin D) known as ERGOCALCIFEROL.
▲/✦ side-effects/warning: *see* CALCIUM; CALCIFEROL.

**cholecalciferol** is one of the natural forms of calciferol (vitamin D), formed in humans by the action of sunlight on the skin. *see* CALCIFEROL.

**Choledyl** (*Parke-Davis*) is a proprietary, non-prescription BRONCHODILATOR, used to treat bronchitis and asthma. Produced in the form of tablets (in two strengths) and as a syrup for dilution (the potency of the syrup once diluted is retained for 14 days), Choledyl is a preparation of choline theophyllinate. It is not recommended for children aged under 3 years.

▲/✿ side-effects/warning: *see* CHOLINE THEOPHYLLINATE.

**cholera vaccine** is a suspension containing non-infective strains of the bacteria that causes cholera, a water- and food-borne disease that causes outbreaks of life-threatening vomiting and diarrhoea. Administration is initially by subcutaneous or intramuscular injection, followed 2 to 4 weeks later by a booster shot. The vaccine cannot guarantee total protection, and travellers should be warned still to take great care over the hygiene of the food and drink they consume. In any case, what protection is afforded lasts only for about 6 months.

**cholestyramine** is a resin which, when taken orally, binds to itself bile salts in the intestines that can then be excreted in the normal way. This is a useful property in the treatment of high blood fat, especially cholesterol, levels (hyperlipidaemia), and of the itching associated with obstruction in the bile ducts. The property can also be utilized in the treatment of diarrhoea following intestinal disease or surgery. Administration is oral in the form of a powder taken with liquids.

▲ side-effects: there may be nausea, heartburn, flatulence with abdominal discomfort, constipation or diarrhoea, and a rash.

✿ warning: cholestyramine should not be administered to patients who suffer from complete blockage of the bile ducts, who are already taking any other drug, or who are pregnant. High dosage may require simultaneous administration of fat-soluble vitamins.
*Related article:* QUESTRAN.

**choline** is a natural compound used in the body in the synthesis of various forms of protein and of the neurotransmitter acetylcholine. It is also essential to the transportation of fats within the body. Because it is synthesized in the body, however, it cannot really be classed as a vitamin (of the B group) as some authorities would specify.

**choline magnesium trisalicylate** is an non-narcotic ANALGESIC with ANTI-INFLAMMATORY properties very similar to aspirin, used to treat the pain and inflammation of rheumatic disease and other musculo-skeletal disorders. Administration is oral in the form of tablets.

▲ side-effects: there may be gastrointestinal problems involving ulceration or bleeding, nausea, and disturbances in hearing and in vision; some patients experience serious sensitivity reactions.

✿ warning: choline magnesium trisalicylate should not be administered to patients who are aged under 12 years, or who have peptic ulcers; it should be administered with caution to those with impaired liver or kidney function, dehydration or any form of allergy, who are pregnant or lactating, who are elderly, or who are already taking oral anticoagulant drugs.
*Related article:* TRILISATE.

**choline salicylate** is a mild ANALGESIC and local ANAESTHETIC, which is used primarily in topical application in the mouth or in the ears. In the mouth it may be used to relieve the pain of teething, of aphthous ulcers or of minor scratches. Administration is in the form of an oral gel or ear-drops.

✹ **warning:** prolonged treatment may result in salicylate poisoning.

*Related articles:* AUDAX; BONJELA; TEEJEL.

**choline theophyllinate** is a modified form of the BRONCHODILATOR theophylline used to treat conditions such as asthma and bronchitis. It is thought to be slightly better tolerated than theophylline. Administration is oral in the form of tablets, sustained-release tablets, or a dilute syrup.

▲ **side-effects:** there may be nausea and gastrointestinal disturbances, and increase or irregularity in the heartbeat, and/or insomnia.

✹ **warning:** treatment should initially be gradually progressive in the quantity administered. Choline theophyllinate should be administered with caution to epileptics, and patients with heart or liver disease, or a peptic ulcer; or who are pregnant or lactating.

*Related articles:* CHOLEDYL; SABIDAL SR 270.

**cho/vac** is an abbreviation for cholera vaccine.

*see* CHOLERA VACCINE.

**Chymar-Zon** (*Armour*) is a proprietary form of an enzymatic preparation used to dissolve the little ligament that suspends the lens of the eye within the eyeball (the zonule of Zinn) in order to facilitate the surgical removal of a lens that has become opaque through cataract. Available only on prescription, Chymar-Zon is

produced as a powder for reconstitution as a medium for injection; the fluid – in which the active constituent is alpha-chymotrypsin – is injected behind the iris a minute or so before the lens is removed, and affects no other part of the eye.

▲/✹ **side-effects/warning:** *see* CHYMOTRYPSIN.

**chymotrypsin** is a protein-digesting enzyme secreted in one form by the pancreas and converted into another within the duodenum by the presence of the other enzyme trypsin. It has more than one therapeutic use. Its primary use is in treating inflammation, especially in conditions of fluid retention (oedema), in which it is thought to work by facilitating the removal of coagulated blood and cellular debris from sites of inflammation. But it is also used very specifically as the medium to dissolve the tiny ligament that suspends the lens within the eyeball in surgery to remove the lens because of cataract. Administration is oral in the form of tablets, or by injection.

▲ **side-effects:** there may be nausea and vomiting, with diarrhoea. Some patients experience sensitivity reactions – which may be serious.

✹ **warning:** chymotrypsin should be administered with caution to patients who are already taking oral anticoagulants. Injection should not take place before testing a patient for sensitivity.

*Related articles:* CHYMAR-ZON; DEANASE D.C.

**Cicatrin** (*Calmic*) is a proprietary ANTIBIOTIC drug, available only on prescription, used by topical application to treat skin infections. Produced in the form of a cream, as a dusting-powder and as an aerosol powder-spray, Cicatrin's major active constituents include the antibiotics neomycin sulphate and bacitracin zinc.

▲/✱ side-effects/warning: *see* BACITRACIN; NEOMYCIN.

**ciclacillin** is an ANTIBIOTIC, a PENICILLIN derivative of ampicillin, used to treat infections of the upper respiratory tract, of the urinary tract, and of the soft tissues. Administration is oral in the form of tablets or a dilute suspension.

▲ side-effects: the drug may cause diarrhoea if given in tablet form; there may be sensitivity reactions ranging from a minor rash to urticaria and joint pains, fever or anaphylactic shock.

✱ warning: ciclacillin should not be administered to patients known to be allergic to penicillins; it should be administered with caution to those with impaired kidney function.

**Cidomycin** (*Roussel*) is a proprietary ANTIBIOTIC, available only on prescription, used to treat many forms of infection, particularly serious gram-negative ones. Produced in ampoules for injection (in two strengths), in vials for the treatment of children, in ampoules for intrathecal injections, as a powder for reconstitution as a medium for injection, as ear- and eye-drops, as an eye ointment, and as a cream and an ointment for topical application, Cidomycin is a preparation of the aminoglycoside gentamicin sulphate.

▲/✱ side-effects/warning: *see* GENTAMICIN.

**Cidomycin Topical** (*Roussel*) is a proprietary ANTIBIOTIC preparation, available only on prescription, used in topical application to treat skin infections. Produced in the form of a water-miscible cream and a paraffin-based ointment, Cidomycin Topical is a preparation of the aminoglycoside gentamicin sulphate.

✱ warning: *see* GENTAMICIN.

**cimetidine** is an ulcer healing drug that reduces the secretion of gastric acid, and is thus used primarily to assist in the healing of peptic ulcers in the stomach and duodenum, stomal ulcer, Zollinger-Ellison syndrome, and reflux oesophagitis. It works by blocking histamine $H_2$ receptors. It is well tolerated, and side-effects are comparatively rare. Administration is oral in the form of tablets or a dilute syrup, or by injection or infusion.

▲ side-effects: the drug may enhance the effects of benzodiazepines or beta-blockers taken simultaneously. In men, because the drug also affects androgen receptors, there may be some minor and temporary feminization. In elderly patients there may be mild (and reversible) confusion.

✱ warning: cimetidine should be administered with caution to patients with impaired liver or kidney function. Treatment of undiagnosed dyspepsia may potentially mask the onset of stomach or duodenal cancer and is therefore undesirable. *Related articles:* ALGITEC; DYSPAMET; TAGAMET.

**cinchocaine** is a local ANAESTHETIC used to relieve pain particularly in dental surgery, but also in topical application to the skin or mucous membranes. It can also be injected into the spinal membranes to effect epidural anaesthesia.

Administration is thus in the form of an ointment or by injection.

▲ side-effects: there may be nausea, vomiting and diarrhoea; some patients experience yawning or excitement. Rarely, there are sensitivity reactions.
*Related article:* NUPERCAINAL.

**cinnarizine** is an ANTIHISTAMINE used primarily as an ANTI-EMETIC in the treatment or prevention of motion sickness and vomiting caused either by chemotherapy for cancer or by infection of the middle or inner ear. But it is also a VASODILATOR that affects the blood vessels of the hands and feet and may also be used to improve circulation in those areas. Administration is oral in the form of tablets. Not recommended for children under 6 years.

▲ side-effects: concentration and speed of thought and movement may be affected. There is commonly drowsiness and dry mouth; there may also be headache, blurred vision and gastrointestinal disturbances.
◆ warning: cinnarizine should be administered with caution to patients with epilepsy, liver disease, glaucoma or enlargement of the prostate gland. Drowsiness may be increased by alcohol consumption.
*Related article:* STUGERON.

**Cinobac** (*Lilly*) is a proprietary ANTIBIOTIC drug, available only on prescription, used primarily to treat infections in the urinary tract. Produced in the form of capsules, Cinobac is a preparation of cinoxacin. It is not recommended for children.
▲/◆ side-effects/warning: CINOXACIN.

**cinoxacin** is an ANTIBIOTIC of the quinolone family used primarily

to treat infections in the urinary tract. Administration is oral in the form of capsules.

▲ side-effects: there may be nausea and vomiting, with gastrointestinal disturbances and weight loss, diarrhoea and cramps. Some patients experience sensitivity reactions, including a rash, dizziness, a headache and tinnitus.
◆ warning: cinoxacin should be administered with caution to patients with even slightly impaired kidney function. It is not recommended for children.
*Related article:* CINOBAC.

**ciprofloxacin** is an ANTIBIOTIC agent of the quinolone family used to treat infections in patients who are allergic to penicillin, or whose strain of bacterium is resistant to standard antibiotics. It is active against Gram-negative bacteria including salmonella, shigella and campylobacter, neisseria and pseudomonas, and to a lesser extent against Gram-positive bacteria of the Streptococcal family. Most anaerobic organisms are not sensitive. This spectrum of activity indicates treatment with ciprofloxacin for infections of the urinary and respiratory tracts, but only when these cases are resistant to more conventional agents. Administration may be oral in the form of tablets or by intravenous infusion.

▲ side-effects: there may be nausea and vomiting, diarrhoea, abdominal and joint pain, dizziness, headache, fatigue and confusion, rashes and pruritus, convulsions, light sensitivity, impairment of liver enzymes and blood components. Drowsiness may impair skilled performance such as driving, and the effects of alcohol may be enhanced.

◆ warning: ciprofloxacin should
be administered with caution
to epileptics, those with a
history of behavioural
disorders, to patients who have
impaired kidney or liver
function, or who are pregnant
or breast-feeding. Not
recommended for children or
adolescents. Severe allergic
reactions have been reported,
especially in those with AIDS.
*Related article:* CIPROXIN.

**Ciproxin** (*Baypharm*) is a
proprietary preparation of the
ANTIBIOTIC drug ciprofloxacin,
one of the quinolones, available
only on prescription, used to treat
a variety of infections when these
are resistant to more
conventional drugs. Produced in
the form of tablets and for
intravenous infusion. Ciproxin is
not recommended for children or
adolescents.
▲/◆ side-effects/warning: *see*
CIPROFLOXACIN.

**cisapride** is a newly developed
MOTILITY STIMULANT acting within
the stomach and small intestine.
It may be used to treat
oesophageal reflux such as that
associated with diseases of the
autonomic system (autonomic
neuropathies) and diabetes. It is
thought to act by releasing
acetylcholine from the nerves
of the stomach and intestine.
It is available in the form of
tablets.
▲ side-effects: there may be
abdominal cramps and pain,
extrapyramidal effects,
diarrhoea, sometimes headache
and light-headedness;
convulsions have been
reported.
◆ warning: in patients with
reduced liver or kidney
function the dose should be
reduced. It should not be given
to pregnant women, children
under 12 years or where

stimulation of the gut might be
dangerous.
*Related articles:* ALIMIX;
PREPULSID.

**cisplatin** is an unusual CYTOTOXIC
drug that contains an organic
complex of platinum. It works by
damaging the DNA of newly-
forming cells, and is used to treat
cancers that are metastatic and
have failed to respond to other
forms of therapy, particularly
cancers of the testes or ovaries.
Side-effects may be severe.
Administration is by injection.
▲ side-effects: there is severe
nausea and vomiting. There
may also be disturbances in
hearing, loss of sensation at
the fingertips, and reduced
blood levels in many normal
factors. Toxic effects may
require withdrawal of
treatment.
◆ warning: cisplatin should be
administered with caution to
patients with impaired kidney
function. Regular, frequent
monitoring of blood levels is
essential, and specialist
consultancy is advised at all
times during treatment.

**Citanest** (*Astra*) is a proprietary
local ANAESTHETIC, available only
on prescription. Produced in vials
(in two strengths) for injection,
Citanest is a preparation of
prilocaine hydrochloride.
▲/◆ side-effects/warning: *see*
PRILOCAINE.

**Citanest with Octapressin**
(*Astra*) is a proprietary local
ANAESTHETIC, available only on
prescription, used as a dental
anaesthetic and as premedication
before surgery. Produced in
cartridges and self-aspirating
cartridges for injection (in two
strengths), Citanest with
Octapressin contains prilocaine
hydrochloride and the minor
VASOCONSTRICTOR felypressin.

▲/✿ side-effects/warning: *see*
PRILOCAINE.

**Citrical** (*Shire*) is a proprietary
MINERAL SUPPLEMENT of calcium,
in the form of CALCIUM
CARBONATE. It is available
without prescription, in the form
of granules in a sachet, to be
taken by mouth.
▲/✿ side-effects/warning: *see*
CALCIUM.

**Claforan** (*Roussel*) is a proprietary
ANTIBIOTIC preparation, available
only on prescription, used to
treat many forms of infection,
including meningitis. Produced
in vials as a powder for reconstitution as a medium for
injection, Claforan is a
preparation of the CEPHALO-
SPORIN cefotaxime.
▲/✿ side-effects/warning: *see*
CEFOTAXIME.

**Clairvan** (*Sinclair*) is a
proprietary respiratory stimulant,
available only on prescription,
used to treat patients about to
lapse into unconsciousness or
coma and who are unable, for one
reason or another, to tolerate the
more usual forms of ventilatory
support. Produced in the form of a
solution to be taken orally, and in
ampoules for injection, Clairvan's
active constituent is ethamivan.
▲/✿ side-effects/warning: *see*
ETHAMIVAN.

**Clarityn** (*Schering-Plough*) is a
proprietary prescription ANTI-
HISTAMINE, with less sedative
properties than many others, used
to treat the symptoms of allergic
disorders such as hay fever and
urticaria (skin rashes). Produced
in the form of tablets, it is a
preparation of loratadine.
▲/✿ side-effects/warning: *see*
LORATADINE.

**clavulanic acid** is a weakly
antibiotic substance, which has
the effect of inhibiting bacterial

resistance in bacteria that have
become resistant to some
penicillin-type antibiotics,
notably amoxicillin and
ticarcillin. It is a potent inhibitor
of bacterial penicillinase enzymes
that can inactivate many
antibiotics of the penicillin
family. It is therefore used in
combination with amoxicillin or
ticarcillin to treat infective
conditions in which the penicillin
alone might be unsuccessful, and
has the additional effect of
extending the activity of the
antibiotic.
*Related article:* AUGMENTIN;
TIMENTIN.

**Clazaril** (*Sandoz*) is an
ANTIPSYCHOTIC, a proprietary
form of clozapine available only
on prescription in the form of
tablets (in two strengths). Subject
to special monitoring for
potentially severe effects on the
blood.
▲/✿ side-effects/warning: *see*
CLOZAPINE.

**clemastine** is an ANTIHISTAMINE
used in the relief of allergic
disorders such as hay fever,
urticaria and some rashes.
Administration is oral in the form
of tablets or a dilute elixir.
▲ side-effects: concentration and
speed of thought and
movement may be affected;
there may be nausea,
headaches, and/or weight gain,
dry mouth, gastrointestinal
disturbances and visual
problems.
✿ warning: clemastine should not
be administered to patients
who are pregnant, or with
glaucoma, urinary retention,
intestinal obstruction,
enlargement of the prostate
gland, or peptic ulcer; it should
be administered with caution
to those with epilepsy or liver
disease.
*Related articles:* ALLER-EZE;
TAVEGIL.

**clindamycin** is a broad-spectrum ANTIBIOTIC used to treat infections of bones and joints, and to assist in the treatment of peritonitis (inflammation of the peritoneal lining of the abdominal cavity). It is notably active against many anaerobic bacteria. Administration is oral in the form of capsules or a dilute suspension, or by injection.

▲ side-effects: if diarrhoea or other symptoms of colitis appear during treatment, administration must be halted at once (see below). There may also be nausea and vomiting.

⚫ warning: clindamycin should not be administered to patients suffering from diarrhoea; and if diarrhoea or other symptoms of colitis appear during treatment, administration must be halted at once. This is because clindamycin greatly alters the normal balance of bacteria in the gut and in a few cases this allows a superinfection by an anaerobe, *Clostridium difficile*, which causes a form of colitis, resulting in potentially severe symptoms. It should be administered with caution to those with impaired liver or kidney function.
*Related article:* DALACIN C; DALACIN T.

**Clinicide** (*De Witt*) is a proprietary, non-prescription preparation used to treat scalp and pubic infestations of lice (pediculosis). Produced in the form of a lotion, Clinicide's active constituent is CARBARYL.

**Clinifeed** (*Roussel*) is a proprietary, non-prescription nutritionally complete feed, used as a dietary supplement for patients whose metabolic processes are unable to break down protein. Produced in four formulations, Clinifeed contains protein, carbohydrate, fat and vitamins and minerals, but it is free of gluten. It is unsuitable for children aged under 12 months.

**Clinitar** (*Smith & Nephew*) is a proprietary, non-prescription, medicated, fragrant shampoo used to treat dandruff and psoriasis: its active constituent is coal tar extract.

▲ / ⚫ side-effects/warning: *see* COAL TAR.

**Clinitar Cream** (*Smith & Nephew Pharmaceuticals*) is a proprietary, non-prescription tar preparation, used in topical application to treat severe non-infective skin conditions such as eczema and psoriasis. Produced in the form of cream and a gel, Clinitar Cream's active constituent is COAL TAR.

**Clinoril** (*Merck, Sharp & Dohme*) is a proprietary, anti-inflammatory, non-narcotic ANALGESIC, available only on prescription, used to treat rheumatic conditions and acute gout. Produced in the form of tablets (in two strengths), Clinoril is a preparation of sulindac.

▲ / ⚫ side-effects/warning: *see* SULINDAC.

**clioquinol** is an ANTISEPTIC compound that contains iodine and is effective against infections by amoebae and some other micro-organisms. Its primary use is to treat infections of the skin and the outer ear. Administration is topical (in the form of drops, creams, ointments and anal suppositories). Systemic use of the drug has been associated with serious toxicity of the optic nerve, causing blindness.

▲ side-effects: some patients experience sensitivity reactions.

⚫ warning: prolonged or excessive use encourages the onset of fungal infection. The

drug stains skin and fabric.
*Related article:* LOCORTEN-
VIOFORM.

**clobazam** is an ANXIOLYTIC drug,
one of the BENZODIAZEPINES, used
to treat anxiety in the short term,
and sometimes to assist in the
treatment of some forms of
epilepsy. Administration is oral in
the form of capsules.
▲ side-effects: concentration and
speed of thought and movement
may be affected; the effects of
alcohol consumption may be
enhanced. There is often
drowsiness and dry mouth;
there may also be dizziness,
headache, and shallow
breathing, and sensitivity
reactions may occur.
● warning: clobazam should be
administered with caution to
patients with depressed
respiration, closed angle
glaucoma, or impaired kidney
or liver function; who are in the
last stages of pregnancy; or
who are elderly or debilitated.
Prolonged use and abrupt
withdrawal of treatment should
be avoided.
*Related article:* FRISIUM.

**clobetasol propionate** is an
extremely powerful
CORTICOSTEROID, used in topical
application on severe non-
infective skin inflammations such
as eczema, especially in cases
where less powerful steroid
treatments have failed.
Administration is in the form of an
aqueous cream, a paraffin-based
ointment or an alcohol-based
scalp lotion.
▲ side-effects: topical application
may result in local thinning of
the skin, with possible
whitening, and an increased
local growth of hair. Some
young patients experience the
outbreak of a kind of
inflammatory dermatitis on the
face or at the site of
application.

● warning: as with all
corticosteroids, clobetasol
propionate treats the symptoms
of inflammation but has no
effect on any underlying
infection. Undetected infection
may thus become worse even as
its effects are masked by the
steroid. The steroid should not
in any case be administered to
patients with untreated skin
lesions; use on the face is best
avoided.
*Related articles:* DERMOVATE;
DERMOVATE-NN.

**clobetasone butyrate** is a
powerful CORTICOSTEROID, used in
topical application on severe non-
infective skin inflammations such
as eczema, especially in cases
where less powerful steroid
treatments have failed.
Administration is in the form of a
water-miscible cream, and a
paraffin-based ointment.
▲ side-effects: topical application
may result in local thinning of
the skin, with possible
whitening, and an increased
local growth of hair. Some
young patients experience the
outbreak of a kind of
inflammatory dermatitis on the
face or at the site of
application.
● warning: as with all
corticosteroids, clobetasone
butyrate treats the symptoms
of inflammation but has no effect
on any underlying infection.
Undetected infection may thus
become worse even as its effects
are masked by the steroid. The
steroid should not in any case
be administered to patients
with untreated skin lesions; use
on the face is best avoided.
*Related articles:* EUMOVATE;
TRIMOVATE.

**clofazimine** is a drug used as part
of the treatment of the major form
of leprosy, in combination with
dapsone and rifampicin. That the

treatment requires no fewer than three drugs is due to the increasing resistance shown by the leprotic bacterium. Administration is oral in the form of capsules.

▲ side-effects: there may be nausea and giddiness, diarrhoea and headache. High dosage may cause the skin and the urine to take on a reddish tinge and a blue-black discoloration of skin lesions.

✿ warning: clofazimine should be administered with caution to patients with impaired kidney or liver function. Regular tests on both functions are essential.

**clofibrate** is a hypolipidaemic drug used to reduce the level of fats (lipids) such as cholesterol in the bloodstream in patients with hyperlipidaemia. It works by altering the metabolism of fats. Generally, it is administered only to patients in whom a strict and regular dietary regime is not having the desired effect, although during treatment such a regime should additionally be adhered to. Administration is oral in the form of capsules.

▲ side-effects: there may be nausea and abdominal pain; rarely, there may be itching or urticaria. In men, impotence occasionally occurs.

✿ warning: clofibrate should not be administered to patients with severely impaired kidney or liver function, disease of the gall bladder, or associated blood disorders, or who are pregnant.
*Related article:* ATROMID-S.

**Clomid** (*Merrell Dow Pharmaceuticals*) is a proprietary HORMONE preparation, available only on prescription, used to treat infertility due to ovulatory failure. Produced in the form of tablets, Clomid is a preparation of the anti-oestrogen clomiphene

citrate, and should be administered only under specialist supervision.
▲ / ✿ side-effects/warning: *see* CLOMIPHENE CITRATE.

**clomiphene citrate** is a substance that is an anti-oestrogen: although it is not actually an androgen (a male sex hormone), it neutralizes the effect of any oestrogen (female sex hormone) present. This property can be useful in treating infertility in women whose condition is linked to the persistent presence of oestrogens and a consequent failure to ovulate. Administration is oral in the form of tablets.

▲ side-effects: multiple births are not uncommon following successful treatment. Hot flushes, nausea, vomiting, visual disturbances, dizziness and insomnia, breast tenderness, weight gain, rashes and hair loss may occur.

✿ warning: clomiphene citrate should not be administered to patients with ovarian cysts, cancer of the womb lining, liver disease, or with abnormal uterine bleeding, or who are pregnant.
*Related articles:* CLOMID; SEROPHENE.

**clomipramine hydrochloride** is an ANTIDEPRESSANT drug that has mild sedative properties. It is used primarily to treat depressive illness, but can be used to assist in treating phobic or obsessional states, and to try to reduce the incidence of cataplexy in narcoleptic patients. Administration is oral in the form of capsules, sustained-release tablets, and a dilute syrup, or by injection.

▲ side-effects: concentration and speed of thought and movement are affected; there is also dry mouth. There may also be blurred vision, difficulty in urinating, sweating, and irregular heartbeat, behavioural disturbances, a rash, a state of confusion, and/or a loss of libido. Rarely, there are also blood deficiencies.

⯐ warning: clomipramine hydrochloride should not be administered to patients with heart disease; it should be administered with caution to those with diabetes, epilepsy, liver or thyroid disease, glaucoma, or urinary retention; or who are pregnant or lactating. Withdrawal of treatment must be gradual.
*Related article:* ANAFRANIL.

**clomocycline sodium** is a broad-spectrum ANTIBIOTIC, one of the TETRACYCLINES, used to treat many forms of infection caused by several types of micro-organism. It is used particularly to treat infections of the urinary tract, the respiratory tract, and genital organs, and acne. Administration is oral in the form of capsules.

▲ side-effects: there may be nausea and vomiting, with diarrhoea. Occasionally there is sensitivity to light or other sensitivity reaction.

⯐ warning: clomocycline sodium should not be administered to patients who are aged under 12 years, who are pregnant, or with impaired kidney function; it should be administered with caution to those who are lactating.
*Related article:* MEGACLOR.

**clonazepam** is a drug related to DIAZEPAM and the BENZO-DIAZEPINES, but it is in effect an ANTICONVULSANT drug used to treat all forms of epilepsy. Administration is oral in the form of tablets.

▲ side-effects: concentration and speed of thought and movement are affected; in susceptible

patients the degree of sedation may be marked. It also enhances the effects of alcohol consumption. There may also be dizziness, fatigue and muscular weakness. Again in susceptible patients, there may be mood changes.

⯐ warning: clonazepam should be administered with caution to patients who are lactating. The drug is more sedative than most drugs used to treat epilepsy.
*Related article:* RIVOTRIL.

**clonidine hydrochloride** is an ANTIHYPERTENSIVE drug used to treat moderate to severe high blood pressure (hypertension). Although controversial, use of the drug has also been extended to assisting in the prevention of migraine attacks. It is thought to work by reducing release of the neurotransmitter NORADRENALINE both in the brain and in blood vessels. Administration is oral in the form of tablets and sustained-release capsules, or by injection.

▲ side-effects: there is sedation and dry mouth; there may also be fluid retention (oedema), a reduced heart rate, and depression.

◗ warning: clonidine hydrochloride should not be administered to patients who have a history of depression. Treatment must be withdrawn gradually (in order to avoid a hypertensive crisis).
*Related article:* CATAPRES.

**clopamide** is a DIURETIC, one of the THIAZIDES, used to treat fluid retention in the tissues (oedema) and high blood pressure (hypertension). Because all thiazides tend to deplete body reserves of potassium, clopamide may be administered in combination either with potassium supplements or with diuretics that are

**C**

complementarily potassium-sparing. Administration is oral in the form of tablets.

▲ side-effects: there may be tiredness and a rash. In men, impotence may occur that is reversible on cessation of treatment.

◆ warning: clopamide should not be administered to patients with kidney failure or urinary retention, or who are lactating. It should be administered with caution to those who are pregnant. The drug may aggravate conditions of diabetes or gout.
*Related articles:* BRINALDIX K; VISKALDIX.

**Clopenthixol** is an alternative proprietary name for the powerful ANTIPSYCHOTIC drug zuclopenthixol.
*see* ZUCLOPENTHIXOL.

**Clopixol** (*Lundbeck*) is a proprietary ANTIPSYCHOTIC drug, available only on prescription, used to treat and restrain psychotic patients, particularly more aggressive or agitated schizophrenics. Clopixol is produced in several forms. Preparations of zuclopenthixol dihydrochloride are available as tablets (in three strengths) called Clopixol; zuclopenthixol decanoate is prepared as oily injections in two strengths, the weaker called Clopixol and the stronger called Clopixol Conc.); and of zuclopenthixol acetate as an oily injection called Clopixol Acuphase. The preparations differ in their duration of action and may be used according to the length of treatment intended.
▲/◆ side-effects/warning: *see* ZUCLOPENTHIXOL.

**clorazepate dipotassium** is an ANXIOLYTIC drug, one of the BENZODIAZEPINES, used to treat anxiety in the short term.

Administration is oral in the form of capsules.

▲ side-effects: concentration and speed of thought and movement may be affected; the effects of alcohol consumption may be enhanced. There is often drowsiness and dry mouth; there may also be dizziness, headache, and shallow breathing, and sensitivity reactions may occur.

◆ warning: clorazepate dipotassium should not be administered to patients with depressed respiration; it should be administered with caution to those with glaucoma, or impaired kidney or liver function; who are in the last stages of pregnancy; or who are elderly or debilitated. Prolonged use and abrupt withdrawal of treatment should be avoided.
*Related article:* TRANXENE.

**clotrimazole** is an ANTIFUNGAL drug used in topical application to treat fungal infection on the skin and mucous membranes (especially the vagina, the outer ear and the toes). Administration is in the form of a water-miscible cream, a dusting-powder, a spray, vaginal inserts (pessaries), and a lotion (solution).

▲ side-effects: rarely, there is a burning sensation or irritation; a very few patients experience sensitivity reactions.
*Related article:* CANESTEN.

**cloxacillin** is an ANTIBIOTIC of the penicillin family, used primarily to treat forms of infection which other penicillins are incapable of countering, due to the production of the enzyme penicillinase by the bacteria concerned. However, cloxacillin is not inactivated by the penicillinase enzymes produced, for example, by certain Staphylococci. It is therefore classed as a penicillinase-resistant penicillin. Administration is oral in the form of capsules and a dilute syrup, and by injection.

▲ side-effects: there may be sensitivity reactions ranging from a minor rash to urticaria and joint pains, fever or anaphylactic shock.

✦ warning: cloxacillin should not be administered to patients who are known to be allergic to penicillins; it should be administered with caution to those with impaired kidney function.
*Related articles:* AMPICLOX; ORBENIN.

**clozapine** is an ANTIPSYCHOTIC drug used for the treatment of schizophrenia in patients who do not respond to, or can not tolerate, conventional therapy. Because clozapine can cause serious blood disorders (leucocytopenia and agranulocytosis), its use is restricted to use in patients registered with the Sandoz Clozaril Patient Monitoring Service. It is available only on prescription, and is available in the form of tablets.

▲ side-effects: potentially very serious effects on the blood (agranulocytosis and neutropenia), extrapyramidal symptoms, over salivation after initial dry mouth, tachycardia (speeding of the heart), postural hypotension (fall in blood pressure on standing up), gastrointestinal disturbances, difficulties in focussing of the eyes, changes in heart rhythms; and more rarely a number of other disturbances.

✦ warning: because of its effects on the blood (especially to depress the white cell count) this drug may only be used on registration with, and concurrent monitoring by, the special patient monitoring service. Any infections in the patient should be reported. Use of clozapine should be avoided in children, those with liver or kidney function impairment, epilepsy, cardiovascular disorders, in those with enlarged prostate gland, glaucoma, and certain gastrointestinal disorders. It should not be used in patients with a history of drug-induced neutropenia (lowered neutrophil white blood cell count) or agranulocytosis (lowered blood platelet count); bone marrow disorders, alcohol or drug induced psychoses; breast feeding or pregnancy; severe depression of the central nervous system or coma.

**coal tar** is a black, viscous liquid obtained by the distillation of coal: it has both anti-itching and keratolytic properties, and works by speeding up the rate at which the surface scale of skin is lost naturally. Therapeutically employed primarily to treat psoriasis and eczema, coal tar is used in solution in which the concentration is decided by each individual patient's condition and response. It is a constituent in many non-proprietary and proprietary formulations, especially pastes, some of which are not suitable for the treatment of facial conditions.

▲ side-effects: some patients experience skin irritation and an acne-like rash. Rarely, there is sensitivity to light.

✦ warning: avoid contact with broken or inflamed skin. Coal tar stains skin, hair and fabric.
*Related articles:* ALPHOSYL; BALTAR; CARBO-CORT; CARBO-DOME; CLINITAR; COCOIS; COLTAPASTE; GELCOTAR; GENISOL; IONIL T; POLYTAR; PRAGMATAR; PSORIDERM;

PsoriGel; Tarband;
Tarcortin; T/Gel.

**Cobadex** (*Cox Pharmaceuticals*) is
a proprietary CORTICOSTEROID
preparation, available only on
prescription, used to treat mild
inflammatory skin conditions,
and itching in the anal and vulval
regions. Produced in the form of a
water-miscible cream (in two
strengths), Cobadex contains the
steroid hydrocortisone and the
antifoaming agent DIMETHICONE.
▲/ ✿ side-effects/warning: *see*
HYDROCORTISONE.

**Cobalin-H** (*Paines & Byrne*) is a
proprietary VITAMIN preparation,
available on prescription only to
private patients. Produced in
ampoules for injection, Cobalin-H
is a preparation of
hydroxocobalamin (vitamin B₁2).
▲/ ✿ side-effects/warning: *see*
HYDROXOCOBALAMIN.

**Co-betaloc** (*Astra*) is a
proprietary compound
ANTIHYPERTENSIVE drug,
available only on prescription,
used to treat high blood pressure.
Produced in the form of tablets,
Co-betaloc contains the BETA-
BLOCKER metoprolol tartrate and
the THIAZIDE DIURETIC
hydrochlorothiazide. It is not
recommended for children.
▲/ ✿ side-effects/warning: *see*
HYDROCHLOROTHIAZIDE;
METOPROLOL.

**Co-betaloc SA** (*Astra*) is a
proprietary compound
ANTIHYPERTENSIVE drug,
available only on prescription,
used to treat high blood pressure.
Produced in the form of tablets,
Co-betaloc SA contains the BETA-
BLOCKER metoprolol tartrate (in a
form that guarantees sustained
release) and the THIAZIDE
DIURETIC hydrochlorothiazide.
▲/ ✿ side-effects/warning: *see*
HYDROCHLOROTHIAZIDE;
METOPROLOL.

**cocaine** is a central
nervous system STIMULANT that
rapidly causes dependence
(addiction). Therapeutically it is
used mainly as a local
ANAESTHETIC for topical
application, particularly (as
cocaine hydrochloride, with or
without the atropine derivative
homatropine) in eye-drops. Its use
as an analgesic, and especially as
a constituent in elixirs prescribed
to treat pain in terminal care
(including the BROMPTON
COCKTAILS), is now virtually
discontinued.

**co-codamol** is a compound
ANALGESIC combining the OPIATE
codeine phosphate with
paracetamol in a ratio of 8:500
(mg). As a compound it forms a
constituent in a large number of
proprietary analgesic
preparations.
▲/ ✿ side-effects/warning: *see*
CODEINE PHOSPHATE;
PARACETAMOL.
*Related articles:* PARACODAL;
PARAKE; METOCODINE;
PANADEINE.

**co-codaprin** is a compound
ANALGESIC combining the OPIATE
codeine phosphate with aspirin in
a ratio of 8:400 (mg). As a
compound it forms a constituent
in a number of proprietary
analgesic preparations, but
although it has the advantages of
both drugs, it also has the
disadvantages.
▲/ ✿ side-effects/warning: *see*
ASPIRIN; CODEINE
PHOSPHATE.
*Related article:* CODIS.

**Cocois** (*Bioglan*) is a proprietary,
non-prescription preparation used
to treat eczema and psoriasis.
Produced in the form of an
ointment, the major active
constituents are coal tar solution,
SALICYLIC ACID and SULPHUR.
▲/ ✿ side-effects/warning: *see*
COAL TAR.

**Codalex** (*Regent*) is a LAXATIVE, a proprietary form of danthron as co-danthramer (danthron and poloxamer '188'). Available only on prescription, the preparation is available as a suspension, and a stronger suspension called Codalex Forte.
▲/✦ side-effects/warning: *see* DANTHRON.

**Codanin** (*Whitehall Laboratories*) is a proprietary, non-prescription ANALGESIC produced in the form of tablets and as a powder. It is a preparation of codeine phosphate and paracetamol.
▲/✦ side-effects/warning: *see* CODEINE PHOSPHATE; PARACETAMOL.

**co-danthrusate** is a non-proprietory compound LAXATIVE combining the stimulant laxative danthron together with poloxamer '188'. It is available in the form of capsules.
▲/✦ side-effects/warning: *see* DANTHRON.
*Related article:* NORMAX.

**codeine phosphate** is an OPIATE, a narcotic ANALGESIC that also has the properties of a cough suppressant. As an analgesic, codeine is a common, but often minor, constituent in non-proprietary and proprietary preparations to relieve pain (the majority of which are not available from the National Health Service), although some authorities dislike any combined form that contains codeine. Even more authorities disapprove of the drug's use as a cough suppressant. The drug also has the capacity to reduce intestinal motility (and so treat diarrhoea). Administration is oral or by injection.
▲ side-effects: tolerance occurs readily, although dependence (addiction) is relatively unusual. Constipation is

common. There may be sedation and dizziness, especially following injection. The effects of alcohol consumption may be enhanced.
✦ warning: codeine phosphate should not be administered to patients who suffer from depressed breathing, or who are aged under 12 months.
*Related articles:* ANTOIN; BENYLIN EXPECTORANT; CO-CODAMOL; CO-CODAPRIN; CODIS; DIARREST; DIMOTANE WITH CODEINE; FORMULIX; GALCODINE; HYPON; KAODENE; MEDOCODENE; MIGRALEVE; MYOLGIN; NEURODYNE; PANADEINE; PARACODOL; PARADENE; PARAHYPON; PARAKE; PARAMOL; PARDALE; PHENSEDYL; PROPAIN; SOLPADEINE; SOLPADOL; SYNDOL; TERCODA; TERPOIN; TYLEX; UNIFLU; VEGANIN.

**co-dergocrine mesylate** is a VASODILATOR that affects the blood vessels of the brain. It is sometimes claimed to improve brain function, but clinical results of psychological tests during and following treatment have neither proved nor disproved that claim, and patients with senile dementia seem to derive little, if any, benefit. It is for the treatment of senile dementia that the drug is most frequently prescribed.
▲ side-effects: there may be nausea and vomiting, flushing, a blocked nose, and a rash. Low blood pressure may cause dizziness on standing up from a lying or sitting position.
✦ warning: co-dergocrine mesylate should be administered with caution to patients who have a particularly slow heart rate.
*Related article:* HYDERGINE.

**Codis** (*Reckitt & Colman*) is a proprietary compound ANALGESIC, which is not available from the

National Health Service. Used to relieve pain and high body temperature, and produced in the form of soluble (dispersible) tablets, Codis contains a combination of ASPIRIN with CODEINE PHOSPHATE (a combination itself known as co-codaprin). It is not recommended for children.

▲/✿ side-effects/warning: *see* CO-CODAPRIN.

**co-dydramol** is a compound ANALGESIC, available on prescription, combining the NARCOTIC dihydrocodeine with paracetamol in a ratio of 10:500 (mg). As a compound it forms a constituent of proprietary analgesic preparations, but although it has the advantages of both drugs, it also has the disadvantages. Since it is a narcotic analgesic, dihydrocodeine is particularly dangerous in overdose, when it requires rapid hospitalization for the subject.

▲/✿ side-effects/warning: *see* DEXTROPROPOXYPHENE; PARACETAMOL.
*Related article:* COSALGESIC.

**Cogentin** (*Merck, Sharp & Dôhme*) is a proprietary preparation of the ANTICHOLINERGIC drug benztropine mesylate, available only on prescription, used in the treatment of parkinsonism (*see* ANTIPARKINSONISM) and to control tremors within drug-induced states involving involuntary movement (dyskinesia). Produced in the form of tablets and in ampoules for injection, Cogentin is not recommended for children aged under 3 years.

▲/✿ side-effects/warning: *see* BENZTROPINE MESYLATE.

**colchicine** is a drug derived from the meadow saffron plant, used to treat gout, particularly as an introductory measure to prevent acute gout attacks during initial treatment with other drugs that reduce blood levels of uric acid. Administration is oral in the form of tablets.

▲ side-effects: there is often nausea, vomiting and abdominal pain. High or excessive dosage may lead to gastrointestinal bleeding and diarrhoea, and even kidney damage. Prolonged treatment may eventually result in blood deficiencies and hair loss in some patients.

✿ warning: colchicine should be administered with caution to patients with heart or gastrointestinal disease, or who have impaired kidney function, who are pregnant or lactating, or who are elderly or debilitated.

**Coldrex** (*Sterling Health*) is a proprietary, non-prescription cold relief preparation produced in the form of tablets and as a powder. It contains paracetamol, phenylephrine and ascorbic acid. The tablet formulation also contains caffeine.

▲/✿ side-effects/warning: *see* ASCORBIC ACID; CAFFEINE; PARACETAMOL; PHENYLEPHRINE.

**Colestid** (*Upjohn*) is a proprietary form of the resin colestipol hydrochloride, available only on prescription, used to treat high levels of fats (hyperlipidaemia) in the blood. Produced in the form of granules (to be taken orally with liquid), Colestid is not recommended for children.

▲/✿ side-effects/warning: *see* COLESTIPOL HYDROCHLORIDE.

**colestipol hydrochloride** is a resin which, when taken orally, binds to itself bile salts in the intestines that can then be excreted in the normal way. This is a useful property in the treatment of high blood fat (especially cholesterol) levels and of the itching associated with obstruction in the bile ducts. The property can also be utilized in the treatment of diarrhoea following intestinal disease or surgery. Administration is oral in the form of granules to be taken with liquid.

▲ side-effects: there may be nausea, heartburn, flatulence with abdominal discomfort, constipation or diarrhoea, and a rash.

◆ warning: colestipol hydrochloride should not be administered to patients with complete blockage of the bile ducts, who are already taking any other drug, or who are pregnant. High dosage may require simultaneous administration of fat-soluble vitamins.
*Related article:* COLESTID.

**Colifoam** (*Stafford-Miller*) is a proprietary CORTICOSTEROID, available only on prescription, used to treat inflammation in the rectum and piles (haemorrhoids). Produced in the form of foam and applied with an aerosol, Colifoam is a preparation of the steroid hydrocortisone acetate. It is not recommended for children.

▲ / ◆ side-effects/warning: *see* HYDROCORTISONE.

**colistin** is a comparatively toxic ANTIBIOTIC of the polymyxin type that is used in topical application (in the form of colistin sulphate) to treat infections of the skin, and particularly the ears. However, in certain conditions and under strict supervision, the drug may be administered orally (primarily to sterilize the bowel, it is not absorbed) or by injection (primarily to treat urinary infection).

▲ side-effects: there may be breathlessness, vertigo, numbness round the mouth, and muscular weakness. Treatment by injection may cause symptoms of nerve or kidney disease.

◆ warning: colistin should not be administered to patients who suffer from the neuromuscular disease myasthenia gravis; it should be administered with caution to those who suffer from impaired kidney function. Dosage by injection is in millions of units.
*Related article:* COLOMYCIN.

**Colofac** (*Duphar*) is a proprietary ANTICHOLINERGIC drug available only on prescription, used to treat gastrointestinal disturbance caused by spasm of the muscles of the intestinal walls (irritable bowel syndrome). Produced in the form of tablets and as a sugar-free suspension, Colofac is a preparation of the ANTISPASMODIC drug mebeverine hydrochloride. It is not recommended for children aged under 10 years.

▲ / ◆ side-effects/warning: *see* MEBEVERINE HYDROCHLORIDE.

**Cologel** (*Lilly*) is a proprietary, non-prescription LAXATIVE, which is not available from the National Health Service. Used to treat constipation that results from inadequate fibre intake, it acts as a bulking agent to form a mass of faecal material that stimulates bowel movement. Produced in the form of sugar-free syrup for dilution (the potency of the syrup once diluted is retained for 14 days), Cologel is a preparation of METHYLCELLULOSE.

**Colomycin** (*Pharmax*) is a proprietary form of the ANTIBIOTIC colistin sulphate, available only on prescription. In powder form, it is used mainly in topical application to treat skin infections, burns and wounds. It is also produced in the form of tablets, and as a syrup for dilution (the potency of the syrup once diluted is retained for 14 days), and (in the form of colistin sulphomethate sodium) as a powder for reconstitution as a medium for injection.

▲/✿ side-effects/warning: *see* COLISTIN.

**Colostomy Plus** (*Shannon*) is a proprietary, non-prescription deodorant, used to freshen and sanitize the appliance or bag attached to a stoma (an outlet on the skin surface following the surgical curtailment of the intestines).

**Colpermin** (*Tillotts*) is a proprietary, non-prescription SMOOTH MUSCLE RELAXANT, used to treat gastrointestinal disturbance caused by spasm of the muscles of the intestinal walls. Produced in the form of capsules, Colpermin is a preparation of peppermint oil. It is not recommended for children.

▲/✿ side-effects/warning: *see* PEPPERMINT OIL.

**Coltapaste** (*Smith & Nephew*) is a proprietary, non-prescription form of impregnated bandaging, used to dress and treat serious non-infective skin diseases (such as eczema and psoriasis). The bandaging is impregnated with COAL TAR and ZINC paste.

**Colven** (*Reckitt & Colman*) is a proprietary ANTICHOLINERGIC SMOOTH MUSCLE RELAXANT, available only on prescription, used to treat gastrointestinal disturbance caused by spasm of the muscles of the intestinal walls. Produced in the form of effervescent granules in sachets, Colven is a preparation of the ANTISPASMODIC drug mebeverine

hydrochloride with the ANTIDIARRHOEAL bulking agent ispaghula husk. It is not recommended for children.

▲/✿ side-effects/warning: *see* ISPAGHULA HUSK; MEBEVERINE HYDROCHLORIDE.

**Combantrin** (*Pfizer*) is a proprietary broad-spectrum ANTHELMINTIC preparation, available only on prescription, used to treat infestations by roundworm, threadworm, hookworm and whipworm. Produced in the form of tablets, Combantrin is a preparation of pyrantel embonate. It is not recommended for children aged under 6 months.

▲/✿ side-effects/warning: *see* PYRANTEL.

**Comfeel** (*Coloplast*) is a proprietary, non-prescription barrier cream, used for the protection, freshening and sanitization of a stoma (an outlet in the skin surface following the surgical curtailment of the intestines).

**Comox** (*Norton*) is a proprietary broad-spectrum ANTIBIOTIC drug, available only on prescription, used to treat infections of the urinary tract, the sinuses or the middle ear, and diseases such as typhoid fever or exacerbations of chronic bronchitis. Produced in the form of tablets (in two strengths, the stronger under the name Comox Forte), as soluble (dispersible) tablets, and as a suspension for children, Comox is a compound of the SULPHONAMIDE sulphamethoxazole and trimethoprim – a compound itself known as CO-TRIMOXAZOLE.

▲/✿ side-effects/warning: *see* SULPHAMETHOXAZOLE; TRIMETHOPRIM.

**Complement Continus** (*Napp*) is a proprietary, non-prescription VITAMIN preparation, which is not available from the National Health Service. Produced in the form of sustained-release tablets, Complement Continus contains PYRIDOXINE hydrochloride (vitamin B₆). It is not recommended for children.

**Comprecin** *(P-D)* is a proprietary ANTIBIOTIC preparation available only on prescription, used to treat gonorrhoea and bacterial dysentery and infections of the urinary tract and skin. Produced in the form of tablets, Comprecin is a preparation of the quinolone antibiotic enoxacin. It is not recommended for use in children.
▲/✿ side-effects/warning: *see* enoxacin.

**Concavit** *(Wallace)* is a proprietary, non-prescription multivitamin compound, which is not available from the National Health Service. Produced in the form of capsules, as drops and as a syrup, Concavit contains RETINOL (vitamin A), several forms of vitamin B (THIAMINE, RIBOFLAVINE, PYRIDOXINE, CYANOCOBALAMIN, NICOTINAMIDE and PANTOTHENIC ACID), ASCORBIC ACID (vitamin C), CALCIFEROL (vitamin D), and TOCOPHEROL (vitamin E).

**Concordin** *(Merck, Sharp & Dohme)* is a proprietary ANTIDEPRESSANT available only on prescription, used to treat depressive illness and especially in apathetic or withdrawn patients. Produced in the form of tablets (in two strengths), Concordin is a preparation of protriptyline hydrochloride. It is not recommended for children.
▲/✿ side-effects/warning: *see* PROTRIPTYLINE.

**Condyline** *(Brocades)* is a proprietary, non-prescription compound OINTMENT for topical application, intended to treat and

remove penile warts. Condyline is a preparation of the KERATOLYTIC salicylic acid and the highly acidic substance podophyllotoxin. It should not be used for facial warts.
▲/✿ side-effects/warning: *see* SALICYLIC ACID; PODOPHYLLIN.

**Congesteze** *(Schering-Plough)* is a proprietary nasal and respiratory DECONGESTANT. Congesteze contains the ANTIHISTAMINE azatadine maleate together with pseudoephedrine, a SYMPATHOMIMETIC with VASOCONSTRICTOR properties. Produced in the form of tablets, a syrup (once diluted potent for 28 days), and a syrup for children (Pediatric syrup).
▲/✿ side-effects/warning: *see* AZATADINE; PSEUDOEPHEDRINE.

**Conjuvac Mite** *(Dome/Hollister-Stier)* is a proprietary preparation of allergens associated with the house dust mite, for use in desensitizing patients who are allergic to it. Available only on prescription and administered by injection, Conjuvac Mite is produced in sets of treatment or for maintenance.
✿ warning: close medical supervision is required for a minimum of 2 hours after the injection; administration should take place in locations where emergency facilities for full cardio-respiratory resuscitation are immediately available. Patients should not have had a large meal before treatment.

**Conjuvac Two Grass** *(Dome/Hollister-Stier)* is a proprietary set of two grass pollen preparations (Timothy and Cocksfoot) for use in desensitizing patients who are allergic to such pollen (and so suffer from hay fever). Available only on prescription and administered by injection, Conjuvac pollen preparations are of carefully annotated different allergenic extracts, so that the process of desensitization, as regulated by a doctor, can be progressive.

● warning: close medical supervision is required for a minimum of 2 hours after the injection; administration should take place in locations where emergency facilities for full cardio-respiratory resuscitation are immediately available. Patients should not have had a large meal before treatment.

**Conotrane** (*Boehringer Ingelheim*) is a proprietary, non-prescription ANTISEPTIC preparation, used to treat rash and sores and for skin protection. Produced in the form of cream, Conotrane is a preparation of BENZALKONIUM CHLORIDE and dimethicone '350' and a fragrance.

**Conova 30** (*Gold Cross*) is a proprietary low-oestrogen combined ORAL CONTRACEPTIVE, available only on prescription. Produced in the form of tablets, Conova 30 is a preparation of the PROGESTOGEN ethynodiol diacetate and the OESTROGEN ethinyloestradiol.

▲ / ● side-effects/warning: see ETHINYLOESTRADIOL.

**Contac 400** (*Menley & James*) is a proprietary, non-prescription cold relief preparation. It contains the ANTIHISTAMINE chlorpheniramine and the DECONGESTANT propanolamine.

▲ / ● side-effects/warning: see CHLORPHENIRAMINE.

**\*contraceptives** are the means of preventing conception. Methods that involve drugs include oral contraceptives (the 'Pill') which

contain either a hormonal combination of a PROGESTOGEN and an OESTROGEN or just a progestogen; and SPERMICIDAL preparations, which contain drugs that kill sperm and/or prevent motility within the vagina or cervix. Spermicides are for use in combination with barrier methods of contraceptives (such as a condom or diaphragm), and a new spermicide-impregnated sponge to be inserted into the vagina is now available over the counter. A progestogen-only injection is prescribed by some doctors, and is renewable at intervals of three months. Post-coital contraception is also possible in an emergency, and consists of high-dose oestrogen preparations. All contraceptives that involve the use of drugs produce side-effects, and a form that is ideally suited to a patient is not always possible.
*see* ORAL CONTRACEPTIVES.

**Coparvax** (*Calmic*) is a proprietary preparation of a VACCINE available only on prescription, used to prompt the immune system to form antibodies and so assist in the treatment of malignant effusions in the abdominal or chest cavity. Produced in the form of powder for reconstitution as a medium for injection, Coparvax's active constituent is inactivated Corynebacterium parvum bacteria.

▲ / ● side-effects/warning: see CORYNEBACTERIUM PARVUM VACCINE.

**Copholco** (*Radiol Chemicals*) is a proprietary, non-prescription EXPECTORANT and cough mixture, which is not available from the National Health Service. Produced in the form of a linctus, Copholco is a preparation that includes the OPIATE pholcodine and MENTHOL. It is not

recommended for children aged
under 5 years.
▲/ ❋ side-effects/warning: *see*
PHOLCODINE.

**Coppertone Supershade 15**
(*Scholl*) is a proprietary, non-
prescription sunscreening
preparation, used to help protect
the skin from ultraviolet
radiation, as in radiotherapy.
Produced in the form of a lotion,
Coppertone Supershade 15
contains para-AMINOBENZOIC ACID
ester and OXYBENZONE.

**co-proxamol** is a compound
ANALGESIC combining the
NARCOTIC dextropropoxyphene
with paracetamol in a ratio of
32.5:325 (mg). As a compound it
forms a constituent in a number
of proprietary analgesic
preparations, but although it has
the advantages of both drugs, it
also has the disadvantages. Since
it is a narcotic analgesic,
dextropropoxyphene is
particularly dangerous in
overdose, when it requires rapid
hospitalization for the subject.
▲/ ❋ side-effects/warning: *see*
DEXTROPROPOXYPHENE;
PARACETAMOL.
*Related articles:*
COSALGESIC; DISTALGESIC;
PAXALGESIC.

**Coracten** (*Evans*) is a proprietary
preparation of the CALCIUM-
ANTAGONIST nifedipine. Available
only on prescription, it is used to
treat angina pectoris (heart pain)
and high blood pressure
(hypertension). Produced in the
form of sustained-release
capsules.
▲/ ❋ side-effects/warning: *see*
NIFEDIPINE.

**Cordarone X** (*Labaz*) is a
proprietary ANTIARRHYTHMIC
drug, available only on
prescription, used to treat
heartbeat irregularities.

Produced in the form of tablets (in
two strengths) and in ampoules
for injections, Cordarone X is a
preparation of amiodarone
hydrochloride.
▲/ ❋ side-effects/warning: *see*
AMIODARONE.

**Cordilox** (*Abbott*) is a proprietary
ANTIARRHYTHMIC,
ANTIHYPERTENSIVE drug,
available only on prescription,
used to treat heartbeat
irregularities, angina pectoris
(heart pain) and high blood
pressure (hypertension).
Produced in the form of tablets (in
four strengths, the strongest
under the name Cordilox 160) and
in ampoules for injection,
Cordilox is a preparation of the
calcium antagonist verapamil
hydrochloride. It is not
recommended for the treatment of
angina in children.
▲/ ❋ side-effects/warning: *see*
VERAPAMIL HYDROCHLORIDE.

**Corgard** (*Squibb*) is a proprietary
BETA-BLOCKER ANTIHYPERTENSIVE
drug, available only on
prescription, used to treat
heartbeat irregularities, angina
pectoris (heart pain), and high
blood pressure (hypertension), to
prevent migraine, and to assist in
the treatment of excess levels of
thyroid hormones in the blood
(thyrotoxicosis). Produced in the
form of tablets (in two strengths),
Corgard is a preparation of
nadolol. It is not recommended for
children.
▲/ ❋ side-effects/warning: *see*
NADOLOL.

**Corgaretic** (*Squibb*) is a
proprietary compound
ANTIHYPERTENSIVE drug,
available only on prescription,
used to treat high blood pressure
(hypertension). Produced in the
form of tablets (in two strengths,
under the names Corgaretic 40
and Corgaretic 80), it is a

combination of the BETA-BLOCKER nadolol and the THIAZIDE DIURETIC bendrofluazide. It is not recommended for children.

▲/✚ side-effects/warning: see BENDROFLUAZIDE; NADOLOL.

**Corlan** (*Glaxo*) is a proprietary CORTICOSTEROID, available only on prescription, used in topical application to treat ulcers and sores in the mouth. Produced in the form of lozenges, Corlan's active constituent is the steroid hydrocortisone.

▲/✚ side-effects/warning: see HYDROCORTISONE.

**Coro-nitro Spray** (*MCP Pharmaceuticals*) is a proprietary, non-prescription VASODILATOR used to treat and prevent angina pectoris (heart pain). Produced in the form of an aerosol spray in metered doses, for application on or under the tongue, Coro-nitro Spray is a preparation of glyceryl trinitrate. It is not recommended for children.

▲/✚ side-effects/warning: see GLYCERYL TRINITRATE.

**Corsodyl** (*ICI*) is a proprietary, non-prescription ANTISEPTIC preparation, used in topical application to treat inflammations and infections of the mouth. Produced in the form of a gel and as a mouth-wash, Corsodyl is a preparation of CHLORHEXIDINE gluconate.

**\*corticosteroids** are steroid hormones secreted by the cortex (outer part) of the adrenal glands, or synthetic substances that closely resemble them. There are two main types: glucocorticoids and mineralocorticoids. The latter assist in maintaining the salt and water balance of the body. The glucocorticoids are potent anti-inflammatory agents, frequently used to treat inflammatory and/or allergic reactions of the skin. Such reactions are sometimes complicated by a co-existing infection, and so many drug companies produce compound preparations containing both an antibiotic (or an antifungal) and an anti-inflammatory corticosteroid. Caution must be exercised in their use because the corticosteroid diminishes the patient's immune response to the infective agent, placing even greater reliance on the antibiotic or antifungal agent. Absorption of a high dose of corticosteroid over a period of time may also cause other undesirable systemic side-effects, such as peptic ulceration, brittle bones, muscle disorders, stunting of growth in children and accumulation of tissue fluids.

**corticotrophin,** or adrenocorticotrophic hormone (ACTH), is a hormone produced and secreted by the pituitary gland in order to control the production and secretion of other hormones – CORTICOSTEROIDS – in the adrenal glands, generally as a response to stress. Therapeutically, corticotrophin may be administered to make up for hormonal deficiency in the pituitary gland, to cause the production of extra corticosteroids in the treatment of inflammatory conditions such as rheumatism and asthma, or to test the function of the adrenal glands.

**cortisol** is another name for the CORTICOSTEROID hormone hydrocortisone.

▲/✚ side-effects/warning: see HYDROCORTISONE.

**cortisone acetate** is a CORTICOSTEROID hormone that has the properties both of glucocorticoids and of mineralocorticoids. It can thus theoretically be used both to treat inflammatory conditions caused, for instance, by allergy or rheumatism, and to make up for hormonal deficiency (especially relating to the salt and water balance in the body) following surgical removal of the adrenal glands. In practice, however, it is not generally used for the suppression of inflammation because it has a tendency to cause fluid retention. Administration is oral in the form of tablets.

▲ side-effects: treatment of susceptible patients may engender euphoria, or a state of confusion or depression. Rarely, there is peptic ulcer.

✦ warning: cortisone acetate should not be administered to patients with psoriasis. It should be administered with caution to the elderly (in whom overdosage can cause osteoporosis, 'brittle bones'), those with kidney disease peptic ulcer, hypertension, glaucoma, epilepsy or diabetes, or who are pregnant. In children, administration of cortisone acetate may lead to stunting of growth. The effects of potentially serious infections may be masked by the drug during treatment. Withdrawal of treatment must be gradual.

*Related articles:* CORTISTAB; CORTISYL.

**Cortistab** (*Boots*) is a proprietary preparation of the CORTICO-STEROID hormone cortisone acetate, available only on prescription, used less commonly now in replacement therapy to make up hormonal deficiency following surgical removal of one or both of the adrenal glands; it is even less commonly used to treat allergic and rheumatic inflammation. It is produced in the form of tablets (in two strengths).

▲/✦ side-effects/warning: *see* CORTISONE ACETATE.

**Cortisyl** (*Roussel*) is a proprietary preparation of the CORTICO-STEROID hormone cortisone acetate, available only on prescription, used less commonly now in replacement therapy to make up hormonal deficiency following surgical removal of one or both of the adrenal glands. Produced in the form of tablets, it is not recommended for children.

▲/✦ side-effects/warning: *see* CORTISONE ACETATE.

**Corwin** (*Stuart*) is a SYMPATHOMIMETIC used as a stimulant of the force of the heart's beat. It is a proprietary form of xamoterol available only on prescription. The preparation is in the form of tablets.

▲/✦ side-effects/warning: *see* XAMOTEROL.

**Corynebacterium parvum vaccine** is a suspension of inactivated Corynebacterium parvum bacteria prepared as a VACCINE, which may be injected into a body cavity in order to promote the formation of antibodies that then assist in the treatment of malignant effusions. It is known as an immuno-stimulant.

▲ side-effects: there is high body temperature; there may also be nausea and vomiting, with abdominal pain.

✦ warning: injection of the vaccine should not take place within 10 days of surgery on the chest wall.

*Related article:* COPARVAX.

**Cosalgesic** (*Cox*) is a proprietary ANALGESIC available only on prescription to private patients. Used to relieve pain anywhere in the body, and produced in the form of tablets, Cosalgesic is a preparation of the narcotic-like analgesic dextropropoxyphene together with paracetamol. This compound combination is known as CO-PROXAMOL). It is not recommended for children.

▲/ ✪ side-effects/warning: *see* DEXTROPROPOXYPHENE; PARACETAMOL.

**Cosmegen Lyovac** (*Merck, Sharp & Dohme*) is a proprietary CYTOTOXIC drug that also has ANTIBIOTIC properties. Available only on prescription, it is used mainly to treat cancers in children, and is produced in the form of a powder for reconstitution as a medium for injection. It may also be used as an immunosuppressant during or following transplant surgery in order to limit tissue rejection. Cosmegen Lyovac is a preparation of actinomycin D.

▲/ ✪ side-effects/warning: *see* ACTINOMYCIN D.

**Cosuric** (*DDSA Pharmaceuticals*) is a proprietary form of the XANTHINE-OXIDASE INHIBITOR allopurinol, used to treat high levels of uric acid in the bloodstream (which may cause gout). Available only on prescription, Cosuric is produced in the form of tablets (in two strengths).

▲/ ✪ side-effects/warning: *see* ALLOPURINOL.

**Cotazym** (*Organon*) is a proprietary, non-prescription preparation of digestive enzymes, pancreatin, used to make up a deficiency of digestive juices normally supplied by the pancreas. This may be required following surgery on the alimentary canal or be necessitated by disease. It is produced in the form of capsules to be sprinkled on food.

▲/ ✪ side-effects/warning: *see* PANCREATIN.

**co-trimoxazole** is the name for an ANTIBIOTIC combination of the SULPHONAMIDE sulphamethoxazole and the similar but not related trimethoprim (a folic acid inhibitor). At one time it was thought that each agent enhanced the action of the other, giving a combined effect greater than the sum of the two. While there is in fact little evidence to support this, the combination remains a very useful antibiotic preparation. It is used to treat and to prevent the spread of infections of the urinary tract, the nasal passages and upper respiratory tract, and the bones and joints, and such diseases as typhoid fever or gonorrhoea (particularly in patients allergic to penicillin); it is the active constituent of many proprietary antibiotic preparations. Administration is oral in the form of tablets or suspension, or by injection or infusion. Side-effects are largely due to the sulphonamide.

▲ side-effects: there may be nausea and vomiting; rashes are not uncommon.
  Blood disorders may occur.

✪ warning: co-trimoxazole should not be administered to patients who are pregnant or with blood disorders, jaundice, or impaired liver or kidney function. It should be administered with caution to infants under 6 weeks and those who are elderly or lactating. Adequate fluid intake must be maintained. Prolonged treatment requires regular blood counts.
  *Related articles:* BACTRIM; CHEMOTRIM; COMOX; FECTRIM; LARATRIM; SEPTRIN.

*\*counter-irritants* are preparations that are applied topically to produce an irritation of the sensory nerve endings,

which offsets underlying muscle or joint pain.

**Covermark** (*Stiefel*) is the name of a proprietary, non-prescription brand of camouflaging preparations designed for topical application to mask scars and other skin disfigurements. Produced in the form of a cream rouge (in three shades), a spotstick (in seven shades), a grey toner (as a cream), a masking or covering cream (in ten shades), a shading cream and a finishing powder, they may be obtained on prescription if the skin disfigurement is the result of surgery or is giving rise to emotional disturbance.

**Coversyl** (*Servier*) is a proprietary form of the ANTIHYPERTENSIVE drug perindopril tert-butylamine. It is used to treat high blood pressure (hypertension), with a DIURETIC or CARDIAC GLYCOSIDE. It is available only on prescription in the form of tablets (in two strengths).
▲/❋ side-effects/warning: *see* PERINDOPRIL.

**Cradocap** (*Napp*) is a proprietary, non-prescription ANTISEPTIC, used to treat the infants' skin conditions cradle cap or scurf cap. Produced in the form of a shampoo, Cradocap represents a 10% solution of CETRIMIDE.

**Cremalgin** (*Berk*) is a proprietary, non-prescription COUNTER-IRRITANT which, in the form of a cream applied to the skin, produces an irritation of sensory nerve endings that offsets the pain of underlying muscle or joint ailments. It contains various vegetable extracts and alcohol esters.
❋ warning: cremalgin should not be used on inflamed or broken skin, or on mucous membranes.

**Creon** (*Duphar*) is a proprietary, non-prescription preparation of digestive enzymes, pancreatin, used to make up a deficiency of digestive juices normally supplied by the pancreas. This may be required following surgery on the alimentary canal or be necessitated by disease. It is produced in the form of capsules.
▲/❋ side-effects/warning: *see* PANCREATIN.

**cristantaspase** is the ENZYME asparaginase used almost exclusively to treat the disease effecting the white blood cells, acute lymphoblastic leukaemia.
▲ side-effects: there may be nausea, vomiting, central nervous system depression, and changes in liver function and blood lipids (requiring careful monitoring including of the urine for glucose).
❋ warning: anaphylaxis.
*Related article:* ERWINASE.

**crotamiton** is a drug used both to relieve itching and to kill parasitic mites on the skin (as in scabies). It is applied to the skin in the form of a lotion or a cream, usually following a bath; the application should be left in position for as long as possible – ideally 24 hours for treatment of parasitic mites – before being washed off.
❋ warning: crotamiton should not be used on broken skin or near the eyes.

**crystal violet** is another name for gentian violet.
*see* GENTIAN VIOLET.

**Crystapen** (*Glaxo*) is a proprietary ANTIBIOTIC, available only on prescription, used to treat infections of the skin, of the middle ear, and of the respiratory tract (such as tonsillitis), and certain severe systemic infections (such as meningitis). Produced as a powder for reconstitution in any of three forms suited to specific sites of injection, Crystapen is a preparation of benzylpenicillin sodium.

▲/✦ side-effects/warning: see BENZYLPENICILLIN.

**Crystapen V** (*Glaxo*) is a proprietary ANTIBIOTIC, available only on prescription, used to treat many forms of infection, and to prevent rheumatic fever. Produced in the form of a syrup (in two strengths) for dilution (the potency of the syrup once diluted is retained for 7 days), Crystapen V is a preparation of phenoxymethylpenicillin.

▲/✦ side-effects/warning: see PHENOXYMETHYLPENICILLIN.

**Cuplex** (*Smith & Nephew*) is a proprietary, non-prescription preparation used to remove warts and hard skin (a keratolytic). Produced in the form of a gel, Cuplex's active constituents are salicylic acid and lactic acid.

**cyanocobalamin** is a form of VITAMIN $B_{12}$ found in most normal diets - in eggs, diary products and meats - and is essential for the functioning of nerve cells and the growth of red blood cells. Really strict vegetarians who eat no animal products whatever may eventually suffer from deficiency of this vitamin in a condition that is a form of anaemia; the condition is also found in patients who for one reason or another cannot absorb food properly. Therapeutically, however, cyanocobalamin has recently been replaced by HYDROXO-COBALAMIN as the version of the vitamin for medical use. Supplements of vitamin $B_{12}$ are administered mainly by injection (because vitamin $B_{12}$ deficiency arises most often through malabsorption - possibly following gastrectomy - which

renders oral administration futile). But whereas hydroxocobalamin can be retained in the body for more than 3 months following injection, cyanocobalamin must be re-injected at least once a month.
*Related articles:* BC 500; CALCIMAX; CE-COBALIN; CONCAVIT; CYTACON; CYTAMEN; HEPACON; KETOVITE; OCTOVIT; SOLIVITO.

**cyclandelate** is a VASODILATOR that specifically affects the blood vessels of the brain. It is sometimes claimed to improve brain function, but clinical results of psychological tests during and following treatment have neither proved nor disproved that claim, and patients suffering from senile dementia seem to derive little benefit if any. It is to assist in the treatment of senile dementia that the drug is most prescribed, although it can also be used to improve circulatory disorders of the limbs.
▲ side-effects: there may be nausea and flushing; high doses may cause dizziness.
✦ warning: cyclandelate should not be administered to patients who are suffering from brain injury.
*Related articles:* CYCLOBRAL; CYCLOSPASMOL.

**Cyclimorph** (*Calmic*) is a proprietary form of the narcotic ANALGESIC morphine tartrate together with the anti-emetic ANTIHISTAMINE cyclizine tartrate, and is on the controlled drugs list. Used to treat moderate to severe pain, especially in serious conditions of fluid within the lungs, it is produced in ampoules (in two strengths, under the names Cyclimorph-10 and Cyclimorph-15) for injection. It is not recommended for children or for those in terminal care because of the anti-emetic content.

▲/❋ side-effects/warning: *see*
CYCLIZINE; MORPHINE.

**cyclizine** is an ANTIHISTAMINE
used primarily as an ANTI-EMETIC
in the treatment or prevention of
motion sickness and vomiting
caused either by chemotherapy
for cancer or by infection of the
middle or inner ear.
Administration (as cyclizine
hydrochloride, cyclizine lactate
or cyclizine tartrate) is oral in the
form of tablets, or by injection.
▲ side-effects: concentration and
speed of thought and
movement may be affected.
There is commonly drowsiness
and dry mouth; there may also
be headache, blurred vision
and gastrointestinal
disturbances.
❋ warning: cyclizine should be
administered with caution to
patients with epilepsy, liver
disease, glaucoma or
enlargement of the prostate
gland. Drowsiness may be
increased by alcohol
consumption.
*Related articles:* CYCLIMORPH;
DICONAL; MIGRIL; VALOID.

**cyclobarbitone calcium** is a
HYPNOTIC BARBITURATE used only
when absolutely necessary, to
treat severe and intractable
insomnia. Administration is oral
in the form of tablets. The
proprietary form is on the
controlled drugs list.
▲ side-effects: concentration and
the speed of thought and
movement are affected. There
may be drowsiness, dizziness
and shallow breathing, with
headache. Some patients
experience hypersensitivity
reactions. (The drug enhances
the effects of alcohol
consumption.)
❋ warning: cyclobarbitone
calcium should not be
administered to patients whose
insomnia is caused by pain,

who have porphyria, who are
pregnant or lactating, who are
elderly or debilitated, or who
have a history of drug
(including alcohol) abuse. It
should be administered with
caution to those with kidney,
liver, or lung disease. Use of
the drug should be avoided as
far as possible. Repeated doses
are cumulative in effect, and
may lead to real sedation;
abrupt withdrawal of
treatment, on the other hand,
may cause serious withdrawal
symptoms. Tolerance and
dependence (addiction) occur
readily.

**Cyclobral** (*Norgine*) is a
proprietary, non-prescription
VASODILATOR, used to improve
blood circulation to the brain
(particularly to assist in the
treatment of senile dementia) and
to the extremities. Produced in
the form of capsules, Cyclobral is
a preparation of cyclandelate.
▲/❋ side-effects/warning: *see*
CYCLANDELATE.

**cyclofenil** is an anti-OESTROGEN.
Although it is not actually an
androgen (a male sex hormone), it
neutralizes the effect of any
oestrogen (female sex hormone)
present. This property can be
useful in treating infertility or
sparse or infrequent menstrual
periods in women whose
condition is linked to the
persistent presence of oestrogens
and a consequent failure to
ovulate. Administration is oral in
the form of tablets.
▲ side-effects: there may be
nausea and hot flushes, with
abdominal discomfort; rarely,
there is jaundice.
❋ warning: cyclofenil should not
be administered to patients
with ovarian cysts, cancer of
the womb lining, or liver
disease, or who are pregnant.
*Related article:* REHIBIN.

**Cyclogest** (*Hoechst*) (Cox Pharmaceuticals) is a proprietary preparation of the female sex HORMONE progesterone, available only on prescription, used to treat premenstrual problems and depression after childbirth. It is produced in the form of (vaginal or anal) suppositories (in two strengths).

▲/✿ side-effects/warning: *see* PROGESTERONE.

**cyclopenthiazide** is a DIURETIC, one of the THIAZIDES, used to treat fluid retention in the tissues (oedema) and high blood pressure (hypertension). Because all thiazides tend to deplete body reserves of potassium, cyclopenthiazide may be administered in combination either with potassium supplements or with diuretics that are complementarily potassium-sparing. Administration is oral in the form of tablets.

▲ side-effects: there may be tiredness and a rash. In men, temporary impotence may occur; this is reversible on stopping treatment.

✿ warning: cyclopenthiazide should not be administered to patients with kidney failure or urinary retention, or who are lactating. It should be administered with caution to those who are pregnant. It may aggravate conditions of diabetes or gout.
*Related articles:* NAVIDREX; NAVISPARE.

**cyclopentolate hydrochloride** is an ANTICHOLINERGIC drug that is used in eye-drops to dilate the pupil and paralyse the ciliary muscle (which alters the curvature of the lens). Used to prepare a patient for ophthalmic examination and, less commonly, to assist in the treatment of eye inflammations, cyclopentolate's

action may last for up to 24 hours.

▲ side-effects: vision may be affected to some degree for the duration of the drug's action. Susceptible patients may experience raised intra-ocular pressure.

✿ warning: cyclopentolate hydrochloride should be administered with caution to patients with pressure within the eyeball. Contact dermatitis may appear where the drug touches the skin.
*Related articles:* MINIMS; MYDRILATE; OPULETS.

**cyclophosphamide** is a CYTOTOXIC drug that is widely used in the treatment of some forms of leukaemia and lymphoma, and some solid tumours. It works by interfering with the DNA of new cells, so preventing normal cell replication, but it remains inactive until metabolised by the liver. The drug may also be used as an IMMUNOSUPPRESSANT to limit tissue rejection during and following transplant surgery, or to assist in the treatment of complicated rheumatoid arthritis. Administration is oral in the form of tablets, or by injection, and should be accompanied by increased fluid intake.

▲ side-effects: there is commonly nausea and vomiting; there is often also hair loss.

✿ warning: cyclophosphamide should be administered with caution to patients with impaired kidney function. It may in susceptible patients cause an unpleasant form of cystitis (inflammation of the bladder): greatly increased fluid intake or the simul-taneous administration of the synthetic drug mesna may help to avoid the problem. Prolonged treatment may cause an early menopause in women, and men may be

rendered permanently sterile early in treatment.
*Related article:* ENDOXANA.

**Cyclo-progynova** (*Schering*) is a proprietary preparation of female sex hormones, available only on prescription, used to treat menopausal problems. Produced in the form of tablets (in two strengths, under the names Cyclo-progynova and Cyclo-progynova), Cyclo-progynova is a combination of the OESTROGEN oestradiol valerate and the PROGESTOGEN norgestrel (or its stronger analogue, levonorgestrel).
▲/ ✹ side-effects/warning: *see*
LEVONORGESTREL;
NORGESTREL; OESTRADIOL.

**cyclopropane** is a gas used as an inhalant general ANAESTHETIC for both induction and maintenance of general anaesthesia. It has some MUSCLE RELAXANT properties too, although in practice a muscle relaxant drug is usually administered simultaneously. However, it has the great disadvantage of being potentially explosive in air, and must be used via closed-circuit systems.
▲ side-effects: although recovery afterwards is rapid, there may be vomiting and agitation.
✹ warning: cyclopropane causes respiratory depression, and some form of assisted pulmonary ventilation may be necessary during anaesthesia.

**cycloserine** is an ANTIBIOTIC drug used specifically in the treatment of tuberculosis that proves to be resistant to the powerful drugs ordinarily used first, or in cases where those drugs are not tolerated. Administration is oral in the form of capsules.
▲ side-effects: there may be headache, dizziness, and drowsiness; possible sensitivity reactions include a rash or, rarely, convulsions.

✹ warning: cycloserine should not be administered to patients with epilepsy, alcoholism, depressive illness, anxiety or psychosis; it should be administered with caution to those with impaired kidney function.

**Cyclospasmol** (*Brocades*) is a proprietary, non-prescription VASODILATOR, used to improve blood circulation to the brain (particularly to assist in the treatment of senile dementia) and to the extremities. Produced in the form of capsules, as tablets and as a suspension for dilution (the potency of the suspension once dilute is retained for 14 days), Cyclospasmol is a preparation of cyclandelate.
▲/ ✹ side-effects/warning: *see*
CYCLANDELATE.

**cyclosporin** is a powerful IMMUNOSUPPRESSANT that is particularly used to limit tissue rejection during and following transplant surgery. Unusually, it has very little effect on the blood-cell producing capacity of the bone-marrow. Administration is oral in the form of an oily solution, or by dilute intravenous infusion.
▲ side-effects: treatment may result in impaired liver and kidney function, with gastrointestinal disturbances; some patients experience tremor or excessive hair growth.
✹ warning: treatment with cyclosporin inevitably leaves the body much more open to infection, in that part of the immune system – its defence mechanism against microbial invasion – is rendered non-functional. It should be administered with caution to patients who are breast-feeding.
*Related article:* SANDIMMUN.

145

**Cyklokapron** (*Kabi Vitrum*) is a proprietary HAEMOSTATIC, available only on prescription, used to staunch blood flow (for instance in menstruation, or following the extraction of a tooth, in haemophiliac patients). Produced in the form of tablets, as a syrup (the potency of the syrup once dilute is retained for 14 days) and in ampoules for injection, Cyklokapron is a preparation of the styptic tranexamic acid.
▲/ ❋ side-effects/warning: *see* TRANEXAMIC ACID.

**Cymevene** (*Syntex*) is an ANTIVIRAL drug, a proprietary form of ganciclovir, available only on prescription to treat life-treatening viral infections.
▲/ ❋ side-effects/warning: *see* GANCICLOVIR

**cyproheptadine hydrochloride** is a powerful ANTIHISTAMINE, which has the unusual distinction of inhibiting not only allergic responses resulting from the release of histamine in the body, but also those allergic responses resulting from the similar release of serotonin. Cyproheptadine is thus capable of treating a much wider range of allergic symptoms than almost any other anti-histamine. Moreover, it is sometimes also used to treat migraine and – under medical supervision – to stimulate the appetite (especially in children). Administration is oral in the form of tablets or a dilute syrup.
▲ side-effects: there may be a sedative effect (or, in susceptible patients – especially children – excitement), a headache, and/or weight gain; some patients experience dry mouth, blurred vision, gastrointestinal disturbances and/or urinary retention.
❋ warning: cyproheptadine hydrochloride should be administered with caution to patients with epilepsy, glaucoma, liver disease or enlargement of the prostate gland.
*Related article:* PERIACTIN.

**Cyprostat** (*Schering*) is a proprietary preparation of the drug cyproterone acetate, available only on prescription, used to treat cancer of the prostate gland. In combination with the administration of OESTROGENS, Cyprostat works by neutralizing the effects of the male sex hormones (androgens) that contribute to the cancer. It is produced in the form of tablets.
▲/ ❋ side-effects/warning: *see* CYPROTERONE ACETATE.

**cyproterone acetate** is an anti-androgen, a drug that neutralizes or otherwise modifies the effects of male sex hormones (androgens) in the body. It is used in the treatment of cancer of the prostate gland, a cancer that advances because of the presence of androgens; in the treatment of masculinization in women, whose symptoms may for example be excessive hair growth or acne; and in the treatment of hypersexuality or sexual deviation in men, in whom the drug causes a condition of reversible sterility through a reduction in the formation of sperm and the creation of non-viable forms of sperm. Administration is oral in the form of tablets.
▲ side-effects: concentration and speed of thought and movement are affected, with fatigue and lethargy. Hormonal effects include changes in hair growth patterns and in men the growth of the breasts. Rarely, there is osteoporosis ('brittle bones').
❋ warning: cyproterone acetate should not be administered to patients with non-sex-linked cancers, liver disease, or severe

depression; who have a history of thrombosis; who are pregnant; or who are adolescent boys (in whom bone growth and testicular development may be arrested). It should be administered with caution to those with diabetes or insufficient secretion of adrenal hormones, or who are lactating. Regular checks on liver function, adrenal gland function, and blood levels of glucose are essential. The drug has no effect on patients who are chronic alcoholics due to its interaction with alcohol.
*Related articles:* ANDROCUR; CYPROSTAT.

**Cytacon** (*Duncan, Flockhart*) is a proprietary, non-prescription VITAMIN preparation, which is not available from the National Health Service. It is used to treat vitamin deficiency disorders (including anaemia), especially those caused by the malabsorption of food. Produced in the form of tablets and as an elixir, Cytacon is a preparation of CYANOCOBALAMIN (vitamin $B_{12}$).

**Cytamen** (*Duncan Flockhart*) is a proprietary VITAMIN preparation, available on prescription only to private patients, used to treat different forms of anaemia. Produced in ampoules for injection, Cytamen is a preparation of CYANOCOBALAMIN (vitamin $B_{12}$).

**cytarabine** is an ANTICANCER drug used primarily in the treatment of leukaemia. It works by combining with new-forming cells in a way that prevents normal cell replication (it is cytostatic rather than cytotoxic). Administration is by injection.
▲ side-effects: there is commonly nausea and vomiting; there is often also hair loss.

✦ warning: cytarabine has a severely depressive effect upon the blood-cell forming capacity of the bone-marrow: constant blood counts are essential. Treatment may cause sterility in men and an early menopause in women if prolonged. Leakage of the drug into the tissues at the site of injection or infusion may cause tissue damage.
*Related articles:* ALEXAN; CYTOSAR.

**Cytosar** (*Upjohn*) is a proprietary ANTICANCER drug, available only on prescription, used to treat acute forms of leukaemia. Produced in the form of a powder for reconstitution as a medium for injection (in vials in two strengths, with or without diluent), Cytosar is a preparation of the cytostatic drug cytarabine.
▲/✦ side-effects/warning: *see* CYTARABINE.

**Cytotec** (*Searle*) is a proprietary form of the synthetic PROSTAGLANDIN analogue misoprostol, available only on prescription, used to treat gastric and duodenal ulcers.
▲/✦ side-effects/warning: *see* MISOPROSTOL.

**\*cytotoxic** drugs are used mainly in the treatment of cancer (and thus form a major group of the ANTICANCER drugs). They have the essential property of preventing normal cell replication, and so inhibiting the growth of tumours or of excess cells in body fluids. There are several mechanisms by which they do this. However, in every case they inevitably also affect the growth of normal healthy cells and cause toxic side-effects, generally in the form of nausea and vomiting, with hair loss. Most used cytotoxic drugs are the alkylating agents, which work by interfering with the action of DNA in cell replication; they include CYCLOPHOSPHAMIDE, CHLORAMBUCIL, BUSULPHAN, LOMUSTINE, MELPHALAN, THIOTEPA and CISPLATIN. The VINCA ALKALOIDS damage part of the metabolic features of new-forming cells; they too are effective cytotoxic drugs but tend to have severely limiting neural side-effects. Some cytotoxic drugs have additional antibiotic properties: such drugs include DOXORUBICIN, ACTINOMYCIN D, EPIRUBICIN and BLEOMYCIN. Not all cytotoxic drugs are used in cancer treatment; some, for example AZATHIOPRINE, are used as immunosuppressants to limit tissue rejection during and following transplant surgery.

**dacarbazine** is a CYTOTOXIC drug that is used comparatively rarely because of its high toxicity. But in combination with other ANTICANCER drugs it may be used to treat the skin (mole) cancer melanoma, some soft-tissue sarcomas, and the lymphatic cancer Hodgkin's disease. Administration is by injection.

▲ side-effects: there may be severe nausea and vomiting, progressive deafness, and symptoms of kidney dysfunction. The blood-forming capacity of the bone-marrow is generally suppressed (and treatment should not be repeated within 4 weeks). Skin disorders are not uncommon.

✿ warning: an anti-emetic should be administered simultaneously to lessen the risk of nausea and vomiting. Monitoring of kidney function and the sense of hearing is essential. Care must be taken in handling the drug: it is a skin irritant.
*Related article:* DTIC-Dome.

**Dactinomycin** is an alternative form of the name of actinomycin D, a drug that is both ANTIBIOTIC and CYTOTOXIC.
*see* ACTINOMYCIN D.

**Daktacort** (*Janssen*) is a proprietary cream for topical application, available only on prescription, that contains the CORTICOSTEROID hydrocortisone and the ANTIFUNGAL agent miconazole nitrate in a water-miscible base. It is used to treat skin inflammation in which fungal infection is also present.
▲/✿ side-effects/warning: *see* MICONAZOLE.

**Daktarin** (*Janssen*) is a proprietary ANTIFUNGAL drug, available only on prescription, used to treat both systemic and skin-surface fungal infections.

Produced in the form of tablets and as a solution for infusion (after dilution), Daktarin is a preparation of the imidazole antifungal MICONAZOLE. Three other versions are available without prescription, in the form of a sugar-free gel for oral treatment, and a water-miscible cream and a spray powder in an aerosol for topical application.
▲/✿ side-effects/warning: *see* MICONAZOLE.

**Dalacin** (*Upjohn*) is a proprietary ANTIBIOTIC, available only on prescription, used to treat staphylococcal infections of bones and joints, and peritonitis (inflammation of the peritoneal lining of the abdominal cavity). Produced in the form of capsules (in two strengths), as a paediatric suspension for dilution (the potency of the suspension once diluted is retained for 14 days), and in ampoules for injection, (Dalacin C). It is also available as a topical lotion used to treat acne (DALACIN T). Dalacin is a preparation of clindamycin. Side-effects are potentially severe.
▲/✿ side-effects/warning: *see* CLINDAMYCIN.

**Dalacin T** (*Upjohn*) is a proprietary ANTIBIOTIC, available only on prescription, used to treat acne. Produced in the form of a solution for topical application, it is a preparation of clindamycin as phosphate in an alcoholic basis.
▲/✿ side-effects/warning: *see* CLINDAMYCIN.

**Dalivit** (*Paines & Byrne*) is a proprietary, non-prescription MULTIVITAMIN compound, which is not available from the National Health Service. Produced in the form of tablets, and as oral drops, Dalivit contains RETINOL (vitamin A), many forms of vitamin B (THIAMINE, RIBOFLAVINE, PYRIDOXINE, NICOTINAMIDE and

PANTOTHENIC ACID), ASCORBIC ACID (vitamin C), and CALCIFEROL (vitamin D).

**Dalmane** (*Roche*) is a proprietary HYPNOTIC, available on prescription only to private patients, used to treat insomnia in cases where some degree of daytime sedation is acceptable. Produced in the form of capsules (in two strengths), Dalmane is a preparation of the long-acting BENZODIAZEPINE flurazepam.
▲/● side-effects/warning: *see* FLURAZEPAM.

**danazol** is a derivative of the PROGESTOGEN ethisterone that inhibits the release of gonadotrophins from the pituitary gland, thus in turn preventing the release of sex HORMONES. It is used to treat conditions such as precocious puberty, endometriosis (the presence of areas of womb-lining – endometrium – outside the womb, within the abdominal cavity), gynaecomastia (the development of feminine breasts on a male), and menorrhagia (excessive menstrual flow). Administration is oral in the form of capsules.
▲ side-effects: there may be nausea, backache and muscle spasm, dizziness and flushing, a rash, and hair loss; in women patients there may be a mild form of masculinization (possibly including a deepening of the voice, and acne).
● warning: danazol should not be administered to patients who are pregnant; it should be administered with caution to those with impaired heart, liver or kidney function, diabetes, epilepsy or migraine, or who are lactating. Non-hormonal contraceptive methods should be used where applicable.
*Related article:* DANOL.

**Daneral SA** (*Hoechst*) is a proprietary, non-prescription ANTIHISTAMINE used to treat the symptoms of allergy, such as hay fever or urticaria. Produced in the form of sustained-release tablets, Daneral SA is a preparation of pheniramine maleate.
▲/● side-effects/warning: *see* PHENIRAMINE MALEATE.

**Danol** (*Winthrop*) is a proprietary preparation of the HORMONAL drug danazol, a derivative of the PROGESTOGEN ethisterone that inhibits the release of gonadotrophins from the pituitary gland, thus in turn preventing the release of sex hormones. Available only on prescription, it is used to treat conditions such as precocious puberty, endometriosis (the presence of areas of womb-lining – endometrium – outside the womb, within the abdominal cavity), gynaecomastia (the development of feminine breasts on a male), and menorrhagia (excessive menstrual flow). It is produced in the form of capsules (in two strengths, the weaker under the name Danol-).
▲/● side-effects/warning: *see* DANAZOL.

**danthron** is a powerful stimulant LAXATIVE which works by increasing the muscular activity of the intestinal walls. Used for constipation in geriatric practice, particularly analgesic-induced constipation in the terminally ill (in all ages), and in cardiac failure and coronary thrombosis to avoid strain.
▲ side-effects: the urine may be coloured red. Prolonged use of such a stimulant may cause severe intestinal problems in terms of motility and absorption.
● warning: danthron should not be taken by any patient who is breast-feeding (because it may

be excreted in breast milk).
Prolonged contact with the
skin may cause irritation and
excoriation.
*Related articles:* CODALEX; CO-
DANTHRUSATE; NORMAX.

**Dantrium** (*Norwich Eaton*) is a
proprietary SKELETAL MUSCLE
RELAXANT, available only on
prescription, used to treat long-
term rigidity of muscles in
disorders such as multiple
sclerosis, cerebral palsy and
similar conditions resulting from
stroke or spinal injury. It is also
used in emergencies (in
combination with MANNITOL) to
treat anaesthetized patients who
enter the potentially lethal state
of hyperthermia. Produced in the
form of capsules (in two
strengths), and as a powder for
reconstitution as a medium for
intravenous injection (under the
name Dantrium Intravenous),
Dantrium represents a
preparation of dantrolene sodium.
▲/● side-effects/warning: *see*
DANTROLENE SODIUM.

**dantrolene sodium** is a SKELETAL
MUSCLE RELAXANT used to treat
long-term rigidity of muscles in
disorders such as multiple
sclerosis, cerebral palsy and
similar conditions resulting from
stroke or spinal injury. It is also
used in emergencies (in
combination with the diuretic
MANNITOL) to treat anaesthetized
patients who enter the potentially
lethal state of hyperthermia.
Administration is oral in the
form of capsules, or by
injection.
▲ side-effects: concentration and
speed of reaction are initially
affected. There may be
drowsiness, dizziness,
weakness and general malaise;
some patients experience
diarrhoea. Rarely there is a
rash, urinary difficulty, or
muscle pain.

● warning: dantrolene sodium
should not be administered to
children; it should be
administered with caution to
patients who suffer from
impaired heart, liver or lung
function. Full therapeutic
effect of the drug administered
orally may take up to 6 weeks
to develop – if no effect is
manifest then, treatment
should be discontinued.
Leakage into the tissues from
the site of injection may cause
severe symptoms.
*Related article:* DANTRIUM.

**Daonil** is a proprietary
preparation of the
SULPHONYLUREA glibenclamide,
available only on prescription,
used to treat adult-onset diabetes
mellitus. It works by augmenting
what remains of insulin
production in the pancreas, and is
produced in the form of tablets (at
twice the strength of SEMI-DAONIL
tablets).
▲/● side-effects/warning: *see*
GLIBENCLAMIDE.

**dapsone** is an ANTIBIOTIC
compound used specifically to
treat leprosy (in both lepromatous
and tuberculoid forms); it is also
sometimes used to treat severe
forms of dermatitis or, in
combination with the enzyme-
inhibitor pyrimethamine (under
the trade name Maloprim), to
prevent tropical travellers from
contracting malaria.
Administration is oral in the form
of tablets, or by injection.
▲ side-effects: side-effects are
rare at low doses (as for
leprosy), but with higher
dosage there may be nausea,
vomiting and headache,
insomnia and increased heart
rate, severe weight loss,
anaemia, hepatitis, neuropathy
or agranulocytosis .
● warning: dapsone should be
administered with caution to
patients with anaemia,

porphyria, glucose-6-phosphate dehydrogenase deficiency, heart or lung disease or who are pregnant or lactating.
*Related article:* MALOPRIM.

**Daranide** (*Merck, Sharp & Dohme*) is a proprietary preparation of the drug dichlorphenamide, available only on prescription, used to treat glaucoma. It is a weak DIURETIC and works by reducing the fluid within the aqueous humour in the eyeball, but there are some potentially troublesome side-effects. Daranide is produced in the form of tablets.
▲/✿ side-effects/warning: *see* DICHLORPHENAMIDE.

**Daraprim** (*Wellcome*) is a proprietary, non-prescription ANTIMALARIAL drug used in combination with other antimalarials to prevent tropical travellers from contracting malaria. It is not recommended as the sole agent of prevention. It works by interfering with the cellular composition of the parasitic organism that causes malaria, but treatment must be continued for 4 weeks after leaving the area of exposure. A preparation of pyrimethamine, Daraprim is not recommended for children aged under 5 years.
▲/✿ side-effects/warning: *see* PYRIMETHAMINE.

**Davenol** (*Wyeth*) is a proprietary, non-prescription cough linctus that is not available from the National Health Service. Orange-flavoured, it contains the BRONCHODILATOR ephedrine hydrochloride, the OPIATE cough suppressant pholcodine, and the antihistamine carbinoxamine maleate, and is produced as a syrup for dilution (the potency of the dilute linctus is retained for 15 days).

▲/✿ side-effects/warning: *see* EPHEDRINE HYDROCHLORIDE; PHOLCODINE.

**Day Nurse** (*Beecham Health Care*) is a proprietary, non-prescription cold relief preparation produced in the form of tablets and as a syrup. It contains paracetamol, the DECONGESTANT phenyl-propanolamine and the ANTITUSSIVE dextromethorphan.
▲/✿ side-effects/warning: *see* PARACETAMOL; PHENYLPROPANOLAMINE; DEXTROMETHORPHAN.

**DDAVP** (*Ferring*) is a proprietary preparation of the antidiuretic hormone vasopressin in the form of its analogue DESMOPRESSIN. Available only on prescription, it is administered primarily to diagnose or to treat pituitary-originated diabetes insipidus, although it can be used for some other diagnostic tests and even (in specialist centres) to boost blood concentration of blood-clotting factors in haemophiliac patients. It is produced in ampoules for injection, and in the form of nose-drops.
▲/✿ side-effects/warning: *see* VASOPRESSIN.

**Deanase D.C.** (*Consolidated*) is a proprietary, non-prescription preparation of the enzyme deoxyribonuclease, used to treat inflammation (particularly of veins, or in and around the eye), bruising or swelling. Thought to work by promoting the removal of coagulated blood, dead tissue and exudate, Deanase is also used to treat bronchitis. It is produced in the form of tablets, and also as Deanase (consolidated) powder for reconstitution as a medium for injection, solution, instillation or inhalation. Deanase is not recommended for children.

▲ side-effects: *see*
DEOXYRIBONUCLEASE.

**Debrisan** (*Pharmacia*) is a
proprietary DEXTRAN-derivative,
available only on prescription,
used in the form of powder or
paste (applied topically in a
dressing) as an absorbent for open
wounds and surface ulcers that
are seeping or suppurating.

**debrisoquine** is an
ANTIHYPERTENSIVE drug that
works by inhibiting the release in
the body of the neurotransmitter
NORADRENALINE. In combination
with a DIURETIC (such as a
thiazide) or a BETA-BLOCKER,
debrisoquine is used to treat
moderate to severe high blood
pressure (hypertension),
especially when other forms of
treatment have failed.
Administration is oral in the form
of tablets.
▲ side-effects: there may be low
blood pressure (hypotension),
nasal congestion and fluid
retention leading to weight
gain, and failure of ejaculation
in men.
● warning: debrisoquine should
not be administered to patients
with disease of the adrenal
glands or with kidney failure;
it should be administered with
caution to those who are
pregnant. Resultant low blood
pressure, especially on rising
from sitting or lying down, may
cause falls in the elderly.
*Related article:* DECLINAX.

**Decadron** (*Merck, Sharp &
Dohme*) is a proprietary
CORTICOSTEROID preparation,
available only on prescription,
used to treat inflammation
especially in rheumatic or
allergic conditions. Produced in
the form of tablets, it comprises
the glucocorticoid steroid
dexamethasone.
▲/● side-effects/warning: *see*
DEXAMETHASONE.

**Decadron Injection** (*Merck,
Sharp & Dohme*) is a proprietary
CORTICOSTEROID preparation
(produced in vials), available only
on prescription, used primarily in
emergencies to replace steroid
loss; but the injection –
comprising dexamethasone
sodium phosphate – can also be
used to treat inflammation in the
joints or in soft tissues.
▲/● side-effects/warning: *see*
DEXAMETHASONE.

**Decadron Shock-pak** (*Merck,
Sharp & Dohme*) is a proprietary
CORTICOSTEROID preparation of
dexamethasone sodium phosphate
(produced in greater
concentration and larger vials
than Decadron Injection),
available only on prescription,
used in emergencies to replace
steroid loss and thus to assist in
the treatment of shock.
Administered by intravenous
injection, it is not recommended
for children.
▲/● side-effects/warning: *see*
DEXAMETHASONE.

**Deca-Durabolin** (*Organon*) is a
proprietary form of the anabolic
steroid nandrolone, available
only on prescription, used to
assist the metabolic synthesis of
protein in – that is, build up – the
body following major surgery or
long-term debilitating disease, or
to treat osteoporosis ('brittle
bones'). Sometimes administered
also to treat sex-hormone-linked
cancers, it is additionally used in
the treatment of certain forms of
anaemia, although how it works
in this respect – and even whether
it works – remains the subject of
some debate: variations in patient
response are wide. It is produced
in ampoules or syringes for
intramuscular injection.
▲/● side-effects/warning: *see*
NANDROLONE.

**Deca-Durabolin 100** (*Organon*) is
a form of Deca-Durabolin

containing NANDROLONE
decanoate, used to treat certain
forms of anaemia.
see DECA-DURABOLIN.

**Declinax** (*Roche*) is a proprietary
ANTIHYPERTENSIVE drug,
available only on prescription,
used to treat moderate to severe
high blood pressure
(hypertension), especially when
other forms of treatment have
failed. Administered in
combination with a DIURETIC or a
BETA-BLOCKER, Declinax works by
inhibiting the release in the body
of the neurotransmitter
NORADRENALINE. It represents a
preparation of debrisoquine, is
produced in the form of tablets,
and is not recommended for
children.
▲/✆ side-effects/warning: see
    DEBRISOQUINE.

*****decongestants** are drugs
administered to relieve or reduce
nasal congestion. Generally
applied in the form of nose-drops
or as a nasal spray – although
some are administered orally –
most decongestants are
SYMPATHOMIMETIC drugs, which
work by constricting the blood
vessels within the mucous
membranes of the nasal cavity, so
reducing the membranes'
thickness and creating more room
for drainage and ventilation.
Nasal congestion caused by
allergy, as in hay fever, however,
is usually dealt with by using
ANTIHISTAMINES, which inhibit
the allergic response, or
CORTICOSTEROIDS, which inhibit
the allergic response and reduce
any inflammation.

**Decortisyl** (*Roussel*) is a
proprietary CORTICOSTEROID
preparation, available only on
prescription, used to treat
inflammation especially in
rheumatic or allergic conditions.
Produced in the form of tablets, it

contains the glucocorticoid
steroid prednisone. It is not
recommended for children aged
under 12 months.
▲/✆ side-effects/warning: see
    PREDNISONE.

**dehydrocholic acid** is a drug that
is administered after surgery on
or near the bile ducts. It
stimulates the production of thin,
watery bile that then flushes the
common bile duct, washing away
any small calculi (stones) that
may remain. It may also be used
to clear the gall bladder in
preparation for X-ray or
endoscope examination.
Administration is oral in the form
of tablets.
✆ warning: dehydrocholic acid
    should not be administered to
    patients with completely
    blocked bile ducts, chronic
    liver disease or hepatitis.

**Delfen** (*Ortho-Cilag*) is a
proprietary, non-prescription
SPERMICIDAL preparation, for use
only in combination with barrier
methods of contraception (such as
a condom or diaphragm).
Produced in the form of a foam in
an aerosol, Delfen is a
preparation of the alcohol ester
nonoxinol.

**Delial Factor 10** (*Bayer*) is a
proprietary, non-prescription
preparation containing
constituents that are able to help
protect the skin from ultraviolet
radiation. Patients whose skin
condition is such as to require
this sort of protection, or who are
undergoing therapies that might
require it, may be prescribed
Delial Factor 10 at the discretion
of their doctors. It is produced in
the form of a cream and a lotion
(milk) for topical application.

**Delimon** (*Consolidated*) is a
proprietary, compound non-
narcotic ANALGESIC, available on

prescription only to private patients. Used for the relief of pain anywhere in the body, Delimon's major active constituent is paracetamol.

▲/● side-effects/warning: see PARACETAMOL.

**Deltacortril** (*Pfizer*) is a proprietary CORTICOSTEROID preparation, available only on prescription, used to treat allergic conditions, inflammation or collagen disorders requiring systemic treatment with corticosteroids. Produced in the form of tablets in two strengths, (also under the name Deltacortril Enteric), it contains the glucocorticoid steroid prednisolone.

▲/● side-effects/warning: see PREDNISOLONE.

**Deltalone** (*DDSA Pharmaceuticals*) is a proprietary CORTICOSTEROID preparation, available only on prescription, used to treat inflammation especially in rheumatic and allergic conditions. Produced in the form of tablets (in two strengths), it contains the glucocorticoid steroid prednisolone.

▲/● side-effects/warning: see PREDNISOLONE.

**Delta-Phoricol** (*Wallace*) is a proprietary CORTICOSTEROID preparation, available only on prescription, used to treat inflammation especially in rheumatic and allergic conditions. Produced in the form of tablets, it contains the glucocorticoid steroid prednisolone.

▲/● side-effects/warning: see PREDNISOLONE.

**Deltastab** (*Boots*) is a proprietary CORTICOSTEROID preparation, available only on prescription, used to treat inflammation

especially in allergic and rheumatic conditions, particularly those affecting the joints, and collagen disorders. It may also be used for systemic corticosteroid therapy. Produced in the form of tablets (in two strengths), and in vials for injection (as an aqueous solution), it contains the glucocorticoid steroid prednisolone.

▲/● side-effects/warning: see PREDNISOLONE.

**demecarium bromide** is a drug used to treat glaucoma. Applied (in solution) in the form of eye-drops, it works by reducing the formation of aqueous humour within the eyeball.

▲ side-effects: some patients experience a burning sensation in eyes treated for a short time following administration (which may in turn be treated with analgesics). Possible sensitivity reactions include nausea and sweating.

● warning: demecarium bromide should not be administered to patients with peptic ulcers, asthma, or a slow heart rate.

**demeclocycline hydrochloride** is a broad-spectrum ANTIBIOTIC, one of the TETRACYCLINES, used to treat infections of many kinds. Administration is oral in the form of tablets and capsules.

▲ side-effects: there may be nausea and vomiting, with diarrhoea. Some patients experience a sensitivity to light. Rarely, there are allergic reactions.

● warning: demeclocycline hydrochloride should not be administered to patients with kidney failure, who are pregnant, or who are aged under 12 years. It should be administered with caution to those who are lactating, or with impaired liver function.

*Related articles:* DETECLO; LEDERMYCIN; TETRACYCLINE.

**Demser** *(Merck, Sharp & Dohme)* is a proprietary ANTIHYPERTENSIVE drug, available only on prescription, used to treat symptoms of a disorder of the adrenal glands (phaeochromocytoma) and certain acute forms of high blood pressure (hypertension). Produced in the form of capsules, and usually administered only in hospitals and clinics, Demser is a preparation of the unusual drug metirosine.
▲/ ● side-effects/warning: *see* METIROSINE.

**De-Nol** *(Brocades)* is a proprietary, non-prescription preparation of tripotassium dicitratobismuthate (an inert bismuth compound), which promotes the healing of peptic ulcers in the stomach and duodenum. It is thought to work by forming a protective coating over the ulcer under which the ulcer is then able to heal. It is produced in the form of an elixir with what has been described as a pungent ammoniacal odour.
● warning: because the elixir may need time to achieve a coating over an ulcer, it is advised that food and drink should be avoided for two hours before and for half an hour after administration.

**De-Noltab** *(Brocades)* is a proprietary, non-prescription preparation of tripotassium dicitratobismuthate (an inert bismuth compound), which promotes the healing of peptic ulcers in the stomach and duodenum. It is thought to work by forming a protective coating over the ulcer under which the ulcer is then able to heal. It is produced in the form of tablets (which are said to be more palatable than the liquid form, DE-NOL).

● warning: because the tablets may need time to achieve a coating over an ulcer, it is advised that food and drink should be avoided for two hours before and for half an hour after administration.

**deoxycortone pivalate** is a CORTICOSTEROID administered therapeutically to make up for a deficiency of mineralocorticoids (the kind of corticosteroids that regulate salt and water, sodium and potassium levels in the body) resulting from a disorder of the adrenal glands.
▲ side-effects: there may be sodium and water retention leading to weight gain, high blood pressure (hypertension) and muscle weakness. Some patients experience psychological symptoms, such as euphoria or mild confusion.
● warning: deoxycortone pivalate administered to children may restrict growth; administered to pregnant women it may prevent adrenal development in the fetus. As with all corticosteroids, administration may also mask the effects of infection, which may then spread undiagnosed and unchecked. Prolonged usage may cause severe physical symptoms.

**deoxyribonuclease** is an enzyme used therapeutically as an ANTIINFLAMMATORY (particularly in the veins, or in and around the eye), bruising and swelling. It is thought to work by promoting the removal of coagulated blood, dead tissue and exudate, and is administered orally in the form of tablets, topically in the form of an instillation or by inhalation from an aerosol, or by injection.
▲ side-effects: local injection may cause skin irritation; inhalation may give rise to irritation in the throat.

Prolonged use may evoke sensitivity reactions.
*Related article:* DEANASE.

**Depixol** (*Lundbeck*) is a proprietary ANTIPSYCHOTIC drug, available only on prescription, used to tranquillize patients suffering from psychosis (including schizophrenia), especially patients with forms of psychosis that render them apathetic and withdrawn. It may also be used in the short term to treat severe anxiety. Produced in the form of tablets, or in ampoules for injection (in two strengths, the stronger under the name Depixol Conc.), Depixol is a preparation of flupenthixol.
▲/✿ side-effects/warning: *see* FLUPENTHIXOL.

**Depo-Medrone** (*Upjohn*) is a proprietary CORTICOSTEROID preparation, available only on prescription, used to treat inflammation and relieve allergic disorders (such as rheumatoid arthritis, osteoarthrosis, hay fever and asthma), and sometimes used additionally to treat shock. Produced in vials and pre-prepared syringes for intramuscular depot injection, Depo-Medrone is a preparation of the steroid methylprednisolone acetate (in aqueous solution).
▲/✿ side-effects/warning: *see* METHYLPREDNISOLONE.

**Depo-Medrone with Lidocaine** (*Upjohn*) is a proprietary CORTICOSTEROID preparation, available only on prescription, used to treat inflammation in the joints (as in rheumatic disease). Produced in vials for intra-articular injection, Depo-Medrone with Lidocaine is a preparation of the steroid methylprednisolone acetate (in aqueous solution) containing the local ANAESTHETIC lignocaine hydrochloride.

▲/✿ side-effects/warning: *see* LIGNOCAINE; METHYLPREDNISOLONE.

**Deponit** (*Schwarz*) is a proprietary, non-prescription, self-adhesive skin-coloured dressing (patch) containing the VASODILATOR glyceryl trinitrate, which, when placed on the chest wall, is absorbed through the skin and helps to give lasting relief from attacks of angina pectoris (heart pain). Patches are replaced daily, and each should be sited in a surface location different from the preceding patch. Deponit is not recommended for children.
▲/✿ side-effects/warning: *see* GLYCERYL TRINITRATE.

**Depo-provera** (*Upjohn*) is a proprietary HORMONE preparation of the synthetic PROGESTOGEN medroxyprogesterone acetate in aqueous suspension, available only on prescription. It has three major uses: as a long-lasting contraceptive preparation, administered as an intramuscular injection every 3 months; as a relatively non-masculinizing hormonal supplement in women whose progestogen level requires boosting, such as at the menopause, or to treat recurrent miscarriage; and (in higher doses) to treat sex-hormone-linked cancer (such as cancer of the breast or of the womb-lining). It is produced in vials (in two strengths).
▲/✿ side-effects/warning: *see* MEDROXYPROGESTERONE.

**Depostat** (*Schering*) is a proprietary preparation of the synthetic HORMONE PROGESTOGEN gestronol hexanoate, available only on prescription, used in women to treat sex-hormone-linked cancers (such as cancer of the breast or of the womb-lining), or in men to treat benign enlargement of the prostate gland or malignant enlargement of the kidneys. It is produced in ampoules for intramuscular injection.

▲/✿ side-effects/warning: see GESTRONOL HEXANOATE.

**Dequacaine** (*Farley*) is the name of a proprietary non-prescription lozenge containing the local ANAESTHETIC benzocaine together with the ANTIFUNGAL agent DEQUALINIUM CHLORIDE, to be sucked slowly until it dissolves, so affording relief from the pain of mouth ulcers or other oral lesions.

✿ warning: see BENZOCAINE.

**Dequadin** (*Farley*) is the name of a proprietary, non-prescription lozenge containing the mild ANTIFUNGAL agent dequalinium chloride, to be sucked slowly until it dissolves, so treating oral infections.

**dequalinium chloride** is a mild ANTIFUNGAL agent that also has some antibacterial properties. It is used primarily to treat fungal infections of the mouth and throat (such as thrush). Administration is oral in the form of lozenges, or topical in the form of a paint.
*Related article:* DEQUADIN.

**Derbac-C** (*International Labs*) is a proprietary, non-prescription drug used to treat infestations of the scalp and pubic hair by lice (pediculosis). Produced in the form of a shampoo, Derbac-C (also called Derbac Shampoo) is a preparation of the pediculicide carbaryl.

▲/✿ side-effects/warning: see CARBARYL.

**Derbac-M** (*International Labs*) is a proprietary, non-prescription drug used to treat infestations of the scalp and pubic hair by lice (pediculosis), or of the skin by the itch-mite (scabies). Produced in the form of a lotion, Derbac-M is a preparation of the insecticide malathion.

✿ warning: see MALATHION.

**Derbac Shampoo** is another name for Derbac-C.
*see* DERBAC-C.

**Dermacolor** (*Fox*) is the name of a proprietary, non-prescription camouflage cream, in any of 30 shades, designed for use in masking scars and other skin disfigurements; there is an additional fixing powder (in 5 shades). It may be obtained on prescription if the skin disfigurement is the result of surgery or is giving rise to emotional disturbance.

**Dermalex** (*Labaz*) is a proprietary, non-prescription skin lotion and emollient (soother and softener), used to treat nappy rash and to prevent bedsores. Its major active constituent is the antiseptic hexachlorophane. It is not recommended for children aged under 2 years.

▲/✿ side-effects/warning: see HEXACHLOROPHANE.

**Dermovate** (*Glaxo*) is an extremely powerful CORTICOSTEROID preparation for topical application, available only on prescription, used (in the short term only) to treat severe exacerbations in serious inflammatory skin disorders such as discoid lupus erythematosus. Produced in the form of a water-miscible cream for dilution (the potency of the cream once dilute is retained for 14 days), as an ointment in an anhydrous base for dilution with liquid paraffin (the potency of the ointment once dilute is retained for 14 days), and as a scalp application in an alcohol base, Dermovate is in all forms a preparation of the steroid clobetasol propionate.

▲ / ✿ side-effects/warning: *see*
CLOBETASOL PROPIONATE.

**Dermovate-NN** (*Glaxo*) is a
combined ANTIBIOTIC,
ANTIFUNGAL and CORTICOSTEROID
preparation for topical
application, available only on
prescription, used (in the short-
term only) to treat severe
exacerbations in serious,
inflammatory skin disorders such
as discoid lupus erythematosus.
Produced in the form of a cream,
and as an ointment in an
anhydrous base for dilution with
white soft paraffin (the potency of
the ointment once diluted is
retained for 14 days), Dermovate-
NN is in both forms a preparation
of the steroid clobetasol
propionate with the broad-
spectrum antibiotic neomycin
sulphate and the antifungal agent
nystatin.

▲ / ✿ side-effects/warning: *see*
NEOMYCIN; NYSTATIN.

**\*desensitizing vaccines** are
preparations of particular
allergens (substances to which a
patient has an allergic reaction).
They are administered to reduce
the degree of allergic reaction the
patient suffers when exposed to
the allergen. For example,
preparations of grass pollens are
administered for the treatment of
hay fever. The mechanism by
which they work is unclear.
   ✿ warning: administration
   should be under close medical
   supervision.

**Deseril** (*Sandoz*) is a proprietary
preparation of the potentially
dangerous drug methysergide,
available only on prescription
(and generally only in hospitals
under strict medical supervision).
It is used primarily to prevent
severe recurrent migraine and
similar headaches in patients for
whom other forms of treatment
have failed. But the drug may also

be used to treat patients who
suffer from tumours of the
intestinal glands that have
metastasized to the liver: the liver
then produces excess serotonin in
the bloodstream – and it is the
symptoms of that excess that
methysergide treats. Deseril is
produced in the form of tablets.

▲ / ✿ side-effects/warning: *see*
METHYSERGIDE.

**Desferal** (*Ciba*) is a proprietary
form of the CHELATING AGENT
desferrioxamine mesylate,
available only on prescription,
used to treat iron poisoning (by
ingestion or through anaemia)
and the symptoms associated with
it (vomiting of blood, diarrhoea,
bleeding from the anus and low
blood pressure, then if untreated,
liver, pancreas and endocrine
gland damage, a bronze
coloration of the skin, and a form
of diabetes). It is produced as a
powder for reconstitution as a
medium for injection.

▲ / ✿ side-effects/warning: *see*
DESFERRIOXAMINE
MESYLATE.

**desferrioxamine mesylate** is a
CHELATING AGENT used to treat
iron poisoning (by ingestion or
through anaemia) and the
symptoms associated with it
(vomiting of blood, diarrhoea,
bleeding from the anus and low
blood pressure, then if untreated,
liver, pancreas and endocrine
gland damage, a bronze
coloration of the skin, and a form
of diabetes). Administration is
oral (in water) following initial
emptying of the stomach either by
induction of vomiting or by
stomach pump; absorbed iron can
also be chelated by an
intramuscular injection of
desferrioxamine mesylate.
   ▲ side-effects: there may be pain
   at the site of injection.
   ✿ warning: over-rapid injection
   of the drug can lead to
   sensitivity reactions and low

D

blood pressure (hypotension). *Related article:* DESFERAL.

**desipramine hydrochloride** is an ANTIDEPRESSANT drug of a type that has fewer sedative properties than many others. Used to treat depressive illness, it is thus suited more to the treatment of withdrawn and apathetic patients than to those who are agitated and restless. Administration is oral in the form of tablets.

▲ side-effects: dry mouth, drowsiness, blurred vision, constipation and urinary retention are all fairly common; there may also be heartbeat irregularities accompanying low blood pressure (hypotension). Concentration and speed of reaction are affected. Elderly patients may enter a state of confusion; younger patients may experience behavioural disturbances. Not recommended for children. There may be alteration in blood sugar levels, and weight gain.

❀ warning: desipramine hydrochloride should not be administered to patients with heart disease or liver failure; it should be administered with extreme caution to those with epilepsy, psychoses or glaucoma, or who are pregnant. Treatment may take up to four weeks to achieve full effect; premature withdrawal of treatment thereafter may cause the return of symptoms. *Related article:* PERTOFRAN.

**desmopressin** is one of two major forms of the antidiuretic hormone vasopressin, which reduces urine production. It is used primarily to diagnose or to treat pituitary-originated diabetes insipidus, although it can be used for some other diagnostic tests and even (in specialist centres) to boost blood concentration of blood-clotting factors in haemophiliac patients. Administration is topical in the form of nose-drops, or by injection. Dosage is adjusted to individual patient response (with special care being taken in patients with hypertension or who are pregnant).

▲ / ❀ side-effects/warning: see VASOPRESSIN.

**desogestrel** is a PROGESTERONE, used as a constituent of the combined ORAL CONTRACEPTIVES that combine an OESTROGEN with a progesterone.

▲ / ❀ warning/side-effects: see PROGESTERONE. *Related articles:* MERCILON; MINULET.

**desonide** is a powerful CORTICOSTEROID, used in topical application on severe skin inflammations (such as eczema), especially in cases where less powerful steroid treatments have failed. Administration is in the form of a dilute aqueous cream or a dilute paraffin-based ointment.

▲ side-effects: topical application may result in the thinning of skin, with possible whitening, and an increased local growth of hair. Some young patients experience the outbreak of a kind of inflammatory dermatitis on the face or at the site of application.

❀ warning: as with all corticosteroids, desonide treats the symptoms of inflammation but has no effect on any underlying infection; undetected infection may thus become worse even as its effects are masked by the steroid. Desonide should not in any case be administered to patients who suffer from untreated skin lesions; use on the face should also be avoided;

caution is advised in treatment for children.
*Related article:* TRIDESILON.

**desoxymethasone** is a CORTICOSTEROID hormone. It is related to HYDROCORTISONE and may be administered, if necessary, in combination with anti-bacterials, to treat inflammatory conditions of the skin and in allergic skin disorders. Administration is normally to the skin in the form of creams and lotions.

▲/● side-effects/warning: treatment with the drug may suppress symptoms of an infection until the infection is far advanced (which may in some cases present its own dangers); treatment should therefore be made as aseptic as possible, and infected areas must not be treated. Withdrawal of treatment must be gradual. Application to the skin is unlikely to give sufficient absorption for the more serious systemic side-effects, but there may be local changes to the area treated such as acne, hair growth, and thinning of the skin.
*Related article:* STIEDEX.

**Destolit** (*Merrell*) is a proprietary preparation of the acidic drug ursodeoxycholic acid, used to dissolve relatively small, light, cholesterol gallstones. X-ray monitoring of treatment is required to supervise progress. The course may last for up to two years, and treatment must be continued for at least three months after stones have been dissolved. Destolit is produced in the form of tablets.

▲/● side-effects/warning: *see* URSODEOXYCHOLIC ACID.

**Deteclo** (*Lederle*) is a proprietary compound ANTIBIOTIC preparation, available only on prescription, used to treat many kinds of infection, but especially those of the respiratory tract, the ear, nose and throat, the gastrointestinal tract and the genito-urinary tract, and the soft tissues. Deteclo consists of a combination of TETRACYCLINES – chlortetracycline hydrochloride, tetracycline hydrochloride and demeclocycline hydrochloride – and is produced in the form of tablets. It should not be used for children under the age of 12 years, and should not be given to pregnant women or patients with kidney disease.

▲/● side-effects/warning: *see* CHLORTETRACYCLINE; DEMECLOCYCLINE HYDROCHLORIDE; TETRACYCLINE.

**dexamethasone** is a synthesized CORTICOSTEROID used, as are most corticosteroids, in the treatment of non-infective inflammation. Accordingly, it is used to treat many conditions, ranging from the suppression of allergic disorders and shock (in the form of dexamethasone or dexamethasone sodium phosphate), and the relief of pain in inflamed joints and tissues (as dexamethasone sodium phosphate), to the soothing of eye inflammations (as dexamethasone) or nasal congestion (as dexamethasone isonicotinate). Administration is in the form of tablets, eye-drops and ointment, and by injection or infusion.

▲ side-effects: systemic treatment of susceptible patients may engender a euphoria – or a state of confusion or depression. Rarely, there is peptic ulceration. Treatment of eye inflammations may in susceptible patients lead to a form of glaucoma (and should therefore be carried out under careful supervision).

● warning: dexamethasone
should not be administered to
patients with psoriasis; it
should be administered with
caution to the elderly (in whom
overdosage can cause
osteoporosis, 'brittle bones'). In
children, administration of
dexamethasone may lead to
stunting of growth. As with all
corticosteroids, dexamethasone
treats only inflammatory
symptoms; an undetected and
potentially serious infection
may have its effects masked by
the drug until it is well
established.
*Related articles:* DECADRON;
DECADRON SHOCK-PAK; DEXA-
RHINASPRAY; MAXIDEX;
MAXITROL; OPTOMIZE;
ORADEXON; SOFRADEX.

**dexamphetamine sulphate** is an
amphetamine, a powerful
STIMULANT drug, used primarily to
treat narcolepsy (a condition
marked by irresistible attacks of
sleep during the daytime),
although it is sometimes also used
under specialist supervision to
treat children who are medically
hyperactive. Tolerance and
dependence (addiction) are major
hazards. Administration is oral in
the form of tablets and sustained-
release capsules.
▲ side-effects: tolerance and
dependence (addiction) occur
readily. There may also be
agitation, insomnia, headache
and dizziness. Some patients
experience heartbeat
irregularities, dry mouth,
diarrhoea or constipation.
There may also be tremor and a
personality change. In
children, drastic weight loss
may be accompanied by
inhibition of growth. Overdoses
may result in psychoses,
convulsions, or even death.
● warning: dexamphetamine
sulphate should not be
administered to patients who

suffer from cardiovascular
disease, glaucoma, or an excess
of thyroid hormones in the
bloodstream (thyrotoxicosis); it
should be administered with
caution to those with impaired
kidney function, anorexia,
insomnia, an unstable
personality or during
pregnancy.
*Related articles:* DEXEDRINE;
DUROPHET.

**Dexa-Rhinaspray** (*Boehringer
Ingelheim*) is a proprietary nasal
inhalation, available only on
prescription, used to treat hay
fever (allergic rhinitis). Produced
in a metered-dose aerosol, it
represents a preparation of the
CORTICOSTEROID dexamethasone
isonicotinate together with the
ANTIBIOTIC neomycin sulphate and
the SYMPATHOMIMETIC
tramazoline hydrochloride. It is
not recommended for children
aged under 5 years.
▲/● side-effects/warning: *see*
DEXAMETHASONE; NEOMYCIN.

**Dexedrine** (*Smith, Kline &
French*) is a proprietary
preparation of the powerful
stimulant drug dexamphetamine
sulphate, which is on the
controlled drugs list. It is used
primarily to treat narcolepsy (a
condition marked by irresistible
attacks of sleep during the
daytime), although it is sometimes
also used under specialist
supervision to treat children who
are medically hyperactive.
Tolerance and dependence
(addiction) are major hazards.
Produced in the form of tablets, it
is not generally recommended for
children.
▲/● side-effects/warning: *see*
DEXAMPHETAMINE SULPHATE.

**dexfenfluramine
hydrochloride** is an APPETITE
SUPPRESSANT drug used for the
treatment of severe obesity. It is

the dextro-isomer of the powerful appetite suppressant drug FENFLURAMINE. Dexfenfluramine is a sedative, rather than a stimulant as with most other appetite suppressants, and may affect a patient's thought and movement, and is potentially addictive (although dependence is rare). It is available in the form of capsules.

▲ side-effects: there may be depression; drowsiness, with headache, vertigo and diarrhoea and other gastrointestinal disturbances, sleep disturbances, rashes, reduction in libido. Sometimes there is insomnia, dry mouth, fluid retention, increased frequency of urination. Treatment is only in the short term, tolerance and/or dependence may occur; dosage should be tapered off gradually to avoid withdrawal depression.

✿ warning: avoid administering to patients with a history of depressive illness, drug abuse or alcoholism, epilepsy, and personality disorders, or who are pregnant or breast-feeding. Not recommended for children.
*Related article:* ADIFAX.

**dextran** is a carbohydrate chemically consisting of glucose units, used in solution as a plasma substitute – that is, as a substitute for the straw-coloured fluid in which blood cells are normally suspended. It is most used in infusion to increase a patient's overall volume of blood following drastic haemorrhage or other forms of shock (such as burns or septicaemia). Generally, administration is on an emergency basis only, until properly tissue-matched blood can be infused. Even so, dextran in a patient's circulation may interfere with the cross-matching process and such tissue-typing should

ideally take place first. There are two major preparations of dextran: dextran 40 and dextran 70. Dextran 40 represents a 10% concentration in glucose or saline solution, and is used mostly to improve blood flow in the limbs and extremities (so treating ischaemic conditions and preventing thrombosis or embolism). Dextran 70 represents a 6% concentration in glucose or saline solution, and is used mostly as outlined initially above to expand a patient's overall blood volume. There is also a proprietary form of dextran 110 which is to all intents and purposes very much the same as dextran 70.

▲ side-effects: rarely, there are hypersensitivity reactions.

✿ warning: dextran should not be administered to patients with severe congestive heart failure or kidney failure, or who may experience blood clotting difficulties.
*Related articles:* DEXTRAVEN 110; GENTRAN; LOMODEX; MACRODEX; RHEOMACRODEX.

**Dextraven 110** (*CP Pharmaceuticals*) is a proprietary preparation of dextran 110, available only on prescription, used in infusion to boost the overall volume of a patient's blood circulation in emergency circumstances. It is produced in flasks (bottles).

▲/✿ side-effects/warning: *see* DEXTRAN.

**Dextrolyte** (*Cow & Gate*) is a proprietary, non-prescription sodium supplement, used to treat mild or moderate degrees of sodium depletion in the body (as may happen in cases of dehydration or in illnesses – particularly kidney disease – in which salt is lost in some quantity). Dextrolyte is produced in the form of a solution (for

swallowing) containing SODIUM
CHLORIDE (salt), POTASSIUM
CHLORIDE, GLUCOSE and SODIUM
LACTATE.

**dextromethorphan** is an
ANTITUSSIVE, an opiate that is
used singly or in combination
with other drugs in linctuses,
syrups or lozenges to relieve dry
or painful coughs.
▲ side-effects: constipation is a
comparatively common side-
effect.
✦ warning: dextromethorphan
should not be administered to
patients who suffer from liver
disease. Used as a linctus, it
may cause sputum retention
which may be injurious to
patients with asthma, chronic
bronchitis or bronchiectasis
(two conditions for which
linctuses are commonly
prescribed).
*Related articles:* ACTIFED
COMPOUND LINCTUS;
TANCOLIN.

**dextromoramide** is a synthesized
derivative of morphine, and like
morphine used as a narcotic
ANALGESIC to counter severe and
intractable pain, particularly in
the final stages of terminal illness.
Proprietary forms are on the
controlled drugs list because, also
like morphine, dextro-
moramide is potentially addictive.
▲ side-effects: shallow breathing,
urinary retention,
constipation, and nausea are
all common; tolerance and
dependence (addiction) occur
fairly readily. There may also
be drowsiness, and pain at the
site of injection (where there
may also be tissue damage).
✦ warning: dextromoramide
should not be administered to
patients who suffer from head
injury or intracranial pressure;
it should be administered with
caution to those with impaired
kidney or liver function,

asthma, depressed respiration,
insufficient secretion of thyroid
hormones (hypothyroidism) or
low blood pressure
(hypotension), or who are
pregnant or lactating. Dosage
should be decreased for the
elderly or debilitated.
*Related article:* PALFIUM.

**dextropropoxyphene** is a weak
ANALGESIC, which is nevertheless
similar to a narcotic, used to treat
pain anywhere in the body. It is
usually combined with other
analgesics (especially
paracetamol or aspirin) for
compound effect. Administration
of the drug alone is oral in the
form of capsules.
▲ side-effects: shallow breathing,
urinary retention,
constipation, and nausea are
all common; in high overdosage
tolerance and dependence
(addiction) occur fairly readily,
leading possibly to psychoses
and convulsions.
✦ warning: dextropropoxyphene
should not be administered to
patients who suffer from head
injury or intracranial pressure;
it should be administered with
caution to those with impaired
kidney or liver function,
asthma, depressed respiration,
insufficient secretion of thyroid
hormones (hypothyroidism) or
low blood pressure
(hypotension), or who are
pregnant or lactating. Dosage
should be decreased for the
elderly or debilitated.
*Related articles:* COSALGESIC;
DISTALGESIC; DOLOXENE.

**dextrose** , or dextrose
monohydrate, is another term for
glucose.
*see* GLUCOSE.

**dextrothyroxine sodium** is a
drug that was formerly used to
reduce high levels of fats (lipids)
in the blood, in patients for whom

simple dietary measures were not sufficient. Although the drug does reduce cholesterol levels, it also has the effect of increasing the heart rate which, for patients with heart disease (as many patients with high blood fat levels are), could lead to angina pectoris (heart pain). Administration is/was oral in the body.

▲ side-effects: the heart rate is increased.

✸ warning: dextrothyroxine sodium should not be administered to patients with heart disease involving deficient blood supply to the heart, or from severe liver or kidney disease.

**DF118** (*Duncan, Flockhart*) is a proprietary narcotic ANALGESIC available on prescription only to private patients, used to treat moderate to severe pain anywhere in the body. Produced in the form of tablets and as an elixir for dilution (the potency of the elixir once dilute is retained for 14 days) and in ampoules (as a controlled drug) for injection, DF118 is a preparation of the narcotic dihydrocodeine tartrate.

▲/✸ side-effects/warning: see DIHYDROCODEINE TARTRATE.

**Diabinese** (*Pfizer*) is a proprietary SULPHONYLUREA, available only on prescription, which has the effect of reducing blood levels of glucose by promoting the secretion of INSULIN within the pancreas. It is thus useful in treating the hyperglycaemia that is associated with adult-onset diabetes mellitus (in which the pancreas still has some capacity for insulin production). Produced in the form of tablets (in two strengths), Diabinese represents a preparation of chlorpropamide.

▲/✸ side-effects/warning: see CHLORPROPAMIDE.

**Dialamine** (*Scientific Hospital Supplies*) is a proprietary, non-

prescription nutritional supplement for patients who need extra amino acids (perhaps following kidney failure). Produced in the form of a powder for reconstitution as an orange-flavoured liquid, Dialamine contains essential amino acids, carbohydrate, ascorbic acid (vitamin C), minerals and trace elements.

**Diamicron** (*Servier*) is a proprietary SULPHONYLUREA, available only on prescription, which has the effect of reducing blood levels of glucose by promoting the secretion of INSULIN within the pancreas. It is useful in treating the hyperglycaemia that is associated with adult-onset diabetes mellitus (in which the pancreas still has some capacity for insulin production). Produced in the form of tablets, Diamicron is a preparation of gliclazide.

▲/✸ side-effects/warning: see GLICLAZIDE.

**diamorphine** is the chemical name of heroin, a white crystalline powder that is a derivative of morphine. Like morphine, it is a powerful NARCOTIC ANALGESIC useful in the treatment of moderate to severe pain, although it has a shorter duration of effect; and like morphine it is also sometimes used – generally in the form of diamorphine hydrochloride – as a cough suppressant in compound linctuses (especially in the treatment of terminal lung cancer). Again like morphine, its use quickly tends to tolerance and then dependence (addiction). Administration is oral in the form of tablets or an elixir, or by injection.

▲ side-effects: there may be euphoria, depending on dosage. There may also be constipation and low blood pressure. In some patients there is respiratory depression with high dosage.

♣ warning: diamorphine should not be administered to patients with renal or liver disease; it should be administered with caution to those with asthma (because it tends to cause sputum retention).

**Diamox** (*Lederle*) is a proprietary DIURETIC, available only on prescription, used to treat an accumulation of fluid in the tissues (oedema), especially in association with congestive heart failure, to assist in the prevention of epileptic seizures, and to treat the symptoms of premenstrual syndrome. Like many diuretics, it may additionally be used in the treatment of glaucoma, having the effect of reducing the moisture of the aqueous humour in the eyeball. Produced in the form of tablets, as capsules (under the trade name Diamox Sustets), and as a powder for reconstitution as a medium for injection or infusion, Diamox is a preparation of acetazolamide. It is not recommended for children.
▲/♣ side-effects/warning: *see* ACETAZOLAMIDE.

**Diarrest** (*Galen*) is a proprietary drug, available only on prescription, which is a preparation of the OPIATE codeine phosphate together with sodium and potassium salts as supplements to replace minerals lost through vomiting or diarrhoea. (The opiate has the capacity to reduce intestinal motility.) Diarrest is produced in the form of a liquid (for swallowing); prolonged use must be avoided.
▲/♣ side-effects/warning: *see* CODEINE PHOSPHATE.

**Diatensec** (*Gold Cross*) is a proprietary DIURETIC, available only on prescription, used to treat

the symptoms of cirrhosis of the liver or of kidney disease, and to assist in the treatment of high blood pressure (hypertension), especially in association with congestive heart failure or diabetes mellitus. Produced in the form of tablets, it is a preparation of the mild but potassium-sparing diuretic spironolactone.
▲/♣ side-effects/warning: *see* SPIRONOLACTONE.

**Diazemuls** (*KabiVitrum*) is a proprietary ANXIOLYTIC drug, available only on prescription, used to treat anxiety in the short- or long-term, to relieve insomnia, and to assist in the treatment of alcohol withdrawal symptoms and migraine. It may be used additionally to provide sedation for very minor surgery or as a premedication prior to surgical procedures and, because it also has some SKELETAL MUSCLE RELAXANT properties, to treat the spasm of tetanus or poisoning, or to relieve the bronchospasm of severe conditions of asthma. Continued use results in tolerance and may lead to dependence (addiction). Produced as an emulsion in ampoules for injection, Diazemuls is a preparation of the BENZODIAZEPINE diazepam.
▲/♣ side-effects/warning: *see* DIAZEPAM.

**diazepam** is an ANXIOLYTIC drug, one of the BENZODIAZEPINES, used to treat anxiety in the short- or long-term, to relieve insomnia, and to assist in the treatment of alcohol withdrawal symptoms and migraine. It may be used additionally to provide sedation for very minor surgery or as a premedication prior to surgical procedures and, because it also has some SKELETAL MUSCLE RELAXANT properties, to treat the spasm of tetanus or poisoning, or to relieve the bronchospasm of

severe conditions of asthma.
Continued use results in
tolerance and may lead to
dependence (addiction),
especially in patients with a
history of drug (including
alcohol) abuse. Administration is
oral in the form of tablets or
capsules or a dilute elixir, topical
as anal suppositories, or by
injection.

▲ side-effects: there may be
drowsiness, dizziness,
headache, dry mouth,
urinary retention, and
shallow breathing; hyper-
sensitivity reactions may
occur.

✦ warning: concentration and
speed of thought and
movement are often affected;
the effects of alcohol consumption may also be
enhanced. Diazepam should be
administered with caution to
patients with respiratory
difficulties, glaucoma, or
kidney or liver damage; who
are in the last stages of pregnancy; or who are elderly or
debilitated. Prolonged use of
the drug or abrupt withdrawal
from treatment should be
avoided.
*Related articles:* ALUPRAM;
ATENSINE; DIAZEMULS;
EVACALM; SOLIS; STESOLID;
TENSIUM; VALIUM.

**diazoxide** is a hypoglycaemic drug
used to treat chronic conditions
involving a deficit of glucose in
the bloodstream (as occurs, for
example, if a pancreatic tumour
causes excessive secretion of
insulin). It is also useful in
treating an acute hypertensive
crisis (apoplexy). Administration
is by injection.

▲ side-effects: there may be
nausea and vomiting, an
increased heart rate with low
blood pressure (hypotension),
loss of appetite accumulation
of fluid in the tissues (oedema),

arrhythmias, and hyper-
glycaemia.

✦ warning: diazoxide should be
administered with caution to
patients with reduced blood
supply to the heart or impaired
kidney function, or who are
pregnant or in labour. During
prolonged treatment, regular
monitoring of blood
constituents and pressure is
essential.
*Related article:* EUDEMINE.

**Dibenyline** (*Smith, Kline &
French*) is a proprietary
VASODILATOR used (in
combination with a BETA-
BLOCKER) in the treatment of the
high blood pressure (*see*
ANTIHYPERTENSIVE) caused by
tumours in the adrenal glands
and the resulting secretion of the
hormones adrenaline and
noradrenaline. Under specialist
supervision it may be used to
treat urinary retention due to
nerve damage in the bladder.
Produced in the form of capsules
and in ampoules for injection,
Dibenyline is a preparation of
phenoxybenzamine
hydrochloride.

▲ / ✦ side-effects/warning: *see*
PHENOXYBENZAMINE
HYDROCHLORIDE.

**Dicapen** (*Leo*) is a proprietary
combination of the ANTIBIOTIC
ampicillin, and sulbactam; an
inhibitor of the bacterial
penicillinase enzyme normally
responsible for inactivation of
ampicillin. Dicapen is available
only on prescription.

▲ / ✦ side-effects/warning: *see*
AMPICILLIN.

**dichloralphenazone** is a
HYPNOTIC drug used to treat
insomnia, particularly in children
or elderly patients. Prolonged use
leads to tolerance and dependence
(addiction). Administration is
oral in the form of tablets or a
dilute elixir.

▲ side-effects: there is commonly drowsiness, dizziness headache and dry mouth. More rarely there may be gastrointestinal disturbance or a rash.

✷ warning: concentration and speed of movement and thought are affected. Dichloralphenazone should be administered with caution to patients with lung disease, who are pregnant or lactating, or who have a history of drug abuse. Dosage should be reduced for elderly or debilitated patients, or for those with impaired liver or kidney function, cardiac disease or gastritis. Keep the drug off the skin and the mucous membranes.
*Related article:* WELLDORM.

**dichlorphenamide** is a drug that has the effect of a DIURETIC; in particular, it reduces the fluid (aqueous humour) in the eyeball, and is therefore used to treat glaucoma. Administration is oral in the form of tablets.

▲ side-effects: there may be tingling in the nerve endings, drowsiness, headache, constipation, loss of appetite and a low potassium blood level. Some patients experience depression.

✷ warning: side-effects are marked in elderly patients.
*Related article:* DARANIDE.

**diclofenac sodium** is a non-steroidal, ANTI-INFLAMMATORY, non-narcotic ANALGESIC drug used to treat pain and inflammation in rheumatic disease and other musculo-skeletal disorders (such as arthritis and gout). Administration is oral in the form of tablets, topical in the form of anal suppositories, or by injection.

▲ side-effects: there may be nausea and gastrointestinal disturbance (to avoid which a patient may be advised to take the drug with food or milk), headache and ringing in the ears (tinnitus). Some patients experience sensitivity reactions (such as a rash or the symptoms of asthma). Fluid retention and/or blood disorders may occur.

✷ warning: diclofenac sodium should be administered with caution to patients with gastric ulcers, impaired kidney or liver function, or allergic disorders particularly induced by aspirin or anti-inflammatory drugs, or to those who are pregnant.
*Related article:* VOLTAROL.

**dicobalt edetate** is used solely as an antidote to poisoning with cyanides – it is actually toxic in the absence of cyanides. Administration is by intravenous injection.

▲ side-effects: the heart rate is increased and the blood pressure reduced; there may be vomiting.
*Related article:* KELOCYANOR.

**Diconal** (*Calmic*) is a proprietary narcotic ANALGESIC, which is on the controlled drugs list. Used to treat moderate to severe pain, and produced in the form of tablets, Diconal represents a compound of the narcotic and OPIATE dipipanone hydrochloride together with the ANTIHISTAMINE and ANTINAUSEANT cyclizine hydrochloride. It is not recommended for children.

▲ / ✷ side-effects/warning: *see* CYCLIZINE; DIPIPANONE.

**dicyclomine hydrochloride** is a synthetic ANTICHOLINERGIC ANTISPASMODIC used primarily to assist in the treatment of gastrointestinal disorders caused by spasm (rigidity) in the muscular walls of the stomach or intestines. Administration is oral in the form of tablets, gel, or dilute syrup.

▲ side-effects: there is commonly dry mouth and thirst; there may also be visual disturbances, flushing, irregular heartbeat and constipation. Rarely, there may be high temperature accompanied by delirium.

◆ warning: dicyclomine hydrochloride should not be administered to patients with glaucoma; it should be administered with caution to those with heart problems and rapid heart rate, ulcerative colitis, urinary retention or enlargement of the prostate gland; who are elderly; or who are lactating.
*Related articles:* KOLANTICON; MERBENTYL.

**Dicynene** (*Delandale*) is a proprietary HAEMOSTATIC drug, available only on prescription, used to treat haemorrhage from small blood vessels or to relieve excessive menstrual flow. Produced in the form of tablets (in two strengths) and in ampoules for injection (in two strengths), Dicynene represents a preparation of ethamsylate.
▲ / ◆ side-effects/warning: *see* ETHAMSYLATE.

**Didronel** (*Norwich Eaton*) is a proprietary form of the drug DISODIUM ETIDRONATE, which reduces the rate of bone calcium turnover in treating the condition known as Paget's disease of bone and to treat high calcium levels associated with malignant tumours. Available only on prescription, Didronel is produced in the form of tablets. It is also available as Didronel IV, a preparation for injection. Didrodel is not recommended for children.
▲ / ◆ side-effects/warning: *see* DISODIUM ETIDRONATE.

**dienoestrol** is a synthetic OESTROGEN, a female sex hormone used in the form of a cream to make up hormonal deficiency in and around the vagina (especially following the menopause). Dosage should be adjusted to be the minimum that still retains effect, and should be discontinued as soon as possible, in order to minimize the absorption of the oestrogen.
▲ side-effects: absorption may result in weight gain through sodium and fluid retention; there may also be nausea and headache, and a rash.
◆ warning: absorption of oestrogen following prolonged use may eventually lead to increased risk of thrombosis or even of endometrial cancer.
*Related article:* ORTHO DIENOESTROL.

**diethylcarbamazine citrate** is an ANTHELMINTIC, specifically an antifilarial agent used to treat infestation by filarial worm parasites (such as those that cause elephantiasis, lymphangitis, loiasis and onchocerciasis). Side-effects are inevitable but are generally treated in turn with other drugs; close monitoring is essential throughout treatment, particularly at first. Several courses of treatment may be necessary. Administration is oral in the form of tablets.
▲ side-effects: there may be nausea and vomiting, with headache. Skin and eye inflammations may be aggravated.
◆ warning: the destruction of the worm-parasites causes the release of antigens and the corresponding allergic response which manifest themselves in skin irritation and inflammation, and visual disturbances because the eyes are also affected. Antihistamines and

corticosteroids may be prescribed to deal with these.
*Related article:* BANOCIDE.

**diethyl ether** is the now old-fashioned 'ether' used as a general ANAESTHETIC. Powerful as it is, it is now unpopular both because it is flammable and explosive in the presence of oxygen, and because it tends to cause nausea and vomiting in a patient. All the same, it is an effective anaesthetic under the influence of which body processes – in particular the heart rhythm – are generally well maintained.

**diethylpropion hydrochloride** is a drug used under medical supervision to aid slimming regimes because it acts to suppress the appetite. But it is also a stimulant and potentially represents the basis for drug abuse, although the stimulant action may in fact be useful in the treatment of lethargic and/or depressed patients. Proprietary preparations are therefore on the controlled drugs list. Administration is oral in the form of sustained-release tablets.
▲ side-effects: there is commonly rapid heart rate, nervous agitation and insomnia, tremor, gastrointestinal disturbance, dry mouth, dizziness and headache. Tolerance and dependence may occur. Susceptible patients may undergo psychotic episodes.
● warning: diethylpropion hydrochloride should not be administered to patients who suffer from glaucoma or any medical condition (such as thyrotoxicosis) that disposes towards excitability; it should be administered with caution to those with heart disease, diabetes, epilepsy, peptic ulcer, depression or unstable personality, and to those with

a history of alcohol or drug abuse.
*Related articles:* APISATE; TENUATE DOSPAN.

**Difflam** (*Riker*) is a proprietary, non-prescription preparation of the ANALGESIC benzydamine hydrochloride. It is produced both as a cream, which, when applied to the skin, produces an irritation of sensory nerve endings that offsets the pain of underlying muscle or joint ailments, and as a mouthwash or spray to relieve the pain of mouth ulcers and other sores or inflammations in the mouth or throat. Prolonged use in any form should be avoided.
▲ / ● side-effects/warning: *see* BENZYDAMINE HYDROCHLORIDE.

**Diflucan** (*Pfizer*) is a proprietary ANTIFUNGAL drug available only on prescription, used to treat candidiasis (thrush) of the vagina or mouth. Produced in the form of capsules in two strengths, it is an orally active preparation of fluconazole.
▲ / ● side-effects/warning: *see* FLUCONAZOLE.

**diflucortolone valerate** is a powerful and popular CORTICOSTEROID, used in topical application on severe non-infective skin inflammations (such as eczema), especially in cases where less powerful steroid treatments have failed. Administration is in the form of a dilute water-miscible cream, a dilute hydrous ointment (or oily cream), or an anhydrous paraffin-based ointment.
▲ side-effects: topical application may result in the local thinning of skin, with possible whitening, and an increased local growth of hair. Some young patients experience the outbreak of a kind of inflammatory dermatitis on the

face or at the site of
application.

⚘ warning: as with all
corticosteroids, diflucortolone
valerate treats the symptoms of
inflammation but has no effect
on any underlying infection;
undetected infection may thus
become worse even as its
effects are masked by the
steroid. The drug should not in
any case be administered to
patients with untreated skin
lesions; use on the face should
be avoided. Not for use in
children under 4.
*Related article:* NERISONE.

**diflunisal** is a non-steroidal, ANTI-
INFLAMMATORY, non-narcotic
ANALGESIC drug derived from
aspirin, used to treat pain and
inflammation especially in
rheumatic disease and other
musculo-skeletal disorders.
Administration is oral in the form
of tablets.

▲ side-effects: there may be
nausea and gastrointestinal
disturbance (to avoid which a
patient may be advised to take
the drug with food or milk),
headache and ringing in the
ears (tinnitus). Some patients
experience sensitivity
reactions (such as the
symptoms of asthma). Fluid
retention and/or blood
disorders may occur.

⚘ warning: diflunisal should be
administered with caution to
patients with gastric ulcers,
impaired kidney or liver
function, or allergic disorders
particularly those induced
by aspirin or anti-inflammatory
agents, or those who
are pregnant or
lactating.
*Related article:* DOLOBID.

**Digibind** (*Wellcome*) is an antidote
to overdosage of the heart
stimulant digoxin, representing
digoxin-specific antibody

fragments for emergency
injection.
*see* DIGOXIN.

**Digitalin Nativelle** (*Lewis*) is a
proprietary form of the powerful
heart stimulant digitoxin (a
CARDIAC GLYCOSIDE), available
only on prescription, used to treat
heart failure and severe heartbeat
irregularity. It is produced in the
form of tablets and as an elixir
(the use of which requires some
counselling).

▲ / ⚘ side-effects/warning: *see*
DIGITOXIN.

**digitoxin** is the most powerful
heart stimulant derived from the
leaf of the digitalis plant, and is a
CARDIAC GLYCOSIDE. The effect is
to regularize and strengthen a
heartbeat that is either too fast or
too slow. Useful as it is, however,
the drug has common toxic side-
effects, the severity of which
depends on each individual
patient's specific condition.
Monitoring of kidney function
is particularly advisable.
Digitoxin is administered orally
in the form of tablets or an
elixir.

▲ side-effects: there is commonly
a loss of appetite, nausea and
vomiting, with a consequent
weight loss (resulting in some
cases in anorexia). There may
also be visual disturbances.
Overdosage may lead to heart
block.

⚘ warning: digitoxin should be
administered with caution to
patients who suffer from undersecretion of thyroid hormones
(hypothyroidism) or who have
recently undergone a heart
attack. Dosage should be
reduced for the elderly and for
those with impaired kidney
function. Regular monitoring
of the blood potassium level is
also recommended.
*Related article:* DIGITALIN
NATIVELLE.

**digoxin** is a heart stimulant derived from the leaf of the digitalis plant, and is a CARDIAC GLYCOSIDE. The effect is to regularize and strengthen a heartbeat that is either too fast or too slow. Useful as it is, however, the drug has common toxic side-effects, the severity of which depends on each individual patient's specific condition. Monitoring of kidney function is particularly advisable. (Overdosage can be corrected by the administration of an antidote called Digibind.) Digoxin is administered orally in the form of tablets or an elixir, or by injection.

▲ side-effects: there is commonly a loss of appetite, nausea and vomiting, with a consequent weight loss (resulting in some cases in anorexia). There may also be visual disturbances. Overdosage may lead to heart block.

✿ warning: digoxin should be administered with caution to patients who suffer from under-secretion of thyroid hormones (hypothyroidism) or who have recently undergone a heart attack. Dosage should be reduced for the elderly and for those with impaired kidney function. Regular monitoring of the blood potassium level is also recommended.
*Related article:* LANOXIN.

**Dihydergot** (*Sandoz*) is a proprietary preparation, available only on prescription, which is used specifically either to treat or to prevent migraine attacks (prevention demands a regular regimen for administration, whether or not attacks occur). It also has ANTINAUSEANT properties. Produced in the form of tablets, as an oral solution, and in ampoules for injection, Dihydergot is a preparation of the ergotamine derivative

dihydroergotomine mesylate
▲/ ✿ side-effects/warning: *see* DIHYDROERGOTAMINE MESYLATE.

**dihydrocodeine tartrate** is a NARCOTIC ANALGESIC that is similar to CODEINE. It is used to relieve pain, especially in cases where continued mobility is required, although it may cause some degree of dizziness and constipation. It is commonly used before and after surgery. Administration is oral in the form of tablets or a dilute elixir, or by injection.

▲ side-effects: there is dizziness, headache, and sedation; often there is also nausea and constipation. The effects of alcohol consumption may be increased.

✿ warning: dihydrocodeine tartrate should not be administered to patients with respiratory depression, obstructive airways disease, or to children aged under 12 months. Tolerance and dependence (addiction) readily occur.
*Related article:* DF 118.

**dihydroergotomine mesylate** is an anti-migraine drug, a derivative of ergotamine, which also has ANTINAUSEANT properties. It is used specifically either to treat or to prevent migraine attacks (prevention demands a regular regimen for administration whether or not attacks occur), and is administered orally in the form of tablets or a solution, or by injection.

▲ side-effects: there may be nausea and vomiting, with headache, and paraesthesia, and possibly vascular spasm.

✿ warning: dihydroergotomine mesylate should not be administered to patients with any infection or circulatory

disorders of the limbs, or who are pregnant or lactating; it should be administered with caution to those with heart, liver or kidney disease, or an excess of thyroid hormones in the bloodstream (thyrotoxicosis).
*Related article:* DIHYDERGOT.

**dihydrotachysterol** is a synthetic form of CALCIFEROL (vitamin D), used to make up body deficiencies. Calcium levels in the body should be regularly monitored during treatment. Administration is oral in the form of tablets and a solution.
❋ warning: overdosage may cause kidney damage. Although an increased amount of vitamin D is necessary during pregnancy, high body levels while lactating may also cause high levels of calcium in the breast-fed infant.
*Related articles:* A.T. 10; PARAMOL; TACHYROL.

**Dijex** (*Crookes*) is a proprietary, non-prescription ANTACID, which is not available from the National Health Service. A compound used to reduce stomach acidity and aid digestion, it contains ALUMINIUM HYDROXIDE and MAGNESIUM CARBONATE, and is produced in the form of tablets and as an oral liquid.

**diloxanide furoate** is an AMOEBICIDAL drug used to treat chronic infection of the intestine by amoebae, causing amoebic dysentery. Administration is oral in the form of tablets; the drug is given in combination with the antibiotic metronidazole in acute cases.
▲ side-effects: there is usually flatulence; there may also be vomiting, itching (pruritus) and/or urticaria.
❋ warning: treatment with diloxanide furoate alone

usually lasts 10 days; with metronidazole 15 days.
*Related article:* FURAMIDE.

**diltiazem hydrochloride** is a VASODILATOR that is a CALCIUM-ANTAGONIST drug used in the prevention and treatment of angina pectoris (heart pain), especially in cases where BETA-BLOCKERS are not tolerated or have been ineffective. Administration is oral, in some cases in the form of sustained-release tablets.
▲ side-effects: there may be severely slowed heart rate and low blood pressure, with an accumulation of fluid (oedema) at the ankles. Occasionally, there may be nausea and headache, depression, and rashes.
❋ warning: diltiazem hydrochloride should not be administered to patients with slow heart rate or progressive heart disease, or who are pregnant; it should be administered with caution to those with impaired liver or kidney function.
*Related articles:* BRITIAZEM, DILTIAZEM, ADIZEM-60, ADIZEM-SR, TILDIEM.

**Dimelor** (*Lilly*) is a proprietary SULPHONYLUREA, available only on prescription, which has the effect of reducing blood levels of glucose by promoting the secretion of INSULIN within the pancreas. It is thus useful in treating the hyperglycaemia that is associated with adult-onset diabetes mellitus (in which the pancreas still has some capacity for insulin production). Produced in the form of tablets, Dimelor is a preparation of acetohexamide.
▲ / ❋ side-effects/warning: *see* ACETOHEXAMIDE.

**dimenhydrinate** is an ANTIHISTAMINE that is effective in quelling nausea, and useful in preventing vomiting caused by travelling in a moving vehicle, by pregnancy, or by chemotherapy or radiation sickness. It is also used to assist in the treatment of the vertigo and loss of balance that accompanies infections of the middle or inner ear. Administration is oral in the form of tablets.

▲ side-effects: there may be dry mouth, drowsiness and headache, with blurred vision. Some patients experience gastrointestinal disturbances.

✿ warning: dimenhydrinate should be administered with caution to patients who suffer from liver disease, epilepsy, enlargement of the prostate gland or glaucoma, and during pregnancy. Concentration and speed of thought and movement are affected – and these symptoms may be made worse by alcohol consumption. *Related article:* DRAMAMINE.

**dimercaprol** is a CHELATING AGENT used as an antidote to poisoning with antimony, arsenic, bismuth, gold, mercury or thallium. Administration is by injection.

▲ side-effects: there is an increase in heart rate and blood pressure, sweating, weeping and agitation, nausea and vomiting, constriction of the throat and chest, and a burning sensation all temporary unless too high a dosage is administered.

**dimethicone** is a water-repellent silicone used as an antifoaming agent and, when taken orally, thought to reduce flatulence while protecting mucous membranes. It is also a constituent in many barrier creams intended to protect against irritation or chapping (as in nappy rash). Not for use on acutely inflamed or weeping skin.

*Related articles:* ALTACAPS; ALTACITE PLUS; ANDURSIL; ASILONE; KOLANTICON; MAALOX; PIPTALIN; POLYCROL; SILOXYL; SIOPEL; VASOGEN.

**dimethindene maleate** is an ANTIHISTAMINE, used to treat the symptoms of allergic conditions such as hay fever and urticaria; it is also used, in combination with other drugs, in expectorants to loosen a dry cough. Administration is oral in the form of sustained-release tablets.

▲ side-effects: sedation may affect patients' capacity for speed of thought and movement; there may be nausea, headaches and/or weight gain, dry mouth, gastrointestinal disturbances and visual problems.

✿ warning: dimethindene maleate should not be administered to patients who are pregnant, or with glaucoma, urinary retention, intestinal obstruction, enlargement of the prostate gland, or peptic ulcer; it should be administered with caution to those with epilepsy or liver disease.

*Related articles:* FENOSTIL RETARD; VIBROSIL.

**Dimotane** (*Robins*) is a proprietary, non-prescription ANTIHISTAMINE, used to treat the symptoms of allergic conditions such as hay fever and urticaria. Produced as tablets, as sustained-release tablets (under the name Dimotane LA), and as an elixir for dilution (the potency of the elixir once dilute is retained for 14 days), Dimotane is a preparation of brompheniramine maleate.

▲/✿ side-effects/warning: *see* BROMPHENIRAMINE MALEATE.

**Dimotane Expectorant** (*Robins*) is a proprietary, non-prescription EXPECTORANT, which is not

available from the National Health Service. Intended to promote the expulsion of excess bronchial secretions, it contains the ANTIHISTAMINE brompheniramine maleate and the VASOCONSTRICTOR phenylephrine hydrochloride, and is produced as a sugar-free elixir for dilution (the potency of the elixir once diluted is retained for 14 days).
▲/● side-effects/warning: *see* BROMPHENIRAMINE MALEATE; PHENYLEPHRINE.

**Dimotane Plus** (*Robins*) is a proprietary, non-prescription oral preparation intended to clear a stuffed nose. It represents a combination of the ANTIHISTAMINE brompheniramine maleate and the SYMPATHOMIMETIC pseudoephedrine hydrochloride, and is produced as a sugar-free liquid (in two strengths, the weaker labelled for children) for dilution with glycerol (the potency of the liquid once diluted is retained for 14 days). It is also available in the form of sustained-release tablets, under the trade name Dimotane Plus LA.
▲/● side-effects/warning: *see* BROMPHENIRAMINE MALEATE; EPHEDRINE HYDROCHLORIDE.

**Dimotane with Codeine** (*Robins*) is a proprietary, non-prescription cough linctus, which is not available from the National Health Service. Intended both to promote the expulsion of excess bronchial secretions and to suppress a cough, it contains the OPIATE codeine phosphate, the ANTIHISTAMINE brompheniramine maleate and the SYMPATHOMIMETIC pseudo-ephedrine hydrochloride, and is produced as a sugar-free elixir (in two strengths, the weaker labelled for children) for dilution with glycerol (the potency of the elixir once diluted is retained for 14 days).

▲/● side-effects/warning: *see* BROMPHENIRAMINE MALEATE; CODEINE PHOSPHATE; EPHEDRINE HYDROCHLORIDE.

**Dimotapp** (*Robins*) is a proprietary, non-prescription oral preparation intended to clear a stuffed nose; it is not available from the National Health Service. It contains the ANTIHISTAMINE brompheniramine maleate, the sympathomimetic VASOCONSTRICTOR phenylephrine hydrochloride, and the SYMPATHOMIMETIC phenylpropanolamine, and is produced as a sugar-free elixir (in two strengths, the weaker labelled for children) for dilution (the potency of the elixir once diluted is retained for 14 days), and in the form of sustained-release tablets (under the trade name Dimotapp LA).
▲/● side-effects/warning: *see* BROMPHENIRAMINE MALEATE; PHENYLEPHRINE; PHENYLPROPANOLAMINE.

**Dimyril** (*Fisons*) is a proprietary cough linctus, which is available on prescription only to private patients. It represents a preparation of the cough suppressant isoaminile citrate, and is produced in the form of a syrup for dilution (the potency of the syrup once dilute is retained for 14 days).
▲/● side-effects/warning: *see* ISOAMINILE CITRATE.

**Dindevan** (*Duncan, Flockhart*) is a proprietary ANTICOAGULANT, available only on prescription, used primarily to treat deep-vein thrombosis. Produced in the form of tablets (in three strengths), Dindevan is a preparation of phenindione, and produces sensitivity reactions in a number of patients.
▲/● side-effects/warning: *see* PHENINDIONE.

**Dinneford's** (*Beecham Health Care*) is a proprietary, non-prescription magnesia gripe mixture. It contains citric acid, sucrose, ALCOHOL and the ANTACIDS sodium bicarbonate and magnesium carbonate.

▲/● side-effects/warning: *see* SODIUM BICARBONATE; MAGNESIUM CARBONATE.

**dinoprost** is PROSTAGLANDIN F2 alpha, which has the effect of causing contractions in the muscular walls of the womb. It is used virtually solely to induce termination of pregnancy (abortion). Administration is by injection, generally into the amniotic sac that surrounds the foetus, and occasionally by intravenous infusion.

▲ side-effects: there may be nausea, vomiting, flushing and shivering, headache and dizziness, a raised temperature and diarrhoea. These effects are all related to the dosage, and are especially liable to occur if treatment is (unusually) by intravenous infusion.

● warning: dinoprost should not be administered to patients with uterine muscular disorders or infections, or in whom there is some obstruction between the womb and the outside world or signs of foetal distress. It should be administered with caution to those with asthma or glaucoma, or in whom there is more than one foetus. Overdosage may cause rupture of the womb.
*Related article:* PROSTIN F2 ALPHA.

**dinoprostone** is the PROSTA-GLANDIN E2, which has the effect of causing contractions in the muscular walls of the womb. It is used virtually solely to induce or to assist in termination of

pregnancy (abortion). Administration is oral in the form of tablets, topical in the form of a gel or vaginal inserts, or by injection, generally into the amniotic sac that surrounds the foetus.

▲ side-effects: there may be nausea, vomiting, flushing and shivering, headache and dizziness, a raised temperature and diarrhoea. These effects are all related to the dosage, and are especially liable to occur if treatment is (unusually) by intravenous infusion.

● warning: dinoprostone should not be administered to patients with uterine muscular disorders or uterine or vaginal infections, or in whom there is an obstruction or signs of foetal distress. It should be administered with caution to those with asthma or glaucoma, or in whom there is more than one foetus.
*Related article:* PREPIDIL; PROSTIN E2.

**Diocalm** (*Beecham Health Care*) is a proprietary, non-prescription ANTIDIARRHOEAL preparation, containing the OPIATE morphine and attapulgite (magnesium aluminium silicate).

▲/● side-effects/warning: *see* MORPHINE.

**Dioctyl** (*Medo*) is a proprietary, non-prescription LAXATIVE used to relieve constipation and also to evacuate the rectum prior to abdominal X-ray procedures. Produced in the form of tablets, and as a syrup (in two strengths, the weaker for children) for dilution (the potency of the syrup once diluted is retained for 14 days), Dioctyl is a prepar-ation of DIOCTYL SODIUM SULPHOSUCCINATE (also called docusate sodium).

**Dioctyl Ear Drops** (*Medo*) is a proprietary, non-prescription preparation of DIOCTYL in the form of ear-drops, used for the dissolution and removal of ear wax. Not for patients with perforated ear drum. Dioctyl Ear Drops is a preparation of dioctyl sodium sulpho-succinate (also called docusate sodium).

**dioctyl sodium sulphosuccinate** , or docusate sodium, is primarily a LAXATIVE, which is used not only to relieve constipation but also to evacuate the rectum prior to abdominal X-rays. It is a constituent of many proprietary compound laxatives because it appears to have few, if any, side-effects. It works as a surfactant, applying a very thin film of low surface tension (like a detergent) over the intestinal wall surface. Dioctyl sodium sulphosuccinate is also used in the form of ear-drops to dissolve and remove ear wax; again it is a constituent in many proprietary ear-drop preparations.
*Related articles:* DIOCTYL; DIOCTYL EAR DROPS; FLETCHER'S ENEMETTE; MOLCER; NORMAX; SOLIWAX; WAXSOL.

**Dioderm** (*Dermal*) is a proprietary, water-miscible, CORTICOSTEROID cream for topical application, used to treat mild inflammation of the skin. Available only on prescription, its major active constituent is the steroid hydrocortisone.
▲/● side-effects/warning: *see* HYDROCORTISONE.

**Dioralyte** (*Armour*) is a proprietary, non-prescription, sodium supplement, used to treat mild or moderate degrees of sodium depletion (as may happen in cases of dehydration or in illnesses – particularly in kidney disease – in which salt is lost in some quantity). Dioralyte is produced in the form of sachets containing a powder for solution, consisting of a compound of SODIUM CHLORIDE, POTASSIUM CHLORIDE, SODIUM BICARBONATE and GLUCOSE; flavours are plain, cherry or pineapple.

**Diovol** (*Pharmax*) is a proprietary, non-prescription ANTACID used to relieve acid stomach and flatulence, and to assist digestion in patients with peptic ulcers or hiatus hernia. Produced in the form of tablets for chewing or sucking, and as a mint- or fruit-flavoured suspension, Diovol is a compound preparation of ALUMINIUM HYDROXIDE together with the antifoaming agent DIMETHICONE. It is not recommended for children aged under 6 years.

**Dipentum** (*Pharmacia*) is a proprietary form of the drug olsalazine sodium, used to treat patients who suffer from ulcerative colitis, but who are unable to tolerate the more commonly used drug sulphasalazine. Available only on prescription, Dipentum is produced in the form of capsules.
▲/● side-effects/warning: *see* OLSALAZINE SODIUM.

**diphenhydramine hydrochloride** is an ANTIHISTAMINE, one of the first to be discovered, used to treat allergic conditions such as hay fever and urticaria, some forms of dermatitis, and some sensitivity reactions to drugs. Its additional sedative properties are useful in the treatment of some allergic conditions, but the fact that it is also an ANTINAUSEANT makes it useful in the treatment or prevention of travel sickness, vertigo, and infections of the inner and middle ears too. Administration is oral in the form of capsules.

▲ side-effects: sedation may affect patients' capacity for speed of thought and movement; there may be headache and/or weight gain, dry mouth, gastrointestinal disturbances and visual problems.

❋ warning: diphenhydramine hydrochloride should not be administered to patients with glaucoma, urinary retention, intestinal obstruction, enlargement of the prostate gland, or peptic ulcer, or who are pregnant; it should be administered with caution to those who suffer from epilepsy or liver disease.
*Related articles:* BENADRYL; BENYLIN EXPECTORANT; HISTALIX.

**diphenoxylate hydrochloride** is a powerful ANTIDIARRHOEAL drug, an OPIATE used to treat chronic diarrhoea. It works by reducing the speed at which material travels along the intestines. Overdosage is uncommon but does occur, particularly in young children – however, the symptoms of overdosage (chiefly sedation) do not appear until some 48 hours after treatment, so monitoring of patients for at least that time is necessary. Because long-term treatment with diphenoxylate hydrochloride is liable to induce dependence (addiction), the drug is usually administered in combination with the belladonna alkaloid ATROPINE, which reduces its potential for abuse. Administration is oral in the form of tablets or as a sugar-free dilute liquid.

▲ side-effects: overdosage causes sedation. Prolonged usage may lead to impaired gastrointestinal function and eventual dependence. The presence of atropine may cause dry mouth, thirst and some visual disturbance in susceptible patients.

❋ warning: fluid intake must be maintained during treatment. In elderly patients, monitoring is essential to detect possible faecal impaction. The drug should not be used in patients with gastrointestinal obstruction or jaundice. Care should be taken in patients with ulcerative colitis, or hepatic disorders
*Related article:* LOMOTIL.

**diphenylpyraline hydrochloride** is an ANTIHISTAMINE used to treat allergic conditions such as hay fever and urticaria, some forms of dermatitis, and some sensitivity reactions to drugs. Its additional sedative properties are useful in the treatment of some allergic conditions. Administration of the drug is oral in the form of sustained-release capsules (spansules) or tablets.

▲ side-effects: sedation may affect patients' capacity for speed of thought and movement; there may be nausea, headache and/or weight gain, dry mouth, gastrointestinal disturbances and visual problems.

❋ warning: diphenylpyraline hydrochloride should not be administered to patients with glaucoma, urinary retention, intestinal obstruction, enlargement of the prostate gland, or peptic ulcer, or who are pregnant; it should be administered with caution to those who suffer from epilepsy or liver disease.
*Related articles:* ESKORNADE; HISTRYL; LERGOBAN.

**diphtheria antitoxin** is a preparation of antibodies to the toxin produced by the diphtheria bacteria, *Corynebacterium diphtheriae*, as this toxin is the major factor in the lethal complications of diphtheria infections. The antibodies are prepared in horses, and once used in patients carry the risk of sensitization of the patient to horse proteins. The antitoxin absorbed onto a carrier, usually aluminium hydroxide, causes active immunity in the patient. It is the mainstay of treatment of suspected and proven cases of diphtheria. Prior tests for sensitization should be carried out.

**diphtheria-pertussis-tetanus (DPT) vaccine** is a combination of VACCINES against diphtheria, whooping cough and tetanus used for the routine immunization of infants at the ages of 3 months, 4 + months and 6 months. Repeat vaccination with this triple vaccine is not usual, although the booster vaccinations of the diphtheria and tetanus vaccines are relatively common. *see* DIPHTHERIA VACCINE; PERTUSSIS VACCINE; TETANUS VACCINE.

**diphtheria-tetanus vaccine** is a combination of VACCINES against diphtheria and tetanus used for the routine immunization of infants at the ages of 3 months, 4 + months and 6 months in children whose parents do not wish them to have the triple vaccine that additionally contains pertussis (whooping cough) vaccine. This double vaccine is also used as a booster shot for children at the age of school entry.

**diphtheria vaccine** is a VACCINE preparation of an inactivated, yet still antigenic, toxin (or toxoid) of the diphtheria bacteria, *Corynebacterium diphtheriae*. Available only on prescription, the vaccine is produced in ampoules for injection. However, far more commonly, it is administered as one constituent in a triple vaccine (additionally against whooping cough – known

as pertussis – and tetanus, often called the DPT vaccine) or, when patients do not want vaccination against whooping cough, in a double vaccine (with TETANUS VACCINE). Reinforcing doses of diphtheria vaccine are required.

**dipipanone** is a rapidly-acting and powerful OPIATE, narcotic, ANALGESIC drug, which is used in combination with an ANTINAUSEANT drug (the antihistamine cyclizine) for the relief of acute moderate to severe pain. Its proprietary form is on the controlled drugs list and is not recommended for children. Administration (in the form of dipipanone hydrochloride) is oral as tablets.

▲ side-effects: the mouth may become dry, vision may blur, and the patient may become drowsy. Tolerance may rapidly be followed by dependence (addiction).

✦ warning: dipipanone should not be administered to patients who have any blockage of the respiratory passages or any form of depressed breathing; it should be administered with caution to those with severely impaired kidney or liver function, or who are pregnant. The consumption of alcohol must be avoided during treatment.
*Related article:* DICONAL.

**dipivefrine** is a derivative of the HORMONE (catecholamine) adrenaline, which is in fact converted internally into adrenaline; it is used – like adrenaline – in ophthalmic treatment to reduce the formation of aqueous humour in the eyeball and to promote its drainage away, so lessening intra-ocular pressure and relieving the main symptoms of glaucoma. However, the drug should not be used in cases of closed-angle glaucoma or soft lens. Treatment may cause transient stinging and mild sensitivity reactions. Administration (in the form of a mild solution of dipivefrine hydrochloride) is topical in the form of eye-drops.

▲/✿ side-effects/warning: see ADRENALINE.
*Related article:* PROPINE.

**dipotassium clorazepate** is a drug better known simply as clorazepate.
*see* CLORAZEPATE.

**Diprivan** (*ICI*) is a proprietary form of the general ANAESTHETIC propofol, used primarily for the induction of anaesthesia at the start of a surgical operation, but sometimes also for its maintenance thereafter. Available only on prescription, it is produced as an emulsion in ampoules for injection.

▲/✿ side-effects/warning: see PROPOFOL.

**Diprobase** (*Kirby-Warrick*) is a proprietary, non-prescription form of OINTMENT used as a base for medications; it is a combination of paraffins (and is intended for particular use with DIPROSONE).

**Diprosalic** (*Kirby-Warrick*) is a proprietary CORTICOSTEROID preparation, available only on prescription, used to treat severe, non-infective skin inflammations such as eczema, particularly in patients who are not responding to less powerful steroids. Produced in the form of an ointment and an alcohol-based lotion for topical application, Diprosalic is a compound preparation of the steroid betamethasone dipropionate together with the ANTI-BACTERIAL/ANTIFUNGAL drug salicylic acid.

▲/✿ side-effects/warning: see BETAMETHASONE DIPROPIONATE; SALICYLIC ACID.

**Diprosone** (*Kirby-Warrick*) is a proprietary CORTICOSTEROID preparation, available only on prescription, used to treat severe, non-infective skin inflammation such as eczema. particularly in patients who are not responding to less powerful steroids. Produced in the form of a water-miscible cream, as an ointment and as an alcohol-based lotion for topical application, Diprosone is a preparation of the steroid betamethasone dipropionate.

▲/✿ side-effects/warning: see BETAMETHASONE DIPROPIONATE.

**dipyridamole** is a drug used to prevent thrombosis, but does not have the usual action of an ANTICOAGULANT. Instead it works by inhibiting the adhesiveness of blood platelets so that they stick neither to themselves nor to the walls of valves or tubes surgically inserted. Administration is oral in the form of tablets, or by injection.

▲ side-effects: there may be nausea and diarrhoea, with a throbbing headache. Blood pressure may fall.

✿ warning: treatment may make low blood pressure (hypotension) or migraine worse. Care is required in patients suffering from angina pectoris or other heart conditions associated with poor cardiovascular blood flow.
*Related article:* PERSANTIN.

**Dirythmin IV** (*Astra*) is a proprietary form of DIRYTHMIN SA prepared in a form suitable for intravenous injection. The method of administration is, however, long and complicated.
*see* DISOPYRAMIDE.

**Dirythmin SA** (*Astra*) is a proprietary ANTIARRHYTHMIC drug, available only on prescription, used to regularize the heartbeat especially following a heart attack. Produced in the form of sustained-release tablets ('Durules'), it is a preparation of disopyramide phosphate. It is not recommended for children.

▲/● side-effects/warning: *see* DISOPYRAMIDE.

**Disadine DP** (*Stuart*) is a proprietary, non-prescription form of the compound DISINFECTANT povidone-iodine, prepared as a powder within an aerosol. For topical application, it is used to treat or prevent infection of the skin following injury or surgery, or to cleanse bedsores.

**Disalcid** (*Riker*) is a proprietary, non-narcotic ANALGESIC, available only on prescription, used to relieve pain – particularly the pain of rheumatic disease in and around the joints. Produced in the form of tablets, it represents a preparation of the aspirin-like drug salsalate, and is not recommended for children.

▲/● side-effects/warning: *see* SALSALATE.

*disinfectants are agents that destroy micro-organisms, or inhibit their activity to a level such that they are less or no longer harmful to health. The term is applied to agents used on inanimate objects as well as to those used to treat the skin and living tissue, and in the latter case is often used synonymously with ANTISEPTIC.

**Disipal** (*Brocades*) is a proprietary ANTICHOLINERGIC drug, available only on prescription, used in ANTIPARKINSONISM treatment to relieve some of the symptoms of parkinsonism, specifically the tremor of the hands, the overall rigidity of the posture, and the tendency to produce an excess of saliva. (The drug also has the capacity to treat these conditions in some cases where they are produced by drugs.) It is thought to work by compensating for the lack of dopamine in the brain that is the major cause of such parkinsonian symptoms. Produced in the form of tablets, Disipal is a preparation of orphenadrine hydrochloride. Counselling of patients is advised.

▲/● side-effects/warning: *see* ORPHENADRINE HYDROCHLORIDE.

**Di-sipidin** (*Paines & Byrne*) is a proprietary preparation of a pituitary extract in powder form, used as snuff by patients who suffer from diabetes insipidus and urinary incontinence. It is available only on prescription, and presented in the form of insufflation capsules.

▲ side-effects: there may be nausea, internal muscular cramps, constriction of the coronary arteries and an urge to defecate. Some patients experience the symptoms of hay fever or asthma.

● warning: Di-sipidin should not be administered to patients who suffer from high blood pressure (hypertension) or chronic nephritis. Dosage of Di-sipidin should initially be adjusted according to individual response: optimum response level should then become the maintenance level.

**disodium etidronate** is a drug used virtually solely to treat the condition known as Paget's disease of bone (osteitis deformans: a severely and continuously painful condition in which the larger bones of the body thicken while their structure becomes disorganized).

It may also be used to treat high calcium levels associated with malignant tumours. It works by inhibiting the demineralization process inherent in the disease through chelating calcium. Treatment may last for 6 months. Administration is oral in the form of tablets. Dietary counselling of patients is advised, particularly with regard to avoiding calcium-containing food products during oral treatment.

▲ side-effects: there may be nausea and diarrhoea. High dosage increases both bone pain and the risk of fractures. A short lived loss of the sense of taste has been reported.

✿ warning: disodium etidronate should be administered with caution to patients with impaired kidney function or intestinal inflammation. Treatment should be withdrawn if the patient suffers a fracture.
*Related article:* DIDRONEL.

**disodium pamidronate** is a drug used to treat disorders of bone metabolism due to HORMONE disorders, and is indicated in the treatment of tumour-induced high blood calcium levels (hypercalcaemia), and is administered by slow intravenous infusion.

▲/✿ side-effects/warning: avoid in patients with severe kidney damage; convulsions may occur due to electrolyte disturbances; short-lived increases in body temperature have been reported.
*Related article:* AREDIA.

**disopyramide** is an ANTIARRHYTHMIC drug used to regularize the heartbeat especially following a heart attack. Dosage must be adjusted to suit the response of each individual patient. Administration (as disopyramide

or as disopyramide phosphate) is oral in the form of capsules, sustained-release capsules or sustained-release tablets, or by slow intravenous injection that has to be monitored using an electrocardiograph (and followed by further dosage by mouth or by infusion).

▲ side-effects: there may be slow heart rate and low blood pressure (hypotension). Many patients experience dry mouth, blurred vision and urinary retention. Rarely, there is heart block.

✿ warning: disopyramide should be administered with caution to patients with depressed heart function (i.e. heart failure and impaired cardiac output) reduced kidney function, or glaucoma.
*Related articles:* DIRYTHMIN IV; DIRYTHMIN SA; RYTHMODAN.

**Disprin** (*Reckitt & Colman*) is a proprietary, non-prescription, non-narcotic ANALGESIC containing paracetamol.
▲/✿ side-effects/warning: *see* PARACETAMOL.

**Disprol** (*Reckitt & Colman*) is a proprietary, non-prescription, non-narcotic ANALGESIC for children which also helps to reduce high body temperature. Produced in the form of a sugar-free suspension, it is a preparation of paracetamol. Even as a paediatric preparation, however, it is not recommended for children aged under 3 months.
▲/✿ side-effects/warning: *see* PARACETAMOL.

**Distaclor** (*Dista*) is a proprietary, broad-spectrum ANTIBIOTIC, available only on prescription, used to treat a wide range of bacterial infections, particularly of the skin and soft tissues, urinary tract, upper respiratory tract, and middle ear. Produced in the form of capsules and as a suspension (in two strengths) for dilution (the potency of the suspension once diluted is retained for 14 days), Distaclor is a preparation of the CEPHALOSPORIN CEFACLOR.

▲/✿ side-effects/warning: *see* CEFACLOR.

**Distalgesic** (*Dista*) is a proprietary ANALGESIC available only on prescription to private patients. Used to relieve pain anywhere in the body, and produced in the form of tablets, Distalgesic is a preparation of the narcotic-like analgesic dextropropoxyphene together with paracetamol. This compound combination is known as CO-PROXAMOL). It is not recommended for children.

▲/✿ side-effects/warning: *see* DEXTROPROPOXYPHENE; PARACETAMOL.

**Distamine** (*Dista*) is a proprietary preparation, available only on prescription, used specifically to relieve the pain of rheumatoid arthritis, and potentially to halt the progress of the disease. Patients should be warned that treatment may take up to 12 weeks for any improvement to be manifest, and up to a year before full effect is achieved. The drug may also be used as a long-term CHELATING AGENT to treat poisoning by the metals copper or lead. Produced in the form of tablets (in three strengths), Distamine is a preparation of the penicillin derivative peni-cillamine.

▲/✿ side-effects/warning: *see* PENICILLAMINE.

**Distaquaine V-K** (*Dista*) is a proprietary preparation of the penicillin-type ANTIBIOTIC phenoxymethylpenicillin, used mainly to treat infections of the throat, middle ear and some skin

conditions. Available only on prescription, it is produced in the form of tablets (in two strengths) or as an elixir (in three strengths) for dilution (the potency of the elixir once diluted is retained for 7 days).

▲/✿ side-effects/warning: *see* PHENOXYMETHYLPENICILLIN.

**distigmine bromide** is an anti-cholinesterase drug that enhances the transmission of neural impulses from the brain to the muscles. It is primarily used, perhaps surprisingly, as a PARASYMPATHOMIMETIC to treat urinary retention caused by lesions in the brain or following surgery; but it may also be used to treat constipation due to paralytic ileus, and also to treat the systemic neuromuscular transmission disorder myasthenia gravis. Administration is oral in the form of tablets, or by injection.

▲ side-effects: there may be nausea and vomiting, sweating and blurred vision, slow heart rate and colic.

✿ warning: distigmine bromide should not be administered to patients who suffer from urinary or intestinal blockage, or who have recently had a heart attack; it should be administered with caution to those with parkinsonism, epilepsy, cardiovascular disease, overactivity of the thyroid glands or asthma, or who are elderly or pregnant. *Related article*: UBRETID.

**Distran** (*Whitehall Laboratories*) is a proprietary, non-prescription DECONGESTANT, produced in the form of tablets and as a nasal spray. The nasal spray contains oxymetazoline, and the tablets contain caffeine, aspirin, phenylephrine and the ANTI-HISTAMINE chlorpheniramine.

▲/✿ side-effects/warning: *see*

ASPIRIN; CAFFEINE; CHLORPHENIRAMINE; OXYMETAZOLINE; PHENYLEPHRINE.

**disulfiram** is a drug that, in combination with the consumption of even small quantities of alcohol, gives rise to unpleasant, even dangerous, reactions – such as flushing, headache, palpitations, nausea and vomiting. This is because disulfiram and alcohol together cause an accumulation in the body of acetaldehyde. The drug is quite well known under its proprietary name. Administration is oral in the form of tablets.

▲ side-effects: taken with a large amount of alcohol, the drug may cause low blood pressure, serious heartbeat irregularities, and eventual collapse.

✺ warning: disulfiram should not be administered to patients with heart disorders, or during pregnancy, or to patients with drug dependence or mental illness. Simultaneous use of medications containing forms of alcohol should also be avoided.
*Related article:* ANTABUSE.

**dithranol** is the most powerful drug presently used to treat chronic or milder forms of psoriasis in topical application. For about an hour at a time, lesions are covered with a dressing on which there is a preparation of the drug in mild solution. Concentration is adjusted not only to suit individual response but also in relation to each patient's tolerance of the associated skin irritation. Healthy skin (and the eyes) must be avoided. The drug may be used in combination with others that have a moisturizing effect.

▲ side-effects: irritation and a local sensation of burning are common.

✺ warning: dithranol is not suitable for the treatment of acute forms of psoriasis. The drug stains skin, hair and fabrics.
*Related articles:* ANTHRANOL; ANTRADERM; DITHROCREAM; DITHROLAN; PSORADRATE; PSORIN.

**dithranol triacetate**, as a salt of dithranol, is used for the same purpose – the treatment of psoriasis – but is less effective and may be compared in this respect with COAL TAR.
▲ / ✺ side-effects/warning: *see* DITHRANOL.
*Related article:* EXOLAN.

**Dithrocream** (*Dermal*) is a proprietary, non-prescription preparation of the powerful drug dithranol, in dilute solution, used in topical application on dressings to treat chronic and mild forms of psoriasis. It is produced in the form of a water-miscible cream (in four strengths).
▲ / ✺ side-effects/warning: *see* DITHRANOL.

**Dithrolan** (*Dermal*) is a proprietary, non-prescription preparation of the powerful drug dithranol, in dilute solution, together with the ANTIBACTERIAL/ ANTIFUNGAL drug salicylic acid, and is used in topical application on dressings to treat chronic and mild forms of psoriasis. It is produced in the form of a paraffin-based ointment for dilution (the potency of the ointment once dilute is retained for 14 days).
▲ / ✺ side-effects/warning: *see* DITHRANOL; SALICYLIC ACID.

**Diumide-K Continus** (*Degussa*) is a proprietary DIURETIC, available only on prescription, used to treat the accumulation of fluid in the tissues (oedema) associated with heart, liver or kidney disorders, especially in cases where a potassium supplement is deemed necessary. Produced in the form of tablets, Diumide-K Continus is a compound preparation of the diuretic frusemide together with POTASSIUM CHLORIDE.

▲/✿ side-effects/warning: *see* FRUSEMIDE.

**Diuresal** (*Lagap*) is a proprietary DIURETIC, available only on prescription, used to treat the accumulation of fluid in the tissues (oedema) associated with heart, liver or kidney disorders. Produced in the form of tablets and in ampoules for injection, Diuresal is a preparation of frusemide.

▲/✿ side-effects/warning: *see* FRUSEMIDE.

**\*diuretics** are drugs that rid the body of fluids, generally by promoting their excretion in the form of urine. Accumulation of fluid in the tissues (oedema) is a common symptom of many disorders, particularly chronic disorders of the heart, liver, kidneys or lungs. Treatment with diuretics can thus assist in remedying such disorders. Salt and water retention also occurs in high blood pressure (hypertension), and diuretics are particularly used to treat that condition (as ANTIHYPERTENSIVE therapy), often in combination with a potassium supplement. Some diuretics are also useful in reducing the aqueous content of the eyeballs, so relieving internal pressure (as in glaucoma). Diuretics are commonly also used for premedication prior to surgery. Best-known and most used diuretics are the thiazides; other non-thiazide diuretics include ACETAZOLAMIDE, FRUSEMIDE, SPIRONOLACTONE and TRIAMTERENE.
*see* THIAZIDES.

**Diurexan** (*Merck*) is a proprietary DIURETIC, available only on prescription, used mainly to relieve the accumulation of fluids in the tissues (oedema) due to heart failure, and in lower dosages or in combination, to relieve high blood pressure (*see* ANTIHYPERTENSIVE). Produced in the form of tablets, Diurexan is a preparation of the THIAZIDE xipamide. It is not recommended for children.

▲/✿ side-effects/warning: *see* XIPAMIDE.

**Dixarit** (*WB Pharmaceuticals*) is a proprietary preparation of the ANTIHYPERTENSIVE drug clonidine hydrochloride, used in low dosage sometimes to try to prevent recurrent migraine and similar headaches, and to relieve flushing during the menopause in women. It is produced in the form of tablets, and is not recommended for children.

▲/✿ side-effects/warning: *see* CLONIDINE HYDROCHLORIDE.

**dobutamine hydrochloride** is a SYMPATHOMIMETIC drug used to treat cardiogenic shock and other serious heart disorders. It works by increasing the heart's force of contraction without affecting the heart rate. Administration is by injection or infusion.

▲ side-effects: the heart rate following treatment may increase too rapidly and result in high blood pressure (hypertension).
✿ warning: dobutamine hydrochloride should be administered with caution to patients with severe low blood pressure (hypotension).
*Related article:* DOBUTREX.

**Dobutrex** (*Lilly*) is a proprietary preparation of the SYMPATHO-

MIMETIC drug dobutamine hydrochloride, used to treat cardiogenic shock and other serious heart disorders. Available only on prescription, Dobutrex is produced in the form of a medium for intravenous infusion.

▲/✥ side-effects/warning: *see* DOBUTAMINE HYDROCHLORIDE.

**docusate sodium** is an alternative term for dioctyl sodium sulphosuccinate, a constituent in many LAXATIVES. *see* DIOCTYL SODIUM SULPHOSUCCINATE.

**Dolmatil** (*Squibb*) is a proprietary ANTIPSYCHOTIC drug used to treat the symptoms of schizophrenia. In low doses it increases an apathetic, withdrawn patient's awareness and tends to generate a true consciousness of events. In high doses it is used also to treat other conditions that may cause tremor, tics, involuntary movements or involuntary utterances (such as the relatively uncommon Giles de la Tourette syndrome). Produced in the form of tablets, Dolmatil is a preparation of sulpiride. It is not recommended for children aged under 14 years.

▲/✥ side-effects/warning: *see* SULPIRIDE.

**Dolobid** (*Morson*) is a proprietary, ANTI-INFLAMMATORY, non-narcotic ANALGESIC, available only on prescription, used to treat the pain of rheumatic disease and other musculo-skeletal disorders. Produced in the form of tablets (in two strengths), Dolobid is a preparation of the aspirin-like, anti-inflammatory drug diflunisal. It is not recommended for children.

▲/✥ side-effects/warning: *see* DIFLUNISAL.

**Doloxene** (*Lilly*) is a proprietary, narcotic analgesic, available on prescription only to private

patients, used to treat mild to moderate pain anywhere in the body. Produced in the form of capsules, Doloxene is a preparation of the OPIATE-like dextropropoxyphene napsylate. It is not recommended for children.

▲/✥ side-effects/warning: *see* DEXTROPROPOXYPHENE.

**Doloxene Compound** (*Lilly*) is a proprietary compound ANALGESIC, available on prescription only to private patients, used to treat mild to moderate pain anywhere in the body. Produced in the form of capsules, Doloxene represents a preparation of the OPIATE-like dextropropoxyphene napsylate, together with aspirin and caffeine. It is not recommended for children.

▲/✥ side-effects/warning: *see* ASPIRIN; CAFFEINE; DEXTROPROPOXYPHENE.

**Domical** (*Berk*) is a proprietary ANTIDEPRESSANT drug, available only on prescription, administered to treat depressive illness (and especially in cases where some degree of sedation is deemed necessary). Like many such drugs, it is also used to treat bedwetting by children at night. Produced in the form of tablets (in three strengths), Domical is a preparation of amitriptyline.

▲/✥ side-effects/warning: *see* AMITRIPTYLINE.

**domperidone** is an ANTI-EMETIC drug that is thought to work by inhibiting the action of the substance DOPAMINE in the brain; this can be useful in patients undergoing treatment with CYTOTOXIC drugs. It is also used to prevent vomiting in patients treated for parkinsonism with levodopa or bromocriptine. Administration is oral in the form of tablets or in suspension, or as anal suppositories.

▲ side-effects: occasionally, spontaneous lactation in women or the development of feminine breasts in men may occur.

✿ warning: domperidone should be administered with caution to those who suffer from impaired kidney function, who are pregnant or lactating. Prolonged treatment is not desirable.
*Related article:* MOTILIUM.

**Dopacard** (*Fisons*) is a SYMPATHOMIMETIC used as a stimulant of the force of the heart's beat. It is a proprietary form of dopamine hydrochloride available only on prescription. The preparation is in ampoules for intravenous infusion.

▲/✿ side-effects/warning: *see* DOPEXAMINE HYDROCHLORIDE.

**Dopamet** (*Berk*) is a proprietary ANTIHYPERTENSIVE drug, available only on prescription, used (generally in combination with a DIURETIC) to treat moderate to severe high blood pressure (hypertension). Produced in the form of tablets, Dopamet is a preparation of methyldopa.

▲/✿ side-effects/warning: *see* METHYLDOPA.

**dopamine** is a NEUROTRANSMITTER substance (a catecholamine), which is an intermediate in the synthesis of noradrenaline, acts as a neurotransmitter (relaying nerve 'messages'), and is particularly concentrated in the brain and in the adrenal glands. It is possible that some psychoses may in part be caused by abnormalities in the metabolism of dopamine because drugs that antagonize its activity as a neurotransmitter (such as chlorpromazine) tend to relieve

schizophrenic symptoms. It may be administered therapeutically (in the form of dopamine hydrochloride) in the treatment of the cardiogenic shock associated with a heart attack or in those who have undergone heart surgery. Administration is by injection or infusion.

▲ side-effects: there may be nausea and vomiting, with changes in heart rate and blood pressure – the fingertips and toes may become cold.

✿ warning: dopamine hydrochloride should not be administered to patients who suffer from disruptive disorder of the adrenal glands (phaeochromocytoma) or from heartbeat irregularities involving very rapid heart rate. Dosage to treat shock after a heart attack need only be low.
*Related articles:* INTROPIN; SELECT-A-JET DOPAMINE.

**dopexamine hydrochloride** is a SYMPATHOMIMETIC drug used for the treatment of heart conditions where moderate stimulation of the force of heart beat is required. It is available in the form of solution for intravenous infusion.

▲ side-effects: there may be stimulation of the rate of heart beat (sometimes excessive tachycardia), irregular heart beats; also angina pain, nausea, vomiting, and muscle tremor.

✿ warning: it should not be used in patients with certain heart outlet obstructions, with low blood platelets, and with certain endocrine disorders (phaeochromocytoma).
*Related article:* DOPACARD.

**Dopram** (*Robins*) is a proprietary preparation of the respiratory stimulant drug doxapram hydrochloride, available only on prescription, used in some

instances to relieve severe
respiratory difficulties in patients
with chronic disease of the
respiratory tract or who undergo
respiratory depression following
major surgery, particularly in
cases where ventilatory support is
for one reason or another not
applicable. It is produced in flasks
(bottles) for infusion (in dextrose
solution) or in ampoules for
injection.
▲/✚ side-effects/warning: see
    DOXAPRAM HYDROCHLORIDE.

**Dor** (*Simpla*) is a proprietary, non-
prescription deodorant solution
used (in drops) to freshen and
sanitize the appliance (bag)
placed over a stoma (an outlet, in
the skin surface, of the surgical
curtailment of the intestines or of
the ureters).

**Doralese** (*Bridge*) is a proprietary
ANTIHYPERTENSIVE drug,
available only on prescription,
and often used in combination
with other antihypertensives.
Produced in the form of tablets,
Doralese is a preparation of (the
alpha-blocker) indoramin
hydrochloride.
▲/✚ side-effects/warning: see
    INDORAMIN.

**Dormonoct** (*Roussel*) is a
proprietary HYPNOTIC drug,
available only on prescription,
used in the short term to treat
insomnia. Produced in the form of
tablets, it is a preparation of the
BENZODIAZEPINE loprazolam
mesylate. It is not recommended
for children.
▲/✚ side-effects/warning: see
    LOPRAZOLAM.

**dothiepin hydrochloride** is an
ANTIDEPRESSANT drug used to
treat depressive illness, especially
in cases where some degree of
sedation is deemed to be
necessary. Administration is oral
in the form of capsules or tablets.

▲ side-effects: concentration and
speed of reaction are
commonly affected; there
may also be dry mouth and
blurred vision, difficulty in
urinating, a rash, sweating
and irregular heartbeat.
Some patients experience
behavioural disturbance, a
state of confusion and/or a
loss of libido. Rarely, there
are also blood deficiencies.
✚ warning: dothiepin
hydrochloride should not be
administered to patients with
heart disease or psychosis; it
should be administered with
caution to those who are
pregnant or lactating, and to
those with epilepsy, diabetes,
liver or thyroid disease,
glaucoma, or urinary
retention. Withdrawal of
treatment must be gradual.
*Related article:* PROTHIADEN.

**Double Check** (*Family Planning
Sales*) is a proprietary, non-
prescription, SPERMICIDAL
preparation, for use only in
combination with barrier methods
of contraception (such as a
condom). Produced in the form of
vaginal inserts (pessaries),
Double Check is a preparation of
an alcohol ester.

**doxapram hydrochloride** is a
respiratory stimulant drug, used
with care in some instances, to
relieve severe respiratory
difficulties in patients who suffer
from chronic disease of the
respiratory tract or who undergo
respiratory depression following
major surgery, particularly in
cases where ventilatory support is
not applicable. Administration is
by injection or by infusion (in
dextrose solution).

▲ side-effects: the blood pressure
and heart rate may increase;
some patients experience
dizziness.
✚ warning: doxapram
hydrochloride should not be

administered to patients who suffer from very high blood pressure (hypertension), from cardiovascular disease, from an excess of thyroid hormones in the blood (thyrotoxicosis), or from severe asthma; it should be administered with caution to those who suffer from epilepsy or who are taking antidepressant drugs that affect mood.
*Related article:* DOPRAM.

**doxazosin** is an ANTI-HYPERTENSIVE drug that is an ALPHA-BLOCKER, used for the treatment of high blood pressure (hypertension), when it may be combined with treatment by DIURETICS and BETA-BLOCKERS. It is available in the form of tablets.
▲ side-effects: these include headache, dizziness, postural hypotension (fall in blood pressure on standing) fatigue and oedema.
● warning: initial dose needs careful adjustment, due to postural hypotension.
*Related article:* CARDURA.

**doxepin** is an ANTIDEPRESSANT drug used to treat depressive illness, especially in cases where some degree of sedation is deemed to be necessary. Administration is oral in the form of capsules (comprising doxepin hydro-chloride).
▲ side-effects: concentration and speed of reaction are commonly affected; there may also be dry mouth and blurred vision, difficulty in urinating, a rash, sweating and irregular heartbeat. Some patients experience behavioural disturbance, a state of confusion and/or a loss of libido. Rarely, there are also blood deficiencies.
● warning: doxepin hydrochloride should not be administered to patients with

heart disease or psychosis; it should be administered with caution to those who are pregnant or lactating, and to those with epilepsy, diabetes, liver or thyroid disease, glaucoma, or urinary retention. Withdrawal of treatment must be gradual.
*Related article:* SINEQUAN.

**doxorubicin hydrochloride** is a powerful and widely used CYTOTOXIC drug, which also has ANTIBIOTIC properties, used especially to treat leukaemia. Administration is by fast-running infusion (usually at intervals of 21 days, although a lower dose taken weekly may result in fewer toxic side-effects).
▲ side-effects: nausea and vomiting, hair loss and reduction in the blood-cell forming capacity of the bone-marrow are all fairly common side-effects. Rarely, there is also an increased heart rate. In the treatment of bladder tumours, side-effects may include urgency or difficulty in urinating, and possible reduction in bladder capacity.
● warning: doxorubicin hydrochloride should be administered with caution to patients with heart disease and liver damage, who are elderly, or who are receiving radiotherapy in the cardiac region. Heart monitoring is essential throughout treatment: high doses tend to cause eventual heart dysfunction. Leakage of the drug from the site of infusion into the tissues may cause tissue damage.
*Related article:* DOXORUBICIN RAPID DISSOLUTION.

**Doxorubicin Rapid Dissolution** (*Farmitalia Carlo Erba*) is a proprietary antibiotic drug that is CYTOTOXIC. It is therefore used to treat cancer (particularly leukaemia, lymphoma and certain solid tumours). Available only on prescription, it is produced in the form of powder for reconstitution as a medium for fast-running infusion (generally at three-week intervals). Its active constituent is doxorubicin hydrochloride. This preparation was formerly available as Adriamycin. Also available as Doxorubicin Solution for Injection.

▲/✷ side-effects/warning: see
DOXORUBICIN
HYDROCHLORIDE.

**doxycycline** is a broad-spectrum ANTIBIOTIC, one of the TETRACYCLINES, used to treat infections of many kinds, notably chlamydial infections (including urethritis and psittacosis), myocaplasmal (pneumonia) infections and exacerbations of chronic bronchitis due to *Haemophilus influenzae*. Administration is oral in the form of tablets and capsules, soluble (dispersible) tablets for solution, and as a dilute syrup. Unlike most tetracyclines it is relatively non-toxic to the kidney.

▲ side-effects: there may be nausea and vomiting, with diarrhoea. Some patients experience a sensitivity to light. Rarely, there are allergic reactions.

✷ warning: doxycycline should be administered with care to patients who are pregnant, or who are aged under 12 years. It should be administered with care to patients who are lactating.
*Related articles:* NORDOX;
VIBRAMYCIN.

**Dozie** (*RP Drugs*) is a proprietary ANTIPSYCHOTIC drug, available only on prescription, used to treat psychosis (especially schizophrenia or the hyperactive,

euphoric condition, mania) and to tranquillize patients undergoing behavioural disturbance. It may also be used in the short term to treat severe anxiety. Produced in the form of a sugar-free liquid (for swallowing, in two strengths), Dozie is a preparation of the powerful drug haloperidol.

▲/✷ side-effects/warning: see
HALOPERIDOL.

**Dramamine** (*Searle*) is a proprietary, non-prescription ANTI-EMETIC, used to treat nausea and vomiting, to prevent forms of motion sickness, and to relieve the loss of balance and vertigo experienced by patients with infections of the middle or inner ear or who have radiation sickness. Produced in the form of tablets, Dramamine is a preparation of dimenhydrinate. It is not recommended for children aged under 12 months.

▲/✷ side-effects/warning: see
DIMENHYDRINATE.

**Drapolene** (*Wellcome*) is a proprietary, non-prescription, ANTISEPTIC cream used primarily to treat nappy rash, although it can also be used to dress abrasions and minor wounds. It contains the antiseptics BENZALKONIUM CHLORIDE and CETRIMIDE in very dilute solution.

**Driclor** (*Stiefel*) is a proprietary medicated ANTIPERSPIRANT, available only on prescription, used to treat abnormally heavy sweating (hyperhidrosis) of the armpits, hands and feet. Produced in a roll-on bottle, Driclor represents a 20% solution of aluminium chloride.

▲/✷ side-effects/warning: see
ALUMINIUM CHLORIDE.

**Drogenil** (*Schering-Plough*) is an anti-androgen HORMONE ANTAGONIST, and is a proprietary form of flutamide available only on prescription. The preparation is available as tablets.

▲/✿ side-effects/warning: *see*
FLUTAMIDE.

**Droleptan** (*Janssen*) is a
proprietary preparation of the
powerful tranquillizer droperidol,
available only on prescription,
used primarily in emergencies to
subdue or soothe psychotic
(particularly manic) patients
during behavioural disturbances,
although it is also used on
patients about to undergo certain
diagnostic procedures that may
be difficult or painful, because it
promotes a sensation of
dispassionate detachment. It is
produced in the form of tablets, as
a sugar-free liquid for dilution
(the potency of the liquid once
dilute is retained for 14 days), and
in ampoules for injection.
▲/✿ side-effects/warning: *see*
DROPERIDOL.

**droperidol** is a powerful
TRANQUILLIZER and ANTI-
PSYCHOTIC, used primarily in
emergencies to subdue or soothe
psychotic (particularly manic)
patients during behavioural
disturbances, although it is also
used on patients about to undergo
certain diagnostic procedures
that may be difficult or painful,
because it promotes a sensation of
dispassionate detachment.
Administration is oral in the form
of tablets or as a sugar-free dilute
liquid, or by injection.
▲ side-effects: concentration and
speed of reaction is usually
affected. There may also be
restlessness, insomnia and
nightmares, rashes and
jaundice, dry mouth,
gastrointestinal disturbances,
difficulties in urinating, and
blurred vision. Muscles in the
neck and back, and sometimes
in the arms, may undergo
spasms. Rarely, there is weight
loss and impaired kidney
function.
✿ warning: droperidol should not
be administered to patients

with a reduction in the bone-
marrow's capacity to produce
blood cells, or with certain
types of glaucoma. It should be
administered only with caution
to those with heart or vascular
disease, kidney or liver disease,
parkinsonism, or depression; or
who are pregnant or lactating.
*Related articles:* DROLEPTAN;
THALAMONAL.

**drostanolone propionate** is a
synthesized steroid that has many
of the properties of an ANDROGEN
(a male sex hormone) and of an
anabolic steroid, used
therapeutically to treat the sex-
hormone-related cancer of the
breast in women. Administration
is by injection.
▲ side-effects: there is usually a
degree of masculinization,
involving at least menstrual
irregularity. High levels of
calcium in the blood are also
usual. There may be acne and
fluid retention leading to
weight gain.
✿ warning: drostanolone
propionate should not be
administered to patients with
impaired liver function or who
are pregnant; it should be
administered with caution to
those with impaired heart or
kidney function, epilepsy,
diabetes, high blood pressure
(hypertension) or migraine. In
patients young enough still to
be growing, bone development
should be monitored.

**Dryptal** (*Berk*) is a proprietary
DIURETIC, available only on
prescription, used to treat fluid
retention in the tissues (oedema)
and mild to moderate high blood
pressure (*see* ANTIHYPERTENSIVE).
In high dosage it may also be used
to assist a failing kidney.
Produced in the form of tablets (in
two strengths, the stronger for
hospital use only), Dryptal is a
preparation of the powerful but

short-acting diuretic frusemide.

▲/✿ side-effects/warning: *see*
FRUSEMIDE.

**DTIC-Dome** (*Bayer*) is a
proprietary CYTOTOXIC drug,
available only on prescription,
used (infrequently) to treat the
skin (mole) cancer melanoma,
some soft-tissue sarcomas, and the
lymphatic cancer Hodgkin's
disease. Produced in vials for
injection, DTIC-Dome is a
preparation of dacarbazine.

▲/✿ side-effects/warning: *see*
DACARBAZINE.

**Dubam** (*Norma*) is a proprietary,
non-prescription COUNTER-
IRRITANT compound which, in the
form of an aerosol spray applied
to the skin, produces an irritation
of sensory nerve endings that
offsets the pain of underlying
muscle or joint ailments. It
contains several salts of SALICYLIC
ACID in solution.

**Dulcolax** (*Boehringer Ingelheim*)
is a proprietary, non-prescription
LAXATIVE, which is not available
from the National Health Service.
Produced in the form of tablets
and as anal suppositories (in two
strengths), it is a preparation of
the stimulant laxative bisacodyl.
It is not recommended for
children.

▲/✿ side-effects/warning: *see*
BISACODYL.

**Duofilm** (*Stiefel*) is a proprietary,
non-prescription, liquid
preparation intended to remove
warts, particularly verrucas (on
the soles of the feet). For daily
topical application, avoiding
normal skin surfaces, it is a
compound in which the major
active constituent is SALICYLIC
ACID.

**Duogastrone** (*Winthrop*) is a
proprietary ANTACID that has
ANTI-INFLAMMATORY and

ANALGESIC properties. Available
only on prescription, it is used to
treat duodenal ulcer. It is
produced in the form of capsules
especially formulated for release
in the duodenum, and contains
carbenoxolone sodium, which is
thought to create a protective
coating over the mucous lining of
the duodenum. It is not
recommended for children.

▲/✿ side-effects/warning: *see*
CARBENOXOLONE SODIUM.

**Duovent** (*Boehringer Ingelheim*) is
a proprietary compound
BRONCHODILATOR, available only
on prescription, used to treat
bronchospasm in asthma and
chronic bronchitis. Produced in a
metered-dose aerosol with
mouthpiece, it is a combination of
the SYMPATHOMIMETIC fenoterol
hydrobromide together with the
ANTICHOLINERGIC drug
ipratropium bromide. It is not
recommended for children aged
under 6 years.

▲/✿ side-effects/warning: *see*
FENOTEROL; IPRATROPIUM.

**Duphalac** (*Duphar*) is a
proprietary, non-prescription
LAXATIVE, which is not available
from the National Health Service.
It works by maintaining a volume
of fluid within the intestines
through osmosis, so lubricating
the faeces and reducing levels of
ammonia-producing organisms.
Produced in the form of a syrup,
Duphalac is a preparation of the
semi-synthetic disaccharide
lactulose.

▲/✿ side-effects/warning: *see*
LACTULOSE.

**Duphaston** (*Duphar*) is a
proprietary preparation of the
PROGESTOGEN dydrogesterone, an
analogue of the sex hormone
PROGESTERONE. Available only on
prescription, it is used to treat
many conditions of hormonal
deficiency in women, including

menstrual difficulty, premenstrual syndrome, displacement of womb-lining tissue (endometriosis), recurrent miscarriage and infertility. It is produced in the form of tablets.

▲/● side-effects/warning: see DYDROGESTERONE.

**Durabolin** (*Organon*) is a proprietary form of the anabolic STEROID nandrolone, available only on prescription, used to assist the metabolic synthesis of protein, e.g., in building up the body following major surgery or long-term debilitating disease, or to treat osteoporosis ('brittle bones'). Sometimes administered also to treat sex-hormone-linked cancers, it is additionally used in the treatment of certain forms of anaemia, although how it works in this respect – and even whether it works – remains the subject of some debate: variations in patient response are wide. It is produced in ampoules or syringes for intramuscular injection.

▲/● side-effects/warning: see NANDROLONE.

**Duracreme** (*Family Planning Sales*) is a proprietary, non-prescription, SPERMICIDAL preparation, for use only in combination with barrier methods of contraception (such as a condom). Produced in the form of a cream, its active constituent is an alcohol ester.

**Duragel** (*LRC Products*) is a proprietary, non-prescription, SPERMICIDAL preparation, for use only in combination with barrier methods of contraception (such as a condom). Produced in the form of a gel, its active constituent is an alcohol ester.

**Duromine** (*Riker*) is a proprietary preparation of phentermine, which, as a strong stimulant drug, is on the controlled drugs list.

Used as an APPETITE SUPPRESSANT in the medical treatment of obesity, it is produced in the form of sustained-release tablets (in two strengths), and is not recommended for children.

▲/● side-effects/warning: see PHENTERMINE.

**Durophet** (*Riker*) is a proprietary preparation of amphetamine and dexamphetamine, and is on the controlled drugs list. It is an immensely powerful stimulant, and is used primarily to treat narcolepsy (a condition marked by irresistible attacks of sleep during the daytime), although it is sometimes also used to treat children who are medically hyperactive. Tolerance and dependence are major hazards. Produced in the form of sustained-release capsules (in three strengths), Durophet is not generally recommended for children.

▲/● side-effects/warning: see DEXAMPHETAMINE SULPHATE.

**Duvadilan** (*Duphar*) is a proprietary VASODILATOR that affects principally the blood vessels of the feet and hands, but it also affects the blood supply to the brain. It is therefore used to relieve the symptoms of both cerebral and peripheral vascular disease. The drug also has the effect of inhibiting contractions of the womb, and is thus additionally used to prevent or stall premature labour. A preparation of isoxsuprine hydrochloride, it is produced in the form of ampoules for injection.

▲/● side-effects/warning: see ISOXSUPRINE HYDROCHLORIDE.

**Dyazide** (*Smith, Kline & French*) is a proprietary compound DIURETIC, available only on

**D**

prescription, used to treat severe fluid retention in the tissues (oedema) and mild to moderate high blood pressure (hypertension). Produced in the form of tablets, Dyazide is a preparation of two powerful diuretics, triamterene and (the THIAZIDE) hydro-chlorothiazide.

▲/✿ side-effects/warning: *see* HYDROCHLOROTHIAZIDE; TRIAMTERENE.

**dydrogesterone** is a PROGESTOGEN, an analogue of the sex hormone PROGESTERONE, and is used to treat many conditions of hormonal deficiency in women, including menstrual difficulty, premenstrual syndrome, displacement of womb-lining tissue (endometriosis), recurrent miscarriage and infertility. Administration is oral in the form of tablets.

▲ side-effects: there may be breast tenderness and irregular menstruation, fluid retention and consequent weight gain, a change in libido, and gastrointestinal disturbances. Some patients also experience acne or urticaria.

✿ warning: dydrogesterone should not be administered to patients who suffer from cancer of the breast, thrombosis, or undiagnosed bleeding from the vagina; it should be administered with caution to those with diabetes, heart, liver or kidney disease, or high blood pressure (hypertension), or who are lactating.
*Related article:* DUPHASTON.

**Dynese** (*Galen*) is a proprietary, non-prescription ANTACID, which

is not available from the National Health Service. Produced in the form of a (mint- or orange-flavoured) suspension, it is a preparation of the complex MAGALDRATE, and is not recommended for children aged under 6 years.

**Dyspamet** (*Bridge*) is a proprietary form of the drug cimetidine, and is used for the treatment of peptic ulcers and gastro-oesophageal reflux disease. It is produced in the form of chewable tablets called Chewtab, and as a suspension.

▲/✿ side-effects/warning: *see* CIMETIDINE.

**Dytac** (*Smith, Kline & French*) is a proprietary DIURETIC, available only on prescription, used to treat fluid retention in the tissues (oedema) especially when caused by kidney or liver disease, or by congestive heart failure. Produced in the form of capsules, Dytac is a preparation of the powerful potassium-sparing diuretic triamterene. It is not recommended for children.

▲/✿ side-effects/warning: *see* TRIAMTERENE.

**Dytide** (*Smith, Kline & French*) is a proprietary compound DIURETIC, available only on prescription, used to treat fluid retention in the tissues (oedema). Produced in the form of capsules, Dytide represents a preparation of the powerful potassium-sparing diuretic triamterene together with the THIAZIDE diuretic benzthiazide. It is not recommended for children.

▲/✿ side-effects/warning: *see* BENZTHIAZIDE; TRIAMTERENE.

**E45 Cream** (*Crookes*) is a
proprietary, non-prescription skin
emollient (softener and soother)
containing a mixture of paraffins
and fats, including wool fat.
  ✳ warning: wool fat causes
    sensitivity reactions in some
    patients.

**Ebufac** (*DDSA Pharmaceuticals*)
is a proprietary, non-narcotic
ANALGESIC that has additional
ANTI-INFLAMMATORY properties.
Available only on prescription,
Ebufac is used to relieve pain –
particularly the pain of rheumatic
disease and other musculo-
skeletal disorders – and is
produced in the form of tablets
consisting of a preparation of
ibuprofen.
  ▲/✳ side-effects/warning: *see*
    IBUPROFEN.

**Econacort** (*Squibb*) is a
proprietary preparation that
combines the CORTICOSTEROID
hydrocortisone with the
ANTIFUNGAL econazole nitrate.
Available only on prescription
and produced in the form of a
cream for topical application,
Econacort is used to treat
inflammation in which fungal
infection is also diagnosed. The
cream, applied sparingly, should
be massaged into the skin;
prolonged use should be avoided.
  ▲/✳ side-effects/warning: *see*
    ECONAZOLE NITRATE.

**econazole nitrate** is a broad-
spectrum ANTIFUNGAL agent, one
of the IMIDAZOLES, used
particularly in topical
applications to treat fungal
infections of the skin or mucous
membranes, such as vaginal
candidiasis. Administration is in
the form of creams or ointments,
as vaginal inserts (pessaries or
tampons), or as lotions, sprays or
dusting-powders.
  ▲ side-effects: there may be local
    skin irritation, even to the
    extent of a burning sensation
    and redness.

  *Related articles:* ECOSTATIN;
  GYNO-PEVARYL; PEVARYL.

**Econocil VK** (*DDSA
Pharmaceuticals*) is a proprietary
preparation of the penicillin-type
ANTIBIOTIC phenoxymethyl-
penicillin. It is effective orally,
and used mainly to treat
infections of the middle ear and
throat, and some skin conditions.
Available only on prescription, it
is produced in the form of
capsules and tablets (in two
strengths).
  ▲/✳ side-effects/warning: *see*
    PHENOXYMETHYLPENICILLIN.

**Economycin** (*DDSA
Pharmaceuticals*) is a proprietary
ANTIBIOTIC, available only on
prescription, used to treat many
kinds of infection, but especially
those of the respiratory tract, ear,
nose and throat, gastrointestinal
tract, urinary tract, and soft
tissues. Produced in the form of
capsules and tablets, Economycin
is a preparation of the
TETRACYCLINE tetracycline
hydrochloride.
  ▲/✳ side-effects/warning: *see*
    TETRACYCLINE.

**Econosone** (*DDSA
Pharmaceuticals*) is a proprietary
CORTICOSTEROID preparation,
available only on prescription,
used to treat inflammation
especially in cases where it is
caused by allergy. Produced in
the form of tablets (in two
strengths), it is a form of the
steroid prednisone.
  ▲/✳ side-effects/warning: *see*
    PREDNISONE.

**Ecostatin** (*Squibb*) is a
proprietary, non-prescription
ANTIFUNGAL preparation of
econazole nitrate, used primarily
to treat yeast infections of the
skin and mucous membranes,
especially in the urogenital areas.
It is produced (in solution) in the

form of a water-miscible cream, as a lotion, as a spray for topical application, as a dusting-powder, as a talc-based powder in a spray container, and as vaginal inserts (pessaries). Treatment should continue for at least a fortnight after lesions have disappeared.

▲ side-effects: see ECONAZOLE NITRATE.

**ecothiopate iodide** is a miotic drug (that is, it causes the pupil of the eye to contract) used to reduce pressure in the eyeball and so relieve the symptoms of glaucoma. It is an anticho-linesterase and is more powerful than some other drugs used for the purpose, and its duration of effect longer, but associated side-effects prevent its common use. Administration is in the form of eye-drops.

▲ side-effects: there may be irritation on initial administration. Some patients then experience an ache across the eyebrow and blurred vision (because the accommodation of the eye is affected). But there is also a risk of cataract and/or blockage of the tear-ducts.

● warning: ecothiopate iodide should not be administered to patients who suffer from retinal damage, inflammation in the eye, or asthma, or who are already taking muscle relaxant drugs.
*Related article:* PHOSPHOLINE IODIDE.

**Eczederm** (*Quinoderm*) is a proprietary, non-prescription skin emollient (softener and soother) in the form of a cream that contains CALAMINE (zinc carbonate) and starch, of use in the treatment of eczematous dermatoses.

**Edecrin** (*Merck, Sharp & Dohme*) is a proprietary DIURETIC, available only on prescription,

used to treat fluid retention within the tissues (oedema), especially when related to congestive heart failure or liver or kidney disorders. Produced in the form of tablets, and in vials for injection, Edecrin is a preparation of ethacrynic acid. The tablets are not recommended for children aged under 2 years; the injection is not suitable for children.

▲/● side-effects/warning: see ETHACRYNIC ACID.

**edrophonium chloride** is a drug that has the effect of enhancing the transmission of neural impulses between the nerves and the muscles they serve because it is an anticholinesterase that prolongs the duration of the neurotransmitter. But its effect is of only very brief duration, and so it is used mainly for the diagnosis of neural disorders such as myasthenia gravis, and to check on the efficacy of cholinergic drugs prescribed to treat them. Administration is by injection.

▲ side-effects: there may be nausea and vomiting with an excess of saliva in the mouth, diarrhoea and abdominal cramps. High dosage may cause gastrointestinal disturbance and sweating; and overdosage may result in urinary and faecal incontinence, loss of coordination in vision, nervous agitation and weakness amounting to paralysis.

● warning: edrophonium chloride should not be administered to patients who suffer from intestinal or urinary blockage. It should be administered only with caution to those with asthma, epilepsy, parkinsonism, slow heart rate or low blood pressure (hypotension); who have recently had a heart

attack; or who are pregnant.
Some doctors administer
atropine (or a similar drug)
simultaneously to forestall
some side-effects.
*Related article:* TENSILON.

**Efalith** (*Scotia*) is a proprietary
ointment used to treat
seborrhoeic dermatitis. Available
only on prescription, the
preparation contains lithium
succinate and zinc sulphate as its
active ingredients.
▲/✿ side-effects/warning: not
    advised for patients with
    psoriasis.

**Efcortelan** (*Glaxo*) is a
proprietary preparation of the
CORTICOSTEROID hydrocortisone,
available only on prescription,
used to treat inflammation
especially where it is caused by
allergy, to relieve itching in the
urogenital areas, or to promote
the healing of dermatitis. It is
produced in the form of a cream,
and as an ointment.
▲/✿ side-effects/warning: *see*
    HYDROCORTISONE.

**Efcortelan Soluble** (*Glaxo*) is a
proprietary preparation of the
CORTICOSTEROID hydrocortisone,
available only on prescription,
used to treat inflammation
especially where it is caused by
allergy, to treat shock, or to make
up a deficiency of steroid
hormones in a patient. It is
produced in the form of a powder
for reconstitution (in water) as a
medium for injection.
▲/✿ side-effects/warning: *see*
    HYDROCORTISONE.

**Efcortesol** (*Glaxo*) is a proprietary
preparation of the CORTICO-
STEROID hydrocortisone, available
only on prescription, used to treat
inflammation especially where it
is caused by allergy, to treat
shock, or to make up a deficiency
of steroid hormones in a patient.
It is produced in ampoules for
injection.

▲/✿ side-effects/warning: *see*
    HYDROCORTISONE.

**Effercitrate** (*Typharm*) is a
proprietary, non-prescription
alkalizing agent used to render a
patient's urine alkaline in cases
of cystitis (inflammation and/or
infection of the bladder).
Produced in the form of tablets
for effervescent solution,
it represents a compound of citric
acid and potassium bicarbonate.
It is not recommended for
children aged under 12
months.
▲ side-effects: there may be mild
    diuresis, reduction in blood
    potassium levels and gastric
    irritation.
✿ warning: Effercitrate should
    not be administered to patients
    who suffer from ulceration or
    obstruction of the small
    intestine; it should be
    administered with caution to
    those with impaired kidney
    function.

**Effico** (*Pharmax*) is a proprietary,
non-prescription tonic, which is
not available from the National
Health Service. Used primarily to
stimulate the appetite, Effico
contains the stimulant CAFFEINE,
vitamin B in the form of THIAMINE
hydrochloride and NICOTINAMIDE,
and an infusion of gentian. It is
produced in the form of a syrup
for dilution (the potency of the
syrup once dilute is retained for
14 days).

**Efudix** (*Roche*) is a proprietary
CYTOTOXIC drug, available only on
prescription, used in the form of a
cream for topical application to
treat malignant skin lesions.
Consisting of a preparation of the
drug fluorouracil, it works by
being incorporated into new-
forming cells and so preventing
normal cell reproduction.
▲/✿ side-effects/warning: *see*
    FLUOROURACIL.

**Elantan** (*Schwarz*) is a proprietary preparation of the VASODILATOR isosorbide mononitrate, available only on prescription, used to prevent or treat angina pectoris (heart pain). Produced in the form of tablets (in three strengths, the stronger under the names Elantan 20 and Elantan 40), and also as sustained-release capsules under the name Elantan LA50. It is not recommended for children.
▲/ ✿ side-effects/warning: *see* ISOSORBIDE MONONITRATE.

**Elavil** (*DDSA Pharmaceuticals*) is a proprietary ANTIDEPRESSANT drug, available only on prescription, administered to treat depressive illness (and especially in cases where some degree of sedation is deemed necessary). Like many such drugs, it has also been used to treat bedwetting by children at night although this use is now becoming less common. Produced in the form of tablets (in two strengths), Elavil is a preparation of amitriptyline hydrochloride.
▲/ ✿ side-effects/warning: *see* AMITRIPTYLINE.

**Eldepryl** (*Britannia*) is a proprietary preparation of the drug selegiline, available only on prescription, used to assist in the treatment of the symptoms of parkinsonism (*see* ANTI-PARKINSONISM). It has the effect of reducing the breakdown of dopamine in the brain, and is used in combination with the amino acid LEVODOPA (which is converted to dopamine in the brain) to supplement and extend levodopa's action through its action as a monoamine oxidase inhibitor (MAO INHIBITOR). In many patients it has the additional effect of lessening some side-effects. It is produced in the form of tablets.
▲/ ✿ side-effects/warning: *see* SELEGILINE.

**Eldisine** (*Lilly*) is a proprietary CYTOTOXIC drug, available only on prescription, used to treat leukaemia, lymphomas and some solid tumours (such as cancer of the breast or lung). Produced in the form of a powder for reconstitution as a medium for injection, Eldisine is a preparation of the VINCA ALKALOID vindesine sulphate.
▲/ ✿ side-effects/warning: *see* VINDESINE SULPHATE.

**Elemental 028** (*Scientific Hospital Supplies*) is a proprietary nutritional supplement for patients who are severely undernourished or who are suffering from some problem with the absorption of food (such as following gastrectomy); it may also be used to feed patients who require a liquid diet through injury or disease. Produced in the form of orange-flavoured or plain powder in sachets for solution in water, Elemental 028 contains amino acids, carbohydrate, fats, VITAMINS and minerals. It is not suitable for children aged under 12 months.

**Elohes 6%** (*Oxford Nutrition*) is a proprietary form of the plasma substitute, hetastarch 6%, available only on prescription. It is used in an infusion with saline (sodium chloride) as a means of increasing overall blood volume in patients whose blood volume is dangerously low through shock, particularly in cases of severe burns or septicaemia.
▲/ ✿ side-effects/warning: *see* HETASTARCH.

**Eltroxin** (*Glaxo*) is a proprietary preparation of the thyroid hormone thyroxine, used to make up a hormonal deficiency, and to treat associated symptoms (myxoedema). It is produced in the form of tablets (in two strengths) containing thyroxine

sodium, and has a delayed effect and cumulative action.
▲/✦ side-effects/warning: *see* THYROXINE SODIUM.

**Eludril** (*Concept*) is a proprietary, non-prescription mouth-wash, which has ANTIBACTERIAL and ANTIFUNGAL properties and inhibits the formation of plaque on the teeth. It is also used in the treatment of gum disease and mouth ulcers. Containing the ANTISEPTIC chlorhexidine gluconate and chlorbutol, Eludril is not recommended for children aged under 6 years. An aerosol spray version is also available.
▲/✦ side-effects/warning: *see* CHLORHEXIDINE.

**Emblon** (*Berk*) is a proprietary preparation of the powerful drug tamoxifen, available only on prescription, which, because it inhibits or blocks the effect of OESTROGENS, is used primarily to treat cancers that depend on the presence of oestrogen in women, particularly breast cancer. But it may also be used (under strict medical supervision) to treat certain conditions of infertility in which the presence of oestrogens may be preventing other hormonal activity. It is produced in the form of tablets (in two strengths).
▲/✦ side-effects/warning: *see* TAMOXIFEN.

**Emcor** (*Merck*) is a proprietary form of the BETA-BLOCKER bisoprolol fumarate available only on prescription, used as an ANTIHYPERTENSIVE to treat hypertension and also angina pectoris (heart pain). Available in the form of tablets.
▲/✦ side-effects/warning: *see* PROPRANOLOL.

**empronium bromide** is a powerful ANTICHOLINERGIC drug used to treat patients who suffer

from excessive frequency of urination or from incontinence. It works by acting on the muscles at the base of the bladder both to inhibit the involuntary release of urine and to expand the bladder's overall capacity. However, empronium is poorly absorbed by the stomach and intestines, and even before reaching that stage may cause ulceration of the gums, mouth, throat or oesophagus unless sufficient fluid is taken simultaneously.
▲ side-effects: there may be dry mouth and difficulty in swallowing; the pupils may be dilated, causing blurred vision and sensitivity to light; pressure may increase inside the eyeballs. Flushing may be followed by heart rate disturbance and heartbeat irregularities. There may also be constipation. Rarely, there is fever.
✦ warning: empronium bromide should not be administered to patients with disorders of or injury to the oesophagus, or from glaucoma; it should be administered with caution to those with abnormal retention of food in the stomach, or enlargement of the prostate gland. It is essential that adequate fluid intake is maintained, or ulceration may occur.

**Emeside** (*L A B*) is a proprietary preparation of the ANTI-EPILEPTIC drug ethosuximide, available only on prescription, used to treat and suppress petit mal ('absence') seizures – the mild form of epilepsy. Produced in the form of capsules and as a blackcurrant- or orange-flavoured syrup for dilution (the potency of the syrup once diluted is retained for 14 days), Emeside's effects should be monitored following the initiation of treatment so that an optimum treatment level can be established.

▲/❋ side-effects/warning: *see* ETHOSUXIMIDE.

**emetic** is any agent that causes vomiting. Emetics are used mostly to treat poisoning by non-acidic, non-corrosive substances, especially drugs in overdose. Some affect the vomiting centre in the brain; others irritate the stomach nerves. Among the best-known and most-used is IPECACUANHA, but several drugs similarly used as constituents in expectorant preparations can in higher concentrations also cause effective emesis.

**Emla** (*Astra*) is a proprietary local ANAESTHETIC in the form of a cream for topical application. Available only on prescription, it is used primarily to relieve localized pain (caused, for example, by skin disease or sensitivity reaction), but it may also be used to prepare patients for a painful injection. It is a combined preparation of the anaesthetics lignocaine and prilocaine, and is presented in a pack that includes dressings.

▲/❋ side-effects/warning: *see* LIGNOCAINE; PRILOCAINE.

**Emulsiderm** (*Dermal*) is a proprietary, non-prescription skin emollient (softener and soother) in the form of a liquid emulsion that contains benzalkonium chloride and liquid paraffin. It can be rubbed into the skin or added to a bath.

❋ warning: *see* BENZALKONIUM CHLORIDE.

**emulsifying ointment** is a non-proprietary formulation comprising a combination of wax together with white soft paraffin and liquid paraffin. It is used as a base for medications that require topical application.

**enalapril** is an ANTIHYPERTENSIVE drug used to treat all forms of high blood pressure (hypertension), especially when more standard forms of therapy have failed or are not tolerated, and to assist in the treatment of congestive heart failure. It works by inhibiting the action of a certain peptide in the blood (angiotensin), which normally constricts the blood vessels. Administration (in the form of enalapril maleate) is oral, as tablets; some patients may require simultaneous administration of a DIURETIC (such as a THIAZIDE).

▲ side-effects: there may be a dry cough, headache, fatigue, dizziness, nausea, an alteration in the sense of taste, muscle cramps, diarrhoea, low blood pressure and renal failure. Some patients develop a rash.

❋ warning: enalapril should be administered with caution to patients with impaired kidney function, or who are pregnant. The initial dose may cause a rapid fall in blood pressure to low blood pressure (hypotension), especially in patients who are also taking diuretics or who are dehydrated.
*Related article:* INNOVACE.

**En-De-Kay** (*Stafford-Miller*) is a proprietary, non-prescription form of fluoride supplement for administration in areas where the water supply is not fluoridated, especially to growing children. Produced in the form of tablets (in three strengths, labelled for children of different ages), as a sugar-free liquid to be used in drops, and as a mouth-wash for dilution, En-De-Kay's active constituent is SODIUM FLUORIDE.

**Endobulin** (*Immuno*) is an IMMUNOGLOBULIN, a proprietary form of human normal immunoglobulin (HNIG) available only on prescription, and used as replacement therapy for patients with deficient gammaglobulin. The preparation is in a form for intravenous use.

▲/✿ side-effects/warning: see HNIG.

**Endoxana** (*Boehringer Ingelheim*) is a proprietary CYTOTOXIC drug, available only on prescription, used in the treatment of leukaemia, lymphomas and some solid tumours. It works by disrupting the DNA in new-forming cells and so preventing normal cell reproduction. Produced in the form of tablets (in two strengths) and as a powder for reconstitution as a medium for injection, Endoxana is a preparation of cyclophosphamide; it is sometimes prescribed in combination with the drug MESNA. It is not recommended for children.

▲/✿ side-effects/warning: see CYCLOPHOSPHAMIDE.

**Enduron** (*Abbott*) is a proprietary DIURETIC, available only on prescription, used to treat an accumulation of fluid within the tissues (oedema) and high blood pressure (hypertension). Produced in the form of tablets, Enduron is a preparation of the THIAZIDE methyclothiazide.

▲/✿ side-effects/warning: see METHYCLOTHIAZIDE.

**Ener-G** (*General Designs*) is a proprietary, non-prescription, gluten-free brown rice bread, for patients whose metabolisms are unable to tolerate the compound cereal protein gluten (as with coeliac disease). The bread is made without milk, eggs, wheat, soya or refined sugar.

**enflurane** is a volatile general ANAESTHETIC usually given to supplement nitrous oxide-oxygen

mixtures (in a concentration of between 1 and 5%) for the induction and maintenance of anaesthesia during major surgery. Only a small proportion of the drug is metabolized by a patient, making it particularly safe for repeated use. Administration is by inhalation through a calibrated vaporizer.

▲ side-effects: reduced heart function results in low blood pressure.

✿ warning: enflurane slows both the heart and the breathing rate. Shallow breathing may tend to build up carbon dioxide levels in the body. The drug should not be administered to patients who have respiratory disorders.
*Related article:* ETHRANE.

**enoxacin** is an antibiotic drug of the quinolone family, used to treat infections of the urinary tract and skin, gonorrhoea and bacterial dysentery. Administration is oral in the form of tablets.

▲ side-effects: there may be nausea and vomiting, with gastro-intestinal disturbances and weight loss, diarrhoea and cramps. Some patients experience sensitivity reactions including a rash, dizziness, headache and ringing in the ears.

✿ warning: enoxacin should be administered with caution to patients with even slightly impaired kidney function.

**enoximone** is a PHOSPHO-DIESTERASE INHIBITOR, used to treat congestive heart failure, especially where other drugs have been unsuccessful. It is available only on prescription, and is administered by intravenous injection or infusion.

▲ side-effects: there may be irregular or extra heart beats, speeding of the heart, hypotension, headache, nausea and vomiting, insomnia, chills and fever, diarrhoea, retention of urine, and pain in the limbs.

✤ warning: enoximone should be given with care to patients with certain forms of heart failure and vascular disease. The blood pressure and electrocardiogram should be monitored. A smaller dose may be indicated in patients with kidney disease.

*Related article:* PERFAN.

**Enrich** (*Abbott*) is a proprietary nutritional supplement for patients who are severely undernourished (such as with anorexia nervosa) or who are suffering from some problem with the absorption of food (such as following gastrectomy); it may also be used to feed patients who require a liquid diet through injury or disease. Produced in the form of a lactose- and gluten-free liquid in cans, Enrich contains protein, carbohydrate (including dietary fibre), fats, vitamins and minerals. It is not suitable for children aged under 12 months, or as a sole source of nutrition for children under 5 years.

**Ensure** (*Abbott*) is a proprietary nutritional supplement for patients who are severely undernourished (such as with anorexia nervosa) or who are suffering from some problem with the absorption of food (such as following gastrectomy); it may also be used to feed patients who require a liquid diet through injury or disease. Produced in the form of a lactose- and gluten-free liquid in cans and bottles (or as a powder for reconstitution in identical form), Ensure contains protein, carbohydrate, fats, vitamins and minerals, and comes in vanilla, coffee and eggnog flavours. It is not suitable for children aged under 12 months. A

version with a higher proportion of protein, carbohydrate and fats is also available (under the name Ensure Plus).

**Enteromide** (*Consolidated*) is a proprietary ANTIBIOTIC drug, available only on prescription, formerly used to treat inflammation and infection of the intestines, to relieve food poisoning, or to reduce bacterial levels in the intestines before surgery or examination, but now used less commonly. Produced in the form of tablets, Enteromide is a preparation of the poorly absorbed SULPHONAMIDE drug calcium sulphaloxate.

▲/✤ side-effects/warning: *see* CALCIUM SULPHALOXATE.

**Enterosan** (*Windsor Pharmaceuticals*) is a proprietary, non-prescription ANTIDIARRHOEAL preparation containing morphine, KAOLIN and belladonna.

▲/✤ side-effects/warning: *see* BELLADONNA; MORPHINE.

**Entrotabs** (*Wallis*) is a proprietary, non-prescription, ANTIDIARRHOEAL preparation containing the ANTACIDS aluminium hydroxide and magnesium aluminium silicate (attapulgite), and the fruit substance pectin.

▲/✤ side-effects/warning: *see* ALUMINIUM HYDROXIDE.

***enzymes** are substances within the body that play an essential part in metabolism since they act as catalysts in speeding the rate of specific necessary biochemical reactions. Some drugs exert their actions through inhibiting or increasing the activity of these natural components of the body, and in rarer instances enzymes are administered to patients in which case they are regarded as drugs since these chemicals are now foreign to the body.

Examples of the former are the ANTIDEPRESSANT drugs MAO INHIBITORS, and of the latter CRISTANASPASE.

**Epanutin** (*Parke-Davis*) is a proprietary ANTICONVULSANT drug, available only on prescription, used to treat and prevent grand mal (tonic-clonic) and partial (focal) epileptic seizures. It is sometimes alternatively used to treat or prevent attacks of migraine or trigeminal (facial) neuralgia. Produced in the form of capsules (in three strengths), as chewable tablets (under the name Epanutin Infatabs), and as a suspension for dilution (the potency of the suspension once dilute is retained for 14 days), Epanutin is a preparation of the effective but non-hypnotic drug phenytoin.

▲/✹ side-effects/warning: *see* PHENYTOIN.

**Epanutin Ready Mixed Parenteral** (*Parke-Davis*) is a form of the proprietary ANTICONVULSANT drug EPANUTIN, which is administered to treat the emergency epileptic condition status epilepticus. It may, however, also be used to prevent convulsive seizures during neurosurgical operations and, perhaps more mundanely, to treat and regularize heartbeat irregularities. Produced in ampoules for injection, it is a solution of phenytoin sodium with propylene glycol. Not recommended for children.

▲/✹ side-effects/warning: *see* PHENYTOIN.

**ephedrine hydrochloride** is a SYMPATHOMIMETIC drug used as a VASOCONSTRICTOR and BRONCHODILATOR, used mainly in the treatment of asthma, chronic bronchitis and similar conditions (especially allergy-based ones). (This is also the major use of the closely related drug pseudo-ephedrine.) Its effect as a vasoconstrictor is sometimes utilized to counteract the fall in blood pressure in the blood vessels of the hands and feet that may occur in general anaesthesia. Other uses are in treating whooping cough, in inhibiting urinary incontinence in adults and bed-wetting by children, to treat nasal congestion, and to dilate the pupil of the eye for ophthalmic examination or surgery. Administration is oral in the form of tablets or as an elixir, or topical in the form of nose-drops.

▲ side-effects: there may be changes in heart rate and blood pressure, anxiety, restlessness, tremor, insomnia, dry mouth, and cold finger-tips and toes. Used as a nasal decongestant, there may be local irritation.

✹ warning: ephedrine hydrochloride should not be administered to patients who are already taking drugs that affect the action of the heart; it should be administered with caution to those with diabetes, reduced blood supply to the heart, high blood pressure (hypertension), disorder of the thyroid gland, and during pregnancy and lactation. Prolonged use as a broncho-dilator or as a nasal decongestant may eventually result in tolerance.

*Related articles:* CAM; DAVENOL; EXPULIN; EXPURHIN; FRANOL; FRANOL PLUS; HAYMINE; LOTUSSIN; NORADRAN; PHENSEDYL.

**Ephynal** (*Roche*) is a proprietary, non-prescription form of vitamin E (TOCOPHEROL) supplement, used to make up for vitamin deficiency. It is produced in the form of tablets (in four strengths) consisting of a preparation of alpha tocopheryl acetate.

**Epifoam** (*Stafford-Miller*) is a proprietary CORTICOSTEROID preparation with mild local ANAESTHETIC properties, available only on prescription, in the form of a foam for topical application in the perineal region of the body (the vulva in women, between the anus and the scrotum in men), especially on women patients who have undergone an episiotomy during childbirth. It is a combination of the steroid hydrocortisone and the mild local anaesthetic pramoxine hydrochloride, and is applied on a pad.
▲/✿ side-effects/warning: *see* HYDROCORTISONE.

**Epifrin** (*Allergan*) is a proprietary preparation of the natural hormone adrenaline hydrochloride, available only on prescription. It is used (in very dilute solution) in the form of eye-drops as a SYMPATHOMIMETIC to treat glaucoma. Prolonged use should be avoided.
▲/✿ side-effects/warning: *see* ADRENALINE.

**Epilim** (*Labaz*) is a proprietary ANTICONVULSANT drug, available only on prescription, used to treat all forms of epilepsy. Considerable monitoring of body functions is necessary during treatment for the first 6 months. Produced in the form of crushable tablets, as enteric-coated tablets (in two strengths), as a sugar-free liquid, and as a syrup for dilution (the potency of the syrup once dilute is retained for 14 days), Epilim is a preparation of the carboxylic acid derivative sodium valproate.
▲/✿ side-effects/warning: *see* SODIUM VALPROATE.

**epirubicin hydrochloride** is an ANTIBIOTIC and CYTOTOXIC drug, and is used both to treat cancer and as an IMMUNOSUPPRESSANT following tissue grafting or transplantation in order to prevent tissue rejection. Dosage is critical to each individual patient. Administration is by injection.
▲ side-effects: hair loss is common, even to total baldness; there may be inflammation of the mucous lining of the mouth (stomatitis), nausea and vomiting. There is also increased sensitivity to radiotherapy (which in most cases should be avoided).
✿ warning: suppression of the bone-marrow's function of producing red blood cells is inevitable, and regular blood counts are essential. The drug is also a skin irritant.
*Related article:* PHARMORUBICIN.

**Epodyl** (*ICI*) is a proprietary CYTOTOXIC drug, available only on prescription, used primarily in the treatment of recurrent but only mildly malignant tumours of the bladder. Produced in the form of a liquid solution for instillation into the bladder (for retention there for at least one hour), Epodyl is a preparation of ethoglucid.
▲/✿ side-effects/warning: *see* ETHOGLUCID.

**epoetin** is a synthesized form of human erythropoietin used to treat anaemia known to be associated with chronic renal failure in dialysis patients. Used in a form for intravenous administration.
▲ side-effects: cardiovascular symptoms including high blood pressure (hypertension) and cardiac complications; anaphylactic reactions, flu-like symptoms, skin reactions; oedema.
✿ warning: it should be administered with caution to patients with uncontrolled

hypertension or an abnormal blood picture (haemoglobin levels and blood pressure should be monitored); in patients with a history of convulsions, vascular disease, liver failure, and malignant diseases. Iron supplements may be required in addition.
*Related articles:* EPREX; RECORMON.

**Epogam** (*Scotia*) is a proprietary preparation containing gamolenic acid in evening primrose oil. It is used for the relief of atopic eczema. It is available only on prescription in the form of capsules.
▲/✿ side-effects/warning: *see* GAMOLENIC ACID.

**epoprostenol**, or prostacyclin, is a prostaglandin present in the walls of blood vessels. Administered therapeutically, by intravenous infusion, it constitutes an ANTICOAGULANT that inhibits blood coagulation by preventing the aggregation of platelets, in addition having the effect of a VASODILATOR. Its major uses are to preserve platelet function in heart by-pass operations, and to act as a substitute for HEPARIN if required during kidney dialysis.
▲ side-effects: there is commonly flushing and low blood pressure (hypotension); there may also be headache. High dosage may cause pallor and sweating.
✿ warning: epoprostenol's half-life is only about 3 minutes, so the drug must be administered in continous intravenous infusion. Blood count monitoring is essential, especially when there is simultaneous administration of heparin.
*Related article:* FLOLAN.

**Eppy** (*Smith & Nephew*) is a proprietary preparation of the hormone adrenaline, available

only on prescription. It is used (in very dilute solution) in the form of eye-drops as a SYMPATHO-MIMETIC to treat glaucoma. Prolonged use should be avoided.
▲/✿ side-effects/warning: *see* ADRENALINE.

**Eprex** (*Cilag*) is a proprietary form of EPOETIN (synthesised human erythropoitin) used to treat anaemia known to be associated with chronic renal failure in dialysis patients. Available only on prescription, the preparation is available in a form for intravenous administration.
▲/✿ side-effects/warning: *see* EPOITIN.

**Equagesic** (*Wyeth*) is a proprietary compound ANALGESIC, which is on the controlled drugs list and is not available from the National Health Service. Used primarily in the short-term treatment of rheumatic pain or the symptoms of other musculo-skeletal disorders, and produced in the form of tablets, Equagesic contains the (potentially addictive) TRANQUILLIZER meprobamate, the SKELETAL MUSCLE RELAXANT ethoheptazine citrate, and aspirin. It is not recommended for children. There are interactions with a wide variety of drugs including alcohol and nervous system depressants.
▲/✿ side-effects/warning: *see* ASPIRIN; MEPROBAMATE.

**Equanil** (*Wyeth*) is a proprietary ANXIOLYTIC drug that is on the controlled drugs list. Used in the short-term treatment of nervous anxiety and associated muscular tension, and produced in the form of tablets (in two strengths), Equanil is a preparation of the potentially addictive, TRANQUILLIZER meprobamate. It is not recommended for children, and is contraindicated in acute porphyria and alcoholism.

▲/✿ side-effects/warning: *see* MEPROBAMATE.

**Eradacin** (*Sterling Research*) is a proprietary preparation of the ANTIBIOTIC drug acrosoxacin, one of the quinolones, and is available only on prescription. It is used to treat the sexually transmitted disease gonorrhoea in patients who are allergic to penicillin, or whose strain of gonorrhoea is resistant to penicillin-type antibiotics. Produced in the form of capsules, Eradacin is not recommended for children.
   ▲/✿ side-effects/warning: *see* ACROSOXACIN.

**ergocalciferol** is one of the two natural forms of calciferol (vitamin D) formed in plants by the action of sunlight. It is in fact vitamin $D_2$, but in medicine it is usually referred to as ERGOCALCIFEROL or simply CALCIFEROL.
   ▲/✿ side-effects/warning: *see* CALCIFEROL.
   *Related articles:* CALCIUM AND ERGOCALCIFERAL TABLETS; CHOCOVITE.

**ergometrine maleate** is an alkaloid VASOCONSTRICTOR and uterine stimulant drug administered to women in childbirth during the third stage of labour: the delivery of the placenta. A measure to prevent excessive postnatal bleeding. The drug is generally administered by injection when the baby is half-way delivered, although it is produced also in the form of tablets.
   ▲ side-effects: there may be nausea and vomiting, with temporary high blood pressure.
   ✿ warning: ergometrine maleate must not in any circumstances be administered to patients who are still in the first and early second stages of labour; it should not be administered

to those with vascular disease, or impaired kidney, liver or lung function. Caution must be exercised in administration to those with heart disease and high blood pressure (hypertension) or with any infection, who have toxaemia of pregnancy, or who have just undergone a multiple birth.
   *Related article:* SYNTOMETRINE.

**ergotamine tartrate** is a drug administered to patients who suffer from migraine, which is not relieved by the ordinary forms of pain-killing drug. A vegetable alkaloid, it is most effectively administered during the aura – the initial symptoms – of an attack, and probably works by constricting the cranial arteries. However, although the pain may be relieved, other symptoms, such as the visual disturbances and nausea, may not (although other drugs may be administered to treat those separately). Repeated treatment may in some patients eventually lead to habituation (addiction); in others it may cause ergot poisoning, resulting in gangrene of the fingers and toes, and confusion. Administration is oral in the form of tablets either for swallowing or to be held under the tongue to dissolve, or as an aerosol inhalant; one proprietary compound preparation is in the form of anal suppositories.
   ▲ side-effects: there may be abdominal pain and muscle cramps that may lead to nausea and vomiting. Overdosage or rapid withdrawal of the drug may in turn cause headache.
   ✿ warning: ergotamine tartrate should not be administered to patients who suffer from vascular disease or any infection, or who are pregnant or lactating. It should be administered with caution to those with kidney, liver or

heart disease, or with thyroid gland overactivity. Dosage should be carefully monitored; treatment should not be repeated within 4 days. It should never be administered on a prophylactic (preventative) basis. Treatment should be withdrawn at once if the patient experiences tingling or numbness at the extremities.
*Related articles:* CAFERGOT; LINGRAINE; MEDIHALER-ERGOTAMINE; MIGRIL.

**Ermysin** (*Britannia*) is a proprietary ANTIBIOTIC, available only on prescription, used to treat many forms of infection (particularly pneumonia and legionnaires' disease) and to prevent others (particularly sinusitis, diphtheria and whooping cough), and as an alternative to penicillin-type antibiotics in patients who are allergic or whose infections are resistant. Produced in the form of tablets (in two strengths), Ermysin is a preparation of the macrolide erythromycin. It is not recommended for children.
▲ / ● side-effects/warning: *see* ERYTHROMYCIN.

**Ervevax** (*Smith, Kline & French*) is a proprietary VACCINE against German measles (rubella) in the form of a solution containing live but attenuated viruses of the Wistar RA27/3 strain. Available only on prescription, it is administered in the form of injection.

**Erwinase** (*Porton*) is a proprietary form of the ENZYME cristantaspase, available only on prescription. Available in the form of a powder for reconstitution.
▲ / ● side-effects/warning: *see* CRISTANASPASE.

**Erycen** (*Berk*) is a proprietary ANTIBIOTIC, available only on prescription, used to treat many forms of infection (particularly pneumonia and legionnaires' disease) and to prevent others (particularly sinusitis, diphtheria and whooping cough), and as an alternative to penicillin-type antibiotics in patients who are allergic or whose infections are resistant. Produced in the form of tablets (in two strengths) and a suspension, Erycen is a preparation of the macrolide erythromycin. It is not recommended for children.
▲ / ● side-effects/warning: *see* ERYTHROMYCIN.

**Erymax** (*Parke-Davis*) is a proprietary ANTIBIOTIC, available only on prescription, used to treat many forms of infection (particularly pneumonia and legionnaires' disease) and to prevent others (particularly sinusitis, diphtheria and whooping cough), and as an alternative to penicillin-type antibiotics in patients who are allergic or whose infections are resistant. Produced in the form of capsules, Erymax is a preparation of the macrolide erythromycin. Also available is Erymax sprinkle, a preparation produced in the form of capsules whose contents may be sprinkled on soft food for use in children.
▲ / ● side-effects/warning: *see* ERYTHROMYCIN.

**Erythrocin** (*Abbott*) is a proprietary ANTIBIOTIC, available only on prescription, used to treat many forms of infection (particularly pneumonia and legionnaires' disease) and to prevent others (particularly sinusitis, diphtheria and whooping cough), and as an alternative to penicillin-type antibiotics in patients who are allergic or whose infections are resistant. Produced in the form of tablets (in two strengths), and as a powder for reconstitution as a medium for injection, Erythrocin is a preparation of salts of the macrolide erythromycin. The tablets are not recommended for children.

▲ / ✿ side effects/warning: *see* ERYTHROMYCIN.

**Erythromid** (*Abbott*) is a proprietary ANTIBIOTIC, available only on prescription, used to treat many forms of infection (particularly pneumonia and legionnaires' disease) and to prevent others (particularly sinusitis, diphtheria and whooping cough), and as an alternative to penicillin-type antibiotics in patients who are allergic or whose infections are resistant. Produced in the form of tablets (in two strengths, the stronger under the name Erythromid DS), Erythromid is a preparation of the macrolide erythromycin. It is not recommended for children.

▲ / ✿ side-effects/warning: *see* ERYTHROMYCIN.

**erythromycin** is a macrolide ANTIBIOTIC with a similar spectrum of action to penicillin, but a different mechanism of action: it inhibits microbial protein synthesis at the ribosome level. It is effective against many gram-positive bacteria including streptococci (soft tissue and respiratory tract infections), mycoplasma (pneumonia), legionella (legionnaire's disease) and chlamydia (urethritis). It is also used as prophylaxis (preventative therapy) for diphtheria and whooping cough. Erythromycin's principal use is as an alternative to penicillin in individuals who are allergic to penicillin. Bacterial resistance is unfortunately not uncommon. Administration is oral in the form

of tablets, as capsules, or as a dilute suspension (mixture), or by injection. Tablets have to be enteric- or film-coated because the drug is inactivated by gastric secretions.

▲ side-effects: large doses may cause nausea and vomiting, and possibly diarrhoea.

✿ warning: one salt of erythromycin (the estolate), a constituent in a proprietary suspension, should not be administered to patients with liver disease; all forms of the drug should be administered with caution to those with impaired liver function.
*Related articles:* ARPIMYCIN; ER/CEN; ERYMAX; ERYTHROCIN; ERYTHROMID; ERYTHROPED; ILOSONE; RETCIN; STIEMYCIN.

**Erythroped** (*Abbott*) is a proprietary ANTIBIOTIC, available only on prescription, used to treat many forms of infection (particularly pneumonia and legionnaires' disease) and to prevent others (particularly sinusitis, diphtheria and whooping cough), and as an alternative to penicillin-type antibiotics in patients who are allergic or whose infections are resistant. Produced in the form of a suspension (in three strengths) for dilution (the potency of the suspension once diluted is retained for 5 days), as sugar-free granules in sachets for solution, and as tablets (under the name Erythroped A), Erythroped is a preparation of salts of the macrolide erythromycin.

▲ / ✿ side-effects/warning: *see* ERYTHROMYCIN.

**Esbatal** (*Calmic*) is a proprietary ANTIHYPERTENSIVE drug, available only on prescription, used to treat very high blood pressure (hypertension). Produced in the form of tablets (in two strengths), it is a preparation of bethanidine sulphate.

▲/❋ side-effects/warning: *see*
BETHANIDINE SULPHATE.

**Esidrex** (*Ciba*) is a proprietary
DIURETIC, available only on
prescription, used to treat an
accumulation of fluid in the
tissues (oedema) and high blood
pressure (hypertension). Produced
in the form of tablets (in two
strengths), Esidrex is a
preparation of the THIAZIDE
hydrochlorothiazide.
▲/❋ side-effects/warning: *see*
HYDROCHLOROTHIAZIDE.

**Esidrex K** (*Ciba*) is a proprietary
DIURETIC, available only on
prescription, used to treat an
accumulation of fluid in the
tissues (oedema) and high blood
pressure (hypertension). Produced
in the form of double-layered
tablets, Esidrex K is a preparation
of the THIAZIDE hydrochlorothiazide (which is potassium-
depleting) with the potassium
supplement POTASSIUM CHLORIDE.
▲/❋ side-effects/warning: *see*
HYDROCHLOROTHIAZIDE.

**Eskamel** (*Smith, Kline & French*)
is a proprietary, non-prescription
cream used to treat acne. It
contains the KERATOLYTIC agent
resorcinol together with SULPHUR.
❋ warning: *see* RESORCINOL.

**Eskornade** (*Smith, Kline &
French*) is a proprietary, non-
prescription nasal DECONGESTANT,
which is not available from the
National Health Service. It is used
particularly to treat the symptoms
of the common cold, sinusitis and
flu. Produced in the form of
spansules (sustained-release
capsules) and as a sugar-free syrup
for dilution (the potency of the
syrup once dilute is retained for 14
days), Eskornade is a combination
of the SYMPATHOMIMETIC
phenylpropanolamine
hydrochloride with the
ANTIHISTAMINE diphenylpyraline
hydrochloride. In the form

of spansules, (sustained-
release capsules), the preparation
is not recommended for
children.
▲/❋ side-effects/warning: *see*
DIPHENYLPYRALINE
HYDROCHLORIDE;
PHENYLPROPANOLAMINE
HYDROCHLORIDE.

**Esoderm** (*Napp*) is a proprietary,
non-prescription preparation of
the drug lindane, used to treat
parasitic infestation by lice
(pediculosis) or by itchmites
(scabies) on the skin surface,
particularly under the hair.
However, strains of head-lice
resistant to lindane have recently
emerged, and the drug is not now
recommended for use on the scalp.
It is produced in the form of a
(flammable) alcohol-based lotion,
and as a cream shampoo.
▲/❋ side-effects/warning: *see*
LINDANE.

**Estracyt** (*Lundbeck*) is a
proprietary CYTOTOXIC drug,
available only on prescription, an
OESTROGEN used to treat cancer of
the prostate gland. Because this
type of cancer is sex-hormone-
linked (with respect to androgens,
male sex hormones),
administration of a female sex
hormone – although it produces
some feminization – is an effective
counter-measure. Produced in the
form of capsules (not to be taken
with milk or with any other dairy
product), Estracyt is a
preparation of estramustine
phosphate.
▲/❋ side-effects/warning: *see*
ESTRAMUSTINE PHOSPHATE.

**Estradurin** (*Lundbeck*) is a
proprietary CYTOTOXIC drug,
available only on prescription, a
compound OESTROGEN used to
treat cancer of the prostate gland.
Because this type of cancer is sex-
hormone-linked (with respect to
androgens, male sex hormones),

administration of female sex hormones – although it produces some feminization – is an effective counter-measure. Produced in vials for injection, Estradurin is a combination of the oestrogen preparation polyestradiol phosphate with the local ANAESTHETIC mepivacaine and the B vitamin NICOTINAMIDE.

▲/✿ side-effects/warning: *see* POLYESTRADIOL PHOSPHATE.

**estramustine phosphate** is a CYTOTOXIC drug, an OESTROGEN used to treat cancer of the prostate gland. Because this type of cancer is sex-hormone-linked (with respect to androgens, male sex hormones), administration of a female sex hormone – although it produces some feminization – is an effective counter-measure. Administration is oral in the form of capsules.

▲ side-effects: there is commonly nausea and vomiting, and sodium retention with a consequent weight gain. The breasts may develop. The blood-producing capacity of the bone-marrow is impaired. And there is hair loss.

✿ warning: treatment causes sterility; prolonged treatment may increase a disposition towards leukaemia especially if there is simultaneous irradiation treatment. Estramustine phosphate should be administered with caution to patients who suffer from diabetes, epilepsy, severe migraine, kidney or heart disease, or high blood pressure (hypertension). Blood count monitoring is essential. *Related article:* ESTRACYT.

**Estrapak 50** (*Ciba*) is a HORMONE preparation containing female sex hormones, used to treat menopausal symptoms. Available only on prescription, the preparation takes the form of a

calender pack containing both self-adhesive dressings (which are applied to unbroken areas of skin below the waist) and tablets to be taken by mouth. The tablets contain the PROGESTOGEN norethisterone, and the tablets the OESTROGEN oestradiol, which is absorbed through the skin.

▲/✿ side-effects/warning: *see* NORETHISTERONE; OESTRADIOL.

**Estrovis** (*Parke-Davis*) is a proprietary preparation of the synthetic OESTROGEN quinestrol, available only on prescription, formerly used to inhibit or suppress lactation in women following childbirth. (Such use was almost entirely discontinued when an association was made between the use of oestrogens and some forms of thrombosis.) Estrovis is produced in the form of tablets.

▲/✿ side-effects/warning: *see* QUINESTROL.

**ethacrynic acid** is a DIURETIC used to treat fluid retention in the tissues (oedema) or to assist a failing kidney by promoting the excretion of urine. Administration is oral in the form of tablets (effective in 1 hour, full diuresis in 6 hours) or by injection (peak effect in half an hour). Patients with kidney failure may require large doses – but large doses imply worse side-effects, especially if the doses are applied intravenously.

▲ side-effects: there may be a rash. High doses administered to patients who suffer from kidney failure may cause deafness, ringing in the ears (tinnitus) and gastrointestinal disturbances.

✿ warning: ethacrynic acid should not be administered to patients who suffer from cirrhosis of the liver; it should be administered with caution to those who are pregnant.

Treatment may aggravate existing conditions of diabetes, gout or those involving the prostrate gland.
*Related article:* EDECRIN.

**ethambutol hydrochloride** is an ANTIBIOTIC that is one of the major forms of treatment for tuberculosis. Even so, it is used generally in combination (to cover resistance and for maximum effect) with other antitubercular drugs such as isoniazid or rifampicin. Treatment lasts for between 6 and 9 months depending on severity and on the specific drug combination, but the use of ethambutol tends to imply the shorter duration. The drug is also used to prevent the contraction of tuberculosis by relatives. Administration is oral in the form of tablets or as a powder.
▲ side-effects: side-effects are rare, and are mostly in the form of visual disturbances (such as loss of acuity or colour-blindness) which should prove temporary if treatment is withdrawn. A regular ophthalmic check is advised during treatment.
✺ warning: ethambutol hydrochloride should not be administered to children aged under 6 years, to patients who are elderly, or to those who suffer from nervous disorders of the eyes. It should be avoided in patients with poor kidney function.
*Related articles:* MYAMBUTOL; MYNAH.

**ethamivan** is a respiratory stimulant drug, used to relieve severe respiratory difficulties in patients who have been gassed (particularly with carbon dioxide), who suffer from chronic disease of the respiratory tract, or who undergo respiratory depression following major surgery – especially in cases

where for one reason or another ventilatory support is not applicable. Administration is oral in the form of a solution (intended for paediatric use), or by injection.
▲ side-effects: there may be nausea, restlessness and tremor, leading possibly to convulsions and heartbeat irregularities.
✺ warning: ethamivan should not be administered to patients who have respiratory failure due to drug overdose or neurological disease, or with coronary artery disease, severe asthma, or an excess of thyroid hormones in the blood (thyrotoxicosis). It should be administered with caution to those with severe high blood pressure (hypertension) or a reduced supply of blood to the heart.
*Related article:* CLAIRVAN.

**ethamsylate** is a drug that reduces bleeding, although how it does so is not perfectly understood – it may correct abnormal adhesion by the blood platelets on the fibrin matrix (so coagulating the blood). As a HAEMOSTATIC, it is used particularly to treat haemorrhage from small blood vessels or to relieve excessive menstrual flow. Administration is oral in the form of tablets, or by injection.
▲ side-effects: there may be nausea with headache; some patients come out in a rash.
✺ warning: ethamsylate should not be administered to patients who are known to have platelet deficiency in the blood.
*Related article:* DICYNENE.

**ethanol**, or ethyl alcohol, is the form of alcohol found in alcoholic drinks, produced by the fermentation of sugar by yeast.
*see* ALCOHOL.

**ethanolamine oleate** is a drug used in sclerotherapy – a technique to treat varicose veins by the injection of an irritant solution. The resultant inflammation of the vein promotes the obliteration of the vein by thrombosis. Leakage of the drug into the tissues at the site of injection may cause severe tissue damage.

▲ side-effects: some patients experience sensitivity reactions.

✷ warning: ethanolamine oleate should not be injected into patients whose varicose veins are already inflamed or so painful as to prevent walking, who are obese, or who are taking oral contraceptives.

**ethinyloestradiol** is a major female sex HORMONE, a synthetic OESTROGEN, used to make up hormonal deficiencies – sometimes in combination with a PROGESTOGEN – to treat menstrual, menopausal or other gynaecological problems (such as oestrogen-related infertility). It is also a constituent of many ORAL CONTRACEPTIVES. Administration is oral in the form of tablets.

▲ side-effects: there may be nausea and vomiting. A common effect is weight gain, generally through fluid or sodium retention in the tissues. The breasts may become tender and enlarge slightly. There may also be headache and/or depression; sometimes a rash breaks out.

✷ warning: ethinyloestradiol should not be administered to patients who have cancers proved to be sex-hormone-linked, who have a history of thrombosis or inflammation of the womb, or who have porphyria or impaired liver function. Prolonged treatment increases the risk of cancer of the endometrium (the lining of

the womb). Caution should be exercised in administering ethinyloestradiol to patients who are diabetic or epileptic, who have heart or kidney disease, who are pregnant or lactating, or who have high blood pressure (hypertension) or recurrent severe migraine.
*Related articles:* BiNovum; BREVINOR; CONOVA 30; FEMODENE; FEMODENE ED; LOESTRIN; LOGYNON; MARVELON; MERCILON; MICROGYNON 30; MINULET; NEOCON-1/35; NORIMIN; OVRAN; OVRANETTE; OVYSMEN; PC4; SYNPHASE; TRINORDIOL; TRI-NOVUM.

**ethoglucid** is a CYTOTOXIC drug used primarily in the treatment of recurrent but only mildly malignant tumours of the bladder. It works by damaging the DNA of newly-forming cells, thus preventing normal cell replication. Administration is by instillation into the bladder of a solution that remains in the bladder for as long as possible (at least an hour); treatment is commonly once a week for 3 months, then once a month for 12.

▲ side-effects: treatment may cause frequency of, or difficulty in, urinating. Almost all males are rendered sterile.

✷ warning: blood count monitoring is essential; a reduction in the blood level of white blood cells is to be expected.
*Related article:* EPODYL.

**ethosuximide** is an ANTICONVULSANT drug used to treat and suppress petit mal ('absence' and myoclonic) seizures – the mild form of epilepsy. It may be used singly or in combination with other drugs, and is particularly useful in successfully treating some patients on whom other anticonvulsants have no

effect. Dosage must be adjusted to the optimum level for each individual patient.
Administration is oral in the form of capsules or as a dilute elixir.

▲ side-effects: there may be gastrointestinal disturbances, drowsiness, headache and/or dizziness; some patients experience depression or euphoria. Rarely, there are haematological disorders or psychotic states.

✿ warning: ethosuximide should not be administered to patients with porphyria. Withdrawal of treatment, if undertaken, must be gradual. Special monitoring of blood levels of the drug are required for a patient who is pregnant or lactating.
*Related articles:* EMESIDE, ZARONTIN.

**Ethrane** (*Abbott*) is a proprietary preparation of the general ANAESTHETIC enflurane, usually administered to supplement nitrous oxide-oxygen mixtures for the induction and maintenance of anaesthesia during major surgery. It is produced in gas bottles for administration through a calibrated vaporizer.
▲/✿ side-effects/warning: *see* ENFLURANE.

**ethyl alcohol**, or ETHANOL, is the form of alcohol found in alcoholic drinks, produced by the fermentation of sugar by yeast. *see* ALCOHOL.

**etodolac** is a non-steroidal, ANTI-INFLAMMATORY, non-narcotic ANALGESIC used primarily to treat rheumatoid arthritis. Administration is oral in the form of tablets and capsules.
▲ side-effects: there may be gastrointestinal disturbance (which may be decreased by taking the drug with food). Some patients experience sensitivity reactions, such as a

rash, and CNS side-effects, including headaches, vertigo or hearing disturbances. There may be fluid retention and consequent weight gain. Blood disorders have occurred.

✿ warning: etodolac should not be administered to patients known to be allergic to aspirin, who suffer from peptic ulcer or from gastrointestinal bleeding, or who are pregnant or lactating. It should be administered with caution to those who suffer from impaired kidney or liver function.
*Related articles:* LODINE; RAMODAR.

**etomidate** is a general ANAESTHETIC used specifically for the initial induction of anaesthesia. Recovery after treatment is rapid and without any hangover effect, and it causes less of a fall in blood pressure than many other anaesthetics. But there is pain on injection, when there may also be simultaneous extraneous muscle movements.

▲ side-effects: repeated doses may suppress the secretion of corticosteroid hormones by the adrenal glands.

✿ warning: pain on injection may be overcome by prior administration of suitable premedication (such as a narcotic analgesic). Intravenous injection must be carried out with caution in order to avoid thrombophlebitis.
*Related article:* HYPNOMIDATE.

**etoposide** is an ANTICANCER drug used primarily to treat small cell lung cancer, or cancer of the testes that proves resistant to other forms of therapy; it may also be used to treat some lymphomas. A unique drug, it works in much the same way as the VINCA ALKALOIDS in disrupting a specific phase in cell replication, thus preventing further growth. Administration is oral in the form of capsules, or by injection.

▲ side-effects: there is commonly nausea and vomiting, and hair loss. The capacity of the bone-marrow for producing red blood cells is reduced: regular blood count monitoring is essential. High dosage may cause loss of sensation at the extremities and other neural symptoms.

✺ warning: the use of etoposide must be closely monitored in relation to each individual patient's tolerance of the toxicity of the drug.
*Related article:* VEPESID.

**etretinate** is a powerful drug, a derivative of RETINOL (vitamin A), used in the treatment of severe psoriasis and complex skin conditions involving keratinization. Treatment may take up to 4 weeks to achieve full effect, but should be continued on a strict regime for between 6 and 9 months; more prolonged treatment is not recommended, although a second course of treatment may be begun after an interval of 3 or 4 months if necessary. It should be prescribed only by a consultant dermatologist, and treatment take place under clinical supervision. Administration is oral in the form of capsules.

▲ side-effects: there is commonly dryness of the mouth with cracking of the lips. Sometimes there is also hair loss, generalized itching, and nose-bleeds. Fat levels in the blood may rise.

✺ warning: etretinate should not be administered to patients who are pregnant (it may cause congenital abnormality in the foetus) or likely to become pregnant; contraception must

be practised by women patients for a year after completion of a course of treatment.
*Related article:* TIGASON.

**Eudemine** (*Allen & Hanburys*) is a proprietary preparation of the hyperglycaemic drug diazoxide, available only on prescription, used to treat chronic conditions involving a deficiency of glucose in the bloodstream. Such a condition might occur, for example, if a pancreatic tumour caused excessive secretion of insulin. Also useful in treating an acute hypertensive crisis (apoplexy), Eudemine is produced in the form of tablets and in ampoules for rapid intravenous injection.

▲ / ✺ side-effects/warning: *see* DIAZOXIDE.

**Euglucon** (*Roussel*) is a pro-prietary form of the SULPHO-NYLUREA drug glibenclamide, used to treat adult-onset diabetes; it works by promoting insulin secretion in whatever remains of the capacity of the pancreas for it, and increasing the number of insulin receptors. Available only on prescription, Euglucon is produced in the form of tablets (in two strengths).

▲ / ✺ side-effects/warning: *see* GLIBENCLAMIDE.

**Eugynon 30** (*Schering*) is a combination ORAL CONTRA-CEPTIVE, available only on prescription, that combines the OESTROGEN ethinyloestradiol with the PROGESTOGEN levonorgestrel in a ratio of 30:250. It is produced in packs of 21 tablets corresponding to one complete menstrual cycle.

▲ / ✺ side-effects/warning: *see* ETHINYLOESTRADIOL; LEVONORGESTREL.

**Eumovate** (*Glaxo*) is a proprietary CORTICOSTEROID preparation, available only on prescription,

used in topical application to
treat non-infective inflammation,
especially in cases where less
powerful steroid treatments have
failed. Produced in the form of a
water-miscible cream and an
anhydrous ointment to treat
inflammatory skin disorders, such
as eczema and some types of
dermatitis, and in the form of eye-
drops (in two preparations, one
additionally containing the
ANTIBIOTIC NEOMYCIN sulphate
under the name Eumovate-N) to
treat ophthalmic inflammations,
Eumovate is a preparation of the
steroid clobetasone butyrate.
▲/◆ side-effects/warning: see
  CLOBETASONE BUTYRATE.

**Eurax** (*Geigy*) is a proprietary,
non-prescription form of the drug
crotamiton, used to treat itching,
especially in relation to the
effects of infestation by the itch-
mite (scabies). It is produced in
the form of a lotion and a cream.
Another version is available (only
on prescription) additionally
containing the CORTICOSTEROID
hydrocortisone, and used also to
treat itching that results from
skin inflammation.
▲/◆ side-effects/warning: see
  CROTAMITON;
  HYDROCORTISONE.

**Evacalm** (*Unimed*) is a
proprietary ANXIOLYTIC drug,
available on prescription only to
private patients, used to treat
anxiety and insomnia, or to assist
in the treatment of acute alcohol
withdrawal symptoms. Produced
in the form of tablets (in two
strengths), Evacalm is a
preparation of the long-acting
BENZODIAZEPINE diazepam.
▲/◆ side-effects/warning: see
  DIAZEPAM.

**Evadyne** (*Ayerst*) is a proprietary
ANTIDEPRESSANT drug, available
only on prescription, used to treat
depression with the added

complication of anxiety. Produced
in the form of tablets (in two
strengths), Evadyne is a
preparation of butriptyline. It is
not recommended for children.
▲/◆ side-effects/warning: see
  BUTRIPTYLINE.

**Exelderm** (*ICI*) is a proprietary
ANTIFUNGAL cream, available only
on prescription, used for topical
application to skin infections,
such as athlete's foot or thrush.
The cream should be massaged
into the skin; treatment should
continue for at least a fortnight
after lesions have disappeared.
Exelderm is a preparation of the
IMIDAZOLE sulconazole nitrate.
▲/◆ side-effects/warning: see
  SULCONAZOLE NITRATE.

**Exirel** (*Pfizer*) is a proprietary
BRONCHODILATOR, available only
on prescription, used to treat
conditions such as asthma and
chronic bronchitis. Produced in
the form of capsules (in two
strengths), and as an aerosol
inhalant, Exirel is a preparation
of the SYMPATHOMIMETIC
pirbuterol. It is not recommended
for children aged under 6 years.
▲/◆ side-effects/warning: see
  PIRBUTEROL.

**Ex-Lax** (*Intercare*) is a proprietary,
non-prescription LAXATIVE
produced in the form of chocolate
and as tablets. It contains
phenolphthalein.
▲/◆ side-effects/warning: see
  PHENOLPHTHALEIN.

**Exolan** (*Dermal*) is a proprietary,
non-prescription preparation of
the drug dithranol triacetate in
mild solution, used to treat
psoriasis. It is produced in the
form of a water-miscible cream for
topical application.
▲/◆ side-effects/warning: see
  DITHRANOL.

*****expectorant** is a medicated
liquid intended to increase the
viscosity of sputum and so make it

easier to cough up phlegm; expectorants are used particularly in the case of bronchial congestion. (They are not the same as linctuses, which merely comprise liquids thick and soothing enough to relieve sore throats or to loosen a cough. Nor is an expectorant necessarily an elixir, which disguises a potentially horrible taste with a sweetening substance like glycerol or alcohol.) Many expectorants work by irritating the lining of the stomach, so stimulating the reflex secretion of sputum by the glands in the mucous membranes of the upper respiratory tract. In high dosage, most expectorants can be used as EMETICS (to provoke vomiting).

**Expulin** (*Galen*) is a proprietary, non-prescription cough linctus that is not available from the National Health Service. It is produced as a linctus in two strengths (the weaker labelled as a paediatric version) for dilution (the potency of the linctus once dilute is retained for 14 days), and is a combination of the OPIATE pholcodine, the SYMPATHOMIMETIC ephedrine hydrochloride, the ANTIHISTAMINE chlorpheniramine maleate, and GLYCEROL and menthol. Even the paediatric linctus is not recommended for children aged under 3 months.

▲/ ◈ side-effects/warning: *see* CHLORPHENIRAMINE; EPHEDRINE HYDROCHLORIDE; PHOLCODINE.

**Expurhin** (*Galen*) is a proprietary, non-prescription nasal DECONGESTANT for children, which is not available from the National Health Service. It is used to relieve all forms of congestion in the upper respiratory tract. Produced in the form of a sugar-free linctus, Expurhin is a combination of the SYMPATHOMIMETIC ephedrine hydrochloride together with the ANTIHISTAMINE chlorpheniramine maleate and MENTHOL. Even as a paediatric linctus, it is not recommended for children aged under 3 months.

▲/ ◈ side-effects/warning: *see* CHLORPHENIRAMINE; EPHEDRINE HYDROCHLORIDE.

**Exterol** (*Dermal*) is a proprietary, non-prescription preparation of a urea-hydrogen peroxide complex designed to dissolve and wash out wax in the ears. To be held in the ear with cotton wool for as long as possible, Exterol is produced in the form of ear-drops also containing GLYCEROL.

**Fabahistin** (*Bayer*) is a proprietary ANTIHISTAMINE, available only on prescription, used to treat allergic symptoms in such cases as hay fever and urticaria. Produced in the form of tablets Fabahistin's active constituent is mebhydrolin.
▲/● side-effects/warning: see MEBHYDROLIN.

**Fabrol** (*Zyma*) is a proprietary MUCOLYTIC, available on prescription only to private patients. Used to reduce the viscosity of sputum and thus facilitate expectoration in patients with asthma or bronchitis, Fabrol is produced in the form of sachets of granules (for solution in water) consisting of a preparation of acetylcysteine.
▲/● side-effects/warning: see ACETYLCYSTEINE.

**Fansidar** (*Roche*) is a proprietary ANTIMALARIAL drug, available only on prescription, used – following a course of quinine – to treat patients who are seriously ill with malaria, particularly with strains resistant to the standard drug chloroquine. (A very few strains are resistant also to Fansidar.) It has been used prophylactically to try to prevent tropical travellers from contracting the disease, but is not now recommended for this purpose. Produced in the form of tablets, Fansidar is a compound of (the antimalarial) pyrimethamine together with the SULPHONAMIDE sulfadoxine. Dosage is critical, and must be carefully monitored.
▲/● side-effects/warning: see PYRIMETHAMINE.

**Farlutal** (*Farmitalia Carlo Erba*) is a proprietary preparation of the synthetic PROGESTOGEN (female sex hormone) medroxyprogesterone acetate, available only on prescription, used in women primarily to support drug treatments against breast cancer or cancer of the womb, or occasionally cancer of the kidney. In men it may be used to treat cancer of the prostate. Produced in the form of tablets (in any of three strengths) and in vials for injection, Farlutal should not be administered in high doses.
▲/● side-effects/warning: see MEDROXYPROGESTERONE ACETATE.

**Fasigyn** (*Pfizer*) is a proprietary drug with ANTIBIOTIC and ANTIPROTOZOAL properties, available only on prescription, used to treat infections by anaerobic bacteria and protozoa, particularly in the gut, the vagina or on the gums, and to ensure asepsis during surgery. Produced in the form of tablets, Fasigyn is a preparation of the nitroimidazole drug tinidazole.
▲/● side-effects/warning: see TINIDAZOLE.

**Faverin** (*Duphar*) is a proprietary form of the ANTIDEPRESSANT drug fluvoxamine maleate, which has less sedative effects than some drugs of this type. Available only on prescription, it is available as tablets in two strengths.
▲/● side-effects/warning: see FLUVOXAMINE MALEATE.

**Fe-Cap** (*MCP Pharmaceuticals*) is a proprietary, non-prescription preparation of the drug ferrous glycine sulphate, used as an IRON supplement in the treatment of iron deficiency anaemia, and produced in the form of capsules. It should not be taken simultaneously with tetracycline antibiotics.
▲/● side-effects/warning: see FERROUS GLYCINE SULPHATE.

**Fe-Cap C** (*MCP Pharmaceuticals*) is a proprietary, non-prescription mineral-and-VITAMIN compound, consisting of capsules containing iron in the form of FERROUS GLYCINE SULPHATE together with ASCORBIC ACID (vitamin C).

**Fe-Cap Folic** (*MCP Pharmaceuticals*) is a proprietary, non-prescription mineral-and-VITAMIN compound used primarily as an iron supplement in the treatment of iron deficiency anaemia, and prophylactically during pregnancy. Produced in the form of capsules, Fe-Cap Folic is a preparation of ferrous glycine sulphate with FOLIC ACID (a vitamin of the B complex). It is not recommended for children, and should not be taken simultaneously with tetracycline antibiotics.

▲/✿ side-effects/warning: *see* FERROUS GLYCINE SULPHATE.

**Fectrim** (*DDSA Pharmaceuticals*) is a proprietary ANTIBIOTIC combination available only on prescription, used especially in infections of the urinary tract, infections of the respiratory tract, such as sinusitis and bronchitis, and infections of the bones and joints. Produced in the form of soluble (dispersible) tablets (in any of three strengths), Fectrim is a preparation of the compound drug co-trimoxazole, made up of the SULPHONAMIDE SULPHAMETHOXAZOLE together with the antibacterial agent TRIMETHOPRIM.

▲/✿ side-effects/warning: *see* CO-TRIMOXAZOLE.

**Fefol** (*Smith, Kline & French*) is a proprietary, non-prescription mineral-and-VITAMIN compound used primarily as an IRON supplement during pregnancy. Produced in the form of spansules (sustained-release capsules), Fefol is a preparation of ferrous sulphate together with FOLIC ACID (a vitamin of the B complex). It is not recommended for children, and should not be

simultaneously with tetracycline antibiotics.

▲/✿ side-effects/warning: *see* FERROUS SULPHATE.

**Fefol-Vit** (*Smith, Kline & French*) is a proprietary, non-prescription mineral-and-VITAMIN compound used primarily as a supplement during pregnancy. Produced in the form of spansules (sustained-release capsules), Fefol-Vit represents a preparation of ferrous sulphate together with THIAMINE (vitamin B₁), RIBOFLAVINE (vitamin B₂), PYRIDOXINE (vitamin B₆), NICOTINAMIDE (of the B complex), FOLIC ACID (of the B complex) and ASCORBIC ACID (vitamin C). It is not recommended for children, and should not be taken simultaneously with tetracycline antibiotics.

▲/✿ side-effects/warning: *see* FERROUS SULPHATE.

**Fefol Z** (*Smith, Kline & French*) is a proprietary, non-prescription mineral-and-VITAMIN compound used primarily as an IRON and ZINC supplement during pregnancy. Produced in the form of spansules (sustained-release capsules), Fefol is a preparation of ferrous sulphate together with FOLIC ACID (a vitamin of the B complex) and zinc sulphate. It is not recommended for children, and should not be taken simultaneously with tetracycline antibiotics.

▲/✿ side-effects/warning: *see* FERROUS SULPHATE.

**Feldene** (*Pfizer*) is a proprietary, NON-STEROIDAL ANTI-INFLAMMATORY DRUG available only on prescription, used to treat gout, arthritic and rheumatic pain, and other musculo-skeletal disorders. Produced in the form of capsules (in two strengths), soluble (dispersible) tablets (in two strengths), as a gel, and as anal suppositories, Feldene's active constituent is piroxicam. It is not recommended for children.

▲/ ✿ side-effects/warning: *see* PIROXICAM.

**Feminax** (*Nicholas Kiwi*) is a proprietary, non-prescription ANALGESIC preparation, produced specifically for the relief of menstrual pain. Produced in the form of tablets, it contains paracetamol, codeine, caffeine, and the atropine-like drug hyoscine.

▲/ ✿ side-effects/warning: *see* CAFFEINE; CODEINE PHOSPAHTE; HYOSCINE; PARACETAMOL.

**Femodene** (*Wyeth*) is a an ORAL CONTRACEPTIVE, available only on prescription, that combines the PROGESTERONE gestodene with the OESTROGEN ethinyloestradiol. It is produced in packs of 21 tablets representing one complete menstrual cycle.

▲/ ✿ side-effects/warning: *see* GESTODENE, ETHINYLOESTRADIOL.

**Femodene ED** (*Wyeth*) is a an ORAL CONTRACEPTIVE, available only on prescription, that combines the PROGESTERONE gestodene with the OESTROGEN ethinyloestradiol. It is produced in packs of 28 tablets representing one complete menstrual cycle, with 21 tablets containing the active constituents.

▲/ ✿ side-effects/warning: *see* GESTODENE, ETHINYLOESTRADIOL.

**Femulen** (*Gold Cross*) is a proprietary ORAL CONTRACEPTIVE, available only on prescription, which consists of a preparation of the PROGESTOGEN ethynodiol acetate. It is produced in the form of tablets, and comes in a calendar pack of 28 corresponding to one complete menstrual cycle.

**Fenbid** (*Smith, Kline & French*) is a proprietary, ANTI-

INFLAMMATORY, non-narcotic ANALGESIC, available only on prescription, used to treat pain of all kinds, especially pain from arthritis and rheumatism, and other musculo-skeletal disorders. Produced in the form of spansules (sustained-release capsules), Fenbid's active constituent is ibuprofen. It is not recommended for children or patients suffering from peptic ulcer.

▲/ ✿ side-effects/warning: *see* IBUPROFEN.

**fenbufen** is an ANTI-INFLAMMATORY, non-narcotic ANALGESIC drug with effects similar to those of aspirin. It is used chiefly in the treatment of pain from rheumatoid arthritis and osteoarthritis.

▲ side-effects: there may be a skin rash; rarely, there is an allergic response, headache, disturbance of the sense of balance, gastrointestinal bleeding (though less than with some others of this class) or kidney dysfunction.

✿ warning: fenbufen should not be administered to patients who are pregnant or lactating; who are allergic to aspirin or other anti-inflammatory drugs; or who are already taking aspirin or an anticoagulant. *Related article:* LEDERFEN; TRAXAM.

**fenfluramine hydrochloride** is a drug used to aid slimming regimes because it acts as an appetite suppressant. Not a stimulant – unlike most other appetite suppressants – fenfluramine hydrochloride instead has sedative properties that may affect a patient's intricacy of thought and movement, and is potentially addictive (although dependence is rare).

▲ side-effects: there may be depression; sedation, with headache, vertigo and gastric upsets, is not uncommon.

Sometimes there is insomnia, dry mouth, fluid retention, increased frequency of urination and speeding of the heart rate. Treatment is only in the short term, tolerance and/or dependence may occur; dosage should be tapered off gradually to avoid withdrawal depression.

◆ warning: fenfluramine hydrochloride may affect mental concentration; it enhances the effect of alcohol.
*Related articles:* ADIFAX; PONDERAX.

**fenofibrate** is used to reduce the level of fats (lipids) such as cholesterol in the bloodstream when these are raised (hyperlipidaemia). It works by inhibiting lipid synthesis. Generally, it is administered only to patients in whom a strict and regular dietary regime is not having the desired effect, although during treatment such a regime should additionally be carried out. Administration is oral in the form of capsules.

▲ side-effects: there may be nausea and abdominal pain; rarely, there may be itching or urticaria. In men, impotence occasionally occurs.

◆ warning: fenofibrate should not be administered to patients with severely impaired kidney or liver function, disease of the gall bladder, or associated blood disorders, or who are pregnant.
*Related article:* LIPANTIL.

**fenoprofen** is an ANTI-INFLAMMATORY, non-narcotic ANALGESIC drug with effects similar to those of aspirin. It is used particularly in the treatment of pain from rheumatoid arthritis and osteoarthritis, and to reduce fever.

▲ side-effects: there may be a skin rash; rarely, there is an allergic response or

gastrointestinal bleeding.

◆ warning: fenoprofen should not be administered to patients who are suffering from gastric or intestinal bleeding (as with a peptic ulcer); who are pregnant or lactating; who are allergic to aspirin or other anti-inflammatory drugs; who have reduced kidney function; who are asthmatic; or who are already taking aspirin, an anticoagulant or a drug to control the blood level of glucose.
*Related articles:* FENOPRON; PROGESIC.

**Fenopron** (*Dista*) is a proprietary, ANTI-INFLAMMATORY, non-narcotic ANALGESIC drug available only on prescription, used to relieve pain – particularly arthritic and rheumatic pain – and to treat other musculo-skeletal disorders. Its active constituent is fenoprofen, and it is produced in the form of tablets (in either of two strengths). Not recommended for children, Fenopron should not be administered to patients with a peptic ulcer, gastrointestinal haemorrhage or asthma, or who are pregnant or lactating.
▲/◆ side-effects/warning: *see* FENOPROFEN.

**Fenostil Retard** (*Zyma*) is a proprietary, non-prescription ANTIHISTAMINE used to treat allergic symptoms in such cases as hay fever. Produced in the form of tablets, Fenostil Retard's active constituent is dimethindene maleate.
▲/◆ side-effects/warning: *see* DIMETHINDENE MALEATE.

**fenoterol** is a SYMPATHOMIMETIC drug used as a BRONCHODILATOR to treat asthmatic attacks and other respiratory problems caused by airway obstruction. Administration is by aerosol spray, nebulizer or ventilator; less commonly, injection or infusion is used.

▲ side-effects: there may be tremor of the hands, nervous tension and headache; the heart rate may increase; the potassium level in the bloodstream may drop (hypokalaemia), following an injected dose.

● warning: fenoterol should not be administered to patients who have heart disease or high blood pressure (hypertension); or who are pregnant. Elderly patients should be given a reduced dosage. Diabetics may be treated by intravenous infusion, with careful monitoring of blood sugar levels.

*Related article:* BEROTEC.

**fentanyl** is a NARCOTIC ANALGESIC, used primarily for analgesia during surgery and to supplement other anaesthetics; it may be used also to slow the breathing of an anaesthetized patient. As a narcotic, its proprietary forms are on the controlled drugs list.

▲ side-effects: post-operatively there may be respiratory depression, low blood pressure, slowing of the heart, and nausea (with or without vomiting).

● warning: fentanyl should not be administered to patients whose respiration is already impaired by disease or those with myasthenia gravis, hypothyroidism or chronic liver disease. Use on a mother during childbirth may cause respiratory depression in the newborn. Elderly patients should be given a reduced dosage.

*Related articles:* SUBLIMAZE; THALAMONAL.

**Fentazin** (*Allen & Hanburys*) is a powerful, proprietary ANTIPSYCHOTIC drug, available

only on prescription, used to treat and tranquillize patients who are undergoing behavioural disturbances, or who are psychotic, particularly schizophrenic. It is also used to treat severe anxiety, or as an ANTI-EMETIC sedative prior to surgery. Produced in the form of tablets (in three strengths), Fentazin is a preparation of perphenazine. It is not recommended for children.

▲/● side-effects/warning: *see* PERPHENAZINE.

**Feospan** (*Smith, Kline & French*) is a proprietary, non-prescription preparation of the drug ferrous sulphate, used as an IRON supplement in the treatment of iron deficiency anaemia, and produced in the form of spansules (sustained-release capsules). It is not recommended for children aged under 12 months, and should not be taken simultaneously with tetracycline antibiotics.

▲/● side-effects/warning: *see* FERROUS SULPHATE.

**Ferfolic SV** (*Sinclair*) is a proprietary, mineral-and-VITAMIN compound, available only on prescription, used primarily as an IRON supplement in the treatment of iron deficiency anaemia, and prophylactically during pregnancy. Produced in the form of tablets, Ferfolic SV represents a preparation of ferrous gluconate together with FOLIC ACID (a vitamin of the B complex). It is not recommended for children, and should not be taken simultaneously with tetracycline antibiotics.

▲/● side-effects/warning: *see* FERROUS GLUCONATE.

**Fergon** (*Winthrop*) is a proprietary, non-prescription preparation of the drug ferrous gluconate, used as an IRON supplement in the treatment of

iron deficiency anaemia, and
produced in the form of tablets. It
is not recommended for children
aged under 6 years, and should
not be taken simultaneously with
tetracycline antibiotics.
▲/✿ side-effects/warning: see
    FERROUS GLUCONATE.

**Ferrocap** (*Consolidated
Chemicals*) is a proprietary, non-
prescription preparation of the
drug ferrous fumarate and
THIAMINE hydrochloride, used as
an IRON supplement in the
treatment of iron deficiency
anaemia, and produced in the
form of capsules. It is not
recommended for children aged
under 6 years, and should not be
taken simultaneously with
tetracycline antibiotics.
▲/✿ side-effects/warning: see
    FERROUS FUMARATE.

**Ferrocap-F 350** (*Consolidated
Chemicals*) is a proprietary, non-
prescription mineral-and-VITAMIN
compound used primarily as an
IRON supplement prophylactically
during pregnancy. Produced in the
form of capsules, Ferrocap-F
350 is a preparation of ferrous
fumarate with FOLIC ACID (a
vitamin of the B complex). It is
not recommended for children,
and should not be taken
simultaneously with tetracycline
antibiotics.
▲/✿ side-effects/warning: see
    FERROUS FUMARATE.

**Ferrocontin Continus** (*Degussa*)
is a proprietary, non-prescription
preparation of the drug ferrous
glycine sulphate, used as an IRON
supplement in the treatment of
iron deficiency anaemia, and
produced in the form of tablets. It
is not recommended for children,
and should not be taken
simultaneously with tetracycline
antibiotics.
▲/✿ side-effects/warning: see
    FERROUS GLYCINE SULPHATE.

**Ferrocontin Folic Continus**
(*Degussa*) is a proprietary, non-
prescription mineral-and-VITAMIN
compound used primarily as an
IRON supplement in the treatment
of iron deficiency anaemia, and
prophylactically during
pregnancy. Produced in the form
of tablets, Ferrocontin Folic
Continus is a preparation of
ferrous glycine sulphate with
FOLIC ACID (a vitamin of the B
complex). It is not recommended
for children, and should not be
taken simultaneously with
tetracycline antibiotics.
▲/✿ side-effects/warning: see
    FERROUS GLYCINE SULPHATE.

**Ferrograd** (*Abbott*) is a
proprietary, non-prescription
preparation of the drug ferrous
sulphate, used as an IRON
supplement in the treatment of
iron deficiency anaemia, and
produced in the form of sustained-
release capsules. It is not
recommended for children, and
should not be taken
simultaneously with tetracycline
antibiotics, or by patients with
diverticular disease or intestinal
obstruction.
▲/✿ side-effects/warning: see
    FERROUS SULPHATE.

**Ferrograd C** (*Abbott*) is a
proprietary, non-prescription
mineral-and-VITAMIN compound
used primarily as an IRON
supplement in the treatment of
iron deficiency anaemia.
Produced in the form of sustained-
release capsules, Ferrograd C is a
preparation of ferrous sulphate
with ASCORBIC ACID (vitamin C). It
is not recommended for children,
and should not be taken by
patients with diverticular disease
or from intestinal obstruction.
▲/✿ side-effects/warning: see
    FERROUS SULPHATE.

**Ferrograd Folic** (*Abbott*) is a
proprietary, non-prescription
mineral-and-VITAMIN compound

used primarily as an IRON
supplement in the treatment of
iron deficiency anaemia.
Produced in the form of sustained-
release capsules, Ferrograd Folic
is a preparation of ferrous
sulphate with FOLIC ACID (a
vitamin of the B complex). It is
not recommended for children,
and should not be taken by
patients with diverticular disease,
intestinal obstruction, or a
dietary deficiency of
CYANOCOBALAMIN (vitamin $B_{12}$).
▲/ ● side-effects/warning: *see*
FERROUS SULPHATE.

**Ferromyn** (*Calmic*) is a
proprietary, non-prescription
preparation of the drug ferrous
succinate, used as an IRON
supplement in the treatment of
iron deficiency anaemia, and
produced in the form of tablets
and as an elixir. It should not be
taken simultaneously with
tetracycline antibiotics or
antacids.
▲/ ● side-effects/warning: *see*
FERROUS SUCCINATE.

**ferrous fumarate** is an IRON-rich
drug used to restore iron to the
blood in cases of iron deficiency
anaemia. Once a patient's blood
haemoglobin level has reached
normal, treatment should
continue for at least 3 months to
replenish fully the stores of iron
in the body. Some preparations
combine ferrous fumarate with
various vitamins, for use
particularly as supplements
during pregnancy.
▲ side-effects: large doses may
cause gastrointestinal upset
and diarrhoea; there may be
vomiting. Prolonged treatment
may result in constipation.
● warning: ferrous fumarate
should not be administered to
patients already taking
tetracycline antibiotics or
antacids; or to patients with a
peptic ulcer.

*Related articles:* B.C. 500 WITH
IRON; FERROCAP; FERROCAP-F
350; FERSADAY; FERSAMAL;
FOLEX-350; GALFER; GALFER
F.A.; GALFER-VIT; GIVITOL;
METERFOLIC; PREGADAY.

**ferrous gluconate** is an IRON-rich
drug used to restore iron to the
blood in cases of iron deficiency
anaemia. Once a patient's blood
haemoglobin level has reached
normal, treatment should
continue for at least 3 months to
replenish the stores of iron
in the body. Some preparations
combine ferrous gluconate with
various VITAMINS, for use
particularly as supplements
during pregnancy.
▲ side-effects: large doses may
cause gastrointestinal upset
and diarrhoea; there may be
vomiting. Prolonged treatment
may result in constipation.
● warning: ferrous gluconate
should not be administered to
patients already taking
tetracycline antibiotics.
*Related articles:* FERFOLIC SV;
FERGON.

**ferrous glycine sulphate** is a
drug used to restore IRON to the
blood in cases of iron deficiency
anaemia. Once a patient's blood
haemoglobin level has reached
normal, treatment should
continue for at least 3 months to
replenish fully the stores of iron
in the body. Some preparations
combine ferrous glycine sulphate
with various VITAMINS, for use
particularly as supplements
during pregnancy.
▲ side-effects: large doses may
cause gastrointestinal upset
and diarrhoea; there may be
vomiting. Prolonged treatment
may result in
constipation.
● warning: ferrous glycine
sulphate should not be
administered to patients
already taking tetracycline
antibiotics.

*Related articles:* FE-CAP;
FE-CAP FOLIC; FERROCONTIN
CONTINUS; FERROCONTIN FOLIC
CONTINUS; KELFERON;
KELFOLATE; PLESMET.

**ferrous succinate** is an IRON-rich
drug used to restore iron to the
blood in cases of iron deficiency
anaemia. Once a patient's blood
haemoglobin level has reached
normal, treatment should
continue for at least 3 months to
replenish fully the stores of iron
in the body.
▲ side-effects: large doses may
cause gastrointestinal upset
and diarrhoea; there may be
vomiting. Prolonged treatment
may result in constipation.
✿ warning: ferrous succinate
should not be administered to
patients already taking
tetracycline antibiotics or
antacids.

**ferrous sulphate** is a drug used to
restore IRON to the blood in cases
of iron deficiency anaemia. Once
a patient's blood haemoglobin
level has reached normal,
treatment should nevertheless
continue for at least 3 months to
replenish fully the stores of iron
in the body. Some preparations
combine dried ferrous sulphate
with various vitamins, or with
zinc, for use particularly as tonic
supplements.
▲ side-effects: large doses may
cause gastrointestinal upset
and diarrhoea; there may be
vomiting. Prolonged treatment
may result in constipation.
✿ warning: ferrous sulphate
should not be administered to
patients already taking
tetracycline antibiotics.
*Related articles:* FEFOL; FEFOL-
VIT; FEFOL Z; FEOSPAN;
FERROGRAD; FERROGRAD C;
FERROGRAD FOLIC; FESOVIT;
FESOVIT Z; FOLICIN; IRONORM;
PREGNAVITE FORTE F; SLOW-FE;
SLOW-FE FOLIC.

**Fersaday** (*Duncan, Flockhart*) is a
proprietary, non-prescription
preparation of the drug ferrous
fumarate. Used as an IRON
supplement in the treatment of
iron deficiency anaemia, it is
produced in the form of tablets. It
is not recommended for children,
and should not be taken
simultaneously with tetracycline
antibiotics or antacids.
▲/✿ side-effects/warning: *see*
FERROUS FUMARATE.

**Fersamal** (*Duncan, Flockhart*) is a
weaker version of Fersaday,
permitting its administration to
children. In addition to tablets, it
is produced in the form of a syrup.
Like Fersaday, Fersamal should
not be taken simultaneously with
tetracycline antibiotics or
antacids.
*see* FERSADAY.

**Fertiral** (*Hoechst*) is a proprietary,
preparation of GONADOTROPHIN-
RELEASING HORMONE, available
only from clinics and hospitals,
used to treat women for infertility
or lack of menstruation
(amenorrhoea) due to hormonal
insufficiency. In such cases, it is
sometimes additionally used to
try to determine whether it is the
pituitary gland or the
hypothalamus that is at fault, but
with little success.
Administration is by pulsed
infusion.
▲ side-effects: rarely, there is
abdominal pain, with headache
and nausea; there may be
irritation at the site of
infusion.
✿ warning: Fertiral should not be
administered to patients with
cysts on the lining of the womb
or on an ovary. Maximum
duration of treatment is 6
months.

**Fesovit** (*Smith, Kline & French*) is
a proprietary, non-prescription
compound of the drug ferrous

sulphate together with ASCORBIC ACID (vitamin C) and several forms of VITAMIN B. It is not available from the National Health Service. Used as a mineral-and-vitamin supplement in the treatment of iron deficiency anaemia, it is produced in the form of spansules (sustained-release capsules). It is not recommended for children aged under 12 months, and should not be taken simultaneously with tetracycline antibiotics.

▲/✿ side-effects/warning: *see* FERROUS SULPHATE.

**Fesovit Z** (*Smith, Kline & French*) is a proprietary, non-prescription compound of the drug ferrous sulphate with ZINC SULPHATE, ASCORBIC ACID (vitamin C) and several forms of VITAMIN B. It is not available from the National Health Service. Used as a mineral-and-vitamin supplement in the treatment of iron deficiency anaemia, it is produced in the form of spansules (sustained-release capsules). It is not recommended for children aged under 12 months, and should not be taken simultaneously with tetracycline antibiotics.

▲/✿ side-effects/warning: *see* FERROUS SULPHATE.

**\*fibrinolytic** drugs act to break up or dissolve blood clots, and are used to treat conditions such as thrombosis and embolism. Examples include STREPTOKINASE and UROKINASE.

**figs elixir** is a non-proprietary, compound LAXATIVE used to relieve mild constipation. It is not available from the National Health Service. Made up as a syrup, it contains the powerful stimulant laxatives CASCARA and SENNA. Prolonged use should be avoided; treatment of children is not advised.

**Finalgon** (*Boehringer Ingelheim*) is a proprietary, non-prescription ointment, which, when smoothed on to the skin using an applicator, produces an irritation of sensory nerve endings that offsets the pain of underlying muscle or joint ailments.

✿ warning: Finalgon should not be used on inflamed or broken skin, or on mucous membranes.

**Fisherman's Friend** (*Lofthouse of Fleetwood*) is a proprietary, non-prescription lozenge for the relief of cold symptoms. It contains liquorice, MENTHOL and aniseed oil.

**Flagyl** (*May & Baker*) is a proprietary form of the drug metronidazole, which has both ANTIPROTOZOAL and ANTIBIOTIC (specifically against anaerobic bacteria) properties. It is available only on prescription and is used to treat anaerobic infections that may occur following colonic or gynaecological trauma or surgery. Brain abscess and Vincent's infections of the gums or throat are other bacterial infections it may also be used to treat. Flagyl's antiprotozoal activity is effective against the organisms that cause amoebic dysentery, giardiasis and trichomoniasis. It is produced in the form of capsules (in two strengths); in the form of a suspension for dilution it is called Flagyl S. Simultaneous treatment with anticoagulants or barbiturates should be avoided as should the consumption of alcohol.

▲/✿ side-effects/warning: *see* METRONIDAZOLE.

**Flagyl Compak** (*May & Baker*) is a proprietary combination of the ANTIPROTOZOAL drug, metronidazole and the ANTIFUNGAL nystatin. Available only on prescription, it is used to treat mixed infections of the vagina,

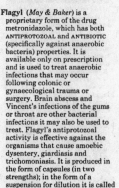

FLAGYL S                                                FLECAINIDE ACETATE

including trichomoniasis and
candidiasis.
▲/◉ side-effects/warning: *see*
METRONIDAZOLE.

**Flagyl S** (*May & Baker*) is a
proprietary form of the
AMOEBICIDAL drug metronidazole,
available only on prescription,
used to treat amoebic dysentery,
infection by the organism
Entamoeba histolytica, and
abscesses on the liver; it is also
used to treat acute inflammation
of the gums (for which purpose it
is not recommended for children
aged under 12 months). Flagyl S is
produced in the form of a
suspension for dilution.
Simultaneous treatment with
anticoagulants or barbiturates
should be avoided; during
treatment patients should not
consume alcohol.
▲/◉ side-effects/warning: *see*
METRONIDAZOLE.

**Flagyl 400** (*May & Baker*) is a
proprietary form of the drug
metronidazole, available only on
prescription, used to treat
protozoan or bacterial infections
(such as trichomoniasis and non-
specific vaginitis). It is produced
in the form of tablets.
▲/◉ side-effects/warning: *see*
METRONIDAZOLE.

**Flamazine** (*Smith & Nephew*) is a
proprietary ANTIBACTERIAL cream,
available only on prescription,
used to treat wounds, burns and
ulcers, bedsores and skin-graft
donor sites. It is a preparation of
silver sulphadiazine in a water-
soluble base.
▲/◉ side-effects/warning: *see*
SILVER SULPHADIAZINE.

**flavoxate hydrochloride** is a
form of drug used to treat
problems of frequent urination,
incontinence, and associated
pain. Administration is oral, in
the form of tablets.

▲ side-effects: there may be
ulceration of the oesophagus;
reduced secretion of digestive
juices in the stomach, and
diarrhoea. Vision may blur;
there may be a pressure
build-up in the eyeballs
(glaucoma), headache,
nausea, fatigue and dry
mouth.
◉ warning: flavoxate
hydrochloride should not be
administered to patients who
suffer from infection or
muscular disorder in the
oesophagus, or from ulceration
of the intestinal walls.
*Related article:* URISPAS.

**Flaxedil** (*May & Baker*) is a
proprietary SKELETAL MUSCLE
RELAXANT, available only on
prescription, of the type known as
competitive or non-depolarising.
It is used during surgical
operations, but only after the
patient has been rendered
unconscious. Produced in
ampoules for injection, Flaxedil's
active constituent is gallamine
triethiodide.
▲/◉ side-effects/warning: *see*
GALLAMINE TRIETHIODIDE.

**flecainide acetate** is a drug used
to slow and regularize the
heartbeat. Administration is
usually first by slow intravenous
injection, followed if necessary by
infusion and then orally in the
form of tablets. It is not
recommended for children.
▲ side-effects: there may be
dizziness and visual
disturbances; rarely, there is
nausea and vomiting.
◉ warning: flecainide acetate
should not be administered to
patients who suffer from heart
disease. Special care must be
taken with patients who are
pregnant, who use a pacemaker
device, or who suffer from
impaired kidney function.
*Related article:* TAMBOCOR.

226

**Fletcher's Arachis Oil** (*Pharmax*) is a proprietary, non-prescription form of enema, designed to soften and lubricate impacted faeces within the rectum. It comprises a preparation of ARACHIS OIL that should be warmed before use.

**Fletcher's Enemette** (*Pharmax*) is a proprietary, non-prescription form of enema, designed to soften and lubricate impacted faeces within the rectum. Commonly used before and after childbirth, and prior to rectal surgery or examination, it comprises a preparation of DIOCTYL SODIUM SULPHOSUCCINATE (docusate sodium) with GLYCEROL, MACROGOL and sorbic acid. It is not recommended for children aged under 3 years.

**Fletcher's Magnesium Sulphate** (*Pharmax*) is a proprietary, non-prescription form of enema, used in hospitals for rapid bowel evacuation to relieve pressure on a patient's cerebrospinal fluid before or during neurosurgery. It comprises an aqueous preparation of MAGNESIUM SULPHATE.

**Fletcher's Phosphate** (*Pharmax*) is a proprietary, non-prescription form of enema, commonly used before and after childbirth, and prior to rectal surgery or examination. It comprises an aqueous preparation of sodium and phosphates, and should not be administered to patients who have increased absorptive capacity in the colon.

**Flexical** (*Mead Johnson*) is a proprietary, non-prescription, gluten-free powder (for reconstitution) that represents a complete nutritional diet for patients who are severely undernourished (such as with anorexia nervosa) or who are suffering from some problem with the absorption of food (such as following gastrectomy). Also lactose-free, Flexical contains protein, carbohydrate, fats, vitamins and minerals; it is not suitable for children aged under 12 months, and should not constitute the sole source of nourishment for children of any age.

**Flolan** (*Wellcome*) is a proprietary form of the ANTICOAGULANT epoprostenol, a PROSTAGLANDIN prostacyclin, used to prevent aggregation of blood platelets, and hence formation of clots, during or following cardiac surgery, and as such may be used as an alternative or together with HEPARIN in kidney dialysis. Available only on prescription, Flolan is produced in the form of powder for reconstitution in a diluent as a medium for infusion. ▲/✸ side-effects/warning: *see* EPOPROSTENOL.

**Florinef** (*Squibb*) is a proprietary form of the hormonal substance fludrocortisone acetate, available only on prescription. A mineralocorticoid, it is used to make up a body deficiency in mineralocorticoids (which are essential for the balance of salt and water in the body) resulting from a malfunctioning of the adrenal glands. Florinef is produced in the form of tablets. ▲/✸ side-effects/warning: *see* FLUDROCORTISONE ACETATE.

**Floxapen** (*Beecham*) is a proprietary ANTIBIOTIC, available only on prescription, used to treat bacterial infections of the skin and of the ear, nose and throat, and especially staphylococcal infections that prove to be resistant to penicillin. Produced in the form of capsules (in two strengths), syrup for dilution (in two strengths; the potency of the diluted syrup is retained for 14 days), and as a powder for reconstitution as injections, Floxapen's active constituent in each case is the penicillinase-resistant penicillin flucloxacillin, or one of its salts.

▲/✿ side-effects/warning: see FLUCLOXACILLIN.

**Flu-Amp** (*Generics*) is a proprietary compound ANTIBIOTIC available only on prescription used to treat bacterial infections particularly of the urinary tract, the middle ear and the upper respiratory tract. Produced in the form of capsules, Flu-Amp contains the penicillin ampicillin, together with the broad-spectrum penicillinase-resistant flucloxacillin (which can treat infections that prove to be resistant to penicillin).

▲/✿ side-effects/warning: see AMPICILLIN; FLUCLOXACILLIN.

**Fluanxol** (*Lundbeck*) is a proprietary ANTIDEPRESSANT, available only on prescription, used to treat depressive illness. Produced in the form of tablets (in two strengths), it represents a preparation of flupenthixol, and is not recommended for children.

▲/✿ side-effects/warning: see FLUPENTHIXOL.

**fluclorolone acetonide** is a powerful CORTICOSTEROID drug, used in very mild solution to treat severe non-infective inflammations of the skin, particularly eczema that is unresponsive to less powerful drugs, and psoriasis. Administration is as a cream or ointment for topical use.

▲ side-effects: side-effects depend to some extent on the area of the skin treated. If infection is present, it may spread although the symptoms may not be experienced by the patient. Prolonged treatment may cause thinning of the skin, yet increase hair growth; dermatitis or acne may present. These side-effects may be worse in children.

✿ warning: like all topical corticosteroids, fluclorolone acetonide treats symptoms and does not cure underlying disorders.

*Related article:* TOPILAR.

**flucloxacillin** is an ANTIBIOTIC of the penicillin family. Similar to penicillin, it is active against many gram-positive bacteria, but its principal attribute is that it is generally resistant to the enzymes secreted by penicillin-resistant stapylococcus aureus, called penicillinases (which can inactivate many penicillins). It is used to treat bacterial infections of the skin and of the ear, nose and throat, and especially staphylococcal infections that prove to be resistant to penicillin. Administration is in the form of capsules, dilute syrup and injection.

▲ side-effects: there may be sensitivity reactions, including high temperature; in some patients there is diarrhoea.

✿ warning: flucloxacillin should not be administered to patients who have a history of allergy to antibiotic substances, or who suffer from impairment of kidney function.

*Related articles:* FLOXAPEN; LADROPEN; STAFOXIL; STAPHCIL.

**fluconazole** is an ANTIFUNGAL drug of the triazole family, used in the treatment of fungal infections of the mucous membranes of the vagina or mouth.

▲ side-effects: may cause nausea, abdominal discomfort and headaches.

● warning: it should not be
administered to patients with
kidney dysfunction or during
pregnancy.
*Related article:* DIFLUCAN.

**flucytosine** is an ANTIFUNGAL
drug used to treat systemic
infections by yeasts – infections
such as systemic candidiasis.
Administration is oral or by
intravenous infusion.
▲ side-effects: there may be
diarrhoea, with nausea and
vomiting; rashes may occur.
White blood cell numbers may
be lowered.
● warning: flucytosine should be
administered only with caution
to patients who suffer from
impaired function of the
kidneys or liver, or from blood
disorders; or who are pregnant
or lactating. During treatment
there should be regular blood
counts and liver-function tests.
*Related article:* ALCOBON.

**fludrocortisone acetate** is a
hormonal substance, a
mineralocorticoid used to make
up a body deficiency of
mineralocorticoids (which are
essential to the balance of salt
and water in the body) resulting
from a malfunctioning of the
adrenal glands.
▲ side-effects: there may be high
blood pressure, sodium and
water retention, and potassium
deficiency; there may also be
muscular weakness.
● warning: side-effects with
fludrocortisone are more
marked than with some other
mineralocorticoids; in
combination with
glucocorticoids (the other type
of corticosteroids), however,
effects are minimal.
*Related article:* FLORINEF.

**flumazenil** is a BENZODIAZEPINE
antagonist used to reverse the
central sedative effects of

benzodiazepines in anaesthesia,
intensive care and diagnostic
procedures. Administration is by
slow intravenous infusion or
injection.
▲ side-effects: nausea, vomiting
and flushing; agitation, anxiety
and fear if wakening is too
rapid, occasionally
convulsions. With intensive-
care patients, transient
increase in blood pressure and
heart rate.
● warning: flumazenil should be
given with caution to high-risk
or anxious patients and
following major surgery, those
with impaired liver function,
or epileptics who have received
prolonged benzodiazepine
therapy.
*Related article:* ANEXATE

**flunisolide** is an ANTI-ALLERGIC
drug used to combat hay fever
and other forms of nasal allergy.
Administration is by nasal spray.
It is not recommended for
children.
▲ side-effects: sneezing may
occur immediately after
administration.
● warning: as a CORTICOSTEROID,
flunisolide treats only the
symptoms and does not treat
any underlying disorder.
Initially undetected infection
may thus spread, its symptoms
suppressed by the drug.
Prolonged use should be
avoided.
*Related article:* SYNTARIS.

**flunitrazepam** is a BENZO-
DIAZEPINE drug used as a
HYPNOTIC to treat insomnia in
cases where some degree of
sedation during the daytime is
acceptable. Doses may have
residual effects that make the
overall treatment cumulative.
Administration is oral, in the
form of tablets.
▲ side-effects: there may be
drowsiness and dry mouth.
Hypersensitivity reactions

sometimes occur. Prolonged use may result in tolerance and eventual dependence (addiction).

✦ warning: there may be a hangover following prolonged use; abrupt withdrawal is thus to be avoided. Patients should not drink alcohol. Dosage should be reduced for the elderly and the debilitated. Flunitrazepam should be administered with caution to patients who have kidney or liver damage; or who are pregnant or lactating. *Related article:* ROHYPNOL.

**fluocinolone acetonide** is a powerful CORTICOSTEROID drug, used in very dilute solution to treat severe non-infective inflammations of the skin. Administration is as a cream, gel, or ointment for topical use.

▲ side-effects: side-effects depend to some extent on the area of the skin treated. If infection is present, it may spread although the symptoms may not be experienced by the patient. Prolonged treatment may cause thinning of the skin, yet increase hair growth; dermatitis or acne may be present. These side-effects may be worse in children.

✦ warning: like all topical corticosteroids, fluocinolone acetonide treats symptoms and does not cure underlying disorders. *Related article:* SYNALAR.

**fluocinonide** is a powerful CORTICOSTEROID drug, used in very dilute solution to treat severe non-infective inflammations of the skin, particularly eczema that is unresponsive to less powerful drugs, and some allergic skin conditions. Administration is as a cream or ointment for topical use.

▲ side-effects: side-effects depend to some extent on the area of the skin treated. If infection is

present, it may spread although the symptoms may not be experienced by the patient. Prolonged treatment may cause thinning of the skin, yet increase hair growth; dermatitis or acne may present. These side-effects may be worse in children.

✦ warning: like all topical corticosteroids, fluocinonide treats symptoms and does not cure underlying disorders. *Related article:* METOSYN.

**fluocortolone** is a powerful CORTICOSTEROID drug, used in very dilute solution to treat severe, non-infective inflammations of the skin, particularly eczema that is unresponsive to less powerful drugs. Administration is as a cream or ointment for topical use.

▲ side-effects: side-effects depend to some extent on the area of the skin treated. If infection is present, it may spread although the symptoms may not be experienced by the patient. Prolonged treatment may cause thinning of the skin, yet increase hair growth; dermatitis or acne may present. These side-effects may be worse in children.

✦ warning: like all topical corticosteroids, fluocortolone treats symptoms and does not cure underlying disorders. *Related articles:* ULTRADIL PLAIN; ULTRALANUM.

**Fluor-a-day Lac** (*Dental Health Promotion*) is a proprietary, non-prescription form of fluoride supplement for administration in areas where the water supply is not fluoridated, especially to growing children. Produced in the form of tablets to be dissolved in the mouth, Fluor-a-day Lac's active constituent is SODIUM FLUORIDE.

**fluorescein sodium** is a proprietary diagnostic medium, a water-soluble dye used to distinguish foreign bodies or injured areas in the surface of an eyeball. Alternatively, it may be injected into a retinal vein to check the retinal circulation. When light is shone on the dye, it shows up a brilliant green.
*Related articles:* MINIMS FLUORESCEIN SODIUM; OPULETS.

**Fluorigard** (*Hoyt*) is a proprietary, non-prescription form of fluoride supplement for administration in areas where the water supply is not fluoridated, especially to growing children. Produced in the form of tablets to be dissolved in the mouth (in two strengths, and in assorted flavours and colours), as drops, and as a mouth wash, Fluorigard's active constituent is SODIUM FLUORIDE.

**fluorometholone** is a CORTICOSTEROID drug used primarily in the treatment of local eye inflammations in cases where the inflammation is not caused by infection.
Administration is as eye-drops.
▲ side-effects: very rarely, and following weeks of treatment, there may be an acute, temporary form of glaucoma in certain patients who are predisposed to it.
✦ warning: as with all corticosteroids, fluorometholone treats only the symptoms and does not treat any underlying disorder. An undetected or misdiagnosed infection may thus get worse although the symptoms may be suppressed.
*Related articles:* FML; FML-NEO.

**fluorouracil** is an ANTICANCER drug used primarily to treat gastrointestinal cancers or malignant skin lesions, or in combination with other drugs to treat breast cancer.
Administration is oral in the form of capsules, by injection, or as a cream.
▲ side-effects: gastric upsets with nausea and vomiting are common; there may also be hair loss (even to total baldness).
✦ warning: as with all CYTOTOXIC drugs, fluorouracil causes depression of the bone-marrow's function of providing red blood cells; anaemia and some loss of immunity may result. There should be regular blood counts.
*Related articles:* EFUDIX; FLUORO-URACIL.

**Fluoro-uracil** (*Roche*) is a proprietary ANTICANCER drug, available only on prescription, used primarily to treat gastrointestinal cancers or malignant skin lesions, or in combination with other drugs to treat breast cancer. Produced in the form of capsules or in ampoules for injection, Fluoro-uracil represents a preparation of the cytotoxic drug fluorouracil.
▲/✦ side-effects/warning: *see* FLUOROURACIL.

**fluoxetine hydrochloride** is an ANTIDEPRESSANT drug used to treat depressive illness. It has the advantage over some other antidepressant drugs that it works by inhibiting uptake of serotonin, and so has relatively less sedative and ANTI-CHOLINERGIC side-effects. It is used as tablets.
▲ side-effects: it may impair performance of skilled tasks such as driving; may cause a rash (if so discontinue treatment), convulsions, fever, headache, tremor, nausea, vomiting, diarrhoea (which may be severe), anorexia with weight loss, slowing of the

heart, hypothermia, sexual dysfunction; and occasionally blood disorders, vaginal bleeding on withdrawal, and confusion.

● warning: it should be given with caution to patients with liver or kidney damage, and those who have epilepsy, diabetes, or who are pregnant. It should be avoided in lactating women. MAO inhibitors should not be used until at least five weeks after discontinuing fluoxetine hydrochloride.
*Related article:* PROZAC.

**flupenthixol** is a powerful ANTIDEPRESSANT drug used (mainly in the form of its salts) to treat and soothe depressive illness, psychosis (such as schizophrenia), and severe anxiety.

▲ side-effects: there may be insomnia with restlessness.

● warning: flupenthixol should not be administered to patients who are excitable or overactive, and should be administered only with extreme caution to patients who suffer from heart, vascular, kidney, or liver disease, or parkinsonism, and who are pregnant or lactating. Dosage should be reduced for the elderly; it is not suitable for children.
*Related articles:* DEPIXOL; FLUANXOL.

**fluphenazine** is a powerful ANTIPSYCHOTIC drug used (mainly in the form of its salts) to treat and tranquillize psychosis (such as schizophrenia), and to relieve severe anxiety in the short term.

▲ side-effects: there may be drowsiness, pallor and hypothermia, insomnia, depression and, sometimes, restlessness and nightmares. Rashes and jaundice may

occur, and there may be dry mouth, constipation, difficulty in urination, and blurred vision. The heart rate may be raised or lowered on administration by injection.

● warning: fluphenazine should be administered only with extreme caution to patients who suffer from heart or vascular disease, from kidney or liver disease, from parkinsonism, or from depression; or who are pregnant or lactating. Dosage should be reduced for the elderly; it is not suitable for children.
*Related articles:* MODECATE; MODITEN.

**flurandrenolone** is a powerful CORTICOSTEROID drug, used in very dilute solution to treat severe, non-infective inflammations of the skin, particularly eczema that is unresponsive to less powerful drugs. Administration is as a cream or ointment for topical use. One proprietary form combines it with an antibacterial, antifungal agent.

▲ side-effects: side-effects depend to some extent on the area of the skin treated. If infection is present, it may spread although the symptoms may not be experienced by the patient. Prolonged treatment may cause thinning of the skin, yet increase hair growth; dermatitis or acne may present. These side-effects may be worse in children.

● warning: like all topical corticosteroids, flurandrenolone by itself treats symptoms and does not cure underlying disorders.
*Related article:* HAELAN.

**flurazepam** is a BENZODIAZEPINE drug used as a HYPNOTIC to treat insomnia in cases where some degree of sedation during the daytime is acceptable. Doses may have residual effects that make the overall treatment cumulative. Administration is oral, in the form of capsules.

▲ side-effects: there may be drowsiness and dry mouth. Hypersensitivity reactions sometimes occur. Prolonged use may result in tolerance and eventual dependence (addiction).

● warning: there may be a hang-over following prolonged use; abrupt withdrawal is thus to be avoided. Patients should not drink alcohol. Dosage should be reduced for the elderly and the debilitated. Flurazepam should be administered with caution to patients who have kidney or liver damage; or who are pregnant or lactating; or who have obstructive lung disease or respiratory depression.
*Related article:* DALMANE.

**flurbiprofen** is a non-steroidal ANTI-INFLAMMATORY non-narcotic ANALGESIC with effects similar to those of aspirin. It is used particularly in the treatment of pain from rheumatoid arthritis and osteoarthritis, or from ankylosing spondylitis. It is not recommended for children.

▲ side-effects: there may be a skin rash; rarely, there is an allergic response or gastrointestinal bleeding.

● warning: flurbiprofen should not be administered to patients who are suffering from gastric or intestinal bleeding (as with a peptic ulcer); who are pregnant or lactating; who are allergic to aspirin or other anti-inflammatory drugs; who have reduced kidney function; who are asthmatic; or who are already taking aspirin, an anticoagulant or a drug to

control the blood level of glucose.
*Related article:* FROBEN.

**fluspirilene** is a powerful ANTI-PSYCHOTIC drug used to treat and tranquillize psychosis (such as schizophrenia).

▲ side-effects: there may be drowsiness, pallor and hypothermia, insomnia, depression and, frequently, restlessness and sweating. Rashes and jaundice may occur, and there may be dry mouth, constipation, difficulty in urination, and blurred vision. Prolonged usage may cause tissue damage (in the form of nodules) at the site of injection.

● warning: fluspirilene should be administered only with extreme caution to patients who suffer from heart or vascular disease, from kidney or liver disease, from parkinsonism, from epilepsy, or from depression; or who are pregnant or lactating. Dosage should be reduced for the elderly; it is not suitable for children.
*Related article:* REDEPTIN.

**flutamide** is a HORMONE ANTAGONIST drug, an anti-androgen, used for the treatment of prostate cancer. It is available in the form of tablets.

▲ side-effects: there may be gynaecomastia (growth of breasts), diarrhoea, nausea and vomiting, increased appetite, tiredness and sleep disturbances, decreased libido, gastrointestinal and chest pain, blurred vision, oedema, rashes, blood disturbances.

● warning: avoid administration to patients suffering cardiac and hepatic diseases.
*Related article:* DROGENIL.

**Fluvirin** (*Servier*) is the name of a series of proprietary flu VACCINES, all comprising inactivated surface antigens of different strains of the influenza virus. None is recommended for children aged under 4 years.

▲ side-effects: rarely, there is local reaction together with headache and high temperature.

✤ warning: like any flu vaccine, Fluvirin cannot control epidemics and should be used only – in what seems to be the appropriate strain – on people who are at high risk: the elderly, patients with cardiovascular problems, and medical staff. Fluvirin should not be administered to patients who are allergic to egg or chicken protein (in which vaccine viruses are cultured), or who are pregnant.

**fluvoxamine maleate** is an ANTIDEPRESSANT drug used to treat depressive illness. It has the advantage over some other antidepressant drugs in that it works by inhibiting uptake of serotonin, and so has relatively less sedative side effects, though it may have gastrointestinal actions. It is used as tablets.

▲ side-effects: it may impair performance of skilled tasks such as driving; may cause a rash (if so discontinue treatment), convulsions, fever, headache, tremor, nausea, vomiting, diarrhoea (which may be severe), anorexia with weight loss, slowing of the heart, hypothermia, sexual dysfunction; and occasionally blood disorders, vaginal bleeding on withdrawal, and confusion. May enhance the effects of alcohol.

✤ warning: it should be given with caution to patients with liver or kidney damage, and those who have epilepsy, diabetes, or who are pregnant. It should be avoided in lactating women. MAO

inhibitor anti-depressant drugs should not be used until at least five weeks after discontinuing fluvoxamine maleate.
*Related article:* FAVERIN.

**FML** (*Allergan*) is a proprietary form of ANTI-INFLAMMATORY eye-drops, available only on prescription, used in cases where the inflammation is not caused by infection. The active constituent of FML is the CORTICOSTEROID fluorometholone.
▲/✤ side-effects/warning: *see* FLUOROMETHOLONE.

**FML-Neo** (*Allergan*) is a proprietary form of ANTIBIOTIC eye-drops, available only on prescription, used in cases where the inflammation is not primarily caused by infection. The active constituents of FML-Neo are the CORTICOSTEROID fluorometholone and the aminoglycoside antibiotic neomycin.
▲/✤ side-effects/warning: *see* NEOMYCIN.

**Folex-350** (*Rybar*) is a proprietary, non-prescription mineral-and-VITAMIN compound, used primarily as an IRON supplement prophylactically during pregnancy. Produced in the form of tablets, Folex-350 represents a preparation of ferrous fumarate together with FOLIC ACID (a vitamin of the B complex). It is not recommended for children, and should not be taken simultaneously with tetracycline artibiotics.
▲/✤ side-effects/warning: *see* FERROUS FUMARATE.

**folic acid** is a VITAMIN of the B complex – also known as pteroylglutamic acid – important in the synthesis of nucleic acids (DNA and RNA). Its importance is parallel with that of CYANOCOBALAMIN (vitamin $B_{12}$), for both are linked to the processes of cell division. Food sources of folic acid include liver and vegetables; consumption is particularly necessary during pregnancy. Deficiency leads to a form of anaemia, which is usually rapidly remedied by a compensatory injection, although treatment (including supplements of cyanocobalamin (vitamin $B_{12}$)) should continue for some months to replenish body stores.

🌢 warning: treatment with folic acid generally also indicates parallel treatment with cyanocobalamin (vitamin $B_{12}$); one without the other may cause various forms of anaemia, and even lead to degeneration of the spinal cord. Folic acid should not be administered to those with malignant disease unless certain forms of anaemia are an important complication.
*Related articles:* FE-CAP FOLIC; FEFOL; FERROCAP-F 350; FERROCONTIN FOLIC CONTINUS; FERROGRAD FOLIC; FOLEX-350; GALFER F.A.; KELFOLATE; PREGADAY; SLOW-FE FOLIC.

**Folicin** (*Paines & Byrne*) is a proprietary, mineral-and-VITAMIN compound, available only on prescription, used primarily as an IRON supplement during pregnancy. In addition to iron (in the form of dried ferrous sulphate), Folicin contains FOLIC ACID (a vitamin of the B complex), copper sulphate and manganese sulphate. It is not recommended for children, and should not be taken simultaneously with tetracycline antibiotics.
▲/🌢 side-effects/warning: *see* FERROUS SULPHATE.

**folinic acid** is a derivative of FOLIC ACID (a VITAMIN of the B complex), and is used therapeutically to suppress the toxic effects of certain ANTICANCER drugs, especially METHOTREXATE, and to

treat some forms of anaemia. Administration is oral in the form of tablets, or by injection or infusion.

🌢 warning: treatment with folinic acid may, just as treatment with folic acid, require complementary treatment with CYANOCOBALAMIN (vitamin $B_{12}$) in order to avoid further deficiency disorders.
*Related article:* CALCIUM LEUCOVORIN.

**Forane** (*Abbott*) is a proprietary preparation of the general ANAESTHETIC isoflurane, produced as a gas to be used in solution with oxygen or nitrous oxide-oxygen. It is available on prescription only.
▲/🌢 side-effects/warning: *see* ISOFLURANE.

**Forceval** (*Unigreg*) is a proprietary, non-prescription mineral-and-VITAMIN compound, which is not available from the National Health Service. Used as a supplement to make up body deficiencies, and produced in the form of gelatin capsules in either of two strengths (the weaker one under the trade name Forceval Junior), Forceval contains almost all the vitamins, plus calcium, copper, iodine, phosphorus, potassium and zinc.

**Forceval Protein** (*Unigreg*) is a proprietary, non-prescription, gluten-free powder (for reconstitution), which represents a complete nutritional diet for patients who are severely undernourished (such as with anorexia nervosa) or who are suffering from some problem with the absorption of food (such as following gastrectomy). Also lactose- and galactose-free, Forceval Protein contains protein, carbohydrate, vitamins and minerals; it is produced in sachets and tins, and in various flavours. Not suitable for children aged

**F**

under 12 months, it should not constitute the sole source of nourishment for children aged under 5 years.

**formaldehyde** is a powerful KERATOLYTIC agent, used in mild solution to dissolve away layers of toughened or warty skin, especially in the treatment of verrucas (plantar warts) on the soles of the feet. Treatment of normal skin should be avoided.
▲ side-effects: formaldehyde solutions may sensitize the skin and become irritant.
✿ warning: effects of treatment are not always predictable. The smell is unpleasantly acrid. *Related article:* VERACUR.

**Formula MCT (1)** (*Cow & Gate*) is a proprietary, non-prescription powder for reconstitution, which is a low-protein, high-calorie dietary supplement for patients who suffer from failure of the liver or cystic fibrosis of the pancreas, or following intestinal surgery, when the need is to provide amino acids and protein in a readily available form that does not rely on breakdown by the body. Formula MCT (1) contains triglycerides (fatty acids), protein, carbohydrate, minerals and electrolytes. It does not, however, form a complete diet.

**Formula S** (*Cow & Gate*) is a proprietary, non-prescription, gluten-free powder for reconstitution, which is a complete nutritional diet for patients who for one reason or another cannot tolerate cow's milk; it is lactose-free, and also fructose- and sucrose-free. Formula S contains protein, carbohydrate, fats, vitamins and minerals in appropriate ratios when used in 8 times its own volume of water.

**Formulix** (*Cilag*) is a proprietary compound ANALGESIC, available only on prescription to private patients, used as a painkiller. Produced in the form of tablets, it is a preparation of the OPIATE codeine phosphate and paracetamol that contains more codeine than the usual compound preparation known as CO-CODAMOL, and is not recommended for children under 3 years of age. The preparation is in the form of an elixir.
▲/✿ side-effects/warning: *see* CODEINE PHOSPHATE; PARACETAMOL.

**Fortical** (*Cow & Gate*) is a proprietary, non-prescription, gluten-free liquid, which is not available from the National Health Service. It is a carbohydrate-based supplement for patients with kidney failure, liver cirrhosis, or any other condition that requires a high-calorie, low-electrolyte diet requiring minimum absorption. It is available in six flavours.

**Fortisip** (*Cow & Gate*) is a bland, proprietary, non-prescription, gluten-free liquid, which is a complete nutritional diet for patients who are severely undernourished (such as with anorexia nervosa) or who are suffering from some problem with the absorption of food, such as following gastrectomy. Produced in two strengths, Fortisip contains protein, carbohydrate, fats, minerals and vitamins; as the slightly stronger Fortisip Energy Plus, the liquid is produced in three flavours. Neither form is suitable for children aged under 12 months.

**Fortison** (*Cow & Gate*) is a bland, proprietary, non-prescription, gluten-free liquid that is a complete nutritional diet for patients who are severely undernourished (such as with anorexia nervosa) or who are suffering from some problem with the absorption of food, such as following gastrectomy. Produced in two strengths (Standard, and Energy Plus) and with a choice of protein types, Fortison contains protein, carbohydrate, fats, minerals and vitamins. It is not suitable for children aged under 12 months.

**Fortral** (*Sterling Research*) is a proprietary, narcotic ANALGESIC, a controlled drug, which is not available from the National Health Service. Produced in the form of tablets, capsules, ampoules for injection, and anal suppositories, its active constituent is the OPIATE pentazocine. Fortral suppositories are not recommended for children; as tablets and capsules Fortral is not recommended for children aged under 6 years; and as injections Fortral is not recommended for children aged under 12 months.
▲/✿ side-effects/warning: *see* PENTAZOCINE.

**Fortum** (*Glaxo*) is a proprietary, broad-spectrum ANTIBIOTIC, available only on prescription, used to treat bacterial infections, particularly infections of the respiratory tract, the ear, nose or throat, the skin, bones and joints, and more serious infections such as septicaemia and meningitis. Produced in the form of powder for reconstitution as a medium for injection or infusion, Fortum is a preparation of the CEPHALOSPORIN ceftazidime.
▲/✿ side-effects/warning: *see* CEFTAZIDIME.

**Fortunan** (*Allen & Hanburys*) is a powerful proprietary, ANTIPSYCHOTIC drug, available only on prescription, used as a major TRANQUILLIZER to treat patients with behavioural disturbances, or who are psychotic, particularly

schizophrenic. More mundanely, it may be used in the short term to treat severe anxiety. Produced in the form of tablets (in five strengths), Fortunan is a preparation of haloperidol.
▲/✿ side-effects/warning: *see* HALOPERIDOL.

**foscarnet sodium** is an ANTIVIRAL agent that has been recently introduced. It is used to treat cytomegaloviral retinitis in patients with AIDS when the more usual anti-viral drug ganciclovir is inappropriate. Administration is by intravenous infusion.
▲ side-effects: there may be various blood cell deficiencies, effects on the functioning of the liver and gastrointestinal disturbances.
✿ warning: foscarnet sodium should be not administered to patients who have impaired kidney function, or who are pregnant. Contraception must be maintained during treatment and breast-feeding must be avoided.
*Related article:* FOSCAVIR.

**Foscavir** (*Astra*) is an ANTIVIRAL drug, a proprietary form of foscarnet sodium, available only on prescription to treat life-threatening viral infections especially of the eye in AIDS.
▲/✿ side-effects/warning: *see* FOSCARNET SODIUM.

**fosfestrol tetrasodium** is a drug that is converted in the body to the OESTROGEN (female sex HORMONE) STILBOESTROL. It may be used as part of hormone replacement therapy for menopausal women, to treat menstrual difficulties, or be used in men to treat cancer of the prostate gland.
▲ side-effects: there may be fluid retention in the tissues (oedema), high blood pressure (hypertension), a high level of

calcium in the bloodstream, and gastrointestinal upsets with nausea and vomiting. There is a greatly increased risk of thrombosis.

❋ warning: fosfestrol tetrasodium should not be administered to patients who are pregnant, diabetic or epileptic, or who have heart or kidney disease. In men, fosfestrol tetrasodium has a marked feminizing effect, resulting in impotence.
Related article: HONVAN.

**Fosfor** (*Consolidated Chemicals*) is a proprietary, nutritional supplement consisting of a phosphoryl compound. It is produced in the form of a syrup (non-prescription, but not available from the National Health Service) and in ampoules for injection (prescription only) or infusion in solution.

**fosinopril** is an ANTIHYPERTENSIVE drug used to treat hypertension (high blood pressure), especially when more standard forms of therapy have failed or are not tolerated. It works by inhibiting the formation of a certain peptide in the blood (angiotensin) that normally constricts the blood vessels. Administration is oral, as tablets; some patients may require simultaneous administration of other antihypertensive drugs.

▲ side-effects: there may be a dry cough, headache, nervousness, fatigue, dizziness, nausea, an alteration in the sense of taste, abdominal pain, diarrhoea, low blood pressure and renal failure.

❋ warning: fosinopril should be administered with caution to patients with impaired kidney function, or who are pregnant. Stop diuretic therapy before giving fosinopril, and resume after 4 weeks. If diuretic cannot be stopped, close

medical supervision is required for several hours.
Related article: STARIL.

**Fragmin** (*Kabi*) is a proprietary ANTICOAGULANT, available only on prescription, used to prevent clotting in the extracorporeal circulation. Produced in ampoules for injection, Fragmin is a preparation of the low molecular weight heparin.
▲/❋ side-effects/warning: see HEPARIN.

**framycetin** is an aminoglycoside ANTIBIOTIC, largely restricted to oral and topical usage due to its toxicity. It is not absorbed from the gastrointestinal tract and therefore when given orally the aim is to kill off sensitive bacteria in the gut prior to intestinal surgery. As with all amino-glycoside antibiotics, framycetin is active against some gram-positive and many gram-negative bacteria. Preparations of framycetin most commonly involve its sulphate form.
▲ side-effects: hypersensitive reactions may occur; there may be temporary kidney malfunction.
❋ warning: oral administration may cause malabsorption of nutrients; application to large areas of the skin may damage the organs of the ears. Framycetin should not be administered to patients who are pregnant, or to those with myasthenia gravis.
Related articles: FRAMYCORT; FRAMYGEN; SOFRAMYCIN.

**Framycort** (*Fisons*) is a proprietary compound, available only on prescription, combining the aminoglycoside ANTIBIOTIC framycetin sulphate with the fairly potent CORTICOSTEROID hydrocortisone acetate. It is used in the form of an ointment to treat skin infections, particularly on the face or in the urogenital area; as eye-drops to treat bacterial infections such as conjunctivitis; and as ear-drops for the treatment of bacterial infections of the outer ear.

▲/✚ side-effects/warning: see FRAMYCETIN.

**Framygen** (*Fisons*) is a proprietary ANTIBIOTIC, available only on prescription, used in the form of eye ointment and eye-drops to treat infections on and around the eyes; as ear-drops to treat infections of the outer ear; and as a cream to treat bacterial skin infections. In all versions, its active constituent is the aminoglycoside framycetin sulphate in very mild solution.

▲/✚ side-effects/warning: see FRAMYCETIN.

**Franol** (*Winthrop*) is a proprietary BRONCHODILATOR combined with a SMOOTH MUSCLE RELAXANT. The bronchodilator is ephedrine hydrochloride, and the muscle relaxant is theophylline. It is produced in the form of tablets, and may be used to treat asthma and chronic bronchitis.

▲/✚ side-effects/warning: see EPHEDRINE HYDROCHLORIDE; PHENOBARBITONE; THEOPHYLLINE.

**Franol Plus** (*Winthrop*) is a proprietary BRONCHODILATOR combined with a SMOOTH MUSCLE RELAXANT and an ANTIHISTAMINE. The bronchodilator is ephedrine hydrochloride, and the muscle relaxant is theophylline. It is produced in the form of tablets, and is used to treat asthma and chronic bronchitis.

▲/✚ side-effects/warning: see BARBITURATE; EPHEDRINE HYDROCHLORIDE; PHENOBARBITONE; THEOPHYLLINE.

**FreAmine II** (*Boots*) is a proprietary form of high-calorie nutritional supplement intended

for injection or infusion, available only on prescription. Produced in two strengths, it contains amino acids, nitrogen, phosphate and electrolytes.

**FreAmine III** (*Boots*) is a proprietary form of high-calorie, nutritional supplement intended for injection or infusion, available only on prescription. Produced in two strengths, it contains amino acids, nitrogen, phosphate and electrolytes.

**Fresubin** (*Fresenius Dylade*) is a bland, proprietary, non-prescription, gluten-free liquid. It is a complete nutritional diet for patients who are severely undernourished (as with anorexia nervosa) or who are suffering from some problem with the absorption of food, such as following gastrectomy. Produced in four flavours and three sizes, Fresubin contains protein, carbohydrate, fats, minerals and vitamins. It is not suitable for children aged under 12 months.

**Frisium** (*Hoechst*) is a proprietary form of the BENZODIAZEPINE clobazam, used primarily as an ANXIOLYTIC to treat anxiety, nervous tension and restlessness. It may also be used to assist in the treatment of epilepsy. Available on prescription only to private patients, Frisium is produced in the form of capsules. It is not recommended for children aged under 3 years.

▲/✚ side-effects/warning: see CLOBAZAM.

**Froben** (*Boots*) is a proprietary, non-steroid, non-narcotic ANALGESIC available only on prescription, used to relieve pain – particularly arthritic and rheumatic pain – and to treat other musculo-skeletal disorders. Its active constituent is flurbiprofen, and it is produced in the form of tablets, as sustained-release capsules (Froben SR), and as anal suppositories. Not recommended for children, Froben should not be administered to patients with a peptic ulcer or gastrointestinal bleeding; special care is necessary in the treatment of patients who are pregnant or lactating; whose kidneys are not fully functional; or who have asthma.

▲/◈ side-effects/warning: *see* FLURBIPROFEN.

**fructose** is a simple sugar which with glucose together makes up the carbohydrate sucrose – the usual form of sugar, found in cane sugar and sugar-beet. By itself, fructose is a constituent in honey and in certain fruits (such as figs), and as part of a normal diet is used to create energy in the body through glycolysis in the liver. This is significant particularly for diabetics, for fructose does not require insulin for metabolism – unlike glucose. Fructose is accordingly available, without prescription, for patients who suffer from glucose or galactose intolerance.

**Frumil** (*Berk*) is a proprietary compound DIURETIC, available only on prescription, used to treat accumulation of fluids within the tissues (oedema) due to heart, kidney or liver disease. Produced in the form of tablets (2 strengths), Frumil combines the potassium-sparing diuretic amiloride hydrochloride with the powerful diuretic frusemide. It is not recommended for children.

▲/◈ side-effects/warning: *see* AMILORIDE; FRUSEMIDE.

**frusemide** is a powerful DIURETIC which works by inhibiting absorption in part of the kidney known as the loop of Henle. It is used to treat fluid retention in the tissues (oedema) and high blood pressure (*see* ANTIHYPERTENSIVE), and to assist a failing kidney. Administration is oral in the form of tablets, or by injection or infusion.

▲ side-effects: the diuretic effect corresponds to dosage; large doses may cause deafness or ringing in the ears (tinnitus). There may be skin rashes.

◈ warning: frusemide should not be administered to patients with kidney damage or who are pregnant, who have gout, diabetes, an enlarged prostate gland, or cirrhosis of the liver. Treatment may cause a deficiency of potassium and sodium in the bloodstream (hypokalaemia, hyponatraemia).
*Related articles:* DIUMIDE-K CONTINUS; DIURESAL; FRUMIL; FRUSENE; FRUSETIC; FRUSID; LASIKAL; LASILACTONE; LASIPRESSIN.

**Frusene** (*Radiol*) is a proprietary compound DIURETIC, available only on prescription, used to treat accumulation of fluids within the tissues (oedema) due to heart or liver disease. Produced in the form of tablets, Frusene combines the potassium-sparing diuretic triamterine with the powerful diuretic frusemide. It is not recommended for children.

▲/◈ side-effects/warning: *see* FRUSEMIDE; TRIAMTERINE.

**Frusetic** (*Unimed*) is a proprietary DIURETIC, available only on prescription, used to treat accumulation of fluids within the tissues (oedema) due to heart or liver disease. Produced in the form of tablets, Frusetic is a preparation of the powerful diuretic frusemide. It is not recommended for children.

▲/◈ side-effects/warning: *see* FRUSEMIDE.

**Frusid** (*DDSA Pharmaceuticals*) is a proprietary DIURETIC, available only on prescription, used to treat accumulation of fluids within the tissues (oedema) due to heart or liver disease. Produced in the form of tablets, Frusid is a preparation of the powerful diuretic frusemide. It is not recommended for children.
▲/ ✪ side-effects/warning: *see* FRUSEMIDE.

**FSH** is an abbreviation for follicle-stimulating hormone, a HORMONE secreted by the anterior pituitary gland that in women causes the monthly ripening in one ovary of a follicle and stimulates ovulation, and that in men stimulates the production of sperm in the testes. It may be injected therapeutically to make up for a deficiency in the natural hormone, as long as careful biochemical monitoring ensues thereafter.
▲ side-effects: there may be local sensitivity reactions.
✪ warning: FSH should be administered to women with care in order to avoid over-stimulation of an ovary which might lead to multiple pregnancy or enlargement and possible rupture. Dosage depends on individual response.
*Related articles:*
GONADOTROPHIN FSH; METRODIN; PERGONAL.

**Fucibet** (*Leo*) is a proprietary compound, available only on prescription, combining the potent CORTICOSTEROID betamethasone with the ANTIBIOTIC fusidic acid. It is used to treat eczema in which bacterial infection is deemed to be present, and is produced in the form of a cream.
▲/ ✪ side-effects/warning: *see* FUSIDIC ACID.

**Fucidin** (*Leo*) is a proprietary,

narrow-spectrum ANTIBIOTIC, available only on prescription, used mainly against staphylococcal infections – especially infections of the skin and bone, as well as abscesses – that prove to be resistant to penicillin. It is produced in many forms: as tablets, as a suspension, as powder for reconstitution as a medium for infusion, as a gel (with or without a special applicator), as a cream, as an ointment, or as an gauze dressing (called Fucidin Intertulle) all for use as indicated by the location of the infection, and all containing as their active constituent either fusidic acid or one of its salts (particularly sodium fusidate).
▲/ ✪ side-effects/warning: *see* FUSIDIC ACID.

**Fucidin H** (*Leo*) is a proprietary compound, available only on prescription, combining the ANTIBIOTIC sodium fusidate with the CORTICOSTEROID hydrocortisone, and used to treat skin inflammation considered to involve bacterial infection. It is produced in the form of an ointment, a cream and a gel.
▲/ ✪ side-effects/warning: *see* FUSIDIC ACID.

**Fucithalmic** (*Leo*) is a proprietary, narrow-spectrum ANTIBIOTIC, available only on prescription, used mainly against staphylococcal infections that prove to be resistant to penicillin. It is produced in the form of eye-drops, as a solution of the active ingredient, fusidic acid, in a gel.
▲/ ✪ side-effects/warning: *see* FUSIDIC ACID.

**Fulcin** (*ICI*) is a proprietary ANTIFUNGAL drug, available only on prescription, used to treat fungal infections of the scalp, skin and nails. Produced in the form of tablets (in two strengths) and as a suspension, Fulcin is a

preparation of the drug
griseofulvin. Treatment may be
required to continue over several
weeks.
▲/✿ side-effects/warning: *see*
GRISEOFULVIN.

**Full Marks** (*Napp*) is a
preparation for the treatment of
lice, whose active ingredient is
phenothrin, a pyrethroid, which
is effective in killing lice though
less so their eggs. Available
without prescription, the
preparation is available as a
fragrant shampoo, which should
be left in contact with scalp for at
least 5 minutes.

**\*fungicidal drugs** act to destroy
fungal infection, and are also
known as an antimycotic or
antifungal drugs.
*see* ANTIFUNGAL DRUGS.

**Fungilin** (*Squibb*) is a proprietary
form of the ANTIFUNGAL drug
amphotericin. Available only on
prescription, Fungilin is produced
in the form of tablets and as a
suspension, as lozenges and as an
ointment, and used in the
appropriate form to treat fungal
infections, especially candidiasis
(thrush) of the mouth, gastrointestinal tract, vagina and skin.
▲/✿ side-effects/warning: *see*
AMPHOTERICIN.

**Fungizone** (*Squibb*) is a
proprietary form of the
ANTIFUNGAL drug amphotericin.
Available only on prescription,
Fungizone is produced in the form
of powder for reconstitution as a
nedium for intravenous infusion,
and used to treat systemic fungal
infections.
▲/✿ side-effects/warning: *see*
AMPHOTERICIN.

**Furadantin** (*Norwich Eaton*) is a
proprietary ANTIBIOTIC drug,
available only on prescription,
used to treat infections of the

urinary tract. It is produced in
the form of tablets (in two
strengths) and as a suspension,
the active constituent of which is
nitrofurantoin.
▲/✿ side-effects/warning: *see*
NITROFURANTOIN.

**Furamide** (*Boots*) is a proprietary
form of the AMOEBICIDAL drug
diloxanide furoate, available only
on prescription, used to treat
chronic infection by the organism
*Entamoeba histolytica* where cysts
are discernible in the faeces. It is
produced in the form of tablets.
▲/✿ side-effects/warning: *see*
DILOXANIDE FUROATE.

**fusidic acid** is a narrow-spectrum
ANTIBIOTIC used most commonly
in combination with other
antibiotics to treat
staphylococcal infections –
especially skin infections,
abscesses and infections of bone –
that prove to be resistant to
penicillin. The drug works by
inhibiting protein synthesis at the
ribosome level in sensitive
organisms (gram-positive
bacteria). Administration is oral
in the form of tablets and as a
suspension, or by infusion, and by
application in the form of a cream
or gel. It is also used in the form
of sodium fusidate.
▲ side-effects: there may be
nausea with vomiting; a rash
may occur. Some patients
experience temporary kidney
dysfunction.
✿ warning: regular monitoring of
liver function is essential
during treatment.
*Related articles:* FUCIDIN;
FUCIDIN H; FUCITHALMIC;
SODIUM FUSIDATE.

**Fybogel** (*Reckitt*) *Colman*) is a
proprietary form of the type of
LAXATIVE known as a bulking
agent, which works by increasing
the overall mass of faeces within
the rectum, so stimulating bowel

movement. It is used also to soothe the effects of diverticular disease and irritable colon. In the case of Fybogel, the agent involved is ispaghula husk, presented in the form of effervescent grains in sachets for swallowing with water.

▲/ ◉ side-effects/warning: *see* ISPAGHULA HUSK.

**Fybranta** (*Norgine*) is a proprietary form of the type of LAXATIVE known as a bulking agent, which works by increasing the overall mass of faeces within the rectum, so stimulating bowel movement. It is used also to soothe the effects of diverticular disease and irritable colon. In the case of Fybranta, the agent involved is bran, presented in the form of tablets to be chewed and swallowed.

▲/ ◉ side-effects/warning: *see* BRAN.

**Galactomin** (*Cow & Gate*) is the name of a proprietary series of powdered formulas representing nutritional supplements for patients whose metabolisms cannot tolerate certain sugars. They contain proteins, fats, carbohydrates, minerals and vitamins but are galactose-free. In the three preparations available (Formulas 17, 18 and 19), Formula 18 may be regarded as standard; Formula 17 has a higher fat content; and Formula 19 has fructose as its carbohydrate.

**Galcodine** (*Galen*) is a proprietary ANTITUSSIVE, available only on prescription, used to encourage the loosening of a dry, painful cough. Produced in the form of an orange-flavoured sugar-free linctus (in two strengths, the weaker under the name Galcodine Paediatric) for dilution (the potency of the dilute linctus is retained for 14 days), galcodine is a preparation of the OPIATE codeine phosphate. It is not recommended for children aged under 12 months.
▲/✿ side-effects/warning: *see* CODEINE PHOSPHATE.

**Galenomycin** (*Galen*) is a proprietary ANTIBIOTIC, available only on prescription, used to treat infections of the soft tissues and the respiratory tract. Produced in the form of tablets, Galenomycin is a preparation of the TETRACYCLINE oxytetracycline dihydrate. It is not recommended for children.
▲/✿ side-effects/warning: *see* OXYTETRACYCLINE.

**Galenphol** (*Galen*) is a proprietary cough suppressant, available only on prescription, used to encourage the loosening of a dry, painful cough. Produced in the form of an aniseed-flavoured sugar-free linctus (in three strengths, the weakest under the name Galenphol Linctus Paediatric, the strongest under the name Galenphol Linctus Strong) for dilution (the potency of the dilute linctus is retained for 14 days), Galenphol is a preparation of the OPIATE pholcodine.
▲/✿ side-effects/warning: *see* PHOLCODINE.

**Galfer** (*Galen*) is a proprietary, non-prescription IRON supplement, used particularly to treat certain forms of anaemia. Produced in the form of capsules, and as a syrup, Galfer is a preparation of ferrous fumarate.
▲/✿ side-effects/warning: *see* FERROUS FUMARATE.

**Galfer F.A.** (*Galen*) is a proprietary, non-prescription IRON-AND-VITAMIN supplement, used particularly to prevent iron deficiency or vitamin B deficiency (as sometimes occurs during pregnancy). Produced in the form of capsules, Galfer F.A. is a compound of ferrous fumarate and folic acid.
▲/✿ side-effects/warning: *see* FERROUS FUMARATE; FOLIC ACID.

**Galfer-Vit** (*Galen*) is a proprietary IRON-AND-VITAMIN supplement that is not available from the National Health Service. It is used to treat certain forms of anaemia in which there is simultaneous vitamin deficiency. Produced in the form of capsules, Galfervit is a compound of various forms of vitamin B (THIAMINE, RIBOFLAVINE, PYRIDOXINE and NICOTINAMIDE) and ASCORBIC ACID (vitamin C) with ferrous fumarate.
▲/✿ side-effects/warning: *see* FERROUS FUMARATE.

**gallamine triethiodide** is a SKELETAL MUSCLE RELAXANT of the type known as competitive or non-depolarizing. It is used during surgical operations to achieve long-duration paralysis. Administration is by injection, but only after the patient has been rendered unconscious.

▲ side-effects: there may be a precipitate deceleration in the heart rate.

✸ warning: gallamine triethiodide should not be administered to patients with impaired function of the kidneys. Respiration should be assisted throughout treatment. *Related article:* FLAXEDIL.

**Galpseud** (*Galen*) is a proprietary, non-prescription form of nasal DECONGESTANT administered orally. It is produced as tablets and as an orange-flavoured sugar-free linctus for dilution (the potency of the linctus once dilute is retained for 14 days), and is a preparation of the SYMPATHO-MIMETIC ephedrine derivative pseudoephedrine hydrochloride.

▲/✸ side-effects/warning: *see* EPHEDRINE HYDROCHLORIDE.

**Gamanil** (*Merck*) is a proprietary ANTIDEPRESSANT drug, available only on prescription, used to treat depressive illness and associated symptoms. Produced in the form of tablets, Gamanil represents a preparation of lofepramine hydrochloride. It is not recommended for children.

▲/✸ side-effects/warning: *see* LOFEPRAMINE.

**Gamimune-N** (*Cutter*) is a proprietary preparation of human normal immunoglobulin (HNIG) as a solution in maltose, used by intravenous infusion to confer immediate immunity to such diseases as hepatitis A virus, measles (rubeola), and at least to some degree German measles (rubella), particularly in patients who cannot tolerate the administration of live (though

weakened) viruses in vaccination therapies. Gamimune-N is primarily used as replacement therapy in patients born with certain immunodeficient conditions. It is available only on prescription, in vials (in three strengths).

✸ warning: *see* HNIG.

**Gammabulin** (*Immuno*) is a proprietary preparation of human normal immunoglobulin (HNIG) as an aqueous solution, used by intramuscular injection to confer immediate immunity to such diseases as hepatitis A virus, measles (rubeola) and at least to some degree German measles (rubella), particularly in patients who cannot tolerate the administration of live (though weakened) viruses in vaccination therapies. It is available only on prescription, in vials.

✸ warning: *see* HNIG.

**gamolenic acid** is used in preparations taken by mouth for the relief of eczema and atopic dermatitis.

▲ side-effects: sometimes nausea, headache, indigestion.

✸ warning: epilepsy, and concurrent treatment with drugs such as phenothiazines. *Related article:* EPOGRAM.

**ganciclovir** is an ANTIVIRAL agent related to ACYCLOVIR, but it is more toxic. Therefore its use is restricted to treat life-threatening cytomegalovirus infections in immunocompromised patients. It works by inhibiting the action of two virally coded enzymes in cells used by the virus to replicate itself. To be effective, however, treatment of an infection must begin early. Administration is by intravenous infusion.

▲ side-effects: there may be various blood cell deficiencies; sore throat and swelling of the face; fever and rash; effects on liver function, gastrointestinal disturbances; and a number of other reactions.

● **warning:** ganciclovir should be administered with caution to patients who are pregnant and contraception must be maintained during treatment. It should not be given to patients who are breast-feeding, or who have impaired kidney function. Ganciclovir must be avoided where sensitivity to acyclovir has been seen, or where there is an abnormal blood picture. Blood monitoring is necessary.
*Related article:* CYMEVENE.

**Ganda** (*Smith & Nephew*) is a proprietary compound of the powerful ANTIHYPERTENSIVE drug guanethidine monosulphate together with the hormone adrenaline, available only on prescription, used as eye-drops to treat glaucoma (or occasionally thyrotoxicosis). Both of the drugs contained are effective in relieving intra-ocular pressure, but guanethidine also has the effect of prolonging the action of adrenaline. Ganda drops are produced in four strengths.
▲/● side-effects/warning: *see* ADRENALINE; GUANETHIDINE MONOSULPHATE.

**Gantrisin** (*Roche*) is a proprietary ANTIBACTERIAL drug, available only on prescription, used primarily to treat infections of the urinary tract, but also to relieve lesser infections of the skin and soft tissues and the respiratory tract, and to treat bacillary dysentery. Produced in the form of tablets and as a syrup, Gantrisin is a preparation of the SULPHONAMIDE sulphafurazole.

**Garamycin** (*Kirby-Warrick*) is a proprietary ANTIBIOTIC, available only on prescription, used primarily in the form of drops to treat bacterial infections of the ear or eye. Garamycin is a preparation of the aminoglycoside gentamicin.
▲/● side-effects/warning: *see* GENTAMICIN.

**Gardenal sodium** (*May & Baker*) is a proprietary form of the ANTICONVULSANT BARBITURATE phenobarbitone, and is on the controlled drugs list. Produced in vials for injection, it is used to treat all forms of epilepsy, although it should be administered with extreme caution to children or the elderly.
▲/● side-effects/warning: *see* PHENOBARBITONE.

**Gastrese LA** (*Wyeth*) is a proprietary ANTINAUSEANT, used to treat digestive disturbances resulting in nausea, and for nausea and vomiting after radiation or cytotoxic drug therapy. Available only on prescription, the active constituent, metoclopramide hydrochloride, works by reducing nausea and vomiting and allowing the passage of absorbable nutrients in food in the stomach down into the intestines. It is produced in the form of sustained-release tablets. It is not recommended for patients less than 20 years of age.
▲/● side-effects/warning: *see* METOCLOPRAMIDE.

**Gastrils** (*Jackson*) is a proprietary, non-prescription ANTACID (used for the relief of indigestion and flatulence), which is not available from the National Health Service. Produced in the form of mint- or fruit-flavoured pastilles, Gastrils contain ALUMINIUM HYDROXIDE and magnesium carbonate.
▲/● side-effects/warning: *see* MAGNESIUM CARBONATE.

**Gastrobid Continus** (*Napp*) is a proprietary ANTINAUSEANT, used to treat digestive disturbances

resulting in nausea; and for
nausea, severe indigestion and
vomiting after radiation or
cytotoxic drug therapy. Available
only on prescription, the active
constituent, metoclopramide
hydrochloride, works by reducing
nausea and vomiting and allowing
the passage of absorbable
nutrients in food in the stomach
down into the intestines. It is
produced in the form of sustained-
release tablets. It is not
recommended for patients less
than 20 years of age.
▲/◎ side-effects/warning: *see*
METOCLOPRAMIDE.

**Gastrocote** (*MCP
Pharmaceuticals*) is a proprietary,
non-prescription ANTACID (used
for the relief of indigestion and
flatulence), produced in the form
of tablets containing ALUMINIUM
HYDROXIDE, SODIUM BICARBONATE
and magnesium trisilicate. It is
not recommended for children
aged under 6 years.
◎ warning: *see* MAGNESIUM
TRISILICATE.

**Gastromax** (*Farmitalia Carlo
Erba*) is a proprietary
ANTINAUSEANT, used to treat
digestive disturbances resulting
in nausea; and for nausea, severe
indigestion and vomiting after
radiation or cytotoxic drug
therapy. Available only on
prescription, the active
constituent, metoclopramide
hydrochloride, works by reducing
nausea and vomiting and allowing
the passage of absorbable
nutrients in food in the stomach
down into the intestines. It is
produced in the form of sustained-
release capsules. It is not
recommended for patients less
than 20 years of age.
▲/◎ side-effects/warning: *see*
METOCLOPRAMIDE.

**Gastron** (*Winthrop*) is a
proprietary, non-prescription
ANTACID (used for the relief of

indigestion and flatulence),
produced in the form of tablets
containing ALUMINIUM
HYDROXIDE, SODIUM BICARBONATE
and magnesium trisilicate. It is
not recommended for children.
◎ warning: *see* MAGNESIUM
TRISILICATE.

**Gastrovite** (*MCP
Pharmaceuticals*) is a proprietary,
non-prescription mineral-
and-VITAMIN compound, which is
not available from the National
Health Service. The minerals are
IRON and CALCIUM, in the form of
ferrous glycine sulphate and
caicium gluconate, and the
vitamins are ASCORBIC ACID
(vitamin C) and ERGOCALCIFEROL
(vitamin D).
▲/◎ side-effects/warning: *see*
CALCIUM GLUCONATE;
FERROUS GLYCINE SULPHATE.

**Gastrozepin** (*Boots*) is a
proprietary preparation of the
ANTICHOLINERGIC drug
pirenzepine, available only on
prescription, used to treat gastric
and duodenal ulcers. It works by
inhibiting the formation and
secretion of stomach acids.
Produced in the form of tablets, it
is not recommended for children.
▲/◎ side-effects/warning: *see*
PIRENZEPINE.

**Gaviscon** (*Reckitt & Colman*) is a
proprietary, non-prescription
ANTACID (used for the relief of
indigestion and flatulence),
produced in the form of chewable
tablets containing alginic acid,
ALUMINIUM HYDROXIDE, SODIUM
BICARBONATE, magnesium
trisilicate and various sugars.
There is also a liquid version that
contains sodium alginate, sodium
bicarbonate and calcium
carbonate.
  Infabt Gaviscon is also
available in the form of a powder,
which is sugar-free and contains
sodium alginate, magnesium

**G**

alginate, aluminium hydroxide with colloidal silica and mannitol. It should not be given to premature infants or to those where excessive water loss is likely (e.g. fever, diarrhoea, vomiting).

❋ **warning:** *see* CALCIUM CARBONATE; MAGNESIUM TRISILICATE.

**Gee's linctus** is a less formal name for the non-proprietary, opiate squill cough linctus.
*see* OPIATE SQUILL LINCTUS AND PASTILLES.

**Gee's pastilles** is a less formal name for the non-proprietary, opiate squill cough pastilles.
*see* OPIATE SQUILL LINCTUS AND PASTILLES.

**gelatin** is hydrolized animal protein. Therapeutically, gelatin is used as a short-term medium for expanding overall blood volume in patients whose blood volume is dangerously low or whose blood is abnormally liable to clot, as a nutritional supplement in the form of a jelly, and in the form of an absorbent sponge as a HAEMOSTATIC.

▲ **side-effects:** some patients suffer serious hypersensitivity reactions.

❋ **warning:** gelatin as a medium to expand the blood volume should not be administered to patients with severe congestive heart failure, with disorders of the blood coagulation mechanism, or with severely impaired function of the kidneys.
*Related articles:* GELOFUSINE; HAEMACCEL.

**Gelcotar** (*Quinoderm*) is a proprietary preparation of the ANTISEPTIC COAL TAR, used both to treat skin conditions such as dandruff, dermatitis, eczema and psoriasis, and to remove

medicated pastes and dressings following treatment. It is produced in the form of a water-miscible gel (with pine tar) and as a liquid shampoo (with cade oil).

**Gelofusine** (*Consolidated*) is a proprietary form of gelatin, the hydrolized animal protein. In a special refined (partly degraded) form available only on prescription, it is used in infusion with saline (sodium chloride) as a means of expanding overall blood volume in patients whose blood volume is dangerously low through shock, (particularly in cases of severe burns or septicaemia. It is produced in bottles (flasks) for infusion.

▲/❋ **side-effects/warning:** *see* GELATIN.

**Gelusil** (*Warner-Lambert*) is a proprietary, non-prescription ANTACID (used for the relief of indigestion and flatulence), which is not available from the National Health Service. It is produced in the form of tablets that can be chewed or sucked, containing ALUMINIUM HYDROXIDE and magnesium trisilicate.

❋ **warning:** *see* MAGNESIUM TRISILICATE.

**gemeprost** is a PROSTAGLANDIN, used during induction of pregnancy and earlier in operative procedures, by administration to the cervix by pessary to cause dilation.

▲ **side-effects:** vaginal bleeding and uterine pain; nausea, vomiting, flushing and shivering, headache and dizziness, a raised temperature and diarrhoea.

❋ **warning:** gemeprost should not be administered to patients with certain uterine disorders or infections. It should be administered with caution to those with asthma or glaucoma.
*Related article:* CERVAGEM.

**gemfibrozil** is a drug used to reduce high levels of fat in the bloodstream (hyperlipidaemia), particularly cholesterol. Administration is oral in the form of capsules.

▲ side-effects: gastrointestinal disturbances are not uncommon. There may also be dizziness, blurred vision and an itching rash. Some patients experience muscle pain, or pain in the fingertips and toes.

✿ warning: gemfibrozil should not be administered to patients with gallstones, impaired function of the liver, alcoholism, or who are pregnant. Before and during treatment there should be blood counts (and specifically to check on the lipid profile), monitoring of kidney function, and an ophthalmic examination.
*Related article:* LOPID.

**\*general anaesthetic:** *see* ANAESTHETIC.

**Genisol** (*Fisons*) is a proprietary preparation of the ANTISEPTIC COAL TAR, used to treat skin conditions such as dandruff, dermatitis, eczema and psoriasis. It is produced in the form of a liquid shampoo for weekly application.

**Genotropin** (*Kabi*) is a HORMONE, a proprietary form of somatropin, used to treat small stature, and deficiencies of other hormones. It is available only on prescription. The preparation is in the form of a powder for reconstition for injection.
▲/✿ side-effects/warning: *see* SOMATROPIN.

**gentamicin** is a broad-spectrum ANTIBIOTIC, the most widely used of the aminoglycoside family, with activity against gram-positive bacteria but used primarily against serious infections caused by gram-negative bacteria. It is not orally absorbed and is therefore given by injection or infusion for the treatment of, for example, septicaemia, meningitis and infections of the heart (usually in conjunction with penicillin), the kidney and the prostate gland. Because of its toxicity to the ear (ototoxicity), potentially resulting in deafness, and its toxicity to the kidney (nephrotoxicity), treatment should be limited in duration. It is also available in the form of drops, creams and ointments for topical application.

▲ side-effects: prolonged or high dosage may be damaging to the ear, causing deafness and balance disorders; treatment must be discontinued if this occurs; there may also be reversible kidney damage.

✿ warning: gentamicin should not be administered to patients who are pregnant or who suffer from myasthenia gravis. It should be administered with caution to those with Parkinsonism. As the drug is excreted by the kidney, great care must be taken in patients with impaired kidney function. In such cases, and/or where dosage is high or prolonged, regular checks on gentamicin concentrations in the blood must be carried out.
*Related articles:* CIDOMYCIN; GARAMYCIN; GENTICIN; GENTISONE HC; MINIMS GENTAMICIN.

**gentian mixture** is a non-proprietary formulation of simple and aromatic constituents intended to stimulate the appetite. (The main active constituent, however, is said to be suggestion.) There are two forms of gentian mixture – an 'acid' formulation, and an 'alkaline'.

Both contain a solution of the herb gentian in infusion in chloroform water. The acid mixture additionally contains the stomach acid hydrochloric acid; the alkaline contains SODIUM BICARBONATE.

**gentian violet**, or crystal violet, is an ANTISEPTIC dye used to treat certain bacterial and fungal skin infections, or abrasions and minor wounds. Administration is mostly in the form of ointment, paint or lotion, but can in dilute solution be oral or as vaginal inserts (pessaries). The dye is also used to stain specimens for examination under a microscope. A non-proprietary antiseptic paint, used particularly to prepare skin for surgery, combines gentian violet with another dye, brilliant green.

▲ side-effects: rarely, there may be nausea and vomiting, with diarrhoea.

✦ warning: gentian violet is a dye: it stains clothes as well as skin.

**Genticin** (*Nicholas*) is a proprietary ANTIBIOTIC, available only on prescription, used to treat a number of serious gram-negative bacterial infections, but especially those of the urinary tract and of the skin. Produced in vials or ampoules for injection (in two strengths) as a (water-miscible) cream or an (anhydrous greasy) ointment applied topically to treat skin infections, and as eye- or ear-drops, Genticin is a preparation of the aminoglycoside gentamicin.

▲/✦ side-effects/warning: *see* GENTAMICIN.

**Genticin HC** (*Nicholas*) is a proprietary compound ANTIBIOTIC, available only on prescription, used in the form of a cream and as an ointment to treat skin infections and to reduce the symptoms of allergic skin conditions. It is a preparation of the aminoglycoside antibiotic gentamicin sulphate with the anti-inflammatory CORTICO-STEROID hydrocortisone acetate.

▲/✦ side-effects/warning: *see* GENTAMICIN.

**Gentisone HC** (*Nicholas*) is a proprietary compound ANTIBIOTIC, available only on prescription, used in the form of ear-drops to treat bacterial infections of the outer or middle ear. It is a preparation of the amino-glycoside gentamicin sulphate with the CORTICOSTEROID hydrocortisone acetate. Because of gentamicin's toxicity to the ear this preparation should not be used in cases where the ear drum is perforated.

▲/✦ side-effects/warning: *see* GENTAMICIN.

**Gentran** (*Travenol*) is a proprietary form of the plasma substitute dextran, available only on prescription, used in infusion with either saline (sodium chloride) or glucose to make up a deficiency in the overall volume of blood in a patient, or to prevent thrombosis following surgery. Produced in flasks (bottles) for infusion, there is a choice of two concentrations: Gentran 40 and Gentran 70.

▲/✦ side-effects/warning: *see* DEXTRAN.

**Gestanin** (*Organon*) is a proprietary form of the PROGESTOGEN allyloestrenol, available only on prescription, used to treat recurrent miscarriage or failure of a blastocyst to implant in the uterine wall following conception. It is produced in the form of tablets.

▲/✦ side-effects/warning: *see* ALLYLOESTRENOL.

**gestodene** is a PROGESTERONE, used as a constituent of the combined ORAL CONTRACEPTIVES that combine an OESTROGEN with a progesterone.
▲/● side-effects/warning: *see* PROGESTERONE.
*Related articles:* FEMODENE; FEMODENE ED.

**Gestone** (*Paines & Byrne*) is a proprietary form of the PROGESTOGEN progesterone, available only on prescription, used to treat recurrent miscarriage, premenstrual symptoms or abnormal bleeding from the womb. It is produced in ampoules for deep intramuscular injection (in three strengths).
▲/● side-effects/warning: *see* PROGESTERONE.

**gestronol hexanoate** is a synthetic PROGESTOGEN used primarily in women to treat cancer of the breast or of the uterine lining (endometrium), but used also in men to treat (malignant) enlargement of the kidneys or (benign) enlargement of the prostate gland.
▲ side-effects: there may be breast tenderness, menstrual irregularity and an alteration in libido; fluid retention and consequent weight gain are not uncommon; there may also be nausea, gastrointestinal disturbances and sensitivity reactions such as acne and urticaria.
● warning: gestronol hexanoate should not be administered to patients with undiagnosed vaginal bleeding or with thrombosis; it should be administered with caution to those who suffer from heart, liver or kidney disease, from diabetes, or who are lactating.
*Related article:* DEPOSTAT.

**Givitol** (*Galen*) is a proprietary, non-prescription, IRON-and-VITAMIN supplement, which is not available from the National Health Service. Produced in the form of capsules, Givitol contains iron in the form of FERROUS FUMARATE, vitamin B in the forms of THIAMINE, RIBOFLAVINE, PYRIDOXINE and NICOTINAMIDE, and ASCORBIC ACID (vitamin C).

**Glandosane** (*Dylade*) is a proprietary, non-prescription form of artificial saliva, produced in an aerosol for spraying on to the membranes of the mouth and throat in conditions that make the mouth abnormally dry. There are neutral and flavoured versions. Constituents include CARMELLOSE SODIUM, SORBITOL, salt (sodium chloride), MAGNESIUM CHLORIDE and POTASSIUM CHLORIDE.

**Glauline** (*Smith & Nephew*) is a proprietary BETA-BLOCKER, available only on prescription, used in the form of eye-drops to treat glaucoma and other conditions involving pressure within the eyeball. Produced in three strengths, Glauline drops represent a preparation of metipranolol, and are not recommended for children.
▲/● side-effects/warning: *see* METIPRANOLOL.

**glibenclamide** is a drug used to treat (adult-onset) diabetes mellitus. It is one of the SULPHONYLUREAS, which work by augmenting insulin production in the pancreas (as opposed to compensating for its absence). Administration is oral in the form of tablets.
▲ side-effects: there may be some sensitivity reaction (such as a rash).
● warning: glibenclamide should not be administered to patients with liver or kidney damage, with endocrine disorders, or who are under stress; who are

pregnant or lactating; or who are already taking corticosteroids or oral contraceptives, oral anticoagulants, or aspirin and other antibiotics.
*Related articles:* DAONIL; EUGLUCON; LIBANIL; MALIX; SEMI-DAONIL.

**Glibenese** (*Pfizer*) is a proprietary form of the SULPHONYLUREA glipizide, available only on prescription, used to treat adult-onset diabetes mellitus. It works by augmenting what remains of insulin production in the pancreas, and is produced in the form of tablets.
▲/● side-effects/warning: *see* GLIPIZIDE.

**glibornuride** is a drug used to treat (adult-onset) diabetes mellitus. It is one of the SULPHONYLUREAS, which work by augmenting insulin production in the pancreas (as opposed to compensating for its absence). Administration is oral in the form of tablets.
▲ side-effects: there may be some sensitivity reaction (such as a rash).
● warning: glibornuride should not be administered to patients with liver or kidney damage, with endocrine disorders, or who are under stress; who are pregnant or lactating; or who are already taking corticosteroids or oral contraceptives, oral anticoagulants, or aspirin and other antibiotics.
*Related article:* GLUTRIL.

**gliclazide** is a drug used to treat (adult-onset) diabetes mellitus. It is one of the SULPHONYLUREAS, which work by augmenting insulin production in the pancreas (as opposed to compensating for its absence). Administration is oral in the form of tablets.

▲ side-effects: there may be some sensitivity reaction (such as a rash).
● warning: gliclazide should not be administered to patients with liver or kidney damage, with endocrine disorders, or who are under stress; who are pregnant or lactating; or who are already taking corticosteroids or oral contraceptives, oral anticoagulants, or aspirin and other antibiotics.
*Related article:* DIAMICRON.

**glipizide** is a drug used to treat (adult-onset) diabetes mellitus. It is one of the SULPHONYLUREAS, which work by augmenting insulin production in the pancreas (as opposed to compensating for its absence). Administration is oral in the form of tablets.
▲ side-effects: there may be some sensitivity reaction (such as a rash).
● warning: glipizide should not be administered to patients with liver or kidney damage, with endocrine disorders, or who are under stress; who are pregnant or lactating; or who are already taking corticosteroids or oral contraceptives, oral anticoagulants, or aspirin and other antibiotics.
*Related articles:* GLIBENESE; MINODIAB.

**gliquidone** is a drug used to treat (adult-onset) diabetes mellitus. It is one of the SULPHONYLUREAS, which work by augmenting insulin production in the pancreas (as opposed to compensating for its absence). Administration is oral in the form of tablets.
▲ side-effects: there may be some sensitivity reaction (such as a rash).
● warning: gliquidone should not be administered to patients with liver or kidney damage,

with endocrine disorders, or who are under stress; who are pregnant or lactating; or who are already taking corticosteroids or oral contraceptives, oral anticoagulants, or aspirin and other antibiotics.
*Related article:* GLURENORM.

**globulin** is any of a group of simple proteins that are present in blood and act either as antibodies (immunoglobulins) or as the means of transport for certain minerals and fats (lipids) around the body. Soluble in saline solution, globulins can be coagulated by heat.
*Related article:* HNIG.

**glucagon** is a HORMONE produced and secreted by the pancreas to cause an increase in blood sugar levels. In most people it is part of a balancing mechanism complementary to INSULIN, which has the opposite effect. Therapeutically, glucagon is thus administered to patients with low blood sugar levels (hypoglycaemia). Administration is by injection.

**Glucophage** (*Lipha*) is a proprietary form of the drug metformin hydrochloride, available only on prescription, used to treat adult-onset diabetes. It works by increasing absorption and utilization in the body of glucose, to make up for the reduction in insulin available from the pancreas, and is produced in the form of tablets (in two strengths).
▲/● side-effects/warning: *see* METFORMIN HYDROCHLORIDE.

**Glucoplex** (*Geistlich*) is a proprietary form of high-energy, nutritional supplement intended for infusion into patients who are unable to take food via the alimentary tract. Produced in two

strengths (under the names Glucoplex 1000 and Glucoplex 1600), its major constituent is the carbohydrate GLUCOSE.

**glucose**, or dextrose, is a simple sugar that represents an important source of energy for the body – and the sole source of energy for the brain. Following digestion, it is stored in the liver and muscles in the form of glycogen, and its breakdown into glucose again in the muscles produces energy. The level of glucose in the blood is critical: harmful symptoms occur if the level is too high or too low. Therapeutically, it may be administered as a dietary supplement in conditions of low blood sugar level, to treat abnormally high acidity of body fluids (acidosis), or to increase glucose levels in the liver following liver damage. Oral administration of a glucose solution is a good way of making up a deficiency of water or of carbohydrate in the body. The more common form of administration is by infusion.
▲ side-effects: injections of glucose may irritate vascular walls and so tend to promote thrombosis and inflammation.

**Glurenorm** (*Winthrop*) is a proprietary form of the SULPHONYLUREA gliquidone, available only on prescription, used to treat adult-onset diabetes mellitus. It works by augmenting what remains of insulin production in the pancreas, and is produced in the form of tablets.
▲/● side-effects/warning: *see* GLIQUIDONE.

**glutaraldehyde** is a DISINFECTANT much like formaldehyde, but stronger and faster-acting. It is used mostly to sterilize medical and surgical equipment, but may alternatively be used therapeutically (in solution) to treat skin conditions such as warts (particularly verrucas on the soles of the feet) and to remove hard, dead skin.

⊕ warning: effects of treatment are not always predictable. Skin treated may become sensitized.
*Related article:* NOVARUCA.

**Glutarol** (*Dermal*) is a proprietary, non-prescription solution for topical application containing the KERATOLYTIC glutaraldehyde, used to treat warts and to remove hard, dead skin.

⊕ warning: *see* GLUTARALDEHYDE.

**Glutenex** (*Cow & Gate*) is the name of a proprietary, non-prescription, brand of gluten-free biscuits made without milk, produced for patients with coeliac disease and similar conditions.

**Glutril** (*Roche*) is a proprietary form of the SULPHONYLUREA glibornuride, available only on prescription, used to treat adult-onset diabetes mellitus. It works by augmenting what remains of insulin production in the pancreas, and is produced in the form of tablets.

▲/⊕ side-effects/warning: *see* GLIBORNURIDE.

**glycerol**, or **glycerin(e)**, is a mixture of hydrolized fat and oils. A colourless viscous liquid, it is used therapeutically as a constituent in many emollient skin preparations, as a sweetening agent for medications, and as a LAXATIVE in the form of anal suppositories. Taken orally, glycerol has the short-term effect of reducing pressure within the eyeballs (which may be useful for patients with glaucoma).

**glyceryl trinitrate** is a powerful VASODILATOR that is extremely effective in treating the symptoms

of angina pectoris (heart pain). It works by dilating the veins returning blood to the heart, thus reducing the pressure within the heart and and reducing its workload at the same time. Short-acting, glyceryl trinitrate's effect is generally extended through its preparation in sustained-release capsules to be kept under the tongue; administration is in an aerosol as a spray, by intravenous injection, or in ointments and dressings to be placed on the surface of the chest for absorption through the skin.

▲ side-effects: there may be headache and dizziness; some patients experience an increase in heart rate.

⊕ warning: glyceryl trinitrate should be administered with caution to patients who suffer from low blood pressure (hypotension) and associated conditions.
*Related articles:* CORO-NITRO SPRAY; DEPONIT; GTN 300 MCG; NITROCINE; NITROCONTIN CONTINUS; NITROLINGUAL SPRAY; NITRONAL; PERCUTOL; SUSCARD BUCCAL; SUSTAC; TRANSIDERM-NITRO; TRIDIL.

**Glyconon** (*DDSA Pharmaceuticals*) is a proprietary form of the SULPHONYLUREA tolbutamide, available only on prescription, used to treat adult-onset diabetes mellitus. It works by augmenting what remains of insulin production in the pancreas, and is produced in the form of tablets.

▲/⊕ side-effects/warning: *see* TOLBUTAMIDE.

**glycopyrronium bromide** is an ANTICHOLINERGIC drug used to assist in the treatment of gastrointestinal disturbances caused by spasm in the muscles of the intestinal walls. Administration is oral in the form of tablets.

▲ side-effects: dry mouth and difficulty with swallowing is not uncommon; there may also be pressure within the eyeballs, dilation of the pupils and consequent sensitivity to light. The heartbeat may become irregular. Urinating may also become difficult. Rarely, there is high temperature and a state of confusion.

❁ warning: glycopyrronium bromide should not be administered to patients who suffer from glaucoma; it should be administered with caution to those who suffer from heart disease, intestinal bleeding, enlargement of the prostate gland, or urinary retention, those who are lactating, or those who are elderly.
*Related article:* ROBINUL.

**Glykola** *(Sinclair)* is a proprietary, non-prescription, IRON supplement, which is not available from the National Health Service. Produced in the form of an elixir for dilution (the potency of the elixir once dilute is retained for 14 days), Glykola contains iron (in the form of ferric chloride), caffeine, calcium and kola extract.

**Glymese** *(DDSA Pharmaceuticals)* is a proprietary form of the SULPHONYLUREA chlorpropamide, available only on prescription, used to treat adult-onset diabetes mellitus. It works by augmenting what remains of insulin production in the pancreas, but because it also has a marked effect in decreasing frequency of urination, it is sometimes also used to treat the condition diabetes insipidus. Glymese is produced in the form of tablets.
▲ / ❁ side-effects/warning: *see* CHLORPROPAMIDE.

**glymidine** is a drug used to treat (adult-onset) diabetes mellitus. Although its effect is that of the

SULPHONYLUREAS, which work by augmenting insulin production in the pancreas (as opposed to compensating for its absence), it is not actually a sulphonylurea and may be used with caution in patients with known sensitivity to those drugs. Administration is oral in the form of tablets.
▲ side-effects: there may be some sensitivity reaction (such as a rash).
❁ warning: glymidine should not be administered to patients with liver or kidney damage, with endocrine disorders, or who are under stress; who are pregnant or lactating; or who are already taking corticosteroids or oral contraceptives, oral anticoagulants, or aspirin and other antibiotics

**Glypressin** *(Ferring)* is a proprietary preparation of the drug terlipressin, a derivative of the HORMONE VASOPRESSIN. Available only on prescription, Glypressin is used to treat the haemorrhaging of varicose veins in the oesophagus (the tubular channel for food between throat and stomach). It is produced in vials for dilution and injection.
▲ / ❁ side-effects/warning: *see* TERLIPRESSIN.

**gold**, in the form of its salts (in particular sodium aurothiomalate), is used therapeutically in the treatment of rheumatoid arthritis. Not an anti-inflammatory ANALGESIC like other treatments, however, gold works slowly so that full effects are achieved only after four or five months. Improvement then is significant, not only in the reduction of joint inflammation but also in associated inflammations. Administration is by injection. Gold is also, although increasingly rarely, used in dentistry, occasionally for fillings, but more commonly (as alloys) in crowns, inlays and bridges.

▲ / ◍ side-effects/warning: *see* SODIUM AUROTHIOMALATE.

**Goldstar** (*Longdon*) is a proprietary form of supportive, thigh-length stocking used to give early preventive treatment for varicose veins especially during pregnancy. It is lightweight and elasticated, and available in pairs in different sizes.

**Golytely** is a BOWEL CLEANSING SOLUTION containing macrogol (polyethylene glycol), along with sodium and potassium salts. It is used prior to colonic surgery, colonoscopy or barium enema to ensure the bowel is free of solid contents.

▲ / ◍ side-effects/warning: *see* BOWEL CLEANSING SOLUTIONS.

**gonadorelin** is the chemical name of gonadotrophin-releasing hormone.
*see* GONADOTROPHIN-RELEASING HORMONE.

**gonadotrophin** is any of a number of HORMONES produced and secreted by the pituitary gland that act on the ovary in women or on the testes in men to promote the production in turn of other sex hormones and of eggs (ova) or sperm. The major gonadotrophins are follicle-stimulating hormone (FSH) and luteinizing hormone (LH). Either may be injected in order to make up hormonal deficiency and so treat infertility.

**gonadotrophin-releasing hormone**, or gonadorelin, is the HORMONE that acts on the pituitary gland to release the GONADOTROPHINS, which in turn stimulate the production and secretion of sex hormones – such as luteinizing hormone and

follicle-stimulating hormone – and sperm and ova. Its therapeutic use is limited mostly to diagnostic purposes (in assessing pituitary function), but it is sometimes injected in women to make up a hormonal deficiency and so treat infertility or absence of menstruation, or in boys to treat undescended testicles.

▲ side-effects: rarely there may be headache, abdominal pain and nausea; the site of infusion may become painful.

◍ warning: administration of gonadorelin to treat infertility or absence of menstruation has to be by pulsed subcutaneous infusion, a form of treatment generally available only in a specialist endocrine unit.
*Related articles:* FERTIRAL; HRF; RELEFACT.

**Gonadotraphon FSH** (*Paines & Byrne*) is a proprietary preparation of follicle-stimulating HORMONE (FSH) in the form of serum GONADOTROPHIN taken from pregnant mares. It is used to treat the absence of menstruation in adolescent girls, and to treat women suffering from specific hormonal deficiency for infertility. Available only on prescription, it is produced in powdered form for reconstitution with solvent as a medium for injection.

**Gonadotraphon LH** (*Paines & Byrne*) is a proprietary preparation of the HORMONE human chorionic GONADOTROPHIN (HCG), available only on prescription, used to treat undescended testicles in boys, and to treat women suffering from specific hormonal deficiency for infertility. It is produced in powdered form for reconstitution with a solvent as a medium for injection.

▲ / ◍ side-effects/warning: *see* HCG.

**Graneodin** (*Squibb*) is a proprietary ANTIBIOTIC, available only on prescription, used to treat bacterial infections of the head and face, and particularly of the eye. Produced in the form of an ointment for topical application, Graneodin contains the aminoglycoside neomycin sulphate.

▲/✿ side-effects/warning: *see* NEOMYCIN.

**Gregoderm** (*Unigreg*) is a proprietary ANTIBIOTIC, ANTIFUNGAL preparation, available only on prescription, used to treat inflammation of the skin in which infection is also present. Produced in the form of an ointment for topical application, Gregoderm is a compound of the aminoglycoside antibiotic neomycin sulphate and the antibiotic polymyxin B sulphate and the antifungal nystatin; together with the CORTICOSTEROID hydrocortisone.

▲/✿ side-effects/warning: *see* NEOMYCIN; NYSTATIN; POLYMYXIN B SULPHATE.

**griseofulvin** is a powerful ANTIFUNGAL drug that during treatment – which may be prolonged – is deposited selectively in the skin, hair and nails, and thus prevents further fungal invasion. It is most commonly used for large-scale infections, or to treat infections that prove intractable to other drugs, but can be used equally successfully on ringworm or localized tinea infections (such as athlete's foot). Administration is oral in the form of tablets or as a suspension.

▲ side-effects: there may be headache, with nausea and vomiting; some patients experience a sensitivity to light. Rarely, there may be a rash (which may be mild or serious).

✿ warning: griseofulvin should not be administered to patients who suffer from liver failure or from porphyria, or who are pregnant or taking oral contraceptives. Avoid alcohol during the period of treatment. *Related articles:* FULCIN; GRISOVIN.

**Grisovin** (*Glaxo*) is a proprietary ANTIFUNGAL drug, available only on prescription, used to treat infections of the scalp, skin and nails. Produced in the form of tablets (in two strengths), Grisovin is a preparation of the drug griseofulvin. Treatment may be required to continue over several weeks.

▲/✿ side-effects/warning: *see* GRISEOFULVIN.

**GTN 300 mcg** (*Martindale*) is a proprietary, non-prescription preparation of the powerful VASODILATOR glyceryl trinitrate, used to treat angina pectoris (heart pain). It is produced in the form of tablets, of the size specified by its name.

▲/✿ side-effects/warning: *see* GLYCERYL TRINITRATE.

**guanethidine monosulphate** is an ANTIHYPERTENSIVE drug, used in the treatment of high blood pressure (hypertension), often in combination with a DIURETIC (such as a thiazide) or a beta-blocker. It is also used to relieve pressure within the eyeball in the treatment of glaucoma, for which its effect is often enhanced by the simultaneous administration of the hormone adrenaline.

▲ side-effects: initial treatment may cause a reduction in heart rate; blood pressure may remain low during periods of rest. There may be muscle weakness and diarrhoea, fluid retention and nasal congestion.

✿ warning: guanethidine monosulphate should not be administered to patients with

Renal failure; it should be administered with caution to those who are elderly or pregnant. In the treatment of low blood pressure, dosage is adjusted according to individual response, and may be high.
*Related articles:* GANDA; ISMELIN.

**Guanor expectorant** (*RP Drugs*) is a proprietary, non-prescription EXPECTORANT and ANTITUSSIVE, which is not available from the National Health Service. Produced in the form of a syrup, its active constituents include AMMONIUM CHLORIDE, SODIUM CITRATE, DIPHENHYDRAMINE HYDROCHLORIDE and menthol.

**guar gum** is a natural, soluble, high-fibre bulking agent which, when consumed in some quantity, has the effect of evening out the peaks and troughs of blood glucose levels, which normally correspond to meals and the intervals between them. It is therefore used mainly to assist the treatment of patients with too low or too high blood glucose levels – as happens particularly in diabetes mellitus.
▲ side-effects: there is commonly flatulence with abdominal distension; occasionally guar gum itself causes intestinal obstruction.
✳ warning: guar gum should not be used in patients who suffer from intestinal obstruction. An adequately high fluid intake must be maintained. Counselling on this and on dosage is advised.
*Related articles:* GUAREM; GUARINA.

**Guarem** (*Rybar*) is a proprietary, non-prescription preparation of guar gum, used to assist in the treatment of patients with too low or too high a blood sugar level (as

in diabetes). A high-fibre bulking agent, guar gum has the effect of evening out the peaks and troughs of glucose levels that normally correspond to meals and the intervals between them. Not recommended for children, Guarem is produced in sachets of granules for solution.
▲/✳ side-effects/warning: *see* GUAR GUM.

**Guarina** (*Norgine*) is a proprietary, non-prescription preparation of guar gum, used to assist in the treatment of patients with too low or too high a blood sugar level (as in diabetes). A high-fibre bulking agent, guar gum has the effect of evening out the peaks and troughs of glucose levels that normally correspond to meals and the intervals between them. Not recommended for children, Guarina is produced in sachets of granules for solution or for sprinkling over food.
▲/✳ side-effects/warning: *see* GUAR GUM.

**Gynatren** (*Cabot*) is a proprietary preparation of certain bacilli that ordinarily reside in the alimentary tract and vagina, consisting of a form of VACCINE used to treat recurrent vaginal infections, particularly trichomaniasis. Available only on prescription, it is produced in ampoules for intramuscular injection, and administered in 3 doses over four weeks.

**Gyno-Daktarin** (*Janssen*) is a series of proprietary preparations of the ANTIFUNGAL drug miconazole nitrate, used to treat yeast infections of the vagina or vulva (such as thrush). All are available only on prescription. There is an intravaginal cream (with its own applicator), vaginal inserts (pessaries), coated tampons, an 'ovule' (which is a vaginal capsule, and marketed under the name Gyno-Daktarin 1), and a Combipack combining the cream and the pessaries.

▲/✿ side-effects/warning: *see* MICONAZOLE.

**Gynol II** (*Ortho-Cilag*) is a proprietary, non-prescription form of SPERMICIDAL jelly used to reinforce barrier methods of contraception. It is a preparation of an alcohol ester.

**Gyno-Pevaryl** (*Ortho-Cilag*) is a series of proprietary preparations of the ANTIFUNGAL drug econazole nitrate, used to treat yeast infections of the vagina or vulva (like thrush). All are available only on prescription. There is a cream for topical application to the anogenital area, vaginal inserts (pessaries, in two formulations, one under the name Gyno-Pevaryl 1), and a Combipack combining the cream and one or other formulation of the pessaries.

▲/✿ side-effects/warning: *see* ECONAZOLE NITRATE.

**Gypsona** (*Smith & Nephew*) is aproprietary form of bandaging impregnated with plaster of Paris, used primarily for the immobilization of a fracture. Soaking the bandage causes the plaster to set hard.

**Haelan** (*Dista*) is a proprietary preparation of the CORTICOSTEROID drug flurandrenolone, available only on prescription, used in the form of a water-miscible cream or an anhydrous ointment as a topical application to treat severe non-infective inflammations of the skin. It is particularly used to treat eczema that is unresponsive to less powerful drugs. In both cream and ointment forms, Haelan is produced in one strength, and in another version that additionally contains the antibacterial, antifungal agent CLIOQUINOL (under the name Haelan-C). There is also an impregnated tape for use as a poultice (marketed under the name Haelan Tape, but not available from the National Health Service).
▲/ ✿ side-effects/warning: *see* FLURANDRENOLONE.

**Haemaccel** (*Hoechst*) is a proprietary form of gelatin, the hydrolized animal protein. In a special refined (partly degraded) form available only on prescription, it is used in infusion with saline (sodium chloride) as a means of expanding overall blood volume in patients whose blood volume is dangerously low through shock, particularly in cases of severe burns or septicaemia. It is produced in bottles (flasks) for infusion.
▲/ ✿ side-effects/warning: *see* GELATIN.

**haemostatics** are agents that prevent or stop bleeding, known also as styptics. Haemostatics are used mostly to treat disorders in which bleeding is prolonged and potentially dangerous, such as haemophilia. Best-known and most-used are probably PHYTOMENADIONE (of which injections or infusions have to be given very slowly) and the coagulant enzyme-precursor thromboplastin.

**Halciderm** (*Squibb*) is a proprietary preparation, in the form of a water-miscible cream for topical application, of the extremely powerful CORTICOSTEROID halcinonide. Available only on prescription, it is used to treat severe non-infective inflammation of the skin, particularly eczema that is unresponsive to less powerful drugs.
▲/ ✿ side-effects/warning: *see* HALCINONIDE.

**halcinonide** is a powerful CORTICOSTEROID drug, used in very dilute solution to treat severe non-infective inflammations of the skin, particularly eczema that is unresponsive to less powerful drugs. Administration is in the form of a water-miscible cream for topical application.
▲ side-effects: side-effects depend to some extent on the area of skin treated. Prolonged treatment may cause thinning of the skin, yet increase hair growth; there may be acne or dermatitis. These side-effects may be worse in children.
✿ warning: like all topical corticosteroids, halcinonide by itself treats symptoms and does not cure underlying disorders. If infection is present, it may worsen although the symptoms may be suppressed by the drug.
*Related article:* HALCIDERM.

**Halcion** (*Upjohn*) is a proprietary TRANQUILLIZER and HYPNOTIC, available only on prescription, used primarily to treat insomnia, particularly in elderly patients. Produced in the form of tablets (in two strengths), Halcion is a preparation of the BENZODIAZEPINE triazolam. It is not recommended for children.
▲/ ✿ side-effects/warning: *see* TRIAZOLAM.

**Haldol** (*Janssen*) is a proprietary form of the powerful ANTIPSYCHOTIC drug haloperidol. Available only on prescription, it is used to treat and tranquillize psychosis (such as schizophrenia), in which it is particularly suitable for treating manic forms of behavioural disturbance. It may be used alternatively to treat anxiety in the short term, as a premedication before surgery, or to control patients in delirium tremens or with alcohol withdrawal problems. Haldol is produced in the form of tablets (in two strengths), as a liquid to take orally (in two strengths, under the name Haldol Oral Liquid), and in ampoules for injection.
▲/✿ side-effects/warning: *see* HALOPERIDOL.

**Haldol Decanoate** (*Janssen*) is another form of HALDOL, available only on prescription, it is an ANTIPSYCHOTIC used to treat and tranquillize forms of psychosis on a long-term maintenance basis. Its active constituent is the decanoate salt of haloperidol. Produced in ampoules (in two strengths) for injection, it is not recommended for children.
▲/✿ side-effects/warning: *see* HALOPERIDOL.

**Half-Inderal LA** (*ICI*) is a preparation of Inderal-LA at half strength, produced in the form of sustained-release capsules of the BETA-BLOCKER PROPRANOLOL hydrochloride.
*see* INDERAL-LA.

**halibut-liver oil** is an excellent source of retinol (vitamin A). A non-proprietary preparation is available in the form of tablets, but should not be taken without initial medical diagnosis; retinol deficiency is very rare, and treatment should be monitored in order to avoid the potentially unpleasant side-effects of excess vitamin A in the body.
▲/✿ side-effects/warning: *see* RETINOL.

**haloperidol** is a powerful ANTIPSYCHOTIC drug used to treat and tranquillize psychosis (such as schizophrenia), in which it is particularly suitable for treating manic forms of behavioural disturbance, especially in order to effect emergency control. The drug may also be used to treat severe anxiety in the short term. Administration is oral in the form of capsules, tablets, a liquid or an elixir, or by injection (which may be short-acting or 'depot').

▲ side-effects: patients should be warned before treatment that their judgement and powers of concentration may become defective under treatment. There may be restlessness, insomnia and nightmares; rashes and jaundice may occur; and there may be dry mouth, gastrointestinal disturbance, difficulties in urinating, and blurred vision. Muscles in the neck and back, and sometimes the arms, may undergo spasms. Rarely, there is weight loss and impaired kidney function.

✿ warning: haloperidol should not be administered to patients who suffer from a reduction in the bone-marrow's capacity to produce blood cells, or from certain types of glaucoma. It should be administered only with caution to those with heart or vascular disease, kidney or liver disease, parkinsonism, or depression; or who are pregnant or lactating. It is not recommended for children.
*Related articles:* DOZIC; FORTUNAN; HALDOL; HALDOL DECANOATE; SERENACE.

**halothane** is a powerful general ANAESTHETIC that is widely used both for induction and for maintenance of anaesthesia during surgical operations. Used in combination with oxygen or nitrous oxide-oxygen mixtures, halothane vapour is non-irritant and even pleasant to inhale, does not induce coughing, and seldom causes post-operative vomiting. Administration is through a calibrated vaporizer in order to control concentration.

▲ side-effects: there may be liver damage. Repetition of anaesthesia by halothane is inadvisable within 3 months.

✺ warning: halothane causes a slowing of the heart rate and shallowness of breathing; both must be monitored during anaesthesia to prevent high levels of carbon dioxide or dangerously slow pulse and low blood pressure. The vapour is not good as a muscle relaxant, and muscle relaxants may have to be used in addition during specific types of surgery.

**Halycitrol** (*L A B*) is a proprietary, non-prescription preparation of retinol (vitamin A) and calciferol (vitamin D), which is not available from the National Health Service. Produced in the form of an emulsion, it is used to treat deficiency of either vitamin, or both, but should be taken only under medical supervision because both vitamins in excess can cause unpleasant side-effects.

▲/✺ side-effects/warning: see CALCIFEROL; RETINOL.

**hamamelis** is a natural soothing agent, derived from the witch hazel plant, used mostly to relieve the pain of piles (haemorrhoids). Administration is in the form of anal suppositories; some versions also contain the mild astringent ZINC OXIDE.

**Hamarin** (*Nicholas*) is a proprietary form of the XANTHINE-OXIDASE INHIBITOR allopurinol,

used to treat high levels of uric acid in the bloodstream (which may otherwise cause gout or kidney stones). Available only on prescription, Hamarin is produced in the form of tablets (in two strengths). It is not recommended for children.

▲/✺ side-effects/warning: see ALLOPURINOL.

**Harmogen** (*Abbott*) is a proprietary OESTROGEN, available only on prescription, formerly commonly used to treat symptoms that occur with falling natural levels of oestrogen in women following the menopause. (Now, however, it is far more usual to prescribe an oestrogen-progestogen compound.) Produced in the form of tablets, Harmogen is a preparation of piperazine oestrone sulphate.

▲/✺ side-effects/warning: see PIPERAZINE OESTRON SULPHATE.

**Hartmann's solution** is another description of sodium lactate in a preparation suitable for intravenous infusion.
see SODIUM LACTATE.

**Haymine** (*Pharmax*) is a proprietary, non-prescription nasal DECONGESTANT, which is not available from the National Health Service. Unlike most nasal decongestants, however, it is produced in the form of tablets (for swallowing) and is a compound of the ANTIHISTAMINE chlorpheniramine maleate together with the BRONCHODILATOR ephedrine hydrochloride.

▲/✺ side-effects/warning: see CHLORPHENIRAMINE; EPHEDRINE HYDROCHLORIDE.

**HBIG**, or hepatitis B immunoglobulin, when injected or infused into the body, confers immediate immunity to the potentially dangerous effects of the disease caused by the hepatitis B virus. Prepared from the blood plasma of recent patients, it is used specifically to immunize personnel in medical laboratories and hospitals who may be infected, and to treat babies of mothers infected by the virus during pregnancy. In normal circumstances, however, immunization is with HEPATITIS B VACCINE.

**HCG** is an abbreviation for human chorionic gonadotrophin, a HORMONE produced by the placenta during pregnancy. Excreted in the urine, its presence there is the basis of most pregnancy tests. Therapeutically, HCG is used in women to treat sterility that is due to lack of ovulation, or to relieve pre-menstrual tension. In men it is used to treat undescended testes or delayed puberty. Administration is by intramuscular injection.

▲ side-effects: there may be headache and tiredness, mood changes and (especially in male patients) weight gain through the accumulation of fluid in the tissues (oedema).

✪ warning: all treatment with HCG must be under the most rigorously controlled monitoring: in women there is a risk of ovarian rupture, and in men a hormonal balance must be created and maintained. HCG should be administered with caution to patients who suffer from asthma, epilepsy or migraine, or from impairment of heart or liver function.
Related articles:
GONADOTRAPHON LH; PROFASI.

**Hedex** (*Sterling Health*) is a proprietary, non-prescription, non-narcotic ANALGESIC produced in the form of tablets and as a soluble powder. It contains paracetamol.
▲/✪ side-effects/warning: see PARACETAMOL.

**Hedex Plus** (*Sterling Health*) is a proprietary, non-prescription combination ANALGESIC produced in the form of capsules. It contains paracetamol, caffeine and codeine.
▲/✪ side-effects/warning: see CAFFEINE; CODEINE; PARACETAMOL.

**Hemabate** (*Upjohn*) is a proprietary form of the drug carboprost, it is sometimes used for post-partum haemorrhage where other drugs have proved to be ineffective. Available only on prescription, the preparation is in a form for deep intramuscular injection.
▲/✪ side-effects/warning: see CARBOPROST.

**Heminevrin** (*Astra*) is a proprietary SEDATIVE, available only on prescription, used to treat insomnia, states of confusion or agitation in the elderly, and (under rigorous monitoring) acute alcohol withdrawal symptoms. Produced in the form of capsules, as a sugar-free syrup for dilution (the potency of the syrup once dilute is retained for 14 days), and in flasks (bottles) for intravenous infusion, Heminevrin is a preparation of chlormethiazole. Not recommended for children.
▲/✪ side-effects/warning: see CHLORMETHIAZOLE.

**Hepacon** (*Consolidated*) is the name of a series of preparations of CYANOCOBALAMIN (vitamin $B_{12}$) or analogues (including folic acid and/or liver extract), intended to make up body deficiency in the vitamin. Such a deficiency is most commonly caused by malabsorption through disease or surgery (and is now more often remedied through the use of HYDROXOCOBALAMIN than through cyanocobalamin), but may also be caused by extreme forms of vegetarianism. All forms of Hepacon are produced in ampoules for injection, but are available on prescription only to private patients.

**Hepacon-Plex** (*Consolidated*) is a proprietary VITAMIN B compound, available on prescription only to private patients, used to make up vitamin deficiency. Produced in the form of ampoules for injection, Hepacon-Plex contains many forms of the vitamin: THIAMINE, RIBOFLAVINE, PYRIDOXINE, CYANOCOBALAMIN, NICOTINAMIDE and PANTOTHENIC ACID.

**heparin** is a natural ANTICOAGULANT in the body, manufactured mostly by the liver and certain leukocytes (white cells). For therapeutic use it is purified after extraction. Administration is generally by injection, to prevent or treat thrombosis and similar conditions, but its effect is short-lived and treatment may have to be repeated at intervals of less than 6 hours, or may have to be by constant infusion.
▲ side-effects: should haemorrhage occur, it may be difficult to stop the bleeding for a time – although because heparin is so short-acting, merely discontinuing treatment is usually effective fairly quickly. There may be sensitivity reactions. Prolonged use may cause a loss of calcium from the bones and of hair from the head.
❀ warning: heparin should not be administered to patients with haemophilia, peptic ulcer, very high blood pressure (hypertension) or who have kidney disease, or who have

recently undergone eye surgery. It should be administered with caution to those who are pregnant.
*Related articles:* CALCIPARINE; FRAGMIN; MINIHEP; MINIHEP; MONOPARIN; MULTIPARIN; PUMP-HEP; UNIHEP; UNIPARIN; UNIPARIN CALCIUM.

**Heparinised Saline** (*Paines & Byrne*) is a proprietary solution (available only on prescription) containing the ANTICOAGULANT HEPARIN sodium, used to wash and rinse the interior surfaces of catheters, cannulas and other medical forms of tubing to ensure that they remain unobstructed while carrying out their functions. The solution has no therapeutic use.

**hepatitis B vaccine** consists of an inactivated hepatitis B virus surface antigen derived from the blood plasma of a human carrier, or prepared biosynthetically, and adsorbed on to alum in suspension. It is used on patients with a high risk of infection from the hepatitis B virus mostly through contact with a carrier. Administration is by intramuscular injection in the arm or thigh; the usual regimen per patient is 3 doses, at intervals of one month and six months.
❀ warning: vaccination does not guarantee the avoidance of infection: commonsense precautions against infection should still be observed in relation to known carriers.

**Hep-Flush** (*Burgess*) is a proprietary solution (available only on prescription) containing the ANTICOAGULANT HEPARIN sodium, used to wash and rinse the interior surfaces of catheters, cannulas and other medical forms of tubing to ensure that they remain unobstructed while carrying out their functions. The solution has no therapeutic use.

**Hepsal** (*CP Pharmaceuticals*) is a proprietary solution (available only on prescription) containing the ANTICOAGULANT HEPARIN sodium, used to wash and rinse the interior surfaces of catheters, cannulas and other medical forms of tubing to ensure that they remain unobstructed while carrying out their functions. The solution has no therapeutic use.

**heroin** is a more familiar term for the narcotic ANALGESIC drug diamorphine.
*see* DIAMORPHINE.

**Herpid** (*Boehringer Ingelheim*) is a proprietary form of the ANTIVIRAL drug idoxuridine, prepared in a solution of dimethyl sulphoxide, used to treat skin infections by the viral organisms Herpes simplex (such as cold sores or genital sores) and Herpes zoster (shingles). Available only on prescription, Herpid is produced as a paint for topical application (with a brush).
● warning: *see* IDOXURIDINE.

**Hespan** (*American Hospital Supply*) is a proprietary form of the plasma substitute hetastarch. Available only on prescription, it is used in infusion with saline (sodium chloride) as a means of expanding overall blood volume in patients whose blood volume is dangerously low through shock, particularly in cases of severe burns or septicaemia. It is produced in flexible bags for infusion.
▲/● side-effects/warning: *see* HETASTARCH.

**hetastarch** is a plasma substitute, administered more commonly as an emergency measure until tissue-matched blood is available, that is used in infusion with saline (sodium chloride) as a means of expanding overall blood volume in patients whose blood

volume is dangerously low through shock, particularly in cases of severe burns or septicaemia.
▲ side-effects: very rarely, there are sensitivity reactions.
● warning: hetastarch should not be administered to patients with congestive heart failure, kidney failure, or disorders of the blood that are likely to cause coagulation problems. Ideally, there should be cross-matching of blood samples before infusion.
*Related article:* ELOHES 6%; HESPAN.

**Hewletts Antiseptic Cream** (*Astra*) is a proprietary ANTISEPTIC cream for topical application on minor abrasions or burns. Available without prescription, it contains boric acid, hydrous wool fat and zinc oxide.

**hexachlorophane** is a powerful DISINFECTANT used on the skin, particularly of the face. In the form of a cream it is effective against scabies, and is a good substitute for soap in cases of acne or facial infection. It is also produced as a dusting-powder (which may help to prevent the onset of bedsores).
▲ side-effects: there are occasionally sensitivity reactions, and even more rarely an increased sensitivity to light.
● warning: hexachlorophane should not be used on areas of raw or abraded skin, and particularly not on raw areas of the skin of infants (in whom neural damage may occur). It is advisable to avoid using hexachlorophane routinely.
*Related article:* STER-ZAC.

**hexamine** is an ANTIBIOTIC that was formerly used to treat infections of the urinary tract. It is now generally considered to be too limited in its action – it limits only bacterial infection, requires the urine to be made to be acidic, and has many potentially unpleasant side-effects. Administration of its one proprietary form is oral, as tablets.

▲ side-effects: there may be bladder irritation, with frequent and painful urination, and possibly blood in the urine; there may also be gastrointestinal disturbances and rashes.

● warning: hexamine should not be administered to patients with impaired kidney or liver function, or who are dehydrated.
*Related article:* HIPREX.

**hexetidine** is a mouthwash or gargle used for routine oral hygiene, to cleanse and freshen the mouth.
*Related article:* ORALDENE.

**Hexopal** (*Winthrop*) is a proprietary, non-prescription VASODILATOR, used to treat circulatory disorders of the extremities, chilblains, and arteriosclerosis in the fingers and toes. It should be administered with caution to those with diabetes mellitus. Produced in the form of tablets (in two strengths, the stronger under the name Hexopal Forte) and as a sugar-free syrup for dilution (the resultant suspension retains its potency for 14 days), Hexopal contains two forms of vitamin B, INOSITOL and NICOTINIC ACID.

**HGH** is an abbreviation for human growth HORMONE, a hormone produced and secreted by the pituitary gland, which promotes growth in the long bones of the limbs and increases protein synthesis. (It is also called somatotropin.) For therapeutic use, the human form is necessary, since unlike some other hormones the form from slaughterhouse animals is not active. It is not viable to extract HGH from human pituitary glands, but genetic engineering produced a form of the hormone using sequences of DNA to create forms similar or identical to hormone of human sequence. This source of hormone now allows the use of preparations to treat dwarfism and other problems of short stature due to hormone deficiency.
▲/● side-effects/warning: *see* SOMATREM.

**Hibidil** (*ICI*) is a proprietary, non-prescription skin DISINFECTANT used to treat wounds and burns, and to provide asepsis during childbirth. Produced in the form of a solution in sachets, for further dilution as required, Hibidil is a preparation of chlorhexidine gluconate.
▲/● side-effects/warning: *see* CHLORHEXIDINE.

**Hibiscrub** (*ICI*) is a proprietary, non-prescription DISINFECTANT used instead of soap to wash skin and hands before surgery. Produced in the form of a solution, Hibiscrub is a preparation of chlorhexidine gluconate in a surfactant liquid (a liquid with low surface tension, like a detergent).
▲/● side-effects/warning: *see* CHLORHEXIDINE.

**Hibisol** (*ICI*) is a proprietary, non-prescription DISINFECTANT, used to treat minor wounds and burns on the skin and hands. Produced in the form of a solution, Hibisol is a preparation of chlorhexidine gluconate in isopropyl alcohol solvent together with emollients.
▲/● side-effects/warning: *see* CHLORHEXIDINE.

**Hibitane** (*ICI*) is the name of a series or proprietary non-prescription forms of

DISINFECTANT, all based on solutions of chlorhexidine gluconate or other chlorhexidine salts. The standard form is that of a powder, used either to prepare solutions of chlorhexidine or powdered antiseptic compounds. There are two solutions: Hibitane 5% Concentrate (for skin disinfection, following further dilution in water or alcohol) and Hibitane Gluconate 20% (for cavities and the bladder, and to treat urethral infections). Hibitane Obstetric is a water-miscible cream used to lubricate the vulva during labour and childbirth. Another cream, Hibitane Antiseptic, is used to treat minor wounds and burns by topical application.

▲/ ⊕ side-effects/warning: see CHLORHEXIDINE.

**Hioxyl** (*Quinoderm*) is a proprietary, non-prescription DISINFECTANT used to treat bedsores and leg ulcers, minor wounds and burns. Produced in the form of a cream for topical application, Hioxyl is a preparation of the antiseptic HYDROGEN PEROXIDE.

**Hiprex** is a proprietary, non-prescription ANTIBIOTIC used to treat infections of the urinary tract, and to prevent infection following urological surgery. Produced in the form of tablets, Hiprex is a compound of the now less commonly used drug hexamine together with hippuric acid (which renders the urine acidic enough for hexamine to be effective).

▲/ ⊕ side-effects/warning: see HEXAMINE.

**Hirudoid** (*Panpharma*) is a proprietary, non-prescription VASODILATOR and ANTICOAGULANT intended to improve the blood circulation in conditions such as varicose veins, chilblains and

bruising, and produced in the form of a cream or a gel for topical application. Its active constituent is a derivative of the anticoagulant heparin.

▲/ ⊕ side-effects/warning: see HEPARIN.

**Hismanal** (*Janssen*) is a proprietary form of the ANTIHISTAMINE drug astemizole, with less sedative properties than many others, used to treat the symptoms of allergic disorders such as hay fever and urticaria (skin rashes). Produced in the form of tablets and as a sugar-free suspension, it can be sold without prescription for the treatment of hay fever in subjects over twelve years old.

▲/ ⊕ side-effects/warning: see ASTEMIZOLE.

**Histalix** (*Wallace*) is a proprietary, non-prescription EXPECTORANT and ANTITUSSIVE, which is not available from the National Health Service. Produced in the form of a syrup, its active constituents include AMMONIUM CHLORIDE, SODIUM CITRATE, DIPHENHYDRAMINE HYDRO-CHLORIDE and MENTHOL.

**Histryl** (*Smith, Kline & French*) is a proprietary ANTIHISTAMINE drug used primarily to treat allergic symptoms such as hay fever and urticaria. Produced in the form of spansules (sustained-release capsules) in two strengths (the weaker under the name Histryl Paediatric Spansule), it is a preparation of diphenylpyraline hydrochloride. Histryl, even in its paediatric form, is not recommended for children aged under 7 years.

▲/ ⊕ side-effects/warning: see DIPHENYLPYRALINE HYDROCHLORIDE.

**HNIG** is an abbreviation for human normal immunoglobulin, an injection of which –

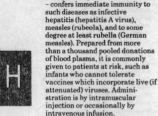

incorporating antibodies in serum – confers immediate immunity to such diseases as infective hepatitis (hepatitis A virus), measles (rubeola), and to some degree at least rubella (German measles). Prepared from more than a thousand pooled donations of blood plasma, it is commonly given to patients at risk, such as infants who cannot tolerate vaccines which incorporate live (if attenuated) viruses. Administration is by intramuscular injection or occasionally by intravenous infusion.

● warning: HNIG should not be administered within 2 weeks following vaccination with live viruses, or within 3 months before vaccination with live viruses is to be given (except in specific circumstances relating to the likelihood of convulsions in patients known to be at risk from them).

*Related article:* ENDOBULIN: VENOGLUBULIN.

**Hollister** (*Abbott*) is the name of a series of proprietary non-prescription products for the care, freshening and sanitization of a stoma (an outlet in the skin surface that is the consequence of the surgical curtailment of the intestines). There is a medicated adhesive spray (for retaining an appliance or bag over the stoma) and a corresponding adhesive remover spray; and there are three skin applications for protection and cleanliness: a paste, a powder, and a gel.

**Honvan** (*WB Pharmaceuticals*) is a proprietary preparation of fosfestrol tetrasodium, a drug that is converted in the body to the OESTROGEN (female sex hormone) STILBOESTROL. Available only on prescription, it may be used in women as part of hormone replacement therapy during and following the menopause or to

treat menstrual difficulties, or used in men to treat cancer of the prostate gland. It is produced in the form of tablets, and in ampoules for injection.

▲/● side-effects/warning: *see* FOSFESTROL TETRASODIUM.

**\*hormone antagonists** are a class of drugs mainly acting to prevent the action of the hormone at its receptors by competing for that site, for example TAMOXIFEN at oestrogen receptors and FLUTAMIDE at androgen receptors; though sometimes acting through other receptors to prevent release of a hormone (for example OCTREOTIDE against the release of hormones from carcinoid tissue).

**\*hormones** are body substances produced and secreted by glands into the bloodstream, where they are carried to specific organs and areas of tissue on which they have a specific effect. Major types of hormone include CORTICOSTEROIDS (produced mainly in the cortex of adrenal glands), ADRENALINE and NORADRENALINE from the medulla of the adrenal gland, thyroid hormones (produced by the thyroid gland), the sex hormones (produced mainly by the ovaries or the testes), the pancreatic hormones (such as INSULIN), and the hormones that cause the secretion or production of these hormones, e.g. GONADOTROPHIN-RELEASING HORMONE. Most hormones can be administered therapeutically to make up hormonal deficiency, sometimes in synthetic form.

**Hormonin** (*Carnrick*) is a proprietary combination of three natural female sex HORMONES – oestradiol (the main ovarian hormone), oestriol and oestrone – used to make up hormone deficiencies and to treat associated symptoms, especially

during or following the
menopause. Available only on
prescription, Hormonin is
produced in the form of tablets.
▲/⊕ side-effects/warning: *see*
OESTRADIOL; OESTRIOL.

**HRF** (*Ayerst*) is a proprietary
preparation of GONADOTROPHIN-
RELEASING HORMONE, available
only on prescription, and
produced in the form of powder for
reconstitution as a medium for
injection or infusion. It is used as
a diagnostic aid in assessing the
functioning of the pituitary gland
and its secretions. The
administration of HRF in stepped
increasing dosages enables the
threshold of pituitary response to
be indicated through the
monitoring of its subsequent
effects.

**HTIG** is an abbreviation for human
tetanus immunoglobulin, a
specific form of immunoglobulin
(antibodies in serum), used mostly
as an added precaution to treat
patients with contaminated
wounds. (It is generally only a
precautionary measure because
almost everybody today has
established immunity through
vaccination from an early age,
and vaccination is in any case
readily available for those at risk.)
Administration is by
intramuscular injection. It is
available only on prescription.

**Human Actraphane** (*Novo*) is a
proprietary preparation of mixed
human insulins, available only on
prescription, used to treat and
maintain diabetic patients.
Produced in vials for injection,
Human Actraphane contains both
isophane and neutral insulins in a
ratio of 70% to 30%, respectively.
▲/⊕ side-effects/warning: *see*
INSULIN.

**Human Actrapid** (*Novo*) is a
proprietary, non-prescription
preparation of synthesized neutral

human insulin, used to treat and
maintain diabetic patients. It is
produced in vials for injection,
and in cartridges for use with a
special injector (under the name
Human Actrapid Penfill).
▲/⊕ side-effects/warning: *see*
INSULIN.

**human albumin solution** is a
solution containing the blood
protein ALBUMIN, and is derived
from blood plasma, serum or
placentas, with at least 95% of the
protein in the form of albumin.
Since only certain soluble
proteins and electrolytes are
present (clotting factors, their
antibodies, and also
cholinesterases have been
removed), the preparations may be
given regardless of blood group of
the patient. Preparations may be
used in states associated with low
blood proteins (hypopro-
teinaemia), such as after burns or
surgery. Human albumin solution
is available in the form of either
concentrated or isotonic solutions
for intravenous infusion.
▲ side-effects: chills, nausea,
fever; especially if infusion is
rapid.
⊕ warning: do not use in severe
anaemia or in cardiac failure.
Caution is required in a wide
variety of conditions including
cardiovascular diseases.
*Related articles:* ALBUMIN
SOLUTION; ALBUMINAR;
BUMINATE; HUMAN ALBUMIN
SOLUTION.

**Human albumin
solution** (*Immuno*) is a
proprietary form of HUMAN
ALBUMIN SOLUTION used to treat
low blood protein
(hypoproteinaemia) especially
after burns and surgery. The
preparation, which is available
only on prescription, is available
in vials for intravenous infusion,
both in isotonic and concentrated
forms.

▲/ ✿ side-effects/warning: *see*
HUMAN ALBUMIN SOLUTION.

**Human Initard 50/50** (*Nordisk
Wellcome*) is a proprietary
preparation of mixed human
insulins, available only on
prescription, used to treat and
maintain diabetic patients.
Produced in vials for injection,
Human Initard 50/50 contains
both isophane and neutral
insulins in equal proportions.
▲/ ✿ side-effects/warning: *see*
INSULIN.

**Human Insulatard** (*Nordisk
Wellcome*) is a proprietary, non-
prescription preparation of
human isophane insulin, used to
treat and maintain diabetic
patients. It is produced in vials
for injection.
▲/ ✿ side-effects/warning: *see*
INSULIN.

**Human Mixtard 30/70** (*Nordisk
Wellcome*) is a proprietary, non-
prescription preparation of mixed
human insulins, used to treat and
maintain diabetic patients.
Produced in vials for injection,
Human Mixtard contains both
isophane and neutral insulins in a
ratio of 70% to 30%, respectively.
▲/ ✿ side-effects/warning: *see*
INSULIN.

**Human Monotard** (*Novo*) is a
proprietary, non-prescription
preparation of human insulin zinc
suspension, used to treat and
maintain diabetic patients. It is
produced in vials for injection.
▲/ ✿ side-effects/warning: *see*
INSULIN.

**Human Protaphane** (*Novo*) is a
proprietary, non-prescription
preparation of human isophane
insulin, used to treat and
maintain diabetic patients. It is
produced in vials for injection,
and as Human Protaphane Perfill
injection to be used with special
devices (Novopen devices).

▲/ ✿ side-effects/warning: *see*
INSULIN.

**Human Ultratard** (*Novo*) is a
proprietary, non-prescription
preparation of human insulin zinc
suspension, used to treat and
maintain diabetic patients. It is
produced in vials for injection.
▲/ ✿ side-effects/warning: *see*
INSULIN.

**Human Velosulin** (*Nordisk
Wellcome*) is a proprietary, non-
prescription preparation of
synthesized neutral human
insulin, used to treat and
maintain diabetic patients. It is
produced in vials for injection.
▲/ ✿ side-effects/warning: *see*
INSULIN.

**Humatrope** (*Lilly*) is a HORMONE,
a proprietary form of somatropin,
used to treat small stature, and
deficiencies of other hormones. It
is available only on prescription.
The preparation is in the form of
a powder for reconstition for
injection.
▲/ ✿ side-effects/warning: *see*
SOMATROPIN.

**Humegon** (*Organon*) is a HORMONE
preparation, and is a proprietary
form of the GONADOTROPHIN,
follicle-stimulating hormone
(FSH) together with luteinising
hormone (LH), called collectively
menotropin. It is used to treat
infertile women with proven
hypopituitarism and who do not
respond to CLOMIPHENE CITRATE
(another drug commonly used to
treat infertility). Available only
on prescription in a form for
injection in two strengths.
▲/ ✿ side-effects/warning: *see*
MENOTROPIN.

**Humiderm** (*BritCair*) is a
proprietary, non-prescription skin
emollient (softener and soother),
used to treat dry skin. Produced
in the form of a cream, the major

constituents are pyrrolidone carboxilic acid and a moisturizer.

**Humotet** (*Wellcome*) is a proprietary, preparation of anti-tetanus immunoglobulin (HTIG), available only on prescription, used mostly as an added precaution to treat patients with contaminated wounds. (It is generally only a precautionary measure because almost everybody today has established immunity through vaccination from an early age, and vaccination is in any case readily available for those at risk.) It is produced in vials for intramuscular injection.

**Humulin I** (*Lilly*) is a proprietary, non-prescription preparation of human isophane insulin, used to treat and maintain diabetic patients. It is produced in vials for injection.
▲/ ● side-effects/warning: *see* INSULIN.

**Humulin M1** (*Lilly*) is a proprietary, non-prescription preparation of mixed human insulins, used to treat and maintain diabetic patients. Produced in vials for injection, Humulin M1 contains both isophane and neutral insulins in a ratio of 90% to 10%, respectively.
▲/ ● side-effects/warning: *see* INSULIN.

**Humulin M2** (*Lilly*) is a proprietary, non-prescription preparation of mixed human insulins, used to treat and maintain diabetic patients. Produced in vials for injection, Humulin M2 contains both isophane and neutral insulins in a ratio of 80% to 20%, respectively.
▲/ ● side-effects/warning: *see* INSULIN.

**Humulin M3** (*Lilly*) is a proprietary, non-prescription preparation of mixed human

insulins, used to treat and maintain diabetic patients. Produced in vials for injection, Humulin M3 contains human isophane insulin (30% soluble/ 70% isophane).
▲/ ● side-effects/warning: *see* INSULIN.

**Humulin M4** (*Lilly*) is a proprietary, non-prescription preparation of mixed human insulins, used to treat and maintain diabetic patients. Produced in vials for injection, Humulin M4 contains human isophane insulin (40% soluble/ 60% isophane).
▲/ ● side-effects/warning: *see* INSULIN.

**Humulin S** (*Lilly*) is a proprietary, non-prescription preparation of synthesized neutral human insulin, used to treat and maintain diabetic patients. It is produced in vials for injection.
▲/ ● side-effects/warning: *see* INSULIN.

**Humulin Zn** (*Lilly*) is a proprietary, non-prescription preparation of human insulin zinc suspension, used to treat and maintain diabetic patients. It is produced in vials for injection.
▲/ ● side-effects/warning: *see* INSULIN.

**Hyalase** (*CP Pharmaceuticals*) is a proprietary form of the enzyme hyaluronidase, available only on prescription, used to increase the permeability of subcutaneous tissues or muscles into which drugs can be injected. It is produced in the form of a powder for reconstitution as a medium also for injection.
▲/ ● side-effects/warning: *see* HYALURONIDASE.

**hyaluronidase** is an enzyme that has the power to loosen the chemical bonds between certain structures within connective tissue – and is thus used to increase the permeability of subcutaneous tissues or muscles into which drugs can be injected. In this way, the resorption of excess fluid (such as blood) into the tissues can additionally be promoted. Administration of hyaluronidase is itself by injection or infusion.

▲ side-effects: sometimes there are sensitivity reactions.

✱ warning: hyaluronidase should not be administered to patients who are to receive intravenous injection, who have recently received bites or stings, or who have any kind of infection at or near the site of injection.
*Related article:* HYALASE.

**Hycal** (*Beecham*) is a proprietary, non-prescription nutritional supplement intended for patients who require a high-energy low-fluid diet low in electrolytes (as with kidney or liver disease). Gluten-free, Hycal contains mostly carbohydrate in the form of corn syrup solids; it is also protein-free and lactose-, fructose- and sucrose-free, and is produced in four flavours.

**Hydergine** (*Sandoz*) is a proprietary form of the powerful drug co-dergocrine mesylate, used primarily to assist in the management of elderly patients with mild to moderate dementia. Hydergine works by enhancing the oxidative capacity of cells. Available only on prescription, it is produced in the form of tablets (in two strengths), and is not recommended for children.

▲ / ✱ side-effects/warning: *see* CO-DERGOCRINE MESYLATE.

**hydralazine** is a VASODILATOR used to treat heart conditions both acute and chronic: acute in the form of a high blood pressure crisis (apoplexy), and chronic in

the form of long-term high blood pressure (in which case simultaneous treatment is administered with a BETA-BLOCKER or a DIURETIC). Administration is oral in the form of tablets, and by injection or infusion.

▲ side-effects: there may be nausea and vomiting. Prolonged high-dosage therapy may cause a vivid red rash.

✱ warning: administered by itself, hydralazine over any length of time causes an increase in the heart rate and fluid retention (oedema). Conversely, the reduction of blood pressure may be unexpectedly swift and severe, and require further treatment.
*Related article:* APRESOLINE.

**hydrargaphen** is an ANTI-MICROBIAL used in vaginal inserts (pessaries) to treat various kinds of infection in the vagina or in the womb. Treatment is usually of two pessaries nightly for a fortnight after menstruation.

✱ warning: hydrargaphen must not be used in patients who have an intrauterine device containing copper.
*Related article:* PENOTRANE.

**Hydrea** (*Squibb*) is a proprietary CYTOTOXIC drug, available only on prescription, used to treat certain forms of chronic leukaemia. It works by reacting with cellular DNA. Produced in the form of capsules, Hydrea is a preparation of hydroxyurea.

▲ / ✱ side-effects/warning: *see* HYDROXYUREA.

**Hydrenox** (*Boots*) is a proprietary DIURETIC, available only on prescription, used to treat an accumulation of fluid in the tissues (oedema) and high blood pressure (*see* ANTIHYPERTENSIVE). Produced in the form of tablets, Hydrenox is a preparation of the

THIAZIDE hydroflumethiazide.
▲/✚ side-effects/warning: see
HYDROFLUMETHIAZIDE.

**Hydrocal** (*Bioglan*) is a
proprietary CORTICOSTEROID
cream for topical application,
used mostly to treat mild
inflammation of the skin and to
assist in the treatment of eczema.
Available only on prescription,
Hydrocal is a compound
preparation of the steroid
hydrocortisone, together with
CALAMINE.
▲/✚ side-effects/warning: see
HYDROCORTISONE.

**hydrochlorothiazide** is a
THIAZIDE DIURETIC drug used to
treat an accumulation of fluid in
the tissues (oedema) and high
blood pressure (see ANTI-
HYPERTENSIVE). Administration is
oral in the form of tablets.
▲ side-effects: there may be
tiredness and a rash. In men,
temporary impotence may
occur. Rarely, there is a
sensitivity to light.
✚ warning: hydrochlorothiazide
should not be administered to
patients who suffer from
urinary retention or kidney
failure, or who are lactating. It
should be administered with
caution to those who are
pregnant. It may aggravate
conditions of diabetes or gout.
(Potassium supplements may
be required.)
*Related articles:* DYAZIDE;
ESIDREX; HYDROSALURIC.

**hydrocortisone** is a CORTICO-
STEROID hormone, a derivative of
cortisone, produced and secreted
by the adrenal glands. Sometimes
known as cortisol, it is highly
important both for the normal
metabolism of carbohydrates in
the diet and for the neuromuscular response to stress.
Other than to make up hormonal
deficiency, hydrocortisone may be

administered therapeutically to
treat any kind of inflammation
(sometimes in combination with
ANTIBACTERIAL drugs), including
arthritis, and to treat allergic
conditions (especially in
emergencies). Administration is
in many forms.
▲/✚ side-effects/warning:
prolonged or high-dosage
treatment may lead to
peptic ulcers, muscle
disorders, bone disorders
and (in children) stunting of
growth. Another potential
result is the onset of adult-
type diabetes. In the elderly
there may be brittle bones
and mental disturbances,
particularly depression or
euphoria. In addition,
treatment with the drug
may suppress symptoms of
an infection until the
infection is far advanced
(which may in some cases
present its own dangers);
treatment should therefore
be made as aseptic as
possible, and infected areas
must not be treated.
Withdrawal of treatment
must be gradual.
*Related articles:*
ALPHADERM; ALPHOSYL HC;
BARQUINOL HC; CALMURID
HC; CANESTEN HC; CARBO-
CORT; CHLOROMYCETIN
HYDROCORTISONE; COBADEX;
COLIFOAM; CORLAN;
DAKTACORT; DIODERM;
ECONACORT; EFCORTELAN;
EFCORTELAN SOLUBLE;
EFCORTESOL; EPIFOAM;
EURAX-HYDROCORTISONE;
FRAMYCORT; FUCIDIN H;
GENTICIN HC; GREGODERM;
HYDROCAL;
HYDROCORTISTAB;
HYDROCORTISYL;
HYDROCORTONE; MILDISON;
NEO-CORTEF; NYBADEX;
NYSTAFORM-HC;
QUINOCORT; QUINODERM;
SENTIAL; SOLU-CORTEF;

TERRA-CORTRIL; TIMODINE; TRI-CITATRIN; VIOFORM-HYDROCORTISONE.

**hydrocortisone acetate** is a HYDROCORTISONE salt used as an ANTI-INFLAMMATORY to treat local inflammation of the joints or of the soft tissues. Produced in the form of an aqueous suspension, it is administered by injection. In the treatment of inflamed joints, injection may be into the joint itself or into the synovial capsule that acts as a shock-absorber within the joint.
▲/● side-effects/warning: see HYDROCORTISONE.
Related articles: CHLOROMYCETIN HYDROCORTISONE; HYDROCORTISTAB; FRAMYCORT; NEO-CORTEF.

**hydrocortisone butyrate** is a HYDROCORTISONE salt used as an ANTI-INFLAMMATORY to treat severe inflammation of the skin that have failed to respond to treatment with less powerful drugs (as may occur with some forms of eczema). Administration is topical in the form of cream, ointment or lotion.
▲/● side-effects/warning: see HYDROCORTISONE.
Related article: LOCOID.

**hydrocortisone sodium phosphate** is a HYDROCORTISONE salt used to treat deficiency of the HORMONE hydrocortisone. Administration is by injection, optionally diluted.
▲/● side-effects/warning: see HYDROCORTISONE.
Related article: EFCORTESOL.

**hydrocortisone sodium succinate** is a HYDROCORTISONE salt used primarily to treat deficiency of the HORMONE hydrocortisone, but also as an ANTI-INFLAMMATORY to treat inflammation and lesions in and around the mouth. Administration is by injection, optionally diluted, or in the form of lozenges.
▲/● side-effects/warning: see HYDROCORTISONE.
Related articles: CORLAN; EFCORTELAN SOLUBLE; SOLU-CORTEF.

**Hydrocortistab** (Boots) is a proprietary, ANTI-INFLAMMATORY drug, available only on prescription, in which the active constituent is the CORTICOSTEROID hormone hydrocortisone. Produced in the form of tablets and in vials for injection, Hydrocortistab is used to treat inflammation in rheumatic or collagen disorders and in allergic conditions. Produced in the form of a cream and an ointment, Hydrocortistab is used to treat severe skin inflammations, such as eczema and various forms of dermatitis.
▲/● side-effects/warning: see HYDROCORTISONE.

**Hydrocortisyl** (Roussel) is a proprietary, ANTI-INFLAMMATORY drug, available only on prescription, in which the active constituent is the corticosteroid hormone hydrocortisone. Produced in the form of a cream and an ointment, Hydrocortisyl is used to treat severe skin inflammations, such as eczema and various forms of dermatitis.
▲/● side-effects/warning: see HYDROCORTISONE.

**Hydrocortone** (Merck, Sharp & Dohme) is a proprietary form of the CORTICOSTEROID hormone hydrocortisone, used to make up hormonal deficiency and to treat inflammation, shock, and certain allergic conditions. Available only on prescription, Hydrocortone is produced in the form of tablets (in two strengths).
▲/● side-effects/warning: see HYDROCORTISONE.

**hydroflumethiazide** is a DIURETIC drug used primarily to treat an accumulation of fluid in the tissues (oedema) and high blood pressure (*see* ANTIHYPERTENSIVE). In combination with the weaker diuretic spironolactone (which helps to replace lost potassium), it may be used also to treat congestive heart failure.

▲ side-effects: there may be tiredness and a rash. In men, temporary impotence may occur.

✹ warning: hydroflumethiazide should not be administered to patients who suffer from urinary retention or kidney failure, or who are lactating. It should be administered with caution to those who are pregnant. It may aggravate conditions of diabetes or gout. (In treatment with hydroflumethiazide alone, potassium supplements may be required.)
*Related articles:* ALDACTIDE 50; HYDRENOX.

**hydrogen peroxide** is a general DISINFECTANT used in solution and as a cream to cleanse and deodorize wounds and ulcers, to clean ears in the form of ear-drops, and as a mouth wash and gargle for oral hygiene. Some preparations available require further dilution: a 6% solution is the maximum concentration recommended for use on the skin. Stronger solutions will bleach fabric.
*Related article:* HIOXYL.

**Hydromet** (*Merck, Sharp & Dohme*) is a proprietary ANTIHYPERTENSIVE compound, available only on prescription, used to treat moderate to very high blood pressure. Produced in the form of tablets, Hydromet consists of the powerful drug methyldopa (which acts directly on the central nervous system but

may cause fluid retention) with the THIAZIDE hydrochlorothiazide (which has complementary DIURETIC properties).

▲/✹ side-effects/warning: *see* HYDROCHLOROTHIAZIDE; METHYLDOPA.

**Hydromol** (*Quinoderm Ltd*) is a proprietary, non-prescription skin emollient (softener and soother), used to treat dry skin. Produced in the form of a cream, the major constituents are liquid paraffin and a moisturizer.

**HydroSaluric** (*Merck, Sharp & Dohme*) is a proprietary DIURETIC, available only on prescription, used to treat an accumulation of fluid within the tissues (oedema) and high blood pressure (*see* ANTIHYPERTENSIVE). Produced in the form of tablets (in two strengths), HydroSaluric is a preparation of the THIAZIDE hydrochlorothiazide.

▲/✹ side-effects/warning: *see* HYDROCHLOROTHIAZIDE.

**hydrotalcite** is an ANTACID complex that is readily dissociated internally for rapid relief of dyspepsia, and has deflatulent properties. Administration is oral in the form of tablets that can be chewed, or in suspension. It is not recommended for children aged under 6 years.
*Related article:* ALTACITE.

**hydrous wool fat ointment**, or lanolin, is a greasy preparation of hydrous wool fat in a yellow soft paraffin base. It is used as a protective barrier cream on cracked, dry or thin skin, encourages hydration, and has mild ANTI-INFLAMMATORY properties.

✹ warning: some people are sensitive to wool fat preparations; for them, local reaction may be comparatively severe.

**hydroxocobalamin** is a form of
VITAMIN B<sub>12</sub> that has recently
replaced CYANOCOBALAMIN as the
version of the vitamin for
therapeutic use. Supplements of
vitamin B<sub>12</sub> are administered only
by injection (because vitamin B<sub>12</sub>
deficiency arises most often
through malabsorption, which
renders oral administration
futile), and hydroxocobalamin
can be retained in the body for
more than 3 months following
injection – far longer than the
formerly standard preparation.
This factor is particularly
significant in that treatment,
once begun, is usually for life.
*Related articles:* COBALIN-H; NEO-
CYTAMEN.

**hydroxychloroquine sulphate** is
a drug used primarily to treat
rheumatoid arthritis and forms of
the skin disease lupus
erythematosus, but also to
prevent and treat malaria. Its
treatment of rheumatic disease is
effective, but may take up to 6
months to become so; then, the
drug improves not only
inflammation in the joints but
assists circulatory problems and
halts erosion of bone surfaces.
Because it takes such a time to
have such an effect, other forms
of treatment are generally tried
first – but treatment must be
begun before joint damage is
irreversible.
▲ side-effects: there may be
   visual disturbances –
   ophthalmic monitoring is
   essential throughout treatment
   to avoid permanent damage.
   There may also be
   gastrointestinal disturbances,
   headache, hair loss, ringing in
   the ears (tinnitus) and/or skin
   reactions. Rarely, there are
   blood disorders, sensitivity to
   light, or even psychological
   disturbances.
⦿ warning: hydroxychloroquine
   sulphate should not be

administered to patients who
have defects or disease in the
retina of the eye (in prolonged
courses of treatment the drug
may be toxic to the eyes), who
are known to be sensitive to
quinine, or who are already
taking drugs containing gold
(for rheumatism). It should be
administered with caution to
those who are pregnant,
elderly, or young; or who suffer
from impaired liver or kidney
function, psoriasis, porphyria,
or severe gastrointestinal
disorder.
*Related article:* PLAQUENIL.

**hydroxyethyl cellulose** is a
constituent of artificial tear
medium, used in conditions where
there is dryness of the eyes due to
disease (for instance some cases
of rheumatoid arthritis). It is
available in the form of eye-drops.
*Related article:* MINIMS
ARTIFICIAL TEARS.

**hydroxyprogesterone
hexanoate** is a PROGESTOGEN
used primarily to prevent a
miscarriage in a pregnant woman
with a history of miscarriages.
Administration is by
intramuscular injection once a
week for the first half of the
pregnancy.
▲ side-effects: there may be
   tenderness of the breasts and
   menstrual disorders, skin
   conditions such as acne and
   urticaria, gastrointestinal
   disturbances, and weight gain
   through the accumulation of
   fluid in the tissues (oedema).
   Rarely, there is pain at the site
   of injection.
⦿ warning: hydroxyprogesterone
   hexanoate should not be
   administered to patients with
   vaginal haemorrhage or cancer
   of the breast, or who have a
   history of thrombosis; it should
   be administered with caution
   to those who are diabetic, who

have heart, liver or kidney disease, who suffer from high blood pressure (hypertension), or who are lactating.

*Related article:* PROLUTON DEPOT.

**hydroxyurea** is a CYTOTOXIC drug used to treat certain forms of chronic leukaemia. It works by reacting with cellular DNA. Administration is oral in the form of capsules.

▲ side-effects: there is commonly nausea and vomiting (which may be separately treated); there may also be skin reactions and hair loss.

✿ warning: like all cytotoxic drugs, hydroxyurea may cause life-threatening toxicity: dosage must be the minimum possible still to be effective. The major toxic effect is to suppress the blood-forming function of the bone-marrow.

*Related article:* HYDREA.

**hydroxyzine hydrochloride** is an ANXIOLYTIC drug, an ANTIHISTAMINE used to treat anxiety in association with skin disorders diagnosed to be caused by stress. It can also be used for either purpose singly. Administration is oral in the form of tablets or as a syrup.

▲ side-effects: drowsiness is fairly common; there is sometimes also neural dysfunction and, with high doses, involuntary movements.

✿ warning: hydroxyzine hydrochloride should not be administered to patients who are pregnant or who are alcoholic; all patients should be warned prior to treatment that their speed of thought and reaction may be impaired by treatment.

*Related article:* ATARAX.

**Hygroton** (*Geigy*) is a proprietary DIURETIC, available only on prescription, used to treat an accumulation of fluid within the tissues (oedema) and high blood pressure (*see* ANTIHYPERTENSIVE). Produced in the form of tablets (in two strengths), Hygroton is a preparation of the THIAZIDE-like drug chlorthalidone.

▲/✿ side-effects/warning: *see* CHLORTHALIDONE.

**Hygroton-K** (*Geigy*) is a proprietary DIURETIC, available only on prescription, used to treat an accumulation of fluid within the tissues (oedema) and high blood pressure (*see* ANTIHYPERTENSIVE). Produced in the form of sustained-release tablets, Hygroton-K is a compound preparation of the THIAZIDE-like drug chlorthalidone with the potassium supplement POTASSIUM CHLORIDE.

▲/✿ side-effects/warning: *see* CHLORTHALIDONE.

**hyoscine**, also known as scopolamine (in the USA), is a powerful alkaloid drug derived from plants of the belladonna family. By itself it is an effective SEDATIVE and HYPNOTIC – it is often used together with the OPIATE papaveretum as a premedication prior to surgery – and an ANTI-EMETIC (in which capacity it is found in travel-sickness medications). In the form of its bromide salts, hyoscine has additional ANTISPASMODIC properties without the side-effects usually associated with other antispasmodic drugs that directly affect the central nervous system (and is thus particularly useful in treating disorders of the muscular walls of the stomach and intestines, or during labour). It is also used (in solution) in ophthalmic treatments to paralyse the muscles of the pupil of the eye either for surgery or to rest the eye following surgery. Administration is oral in the form of tablets, by injection, or as eye-drops.

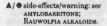

▲ side-effects: there may be drowsiness, dizziness and dry mouth; sometimes there is also blurred vision and difficulty in urinating.

✿ warning: hyoscine (or its bromide salts) should not be administered to patients with glaucoma; it should be administered with caution to those with heart or intestinal disease, or urinary retention, or who are elderly.
*Related articles:* BUSCOPAN; OMNOPON-SCOPOLAMINE; SCOPODERM TTS.

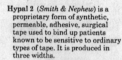

**Hypal 2** (*Smith & Nephew*) is a proprietary form of synthetic, permeable, adhesive, surgical tape used to bind up patients known to be sensitive to ordinary types of tape. It is produced in three widths.

**Hypercal** is an ANTIHYPERTENSIVE drug consisting of Rauwolfia alkaloids – derivatives of the plant Rauwolfia serpentina – which act by depressing certain functions of the central nervous system. It is used to treat high blood pressure (hypertension). Available only on prescription, Hypercal is produced in the form of tablets.
▲ / ✿ side-effects/warning: *see* RAUWOLFIA ALKALOIDS.

**Hypercal-B** is an ANTI-HYPERTENSIVE drug consisting of Rauwolfia alkaloids – derivatives of the plant Rauwolfia serpentina (which act by depressing certain functions of the central nervous system) – together with the BARBITURATE amylobarbitone. Accordingly, it may be used to treat high blood pressure (hypertension), although because it contains a barbiturate it is on the controlled drugs list and its use is becoming rare.
It is produced in the form of tablets.

▲ / ✿ side-effects/warning: *see* AMYLOBARBITONE; RAUWOLFIA ALKALOIDS.

**Hypnomidate** (*Janssen*) is a proprietary general ANAESTHETIC used primarily for initial induction of anaesthesia. Available only on prescription, it is produced in ampoules for injection (in two strengths, the stronger for dilution), and is a preparation of etomidate. It should not be allowed to come into contact with plastic equipment.
▲ / ✿ side-effects/warning: *see* ETOMIDATE.

\*hypnotics are a type of drug that induce sleep by direct action on various centres of the brain. They are used mainly to treat insomnia, and to calm patients who are mentally ill. Best-known and most-used hynotics are the BENZODIAZEPINES (such as diazepam and nitrazepam), which are for several reasons safer than using derivatives of chloral (such as chloral hydrate) or the BARBITURATES (such as amylobarbitone), which may cause dependence (addiction). Some cause a hangover effect the following morning.

**Hypnovel** is a proprietary preparation of the powerful BENZODIAZEPINE midazolam, available only on prescription, used mainly for sedation, particularly as a premedication prior to surgery, for the initial induction of anaesthesia, or for the short-term anaesthesia required for endoscopy or minor surgical examinations. Its effect is often accompanied by a form of amnesia. It is produced in ampoules for infusion (in two strengths).

\*hypoglycaemic drugs reduce the levels of glucose (sugar) in the bloodstream, and are used mainly in the treatment of diabetes mellitus of adult onset, when there is still some residual capacity in the pancreas for the production of INSULIN. The major type of hypoglycaemic drug is provided by the SULPHONYLUREAS (such as CHLORPROPAMIDE and GLIBENCLAMIDE), but the biguanide metformin hydrochloride is effective, as is the administration in quantity of GUAR GUM.

**Hypon** (*Calmic*) is a proprietary, non-prescription compound ANALGESIC preparation, which is not available from the National Health Service. Produced in the form of tablets, Hypon is a combination of aspirin, the stimulant caffeine, and the OPIATE codeine phosphate. It is not recommended for children.
▲/ ● side-effects/warning: *see* ASPIRIN; CAFFEINE; CODEINE PHOSPHATE.

**Hypotears** (*Cooper Vision*) is a proprietary, non-prescription compound of polyethylene glycol with POLYVINYL ALCOHOL, used to supplement the film of tears over the eye when the mucus that normally constitutes that film is intermittent or missing through disease or disorder. It is produced in the form of drops to be used every 3 to 4 hours (or as required).

\*hypotensive is a term used similarly to antihypertensive. *see* ANTIHYPERTENSIVE.

**Hypovase** (*Pfizer*) is a proprietary ANTIHYPERTENSIVE drug, available only on prescription, used to treat both high blood pressure (hypertension) and congestive heart failure. Produced in the form of tablets (in four strengths), Hypovase is a preparation of prazosin hydrochloride, which acts only on the muscles of the smaller arteries. It is not recommended for children.
▲/ ● side-effects/warning: *see* PRAZOSIN.

**Hypurin Isophane** (*CP Pharmaceuticals*) is a proprietary, non-prescription preparation of highly purified beef isophane insulin, used to treat and maintain diabetic patients. It is produced in vials for injection.
▲/ ● side-effects/warning: *see* INSULIN.

**Hypurin Lente** (*CP Pharmaceuticals*) is a proprietary, non-prescription preparation of highly purified beef INSULIN zinc suspension, used to treat and maintain diabetic patients. It is produced in vials for injection.
▲/ ● side-effects/warning: *see* INSULIN.

**Hypurin Neutral** (*CP Pharmaceuticals*) is a proprietary, non-prescription preparation of highly purified beef neutral insulin, used to treat and maintain diabetic patients. It is produced in vials for injection.
▲/ ● side-effects/warning: *see* INSULIN.

**Hypurin Protamine Zinc** (*CP Pharmaceuticals*) is a proprietary, non-prescription preparation of highly purified beef protamine zinc insulin, used to treat and maintain diabetic patients. It is produced in vials for injection.
▲/ ● side-effects/warning: *see* INSULIN.

**Ibular** (*Lagap*) is a proprietary, ANTI-INFLAMMATORY, non-narcotic ANALGESIC, available only on prescription, used to treat the pain of rheumatic and other musculo-skeletal disorders. Produced in the form of tablets, Ibular is a preparation of ibuprofen.

▲/● side-effects/warning: see IBUPROFEN.

**ibuprofen** is a non-steroidal, ANTI-INFLAMMATORY, non-narcotic ANALGESIC drug used primarily to treat the pain of rheumatism and other musculo-skeletal disorders, but also used sometimes to treat other forms of pain, including menstrual pain (dysmenorrhoea). In its anti-inflammatory capacity it is not as powerful as many other drugs, however, and dosage tends to be high to compensate. Administration is oral in the form of tablets or sustained-release capsules, or as a syrup.

▲ side-effects: administration with or following meals reduces the risk of gastrointestinal disturbance and nausea. But there may be headache, dizziness and ringing in the ears (tinnitus), and some patients experience sensitivity reactions or blood disorders. Occasionally, there is fluid retention.

● warning: ibuprofen should be administered with caution to patients with impaired liver or kidney function, gastric ulcers, or severe allergies (including asthma), or who are pregnant.
*Related articles:* APSIFEN; BRUFEN; EBUFAC; FENBID; IBULAR; JUNIFEN; MOTRIN; NUROFEN; PAXOFEN; PROFLEX.

**Ichthaband** (*Seton*) is a proprietary form of bandaging impregnated with ZINC PASTE (15%) and ichthammol (2%), used to treat and dress chronic forms of eczema.

▲/● side-effects/warning: see ICHTHAMMOL.

**ichthammol** is a thick, dark brown liquid derived from bituminous oils, used for its mildly ANTISEPTIC properties in ointments or in glycerol solution for the topical treatment of ulcers and inflammation on the skin. Milder than COAL TAR, ichthammol is useful in treating the less severe forms of eczema. A popular mode of administration is in an impregnated bandage with ZINC PASTE.

▲ side-effects: some patients experience skin irritation; the skin may become sensitized.

● warning: ichthammol must not be placed in contact with broken skin surfaces.
*Related articles:* ICHTHABAND; ICHTHOPASTE.

**Ichthopaste** (*Smith & Nephew*) is a proprietary form of bandaging impregnated with ZINC PASTE (6%) and ichthammol (2%), used to treat and dress chronic forms of eczema.

▲/● side-effects/warning: see ICHTHAMMOL.

**idarubicin hydrochloride** is a powerful CYTOTOXIC drug, which also has ANTIBIOTIC properties, used especially to treat leukaemia. It is a recently introduced agent with properties similar to doxorubicin. Administration is by fast-running infusion.

▲ side-effects: there may be nausea and vomiting, hair loss and reduction in the blood-cell forming capacity of the bone-marrow are all fairly common side-effects.

● warning: idarubicin hydrochloride should be administered with caution to patients with heart disease, who are elderly, or who are receiving radiotherapy in the

cardiac region. Heart
monitoring is essential
throughout treatment: high
doses tend to cause eventual
heart dysfunction. Leakage of
the drug from the site of
infusion into the tissues may
cause tissue damage.
*Related articles:* DOXORUBICIN;
ZAVEDOS.

**Idoxene** (*Spodefell*) is a
proprietary ANTIVIRAL eye
ointment, available only on
prescription, used to treat local
viral infections, particularly of
herpes simplex. It is a preparation
of idoxuridine.
▲/● side-effects/warning: *see*
IDOXURIDINE.

**idoxuridine** is an ANTIVIRAL drug
used primarily in very mild
solution to treat infections caused
by herpes viruses in and around
the mouth or eye. In a solution of
dimethyl sulphoxide, however, it
is alternatively used to treat
herpes zoster skin infections. It
inhibits the multiplication of the
virus by interfering with viral
DNA synthesis. Administration is
as a paint for topical application,
as eye-drops or as eye ointment.
● warning: because idoxuridine
contains iodine, treatment may
cause initial irritation and/or
stinging.
*Related articles:* HERPID;
IDOXENE; IDURIDIN; KERECID;
VIRUDOX.

**Iduridin** (*Ferring*) is a proprietary
ANTIVIRAL drug, available only on
prescription, used to treat
infections of the skin by herpes
simplex (cold sores, fever sores) or
by herpes zoster (shingles).
Produced in the form of a lotion
or paint, for topical application
either with a dropper or its own
applicator, Iduridin is a solution
of idoxuridine in the organic
solvent dimethyl sulphoxide
(DMSO).
● warning: *see* IDOXURIDINE.

**ifosfamide** is a CYTOTOXIC drug
used to treat cancers, especially
sarcomas, lymphomas, and cancer
of the testicles. It works by
interfering with cellular DNA,
thus inhibiting cell replication.
Administration is by injection or
infusion, often simultaneously
with the synthetic drug MESNA,
which reduces the toxic side-
effects (and particularly prevents
cystitis).
▲ side-effects: cystitis, leading to
blood in the urine, is not
uncommon (unless mesna is
administered simultaneously).
There may also be nausea
and vomiting, and hair
loss.
● warning: prolonged treatment
may cause sterility in men and
an early menopause in women;
prolonged treatment has also
been associated with the
incidence of leukaemia
following simultaneous
irradiation treatment. Blood
count monitoring is essential.
Dosage should be the minimum
still to be effective.
*Related article:* MITOXANA.

**Ilosone** (*Dista*) is a proprietary
macrolide ANTIBIOTIC, available
only on prescription, used to treat
many serious infections (such as
legionnaires' disease and
inflammation of the prostate
gland) and to prevent others (such
as diphtheria or whooping
cough), but more commonly in the
treatment of infections of the
upper respiratory tract or of
infected wounds, especially in
patients who are allergic to
penicillin-type antibiotics.
Produced in the form of capsules,
tablets, and as a suspension (in
two strengths, the stronger under
the name Ilosone Suspension
Forte) for dilution (the potency of
the suspension once diluted is
retained for 14 days), Ilosone in
every form is a preparation of
erythromycin estolate.

▲/❋ side-effects/warning: *see*
ERYTHROMYCIN.

**Ilube** (*Duncan Flockhart*) is a
proprietary preparation of the
mucolytic agent acetylcysteine,
available only on prescription,
used to treat a deficiency of tears
in the eyes – a deficiency that can
lead to eye dryness and
inflammation. It works by
breaking down mucus around the
eye into a film of tears.
Administered as eye-drops, Ilube
also contains a small proportion
of the synthetic tear fluid
hypromellose.
▲/❋ side-effects/warning: *see*
ACETYLCYSTEINE.

**Imbrilon** (*Berk*) is a proprietary,
ANTI-INFLAMMATORY, non-narcotic
ANALGESIC, available only on
prescription, used to treat the
pain of rheumatic and other
musculo-skeletal disorders
(including gout). Produced in the
form of capsules (in two
strengths), and as anal
suppositories, Imbrilon is a
preparation of indomethacin. It is
not recommended for children.
▲/❋ side-effects/warning: *see*
INDOMETHACIN.

**Imferon** (*CP Pharmaceuticals*) is a
proprietary preparation of IRON
and DEXTRAN, a nutritive plasma-
and-iron supplement administered
in infusion or by injection to
patients who are in need of
substantial replacement of both,
and who, perhaps because of
malabsorption, cannot be given
iron orally. Administration by
infusion is slow – over 6 to 8
hours.
❋ warning: stringent tests must
first be carried out to ensure
that the patient will not suffer
any allergic reaction: if
hypersensitivity reactions do
occur, they are usually violent.
For this reason, treatment by
infusion must be supervised

throughout and for a time
afterwards; there must also be
full facilities for emergency
cardio-respiratory
resuscitation immediately
available. Imferon should not
be administered to patients
with severe disease of the
kidneys or liver, and should
not be administered by
infusion to asthmatic patients.

\*imidazoles are a group of broad-
spectrum ANTIFUNGAL drugs
active against most fungi and
yeasts. The most common
conditions that they are used to
treat are vaginal infections (such
as candidiasis, or thrush) and
infections of the skin surface and
mucous membranes, the hair and
the nails. Best-known and most-
used imidazoles include
clotrimazole, miconazole,
ketoconazole and econazole.
Miconazole and ketoconazole
may be used systemically,
although the latter can cause
serious toxicity to the liver
(hepatoxicity) and systemic use
should be reserved for serious
infections.
*see* CLOTRIMAZOLE; ECONAZOLE
NITRATE; KETOCONAZOLE;
MICONAZOLE.

**imipramine** is an
ANTIDEPRESSANT drug of a type
that has fewer sedative properties
than many others. It is thus suited
more to the treatment of
withdrawn and apathetic patients
than to those who are agitated
and restless. As is the case with
many such drugs, imipramine can
also be used to treat bedwetting
at night by children (aged over 7
years). Administration is oral in
the form of tablets or as a syrup,
or by injection.
▲ side-effects: dry mouth,
drowsiness, blurred vision,
constipation and urinary
retention are all fairly
common; there may also be

heartbeat irregularities accompanying low blood pressure (hypotension). Concentration and speed of reaction are affected. Elderly patients may enter a state of confusion; younger patients may experience behavioural disturbances. There may be alteration in blood sugar levels, and weight gain. Rarely, there is a black tongue, convulsions, or a more serious change in the composition of the blood.

✿ warning: imipramine should not be administered to patients with heart disease or liver failure; it should be administered with extreme caution to those who suffer from epilepsy, psychoses or glaucoma, or who are pregnant. Treatment may take up to four weeks to achieve full effect; premature withdrawal of treatment thereafter may cause the return of symptoms. *Related article:* TOFRANIL.

**Immravax** (*Mewrieux*) is the MMR VACCINE used to treat children in the prevention of measles/mumps/rubella (German measles). It is available only on prescription, and is made available by Local Health Authorities.

▲/ ✿ side-effects/warning: *see* MMR VACCINE.

*****immunization** against specific diseases is effected by either of two means. Active immunity is conferred by vaccination, in which live antigens that have been rendered harmless (attenuated), or dead ones (inactivated), are injected into the bloodstream so that the body's own defence mechanisms are required to deal with them (by manufacturing antibodies) and with anything like them that they encounter again. This method

gives long-lasting but impermanent protection (and there is a slight risk of allergic reaction or toxic effect). Passive immunity is conferred by the injection of a quantity of blood serum already containing antibodies (immunoglobulins), or of the purified, specific immunoglobulins themselves; this method gives immediate but short-lived protection, and carries the risk of sensitizing the individual to future exposure to similar injections.
*see* IMMUNOGLOBULINS; VACCINES.

*****immunocompromised** is a term that refers to a host whose immune defences are very much lower than normal due to either a congenital or acquired condition. The commonest deficiencies are: of the white cells, neutrophils, which are the first line of defence in acute infections; of the white cells, macrophages, and T lymphocytes, which are involved in cell-mediated killing of foreign or 'parasitized' host cells; and of the antibodies, which neutralize and bind to foreign antigens. Examples of immunocompromised hosts are patients receiving immunosuppressant drugs to prevent rejection of transplanted organs. Individuals suffering from leukaemia, or being treated with high doses of cytotoxic drugs to treat cancer, will also be immunocompromised, as will individuals with AIDS. In any of these circumstances 'opportunistic' infections are apt to occur where microbes which normally pose little threat to the healthy become highly invasive and pose a serious threat. Prophylaxis with antibiotics may be required, and once infections are established they are much more difficult to eradicate even with vigorous antibiotic treatment.

**\*immunoglobulins** are proteins of a specific structure, which act as antibodies in the bloodstream. Created in response to the presence of a specific antigen, immunoglobulins circulate with the blood to give systemic defence and protection as part of the immune system. Immunoglobulin deficiencies are often associated with increased risk of infection. Classified according to a differentiation of class and function, immunoglobulins may be administered therapeutically by injection or infusion to confer immediate (passive) immunity.
*see* IMMUNIZATION.
*Related article:* HNIG.

**\*immunostimulants** are used to treat the presence of malignant fluids inside body cavities. A preparation of inactivated bacteria of the species Corynebacterium parvum, for example, may be injected into the lung (pleural) cavity of the chest or the abdominal (peritoneal) cavity to treat the presence of such fluids (effusions) there. The effect is to increase the local effect of antibacterial activity by the immune system.
*Related article:* COPARVAX.

**\*immunosuppressants** are drugs used to inhibit the body's resistance to the presence of infection or foreign bodies. In this capacity, such drugs may be used to suppress tissue rejection following donor grafting or transplant surgery (although there is then the risk of unopposed infection). But immunosupressant drugs are even more commonly used in a different capacity - to treat auto-immune disease (when the body's immune system is for some reason triggered into its defence mode against part of the body itself). And in this respect, immuno-suppressant drugs may be used to treat cancers or disorders such as rheumatoid arthritis or lupus erythematosus. Best-known and most-used among immuno-suppressants administered both for tissue rejection prevention and to treat auto-immune disease are the non-steroids azathioprine, chlorambucil, cyclophosphamide, methotrexate and cyclosporin, and all the CORTICOSTEROID drugs.
*see* AZATHIOPRINE; CHLORAMBUCIL; CYCLOPHOSPHAMIDE; CYCLOSPORIN; METHOTREXATE.

**Imodium** (*Janssen*) is a proprietary ANTIDIARRHOEAL drug, available only on prescription, which works by reducing intestinal activity and fluid loss. Produced in the form of capsules, and as a syrup, Imodium is a preparation of the OPIATE loperamide hydrochloride. It is not recommended for children aged under 4 years.
▲/✚ side-effects/warning: *see* LOPERAMIDE HYDROCHLORIDE.

**Imperacin** (*ICI*) is a proprietary, broad-spectrum ANTIBIOTIC, available only on prescription, used to treat serious infections by bacteria and other micro-organisms (such as chlamydia and rickettsia), and to relieve severe acne. Produced in the form of tablets, Imperacin is a preparation of the TETRACYCLINE oxytetracycline dihydrate. It is not recommended for children.
▲/✚ side-effects/warning: *see* OXYTETRACYCLINE.

**Imunovir** (*Burgess*) is a proprietary preparation of the ANTIVIRAL drug inosine pranobex, available only on prescription, used to treat herpes simplex infections and warts in mucous membranes and adjacent skin, particularly in or on the genitalia. It is produced in the form of tablets.

▲/● side-effects/warning: *see*
INOSINE PRANOBEX.

**Imuran** (*Wellcome*) is a
proprietary preparation of the
CYTOTOXIC drug azathioprine,
used to suppress tissue rejection
following donor grafting or
transplant surgery, particularly
in cases where corticosteroids
have already been used
excessively and/or failed to be
fully effective. Available only on
prescription, Imuran is produced
in the form of tablets (in two
strengths), and as a powder for
reconstitution as a medium for
injection.
▲/● side-effects/warning: *see*
AZATHIOPRINE.

**indapamide** is a DIURETIC, a
THIAZIDE-like compound used to
treat high blood pressure (*see*
ANTIHYPERTENSIVE). It works by
promoting fluid in the kidneys,
and it may also have some
beneficial actions on the blood
vessels; and is claimed to be
especially beneficial to patients
with diabetes mellitus.
Administration is oral in the form
of tablets.
▲ side-effects: there may be
nausea and a headache; slight
weight loss is to be expected.
● warning: indapamide should
not be administered to patients
with impaired kidney or liver
function, and should be
administered with caution to
those who are pregnant. Its
proprietary form is not
recommended for children.
*Related article:* NATRILIX.

**Inderal** (*ICI*) is a proprietary
BETA-BLOCKER, available only on
prescription, used to treat angina
pectoris (heart pain), myocardial
infarction, heart arrhythmias,
high blood pressure
(hypertension) and anxiety; to try
to prevent migraine attacks; and
to assist in the treatment of

excess thyroid hormones in the
blood (thyrotoxicosis). Produced
in the form of tablets (in four
strengths), and in ampoules for
injection; as sustained-release
capsules (in two strengths, Inderal
LA and the weaker Half-Inderal
LA), and as tablets (in five
strengths). Inderal is a
preparation of propranolol
hydrochloride.
▲/● side-effects/warning: *see*
PROPRANOLOL.

**Inderal-LA** (*ICI*) is a proprietary
BETA-BLOCKER, available only on
prescription, used to treat angina
pectoris (heart pain), the
symptoms of the congenital heart
disorder Fallot's tetralogy, high
blood pressure (hypertension) and
anxiety; to try to prevent migraine
attacks; and to assist in the
treatment of excess thyroid
hormones in the blood
(thyrotoxicosis). Produced in the
form of sustained-release capsules
(in two strengths, the weaker
under the name Half-Inderal LA),
and as tablets (in four strengths),
Inderal-LA is a preparation of
propranolol hydrochloride. In the
treatment of most of the disorders
listed above, Inderal-LA is not
recommended for children.
▲/● side-effects/warning: *see*
PROPRANOLOL.

**Inderetic** (*ICI*) is a proprietary
ANTIHYPERTENSIVE drug, available
only on prescription, used to treat
mild to moderate high blood
pressure (hypertension). Produced
in the form of capsules, Inderetic
is a preparation that combines the
BETA-BLOCKER propranolol
hydrochloride with the THIAZIDE
diuretic bendrofluazide. It is not
recommended for children.
▲/● side-effects/warning: *see*
BENDROFLUAZIDE;
PROPRANOLOL.

**Inderex** (*ICI*) is a proprietary
ANTIHYPERTENSIVE drug, available
only on prescription, used to treat

mild to moderate high blood pressure (hypertension). Produced in the form of sustained-release capsules, Inderex is a preparation that combines the beta-blocker propranolol hydrochloride with the THIAZIDE diuretic bendrofluazide. It is not recommended for children.
▲/● side-effects/warning: *see* BENDROFLUAZIDE; PROPRANOLOL.

**Indian hemp** is the name of the plant from which the psychedelic drug cannabis is prepared.
*see* CANNABIS.

**Indocid** (*Morson*) is a proprietary, ANTI-INFLAMMATORY, non-narcotic ANALGESIC, available only on prescription, used to treat the pain of rheumatic and other musculo-skeletal disorders (including gout and degenerative bone diseases). Produced in the form of capsules (in two strengths), and as sustained-release capsules (under the name Indocid-R), as anal suppositories, and as a sugar-free suspension, Indocid is a preparation of indomethacin. It is not recommended for children.
▲/● side-effects/warning: *see* INDOMETHACIN.

**Indoflex** (*Unimed*) is a proprietary, anti-inflammatory ANALGESIC, available only on prescription, used to treat the pain of rheumatic and other musculo-skeletal disorders (including gout and degenerative bone diseases). Produced in the form of capsules, Indoflex is a preparation of indomethacin. It is not recommended for children.
▲/● side-effects/warning: *see* INDOMETHACIN.

**indomethacin** is a non-steroidal, ANTI-INFLAMMATORY, non-narcotic ANALGESIC drug used to treat rheumatic and muscular pain

caused by inflammation and/or bone degeneration particularly at the joints. Administration is mostly oral in the form of tablets, capsules, sustained-release capsules or as a liquid, but its use in anal suppositories is especially effective for the relief of pain overnight and stiffness in the morning. Some proprietary preparations are not recommended for children.
▲ side-effects: all drugs of this type are prone to give gastro-intestinal discomfort. During treatment, concentration and speed of reaction may be affected; there may also be headache and dizziness, although further mental effects (including depression and confusion) are rare. Some patients experience ringing in the ears (tinnitus) blood disorders, and high blood pressure (hypertension). There may be visual disturbances, tingling in the toes and fingertips and (following the use of suppositories) anal itching.
● warning: indomethacin should not be administered to patients who suffer from peptic ulcers or who are sensitive to aspirin. It should be administered with caution to those who suffer from allergic conditions (such as asthma), from epilepsy, from psychological disturbances, or from impaired function of the liver or kidneys, who are elderly, or who are pregnant. Blood counts and ophthalmic checks are advised during prolonged treatment. Suppositories should not be used by patients with anorectal infections or piles (haemorrhoids).
*Related articles:* ARTRACIN; IMBRILON; INDOCID; INDOFLEX; INDOMOD; MOBILAN; RHEUMACIN LA; SLO-INDO.

**Indomod** (*Benzon*) is a
proprietary, ANTI-INFLAMMATORY,
non-narcotic ANALGESIC,
available only on prescription,
used to treat the pain of
rheumatic and other musculo-
skeletal disorders (including gout,
bursitis and tendonitis). Produced
in the form of sustained-release
capsules (in two strengths),
Indomod is a preparation of
indomethacin. It is not
recommended for children.
▲/✿ side-effects/warning: *see*
INDOMETHACIN.

**indoramin** is an ANTI-
HYPERTENSIVE drug, used usually
in combination with a THIAZIDE
diuretic or a BETA-BLOCKER to
treat high blood pressure
(hypertension). It works by
selective vasodilation of the
arteries. Administration is oral in
the form of tablets.
▲ side-effects: there is usually
drowsiness and dizziness; there
may also be dry mouth and
nasal congestion. Some
patients experience depression.
✿ warning: indoramin should not
be administered to patients
who suffer well-established
heart failure; it should be
administered with caution to
those with impaired kidney or
liver function, parkinsonism or
epilepsy, or who are elderly.
Concentration and speed of
reaction may be affected.
*Related article:* BARATOL;
DORALESE.

**\*influenza vaccines** are
recommended only for persons at
high risk of catching known
strains of influenza. This is
because the influenza viruses A
and B are constantly changing in
physical form, and antibodies
manufactured in the body to deal
with one strain at one time will
have no effect at all on the same
strain at another time.
Consequently, it is only possible

to provide vaccine for any single
strain once it has already shown
itself to be endemic. Moreover,
during times when no influenza
strain is endemic, vaccination
against influenza is positively
discouraged. The World Health
Organisation makes an annual
recommendation on the strains of
virus for which stocks of vaccine
should be prepared.
Administration is by injection of
surface-antigen vaccine: a single
dose for adults (unless the specific
strain is in the process of
changing again and two slightly
different doses are required), two
doses over 5 weeks or so for
children. As the vaccines are
prepared from virus strains grown
in chicken embryos, the vaccines
should not be given to individuals
known to be sensitive to eggs.
*Related articles:* FLUVIRIN;
INFLUVAC SUB-UNIT; MFV-JECT.

**Influvac Sub-unit** (*Duphar*) is the
name of a series of proprietary flu
vaccines consisting of inactivated
surface antigens of the influenza
virus. None is recommended for
children aged under 4 years.
▲ side-effects: rarely, there is
local reaction together with
headache and high
temperature.
✿ warning: like any flu vaccine,
Influvac Sub-unit cannot
control epidemics and should
be used only – in what seems to
be the appropriate strain – to
treat people who are at high
risk: the elderly, patients with
cardiovascular problems, and
medical staff. Influvac Sub-unit
should not be administered to
patients who are allergic to egg
or chicken protein (in which
vaccine viruses are cultured),
or who are pregnant.

**\*inhalations** of steaming vapours,
whether or not they contain
volatile substances such as
menthol or eucalyptus, are useful

in combating nasal congestion (rhinitis, sinusitis) and bronchitis chiefly (if not solely) because they encourage the breathing in of warm, moist air.

**Initard 50/50** (*Novo Nordisk*) is a proprietary, non-prescription preparation of mixed pork insulins used to treat and maintain diabetic patients. Produced in vials for injection, Initard 50/50 contains both neutral and isophane insulins in equal proportions.
▲/● side-effects/warning: *see* INSULIN.

**Initard 50/50, Human:** *see* HUMAN INITARD 50/50.

**Innovace** (*Merck, Sharp & Dohme*) is a proprietary preparation of the ANTIHYPERTENSIVE drug enalapril maleate, used to treat all forms of high blood pressure (hypertension), and to assist in the treatment of congestive heart failure. Produced in the form of tablets (in four strengths), it is not recommended for children.
▲/● side-effects/warning: *see* ENALAPRIL.

**inosine pranobex** is an ANTIVIRAL drug introduced recently, used primarily to treat herpes simplex infections in mucous membranes and adjacent skin, particularly in or on the genitalia; it is also effective in removing warts in similar areas. Administered in the form of tablets, it works partly by increasing the local activity of the body's own immune system.
▲ side-effects: uric acid levels rise in the blood and in the urine.
● warning: inosine pranobex should not be administered to patients with impaired kidney function or high blood levels of uric acid (as with gout).
*Related article:* IMUNOVIR.

**inositol** is a compound substance resembling a type of sugar. Present in many foods,

particularly in cereals, it is sometimes classified as a member of the vitamin B complex – but unlike true vitamins it can be synthesized in the bodies of most animals, and there is no evidence that it is in any way vital to human life and metabolism. Therapeutically, it is used only in combination with the genuine vitamin B NICOTINIC ACID: inositol nicotinate is a VASODILATOR used mainly to treat circulatory problems of the hands and feet.
▲ side-effects: there may be nausea and vomiting, flushing, and dizziness.
● warning: inositol nicotinate should be administered with caution to patients with diabetes mellitus.
*Related article:* HEXOPAL.

**Instant Carobel** (*Cow & Gate*) is a proprietary, non-prescription powder, used to thicken liquid and semi-liquid diets in the treatment of vomiting. Carobel is a preparation of carob seed flour.

**Instillagel** (*Rimmer*) is a proprietary compound preparation, available only on prescription, in the form of a water-miscible gel produced in disposable syringes that combines a local anaesthetic with a powerful disinfectant. It is used primarily to treat painful inflammations of the urethra: the compound is instilled into the urethra after external cleansing. But it may also be used to disinfect and lubricate medical equipment following such procedures as catheterization and cystoscopy. The anaesthetic constituent is lignocaine hydrochloride; the major antiseptic constituent is chlorhexidine gluconate.
▲/● side-effects/warning: *see* CHLORHEXIDINE.

**Insulatard** (*Novo Nordisk*) is a proprietary, non-prescription preparation of pork isophane

insulin, used to treat and
maintain diabetic patients. It is
produced in vials for injection.
▲/ ✪ side-effects/warning: *see*
INSULIN.

**Insulatard, Human:** *see* HUMAN
INSULATARD.

insulin is a protein hormone
produced and secreted by the
islets of Langerhans within the
pancreas. It has the effect of
reducing the level of glucose
(sugar) in the bloodstream, and is
meant as one half of a balancing
mechanism with the opposing
hormone glycogen (which
increases blood sugars). Its
absence (in the disorder called
diabetes mellitus) therefore
results in high levels of blood
sugar that can rapidly lead to
severe symptoms, and potentially
coma and death. Most diabetics
therefore take some form of
insulin on a regular (daily) basis,
generally by injection, although
oral administration is becoming
popular. Modern genetic
engineering has permitted the
production of quantities of the
human form of insulin that are
now replacing the former insulins
extracted from oxen (beef insulin)
or pigs (pork insulin). There is
also a difference in absorption
time between insulin with an acid
pH (acid insulin injection) and
neutral insulin. Other insulin
preparations are intermediate-
acting (and require administration twice daily, on a
'biphasic' basis) or long-acting
(and require only once-daily
administration). These include
insulin zinc suspension (long-
acting) and isophane insulin
(suitable for the initiation of
biphasic regimes). Many diabetic
patients use more than one type
of insulin in proportions directly
related to their own specific
needs.
*Related articles:* HUMULIN M1;
HUMULIN M2; PENMIX 30/70.

**Intal** (*Fisons*) is a proprietary
preparation of sodium
cromoglycate, available only on
prescription, used in the form of
an inhalant to prevent asthma
attacks. The drug is thought to
work by effectively inhibiting the
release of histamine and other
mediators in the membranes of
the bronchial passages. Intal is
produced in several modes both in
liquid form and as a powder: in an
aerosol (in two strengths), as a
breath-actuated autohaler, in an
automatic insufflator and in
solution for a power-operated
nebuliser. Under the trade name
Intal Compound, sodium
cromoglycate is combined with
the BETA-RECEPTOR STIMULANT
isoprenaline sulphate, and
produced in the form of
inhalation cartridges (Spincaps),
which is not usually
recommended.
▲/ ✪ side-effects/warning: *see*
ISOPRENALINE; SODIUM
CROMOGLYCATE.

**Integrin** (*Sterling Research*) is a
powerful drug, available only on
prescription, used to treat and
tranquillize patients who are
undergoing behavioural
disturbances (states both of
apathetic withdrawal and of
hyperactive mania), or who are
psychotic (particularly
schizophrenic). More mundanely,
it is used to treat severe anxiety
in the short term. Produced in the
form of capsules and tablets,
Integrin is a preparation of the
antipsychotic drug oxypertine. It
is not recommended for children.
▲/ ✪ side-effects/warning: *see*
OXYPERTINE.

*interferons are proteins
produced in tiny quantities by
cells infected by a virus; they
have the ability to inhibit further
growth by the virus. Genetic
engineering, including the use of
bacteria as host cells, has enabled

interferons to be mass-produced – but they have not turned out to be the ultimate weapon against viruses that it was thought they would be. But because they have specific and complex effects on cells, cell function and immunity, interferons are now undergoing trials in the treatment of cancers (particularly lymphomas and certain solid tumours).

▲ side-effects: symptoms of severe fever are common; there may also be lethargy and/or depression. The blood-producing capacity of the bone marrow may be reduced. Some patients experience high or low blood pressure, and heartbeat irregularities.

✿ warning: regular blood counts are essential during treatment, particularly to check on levels of white blood cells that contribute to the immune system.

**Intralgin** (*Riker*) is a proprietary COUNTER-IRRITANT and local ANAESTHETIC non-prescription gel, which, when applied topically, produces an irritation of sensory nerve endings that offsets the pain of underlying muscle or joint ailments. The gel is an alcohol-based preparation of a SALICYLIC ACID-like compound and BENZOCAINE in dilute solution.

**Intralipid** (*KabiVitrum*) is a proprietary form of high-energy nutritional supplement intended for infusion into patients who are unable to take food via the alimentary canal. Produced in two strengths (under the trade names Intralipid 10% and Intralipid 20%), its major constituent is fat emulsion derived from soya bean oils and from eggs.

**Intraval Sodium** (*May & Baker*) is a proprietary general ANAESTHETIC, available only on

prescription, used mainly for the induction of anaesthesia or for short-duration effect during minor surgical procedures. Produced in the form of a powder for reconstitution as a medium for injections (in two strengths), and in ampoules and bottles (flasks), Intraval Sodium is a preparation of thiopentone sodium.

▲/✿ side-effects/warning: *see* THIOPENTONE SODIUM.

**Intron A** (*Kirby-Warrick*) is a proprietary preparation of interferon (in the form of alpha interferon), available only on prescription, and used mainly to treat leukaemia. Administration is by injection. As with virtually all anticancer drugs, some side-effects are inevitable.

▲/✿ side-effects/warning: *see* INTERFERONS.

**Intropin** (*American Hospital Supply*) is a proprietary preparation of the powerful SYMPATHOMIMETIC drug dopamine hydrochloride, used to treat cardiogenic shock following a heart attack or during heart surgery. Dosage is critical – too much *or* too little may have harmful effects. It is produced in the form of a liquid (in two strengths) for dilution and infusion.

▲/✿ side-effects/warning: *see* DOPAMINE.

**iodine** is an element required in small quantities in the diet for healthy growth and development. More mundanely, iodine is still commonly used as an ANTISEPTIC (either as aqueous iodine solution or as POVIDONE-IODINE).

▲ side-effects: there may be sensitivity reactions.

**Iodosorb** (*Stuart*) is a proprietary ANTISEPTIC drug, available only on prescription, and is an absorbent material that cleans, dries and removes dead skin from leg ulcers and open bedsores. Applied to the site as a powder or ointment, it should be covered with a sterile dressing changed daily. Iodosorb powder is based on a form of iodine, and is produced in sachets.

**Ionamin** (*Lipha*) is a proprietary preparation of the stimulant drug phentermine used, in the short term only, to assist in the medical treatment of obesity. On the controlled drugs list, Ionamin is produced in the form of sustained-release capsules (in two strengths). It is not recommended for children aged under 6 years.
▲/ ✷ side-effects/warning: *see* PHENTERMINE.

**Ionax Scrub** (*Alcon*) is a proprietary, non-prescription gel and is a preparation of the ANTISEPTIC BENZALKONIUM CHLORIDE together with abrasive polyethylene granules within a foaming aqueous-alcohol base. It is used to treat acne, or to cleanse the skin before the application of further acne treatments.

**Ionil T** (*Alcon*) is a proprietary preparation of the ANTISEPTICS BENZALKONIUM CHLORIDE and COAL TAR together with the astringent antifungal drug SALICYLIC ACID, all within an alcohol base. It is used to treat seborrhoeic dermatitis of the scalp, and is accordingly produced as a shampoo. If required for strictly medical reasons it is available on prescription.

**ipecacuanha** is a plant extract that is an irritant to the digestive system. It is a powerful emetic (used to clear the stomach in some instances of non-corrosive poisoning), but in smaller doses it is also used in non-proprietary mixtures and in proprietary tinctures and syrups as an expectorant.

✷ warning: high dosage can cause severe gastric upset.

**Ipral** (*Squibb*) is a proprietary ANTIBIOTIC, available only on prescription, used to treat infections of the upper respiratory tract (particularly bronchitis and bronchial pneumonia) and of the urinary tract. Produced in the form of tablets (in two strengths), Ipral is a preparation of the antibacterial drug trimethoprim.
▲/ ✷ side-effects/warning: *see* TRIMETHOPRIM.

**ipratropium** is an ANTI-CHOLINERGIC drug that has the properties of a BRONCHODILATOR, and is (in the form of ipratropium bromide) accordingly used to treat restriction of the air passages of the upper respiratory tract, especially in chronic bronchitis. Administration is by inhalation, from an aerosol or from a nebuliser.
▲ side-effects: There may be dryness of mouth. Rarely, there is urinary retention and/or constipation.
✷ warning: ipratropium should be administered with caution to patients with glaucoma or enlargement of the prostate gland. It is advised that treatment should be initiated under hospital supervision; patients on their own should be careful not to exceed the prescribed dose, and should be scrupulous in observing the manufacturer's directions. *Related article:* ATROVENT; RINATEC.

**iprindole** is an ANTIDEPRESSANT. drug of a type that has fewer sedative properties than many others. In the treatment of depressive illness it is thus suited more to the treatment of withdrawn and apathetic patients than to those who are agitated and restless. Administration is oral in the form of tablets.

▲ side-effects: dry mouth, drowsiness, blurred vision, constipation and urinary retention are all fairly common; there may also be minor heartbeat irregularities accompanying low blood pressure (hypotension). Concentration and speed of reaction are likely to be affected.

● warning: iprindole should not be administered to patients with heart disease or liver failure; it should be administered with extreme caution to those with epilepsy, psychoses or glaucoma, or who are pregnant. Treatment may take up to four weeks to achieve full effect; premature withdrawal of treatment thereafter may cause the return of symptoms.
*Related article:* PRONDOL.

**iproniazid** is an ANTIDEPRESSANT drug, a MAO INHIBITOR (mono amine oxidase inhibitor, or MAOI) used accordingly to treat depressive illness. Administration is oral in the form of tablets. It is not suitable for children.
▲ side-effects: dizziness is fairly common. There may also be headache, dry mouth, blurred vision and tremor; some patients experience constipation and difficulty in urinating; a rash may break out. Susceptible patients may undergo psychotic episodes.
● warning: iproniazid should not be administered to patients with disease of the liver or the blood vessels, or epilepsy. Treatment with this drug requires the strict avoidance of certain foods (particularly cheese, pickled fish or meat extracts), of alcohol, and of certain other medications; professional counselling on this subject is utterly essential.

Withdrawal of treatment should be gradual.

**iron** is a metallic element essential to the body in several ways, and especially important in its role as transporter of oxygen around the body (in the form of the red blood cell constituent oxyhaemoglobin); it is also retained in the muscles. Dietary deficiency of iron leads to any of several forms of anaemia: good food sources include meats, particularly liver. Iron is administered therapeutically mostly to make up a dietary deficiency (and so treat anaemia). Supplements may be administered orally (in the form of FERROUS FUMARATE, FERROUS GLUCONATE, FERROUS GLYCINE SULPHATE, FERROUS SUCCINATE, FERROUS SULPHATE, and other salts) or by injection or infusion (in the form of iron dextran and other preparations). There are also many iron-and-vitamin supplements available to prevent deficiencies of either (particularly during pregnancy).

**Ironorm** (*Wallace*) is three preparations of a mineral-and-VITAMIN compound. Available without prescription is a tonic (or elixir) containing IRON (in the form of ferric ammonium citrate), calcium, PHOSPHORUS, most forms of vitamin B, and liver extract. Available only on prescription are capsules containing iron (in the form of FERROUS SULPHATE), several forms of vitamin B, ascorbic acid (vitamin C) and fractionated liver. Also available only on prescription are ampoules of the plasma-and-iron infusion fluid, iron dextran complex.

**Ismelin** (*Ciba/Zyma*) is a proprietary preparation of the antihypertensive drug guanethidine monosulphate, available only on prescription. It is produced in two entirely different forms for two entirely different purposes by two manufacturers – but under the same trade name. In the form of tablets (in two strengths) and in ampoules for injection, Ismelin is used to treat moderate to severe high blood pressure (hypertension) and is administered simultaneously with either a DIURETIC (such as a thiazide) or a BETA-BLOCKER. In the form of eye-drops, Ismelin is used to relieve pressure within the eyeball in the treatment of glaucoma, for which its effect is often enhanced by the simultaneous administration of the hormone ADRENALINE.

▲/ ✹ side-effects/warning: *see* GUANETHIDINE MONOSULPHATE.

**Ismo** (*MCP Pharmaceuticals*) is a proprietary VASODILATOR, available only on prescription, used to assist in the treatment of congestive heart failure and to prevent attacks of angina pectoris (heart pain). Produced in the form of tablets (in three strengths) and as sustained-release tablets (Ismo Retard), it is a preparation of isosorbide mononitrate, and is not recommended for children.

▲/ ✹ side-effects/warning: *see* ISOSORBIDE MONONITRATE.

**isoaminile citrate** is a drug that suppresses a cough (ANTITUSSIVE); such drugs are used medically only when absolutely necessary, and when sputum retention is guaranteed to do no harm. Administration is oral in the form of a linctus.
▲ side-effects: constipation is often associated with treatment.
✹ warning: isoaminile citrate should not be administered to patients with any impairment of airflow in the respiratory passages (as in asthma), or who would find sputum retention a hazard (as in chronic bronchitis).

*Related article:* DIMYRIL; ISOAMINILE LINCTUS.

**isoaminile linctus** is a non-proprietary preparation of isoaminile citrate, available only on prescription, used only under specific circumstances to treat a dry or persistent and painful cough (ANTITUSSIVE). It is produced in the form of a syrup for dilution (the potency of the syrup once dilute is retained for 14 days).
▲/ ✹ side-effects/warning: *see* ISOAMINILE CITRATE.

**Isocal** (*Mead Johnson*) is a proprietary, non-prescription, gluten-free liquid, which is a complete nutritional diet for patients who are severely undernourished (such as with anorexia nervosa) or who have some problem of absorption of food (such as following gastrectomy). Also lactose-free, Isocal contains protein, carbohydrate and fats, with vitamins and minerals, but is unsuitable as the sole source of nutrition for children, and unsuitable altogether for children aged under 12 months.

**isocarboxazid** is an ANTIDEPRESSANT drug, an MAO INHIBITOR (mono amine oxidase inhibitor, or MAOI) used accordingly to treat depressive illness. Administration is oral in the form of tablets. It is not suitable for children.
▲ side-effects: dizziness is fairly common. There may also be headache, dry mouth, blurred vision and tremor; some patients experience constipation and difficulty in urinating; a rash may break out. Susceptible patients may undergo psychotic episodes.
✹ warning: isocarboxazid should not be administered to patients with disease of the liver or the

blood vessels, or epilepsy. Treatment with this drug requires the strict avoidance of certain foods (particularly cheese, pickled fish or meat extracts), of alcohol, and of certain other medications; professional counselling on this subject is utterly essential. Withdrawal of treatment should be gradual.
*Related article:* MARPLAN.

**isoconazole** is an ANTIFUNGAL drug, one of the IMIDAZOLES, used particularly to treat fungal infections of the vagina and anogenital area. Administration is in the form of a cream or as vaginal tablets (pessaries), usually as a single-dose treatment. It is not recommended for children.
▲ side-effects: there may be local irritation, and even a temporary burning sensation.
*Related article:* TRAVOGYN.

**isoetharine** is a SYMPATHOMIMETIC drug (and mild VASOCONSTRICTOR) used primarily to treat the bronchospasm of asthma and chronic bronchitis. Administration (in the form of isoetharine hydrochloride or isoetharine mesylate) is oral in the form of sustained-release tablets, or topical (in combination) as an aerosol inhalant.
▲ side-effects: there may be headache, nervous tension, tremor of the hands, sweating, increased heart rate and heartbeat irregularities, and a decrease in blood potassium levels.
✵ warning: isoetharine hydrochloride should be administered with caution to patients with heart disease or excessive secretion of thyroid hormones (hyperthyroidism), who are diabetic (in which case regular blood sugar counts are

essential during treatment), or who are pregnant or elderly.
*Related articles:*
BRONCHILATOR; NUMOTAC.

**isoflurane** is a GENERAL ANAESTHETIC related to ENFLURANE, produced as a gas to be used in solution with oxygen or nitrous oxide-oxygen. Administration is through a specially calibrated vaporiser. It is used particularly for the initial induction of anaesthesia.
▲ side-effects: there may be an increase in heart rate accompanied by a fall in blood pressure (especially in younger patients).
✵ warning: treatment depresses respiration. The drug also produces muscle relaxation, and/or enhances the effect of muscle-relaxant drugs administered simultaneously.
*Related article:* FORANE.

**Isogel** (*Allen & Hanburys*) is a proprietary form of the type of laxative known as a bulking agent, which works by increasing the overall mass of faeces within the rectum, so stimulating bowel movement. It is thus used both to relieve constipation and to relieve diarrhoea, and also in the control of faecal consistency for patients with a colostomy. Produced in the form of granules for solution in water, Isogel is a preparation of ispaghula husk.
▲/✵ side-effects/warning: *see* ISPAGHULA HUSK.

**isometheptene mucate** is a SYMPATHOMIMETIC drug used in combination with a sedative (such as dichloralphenazone) to treat migraine attacks. Administration is oral in the form of capsules.
▲ side-effects: there may be dizziness associated with peripheral disturbances in blood circulation.

● warning: the combination
should not be administered to
patients with glaucoma; it
should be administered with
caution to those with
cardiovascular disease, or
those on MAO INHIBITOR
therapy.
*Related article:* MIDRID.

**Isomil** (*Abbott*) is a proprietary,
non-prescription, gluten-free
powder that when reconstituted is
a complete nutritional diet for
patients – especially infants –
who are unable to tolerate milk
or milk sugars. Also, therefore,
milk protein-free and lactose-
free, Isomil contains protein,
carbohydrate and fats,
plus vitamins and
minerals.

**isoniazid** is an ANTITUBERCULAR
drug used, as is normal in the
treatment of tuberculosis, in
combination with other
antibacterial drugs to defeat
bacterial resistance. It is also
administered to prevent the
contraction of tuberculosis by
close associates of an infected
patient. Administration is oral
in the form of tablets or as a
non-proprietary elixir, or by
injection.
▲ side-effects: there may be
nausea with vomiting. High
dosage may lead to sensitivity
reactions, including a rash,
and in susceptible patients to a
peripheral neuritis leading to
loss of sensation in the hands
and feet, convulsions and/or
psychotic episodes.
● warning: isoniazid should not
be administered to patients
with liver disease induced by
drug treatment; it should be
administered with caution to
those with impaired kidney or
liver function, epilepsy or
alcoholism, or who are
lactating.
*Related article:* RIMIFON.

**isoprenaline** is a synthetic
substance closely related to
the hormone ADRENALINE. In
the form of isoprenaline
sulphate it is a BETA-
RECEPTOR STIMULANT and
VASODILATOR produced as an
inhalant or in the form of
tablets to be held under the
tongue, that is used primarily
to treat the bronchospasm of
asthma and chronic
bronchitis. In the form of
isoprenaline hydrochloride,
this SYMPATHOMIMETIC is
administered by injection to
stimulate the heart in
emergencies when the rate is
very low and in some disease
states.
▲ side-effects: there may be
headache, nervous tension,
tremor of the hands, sweating,
increased heart rate and
heartbeat irregularities, and a
decrease in blood potassium
levels. Administration as an
inhalant results in few of these
side-effects.
● warning: isoprenaline should
be administered with caution
to patients with heart disease
or excessive secretion of
thyroid hormones
(hyperthyroidism), who are
diabetic (in which case regular
blood sugar counts are
essential during treatment),
or who are pregnant or
elderly.
*Related articles:* MEDIHALER-
ISO; SAVENTRINE.

**Isopto** (*Alcon*) is a series of
proprietary preparations of
various drugs, all available only
on prescription. Each preparation
of Isopto is used in the form of
eye-drops, used variously to treat
infections such as conjunctivitis,
blepharitis, and glaucoma, and to
facilitate inspection of the eye.
The range includes the
preparation Isopto Cetamide
(comprising the sulphonamide

sulphacetamide sodium and the synthetic tear medium hypromellose).

▲/● side-effects/warning: *see* PRIMARY CONSTITUENTS LISTED ABOVE.

**Isordil** (*Ayerst*) is a proprietary, non-prescription VASODILATOR used to treat acute congestive heart failure, to assist in the treatment of chronic congestive heart failure, and to prevent attacks of angina pectoris (heart pain). Produced in the form of tablets (in three strengths) and as sustained-release capsules (under the trade name Isordil Tembids), it is a preparation of isosorbide dinitrate, and is not recommended for children.

▲/● side-effects/warning: *see* ISOSORBIDE DINITRATE.

**isosorbide dinitrate** is a VASODILATOR used to treat acute congestive heart failure, to assist in the treatment of chronic congestive heart failure, and to prevent attacks of angina pectoris (heart pain). Administration is oral in the form of tablets (for swallowing, chewing, or holding under the tongue) or as sustained-release capsules, or by infusion.

▲ side-effects: there may be headache, with flushing and dizziness; the heart rate may increase.

● warning: isosorbide dinitrate should be administered with extreme caution to patients with low blood pressure (hypotension) or severe forms of anaemia. Monitoring of heart function during treatment is advisable. *Related articles:* CEDOCARD; ISORDIL; SONI-SLO; SORBICHEW; SORBID SA; SORBITRATE; VASCARDIN.

**isosorbide mononitrate** is a VASODILATOR used to assist in the treatment of chronic congestive

heart failure, and to prevent attacks of angina pectoris (heart pain). Administration is oral in the form of tablets.

▲ side-effects: there may be headache, with flushing and dizziness; the heart rate may increase.

● warning: isosorbide mononitrate should be administered with caution to patients who have low blood pressure (hypotension). Monitoring of heart function during treatment is advisable. *Related articles:* ELANTAN; ISMO; ISOTRATE; MONIT; MONO-CEDOCARD 20.

**Isotrate** (*Thames*) is a proprietary VASODILATOR, available only on prescription, used to prevent attacks of angina pectoris (heart pain). Produced in the form of tablets, it is a preparation of isosorbide mononitrate. It is not recommended for children.

▲/● side-effects/warning: *see* ISOSORBIDE MONONITRATE.

**isotretinoin** is a powerful drug of fairly recent provenance, derived from RETINOL (vitamin A), and used for the systemic treatment of severe acne that has failed to respond to more usual therapies. Full medical supervision is required during treatment, which may last for three or four months – during which (from about the second to the fourth week) there may actually be an exacerbation of the acne; if treatment fails, repeat courses should not be given. Administration is oral in the form of capsules (generally from hospitals only).

▲ side-effects: dry lips and mucous membranes, sore eyes, and joint and muscle pains are not uncommon; there may also be nose-bleeds and temporary hair loss.

● warning: isotretinoin should not be administered to patients who are pregnant or likely to

become so – the drug may cause congenital abnormalities in a foetus; effective contraceptive measures should be continued for at least one month after treatment has ceased. Blood fat levels and liver function should be regularly checked.
*Related article:* ROACCUTANE.

**isoxsuprine hydrochloride** is a SYMPATHOMIMETIC VASODILATOR that affects principally the blood vessels of the hands and feet, but also affects the blood supply to the brain. It is therefore used to relieve the symptoms of both cerebral and peripheral vascular disease. The drug also has the effect of inhibiting contractions of the womb, and is thus additionally used to prevent or stall premature labour. Administration is oral in the form of tablets and sustained-release capsules, or by injection or infusion.
▲ side-effects: flushing and an increase in heart rate with some heartbeat irregularity are not uncommon; there may also be nausea and vomiting.
✦ warning: isoxsuprine hydrochloride should not be administered to patients who have recently had bleeding from an artery, with heart disease or severe anaemia, or who towards the end of a pregnancy have any infection. Administration to stall or prevent premature labour may cause low blood pressure (hypotension) in the foetus.
*Related article:* DUVADILAN.

**ispaghula husk** is a high-fibre substance used as a LAXATIVE because it is an effective bulking agent – it increases the overall mass of faeces within the rectum, so stimulating bowel movement. It is also particularly useful in soothing the symptoms of

diverticular disease and irritable colon. Administration is oral, generally in the form of granules or a powder for solution in water.
▲ side-effects: there may be flatulence, so much as to distend the abdomen.
✦ warning: preparations of ispaghula husk should not be administered to patients with obstruction of the intestines, or failure of the muscles of the intestinal wall; it should be administered with caution to those with ulcerative colitis. Fluid intake during treatment should be higher than usual.
*Related articles:* AGIOLAX; FYBOGEL; ISOGEL; METAMUCIL; REGULAN.

**isradipine** is a CALCIUM ANTAGONIST drug, used as an ANTIHYPERTENSIVE to treat raised blood pressure (hypertension). It is available in the form of tablets.
▲ side-effects: these include flushing, dizziness, headache, palpitations and elevated heart rate, and oedema. Occasionally hypotension (lowered blood pressure) may occur, as well as rashes, gastrointestinal disturbances, weight gain and fatigue.
✦ warning: the dose should be reduced when treating patients with impaired liver or kidney function, and avoided in pregnancy. It should be given with caution to patients fitted with a pacemaker or with some types of heart defect.
*Related article:* PRESCAL.

**Istin** (*Pfizer*) is a proprietary form of the CALCIUM ANTAGONIST amlodipine, used as an ANTIHYPERTENSIVE to treat raised blood pressure (hypertension) and to prevent angina (heart pain). Available only on prescription, as amlodipine besylate, in tablets in two strengths.
▲ / ✦ side-effects/warning: *see* AMLODIPINE

**itraconazole** is a broad-spectrum ANTIFUNGAL drug of the triazole family. Orally absorbed, it is used to treat resistant forms of candidiasis (thrush, or moniliasis) of the vagina or vulva and for dermatophyte infections of the skin, or finger-nails by tinea organisms, including ringworm and athlete's foot. Itraconazole is broken down in the liver and should therefore not be given to individuals with impaired liver function.

▲ side-effects: nausea and gastrointestinal disturbance causing abdominal pains and dyspepsia may occur; there may also be headaches.

✺ warning: itraconazole should not be used with a patient with impaired liver function, in pregnancy or when lactating.

**ivermectin** is an ANTIFUNGAL drug that is not available in the United Kingdom. Ivermectin is used to treat the tropical disease onchocerciasis – infestation by the filarial worm-parasite Onchocerca volvulus. The destruction of the worms, however, releases antigens into the bloodstream and causes an allergic response, generally requiring the simultaneous administration of antihistamines or CORTICOSTEROIDS to control it. More than one course of treatment with ivermectin may be necessary to deal with the infestation.

▲ side-effects: headache, with nausea and vomiting, is not uncommon; the dermatitis associated with onchocerciasis may temporarily be aggravated, as may any associated conjunctivitis or other eye inflammation.

✺ warning: close medical supervision is essential during treatment.

**Jacksons** (*Ernest Jackson*) are proprietary, non-prescription throat lozenges. They contain acetic acid, camphor, bonzoic acid and menthol.

**Jectofer** (*Astra*) is a proprietary compound of iron sorbitol and citric acid, available only on prescription, used to replace IRON in patients with iron-deficiency anaemia. It is produced as a dark brown liquid for intramuscular injection.
▲ side-effects: rarely, there are heartbeat irregularities.
✿ warning: Jectofer should not be administered to patients with liver or kidney disease.

**Jexin** (*Duncan, Flockhart*) is a proprietary SKELETAL MUSCLE RELAXANT, available only on prescription, of the type known as competitive or non-depolarizing. It is used during surgical operations, but only after the patient has been rendered unconscious. Produced in ampoules for injection, Jexin's active constituent is tubocurarine chloride.
▲/✿ side-effects/warning: *see* TUBOCURARINE.

**Joy-Rides** (*Stafford-Miller*) is a proprietary, non-prescription ANTICHOLINERGIC formulation for the treatment of motion sickness. It contains the atropine-like drug hyoscine.
▲/✿ side-effects/warning: *see* HYOSCINE.

**Junifen** (*Boots*) is a proprietary, non-narcotic ANALGESIC, which has valuable additional anti-inflammatory properties. Available only on prescription, Junifen is used to relieve fever and moderate pain in children. It is produced in the form of a suspension for taking by mouth. It is a preparation of ibuprofen. Not recommended for children under one year.
▲/✿ side-effects/warning: *see* IBUPROFEN.

**Juvela** (*G F Dietary Supplies*) is a proprietary, non-prescription brand of gluten-free bread- and cake-mix, produced for patients with coeliac disease and other forms of gluten sensitivity. There is also a low-protein milk-free version for patients suffering from defects of protein metabolism such as phenylketonuria (PKU).

**Kabiglobulin** (*KabiVitrum*) is a proprietary preparation of human normal immunoglobulin (HNIG), part of the plasma of the blood that is directly concerned with immunity. Administered by intramuscular injection, Kabiglobulin is used to protect patients at risk from contact with hepatitis A virus, measles (rubeola) or at least to some degree rubella (German measles), or to replace some measure of immunity in patients who have suffered serious shock (as for example with large-scale burns).
 warning: see HNIG.

**Kabikinase** (*KabiVitrum*) is a proprietary form of the effective fibrinolytic drug streptokinase, used to treat and prevent blood clots, particularly in relation to all types of thrombosis. It is produced in the form of powder for reconstitution as a medium for injection.
▲/ side-effects/warning: see STREPTOKINASE.

**Kalspare** (*Armour*) is a proprietary compound DIURETIC, available only on prescription, used to treat the accumulation of fluids within the tissues (oedema). Produced in the form of tablets, it combines the THIAZIDE-related diuretic chlorthalidone with a second diuretic triamterene that has the complementary effect of retaining potassium in the body.
▲/ side-effects/warning: see CHLORTHALIDONE; TRIAMTERENE.

**Kalten** (*Stuart*) is a proprietary compound BETA-BLOCKER, available only on prescription, used to treat heartbeat irregularities and severe high blood pressure. Produced in the form of capsules, it combines the beta-blocker atenolol with a thiazide DIURETIC (HYDROCHLOROTHIAZIDE) and a complementary potassium-sparing diuretic (AMILORIDE hydrochloride). It is not recommended for children.
▲/ side-effects/warning: see ATENOLOL.

**Kamillosan** (*Norgine*) is a proprietary, non-prescription, water-based OINTMENT, used to treat and soothe nappy rash, cracked nipples and chapping on the hands. Its active constituents are various essences of chamomile.

**kanamycin** is a broad-spectrum ANTIBIOTIC of the aminoglycoside family, with activity against gram-positive bacteria but used primarily against serious infections caused by gram-negative bacteria. It is not orally absorbed and is therefore given by injection or infusion for the treatment of, for example, septicaemia, meningitis and infections of the heart (usually in conjunction with penicillin), the kidney and the prostate gland. Because of its toxicity to the ear (ototoxicity) potentially resulting in deafness, and its toxicity to the kidney (nephrotoxicity), treatment should be limited in duration. Because of the relatively frequent occurrence of bacterial resistance in some coliform bacteria, kanamycin has largely been replaced by gentamicin.
▲ side-effects: prolonged or high dosage may be damaging to the ear, causing deafness and balance disorders; treatment must be discontinued if this occurs; there may also be reversible kidney damage.
 warning: kanamycin should not be administered to patients who are pregnant or who suffer from myasthenia gravis. It should be administered with caution to those with Parkinsonism. As the drug is

excreted by the kidney, great care must be taken in patients with impaired kidney function. In such cases, and/or where dosage is high or prolonged, regular checks on kanamycin concentrations in the blood must be carried out.
*Related article:* KANNASYN.

**Kannasyn** (*Winthrop*) is a proprietary form of the aminoglycoside ANTIBIOTIC kanamycin sulphate, available only on prescription, used to treat serious bacterial infections. It is produced in the form of solution and as powder for reconstitution, in both cases for injection.
▲/● side-effects/warning: *see* KANAMYCIN.

**Kaodene** (*Boots*) is a proprietary, non-prescription, liquid preparation used to treat diarrhoea, containing the adsorbent kaolin with the opiate codeine phosphate. Not recommended for children aged under 5 years or patients with chronic liver disease (because it may cause sedation), Kaodene should also be used with caution by the elderly (in whom it may cause faecal impaction and constipation). In particular, fluid intake should be increased to more than normal. Prolonged use should be avoided.
▲/● side-effects/warning: *see* CODEINE PHOSPHATE.

**kaolin** is a white clay (china clay) which, when purified (and sometimes powdered), is used as an adsorbent particularly in ANTIDIARRHOEAL preparations (with or without opiates such as CODEINE PHOSPHATE or MORPHINE) but also to treat food poisoning and some digestive disorders. Occasionally used in poultices, it is additionally found in some dusting powders.
*Related articles:* KAODENE; KAOPECTATE; KLN.

**Kaopectate** (*Upjohn*) is a proprietary, non-prescription suspension of the ANTI-DIARRHOEAL adsorbent KAOLIN, in a form suitable for dilution (the potency of the dilute mixture is retained for 14 days) before being taken orally. During treatment, fluid intake should be increased to more than normal.

**Karvol** (*Crookes*) is a proprietary, non-prescription inhalant, which is not available from the National Health Service. It may be used to treat symptoms associated with infections of the nose and upper respiratory tract. Containing MENTHOL, THYMOL and several other extracts from plant oils, Karvol capsules may be crushed in a handkerchief or infused in hot water for the essences to be inhaled. It is not recommended for children.

**Kay-Cee-L** (*Geistlich*) is a proprietary, non-prescription form of potassium supplement, used to treat patients with deficiencies and to replace potassium in patients taking potassium-depleting drugs such as CORTICOSTEROIDS. It is produced in the form of a red syrup (not for dilution) containing potassium chloride.

**Kefadol** (*Dista*) is a proprietary ANTIBIOTIC, available only on prescription, used to treat both gram-positive and gram-negative bacterial infections. It may be used to prevent infections following abdominal surgery. Produced in the form of a powder for reconstitution as injections, Kefadol is a compound of the CEPHALOSPORIN cephamandole with sodium carbonate.
▲/● side-effects/warning: *see* CEPHAMANDOLE.

**Keflex** (*Lilly*) is a proprietary ANTIBIOTIC, available only on prescription, used to treat

sensitive bacterial infections.
Produced in the form of capsules
(in two strengths), tablets (in two
strengths) and as chewy tablets
(in two strengths), Keflex is a
preparation of the orally active
CEPHALOSPORIN cephalexin.
▲ / ✪ side-effects/warning: *see*
CEPHALEXIN.

**Keflin** (*Lilly*) is a proprietary
ANTIBIOTIC, available only on
prescription, used to treat
sensitive bacterial infections, but
also to prevent infection
following surgery. Produced in
the form of powder for
reconstitution as injections,
Keflin is a preparation of the
CEPHALOSPORIN cephalothin.
▲ / ✪ side-effects/warning: *see*
CEPHALOTHIN.

**Kefzol** (*Lilly*) is a proprietary
ANTIBIOTIC, available only on
prescription, used to treat
bacterial infections, but also to
provide freedom from infection
during surgery. Produced in the
form of powder for reconstitution
as injections, Kefzol is a
preparation of the
CEPHALOSPORIN cephazolin.
▲ / ✪ side-effects/warning: *see*
CEPHAZOLIN.

**Kelferon** (*MCP Pharmaceuticals*)
is a proprietary, non-prescription
preparation of the drug ferrous
glycine sulphate, used as an IRON
supplement in the treatment of
iron-deficiency anaemia, and
produced in the form of tablets.
▲ / ✪ side-effects/warning: *see*
FERROUS GLYCINE SULPHATE.

**Kelfizine W** (*Farmitalia Carlo
Erba*) is a proprietary ANTIBIOTIC,
available only on prescription,
used primarily to treat chronic
bronchitis and infections of the
urinary tract. Produced in the
form of tablets, Kelfizine W is a
preparation of the SULPHONAMIDE
sulfametopyrazine.

▲ / ✪ side-effects/warning: *see*
SULFAMETOPYRAZINE.

**Kelfolate** (*MCP Pharmaceuticals*)
is a proprietary, non-prescription
compound of iron-rich FERROUS
GLYCINE SULPHATE and FOLIC ACID
(a vitamin of the B complex), used
to prevent iron and vitamin
deficiency during pregnancy.
▲ side-effects: there may be
gastrointestinal upsets with
diarrhoea following large
doses.
✪ warning: prolonged
administration may cause
constipation.

**Kelocyanor** (*Lipha*) is a
proprietary CHELATING AGENT,
available only on prescription,
that is an emergency antidote to
cyanide poisoning. It is produced
in the form of ampoules for
injection, containing dicobalt
edetate in glucose solution.
▲ side-effects: *see* DICOBALT
EDETATE.

**Kemadrin** (*Wellcome*) is a
proprietary preparation of the
ANTICHOLINERGIC procyclidine
hydrochloride, available only on
prescription, used in the
treatment of parkinsonism and to
control tremors within drug-
induced states involving
involuntary movement (*see*
ANTIPARKINSONISM). Produced in
the form of tablets and in
ampoules for injection, Kemadrin
is not recommended for children.
▲ / ✪ side-effects/warning: *see*
PROCYCLIDINE.

**Kemicetine** (*Farmitalia Carlo
Erba*) is a proprietary, broad-
spectrum ANTIBIOTIC, available
only on prescription. Produced in
the form of powder for
reconstitution as injections,
Kemicetine is a preparation of the
powerful drug chloramphenicol
which, because of its potential
toxicity, is generally used
systemically only to treat life-
threatening infections.

▲/✿ side-effects/warning: *see* CHLORAMPHENICOL.

**Kenalog** (*Squibb*) is a proprietary form of the anti-inflammatory glucocorticoid (corticosteroid) drug triamcinolone acetonide, available only on prescription. Produced in the form of pre-filled hypodermics, Kenalog is used in two different ways in order to achieve either of two distinct purposes: intramuscular injection relieves allergic states (such as hay fever or pollen induced asthma) and some collagen disorders, and can reduce severe dermatitis; injection directly into a joint relieves pain, swelling and stiffness (such as with rheumatoid arthritis, bursitis and tenosynovitis). It is not recommended for children aged under 6 years.

▲/✿ side-effects/warning: *see* TRIAMCINOLONE ACETONIDE.

**keratolytics** are drugs and preparations intended to clear the skin of thickened, horny patches (hyperkeratoses) and scaly areas, as occur in some forms of eczema, ichthyosis and psoriasis, and in the treatment of acne. The standard, classic keratolytic is salicylic acid, generally used in very mild solution. Others include ichthammol, coal tar, etretinate and dithranol (which is the most powerful), several of which can usefully be applied in the form of paste inside an impregnated bandage.

*Related articles:* COAL TAR; DITHRANOL; ETRETINATE; ICHTHAMMOL; SALICYLIC ACID; ZINC PASTE.

**Kerecid** (*Smith, Kline & French*) is a proprietary preparation, available only on prescription, used to treat herpes simplex infections of the eye. Containing a mild solution of the antiviral agent idoxuridine, it is produced

in the form of eye-drops (with polyvinyl alcohol) for use during the day.

✿ warning: *see* idoxuridine.

**Keri** (*Westwood*) is a proprietary, non-prescription lotion used to soften dry skin and to relieve itching. Active constituents include liquid paraffin and lanolin oil. It is produced in a pump pack, and is intended to be massaged into the skin.

**Kerlone** (*Lorex*) is a proprietary BETA-BLOCKER, available only on prescription, used to treat high blood pressure (*see* ANTI-HYPERTENSIVE). It is produced in the form of tablets consisting (as an antihypertensive) of a preparation of betaxolol hydrochloride. Kerlone is not recommended for children; dosage should be reduced for the elderly (at least initially), and in patients with kidney impairment.

▲/✿ side-effects/warning: *see* BETAXOLOL HYDROCHLORIDE.

**Keromask** (*Innoxa*) is the name of a proprietary, non-prescription camouflage cream, in two shades, designed for use in masking scars and other skin disfigurements; there is an additional finishing powder. It may be obtained on prescription if the skin disfigurement is the result of surgery or is giving rise to emotional disturbance.

**Kest** (*Berk*) is a proprietary, non-prescription LAXATIVE, which is not available from the National Health Service. Produced in the form of tablets containing MAGNESIUM SULPHATE and phenolphthalein, Kest is not recommended for children.

▲ side-effects: laxative effects may continue for several days; there may be dysfunction of the kidneys, leading possibly to discoloration of the urine. A mild skin rash may appear.

**Ketalar** (*Parke-Davis*) is a proprietary preparation of the general ANAESTHETIC ketamine, in the form of ketamine chloride. Available only on prescription, Ketalar is produced as vials for injection (in three strengths).
▲ / ✿ side-effects/warning: *see* KETAMINE.

**ketamine** is a general ANAESTHETIC that is used mainly for surgery on children, in whom hallucinogenic side-effects seem to appear less often than in adults. Ketamine has a good reputation for increasing muscle tone, maintaining good air passage, and having fair analgesic qualities in doses too low for actual anaesthesia (and the hallucinations can be avoided through the simultaneous use of other drugs). Administration is either by intramuscular injection or by intravenous infusion.
▲ side-effects: transient hallucinations may occur. Recovery is relatively slow.
✿ warning: ketamine should not be administered to patients who suffer from high blood pressure (hypertension) or who are mentally ill.
*Related article:* KETALAR.

**ketazolam** is an ANXIOLYTIC drug, one of the BENZODIAZEPINES, used to treat chronic states of anxiety. Dosage must be measured to each patient's individual response. It is also sometimes used to relieve muscle spasm and as a muscle relaxant.
▲ side-effects: drowsiness and lethargy are common, with or without dizziness; there may be a dry mouth and headache. Occasionally there is a hypersensitivity reaction.
✿ warning: sedative effects may inhibit intricate movement or rapid reaction, and may

increase the effect of alcohol. Dosage should be reduced for the elderly and for patients with impaired functioning of the kidneys or liver.

**ketoconazole** is a broad-spectrum ANTIFUNGAL agent, an imidazole that is effective when taken orally, used to treat deep-seated fungal infections (mycoses) or superficial ones that have not responded to other treatment. In particular, ketoconazole is used to treat resistant candidiasis (thrush, or moniliasis) and serious dermatophytic infections of the skin or fingernails.
▲ side-effects: liver damage may occur – and to a serious extent; rarely there may be an itching skin rash, or nausea.
✿ warning: ketoconazole should not be administered to patients who have impaired liver function, or who are pregnant. Because it may cause serious liver toxicity it should not be used for minor fungal infections.
*Related article:* NIZORAL.

**ketoprofen** is a non-steroid, ANTI-INFLAMMATORY, non-narcotic ANALGESIC drug, used to treat rheumatic and muscular pain caused by inflammation, and to treat gout. It is produced in the form of capsules and anal suppositories. In all forms, the drug should be taken with food in order to avoid possible gastrointestinal upset.
▲ side-effects: there may be gastrointestinal upset; suppositories may cause irritation.
✿ warning: use with caution in the presence of gastric ulceration, liver or kidney damage, allergic disorders or pregnancy. It tends to enhance the effect of anticoagulant drugs. Dosage should be closely monitored.

*Related articles:* ALRHEUMAT;
ORUDIS; ORUVAIL.

**ketotifen** is an effective
ANTIHISTAMINE used primarily to
prevent asthmatic attacks,
although it may alternatively be
used to treat other allergic
disorders. Taken orally, it may
require up to a month to become
fully operational, and may in the
meantime cause some minor but
inconvenient side-effects.
Administration should be
simultaneous with a meal.
▲ side-effects: ketotifen may
cause drowsiness and dryness
in the mouth; the ability to
drive a vehicle or operate
machinery may be affected.
● warning: consumption of
alcohol should be avoided
during treatment.
*Related article:* ZADITEN.

**Ketovite** (*Paines & Byrne*) is a
proprietary MULTIVITAMIN
supplement, available only on
prescription, used as an adjunct
in synthetic diets. Produced in the
form of tablets and a liquid, both
forms are intended to be taken
daily following a specified
regimen. The tablets contain
THIAMINE (vitamin B₁),
RIBOFLAVINE (vitamin B₂),
PYRIDOXINE (vitamin B₆),
CYANOCOBALAMIN (vitamin B₁₂),
NICOTINAMIDE (of the vitamin B
complex), FOLIC ACID (of the B
complex), ASCORBIC ACID (vitamin
C) and other useful factors; the
sugar-free liquid contains
RETINOL (vitamin A), and a form
of CALCIFEROL (vitamin D) in a
purified water base.

**Kiditard** (*Delandale*) is a
proprietary ANTIARRHYTHMIC
drug, available only on
prescription, used to treat
heartbeat irregularities and to
prevent speeding up of the heart
rate. Produced in the form of
capsules – the interval between

doses being the regulating factor
to suit each individual patient –
Kiditard is a preparation of
quinidine bisulphate. It is not
recommended for children.
▲/● side-effects/warning: *see*
QUINIDINE.

**Kinidin Durules** (*Astra*) is a
proprietary ANTIARRHYTHMIC
drug, available only on
prescription, used to treat
heartbeat irregularities and to
prevent speeding up of the heart
rate. Produced in the form of
tablets – the interval between
doses being the regulating factor
to suit each individual patient –
Kinidin Durules is a preparation
of quinidine bisulphate. It is not
recommended for children.
▲/● side-effects/warning: *see*
QUINIDINE.

**Klean-Prep** (*Norgine*) is a BOWEL
CLEANSING SOLUTION containing
macrogol (polyethylene glycol),
along with sodium and potassium
salts. It is used prior to colonic
surgery, colonoscopy or barium
enema to ensure the bowel is free
of solid contents.
▲/● side-effects/warning: *see*
BOWEL CLEANSING
SOLUTIONS.

**KLN** (*Ashe*) is a proprietary, non-
prescription mixture of the
mineral adsorbent KAOLIN with
the gelatinous adsorbent pectin
and the alkaline diuretic SODIUM
CITRATE. Prepared as a liquid for
oral intake, KLN is used to treat
diarrhoea. During the course of
treatment with KLN, fluid intake
by the patient should be increased
to more than normal.

**Kloref** (*Cox*) is a proprietary, non-
prescription form of POTASSIUM
supplement, used to treat patients
with deficiencies and to replace
potassium in patients taking
potassium-depleting drugs such as
CORTICOSTEROIDS. It is produced

in the form of effervescent tablets and (under the name Kloref-S) sachets of granules containing potassium chloride, potassium bicarbonate and betaine hydrochloride.

**Kolanticon** (*Merrell Dow*) is a proprietary, non-prescription, anticholinergic drug, which is not available from the National Health Service. An ANTACID, it is used to treat hyperacidity in the stomach and intestines, peptic ulcer, flatulence, and gastro-intestinal spasm. Produced in the form of a gel, Kolanticon is a sugar-free compound of dicyclomine hydrochloride, dimethicone, ALUMINIUM HYDROXIDE and MAGNESIUM oxide, for dilution with purified water (the potency of the dilute gel is retained for 14 days).

▲/✿ side-effects/warning: *see* DICYCLOMINE HYDROCHLORIDE.

**Konakion** (*Roche*) is a proprietary form of VITAMIN K – or phytomenadione – used to treat newborn infants in need of the vitamin, and to treat patients deficient in the vitamin because of fat malabsorption. It is produced in the form of (non-prescription) tablets, and ampoules for injection (available in two strengths, only on prescription).

**Kwells** (*Nicholas-Kiwi*) is a proprietary, ANTCHOLINERGIC, non-prescription, anti-motion sickness preparation containing hyoscine.
▲/✿ side-effects/warning: *see* HYOSCINE.

**labetalol hydrochloride** is a mixed BETA-BLOCKER and ALPHA-BLOCKER used to treat high blood pressure (hypertension) and to control blood pressure during surgery. Administration is oral in the form of tablets, and by injection. It is not recommended for children.

▲ side-effects: there may be lethargy and debility, headache and/or tingling of the scalp; rashes may break out. Higher dosages may lead to low blood pressure (hypotension).

✤ warning: labetalol hydrochloride should be administered with caution to patients who have heart failure, who are already taking drugs to control the heart rate, or who have a history of bronchospasm.
*Related article:* LABROCOL; TRANDATE.

**Labiton** (*L A B*) is a proprietary, non-prescription tonic, which is not available from the National Health Service. Used primarily to stimulate the appetite, Labiton contains the stimulant CAFFEINE, vitamin B in the form of THIAMINE, extract of kola nut, and ethyl alcohol. It is not recommended for children.

✤ warning: labiton should not be taken by patients who are already taking drugs that directly affect the central nervous system, or who have liver disease.

**Labophylline** (*LAB*) is a proprietary, non-prescription BRONCHODILATOR, used to treat asthmatic bronchospasm and chronic bronchitis. Produced in a form for injection or slow intravenous infusion. It is a preparation of the drug theophylline.

▲/✤ side-effects/warning: *see* THEOPHYLLINE.

**Laboprin** (*L A B*) is a proprietary, non-prescription preparation of the non-narcotic ANALGESIC aspirin, which is not available from the National Health Service. Produced in the form of tablets, Laboprin also contains the essential amino acid lysine. It is not recommended for children.

▲/✤ side-effects/warning: *see* ASPIRIN.

**Labosept** (*L A B*) is a proprietary, non-prescription form of pastilles used to treat mild fungal or bacterial infections of the mouth. The pastilles, to be sucked slowly, are not available from the National Health Service; their active constituent is the ANTISEPTIC drug DEQUALINIUM CHLORIDE.

**Labrocol** (*Lagap*) is a proprietary form of the mixed BETA-BLOCKER and ALPHA-BLOCKER labetalol hydrochloride, available only on prescription, used to treat high blood pressure (*see* ANTI-HYPERTENSIVE) and to control the heart rate during surgery. Produced in the form of tablets (in three strengths), Labrocol is not recommended for children.

▲/✤ side-effects/warning: *see* LABETALOL HYDROCHLORIDE.

**lachesine chloride** is an ANTICHOLINERGIC drug used to dilate the pupil of the eye, generally in order that the eye may be examined by an ophthalmologist, but sometimes to treat an inflammation in the eye or the eye muscle. It is useful in treating patients who are hypersensitive to other mydriatic drugs. Administration is in the form of eye-drops.

✤ warning: its dilating action is persistent, and prolonged treatment risks the precipitation of glaucoma. Driving may be difficult following mydriatic treatment.

**Lacri-Lube** (*Allergan*) is a proprietary, non-prescription form of liquid paraffin used as a lubricant for the eyes in patients whose tear glands are not functioning effectively. Produced in the form of an ointment, Lacri-Lube also contains HYDROUS WOOL FAT.
▲/✤ side-effects/warning: *see* LIQUID PARAFFIN.

**Lacticare** (*Stiefel*) is a proprietary, non-prescription skin emollient (softener and soother), used to treat chronic conditions of dry skin. Produced in the form of a lotion for topical application, Lacticare contains the simple sugar lactic acid and a moisturizer.

**lactulose** is a LAXATIVE that works by causing a volume of fluid to be retained in the colon through osmosis. Its action also discourages the increase of ammonia-producing microbes – although it may take up to 48 hours to have full effect.
▲ side-effects: rarely, there is nausea and vomiting.
✤ warning: lactulose should not be administered to patients with any form of intestinal obstruction. Because lactulose is itself a form of sugar, patients who have blood sugar level abnormalities should be checked before being treated.
*Related article:* DUPHALAC.

**Ladropen** (*Berk*) is a proprietary ANTIBIOTIC, available only on prescription, used to treat gram-positive bacterial infections of the skin and of the ear, nose and throat, and especially staphylococcal infections that prove to be resistant to penicillin. Produced in the form of capsules (in two strengths), Ladropen is a preparation of flucloxacillin. It is not suitable for children.

▲/✤ side-effects/warning: *see* FLUCLOXACILLIN.

**Lamprene** (*Geigy*) is a proprietary preparation of the phenazine drug clofamizine, used to halt the progress of leprosy. Available only on prescription and produced in the form of gelatin capsules, Lamprene is not recommended for children.
▲/✤ side-effects/warning: *see* CLOFAZIMINE.

**lanatoside C** is a CARDIAC GLUYCOSIDE drug that acts as a heart stimulant, used to treat heart failure and severe heartbeat irregularity. Administration is oral in the form of tablets; ingestion into the body causes the conversion of lanatoside C into another glycoside, digoxin.
▲/✤ side-effects/warning: *see* DIGOXIN.
*Related article:* CEDILANID.

**Lanitop** (*Roussel*) is a proprietary form of the CARDIAC GLYCOSIDE heart stimulant medigoxin, available only on prescription, used to treat congestive heart failure and severe heartbeat irregularity. It is produced in the form of tablets.
▲/✤ side-effects/warning: *see* MEDIGOXIN.

**lanolin** (hydrous wool fat) is a non-proprietary skin emollient (softener and soother) commonly used also as a base for other medications. It has some antibacterial properties, but in some patients can cause a sensitivity reaction (in the form usually of an eczematous rash).

**Lanoxin** (*Wellcome*) is a proprietary form of the powerful heart stimulant digoxin (a CARDIAC GLYCOSIDE), available only on prescription, used to treat heart failure and severe heartbeat irregularity. It is produced in the

form of tablets (in several strengths, under the names Lanoxin, Lanoxin 125 and Lanoxin PG), as an elixir (under the name Lanoxin PG Elixir) and in ampoules for injection (under the name Lanoxin Injection).
▲/ ✿ side-effects/warning: see DIGOXIN.

**Lanvis** (*Calmic*) is a proprietary CYTOTOXIC drug, available only on prescription, used to treat acute forms of leukaemia. An antimetabolite, it works by incorporating itself into new-forming cells or by combining with intracellular enzymes. Produced in the form of tablets, Lanvis is a preparation of thioguanine.
▲/ ✿ side-effects/warning: see THIOGUANINE.

**Laractone** (*Lagap*) is a proprietary DIURETIC drug, available only on prescription, used to treat accumulation of fluids within the tissues (oedema), particularly when due to cirrhosis of the liver. Produced in the form of tablets (in two strengths), Laractone is a preparation of the weak potassium-sparing diuretic spironolactone.
▲/ ✿ side-effects/warning: see SPIRONOLACTONE.

**Laraflex** (*Lagap*) is a proprietary, non-steroidal, ANTI-INFLAMMATORY non-narcotic ANALGESIC, available only on prescription, used to relieve pain – particularly rheumatic and arthritic pain – and to treat other musculo-skeletal disorders. Its active constituent is naproxen, and it is produced in the form of tablets (in two strengths). Not recommended for children, Laraflex should not be administered to patients with a peptic ulcer, gastrointestinal haemorrhage or asthma, or who are pregnant or lactating.

▲/ ✿ side-effects/warning: see NAPROXEN.

**Larapam** (*Lagap*) is a proprietary, non-steroidal, ANTI-INFLAMMATORY non-narcotic ANALGESIC, available only on prescription, used to relieve pain – particularly rheumatic and arthritic pain – and to treat other musculo-skeletal disorders. Its active constituent is piroxicam, and it is produced in the form of tablets (in two strengths). Not recommended for children, Larapam should not be administered to patients with a peptic ulcer, gastrointestinal haemorrhage or asthma, or who are pregnant or lactating.
▲/ ✿ side-effects/warning: see PIROXICAM.

**Laratrim** (*Lagap*) is a proprietary, broad-spectrum ANTIBIOTIC, available only on prescription, used to treat infections of the urinary tract, the sinuses or the middle ear, an inflamed prostate gland, or exacerbated chronic bronchitis. Produced in the form of tablets (Laratrim Forte) and as a suspension (in two strengths, Laratrim Paediatric Suspension and Laratrim Adult Suspension), Laratrim is a compound combination of the drug trimethoprim and the SULPHO-NAMIDE sulphamethoxazole.
▲/ ✿ side-effects/warning: see CO-TRIMOXAZOLE.

**Largactil** (*May & Baker*) is a proprietary preparation of the powerful PHENOTHIAZINE drug chlorpromazine hydrochloride, used primarily to treat patients who are undergoing behavioural disturbances (as a major TRANQUILLIZER), or who are psychotic (as an ANTIPSYCHOTIC), particularly schizophrenic. It is also used to treat severe anxiety, or as an anti-emetic sedative prior to surgery. Available only on prescription, Largactil is produced in the form of tablets (in three strengths), as a syrup (under the name Largactil Syrup), as a suspension (under the name Largactil Forte Suspension), as anal suppositories (under the name Largactil Suppositories), and in ampoules for injection (under the name Largactil Injection). In the form of the suppositories and the ampoules for injection Largactil is not recommended for use with children.

▲/✚ side-effects/warning: see
    CHLORPROMAZINE
    HYDROCHLORIDE.

**Lariam** (*Roche*) is a proprietary ANTIMALARIAL preparation of the drug mefloquine, available only on prescription, used to prevent or treat falciprarum malaria where this is common and where there is chloroquine resistance. Available in the form of tablets.

▲/✚ side-effects/warning: see
    MEFLOQUINE.

**Larodopa** (*Roche*) is a proprietary form of the powerful drug levodopa, used in ANTI-PARKINSONISM treatment. It is particularly good at relieving the rigidity and slowness of movement associated with the disease, although it does not always improve the tremor. Produced in the form of tablets, Larodopa is not recommended for children.

▲/✚ side-effects/warning: see
    LEVODOPA.

**Lasikal** (*Hoechst*) is a proprietary compound DIURETIC drug, available only on prescription, used to treat accumulation of fluids in the tissues (oedema) in cases where extra potassium is also required. Produced in the form of two-layered tablets (consisting of a sustained-release matrix), Lasikal combines the

diuretic frusemide with POTASSIUM CHLORIDE. It is not suitable for children.

▲/✚ side-effects/warning: see
    FRUSEMIDE.

**Lasilactone** (*Hoechst*) is a proprietary compound DIURETIC, available only on prescription, used to treat accumulation of fluids within the tissues (oedema) in cases that have failed to respond to other forms of treatment. Produced in the form of capsules, Lasilactone combines the weak diuretic spironolactone with the powerful diuretic frusemide. It is not recommended for children.

▲/✚ side-effects/warning: see
    FRUSEMIDE;
    SPIRONOLACTONE.

**Lasipressin** (*Hoechst*) is a proprietary ANTIHYPERTENSIVE compound, available only on prescription, used to treat mild to moderate high blood pressure (hypertension). Produced in the form of tablets, Lasipressin contains the BETA-BLOCKER penbutolol sulphate with the DIURETIC frusemide.

▲/✚ side-effects/warning: see
    FRUSEMIDE; PENBUTOLOL
    SULPHATE.

**Lasix** (*Hoechst*) is a proprietary DIURETIC drug, available only on prescription, used to treat accumulation of fluids in the tissues (oedema), particularly when due to heart, kidney or liver disease, or associated with high blood pressure (hypertension). Produced in the form of tablets (in three strengths, the third under the name Lasix 500 for use in hospitals only), as a syrup for children (under the name Lasix Paediatric Liquid), and in ampoules for injection (under the name Lasix Injection, and intended particularly to treat conditions associated with cirrhosis of the liver).

▲ / ● side-effects/warning: *see* FRUSEMIDE.

**Lasix + K** (*Hoechst*) is a proprietary compound DIURETIC drug, available only on prescription, used to treat accumulation of fluids in the tissues (oedema) in cases where extra potassium is also required. Produced in the form of pairs of tablets (the one being the potassium supplement within a sustained-release matrix), Lasix + K combines the diuretic frusemide with POTASSIUM CHLORIDE. It is not suitable for children.

▲ / ● side-effects/warning: *see* FRUSEMIDE.

**Lasma** (*Pharmax*) is a proprietary, non-prescription BRONCHO-DILATOR, used to treat asthmatic bronchospasm, emphysema and chronic bronchitis. Produced in the form of sustained-release tablets, Lasma is a preparation of the xanthine drug theophylline. It is not recommended for children.

▲ / ● side-effects/warning: *see* THEOPHYLLINE.

**Lasonil** (*Bayer*) is a proprietary, non-prescription ointment used to soothe and treat piles (haemorrhoids) and anal itching. It contains heparinoids (which promote the resorption of fluids accumulating in the tissues) together with the absorptive agent hyaluronidase.

**Lassar's paste** is a non-proprietary formulation of ZINC OXIDE, salicylic acid and starch in white soft paraffin. Applied topically, it is used to treat hard, layered, dead skin. The compound must not be put on broken or inflamed skin.

**latamoxef disodium** is a third-generation CEPHALOSPORIN ANTIBIOTIC used to treat many

bacterial infections. Unlike early cephalosporins it has effective activity against many gram-negative bacteria. Administration is by injection.

▲ side-effects: there may be hypersensitivity reactions, effects on the white cells of the blood (on which it may have an anticoagulating influence). Rarely there is diarrhoea.

● warning: latamoxef should be used with caution in patients taking anticoagulants and with bleeding tendencies; it should be administered with caution to those known to have penicillin sensitivity, and not at all to those with known sensitivity to cephalosporins. Dosage should be reduced in patients with impaired liver function.

**\*laxatives** are preparations that promote defecation and so relieve constipation. There are several types. One major type is represented by faecal softeners (which soften the faeces for easier evacuation): they include LIQUID PARAFFIN. Another type is the bulking agent (which increases the overall volume of the faeces in the rectum and thus stimulates bowel movement): bulking agents are mostly what is also called fibre, and include BRAN, ISPAGHULA HUSK, METHYLCELLULOSE and STERCULIA. A third type is the stimulant laxative, which acts on the intestinal muscles to increase motility: many old-fashioned remedies are stimulants of this kind, including CASCARA, CASTOR OIL, FIGS ELIXIR, and SENNA – but there are modern variants too, such as BISACODYL, DANTHRON, DIOCTYL SODIUM SULPHO-SUCCINATE (docusate sodium) and SODIUM PICOSULPHATE. Some laxatives work by bringing in water from surrounding tissues, so increasing overall liquidity:

such osmotic laxatives include MAGNESIUM HYDROXIDE, MAGNESIUM SULPHATE and LACTULOSE. Suppositories and enemas also aid in promoting defecation.

**Laxoberal** (*Windsor*) is a proprietary, non-prescription LAXATIVE, which is not available from the National Health. A stimulant laxative, Laxoberal is produced in the form of a liquid containing sodium picosulphate.
▲/ ● side-effects/warning: *see* SODIUM PICOSULPHATE.

**Ledclair** (*Sinclair*) is a proprietary CHELATING AGENT, an antidote to poisoning from heavy metals, especially by lead, available only on prescription. Produced in liquid form in ampoules for injection, and as a cream for topical use on areas of skin that have become broken or sensitive through contact with the metals, Ledclair's active constituent is sodium calciumedetate.
▲/ ● side-effects/warning: *see* SODIUM CALCIUMEDETATE.

**Ledercort** (*Lederle*) is a proprietary form of the anti-inflammatory glucocorticoid (CORTICOSTEROID) drug triamcinolone, available only on prescription. Produced in the form of tablets (in two strengths) and, as triamcinolone acetonide, as a water-based cream and an anhydrous ointment, Ledercort treats inflammations of the skin (such as severe eczema), and particularly inflammations arising as a result of allergy.
▲/ ● side-effects/warning: *see* TRIAMCINOLONE; TRIAMCINOLONE ACETONIDE.

**Lederfen** (*Lederle*) is a proprietary, non-steroid, ANTI-INFLAMMATORY non-narcotic ANALGESIC, available only on prescription, used to relieve pain

– particularly rheumatic and arthritic pain – and to treat other musculo-skeletal disorders. Its active constituent is fenbufen, and it is produced in the form of tablets (in two strengths) and capsules (under the name Lederfen Capsules). Not recommended for children, Lederfen should not be administered to patients with a peptic ulcer, gastrointestinal haemorrhage or asthma, or who are pregnant or lactating.
▲/ ● side-effects/warning: *see* FENBUFEN.

**Ledermycin** (*Lederle*) is a proprietary ANTIBIOTIC, available only on prescription, used to treat infections of soft tissues, particularly of the upper respiratory tract. Produced in the form of tablets (in two strengths, the stronger under the name Ledermycin Tablets), Ledermycin is a preparation of the TETRACYCLINE demeclocycline hydrochloride.
▲/ ● side-effects/warning: *see* DEMECLOCYCLINE HYDROCHLORIDE.

**Lederspan** (*Lederle*) is a proprietary CORTICOSTEROID drug, available only on prescription, used to treat inflammation of the joints and the soft tissues. Produced in the form of a suspension in vials for injection (in two concentrations), Lederspan's active constituent is the corticosteroid triamcinolone hexacetonide.
▲/ ● side-effects/warning: *see* TRIAMCINOLONE HEXACETONIDE.

**Lem-sip** (*Nicholas-Kiwi*) is a proprietary, non-prescription cold relief preparation containing the non-narcotic ANALGESIC paracetamol, the SYMPATHOMIMETIC phenylephrine, sodium citrate and ascorbic acid.

▲/✿ side-effects/warning: *see*
ASCORBIC ACID;
PARACETAMOL;
PHENYLEPHRINE; SODIUM
CITRATE.

**Lenium** (*Winthrop*) is a
proprietary, non-prescription
cream shampoo containing
SELENIUM SULPHIDE, a salt
thought to act as an antidandruff
agent. Lenium should not be used
within 48 hours of a hair colorant
or a permanent wave.

**Lentard MC** is a proprietary, non-
prescription preparation of the
protein hormone insulin, in the
form of insulin zinc suspension,
used to treat diabetic patients.
Containing highly purified bovine
and porcine insulin, Lentard
MC's effect is of intermediate
duration, intended to maintain
background residual levels of the
hormone. It is produced in vials
for injection.
▲/✿ side-effects/warning: *see*
INSULIN.

**Lentizol** (*Parke-Davis*) is a
proprietary ANTIDEPRESSANT,
available only on prescription,
used to treat depressive illness,
and particularly in cases where
some degree of sedation is called
for. Produced in the form of
capsules (in two strengths),
Lentizol is a preparation of the
TRICYCLIC amitriptyline
hydrochloride, and is
not recommended for
children.
▲/✿ side-effects/warning: *see*
AMITRIPTYLINE.

**Leo K** (*Leo*) is a proprietary, non-
prescription form of POTASSIUM
supplement, used to treat patients
with deficiencies and to replace
potassium in patients being
treated with potassium-depleting
drugs such as
CORTICOSTEROIDS. It is produced
in the form of tablets containing
potassium chloride.

▲/✿ side-effects/warning: *see*
POTASSIUM CHLORIDE.

**Lergoban** (*Riker*) is a proprietary,
non-prescription ANTIHISTAMINE
drug used to treat various allergic
conditions, particularly
conditions of the nose (hay fever)
and skin (urticaria). Produced in
the form of tablets, Lergoban is a
preparation of diphenylpyraline
hydrochloride. It is not
recommended for children.
▲/✿ side-effects/warning: *see*
DIPHENYLPYRALINE
HYDROCHLORIDE.

**Leukeran** (*Calmic*) is a
proprietary CYTOTOXIC drug,
available only on prescription,
used to treat various forms of
cancer, particularly leukaemia,
ovarian cancer and certain
lymphomas. Produced in the form
of tablets (in two strengths),
Leukeran is a preparation of
chlorambucil.
▲/✿ side-effects/warning: *see*
CHLORAMBUCIL.

**levamisole** is an ANTHELMINTIC
drug used specifically to treat
infestation by roundworms.
Effective, it is also well tolerated
and side-effects are rare.
Occasionally there may be mild
nausea.

**levobunolol hydrochloride** is a
BETA-BLOCKER used in the form of
eye-drops to treat glaucoma. It is
thought to work by slowing the
rate of production of the aqueous
humour in the eyeball, but it may
be absorbed and have systemic
effects as well.
▲ side-effects: there may be
periods in which the eyes
temporarily become dry; at
such times there may be
infections such as
conjunctivitis.
✿ warning: because systemic
absorption may occur,
levobunolol hydrochloride

should be administered with caution to patients with slow heart rate, heart failure or asthma.

*Related article:* BETAGEN.

**levodopa** is an immensely powerful ANTIPARKINSONISM drug used to treat parkinsonism (but not the symptoms of parkinsonism induced by drugs). Effective in reducing the slowness of movement and rigidity associated with parkinsonism, levodopa is not so successful in controlling the tremor. Administration is in the form of capsules or tablets, often combined with another form of drug that inhibits the conversion of levodopa to dopamine outside the brain. It is the presence of such an inhibitor that may produce involuntary movements. Initial dosage should be minimal and increase gradually; intervals between doses may be critical to each individual patient. Treated with levodopa a patient may be expected to improve quality of life for 6 to 18 months, and for that improvement to obtain for up to another 2 years; thereafter a slow decline is to be expected.

▲ side-effects: there may be nausea, dizziness, irregularity of the heart rate, insomnia and restlessness, and discoloration of the urine. Psychiatric symptoms and involuntary movements may direct dosage quantities.

● warning: levodopa should not be administered to patients with a specific form of glaucoma; it should be administered with caution to those with heart disease, psychiatric illness, diabetes or peptic ulcers. Monitoring of heart, blood, liver and kidney functions is advisable during prolonged treatment; some check on psychological

disposition should also be made.

*Related articles:* BROCADOPA; LARODOPA; MADOPAR; SINEMET.

**levonorgestrel** is a female sex hormone, a PROGESTOGEN used especially in ORAL CONTRACEPTIVES – in which it may or may not be combined with an OESTROGEN. It is occasionally alternatively used, also in combination with oestrogens, in hormone replacement therapy in menopausal women. The hormone NORGESTREL is a weaker form of levonorgestrel.

▲ side-effects: there may be nausea and vomiting, with a headache; menstrual irregularities and breast tenderness are common, but there may also be weight gain and depression. Some patients experience skin disorders.

● warning: levonorgestrel should not be administered to patients who are pregnant, or with vascular or liver disease, cancer of the liver or of the breast, or vaginal bleeding. It should be administered with caution to those with heart disease or high blood pressure (hypertension), diabetes or migraine.

*Related articles:* EUGYNON 30; LOGYNON; MICROGYNON 30; MICROVAL; Norgeston; OVRAN; OVRANETTE; SCHERING PC4; TriNORDIOL.

**Levophed** (*Winthrop*) is a proprietary VASOCONSTRICTOR, a sympathomimetic used in emergencies to raise the blood pressure in cases of dangerously low blood pressure or even cardiac arrest. Available only on prescription, Levophed is produced in ampoules (in two strengths) for injection or infusion following dilution, and is a preparation of noradrenaline acid tartrate.

▲ / ✸ side-effects/warning: see
NORADRENALINE.

**levorphanol** is a narcotic
ANALGESIC used to treat severe
pain. Because it is a narcotic, its
prolonged use may lead to
dependence (addiction) and the
proprietary form of the drug is
therefore on the controlled drugs
list. Nevertheless it causes fewer
sedative effects than many other
narcotics, and is administered (as
levorphanol tartrate) orally in the
form of tablets, or by injection.
▲ side-effects: breathing may
become shallow, and coughing
be suppressed. Commonly there
is also constipation and urine
retention, with or without
nausea. There may be pain at
the site of injection.
✸ warning: levorphanol should
not be administered to patients
who suffer from respiratory
difficulties (such as asthma),
from head injury or from
pressure within the skull; it
should be administered with
extreme caution to patients
with low blood pressure
(hypotension), thyroid
problems, or impaired kidney
or liver function. Dosage
should be reduced for elderly
or debilitated patients.

**Lexotan** (*Roche*) is a proprietary
ANXIOLYTIC drug, available on
prescription only to private
patients, used to treat anxiety in
the short term. Produced in the
form of tablets (in two strengths),
Lexotan is a preparation of the
BENZODIAZEPINE bromazepam. It
is not recommended for children.
▲ / ✸ side-effects/warning: see
BROMAZEPAM.

**Lexpec** (*RP Drugs*) is a
proprietary preparation of the
VITAMIN B folic acid, available
only on prescription, used to treat
body deficiency of the vitamin (as
occurs in certain types of

anaemia). It is produced in the
form of a syrup. Two further
versions are also available, both
including iron (in the form of
ferric ammonium citrate), under
the names Lexpec with Iron and
Lexpec with Iron-M, and intended
as mineral-and-vitamin
supplements for use in treating
anaemia during pregnancy.
▲ side-effects: the iron
preparations may cause nausea
or constipation, and should be
drunk through a straw because
the syrup can cause a
discoloration of the teeth.
✸ warning: the iron preparations
should not be taken by patients
who are already being treated
with tetracycline antibiotics.

**Libanil** (*Approved Prescription
Services*) is a proprietary
preparation of the
SULPHONYLUREA glibenclamide,
used to treat adult-onset diabetes;
it works by promoting the
formation of insulin in whatever
remains of the capacity of the
pancreas for it, and increasing the
number of insulin receptors.
Available only on prescription,
Libanil is produced in the form of
tablets (in two strengths).
▲ / ✸ side-effects/warning: see
GLIBENCLAMIDE.

**Librium** (*Roche*) is a proprietary
form of the BENZODIAZEPINE
chlordiazepoxide, used to treat
anxiety, insomnia in the short
term, and symptoms of acute
alcohol withdrawal. Available on
prescription only to private
patients, Librium is produced in
the form of tablets (in three
strengths), capsules (in two
strengths) and powder for
reconstitution as a medium for
injection. It is not recommended
for children.
▲ / ✸ side-effects/warning: see
CHLORDIAZEPOXIDE.

**Lidocaton** is a proprietary
preparation of the local

ANAESTHETIC lignocaine, used in cartridges for dental surgery.
▲/● side-effects/warning: *see* LIGNOCAINE.

**lidoflazine** is a CALCIUM ANTAGONIST and VASODILATOR used to reduce blood pressure and prevent recurrent attacks of angina pectoris (heart pain). Administration is oral in the form of tablets.
▲ side-effects: the heart rate is increased. There may be headache, dizziness and ringing in the ears (tinnitus); some patients have nightmares. Gastrointestinal disturbance may occur.
● warning: lidoflazine should not be administered to patients who are pregnant.

**Liga** (*Cow and Gate*) are egg and gluten-free rusks available without prescription for people requiring a gluten-free diet.

**lignocaine** is primarily a local ANAESTHETIC, the medium of choice for very many topical or minor surgical procedures, especially in dentistry (because it is absorbed directly through mucous membranes). It is, for example, used on the throat to prepare a patient for bronchoscopy. For general anaesthesia it may be combined with adrenaline. But it is also administered in the treatment of heart conditions involving heartbeat irregularities, and is effective in safely slowing the heart rate (particularly after a heart attack). Administration is (in the form of a solution of lignocaine hydrochloride) by infiltration, injection or infusion, or topically as a gel, an ointment, a spray, a lotion, or as eye-drops.
▲ side-effects: there is generally a slowing of the heart rate and a fall in blood pressure. Some patients under anaesthetic

become agitated, others enter a state of euphoria.
● warning: lignocaine should not be administered to patients with the neuromuscular disease myasthenia gravis; it should be administered with caution to those with heart or liver failure (in order not to cause depression of the central nervous system and convulsions), or from epilepsy. Dosage should be reduced for the elderly and the debilitated. Full facilities for emergency cardio-respiratory resuscitation should be on hand during anaesthetic treatment.
*Related articles:* DEPO-MEDRONE WITH LIDOCAINE; INSTILLAGEL; LIDOCATON; LIGNOSTAB; MINIMS LIGNOCAINE AND FLUORESCEIN; NEO-LIDOCATON; XYLOCAINE; XYLOCARD; XYLOTOX.

**Lignostab** is a proprietary preparation of the local ANAESTHETIC lignocaine, used in cartridges for dental surgery.
▲/● side-effects/warning: *see* LIGNOCAINE.

**Limbitrol** (*Roche*) is a proprietary compound ANTIDEPRESSANT, available on prescription only to private patients, used to treat depressive illness and associated anxiety. Produced in capsules (in two strengths, under the names Limbitrol 5 and Limbitrol 10), Limbitrol's active constituents are amitriptyline and chlordiazepoxide. It is not recommended for the elderly or for children.
▲/● side-effects/warning: *see* AMITRIPTYLINE; CHLORDIAZEPOXIDE.

**Limclair** (*Sinclair*) is a proprietary preparation of trisodium edetate, available only on prescription, used to treat the symptoms of an excess of calcium in the blood (hypercalcaemia). It is produced in ampoules for injection.

▲/◉ side-effects/warning: *see* TRISODIUM EDETATE.

**Limone** (*CliniMed*) is a proprietary, non-prescription deodorant spray, used to freshen and sanitize the appliance or bag that is attached to a stoma (an outlet on the skin surface) following ileostomy or colostomy (surgical curtailment of the intestines).

**Lincocin** (*Upjohn*) is a proprietary ANTIBIOTIC, available only on prescription, used to treat serious infections of the tissues and bones (particularly infections that prove to be resistant to penicillin). Produced in the form of capsules, as a syrup for dilution (the potency of the syrup once diluted is retained for 14 days) and in ampoules for injection, Lincocin is a preparation of lincomycin.

▲/◉ side-effects/warning: *see* LINCOMYCIN.

**lincomycin** is an ANTIBIOTIC, which used less commonly than it once was (because of side-effects) to treat infections of bones and joints, and peritonitis (inflammation of the peritoneal lining of the abdominal cavity due to gram-positive cocci or anaerobic bacteria). Administration is oral in the form of capsules and as a dilute syrup, or by injection or infusion.

▲ side-effects: if diarrhoea or other symptoms of colitis appear during treatment, administration must be halted at once (*see below*). There may be nausea and vomiting.

◉ warning: lincomycin should not be administered to patients suffering from diarrhoea; if diarrhoea or other symptoms of

colitis appear during treatment, administration must be halted at once. This is because lincomycin's disturbance of the balance of intestinal micro-organisms disposes towards a superinfection with the anaerobic bacterium *Clostridium difficile*, which causes a severe pseudomembranous colitis (particularly in adult/elderly females). It should be administered with caution to patients with impaired liver or kidney function.
*Related article:* LINCOCIN.

*****linctuses** are medicated syrups, thick and soothing enough to relieve sore throats or loosen a cough. (A linctus is not the same as an expectorant, however, which is intended to increase the viscosity of sputum and so make it easier to cough up. Nor is it necessarily an elixir, which disguises a potentially horrible taste with a sweetening substance like glycerol or alcohol.)

**lindane**, or gamma benzene hexachloride, is a drug used to treat parasitic infestation by lice (pediculosis) or by itch-mites (scabies) on the skin surface, particularly under the hair. However, strains of head-lice resistant to lindane have recently emerged, and the drug is now not recommended for use on the scalp. Administration is topical in the form of a lotion or a shampoo, to be left wet as long as possible.

▲ side-effects: side-effects are rare, but a few patients suffer minor skin irritation.

◉ warning: keep lindane away from the eyes.
*Related articles:* ESODERM; QUELLADA.

**Lingraine** (*Winthrop*) is a proprietary anti-migraine drug, available only on prescription.

Produced in the form of tablets, Lingraine is a preparation of the ergot-derived alkaloid ergotamine tartrate. It is not recommended for children.

▲/● side-effects/warning: *see* ERGOTAMINE TARTRATE.

**liniments** are medicated lotions for rubbing into the skin; many contain alcohol and/or camphor, and are intended to relieve minor muscle indispositions. Some liniments are alternatively produced for application on a surgical dressing.

**Lioresal** (*Ciba*) is a proprietary SKELETAL MUSCLE RELAXANT, available only on prescription, used to treat muscle spasm caused by injury or disease in the central nervous system. Produced in the form of tablets and as a sugar-free liquid for dilution (the potency of the diluted liquid is retained for 14 days), Lioresal is a preparation of baclofen.

▲/● side-effects/warning: *see* BACLOFEN.

**liothyronine sodium** is a form of the natural thyroid HORMONE triiodothyronine, used to make up a hormonal deficiency (hypothyroidism) and to treat the associated symptoms (myxoedema). It may also be used in the treatment of goitre and of thyroid cancer. Liothyronine sodium is rapidly absorbed by the body and is administered by intravenous injection in emergency treatment of hypothyroid coma. In other circumstances, administration is oral in the form of tablets, or by injection.

▲ side-effects: there may be an increase in the heart rate, heartbeat irregularities and angina; some patients experience headache, muscle cramp, flushing and sweating; there may also be diarrhoea. Dramatic weight loss occurs in some patients.

● warning: liothyronine sodium should not be administered to patients with cardiovascular disease or angina pectoris (heart pain), or impaired secretion from the adrenal glands.

*Related article:* TERTROXIN.

**Lipantil** (*Bristol-Myers*) is a proprietary preparation of the drug fenofibratebezafibrate, available only on prescription, used to treat high levels of fats (lipids) such as cholesterol in the bloodstream (hyperlipidaemia). It works by inhibiting production of fat. Produced in the form of capsules, it is not recommended for children.

▲/● side-effects/warning: *see* FENOFIBRATE.

**Lipobase** (*Brocades*) is a proprietary, non-prescription skin emollient (softener and soother), used to treat dry conditions of the skin (especially in alternation with corticosteroid preparations). Produced in the form of cream, Lipobase contains stearyl alcohol in a paraffin base, and is a base in which other medications can be applied topically.

**Lipostat** (*Squibb*) is a newly developed drug that is used to lower lipid (fat) levels in the blood where this is markedly elevated (hyperlipidaemia). It is used in patients who do not respond to, or who are intolerant of, other therapy. It is a proprietary form of pravastin available only on prescription. The preparation is available as tablets in two strengths.

▲/● side-effects/warning: *see* PRAVASTIN.

**Lipotriad** (*Lewis*) is a proprietary, non-prescription MULTIVITAMIN compound, which is not available from the National Health Service. Produced in the form of capsules and as an elixir, Lipotriad contains THIAMINE (vitamin B₁), RIBOFLAVINE (vitamin B₂), PYRIDOXINE (vitamin B₆), HYDROXOCOBALAMIN (vitamin B₁₂), NICOTINAMIDE, INOSITOL (both of the B complex) and other metabolic constituents. It is not recommended for children.

**liquid paraffin** is an old-fashioned but effective LAXATIVE, used in many households to relieve constipation. It is a constituent of a number of proprietary laxatives and some non-proprietary formulations. But it can also be used as a tear-substitute, administered as an eye ointment for patients whose lachrymal apparatus is dysfunctioning.

▲ side-effects: little is absorbed in the intestines: seepage of the paraffin may thus occur from the anus, causing local irritation. Prolonged use may interfere with the internal absorption of fat- soluble vitamins.

✿ warning: prolonged or continuous use of liquid paraffin as a laxative is to be avoided.
*Related articles:* AGAROL; LACRI-LUBE; PETROLAGAR.

**Liquifilm Tears** (*Allergan*) is a proprietary, non-prescription tear-substitute, used to lubricate the eyes of patients whose lachrymal apparatus is not working properly. Produced in the form of eye drops, Liquifilm Tears is a solution of POLYVINYL ALCOHOL.

**Liquigen** (*Scientific Hospital Supplies*) is a proprietary, non-prescription gluten-free milk substitute, produced for patients recovering from intestinal surgery or with chronic disease of the liver or of the pancreas; it may also be used for patients on the special diet associated with

epilepsy. Produced in the form of an emulsion, Liquigen is a preparation of neutral lipids.

**liquorice, deglycyrrhizinized,** is a constituent of some compound drugs used to treat peptic ulcers particularly in the stomach, but also in the duodenum.

**lisinopril** is an ANTIHYPERTENSIVE drug used to treat all forms of high blood pressure (hypertension), especially when more standard forms of therapy have failed or are not tolerated, and to assist in the treatment of congestive heart failure. It works by inhibiting the formation of a certain peptide in the blood (angiotensin), which normally constricts the blood vessels. Administration is oral, as tablets; some patients may require simultaneous administration of other antihyperensive drugs.

▲ side-effects: there may be a dry cough, headache, nervousness, fatigue, dizziness, nausea, an alteration in the sense of taste, muscle cramps, acid stomach, diarrhoea, low blood pressure and renal failure, rhinitis, insomnia; chest, back, and abdominal pains; sinusitis, paraesthesia. Some patients develop a rash.

✿ warning: lisinopril should be administered with caution to patients with impaired kidney function, or who are pregnant. The initial dose may cause a rapid fall in blood pressure to low blood pressure (hypotension), especially in patients who are also taking diuretics or who are dehydrated.
*Related articles:* CARACE; ZESTRIL.

**Liskonum** (*Smith, Kline & French*) is a proprietary drug, available only on prescription, used to treat mania and to prevent manic-depressive illnesses. Produced in the form of sustained-release tablets, Liskonum is a preparation of lithium carbonate. It is not recommended for children.

▲/● side-effects/warning: see LITHIUM.

**Litarex** (*CP Pharmaceuticals*) is a proprietary drug, available only on prescription, used to treat acute mania and to prevent manic-depressive illnesses. Produced in the form of sustained-release tablets, Litarex is a preparation of lithium citrate. It is not recommended for children.

▲/● side-effects/warning: see LITHIUM.

**lithium**, in the form of lithium carbonate or lithium citrate, is effective in preventing the euphoric or hyperactive form of psychosis that is mania, and in preventing manic-depressive illness. How it works remains imperfectly understood, but its use is so successful that the side-effects caused by its toxicity are deemed to be justified. Administration is oral in the form of tablets and sustained-release tablets.

▲ side-effects: many long-term patients experience nausea, thirst and excessive urination, gastrointestinal disturbance, weakness and tremor. There may be fluid retention and consequent weight gain. Visual disturbances and increasing gastric problems indicate lithium intoxication.

● warning: lithium should not be administered to patients with heart disease, impaired kidney function or imperfect sodium balance in the bloodstream. It should be administered with caution to those who are pregnant or lactating, or who are elderly. Prolonged treatment may cause kidney

and thyroid gland dysfunction; prolonged overdosage causes eventual brain disease, convulsions, coma, and finally death. Consequently, blood levels of lithium must be regularly checked for toxicity; thyroid function must be monitored; and there must be adequate intake of fluids and sodium.

*Related articles:* CAMCOLIT; LISKONUM; LITAREX; PHASAL; PRIADEL.

**Lobak** (*Sterling Research*) is a proprietary, non-narcotic ANALGESIC, available on prescription only to private patients, used to treat painful muscle spasm. Produced in the form of tablets, Lobak represents a preparation of paracetamol together with the SKELETAL MUSCLE RELAXANT chlormezanone. It is not recommended for children.

▲/● side-effects/warning: see CHLORMEZANONE; PARACETAMOL.

**Locabiotal** (*Servier*) is a proprietary ANTIBIOTIC, available only on prescription, used to treat infection and inflammation in the nose and throat. Produced in an aerosol with a nose and mouth adaptor, Locabiotal is a preparation of fusafungine. It is not recommended for children aged under 3 years.

\*local anaesthetic: see ANAESTHETIC.

**Locasol New Formula** (*Cow & Gate*) is a proprietary, non-prescription nutritional formulation, used instead of milk in diets for people who suffer from calcium intolerance. Produced in the form of powder, Locasol New Formula is a preparation of protein, carbohydrate, fat, lactose, vitamins and minerals.

**Lockets** (*Mars*) are a proprietary, non-prescription cold relief preparation containing honey, GLYCEROL, citric acid, menthol and eucalyptus.

▲/✤ side-effects/warning: *see* MENTHOL.

**Locobase** (*Brocades*) is a proprietary, non-prescription skin emollient (softener and soother), used to treat dry conditions of the skin (especially in alternation with corticosteroid preparations). Produced in the form of a water-miscible cream and an anhydrous ointment, Locobase is a base in which other medications can be applied topically to the skin.

**Locoid** (*Brocades*) is a proprietary CORTICOSTEROID, available only on prescription, used to treat serious non-infective inflammatory skin conditions, such as eczema. Produced in the form of a water-miscible cream, in a fatty cream base (under the name Lipocream), ointment and a scalp lotion, Locoid is a preparation of the steroid hydrocortisone butyrate. Another version of Locoid additionally containing the broad-spectrum ANTIBIOTIC chlorquinaldol is also available (under the name Locoid C), produced in the form of a cream and an ointment.

▲/✤ side-effects/warning: *see* HYDROCORTISONE BUTYRATE.

**Locorten-Vioform** (*Ciba*) is a proprietary ANTIBACTERIAL and ANTIFUNGAL, available only on prescription, used to treat mild infections of the outer ear. Produced in the form of ear-drops, Locorten-Vioform is a compound of clioquinol and the minor CORTICOSTEROID flumethasone pivalate.

▲/✤ side-effects/warning: *see* CLIOQUINOL.

**Lodine** (*Ayerst*) is a proprietary, ANTI-INFLAMMATORY, non-narcotic ANALGESIC, available only on prescription, used to treat the pain of rheumatism and of other musculo-skeletal disorders. Produced in the form of capsules, Lodine is a preparation of etodolac. It is not recommended for children.

▲/✤ side-effects/warning: *see* ETODOLAC.

**Loestrin** (*Parke-Davis*) is an ORAL CONTRACEPTIVE, available only on prescription, that combines the OESTROGEN ethinyloestradiol with the PROGESTOGEN norethisterone acetate. It is produced in packs of 21 tablets (in two strengths, under the names Loestrin 20 and Loestrin 30) representing one complete menstrual cycle.

▲/✤ side-effects/warning: *see* ETHINYLOESTRADIOL; NORETHISTERONE.

**Lofenalac** (*Bristol-Myers*) is a proprietary, non-prescription nutritional supplement, used to nourish patients with amino-acid abnormalities (such as phenylketonuria). Produced in the form of a powder, Lofenalac contains protein, carbohydrate, fats, vitamins and minerals. It is gluten-, sucrose- and lactose-free.

**lofepramine** is an ANTI-DEPRESSANT drug of a type that has fewer sedative properties than many others. Used to treat depressive illness, it is thus suited more to the treatment of withdrawn and apathetic patients than to those who are agitated and restless. Administration is oral in the form of tablets.

▲ side-effects: dry mouth, drowsiness, blurred vision, constipation and urinary retention are all fairly common; there may also be heartbeat irregularities accompanying low blood pressure (hypotension). Concentration and speed of reaction are affected. Elderly patients may enter a state of confusion; younger patients may experience behavioural disturbances. There may be alteration in blood sugar levels, and weight gain.

✿ warning: lofepramine should not be administered to patients with heart disease or liver failure; it should be administered with extreme caution to those with epilepsy, psychoses or glaucoma, or who are pregnant. Treatment may take up to four weeks to achieve full effect; premature withdrawal of treatment thereafter may cause the return of symptoms.
*Related article:* GAMANIL.

**Logynon** (*Schering*) is an ORAL CONTRACEPTIVE, available only on prescription, that combines the OESTROGEN ethinyloestradiol with the PROGESTOGEN levonorgestrel. It is produced in packs either of 21 tablets or (under the name Logynon ED) of 28 tablets, both representing one complete menstrual cycle.

▲/✿ side-effects/warning: *see* ETHINYLOESTRADIOL; LEVONORGESTREL.

**Lomodex** (*CP Pharmaceuticals*) is a proprietary form of the plasma substitute dextran, available only on prescription, used in infusion with either saline (sodium chloride) or glucose to make up a deficiency in the overall volume of blood in a patient, or to prevent thrombosis following surgery. Produced in flasks (bottles) for infusion, there is a choice of two concentrations: Lomodex 40 and Lomodex 70.

▲/✿ side-effects/warning: *see* DEXTRAN.

**Lomotil** (*Gold Cross*) is a proprietary ANTIDIARRHOEAL drug, available only on prescription, which acts by

reducing intestinal activity and fluid loss from the intestines. Produced in the form of tablets and as a sugar-free liquid for dilution (with glycerol: the potency of the diluted liquid is retained for 14 days), Lomotil is a preparation of the OPIATE diphenoxylate hydrochloride and the ANTI-CHOLINERGIC belladonna alkaloid, atropine sulphate (a combination called cophenotrope). It is not recommended for children aged under 2 years.

▲/✿ side-effects/warning: *see* ATROPINE SULPHATE; DIPHENOXYLATE HYDROCHLORIDE.

**lomustine** is a CYTOTOXIC drug that is used particularly to treat Hodgkin's disease (cancer of the lymphatic tissues) and some solid tumours. It works by disrupting cellular DNA, so inhibiting cell replication, and is administered orally in the form of capsules at intervals of between 4 and 6 weeks.

▲ side-effects: there is commonly nausea and vomiting. The blood-producing capacity of the bone-marrow is impaired (although the effect is delayed – which is why there should be a good interval between doses). There may be hair loss.

✿ warning: prolonged use may cause sterility in men and an early menopause in women; in both sexes it may lead to permanent bone-marrow damage. Prolonged treatment has also been associated with the incidence of leukaemia following simultaneous irradiation treatment. Blood count monitoring is essential. Dosage should be the minimum still to be effective.
*Related article:* CCNU.

**Loniten** (*Upjohn*) is a proprietary VASODILATOR, available only on prescription, used – in

combination with a DIURETIC
(such as a thiazide) and a BETA-
BLOCKER – to treat severe high
blood pressure (hypertension).
Produced in the form of tablets (in
three strengths), Loniten is a
preparation of minoxidil.
▲/✤ side-effects/warning: see
MINOXIDIL.

**loperamide hydrochloride** is an
ANTIDIARRHOEAL drug which acts
on the nerves of the intestine to
inhibit peristalsis – the waves of
muscular activity that force along
the intestinal contents – so
reducing motility, and also
decreases fluid loss from the
intestines. Although loperamide
is an OPIATE, even prolonged
treatment is unlikely to cause
dependence; it also has fewer
sedative effects on patients than
other opiates used to treat
chronic diarrhoea.
Administration is oral in the form
of capsules or as a dilute syrup.
▲ side-effects: there may be a
rash.
✤ warning: loperamide
hydrochloride should be
administered with caution to
patients who are elderly, in
whom it may cause faecal
impaction. Prolonged use
should be avoided in order not
to wear out the muscles on
which the drug has its effect,
causing irritable bowel
syndrome. Adequate fluid
intake must be maintained.
*Related articles:* ARRET;
IMODIUM.

**Lopid** (*Parke-Davis*) is a
proprietary preparation of the
drug gemfibrozil, available only
on prescription, used to treat high
levels of cholesterol or other
lipids (fats) in the blood
(hyperlipidaemia). Lopid works
by inhibiting the uptake of fats by
the liver. Produced for oral
adminstration in the form of
capsules, Lopid is not
recommended for children.

▲/✤ side-effects/warning: see
GEMFIBROZIL.

**loprazolam** is a HYPNOTIC drug,
one of the BENZODIAZEPINES, used
as a tranquillizer to treat
insomnia. Administration is oral
in the form of tablets.
▲ side-effects: concentration and
speed of reaction are affected.
There may also be drowsiness,
dry mouth and dizziness;
elderly patients may enter a
state of confusion. Some
patients experience sensitivity
reactions. Prolonged use may
eventually result in tolerance,
and finally dependence.
✤ warning: loprazolam should
not be administered to patients
with acute pulmonary
insufficiency (lung disease or
shallow breathing) or with
myasthenia gravis; it should be
administered with caution to
those with impaired liver or
kidney function, who are
pregnant or lactating, or who
are elderly and debilitated.
*Related article:* DORMONOCT.

**Lopresor** (*Geigy*) is a proprietary
preparation of the BETA-BLOCKER
metoprolol tartrate, available
only on prescription, used to
control and regulate the heart
rate and to treat high blood
pressure (hypertension), angina
pectoris (heart pain), or an excess
of thyroid hormones in the blood
(thyrotoxicosis). It is produced in
the form of tablets (in two
strengths). A stronger form is also
produced (under the name
Lopresor SR). None of these is
recommended for children.
▲/✤ side-effects/warning: see
METOPROLOL.

**Lopresoretic** (*Geigy*) is a
proprietary ANTIHYPERTENSIVE
compound, available only on
prescription, used to treat mild to
moderate high blood pressure
(hypertension). Produced in the

form of tablets, Lopresoretic is a preparation of the BETA-BLOCKER metoprolol tartrate together with the THIAZIDE DIURETIC chlorthalidone. It is not recommended for children.

▲/● side-effects/warning: *see* CHLORTHALIDONE; METOPROLOL.

**loratadine** is a relatively new ANTIHISTAMINE used to treat the symptoms of allergic disorders such as hay fever and urticaria (skin rashes). It joins a new class of drugs, which have little sedative effect. Administration is oral in the form of tablets.

▲ side-effects: side-effects are comparatively uncommon, but there may be headache. There may also be sufficient drowsiness to counter-indicate driving or operating machinery.

● warning: loratadine should be administered with caution to patients with epilepsy, glaucoma, liver disease or enlargement of the prostate gland, in pregnancy. Not recommended for children or the elderly.
*Related article:* CLARITYN.

**lorazepam** is an ANXIOLYTIC and ANTIDEPRESSANT drug, one of the BENZODIAZEPINES, used to treat mental stress ranging from anxiety to severe panic, including depressive illness. It may also be used to treat insomnia. Administration is oral in the form of tablets, or by injection.

▲ side-effects: concentration and speed of reaction are affected. Drowsiness, dizziness, headache, dry mouth and shallow breathing are all fairly common. Elderly patients may enter a state of confusion. Sensitivity reactions may occur. The drug may enhance the effects of alcohol consumption.

● warning: lorazepam should be administered with caution to patients with respiratory difficulties, glaucoma, or kidney or liver damage; who are in the last stages of pregnancy or are lactating; or who are elderly or debilitated. Prolonged use or abrupt withdrawal of the drug should be avoided.
*Related articles:* ALMAZINE; ATIVAN.

**lormetazepam** is a HYPNOTIC drug, one of the BENZODIAZEPINES, used as a TRANQUILLIZER to treat insomnia (especially in the elderly). Administration is oral in the form of tablets.

▲ side-effects: concentration and speed of reaction are affected. There may also be drowsiness, dry mouth and dizziness. Some patients experience sensitivity reactions. Prolonged use may eventually result in tolerance, and finally dependence.

● warning: lormetazepam should be administered with caution to patients with lung disease or shallow breathing, or impaired liver or kidney function, who are pregnant or lactating, or who are elderly and debilitated.
*Related article:* NOCTAMID.

**Loron** (*Boehringer Mannheim*) is a recently introduced proprietary form of the drug SODIUM CHLODRONATE, which is used to treat high calcium levels associated with malignant tumours. Available only on prescription it is produced in a form suitable for intravenous infusion and as capsules.

▲/● side-effects/warning: *see* SODIUM CHLODRONATE.

**Losec** (*Astra*) is a anti-ulcer drug, and is a proprietary form of omeprazole available only on prescription in the form of capsules.

▲/✦ side-effects/warning: *see* OMEPRAZOLE.

**\*lotions** are medicated liquids used to bathe or wash skin conditions, the hair or the eyes. In many cases lotions should be left wet after application for as long as possible.

**lotio rubra** is a non-proprietary formulation of ZINC SULPHATE in solution with amaranth, used as a lotion to clean and dress ulcers.

**Lotussin** (*Searle*) is a proprietary, non-prescription, ANTIHISTAMINE, EXPECTORANT and cough mixture, which is not available from the National Health Service. Produced in the form of a syrup for dilution (the potency of the mixture once dilute is retained for 14 days), Lotussin is a compound of the cough suppressant dextromethorphan hydrobromide, the antihistamine diphenhydramine hydrochloride, the SYMPATHOMIMETIC ephedrine hydrochloride and the expectorant guaiphenesin. It is not recommended for children aged under 12 months.

▲/✦ side-effects/warning: *see* DEXTROMETHORPHAN; DIPHENHYDRAMINE HYDROCHLORIDE; EPHEDRINE HYDROCHLORIDE.

**LSD**, or lysergide (lysergic acid diethylamide), is a powerful hallucinogenic drug that was occasionally used therapeutically to assist in the treatment of psychological disorders. Although the drug expands awareness and perception, and creates a false world at the same time, there are many toxic side-effects and its use – apart from being illegal – can lead to severely psychotic conditions in which life itself may be at risk.

This drug is on the controlled drugs list, and is no longer considered by most authorities to be of medical value.

▲ side-effects: use may cause dizziness and sweating, tingling and dilated pupils, gastrointestinal disturbance and anxiety, tremor and loss of delicate control of the muscles.

✦ warning: LSD should be used only to treat cases for which it is deemed essential. Alteration in the experience of all the senses occurs; psychotic affects are common; confusion and depression may follow.

**Ludiomil** (*Ciba*) is a proprietary ANTIDEPRESSANT, available only on prescription, used to treat depressive illness especially in cases where sedation is deemed additionally to be necessary. Produced in the form of tablets (in four strengths), Ludiomil is a preparation of maprotiline hydrochloride. It is not recommended for children.

▲/✦ side-effects/warning: *see* MAPROTILINE HYDROCHLORIDE.

**Lugol's solution** is a non-proprietary solution of iodine and potassium iodide in water (and is also known as aqueous iodine solution). It is used as an iodine supplement for patients suffering from an excess of thyroid hormones in the bloodstream (thyrotoxicosis), especially prior to thyroid surgery.

▲/✦ side-effects/warning: *see* IODINE.

**Lurselle** (*Merrell Dow*) is a proprietary form of the drug probucol, available only on prescription, used to treat high levels of cholesterol or other lipids (fats) in the blood. Produced in the form of tablets, Lurselle is not recommended for children.

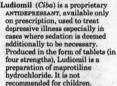

▲/● side-effects/warning: *see*
PROBUCOL.

**Lyclear** (*Wellcome*) is a
preparation for the treatment of
lice, whose active ingredient is
pheremthrin, a pyrethroid, which
is effective in killing lice though
less so their eggs. Available
without prescription, the
preparation is available as a
cream, which should be left in
contact with scalp for at least 10
minutes.

**lymecycline** is a broad-spectrum
ANTIBIOTIC, one of the
TETRACYCLINES, used to treat
infections of many kinds.
Administration is oral in the form
of capsules.
▲ side-effects: there may be
nausea and vomiting, with
diarrhoea. Some patients
experience a sensitivity to
light. Rarely, there are allergic
reactions.
● warning: lymecycline should
not be administered to patients
with kidney failure, who are
pregnant, or who are aged
under 12 years. It should be
administered with caution to
those who are lactating, or who
have impaired liver function.
*Related article:* TETRALYSAL.

**lynoestrenol** is a PROGESTOGEN
used in combination ORAL
CONTRACEPTIVES that contain
both a progestogen and an
OESTROGEN. Administration is
oral in the form of tablets.
▲ side-effects: the combined oral
contraceptive may cause
nausea and vomiting, with
headache; there may be breast
tenderness, slight weight gain
and a change in libido. Some
women experience high blood
pressure (hypertension), a
tendency to thrombosis, and/or
reduced menstrual flow.
Rarely, there is impaired liver
function or a sensitivity to
light.

● warning: lynoestrenol in
combination with an oestrogen
should not be administered to
patients with thrombosis, liver
disease, sickle-cell anaemia,
cancer of the womb or of the
breast, an excess of lipids (fats)
in the blood, or severe
migraine; who are pregnant; or
who are bleeding from the
vagina for an undiagnosed
reason. It should be
administered with caution to
those with epilepsy, diabetes,
heart or kidney disease, high
blood pressure (hypertension),
asthma, varicose veins and/or
obesity, or depression. Many
doctors will not prescribe a
combined oral contraceptive
for women aged over 35 years or
who smoke cigarettes.

**lypressin**, or 8-lysine vasopressin,
is one of two major forms of the
antidiuretic HORMONE
vasopressin, used to treat
pituitary-originated diabetes
insipidus. Administration of
lypressin is topical in the form of a
nasal spray.
▲/● side-effects/warning: *see*
VASOPRESSIN.
*Related article:*
SYNTOPRESSIN.

**lysergide** is another chemical
name for lysergic acid
diethylamide, or LSD.
*see* LSD.

**8-lysine vasopressin** is a chemical
name for lypressin.
*see* LYPRESSIN.

**lysuride maleate** is a recently
introduced ANTIPARKINSONISM
drug that is similar to
BROMOCRIPTINE in its actions. It
acts by stimulating those
dopamine receptors still present
in the brain to a suitable extent,
and differs from the older form of
treatment with levodopa in that
the latter is actually converted to

dopamine in the brain. It is particularly useful in patients who cannot tolerate levodopa. It is available in the form of tablets.

▲ side-effects: there may be headache, nausea and vomiting, lethargy and drowsiness, hypotension, rashes, psychotic reactions including hallucinations, occasional rashes, constipation and abdominal pain. Care should be taken driving and operating machinery.

◆ warning: should be administered with caution in patients with a psychotic history, or who have had a pituitary tumour. It should not be given to patients with certain severe cardiovascular disorders.

*Related article:* REVANIL.

**Maalox** (*Rorer*) is a proprietary, non-prescription, compound ANTACID used to treat severe indigestion, heartburn, and gastric or duodenal ulcers. Produced in the form of tablets to be chewed (in two strengths, the stronger under the name Maalox Concentrated Tablets, not available from the National Health Service) and as a suspension (under the name Maalox Suspension), Maalox is a preparation of ALUMINIUM HYDROXIDE together with magnesium hydroxide – both known antacids in their own right. There is also a version of Maalox that incorporates the additional constituent DIMETHICONE, an antifoaming agent; this is produced in the form of a syrup (under the name Maalox Plus Suspension) and as tablets (under the name Maalox Plus Tablets, not available from the National Health Service). None of these preparations is recommended for children.

**Mac** (*Beecham Health Care*) are proprietary, non-prescription throat sweets containing sucrose and glucose syrups, menthol and amylmetacresol.

**Macrodantin** (*Norwich Eaton*) is a proprietary ANTIBIOTIC, available only on prescription, used to treat infections of the urinary tract. It works by interfering with the DNA of specific bacteria. Produced in the form of capsules (in two strengths), Macrodantin is a preparation of the antibacterial nitrofurantoin. It is not recommended for children aged under 30 months.
▲/● side-effects/warning: *see* NITROFURANTOIN.

**Macrodex** (*Pharacia*) is a proprietary form of DEXTRAN 70 intravenous infusion, available only on prescription, used to make up a deficiency in the overall volume of blood in a patient, or to prevent thrombosis following surgery. It is produced in flasks and prepared in a glucose or a saline matrix.
▲/● side-effects/warning: *see* DEXTRAN.

**Macrofix** (*Macarthy*) is a proprietary brand of elasticated tubular stockinette bandaging, produced in various diameters corresponding to average thicknesses of parts of the body.

**macrogol** as a skin emollient (softener and soother) consists of a compound of two water-soluble constituent macrogols; unlike most emollient ointments, therefore, it is readily washed off – a property that is sometimes useful. Macrogol is also present in certain solutions used to cleanse the bowel prior to colonic investigation, surgery or barium enema.
*Related article:* KLEAN-PREP.

**Madopar** (*Roche*) is a proprietary preparation of the powerful drug levodopa in combination with the enzyme inhibitor BENSERAZIDE; it is available only on prescription. Madopar is used to treat parkinsonism, but not the parkinsonian symptoms induced by drugs (*see* ANTIPARKINSONISM). The benserazide prevents too rapid a breakdown of the levodopa (into dopamine), thus allowing more levodopa to reach the brain to make up the deficiency (of dopamine), which is the cause of parkinsonian symptoms. Madopar is produced in the form of capsules (in three strengths), tablets (in two strengths) and as capsules (Madopar CR).
▲/● side-effects/warning: *see* LEVODOPA.

**Madribon** (*Roche*) is a proprietary ANTIBACTERIAL, available only on prescription, used to treat a number of bacterial infections – of the upper respiratory tract, of the ear, nose or throat, the skin, but particularly of the urinary tract. Produced in the form of tablets, Madribon is a preparation of the sulphonamide sulphadimethoxine. It is not recommended for children aged under 2 years.

▲/✿ side-effects/warning: *see* SULPHADIMETHOXINE.

**mafenide** is an ANTIBIOTIC, a SULPHONAMIDE used (as mafenide propionate) to treat infections in and around the eye, and (as mafenide acetate) to treat infectious burns. Administration is thus both in solution as eye-drops, and as a cream.
▲ side-effects: acid levels in the body may become high.
✿ warning: mafenide acetate should be administered with caution to patients with respiratory problems.
*Related article:* SULFOMYL.

**magaldrate** is an ANTACID complex, used to treat severe indigestion; it may be administered after meals and before going to sleep at night. The complex is not recommended for children aged under 6 years.
*Related article:* DYNESE.

**Magnapen** (*Beecham*) is a proprietary compound ANTIBIOTIC, available only on prescription, used to treat severe infection where the causative organism has not been identified, but gram-positive staphylococcal infection is suspected, or where penicillin-resistant bacterial infection is probable. Produced in the form of capsules, as a syrup (under the name Magnapen Syrup), as a powder for reconstitution as a syrup, and in vials for injections (under the name Magnapen Injection),

Magnapen is a preparation of the broad-spectrum penicillin-like antibiotic ampicillin together with the anti-staphylococcal antibiotic flucloxacillin.
▲/✿ side-effects/warning: *see* AMPICILLIN; FLUCLOXACILLIN.

**magnesium** is a metallic element necessary to the body; ingested as a trace element in the diet, it is essential to the bones and important to the functioning of the nerves and muscles. Good dietary sources include green vegetables. Therapeutically, magnesium is used in the form of its salts. Magnesium carbonate, hydroxide, oxide ('magnesia') and trisilicate are ANTACIDS; magnesium sulphate (Epsom salt/salts) is a saline LAXATIVE; magnesium deficiency is usually treated with supplements of magnesium chloride.
▲/✿ side-effects/warning: *see* MAGNESIUM CARBONATE; MAGNESIUM CHLORIDE; MAGNESIUM HYDROXIDE; MAGNESIUM SULPHATE; MAGNESIUM TRISILICATE.

**magnesium carbonate** is a natural ANTACID that also has LAXATIVE properties. As an antacid it is actually comparatively weak, but fairly long-acting. Used to relieve indigestion and to soothe duodenal ulcer pain, it is commonly combined with other antacids. Administration is oral, most commonly in the form of a non-proprietary water-based mixture that also includes sodium bicarbonate.
▲ side-effects: there may be belching – due to the internal liberation of carbon dioxide – and diarrhoea.
✿ warning: magnesium carbonate should be administered with caution to patients with impaired function of the

kidney, or who are taking any other form of drug.
*Related articles:* ALGICON; ALUDROX; ANDURSIL; APP; Bellocarb; CAVED-S; DIJEX; DIOVOL; GASTRILS; NULACIN; POLYCROL; ROTER; SIMECO; TOPAL.

**magnesium chloride** is the form of MAGNESIUM most commonly used to make up a deficiency of the metallic element in the body (as may occur through prolonged diarrhoea or vomiting, or through alcoholism).

**magnesium hydroxide**, or hydrated magnesium oxide ('magnesia'), is a natural ANTACID that also has LAXATIVE properties. As an antacid it is actually comparatively weak, but fairly long-acting. Used to relieve indigestion and to soothe duo-denal ulcer pain, it is sometimes combined with other antacids. Administration is oral in the form of tablets or as an aqueous suspension.
▲ side-effects: there may be diarrhoea.
❋ warning: magnesium hydroxide should be administered with caution to patients with impaired function of the kidney, or who are taking any other form of drug.
*Related articles:* ANDURSIL; CARBELLON; DIOVOL; MAALOX; MUCAINE; MUCOGEL; POLYCROL; SIMECO.

**magnesium sulphate** , or Epsom salt(s), is a LAXATIVE that works by preventing the resorption of water within the intestines. It is sometimes also used as a MAGNESIUM supplement administered to patients whose bodies are deficient in the mineral. And as a paste with glycerol, it is used topically to treat boils and carbuncles.

**magnesium trisilicate** is a natural ANTACID, which also has absorbent properties. As an antacid it is long-acting. Used to relieve indigestion and to soothe peptic ulcer pain, it is sometimes combined with other antacids. Administration is oral in the form of tablets or as an aqueous suspension.
❋ warning: magnesium trisilicate should be administered with caution to patients with impaired function of the kidney, or who are taking any other form of drug.
*Related articles:* BELLOCARB; GASTROCOTE; GASTRON; GAVISCON; GELUSIL; NULACIN; PYROGASTRONE.

**\*major tranquillizer:** *see* TRANQUILLIZER.

**Malarivon** *(Wallace)* is a proprietary ANTIMALARIAL drug, available only on prescription, used both to prevent and to treat malaria. Produced in the form of an elixir, Malarivon is a preparation of the powerful drug chloroquine.
▲/❋ side-effects/warning: *see* CHLOROQUINE.

**Malatex** *(Norton)* is a proprietary, non-prescription agent for sloughing off dead skin or old clots in wounds or ulcers. Produced in the form of a solution, Malatex's active constituents are SALICYLIC ACID and various other natural acids (including benzoic acid and malic acid).

**malathion** is an insecticidal drug used to treat infestations by lice (pediculosis) or by itch-mites (scabies). Administration is topical in the form of a lotion or a shampoo, but treatment should not take place more than once a week for more than three weeks in succession. Some of the proprietary forms are highly inflammable.

✿ warning: avoid contact with the eyes.
*Related articles:* DERBAC-M; PRIODERM; SULEO-M.

**Malix** (*Lagap*) is a proprietary form of the SULPHONYLUREA drug glibenclamide, used to treat adult-onset diabetes; it works by promoting the formation of insulin in whatever remains of the capacity of the pancreas for it, and increasing the number of insulin receptors. Available only on prescription, Malix is produced in the form of tablets (in two strengths).
▲/✿ side-effects/warning: *see* GLIBENCLAMIDE.

**Maloprim** (*Wellcome*) is a proprietary ANTIMALARIAL drug, available only on prescription, used to prevent travellers to tropical areas from contracting the disease. Produced in the form of tablets, Maloprim is a compound of the sulphone dapsone together with the catalytic enzyme-inhibitor pyrimethamine (which is particularly useful in relation to malarial strains resistant to chloroquine). It is commonly used in conjunction with chloroquine. Treatment is weekly, not daily, but must be continued for at least 4 weeks after the patient leaves the tropical area.
▲/✿ side-effects/warning: *see* DAPSONE; PYRIMETHAMINE.

**Manevac** (*Galen*) is a proprietary non-prescription form of the stimulant LAXATIVE senna together with the bulking-agent laxative ispaghula. Produced in the form of granules for solution in water, Agiolax is not recommended for children aged under 5 years.
▲/✿ side-effects/warning: *see* ISPAGHULA HUSK; SENNA.

**mannitol** is a form of sugar that cannot be metabolized. Therapeutically, it is used primarily as a powerful DIURETIC – to treat the accumulation of fluids in the body (oedema), especially in emergency situations (such as drug overdose) – but it may also be used to decrease pressure within the eyeball in acute attacks of glaucoma. Administration is by intravenous infusion.
▲ side-effects: there may be high body temperature with chills.
✿ warning: treatment may in the short term expand the overall blood volume, and should not be administered to patients with heart complaints or fluid on the lungs (pulmonary oedema). An escape of mannitol into the tissues from the site of infusion or from a blood vessel causes inflammation and forms of thrombosis.
*Related article:* OSMITROL.

**Mansil** is a proprietary form of the ANTHELMINTIC drug oxaminiquine, used to treat schistosomiasis (bilharziasis). *see* OXAMINIQUINE.

**Mantadine** (*Du Pont*) is a proprietary preparation of the powerful drug amantadine hydrochloride, available only on prescription, used to treat parkinsonism, but not the parkinsonian symptoms induced by drugs (*see* ANTI-PARKINSONISM). Effective on some patients, but not on others, Mantadine is produced in the form of capsules.
▲/✿ side-effects/warning: *see* AMANTADINE HYDROCHLORIDE.

**Manusept** (*Hough/Hoseason*) is a proprietary, non-prescription ANTISEPTIC, used particularly as a hand cleanser prior to surgery, but also to moisturize dry skin. It consists of a preparation of the alcohol-based disinfectant triclosan in very mild solution.

**\*MAO inhibitors** are one of the two main classes of ANTI-DEPRESSANT. Chemically, they are (usually) hydrazine derivatives. They are used less often than members of the TRICYCLIC group of antidepressants largely because of the dangers of interactions with foodstuffs and other drugs.

**maprotiline hydrochloride** is an ANTIDEPRESSANT drug used to treat depressive illness, particularly in cases where some degree of sedation is called for. Administration is oral in the form of tablets, or by intramuscular or intravenous injection.
▲ side-effects: concentration and intricacy in thought and movement may be reduced. There may be an increased heart rate, sweating and tremor; constipation and difficulty in urinating; blurred vision and rashes; and weight changes and loss of libido. The composition of the blood may alter, especially in blood sugars.
✹ warning: maprotiline hydrochloride should not be administered to patients who have serious heart complaints or have recently had a heart attack, or to those who have manic episodes. It should be administered with caution to patients with epilepsy, diabetes, impaired liver function, heartbeat irregularities, thyroid disorders, glaucoma, or urinary retention; who are pregnant; or who are mentally unstable. Withdrawal of treatment should be gradual.
*Related article:* LUDIOMIL.

**Marcain** (*Astra*) is a proprietary form of the local ANAESTHETIC drug bupivacaine, used particularly when duration of treatment is to be prolonged. Administration is thus most

commonly as a nerve block injection, or as a lumbar puncture or epidural. Available only on prescription, Marcain is produced in ampoules by itself (in four strengths, the strongest under the name Marcain Heavy) and with additional adrenaline (in two strengths, under the name Marcain with Adrenaline).
▲/✹ side-effects/warning: *see* ADRENALINE; BUPIVACAINE HYDROCHLORIDE.

**Marevan** (*Duncan, Flockhart*) is a proprietary ANTICOAGULANT, available only on prescription, used to prevent or treat thrombosis. Produced in the form of tablets (in three strengths), Marevan is a preparation of warfarin; it is not recommended for children.
▲/✹ side-effects/warning: *see* WARFARIN.

**Marplan** (*Roche*) is a proprietary ANTIDEPRESSANT drug, available only on prescription, used to treat depressive illness. Produced in the form of tablets, Marplan is a preparation of the potentially dangerous drug isocarboxazid (which requires a careful dietary regimen to accompany treatment). It is not suitable for children.
▲/✹ side-effects/warning: *see* ISOCARBOXAZID.

**Marvelon** (*Organon*) is a proprietary ORAL CONTRACEPTIVE pill, available only on prescription, of the type that combines an OESTROGEN and a PROGESTOGEN. In this case the oestrogen is ethinyloestradiol, and the progestogen is DESOGESTREL.
▲/✹ side-effects/warning: *see* ETHINYLOESTRADIOL.

**Mass Cream** (*Ortho-Cilag*) is a proprietary, non-prescription cream used as an emollient (softener and soother) for the nipples of women about to give birth and during lactation. Water-miscible, it contains many constituents, including arachis oil, wool fat, stearic acid and potassium hydroxide.

**Maxamaid XP** (*Scientific Hospital Supplies*) is a proprietary, non-prescription, orange-flavoured powder consisting of a virtually complete nutritional supplement for patients with amino-acid abnormalities (such as phenylketonuria). It thus contains amino acids (except phenylalanine), carbohydrate, vitamins and trace elements; it is also gluten-free. Maxamaid XP is not recommended for children aged under 2 years.

**Maxidex** (*Alcon*) is a proprietary compound, available only on prescription, used to treat inflammation of the surface of the eye. Produced in the form of eye-drops, Maxidex is a combination of the CORTICOSTEROID dexamethasone with the water-soluble cellulose derivative hypromellose (the basis of 'artificial tears', a spreading agent).

▲/◆ side-effects/warning: *see* DEXAMETHASONE.

**Maxijul** (*Scientific Hospital Supplies*) is the name of a proprietary, non-prescription series of preparations consisting of nutritional supplements for patients who require a high-energy low-fluid diet. Consisting mostly of polyglucose polymer, sodium and potassium, the standard form of Maxijul is produced as a gluten-, sucrose-, lactose-, galactose- and fructose-free powder. There is also a liquid form (in three flavours, under the name Maxijul Liquid), and a form with less sodium and potassium (under the name Maxijul LE).

**Maxipro HBV Super** (*Scientific Hospital Supplies*) is a proprietary NUTRITIONAL PREPARATION, a non-prescription protein supplement used to treat patients who are undernourished through lack of food or poor internal absorption (particularly those who have undergone gastrectomy). Its major constituent is whey protein. It is used for biochemically proven low protein blood levels (hypoproteinaemia).

**Maxitrol** (*Alcon*) is a proprietary compound, available only on prescription, used to treat inflammation of the surface of the eye. Produced in the form of eye-drops for daytime use, and as an ointment for use overnight, Maxitrol is a combination of the corticosteroid dexamethasone and the ANTIBIOTICS neomycin and polymyxin B sulphate; the eye-drops also contain the water-soluble cellulose derivative hypromellose (the basis of 'artificial tears', a spreading agent).

▲/◆ side-effects/warning: *see* DEXAMETHASONE; NEOMYCIN; POLYMYXIN B SULPHATE.

**Maxolon** (*Beecham*) is a proprietary ANTINAUSEANT, used to treat severe indigestion, flatulence, peptic, gastric or duodenal ulcer, hiatus hernia or gallstones. Available only on prescription, Maxolon's primary constituent – metoclopramide hydrochloride – works by encouraging the flow of absorbable nutrients in food in the stomach down into the intestines. It is produced in the form of tablets, in liquid form (under the name Maxolon Paediatric Liquid), as a syrup (under the name Maxolon Syrup) and in ampoules for injection (under the names Maxolon Injection and Maxolon High Dose).

▲/✿ side-effects/warning: *see* METOCLOPRAMIDE.

**mazindol** is a drug used to aid slimming regimes because it acts as an appetite suppressant. It also has stimulant properties, however, and there is a slight risk of dependence (addiction). Administration is oral in the form of tablets. The drug should be used only in cases where there is genuine medical need for weight loss, and is not recommended for children.

  ▲ side-effects: there may be agitation, insomnia and restlessness, and a increased heart rate; headache and dizziness may occur; there may also be gastrointestinal disturbances. In predisposed patients there may be manic episodes.

  ✿ warning: mazindol is merely an aid to a slimming regime, not a treatment for obesity. Its use should be short-term only. Prolonged treatment may result in dependence (addiction). It should not be administered to patients with glaucoma or from disorders of the thyroid gland, and should be administered with caution to those with epilepsy, diabetes, heart disease or peptic ulcer, or who are unstable psychologically. *Related article:* TERONAC.

**MCT (1)** (*Cow & Gate*) is a proprietary, non-prescription nutritional supplement for patients whose capacity for food absorption has been reduced (for instance following intestinal surgery, with chronic liver disease, or with cystic fibrosis of the pancreas). In the form of a powder for reconstitution, MCT (1) contains protein, carbohydrate, and fats (triglycerides); it is also low in lactose and sucrose-free.

**MCT Oil** (*Bristol-Myers*) is a proprietary, non-prescription form of fats (lipids) used as a nutritional supplement for patients whose metabolism finds fat absorption difficult or impossible (for instance following intestinal surgery, with cirrhosis of the liver, or with cystic fibrosis of the pancreas). MCT Oil is a preparation of triglycerides from fatty acids.

**mebendazole** is an ANTHELMINTIC drug used in the treatment of infections by roundworm, threadworm, whipworm and hookworm. A powerful drug generally well tolerated, it is the treatment of choice for patients of all ages over 2 years.

  ▲ side-effects: side-effects are uncommon, but there may be diarrhoea and abdominal pain.

  ✿ warning: mebendazole should not be administered to patients who are aged under 2 years; it should be administered with caution to those who are pregnant. *Related article:* VERMOX.

**mebeverine hydrochloride** is an ANTISPASMODIC drug used to treat muscle spasm in both the gastrointestinal tract (leading to abdominal pain and constipation) and the uterus or vagina (leading to menstrual problems). Administration is oral in the form of tablets, as a sugar-free liquid concentrate, and as soluble (dispersible) granules, to be taken before food. It is not recommended for children.

  ✿ warning: Mebeverine hydrochloride should not be administered to patients with paralytic ileus. *Related articles:* COLOFAC; COLVEN.

**mebhydrolin** is an ANTIHISTAMINE used to treat allergic conditions such as hay fever and urticaria, some forms of dermatitis, and some sensitivity reactions to drugs. Its additional sedative properties are useful in the treatment of some allergic conditions. Administration is oral in the form of tablets or a dilute suspension (mixture).

▲ side-effects: sedation may affect patients' capacity for speed of thought and movement; there may be nausea, headache and/or weight gain, dry mouth, gastrointestinal disturbances and visual problems.

✿ warning: mebhydrolin should not be administered to patients with glaucoma, urinary retention, intestinal obstruction, enlargement of the prostate gland, or peptic ulcer, or who are pregnant; it should be administered with caution to those with epilepsy or liver disease.
*Related article:* FABAHISTIN.

**mecillinam** is a penicillin-type ANTIBIOTIC, but with a different mechanism of action to most of the penicillins. Unlike the classic penicillins it has little activity against gram-positive bacteria but is active against some gram-negative bacteria. It is used primarily to treat sensitive urinary tract infections and systemic salmonella infections. Administration is in the form of injection.

▲ side-effects: there may be sensitivity reactions ranging from a minor rash to urticaria and joint pains, and (occasionally) to high temperature or anaphylactic shock.

✿ warning: mecillinam should not be administered to patients known to be allergic to penicillins; it should be administered with caution to those with impaired kidney function. Prolonged treatment

requires regular checks on liver and kidney function.
*Related article:* SELEXIDIN.

**meclozine** is an ANTIHISTAMINE used primarily as an ANTI-EMETIC in the treatment or prevention of motion sickness and vomiting. Administration (as meclozine hydrochloride, generally with a form of vitamin B) is oral in the form of tablets.

▲ side-effects: concentration and speed of thought and movement may be affected. There is commonly dry mouth and drowsiness; there may also be headache, blurred vision and gastrointestinal disturbances.

✿ warning: meclazine should be administered with caution to patients with epilepsy, liver disease, glaucoma or enlargement of the prostate gland. Drowsiness may be increased by alcohol consumption.

**medazepam** is an ANXIOLYTIC drug, one of the BENZO-DIAZEPINES, used primarily to treat chronic anxiety, and less commonly, insomnia. It may also be used to relieve acute alcohol withdrawal symptoms. But it also has the properties of a SKELETAL MUSCLE RELAXANT, and may also be administered to relieve conditions of skeletal muscle spasticity. Administration is oral in the form of capsules.

▲ side-effects: concentration and speed of reaction are affected. Drowsiness, dizziness, headache, dry mouth and shallow breathing are all fairly common. Elderly patients may enter a state of confusion. Sensitivity reactions may occur.

✿ warning: medazepam should be administered with caution to patients with respiratory difficulties, glaucoma, or

**M**

kidney or liver disease; who are in the last stages of pregnancy or are lactating; or who are elderly or debilitated. Prolonged use or abrupt withdrawal of the drug should be avoided.
*Related article:* NOBRIUM.

**Medicoal** (*Lundbeck*) is a proprietary, non-prescription adsorbent preparation for oral administration, used to treat patients suffering from poisoning or a drug overdose. It works by binding the toxic material to itself before being excreted in the normal way. Produced in the form of granules for effervescent solution in water, Medicoal is a preparation of CHARCOAL.

**medigoxin** is a derivative of DIGOXIN, a CARDIAC GLYCOSIDE that acts as a strong heart stimulant, and is thus used to treat heart failure and severe heartbeat irregularity. Administration is oral in the form of tablets.
▲ side-effects: there may be serious effects on the heart rate. Sometimes there is nausea and vomiting, visual disturbances and weight loss.
● warning: medigoxin should be administered with caution to patients who have undergone a recent heart attack, or who have disorders of the thyroid gland. Dosage should be reduced for the elderly.
*Related article:* LANITOP.

**Medihaler-Duo** (*Riker*) is a proprietary BRONCHODILATOR, available only on prescription, used in the form of an inhalant to treat bronchial asthma and chronic bronchitis. Produced in a metered-dosage aerosol, Medihaler-Duo is a compound preparation of the SYMPATHOMIMETICS isoprenaline hydrochloride and phenylephrine bitartrate.

▲/● side-effects/warning: *see* ISOPRENALINE; PHENYLEPHRINE.

**Medihaler-epi** (*Riker*) is a proprietary BRONCHODILATOR, available only on prescription, used in the form of an inhalant to treat bronchial asthma and chronic bronchitis. Produced in a metered-dosage aerosol, Medihaler-epi is a preparation of the SYMPATHOMIMETIC adrenaline acid tartrate.
▲/● side-effects/warning: *see* ADRENALINE.

**Medihaler-Ergotamine** (*Riker*) is a proprietary anti-migraine treatment, available only on prescription, used in the form of an inhalant to treat migraine and recurrent vascular headache. Produced in a metered-dosage aerosol, Medihaler-Ergotamine is a preparation of the vegetable alkaloid ergotamine tartrate.
▲/● side-effects/warning: *see* ERGOTAMINE TARTRATE.

**Medihaler-iso** (*Riker*) is a proprietary BRONCHODILATOR, available only on prescription, used in the form of an inhalant to treat bronchial asthma and chronic bronchitis. Produced in a metered-dosage aerosol (in two strengths, the stronger under the trade name Medihaler-iso Forte), it is a preparation of the SYMPATHOMIMETIC isoprenaline sulphate.
▲/● side-effects/warning: *see* ISOPRENALINE.

**Medilave** (*Martindale*) is a proprietary, non-prescription preparation for topical application, used to relieve pain in sores and ulcers in the mouth. Produced in the form of a gel, Medilave is a preparation of the local ANAESTHETIC benzocaine and the ANTISEPTIC CETYLPYRIDINIUM CHLORIDE, and is not recommended for children aged under 6 months.

▲/● side-effects/warning: *see*
BENZOCAINE.

**Medised** (*Martindale/Panpharma*)
is a proprietary, non-prescription,
compound non-narcotic
ANALGESIC, which is not available
from the National Health Service.
Used to treat pain, especially that
associated with fever and
respiratory congestion, and to
relieve the symptoms of
chickenpox, Medised is produced
in the form of a suspension (which
is not recommended for children
aged under 3 months). Medised is
a combination of the analgesic
paracetamol and the
ANTIHISTAMINE promethazine
hydrochloride.
▲/● side-effects/warning: *see*
PARACETAMOL;
PROMETHAZINE
HYDROCHLORIDE.

**Medocodene** (*Medo*) is a
proprietary, non-prescription
compound ANALGESIC, which is
not available from the National
Health Service. Used to treat pain
anywhere in the body, and
produced in the form of tablets,
Medocodene is a combination of
the analgesic paracetamol and
the OPIATE codeine phosphate (a
combination itself known as co-
codamol). It is not recommended
for children aged under 6 years.
▲/● side-effects/warning: *see*
CODEINE PHOSPHATE;
PARACETAMOL.

**Medomet** (*DDSA
Pharmaceuticals*) is a proprietary
form of the powerful
ANTIHYPERTENSIVE drug
methyldopa, which works by
direct action on the central
nervous system. Available only
on prescription, Medomet is used
– usually in combination with a
DIURETIC drug – to treat moderate
to very high blood pressure
(hypertension), and is produced in
the form of tablets (in two
strengths) and capsules.

▲/● side-effects/warning: *see*
METHYLDOPA.

**Medrone** (*Upjohn*) is a proprietary
preparation of the anti-
inflammatory CORTICOSTEROID
drug methylprednisolone,
available only on prescription,
used to treat arthritis, joint pain
and allergies, and to relieve the
symptoms of severe acne. It is
produced in the form of tablets (in
three strengths).
▲/● side-effects/warning: *see*
METHYLPREDNISOLONE.

**medroxyprogesterone acetate** is
a long-acting female sex hormone,
a PROGESTOGEN most commonly
administered by intramuscular
injection. One of its uses is as an
ORAL CONTRACEPTIVE of a type
that is particularly useful in
being effective for a short period
of time (as for example during the
time a partner's vasectomy takes
to become effective). Prolonged
use in contraception may be
accompanied by potentially
uncomfortable side-effects,
however, although for some
women it may be the only
tolerable method. The drug can
also be used to make up hormonal
deficiency in such conditions as
an absence of menstruation
(amenorrhoea), or to treat the
relatively common condition in
which some womb-lining tissue
that is located outside the womb
in the abdominal cavity continues
to go through the menstrual cycle
(endometriosis). Medroxy-
progesterone acetate can also be
used in the treatment of cancers
of the breast that are related to
the presence of OESTROGENS.
▲ side-effects: there may be
nausea and vomiting, with
headache; there may also be
weight gain, breast tenderness,
depression and skin disorders.
Withdrawal of long-term
treatment may cause
temporary infertility and the

onset of some irregular menstrual cycles.

◆ warning: medroxy-progesterone acetate should not be administered to patients with liver disease, undiagnosed vaginal haemorrhage or sex-hormone-linked cancer; who are pregnant; or who have a history of ectopic pregnancy, of arterial disease or of jaundice. It should be administered with caution to those who suffer from diabetes, heart disease, ovarian cysts, or high blood pressure (hypertension); who have recently given birth; or who have started suffering from migraine since beginning to use oral contraceptive methods.
Related articles: DEPO-PROVERA; FARLUTAL; PROVERA.

**mefenamic acid** is a non-steroidal, ANTI-INFLAMMATORY, non-narcotic ANALGESIC. It is primarily used to treat mild to moderate pain in rheumatic disease and other musculo-skeletal disorders, although it may also be used either to reduce high body temperature (especially in children) or to lessen the pain of menstrual problems.
▲ side-effects: there may be drowsiness and dizziness; some patients experience nausea; gastrointestinal disturbances may eventually result in ulceration. Treatment should be withdrawn if diarrhoea, jaundice, anaemia or sensitivity reactions such as asthma-like symptoms occur.
◆ warning: mefenamic acid should not be administered to patients with inflammations in the intestines, peptic ulcers, or impaired liver or kidney function; or who are pregnant. It should be administered with caution to those with any allergic condition (including

asthma). Prolonged treatment requires regular blood counts.
Related article: PONSTAN.

**mefloquine** is an ANTIMALARIAL drug used to prevent, and to treat infection by one of the three Plasmodium species that cause malaria where there is chloroquine-resistance. It is effective against falciparum malaria, and is used in areas of the world where this is common.
▲ side-effects: there may be nausea and vomiting, with headache, rash and itching; disturbances of the gastrointestinal tract and liver. Susceptible patients may undergo psychotic episodes (treatment should be discontinued).
◆ warning: mefloquine should not be used where there is impaired renal or hepatic function, or where there is a history of behavioural diseases or convulsions. It should not be given to those breast-feeding, avoid if pregnancy is suspected (and 3 months after). Not recommended for young children. Avoid prolonged or frequent treatment.
Related article: LARIAM.

**Mefoxin** (Merck, Sharp & Dohme) is a proprietary, broad-spectrum ANTIBIOTIC, available only on prescription, used to treat bacterial infections and to ensure asepsis during surgery. Produced in the form of a powder for reconstitution as a medium for injection, Mefoxin is a preparation of the CEPHALOSPORIN cefoxitin.
▲ / ◆ side-effects/warning: see CEFOXITIN.

**mefruside** is a DIURETIC, one of the THIAZIDES, used to treat fluid retention in the tissues (oedema) and high blood pressure (hypertension). Because all thiazides tend to deplete body reserves of potassium, mefruside may be administered in combination either with potassium supplements or with diuretics that are complementarily potassium-sparing. Administration is oral in the form of tablets.

▲ side-effects: there may be tiredness and a rash. In men, temporary impotence may occur.

✹ warning: mefruside should not be administered to patients with kidney failure or urinary retention, or who are lactating. It should be administered with caution to those who are pregnant. It may aggravate conditions of diabetes or gout.
*Related article:* BAYCARON.

**Megace** (*Bristol-Myers*) is a proprietary preparation of the PROGESTOGEN megestrol acetate, available only on prescription, used to treat sex-hormone-linked cancers (such as cancer of the breast or of the womb-lining). It is produced in the form of tablets (in two strengths).
▲ / ✹ side-effects/warning: *see* MEGESTROL ACETATE.

**Megaclor** (*Pharmax*) is a proprietary ANTIBIOTIC, available only on prescription, used to treat infections of soft tissues, particularly of the upper respiratory tract, and to relieve the symptoms of acne. Produced in the form of capsules, Megaclor is a preparation of the TETRACYCLINE clomocycline sodium. It is not recommended for children.
▲ / ✹ side-effects/warning: *see* CLOMOCYCLINE SODIUM.

**megestrol acetate** is a female sex hormone, a PROGESTOGEN used primarily to treat forms of cancer in which the presence of OESTROGENS is significant (such

as breast cancer or cancer of the womb-lining). Administration is oral in the form of tablets.

▲ side-effects: side-effects are generally mild, but there may be nausea, fluid retention, and weight gain. Some patients experience irregular menstrual cycles and/or gastrointestinal disturbances.

✹ warning: megestrol acetate should not be administered to patients with breast cancer that is not sex-hormone-linked, or who have undiagnosed vaginal haemorrhage; or who have a history of thrombosis. It should be administered with caution to those with diabetes, heart, liver or kidney disease, or high blood pressure (hypertension); or who are lactating.
*Related article:* MEGACE.

**Megozzones** (*Kirby-Warrick Pharmaceuticals*) are proprietary, non-prescription throat pastilles containing MENTHOL, benzoin and liquorice.

**Melleril** (*Sandoz*) is a proprietary form of the powerful ANTI-PSYCHOTIC drug thioridazine. Available only on prescription, it is used to treat and tranquillize psychosis (such as schizophrenia) in which it is particularly suitable for treating manic forms of behavioural disturbance. It may also be used to treat anxiety in the short term. Melleril is produced in the form of tablets (in four strengths), as a suspension (in two strengths) and as a syrup for dilution (the potency of the syrup once dilute is retained for 14 days).
▲ / ✹ side-effects/warning: *see* THIORIDAZINE.

**melphalan** is a CYTOTOXIC drug used in the treatment of various forms of cancers, especially cancer of the bone-marrow. It works by direct action on the DNA of new-forming cells, so preventing normal cell replication. Administration is oral in the form of tablets, or by injection.

▲ side-effects: there is commonly nausea and vomiting; there is often also hair loss.

✦ warning: prolonged treatment may cause sterility in men and an early menopause in women. Regular and frequent blood counts are essential. Dosage should be reduced for patients with impaired kidney function. Because the effect of the drug on the bone marrow is delayed, treatment may be required only at intervals of between 4 and 6 weeks.
*Related article:* ALKERAN.

**menadiol sodium phosphate** is an analogue of VITAMIN K (phytomenadione), which because it is water-soluble – whereas other forms are only fat-soluble – is primarily used in oral application to treat vitamin deficiency caused by the malabsorption of fats in the diet (perhaps through obstruction of the bile ducts or liver disease). The vitamin is necessary on a regular basis to maintain the presence in the blood of clotting factors and other factors that are responsible for the calcification of bone. Administration is both oral in the form of tablets, and by injection.

✦ warning: menadiol sodium phosphate should be administered with caution to patients who are pregnant.
*Related article:* SYNKAVIT.

**Mengivac (A + C)** *(Merieux)* is a VACCINE, now called meningococcal polysaccharide vaccine, prepared from Neisseria meningitidis (meningococcus) groups A and C. It is designed to give protection against the organism meningococcus, which

can cause serious infection including meningitis. It is advised for travellers intending to go 'rough' to parts of the world where the risk of meningococcal infection is much higher than in the United Kingdom, e.g. parts India and Saudi Arabia and much of Africa . It is recommended for adults and children aged over 18 months by deep subcutaneous or intramuscular injection on prescription.

▲/✦ side-effects/warning: see MENINGOCOCCAL POLYSACCHARIDE VACCINE.

**meningococcal polysaccharide vaccine** is a VACCINE designed to give protection against the organism meningococcus, which can cause serious infection including meningitis. It may be indicated for travellers intending to go 'rough' to parts of the world where the risk of meningococcal infection is much higher than in the United Kingdom, e.g. parts of India and Saudi Arabia and much of Africa. It is recommended for adults and children over either 2 months or 18 months according to manufacturer (transient side-effects are more common below the age of 18 months, and though the serogroup A component is effective over 3 months of age, the response to the C component is transitory). It is available in the form of vials for deep subcutaneous or intramuscular injection.

▲/✦ side-effects/warning: see VACCINE.
*Related article:* AC VAX; MENGIVAC (A + C).

**Menophase** *(Syntex)* is a proprietary compound sex-HORMONE preparation, available only on prescription, used to treat menopausal symptoms. Produced in the form of a calendar pack corresponding to one complete menstrual cycle,

Menophase is a preparation of the PROGESTOGEN norethisterone and the OESTROGEN mestranol.
▲/● side-effects/warning: *see* MESTRANOL; NORETHISTERONE.

**menotropin** is a HORMONE preparation, and is a collective name for combinations of the GONADOTROPHINS including follicle-stimulating hormone (FSH) and luteinising hormone (LH). It can be extracted from post-menopausal urine, and has various suggested uses alone or in combination, including treatment of infertile women with proven hypopituitarism or who do not respond to the drug CLOMIPHENE CITRATE (another drug commonly used to treat infertility). It is available in a form for injection.
▲ side-effects: hyperstimulation of the ovaries, multiple pregnancy, local reactions.
● warning: menotropin should be given with caution to women with ovarian cysts; thyroid, adrenal, or pituitary gland disorders.
*Related articles:* HUMEGON; PERGONAL.

**menthol** is a white, crystalline substance derived from peppermint oil (an essential oil in turn derived from a plant of the mint family). It is used, with or without the volatile substance eucalyptus oil, mostly in inhalations meant to clear nasal or catarrhal congestion in conditions such as rhinitis or sinusitis.
*Related articles:* ARADOLENE; ASPELLIN; BALMOSA; BENGUE'S BALSAM; BENYLIN EXPECTORANT; COPHOLCO; EXPULIN; EXPURHIN; GUANOR EXPECTORANT; HISTALIX; PHYTOCIL; ROWACHOL; SALONAIR; TERCODA; TERPOIN.

**Mentholatum** (*Mentholatum*) is a proprietary, non-prescription preparation for the relief of cold symptoms produced in the form of ANTISEPTIC lozenges, balm, deep heat lotion, and spray. These preparations contain MENTHOL, camphor, eucalyptus oil, METHYL SALYCILATE and amylmetacersol.

**Menzol** (*Kabi*) is a proprietary PROGESTOGEN (ovulation-suppressing SEX HORMONE), available only on prescription, in the form of tablets containing norethisterone, in 8-day and 20-day packs called Planapak. It is used to treat uterine bleeding, abnormally heavy menstruation, and other menstrual problems, and may additionally be used as an effective contraceptive preparation.
▲/● side-effects/warning: *see* NORETHISTERONE.

**mepacrine hydrochloride** is a drug with ANTIPROTOZOAL properties used primarily to treat infection by the intestinal protozoon *Giardia lamblia*; giardiasis occurs throughout the world, particularly in children, and is contracted by eating contaminated food. It has largely been superseded by METRONIDAZOLE. Mepacrine can also be used to assist in the treatment of most forms of malaria. It is available as tablets.

**mepenzolate bromide** is an ANTICHOLINERGIC drug used to assist in the treatment of gastrointestinal disorders that involve muscle spasm of the intestinal wall. Administration is oral in the form of tablets or an elixir.
▲ side-effects: there is commonly dry mouth and thirst; there may also be visual disturbances, flushing, irregular heartbeat and constipation. Rarely, there may be high temperature accompanied by delirium.
● warning: mepenzolate bromide should not be administered to patients with glaucoma; it

should be administered with caution to those with heart problems and rapid heart rate, ulcerative colitis, urinary retention or enlargement of the prostate gland; who are elderly; or who are lactating.
*Related article:* CANTIL.

**Meprate** (*DDSA Pharmaceuticals*) is a proprietary ANXIOLYTIC drug that is on the controlled drugs list. Used in the short-term treatment of nervous anxiety and associated muscular tension, and produced in the form of tablets, Meprate is a preparation of the (potentially addictive) tranquilizer meprobamate. It is not recommended for children.
▲/✿ side-effects/warning: *see* MEPROBAMATE.

**meprobamate** is a minor TRANQUILLIZER and ANXIOLYTIC used to relieve nervous tension and anxiety, particularly that associated with premenstrual syndrome. It may also be used to assist in the treatment of minor forms of neurosis. Prolonged treatment, however, may lead to tolerance and dependence (addiction). Administration is oral in the form of tablets.
▲ side-effects: concentration and speed of thought and movement are affected; the degree of sedation may be marked. There may also be low blood pressure (hypotension), debility, gastrointestinal disturbances, headache, blurred vision and rashes. The effect of alcohol consumption may be enhanced.
✿ warning: meprobamate should not be administered to patients with porphyria, or who are lactating. It should be administered with caution to those with respiratory difficulties, glaucoma, epilepsy, or impaired liver or kidney function, who are in the last stages of pregnancy, or who are

elderly or debilitated. Withdrawal of treatment must be gradual (abrupt withdrawal may cause convulsions).
*Related articles:* EQUAGESIC; EQUANIL; MEPRATE.

**meptazinol** is a powerful synthetic narcotic ANALGESIC, an OPIATE that is used to treat moderate to severe pain, including pain in childbirth or following surgery. The onset of its effect is said to take place within 15 minutes of injection, and the duration is said to be between 2 and 7 hours; however, there are some post-operative side-effects. Administration is also oral in the form of tablets.
▲ side-effects: nausea, vomiting, dizziness, sweating and drowsiness are fairly common. However, unlike most drugs of its type, meptazinol is said not to cause shallow breathing.
✿ warning: meptazinol should not be administered to patients with head injury or intracranial pressure; it should be administered with caution to those with impaired kidney or liver function, asthma, depressed respiration, insufficient secretion of thyroid hormones (hypothyroidism) or low blood pressure (hypotension), or who are pregnant or lactating. Dosage should be decreased for the elderly or debilitated.
*Related article:* MEPTID.

**Meptid** (*Wyeth*) is a proprietary narcotic ANALGESIC, available only on prescription, used to treat moderate to severe pain, particularly during or following surgical procedures (including childbirth). Produced in the form of tablets and in ampoules for injection, Meptid is a preparation of the OPIATE meptazinol, and is not recommended for children.
▲/✿ side-effects/warning: *see* MEPTAZINOL.

**mepyramine** is an ANTIHISTAMINE used to treat the symptoms of allergic conditions such as hay fever and urticaria, and – as an anti-emetic – to treat or prevent nausea and vomiting, especially in connection with motion sickness or the vertigo caused by infection of the middle or inner ear. Administration (as mepyramine maleate) is oral in the form of tablets.

▲ side-effects: sedation may affect patients' capacity for speed of thought and movement; there may be headache and/or weight gain, dry mouth, gastrointestinal disturbances and visual problems.

● warning: mepyramine should not be administered to patients with glaucoma, urinary retention, intestinal obstruction, enlargement of the prostate gland, or peptic ulcer, or who are pregnant; it should be administered with caution to those with epilepsy or liver disease.
*Related article:* ANTHISAN.

**mequitazine** is an ANTIHISTAMINE, used to treat the symptoms of allergic conditions such as hay fever and urticaria. Administration is oral in the form of tablets.

▲ side-effects: concentration and speed of thought and movement may be affected. There may be nausea, headache, and/or weight gain, dry mouth, gastrointestinal disturbances and visual problems.

● warning: mequitazine should not be administered to patients who are pregnant, or who have glaucoma, urinary retention, intestinal obstruction, enlargement of the prostate gland, or peptic ulcer; it should be administered with caution

to those with epilepsy or liver disease.
*Related article:* PRIMALAN.

**Merbentyl** (*Merrell*) is a proprietary ANTICHOLINERGIC drug, available only on prescription, used to treat gastrointestinal disorders that result from muscle spasm in the stomach or intestinal walls. Produced in the form of tablets (in two strengths, the stronger under the name Merbentyl 20) and as a syrup for dilution (the potency of the syrup once dilute is retained for 14 days), Merbentyl is a preparation of dicyclomine hydrochloride and is not recommended for children aged under 6 months.

▲/● side-effects/warning: *see* DICYCLOMINE HYDROCHLORIDE.

**mercaptopurine** is a CYTOTOXIC drug used in the treatment of acute leukaemia. It works by combining with new-forming cells in a way that prevents normal cell replication. Administration is oral in the form of tablets.

▲ side-effects: there is commonly nausea and vomiting; there is often also hair loss.

● warning: prolonged treatment may cause sterility in men and an early menopause in women. Regular blood counts are essential during treatment. Mercaptopurine should be administered with caution to patients who are already taking the drug allopurinol for gout or similar conditions.
*Related article:* PURI-NETHOL.

**Mercilon** (*Organon*) is a an ORAL CONTRACEPTIVE, available only on prescription, that combines the PROGESTERONE desogestrel with the OESTROGEN ethinyloestradiol. It is produced in packs of 21 tablets representing one complete menstrual cycle.

▲ / ◆ warning/side-effects: *see*
    DESOGESTREL;
    ETHINYLOESTRADIOL.

**mercuric oxide** is a substance
used as the basis for an eye
ointment intended for topical
application to treat infections in
and around the eye. It is not now
recommended as a form of
treatment.

**Merieux Inactivated Rabies
Vaccine** is a proprietary
preparation of rabies VACCINE
with two uses. Firstly, it may be
used prophylactically to prevent
individuals who might be at risk
from contracting rabies should
they be bitten by a rabid animal.
Secondly, it may be used after an
unvaccinated individual has been
bitten by a suspected rabid
animal to prevent growth of the
virus. It is the only vaccine which
can be used in this way, post
exposure. The success of such
treatment is related to how soon
after the bite the injections of the
vaccine are given. Ideally they
should be on days 0, 3, 7, 14, 30
and 100. Available only on
prescription, the vaccine is of a
type known as human diploid cell
vaccine and has no known contra-
indications. It is freeze-dried and
produced in vials with a diluent
for injection.
*see* RABIES VACCINE.

**Merieux Tetavax** (*Merieux*) is a
proprietary preparation of
tetanus VACCINE, formed of
tetanus toxin (i.e. a toxoid
vaccine) adsorbed on to a mineral
carrier (in the form of aluminium
hydroxide) and produced in
syringes and in vials for injection.
*see* TETANUS VACCINE.

**Merocaine** (*Merrell*) is a
proprietary, non-prescription
local anaesthetic, used to treat
painful mouth and throat
infections. Produced in the form

of lozenges, Merocaine is a
preparation of the local
anaesthetic benzocaine together
with the minor ANTISEPTIC
CETYLPYRIDINIUM CHLORIDE. It is
not recommended for children.
▲ / ◆ side-effects/warning: *see*
    BENZOCAINE.

**Merocet** (*Merrell*) is a proprietary,
non-prescription mouth-wash,
which is a preparation of the
ANTISEPTIC CETYLPYRIDINIUM
CHLORIDE. Although it can (but
need not) be used in dilute form, it
is not recommended for children
aged under 6 years.

**Merocets** (*Merrell*) are
proprietary, non-prescription
lozenges, which are a preparation
of the ANTISEPTIC
CETYLPYRIDINIUM CHLORIDE, used
in general oral hygiene.

**mersalyl** is a powerful DIURETIC
that is used only when all other
methods of treating fluid
retention have failed or are not
tolerated. The drug is so toxic
that it can be administered only
by intramuscular injection: an
intravenous injection may cause
a fatal fall in blood pressure.
▲ side-effects: there may be
gastrointestinal disturbances;
some patients experience
allergic reactions.
◆ warning: mersalyl should not be
administered to patients
with impaired kidney function;
it should be administered with
caution to those who are
pregnant, who have recently
had a heart attack, who suffer
from heartbeat irregularities,
or who are taking drugs that
stimulate the heart's action.

**mesalazine** is an ANTI-
INFLAMMATORY and
ANTIBACTERIAL drug used in the
long-term treatment of diarrhoea
caused by ulcerative colitis in
patients who are sensitive to the

commonly-prescribed drug
sulphasalazine. Administration is
oral or by suppositories.

▲ side-effects: there may be
nausea, with diarrhoea and
abdominal pain; some patients
experience a headache.

✿ warning: mesalazine should
not be administered to patients
who are allergic to aspirin or
other salicylates; it should be
administered with caution to
those with impaired kidney
function.
*Related articles:* ASACOL;
PENTASA.

**mesna** is a synthetic drug that has
the remarkable property of
reducing the incidence of the
serious form of cystitis
(inflammation of the bladder) that
is a toxic complication of the use
of the CYTOTOXIC drugs CYCLO-
PHOSPHAMIDE and ifosfamide,
without inhibiting the cytotoxic
effects of the drugs. Used
therefore as an adjunct in the
treatment of certain forms of
cancer, mesna is administered by
injection.

▲ side-effects: overdosage may
cause gastrointestinal
disturbances and headache,
with tiredness.
*Related article:* UROMITEXAN.

**mesterolone** is an ANDROGEN, a
male SEX HORMONE produced
mainly in the testes that, with
other androgens, promotes the
development of the secondary
male sexual characteristics.
Therapeutically, it may be
administered to treat hormonal
deficiency (but only following
careful investigation and under
strict medical supervision),
particularly in cases of delayed
puberty and underdevelopment in
boys. Administration is oral in
the form of tablets.

▲ side-effects: there may be fluid
retention in the tissues
(oedema) leading to weight

gain. Increased levels of
calcium in the body may cause
bone growth (and in younger
patients may fuse bones before
fully grown) and the symptoms
of hypercalcaemia. In elderly
patients there may be
(increased) enlargement of the
prostate gland. High doses halt
the production of sperm in men
and cause the visible
masculinization of women.

✿ warning: mesterolone should
not be administered to male
patients with kidney disease,
cancer of the prostate gland or
cancer of the breast, or to
female patients who are
pregnant or lactating; it should
be administered with caution
to those with impaired
function of the heart, liver or
kidney, circulatory disorders
and/or high blood pressure,
epilepsy or diabetes, thyroid
disorders, or migraine.
*Related article:* PRO-VIRON.

**Mestinon** (*Roche*) is a proprietary
form of the drug pyridostigmine
bromide, which has the effect of
increasing the activity of the
neurotransmitter acetylcholine
that transmits the neural
instructions of the brain to the
muscles. It is thus used primarily
to treat the neuromuscular
disease myasthenia gravis, but
may also be used to stimulate
intestinal motility and so promote
defecation. Available only on
prescription, Mestinon is
produced in the form of tablets
and in ampoules for injection.

▲/✿ side-effects/warning: *see*
PYRIDOSTIGMINE.

**mestranol** is a female sex
hormone, a synthetic OESTROGEN,
which is a constituent in several
ORAL CONTRACEPTIVES that
contain relatively high oestrogen
levels in comparison with the
PROGESTOGEN content. It is also
used in some similarly combined

preparations to assist in hormone replacement therapy for women experiencing menopausal problems. Administration is on a regular, calendar basis corresponding to menstrual cycles.

▲ side-effects: there may be nausea and vomiting. Fluid and sodium retention in the tissues may result in overall weight gain. The breasts may become tender and enlarge slightly. The patient may also suffer from a headache and/or depression; sometimes a rash breaks out.

● warning: mestranol should not be taken by patients who have cancers proved to be sex-hormone-linked, who have a history of thrombosis or of inflammation of the womb, or who suffer from porphyria or impaired liver function. It should be taken with caution by patients who are diabetic or epileptic, who have heart or kidney disease, who are lactating, or who have high blood pressure (hypertension) or recurrent severe migraine. Prolonged treatment increases the risk of cancer of the endometrium (the lining of the womb).
*Related articles:* NORINYL-1; ORTHO NOVIN.

**Metabolic Mineral Mixture** (*Scientific Hospital Supplies*) is a proprietary, non-prescription mineral supplement, used to supplement special diets. Produced in the form of a powder, it contains various mineral salts.

**Metamucil** (*Searle*) is a proprietary, non-prescription LAXATIVE of the type known as a bulking agent, which works by increasing the overall mass of faeces within the rectum, so stimulating bowel movement. It is also used to soothe the effects of

diverticular disease and irritable colon, and to control the consistency of faecal material in patients who have had a colostomy. Produced in the form of a gluten-free powder, Metamucil is a preparation of ispaghula husk.

▲/● side-effects/warning: *see* ISPAGHULA HUSK.

**Metanium** (*Bengué*) is a proprietary, non-prescription astringent, used to relieve nappy rash and other macerated skin conditions. Produced in the form of an ointment, Metanium is a preparation of titanium salts in a silicone base.

**metaraminol** is a SYMPATHOMIMETIC drug and as such also has the properties of a VASOCONSTRICTOR. It is used to treat cases of acute low blood pressure (particularly in emergency situations as a temporary measure while preparations are made for blood transfusion). Administration is by injection or infusion.

▲ side-effects: there is a reduction in the flow of blood through the kidneys; there is also an increase in the heart rate and there may be heartbeat irregularities.

● warning: metaraminol should not be administered to patients who are pregnant, or who are undergoing a heart attack. Leakage of the drug at the site of injection or infusion may cause local tissue death.
*Related article:* ARAMINE.

**Metatone** (*Parke-Davis*) is a proprietary, non-prescription tonic, which is not available from the National Health Service: it is used to remedy loss of appetite. Metatone is a preparation of THIAMINE (vitamin $B_1$) and minerals such as calcium, manganese, potassium and sodium in a diluent (the potency of the preparation is retained for 14 days). It is not recommended for children aged under 6 years.

**Metenix** (*Hoechst*) is a proprietary DIURETIC, available only on prescription, used to treat an accumulation of fluid within the tissues (oedema) and high blood pressure (*see* ANTIHYPERTENSIVE). Produced in the form of tablets, Metenix is a preparation of the thiazide-like diuretic metolazone. It is not recommended for children.

▲/✸ side-effects/warning: *see* METOLAZONE.

**Meterfolic** (*Sinclair*) is a proprietary, non-prescription IRON-and-VITAMIN supplement, used particularly to prevent iron deficiency or vitamin B deficiency (as sometimes occurs during pregnancy). Produced in the form of tablets, Meterfolic is a compound of ferrous fumarate and folic acid.

▲/✸ side-effects/warning: *see* FERROUS FUMARATE; FOLIC ACID.

**metformin hydrochloride** is a drug used to treat adult-onset diabetes, particularly in patients who are not totally dependent on additional supplies of INSULIN. It works by increasing the absorption and utilization in the body of glucose, to make up for the reduction in insulin available from the pancreas.
Administration is oral in the form of tablets.

▲ side-effects: there may be nausea and vomiting, with diarrhoea and weight loss. Body uptake of CYANOCOBALAMIN (vitamin B₁₂) or its analogues may be reduced.

✸ warning: metformin hydrochloride should not be administered to patients with

heart, liver or kidney failure, dehydration, alcoholism, or severe infection or trauma; it should be administered with caution to those who are lactating.
*Related articles:* GLUCOPHAGE; ORABET.

**methadone** is a powerful and long-acting narcotic ANALGESIC used both to relieve severe pain and – like several narcotic analgesics – to suppress coughs. One of its principal uses is in the treatment of heroin addicts. Ironically, prolonged use of methadone can also lead to dependence (addiction). Administration (in the form of methadone hydrochloride) is oral in the form of tablets, as a linctus, or by injection.

▲ side-effects: there is commonly constipation, drowsiness and dizziness. High dosage may result in respiratory depression.

✸ warning: methadone should not be administered to patients with liver disease, raised intracranial pressure, or head injury. It should be administered with caution to those with asthma, low blood pressure (hypotension), underactivity of the thyroid gland (hypothyroidism) or impaired liver or kidney function; who are pregnant or lactating; who are taking monoamine oxidase inhibitors; or have a history of drug abuse. Its effect is cumulative. Dosage should be reduced for elderly or debilitated patients.
*Related article:* PHYSEPTONE.

**methenamine** is another name for the somewhat toxic ANTIBACTERIAL ANTISEPTIC hexamine.
*see* HEXAMINE.

**methicillin** is an ANTIBIOTIC of the penicillin family, which was the first of the type to be resistant to the penicillinase enzyme secreted by penicillin-resistant strains of Staphylococcus aureus. It has been largely superseded by orally-active penicillinase-resistant penicillins, e.g. flucloxacillin. Methicillin has to be given by injection or infusion. In recent years the occurrence of methicillin-resistant strains of Staphylococcus has created major problems in hospitals throughout the world.

▲ side-effects: there may be sensitivity reactions ranging from a minor rash to urticaria and joint pains, and (occasionally) to fever or anaphylactic shock.

✿ warning: methicillin should not be administered to patients known to be allergic to penicillins; it should be administered with caution to those with impaired kidney function.
*Related article:* CELBENIN.

**methionine** is an antidote to poisoning by the analgesic paracetamol (which has the greatest toxic effect on the liver). Administration is oral in the form of tablets; dosage depends on the results of blood counts every 4 hours.

**methixene hydrochloride** is a powerful ANTIPARKINSONISM drug, used to relieve some of the symptoms of parkinsonism, specifically the tremor of the hands, the overall rigidity of the posture, and the tendency to produce an excess of saliva. (The drug also has the capacity to treat these conditions in some cases where they are produced by drugs.) It is thought to work by compensating for the lack of dopamine in the brain that is the major cause of such parkinsonian symptoms. Administration – which may be in parallel with the administration of LEVODOPA – is oral in the form of tablets.

▲ side-effects: there may be dry mouth, dizziness and blurred vision, and/or gastrointestinal disturbances. Some patients experience sensitivity reactions and anxiety. Rarely, and in susceptible patients, there may be confusion, agitation and psychological disturbance (at which point treatment must be withdrawn).

✿ warning: methixene hydrochloride should not be administered to patients with not merely tremor but with distinct involuntary movements; it should be administered with caution to those with impaired kidney or liver function, cardiovascular disease, glaucoma, or urinary retention. Withdrawal of treatment must be gradual.
*Related article:* TREMONIL.

**methocarbamol** is a SKELETAL MUSCLE RELAXANT used primarily to relieve muscle spasm in the limbs caused by injury, but also is a constituent in several compound analgesic preparations. It works by direct action on the central nervous system. Administration is oral in the form of tablets, or by injection.

▲ side-effects: concentration and speed of thought and movement is affected. There may be light-headedness, dizziness, drowsiness and/or nausea; or there may be restlessness, anxiety and mild confusion. Some patients experience sensitivity reactions such as a rash. Rarely, there are convulsions.

✿ warning: methocarbamol should not be administered to patients with glaucoma, epilepsy, enlargement of the prostate gland, rapid heart rate or defective bladder sphincter muscles, who have brain damage, or who are in a comatose state. It should be administered only orally to those with impaired kidney function. The drug may increase the effects of alcohol consumption.

*Related articles:* ROBAXIN 750; ROBAXISAL FORTE.

**methohexitone sodium** is a general ANAESTHETIC used for both the induction and the maintenance of general anaesthesia in surgical operations; administration is intravenous (generally in 1% solution). It is less irritant to tissues than some other anaesthetics, and recovery afterwards is quick, but the induction of anaesthesia is not particularly smooth.

▲ side-effects: induction may cause hiccups and involuntary movements. The patient may feel pain on the initial injection.

✱ warning: maintenance of anaesthesia is usually in combination with other anaesthetics. Induction may take up to 60 seconds.

*Related article:* BRIETAL SODIUM.

**methotrexate** is a CYTOTOXIC drug used primarily in the treatment of lymphoblastic leukaemia, but also to treat other lymphomas and the lymphatic cancer Hodgkin's disease, as well as some solid tumours. It works by inhibiting the activity of an enzyme essential to the DNA metabolism in cells, and is administered orally or by injection.

▲ side-effects: there is commonly nausea and vomiting; there may also be hair loss. The capacity of the bone-marrow to produce blood cells is reduced. The drug may also cause inflammation in various body tissues.

✱ warning: methotrexate should not be administered to patients with severely impaired kidney function, or who have fluid within the pleural cavity. Leakage of the drug into the tissues at the site of injection may cause tissue damage. Regular blood counts are essential during treatment.

**methotrimeprazine** is an ANTIPSYCHOTIC drug used to tranquillize patients suffering from schizophrenia and other psychoses, and to calm and soothe patients who are dying. Administration is oral in the form of tablets or by injection.

▲ side-effects: concentration and speed of thought and movement are affected; the effects of alcohol consumption are enhanced. There may be dry mouth and blocked nose, constipation and difficulty in urinating, and blurred vision; menstrual disturbances in women or impotence in men may occur, with weight gain; there may be sensitivity reactions. Some patients feel cold and depressed, and tend to suffer from poor sleep patterns. Blood pressure may be low and the heartbeat irregular. Prolonged high dosage may cause opacity in the cornea and lens of the eyes, and a purple pigmentation of the skin. Treatment by intramuscular injection may be painful.

✱ warning: methotrimeprazine should not be administered to patients with certain forms of glaucoma, whose blood-cell formation by the bone-marrow is reduced, or who are taking drugs that depress certain centres of the brain and spinal cord. It should be administered with caution to those with lung disease, cardiovascular disease, epilepsy,

parkinsonism, abnormal secretion by the adrenal glands, impaired liver or kidney function, undersecretion of thyroid hormones (hypothyroidism), enlargement of the prostate gland or any form of acute infection; who are pregnant or lactating; or who are elderly. Prolonged use requires regular physical checks. Withdrawal of treatment should be gradual.
*Related articles:* NOZINAN; VERACTIL.

**methoxamine hydrochloride** is a SYMPATHOMIMETIC drug that, as such, has the properties of a VASOCONSTRICTOR. It is used primarily to raise the blood pressure of a patient whose blood pressure has dropped because of the induction of anaesthesia. Administration is by injection.

▲ side-effects: there may be headache and a slow heartbeat; the blood pressure may be raised too high.

✿ warning: methoxamine hydrochloride should not be administered to patients with severe heart disease of any kind; it should be administered with caution to those who suffer from overactivity of the thyroid gland (hyperthyroidism), or who are pregnant.
*Related article:* VASOXINE.

**methyclothiazide** is a DIURETIC, one of the THIAZIDES, used to treat fluid retention in the tissues (oedema), and high blood pressure (hypertension). Because all thiazides tend to deplete body reserves of potassium, methyclothiazide may be administered in combination either with potassium supplements or with diuretics that are complementarily potassium-sparing. Administration is oral in the form of tablets.

▲ side-effects: there may be tiredness and a rash. In men, temporary impotence may occur.

✿ warning: methyclothiazide should not be administered to patients with liver or kidney impairment or urinary retention, or who are lactating. It should be administered with caution to those who are pregnant. It may aggravate conditions of diabetes or gout.
*Related article:* ENDURON.

**methyl salicylate** is an non-narcotic ANALGESIC for topical application in solution. It works by producing an irritation of sensory nerve endings within the skin that offsets the pain of underlying muscle or joint pains, and is produced in the form of a non-proprietary liniment and ointment, in addition to several proprietary preparations in the form of a cream or a balsam, for gently massaging in.

✿ warning: preparations of methyl salicylate in the form of an ointment may contain wool fat, which can cause sensitivity reactions in some patients.
*Related articles:* ASPELLIN; BALMOSA; BENGUE'S BALSAM; DUBAM; PHYTEX; SALONAIR.

**methylcellulose** is a high-fibre substance used as a LAXATIVE because it is an effective bulking agent – it increases the overall mass of faeces within the rectum, so stimulating bowel movement. It is also particularly useful in soothing the symptoms of diverticular disease and irritable colon. Moreover, it can additionally be used to treat diarrhoea (as well as constipation) and to assist in the medical treatment of obesity because it reduces the intake of food by producing the sensation of satiety. Administration is oral, generally in the form of tablets, granules for solution, or a mixture.

▲ side-effects: there may be flatulence, so much as to distend the abdomen.

✿ warning: preparations of methylcellulose should not be administered to patients with obstruction of the intestines, or failure of the muscles of the intestinal wall; it should be administered with caution to those with ulcerative colitis. Fluid intake during treatment should be higher than usual.
*Related articles:* CELEVAC; COLOGEL; NILSTIM.

**methylcysteine** is a MUCOLYTIC drug, used to reduce the viscosity of sputum and thus facilitate expectoration (the coughing up of sputum) in patients with disorders of the upper respiratory tract such as asthma and bronchitis. Administration is oral in the form of tablets or, rarely, aerosol spray.
▲ side-effects: side-effects are uncommon, but there may be gastrointestinal disturbance, with nausea, or a rash.
✿ warning: methylcysteine should not be administered to patients with a peptic ulcer; it should be administered with caution to those who are pregnant.
*Related article:* VISCLAIR.

**methyldopa** is a powerful ANTIHYPERTENSIVE drug used, in combination with a diuretic drug, to treat moderate to severe high blood pressure (hypertension). With other antihypertensives that work by direct action on the brain, however, methyldopa is becoming ever more rarely used, although triple combinations involving a diuretic and a beta-blocker in addition to methyldopa remain fairly popular. Administration is oral in the form of capsules, tablets and a suspension, or by injection.
▲ side-effects: there is dry mouth, drowsiness, fluid retention and diarrhoea; there may also be

sedation, depression, impaired liver function, and skin and blood disorders.
✿ warning: methyldopa should not be administered to patients with abnormal secretion of corticosteroids by the adrenal glands or chronic liver disease, or who have a history of depression. It should be administered with caution to those with impaired kidney function. Regular blood counts and tests on liver function are essential during treatment.
*Related articles:* ALDOMET; DOPAMET; HYDROMET; MEDOMET.

**methyldopate hydrochloride** is the form of the ANTIHYPERTENSIVE drug methyldopa that is used for injection.
*see* METHYLDOPA.

**methylphenobarbitone** is a drug used to treat grand mal (tonic-clonic) and focal (partial) seizures of epilepsy. Administered orally in the form of tablets, it is converted in the liver to the powerful SEDATIVE and ANTICONVULSANT BARBITURATE phenobarbitone, with which it shares action and effects.
*see* PHENOBARBITONE.

**methylprednisolone** is a CORTICOSTEROID used primarily to treat the symptoms of inflammation or allergic reaction, but useful also in the treatment of fluid retention in the brain or of shock. Administration (as methylprednisolone, methylprednisolone acetate or methylprednisolone sodium succinate) is oral in the form of tablets, or by injection or infusion.
▲ side-effects: treatment of susceptible patients may engender a euphoria, or a state of confusion or depression. Rarely, the patient suffers from a peptic ulcer.

**M**

● warning: methylprednisolone
should not be administered to
patients with psoriasis; it
should be administered with
caution to the elderly (in whom
overdosage can cause
osteoporosis, 'brittle bones'). In
children, administration of
methylprednisolone may lead
to stunting of growth. The
effects of potentially serious
infections may be masked by
the drug during treatment.
Withdrawal of treatment must
be gradual.
*Related articles:* DEPO-
MEDRONE; DEPO-MEDRONE
WITH LIDOCAINE; MEDRONE;
MIN-I-MIX
METHYLPREDNISOLONE; SOLU-
MEDRONE.

**methyprylone** is a HYPNOTIC
formerly used to treat severe and
intractable insomnia. Repeat
doses are cumulative in effect and
result in dependence (addiction)
so the drug has been included in
the controlled drugs list.
Administration is oral in the form
of tablets. The proprietary
preparation is on the controlled
drugs list.
▲ side-effects: there is a marked
degree of sedation that may
affect concentration and speed
of thought and movement.
There may also be dizziness and
respiratory depression,
headache and sensitivity
reactions (particularly in the
elderly).
● warning: methyprylone should
not be administered to patients
whose insomnia is caused by
pain, who have porphyria, who
are children or elderly or
debilitated, who are pregnant
or lactating, or who have a
history of drug abuse. It should
be administered with caution to
those with respiratory
depression for any reason, or
who have impaired liver or
kidney function. Dosage should

be the least still to be effective;
prolonged treatment should be
avoided. Withdrawal of
treatment should nevertheless
be gradual.

**methysergide** is a potentially
dangerous drug used, generally
under strict medical supervision
in a hospital, to prevent severe
recurrent migraine and similar
headaches in patients for whom
other forms of treatment have
failed. But the drug may also be
used to treat patients with
tumours of the intestinal glands
that have spread to the liver: the
liver then produces excess
serotonin in the bloodstream –
and it is the symptoms of that
excess that methysergide treats.
Administration is oral in the form
of tablets.
▲ side-effects: there is initial
nausea, drowsiness and
dizziness; there may also be
fluid retention and consequent
weight gain, spasm of the
arteries, numbness of the
fingers and toes, increased
heart rate and even
psychological changes.
● warning: methysergide should
not be administered to patients
with heart, lung, liver or
kidney disease, or who suffer
from collagen disorders, or who
are pregnant or lactating. It
should be administered with
caution to those with peptic
ulcer. Withdrawal of treatment
should be gradual, although no
course of treatment should last
for more than 6 months at a
time.
*Related article:* DESERIL.

**metipranolol** is a BETA-BLOCKER
used in the form of eye-drops to
treat glaucoma. It is thought to
work by slowing the rate of
production of the aqueous humour
in the eyeball, but it may be
absorbed and have systemic
effects as well.

▲ side-effects: there may be periods in which the eyes temporarily become dry; at such times there may be infections such as conjunctivitis or blepharitis.

❀ warning: because systemic absorption may occur, metipranolol should be administered with caution to patients with slow heart rate, heart failure or asthma. It should not be administered to patients who have a history of asthmatic symptoms.
Related articles: GLAULINE; MINIMS METIPRANOLOL.

**metirosine** is an ANTI-HYPERTENSIVE drug used, generally under strict medical supervision in a hospital, primarily to treat the symptoms of high blood pressure associated with conditions that result in abnormal secretion of CORTICO-STEROIDS by the adrenal glands due to phaeochromocytoma, or in patients for whom surgery is not possible. It works by inhibiting an enzyme that contributes to the secretion of catecholamines such as adrenaline and noradrenaline (as occurs in situations of stress). Administration is oral in the form of capsules.

▲ side-effects: there is a degree of sedation such that concentration and speed of thought and movement may be affected. There is commonly also severe diarrhoea. Some patients experience sensitivity reactions – which may also be severe.

❀ warning: increased fluid intake during treatment is essential. Regular checks on overall blood volume are advisable.
Related article: DEMSER.

**metoclopramide** is an effective ANTI-EMETIC and ANTINAUSEANT drug, which also has MOTILITY STIMULANT properties, and may be used to prevent vomiting caused by gastrointestinal disorders or by chemotherapy or radiotherapy in the treatment of cancer. It works both by direct action on the vomiting centre of the brain and by actions within the intestinal walls to increase the rate of emptying of the stomach and increase the passage of food products along the intestine. In this respect some newer drugs such as cisapride are effective but with fewer side-effects. Although as an anti-emetic metoclopramide has fewer side-effects than some others (such as the phenothiazine derivatives), newer agents such as ondansetron may now prove more beneficial. Administration (as metoclopramide hydrochloride) is oral in the form of tablets and syrups, or by injection.

▲ side-effects: side-effects are relatively uncommon, especially in male patients. There may, however, be mild neuromuscular symptoms, drowsiness, restlessness and diarrhoea.

❀ warning: metoclopramide should not be administered to patients who have had gastrointestinal surgery within the previous 4 days; it should be administered with caution to those with impaired kidney function, or who are children, pregnant, lactating or elderly. Dosage should begin low and gradually increase. The effects of the drug may mask underlying disorders.
Related articles: GASTRESE LA; GASTROBID CONTINUS; GASTROMAX; MAXOLON; METOX; METRAMID; PARMID; PRIMPERAN.

**metolazone** is a DIURETIC, one of the THIAZIDES, used to treat fluid retention in the tissues (oedema), high blood pressure (hypertension) and mild to moderate heart failure. Because all thiazides tend to deplete body reserves of potassium, metolazone may be administered in combination either with potassium supplements or with diuretics that are complementarily potassium-sparing. Administration is oral in the form of tablets.

▲ side-effects: there may be tiredness and a rash. In men, temporary impotence may occur.

✸ warning: metolazone should not be administered to patients with kidney failure or urinary retention, or who are lactating. It should be administered with caution to those who are pregnant. It may aggravate conditions of diabetes or gout.
*Related article:* METENIX.

**Metopirone** (*Ciba*) is a proprietary form of metyrapone, available only on prescription, used with corticosteroids (glucocorticoids) to treat resistant accumulation of fluid within the tissues (oedema) caused by increased secretion of the mineralocorticoid aldosterone. It may also be used to test the functioning of the pituitary gland. Produced in the form of capsules, Metopirone is not recommended for children.
▲/✸ side-effects/warning: *see* METYRAPONE.

**metoprolol** is a BETA-BLOCKER used to treat high blood pressure (*see* ANTIHYPERTENSIVE), heartbeat irregularities, angina pectoris (heart pain), and the effects of an excess of thyroid hormones in the bloodstream (thyrotoxicosis), to provide emergency relief in a heart attack, and to prevent recurrent attacks of migraine. Administration (as metoprolol tartrate) is oral in the form of tablets and sustained-release tablets, or by injection.
▲ side-effects: there may be some gastrointestinal or slight respiratory disturbance

following oral administration. Some patients experience sensitivity reactions.

✸ warning: as a hypertensive drug, metoprolol tartrate should not be administered to patients with heart disease or asthmatic symptoms; it should be administered with caution to those with impaired kidney function, or who are nearing the end of pregnancy or lactating. Withdrawal of treatment should be gradual.
*Related articles:* BETALOC; CO-BETALOC; LOPRESOR; LOPRESORETIC; METOROS.

**Metoros** (*Geigy*) is a proprietary preparation of the BETA-BLOCKER metoprolol tartrate, available only on prescription, used to control and regulate the heart rate and to treat high blood pressure (hypertension), angina pectoris (heart pain), or an excess of thyroid hormones in the blood (thyrotoxicosis). It is produced in the form of sustained-release tablets in two strengths; the lower dose form is known as Meteros LS.
▲/✸ side-effects/warning: *see* METOPROLOL.

**Metosyn** (*Stuart*) is a proprietary CORTICOSTEROID preparation, available only on prescription, used to treat inflammations of the skin (such as severe eczema) in patients not responding to less potent corticosteroids. Produced in the form of a water-miscible cream, as a paraffin-based ointment, and as a scalp lotion, Metosyn is a preparation of the potent steroid fluocinonide.
▲/✸ side-effects/warning: *see* FLUOCINONIDE.

**Metox** (*Steinhard*) is a proprietary preparation of the ANTI-EMETIC drug metoclopramide hydrochloride, available only on prescription, used to relieve symptoms of nausea and vomiting caused by gastrointestinal disorders, or by chemotherapy or radiotherapy in the treatment of cancer. It is produced in the form of tablets.

▲/ ✚ side-effects/warning: see METOCLOPRAMIDE.

**Metramid** (*Nicholas*) is a proprietary preparation of the ANTI-EMETIC drug metoclopramide hydrochloride, available only on prescription, used to relieve symptoms of nausea and vomiting caused by gastrointestinal disorders, or by chemotherapy or radiotherapy in the treatment of cancer. It is produced in the form of tablets, and is not recommended for children aged under 15 years.

▲/ ✚ side-effects/warning: see METOCLOPRAMIDE.

**metriphonate** is an organophosphorus compound that destroys the blood fluke *Schistosoma haematobium*, which causes a form of bilharzia that is common in North Africa and the Middle East. The disease is contracted by bathing in water contaminated by the larvae of the flukes; adult flukes of this species infest the veins of the bladder, ureter and other pelvic organs, causing severe inflammation. Administration is oral in three doses over four weeks. The drug has largely been superseded by PRAZIQUANTEL.

**Metrodin** (*Serono*) is a proprietary preparation of the pituitary HORMONE follicle-stimulating hormone (FSH), available only on prescription, used primarily to treat women suffering from specific hormonal deficiencies resulting in infertility. The treatment is ordinarily undertaken in specialist centres because monitoring is essential. Produced in the form of a powder for reconstitution as a medium for injection, Metrodin is a form of the hormone prepared from human menopausal urine.

▲/ ✚ side-effects/warning: see FSH.

**Metrolyl** (*Lagap*) is a proprietary drug with ANTIBIOTIC and ANTIPROTOZOAL properties. Available only on prescription it is used to treat many forms of infection including those caused by bacteria (such as non-specific vaginitis), and by protozoa. Produced in the form of tablets (in two strengths), as anal suppositories (in two strengths), and in solution for intravenous infusion, Metrolyl is a preparation of metronidazole.

▲/ ✚ side-effects/warning: see METRONIDAZOLE.

**metronidazole** is an ANTI-MICROBIAL with ANTIBIOTIC and ANTIPROTOZOAL properties. Its antibiotic spectrum is narrow, being limited to activity against strictly anaerobic bacteria. It acts by interfering with DNA replication. The other group of microbes it is active against are the protozoa, specifically *Entamoeba histolytica* (causes amoebic dysentery), *Giardia lamblia* (causes giardiasis, an infection of the small intestine) and *Trichomonas vaginalis* (causes vaginitis). Resistance is rare and this drug has radically improved the success of treating anaerobic infections such as may be found in peritonitis, pelvic abscess, brain abscess and wound infections. One reason for its activity in such situations is its ability to penetrate and remain effective in the presence of pus. Administration is oral in the form of tablets or a suspension, topical in the form of anal suppositories, or by injection or infusion.

▲ side-effects: these are uncommon – but there may be nausea and vomiting, with

drowsiness, headache and gastrointestinal disturbances; gastrointestinal effects may be reduced by taking the drug during or after food. Some patients experience a discoloration of the urine. Prolonged treatment may eventually give rise to neuromuscular disorders or even seizures reminiscent of epilepsy with high doses.
● warning: metronidazole should not be taken regularly on a high-dosage basis. It should be administered with caution to patients with impaired liver function, or who are pregnant or lactating. During treatment patients must avoid alcohol consumption (the presence of alcohol in the body during treatment gives rise to most unpleasant side-effects).
*Related articles:* FLAGYL; FLAGYL COMPAK; FLAGYL S; METROLYL; NIDAZOL; ZADSTAT.

**metronidazole benzoate** is the form in which the ANTIBIOTIC metronidazole is administered in a suspension.
*see* METRONIDAZOLE.

**metyrapone** is a substance that has the effect of inhibiting the production of mineralocorticoids by the adrenal glands. It can thus be used with glucocorticoids to treat resistant fluid retention within the tissues (oedema) caused by increased secretion of the mineralocorticoid aldosterone, and to treat other conditions that result from the abnormal secretion of adrenal hormones (such as Cushing's syndrome). It may also be used to test the functioning of the pituitary gland.
▲ side-effects: there may be nausea and vomiting; in some patients, the overall production and secretion of adrenal hormones is

drastically reduced, causing further symptoms.
● warning: metyrapone should be administered with caution to patients with severe under-secretion of pituitary hormones.
*Related article:* METOPIRONE.

**Mevillin-L** (*Evans*) is a proprietary VACCINE against measles (rubeola), available only on prescription. It is a powdered preparation of live but attenuated measles viruses for administration within a diluent by injection.
▲ side-effects: there may be inflammation at the site of injection. Rarely, there may be high temperature, cough and sore throat, a rash, swelling of the lymph glands and/or pain in the joints.
● warning: mevillin-L should not be administered to patients with any infection, particularly tuberculosis; who are allergic to eggs (the viruses are cultured in chick embryo tissue); who have known immune-system abnormalities; who are pregnant; who are hypersensitive to neomycin or polymyxin; or who are already taking corticosteroid drugs, cytotoxic drugs or are undergoing radiating treatment. It should be administered with caution to those with epilepsy or any other condition potentially involving convulsive fits.

**mexiletine** is an ANTIARRHYTHMIC drug used to reduce the rate of the heartbeat, especially following a heart attack, and especially when the more commonly-used local ANAESTHETIC lignocaine has proved to be ineffective. Administration (in the form of mexiletine hydrochloride) is by injection followed by infusion as necessary. Overdosage is, however, dangerous.

▲ side-effects: there may be slow
heart rate and low blood
pressure; some patients have
neuromuscular reactions such
as tremor or nystagmus (eye-
twitch) and gastrointestinal
disturbances. Rarely, there is a
state of confusion.

✤ warning: mexiletine should not
be administered to patients
who have a slow heart rate,
who have heart block, who are
taking diuretic drugs, or who
suffer from PARKINSONISM.
*Related article:* MEXITIL.

**Mexitil** (*Boehringer Ingelheim*) is a
proprietary ANTIARRHYTHMIC
drug, available only on
prescription. It is a preparation
of mexiletine hydrochloride and is
produced in the form of capsules
(in two strengths), as sustained-
release capsules ('Perlongets',
under the name Mexitil PL),
and in ampoules for injection.
It is not recommended for
children.

▲/✤ side-effects/warning: *see*
MEXILETINE.

**mezlocillin** is a derivative of the
broad-spectrum, penicillin-type
ANTIBIOTIC ampicillin, which has
increased activity against some
important gram-negative bacteria
such as *Klessiella* and
*Pseudomonas*. Administration is
by injection or infusion.

▲ side-effects: there may be
sensitivity reactions ranging
from a minor rash to urticaria
and joint pains, and
(occasionally) to high
temperature and anaphylactic
shock.

✤ warning: mezlocillin should
not be administered to
pregnant women or to patients
known to be allergic to
penicillins; it should be
administered with caution to
those with impaired kidney
function.
*Related article:* BAYPEN.

**MFV-Ject** (*Merieux*) is the name of
a series of proprietary flu
VACCINES consisting of
suspensions containing
inactivated viral material derived
from influenza viruses. It is not
recommended for children.

▲ side-effects: rarely, there is
local reaction together with
headache and high
temperature.

✤ warning: like any flu vaccine,
MFV-Ject cannot control
epidemics and should be used
only against what seems to be
the appropriate viral strain –
on people who are at high risk:
the elderly, patients with
cardiovascular problems, and
medical staff. MFV-Ject should
not be administered to patients
who are allergic to egg or
chicken protein (in which
vaccine viruses are cultured),
or who are pregnant.

**Miacalcic** (*Sandoz*) is a
proprietary synthesized form of
calcitonin (salcatonin), one of the
hormones that regulate blood
levels of calcium in the body.
Available only on prescription. It
is used to treat several types of
serious bone disease, including
cancer, and is produced in
ampoules (in three strengths) for
injection by the subcutaneous,
intramuscular and intravenous
routes.

▲/✤ side-effects/warning: *see*
CALCITONIN; SALCATONIN.

**mianserin** is an ANTIDEPRESSANT
drug used to treat depressive
illness, especially in cases in
which a degree of sedation may be
useful. Administration is oral in
the form of tablets.

▲ side-effects: concentration and
speed of thought and
movement may be affected;
there may also be dry mouth,
blurred vision, difficulty in
urinating, sweating, and
irregular heartbeat; some

357

patients experience a rash, behavioural disturbances, a state of confusion and/or a loss of libido. Treatment must be withdrawn if blood disorders occur: regular blood counts are essential in connection with the use of this drug.

● warning: mianserin should not be administered to patients with heart disease or psychosis, or who are already taking other types of antidepressants, barbiturates, anti-hypertensives or alcohol; it should be administered with caution to those with diabetes, epilepsy, liver or thyroid disease, glaucoma or urinary retention; or who are pregnant or lactating. Withdrawal of treatment must be gradual.
*Related article:* LUDIOMIL.

**Micolette** (*Ayerst*) is a proprietary, non-prescription form of small enema administered rectally to promote defecation, especially pre- or post-operatively or before labour or rectal examination by endoscope. Produced in single-dose disposable packs with a nozzle, Micolette is a preparation that includes sodium citrate, sodium laurylsulphoacetate and GLYCEROL in a viscous solution. It is not recommended for children aged under 3 years.
▲/ ● side-effects/warning: *see* SODIUM CITRATE.

**miconazole** is an ANTI-FUNGAL drug of the imidazole type, used in the treatment of many forms of fungal infection, generally by topical application (for instance, as an oral gel, as a spray powder, or as a water-miscible cream), although tablets are also available for use in oral or intestinal infection and as an injection for systemic infections. The injection contains a castor oil derivative which may cause

sensitivity reactions. In solution, the drug may be used for irrigation of the bladder.
▲ side-effects: rarely, there is irritation of the skin or minor sensitivity reaction. Miconazole may cause nausea and vomiting.
● warning: topical treatment should be continued for more than a week after lesions or other symptoms have healed.
*Related article:* DAKTARIN.

**Micralax** (*Smith, Kline & French*) is a proprietary, non-prescription form of small enema administered rectally to promote defecation, especially before labour or rectal examination by endoscope. Produced in single-dose disposable packs with a nozzle, Micralax is a preparation that includes sodium citrate, sodium alkylsulphoacetate and sorbic acid in a viscous solution. It is not recommended for children aged under 3 years.
▲/ ● side-effects/warning: *see* SODIUM CITRATE.

**Microgynon 30** (*Schering*) is a proprietary combined ORAL CONTRACEPTIVE, available only on prescription, used also (because it is a combination of female sex hormones) to treat menstrual problems. Produced in the form of tablets in a calendar pack, Microgynon 30 is a preparation of the OESTROGEN ethinyloestradiol and the PROGESTOGEN levonorgestrel.
▲/ ● side-effects/warning: *see* ETHINYLOESTRADIOL; LEVONORGESTREL.

**Micro-K** (*Merck*) is a proprietary, non-prescription form of potassium supplement, used to treat patients with deficiencies and to replace potassium in patients taking potassium-depleting drugs such as CORTICOSTEROIDS or the THIAZIDE diuretics. Produced in the form of sustained-release capsules, Micro-K is a preparation of POTASSIUM CHLORIDE.

✢ warning: should not be used in patients with advanced renal failure. Should be discontinued if it produces ulceration or obstruction of the small bowel.

**Micronor** (*Ortho-Cilag*) is a proprietary, progesterone-only ORAL CONTRACEPTIVE, available only on prescription. Produced in the form of tablets in a calendar pack corresponding to one complete menstrual cycle, Micronor is a preparation of the PROGESTOGEN norethisterone.

▲/✢ side-effects/warning: *see* NORETHISTERONE.

**Microval** (*Wyeth*) is a proprietary, progesterone-only CONTRACEPTIVE, available only on prescription. Produced in the form of tablets in a calendar pack corresponding to one complete menstrual cycle, Microval is a preparation of the PROGESTOGEN levonorgestrel.

▲/✢ side-effects/warning: *see* LEVONORGESTREL.

**Mictral** (*Winthrop*) is a proprietary ANTIBIOTIC, available only on prescription, used primarily to treat infections of the urinary tract, including cystisis. Produced in the form of granules in a sachet for solution in water, Mictral's major active constituents are the drug nalidixic acid and sodium citrate. It is not recommended for infants under 3 months.

▲/✢ side-effects/warning: *see* NALIDIXIC ACID.

**Micturin** (*KabiVitrum*) is a proprietary preparation of the ANTICHOLINERGIC drug terodiline hydrochloride, available only on prescription, used to treat excessive frequency of urination

and urinary incontinence. It works mainly by reducing the effect of the parasympathetic nervous system on the bladder, although it also has CALCIUM ANTAGONIST properties. Produced in the form of tablets, it is not recommended for children.

▲/✢ side-effects/warning: *see* TERODILINE HYDROCHLORIDE.

**Midamor** (*Morson*) is a proprietary DIURETIC, available only on prescription, used to treat fluid retention in the tissues (oedema), and to conserve potassium when administered in combination with other diuretics. Produced in the form of tablets, Midamor is a preparation of the potassium-sparing diuretic amiloride hydrochloride; it is not recommended for children.

▲/✢ side-effects/warning: *see* AMILORIDE.

**midazolam** is an ANXIOLYTIC drug, one of the BENZODIAZEPINES, used primarily to provide sedation for minor surgery such as dental operations or as a premedication prior to surgical procedures and, because it also has some SKELETAL MUSCLE RELAXANT properties, to treat some forms of spasm. Prolonged use results in tolerance and may lead to dependence (addiction), especially in patients with a history of drug (including alcohol) abuse. Administration is by injection.

▲ side-effects: there may be drowsiness, dizziness, headache, dry mouth and shallow breathing; hypersensitivity reactions may occur.

✢ warning: concentration and speed of thought and movement are often affected. Midazolam should be administered with caution to patients with respiratory difficulties (it sometimes causes a sharp fall in blood pressure), glaucoma, or kidney or liver disease; who are in especially the last stages of pregnancy; or who are elderly or debilitated. Abrupt withdrawal of treatment should be avoided. *Related articles:* DIAZEPAM; HYPNOVEL.

**Midrid** (*Carnrick*) is a proprietary compound non-narcotic ANALGESIC, available only on prescription, used to treat migraine and other headaches caused by tension. Produced in the form of capsules, Midrid is a preparation of the SYMPATHO-MIMETIC isometheptene mucate, the SEDATIVE dichloralphenazone and the analgesic paracetamol; it is not recommended for prescription to children.

▲/✚ side-effects/warning: *see* DICHLORALPHENAZONE; ISOMETHEPTENE MUCATE; PARACETAMOL.

**Migraleve** (*International Labs*) is a proprietary, non-prescription compound ANALGESIC and ANTIHISTAMINE, used to treat migraine. Produced in the form of tablets, Migraleve is a preparation of the antihistamine buclizine hydrochloride, the analgesic paracetamol and the OPIATE codeine phosphate; tablets without buclizine hydrochloride are also available separately or in a duo-pack. These preparations are not recommended for children aged under 10 years. They should never be prescribed prophylactically.

▲/✚ side-effects/warning: *see* CODEINE PHOSPHATE; PARACETAMOL.

**Migravess** (*Bayer*) is a proprietary, compound non-narcotic ANALGESIC, available only on prescription, used to treat migraine. Produced in the form of tablets (in two strengths, the stronger under the name

Migravess Forte), Migravess is a preparation of the analgesic aspirin together with the ANTI-EMETIC metoclopramide hydrochloride. It is not recommended for children aged under 10 years.

▲/✚ side-effects/warning: *see* ASPIRIN; METOCLOPRAMIDE.

**Migril** (*Wellcome*) is a proprietary, compound non-narcotic ANALGESIC, available only on prescription, used to treat migraine and some other vascular headaches. Produced in the form of tablets, Migril is a preparation of the vegetable alkaloid ergotamine tartrate, the ANTIHISTAMINE cyclizine hydrochloride and the mild stimulant caffeine hydrate. It is not recommended for children.

▲/✚ side-effects/warning: *see* CYCLIZINE; ERGOTAMINE TARTRATE.

**Mildison** (*Brocades*) is a proprietary ANTI-INFLAMMATORY drug, available only on prescription, in which the active constituent is the corticosteroid hormone hydrocortisone. Produced in the form of a cream, Mildison is used to treat severe skin inflammations, such as eczema and various forms of dermatitis.

▲/✚ side-effects/warning: *see* HYDROCORTISONE.

**milrinone** is a PHOSPHO-DIESTERASE INHIBITOR, used to treat congestive heart failure, especially where other drugs have been unsuccessful. It is available only on prescription, and is administered by intravenous injection or infusion.

▲ side-effects: there may be irregular or extra heart beats, speeding of the heart, hypotension, headache, nausea and vomiting, insomnia, chills and fever, diarrhoea, retention

of urine and pain in the limbs.
● warning: milrinone should be
administered with care to
patients with certain forms of
heart failure and vascular
disease. The blood pressure
and electrocardiogram should
be monitored. A smaller dose
may be indicated in patients
with kidney disease.
*Related article:* PRIMACOR.

**Milupa Low Protein
Drink** (*Milupa*) is a proprietary
NUTRITIONAL PREPARATION
containing as a powder; protein,
carbohydrate and fat which are
reconstituted as a drink. It is used
for inherited disorders of amino-
acid metabolism in childhood.
Available without prescription.

**Minafen** (*Cow & Gate*) is a
proprietary, non-prescription,
nutritional preparation, used to
feed infants and young children
who have the amino acid
metabolic abnormality
phenylketonuria (PKU).
Produced in the form of a powder,
Minafen is a preparation of
protein, fat, carbohydrate,
vitamins and minerals, and is low
in the amino acid phenylalanine.
It is not, however, usable as a
complete diet.

**Minamino** (*Consolidated*) is a
proprietary, non-prescription,
vitamin-and-mineral preparation,
which is not available from the
National Health Service.
Produced in the form of a syrup,
Minamino is a preparation of
essential and non-essential amino
acids, B-group VITAMINS and
minerals, together with liver,
spleen and gastric mucosa
extracts. It is used as a vitamin
and MINERAL SUPPLEMENT in the
elderly, and during pregnancy
and lactation.

*mineral supplement is the term
used for salts of essential dietary
minerals, which may be taken,

usually by mouth, to make-up
deficiencies in the diet, or where
there are problems with
absorption of the minerals from
normal foodstuffs. Examples
include CALCIUM, SODIUM,
PHOSPHORUS, POTASSIUM, IRON
and ZINC.

**Minihep** (*Leo*) is a proprietary
ANTICOAGULANT, available only
on prescription, used to treat and
prevent various forms of
thrombosis. Produced in the form
of 'darts' and in ampoules for
subcutaneous injection, Minihep
is a preparation of the natural
anticoagulant heparin sodium,
and is also available as Minihep
Calcium.
▲/ ● side-effects/warning: *see*
HEPARIN.

**Min-i-Jet Adrenaline**
(*International Medication
Systems*) is a proprietary form of
the natural catecholamine
adrenaline, available only on
prescription, used as a
SYMPATHOMIMETIC drug to treat
bronchial asthma, in the
emergency treatment of acute
allergic reactions, and to relieve
the symptoms of heart failure.
Produced in disposable syringes
for injection (straight into the
heart muscle if necessary), Min-i-
Jet Adrenaline is a preparation of
adrenaline hydrochloride.
▲/ ● side-effects/warning: *see*
ADRENALINE.

**Min-I-Jet Sodium
Bicarbonate** (*IMS*) is a
proprietary form of sodium
bicarbonate, available only on
prescription, and used to treat
metabolic acidosis which
sometimes occurs in renal failure
or diabetic ketoacidosis. The
preparation is administered
intravenously from a disposable
syringe.
▲/ ● side-effects/warning: *see*
SODIUM BICARBONATE.

**Min-i-Mix Methylprednisolone** (*International Medication Systems*) is a proprietary CORTICOSTEROID, available only on prescription, used to suppress inflammation or allergic symptoms, to relieve fluid retention around the brain, or to treat shock. Produced in the form of powder for reconstitution as a solution for injection, it is a preparation of methyl-prednisolone sodium succinate.
▲/✹ side-effects/warning: *see* METHYLPREDNISOLONE.

**Min-I-Mix Suxamethonium Chloride** (*IMS*) is a proprietary MUSCLE RELAXANT, available only on prescription, which has an effect for only 5 minutes. It is used to relax muscles during surgical anaesthesia and this facilitates some surgical procedures (e.g. inserting a ventilator into the windpipe). Produced in ampoules for injection, it is a preparation of suxamethonium chloride.
▲/✹ side-effects/warning: *see* SUXAMETHONIUM CHLORIDE.

**Minims Amethocaine** (*Smith & Nephew*) is a proprietary local ANAESTHETIC for topical application, and ophthalmic procedures available only on prescription. Produced in the form of single-dose eye-drops, Minims Amethocaine is a preparation of amethocaine hydrochloride.
▲/✹ side-effects/warning: *see* AMETHOCAINE HYDROCHLORIDE.

**Minims Artificial Tears** (*S & N Pharmaceuticals*) is a proprietary form of medium used to treat chronically sore eyes where there is an impaired tear production. Available without prescription, the preparation contains HYDROXYETHYL CELLULOSE, and comes in the form of eye-drops.

**Minims Atropine Sulphate** (*Smith & Nephew*) is a proprietary ANTICHOLINERGIC mydriatic drug, available only on prescription, used to dilate the pupils and paralyse certain eye muscles for the purpose of ophthalmic examination especially in young children (or occasionally to assist in antibiotic treatment). It is produced in the form of single-dose eye-drops (and indeed is a preparation of the anticholinergic drug atropine sulphate).
▲/✹ side-effects/warning: *see* ATROPINE SULPHATE.

**Minims Benoxinate** (*Smith & Nephew*) is a proprietary local ANAESTHETIC, available only on prescription, used to relieve pain in the eyes especially during minor surgery or ophthalmic examination. Produced in the form of single-dose eye-drops, Minims Benoxinate is a preparation of oxybuprocaine hydrochloride.
▲/✹ side-effects/warning: *see* OXYBUPROCAINE.

**Minims Castor Oil** (*Smith & Nephew*) is a proprietary, non-prescription form of eye-drops consisting of castor oil, for use as a lubricant in removing foreign bodies from the eye.

**Minims Chloramphenicol** (*Smith & Nephew*) is a proprietary ANTIBIOTIC for topical application, available only on prescription, used to treat bacterial infections in the eye. Produced in the form of single-dose eye-drops, Minims Chloramphenicol is a preparation of chloramphenicol.
▲/✹ side-effects/warning: *see* CHLORAMPHENICOL.

**Minims Cyclopentolate** (*Smith & Nephew*) is a proprietary, ANTI-CHOLINERGIC mydriatic drug, available only on prescription, used to dilate the pupils and paralyse certain eye muscles for the purpose of ophthalmic examination (or occasionally to assist in antibiotic treatment). Produced in the form of single-dose eye-drops, it is a preparation of drug cyclopentolate hydrochloride.

▲/ ❋ side-effects/warning: *see* CYCLOPENTOLATE HYDROCHORIDE.

**Minims Fluorescein Sodium** (*Smith & Nephew*) is a proprietary, non-prescription dye used in the diagnosis of certain disorders of the eye – for instance, to locate abrasions and foreign bodies. Produced in the form of single-dose eye-drops, it is a preparation of FLUORESCEIN SODIUM.

**Minims Gentamicin** (*Smith & Nephew*) is a proprietary ANTIBIOTIC, available only on prescription, used to treat bacterial infections in the eye. Produced in the form of single-dose eye-drops, Minims Gentamicin is a preparation of the aminoglycoside gentamicin sulphate.

▲/ ❋ side-effects/warning: *see* GENTAMICIN.

**Minims Homatropine** (*Smith & Nephew*) is a proprietary, ANTI-CHOLINERGIC mydriatic drug, available only on prescription, used to dilate the pupils and paralyse certain eye muscles for the purpose of ophthalmic examination (or occasionally to assist in antibiotic treatment). Produced in the form of single-dose eye-drops, it is a preparation of the ATROPINE derivative homatropine hydrobromide.

**Minims Lignocaine and Fluorescein** (*Smith & Nephew*) is a proprietary local ANAESTHETIC, available only on prescription. Produced in the form of single-dose eye-drops, Minims Lignocaine and Fluorescein is a

preparation of lignocaine hydrochloride together with the diagnostic dye FLUORESCEIN SODIUM.

▲/ ❋ side-effects/warning: *see* LIGNOCAINE.

**Minims Metipranolol** (*Smith & Nephew*) is a proprietary BETA-BLOCKER, available only on prescription, used in the form of eye-drops to treat glaucoma and other conditions involving pressure within the eyeball. Produced in eye-drops of three strengths, it is a preparation of metipranolol, and is not recommended for children.

▲/ ❋ side-effects/warning: *see* METIPRANOLOL.

**Minims Neomycin** (*Smith & Nephew*) is a proprietary ANTIBIOTIC, available only on prescription, used to treat bacterial infections in the eye. Produced in the form of single-dose eye-drops, it is a preparation of the aminoglycoside antibiotic neomycin.

▲/ ❋ side-effects/warning: *see* NEOMYCIN.

**Minims Phenylephrine** (*Smith & Nephew*) is a proprietary, non-prescription SYMPATHOMIMETIC, used to dilate the pupils and paralyse certain eye muscles for the purpose of ophthalmic examination (or occasionally to assist in antibiotic treatment). Produced in the form of single-dose eye-drops, it is a preparation of the sympathomimetic phenylephrine hydrochloride.

▲/ ❋ side-effects/warning: *see* PHENLYEPHRINE.

**Minims Pilocarpine** (*Smith & Nephew*) is a proprietary, PARASYMPATHOMIMETIC miotic drug, available only on prescription, used in the treatment of glaucoma. It works by improving drainage in the trabecular meshwork of the eyeball. Produced in the form of eye-drops (in three strengths), it is a preparation of pilocarpine nitrate.

▲/✹ side-effects/warning: *see* PILOCARPINE.

**Minims Prednisolone** (*Smith & Nephew*) is a proprietary CORTICOSTEROID, available only on prescription, used to treat non-infective inflammatory conditions in and around the eye. Produced in the form of eye-drops, it contains prednisolone sodium phosphate.

▲/✹ side-effects/warning: *see* PREDNISOLONE.

**Minims Rose Bengal** (*Smith & Nephew*) is a proprietary, non-prescription dye used in the diagnosis of certain conditions in the eye, such as the presence of degenerated cells in dry eye syndrome or pressure marks from contact lenses. Produced in the form of single-dose eye-drops, it is a preparation of rose bengal. It is not recommended for children.

**Minims Sodium Chloride** (*Smith & Nephew*) is a proprietary, non-prescription preparation of saline solution used for the irrigation of the eyes, and to facilitate the first-aid removal of harmful substances. It is produced in the form of single-dose eye-drops.

▲/✹ side-effects/warning: *see* SODIUM CHLORIDE.

**Minims Sulphacetamide Sodium** (*Smith & Nephew*) is a proprietary ANTIBIOTIC, available only on prescription, used to treat local infections in the eye. Produced in the form of single-dose eye-drops, it is a preparation of the SULPHONAMIDE sulphacetamide sodium. It is no longer recommended.

▲/✹ side-effects/warning: *see* SULPHACETAMIDE.

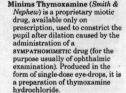

**Minims Thymoxamine** (*Smith & Nephew*) is a proprietary miotic drug, available only on prescription, used to constrict the pupil after dilation caused by the administration of a SYMPATHOMIMETIC drug (for the purpose usually of ophthalmic examination). Produced in the form of single-dose eye-drops, it is a preparation of thymoxamine hydrochloride.

▲/✹ side-effects/warning: *see* THYMOXAMINE.

**Minims Tropicamide** (*Smith & Nephew*) is a proprietary mydriatic drug, available only on prescription, used to dilate the pupils and paralyse certain eye muscles for the purpose of ophthalmic examination (or occasionally to assist in antibiotic treatment). Produced in the form of single-dose eye-drops, it is a preparation of the short-acting ANTICHOLINERGIC drug tropicamide.

▲/✹ side-effects/warning: *see* TROPICAMIDE.

**Minocin** (*Lederle*) is a proprietary broad-spectrum ANTIBIOTIC, available only on prescription, used to treat many forms of infection but particularly those of the urinary tract, the respiratory tract, skin and soft tissue (including acne), and to prevent meningococcal infections. Produced in the form of tablets (in two strengths), Minocin is a preparation of the TETRACYCLINE minocycline hydrochloride. It should not be given to children aged under 12 years or to pregnant women.

▲/✹ side-effects/warning: *see* MINOCYCLINE.

**minocycline** is a broad-spectrum ANTIBIOTIC, a TETRACYCLINE with a wider range of action than other tetracyclines in that it is effective also in treating and preventing certain forms of meningitis. Also unlike most tetracyclines it may be used relatively safely in a patient with impaired renal function. Administration is oral in the form of tablets.

▲ side-effects: there may be nausea and vomiting, with diarrhoea; dizziness and vertigo are not uncommon, especially in female patients. Rarely, there are sensitivity reactions.

✿ warning: minocycline should not be administered to patients who are aged under 12 years, or who are pregnant. It should be administered with caution to those who are lactating or who have impaired liver or kidney function.

*Related articles:* MINOCIN; TETRACYCLINES.

**Minodiab** (*Farmitalia Carlo Erba*) is a proprietary SULPHONYLUREA, available only on prescription, used to treat adult-onset diabetes mellitus. It works by augmenting what remains of insulin production in the pancreas. Produced in the form of tablets (in two strengths), Minodiab is a preparation of glipizide and is not recommended for children.

▲/✿ side-effects/warning: *see* GLIPIZIDE.

**\*minor tranquillizer:** *see* TRANQUILLIZER; ANXIOLYTIC.

**minoxidil** is a powerful ANTIHYPERTENSIVE drug that works primarily by being a VASODILATOR – and has many side-effects. Useful as it is in treating severe high blood pressure (hypertension), particularly when administered simultaneously with a diuretic and a beta-blocker, the drug has come to be employed really only when other vasodilators have failed. Administration is oral in the form of tablets. It can also be used, as a

lotion, to treat male-pattern baldness (men and women). The lotion is flammable, so hands should be washed after application.

▲ side-effects: there are commonly gastrointestinal disturbances and weight gain; there may also be fluid retention, a rise in the heart rate and, in women, breast tenderness. When used topically to the scalp there may be itching and dermatitis.

✿ warning: minoxidil should not be administered to patients with adrenal disorders that cause abnormal secretion of corticosteroid hormones; it should be administered with caution to patients who undergo renal dialysis. The drug may aggravate conditions of heart failure and angina pectoris (heart pain).

*Related articles:* LONITEN; REGAINE.

**Mintec** (*Smith, Kline & French*) is a proprietary, non-prescription ANTISPASMODIC drug, used to treat the discomfort and sensation of distension associated with irritable bowel syndrome. Produced in the form of capsules, Mintec is a preparation of PEPPERMINT OIL; it is not recommended for children.

**Mintezol** (*Merck Sharp & Dohme*) is a proprietary, non-prescription ANTHELMINTIC drug, used to treat intestinal infestations by threadworm and guinea worm, and to assist in the treatment of resistant infections by hookworm, whipworm and roundworm. Produced in the form of tablets, Mintezol is a preparation of thiabendazole.

▲/✿ side-effects/warning: *see* THIABENDAZOLE.

**Minulet** (*Wyeth*) is a an ORAL CONTRACEPTIVE, available only on prescription, which combines the

PROGESTERONE gestodene with the OESTROGEN ethinyloestradiol. It is produced in packs of 21 tablets representing one complete menstrual cycle.

▲/✿ side-effects/warning: see DESOGESTREL; ETHINYLOESTRADIOL.

**Miochol** (*Cooper Vision*) is a proprietary preparation of the PARASYMPATHOMIMETIC drug acetylcholine chloride, available only on prescription, used mainly to contract the pupil of the eye for the purpose of surgery on the iris, the cornea, or other sections of the exterior of the eye. It is produced in the form of a solution for intra-ocular irrigation.

▲/✿ side-effects/warning: see ACETYLCHOLINE CHLORIDE.

**Miol** (Formula M1) (*Brit Cair*) is a proprietary ANTISEPTIC, available only on prescription, used in topical application to treat inflammatory and ulcerative skin conditions. Produced in the form of a cream and a lotion, Miol is a preparation of various antiseptic and antifungal agents.

**Miraxid** (*Leo*) is a proprietary compound, orally active, ANTIBIOTIC preparation, available only on prescription, used to treat particularly gram-negative bacterial infections in the respiratory tract, the ear and the urinary tract. Produced in the form of tablets (in two strengths, the stronger under the name Miraxid 450, which is not recommended for children) and as a suspension for children, Miraxid is a compound preparation of the penicillins pivampicillin and pivmecillinam hydrochloride.

▲/✿ side-effects/warning: see PIVAMPICILLIN; PIVMECILLINAM.

**misoprostol** is a synthetic analogue of the PROSTAGLANDIN E1, ALPROSTADIL. It is used to promote healing of gastric and duodenal ulcers, since it inhibits acid secretion and promotes protective blood flow to the mucosa. It can protect against ulcers caused by non-steroidal, ANTI-INFLAMMATORY drugs, but not dyspepsia.

▲ side-effects: diarrhoea which may be severe, nausea, vomiting, abdominal pain, dyspepsia, abnormal vaginal bleeding.

✿ warning: misoprostol should not be administered to women who are pregnant or contemplating pregnancy. *Related article:* CYTOTEC.

**Mithracin** (*Pfizer*) is a proprietary form of the drug plicamycin, formerly used as a CYTOTOXIC drug in the treatment of cancers but now used mainly in the emergency treatment of hypercalcaemia (excessive levels of calcium in the bloodstream) caused by malignant disease. It is produced in the form of powder for reconstitution as a medium for injection (in combination with other constituents, such as the diuretic mannitol).

▲/✿ side-effects/warning: see PLICAMYCIN.

**mithramycin** is the name formerly used for the drug plicamycin. see PLICAMYCIN.

**mitobronitol** is a CYTOTOXIC drug used primarily to treat leukaemia, particularly the type that involves the bone marrow. It works by interfering with the DNA of new-forming cells, thus preventing normal cell replication. Administration is oral in the form of tablets (generally only in hospitals).

▲ side-effects: there may be nausea and vomiting; there may also be hair loss. The blood-cell producing capacity of the bone-marrow is impaired.

❋ warning: prolonged treatment may cause sterility in men and an early menopause in women; in both sexes it may lead to permanent bone marrow damage. Blood count monitoring is essential. Dosage should be the minimum still to be effective.
*Related article:* MYELOBROMOL.

**mitomycin** is a CYTOTOXIC drug that is of antibiotic origin, and is used to treat cancers of the stomach, duodenum or jejunum, or of the breast. It is a comparatively toxic drug, and may cause severe side-effects such as permanent bone marrow damage. Administration is by injection.

▲ side-effects: there may be nausea and vomiting; there may also be hair loss. The blood-cell producing capacity of the bone marrow is impaired.

❋ warning: prolonged treatment may cause sterility in men and an early menopause in women; in both sexes it may lead to permanent bone marrow, lung and kidney damage. Blood count monitoring is essential. Dosage should be the minimum still to be effective. If spilled, the drug is an irritant to tissues.
*Related article:* MITOMYCIN C KYOWA.

**Mitomycin C Kyowa** (*Martindale*) is a proprietary preparation of the CYTOTOXIC drug mitomycin, available generally for hospital use only, used to treat upper gastrointestinal and breast cancers. Produced in the form of powder for reconstitution as a medium for injection, it is a preparation of mitomycin.

▲/❋ side-effects/warning: *see* MITOMYCIN.

**Mitoxana** (*Boehringer Ingelheim*) is a proprietary preparation of the CYTOTOXIC drug ifosamide, available for hospital use only, and used pretty well always in combination with MESNA to reduce some of the toxic effects. It is produced in the form of powder for reconstitution as a medium for injection.

▲/❋ side-effects/warning: *see* IFOSFAMIDE.

**mitozantrone** is a CYTOTOXIC drug chemically related to doxorubicin. It is used principally to treat breast cancer, although it tends to suppress the blood-cell forming capacity of the bone marrow and to have toxic effects on the heart. Administration is by intravenous infusion.

▲ side-effects: there may be nausea and vomiting; there may also be hair loss. The blood-cell producing capacity of the bone marrow is impaired.

❋ warning: prolonged treatment may cause an early menopause in women; in both sexes it may lead to permanent bone-marrow, lung and kidney damage. Blood count monitoring is essential. Dosage should be the minimum still to be effective.
*Related article:* NOVANTRONE.

**Mixtard 30/70** (*Nordisk Wellcome*) is a proprietary, non-prescription preparation of mixed pork insulins used to treat and maintain diabetic patients. Produced in vials for injection, Mixtard 30/70 is a preparation of both neutral (30%) and isophane (70%) insulins. HUMAN MIXTARD 30/70 is also available.

▲/❋ side-effects/warning: *see* INSULIN.

**MMR vaccine** is a combined VACCINE against measles/mumps/rubella, using live but weakened strains of the viruses. It was introduced with the aim of eliminating rubella (German measles) through largely universal vaccination before entering school. Rarely, the mumps component has been thought to cause a mild viral meningitis, but this is less common than the incidence of viral meningitis complicating natural mumps, and such a complication settles on its own. Less commonly, convulsions and encephalitis (inflammation of the brain) have been associated with the vaccine. This may be related to either the measles or the mumps component. Such complications are again more common after either natural mumps or measles. The vaccine is available from District Health Authorities under a number of names that include: IMMRAVAX; MMR II; PLUSERIX.

▲ side-effects: as with single measles vaccine there may be fever and/or rash about a week after; there may be a swelling of the parotid gland (a salivary gland in the jaw) about two to three weeks after vaccination.

✸ warning: it should not be given to immunocompromised children; to children allergic to neomycin or kanamycin; or who have had an anaphylactic reaction to egg; with acute febrile illness. It should not be given within three months of an immunoglobulin injection.

**MMR II** (*Wellcome*) is the MMR VACCINE used to treat children in the prevention of measles/mumps/rubella (German measles). It is available only on prescription, and is made available by Local Health Authorities.

▲/✸ side-effects/warning: *see* MMR VACCINE.

**Mobilan** (*Galen*) is a proprietary, ANTI-INFLAMMATORY, non-narcotic ANALGESIC, available only on prescription, used to treat the pain of rheumatic and other musculo-skeletal disorders (including gout, bursitis and tendonitis). Produced in the form of capsules (in two strengths), Mobilan is a preparation of indomethacin.

▲/✸ side-effects/warning: *see* INDOMETHACIN.

**Modecate** (*Squibb*) is a proprietary ANTIPSYCHOTIC drug, available only on prescription, used in the long-term maintenance of tranquillization for patients suffering from psychoses (including schizophrenia). Produced in ampoules for injection (in two strengths, the stronger under the trade name Modecate Concentrate), Modecate is a preparation of fluphenazine decanoate. It is not recommended for children.

▲/✸ side-effects/warning: *see* FLUPHENAZINE.

**Moditen** (*Squibb*) is a proprietary ANTIPSYCHOTIC drug, available only on prescription, used in the long-term maintenance, as a major TRANQUILLIZER, for patients suffering from psychoses (including schizophrenia) and patients with behavioural disturbances. It may also be used in the short term to treat severe anxiety. Produced in the form of tablets (in three strengths), Moditen is a preparation of fluphenazine hydrochloride. Ampoules for depot injection are also available (under the name Moditen Enanthate) containing fluphenazine enanthate. Neither of these preparations is recommended for children.

▲/✸ side-effects/warning: *see* FLUPHENAZINE.

**Modrasone** (*Kirby-Warrick*) is a proprietary, ANTI-INFLAMMATORY CORTICOSTEROID drug, available only on prescription, used in topical application to treat severe skin inflammation, such as eczema and various forms of dermatitis. Produced in the form of a cream and as an ointment, Modrasone is a preparation of the corticosteroid alclometasone dipropionate.

▲/✚ side-effects/warning: *see* ALCLOMETASONE DIPROPIONATE.

**Modrenal** (*Sterling Research*) is a proprietary preparation, available only on prescription, of the unusual drug trilostane, which inhibits the production of corticosteroids by the adrenal glands. It is thus used to treat conditions that result from the excessive secretion of adrenal hormones into the bloodstream (such as Cushing's disease). It is produced in the form of capsules, and is not recommended for children.

▲/✚ side-effects/warning: *see* TRILOSTANE.

**Moducren** (*Morson*) is a proprietary, ANTIHYPERTENSIVE, DIURETIC compound preparation, available only on prescription, used to treat mild to moderate high blood pressure (hypertension). Produced in the form of tablets, Moducren is a preparation of the THIAZIDE hydrochlorothiazide, the weak, but potassium-sparing, diuretic amiloride hydrochloride and the BETA-BLOCKER timolol maleate. It is not recommended for children.

▲/✚ side-effects/warning: *see* AMILORIDE; HYDROCHLOROTHIAZIDE; TIMOLOL MALEATE.

**Moduret 25** (*Morson*) is a proprietary DIURETIC, available only on prescription, used to treat congestive heart failure, high blood pressure (*see* ANTI-HYPERTENSIVE) and cirrhosis of the liver. Produced in the form of tablets, it is a compound of the

weak, but potassium-sparing, diuretic amiloride hydrochloride together with the THIAZIDE hydrochlorothiazide. It is not recommended for children.

▲/✚ side-effects/warning: *see* AMILORIDE; HYDROCHLOROTHIAZIDE.

**Moduretic** (*Merck, Sharp & Dohme*) is a proprietary DIURETIC, available only on prescription, used to treat congestive heart failure, high blood pressure (*see* ANTIHYPERTENSIVE) and cirrhosis of the liver. Produced in the form of tablets and as an oral solution, it is a compound of the weak, but potassium-sparing, diuretic amiloride hydrochloride together with the THIAZIDE hydrochlorothiazide. It is not recommended for children.

▲/✚ side-effects/warning: *see* AMILORIDE; HYDROCHLOROTHIAZIDE.

**Mogadon** (*Roche*) is a proprietary HYPNOTIC, available on prescription only to private patients, used to treat insomnia in cases where some degree of daytime sedation is acceptable. Produced in the form of tablets and as capsules, Mogadon is a preparation of the long-acting BENZODIAZEPINE nitrazepam, and is not recommended for children.

▲/✚ side-effects/warning: *see* NITRAZEPAM.

**Molcer** (*Wallace*) is a proprietary, non-prescription form of ear-drops designed to soften and dissolve ear-wax (cerumen), and commonly prescribed for use at home two nights consecutively before syringing of the ears in a doctor's surgery. Its solvent constituent is DIOCTYL SODIUM SULPHO-SUCCINATE (also called docusate sodium).

✚ warning: molcer should not be used if there is inflammation in the ear, or where there is any chance that the eardrum has been perforated.

**Molipaxin** (*Roussel*) is a proprietary ANTIDEPRESSANT, available only on prescription, used to treat depressive illness (especially in cases where there is anxiety). It causes sedation. Produced in the form of capsules (in two strengths) and as a sugar-free liquid, Molipaxin is a preparation of the drug trazodone hydrochloride; it is not recommended for children.
▲/● side-effects/warning: *see* TRAZODONE HYDROCHLORIDE.

**Monaspor** (*Ciba*) is a proprietary ANTIBIOTIC, available only on prescription, used to treat many forms of infection, especially those of the respiratory tract, certain bone and soft tissue infections, and those caused by the organism *Pseudomonas aeruginosa*. It is also sometimes used to ensure asepsis during surgery. Produced in the form of a powder for reconstitution as a medium for injection, Monaspor is a preparation of the CEPHALOSPORIN cefsulodin sodium.
▲/● side-effects/warning: *see* CEFSULODIN.

**Monistat** (*Ortho-Cilag*) is a proprietary ANTIFUNGAL preparation for topical application, available only on prescription, used to treat yeast infections (such as thrush) of the vagina or vulva. Produced in the form of a vaginal cream and vaginal inserts (pessaries), Monistat is a preparation of miconazole nitrate. Not for use in children.
▲/● side-effects/warning: *see* MICONAZOLE.

**Monit** (*Stuart*) is a proprietary VASODILATOR, available only on prescription, used to prevent

attacks of angina pectoris (heart pain). Produced in the form of tablets (in two strengths, the weaker under the name Monit LS) and as sustained-release tablets (Monit SR), Monit is a preparation of isosorbide mononitrate. It is not recommended for children.
▲/● side-effects/warning: *see* ISOSORBIDE MONONITRATE.

**\*monoamine oxidase inhibitor:** *see* MAO INHIBITOR.

**Mono-Cedocard 20** (*Tillotts*) is a proprietary VASODILATOR, available only on prescription, used to prevent attacks of angina pectoris (heart pain). Produced in the form of tablets (in three strengths, under the names Mono-Cedocard 10, Mono-Cedocard 20 and Mono-Cedocard 40), Mono-Cedocard is a preparation of isosorbide mononitrate. It is not recommended for children.
▲/● side-effects/warning: *see* ISOSORBIDE MONONITRATE.

**Monocor** (*Cyanamid*) is a proprietary form of the BETA-BLOCKER bisoprolol fumarate available only on prescription, used as an ANTIHYPERTENSIVE to treat hypertension and also angina pectoris (heart pain). Available in the form of tablets.
▲/● side-effects/warning: *see* PROPRANOLOL.

**Monoparin** (*CP Pharmaceuticals*) is a proprietary ANTICOAGULANT, available only on prescription, used to treat or prevent various forms of thrombosis (e.g. post-operative). Produced in ampoules for subcutaneous and intravenous injection, Monoparin is a preparation of the anticoagulant heparin sodium.
▲/● side-effects/warning: *see* HEPARIN.

**monosulfiram** is a parasiticidal drug used mainly in topical application to treat skin surface infestation by the itch-mite (scabies). In this it is particularly valuable in treating children. Administration is in the form of a dilute spiritous solution (generally applied topically after a hot bath).

▲ side-effects: rarely, there are sensitivity reactions.

● warning: keep the solution away from the eyes. During treatment, patients should avoid alcohol consumption (if absorbed, the drug may give rise to a severe reaction – as does the closely-related drug disulfiram if ingested with alcohol).

**Monotard MC** (*Nova*) is a proprietary, non-prescription, highly purified pork insulin zinc suspension, used to treat and maintain diabetic patients. It is produced in vials for injection.

▲/● side-effects/warning: see INSULIN.

**Monotrim** (*Duphar*) is a proprietary ANTIBIOTIC, available only on prescription, used to treat infections of the upper respiratory tract (particularly bronchitis and bronchial pneumonia) and of the urinary tract. Produced in the form of tablets (in two strengths), as a sugar-free suspension for dilution (the potency of the suspension once diluted is retained for 14 days), and in ampoules for injection, Monotrim is a preparation of the antibacterial drug trimethoprim. It is not recommended for children aged under 6 weeks.

▲/● side-effects/warning: see TRIMETHOPRIM.

**Monovent** (*Lagap*) is a proprietary BETA-RECEPTOR STIMULANT, A BRONCHODILATOR, available only on prescription, used to relieve the bronchial spasm associated with such conditions as asthma and bronchitis. Produced in the form of sustained-release tablets (under the name Monovent SA), and as a syrup for dilution (the potency of the syrup once dilute is retained for 14 days), Monovent is a preparation of terbutaline sulphate.

▲/● side-effects/warning: see TERBUTALINE.

**Monphytol** (*L A B*) is a proprietary, non-prescription ANTIFUNGAL liquid used in topical application to treat skin infections (particularly nail) caused by fungi of the genus Tinea (such as athlete's foot). Produced in the form of a paint, Monphytol is a preparation of various acids and antibacterial agents, including salicylic acid and chlorbutol.

**Morhulin** (*Napp*) is a proprietary, non-prescription skin emollient (softener and soother), used to treat nappy rash and bedsores. Produced in the form of an ointment, Morhulin is a preparation of cod-liver oil and ZINC OXIDE in a wool fat and paraffin base.

● warning: wool fat causes sensitivity reactions in some patients.

**morphine** is a powerful narcotic ANALGESIC, which is the principal alkaloid of opium. It is widely used to treat severe pain and to soothe the associated stress and anxiety; it may be used in treating shock (with care since it lowers blood pressure), in suppressing coughs (although it may cause nausea and vomiting), and in reducing peristalsis (the muscular waves that urge material along the intestines) as a constituent in some antidiarrhoeal mixtures. It is also sometimes used as a premedication prior to surgery, or to supplement anaesthesia during an operation. Tolerance occurs extremely readily; dependence (addiction) may follow. Administration is oral and by injection; given by injection, morphine is more active. Proprietary preparations that contain morphine (in the form of morphine, morphine tartrate, morphine hydrochloride or morphine sulphate) are all on the controlled drugs list.

▲ side-effects: there may be nausea and vomiting, loss of appetite, urinary retention and constipation. There is generally a degree of sedation, and euphoria which may lead to a state of mental detachment or confusion.

● warning: morphine should not be administered to patients with depressed breathing (the drug may itself cause a degree of respiratory depression), or who have intracranial pressure or head injury. It should be administered with caution to those with low blood pressure (hypotension), impaired liver or kidney function, or underactivity of the thyroid gland (hypothyroidism); or who are pregnant or lactating. Dosage should be reduced for the elderly or debilitated. Treatment by injection may cause pain and tissue damage at the site of the injection. Prolonged treatment should be avoided.
*Related articles:* CYCLIMORPH; MST CONTINUS; NEPENTHE; ORAMORPH; SEVREDOL.

**Morsep** (*Napp*) is a proprietary, non-prescription skin emollient (softener and soother), used to treat urinary dermatis and nappy rash. Produced in the form of a cream, Morsep is a preparation of the ANTISEPTIC CETRIMIDE, RETINOL (vitamin A) and CALCIFEROL (vitamin D).

**\*motility stimulants** are a class of drugs, newly recognised, that stimulate stomach emptying and the rate of passage of food products along the small intestine, and may also enhance closure of the oesophageal sphincter thereby reducing reflux passage of stomach contents up into the oesophagus. Under the condition that they are used carefully, such drugs are of benefit because they have anti-nauseant and anti-emetic properties. Older drugs of this class, such as METOCLOPRIMIDE, had dopamine receptor antagonist properties, so they had a wide variety of undesirable effects on the brain. Some recently introduced agents such as CISAPRIDE do not have this action, and are thought to work by acting at receptors for 5-HT (serotonin) to cause release of acetylcholine (*see* NEUROTRANSMITTER) from nerves within the gut wall.

**Motilium** (*Janssen*) is a proprietary preparation of the ANTINAUSEANT and ANTI-EMETIC drug domperidone, available only on prescription. It is thought to work by inhibiting the action of the natural substance dopamine on the vomiting centre of the brain, and may be used to treat nausea and vomiting in gastrointestinal disorders, or during treatment with cytotoxic drugs or radiotherapy. It is produced in the form of tablets, as a sugar-free suspension and as anal suppositories.

▲ / ● side-effects/warning: *see* DOMPERIDONE.

**Motipress** (*Squibb*) is a proprietary mixed ANTIDEPRESSANT-ANTIPSYCHOTIC compound, available only on prescription, used to treat depressive illness and associated anxiety. Produced in the form of tablets, Motipress is a preparation of the

antipsychotic drug fluphenazine hydrochloride and the antidepressant nortriptyline hydrochloride in the ratio 1:20. It is not recommended for children.
▲/✚ side-effects/warning: see
FLUPHENAZINE;
NORTRIPTYLINE.

**Motival** (*Squibb*) is a proprietary mixed ANTIDEPRESSANT-ANTIPSYCHOTIC compound, available only on prescription, used to treat depressive illness and associated anxiety. Produced in the form of tablets, Motival is a preparation of the antipsychotic drug fluphenazine hydrochloride and the antidepressant nortriptyline hydrochloride in the ratio 50:1. It is not recommended for children.
▲/✚ side-effects/warning: see
FLUPHENAZINE;
NORTRIPTYLINE.

**Motrin** (*Upjohn*) is a proprietary, ANTI-INFLAMMATORY, non-narcotic ANALGESIC, available only on prescription, used to treat the pain of rheumatic and other musculo-skeletal disorders. Produced in the form of tablets (in four strengths), Motrin is a preparation of ibuprofen.
▲/✚ side-effects/warning: see
IBUPROFEN.

**Movelat** (*Panpharma*) is a proprietary, CORTICOSTEROID, COUNTER-IRRITANT preparation, which has some ANALGESIC properties. Available only on prescription, it is used in topical application to treat the inflammatory symptoms of arthritis and to relieve muscular back pain and soft tissue pain. Produced in the form of a cream and a gel in an alcohol base, Movelat is a compound that includes corticosteroids and SALICYLIC ACID.

**MST Continus** (*Napp*) is a proprietary narcotic ANALGESIC, which is on the controlled drugs

list. It is used primarily to relieve pain following surgery, or the pain experienced during the final stages of terminal malignant disease. Produced in the form of sustained-release tablets (in four strengths), MST Continus is a preparation of the OPIATE and NARCOTIC morphine sulphate; it is not recommended for children.
▲/✚ side-effects/warning: see
MORPHINE.

**MSUD Aid** (*Scientific Hospital Supplies*) is a proprietary, essential and non-essential, amino acid mixture, used as a nutritional supplement for patients with the congenital abnormality maple syrup urine disease. Produced in the form of a powder containing vitamins, minerals and trace elements, it is isoleucine-, leucine- and valine-free, but does not consist of a complete diet.

**Mucaine** (*Wyeth*) is a proprietary ANTACID, which also has local anaesthetic properties, available only on prescription, used to treat inflammation of the oesophagus and hiatus hernia. Produced in the form of a sugar-free suspension for dilution (the potency of the suspension once dilute is retained for 14 days), Mucaine is a preparation of ALUMINIUM HYDROXIDE mixture and magnesium hydroxide with the ANAESTHETIC oxethazaine. It is not recommended for children.
▲/✚ side-effects/warning: see
OXETHAZAINE.

**Mucodyne** (*Berk*) is a proprietary MUCOLYTIC drug, available on prescription only to private patients, used to reduce the viscosity of sputum and thus facilitate expectoration in patients with asthma or bronchitis. Produced in the form of capsules, as a syrup (in two strengths, the stronger labelled

Forte) for dilution (the potency of the syrup once dilute is retained for 14 days), and as another syrup for children (which is not recommended for children aged under 2 years), Mucodyne is a preparation of carbocisteine.

▲/● side-effects/warning: *see* CARBOCISTEINE.

**Mucogel** (*Pharmax*) is a proprietary, non-prescription ANTACID, used to treat severe indigestion and heartburn and to relieve the symptoms of gastric and duodenal ulcers. Produced in the form of tablets and as a sugar-free suspension, Mucogel is a preparation of ALUMINIUM HYDROXIDE and MAGNESIUM HYDROXIDE. It is not recommended for children.

**\*mucolytic** describes an agent that dissolves or otherwise breaks down mucus. Mucolytic drugs are generally used in an endeavour to reduce the viscosity of sputum in the upper respiratory tract, and thus facilitate expectoration (coughing up sputum). Not all authorities agree that they work, although mucolytic agents are commonly prescribed to treat such conditions as asthma and chronic bronchitis. Best-known and most-used mucolytic agents are CARBOCISTEINE, TYLOXAPOL, BROMHEXINE HYDROCHLORIDE, ACETYLCYSTEINE and METHYLCYSTEINE hydrochloride. Many proprietary preparations are available on prescription only to private patients.

**Multibionta** (*Merck*) is a proprietary MULTIVITAMIN solution, available only on prescription, for addition to infusion solutions to feed patients who for one reason or another cannot be fed via the alimentary canal such as during severe disorders of the gastrointestinal tract, and coma. Produced in

ampoules, Multibionta represents a preparation of RETINOL (vitamin A), THIAMINE (vitamin B₁), RIBOFLAVINE (vitamin B₂), PYRIDOXINE (vitamin B₆), NICOTINAMIDE (of the B complex), dexpanthenol (of the B complex), ASCORBIC ACID (vitamin C) and TOCOPHERYL ACETATE (vitamin E).

**Multilind** (*Squibb*) is a proprietary ANTIFUNGAL preparation, available only on prescription, used in topical application to treat fungal infections, especially forms of candidiasis (such as thrush), and to relieve the symptoms of nappy rash. Produced in the form of an ointment, Multilind is a preparation of the antifungal agent nystatin together with zinc oxide.

▲/● side-effects/warning: *see* NYSTATIN.

**Multiparin** (*CP Pharmaceuticals*) is a proprietary ANTICOAGULANT, available only on prescription, used to treat and prevent various forms of thrombosis. Produced in ampoules for intravenous injection, Multiparin is a preparation of the natural anticoagulant heparin sodium.

▲/● side-effects/warning: *see* HEPARIN.

**\*multivitamin** preparations contain a selection of various VITAMINS. There are a large number of such preparations available, and are mostly used as dietary supplements and for making up vitamin deficiencies. The choice of a particular multivitamin depends on its content; they are not usually available from the National Health Service.

**Multivitamins** (*Evans*) is a proprietary, non-prescription, MULTIVITAMIN preparation, which is not available from the National

Health Service. Produced in the form of tablets, Multivitamins is a preparation of RETINOL (vitamin A), THIAMINE (vitamin B₁), RIBOFLAVINE (vitamin B₂), NICOTINAMIDE (of the B complex), ASCORBIC ACID (vitamin C) and CALCIFEROL (vitamin D).

**mumps vaccine** is a suspension of live, but attenuated, mumps viruses cultured in chick embryo tissue. It is is a VACCINE not recommended for routine use in the United Kingdom, although it is readily available for patients at risk. Administration is by injection. Combined with measles and rubella vaccine it constitutes MMR VACCINE.

**Mumpsvax** (*Morson*) is a proprietary MUMPS VACCINE, available only on prescription. Produced in the form of powder in a single-dose vial with diluent, Mumpsvax is a preparation of live but attenuated viruses that when injected cause the body to provide itself with antibodies against the virus. It is not recommended for children aged under 1 year.

**mupirocin**, or pseudomonic acid, is an ANTIBIOTIC drug, unrelated to any other antibiotic, used in topical application to treat bacterial skin infection. Administration is in the form of a water-miscible cream.
▲ side-effects: topical application may sting.
✸ warning: mupirocin should be administered with caution to patients with impaired kidney function.
*Related article*: BACTROBAN.

**Muripsin** (*Norgine*) is a proprietary, non-prescription compound used to make up a deficiency of hydrochloric acid and other digestive juices in the stomach. Produced in the form of tablets, Muripsin is a preparation

of glutamic acid hydrochloride and the gastric enzyme pepsin.

\*__muscle relaxants__ are agents that reduce tension in or paralyse muscles. They include ANTISPASMODIC drugs or SMOOTH MUSCLE RELAXANTS, which relieve spasm (rigidity) in smooth muscles that are not under voluntary control (such as the muscles of the respiratory tract or of the intestinal walls – or of blood vessels). They also include those drugs that are used in surgical operations to paralyse skeletal muscles that are normally under voluntary control (neuromuscular blocking drugs): such drugs work either by competing with the neurotransmitter acetylcholine at receptor sites between nerve and muscle (non-depolarizing) or by imitating the action of acetylcholine and so producing depolarization block at the receptor sites (depolarizing). Non-depolarizing muscle relaxants include TUBOCURARINE CHLORIDE, GALLAMINE TRIETHIODIDE, ALCURONIUM CHLORIDE and VECURONIUM BROMIDE; depolarizing muscle relaxants include SUXAMETHONIUM CHLORIDE. Antagonists used to reverse the effects of the non-depolarizing drug types once surgery has finished prolong the effect of the other drug type. Patients receiving a muscle relaxant during surgery must have their respiration assisted or controlled. Other drugs again relax skeletal muscle spasm by an action on the spinal cord and these SKELETAL MUSCLE RELAXANTS include mephanesin, baclophen and certain BENZODIAZEPINES.

**mustine hydrochloride** is a CYTOTOXIC drug used principally to treat the lymphatic cancer

Hodgkin's disease. Because it is so toxic, however, mustine is now much less commonly used. Administration is by fast-running infusion.

▲ side-effects: there is severe nausea and vomiting; there is commonly also hair loss. The formation of red blood cells by the bone marrow is reduced.

✿ warning: prolonged treatment may cause sterility in men and an early menopause in women. Regular and frequent blood counts are essential. Leakage of the drug into the tissues at the site of infusion may cause severe tissue damage. The drug must be handled with care: it is caustic to the skin and irritating to the nose.

**Myambutol** (*Lederle*) is a proprietary ANTITUBERCULAR drug, available only on prescription, used for the prevention and treatment of tuberculosis in conjunction with other drugs. Produced in the form of tablets (in two strengths) and as an oral powder, Myambutol is a preparation of ethambutol hydrochloride.

▲ / ✿ side-effects/warning: *see* ETHAMBUTOL HYDROCHLORIDE.

**Mycardol** (*Winthrop*) is a proprietary, non-prescription VASODILATOR, used as an ANTIHYPERTENSIVE drug in the prevention or treatment of angina pectoris (heart pain). Produced in the form of tablets, Mycardol is a preparation of pentaerythritol tetranitrate; it is not recommended for children.

▲ / ✿ side-effects/warning: *see* PENTAERYTHRITOL TETRANITRATE; GLYCERYL TRINITRATE.

**Mycota** (*Crookes Products*) is a proprietary, non-prescription, ANTIFUNGAL preparation, used in topical application to treat skin infections caused by Tinea organisms (such as athlete's foot). Produced in the form of a cream, as a dusting powder, and as an aerosol spray, Mycota is a preparation of undecenoic acid and its salts.

**Mydriacyl** (*Alcon*) is a proprietary, ANTICHOLINERGIC, mydriatic drug, available only on prescription, used to dilate the pupils and paralyse certain eye muscles generally for the purpose of ophthalmic examination (but occasionally to assist in antibiotic treatment). Produced in the form of eye-drops (in two strengths), Mydriacyl is a preparation of tropicamide.

▲ / ✿ side-effects/warning: *see* TROPICAMIDE.

**Mydrilate** (*Boehringer Ingelheim*) is a proprietary, ANTICHOLINERIC, mydriatic drug, available only on prescription, used to dilate the pupils and paralyse certain eye muscles generally for the purpose of ophthalmic examination (but occasionally to assist in antibiotic treatment). Produced in the form of eye-drops (in two strengths), Mydrilate is a preparation of cyclopentolate hydrochloride.

▲ / ✿ side-effects/warning: *see* CYCLOPENTOLATE HYDROCHLORIDE.

**Myelobromol** (*Sinclair*) is a proprietary CYTOTOXIC drug, available only on prescription (and generally only in hospital), used to treat chronic myeloid leukaemia. Produced in the form of tablets, Myelobromol is a preparation of the drug mitobronitol – which has some severe side-effects.

▲ / ✿ side-effects/warning: *see* MITOBRONITOL.

**Mygdalon** (*DDSA Pharmaceuticals*) is a proprietary ANTINAUSEANT, available only on prescription, used to treat nausea and vomiting especially when associated with gastrointestinal disorders, during radiotherapy, or accompanying treatment with CYTOTOXIC drugs. Produced in the form of tablets, Mygdalon is a preparation of metoclopramide hydrochloride.

▲/● side-effects/warning: *see* METOCLOPRAMIDE.

**Myleran** (*Wellcome*) is a proprietary CYTOTOXIC drug, available only on prescription, used to treat chronic myeloid leukaemia. It works by interfering with the DNA of new-forming cells, so preventing normal cell replication. Produced in the form of tablets (in two strengths), Myleran is a preparation of busulphan.

▲/● side-effects/warning: *see* BUSULPHAN.

**Mynah** (*Lederle*) is a proprietary ANTITUBERCULAR drug, available only on prescription, used for the prevention and treatment of tuberculosis in conjunction with other drugs. Produced in the form of tablets (in four strengths, under the names Mynah 200, Mynah 250, Mynah 300 and Mynah 365), it is a compound preparation of ethambutol hydrochloride and isoniazid. It is not recommended for children.

▲/● side-effects/warning: *see* ETHAMBUTOL HYDROCHLORIDE; ISONIAZID.

**Myocrisin** (*May & Baker*) is a proprietary preparation of one of the salts of gold, available only on prescription, used to treat rheumatoid arthritis. Produced in ampoules (in five strengths) for injection, Myocrisin is a preparation of sodium aurothiomalate.

▲/● side-effects/warning: *see* SODIUM AUROTHIOMALATE.

**Myolgin** (*Cox*) is a proprietary, non-prescription, compound ANALGESIC, which is not available from the National Health Service. Used to treat mild to moderate pain, and produced in the form of soluble (dispersible) tablets, Myolgin is a preparation of PARACETAMOL, ASPIRIN, CODEINE PHOSPHATE and CAFFEINE citrate; it is not recommended for children.

**Myotonine Chloride** (*Glenwood*) is a proprietary preparation of the parasympathomimetic drug bethanechol chloride, available only on prescription, used to treat urinary retention. It works by increasing the contraction of the muscle within the walls of the bladder. It is produced in the form of tablets (in two strengths).

▲/● side-effects/warning: *see* BETHANECHOL CHLORIDE.

**Mysoline** (*ICI*) is a proprietary ANTICONVULSANT, available only on prescription, used to treat and prevent epileptic attacks, especially grand mal (tonic-clonic) and partial (focal) seizures (but not petit mal epilepsy). Produced in the form of tablets and an oral suspension, Mysoline is a preparation of primidone.

▲/● side-effects/warning: *see* PRIMIDONE.

**Mysteclin** (*Squibb*) is a proprietary compound preparation with ANTIBIOTIC and ANTIFUNGAL actions, available only on prescription, used to treat infections anywhere in the body, but especially of mucous membranes. Produced in the form of capsules and as tablets, Mysteclin is a preparation of the broad-spectrum antibiotic tetracycline hydrochloride with the antifungal agent nystatin. These preparations are not recommended for children.

▲/● side-effects/warning: *see* AMPHOTERICIN; NYSTATIN; TETRACYCLINE.

**nabilone** is a synthetic cannabinoid (a drug derived from CANNABIS) used to relieve some of the toxic side-effects, particularly the nausea and vomiting, associated with chemotherapy in the treatment of cancer. However, it too has significant side-effects. Administration is oral in the form of capsules.

▲ side-effects: drowsiness, dry mouth and decreased appetite are common; there may also be an increase in the heart rate, dizziness on rising from a sitting or lying position (indicating low blood pressure), and abdominal cramps. Some patients experience psychological effects such as euphoria, confusion, depression, hallucinations and general disorientation. There may be headache, blurred vision and tremors.

✚ warning: nabilone should be administered with caution to patients with severely impaired liver function or unstable personality. Concentration and speed of reaction is affected, and the effects of alcohol may be increased.
*Related article:* CESAMET.

**Nacton** (*Bencard*) is a proprietary, ANTICHOLINERGIC, ANTISPASMODIC drug, available only on prescription, used to assist in the treatment of gastrointestinal disorders, such as peptic ulceration and hyperacidity, arising from muscular spasm of the intestinal walls. As a SMOOTH MUSCLE RELAXANT, it is also sometimes used to treat children for nocturnal bedwetting (because the bladder sphincter muscles have to contract to let urine through). Produced in the form of tablets (in two strengths), Nacton is a preparation of poldine methylsulphate. Other than for reasons stated it is not recommended for children.

▲ / ✚ side-effects/warning: *see* POLDINE METHYLSULPHATE.

**nadolol** is a BETA-BLOCKER used to treat high blood pressure (*see* ANTIHYPERTENSIVE), angina pectoris (heart pain) and heartbeat irregularities. It is sometimes also used to treat the effects of an excess of thyroid hormones in the bloodstream (thyrotoxicosis), or to prevent attacks of migraine. Administration is oral in the form of tablets.

▲ side-effects: the heartbeat may slow more than intended; there may be some gastrointestinal or respiratory disturbance. Fingers and toes may turn cold.

✚ warning: nadolol should not be administered to patients who suffer from heart disease or asthma, and should be administered with caution to those who are nearing the end of pregnancy or who are lactating. Withdrawal of treatment should be gradual.
*Related article:* CORGARD.

**naftidrofuryl oxalate** is a VASODILATOR that affects the blood vessels of the brain and of the extremities. Because it improves blood circulation in the brain, it is thought by some also to improve memory in the elderly. Administration is oral in the form of capsules (in a course of treatment that lasts for at least 3 months), or by injection or infusion.

▲ side-effects: there may be nausea and pain in the small intestine.

✚ warning: naftidrofuryl oxalate should not be administered to patients with heart block.
*Related article:* PRAXILENE.

**nalbuphine hydrochloride** is a narcotic ANALGESIC that is very similar to morphine (although it has fewer side-effects and possibly less addictive potential). Like morphine, it is used primarily to relieve moderate to severe pain, especially during or after surgery. Administration is by injection.

▲ side-effects: shallow breathing, urinary retention, constipation, and nausea are all common; tolerance and dependence (addiction) are possible. There may also be drowsiness and pain at the site of injection (where there may also be tissue damage).

✿ warning: nalbuphine should not be administered to patients who suffer from head injury or intracranial pressure; it should be administered with caution to those with impaired kidney or liver function, asthma, depressed respiration, insufficient secretion of thyroid hormones (hypothyroidism) or low blood pressure (hypotension), or who are pregnant or lactating. Dosage should be reduced for the elderly or debilitated.
Related article: NUBAIN.

**Nalcrom** (*Fisons*) is a proprietary compound mast cell stabiliser, available only on prescription, used to assist in the treatment of allergy to specific foods. Produced in the form of capsules, Nalcrom is a preparation of sodium cromoglycate, a drug that prevents some cellular allergic response. It is not recommended for children aged under 2 years.
▲ / ✿ side-effects/warning: *see* SODIUM CROMOGLYCATE.

**nalidixic acid** is an ANTIBIOTIC used primarily to treat gram-negative infection of the urinary tract. One of the first of the quinolone family of antibiotics, it is not active enough to achieve effective concentrations in the blood; it inhibits DNA coiling and replication in the bacterial cell.

Administration is oral in the form of tablets, as a dilute suspension, or as an effervescent solution.

▲ side-effects: nausea, vomiting, diarrhoea and gastrointestinal disturbance are fairly common, but there may also be sensitivity reactions (such as urticaria or a rash). A very few patients experience visual disturbances and convulsions.

✿ warning: nalidixic acid should not be administered to patients who suffer from epilepsy, have a history of porphyria, or who are aged under 3 months. It should be administered with caution to those with kidney or liver dysfunction or who are lactating. During treatment it is advisable for patients to avoid strong sunlight.
Related articles: MICTRAL; NEGRAM; URIBEN.

**Nalorex** (*Du Pont*) is an antagonist of narcotic ANALGESIC drugs, chemically an OPIATE, and is used in detoxification therapy for formerly opiate-dpendent individuals to help prevent relapse. It is a proprietary form of naltrexone hydrochloride available only on prescription, and is a preparation in the form of tablets.
▲ / ✿ side-effects/warning: *see* NALTREXONE HYDROCHLORIDE.

**naloxone** is a powerful OPIATE antagonist drug used primarily (in the form of naloxone hydrochloride) as an antidote to an overdose of narcotic ANALGESICS. Quick but short-acting, it effectively reverses the respiratory depression, coma and convulsions that follow over-dosage of opiates. Administration is by intramuscular or intravenous injection, and may be repeated at intervals of 2 minutes until there is some response. Also used at the end of operations to reverse respiratory depression caused by narcotic analgesics.

✷ warning: naloxone should not be administered to patients who are physically dependent on narcotics.

*Related article:* NARCAN.

**naltrexone hydrochloride** is an antagonist of narcotic ANALGESIC drugs, chemically an OPIATE, and is used in detoxification therapy for formerly opiate-dependent individuals to help prevent relapse. Since it is an antagonist of dependence-forming opiates (such as heroin), it will precipitate withdrawal symptoms in those already taking opiates. During naltrexone treatment, the euphoric effects of habit-forming opiates are blocked, so helping prevent re-addiction in former addicts. Naltrexone should be used in specialist clinics only. (For overdose with opiates the related drug NALOXONE is normally used.) It is available only on prescription in the form of tablets.

▲ side-effects: in withdrawal of opiate-dependent patients there may be nausea, vomiting, abdominal pain, anxiety, nervousness, difficulty in sleeping, headache, and pain in joints and muscles. There may also be diarrhoea or constipation, sweating, dizziness, chills, irritability, rash, lethargy, and decreased sexual potency. There have been reports of liver and blood abnormalities.

✷ warning: kidney and liver impairment (function tests before and during treatment are advisable). Test for opiate dependence with naloxone, avoid giving to patients currently dependent on opiates, or those with acute hepatic or renal failure.

*Related article:* NALOREX.

**nandrolone** is an anabolic STEROID related to the male sex hormone testosterone (although it has far fewer masculinizing properties), used to assist the metabolic synthesis of protein in the body following major surgery or long-term debilitating disease, or to treat osteoporosis ('brittle bones'). Sometimes also used to treat sex-hormone-linked cancers in women, particularly cancer of the breast, it is additionally used in the treatment of certain forms of anaemia, although how it works in this respect – and even whether it works – remains the subject of some debate: variations in patient response are wide. Administration (in the form of nandrolone decanoate or nandrolone phenylpropionate) is by injection.

▲ side-effects: there may be fluid retention in the tissues, leading to weight gain; blood levels of calcium generally rise. High dosage in women may cause menstrual irregularity and eventual signs of masculinization.

✷ warning: nandrolone should not be administered to patients with impaired liver function, or cancer of the prostate gland (in men) or of the breast, or who are pregnant; it should be administered with caution to those with impaired heart or kidney function, circulatory disorders, high blood pressure (hypertension), diabetes, epilepsy, or recurrent attacks of migraine. Treatment of young patients may affect bone growth.

*Related articles:* DECA-DURABOLIN; DECA-DURABOLIN 100; DURABOLIN.

**Naprosyn** (*Syntex*) is a proprietary, non-steroidal, ANTI-INFLAMMATORY, non-narcotic ANALGESIC, available only on prescription, used to relieve pain – particularly rheumatic and arthritic pain, and that of acute gout – and to treat other musculo-skeletal disorders. Produced in the form of tablets (in two strengths), as a suspension (the potency of the suspension once dilute is retained for 14 days), and as anal suppositories, Naprosyn is a preparation of naproxen. In the form of tablets or suspension it is not recommended for children aged under 5 years; the suppositories are not suitable for children.

▲/ ● side-effects/warning: *see* NAPROXEN.

**naproxen** is a non-steroidal, ANTI-INFLAMMATORY, non-narcotic ANALGESIC used to relieve pain – particularly rheumatic and arthritic pain, and that of acute gout – and to treat other musculo-skeletal disorders. It is also effective in relieving the pain of menstrual disorders and difficulties, in preventing recurrent attacks of migraine, and in reducing high body temperature. Administration (in the form of naproxen or naproxen sodium) is oral in the form of tablets or as a dilute suspension, or by anal suppositories.

▲ side-effects: side-effects are relatively uncommon, but may include gastrointestinal disturbance with nausea; patients may be advised to take the drug with food or milk. Some patients experience sensitivity reactions or fluid retention in the tissues (oedema).

● warning: naproxen should be administered with caution to patients with allergic disorders (such as asthma), impaired liver or kidney function, or gastric ulcers, or who are pregnant.
*Related articles:* LARAFLEX; NAPROSYN; NYCOPREN; SYNFLEX.

**Narcan** (*Du Pont*) is a proprietary drug, available only on prescription, that is most often used to treat the symptoms of acute overdosage of OPIATES such as morphine. Produced in ampoules for injection, Narcan is a preparation of naloxone hydrochloride. A weaker form is available (under the name Narcan Neonatal) for the treatment of respiratory depression in babies born to mothers on whom narcotic analgesics have been used during the birth, or who are drug addicts.

▲/ ● side-effects/warning: *see* NALOXONE.

**\*narcotic** is a description applied to drugs that induce stupor and insensibility. Commonly the term is applied to the opiates (such as MORPHINE and DIAMORPHINE), but it can also be used to describe SEDATIVES and HYPNOTIC drugs and alcohol that act directly on the brain centres to depress their functioning. In law, however, the term describes an addictive drug that is the subject of abuse (especially in the USA).

**\*narcotic analgesic:** *see* ANALGESIC.

**Nardil** (*Parke-Davis*) is a proprietary ANTIDEPRESSANT drug, available only on prescription, used to treat depressive illness. Produced in the form of tablets, Nardil is a preparation of the potentially dangerous drug phenelzine (which requires a careful dietary regimen to accompany treatment because of complex interactions with various foods such as cheese, yeast extract, chocolate etc.). It is not recommended for children.

▲/ ● side-effects/warning: *see* PHENELZINE.

**Narphen** (*Smith & Nephew Pharmaceuticals*) is a proprietary, narcotic ANALGESIC, a controlled

OPIATE consisting of a preparation of phenazocine hydrobromide, used to relieve severe pain and pancreatic or biliary pain. Produced in the form of tablets, Narphen is not recommended for children.
▲/✿ side-effects/warning: *see* PHENAZOCINE.

**Naseptin** (*ICI*) is a proprietary ANTIBIOTIC preparation, available only on prescription, used to treat staphylococcal infections in and around the nostrils. Produced in the form of a cream for topical application, Naseptin is a preparation of the ANTISEPTIC chlorhexidine hydrochloride and the topical antibiotic neomycin sulphate.
▲/✿ side-effects/warning: *see* CHLORHEXIDINE; NEOMYCIN.

**natamycin** is an ANTIBIOTIC, an ANTIFUNGAL drug used to treat candidiasis (thrush), trichomoniasis and fungal infections of the respiratory tract. Administration is in many forms, depending on the site of infection: oral as a sugar-free suspension (sometimes in drops), topical as an aerosol inhalant and as a water-miscible cream, and also as vaginal tablets (pessaries).
✿ warning: diagnosis should preferably be confirmed (through analysis of tissue from the site of infection) before administration.
*Related article:* PIMAFUCIN.

**Natirose** (*Lewis*) is a proprietary VASODILATOR, available only on prescription, used to prevent and treat angina pectoris (heart pain). Produced in the form of tablets, Natirose is a compound preparation of the vasodilator glyceryl trinitrate, the ANALGESIC ethylmorphine hydrochloride, and the MUSCLE RELAXANT hyoscyamine hydrobromide.
▲/✿ side-effects/warning: *see* GLYCERYL TRINITRATE.

**Natrilix** (*Servier*) is a proprietary DIURETIC, available only on prescription, used to treat an accumulation of fluid within the tissues (oedema) and high blood pressure (*see* ANTIHYPERTENSIVE), particularly in cases of diabetes mellitus. Produced in the form of tablets, Natrilix is a preparation of the THIAZIDE-like drug indapamide. It is not recommended for children.
▲/✿ side-effects/warning: *see* INDAPAMIDE.

**Natuderm** (*Burgess*) is a proprietary, non-prescription skin emollient (softener and soother), used to treat dry conditions of the skin. Produced in the form of a cream, Natuderm is a preparation of glycerides, sterols and other lipids, water, waxes and GLYCEROL.

**Natulan** (*Roche*) is a proprietary preparation of the CYTOTOXIC drug procarbazine, available only on prescription, used primarily to treat the lymphatic cancer Hodgkin's disease, but also to assist in the treatment of solid tumours resistant to other therapy. Advice and counselling on diet during treatment is recommended (eating foods such as cheese or meat extracts, or drinking alcohol, for example, is inadvisable). Natulan is produced in the form of capsules.
▲/✿ side-effects/warning: *see* PROCARBAZINE.

**Navidrex** (*Ciba*) is a proprietary DIURETIC, available only on prescription, used to treat high blood pressure (*see* ANTIHYPERTENSIVE) and the accumulation of fluid within the tissues (oedema). Produced in the form of tablets, it is a preparation of the THIAZIDE cyclopenthiazide.
▲/✿ side-effects/warning: *see* CYCLOPENTHIAZIDE.

**Navidrex-K** (*Ciba*) is a proprietary DIURETIC, available only on prescription, used to treat high blood pressure (*see* ANTIHYPERTENSIVE) and the accumulation of fluid within the tissues (oedema). Produced in the form of tablets, it is a preparation of the thiazide cyclopenthiazide (which is potassium-depleting) together with POTASSIUM in a form for sustained release.
▲/✿ side-effects/warning: *see* CYCLOPENTHIAZIDE.

**Navispare** (*Ciba*) is a proprietary DIURETIC available only on prescription, used to treat congestive heart failure, high blood pressure (*see* ANTIHYPERTENSIVE) and cirrhosis of the liver. Produced in the form of tablets, it is a compound of the weak but potassium-sparing diuretic amiloride, together with the THIAZIDE cyclopenthiazide. It is not recommended for children.
▲/✿ side-effects/warning: *see* AMILORIDE; CYCLOPENTHIAZIDE.

**Naxogin 500** (*Farmitalia Carlo Erba*) is a proprietary, non-prescription ANTIPROTOZOAL, used to treat trichomonal infections of the urogenital areas. It may also be useful in the treatment of ulcerative gingivitis due to Vincent's organisms. Produced in the form of tablets, Naxogin 500 is a preparation of nimorazole. Alcohol consumption should be avoided during treatment.
▲/✿ side-effects/warning: *see* NIMORAZOLE.

**Nebcin** (*Lilly*) is a proprietary ANTIBIOTIC, used to treat serious infections in specific organs, such as meningitis, prostatitis, pyelonephritis and endocarditis. Produced in ampoules (in two strengths) for injection, Nebcin is a preparation of the aminoglycoside tobramycin.
▲/✿ side-effects/warning: *see* TOBRAMYCIN.

**nedocromil** is used to prevent recurrent attacks of asthma; it is not useful in treating an acute attack, but is particularly effective in forestalling attacks in patients whose asthma is allergy related, and especially when administered before exercise. Patient response varies, however: so dosage should be adjusted for individually optimal results, and should be regular whether symptoms are present or not. Administration is topical by inhalation from an aerosol.
▲ side-effects: the taste is rather bitter. There may be a tendency to mild nausea and/or headache.
✿ warning: some patients may find that the administration of a bronchodilator (such as salbutamol) some 10 minutes before taking nedocromil may enhance the effects. Should not be taken by pregnant women. *Related article:* TILADE.

**nefopam** is an non-narcotic ANALGESIC used to treat moderate to severe pain, such as that following surgery, or in cancer or toothache. Administration is oral in the form of tablets, or by injection.
▲ side-effects: there may be nausea, dry mouth, nervous agitation and insomnia. A few patients experience blurred vision, drowsiness, headache, an increase in the heart rate and sweating. Rarely, there is discoloration of the urine.
✿ warning: nefopam should not be administered to patients who suffer from convulsive disorders, or who are undergoing a heart attack. It should be administered with caution to those with glaucoma, liver disease or urinary retention. Not

recommended for children.
*Related article:* ACUPAN.

**Negram** (*Sterling Research*) is a
proprietary ANTIBIOTIC, available
only on prescription, used to treat
infections of the urinary tract.
Produced in the form of tablets
and as a sugar-free suspension for
dilution (the potency of the
suspension once diluted is
retained for 14 days), Negram is a
preparation of the drug nalidixic
acid.
▲/✿ side-effects/warning: *see*
NALIDIXIC ACID.

**Neocon-1/35** (*Ortho-Cilag*) is a
combined ORAL CONTRACEPTIVE,
available only on prescription,
which combines the OESTROGEN
ethinyloestradiol with the
PROGESTOGEN norethisterone. It is
produced in packs of 21 tablets
corresponding to one complete
menstrual cycle.
▲/✿ side-effects/warning: *see*
ETHINYLOESTRADIOL;
NORETHISTERONE.

**Neo-Cortef** (*Upjohn*) is a
proprietary compound ANTIBIOTIC
available only on prescription,
used to treat bacterial infections
in the outer ear and inflammation
in the eye. Produced in the form
of ear- or eye-drops and as an
ointment, Neo-Cortef is a
compound preparation of the
antibiotic aminoglycoside
neomycin sulphate with the
CORTICOSTEROID hydrocortisone
acetate.
▲/✿ side-effects/warning: *see*
NEOMYCIN.

**Neo-Cytamen** (*Duncan,
Flockhart*) is a proprietary
vitamin B₁₂ preparation,
available on prescription only to
private patients, used to make up
vitamin B₁₂ deficiency in the body
(pernicious anaemia). Produced in
ampoules (in two strengths) for
injection, Neo-Cytamen is a

preparation of hydroxocobalamin.
▲/✿ side-effects/warning: *see*
HYDROXOCOBALAMIN.

**Neogest** (*Schering*) is a
proprietary, progesterone-only
ORAL CONTRACEPTIVE, available
only on prescription, which is a
preparation of the PROGESTOGEN
norgestrel. On first using
Neogest, an additional form of
contraception is advisable for the
initial fortnight.
▲/✿ side-effects/warning: *see*
NORGESTREL.

**Neo-Lidocaton** is a proprietary
preparation of the local
ANAESTHETIC lignocaine, used in
cartridges for dental surgery.
▲/✿ side-effects/warning: *see*
LIGNOCAINE.

**Neo-Medrone** (*Upjohn*) is a
proprietary, CORTICOSTEROID,
ANTIBIOTIC preparation, available
only on prescription, used for
topical application to treat
inflammatory skin conditions,
particularly those resulting from
allergy, which may be infected.
Produced in the form of a cream,
Neo-Medrone is a preparation of
the steroid methylprednisolone
acetate and the antibiotic
neomycin sulphate.
▲/✿ side-effects/warning: *see*
NEOMYCIN.

**Neo-Mercazole** (*Nicholas*) is a
proprietary preparation of the
drug carbimazole, available only
on prescription, used to treat the
effects of an excess of thyroid
hormones in the bloodstream
(thyrotoxicosis). It works by
inhibiting the formation of
the hormone thyroxine in the
thyroid gland, and is produced in
the form of tablets (in two
strengths, under the names Neo-
Mercazole 5 and Neo-Mercazole
20).
▲/✿ side-effects/warning: *see*
CARBIMAZOLE.

neomycin is a broad-spectrum ANTIBIOTIC drug of the aminoglycoside family that is effective in treating some superficial bacterial infections. Too toxic to be used in intravenous or intramuscular administration, it is nevertheless sometimes also used orally to reduce the levels of bacteria in the colon prior to intestinal surgery or examination, or in the case of liver failure. When given orally it is not absorbed from the gastrointestinal tract. Prolonged or widespread topical application may eventually lead to sensitivity reactions, and/or the development of resistance to certain strains of bacteria. Administration (most often in the form of neomycin sulphate) is oral as tablets or in solution, or topical as nose-drops, ear-drops, eye-drops, ear ointment, eye ointment or nasal spray.

▲ side-effects: prolonged use may eventually lead to temporarily impaired kidney function, malabsorption from the intestines, or to deafness. Prolonged use to treat infection in the outer ear may lead to a fungal superinfection.

◆ warning: neomycin should not be administered to patients with the neuromuscular disease myasthenia gravis, or who are pregnant. Intervals between doses should be increased for patients with impaired kidney function. *Related articles:* AUDICORT; CICATRIN; DERMOVATE-NN; DEXA-RHINASPRAY; GRANEODIN; GREGODERM; MINIMS NEOMYCIN; NEO-CORTEF; NEOSPORIN; NIVEMYCIN; OPTOMIZE; POLYBACTRIN; TRIBIOTIC; TRI-CITATRIN.

Neo-NaClex (*Duncan, Flockhart*) is a proprietary DIURETIC, available only on prescription,

used to treat high blood pressure (*see* ANTIHYPERTENSIVE) and the accumulation of fluid within the tissues (oedema). Produced in the form of tablets, Neo-NaClex is a preparation of the THIAZIDE bendrofluazide.

▲/◆ side-effects/warning: *see* BENDROFLUAZIDE.

Neo-NaClex-K (*Duncan, Flockhart*) is a proprietary DIURETIC, available only on prescription, used to treat high blood pressure (*see* ANTI-HYPERTENSIVE) and the accumulation of fluid within the tissues (oedema). Produced in the form of sustained-release tablets, Neo-NaClex-K is a preparation of the THIAZIDE bendrofluazide (which is potassium-depleting) with a POTASSIUM CHLORIDE supplement.

▲/◆ side-effects/warning: *see* BENDROFLUAZIDE.

Neosporin (*Calmic*) is a proprietary ANTIBIOTIC, available only on prescription, used to treat bacterial infections in the eye. Produced in the form of eye-drops, Neosporin is a compound preparation of the antibiotics neomycin sulphate, polymyxin B sulphate and gramicidin.

▲/◆ side-effects/warning: *see* NEOMYCIN; POLYMYXIN B.

neostigmine is an anti-cholinesterase drug that has the effect of increasing the activity of the neurotransmitter (acetylcholine), which transmits the neural instructions of the brain to the skeletal muscles. It works by inhibiting the 'switching-off' of the neural impulses by the breakdown of acetylcholine by enzymes. Its main use is therefore in the treatment of the neuromuscular disease myasthenia gravis (which causes extreme muscle weakness

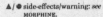

amounting even to paralysis); it is also commonly used to counter the effects of muscle relaxants administered during surgical operations. Occasionally the drug is alternatively used as a PARASYMPATHOMIMETIC to stimulate intestinal motility and so promote defecation. Administration is oral in the form of tablets, or by injection.

▲ side-effects: there may be nausea and vomiting, diarrhoea and abdominal cramps, and an excess of saliva in the mouth. Overdosage may cause gastrointestinal disturbance, an excess of bronchial mucus, sweating, faecal and urinary incontinence, vision disorders, nervous agitation and muscular weakness.

● warning: neostigmine should not be administered to patients with intestinal or urinary blockage; it should be administered with caution to those with epilepsy, asthma, parkinsonism, low blood pressure (hypotension) or a slow heart rate, who have recently suffered a heart attack, or who are pregnant.
*Related article:* PROSIGMIN.

**Nepenthe** (*Evans*) is a proprietary, narcotic ANALGESIC, which, because it is a preparation of the OPIATES anhydrous morphine and opium tincture, is on the controlled drugs list. It is used to relieve severe pain, especially during the final stages of terminal malignant disease, it is produced in the form of a syrup for dilution (the potency of the syrup once dilute is retained for 4 weeks) and in ampoules for injection. Nepenthe solution is not recommended for children aged under 12 months; the injection is not recommended for children aged under 6 years.

▲ / ● side-effects/warning: *see* MORPHINE.

**Nephramine** (*Boots*) is a proprietary nutritional supplement for patients unable to feed or be fed via the alimentary canal. Not a complete diet, however, Nephramine is a selection of essential amino acids in a form suitable for intravenous infusion.

**Nephril** (*Pfizer*) is a proprietary DIURETIC, available only on prescription, used to treat high blood pressure (*see* ANTIHYPERTENSIVE) and the accumulation of fluid within the tissues (oedema). Produced in the form of tablets, Nephril is a preparation of the THIAZIDE polythiazide. It is not recommended for children.

▲ / ● side-effects/warning: *see* POLYTHIAZIDE.

**Nericur** (*Schering*) is a proprietary, non-prescription, topical preparation for the treatment of acne. Produced in the form of a gel (in two strengths), Nericur is a solute preparation of the KERATOLYTIC benzoyl peroxide. It is not recommended for children.

▲ / ● side-effects/warning: *see* BENZOYL PEROXIDE.

**Nerisone** (*Schering*) is a proprietary CORTICOSTEROID preparation, available only on prescription, used to treat serious, non-infective inflammatory skin conditions, such as eczema. Produced in the form of a cream, as an oily cream and as an ointment, Nerisone is a preparation of the steroid diflucortolone valerate. A stronger form is also available in the form of an oily cream and an ointment (under the name Nerisone Forte), which is not recommended for children aged under 4 years.

▲/✿ side-effects/warning: *see*
DIFLUCORTOLONE VALERATE.

**Nestargel** (*Nestlé*) is a
proprietary, non-prescription,
nutritional preparation, used to
thicken foods for patients who
suffer from vomiting and
regurgitation. Produced in the
form of a powder, Nestargel
contains CALCIUM LACTATE and
carob seed flour.

**Nethaprin Expectorant** (*Merrell
Dow*) is a proprietary
EXPECTORANT, available on
prescription only to private
patients, used to treat coughing
and wheezing. Produced in the
form of a syrup, Nethaprin
Expectorant's major active
constituent is the expectorant
agent guaiphenesin. It is not
recommended for children aged
under 6 years.

**Netillin** (*Kirby-Warrick*) is a
proprietary form of the
aminoglycoside ANTIBIOTIC
netilmicin sulphate, available
only on prescription. Used to
treat various serious bacterial
infections, it is produced in
ampoules (in three strengths) for
injection.
▲/✿ side-effects/warning: *see*
NETILMICIN.

**netilmicin** is a broad-spectrum
ANTIBIOTIC, one of the aminoglycosides used (singly or in
combination with other types of
antibiotic) to treat serious
bacterial infections caused by
gram-negative bacteria,
especially those that prove to be
resistant to the more commonly
used aminoglycoside gentamicin.
Administration is by injection.
▲ side-effects: there may be
temporary kidney dysfunction;
any hearing deficit should be
reported.
✿ warning: netilmicin should not
be administered to patients
with the neuromuscular

disease myasthenia gravis, or
who are pregnant. Intervals
between doses should be
increased for patients with
impaired kidney functions.
*Related article:* NETILLIN.

**Neulactil** (*May & Baker*) is a
powerful ANTIPSYCHOTIC drug,
available only on prescription,
used to treat and tranquillize
patients who are undergoing
behavioural disturbances, or who
are psychotic (particularly
schizophrenic); it may also be
used to treat severe anxiety in the
short-term. Produced in the form
of tablets (in three strengths) and
as a strong syrup for dilution (the
potency of the syrup once dilute is
retained for 14 days), Neulactil is
a preparation of the antipsychotic
drug pericyazine.
▲/✿ side-effects/warning: *see*
PERICYAZINE.

**Neurodyne** (*Radiol*) is a
proprietary, non-prescription,
compound ANALGESIC, which is
not available from the National
Health Service. Used to treat pain
anywhere in the body, Neurodyne
is a preparation of paracetamol
and the OPIATE codeine
phosphate. Produced in the form
of capsules, it is not recommended
for children.
▲/✿ side-effects/warning: *see*
CODEINE PHOSPHATE;
PARACETAMOL.

**Neutradonna** (*Nicholas*) is a
proprietary, non-prescription,
ANTACID and ANTISPASMODIC
compound, which is not available
from the National Health Service.
It is used to treat muscle spasm
(rigidity) of the intestinal and
stomach walls and the resulting
gastrointestinal discomfort, and
to relieve acid stomach and
indigestion. Produced in the form
of tablets and as a powder,
Neutradonna is a preparation of
the ANTICHOLINERGIC belladonna

alkaloids and the mild antacid
aluminium sodium silicate. It is
not recommended for children.
▲/✚ side-effects/warning: *see*
BELLADONNA.

*neurotransmitters** are chemical
messengers that, on excitation of
the nerve, are released from nerve
endings to act locally to excite or
inhibit either other nerves or the
cells within organs innervated by
the nerves (such as the heart,
intestine, skeletal muscle, or
glands). Thus neurotransmitters
are rather like HORMONES, but
unlike the latter act locally
rather than on circulation in the
blood. Examples include:
acetylcholine (*see* ACETYCHOLINE
CHLORIDE); DOPAMINE;
NORADRENALINE; serotonin.
*Related article:* HORMONES.

**niacin** is another name for the B
VITAMIN nicotinic acid.
*see* NICOTINIC ACID.

**nicardipine** is a CALCIUM
ANTAGONIST drug used as an
ANTIHYPERTENSIVE to prevent or
treat chronic angina pectoris
(heart pain) and high blood
pressure (hypertension) by means
of its VASODILATOR properties.
Administration (in the form of
nicardipine hydrochloride) is
oral, as capsules.
▲ side-effects: there may be
nausea, headache, dizziness,
flushing and fluid retention in
the fingers and toes; some
patients experience
gastrointestinal disturbances,
palpitations, low blood
pressure (hypotension), an
excess of saliva in the mouth, a
rash, and a frequent urge to
urinate.
✚ warning: nicardipine should
not be administered to patients
with advanced disease of the
aorta; it should be
administered with caution to
those with impaired liver or

kidney function. Treatment
should be stopped if heart pain
occurs.
*Related article:* CARDENE.

**niclosamide** is a synthetic
ANTHELMINTIC drug used to rid
the body of an infestation of
tapeworms. Administration is
oral in the form of tablets.
▲ side-effects: there may be
gastrointestinal disturbance.
✚ warning: side-effects are
minimal, but in case the
tapeworms are multiplying
some doctors prefer to
prescribe an additional anti-
emetic for patients to take on
waking. The dose should be
administered on a relatively
empty stomach, and be
followed by a purgative after
about 2 hours.
*Related article:* YOMESAN.

**nicofuranose** is a derivative of
the B vitamin NICOTINIC ACID,
used therapeutically primarily to
reduce the level of fats (lipids) in
the blood, and therefore to slow
the progression of premature
arteriosclerosis and to treat
vascular disease in the limbs.
Administration is oral in the form
of tablets.
▲/✚ side-effects/warning: *see*
NICOTINIC ACID.
*Related article:* BRADILAN.

**nicotinamide** is a compound
derived from the B vitamin
NICOTINIC ACID that is used
primarily as a constituent in
vitamin supplements, especially
in cases when a large dose is
required (for nicotinamide does
not have as great a VASODILATOR
effect as does nicotinic acid).

**nicotinic acid**, or niacin, is a
VITAMIN of the B complex, a
derivative of pyridine that is
required in the diet, but is also
synthesized in the body to a small
degree from the amino acid

tryptophan. Dietary deficiency results in the disease pellagra (the symptoms of which are dermatitis, diarrhoea and depression), but deficiency is comparatively rare. Good food sources include meat, cereals and yeast extract. Nicotinic acid may be administered therapeutically as a vitamin supplement (in the form of tablets), but its effect as a VASODILATOR prevents high dosage. It is, indeed, more commonly used as a vasodilator, especially in relieving circulatory disorders in the limbs, which it also does by reducing blood levels of fats (lipids) such as cholesterol.

▲ side-effects: there may be nausea and vomiting, flushing and sweating, dizziness and heartbeat irregularities: taking the drug initially in low dosage and with food may reduce these effects – some doctors, however, prescribe aspirin to be taken half an hour before the dose. Sensitivity reactions may occur.

✹ warning: nicotinic acid should not be administered to patients who are pregnant or lactating; it should be administered with caution to those with diabetes, liver disease, peptic ulcers or gout.

**nicotinyl alcohol** is a derivative of the B vitamin NICOTINIC ACID, used therapeutically primarily to reduce the level of fats (lipids) in the blood, and so to treat vascular disease in the limbs. In this it is similar to nicotinic acid, but its effect has longer duration. Administration is oral in the form of tablets and sustained-release tablets.

▲/✹ side-effects/warning: see NICOTINIC ACID.
Related article: RONICOL.

**nicoumalone** is a synthetic ANTI-COAGULANT, used to treat deep-vein thrombosis and conditions in which the blood supply to the

brain is reduced; it is also used to assist heart function following heart surgery, and especially following the implantation of prosthetic heart valves. Administration is oral in the form of tablets.

▲ side-effects: if bleeding starts, it may be difficult to stop.

✹ warning: nicoumalone should not be administered to patients with peptic ulcer (or any other potential source of haemorrhage), bacterial heart disease, or severe high blood pressure (hypertension), or who are pregnant or lactating. It should be administered with caution to those with liver or kidney disease.
Related article: SINTHROME.

**Nidazol** (*Steinhard*) is a proprietary, ANTIBIOTIC AMOEBICIDAL drug, available only on prescription, used to treat infections by anaerobic bacteria and protozoa (particularly in the vagina) and to provide asepsis during surgery involving the large intestine or during gynaecological procedures. Produced in the form of tablets, Nidazol is a preparation of the drug metronidazole.

▲/✹ side-effects/warning: see METRONIDAZOLE.

**nifedipine** is a CALCIUM ANTAGONIST VASODILATOR used primarily to assist in the treatment of angina pectoris (heart pain), coldness and numbness of the arteries of the fingers (Raynaud's phenomenon), and high blood pressure (*see* ANTIHYPERTENSIVE). Administration is oral in the form of capsules or sustained-release tablets.

▲ side-effects: headache, flushing and swelling of the ankles (through fluid retention) are not uncommon; there may also be lethargy or swelling of the gums.

✹ warning: treatment should be halted if heart pain occurs. In late pregnancy the drug may inhibit the onset or stages of labour.

*Related articles:* ADALAT; BETA-ADALAT; CORACTEN; TENIF.

**Niferex** (*Tillotts*) is a proprietary, non-prescription IRON preparation, used to treat iron-deficiency anaemia. Produced in the form of tablets and as an elixir for dilution (the potency of the elixir once dilute is retained for 14 days), Niferex is a polysaccharide-iron complex. An additional preparation in the form of capsules is available (under the name Niferex-150) which is not recommended for children.

▲/✹ side-effects/warning: *see* POLYSACCHARIDE-IRON COMPLEX.

**Night Nurse** (*Beecham Health Care*) is a proprietary, non-prescription, cold relief preparation produced in the form of capsules. It contains the ANALGESIC paracetamol, ALCOHOL, the ANTITUSSIVE dextromethorphan and the ANTIHISTAMINE promethazine, which has a marked sedative activity.

▲/✹ side-effects/warning: *see* DEXTROMETHORPHAN; PARACETAMOL; PROMETHAZINE HYDROCHLORIDE.

**nikethamide** is a respiratory stimulant drug, used to relieve severe respiratory difficulties in patients who have been suffocated (particularly with carbon dioxide), who suffer from chronic disease of the respiratory tract, or who undergo respiratory depression following major surgery – particularly in cases where ventilatory support is not applicable. As a respiratory stimulant, however, nikethamide is now less commonly used (and nikethamide or doxapram is generally the drug of first choice). Administration is by slow intravenous injection, and may be repeated at intervals of between 15 and 30 minutes. It should only be given under expert supervision in a hospital.

▲ side-effects: there may be nausea, restlessness and tremor, leading possibly to convulsions and heartbeat irregularities.

✹ warning: nikethamide should not be administered to patients with respiratory failure resulting from drug overdose or neurological disease, or with coronary artery disease, severe asthma, or an excess of thyroid hormones in the blood (thyrotoxicosis). It should be administered with caution to those with severe high blood pressure (hypertension) or a reduced supply of blood to the heart. Effective dosage is unfortunately close to the level that causes toxic effects, especially convulsions.

**Nilodor** (*Loxley*) is a proprietary, non-prescription deodorant solution, used to freshen and sanitize the appliance or bag that is attached to a stoma (an outlet on the skin surface) following ileostomy or colostomy (surgical curtailment of the intestines).

**Nilstim** (*De Witt*) is a proprietary, non-prescription absorbent agent used, perhaps controversially, to assist in the medical treatment of obesity. The intention is that food consumed is bulked up internally and thus satisfies the patient. Produced in the form of tablets, Nilstim is a preparation in which the active constituent is methylcellulose. It is not recommended for children.

▲/✹ side-effects/warning: *see* METHYLCELLULOSE.

**nimodipine** is a CALCIUM ANTAGONIST used to treat and prevent ischaemic neurological defects following subarachnoid haemorrhage. It is administered as tablets or by intravenous infusion.

▲ side-effects: hypotension, flushing, variable heart rate, headaches, gastrointestinal disorders, nausea.

✹ warning: cerebral oedema and severely raised intracranial pressure; avoid concomitant administration of nimodipine tablets and infusion, other CALCIUM ANTAGONISTS or BETA-BLOCKERS; impaired kidney function or nephrotoxic drugs. *Related article:* NIMOTOP.

**nimorazole** is an ANTIPROTOZOAL agent used to treat protozoal infections (such as giardiasis or trichomoniasis), particularly of the urogenital areas, and especially in cases when the major alternative drug metronidazole has failed. Administration is oral in the form of tablets.

▲ side-effects: there may be nausea and vomiting, drowsiness and vertigo; a rash may appear.

✹ warning: nimorazole should not be administered to patients with severe kidney failure or disease of the central nervous system. In cases of sexually transmitted disease, both partners should be treated even if one presents no symptoms. Alcohol consumption should be avoided during treatment. *Related article:* NAXOGIN 500.

**Nimotop** (*Bayer*) is a proprietary form of the CALCIUM ANTAGONIST nimodipine, available only on prescription to treat and prevent ischaemic neurological defects following subarachnoid haemorrhage. Available as tablets and as an intravenous infusion.

▲ / ✹ warning/side-effects: *see* NIMODIPINE.

**Nipride** (*Roche*) is a proprietary ANTIHYPERTENSIVE drug, available only on prescription (and generally only in hospitals), used to treat high blood pressure (hypertension) or acute or chronic heart failure. Produced in the form of a powder for reconstitution as a medium for infusion, Nipride is a preparation of the VASODILATOR sodium nitroprusside.

▲ / ✹ side-effects/warning: *see* SODIUM NITROPRUSSIDE.

**niridazole** is an ANTHELMINTIC drug used to treat infestations of guinea worms (dracontiasis). In treating guinea worm infestation the drug kills the worms and facilitates their removal from the tissues – but they do still have to be removed physically from the ulcers they cause, and the ulcers require dressing.

▲ side-effects: there may be nausea and anxiety; some patients enter a state of confusion.

✹ warning: niridazole should not be administered to patients with epilepsy; it should be administered with caution to those with impaired liver function.

**Nitoman** (*Roche*) is a proprietary preparation of the powerful drug tetrabenazine, available only on prescription, used to assist a patient to regain voluntary control of movement in Huntington's chorea and related disorders. It is thought to work by reducing the amount of dopamine in the nerve endings of the brain. Produced in the form of tablets, Nitoman is not recommended for children.

▲ / ✹ side-effects/warning: *see* TETRABENAZINE.

**Nitrados** (*Berk*) is a proprietary HYPNOTIC drug, available on prescription only to private patients, used in the short term to treat insomnia in patients for whom a degree of sedation during the daytime is acceptable. Produced in the form of tablets, Nitrados is a preparation of the BENZODIAZEPINE nitrazepam. It is not recommended for children.
▲/✿ side-effects/warning: *see* NITRAZEPAM.

**nitrates** are VASODILATORS that work by relaxing the walls of blood vessels. They are therefore used mainly in the treatment or prevention of angina pectoris (heart pain), heart failure, and high blood pressure (hypertension). Best-known and most-used nitrates include GLYCERYL TRINITRATE, ISOSORBIDE DINITRATE and ISOSORBIDE MONONITRATE. Administration is commonly in the form of tablets to be held under the tongue until dissolved, but aerosol sprays are also numerous; other presentations are as sustained-release tablets, as impregnated dressings, as ointment for topical application on the chest, and in ampoules for injection.

**nitrazepam** is a comparatively mild HYPNOTIC drug, one of the BENZODIAZEPINES used primarily as a TRANQUILLIZER for patients with insomnia, and in whom a degree of sedation during the daytime is acceptable. However, nitrazepam is thought to be potentially habituating (addictive), and continuous use may in any case have cumulative effects, so many doctors now prefer to prescribe other shorter-acting benzodiazepines instead. Administration is oral in the form of tablets, as capsules, or as a suspension (mixture).
▲ side-effects: concentration and speed of reaction are affected. There is commonly drowsiness

and dry mouth; there may also be sensitivity reactions and, in the elderly, a mild state of confusion. Prolonged use may lead to tolerance and a form of dependence (in which there may be insomnia that is worse than before).
✿ warning: nitrazepam should be administered with caution to patients with diseases of the lungs, particularly if respiratory depression is a symptom, who are elderly or debilitated, who have impaired liver or kidney function, or who are pregnant or lactating. The consumption of alcohol enhances the hypnotic effect of the drug. Withdrawal of treatment should be gradual (abrupt withdrawal after prolonged use may give rise to withdrawal symptoms).
*Related articles:* MOGADON; NITRADOS; NOCTESED; REMNOS; SOMNITE; SUREM; UNISOMNIA.

**Nitrocine** (*Schwarz*) is a proprietary VASODILATOR, available only on prescription, used to treat congestive heart failure and angina pectoris (heart pain). Produced in the form of ampoules for injection (to be administered diluted or undiluted), Nitrocine is a preparation of glyceryl trinitrate.
▲/✿ side-effects/warning: *see* GLYCERYL TRINITRATE; NITRATES.

**Nitrocontin Continus** (*Degussa*) is a proprietary, non-prescription VASODILATOR, used to treat angina pectoris (heart pain). Produced in the form of sustained-release tablets (in two strengths), Nitrocontin Continus is a preparation of glyceryl trinitrate. It is not recommended for children.
▲/✿ side-effects/warning: *see* GLYCERYL TRINITRATE; NITRATES.

**nitrofurantoin** is an ANTIBIOTIC used particularly to treat infections of the urinary tract. It is especially useful in treating kidney infections that prove to be resistant to other forms of therapy. Administration is oral in the form of tablets, as capsules, or as a suspension.

▲ side-effects: there may be loss of appetite, nausea, vomiting and diarrhoea; impaired lung function; peripheral neuropathy causing tingling and other sensory disorders in the fingers and toes (patients should report such symptoms). Rarely there is liver damage, allergic skin reactions and blood disorders. Urine may be coloured yellow or brown.

✿ warning: nitrofurantoin should not be administered to patients with impaired kidney function, or who are aged under 1 month. The drug is ineffective in patients whose urine is alkaline. Lung, liver and peripheral nerve function should be monitored in long-term treatment.
*Related articles:* FURADANTIN; MACRODANTIN; URANTOIN.

**nitrofurazone** is an ANTIBACTERIAL drug used primarily in the treatment or prevention of infection on the skin surface, and to prepare skin for grafting, and for some bladder infections. (Occasionally an oral preparation is used to treat the protozoan infection trypanosomiasis.) Administration is thus ordinarily topical, in the form of an ointment.

▲ side-effects: there may be local sensitivity reactions, especially following prolonged use.

✿ warning: nitrofurazone should be administered with caution to patients with impaired kidney function.

**Nitrolingual Spray** (*Lipha*) is a proprietary, non-prescription VASODILATOR, used for the treatment and prevention of angina pectoris (heart pain). Produced in the form of an aerosol spray, Nitrolingual Spray is a preparation of glyceryl trinitrate. It is not recommended for children.

▲/✿ side-effects/warning: *see* GLYCERYL TRINITRATE.

**Nitronal** (*Lipha*) is a proprietary VASODILATOR, available only on prescription, used to treat congestive heart failure and angina pectoris (heart pain). Produced in ampoules for injection (to be administered diluted or undiluted), Nitronal is a preparation of glyceryl trinitrate.

▲/✿ side-effects/warning: *see* GLYCERYL TRINITRATE.

**nitrophenol** is an ANTIFUNGAL drug used in topical application to treat skin infection (such as athlete's foot). Administration is as an alcohol-based paint, using a special applicator.

**Nivaquine** (*May & Baker*) is a proprietary ANTIMALARIAL drug, available only on prescription, used primarily in combination with other drugs (such as tetracycline) for the prevention and treatment of malaria. Some malarial strains are now resistant to the drug. Produced in the form of tablets, as a syrup for dilution (the potency of the elixir once diluted is retained for 14 days), and in ampoules for injection (during emergency treatment only), Nivaquine is a preparation of chloroquine sulphate.

▲/✿ side-effects/warning: *see* CHLOROQUINE.

**Nivemycin** (*Boots*) is a proprietary form of the aminoglycoside ANTIBIOTIC

neomycin sulphate, available only on prescription, used to reduce bacterial levels in the intestines before surgery. Nivemycin is produced in the form of tablets and as an elixir.
▲/✿ side-effects/warning: *see* NEOMYCIN.

**Nizoral** (*Janssen*) is a proprietary ANTIFUNGAL drug, available only on prescription, used to treat both serious systemic and skin-surface fungal infections. Produced in the form of tablets, as a suspension, as a water-miscible cream for topical application and as a shampoo to treat certain forms of dermatitis and dandruff, Nizoral is a preparation of the IMIDAZOLE ketoconazole.
▲/✿ side-effects/warning: *see* KETOCONAZOLE.

**Nobrium** (*Roche*) is a proprietary TRANQUILLIZER, available on prescription only to private patients, used in the short-term treatment of anxiety. Produced in the form of capsules (in two strengths), Nobrium is a preparation of the long-acting BENZODIAZEPINE medazepam. It is not recommended for children.
▲/✿ side-effects/warning: *see* MEDAZEPAM.

**Noctamid** (*Schering*) is a proprietary HYPNOTIC drug, available on prescription only to private patients, used in the short-term treatment of insomnia. Produced in the form of tablets (in two strengths), Noctamid is a preparation of the BENZO-DIAZEPINE lormetazepam. It is not recommended for children.
▲/✿ side-effects/warning: *see* LORMETAZEPAM.

**Noctec** (*Squibb*) is a proprietary HYPNOTIC drug, available only on prescription, used to treat insomnia and for sedation in the elderly. Produced in the form of

capsules, Noctec is a preparation of the powerful SEDATIVE chloral hydrate, and is not recommended for children.
▲/✿ side-effects/warning: *see* CHLORAL HYDRATE.

**Noctesed** (*Unimed*) is a proprietary TRANQUILLIZER, available on prescription only to private patients, used to treat insomnia in cases where some degree of daytime sedation is acceptable. Produced in the form of tablets, Noctesed is a preparation of the long-acting BENZODIAZEPINE nitrazepam.
▲/✿ side-effects/warning: *see* NITRAZEPAM.

**Noltam** (*Lederle*) is a proprietary preparation of the powerful drug tamoxifen, available only on prescription, which, because it inhibits or blocks the effect of OESTROGENS, is used primarily to treat cancers that depend on the presence of oestrogen in women, particularly breast cancer. But it may also be used (under strict medical supervision) to treat certain conditions of infertility in which the presence of oestrogens may be preventing other hormonal activity. It is produced in the form of tablets (in two strengths).
▲/✿ side-effects/warning: *see* TAMOXIFEN.

**Nolvadex** (*ICI*) is a proprietary preparation of the powerful drug tamoxifen, available only on prescription, which because it inhibits or blocks the effect of OESTROGENS, is used primarily to treat cancers that depend on the presence of oestrogen in women, particularly breast cancer. But it may also be used (under strict medical supervision) to treat certain conditions of infertility in which the presence of oestrogens may be preventing other hormonal activity. It is produced in the form of tablets (in three strengths, the stronger ones under the trade names Nolvadex-D and Nolvadex-Forte).

▲/✿ side-effects/warning: *see* TAMOXIFEN.

\*non-narcotic analgesic: *see* ANALGESIC.

\*non-steroidal anti-inflammatory drug is usually abbreviated to NSAID.
*see* ANALGESIC; ANTI-INFLAMMATORY; ANTIRHEUMATIC.

**Noradran** (*Norma*) is a proprietary, non-prescription, ANTIHISTAMINE expectorant and cough mixture, which is not available from the National Health Service. Produced in the form of a syrup, Noradran is a compound that includes the antihistamine diphenhydramine hydrochloride, the SYMPATHO-MIMETIC ephedrine hydrochloride and the EXPECTORANT guaiphenesin. It is not recommended for children aged under 5 years.

▲/✿ side-effects/warning: *see* DIPHENHYDRAMINE HYDROCHLORIDE; EPHEDRINE HYDROCHLORIDE.

**noradrenaline** is a catecholamine – a HORMONE – produced and secreted by the central core (medulla) of the adrenal glands. Like the closely-related ADRENALINE, it represents one contributory element of the sympathetic nervous system in that, as a NEUROTRANSMITTER (transmitting neural impulses between nerves, and between nerves and muscles), it relays a response to stress. In the face of stress, the body thus uses noradrenaline (and adrenaline) to organize constriction of the small blood vessels (vasoconstriction, so increasing blood pressure), increased blood flow through the

heart while the heart rate falls or rises, dilatation of the muscles of the airways, and relaxation of the muscles of the intestinal walls. And it is to effect one or more of these responses that nora-drenaline, as a SYMPATHO-MIMETIC, may be administered therapeutically. In an emergency, for example, noradrenaline (in the form of noradrenaline acid tartrate) may be injected to raise depressed blood pressure.

▲ side-effects: there may be headache, with reduced heart rate and uneven heartbeat.

✿ warning: noradrenaline should not be administered to patients who are undergoing a heart attack, or who are pregnant. Leakage of the hormone into the tissues at the site of injection may cause tissue damage.
*Related article:* LEVOPHED.

**Noratex** (*Norton*) is a proprietary, non-prescription skin emollient (softener and soother), used to treat nappy rash and bedsores. Produced in the form of a cream, it contains wool fat, ZINC OXIDE, KAOLIN and talc.

✿ warning: wool fat causes sensitivity reactions in some patients.

**Norcuron** (*Organon-Teknika*) is a proprietary SKELETAL MUSCLE RELAXANT, of the type known as competitive or non-depolarizing; it is used during surgical operations, but only after the patient has been rendered unconscious. Available only on prescription, and produced in ampoules for injection, Norcuron is a preparation of vecuronium bromide.

✿ warning: *see* VECURONIUM BROMIDE.

**Norditropin** (*Novo Nordiski*) is a HORMONE, a proprietary form of somatropin, used to treat small

stature, and deficiencies of other hormones. It is available only on prescription. The preparation is in the form of a powder for reconstitution for injection.
▲/✦ side-effects/warning: *see* SOMATROPIN.

**Nordox** (*Norton*) is a proprietary, broad-spectrum ANTIBIOTIC, available only on prescription, used to treat infections of many kinds, including acne and chronic prostatitis. Produced in the form of capsules, Nordox is a preparation of the TETRACYCLINE doxycycline.
▲/✦ side-effects/warning: *see* DOXYCYCLINE.

**norethisterone** is a PROGESTOGEN (a sex HORMONE) that is an analogue of testosterone (the major male sex hormone). Like all progestogens, norethisterone opposes or modifies some of the effects of OESTROGENS (female sex hormones), and may be used therapeutically to treat several forms of menstrual disorder, endometriosis, dysfunctional uterine bleeding, and to assist in the treatment of sex-hormone-linked cancer. It is also a constituent in many ORAL CONTRACEPTIVES, which combine an oestrogen and a progestogen. Administration is oral in the form of tablets.
▲ side-effects: there may be fluid and sodium retention (oedema) leading to weight gain; there may also be breast tenderness, a change in libido, irregular menstrual cycles and gastrointestinal disturbance. Headache and depression may occur; some patients take on the yellow coloration of jaundice, or suffer from skin disorders.
✦ warning: norethisterone should not be administered to patients with undiagnosed bleeding from the vagina or

breast cancer, who are pregnant, or who have a history of thrombosis; it should be administered with extreme caution to those with heart, liver or kidney disease, diabetes, asthma, epilepsy, or high blood pressure (hypertension), or who are lactating.
*Related articles:* BINOVUM; BREVINOR; ESTRAPAK 50; MENOPHASE; MENZOL; MICRONOR; NEOCON-1/35; NORIDAY; NORIMIN; NORINYL-1; ORTHO-NOVIN 1/50; OVYSMEN; PRIMOLUT N; SYNPHASE; TRI-NOVUM; UTOVLAN.

**norethisterone acetate** is another form of the PROGESTOGEN norethisterone, used primarily as a constituent in ORAL CONTRACEPTIVES, which combine an OESTROGEN with a progestogen, but also in hormone replacement therapy to treat some menopausal symptoms.
▲/✦ side-effects/warning: *see* NORETHISTERONE.
*Related articles:* LOESTRIN; TRISEQUENS.

**norethisterone enanthate** is another form of the PROGESTOGEN norethisterone, used as a contraceptive and administered by injection to patients who prefer not to – or cannot – use ORAL CONTRACEPTIVE methods or forms of contraception that include an OESTROGEN.
▲/✦ side-effects/warning: *see* NORETHISTERONE.
*Related article:* NORISTERAT.

**Norflex** (*Riker*) is a proprietary SKELETAL MUSCLE RELAXANT, available only on prescription, used to relieve muscle spasm mainly in the muscles of the limbs; it works by direct action on the central nervous system. Produced in the form of ampoules for injection, Norflex is a preparation of orphenadrine citrate. It is not recommended for children.

▲/ ● side-effects/warning: *see* ORPHENADRINE CITRATE.

**Norgeston** (*Schering*) is a proprietary, progesterone-only, ORAL CONTRACEPTIVE, available only on prescription, which is a preparation of the PROGESTOGEN levonorgestrel. It is produced in 35-day calendar packs that correspond to one complete menstrual cycle.

▲/ ● side-effects/warning: *see* LEVONORGESTREL.

**norgestrel** is a female sex hormone, a PROGESTOGEN used in ORAL CONTRACEPTIVES – in which it may or may not be combined with an oestrogen – and, also in combination with oestrogens, to treat menstrual and menopausal disorders. The hormone LEVONORGESTREL is a stronger form of norgestrel.

▲ side-effects: there may be nausea and vomiting, with a headache; menstrual irregularities and breast tenderness are common, but there may also be weight gain and (occasionally) depression. Some patients experience skin disorders.

● warning: norgestrel should not be administered to patients who are pregnant, or with vascular or liver disease, cancer of the liver or of the breast, or undiagnosed bleeding from the vagina. It should be administered with caution to those with heart disease or high blood pressure (hypertension), diabetes, or severe migraine.
*Related articles*: CYCLO-PROGYNOVA; NEOGEST; PREMPAK C; PREMPAK-C.

**Noriday** (*Syntex*) is a proprietary, progesterone-only, ORAL CONTRACEPTIVE, available only on

prescription, which consists of a preparation of the PROGESTOGEN norethisterone. It is produced in 28-day calendar packs that correspond to one complete menstrual cycle.

▲/ ● side-effects/warning: *see* NORETHISTERONE.

**Norimin** (*Syntex*) is a proprietary combined ORAL CONTRACEPTIVE, available only on prescription, that consists of a preparation of the PROGESTOGEN, norethisterone and the OESTROGEN ethinylo-estradiol. It is produced in 21-day calendar packs that correspond to one complete menstrual cycle.

▲/ ● side-effects/warning: *see* ETHINYLOESTRADIOL; NORETHISTERONE.

**Norinyl-1** (*Syntex*) is a proprietary combined ORAL CONTRACEPTIVE, available only on prescription, that consists of a combined preparation of the PROGESTOGEN norethisterone and the OESTROGEN mestranol. It is produced in 21-day calendar packs that correspond to one complete menstrual cycle.

▲/ ● side-effects/warning: *see* MESTRANOL; NORETHISTERONE.

**Norisen** (*Merck*) is a proprietary set of preparations of common allergens, including pollens, moulds, dusts, animal danders, stinging insects and house dust mites, for use in desensitizing patients who are allergic to them. Available only on prescription and administered by injection, Norisen preparations are of carefully annotated different allergenic effect, so that the process of desensitization, as regulated by a doctor, can be progressive. Also available are preparations of 6 varieties of common grass pollen (under the name Norisen Grass) in vials of graded strength. Skin testing solutions are also available on prescription for each extract in the Norisen range.

✚ warning: injections should be administered under close medical supervision and in locations where emergency facilities for full cardio-respiratory resuscitation are immediately available.

**Noristerat** (*Schering*) is a proprietary CONTRACEPTIVE, available only on prescription, that consists of a preparation of the progestogen norethisterone enanthate. It is produced in ampoules for injection for short-term contraception.

▲/✚ side-effects/warning: *see* NORETHISTERONE.

**Norit** (*Dendron*) is a proprietary, non-prescription, adsorbent medium used orally to treat diarrhoea, indigestion and flatulence. Produced in the form of capsules, Norit is a preparation of activated CHARCOAL. It is not recommended for children aged under 2 years.

**Normacol** (*Norgine*) is a proprietary, non-prescription LAXATIVE of the type known as bulking agents, which works by increasing the overall mass of faeces within the rectum, so stimulating bowel movement. It is thus used both to relieve constipation and to relieve diarrhoea, and is used also in the control of faecal consistency for patients with a colostomy. Produced in the form of granules in sachets, Normacol is a preparation of the bulk forming drug sterculia. Two compound preparations are also available, although not from the National Health Service: Normacol Standard granules with added frangula bark, and Normacol Antispasmodic with the added muscle relaxant ALVERINE

CITRATE. None of these preparations is recommended for children aged under 6 years.

**Normasol** (*Schering*) is a proprietary, non-prescription, saline solution, used to clean burns and minor wounds. Produced in the form of a sterile solution, Normasol is a preparation of SODIUM CHLORIDE (saline). An ophthalmic form is also available (under the trade name Normasol Undine) for the washing out of harmful substances and foreign bodies from the eye.

**Normax** (*Innovex*) is a proprietary LAXATIVE, used to treat constipation and to prepare patients for abdominal radiographic procedures. Produced in the form of capsules, Normax is a preparation of the stimulant danthron in the from of co-danthrusate (danthron and poloxamer '188'). It is not recommended for children.

▲/✚ side-effects/warning: *see* DANTHRON.

**Normetic** (*Abbott*) is a proprietary DIURETIC, available only on prescription, used to treat congestive heart failure, high blood pressure (hypertension) and cirrhosis of the liver. Produced in the form of tablets, it is a compound of the weak but diuretic amiloride hydrochloride together with the THIAZIDE hydrochlorothiazide. It is not recommended for children.

▲/✚ side-effects/warning: *see* AMILORIDE; HYDROCHLOROTHIAZIDE.

**Normison** (*Wyeth*) is a proprietary HYPNOTIC drug, available on prescription only to private patients, used (in the short-term) to treat insomnia especially in the elderly, and as a premedication prior to surgery. Produced in the form of capsules (in two strengths), Normison is a preparation of the BENZO-DIAZEPINE temazepam. It is not recommended for children.

▲/⦿ side-effects/warning: *see* TEMAZEPAM.

**nortriptyline** is an ANTI-DEPRESSANT drug, which also has mild sedative properties, used primarily to treat depressive illness. Like several others of its type, however, the drug may also be used to assist in the treatment of nocturnal bedwetting by children (aged over 7 years). Administration is oral in the form of tablets, capsules, or a sugar-free dilute liquid.

▲ side-effects: common effects include a loss of concentration, movement and thought, dry mouth, and blurred vision; there may also be difficulty in urinating, sweating, and irregular heartbeat, behavioural disturbances, a rash, a state of confusion, and/or a loss of libido. Rarely, there are also blood deficiencies.

⦿ warning: nortriptyline should not be administered to patients with heart disease or psychosis; it should be administered with caution to those with diabetes, epilepsy, liver or thyroid disease, glaucoma or urinary retention; or who are pregnant or lactating. Withdrawal of treatment must be gradual. *Related articles:* ALLEGRON; AVENTYL.

**Norval** (*Bencard*) is a proprietary ANTIDEPRESSANT, available only on prescription, used to treat depressive illness especially when associated with anxiety. Produced in the form of tablets (in three strengths), Norval is a preparation of mianserin hydrochloride. It is not recommended for children.

▲/⦿ side-effects/warning: *see* MIANSERIN.

**noscapine** is an OPIATE (although not related to morphine) used as a constituent in proprietary and non-proprietary formulations intended to relieve dry and painful coughs: such formulations are not available from the National Health Service. The drug has some effect as a cough suppressant.

▲ side-effects: there may be constipation

⦿ warning: noscapine should not be administered to patients with liver disease, asthma or chronic bronchitis.

**Novantrone** (*Lederle*) is a proprietary CYTOTOXIC drug, available only on prescription, used to treat certain forms of cancer including breast cancer. It works by reacting with cellular DNA and so disrupting normal cell replication. Produced in vials for intravenous infusion, Novantrone is a preparation of mitozantrone.

▲/⦿ side-effects/warning: *see* MITOZANTRONE; DOXORUBICIN.

**Novaruca** (*Bioglan*) is a proprietary, non-prescription solution for topical application containing the KERATOLYTIC glutaraldehyde, used to treat warts and to remove hard, dead skin. Not for use on facial, anal or perineal warts. The preparation is in the form of a gel.

⦿ warning: *see* GLUTARALDEHYDE.

**Noxyflex S** (*Geistlich*) is a proprietary ANTIMICROBIAL, available only on prescription, used to treat infections of the urinary tract. Produced in the form of a powder for reconstitution as a solution for instillation into the bladder, Noxyflex S is a compound preparation of the ANTI-BACTERIAL/ANTIFUNGAL drug noxythiolin.

▲/✿ side-effects/warning: *see* NOXYTHIOLIN.

**noxythiolin** is an ANTIBIOTIC that has both ANTIBACTERIAL and ANTIFUNGAL properties. A derivative of urea, its primary use is in the treatment of an infected bladder. It is introduced directly into the bladder as an irrigating solution.

✿ warning: because there may be a stinging, burning sensation on initial instillation, the drug is sometimes administered in combination with a local anaesthetic. Administration into a severely infected bladder may cause the formation of clumps of fibrous protein, which pass out with the irrigation fluid.

*Related article:* NOXYFLEX S.

**Nozinan** (*May & Baker*) is a proprietary ANTIPSYCHOTIC drug, available only on prescription, used to treat and sedate patients with schizophrenia and related psychoses, and to relieve anxiety during terminal care. Produced in ampoules for injection, Nozinan is a preparation of metho-trimeprazine hydrochloride. It is not recommended for children.

▲/✿ side-effects/warning: *see* METHOTRIMEPRAZINE.

**\*NSAID** is an abbreviation of non-steroidal ANTI-INFLAMMATORY drug.

*see* ANALGESIC; ANTIRHEUMATIC.

**Nubain** (*Du Pont*) is a proprietary, narcotic ANALGESIC, available only on prescription, used to treat moderate to severe pain, particularly during or following surgical procedures or a heart attack. Produced in ampoules for injection, Nubain is a preparation of the OPIATE nalbuphine hydrochloride. It is not recommended for children.

▲/✿ side-effects/warning: *see* NALBUPHINE HYDROCHLORIDE.

**Nuelin** (*Riker*) is a proprietary, non-prescription BRONCHO-DILATOR, used to treat asthmatic bronchospasm and chronic bronchitis. Produced in the form of tablets (not recommended for children aged under 7 years), as sustained-release tablets (in two strengths under the names Nuelin SA and Nuelin SA 250; not recommended for children aged under 6 years), and as a syrup for dilution (the potency of the liquid once diluted is retained for 14 days; not recommended for children aged under 2 years), Nuelin is a preparation of the drug theophylline.

▲/✿ side-effects/warning: *see* THEOPHYLLINE.

**Nu-K** (*Consolidated*) is a proprietary, non-prescription POTASSIUM supplement, used to make up a blood deficiency of potassium (as may occur in the elderly, in patients with severe diarrhoea, or in patients being treated with diuretics). Produced in the form of sustained-release capsules, Nu-K is a preparation of POTASSIUM CHLORIDE. It is not recommended for children.

**Nulacin** (*Bencard*) is a proprietary, non-prescription ANTACID, which is not available from the National Health Service. It is used to treat peptic ulcers and inflammation of the stomach. Produced in the form of tablets, Nulacin is a compound preparation that includes calcium carbonate, magnesium carbonate, magnesium oxide ('magnesia'), magnesium trisilicate and maltose. It is not recommended for children, and should be avoided because of potential side-effects.

▲/✪ side-effects/warning: *see*
CALCIUM CARBONATE;
MAGNESIUM CARBONATE;
MAGNESIUM TRISILICATE.

**Numotac** (*Riker*) is a proprietary
BRONCHODILATOR, available only
on prescription, used to treat
bronchial asthma and chronic
bronchitis. Produced in the form
of sustained-release tablets,
Numotac is a preparation of the
BETA-RECEPTOR STIMULANT
isoetharine hydrochloride. It is
not recommended for children.
▲/✪ side-effects/warning: *see*
ISOETHARINE.

**Nupercainal** (*Ciba*) is a
proprietary, non-prescription
local ANAESTHETIC, used in topical
application to treat painful skin
conditions. Produced in the form
of an ointment, Nupercainal is a
solute preparation of cinchocaine
hydrochloride.
▲/✪ side-effects/warning: *see*
CINCHOCAINE.

**Nurofen** (*Crookes Healthcare*) is a
proprietary, non-prescription,
non-narcotic ANALGESIC
containing ibuprofen.
▲/✪ side-effects/warning: *see*
IBUPROFEN.

**Nu-Seals Aspirin** (*Lilly*) is a
proprietary, non-prescription,
non-narcotic ANALGESIC, a form of
aspirin used to treat chronic pain
such as that of arthritis and
rheumatism. Produced in the form
of tablets (in two strengths), Nu-
Seals Aspirin is not recommended
for children aged under 12 years.
▲/✪ side-effects/warning: *see*
ASPIRIN.

**Nutracel** (*Travenol*) is a
proprietary form of high-energy
nutritional supplement, available
only on prescription, intended for
infusion into patients who are
unable to take food via the
alimentary tract such as after

total gastrectomy. Produced in
two strengths (under the trade
names Nutracel 400 and Nutracel
800), it is a preparation of
GLUCOSE with MAGNESIUM
CHLORIDE and several other
mineral salts.

**Nutramigen** (*Bristol-Myers*) is a
proprietary, non-prescription,
dietary supplement. Nutritionally
complete, it is intended for
patients who suffer from milk
protein intolerance. Produced in
the form of a powder, Nutramigen
is a preparation of protein,
carbohydrate, fat (corn oil),
vitamins and minerals, and is
lactose-, fructose- and gluten-free.
It is not recommended for infants
aged under 3 months.

**Nutranel** (*Roussel*) is a
proprietary, non-prescription,
dietary supplement. It is intended
for patients who suffer from
malabsorption of food (for
example following gastrectomy).
Produced in the form of a powder,
Nutranel is a preparation of
protein, fat, carbohydrate,
vitamins, minerals and trace
elements, and is low in lactose. It
is not suitable as the sole source
of nutrition for children, and is
unsuitable for infants aged under
12 months.

**Nutraplus** (*Alcon*) is a
proprietary, non-prescription,
skin emollient (softener and
soother), used to treat dry skin.
Produced in the form of a cream
in a water-miscible basis,
Nutraplus is a preparation of the
hydrating substance urea.

**\*nutritional preparations** or
nutritional supplements have
their main place in medicine for
the nutrition of those who cannot
tolerate normal foods for some
reason. Their use is only seen as
essential under certain
circumstances that include after

major bowel surgery and in serious stomach and intestinal disorders, for those allergic to certain food products such as cows' milk, and for those unable to metabolize certain sugars and amino-acids.

**Nutrizym** (*Merck*) is a proprietary, non-prescription form of pancreatic enzymes, pancreatin, used to treat enzymatic deficiency in such conditions as cystic fibrosis and chronic inflammation of the pancreas. Pancrease is produced in the form of capsules.
▲/✿ side-effects/warning: *see* PANCREATIN.

**Nutrizym GR** (*Merck*) is a proprietary non-prescription preparation of pancreatic enzymes, used to treat pancreatic disorders, and particularly the symptoms arising from cystic fibrosis (in which thick mucus obstructs the secretion of pancreatic juices). It is produced in the form of tablets to be taken during or after meals.

**Nybadex** (*Cox*) is a proprietary, anti-inflammatory and ANTIFUNGAL compound, available only on prescription, used to treat skin inflammations in which infection is thought to be present. It is produced in the form of a dilute emulsifying ointment for topical application, and contains the CORTICOSTEROID hydrocortisone with the ANTIBIOTIC nystatin, the antifoaming agent DIMETHICONE and the antiseptic BENZALKONIUM CHLORIDE.
▲/✿ side-effects/warning: *see* HYDROCORTISONE; NYSTATIN.

**Nycopren** (*Lundbeck*) is a proprietary, non-steroidal, ANTI-INFLAMMATORY, non-narcotic ANALGESIC, available only on prescription, used to relieve pain – particularly rheumatic and

arthritic pain, and that of acute gout – and to treat other musculo-skeletal disorders. Produced in the form of tablets (in two strengths), it is a preparation of naproxen.
▲/✿ side-effects/warning: *see* NAPROXEN.

**Nydrane** (*Lipha*) is a proprietary preparation of the ANTI-CONVULSANT drug beclamide, available only on prescription, used to treat grand mal and partial seizures in epilepsy, and associated behavioural disorders. It is produced in the form of tablets.
▲/✿ side-effects/warning: *see* BECLAMIDE.

**Nyspes** (*DDSA Pharmaceuticals*) is a proprietary ANTIFUNGAL preparation, available only on prescription, used to treat yeast infections of the vagina or vulva. Produced in the form of vaginal inserts (pessaries), Nyspes is a preparation of nystatin.
▲/✿ side-effects/warning: *see* NYSTATIN.

**Nystadermal** (*Squibb*) is a proprietary, CORTICOSTEROID, ANTIFUNGAL cream, available only on prescription, used for topical application on areas of inflamed skin, particularly in cases of eczema that have failed to respond to less powerful drugs. Nystadermal is a preparation of the steroid triamcinolone acetonide and the antifungal nystatin.
▲/✿ side-effects/warning: *see* NYSTATIN.

**Nystaform** (*Bayer*) is a proprietary ANTIFUNGAL preparation, available only on prescription, used in topical application to treat fungal (particularly yeast) infections. Produced in the form of a cream and an anhydrous ointment,

Nystaform is a preparation of the antifungal drug nystatin and one of two forms of the ANTISEPTIC chlorhexidine.

▲/● side-effects/warning: see CHLORHEXIDINE; NYSTATIN.

**Nystaform-HC** (*Bayer*) is a proprietary CORTICOSTEROID compound, available only on prescription, used to treat skin inflammations in which fungal and bacterial infections are suspected. Produced in the form of a water-miscible cream and an anhydrous ointment, Nystaform-HC is a preparation of the corticosteroid hydrocortisone, the ANTIFUNGAL drug nystatin, and one of two forms of the (mildly antibacterial) ANTISEPTIC chlorhexidine.

▲/● side-effects/warning: see CHLORHEXIDINE; NYSTATIN.

**Nystan** (*Squibb*) is the name of a proprietary group of ANTIFUNGAL preparations, available only on prescription, used to treat fungal infections (such as candidiasis, thrush). All are forms of the antifungal nystatin. Preparations for oral administration include tablets, a suspension, a gluten-, lactose- and sugar-free suspension, granules for reconstitution with water to form a solution, and pastilles (for treating mouth infections). For vaginal and vulval infections there is a vaginal cream, a gel, and vaginal inserts (pessaries), under the name Nystavescent). A triple pack containing tablets, gel and pessaries is available. A water-miscible cream, gel, ointment and dusting-powder are available for the topical treatment of fungal skin infections.

▲/● side-effects/warning: see NYSTATIN.

**nystatin** is an ANTIFUNGAL drug,

effective both in topical application and when taken orally (when taken by this method it is not absorbed and exerts its antifungal action only in the mouth and gastrointestinal tract), primarily used to treat the yeast infection candidiasis (thrush). Less commonly, it is used to treat other fungal infections, particularly in and around the mouth. Administration is in many forms: tablets, a suspension, a solution, pastilles, vaginal inserts (pessaries), a cream, a gel and an ointment. It is too toxic to be injected systemically.

▲ side-effects: treatment of the vagina may require additional medication to restore the natural acidity of the area. There may be nausea, vomiting or diarrhoea.

● warning: the full course of treatment must be completed, even if symptoms disappear earlier: recurrence of infection is common when treatment is withdrawn too hastily. Fungal infections in the urogenital areas imply simultaneous treatment of the patient's sexual partner. Treatment with pessaries should be continued through menstruation.
*Related articles:* DERMOVATE-NN; GREGODERM; MULTILIND; NYSTAFORM; NYSTAN; NYSTATIN-DOME; TERRA-CORTIL; TINADERM-M; TRI-CITATRIN.

**Nystatin-Dome** (*Bayer*) is a proprietary ANTIFUNGAL preparation, available only on prescription, used to treat intestinal candidiasis (thrush) and oral infections. Produced in the form of a suspension, Nystatin-Dome is a preparation of the antifungal drug nystatin.

▲/● side-effects/warning: see NYSTATIN.

**Octovit** (*Smith, Kline & French*) is a proprietary non-prescription mineral-and-VITAMIN compound, used particularly as an IRON supplement (containing ferrous sulphate). Produced in the form of tablets, Octovit contains – apart from iron – calcium, magnesium and zinc, together with THIAMINE (vitamin B₁), RIBOFLAVINE (vitamin B₂), PYRIDOXINE (vitamin B₆), CYANOCOBALAMIN (vitamin B₁₂), NICOTINAMIDE (of the vitamin B complex), ASCORBIC ACID (vitamin C), CALCIFEROL (vitamin D) and TOCOPHEROL (vitamin E). Octovit should not be used simultaneously with tetracycline antibiotics.
▲/✿ side-effects/warning: *see* FERROUS SULPHATE.

**octoxinol** is a SPERMICIDAL drug used to assist barrier methods of contraception. In mild solution, it is produced as a jelly.
▲ side-effects: very rarely, there may be sensitivity reactions.
*Related article:* STAYCEPT.

**octreotide** is a HORMONE analogue, a long-lasting form of the hypothalamic release-inhibiting hormone somatostatin, which is indicated for the relief of symptoms originating from the release of hormones from carcinoid tumours of the endocrine system, including vipomas, and glucagonomas. It is given by subcutaneous injection.
*Related article:* SANDOSTATIN.

**Ocusert Pilo** (*May & Baker*) is a proprietary form of the PARA-SYMPATHOMIMETIC pilocarpine hydrochloride, used to treat glaucoma. Available only on prescription (in either of two strengths), it is produced in the form of elliptical plastic inserts to be placed under the eyelid (following instructions on the pack), permitting sustained local release of the drug. Ocusert Pilo

is not recommended for children.
▲/✿ side-effects/warning: *see* PILOCARPINE.

**oestradiol** is the main female sex hormone produced and secreted by the ovary. An OESTROGEN, it is used therapeutically to make up hormonal deficiencies – sometimes in combination with a PROGESTOGEN – to treat menstrual, menopausal or other gynaecological problems (such as infertility). Administration is oral in the form of tablets, or by injection.
▲ side-effects: there may be nausea and vomiting. A common effect is weight gain, generally through fluid or sodium retention in the tissues. The breasts may become tender and enlarge slightly. There may also be headache and/or depression; sometimes a rash breaks out.
✿ warning: oestradiol should not be administered to patients who have cancers proved to be sex-hormone-related, who have a history of thrombosis or inflammation of the womb, or who suffer from porphyria or impaired liver function. Prolonged treatment increases the risk of cancer of the endometrium (the lining of the womb). Caution should be exercised in administering oestradiol to patients who are diabetic or epileptic, who have heart or kidney disease, who are pregnant or lactating, or who have high blood pressure (hypertension) or migraine.
*Related articles:* CYCLO-PROGYNOVA; ESTRAPAK 50; HORMONIN; PROGYNOVA; TRISEQUENS; VAGIFEM.

**oestriol** is a female sex hormone produced and secreted by the ovary. An OESTROGEN, it is similar in properties and uses to OESTRADIOL.

*Related articles:* ORTHO-GYNEST; OVESTIN; TRISEQUENS.

**oestrogens** are a group of STEROID hormones that promote the growth and functioning of the female sex organs and the development of female sexual characteristics. In their natural forms they are produced and secreted mainly by the ovary (and to a small extent the adrenal cortex and – in men – the testes). Natural and synthesized oestrogens are used therapeutically, sometimes in combination with PROGESTOGENS, to treat menstrual, menopausal or other gynaecological problems, and as oral contraceptives. Best-known and most used are oestradiol, oestriol, ethinyloestradiol, mestranol and quinestradol.

▲/✿ side-effects/warning: *see* ETHINYLOESTRADIOL; MESTRANOL; OESTRADIOL; OESTRIOL; QUINESTRADOL; QUINESTROL.

**ofloxacin** is an ANTIBIOTIC agent of the quinolone family used to treat infections in patients who are allergic to penicillin, or whose strain of bacterium is resistant to standard antibiotics. It is active against Gram-negative bacteria including salmonella, shigella and chlamydobacter, neisseria and pseudomonas, and to a lesser extent against Gram-positive bacteria of the Streptococcal family. Most anaerobic organisms are not sensitive. This spectrum of activity indicates treatment with ofloxacin for infections of the genito-urinary tract, including both gonorrhoea and non-gonorrhoeal infections (and also some respiratory infections), but only when these cases are resistant to more conventional agents. Administration may be oral in the form of tablets or by intravenous infusion.

▲ side-effects: there may be nausea and vomiting, diarrhoea, gastrointestinal pain, dizziness, headache; fatigue, confusion and sleep disturbances; rashes and pruritus, convulsions, light sensitivity, disturbances of taste and smell; impairment of liver enzymes; bone marrow depression. Drowsiness may impair skilled performance such as driving, and the effects of alcohol may be enhanced. Treatment should be discontinued if psychotic symptoms are observed.

✿ warning: ofloxacin should be administered with caution to epileptics, those with a history of behavioural disorders, to patients who have impaired kidney or liver function, or who are pregnant or breast-feeding. Not recommended for children or adolescents. Severe allergic reactions have been reported, especially in those with AIDS.

*Related article:* TARIVID.

**Oilatum** (*Stiefel*) is a proprietary, non-prescription skin emollient (softener and soother) in the form of a water-based cream containing arachis oil and povidone. Under the same name there is a bath emulsion containing liquid paraffin and wool alcohols, for use as an emollient soaking medium.

**oily cream** is a general term for the kind of cream that is not water-miscible and so does not wash off so easily. Such creams are used as bases for many therapeutic preparations for topical application. Whereas an oily cream is oily, OINTMENTS are deemed to be greasy.

**ointments** is a general term for a group of essentially greasy preparations that are anhydrous and insoluble in water and so do not wash off. Such unguents are used as bases for many therapeutic preparations for topical application (particularly in the treatment of dry lesions or of ophthalmic complaints). Most have a form of paraffin as their base; a few contain lanolin and wool alcohols, to which a small number of patients may be sensitive.

**olive oil** is used therapeutically – always warmed beforehand – either to soften earwax prior to syringing the ears, or to treat the brown, flaking skin that commonly appears on the heads of very young infants (cradle cap) prior to shampooing.

**olsalazine sodium** is an ANTI-INFLAMMATORY and ANTIBACTERIAL used in the treatment of the inflammatory state and chronic diarrhoea caused by ulcerative colitis, in patients who are sensitive to the commonly-prescribed drug sulphasalazine. Administration is oral in the form of capsules.
▲ side-effects: there may be nausea, with diarrhoea and abdominal pain; some patients experience a headache.
✳ warning: olsalazine sodium should not be administered to patients who are allergic to aspirin or other salicylates; it should be administered with caution to those with impaired kidney function.
*Related article:* DIPENTUM.

**omeprazole** is an anti-ulcer drug of a recently developed class that works as an inhibitor of gastric acid secretion through acting as a proton pump inhibitor. It is used for the treatment of benign gastric and duodenal ulcers (including those complicating NSAID therapy), Zollinger-Ellison syndrome and reflux

oesophagitis. Treatment with omeptazole may be tried when there has been a poor response to conventional therapies. The dose may need careful adjustment according to the patient and condition. It is available in the form of capsules.
▲ side-effects: diarrhoea or constipation, flatulence, rashes; headaches have been reported.
✳ warning: use only when the ulcer has been established to be benign, avoid in pregnancy or breast-feeding.
*Related article:* LOSEC.

**Omnopon** (*Roche*) is a proprietary OPIATE, a controlled drug which is a preparation of papaveretum, used primarily as premedication before surgery, but also to relieve severe pain. It is produced in the form of ampoules for injection.
▲/✳ side-effects/warning: *see* PAPAVERETUM.

**Omnopon-Scopolamine** (*Roche*) is a proprietary combination of Omnopon and the powerful alkaloid SEDATIVE hyoscine (also known as scopolamine in the USA). It is a controlled drug, and is used primarily as pre-medication before surgery. It is produced in ampoules for injection.
▲/✳ side-effects/warning: *see* PAPAVERETUM; HYOSCINE.

**Oncovin** (*Lilly*) is a proprietary form of the VINCA ALKALOID vincristine sulphate, available only on prescription, used to treat acute leukaemia, lymphoma and certain sarcomas. It is produced in ampoules or as powder for reconstitution, in both cases for injection.
▲/✳ side-effects/warning: *see* VINCRISTINE SULPHATE.

**ondansetron** is a recently introduced ANTI-EMETIC drug, which gives relief from nausea and vomiting, especially in patients receiving radiotherapy and chemotherapy, and where other drugs are ineffective. It acts by preventing the action of the naturally-occuring HORMONE and NEUROTRANSMITTER serotonin. It is used in those over 4 years of age, and is given as tablets or by slow intravenous injection or infusion

▲ side-effects: headache, constipation, warmth or flushing in the head and over stomach. Hypersensitivity reactions and effects on liver enzymes have been reported.

⬤ warning: do not use in pregnancy or breast-feeding. *Related article:* ZOFRAN.

**One-alpha** (*Leo*) is a proprietary form of the VITAMIN D analogue alfacalcidol, available only on prescription, used after renal osteodystrophy to restore and sustain calcium balance in the body due to e.g. neonatal hypocalcaemia. It is produced in the form of capsules (in two strengths) and as drops (with a diluent to adjust concentration).

▲/⬤ side-effects/warning: *see* ALFACALCIDOL.

**Operidine** (*Janssen*) is a proprietary, narcotic ANALGESIC, a controlled drug used primarily as an analgesic during surgery. Produced in the form of ampoules for injection, Operidine is a preparation of phenoperidine hydrochloride.

▲/⬤ side-effects/warning: *see* PHENOPERIDINE.

**Ophthaine** (*Squibb*) is a proprietary form of local ANAESTHETIC eye-drops, available only on prescription, commonly used during ophthalmic procedures and consisting of a preparation of proxymetacaine hydrochloride.

▲/⬤ side-effects/warning: *see* PROXYMETACAINE.

**opiates** are a group of drugs, derived from opium, that depress certain functions of the central nervous system. In this way, they can relieve pain (and inhibit coughing). They are also used to treat diarrhoea. Therapeutically, the most important opiate is probably morphine which, with its synthetic derivative heroin (diamorphine), is a NARCOTIC; all are potentially habituating (addictive).

▲/⬤ side-effects/warning: *see* BUPRENORPHINE; CODEINE PHOSPHATE; DEXTROMORAMIDE; DIAMORPHINE; DIHYDROCODEINE TARTRATE; MEPTAZINOL; METHADONE; MORPHINE; PAPAVERETUM; PENTAZOCINE; PETHIDINE; PHENAZOCINE; PHENOPERIDINE.

**opium squill linctus and pastilles** are compound formulations not available from the National Health Service, combining several soothing liquids – including camphorated tincture of opium and tolu syrup – into a cough linctus (also known as Gee's linctus) and into a form of cough pastilles (also known as Gee's pastilles) made from that linctus.

**Opilon** (*Parke-Davis*) is a proprietary VASODILATOR, available only on prescription, used to treat neural conditions resulting from poor blood supply, particularly in the hands and feet, and in the ears (such as Raynaud's phenomenon). Produced in the form of tablets and in ampoules for injection (in two strengths), Opilon contains thymoxamine hydrochloride. It is not recommended for children.

▲/⬤ side-effects/warning: *see* THYMOXAMINE.

**opium alkaloids** is another term for opiates.
*see* OPIATES.

**Opticrom** (*Fisons*) is an ANTI-INFLAMMATORY preparation, available only on prescription, used to treat forms of conjunctivitis caused by allergic reactions. Produced in the form of eye-drops and eye ointment, Opticrom contains sodium cromoglycate.
▲/❋ side-effects/warning: *see* SODIUM CROMOGLUCATE.

**Optimine** (*Kirby-Warrick*) is a proprietary non-prescription form of the ANTIHISTAMINE drug azatadine maleate, used to relieve the symptoms of allergic reactions such as hay fever and urticaria. Produced in the form of tablets and as a syrup for dilution, Optimine is not recommended for children aged under 12 months.
▲/❋ side-effects/warning: *see* AZATADINE MALEATE.

**Optomize** (*Stafford-Miller*) is a proprietary, anti-inflammatory and ANTIBACTERIAL ear spray preparation, available only on prescription, used in the treatment of bacterial infections of the outer ear. It contains the CORTICOSTEROID dexamethasone and the antibacterial neomycin sulphate, in the form of a metered spray device.
▲/❋ side-effects/warning: *see* DEXAMETHASONE; NEOMYCIN.

**Opulets** (*Alcon*) is the name of a proprietary eye-drop preparation which consists of a variety of different drugs. Available only on prescription, Opulets Chloramphenicol is used to treat bacterial infections in the eye and contains the ANTIBIOTIC chloramphenicol.
▲/❋ side-effects/warning: *see* CHLORAMPHENICOL.

**Orabase** (*Squibb*) is a proprietary, non-prescription ointment, used to protect sores and ulcers in and on the mouth, or in the vicinity of a stoma (an outlet on the skin surface that following the surgical curtailment of the intestines). Produced in the form of paste, Orabase's active constituent is CARMELLOSE SODIUM.

**Orabet** (*Lagap*) is a proprietary form of the biguanide drug metformin hydrochloride, available only on prescription, used to treat adult-onset diabetes mellitus. It works by increasing the absorption and utilization in the body of glucose, to make up for the reduction in insulin available from the pancreas, and is produced in the form of tablets (in two strengths).
▲/❋ side-effects/warning: *see* METFORMIN HYDROCHLORIDE.

**Orabolin** (*Organon*) is a proprietary steroid preparation, available only on prescription, used to promote protein synthesis after major surgery or debilitating disease.

**Oradexon** (*Organon*) is a proprietary, CORTICOSTEROID, ANTI-INFLAMMATORY drug, available only on prescription, used to treat arthritis, joint pain, and allergies. Produced in the form of tablets (in two strengths) and in ampoules for injection, Oradexon's primary constituent is dexamethasone.
▲/❋ side-effects/warning: *see* DEXAMETHASONE.

**Orahesive** (*Squibb*) is a proprietary, non-prescription preparation, used to protect sores and ulcers in and on the mouth, or in the vicinity of a stoma (an outlet on the skin surface that following the surgical curtailment of the intestines).

Produced in the form of powder, Orahesive's active constituent is CARMELLOSE SODIUM.

**Oral-B fluoride** (*Oral-B Labs*) is a proprietary, non-prescription form of fluoride supplement for administration in areas where the water supply is not fluoridated, especially to growing children. Produced in the form of tablets to be dissolved in the mouth (in two strengths). The active constituent is SODIUM FLUORIDE.

**Oralcer** (*Vitabiotics*) is a proprietary, non-prescription, ANTISEPTIC preparation, used to treat infections and ulcers in the mouth. Produced in the form of lozenges, Oralcer contains clioquinol and ascorbic acid (vitamin C).
▲/ ◈ side-effects/warning: *see* CLIOQUINOL.

**oral contraceptives** are prophylactic preparations taken by women to prevent conception following sexual intercourse, and commonly referred to as the 'pill'. Most contain both an OESTROGEN and a PROGESTOGEN – the oestrogen blocks the release of a ripened egg (ovum) from an ovary, and the progestogen blocks the remaining processes of the menstrual cycle. This type of preparation is known as the combined oral contraceptive, or combined pill, and is taken daily for 3 weeks and stopped for a week during which menstruation occurs. A second form of combined pill (the 'phased formulation') is the biphasic or triphasic pill, in which the hormonal content varies according to the time of the month at which each pill is to be taken, and is reduced to the minimum still to be effective. Other types of pill contain only progestogen. A variant on this is the progestogen injection, which

is renewable every 3 months. All forms may produce side-effects, and a form that is ideally suited to a patient is not always possible. Post-coital contraception is also possible in emergency by use of high-dose oestrogen preparations.
▲/ ◈ side-effects/warning: *see* individual oestrogens and progestogens listed under OESTROGENS and PROGESTOGENS.
*Related articles:* BiNOVUM; BREVINOR; CONOVA 30; DEPO-PROVERA; EUGYNON 30; FEMULEN; LOESTRIN; LOGYNON; MARVELON; MICROGYNON 30; MICRONOR; MICROVAL; NEOCON 1/35; NEOGEST; NORGESTON; NORIDAY; NORIMIN; NORINYL-1; ORTHO-NOVIN 1/50; OVRAN; OVRANETTE; OVYSMEN; PC4; SYNPHASE; TriNORDIOL; TRI-NOVUM.

**Oraldene** (*Warner-Lambert*) is a proprietary, non-prescription, ANTISEPTIC preparation, used to treat sores and ulcers in the mouth. Produced in the form of a mouth-wash, Oraldene's active constituent is hexetidine.

**Oramorph** (*Boehringer Ingelheim*) is a proprietary narcotic ANALGESIC. It is used primarily to relieve pain following surgery, or the pain experienced during the final stages of terminal malignant disease. Produced in the form of an oral solution in two strengths, the more concentrated of which is on the controlled drugs list. It is a preparation of the OPIATE and NARCOTIC morphine sulphate; it is not recommended for children.
▲/ ◈ side-effects/warning: *see* MORPHINE.

**Orap** (*Janssen*) is a powerful proprietary ANTIPSYCHOTIC of complex action, available only on prescription, used with care to

O

treat and tranquillize patients who are psychotic, particularly schizophrenic. Produced in the form of tablets (in three strengths), Orap is a preparation of pimozide.

▲/✿ side-effects/warning: see PIMOZIDE.

**Orbenin** (*Beecham*) is a proprietary ANTIBIOTIC, available only on prescription, used to treat bacterial infections, especially staphylococcal infections that prove to be resistant to penicillin. Produced in the form of capsules (in two strengths), and as powder for reconstitution as injections, Orbenin's active constituent is cloxacillin.

▲/✿ side-effects/warning: see CLOXACILLIN.

**orciprenaline** is a BETA-RECEPTOR STIMULANT so acts both as a BRONCHODILATOR, commonly as an aerosol, and as a SMOOTH MUSCLE RELAXANT. Consequently it is used to treat respiratory problems associated with such conditions as asthma and emphysema, and may also be used to slow premature labour.

▲ side-effects: increased heart rate, reduced blood pressure, flushing and sweating are relatively common; there may also be nausea and vomiting, and/or a tremor.

✿ warning: orciprenaline should not be administered to patients who have heart disease or high blood pressure (hypertension); who have disorders of the thyroid gland or diabetes; who are bleeding; or who are already taking strong drugs of any kind. It should be administered with caution to those who are diabetic or pregnant. Blood pressure and pulse must be monitored constantly.
*Related article:* ALUPENT.

**Orimeten** (*Ciba*) is a powerful proprietary ANTICANCER drug, available only on prescription, used to treat advanced stages of cancer of the breast in women who have reached the menopause. It is also used to treat advanced stages of cancer of the prostate gland in men. Produced in the form of tablets, Orimeten's active constituent is aminoglutethimide.

▲/✿ side-effects/warning: see AMINOGLUTETHIMIDE.

**Orovite** (*Bencard*) is a proprietary, non-prescription, VITAMIN preparation, which is not available from the National Health Service. It is used to treat vitamin deficiencies after illness, infection or operation. Produced in the form of tablets and as an elixir, Orovite contains THIAMINE (vitamin $B_1$), RIBOFLAVINE (vitamin $B_2$), PYRIDOXINE (vitamin $B_6$), NICOTINAMIDE (of the B complex) and ASCORBIC ACID (vitamin C). There is also a granular form (issued under the name Orovite 7) that includes RETINOL (vitamin A) with CALCIFEROL (vitamin D), produced in sachets for solution in water.

**orphenadrine citrate** is a powerful SKELETAL MUSCLE RELAXANT used to treat muscle spasm (rigidity), particularly following injury to a muscle. It works by directly affecting the central nervous system. Administration is oral in the form of tablets, or by injection. Orphenadrine citrate is not suitable for children.

▲ side-effects: there may be dry mouth and gastrointestinal disturbances; visual disturbances may also arise, with dizziness. Rarely, there is increased heart rate and/or a hypersensitive reaction, mental confusion and nervousness.

✿ warning: prolonged use can reduce muscle tone in an affected muscle, leading

eventually to worse disability. The drug should be administered with caution to patients with heart, kidney or liver disease, glaucoma, or urinary retention. Withdrawal of treatment must be gradual. It should not be administered to children.
*Related article:* NORFLEX.

**orphenadrine hydrochloride** is an ANTICHOLINERGIC drug used primarily to treat the symptoms of parkinsonism (whether drug-induced or not) and drug-induced extrapyramidal symptoms (*see* ANTIPARKINSONISM). It thus reduces tremor and rigidity, has a diuretic effect on the excess salivary flow, but can do little to improve slowness or awkwardness in movement. Administration of orphenadrine hydrochloride is oral in the form of tablets or as an elixir, or by injection.
▲ side-effects: there may be dry mouth and gastrointestinal disturbances; visual disturbances may also arise, with dizziness. Rarely, there is increased heart rate and/or a hypersensitive reaction, mental confusion and nervousness.
● warning: prolonged use can reduce muscle tone in an affected muscle, leading eventually to worse disability. The drug should be administered with caution to patients with heart, kidney or liver disease, glaucoma, or urinary retention. Withdrawal of treatment must be gradual. It should not be administered to children.
*Related articles:* BIORPHEN; DISIPAL.

**Ortho-Creme** (*Ortho-Cilag*) is a proprietary, non-prescription, SPERMICIDAL preparation, used as a contraceptive in conjunction with a diaphragm. Produced in the form of cream, Ortho-Creme's active constituent is an alcohol ester.

**Ortho Dienoestrol** (*Ortho-Cilag*) is a proprietary, OESTROGEN hormone preparation, available only on prescription, used to treat infection and irritation of the membranous surface of the vagina. Produced in the form of cream, Ortho Dienoestrol's active constituent is dienoestrol.
▲/● side-effects/warning: *see* DIENOESTROL.

**Orthoforms** (*Ortho-Cilag*) is a proprietary, non-prescription, SPERMICIDAL preparation, used as a contraceptive in conjunction with any of the barrier methods. Produced in the form of pessaries (vaginal inserts), Orthoforms' active constituent is an alcohol ester.

**Ortho-Gynest** (*Cilag*) is a proprietary OESTROGEN preparation, available only on prescription, used to treat vaginal and cervical disorders during the menopause. Produced in the form an intravaginal cream supplied with an applicator, and as pessaries. Ortho-Gynest contains oestriol.
▲/● side-effects/warning: *see* OESTRIOL.

**Ortho-Gyne T** (*Ortho-Cilag*) is a proprietary, intrauterine contraceptive device, available only on prescription. Ortho-Gyne T is a T-shaped plastic carrier with a copper wire, which has an effect on the enzyme activity on the lining of the womb necessary for implantation. The device has to be replaced after three years. Another device, Ortho-Gyne T 380 S, is available only on prescription to private patients, and needs replacement only after four years.

**Ortho-Gynol** (*Ortho-Cilag*) is a
proprietary, non-prescription,
SPERMICIDAL preparation, used as
a contraceptive in conjunction
with a diaphragm (intrauterine
device). Produced in the form of
jelly, Ortho-Gynol's active
constituent is an alcohol ester.

**Ortho Novin 1/50** (*Ortho-Cilag*) is
a proprietary, OESTROGEN-
and-PROGESTOGEN preparation,
available only on prescription,
used as a combined ORAL
CONTRACEPTIVE. Produced in the
form of tablets in a 21 day
calender pack representing one
menstrual cycle, Ortho Novin
1/50 is a preparation of
norethisterone and mestranol.
▲/✿ side-effects/warning: *see*
MESTRANOL;
NORETHISTERONE.

**Orudis** (*May & Baker*) is a
proprietary, ANTI-INFLAMMATORY,
non-narcotic ANALGESIC,
available only on prescription,
used to relieve arthritic and
rheumatic pain and to treat other
musculo-skeletal disorders.
Produced in the form of capsules
(in two strengths) and as anal
suppositories, Orudis's active
constituent is ketoprofen.
▲/✿ side-effects/warning: *see*
KETOPROFEN.

**Oruvail** (*May & Baker*) is a
proprietary, ANTI-INFLAMMATORY,
non-narcotic ANALGESIC,
available only on prescription,
used to relieve arthritic and
rheumatic pain and to treat other
musculo-skeletal disorders.
Produced in the form of capsules
(in two strengths), and as
ampoules for injection, Oruvail's
active constituent is ketoprofen.
▲/✿ side-effects/warning: *see*
KETOPROFEN.

**Osmitrol** (*Travenol*) is a powerful,
proprietary, DIURETIC drug,
available only on prescription,

used to rid the body of
accumulated fluids especially in
emergency situations (such as
following a drug overdose).
Produced in the form of fluid for
intravenous infusion (in three
strengths), Osmitrol is a
preparation of mannitol.
▲/✿ side-effects/warning: *see*
MANNITOL.

**Osmolite** (*Abbott*) is a bland,
proprietary, non-prescription,
gluten- and lactose-free liquid
that is a complete nutritional diet
for adult patients (but not for
children) who are severely
undernourished (such as with
anorexia nervosa) or who are
suffering from some problem with
the absorption of food (such as
following gastrectomy). Produced
in cans, Osmolite contains
protein, carbohydrate, fat,
vitamins and minerals. It is not
suitable for children aged under
12 months.

**Ossopan** (*Sanofi*) is a proprietary
MINERAL SUPPLEMENT of calcium,
in the form of hydoxyapatite. It is
available without prescription,
and is in the form of granules in a
sachet or as tablets.
▲/✿ side-effects/warning: *see*
CALCIUM.

**OsterSoy** (*Farley*) is a
NUTRITIONAL PREPARATION, a
powder, which when
reconstituted, contains protein
(2%), carbohydrate (11%), with
minerals and vitamins. It is
available for pre-school children
who have proven lactose and
sucrose intolerance, for
galactokinase deficiency, and
proven whole cows' milk protein
sensitivity.

**Ostobon** (*Coloplast*) is a
proprietary, non-prescription,
deodorant powder, used to
freshen and sanitize the appliance
or bag that is attached to a stoma

(an outlet on the skin surface) following ileostomy or colostomy (surgical curtailing of the intestines) or ureterostomy (surgical curtailing of the ureter between kidney and bladder).

**Otosporin** (*Calmic*) is a proprietary ANTIBIOTIC preparation, available only on prescription, used to treat infections and inflammation in the outer ear. Produced in the form of ear-drops, Otosporin contains the CORTICOSTEROID hydrocortisone and the antibiotics neomycin sulphate and polymyxin B sulphate.
* warning: *see* CORTICOSTEROIDS; NEOMYCIN; POLYMYXIN B.

**Otrivine** (*Ciba*) is a proprietary, SYMPATHOMIMETIC, nasal DECONGESTANT, available only on prescription, and produced in the form of drops and spray. Otrivine Paediatric drops (at half the strength) are available for children. Otrivine's active constituent is xylometazoline hydrochloride.
▲/* side-effects/warning: *see* XYLOMETAZOLINE HYDROCHLORIDE.

**Otrivine-Antistin** (*Zyma*) is a proprietary, non-prescription, ANTIHISTAMINE drug, used to treat allergic and inflammatory ophthalmic conditions. Produced in the form of eye-drops, Otrivine-Antistin contains antazoline and xylometazoline hydrochloride. It is not recommended for children aged under 2 years.
▲/* side-effects/warning: *see* ANTAZOLINE; XYLOMETAZOLINE HYDROCHLORIDE.

**ouabain** is a CARDIAC GLYCOSIDE that acts as a strong heart stimulant, and is thus used to treat heart failure and severe heartbeat irregularity. Administration is almost always by injection.

▲ side-effects: there may be serious effects on the heart rate. Sometimes there is nausea and vomiting.
* warning: ouabain should be administered with caution to patients who have undergone a recent heart attack, or who suffer from disorders of the thyroid gland. Dosage should be reduced for the elderly. *Related article:* OUABAINE ARNAUD.

**Ouabaine Arnaud** (*Lewis*) is a proprietary heart stimulant drug, a CARDIAC GLYCOSIDE, available only on prescription, used to treat heart attack and severe heartbeat irregularity. Produced in ampoules for injection, Ouabaine Arnaud's active constituent is ouabain.
▲/* side-effects/warning: *see* OUABAIN.

**Ovestin** (*Organon*) is a proprietary OESTROGEN preparation, available only on prescription, used to treat vaginal and cervical disorders during the menopause. Produced in the form of tablets and cream, Ovestin contains oestriol.
▲/* side-effects/warning: *see* OESTRIOL.

**Ovran** (*Wyeth*) is a proprietary OESTROGEN-and-PROGESTOGEN preparation, available only on prescription, used as a combined ORAL CONTRACEPTIVE and to treat menstrual problems. Produced in the form of tablets in a 21 day calender pack representing one menstrual cycle, Ovran contains levonorgestrel and ethinyloestradiol. A lower-dosage version is available under the name Ovran 30.
▲/* side-effects/warning: *see* ETHINYLOESTRADIOL; LEVONORGESTREL.

**Ovranette** (*Wyeth*) is a proprietary OESTROGEN-and-PROGESTOGEN preparation (a lower dosage version of OVRAN), available only on prescription, used as a combined ORAL CONTRACEPTIVE. Produced in the form of tablets in a 21 day calender pack representing one menstrual cycle, Ovranette contains levonorgestrel and ethinyloestradiol.

▲/✿ side-effects/warning: *see* ETHINYLOESTRADIOL; LEVONORGESTREL.

**Ovysmen** (*Ortho-Cilag*) is a proprietary OESTROGEN-and-PROGESTOGEN preparation, available only on prescription, used as a combined ORAL CONTRACEPTIVE. Produced in the form of tablets in a 21 day calender pack representing one menstrual cycle, Ovysmen contains norethisterone and ethinyloestradiol.

▲/✿ side-effects/warning: *see* ETHINYLOESTRADIOL; NORETHISTERONE.

**oxaminiquine** is an ANTHELMINTIC drug that is effective in treating the form of bilharzia (schistosomiasis) caused by the intestinal blood vessel parasite *Schistosoma mansoni*, not uncommon in Africa, the West Indies, and South and Central America. Administration is oral, and toxicity is minimal.

**Oxanid** (*Steinhard*) is a proprietary ANXIOLYTIC or TRANQUILLIZER drug, available only on prescription to private patients, used to treat acute anxiety and attacks of phobic panic. Produced in the form of tablets (in three strengths), Oxanid is a preparation of the BENZODIAZEPINE oxazepam.

▲/✿ side-effects/warning: *see* OXAZEPAM.

**oxatomide** is a relatively new ANTIHISTAMINE, used to treat hay fever, urticaria and other allergic

conditions, particularly those concerned with food intake. Administration is oral in the form of tablets. It is not recommended for children aged under 5 years.

▲ side-effects: there may be headache, dry mouth, gastrointestinal disturbances and/or visual disturbances. High dosage may lead to increased appetite and consequent weight gain.

✿ warning: as with all antihistamines, oxatomide may cause drowsiness, or loss of the ability to concentrate. It should be administered with caution to patients with epilepsy, glaucoma, liver disease, or enlargement of the prostate gland. It may also enhance the effects of alcohol consumption.
*Related article:* TINSET.

**oxazepam** is a short-acting ANXIOLYTIC or TRANQUILLIZER drug, one of the BENZODIAZEPINES used primarily to relieve acute anxiety or an attack of phobic panic. Administration is oral in the form of tablets or capsules.

▲ side-effects: drowsiness usually occurs; there may also be dizziness, headache, dry mouth and shallow breathing. Hypersensitive reactions may occur. Repeated doses are, however, less cumulative in effect than with many other benzodiazepine anxiolytics.

✿ warning: oxazepam may reduce a patient's concentration and intricacy of movement or thought; it may enhance the effects of alcohol consumption. Prolonged use or abrupt withdrawal should be avoided. It should be administered with caution to patients with respiratory difficulties, glaucoma, or kidney or liver damage; who are in the last

stages of pregnancy; or who are elderly or debilitated.
*Related article:* OXANID.

**oxedrine tartrate** is a VASO-CONSTRICTOR, a SYMPATHO-MIMETIC used to treat very low blood pressure (hypotension) or cardiac arrest. Administration is oral in the form of a liquid, or by intramuscular or intravenous injection.
▲ side-effects: there is a risk of speeding the heart rate too much, resulting in high blood pressure (hypertension) or of reflex bradycardia (slowing of the heart rate), and associated headache and palpitations. There may be vomiting, and tingling and coolness of the skin. Prolonged treatment may result in kidney problems.
✿ warning: oxedrine tartrate should not be administered to patients who suffer a heart attack caused by interruption of the blood supply (myocardial infarction), or who are pregnant. An escape of the drug into the tissues at the site of the injection may cause tissue damage.
*Related article:* SYMPATOL.

**oxerutins** are mixtures of vasodilating RUTOSIDES that are thought to reduce the fragility and the permeability of the capillary blood vessels. They are used to treat disorders of the veins, mostly in the legs.

**oxethazaine** is a minor local ANAESTHETIC used in very mild solution within other preparations to relieve incidental local pain. It is for example used in one proprietary antacid.
*Related article:* MUCAINE.

**oxpentifylline** is a drug used to treat circulation problems in the extremities, and the attendant neural effects. Administration is

oral in the form of tablets, or by injection. It is not recommended for children.
▲ side-effects: there may be flushes, dizziness and/or nausea.
✿ warning: oxpentifylline should be administered with caution to patients with low blood pressure (hypotension).
*Related article:* TRENTAL.

**oxprenolol** is a BETA-BLOCKER, a drug used to control and regulate the heart rate and and irregularities in its rhythms (arrhythmias), and to treat high blood pressure (*see* ANTI-HYPERTENSIVE) and angina. It is also used to treat the symptoms of excessive amounts of thyroid hormones in the bloodstream (including goitre). Administration is oral in the form of tablets, or by injection.
▲ side-effects: there may be a slowing of the heartbeat, with coldness of the extremities. Sometimes there is respiratory depression and/or gastrointestinal disturbances.
✿ warning: oxprenolol should not be administered to patients with heart disease or asthma; it should be administered with caution to those with liver or kidney disease, or who are pregnant or lactating. Withdrawal of treatment must be gradual.
*Related articles:* APSOLOX; SLOW-PREN; SLOW-TRASICOR; TRASICOR.

**oxybenzone** is a derivative of aminobenzoic acid used to protect the skin from ultraviolet radiation. It is a constituent in several suntan lotions and barrier creams for topical application.
▲ / ✿ side-effects/warning: *see* AMINOBENZOIC ACID.

**oxybuprocaine** is a widely-used local ANAESTHETIC particularly used in ophthalmic treatments. In

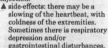

the form of oxybuprocaine hydrochloride, it is administered as eye-drops.

▲ side-effects: there may be initial stinging on application. *Related articles:* MINIMS BENOXINATE; OPULETS.

**oxygen** is an odourless, colourless gas which makes up 20% of the air at usual surface levels. Breathed into the human body through the lungs and taken up by the bloodstream, it combines chemically with glucose (or other sugars) to provide energy for metabolism. Therapeutically, oxygen is administered both to relieve respiratory problems and to maintain metabolic functions. Dosage (that is, concentration) is critical, for too much OR too little may be harmful. Too little prevents body function; too much may eventually inhibit the body's respiratory mechanism altogether. For emergency purposes (when blood gas measurements are not immediately feasible), a 35%-50% oxygen concentration is normally used, administered through a mask. Blood gas measurements should, however, be taken as soon as possible and regularly thereafter in order to achieve an optimum dosage level. Many patients who suffer from respiratory complications need an intermittent supply of oxygen daily: cylinders of oxygen, with a breathing-mask attachment, are available on prescription from the National Health Service for use at home (although counselling is normally given first about the fire risk). Also available are oxygen concentrators.

**oxymetazoline** is a VASOCONSTRICTOR, a potent SYMPATHOMIMETIC used primarily as a nasal decongestant. It works by constricting the blood vessels of the nose, thus in turn constricting the nasal mucous membranes. Administration is in the form of nose-drops or nasal spray.

▲ side-effects: there may be local irritation.

✿ warning: prolonged use may result in tolerance, leading to even worse nasal congestion. Oxymetazoline should be administered with caution to children aged under 3 months. *Related article:* AFRAZINE.

**oxymetholone** is an anabolic STEROID used primarily to treat aplastic anaemia, but also to assist post-operative and convalescent recovery to full metabolic function. Administration is oral in the form of tablets.

▲ side-effects: there may be acne, jaundice and high blood calcium levels, with fluid retention in the tissues (oedema). Prolonged treatment with high doses may in women cause menstrual problems and some degree of masculinization.

✿ warning: the necessarily prolonged high-dosage treatment of anaemias ordinarily produces some masculinizing effects in women; such effects are, however, potentially reversible. Oxymetholone should not be administered to patients with impaired liver function or cancer of the prostate gland, or who are pregnant or lactating. It should be administered with caution to patients who are diabetic or epileptic; who have heart or kidney disease; or who suffer from migraine. Bone growth in children should be monitored for 6 months following treatment. *Related article:* ANAPOLON 50.

**Oxymycin** (*DDSA Pharmaceuticals*) is a proprietary

ANTIBIOTIC, available only on prescription, used to treat many microbial infections, such as severe acne vulgaris and exacerbations of chronic bronchitis. Produced in the form of tablets, Oxymycin's active constituent is the tetracycline oxytetracycline dihydrate.

✚ warning: *see* OXYTETRACYCLINE.

-**oxypertine** is a powerful ANTIPSYCHOTIC drug used to treat and tranquillize psychosis (such as schizophrenia); it is suitable both for manic and hyperactive forms of behavioural disturbance, as well as for apathetic and withdrawal forms. The drug may also be used to treat severe anxiety in the short term. Administration is oral in the form of capsules or tablets.

▲ side-effects: patients should be warned before treatment that their judgement and powers of concentration may become defective under treatment. There may be restlessness, insomnia and nightmares; rashes and jaundice may occur; and there may be dry mouth, constipation, difficulties on urination, and blurred vision.

✚ warning: oxypertine should not be administered to patients who suffer from reduction in the bone marrow's capacity for producing blood cells, or from certain types of glaucoma. It should be administered only with caution to patients with heart or vascular disease, kidney or liver disease, parkinsonism, or depression; or who are pregnant or lactating. Abrupt withdrawal should be avoided. It is not recommended for children.

*Related article:* INTEGRIN.

**oxyphenbutazone** is an ANTI-INFLAMMATORY, non-narcotic, ANALGESIC used to relieve pain in rheumatic and arthritic joints,

and in gout; in solution it is used as an eye ointment to treat local infection. Administration is oral, as eye-drops, or as anal suppositories.

▲ side-effects: oral treatment may cause nausea and dizziness, a rash and/or mouth ulcers.

✚ warning: ophthalmic treatment should not be prolonged.

*Related article:* TANDERIL.

**oxytetracycline** is a broad-spectrum ANTIBIOTIC, one of the TETRACYCLINES, used to treat many serious infections, particularly those of the urogenital organs and skin or mucous membrane, of the bones, and of the respiratory passages. It may also be used to treat acne, although it is not suitable for children aged under 12 years. Administration is oral in the form of tablets or syrup.

▲ side-effects: there may be nausea and vomiting, with diarrhoea; hypersensitivity reactions may occur, as may photosensitivity (sensitivity of the skin and eyes to light), but both are rare.

✚ warning: oxytetracycline should not be administered to patients who are pregnant, or who have kidney failure. It should be administered with caution to patients who are lactating. Some bacterial strains have now become resistant to the drug.

*Related articles:* BERKMYCEN; GALENOMYCIN; IMPERACIN; OXYMYCIN; TERRAMYCIN.

**oxytocin** is a natural HORMONE produced and secreted by the pituitary gland. Although it does not actually initiate the process, it increases the contractions of the womb during labour, and stimulates lactation in the breasts. Therapeutically, it may be administered orally or by injection to induce or assist labour (or abortion), or to stimulate lactation in women who have a hormonal insufficiency (in which case administration is by nasal spray). Sometimes it is additionally used to help stop post-natal bleeding.

▲ side-effects: there may be heartbeat irregularity and cerebral pressure. High doses may lead to violent contractions of the womb which may actually rupture the uterine wall and/or cause harm to the child.

❋ warning: oxytocin should not be administered to patients who suffer from muscular abnormalities of the womb or whose birth canal is obstructed in any way; or in whom the foetus is in evident distress. It should be administered with caution to those who suffer from high blood pressure (hypertension), who are about to undergo a multiple birth, or who have previously had a Caesarean section.

*Related articles:* SYNTOCINON; SYNTOMETRINE.

O

**Pabrinex** (*Paines & Byrne*) is a proprietary VITAMIN preparation, available only on prescription, used to treat vitamin B and C deficiencies associated with acute feverish illnesses, with the effects of alcoholism or of certain drug treatments, or with states of confusion following severe illness or major surgery. It is produced in ampoules (in two strengths) for intramuscular injection, and in ampoules for intravenous injection.

**padimate O** is a sunscreen that is capable of protecting the skin from ultraviolet radiation. For this reason, padimate O is a constituent in a number of suntan lotions. Administration is topical in the form of a solution.
🌑 warning: protection is temporary, and the solution must be applied frequently. Some patients are in any case more sensitive to ultraviolet radiation than others. Padimate O is also flammable, and stains fabric.
*Related article:* SPECTRABAN.

**Paedo-Sed** (*Pharmax*) is a proprietary compound ANALGESIC, available on prescription only to private patients. Used to treat children, Paedo-Sed is a preparation of PARACETAMOL and the HYPNOTIC drug DICHLORAL-PHENAZONE, and is produced in the form of an elixir for dilution (the potency of the elixir once dilute is retained for 14 days).
▲/🌑 side-effects/warning: *see* DICHLORALPHENAZONE; PARACETAMOL.

**Palaprin Forte** (*Nicholas*) is a proprietary, non-prescription, ANTI-INFLAMMATORY, non-narcotic ANALGESIC used to relieve pain particularly rheumatic and arthritic pain   and to treat other musculo-skeletal disorders. Produced in the form of tablets,

Palaprin Forte is a preparation of the aspirin-like analgesic aloxiprin.
▲/🌑 side-effects/warning: *see* ALOXIPIRIN.

**Paldesic** (*RP Drugs*) is a proprietary, non-prescription form of the non-narcotic ANALGESIC paracetamol. It is produced in the form of a syrup and is intended for hospital use only.
▲/🌑 side-effects/warning: *see* PARACETAMOL.

**Palfium** (*MCP Pharmaceuticals*) is a proprietary, narcotic ANALGESIC, which, because it is a preparation of the OPIATE dextromoramide, is on the controlled drugs list. Used to relieve severe pain, especially during the final stages of terminal malignant disease, it is produced in the form of tablets (in two strengths), ampoules (in two strengths) for injection, and anal suppositories (which are not recommended for children).
▲/🌑 side-effects/warning: *see* DEXTROMORAMIDE.

**Paludrine** (*ICI*) is a proprietary, non-prescription drug used in the prevention of malaria (*see* ANTIMALARIAL). Produced in the form of tablets, Paludrine is a preparation of proguanil hydrochloride.
▲/🌑 side-effects/warning: *see* PROGUANIL.

**Pamergan P100** (*Martindale*) is a proprietary narcotic ANALGESIC on the controlled drugs list, used both in the relief of pain and as a premedication prior to surgery, especially obstetrics. Produced in ampoules for injection, Pamergan P100 is a preparation of the narcotic analgesic pethidine hydrochloride and the SEDATIVE ANTIHISTAMINE promethazine hydrochloride.

▲/✿ side-effects/warning: *see* PETHIDINE; PROMETHAZINE HYDROCHLORIDE.

**Pameton** (*Winthrop*) is a proprietary, non-prescription, non-narcotic ANALGESIC, not available from the National Health Service, used to treat pain (especially for patients likely to overdose) and to reduce high body temperature. Produced in the form of tablets, Pameton is a compound preparation of PARACETAMOL and the amino acid METHIONINE (a paracetamol overdose antidote). It is not recommended for children aged under 6 years.

▲/✿ side-effects/warning: *see* METHIONINE; PARACETAMOL.

**Panadeine** (*Winthrop*) is a proprietary, non-prescription, compound ANALGESIC, not available from the National Health Service, used to treat pain and to reduce high body temperature. Produced in the form of tablets, it is a preparation of paracetamol and codeine (a combination known as co-codamol), and is not recommended for children aged under 7 years.

▲/✿ side-effects/warning: *see* CODEINE PHOSPHATE; PARACETAMOL.

**Panadol** (*Winthrop*) is a proprietary, non-prescription, non-narcotic ANALGESIC. Used to treat pain and to reduce high body temperature, it is produced in the form of tablets (of two kinds), as effervescent tablets (under the name Panadol Soluble), and as an elixir for dilution (the potency of the elixir once dilute is retained for 14 days). It is not available from the National Health Service. In all forms it is a preparation of paracetamol, and is not recommended for children aged under 3 months.

▲/✿ side-effects/warning: *see* PARACETAMOL.

**Pancrease** (*Ortho-Cilag*) is a proprietary, non-prescription form of pancreatic enzymes pancreatin, used to treat enzymatic deficiency in such conditions as cystic fibrosis and chronic inflammation of the pancreas. Pancrease is produced in the form of capsules.

▲/✿ side-effects/warning: *see* PANCREATIN.

**pancreatin** is a name given to supplements of pancreatic ENZYME, given by mouth in the treatment of deficiencies due to impaired natural secretion by the pancreas, such as in cystic fibrosis, and also following operations involving removal of pancreatic tissue, such as panreatectomy and gastrectomy. The enzymes are inactivated by the acid of the stomach, so preparations of the enzyme are best taken with food or concurrently with drugs such as ranitidine that decrease acid secretion. It is available also in the form of enteric-coated preparations that overcome some of these problems. The enzymes are also inactivated by heat, so should be mixed with food after its preparation.

▲ side-effects: there may be irritation of the skin around the mouth and anus.

✿ warning: hypersensitivity reactions will occur in patients of known allergic sensitivity. *Related articles:* COTAZYM; CREON; NUTRIZYM; PANCREASE; PANCREX.

**Pancrex** (*Paines & Byrne*) is a proprietary, non-prescription form of pancreatic enzymes pancreatin, used to treat enzymatic deficiency in cystic fibrosis and similar diseases. Pancrex is produced in the form of granules, but (under the name Pancrex V) there are also versions available as a powder, as capsules (in two strengths, the weaker under the name Pancrex V '125'), and as tablets (in two strengths, the stronger under the name Pancrex V Forte).

▲/✸ side-effects/warning: see PANCREATIN.

**pancuronium bromide** is a SKELETAL MUSCLE RELAXANT used primarily under general anaesthesia for medium-duration paralysis. Administration is by injection.

▲ side-effects: paralysis is rapid in onset following injection.

✸ warning: the onset of the paralysis may be accompanied by temporarily increased heart rate: caution should be exercised in relation to patients for whom this might present difficulty. Dosage should be reduced for patients who suffer from impaired kidney function or who are obese.

*Related article:* PAVULON.

**Panmycin** (*Upjohn*) is a proprietary form of the broad-spectrum ANTIBIOTIC tetracycline hydrochloride, available only on prescription. Used to treat many types of microbial infections both systemically and on the skin and in the ears and eyes (especially trachoma). Panmycin is produced as capsules and as a syrup.

▲/✸ side-effects/warning: see TETRACYCLINE.

**Panoxyl 2.5** (*Stiefel*) is a proprietary, non-prescription, topical preparation for the treatment of acne. Produced in the form of an aqueous gel, Panoxyl 2.5 is a solute preparation of the KERATOLYTIC benzoyl peroxide. A stronger version is produced also in the form of an aqueous gel and

additionally as a gel in an alcohol base (under the name Panoxyl 5). And an even stronger preparation is available as an aqueous gel, as a gel in an alcohol base, and as a wash lotion in a detergent base (under the name Panoxyl 10).

▲/✸ side-effects/warning: see BENZOYL PEROXIDE.

**panthenol:** *see* PANTOTHENIC ACID.

**pantothenic acid,** or panthenol, is an organic compound often classified as a VITAMIN of the B complex; it is a coenzyme – a catalyst in the reaction instituted by an enzyme – that assists in the metabolism of fatty acids. Dietary sources are many such as in milk, yeast, fresh vegetables and are plentiful in normal life-styles; deficiency is exceptional. Pantothenic acid has no accepted therapeutic uses, although the calcium salt has been used to treat streptomycin intoxication and rheumatoid conditions. *Related articles:* LIPOTRIAD; MULTIBIONTA; SOLIVITO; VIGRANON B.

**papaveretum** is a compound preparation of alkaloids of opium, about half of which is made up of MORPHINE, the rest consisting of proportions of CODEINE, NOSCAPINE and PAPAVERINE. It is used as a NARCOTIC ANALGESIC primarily during or following surgery, but also as a SEDATIVE prior to an operation. Administration is oral in the form of tablets, or by injection. All proprietary preparations containing papaveretum are on the controlled drugs list: the drug is potentially addictive.

▲ side-effects: there is constipation and urinary retention, shallow breathing and cough suppression; there may also be nausea and vomiting, and drowsiness. Injections may cause pain and

P

tissue damage at the site. Tolerance and dependence (addiction) occur readily.

❀ warning: papaveretum should not be administered to patients who are suffering from head injury or increased intracranial pressure; it should be administered with caution to those with asthma, impaired kidney or liver function, hypotension (low blood pressure), or hypothyroidism (underactivity of the thyroid gland), who are pregnant or breast-feeding, or who have a history of drug abuse. Dosage should be reduced for elderly or debilitated patients.
*Related articles:* OMNOPON; OMNOPON-SCOPOLAMINE.

**papaverine** is an alkaloid of opium, technically an OPIATE, but it is unlike many others in being primarily a SMOOTH MUSCLE RELAXANT, and having little or no ANALGESIC effect. It is consequently used mostly in the treatment of the bronchospasm of asthma or to relieve other spasmodic conditions of smooth muscle, such as in indigestion or in vascular disorders of the limbs. It is present in some cough preparations. Administration is mostly (in the form of papaverine hydrochloride) as a solution for an aerosol spray or as a linctus, in combination with other anti-asthma drugs; it may sometimes be prescribed in the form of tablets.

▲ side-effects: it may cause heartbeat irregularities, gastrointestinal disturbances, headache, sweating, vertigo and skin rash.

❀ warning: papaverine should not be administered to patients with heart disease, especially if it involves heartbeat irregularities, or glaucoma.
*Related articles:* APP;

PAVACOL-D; PHOLCOMED; RYBARVIN.

**paracetamol** is a non-narcotic ANALGESIC used to treat all forms of mild to moderate pain; although it is also effective in reducing high body temperature it has no capacity for relieving inflammation. In many ways it is similar to ASPIRIN – except that it does not cause gastric irritation. It may (in high overdosage or prolonged use) cause liver damage. Many proprietary preparations combine the two analgesics (compound analgesics) although these are not generally recommended. Administration is oral in the form of tablets, capsules or a liquid.

▲ side-effects: there are few side-effects if dosage is low; high overdosage or prolonged use may result in liver dysfunction.

❀ warning: paracetamol should be administered with caution to patients with impaired liver function or who suffer from alcoholism (which causes liver damage).
*Related articles:* CAFADOL; CALPOL; CO-CODAMOL; CO-DYDRAMOL; CO-PROXAMOL; COSALGESIC; DISPROL; DISTALGESIC; FORMULIX; LOBAK; MEDISED; MEDOCODENE; MIDRID; MIGRALEVE; MYOLGIN; NEURODYNE; PAEDO-SED; PALDESIC; PAMETON; PANADEINE; PANADOL; PARACLEAR; PARACODOL; PARADEINE; PARAHYPON; PARAKE; PARAMAX; PARAMOL; PARDALE; PAXALGESIC; PROPAIN; SALZONE; SOLPADEINE; SOLPADOL; SYNDOL; TYLEX; UNIFLU PLUS GREGOVITE C; UNIGESIC; VEGANIN.

**Paraclear** (*Sussex Pharmaceuticals*) is a proprietary, non-prescription, non-narcotic

ANALGESIC produced in the form of soluble tablets. It contains paracetamol.

▲/✦ side-effects/warning: see PARACETAMOL.

**Paracodol** (*Fisons*) is a proprietary, non-prescription, compound ANALGESIC, not available from the National Health Service. Used to treat muscular and rheumatic pain, and produced in the form of tablets for effervescent solution, it is a preparation of paracetamol and codeine phosphate (a combination itself known as co-codamol) and is not recommended for children aged under 6 years.

▲/✦ side-effects/warning: see CODEINE; PARACETAMOL.

**Paradeine** (*Scotia*) is a proprietary, non-prescription compound ANALGESIC, not available from the National Health Service. Used to treat muscular and rheumatic pain, and produced in the form of tablets, Paradeine is a preparation of paracetamol and codeine phosphate, together with the LAXATIVE phenolphthalein.

▲/✦ side-effects/warning: see CODEINE PHOSPHATE; PARACETAMOL; PHENOLPHTHALEIN.

**paraffin** is a hydrocarbon derived from petroleum. Its main therapeutic use is as a base for ointments (in the form of yellow or white soft paraffin). As a mineral oil, liquid paraffin is used as an effective laxative (although prolonged use may have unpleasant side-effects) and as an eye ointment in cases of tear deficiency.

*see* LIQUID PARAFFIN.

**Parahypon** (*Calmic*) is a proprietary, non-prescription compound ANALGESIC, not available from the National

Health Service. Used to relieve most types of pain, and produced in the form of tablets, Parahypon is a preparation of paracetamol and codeine phosphate with the stimulant caffeine. It is not recommended for children aged under 6 years.

▲/✦ side-effects/warning: see CAFFEINE; CODEINE PHOSPHATE; PARACETAMOL.

**Parake** (*Galen*) is a proprietary, non-prescription compound ANALGESIC, not available from the National Health Service. Used both to relieve pain and to reduce high body temperature, and produced in the form of tablets, Parake is a preparation of paracetamol and codeine phosphate (a combination itself known as co-codamol) and is not recommended for children.

▲/✦ side-effects/warning: see CODEINE PHOSPHATE; PARACETAMOL.

**paraldehyde** is a strong-smelling and fast-acting SEDATIVE. It is primarily used in the treatment of severe and continuous epileptic seizures (status epilepticus), and is administered generally by injection although it is sometimes instead administered via the rectum in the form of an enema.

▲ side-effects: a rash is not uncommon. The injections may be painful.

✦ warning: paraldehyde should be administered with caution to patients with lung disease or impaired liver function. Keep away from rubber, plastics or fabric.

**Paramax** (*Beecham*) is a proprietary, non-narcotic, ANALGESIC, available only on prescription, used to relieve the pain of migraine. Produced in the form of tablets and as a sugar-free powder in sachets for effervescent solution, Paramax is a

preparation of paracetamol and the ANTINAUSEANT meto-clopramide hydrochloride. It is not recommended for children.
▲/✚ side-effects/warning: *see* METOCLOPRAMIDE; PARACETAMOL.

**Paramol** (*Duncan, Flockhart*) is a proprietary compound ANALGESIC, available only on prescription to private patients, used as a painkiller and as a cough suppressant. Produced in the form of tablets, Paramol is a preparation of paracetamol and the OPIATE dihydrocodeine tartrate (a combination itself known as CO-DYDRAMOL) and is not recommended for children.
▲/✚ side-effects/warning: *see* DIHYDROCODEINE TARTRATE; PARACETAMOL.

**Paraplatin** (*Bristol-Myers*) is a proprietary CYTOTOXIC drug, available only on prescription, used to treat certain types of solid tumour such as cancer of the ovary. Produced in the form of powder for reconstitution as a medium for injection, Paraplatin is a preparation of the CISPLATIN derivative carboplatin.
▲/✚ side-effects/warning: *see* CARBOPLATIN.

*\*parasympathomimetics* are drugs that have effects similar to those of the parasympathetic nervous system. They work by mimicking the actions of a natural neurotransmitter (e.g. ACETYLCHOLINE CHLORIDE) or by prolonging its duration of action (e.g. NEOSTIGMINE). Important actions include slowing of the heart, vasodilation, construction of the bronchioles, stimulation of the muscles of the intestine and bladder, dilation of the pupil and altering the focusing of the eye. ANTICHOLINERGIC drugs oppose some of these actions.

**Pardale** (*Martindale*) is a proprietary, non-prescription compound ANALGESIC, not available from the National Health Service. Used to relieve headaches and menstrual and rheumatic pain, and produced in the form of tablets, Pardale is a preparation of paracetamol and codeine phosphate together with the mild stimulant caffeine hydrate. It is not recommended for children.
▲/✚ side-effects/warning: *see* CAFFEINE; CODEINE PHOSPHATE; PARACETAMOL.

**Parentrovite** (*Bencard*) is a proprietary VITAMIN preparation, available only on prescription, used to treat vitamin B and C deficiencies associated with acute illnesses such as those that involve high body temperature, that result from alcoholism or from drug treatment, or that accompany states of confusion following severe illness or major surgery. It is produced in ampoules (in two strengths) for intramuscular injection, and in ampoules for intravenous injection.
▲/✚ side-effects/warning: *see* THIAMINE.

**Parfenac** (*Lederle*) is a proprietary, non-steroidal, ANTI-INFLAMMATORY drug, available only on prescription, used in topical application to treat mild inflammation on the skin. Produced in the form of a water-miscible cream, Parfenac is a preparation of bufexamac.
▲/✚ side-effects/warning: *see* BUFEXAMAC.

**Parlodel** (*Sandoz*) is a proprietary preparation of the drug bromocriptine, used primarily to treat parkinsonism but not the parkinsonian symptoms caused by certain drug therapies (*see* ANTIPARKINSONISM). It may also

be used to treat delayed puberty caused by hormonal insufficiency, to relieve certain menstrual disorders, or to reduce or halt lactation. It is produced in the form of tablets (in two strengths) and capsules (in two strengths).
▲/✿ side-effects/warning: see BROMOCRIPTINE.

**Parmid** (*Lagap*) is a proprietary ANTINAUSEANT, available only on prescription, used to treat severe conditions of nausea and vomiting especially when associated with gastrointestinal disorders, during radiotherapy, or accompanying treatment with cytotoxic drugs. Produced in the form of tablets, as a syrup, and in ampoules for injection, Parmid is a preparation of metoclopramide hydrochloride. Use is usually restricted to patients over 20 years of age.
▲/✿ side-effects/warning: see METOCLOPRAMIDE.

**Parnate** (*Smith Kline & French*) is a proprietary ANTIDEPRESSANT drug, available only on prescription. Produced in the form of tablets, Parnate is a preparation of the MAO INHIBITOR tranylcypromine. It is not recommended for children.
▲/✿ side-effects/warning: see TRANYLCYPROMINE.

**Paroven** (*Zyma*) is a proprietary, non-prescription preparation used to treat symptoms of cramps and other manifestations of poor circulation in the veins. Produced in the form of capsules, Paroven is a preparation of oxerutins and is not recommended for children.
▲/✿ side-effects/warning: see OXERUTINS.

**Parstelin** (*Smith Kline & French*) is a proprietary ANTIDEPRESSANT drug, available only on prescription, used to treat depressive illness particularly in association with anxiety. Produced in the form of tablets, Parstelin is a compound preparation of the MAO INHIBITOR tranylcypromine and the ANTI-EMETIC tranquillizer trifluoperazine. It is not recommended for children.
▲/✿ side-effects/warning: see TRANYLCYPROMINE; TRIFLUOPERAZINE.

**Partobulin** (*Immuno*) is a proprietary IMMUNOGLOBULIN of the anti-D type used to prevent rhesus-negative mothers from making antibodies to foetal rhesus-positive cells that may pass into the mother's circulation during childbirth. It should be injected within 3 days of birth, with the object of protecting a future child from haemolytic disease.
▲/✿ side-effects/warning: see IMMUNOGLOBULINS.

**Parvolex** (*Duncan, Flockhart*) is a proprietary form of the amino acid acetylcysteine, available only on prescription, used in emergencies to treat paracetamol overdosage and so to try to limit liver damage. It is produced in ampoules for injection.
▲/✿ side-effects/warning: see ACETYLCYSTEINE.

**Pavacol-D** (*Boehringer Ingelheim*) is a proprietary, non-prescription cough mixture. It is a sugar-free preparation of the OPIATES papaverine hydrochloride and pholcodine for solution with the sugar-substitute sorbitol (the potency of the mixture once dilute is retained for 14 days). It is not recommended for children aged under 12 months.
▲/✿ side-effects/warning: see PAPAVERINE; PHOLCODINE.

**Pavulon** (*Organon-Teknika*) is a proprietary SKELETAL MUSCLE RELAXANT of the type known as

competitive or non-depolarizing.
Available only on prescription, it
is used during surgical
operations, but only after the
patient has been rendered
unconscious. Produced in
ampoules for injection, Pavulon is
a preparation of pancuronium
bromide.

▲/ ● side-effects/warning: *see*
PANCURONIUM BROMIDE.

**Paxadon** (*Steinhard*) is a
proprietary, non-prescription,
VITAMIN B supplement, which is
not available from the National
Health Service. Used to treat
vitamin deficiency and associated
symptoms, Paxadon is a
preparation of PYRIDOXINE
hydrochloride (vitamin B₆). It is
produced in the form of tablets.

▲/ ● side-effects/warning: *see*
PYRIDOXINE

**Paxalgesic** (*Steinhard*) is a
proprietary ANALGESIC available
only on prescription to private
patients. Used to relieve pain
anywhere in the body, and
produced in the form of tablets,
Paralgesic is a preparation of the
narcotic-like analgesic
dextropropoxyphene together
with paracetamol. This compound
combination is known as CO-
PROXAMOL). It is not
recommended for children.

▲/ ● side-effects/warning: *see* CO-
PROXAMOL;
DEXTROPROPOXYPHENE;
PARACETAMOL.

**Paxane** (*Steinhard*) is a
proprietary TRANQUILLIZER and
HYPNOTIC, available only on
prescription only to private
patients, used to treat insomnia in
cases where some degree of
daytime sedation is acceptable for
short-term use only. Produced in
the form of capsules (in two
strengths), Paxane is a
preparation of the long-acting
BENZODIAZEPINE flurazepam.

▲/ ● side-effects/warning: *see*
FLURAZEPAM.

**Paxofen** (*Steinhard*) is a
proprietary, ANTI-INFLAMMATORY,
non-narcotic ANALGESIC,
available only on prescription,
used to treat the pain of
rheumatic and other musculo-
skeletal disorders. Produced in
the form of tablets (in three
strengths), Paxofen is a
preparation of ibuprofen.

▲/ ● side-effects/warning: *see*
IBUPROFEN.

**PC4** (*Schering*) is a proprietary
form of ORAL CONTRACEPTIVE for
use after sexual intercourse has
already taken place. Available
only on prescription as as
occasional emergency measure,
and produced in the form of
tablets, PC4 is a preparation of
the OESTROGEN ethinyloestradiol
and the PROGESTOGEN norgestrel.

▲/ ● side-effects/warning: *see*
ETHINYLOESTRADIOL;
NORGESTREL.

**Pecram** (*Zyma*) is a proprietary
prescription BRONCHODILATOR,
used to treat the symptoms of
asthma and obstructive airways
disease. Produced in the form of
sustained-release tablets, it is a
preparation of aminophylline
hydrate.

▲/ ● side-effects/warning: *see*
AMINOPHYLLINE.

**Ped-El** (*KabiVitrum*) is a
preparation of additional
electrolytes and trace elements
for use in association with Vamin
(proprietary) amino acid solutions
for use as intravenous nutrition.
Available only on prescription,
Ped-El is intended primarily for
paediatric use.
*see* VAMIN.

**\*pediculicidal drugs** kill lice of
the genus Pediculus, which infest
either the body or the scalp – or

both – and cause intense itching. Scratching tends only to damage the skin surface, and may eventually cause weeping lesions or bacterial infection as well. Best-known and most-used pediculicides include malathion and carbaryl; the once commonly used lindane is now no longer recommended for lice on the scalp because resistant strains of lice have emerged. Administration is topical, generally in the form of a lotion; contact between drug and skin should be as long as possible (at least two hours), which is why shampoos are less commonly used.

▲/✿ side-effects/warning: *see* BENZYL BENZOATE; CARBARYL; MALATHION.

**pemoline** is a fairly mild STIMULANT that works by direct action on the brain, and is used primarily to treat debility, lassitude, senility or fatigue. It may also be administered to prevent patients from becoming too drowsy following the administration of other drugs. Administration is oral in the form of tablets, it is not recommended and should not be used to treat depression.

▲ side-effects: concentration and speed of thought and movement may be affected. There may also be sweating and slight headache. High dosage may cause heartbeat irregularities and dizziness, insomnia. agitation.

✿ warning: pemoline should not be administered to patients with heart disease, glaucoma, extrapyramidal disorders, hyperexcitable states.
*Related article:* VOLITAL.

**Penbritin** (*Beecham*) is a proprietary form of the broad-spectrum penicillin ampicillin, available only on prescription. An ANTIBIOTIC used mainly to treat

infections of the respiratory passages, the middle ear and the urinary tract, it is also effective against gonorrhoea. Penbritin is produced in the form of capsules (in two strengths), as tablets for children, as a syrup (in two strengths, for dilution; the potency of the syrup once diluted is retained for 7 days), as a children's suspension for use with a pipette, and as powder for reconstitution as a solution for injections.

▲/✿ side-effects/warning: *see* AMPICILLIN.

**penbutolol sulphate** is a BETA-BLOCKER used as an ANTI-HYPERTENSIVE drug. Administration is in combination with the DIURETIC FRUSEMIDE, and is oral in the form of tablets.

▲ side-effects: the heart rate is slowed; there may also be bronchospasm (causing asthma-like symptoms), gastrointestinal disturbances, and tingling or numbness in the fingers and toes.

✿ warning: penbutolol sulphate should not be administered to patients with any serious form of heart disessase, or asthma. It should be administered with caution to those with impaired liver or kidney function, who are nearing the end of pregnancy, or who are lactating.
*Related article:* LASIPRESSIN.

**Pendramine** (*Degussa*) is a proprietary, non-steroidal, ANTI-INFLAMMATORY drug, available only on prescription, used to relieve the pain and to halt the progress of severe rheumatoid arthritis. The drug may also be used as a long-term chelating agent to treat poisoning by the metals copper or lead (especially in metabolic disorders like Wilson's disease). Produced in the form of tablets (in two strengths),

Pendramine is a preparation of the penicillin-derivative penicillamine.
▲/● side-effects/warning: see PENICILLAMINE.

**Penetrol** (*Crookes Healthcare Prooducts UK*) is a proprietary, non-prescription preparation for the relief of catarrh. Produced in the form of an inhalant and as lozenges, it contains MENTHOL, eucalyptus and peppermint oils.
▲/● side-effects/warning: see PEPPERMINT OIL.

**penicillamine** is a breakdown product of penicillin, which is an extremely effective CHELATING AGENT: it binds various metals (and mineral substances) as it passes through the body before being excreted in the normal way. It is thus used to treat various forms of metallic poisoning – notably copper poisoning in Wilson's disease, lead and mercury poisoning – and can also be used to assist in the treatment of severe rheumatoid arthritis or juvenile chronic arthritis, especially when anti-inflammatory analgesics (such as aspirin) have proved unsuccessful; in the treatment of chronic hepatitis once the acute phase is over. Administration is oral in the form of tablets.
▲ side-effects: there may be nausea, but this can be minimized by taking the drug before food or on going to bed. Between the sixth and twelfth weeks of treatment there is commonly a loss of the sense of taste. There is commonly also a rash. Some patients experience extreme weight loss, mouth ulcers, muscle weakness, fluid retention and/or blood disorders.
● warning: penicillamine should not be administered to patients with the serious skin disorder lupus erythematosus; it should be administered with caution to those with impaired kidney function, or some forms of hypertension (high blood pressure), who are pregnant, who are taking any form of immunosuppressant drug,or who are sensitive to penicillin. Patients should be warned that treatment may take up to 12 weeks for any effect to become apparent, and up to 6 months to achieve its full therapeutic effect. Regular and frequent blood counts and urine analyses are essential.
*Related articles:* DISTAMINE; PENDRAMINE.

**penicillinases** are enzymes, produced by some bacteria, that inhibit or completely neutralize the antibacterial activity of many forms of PENICILLIN. Treatment of infections caused by bacteria that produce penicillinases has generally therefore to be undertaken either with penicillinase-resistant penicillins, such as flucloxacillin, or with other types of antibiotic. Therapeutically, however, penicillinases can be used (in purified form) to treat sensitivity reactions to penicillin, or in tests to identify micro-organisms in blood samples taken from patients who are taking penicillin.

**penicillin G** is a term for the ANTIBIOTIC more commonly known as benzylpenicillin.
see BENZYLPENICILLIN.

**penicillin V** is a term for the ANTIBIOTIC more commonly known as phenoxy-methylpenicillin.
see PHENOXYMETHYLPENICILLIN.

**penicillin VK** is a term for the potassium salt of the ANTIBIOTIC more commonly known as phenoxymethylpenicillin.
see PHENOXYMETHYLPENICILLIN.

**penicillins** are ANTIBIOTIC drugs
that work by interfering with the
synthesis of bacterial cell walls.
The early penicillins were
effective against principally
gram-positive bacteria but also
the gram-negative organisms
(Neisseria) causing gonorrhoea
and meningitis, as well as the
organism causing syphilis. Later
penicillins, e.g. ampicillin and
pipercillin, expanded the
spectrum to a much wider range
of gram-negative organisms. They
are absorbed rapidly by most (but
not all) body tissues and fluids,
perfuse through the kidneys, and
are excreted in the urine. One
great disadvantage of penicillins
is that many patients are allergic
to them – allergy to one means
allergy to them all – and may
have reactions that range from a
minor rash right up to
anaphylactic shock, which may
be fatal. Otherwise they are
remarkably non-toxic. Very high
dosage may rarely cause
convulsions, haemolytic anaemia,
or abnormally high body levels of
sodium or potassium, with
consequent symptoms. Best
known and most used penicillins
include benzylpenicillin
(penicillin G, the first of the
penicillins), phenoxy-
methylpenicillin (penicillin V),
flucloxacillin, ampicillin and
amoxycillin. Those taken orally
tend to cause diarrhoea; and there
is a risk with broad-spectrum
penicillins of allowing a
superinfection to develop.

▲/✿ side-effects/warning: *see*
AMOXYCILLIN; AMPICILLIN;
AZLOCILLIN; BACAMPICILLIN
HYDROCHLORIDE;
BENETHAMINE PENICILLIN;
BENZATHINE PENICILLIN;
BENZYLPENICILLIN;
CARBENICILLIN; CARFECILLIN
SODIUM; CICLACILLIN;
CLOXACILLIN;
FLUCLOXACILLIN;
MECILLINAM; METHICILLIN;
MEZLOCILLIN;
PHENETHICILLIN;
PHENOXYMETHYLPENICILLIN;
PIPERACILLIN;
PIVAMPICILLIN;
PIVMECILLINAM; PROCAINE
PENICILLIN; TALAMPICILLIN
HYDROCHLORIDE;
TICARCILLIN.

**Penidural** (*Wyeth*) is a proprietary
ANTIBIOTIC, available only on
prescription, used to treat many
forms of infection (including
syphilis) and to prevent fresh
episodes of rheumatic fever
following from a streptococcal
sore throat/tonsillitis. Produced
in the form of a suspension for
dilution (the potency of the
suspension once diluted is
retained for 14 days), as drops for
children, and in vials for injection
(under the name Penidural-LA),
Penidural is a preparation of
benzathine penicillin.

▲/✿ side-effects/warning: *see*
BENZATHINE PENICILLIN.

**PenMix 30/70** (*Novo Nordisk*) is a
proprietary, non-prescription
preparation of human isophane
insulin (30% soluble/70%
isophane) used to treat and
maintain diabetic patients. It is
produced in cartridges for
injection for use with Novopen
discs.

▲/✿ side-effects/warning: *see*
INSULIN.

**Penotrane** (*Boehringer Ingelheim*)
is a proprietary ANTISEPTIC that
has ANTIBACTERIAL and
ANTIFUNGAL properties, available
only on prescription, used in
topical application to treat
vaginal infections. Produced in
the form of vaginal inserts
(pessaries), Penotrane is a
preparation of the organic
mercurial compound
hydrargaphen.

▲/✿ side-effects/warning: *see*
HYDRARGAPHEN.

**pentaerythritol tetranitrate** is a powerful VASODILATOR that is extremely effective in preventing and treating the symptoms of angina pectoris (heart pain). It works by dilating the veins returning blood to the heart, thus reducing the pressure within the heart and reducing its workload at the same time. Fairly short-acting, pentaerythritol tetranitrate's effect is generally extended through its preparation in sustained-release capsules to be kept under the tongue; administration is also in the form of tablets.

▲ side-effects: there may be headache, flushes and dizziness; some patients experience an increase in heart rate.

✿ warning: pentaerythritol tetranitrate should be administered with caution to patients with low blood pressure (hypotension) and associated conditions. *Related articles:* CARDIACAP; MYCARDOL.

**pentamidine** is an ANTI-PROTOZOAL drug that is used to treat pneumonia caused by the protozoan micro-organism *Pneumocystis carinii* in patients whose immune system has been suppressed (either following transplant surgery or because of a condition such as AIDS). However, it is not ordinarily available in the United Kingdom. It is administered either by injection or inhalation. Both methods of administration can cause acute episodes of low blood pressure.

**Pentasa** (*Nordic*) is a proprietary form of the drug mesalazine, used to treat patients who suffer from ulcerative colitis, but who are unable to tolerate the more commonly used drug sulpha-salazine. Available only on prescription, Pentasa is produced in the form of slow-release tablets and as a retention enema.
▲ / ✿ side-effects/warning: *see* MESALAZINE.

**pentazocine** is a powerful narcotic ANALGESIC used to treat moderate to severe pain. Much like MORPHINE in effect and action, it is less likely to cause dependence. Administration is oral in the form of capsules and tablets, topical in the form of anal suppositories, or by injection. Treatment by injection has a stronger effect than oral treatment. The proprietary form is on the controlled drugs list.

▲ side-effects: there is sedation and dizziness, with nausea; injection may lead to hallucinations. There is often also constipation. Tolerance and dependence (addiction) may result from prolonged treatment.

✿ warning: pentazocine should not be administered to patients who have recently had a heart attack, with high blood pressure (hypertension), heart failure, respiratory depression or head injury, who are taking any other narcotic analgesic, who are pregnant or have kidney or liver damage. Patients should be warned that hallucinations and other disturbances in thought and sensation may occur, especially following administration by injection. *Related article:* FORTRAL.

**Pentostam** (*Wellcome*) is a proprietary ANTIPROTOZOAL preparation of the drug sodium stibogluconate (an organic compound of antimony), available only on prescription, used to treat skin infections by protozoal micro-organisms of the genus *Leishmania* (leishmaniasis). It is produced in a solution for injection.

▲/ ✪ side-effects/warning: *see*
SODIUM STIBOGLUCONATE.

**Pentovis** (*Parke-Davis; Warner
UK*) is a proprietary female sex
HORMONE preparation, available
only on prescription, used to
make up hormonal deficiency
during and after the menopause.
Produced in the form of capsules,
Pentovis is a preparation of the
OESTROGEN quinestradol.
▲/ ✪ side-effects/warning: *see*
QUINESTRADOL.

**peppermint oil** is used to relieve
the discomfort of abdominal colic
and distension and of severe
indigestion or flatulence. It is
thought to work by direct action
on the smooth muscle of the
intestinal walls. Administration
is oral in the form of capsules.
▲ side-effects: there may be
heartburn and local irritation.
✪ warning: peppermint oil should
not be administered to patients
who suffer from paralytic ileus
or ulcerative colitis; a very few
patients are allergic to
menthol.
*Related articles:* CARBELLON;
COLPERMIN; MINTEC; TERCODA.

**Peptisorbon** (*Merck*) is a
proprietary, non-prescription,
sucrose-, galactose-, fructose- and
gluten-free, lactose-low powder
that is a complete nutritional diet
for patients who have conditions
involving the malabsorption of
food (such as following
gastrectomy). Produced in sachets
for solution, Peptisorbon is a
preparation of amino acids and
peptides, carbohydrate, fats, and
vitamins and minerals. It is not
suitable for children.

**Percutol** (*Rorer*) is a proprietary,
non-prescription VASODILATOR,
used to prevent recurrent attacks
of angina pectoris (heart pain).
Produced in the form of an
ointment for use on a dressing

strapped to the skin surface (on
the chest, arm or thigh), Percutol
is a preparation of glyceryl
trinitrate. It is not recommended
for children.
▲/ ✪ side-effects/warning: *see*
GLYCERYL TRINITRATE.

**Perfan** (*Merrell*) is a PHOSPHO-
DIESTERASE INHIBITOR and is a
proprietary form of enoximone. It
is used in the short-term
treatment of heart failure,
especially where other drugs have
not been successful. Available
only on prescription, it is in a
form for dilution before
administration by intravenous
infusion or injection.
▲/ ✪ side-effects/warning: *see*
ENOXIMONE.

**Pergonal** (*Serono*) is a HORMONE
preparation, and is a proprietary
form of the GONADOTROPHIN,
follicle-stimulating hormone
(FSH) together with luteinising
hormone (LH), called collectively
menotropin. It is used to treat
infertile women with proven
hypopituitarism and who do not
respond to CLOMIPHENE CITRATE
(another drug commonly used to
treat infertility). Available only
on prescription in a form for
injection.
▲/ ✪ side-effects/warning: *see*
MENOTROPIN.

**Periactin** (*Merck, Sharp &
Dohme*) is a proprietary, non-
prescription ANTIHISTAMINE, used
both to treat the symptoms of
allergic disorders like hay fever
and as a tonic for stimulating
appetite. Produced in the form of
tablets and as a syrup for dilution
(the potency of the syrup once
dilute is retained for 14 days),
Periactin is a preparation of
cyproheptadine hydrochloride,
and is not recommended for
children aged under 2 years.
▲/ ✪ side-effects/warning: *see*
CYPROHEPTADINE
HYDROCHLORIDE.

**pericyazine** is an ANTIPSYCHOTIC drug used to tranquillize patients suffering from schizophrenia and other psychoses, particularly during behavioural disturbances. The drug may also be used in the short term to treat severe anxiety. Administration is oral in the form of tablets or a dilute elixir.

▲ side-effects: concentration and speed of thought and movement are affected; the effects of alcohol consumption are increased. There may be dry mouth and blocked nose, constipation and difficulty in urinating, and blurred vision; menstrual disturbances in women or impotence in men may occur, with weight gain; there may be sensitivity reactions. Some patients feel cold and depressed, and tend to suffer from poor sleep patterns. Blood pressure may be low and the heartbeat irregular. Prolonged high dosage may cause opacity in the cornea and lens of the eyes, and a purple pigmentation of the skin. Treatment by intramuscular injection may be painful.

● warning: pericyazine should not be administered to patients with certain forms of glaucoma, whose blood-cell formation by the bone-marrow is reduced, or who are taking drugs that depress certain centres of the brain and spinal cord. It should be administered with caution to those with lung disease, cardiovascular disease, epilepsy, parkinsonism, abnormal secretion by the adrenal glands, impaired liver or kidney function, undersecretion of thyroid hormones (hypothyroidism), enlargement of the prostate gland or any form of acute infection; who are pregnant or lactating; or who are elderly.

Prolonged use requires regular checks on eye function and skin pigmentation. Withdrawal of treatment should be gradual.
*Related article:* NEULACTIL.

**Perifusin** (*Merck*) is a proprietary fluid nutritional preparation, available only on prescription. Produced in the form of a solution for intravenous infusion into patients who cannot be fed via the alimentary canal because of conditions such as coma or prolonged disorders of the gastrointestinal tract. Perifusin is a preparation of amino acids with electrolytes.

**perindopril** is an ANTIHYPERTENSIVE drug used to treat hypertension (high blood pressure), especially when more standard forms of therapy have failed or are not tolerated. It works by inhibiting the formation of a certain peptide in the blood (angiotensin) that normally constricts the blood vessels. Administration is oral, as tablets; some patients may require simultaneous administration of other antihypertensive drugs.

▲ side-effects: there may be a dry cough, headache, fatigue, dizziness, nausea, an alteration in the sense of taste, muscle cramps, diarrhoea, low blood pressure and renal impairment, abdominal pains. Some patients develop a rash.

● warning: perindopril should be administered with caution to patients with impaired kidney function, or who are pregnant. The initial dose may cause a rapid fall in blood pressure to low blood pressure (hypotension), especially in patients who are also taking diuretics or who are dehydrated.
*Related article:* COVERSYL.

**perphenazine** is an ANTIPSYCHOTIC drug used to

tranquillize patients suffering from schizophrenia and other psychoses, particularly during behavioural disturbances. The drug may also be used in the short term to treat severe anxiety, to soothe patients who are dying, as a premedication prior to surgery, and to remedy intractable hiccups. Alternatively, it may be used to relieve nausea and vertigo caused by disorders in the middle or inner ear. Administration is oral in the form of tablets, or by injection.

▲ side-effects: concentration and speed of thought and movement are affected; the effects of alcohol consumption are increased. There may be dry mouth and blocked nose, constipation and difficulty in urinating, and blurred vision; menstrual disturbances in women or impotence in men may occur, with weight gain; there may be sensitivity reactions. Some patients feel cold and depressed, and tend to suffer from poor sleep patterns. Blood pressure may be low and the heartbeat irregular. Prolonged high dosage may cause opacity in the cornea and lens of the eyes, and a purple pigmentation of the skin. Treatment by intramuscular injection may be painful.

● warning: perphenazine should not be administered to patients with certain forms of glaucoma, whose blood-cell formation by the bone-marrow is reduced, or who are taking drugs that depress certain centres of the brain and spinal cord. It should be administered with caution to those with lung disease, cardiovascular disease, epilepsy, parkinsonism, abnormal secretion by the adrenal glands, impaired liver or kidney function, undersecretion of thyroid hormones (hypothyroidism), enlargement of the prostate gland or any form of acute infection; who are pregnant or lactating; or who are elderly. Prolonged use requires regular checks on eye function and skin pigmentation. Withdrawal of treatment should be gradual. It should not be administered to children.
*Related article:* FENTAZIN.

**Persantin** (*Boehringer Ingelheim*) is a proprietary preparation of the unusual drug dipyramidole, available only on prescription, used as an additional treatment with anticoagulants or aspirin in the prevention of thrombosis, especially during or following surgical procedures. It works by inhibiting the adhesiveness of blood platelets so that they stick neither to themselves nor to the walls of valves or tubes surgically inserted. The drug is produced in the form of tablets (in two strengths) and in ampoules for injection.
▲/● side-effects/warning: *see* DIPYRIDAMOLE.

**Pertofran** (*Geigy*) is a proprietary ANTIDEPRESSANT, available only on prescription. Produced in the form of tablets, Pertofran is a preparation of desipramine hydrochloride. It is not recommended for children.
▲/● side-effects/warning: *see* DESIPRAMINE HYDROCHLORIDE.

**pertussis vaccine**, or whooping cough VACCINE, is a suspension of dead pertussis bacteria (*Bordetella pertussis*) that is injected to cause the body's own defence mechanisms to form antibodies and thus provide immunity. It is available on prescription by itself, but it is most commonly administered as one element in the triple vaccination procedure involving diphtheria-pertussis-tetanus (DPT) vaccine. The vaccine remains the subject of some controversy over the number of children who may or may not have been brain-damaged by inoculation. It would in any case be extremely difficult to attribute such damage definitively to the use of the vaccine, and law suits brought to court have had to rely on solely statistical evidence of probability or possibility. However, the statistics do not make for comfortable reading by parents: in the 1980s it was estimated that permanent brain damage might be expected to occur in 1 in 300,000 vaccinations. Obviously, people would prefer to have no risk whatever, but sometimes disregard the fact that the likelihood of catching whooping cough and developing serious neurological complications is statistically greater. Administration is by three injections one month apart.

▲ side-effects: there may be a local reaction of swelling and inflammation around the injection site. Very rarely there is a generalized reaction within 48 hours, with fever being a prominent symptom.

✦ warning: in general, pertussis vaccine should not be administered to children who suffer a severe local or general reaction to the initial dose, or who have a history of brain damage at birth or of cerebral irritation or seizures. It should be administered with extreme caution to children whose relatives have a history of seizures or who appear to have any form of neurological disorder.

see also DIPHTHERIA-PERTUSSIS-TETANUS (DPT) VACCINE.

**Peru balsam** is a mild ANTISEPTIC used in some disinfectant preparations, especially in creams or ointments for topical application for example as soothing agents or in anal suppositories.

**per/vac** is an abbreviation for pertussis vaccine (whooping cough vaccine).
see PERTUSSIS VACCINE.

**pethidine** is a NARCOTIC ANALGESIC used primarily for the relief of moderate to severe pain, especially in labour and childbirth. Its effect is rapid and short-lasting, so its sedative properties are made use of only as a premedication prior to surgery or to enhance the effects of other anaesthetics during or following surgery. Administration (as pethidine hydrochloride) is oral in the form of tablets, or by injection. Proprietary forms are on the controlled drugs list.

▲ side-effects: shallow breathing, urinary retention, constipation and nausea are all fairly common; tolerance and dependence (addiction) are possible. There may also be drowsiness and pain at the site of injection.

✦ warning: pethidine should not be administered to patients with head injury or increased intracranial pressure; it should be administered with caution to those with impaired kidney or liver function, asthma, depressed respiration, insufficient secretion of thyroid hormones (hypothyroidism) or low blood pressure (hypotension), or who are pregnant (except during labour) or breast feeding. Dosage should be reduced for the elderly or debilitated.
*Related articles:* PAMERGAN P100; PETHILORFAN.

**Pethilorfan** (*Roche*) is a proprietary narcotic ANALGESIC on the controlled drugs list; it is used to treat moderate to severe pain, particularly in labour and childbirth. Produced in ampoules for injection, Pethilorfan is a preparation of pethidine hydro-chloride with the respiratory stimulant levallorphan tartrate.
▲/● side-effects/warning: *see* PETHIDINE.

**Petrolagar** (*Wyeth*) is a proprietary, non-prescription LAXATIVE, which is not available from the National Health Service. Produced in the form of a sugar-free emulsion, Petrolagar is a preparation of two forms of LIQUID PARAFFIN.

**Pevaryl** (*Ortho-Cilag*) is a proprietary, non-prescription ANTIFUNGAL drug, used in topical application to treat fungal infections on the skin such as nail infections, and in the genital areas. Produced in the form of a cream, a lotion and a spray-powder in an aerosol unit, Pevaryl is a preparation of econazole nitrate.
▲/● side-effects/warning: ECONAZOLE NITRATE.

**Pharmalgen** (*Pharmacia*) is either one of two preparations – of bee venom or of wasp venom – for use in diagnosing and desensitizing patients who are allergic to them. Available only on prescription, solutions of one or the other venom are administered as injections in increasingly less dilute form so that treatment is progressive.
● warning: injections should be administered under close medical supervision and in locations where emergency facilities for full cardio-respiratory resuscitation are immediately available. Pharmalgen preparations should not be given to patients who are pregnant, feverish or who suffer from asthma.

**Pharmorubicin Rapid Dissolution** (*Farmitalia Carlo Erba*) is a proprietary CYTOTOXIC drug that has ANTIBIOTIC properties. It is available only on prescription, and is used to treat acute leukaemia and various solid tumours. Produced in the form of a powder for reconstitution as a medium for injection, Pharmorubicin is a preparation of epirubicin hydrochloride.
▲/● side-effects/warning: *see* EPIRUBICIN HYDROCHLORIDE.

**Phasal** (*Lagab*) is a proprietary ANTIDEPRESSANT, available only on prescription, used in the treatment and prevention of mania, in the prevention of recurrent manic-depressive bouts, and for aggressive or self-mutilating behaviour. Produced in the form of sustained-release tablets, Phasal is a preparation of the powerful drug lithium carbonate.
▲/● side-effects/warning: *see* LITHIUM.

**phenazocine** is a narcotic ANALGESIC used primarily for the relief of moderate to severe pain, especially pain arising from disorders of the pancreas or of the bile ducts. Administration (as phenazocine hydrobromide) is oral in the form of tablets. The proprietary form is on the controlled drugs list.
▲ side-effects: shallow breathing, urinary retention, constipation and nausea are all fairly common; tolerance and dependence (addiction) are possible. There may also be drowsiness.
● warning: phenazocine should not be administered to patients with head injury or increased intracranial pressure; it should

be administered with caution to those with impaired kidney or liver function, asthma, depressed respiration, insufficient secretion of thyroid hormones (hypothyroidism) or low blood pressure (hypotension), or who are pregnant or lactating. Dosage should be reduced for the elderly or debilitated.
*Related article:* NARPHEN.

**phenazopyridine** is an ANALGESIC that relieves the pain specifically of disorders of the urinary tract such as cystitis and urethritis. It is sometimes used as a constituent in compound antibiotic preparations to treat urinary infections. Administration (as phenazo-pyridine hydrochloride) is oral in the form of tablets.

▲ side-effects: there may be gastrointestinal disturbance, with headache and dizziness. High dosage may cause blood disorders and discolour the urine. Prolonged treatment may increase the risk of urinary stones (calculi).

✿ warning: phenazopyridine hydrochloride should be administered with caution to patients with impaired liver or kidney function.
*Related article:* PYRIDIUM.

**phenelzine** is an ANTIDEPRESSANT drug, one of the MAO INHIBITORS. It is used particularly when treatment with TRICYCLIC antidepressants (such as AMITRIPTYLINE or IMIPRAMINE) has failed, even though phenelzine is one of the safer, less stimulant MAO inhibitors. Treatment with the drug requires a strict dietary regime – in which for example a patient must avoid eating cheese, or meat or yeast extracts, or drinking alcohol – and extreme care in taking any other form of medication. Administration (as phenelzine sulphate) is oral in the form of tablets.

▲ side-effects: concentration and speed of thought and movement may be affected. There may also be dizziness, particularly on standing up from lying or sitting (because of low blood pressure). Much less commonly, there may be headache, dry mouth and blurred vision, difficulty in urinating, constipation and a rash. Susceptible patients may experience agitation, tremor, or even psychotic episodes.

✿ warning: phenelzine should not be administered to patients with liver disease, epilepsy, vascular disease of the heart or brain, or abnormal secretion of hormones by the adrenal glands, or who are children. It should be administered with caution to those who are elderly or debilitated. Counselling – if not supervision – over diet and any other medication is essential. Withdrawal of treatment should be gradual.
*Related article:* NARDIL.

**Phenergan** (*May & Baker*) is a proprietary, non-prescription ANTIHISTAMINE, used to treat the symptoms of allergies such as hay fever and for emergency treatment of reactions to drugs or injected substances. It is produced in the form of tablets (in two strengths), as an elixir for dilution (the potency of the elixir once dilute is retained for 14 days), neither of which is recommended for children aged under 6 months, and (only on prescription) in ampoules for injection, which is not recommended for children aged under 5 years. Phenergan is a preparation of promethazine hydrochloride. Under the name Phenergan Compound Expectorant, a compound linctus is also available, but not from the

National Health Service, which consists of a preparation of promethazine hydrochloride and several LAXATIVE constituents; it too is not recommended for children aged under 5 years.

▲/● side-effects/warning: *see* PROMETHAZINE HYDROCHLORIDE.

**phenethicillin** is a penicillin-type ANTIBIOTIC used to treat and prevent bacterial infection. It has a similar spectrum of activity and usage to phenoxymethyl-penicillin. Administration (as a potassium salt) is oral in the form of capsules or a dilute syrup.

▲ side-effects: there may be sensitivity reactions ranging from a minor rash to urticaria and joint pains, diarrhoea and (occasionally) to high temperature or anaphylactic shock.

● warning: phenethicillin should not be administered to patients who are known to be allergic to penicillins; it should be administered with caution to those with impaired kidney function.

**phenindamine tartrate** is an ANTIHISTAMINE used to treat the symptoms of allergic conditions such as hay fever and urticaria. It has only a mildly depressant action on the brain and so is less sedating than most anti-histamines, and may in fact cause slight stimulation of the central nervous system. Administration is oral in the form of tablets.

▲ side-effects: concentration and speed of thought and movement may be affected; there may be nausea, headache, and/or weight gain, dry mouth, gastrointestinal disturbances and visual problems.

● warning: phenindamine tartrate should not be administered to patients with

glaucoma, urinary retention, intestinal obstruction, enlargement of the prostate gland, or peptic ulcer, or who are pregnant; it should be administered with caution to those with epilepsy or liver disease.
*Related article:* THEPHORIN.

**phenindione** is an ANTI-COAGULANT that is effective when taken orally, used in the treatment and prevention of thrombosis. However, because of the proportion of patients who are sensitive to it, its use has largely been replaced by that of WARFARIN sodium. It remains available: administration is in the form of tablets.

▲ side-effects: there may be sensitivity reactions. Internal haemorrhaging may occur: monitoring is required.

● warning: phenindione should not be administered to patients with kidney or liver disease, severe hypertension (high blood pressure), bacterial endocarditis, or a peptic ulcer; who are regularly taking anabolic steroids, aspirin, barbiturates or phytomenadione (vitamin K) supplements; who are using oral contraceptives; or who are in the first three months or last two months of pregnancy, or have had recent surgery.
*Related article:* DINDEVAN.

**pheniramine maleate** is an ANTIHISTAMINE used to treat the symptoms of allergic conditions such as hay fever and urticaria. Administration is oral in the form of tablets.

▲ side-effects: concentration and speed of thought and movement may be affected; there may be nausea, headache, and/or weight gain, dry mouth, gastrointestinal disturbances and visual problems.

◆ warning: pheniramine maleate should not be administered to patients with glaucoma, urinary retention, intestinal obstruction, enlargement of the prostate gland, or peptic ulcer, or who are pregnant; it should be administered with caution to those with epilepsy or liver disease.
*Related article:* DANERAL SA.

**phenobarbitone** is a powerful BARBITURATE, used as a HYPNOTIC drug to treat insomnia, as an ANXIOLYTIC to relieve anxiety, and as an ANTICONVULSANT in the prevention of recurrent epileptic seizures or the treatment of febrile convulsions. In all uses, prolonged treatment may rapidly result in tolerance and then dependence (addiction). Its use may also cause behavioural disturbances (such as hyperactivity) in children. Administration (as pheno-barbitone or phenobarbitone sodium) is oral in the form of tablets and an elixir, or by injection. All proprietary preparations containing phenobarbitone are on the controlled drugs list.

▲ side-effects: there is drowsiness and lethargy; sometimes there is also depression, muscle weakness and/or sensitivity reactions in the form of skin rashes or blood disorders. Elderly or juvenile patients may experience psychological disturbance.

◆ warning: phenobarbitone should not be administered to patients with porphyria or who are already taking drugs that depress brain function (such as alcohol) on a regular basis; it should be administered with caution to those with impaired kidney or liver function, or who have respiratory disorders, who are elderly or children, or who are lactating.

Withdrawal of treatment should be gradual.
*Related article:* GARDENAL SODIUM.

**phenol**, or carbolic acid, is a very early DISINFECTANT still much used for the cleaning of wounds or inflammation (such as boils and abscesses), the maintenance of hygiene in the mouth, throat or ear, and as a preservative in injections. Administration is topical in solutions, lotions, creams and ointments.

◆ warning: phenol is highly toxic if swallowed in concentrated form.
*Related articles:* CHLORASEPTIC; SECADERM.

**phenolphthalein** is a LAXATIVE that works by irritating the nerve endings in the intestinal walls. Its use is now rare because of an association with blood disorders that affect the composition of the urine, with sensitivity reactions, and with a duration of effect that may continue for several days as the chemical is recycled through the liver. Proprietary preparations that contain phenolphthalein all also contain either other forms of laxative or an antacid.
*Related articles:* AGAROL; ALOPHEN; KEST.

**phenoperidine** is a narcotic ANALGESIC, a morphine-like drug used to relieve pain during surgery and particularly in combination with (to enhance) general ANAESTHETICS; its additional properties as a respiratory depressant are sometimes made use of in the treatment of patients who undergo prolonged assisted respiration. Administration (in the form of phenoperidine hydrochloride) is by injection.

▲ side-effects: shallow breathing, urinary retention, constipation and nausea are all fairly common; tolerance and dependence (addiction) are possible. There may also be drowsiness, and pain at the site of injection.

✦ warning: phenoperidine should not be administered to patients who suffer from head injury or increased intracranial pressure; it should be administered with caution to those with impaired kidney or liver function, insufficient secretion of thyroid hormones (hypothyroidism) or low blood pressure (hypotension), or who are pregnant or lactating. Dosage should be reduced for the elderly or debilitated.
*Related article:* OPERIDINE.

**phenothiazine derivatives,** or phenothiazines, are a group of drugs that are chemically related but are not restricted to a single mode of activity. Many are ANTIPSYCHOTIC drugs, including some of the tranquillizers best known and most used – such as chlorpromazine, promazine, thioridazine, fluphenazine and trifluoperazine. Some of these are used also as ANTI-EMETICS. Others – such as piperazine – are ANTHELMINTICS.

▲/✦ side-effects/warning: *see*
CHLORPROMAZINE;
FLUPHENAZINE;
METHOTRIMEPRAZINE;
PERICYAZINE;
PERPHENAZINE; PIPERAZINE;
PIPOTHIAZINE;
PROCHLORPERAZINE;
PROMAZINE HYDROCHLORIDE;
THIORIDAZINE;
TRIFLUOPERAZINE.

**phenoxybenzamine hydrochloride** is an ALPHA-BLOCKER used in conjunction with either a BETA-BLOCKER and/or a DIURETIC to reduce blood pressure and to improve conditions that result from poor circulation or from abnormal secretion of

hormones by the adrenal glands. By itself it is also sometimes useful in improving urine flow in cases of benign enlargement of the prostate gland. Administration is oral in the form of capsules, or by injection.

▲ side-effects: the heart rate increases; there may be dizziness, particularly on standing up from lying or sitting (because of low blood pressure), with lethargy. There is sometimes nasal congestion and contraction of the pupils. Rarely, there is gastro-intestinal disturbance or ejaculation failure.

✦ warning: phenoxybenzamine hydrochloride should be administered with caution to patients with heart disease, severe arteriosclerosis, or impaired kidney function, or who are elderly.
*Related article:* DIBENYLINE.

**phenoxymethylpenicillin,** or penicillin V, is a widely used ANTIBIOTIC, particularly effective in treating tonsillitis, infection of the middle ear, and some skin infections, and to prevent recurrent streptococcal throat infection which can lead to episodes of rheumatic fever. Administration (as a potassium salt sometimes called phenoxymethylpenicillin VK) is oral in the form of tablets or liquids.

▲ side-effects: there may be sensitivity reactions ranging from a minor rash to urticaria and joint pains, and (occasionally) to high temper-ature or anaphylactic shock.

✦ warning: phenoxymethyl-penicillin should not be administered to patients known to be allergic to penicillins; it should be administered with caution to those with impaired kidney function.

*Related articles:* APSIN V.K.;
CRYSTAPEN V; DISTAQUAINE
V·K; ECONOCIL VK; STABILLIN-
V·K; V-CIL-K.

**Phensedyl** (*May & Baker*) is a
proprietary, non-prescription
ANTITUSSIVE, which is not
available from the National
Health Service. Produced in the
form of a linctus, Phensedyl is a
preparation of the ANTIHISTAMINE
promethazine hydrochloride, the
OPIATE codeine phosphate and the
SYMPATHOMIMETIC ephedrine
hydrochloride as a syrup for
dilution (the potency of the syrup
once dilute is retained for 14
days). It is not recommended for
children aged under 2 years.
▲/❋ side-effects/warning: *see*
CODEINE PHOSPHATE;
EPHEDRINE HYDROCHLORIDE;
PROMETHAZINE
HYDROCHLORIDE.

**Phensic** (*Beecham Health Care*) is
a proprietary, non-prescription
ANALGESIC containing aspirin and
caffeine.
▲/❋ side-effects/warning: *see*
ASPIRIN; CAFFEINE.

**phentermine** is a SYMPATHO-
MIMETIC drug used under medical
supervision and on a short-term
basis to aid weight loss in
moderate to severe obesity
because it acts to suppress the
appetite. Administration is in the
form of sustained-release
capsules.
▲ side-effects: there is commonly
rapid heart rate, nervous
agitation and insomnia,
tremor, gastrointestinal
disturbance, dry mouth,
dizziness and headache.
❋ warning: phentermine should
not be administered to patients
who suffer from glaucoma; it
should be administered with
caution to those with heart
disease, diabetes, epilepsy,
peptic ulcer, or depression.

*Related articles:* DUROMINE;
IONAMIN.

**phentolamine** is an ALPHA-
BLOCKER used to reduce blood
pressure and to improve
conditions that result from poor
circulation, it is particularly
useful in emergency situations
caused by abnormal secretion of
hormones by the adrenal glands,
by internal reactions between
incompatible antidepressant
drugs, or by heart failure. It is also
used to test adrenal function or
diagnose adrenal disorder.
Administration is by injection or
infusion.
▲ side-effects: there is commonly
a rapid heart rate and dizziness,
with low blood pressure
(hypotension). High dosage
may lead to nausea, nasal
congestion and diarrhoea.
*Related article:* ROGITINE.

**phenylbutazone** is an ANTI-
INFLAMMATORY, non-narcotic
ANALGESIC, which, because of its
sometimes severe side-effects, is
used solely in the treatment of
progressive fusion of the synovial
joints of the spine (ankylosing
spondylitis) under medical
supervision in hospitals. Even for
that purpose, it is used only when
all other therapies have failed.
Treatment then, however, may be
prolonged. Administration is oral
in the form of tablets.
▲ side-effects: there may be
gastrointestinal disturbances,
nausea, vomiting, and allergic
reactions such as a rash. Less
often, there is inflammation of
the glands of the mouth, throat
and neck; pancreatitis;
nephritis or hepatitis; or
headache and visual
disturbances. Rarely, there is
severe fluid retention (which
may eventually in susceptible
patients precipitate heart
failure) or serious and
potentially dangerous blood
disorders.

● **warning:** phenylbutazone should not be administered to patients with cardiovascular disease, thyroid disease, or impaired liver or kidney function; who are pregnant; or who have a history of stomach or intestinal haemorrhaging. It should be administered with caution to those who are elderly or ' ctating. Regular and frequent blood counts are essential.
*Related articles:* BUTACOTE; BUTAZONE.

**phenylephrine** is a VASO-CONSTRICTOR, a SYMPATHO-MIMETIC drug used in administration by injection or infusion to increase blood pressure (sometimes in emergency situations until plasma transfusion is available). It is sometimes used in the form of a spray or drops to clear nasal congestion; as eye-drops to dilate the pupil and facilitate ophthalmic examination; or as a constituent in some proprietary preparations produced to treat bronchospasm in conditions such as asthma.
▲ **side-effects:** treatment by injection or infusion causes a rise in the blood pressure, which may in turn cause headache and heartbeat irregularities; there may be vomiting, and a tingling or coolness in the skin. Topical application may promote the appearance of a form of dermatitis. As nasal drops or spray, excessive use may lead to tolerance and worse congestion than previously.
● **warning:** phenylephrine should not be administered to patients with severe hypertension (high blood pressure), or from overactivity of the thyroid gland (hyperthyroidism), who are undergoing a heart attack, or who are pregnant. Leakage

of the drug into the tissues following injection may cause tissue damage.
*Related articles:* BETNOVATE; BETOPTIC; BRONCHILATOR; DIMOTANE EXPECTORANT; DIMOTAPP; ISOPTO; MEDIHALER-DUO; MINIMS PHENYLEPHRINE; SOFRAMYCIN; UNIFLU PLUS GREGOVITE C; VIBROCIL; ZINCFRIN.

**phenylpropanolomine** is a SYMPATHOMIMETIC drug that has a strongly relaxant effect on certain muscles of the body, including especially the muscles of the bladder that contract to allow urine to escape through the urethra. The drug is therefore primarily used under medical supervision to treat urinary incontinence (of the type caused by muscular weakness). However, it is used also to relieve the symptoms of some allergic disorders, such as asthma and hay fever, often when administered with an antihistamine. Administration is oral in the form of sustained-release capsules and a dilute syrup, topical in the form of a nasal or throat spray, and by injection.
▲ **side-effects:** there may be anxiety, restlessness and insomnia, with dry mouth, sweating, and cold extremities; urinary retention may occur. Some patients experience tremor and heartbeat irregularities.
● **warning:** phenylpropanolamine should not be administered to patients with high blood pressure (hypertension), overactivity of the thyroid gland (hyperthyroidism), coronary heart disease or diabetes, or who are taking antidepressant drugs. It should be administered with caution to those who are elderly.
*Related articles:* DIMOTAPP; ESKORNADE; TRIOGESIC.

**phenytoin** is an ANTICONVULSANT drug that is also an ANTI-ARRHYTHMIC. It is consequently used both to treat the severer forms of epilepsy (not including petit mal), and to regularize the heartbeat (especially following the administration of a heart stimulant). The drug is also useful in assisting in the treatment of the neuropathy that sometimes accompanies diabetes. Administration (as phenytoin or phenytoin sodium) is oral in the form of tablets, chewable tablets, capsules and a suspension, or by injection.

▲ side-effects: the heart rate and blood pressure are reduced; asystole (a 'missed beat') may occur. The skin and facial features may coarsen during prolonged treatment; there may also be acne, enlargement of the gums, and/or growth of excess hair. Some patients enter a state of confusion. Nausea and vomiting, headache, blurred vision, blood disorders and insomnia may occur.

✺ warning: phenytoin should not be administered to patients whose heart rate is excessively fast, who have heart block, liver damage or who have already been administered lignocaine hydrochloride. Monitoring of plasma concentration of the drug is essential in the initial treatment of epilepsy in order to establish an optimum administration level. Withdrawal should be gradual. Drug interactions are common. *Related articles:* EPANUTIN; EPANUTIN READY MIXED PARENTERAL.

**pHiso-Med** (*Winthrop*) is a proprietary, non-prescription DISINFECTANT used as a soap or shampoo substitute in acne and seborrhoeic conditions, for bathing mothers and babies in maternity units to prevent cross infection, and for pre-operative hand and skin cleansing. Produced in the form of a solution, pHiso-Med is a preparation of CHLORHEXIDINE gluconate.

✺ warning: skin sensitivity may occur.

**pholcodine** is an OPIATE that is used as an ANTITUSSIVE constituent in cough linctuses or syrups. Although its action on the cough centre of the brain resembles that of other opiates, it has no ANALGESIC effect.

▲ side-effects: there is commonly constipation. High or prolonged dosage may lead to respiratory depression.

✺ warning: pholcodine should not be taken by patients with liver or kidney disease; it should be taken with caution by patients who suffer from asthma or have a history of drug abuse. *Related articles:* COPHOLCO; DAVENOL; EXPULIN; GALENPHOL; PAVACOL-D; PHOLCOMED.

**Pholcomed** (*Medo*) is a proprietary brand of ANTITUSSIVES used to treat an irritable and unproductive cough. Produced in the form of a sugar-free linctus for use by diabetics (in two strengths, under the names Pholcomed-D and Pholcomed Forte Diabetic) and as pastilles (only the last of which preparations is available from the National Health Service), Pholcomed is a compound of the antitussive PHOLCODINE and the MUSCLE RELAXANT PAPAVERINE hydrochloride, both of which are OPIATES. The Forte linctuses are not recommended for children.

▲/✺ side-effects/warning: *see* PAPAVERINE; PHOLCODINE.

**Pholcomed Expectorant** (*Medo*) is a proprietary, non-prescription ANTITUSSIVE, which is not available from the National Health Service. It is a compound preparation of the EXPECTORANT guaiphenesin and the SYMPATHOMIMETIC methylephedrine hydrochloride.

**phosphate infusion** is administered to replace phosphates lost through disease or disorder – as may occur in diabetic emergencies. For infusion, phosphates (usually as the potassium and sodium salts) may be administered in saline or glucose solution.

**phosphates** may be administered orally (with CALCIFEROL) to make up for the phosphate (and vitamin D) deficiency that occurs in vitamin D-resistant rickets. Diarrhoea is a common side-effect. Rarely, phosphates may be administered in order to treat high levels of calcium in the blood, although this may lead to the deposition of calcium in kidney tissues and consequent kidney damage. Phosphates are used as enemas for bowel clearance before radiological procedures, endoscopy and surgery.

**Phosphate-Sandoz** (*Sandoz*) is a proprietary, non-prescription phosphate supplement, which may be required in addition to vitamin D in patients with vitamin D-resistant rickets. Produced in the form of tablets, Phosphate-Sandoz is a preparation of sodium acid phosphate, SODIUM BICARBONATE and potassium bicarbonate.

**\*phosphodiesterase inhibitors** form a relatively new class of drugs, so far used in the short-term treatment of congestive heart failure, especially where other drugs have been unsuccessful. They work by inhibiting the breakdown, and thus enhancing the action of,

intracellular chemical messengers that mediate the actions of several HORMONES and NEUROTRANSMITTERS. In this way they effect the heart in ways that mimic SYMPATHOMIMETICS acting at beta-adrenoceptor. Examples of these drugs include ENOXIMONE and MILRINONE.

**Phospholine Iodide** (*Ayerst*) is a proprietary form of eye-drops, available only on prescription, used to treat severe cases of glaucoma. Phospholine Iodide is a preparation of ecothiopate iodide and is produced in the form of a powder (with diluent) for reconstitution (in four strengths).

▲ / ✿ side-effects/warning: *see* ECOTHIOPATE IODIDE.

**phosphorus** is a non-metallic element whose salts are important to all forms of terrestrial life. In humans, for example, phosphates are concentrated mainly in bones and teeth, but are also essential to the conversion and storage of energy in the body, and are intimately linked with corresponding levels of CALCIUM, POTASSIUM and SODIUM in the bloodstream. Phosphates may also be administered therapeutically to treat deficiency disorders. *see* PHOSPHATES.

**phthalylsulphathiazole** is a SULPHONAMIDE used primarily to treat infection of the intestines, or to act as a disinfectant before intestinal surgery. That it is effective for this purpose is due to the fact that it is poorly absorbed when taken orally – but that it is poorly absorbed means that it is now declining in use in favour of more specific drugs.

▲ side-effects: there may be nausea and vomiting; rarely, there may be rashes, skin disorders and blood deficiencies.

◆ warning: phthalysulpha-
thiazole should not be
administered to patients with
blood disorders or impaired
kidney or liver function, who
are pregnant, or who are aged
under 6 weeks. It should be
administered with caution to
those who are elderly or
lactating. Regular blood
counts are essential during
treatment. An adequate
fluid intake must be
maintained.

*Related article:* THALAZOLE.

**Phyllocontin Continus** (*Napp*) is
a proprietary, non-prescription
BRONCHODILATOR, used to treat
asthma and chronic bronchitis.
Produced in the form of sustained-
release tablets (in three strengths,
the weakest labelled for children,
the strongest labelled Forte),
Phyllocontin Continus is a
preparation of aminophylline.
The two stronger forms of tablets
are not recommended for
children; and the paediatric
tablets are not recommended for
children aged under 12 months.
▲ / ◆ side-effects/warning: *see*
AMINOPHYLLINE.

**Physeptone** (*Calmic*) is a
proprietary, narcotic ANALGESIC
that is on the controlled drugs
list. Used to treat severe pain, and
produced in the form of tablets
and in ampoules for injection,
Physeptone is a preparation of
the OPIATE methadone
hydrochloride; it is not
recommended for children.
▲ / ◆ side-effects/warning: *see*
METHADONE.

**physostigmine** is a vegetable
alkaloid (derived from calabar
beans) used in dilute solution in
the form of eye-drops to treat
glaucoma or to contract the pupil
of the eye after it has been dilated
through the use of ANTI-
CHOLINERGICS such as ATROPINE

for the purpose of ophthalmic
examination. It works by
improving drainage in the tiny
channels of the eye processes. It
is, however, potentially irritant,
causing gastrointestinal
disturbance and excessive
salivation if absorbed, and is most
commonly used in combination
with other drugs, particularly
pilocarpine.

**Phytex** (*Pharmax*) is a
proprietary, non-prescription
ANTIFUNGAL drug, used to treat
fungal infections in the skin and
nails. Produced in the form of a
paint for topical application,
Phytex is a preparation of various
natural acids, including salicylic
acid, together with methyl
salicylate.
▲ / ◆ side-effects/warning:
hypersensitivity reactions
may occur.

**Phytocil** (*Radiol*) is a proprietary,
non-prescription ANTIFUNGAL
drug, used in topical application,
to treat skin infections, especially
athlete's foot. Produced in the
form of a cream, and a powder in
a sprinkler tin, Phytocil is a
compound preparation that
includes several minor antifungal
constituents, including salicylic
acid.
▲ / ◆ side-effects/warning:
hypersensitivity may occur.

**phytomenadione** is the technical
term for vitamin K, a fat-soluble
vitamin essential to the
production of clotting factors in
the blood, and to the metabolism
of the proteins necessary for the
calcification of bone. Good food
sources include vegetable oils,
liver, pork meat and green
vegetables. Deficiency causes a
condition much like haemophilia,
and in children may lead to
irregular bone growth.
Therapeutically, phytomenadione
is administered to make up

deficiency – especially in newborn babies whose intestines have not had to time to obtain the normal bacterial agents that synthesize the vitamin. Administration is oral in the form of tablets, or by very slow intravenous injection.
*Related articles:* KONAKION; VITLIPID.

**PIB** (*Napp*) is a proprietary compound BRONCHODILATOR, available only on prescription, used to treat bronchospasm in asthma and chronic bronchitis. Produced in a metered-dosage aerosol (in two strengths, the stronger under the name PIB Plus), it is a preparation of the SYMPATHOMIMETIC isoprenaline hydrochloride together with the BELLADONNA alkaloid atropine methonitrate. It is not recommended for children.
▲/❦ side-effects/warning: *see* ATROPINE METHONITRATE; ISOPRENALINE.

**Picolax** (*Nordic*) is a proprietary, non-prescription LAXATIVE produced in the form of a sugar-free powder for solution. Picolax is a preparation of the stimulant laxative sodium picosulphate and the ANTACID laxative magnesium citrate.
▲/❦ side-effects/warning: *see* SODIUM PICOSULPHATE.

**pilocarpine** is a PARASYMPATHO-MIMETIC drug used in dilute solution in the form of eye-drops to treat glaucoma or to contract the pupil of the eye after it has been dilated for the purpose of ophthalmic examination. It works by improving drainage in the channels of the eye processes. It is, however, potentially irritant, causing eyeache and blurred vision, and even gastrointestinal disturbance and excessive salivation if absorbed especially to patients under 40 years of age. As pilocarpine hydrochloride or

pilocarpine nitrate, it is commonly used in combination with other drugs, particularly PHYSOSTIGMINE.
*Related articles:* ISOPTO; MINIMS PILOCARPINE; OCUSERT PILO; SNO-PILO.

**Pimafucin** (*Brocades*) is a proprietary ANTIFUNGAL drug, available only on prescription, used to treat fungal infections (such as candidiasis), particularly in the mouth, respiratory tract and vagina. Produced in the form of a vaginal cream, and as a water-miscible cream for topical application to the skin, Pimafucin is a preparation of natamycin.
▲/❦ side-effects/warning: *see* NATAMYCIN.

**pimozide** is an ANTIPSYCHOTIC drug used to tranquillize patients suffering from schizophrenia and other psychoses, including paranoia and mania. It is especially effective in relieving hallucinations. The drug may also be used in the short term to treat severe anxiety. Administration is oral in the form of tablets.
▲ side-effects: concentration and speed of thought and movement are affected; the effects of alcohol consumption are enhanced. There may be dry mouth and blocked nose, constipation and difficulty in urinating, and blurred vision; menstrual disturbances in women or impotence in men may occur, with weight gain; there may be sensitivity reactions. Some patients feel cold and depressed, and tend to suffer from poor sleep patterns. Blood pressure may be low and the heartbeat irregular.
❦ warning: pimozide should not be administered to patients who suffer from certain forms of glaucoma, whose blood-cell formation by the bone-marrow is reduced, or who are taking

drugs that depress certain centres of the brain and spinal cord. It should be administered with caution to those with lung disease, cardiovascular disease, epilepsy, parkinsonism, abnormal secretion by the adrenal glands, impaired liver or kidney function, undersecretion of thyroid hormones (hypothyroidism), enlargement of the prostate gland or any form of acute infection; who are pregnant or lactating; or who are elderly. Prolonged use requires regular checks on eye function and skin pigmentation. Withdrawal of treatment should be gradual.
*Related article:* ORAP.

**pindolol** is a BETA-BLOCKER, a drug used to control and regulate the heart rate and to treat hypertension (high blood pressure). It is also used to treat the symptoms of angina pectoris (heart pain) and to assist in relieving the symptoms of the neuropathy that sometimes accompanies diabetes. Administration is oral in the form of tablets.
▲ side-effects: there may be a slowing of the heartbeat, with coldness of the extremities. Sometimes there is respiratory depression and/or gastrointestinal disturbances.
✿ warning: pindolol should not be administered to patients who have heart disease or asthma; it should be administered with caution to those with liver or especially kidney disease, or who are pregnant or lactating. Withdrawal of treatment must be gradual.
*Related articles:* VISKALDIX; VISKEN.

**pipenzolate bromide** is an ANTICHOLINERGIC drug used to assist in the treatment of

gastrointestinal disorders that involve muscle spasm of the intestinal wall. Administration is oral in the form of tablets, or a suspension.
▲ / ✿ side-effects/warning: *see* under ATROPINE
*Related articles:* PIPTAL; PIPTALIN.

**piperacillin** is a broad-spectrum, penicillin-type ANTIBIOTIC closely related to ampicillin, used to treat many serious or compound forms of bacterial infection, particularly those caused by *Pseudomonas aeruginosa*. Administration is by injection or infusion.
▲ side-effects: there may be sensitivity reactions ranging from a minor rash to urticaria and joint pains, and (occasionally) to high temperature or anaphylactic shock.
✿ warning: piperacillin should not be administered to patients known to be allergic to penicillins; it should be administered with caution to those with impaired kidney function.
*Related article:* PIPRIL.

**piperazine** is an ANTHELMINTIC drug, one of the phenothiazine derivatives, used to treat infestation by roundworms or threadworms. Treatment should take no longer than seven days; in the treatment of some species a single dose is sufficient. Administration (as piperazine citrate, piperazine hydrate or piperazine phosphate) is oral in the form of tablets, a syrup or a dilute elixir.
▲ side-effects: there may be nausea and vomiting, with diarrhoea; there may also be urticaria. Rarely, there is dizziness and lack of muscular co-ordination.
✿ warning: piperazine should not be administered to patients with liver disease or epilepsy; it

446

P

should be administered with caution to those with impaired kidney function, neurological disease or psychiatric disorders.

*Related articles:* ANTEPAR; ASCALIX; PRIPSEN.

**piperazine oestron sulphate** is a female sex hormone, an OESTROGEN used to make up hormonal deficiency during or following the menopause. Administration is oral in the form of tablets.

▲ side-effects: there may be nausea and vomiting. A common effect is weight gain, generally through fluid or sodium retention in the tissues. The breasts may become tender and enlarge slightly. There may also be headache and/or depression; rash, liver function disorders, jaundice.

◆ warning: piperazine oestron sulphate should not be administered to patients who have cancers proved to be sex-hormone-linked, who have a history of thrombosis or inflammation of the womb, or with porphyria or impaired liver function. It should be administered with caution to those who are diabetic or epileptic, who have heart or kidney disease, or who have hypertension (high blood pressure) or recurrent severe migraine. Prolonged treatment may increase the risk of cancer of the endometrium (the lining of the womb).

*Related article:* HARMOGEN.

**piperidolate hydrochloride** is an ANTICHOLINERGIC drug used to assist in the treatment of gastrointestinal disorders that involve muscle spasm of the intestinal wall. Administration is oral in the form of tablets.

▲ side-effects: there is commonly dry mouth and thirst; there may also be visual disturbances,

flushing, irregular heartbeat and difficulty in urination and constipation. Rarely, there may be high temperature accompanied by delirium.

◆ warning: piperidolate hydrochloride should not be administered to patients with glaucoma; it should be administered with caution to those with heart problems and rapid heart rate (tachycardia), ulcerative colitis, urinary retention or enlargement of the prostate gland; who are elderly; or who are lactating.

**Piportil Depot** (*May & Baker*) is a proprietary ANTIPSYCHOTIC drug, available only on prescription, used in maintenance therapy for patients who suffer from psychotic disorders such as chronic schizophrenia and related psychoses. Produced in ampoules for long-acting depot injections, Piportil Depot is a preparation of the PHENOTHIAZINE DERIVATIVE pipothiazine palmitate; it is not recommended for children.

▲/◆ side-effects/warning: see CHLORPROMAZINE.

**pipothiazine palmitate** is an ANTIPSYCHOTIC drug, one of the PHENOTHIAZINE DERIVATIVES used in maintenance therapy for patients who suffer from schizophrenia and other related psychoses. Administration is by injection.

▲/◆ side-effects/warning: see CHLORPROMAZINE.
*Related article:* PIPORTIL DEPOT.

**Pipril** (*Lederle*) is a proprietary, broad-spectrum, penicillin-type ANTIBIOTIC, available only on prescription, used to treat many serious or compound forms of bacterial infection, particularly those caused by *Pseudomonas aeruginosa*. Produced in the form of a powder in vials (in two strengths) and in an infusion bottle, Pipril is a preparation of piperacillin.

▲/✸ side-effects/warning: *see* PIPERACILLIN.

**Piptal** (*MCP Pharmaceuticals*) is a proprietary ANTISPASMODIC drug, available only on prescription, used to assist in the treatment of gastrointestinal disorders arising from muscular spasm of the intestinal walls. Produced in the form of tablets, Piptal is a preparation of the ANTI-CHOLINERGIC drug pipenzolate bromide; it is not recommended for children.

▲/✸ side-effects/warning: *see* PIPENZOLATE BROMIDE.

**Piptalin** (*MCP Pharmaceuticals*) is a proprietary ANTISPASMODIC drug, available only on prescription, used to assist in the treatment of gastrointestinal disorders arising from muscular spasm of the intestinal walls. Produced in the form of a sugar-free suspension for dilution (the potency of the suspension once dilute is retained for 14 days), Piptalin is a preparation of the ANTICHOLINERGIC pipenzolate bromide together with the antifoaming agent DIMETHICONE.

▲/✸ side-effects/warning: *see* PIPENZOLATE BROMIDE.

**pirbuterol** is a BRONCHODILATOR, of the type known as a selective BETA-RECEPTOR STIMULANT, used to treat asthmatic bronchospasm, emphysema and chronic bronchitis. It has fewer cardiac side-effects than some others of its type, and is administered orally in the form of capsules, as a syrup or by aerosol inhalation.

▲ side-effects: there may be headache and nervous tension, associated with tingling of the fingertips and a fine tremor of the muscles of the hands. Administration other than by

inhalation may cause an increase in the heart rate.

✸ warning: pirbuterol should be administered with caution to patients with disorders of the thyroid gland, from heart disease or hypertension (high blood pressure), who are elderly, or who are pregnant. It is important not to exceed the recommended dose.
*Related article:* EXIREL.

**pirenzepine** is a relatively new drug used in the treatment of gastric and duodenal ulcers. It is an ANTICHOLINERGIC drug, but with properties different from many others in this class, and works by inhibiting the receptors in the stomach lining that ordinarily evoke the production of gastric acids and digestive juices from the stomach, so reducing the overall acidity around the ulcerated area. Administration is oral in the form of tablets to be taken before meals.

▲ side-effects: side-effects are uncommon, but there may be dry mouth and slight visual disturbance. Blood disorders have been reported.

✸ warning: in resistant cases it may be used simultaneously with drugs like CIMETIDINE, which are thought to form a protective layer over the healing ulcer.
*Related article:* GASTROZEPIN.

**piretanide** is a DIURETIC used primarily to treat mild to moderate high blood pressure (*see* ANTIHYPERTENSIVE). Administration is oral in the form of sustained-release capsules.

▲ side-effects: side-effects are rare, but there may be nausea and vomiting, with diarrhoea and gastrointestinal disturbances; some patients experience sensitivity reactions such as rashes. High dosage in the elderly may lead to excessive diuresis and consequent circulatory disorders.

● warning: piretanide should not be administered to patients who have any form of electrolyte imbalance; this is because the drug itself tends to cause a reduction in blood potassium. Regular checks on liver and kidney function during treatment are therefore essential.
*Related article:* ARELIX.

**Piriton** (*Allen & Hanburys*) is a proprietary, non-prescription preparation of the ANTIHISTAMINE chlorpheniramine maleate, used to treat allergic conditions such as hay fever and urticaria. It is produced in the form of tablets, as sustained-release tablets ('spandets', not recommended for children), and as a syrup for dilution (the potency of the syrup once dilute is retained for 14 days); it is also produced in ampoules for injection, but in that form is available only on prescription, and is not recommended for children.
▲ / ● side-effects/warning: *see* CHLORPHENIRAMINE.

**piroxicam** is a non-steroidal, ANTI-INFLAMMATORY ANALGESIC used to treat pain and inflammation in rheumatic disease and other musculo-skeletal disorders (such as acute gout). Administration is oral in the form of capsules and soluble (dispersible) tablets, and topical in the form of anal suppositories.
▲ side-effects: there may be nausea and gastrointestinal disturbance, either or both of which may be reduced by taking the drug with milk or food. Some patients experience sensitivity reactions (such as headache, ringing in the ears – tinnitus – and vertigo), fluid retention, and/or blood disorders.

● warning: piroxicam should be administered with caution to patients with allergies, gastric ulceration or impaired liver or kidney function, or who are pregnant. Prolonged high dosage increases the risk of gastrointestinal disturbances.
*Related articles:* FELDENE; LARAPAM.

**Pitressin** (*Parke-Davis Medical*) is a proprietary preparation of argipressin, which is a synthetic version of the hormone vasopressin. Available only on prescription, it is administered primarily to diagnose or to treat pituitary-originated diabetes insipidus, and to treat the haemorrhaging of varicose veins in the oesophagus (the tubular channel for food between throat and stomach). Produced in ampoules for injection (generally in hospitals only).
▲ / ● side-effects/warning: *see* VASOPRESSIN.

**pivampicillin** is a more readily absorbed form of the ANTIBIOTIC ampicillin that is converted in the body to ampicillin after absorption. It has similar actions and uses.
▲ / ● side-effects/warning: *see* AMPICILLIN.
*Related articles:* MIRAXID; PONDOCILLIN.

**pivmecillinam hydrochloride** is a form of the ANTIBIOTIC mecillinam that can be taken orally. It has similar actions and uses.
▲ / ● side-effects/warning: *see* MECILLINAM.
*Related articles:* MIRAXID; SELEXID.

**Piz Buin** (*Ciba*) is a proprietary, non-prescription brand of barrier creams for topical application, containing constituents able to protect the skin from ultraviolet radiation (such as with radiotherapy or as a sunscreen). A lipstick having similar constituents is also available.

**pizotifen** is an ANTIHISTAMINE structurally related to TRICYCLIC antidepressant drugs. It is used to treat and prevent headaches, particularly those in which blood pressure inside the blood vessels plays a part – such as migraine. Administration is oral in the form of tablets and an elixir.

▲ side-effects: concentration and speed of thought and movement may be affected. There may be drowsiness, dry mouth and blurred vision, with constipation and difficulty in urinating; sometimes there is muscle pain and/or nausea. Patients may put on weight.

◆ warning: pizotifen should not be administered to patients with closed-angle glaucoma or urinary retention. The effects of alcohol may be enhanced. *Related article:* SANOMIGRAN.

**PK Aid 1** (*Scientific Hospital Supplies*) is a proprietary, non-prescription nutritional supplement for patients who suffer from amino acid abnormalities (such as phenylketonuria). It contains essential and non-essential amino acids – except phenylalanine. It is produced in the form of a powder.

**PK Aid 3** (*Scientific Hospital Supplies*) is a proprietary, non-prescription nutritional supplement for patient who suffer from amino acid abnormalities (such as phenylketonuria). It contains essential and non-essential amino acids – except phenylalanine.

**PK 2** (*Milupa*) is a proprietary, non-prescription nutritional supplement for patients who suffer from amino acid

abnormalities (such as phenylketonuria). It contains essential and non-essential amino acids – except phenylalanine; with vitamins, minerals and trace elements, and 7.1% sucrose; flavoured with vanilla. It is produced in the form of granules.

**PK 3** (*Milupa*) is a proprietary, non-prescription nutritional supplement for patients who suffer from amino acid abnormalities (such as phenylketonuria). It contains essential and non-essential amino acids – except phenylalanine; with vitamins, minerals and trace elements, and 3.4% sucrose; flavoured with vanilla. It is produced in the form of granules. It is not recommended for children under 8 years.

**P.K.U. Drink** (*Nutricia*) is a proprietary, non-prescription nutritional supplement. It is a whey and butterfat drink providing protein (including the amino acid phenylalanine), lactose and fat.

**Plaquenil** (*Sterling Research*) is a proprietary, ANTI-INFLAMMATORY drug, available only on prescription, used primarily to treat rheumatoid arthritis and forms of the skin disease lupus erythematosus. Treatment of rheumatoid arthritis may take up to 6 months to achieve full effect. The drug is also used in the prevention and treatment of malaria. Produced in the form of tablets, Plaquenil is a preparation of hydroxychloroquine sulphate.

▲/◆ side-effects/warning: *see* HYDROXYCHLOROQUINE.

**Plasma-Lyte** (*Travenol*) is the name of a selection of proprietary infusion fluids for the intravenous nutrition of a patient in whom feeding via the alimentary tract is not possible. All contain glucose in the form of dextrose, and water.

**plasma protein solution** is a solution containing the blood proteins derived from blood plasma, serum or normal placentas. Since only certain soluble proteins and electrolytes are present, and clotting factors, their antibodies, and also cholinesterases have been removed, the preparations may be given regardless of blood group of the recipient. Preparation may be used in states associated with low blood proteins (hypoproteinaemia), such as after burns or surgery. It is available in the form of a concentrated or isotonic solution for intravenous infusion.

▲ side-effects: chills, nausea, fever; especially if infusion is rapid.

✿ warning: do not use in severe anaemia or in cardiac failure. Caution is required in a wide variety of conditions including cardiovascular diseases.
*Related articles:* PLASMA PROTEIN SOLUTION 4.5%; PLASMATEIN 5%.

**Plasma Protein Solution 4.5%** (*SNBTS*) is a non-proprietary form of PLASMA PROTEIN SOLUTION, used to correct hypoproteinaemia, available only on prescription. The preparation is available in bottles for infusion.
▲/✿ side-effects/warning: *see* PLASMA PROTEIN SOLUTION

**Plasmatein 5%** (*Alpha*) is a proprietary form of PLASMA PROTEIN SOLUTION, used to correct hypoproteinaemia, available only on prescription. The preparation is available in bottles for infusion.
▲/✿ side-effects/warning: *see* PLASMA PROTEIN SOLUTION.

**Platet** (*Nicholas*) is a proprietary preparation of the ANTI-INFLAMMATORY, non-narcotic

ANALGESIC drug ASPIRIN, used here to reduce blood platelet adhesion, and thus formation of blood clots (thrombi). It is particularly indicated after problems relating to blocked blood vessels, such as myocardial infarction or cerebrovascular disease. Platet is available without prescription, in the form of effervescent tablets in two strengths (the stronger is named Platet-300).
▲/✿ side-effects/warning: *see* ASPIRIN.

**Plesmet** (*Napp*) is a proprietary, non-prescription preparation of ferrous glycine sulphate, used as an IRON supplement in the treatment of iron-deficiency anaemia, and produced in the form of a syrup for dilution (the potency of the syrup once dilute is retained for 14 days).
▲/✿ side-effects/warning: *see* FERROUS GLYCINE SULPHATE.

**plicamycin**, formerly called mithramycin, is a CYTOTOXIC drug that has ANTIBIOTIC properties. It is no longer used as a cytotoxic drug but now is used solely in the emergency treatment of excessive levels of calcium in the blood caused by malignant disease. Administration is by injection.
▲ side-effects: there may be nausea and vomiting, with hair loss. The blood-cell producing capacity of the bone-marrow is reduced.
✿ warning: the drug is toxic; dosage should be the least that is effective. Regular blood counts are essential during treatment.
*Related article:* MITHRACIN.

**Pluserix** (*Smith Kline & French*) is the MMR VACCINE used to treat children in the prevention of measles/mumps/rubella (German measles). It is available only on prescription, and is made available by Local Health Authorities.

▲/● side-effects/warning: *see* MMR VACCINE.

**pneumococcal vaccine** is a VACCINE against pneumonia, consisting a suspension of polysaccharides from a number of capsular types of pneumococci, administered by subcutaneous or intramuscular injection. Like the influenza vaccine, it is intended really only for those people at risk from infection in a community – and at risk from an identified pneumococcal strain prevalent within that community. Immunity is reckoned to last for about 5 years.

  ● warning: vaccination should not be given to patients who are aged under 2 years, who have any form of infection, or who are pregnant. It should be administered with caution to those with cardiovascular or respiratory disease. Some patients experience sensitivity reactions, which may be serious. Although protection may last for only 5 years, revaccination should be avoided because of the risk of adverse reactions.

**Pneumovax** (*Morson*) is a proprietary form of the pneumococcal vaccine, available only on prescription for the immunization of personnel for whom the risk of contracting pneumococcal pneumonia is unusually high.

  ● warning: see PNEUMOCOCCAL VACCINE.

**podophyllin** is a non-proprietary compound paint for the topical treatment of verrucas (plantar warts) and warts in the ano-genital region. It is a solution of PODOPHYLLUM RESIN, a highly acidic substance.

▲ side-effects: application may cause pain (because of the acidity).

● warning: the paint should not be used on the face. The maximum duration for paint to remain on the skin is 6 hours: it should then be washed off. Avoid areas of normal skin. Do not attempt to treat a large number or a whole area of warts at any one time: the highly acidic drug may be absorbed. Pregnant patients are advised *not* to use the paint. *Related article:* CONDYLINE; POSALFILIN.

**podophyllum resin** is the highly acidic substance from which podophyllin compound paint is derived.

▲/● side-effects/warning: *see* PODOPHYLLIN. *Related articles:* CONDYLINE; POSALFILIN; WARTICON.

**Point-Two** (*Hoyt*) is a proprietary, non-prescription form of fluoride supplement for administration in areas where the water supply is not fluoridated, especially to growing children. Produced in the form of a mouth-wash, Point-Two is a preparation of SODIUM FLUORIDE.

**poldine methylsulphate** is an ANTICHOLINERGIC and ANTISPASMODIC drug used to assist in the treatment of gastrointestinal disorders that involve muscle spasm of the intestinal wall. Administration is oral in the form of tablets.

▲ side-effects: there is commonly dry mouth and thirst; there may also be visual disturbances, flushing, irregular heartbeat and constipation. Rarely, there may be high temperature accompanied by delirium.

● warning: poldine methyl-sulphate should not be administered to patients with glaucoma; it should be

administered with caution to those with heart problems and rapid heart rate, ulcerative colitis, urinary retention or enlargement of the prostate gland; who are elderly; or who are breast feeding.
*Related article:* NACTON.

**poliomyelitis vaccine** is a VACCINE available in two types. Poliomyelitis vaccine, inactivated, is a suspension of dead viruses injected into the body for the body to generate antibodies and so become immune. Poliomyelitis vaccine live, is a suspension of live but attenuated polio viruses (of polio virus types 1, 2 and 3) for oral administration. In the United Kingdom, the live vaccine is the medium of choice, and the administration is generally simultaneous with the administration of the diphtheria-pertussis-tetanus (DPT) vaccine three times during the first year of life, and a booster at school entry age. The inactivated vaccine remains available for those patients for whom there are contra-indications.
💊 warning: poliomyelitis vaccine should not be administered to patients known to have immunodeficiency disorders, who have diarrhoea or cancer, where there is infection, or who are pregnant. Parents of a recently inoculated baby must take extra hygienic precautions when changing its nappies.

**Pollon-eze** (*Janssen*) is a proprietary, non-prescription ANTIHISTAMINE, with less sedative properties than many others, used to treat the symptoms of allergic disorders such as hay fever and urticaria (skin rashes). Produced in the form of tablets, it is a preparation of astemizole.
▲/💊 side-effects/warning: *see* ASTEMIZOLE.

**pol/vac (inact)** is an abbreviation for poliomyelitis vaccine, inactivated.
*see* POLIOMYELITIS VACCINE.

**pol/vac (oral)** is an abbreviation for poliomyelitis vaccine, live (oral).
*see* POLIOMYELITIS VACCINE.

**Polybactrin** (*Calmic*) is a proprietary ANTIBIOTIC, available only on prescription, used either as a powder for reconstitution as a solution for bladder irrigation to treat bladder and urethral infections, or in the form of a powder spray as a topical treatment for minor burns and wounds. In each case, active constituents are polymyxin B sulphate, neomycin sulphate and bacitracin.
▲/💊 side-effects/warning: *see* BACITRACIN; NEOMYCIN; POLYMYXIN B.

**Polycal** (*Cow & Gate*) is a proprietary, non-prescription nutritional supplement for patients with renal failure, liver cirrhosis, disorders of amino acid metabolism and protein intolerance, and who require a high-energy, low-fluid diet. Produced in the form of a powder for solution, Polycal contains glucose, maltose and polysaccharides.

**Polycose** (*Abbott*) is a proprietary, non-prescription nutritional supplement for patients with renal failure, liver cirrhosis, disorders of amino acid metabolism and protein intolerance, and who require a high-energy, low-fluid diet. Produced in the form of a powder for solution, Polycose contains GLUCOSE polymers.

**Polycrol** (*Nicholas*) is a proprietary, non-prescription ANTACID. Used to treat severe indigestion, heartburn, stomach acidity and flatulence, and produced in the form of tablets (in two strengths, the stronger under the name Polycrol Forte) and a sugar-free gel (in two strengths, the stronger under the name Polycrol Forte Gel), Polycrol is a preparation that contains aluminium hydroxide, MAGNESIUM HYDROXIDE, and the antifoaming agent DIMETHICONE. Most of these preparations are not recommended for children aged under 12 months.

**polyestradiol phosphate** is a compound OESTROGEN used to treat cancer of the prostate gland. Because this type of cancer is linked to the presence of androgens (male sex hormones), administration of this female sex hormone – although it produces some symptoms of feminization – is an effective counter-measure. Administration is by injection.
▲ side-effects: there may be nausea and vomiting. A common effect is weight gain, generally through fluid or sodium retention in the tissues. There may also be headache and/or depression; sometimes a rash breaks out.
✿ warning: caution should be exercised in administering polyestradiol to patients who are diabetic or epileptic, who have heart or kidney disease, or who have high blood pressure (hypertension) or recurrent severe migraine.
▲ / ✿ side-effects/warning: *see* ETHINYLOESTRADIOL.

**Polyfax** (*Calmic*) is a proprietary ANTIBIOTIC preparation, available only on prescription, used by topical application to treat infections of the skin and the eye. Produced in the form of an ointment in a paraffin base, and as an eye ointment, Polyfax is a preparation of polymyxin B

sulphate and bacitracin zinc.
▲ / ✿ side-effects/warning: *see* BACITRACIN; POLYMYXIN B.

**polygeline** is a special refined, partly degraded, form of the hydrolyzed animal protein gelatin, used in infusion with saline (sodium chloride) as a means of expanding overall blood volume in patients whose blood volume is dangerously low through shock, particularly in cases of severe burns or septicaemia.
▲ side-effects: rarely, there are hypersensitive reactions.
✿ warning: polygeline should not be administered to patients with congestive heart failure, severely impaired kidney function, or certain blood disorders; ideally, blood samples for cross-matching should be taken before administration.
*Related article:* HAEMACCEL.

**polymyxin B** is an ANTIBIOTIC used to treat several forms of bacterial infection, particularly those of the gram-negative organisms, including *Pseudomonas aeruginosa*. Its use would be more popular were it not so toxic. Because of its toxicity, administration (as polymyxin B sulphate) is usually topical in the form of solutions (as in eye-drops and ear-drops) or ointments, and only rarely by injection or infusion.
▲ side-effects: there may be numbness and tingling in the limbs, blood and protein in the urine, dizziness, breathlessness and overall weakness.
✿ warning: polymyxin B should not be administered to patients with the neuromuscular disease myasthenia gravis; it should be administered with caution to those with impaired kidney function.
*Related articles:* AEROSPORIN; GREGODERM; NEOSPORIN;

Otosporin; Polybactrin; Polyfax; Polytrim; Tribiotic.

**polynoxylin** is a mild ANTIFUNGAL agent. It is used primarily to treat fungal infections of the mouth and throat (such as thrush). Administration is oral in the form of lozenges.
*Related article:* ANAFLEX.

**polysaccharide-iron complex** is an IRON-rich compound used to restore iron to the blood (in the form of haemoglobin) in cases of iron-deficiency anaemia. Once a patient's blood haemoglobin level has reached normal, treatment should nevertheless continue for at least three months to replenish fully the reserves of iron in the body.
▲ side-effects: large doses may cause gastrointestinal upset and diarrhoea; there may be vomiting. Prolonged treatment may result in constipation.
✴ warning: polysaccharide-iron complex should not be administered to patients already taking tetracycline antibiotics.
*Related article:* NIFEREX.

**polystyrene sulphonate resins** are used to treat excessively high levels of potassium in the blood such as dialysis patients. Administration is oral in the form of a solution, or topical in the form of a retention enema (to be retained for as long as 9 hours, if possible). Adequate fluid intake during oral treatment is essential, to prevent impaction of the resins.
▲ side-effects: some patients treated by enema experience rectal ulcers.
✴ warning: resins that contain calcium should be avoided in patients with metastatic cancer or abnormal secretion by the parathyroid glands. Resins that contain sodium

should be avoided by patients with congestive heart failure or impaired kidney function.
*Related articles:* CALCIUM RESONIUM; RESONIUM-A.

**Polytar Emollient** (*Stiefel*) is a proprietary, non-prescription brand of preparations used to treat non-infective skin inflammations, including psoriasis and eczema. The standard form is produced in the form of a bath additive, and is a preparation of ANTISEPTICS and natural oils including COAL TAR and ARACHIS OIL. An alcohol-based shampoo is also available (under the name Polytar Liquid), as is a gelatin-based shampoo (under the name Polytar Plus Liquid).

**polythiazide** is a DIURETIC, one of the THIAZIDES, used to treat fluid retention in the tissues (oedema), hypertension (high blood pressure) and mild to moderate heart failure. Because all thiazides tend to deplete body reserves of potassium, polythiazide may be administered in combination either with potassium supplements or with diuretics that are complementarily potassium-sparing. Administration is oral in the form of tablets.
▲ side-effects: there may be tiredness and a rash. In men, temporary impotence may occur.
✴ warning: polythiazide should not be administered to patients with kidney failure or urinary retention, or who are lactating. It should be administered with caution to those who are pregnant. It may aggravate conditions of diabetes or gout.
*Related article:* NEPHRIL.

**Polytrim** (*Wellcome*) is a proprietary ANTIBIOTIC, available only on prescription, used in the form of eye-drops to treat bacterial infections in the eye. Polytrim is a preparation of the antibiotics trimethoprim and polymyxin B sulphate.

▲/ ✚ side-effects/warning: *see* POLYMYXIN B; TRIMETHOPRIM.

**polyvinyl alcohol** is used as a surfactant tear-distributor, administered in the form of eye-drops to patients whose lachrymal apparatus is dysfunctioning. It works by helping the aqueous layer provided by the lachrymal apparatus (tear fluid) to spread across an eyeball on which the normal mucous surface is patchy or missing.
*Related articles:* HYPOTEARS; LIQUIFILM TEARS; SNO TEARS.

**Ponderax** (*Servier*) is a proprietary APPETITE SUPPRESSANT, available only on prescription, used as a short-term additional treatment in medical therapy for obesity. Produced in the form of sustained-release capsules ('Pacaps'), Ponderax is a preparation of the potentially addictive drug fenfluramine hydrochloride. It is not recommended for children.

▲/ ✚ side-effects/warning: *see* FENFLURAMINE HYDROCHLORIDE.

**Pondocillin** (*Burgess*) is a proprietary ANTIBIOTIC, available only on prescription, used to treat systemic bacterial infections and infections of the upper respiratory tract, of the ear, nose and throat, and of the urogenital tracts. Produced in the form of tablets, as a sugar-free suspension, and as granules in sachets, Pondocillin is a preparation of the broad-spectrum penicillin pivampicillin.

▲/ ✚ side-effects/warning: *see* PIVAMPICILLIN.

**Ponstan** (*Parke-Davis*) is a proprietary, ANTI-INFLAMMATORY, non-narcotic ANALGESIC,

available only on prescription, used to treat pain in rheumatoid arthritis, osteoarthritis and other musculo-skeletal disorders. Produced in the form of capsules, as tablets, as soluble (dispersible) tablets (under the name Ponstan Dispersible), and as a children's suspension for dilution (the potency of the suspension once dilute is retained for 14 days), Ponstan is a preparation of mefenamic acid. None of these products is recommended for children aged under 6 months.

▲/ ✚ side-effects/warning: *see* MEFENAMIC ACID.

**Portagen** (*Bristol-Myers*) is a proprietary, non-prescription powdered nutritionally complete diet, used to treat patients whose metabolisms have difficulty in absorbing fats and are unable to tolerate lactose, such as in liver cirrhosis and after surgery of the intestine. Portagen is a preparation of proteins, glycerides, sucrose, vitamins and minerals, and is glucose- and lactose-free.

**Posalfilin** (*Norgine*) is a proprietary, non-prescription compound OINTMENT for topical application, intended to treat and remove ano-genital warts and verrucas (plantar warts). Posalfilin is a preparation of the KERATOLYTIC salicylic acid and the highly acidic substance PODOPHYLLUM RESIN. It should not be used for facial warts.

▲/ ✚ side-effects/warning: *see* SALICYLIC ACID; PODOPHYLLUM RESIN.

**Potaba** (*Glenwood*) is a proprietary preparation of potassium aminobenzoate, available only on prescription, used to treat scleroderma (hardening and contraction of connective tissue anywhere in the body). Produced in the form of capsules, as tablets

and as a powder in sachets ('envules'), Potaba is not recommended for children. Its therapeutic value is debatable.
▲/✿ side-effects/warning: *see*
POTASSIUM AMINOBENZOATE.

**potassium** is a metallic element that occurs naturally only in compounds. In the body, a highly sensitive balance is maintained between potassium within the cells and sodium in the fluids outside the cells (although chemically the two elements are very similar). Nerve impulses are transmitted by means of an almost instantaneous transference of potassium and sodium across cell membranes that sets up a momentary electric current. Deficiency or excess of potassium thus interferes with the actions of most nerves, and particularly those of the heart. Fluid loss from the body results in potassium loss – and therapeutically most potassium is administered to make up such losses, especially following the use of some potassium-depleting drugs (such as the THIAZIDE DIURETICS or CORTICOSTEROIDS). Compounds most used as potassium supplements are potassium bicarbonate and potassium chloride (the latter being a good substitute for natural salt – sodium chloride).

**potassium aminobenzoate** is a drug most commonly used in the treatment of conditions in which body tissues anywhere in the body become fibrous or hardened (scleroderma), and contract. How it works – and even whether it works – remains the subject of some debate. Administration is oral in the form of capsules, tablets or in solution.
▲ side-effects: there may be nausea. Treatment should be withdrawn if serious weight loss occurs.

✿ warning: potassium aminobenzoate should not be administered to patients who are already taking sulphonamide antibiotics; it should be administered with caution to those with impaired kidney function.
*Related article:* POTABA.

**potassium canrenoate** is a diuretic used to treat the fluid retention associated with heart or liver disease or disorder. Administration is by injection.
▲ side-effects: there may be nausea and vomiting, especially following high doses. Injection may cause pain.
✿ warning: potassium canrenoate should not be administered to patients with high levels of potassium in the blood or impaired kidney function. It should be administered with caution to those who are pregnant.
*Related article:* SPIROCTAN-M.

**potassium chloride** is used primarily as a POTASSIUM supplement to treat conditions of potassium deficiency, especially during or following severe loss of body fluids or treatment with drugs that deplete body reserves. It may also be used as a substitute for natural salt (sodium chloride) in cases where sodium is for one reason or another inadvisable. Administration is oral, or by injection or infusion.
*Related articles:* BRINALDIX K; BURINEX; CENTYL-K; DEXTROLYTE; DIARREST; DIORALYTE; DIUMIDE-K CONTINUS; ESIDREX K; GLANDOSANE; HYGROTON-K; KAY-CEE-L; KLOREF; LASIKAL; LASIX; LEO K; MICRO-K; NAVIDREX-K; NEO-NACLEX-K; NU-K; RAUTRAX; REHIDRAT; RUTHMOL; SANDO-K; SLOW-K.

**potassium citrate** administered orally has the effect of making the urine alkaline instead of acid.

This is of use in relieving pain in some infections of the urinary tract or the bladder. Administration is in the form of tablets or a non-proprietary liquid mixture.

▲ side-effects: there may be mild diuresis. Prolonged high dosage may lead to excessively high levels of potassium in the blood.

✦ warning: potassium citrate should be administered with caution to patients with heart disease or impaired kidney function.
*Related article:* EFFERCITRATE.

**potassium hydroxyquinoline sulphate** is a drug that has both ANTIBACTERIAL and ANTIFUNGAL properties – and is pleasant-smelling with it. It is used mostly as a constituent in anti-inflammatory and antibiotic creams and ointments that also contain corticosteroids, such as preparations used to treat acne. Rarely, it causes sensitivity reactions.
*Related articles:* QUINOCORT; QUINODEEM; QUINOPED.

**potassium perchlorate** was formerly used to treat overactivity of the thyroid gland (hyperthyroidism) and the consequent symptoms (thyrotoxicosis). It works by blocking the uptake of iodine by the thyroid gland, so preventing the production and secretion of thyroid hormones. However, treatment was then proved to be associated with the risk of anaemia, and there are now no proprietary forms available in the United Kingdom.

**potassium permanganate** is a general DISINFECTANT used in solution for cleaning burns and abrasions and maintaining asepsis in wounds that are suppurating or weeping.

✦ warning: avoid splashing mucous membranes, to which it is an irritant. It also stains skin and fabric.

**povidone-iodine** is a complex of iodine on an organic carrier, used as an ANTISEPTIC in topical application to the skin, especially in sensitive areas (such as the vulva), and as a mouth wash. Produced in the form of a gel, a solution, or vaginal inserts (pessaries), it works by slowly releasing the iodine it contains.

▲ side-effects: rarely, there may be sensitivity reactions.

✦ warning: povidone-iodine should not be used during pregnancy or while lactating.
*Related articles:* BETADINE; DISADINE DP; VIDENE.

**practolol** is a BETA-BLOCKER used as an ANTIARRHYTHMIC drug used to treat tachycardia (fast heart rate), especially following a heart attack. It works by inhibiting the contractile capacity of the heart muscle. Administration is by slow intravenous injection.

▲ side-effects: the heart rate and blood pressure are reduced; there may rarely be heart failure and/or bronchospasm (producing asthma-like symptoms).

✦ warning: practolol should not be administered to patients who have already been given the anti-arrhythmic CALCIUM ANTAGONIST verapamil; it should be administered with caution to those who have had long-term respiratory depression.

**Pragmatar** (*Bioglan*) is a proprietary, non-prescription ointment used in topical application to treat chronic eczema and psoriasis. It is a preparation of various mildly KERATOLYTIC and antibiotic agents including SALICYLIC ACID in a water-miscible base.

**pralidoxime mesylate** is an unusual drug that is used virtually solely in combination with the belladonna alkaloid ATROPINE in the treatment of severe poisoning by organophosphoric compounds (such as those used as insecticides). The drug is particularly effective in reversing the dangerous muscular paralysis that may affect the entire body. Diagnosis is critical, in that the use of atropine and pralidoxime mesylate to treat poisoning by other compounds used as insecticides may have no effect whatever and can be dangerous. Administration is by injection; repeated doses may be required.

▲ side-effects: there is drowsiness, dizziness and visual disturbances, muscular weakness, nausea and headache, and rapid heart and breathing rate.

✹ warning: pralidoxime mesylate should be administered with caution to patients with the neuromuscular disease myasthenia gravis, or impaired kidney function.

**pravastin** is a very newly developed drug that is used to lower lipid (fat) levels in the blood where this is markedly elevated (hyperlipidaemia). It is used in patients who do not respond to, or who are intolerant of, other therapy. It acts by inhibiting one of the enzymes that catalyses a step in the synthesis within the body of cholesterol and is available in the form of tablets.

▲ side-effects: there may be constipation or diarrhoea, flatulence, fatigue or insomnia, rash. Raised levels of the enzyme creatine phospho-kinase.

✹ warning: liver function must be monitored. Do not administer in patients with liver disease, or who are pregnant or lactating, or where there is porphyria. Avoid pregnancy during, and for a month after, treatment.
*Related article:* LIPOSTAT.

**Praxilene** (*Lipha*) is a proprietary VASODILATOR that affects principally the blood vessels of the feet and hands, but also affects the blood supply to the brain. It is therefore used to relieve the symptoms of both cerebral and peripheral vascular disease. Produced in the form of capsules, and in ampoules for injection (under the name Praxilene Forte), it is a preparation of naftidrofuryl oxalate, and is not recommended for children.

▲/✹ side-effects/warning: *see* NAFTIDROFURYL OXALATE.

**prazepam** is an ANXIOLYTIC drug, one of the BENZODIAZEPINES, used primarily in the short-term to treat anxiety and states of nervous tension. Administration is oral in the form of tablets.

▲ side-effects: concentration and speed of reaction are affected. Drowsiness, dizziness, headache, dry mouth and shallow breathing are all fairly common. Elderly patients may enter a state of confusion. Sensitivity reactions may occur.

✹ warning: prazepam should be administered with caution to patients with severe respiratory difficulties, muscle weakness, glaucoma, or kidney or liver damage; who are in the last stages of pregnancy or are lactating; who are elderly or debilitated; or who have a history of drug abuse. Prolonged use or abrupt withdrawal of the drug should be avoided.

**praziquantel** is an ANTHELMINTIC, the drug of first choice in treating infections caused by schistosomes, the worms that can colonize the veins of a human host and cause bilharziasis. It is effective against all three human schistosomes. It is also useful in the treatment of tapeworm infestations. Praziquantel is of low toxicity and is active when taken orally. The drug is not marketed in the United Kingdom.

**prazosin** is a VASODILATOR, an ANTIHYPERTENSIVE drug of the ALPHA-BLOCKER class used to treat both high blood pressure (hypertension) and congestive heart failure. It works as a so MUSCLE RELAXANT that is so specific in action that it affects mainly the muscles that surround the smaller arteries. Administration is oral in the form of tablets.

▲ side-effects: blood pressure may be reduced, causing dizziness on standing up from lying or sitting. There may be weakness.

✿ warning: the initial reduction in blood pressure may be precipitous and cause collapse due to hypotension (low blood pressure) (for which reason, extreme caution should be observed in the treatment of patients with impaired kidney function). Later dosage may lead to rapid heart rate.
*Related article:* HYPOVASE.

**Precortisyl** (*Roussel*) is a proprietary CORTICOSTEROID preparation, available only on prescription, used to treat inflammation especially in allergic and rheumatic conditions (particularly those affecting the joints) and collagen disorders. It may also be used for systemic corticosteroid therapy. Produced in the form of tablets (in three strengths, the strongest under the name Precortisyl Forte), its active ingredient is the glucocorticoid steroid prednisolone. It is not

recommended for children aged under 12 months.
▲/✿ side-effects/warning: *see* PREDNISOLONE.

**Predenema** (*Pharmax*) is a proprietary CORTICOSTEROID preparation, available only on prescription, used to treat inflammation of the rectum and anus, and associated with haemorrhoids and ulcerative colitis. Produced in the form of a retention enema, Predenema is a preparation of the glucocorticoid steroid prednisolone meta-sulphobenzoate sodium. It is not recommended for children.
▲/✿ side-effects/warning: *see* PREDNISOLONE.

**Pred Forte** (*Allergen*) is a proprietary CORTICOSTEROID, available only on prescription, used to treat non-infective inflammatory conditions in and around the eye. Produced in the form of eye-drops, it contains prednisolone acetate.
▲/✿ side-effects/warning: *see* PREDNISOLONE.

**Prednesol** (*Glaxo*) is a proprietary CORTICOSTEROID preparation; available only on prescription, used to treat inflammation especially in allergic and rheumatic conditions (particularly those affecting the joints) and collagen disorders. It may also be used for systemic corticosteroid therapy. Produced in the form of tablets, its active ingredient is the glucocorticoid steroid prednisolone disodium phosphate. It is not recommended for children aged under 12 months.
▲/✿ side-effects/warning: *see* PREDNISOLONE.

**prednisolone** is a synthetic CORTICOSTEROID, a glucocorticoid used to treat inflammation especially in rheumatic and

allergic conditions (particularly
those affecting the joints or the
bronchial passages) and collagen
disorders, but also effective in the
treatment of ulcerative colitis, or
rectal or anal inflammation. It
may also be used for systemic
corticosteroid therapy.
Administration (as prednisolone,
prednisolone acetate,
prednisolone sodium phosphate or
prednisolone steaglate) is oral in
the form of tablets, or topical in
the form of creams, lotions and
ointments, as anal suppositories
and a retention enema, or by
injection.
▲ side-effects: treatment of
susceptible patients may
engender a euphoria, or a state
of confusion or depression.
Rarely, there is peptic
ulcer.
✚ warning: prednisolone should
not be administered to patients
with psoriasis; it should be
administered with caution to
the elderly (in whom
overdosage can cause
osteoporosis, 'brittle bones'). In
children, administration of
prednisolone may lead to
stunting of growth. The effects
of potentially serious
infections may be masked by
the drug during treatment.
Withdrawal of treatment must
be gradual.
*Related articles:* ANACAL;
DELTACORTRIL; DELTALONE;
DELTA-PHORICOL; DELTASTAB;
MINIMS PREDNISOLONE;
PRECORTISYL; PREDENEMA;
PRED FORTE; PREDNESOL;
PREDSOL; SCHERIPROCT;
SINTISONE.

**prednisone** is a synthetic
CORTICOSTEROID that is converted
in the body to the glucocorticoid
PREDNISOLONE, and is used to
treat inflammation especially in
rheumatic and allergic conditions
(particularly those affecting the
joints or the bronchial passages).

Administration is oral in the form
of tablets.
▲/✚ side-effects/warning: *see*
PREDNISOLONE.
*Related articles:*
DECORTISYL; ECONOSONE.

**Predsol** (*Glaxo*) is a proprietary
CORTICOSTEROID preparation,
available only on prescription,
used either to treat ulcerative
colitis and inflammations of the
rectum and anus especially in
Crohn's disease, or to treat non-
infected inflammatory ear and eye
conditions. Produced in the form
of a retention enema and anal
suppositories, and as ear- or eye-
drops, Predsol is a preparation of
the glucocorticoid prednisolone
sodium phosphate. Ear- and eye-
drops that additionally contain
the antibiotic neomycin sulphate
are also available (under the
name Predsol-N).
▲/✚ side-effects/warning: *see*
NEOMYCIN; PREDNISOLONE.

**Preferid** (*Brocades*) is a
proprietary form of the
CORTICOSTEROID drug budesonide,
available only on prescription to
treat severe non-infective
inflammation of the skin, for
instance eczema. Available in the
form of a cream and ointment.
▲/✚ side-effects/warning: *see*
BUDESONIDE.

**Prefil** (*Norgine*) is a proprietary,
non-prescription bulking agent,
used orally in the medical
treatment of obesity. It is
intended to work by causing a
patient to feel full. Produced in
the form of granules for solution,
Prefil is a preparation of
sterculia.
▲/✚ side-effects/warning: *see*
STERCULIA.

**Pregaday** (*Duncan, Flockhart*) is a
proprietary, non-prescription
VITAMIN-and-mineral supplement,
used to prevent iron and folic acid

deficiencies in pregnancy.
Produced in the form of tablets,
Pregaday is a preparation of
FERROUS FUMARATE and FOLIC
ACID.

**Pregestimil** (*Bristol-Myers*) is a
proprietary, non-prescription
nutritionally complete dietary
preparation, used by patients
whose metabolisms are unable to
tolerate sucrose, lactose or
protein, and who in addition have
difficulty in absorbing fats
following surgery of the intestine.
Produced in the form of a powder,
Pregestimil is a preparation of
glucose, the milk fat casein, corn
oil, modified starch, vitamins and
minerals, and is gluten-, sucrose-
and lactose-free.

**Pregnavite Forte F** (*Bencard*) is a
proprietary compound IRON and
VITAMIN preparation, which is not
usually available from the
National Health Service. It is
used mainly by patients during
pregnancy to avoid iron and folic
acid deficiency. Produced in the
form of tablets, Pregnavite Forte
F is a preparation of FERROUS
SULPHATE, RETINOL (vitamin A),
THIAMINE (vitamin B₁),
RIBOFLAVINE (vitamin B₂),
PYRIDOXINE (vitamin B₆),
NICOTINAMIDE (of the B complex),
FOLIC ACID, ASCORBIC ACID
(vitamin C), CALCIFEROL (vitamin
D) and calcium phosphate.

**Premarin** (*Ayerst*) is a proprietary
preparation of female sex
HORMONES, available only on
prescription, used to treat vaginal
and cervical disorders during the
menopause. Produced in the form
of tablets (in three strengths) and
as a vaginal cream for topical
application, Premarin is a
preparation of conjugated
oestrogens.

**Premence-28** (*Viabiotics*) is a
proprietary, non-prescription
formulation of nutrients for the

days preceeding menstruation. It
contains, VITAMIN B, magnesium
and IRON.

▲/● side-effects/warning: *see*
MAGNESIUM.

**Prempak C** (*Wyeth*) is a
proprietary HORMONE
preparation, available only on
prescription, used for the
replacement of female sex
hormones in women during and
following the menopause and to
treat atrophic vaginitis or
urethritis. Produced in the form
of tablets (in two strengths),
Prempak is a preparation of
conjugated OESTROGENS together
with the PROGESTOGEN norgestrel.

▲/● side-effects/warning: *see*
NORGESTREL.

**prenylamine** is a VASODILATOR
used primarily to prevent
recurrent attacks of angina
pectoris (heart pain). It works as
a CALCIUM ANTAGONIST by
inhibiting the contractile
capacity of the heart muscle.
Administration is oral in the form
of tablets.

▲ side-effects: there may be
nausea and vomiting, with
diarrhoea. Some patients faint
through a condition
corresponding to rapid
heartbeat combined with low
potassium levels. It should
therefore not be considered as
a first-line drug. Withdrawal
should be gradual.

● warning: prenylamine should
not be administered to patients
with severely impaired liver or
kidney function or severe heart
disease. Blood counts to check
on blood potassium levels are
advisable during treatment.
*Related article:* SYNADRIN.

**Prepidil** (*Upjohn*) is a proprietary
drug of the PROSTAGLANDIN
dinoprostone, available only on
prescription, administered to the
cervix as a vaginal gel, to cause
preinduction dilation.

▲/✹ side-effects/warning: *see*
DINOPROSTONE.

**Prepulsid** (*Janssen*) is a stomach
and intestine MOTILITY
STIMULANT. It is a proprietary
form of cisapride available only
on prescription, and available in
the form of tablets which are
taken 15-30 minutes before
meals.
▲/✹ side-effects/warning: *see*
CISAPRIDE.

**Prescal** (*Ciba*) is a proprietary
form of the CALCIUM ANTAGONIST
isradipine, used as an
ANTIHYPERTENSIVE to treat raised
blood pressure (hypertension).
Available only on prescription, as
tablets.
▲/✹ side-effects/warning: *see*
ISRADIPINE.

**Pressimmune** (*Hoechst*) is a
powerful proprietary
immunosuppressant, available
only on prescription (but
generally only in hospitals).
Synthesized as an antilymphocyte
immunoglobulin from plasma
taken from immunized horses, and
produced in ampoules for
injection, Pressimmune is used to
prevent tissue rejection following
transplant surgery.
▲/✹ side-effects/warning: *see*
IMMUNOGLOBULINS.

**Prestim** (*Leo*) is a proprietary
ANTIHYPERTENSIVE compound,
available only on prescription,
used to treat mild to moderate
high blood pressure
(hypertension). Produced in the
form of tablets (in two strengths,
the stronger under the name
Prestim Forte), it is a preparation
of the BETA-BLOCKER timolol
maleate and the diuretic THIAZIDE
bendrofluazide. It is not
recommended for children.
▲/✹ side-effects/warning: *see*
BENDROFLUAZIDE; TIMOLOL
MALEATE.

**Priadel** (*Delandale*) is a
proprietary drug,
available only on
prescription, used to treat
acute mania and to
prevent manic-depressive
illness. Produced in the
form of a sugar-free liquid,
it is a preparation of
lithium citrate. It is not
recommended for children.
▲/✹ side-effects/warning: *see*
LITHIUM.

**prilocaine** is primarily a local
ANAESTHETIC, the drug of choice
for very minor topical or minor
surgical procedures, especially in
dentistry (because it is absorbed
directly through mucous
membranes). Administration is (in
the form of a solution of
prilocaine hydrochloride) by
injection or topically as a cream.
▲ side-effects: there is generally a
slowing of the heart rate and a
fall in blood pressure. Some
patients under anaesthetic
become agitated, others enter a
state of euphoria. Sometimes
there is respiratory depression
and convulsions.
✹ warning: prilocaine should not
be administered to patients
with the neural disease
myasthenia gravis; it should be
administered with caution to
those with heart or liver
failure (in order not to cause
depression of the central
nervous system and
convulsions), or from epilepsy.
Dosage should be reduced for
the elderly and the debilitated.
Full facilities for emergency
cardio-respiratory
resuscitation should be on
hand during anaesthetic
treatment.
*Related articles:* CITANEST;
CITANEST WITH OCTAPRESSIN;
EMLA.

**Primacor** (*Sterling-Winthrop*) is a
PHOSPHODIESTERASE INHIBITOR
and is a proprietary form of

milrinone. It is used in the short term treatment of heart failure, especially where other drugs have not been successful. Available only on prescription, it is in a form for dilution before administration by intravenous infusion or injection.

▲/✿ side-effects/warning: *see* MILRINONE.

**Primalan** (*May & Baker*) is a proprietary ANTIHISTAMINE, available only on prescription, used to treat allergic symptoms in such conditions as hay fever. Produced in the form of tablets, Primalan is a preparation of the phenothiazine-type antihistamine mequitazine; it is not recommended for children.

▲/✿ side-effects/warning: *see* MEQUITAZINE.

**primaquine** is an ANTIMALARIAL drug used to destroy parasitic forms in the liver which are not destroyed by chloroquine. It is given for two to three weeks following successful killing by chloroquine of all blood cell forms of the malarial parasite. Administration is oral in the form of tablets.

▲ side-effects: there may be nausea and vomiting, anorexia and jaundice. Rarely, there are blood disorders or depression of the bone-marrow's capacity for forming new blood cells.

✿ warning: a blood count is essential before administration to check that a patient has sufficient blood levels of a specific enzyme, without which the presence of the drug may cause blood disorders. Primaquine should be administered with caution to patients who are pregnant.

**Primicor** (*Sterling-Winthrop*) is a PHOSPHODIESTERASE INHIBITOR and is a proprietary form of milrinone. It is used in the short-

term treatment of severe heart failure, especially where other drugs have not been successful. Available only on prescription, it is in a form for dilution before administration by intravenous infusion or injection.

▲/✿ side-effects/warning: *see* MILRINONE.

**primidone** is an ANTICONVULSANT drug used in the treatment of all forms of epilepsy (except absence seizures) and of tremors due to old age or infirmity. It is converted in the body to the BARBITURATE phenobarbitone, and its actions and effects are thus identical to those of that drug.

▲/✿ side-effects/warning: *see* PHENOBARBITONE.
*Related article:* MYSOLINE.

**Primolut N** (*Schering*) is a proprietary HORMONAL preparation, available only on prescription, used primarily to treat dysmenorrhoea and pre-menstrual syndrome, although it can additionally be used to make up a hormonal deficiency during or following the menopause. Produced in the form of tablets, Primolut N is a preparation of the PROGESTOGEN norethisterone.

▲/✿ side-effects/warning: *see* NORETHISTERONE.

**Primoteston Depot** (*Schering*) is a proprietary preparation of the ANDROGEN (male sex hormone) testosterone enanthate, available only on prescription, used to treat hormonal deficiency in men and inoperable breast cancer in women. It is produced in ampoules for long-acting (depot) injection.

▲/✿ side-effects/warning: *see* TESTOSTERONE.

**Primperan** (*Berk*) is a proprietary ANTINAUSEANT, available only on prescription, used to treat nausea and vomiting especially in gastrointestinal disorders, during treatment for cancer with cytotoxic drugs or radiotherapy, or in association with migraine. Produced in the form of tablets, as a sugar-free syrup for dilution (the potency of the syrup once dilute is retained for 14 days) and in ampoules for injection, Primperan is a preparation of metoclopramide hydrochloride. It is not recommended for children aged under 5 years.

▲/✦ side-effects/warning: *see* METOCLOPRAMIDE.

**Prioderm** (*Napp*) is a proprietary, non-prescription drug used to treat infestations of the scalp and pubic hair by lice (pediculosis), or of the skin by the itch-mite (scabies). Produced in the form of a lotion in an alcohol base, and as a cream shampoo, Prioderm is a preparation of the insecticide malathion.

▲/✦ side-effects/warning: *see* MALATHION.

**Pripsen** (*Reckitt & Colman*) is a proprietary, non-prescription ANTHELMINTIC, used to treat infections by threadworm and roundworm. Produced in the form of an oral powder, Pripsen is a preparation of the phenothiazine derivative piperazine phosphate with various stimulant laxatives, and is not recommended for children aged under 3 months.

▲/✦ side-effects/warning: *see* PIPERAZINE.

**Pro-Actidil** (*Wellcome*) is a proprietary, non-prescription ANTIHISTAMINE drug used to treat the symptoms of various allergic conditions, particularly hay fever and urticaria. Produced in the form of sustained-release tablets, Pro-Actidil is a preparation of the antihistamine triprolidine hydrochloride; it is not recommended for children.

▲/✦ side-effects/warning: *see* TRIPROLIDINE.

**Pro-Banthine** (*Gold Cross*) is a proprietary, ANTICHOLINERGIC, ANTISPASMODIC drug, available only on prescription, used to assist in the treatment of gastrointestinal disorders arising from muscular spasm of the intestinal walls. As a SMOOTH MUSCLE RELAXANT, it is also sometimes used to treat children for nocturnal bedwetting (because the bladder sphincter muscles have to contract to let urine through) or with retention enemas. Produced in the form of tablets, Pro-Banthine is a preparation of propantheline bromide.

▲/✦ side-effects/warning: *see* PROPANTHELINE BROMIDE.

**probenecid** is a drug that can be used to inhibit the excretion by the kidneys of penicillin and cephalosporin antibiotics, thus prolonging the antibiotics' effects.

▲ side-effects: side-effects are uncommon, but there may be nausea and vomiting, headache and flushing, dizziness and a rash, and frequent urination. Some patients experience blood disorders.

✦ warning: probenecid should not be administered to patients with blood disorders or kidney stones, who are undergoing an acute attack of gout, or who are already taking salicylate drugs (such as aspirin). It should be administered with caution to patients with peptic ulcer. The drug is ineffective in a patient with impaired kidney function. Initial administration should be accompanied by the administration of colchicine to ward off acute gout attacks. Adequate fluid intake is essential.

**probucol** is a drug used to treat high levels of cholesterol or other lipids (fats) within the bloodstream. It works by inhibiting the uptake of fats by the liver. Administration is oral in the form of tablets.

▲ side-effects: there may be nausea, vomiting, flatulence, abdominal pain and diarrhoea. Rarely there are sensitivity reactions – which may be serious.

✦ warning: probucol should not be administered to patients who are lactating. Pregnancy should be avoided during treatment and for 6 months afterwards.
*Related article:* LURSELLE.

**procainamide** is a BETA-BLOCKER, used as an ANTIARRHYTHMIC drug to treat heartbeat irregularities especially after a heart attack. Administration (as procainamide hydrochloride) is oral in the form of tablets and sustained-release tablets, or by injection.

▲ side-effects: there may be nausea, diarrhoea, high temperature, slow heart rate and rashes. In susceptible patients there may be heart failure and/or skin or blood disorders, especially after prolonged treatment.

✦ warning: procainamide should not be administered to patients with heart failure, heart block, or low blood pressure; it should be administered with caution to those with asthma, the neuromuscular disease myasthenia gravis or impaired kidney function, or who have already received treatment with lignocaine.
*Related articles:* PROCAINAMIDE DURULES; PRONESTYL.

**Procainamide Durules** (*Astra*) is a proprietary ANTIARRHYTHMIC drug, available only on prescription, used to treat heartbeat irregularities especially after a heart attack. Produced in the form of sustained-release

tablets, Procainamide Durules is a preparation of the BETA-BLOCKER procainamide hydrochloride; it is not recommended for children.

▲ / ✦ side-effects/warning: *see* PROCAINAMIDE.

**procaine** is a local ANAESTHETIC now seldom used. Once popular, it has been overtaken by anaesthetics that are longer-lasting and better absorbed through mucous membranes. Because of this poor absorption it cannot be used as a surface anaesthetic. It remains available, however, and may be used for regional anaesthesia or by infiltration, usually in combination with adrenaline. Administration (as procaine hydrochloride) is by injection.

▲ side-effects: rarely, there are sensitivity reactions – which may be serious.

✦ warning: the metabolite of procaine inhibits the action on the body of sulphonamide drugs.

**procaine penicillin** is a penicillin-type ANTIBIOTIC that is essentially a rather insoluble salt of benzylpenicillin. It is primarily used in long-lasting intramuscular (depot) injections to treat conditions such as syphilis and gonorrhoea, but may also be used to treat the equally serious condition gas gangrene following amputation. Benzylpenicillin is released slowly into the blood over a period of days, thus avoiding the need for frequent injections. Administration is by intramuscular injection.

▲ / ✦ side-effects/warning: *see* BENZYLPENICILLIN.

**procarbazine** is a CYTOTOXIC drug used to treat the lymphatic cancer Hodgkin's disease, other lymphatic growths, and some small solid tumours, such as of the bronchus. Administration is oral in the form of capsules.

▲ side-effects: there is a reduction in the capacity of the bone-marrow for producing new blood cells. There may also be nausea, vomiting and hair loss. Treatment should be withdrawn if a rash denoting hypersensitivity appears.

❧ warning: dietary counselling is essential before treatment with procarbazine. Alcohol consumption must be avoided during treatment. Regular blood counts are advisable. A reduced dose should be used in patients with kidney damage. *Related article:* NATULAN.

**prochlorperazine** is a phenothiazine derivative used as an ANTIPSYCHOTIC drug in the treatment of psychosis (such as schizophrenia); as an ANXIOLYTIC in the short-term treatment of anxiety; and as an ANTI-EMETIC in the prevention of nausea caused by gastrointestinal disorder, by chemotherapy and radiotherapy in the treatment of cancer, by motion within a vehicle, or by the vertigo that results from infection of the middle or inner ear. Administration (as prochlor-promazine maleate or prochlorpromazine mesylate) is oral in the form of tablets, sustained-release capsules and syrups, topical in the form of anal suppositories, or by injection.

▲ side-effects: concentration and speed of thought and movement may be affected. High doses may cause neuromuscular disorders, especially in children, the elderly or the debilitated.

❧ warning: prochlorpromazine should not be administered to patients with certain forms of glaucoma, whose blood-cell formation by the bone-marrow is reduced, or who are taking drugs that depress certain centres of the brain and spinal cord. It should be administered with caution to those with lung disease, cardiovascular disease, epilepsy, parkinsonism, abnormal secretion by the adrenal glands, impaired liver or kidney function, undersecretion of thyroid hormones (hypothyroidism), enlargement of the prostate gland, or any form of acute infection; who are pregnant or lactating; or who are elderly. Prolonged treatment requires checks on eye function and skin pigmentation. Withdrawal of treatment should be gradual. *Related articles:* STEMETIL; VERTIGON.

**Proctofibe** (*Roussel*) is a proprietary, non-prescription LAXATIVE, which is not available from the National Health Service. A bulking agent – which works by increasing the overall mass of faeces within the rectum, so stimulating bowel movement – Proctofibe is a preparation of grain fibre and citrus fibre. Produced in the form of tablets, it is not recommended for children aged under 3 years, and counselling is advised before use.

**Proctofoam HC** (*Stafford-Miller*) is a proprietary CORTICOSTEROID compound with ANALGESIC properties, available only on prescription, used to treat, dress and soothe various painful conditions of the anus and rectum. Produced in the form of a foam in an aerosol, Proctofoam HC is a preparation of the corticosteroid hydrocortisone acetate and the ANAESTHETIC pramoxine hydrochloride. It is not recommended for children.

▲/❧ side-effects/warning: *see* HYDROCORTISONE ACETATE.

**Proctosedyl** (*Roussel*) is a proprietary CORTICOSTEROID compound with ANALGESIC properties, available only on prescription, used to treat, dress and soothe various painful conditions of the anus and rectum. Produced in the form of suppositories and as an ointment, Proctosedyl is a preparation that includes the corticosteroid hydrocortisone, the ANAESTHETIC cinchocaine hydrochloride, and the antibiotic framycetin sulphate.

▲/✱ side-effects/warning: *see* CINCHOCAINE; FRAMYCETIN; HYDROCORTISONE.

**procyclidine** is a powerful ANTICHOLINERGIC drug used to relieve some of the symptoms of parkinsonism, specifically the tremor of the hands, the overall rigidity of the posture, and the tendency to produce an excess of saliva. (The drug also has the capacity to treat these conditions in some cases where they are produced by drugs.) It is thought to work by compensating for the lack of dopamine in the brain that is the major cause of such parkinsonian symptoms. Administration – which may be in parallel with the administration of levodopa – is oral in the form of tablets or a syrup or by injection.

▲ side-effects: there may be dry mouth, dizziness and blurred vision, and/or gastrointestinal disturbances. Some patients experience sensitivity reactions and anxiety. Rarely, and in susceptible patients, there may be confusion, agitation and psychological disturbance (at which point treatment must be withdrawn).

✱ warning: procyclidine should not be administered to patients who suffer not merely from tremor but from distinct involuntary movements; it should be administered with caution to those with impaired kidney or liver function, cardiovascular disease, glaucoma, or urinary retention. Withdrawal of treatment must be gradual. *Related articles:* ARPICOLIN; KEMADRIN.

**Profasi** (*Serono*) is a proprietary preparation of human chorionic gonadotrophin (HCG), available only on prescription, used to treat undescended testicles in boys, and to treat women suffering from specific hormonal deficiency for infertility. It is produced in the form of a powder for reconstitution as a medium for injection.

▲/✱ side-effects/warning: *see* HCG.

**proflavine cream** is a non-proprietary formulation that includes beeswax, wool fat, liquid paraffin and some mild antibacterial agents; it is used in topical application as a dressing for minor skin infections, burns and abrasions.

✱ warning: wool fat causes sensitivity reactions in some patients.

**Proflex** (*Lederle*) is a non-narcotic ANALGESIC drug with good ANTI-INFLAMMATORY properties. It is a proprietary form of ibuprofen. Available without prescription, it is used topically as a cream applied to the skin to treat the inflammatory symptoms of arthritis and to relieve soft tissue pain.

▲/✱ side-effects/warning: *see* IBUPROFEN.

**Progesic** (*Lilly*) is a proprietary, non-steroidal, ANTI-INFLAMMATORY, non-narcotic ANALGESIC used to relieve pain – particularly arthritic and rheumatic pain – and to treat other musculo-skeletal disorders.

Available only on prescription, and produced in the form of tablets, Progesic is a preparation of fenoprofen (as a calcium salt). It is not recommended for children.

▲/✿ side-effects/warning: *see* FENOPROFEN.

**progesterone** is a sex HORMONE, a PROGESTOGEN found predominantly in women, but that has a role in the sexual make-up also of men. In women it is produced and secreted mainly by the corpus luteum of the ovary, and is responsible for the preparation of the lining of the womb (the endometrium) once every menstrual cycle to receive a fertilized ovum. Most cycles come and go without fertilization (conception), but if a fertilized ovum does implant in the endometrium, the resultant formation of a placenta ensures the continuation of the supply of progesterone and so prevents further menstrual cycles while the pregnancy lasts. In men, small quantities of progesterone are secreted by the testes and by the adrenal glands. Therapeutically, progesterone is administered to women chiefly to treat premenstrual syndrome, but may also be used to prevent recurrent miscarriage or abnormal bleeding from the vagina. Administration is by anal or vaginal suppositories (pessaries), or by injection.

▲ side-effects: there may be acne, urticaria, fluid retention and consequent weight gain, and gastrointestainal disturbances; there may also be breast tenderness, irregular menstruation and a change in libido. Injection may cause pain.

✿ warning: progesterone should not be administered to patients who suffer from undiagnosed vaginal bleeding or from sex-hormone-linked cancer, or who

have a history of thrombosis. It should be administered with caution to those with high blood pressure (hypertension), diabetes, impaired liver or kidney function, or heart disease.
*Related articles:* CYCLOGEST; GESTONE.

**progestogens** are sex hormones that oppose or modify the action of some OESTROGENS. There are two main groups of progestogens: the natural progestogen PROGESTERONE and those like it (allyloestrenol, dydrogesterone, hydroxyprogesterone and medroxyprogesterone) and the analogues of TESTOSTERONE (such as norethisterone). All are synthesized for therapeutic use – and can therefore be taken orally – to prevent recurrent miscarriage, to relieve the symptoms of premenstrual syndrome or menstrual difficulty, or to treat lack of menstruation (amenorrhoea) or abnormal bleeding from the womb through the vagina. But perhaps the most widely used mode of application is as constituents (with or without accompanying oestrogens) in ORAL CONTRACEPTIVES, because progestogens prevent ovulation.

▲/✿ side-effects/warning: *see* PROGESTERONE.
*Related articles:*
ALLYLOESTRENOL;
DYDROGESTERONE;
HYDROXYPROGESTERONE
HEXANOATE;
LEVONORGESTREL;
LYNOESTRENOL;
MEDROXYPROGESTERONE
ACETATE; NORETHISTERONE;
NORETHISTERONE ACETATE;
NORGESTREL.

**proguanil** is an ANTIMALARIAL drug used to try to prevent the contraction of malaria by travellers in tropical countries. Its effectiveness is not guaranteed, and the traveller is advised to take measures as far as possible to avoid being bitten by mosquitoes. In some areas concurrent prophylactic treatment with chloroquine is advised. Administration (as proguanil hydrochloride) is oral in the form of tablets.

▲ side-effects: there may be mild gastric disorder.

✿ warning: proguanil should be administered with caution to patients who suffer from impaired kidney function.
*Related article:* PALUDRINE.

**Progynova** (*Schering*) is a proprietary OESTROGEN preparation available only on prescription, used to treat vaginal and cervical disorders during the menopause. Produced in the form of tablets (in two strengths), Progynova is a preparation of oestradiol valerate.

▲/✿ side-effects/warning: *see* OESTRADIOL.

**prolintane** is a weak STIMULANT used as a constituent in some proprietary vitamin preparations, and intended to assist in the treatment of fatigue or lethargy. Prolonged or high dosage, however, may lead to a state of arousal or anxiety.
*Related article:* VILLESCON.

**Proluton Depot** (*Schering*) is a proprietary form of the PROGESTOGEN (sex hormone) hydroxyprogesterone hexanoate, available only on prescription, used to treat recurrent miscarriage. It is produced in ampoules (in two strengths) for long-lasting (depot) injection.

▲/✿ side-effects/warning: *see* HYDROXYPROGESTERONE HEXANOATE.

**promazine hydrochloride** is an ANTIPSYCHOTIC drug used to tranquillize agitated patients,

especially patients who are elderly. The drug is also used in the short term to treat severe anxiety, or to soothe patients who are dying. Administration is oral in the form of a suspension, or by injection.

▲ side-effects: concentration and speed of thought and movement are affected; the effects of alcohol consumption are enhanced. There may be dry mouth and blocked nose, constipation and difficulty in urinating, rash, jaundice and blurred vision; menstrual disturbances in women or impotence in men may occur, with weight gain; there may be sensitivity reactions. Some patients feel cold and depressed, and tend to suffer from poor sleep patterns. Blood pressure may be low and the heartbeat irregular. Treatment by intramuscular injection may be painful.

✿ warning: promazine hydrochloride should not be administered to patients with certain forms of glaucoma (closed-angle), whose blood-cell formation by the bone-marrow is reduced, or who are taking drugs that depress certain centres of the brain and spinal cord. It should be administered with caution to those with lung disease, cardiovascular disease, epilepsy, parkinsonism, abnormal secretion by the adrenal glands, impaired liver or kidney function, undersecretion of thyroid hormones (hypothyroidism), enlargement of the prostate gland or any form of acute infection; who are pregnant or lactating; or children. Prolonged use requires regular checks on eye function and skin pigmentation. Withdrawal of treatment should be gradual.
*Related article:* SPARINE.

**promethazine hydrochloride** is a powerful ANTIHISTAMINE that also has HYPNOTIC and ANTITUSSIVE properties. Consequently, although it is used to treat the symptoms of allergic conditions (such as hay fever and urticaria, but additionally including the emergency treatment of anaphylactic shock), it is used also to induce sleep in the treatment of insomnia (especially in children) or as a premedication prior to surgery, and as a cough suppressant in cough linctuses. It may also be used in the treatment of parkinsonism, and as an ANTI-EMETIC in the prevention of nausea due to motion sickness or to ear infection. Its effect is comparatively long-lasting. Administration is oral in the form of tablets and a dilute elixir, or by injection.

▲ side-effects: concentration and speed of thought and movement may be affected. There may be headache, drowsiness and dry mouth, with gastrointestinal disturbances. Some patients experience blurred vision and/or sensitivity reactions on the skin.

✿ warning: promethazine should be administered with caution to patients with epilepsy, glaucoma, liver disease or enlargement of the prostate gland. During treatment, alcohol consumption must be avoided.
Related articles: MEDISED; PAMERGAN P100; PHENERGAN; PHENSEDYL; SOMINEX.

**promethazine theoclate** is a salt of the powerful ANTIHISTAMINE promethazine, used primarily to prevent nausea and vomiting caused by motion sickness or infection of the ear. It is slightly longer-acting than the hydrochloride, but otherwise is similar in every respect.

▲/✿ side-effects/warning: see PROMETHAZINE HYDROCHLORIDE.
Related article: AVOMINE.

**Prominal** (*Winthrop*) is a proprietary form of the BARBITURATE methylpheno-barbitone, and is on the controlled drugs list. Produced in the form of tablets (in three strengths), Prominal is used to treat tonic-clonic and partial seizure epilepsy. It is not recommended for children.
▲/✿ side-effects/warning: see METHYLPHENOBARBITONE.

**Prondol** (*Wyeth*) is a proprietary ANTIDEPRESSANT drug, available only on prescription, used to treat depressive illness and associated symptoms. Produced in the form of tablets (in two strengths), Prondol is a preparation of the TRICYCLIC drug iprindole hydrochloride; it is not recommended for children.
▲/✿ side-effects/warning: see IPRINDOLE.

**Pronestyl** (*Squibb*) is a proprietary ANTIARRHYTHMIC drug, available only on prescription, used to treat irregularities in the heartbeat, especially after a heart attack. Produced in the form of tablets and in vials for injection, Pronestyl is a preparation of the PROCAINE derivative procainamide hydrochloride. It is not recommended for children.
▲/✿ side-effects/warning: see PROCAINAMIDE.

**Propaderm** (*Allen & Hanburys*) is a proprietary brand of CORTICOSTEROID preparations, available only on prescription, used in topical application to treat severe non-infective skin inflammation such as eczema, especially in patients whose conditions have not responded to

less powerful corticosteroids.
Produced in its standard form of a
cream and ointment, Propaderm
is a preparation of the steroid
beclomethasone dipropionate. An
ointment additionally containing
the ANTIBACTERIAL drug
chlortetracycline hydrochloride
(under the name Propaderm-A) is
available for infective skin
inflammation, and a cream and an
ointment additionally containing
the iodine-rich ANTISEPTIC
clioquinol (under the name
Propaderm-C) are also available.
▲/● side-effects/warning: see
   BECLOMETHASONE
   DIPROPIONATE;
   CHLORTETRACYCLINE;
   CLIOQUINOL.

**propafenone hydrochloride** is an
ANTIARRHYTHMIC drug used to
prevent and treat irregularities of
heart beat (arryhythmias), and is
administered as tablets (after
food).
▲ side-effects: there may be
   nausea, vomiting, fatigue,
   dizziness, rash, postural
   hypotension (especially in the
   elderly), diarrhoea,
   constipation, dry mouth,
   blurred vision, occasionally
   heart and blood disorders.
● warning: it should be
   administered with care in the
   elderly, pregnant, or in cases of
   liver impairment. Avoid in
   patients with severe heart
   conditions, electrolyte
   imbalance, and obstructive
   lung disease.
   Related article: ARTHMOL.

**Propain** (*Panpharma*) is a
proprietary, non-prescription
compound ANALGESIC, which is
not available from the National
Health Service. It is used to treat
many forms of pain, including
headache, migraine, muscular
pain and menstrual problems.
Produced in the form of tablets,
Propain is a compound that

includes the OPIATE codeine
phosphate, the ANTIHISTAMINE
diphenhydramine hydrochloride,
the ANALGESIC paracetamol and
the STIMULANT caffeine. It is not
recommended for children.
▲/● side-effects/warning: see
   CAFFEINE; CODEINE
   PHOSPHATE;
   DIPHENHYDRAMINE
   HYDROCHLORIDE;
   PARACETAMOL.

**propamidine isethionate** is an
ANTIBIOTIC drug used specifically
in the form of eye-drops to treat
bacterial infections of the eyelids
(blepharitis) or conjunctiva
(conjunctivitis).
Related article: BROLENE.

**propantheline bromide** is an
ANTICHOLINERGIC drug used to
assist in the treatment of
gastrointestinal disorders that
involve muscle spasm of the
intestinal wall (and by the same
token to increase the duration of
enema retention in patients who
suffer from diarrhoea). It is also
used to treat urinary
incontinence and nocturnal
bedwetting in children.
Administration is oral in the form
of tablets.
▲ side-effects: there is commonly
   dry mouth and thirst; there
   may also be visual
   disturbances, flushing,
   irregular heartbeat, urinary
   retention and constipation.
   Rarely, there may be high
   temperature accompanied by
   delirium.
● warning: propantheline
   bromide should not be
   administered to patients with
   glaucoma; it should be
   administered with caution to
   those with heart problems and
   rapid heart rate, ulcerative
   colitis and other
   gastrointestinal disorders,
   urinary retention or
   enlargement of the prostate

gland; who are elderly; or who are breast feeding.
*Related article:* PRO-BANTHINE.

**Propine** (*Allergan*) is a proprietary SYMPATHOMIMETIC, available only on prescription, used in the form of eye-drops to treat glaucoma by relieving intra-ocular pressure. Propine is a preparation of the ADRENALINE derivative dipivefrine hydrochloride, which passes more readily through the cornea and is then converted to adrenaline. It is not recommended for children.
▲/◆ side-effects/warning: *see* DIPIVEFRINE.

**Pro-Plus** (*Ashe Consumer Products*) is a proprietary, non-prescription preparation of caffeine for use in reducing fatigue.
▲/◆ side-effects/warning: *see* CAFFEINE.

**propofol** is a general ANAESTHETIC used specifically for the initial induction of anaesthesia. Recovery after treatment is rapid and without any hangover effect. Administration is by injection.
▲ side-effects: there may sometimes be pain on injection, which can be overcome by prior administration of suitable premedication (such as a narcotic analgesic). Urine may turn green.
◆ warning: intravenous injection must be carried out with caution in order to avoid thrombophlebitis.
*Related article:* DIPRIVAN.

**propranolol** is a BETA-BLOCKER, used primarily to regularize the heartbeat and to treat and prevent angina pectoris (heart pain) and hypertension (*see* ANTIHYPERTENSIVE). It may additionally be used to relieve the symptoms of excess thyroid hormones in the bloodstream

(thyrotoxicosis), or of migraine, and it is also often used to relieve anxiety (particularly if there is tremor or palpitations). Administration (as propranolol hydrochloride) is oral in the form of tablets and sustained-release capsules, or by injection.
▲ side-effects: the heart rate is slowed; there may also be bronchospasm (causing asthma-like symptoms), gastrointestinal disturbances, and tingling or numbness in the fingers and toes.
◆ warning: propranolol should not be administered to patients with any serious form of heart disease, or asthma. It should be administered with caution to those with impaired liver or kidney function, who are nearing the end of pregnancy, or who are lactating.
*Related articles:* ANGILOL; APSOLOL; BEDRANOL; BEDRANOL S.R.; BERKOLOL; CARTROL; EMCOR; HALF-INDERAL LA; INDERAL; INDERAL-LA; INDERETIC; INDEREX; MONOCOR; SLOPROLOL.

**propylthiouracil** is a drug that prevents the production or secretion of the HORMONE thyroxine by the thyroid gland, so treating an excess in the blood of thyroid hormones and the symptoms that it causes (thyrotoxicosis). Treatment may be on a maintenance basis over a long period (dosage adjusted to optimum effect), or may be merely preliminary to surgical removal of the thyroid gland. Administration is oral in the form of tablets.
▲ side-effects: an itching rash may indicate a need for alternative treatment. There may also be nausea and headache; occasionally there is jaundice or hair loss. Rarely,

there may be a tendency to haemorrhage.

● warning: propylthiouracil should not be administered to patients with obstruction of the upper respiratory tract, and should be administered with extreme caution to patients who are pregnant or lactating.

**Prosigmin** (*Roche*) is a proprietary preparation of neostigmine, available only on prescription. The drug prolongs the action of the natural neurotransmitter ACETYLCHOLINE, and can thus be used both in the diagnosis of disorders of the neurotransmission process caused by disease such as myesthesia gravis or by drug treatments (through a comparison of its effect with the effect of its absence), and as an antidote to muscle relaxants and anaesthetics which block the action of the neurotransmitter (in which case, atropine should be administered simultaneously). It is produced in ampoules (in two strengths) for injection (in the form of neostigmine methylsulphate) and as tablets (as neostigmine bromide).

▲/● side-effects/warning: *see* NEOSTIGMINE.

**Prosobee** (*Bristol-Myers*) is a proprietary food product that is nutritionally a complete diet, for use by patients whose metabolic processes are unable to tolerate milk or lactose. Produced in the form of a liquid concentrate, it is a preparation of protein (soya protein), carbohydrate (corn syrup solids), fat (soya oil, coconut oil), VITAMINS, minerals and trace elements, and is gluten-, sucrose-, fructose- and lactose-free. Prosobee is also produced as a powder containing protein (soya protein), carbohydrate (corn syrup solids), fat (coconut oil,

corn oil) and vitamins and minerals that is also gluten-, sucrose-, fructose- and lactose-free.

**Prosparol** (*Duncan, Flockhart*) is a proprietary nutritional preparation for patients requiring a high energy, low fluid and low electrolyte diet. Produced in the form of an emulsion, Prosparol is a preparation of ARACHIS OIL in water.

**prostacyclin** is a technical term for the drug and naturally occuring compound more commonly known as eoprostenol.
*see* EPOPROSTENOL.

**prostaglandin** is the name given to members of a family of HORMONES having a local action, which are produced naturally by many organs and tissues in the body, both normally and in disease states. Naturally occurring members of the family such as prostaglandin E2 (DINOPROSTONE), prostaglandin F2 alpha (DINOPROST) and prostacyclin (EPOPROSTENOL) are used therapeutically, along with synthetic analogues. The uses of the prostaglandins reflect their high potency in causing such bodily actions as: contraction of the uterus and dilation of the cervix, dilation of blood vessel and prevention of platelet aggregation which leads to blood clots. Similarly, the side-effects of these agents used as drugs reflect other of their powerful actions: such as stimulating the intestine to cause pain, diarrhoea; actions on the brain to cause fever; and prolongation of bleeding.

**Prostin E2** (*Upjohn*) is a proprietary drug of the PROSTAGLANDIN dinoprostone, available only on prescription, used because of its property of causing uterine contractions mainly to induce and augment labour and therapeutic abortion. Produced in the form of tablets, as vaginal tablets (pessaries), as a vaginal gel (in two strengths), and in ampoules (in two strengths) for intravenous injection and in ampoules for extra-amniotic injection (both for hospital use only).

▲/ ✿ side-effects/warning: *see* DINOPROSTONE.

**Prostin F2 alpha** (*Upjohn*) is a proprietary form of the PROSTAGLANDIN F2 alpha, dinoprost, available only on prescription, used because of its property of causing uterine contractions mainly to induce and augment labour and therapeutic abortion. Produced in ampoules for intravenous injection, and in ampoules for intra-amniotic injection (for hospital use only).

▲/ ✿ side-effects/warning: *see* DINOPROST.

**Prostin VR** (*Upjohn*) is a proprietary form of the PROSTAGLANDIN alprostadil, available only on prescription, used to maintain newborn babies born with heart defects (closure of ductus arteriosus) while preparations are rapidly made for corrective surgery in intensive care. Produced in ampoules for dilution before infusion.

▲/ ✿ side-effects/warning: *see* ALPROSTADIL.

**protamine sulphate** is essentially a coagulant, in that its primary use is as an antidote to an overdose of the ANTICOAGULANT heparin. However, it too – in overdosage – has an anti-coagulant effect. Administration is by slow intravenous injection.

▲ side-effects: there is a reduction in heart rate and blood pressure; there is often also flushing.

✿ warning: dosage is critical: administration must be of enough to neutralize the heparin, but not so much as to contribute to further anticoagulation.

**Protaphane, Human:** *see* HUMAN PROTAPHANE.

✤ **Prothiaden** (*Boots*) is a proprietary ANTIDEPRESSANT drug, available only on prescription, used to treat depressive illness especially in cases where some degree of sedation is deemed necessary. Produced in the form of tablets and capsules, Prothiaden is a preparation of dothiepin hydrochloride. It is not recommended for children.

▲/ ✿ side-effects/warning: *see* DOTHIEPIN HYDROCHLORIDE.

**prothionamide** is an ANTITUBERCULAR drug also used to treat leprosy. It is not marketed in the United Kingdom.

**protirelin**, or thyrotrophin-releasing hormone (TRH), is a natural HORMONE produced and secreted by the thalamus; it acts on the pituitary gland in turn to produce and secrete thyrotrophin, a hormone that then causes the production and secretion of yet other hormones in the body. Therapeutically it is used primarily to assess thyroid function in patients who suffer from underactivity of the pituitary gland (hypopituitarism) or from overactivity of the thyroid gland (hyperthyroidism). Administration is oral in the form of tablets, or it can be given by injection.

▲ side-effects: there is commonly nausea. Treatment by injection may cause flushing, dizziness, faintness, a strange taste in the mouth, and a desire to urinate. Occasionally there may be bronchospasm.

P

● warning: protirelin should be
administered with caution to
patients with severe
underactivity of the pituitary
gland or heart failure, or who
are in early pregnancy; oral
administration is advised for
patients with breathing
difficulties.
*Related article:* TRH.

**protriptyline** is an
ANTIDEPRESSANT drug used
because it has a stimulant effect
particularly to treat depressive
illness that disposes towards
apathy and withdrawal.
Administration (as protriptyline
hydrochloride) is oral in the form
of tablets.
▲ side-effects: common effects
include loss of intricacy in
movement or thought, dry
mouth and blurred vision, an
increased heart rate, irregular
heartbeat, and a raised body
temperature; there may also be
difficulty in urinating, a rash,
behavioural disturbances,
insomnia, anxiety, state of
confusion, and/or a loss of
libido. Rarely, there are also
blood deficiencies.
● warning: protriptyline should
not be administered to patients
with heart disease or psychosis,
as it may aggravate tension and
cause insomnia; it should be
administered with caution to
patients with diabetes,
epilepsy, liver or thyroid
disease, glaucoma or urinary
retention; or who are pregnant
or lactating; or who are elderly.
Withdrawal of treatment must
be gradual.
*Related article:* CONCORDIN.

**Pro-Vent** (*Wellcome*) is a
proprietary, non-prescription
BRONCHODILATOR, used to treat the
bronchospasm of asthma,
emphysema and chronic
bronchitis. Produced in the form
of sustained-release capsules, Pro-

Vent is a preparation of the
xanthine drug theophylline. It is
not recommended for children.
▲/● side-effects/warning: *see*
THEOPHYLLINE.

**Provera** (*Upjohn*) is a proprietary
preparation of the PROGESTOGEN
medroxyprogesterone acetate,
available only on prescription,
used as a hormonal supplement in
women whose progestogen level
requires boosting, as at
menopause, and (in higher doses)
to treat sex-hormone-linked
cancer, such as cancer of the
breast or of the womb-lining. It is
produced in tablets (in four
strengths).
▲/● side-effects/warning: *see*
MEDROXYPROGESTERONE.

**Pro-Viron** (*Schering*) is a
proprietary ANDROGEN (male sex
hormone), available only on
prescription, used primarily to
make up hormonal deficiency and
thus treat male infertility.
Produced in the form of tablets,
Pro-Viron is a preparation of
mesterolone.
▲/● side-effects/warning: *see*
MESTEROLONE.

**proxymetacaine** is a widely-used
local ANAESTHETIC with
particular application to
ophthalmic treatments.
Administered in the form of eye-
drops (and as proxymetacaine
hydrochloride) it generally causes
little initial stinging and is
therefore useful for treating
children.
▲ side-effects: there may be slight
stinging on initial application.
*Related article:* OPHTHAINE.

**Prozac** (*Dista*) is a proprietary
form of the ANTIDEPRESSANT drug
fluoxetine hydrochloride, which
has less sedative effects than
some drugs of this type.
Available only on prescription, it
is available as tablets.

▲/● side-effects/warning: *see*
FLUOXETINE
HYDROCHLORIDE.

**pseudoephedrine** is a
VASOCONSTRICTOR, a
SYMPATHOMIMETIC drug that is
also a BRONCHODILATOR, used
mainly in the treatment of
asthma, chronic bronchitis and
similar conditions (especially
allergy-based ones). In all
respects its actions and effects are
identical to those of the closely-
related drug ephedrine
hydrochloride.
▲/● side-effects/warning: *see*
EPHEDRINE HYDROCHLORIDE.
*Related articles:* BENYLIN
EXPECTORANT; CONGESTEZE;
DIMOTANE PLUS; DIMOTANE
WITH CODEINE; GALPSEUD;
SUDAFED.

**pseudomonic acid** is a term for
the drug more commonly known
as mupirocin.
*see* MUPIROCIN.

**Psoradrate** (*Norwich Eaton*) is a
proprietary, non-prescription
preparation, used in topical
application to treat chronic and
mild forms of psoriasis. Produced
in a powder-in-cream base
containing the natural DIURETIC
urea (in three strengths),
Psoradrate is a preparation of
dithranol.
▲/● side-effects/warning: *see*
DITHRANOL.

**Psoriderm** (*Dermal*) is a
proprietary ANTISEPTIC used to
treat non-infective skin
conditions such as psoriasis.
Produced in the form of a cream, a
scalp lotion (used as a shampoo)
and a bath emulsion, Psoriderm's
active constituent is COAL TAR.

**PsoriGel** (*Alcon*) is a proprietary
ANTISEPTIC used to treat non-
infective skin conditions such as
psoriasis and chronic eczema.
Produced in the form of a gel,
PsoriGel is a preparation of a
COAL TAR solution in an emollient
alcohol base.

**Psorin** (*Thames*) is a proprietary,
non-prescription compound
preparation used in topical
application to treat chronic and
mild forms of the troublesome
skin disorder psoriasis. Produced
in the form of an ointment in an
emollient base, Psorin is a
combination of dithranol,
salicylic acid and COAL TAR.
▲/● side-effects/warning: *see*
DITHRANOL; SALICYLIC ACID.

**Pulmadil** (*Riker*) is a proprietary
BRONCHODILATOR, available only
on prescription, used to treat
bronchospasm in asthma and
chronic bronchitis. Produced in a
metered-dosage aerosol, and in
metered-dosage cartridges (under
the name Pulmadil Puto),
Pulmadil is a preparation of the
SYMPATHOMIMETIC rimiterol
hydrobromide.
▲/● side-effects/warning: *see*
RIMITEROL.

**Pulmicort** (*Astra*) is a proprietary
form of the CORTICOSTEROID drug
budesonide, available only on
prescription to prevent asthma
attacks. Available in several
forms, where the standard dose
aerosol inhaler is called
Pulmicort LS, the high dose
inhaler Pulmicort. The inhaling
device is called a Nebuhaler, and
a spacer inhaler device is
available with all dosages.
▲/● side-effects/warning: *see*
BUDESONIDE.

**Pump-Hep** (*Burgess*) is a
proprietary preparation of the
natural ANTICOAGULANT heparin
sodium, available only on
prescription, used to treat and
prevent various forms of
thrombosis. It is produced in
ampoules for intravenous
infusion.

▲/ ✸ side-effects/warning: *see*
HEPARIN.

**Puri-Nethol** (*Wellcome*) is a
proprietary CYTOTOXIC drug,
available only on prescription,
used to treat acute leukaemia,
especially in children. It works by
combining with new-forming cells
in a way that prevents normal cell
replication. Produced in the form
of tablets, Puri-Nethol is a
preparation of mercaptopurine.
▲/ ✸ side-effects/warning: *see*
MERCAPTOPURINE.

**Pyopen** (*Beecham*) is a proprietary
ANTIBIOTIC, available only on
prescription, used mainly to treat
infections of the urinary tract and
upper respiratory tract, and
septicaemia. Produced in the form
of a powder for reconstitution as
a medium for injection, Pyopen is
a preparation of the PENICILLIN
carbenicillin.
▲/ ✸ side-effects/warning: *see*
CARBENICILLIN.

**Pyralvex** (*Norgine*) is a
proprietary, non-prescription,
ANTI-INFLAMMATORY preparation,
used in topical application to
treat inflammation in and around
the mouth. Produced in the form
of a paint, Pyralvex is a
preparation of various glycosides
with the anti-inflammatory
salicylic acid.
▲/ ✸ side-effects/warning: *see*
SALICYLIC ACID.

**pyrantel** is a broad-spectrum
ANTHELMINTIC drug used in the
treatment of infections by
roundworm, threadworm,
hookworm and whipworm.
Administration is oral in the form
of tablets.
▲ side-effects: pyrantel rarely has
side-effects, but it may
occasionally produce mild
nausea.
✸ warning: pyrantel should not
be administered to patients
with liver disease, or to

children aged under 6 months.
*Related article:* COMBANTRIN.

**pyrazinamide** is an ANTI-
BACTERIAL that is one of the major
forms of treatment for
tuberculosis, and particularly
tuberculous meningitis. It is used
generally in combination (to
cover resistance and for
maximum effect) with other drugs
such as isoniazid and rifampicin.
Treatment lasts for between 6 and
9 months, depending on the
severity of the condition and on
the specific drug combination.
Because pyrazinamide is active
only against dividing forms of
*Mycobacterium tuberculosis* it is
most effective in the early stages
of treatment, i.e. the first few
months. Administration is oral in
the form of tablets.
▲ side-effects: there may be
symptoms of liver malfunction,
including high temperature,
severe weight loss and
jaundice. There may be nausea
and vomiting, sensitivity
reactions such as urticaria,
and/or blood disorders.
✸ warning: pyrazinamide should
not be administered to patients
with liver disease; it should be
administered with caution to
patients with impaired liver
function, porphyria, diabetes
or gout. Regular checks on
liver function are essential.
*Related article:* ZINAMIDE.

**Pyridium** (*Parke-Davis*) is a
proprietary, non-prescription
preparation, used to relieve pain
stemming from disorder in the
urinary tract. Produced in the
form of tablets, Pyridium is a
preparation of phenazopyridine
hydrochloride; it is not
recommended for children.
▲/ ✸ side-effects/warning: *see*
PHENAZOPYRIDINE.

**pyridostigmine** is a drug that has
the effect of increasing the
activity of the neurotransmitters

which transmit the neural instructions of the brain to the muscles. It works by inhibiting the 'switching-off' of the neural impulses as they pass from one nerve cell to another, therefore increasing transmission. Its main use is in the treatment of the neuromuscular disease myasthenia gravis (which causes extreme muscle weakness amounting even to paralysis); it is also used to reverse the effects of muscle relaxants administered during surgical operations. Occasionally the drug is used to stimulate intestinal motility and so promote defecation. Administration is oral in the form of tablets, or by injection.

▲ side-effects: there may be nausea and vomiting, diarrhoea and abdominal cramps, and an excess of saliva in the mouth. Overdosage may cause gastrointestinal disturbance, an excess of bronchial mucus, sweating, faecal and urinary incontinence, vision disorders, excessive dreaming, nervous agitation and muscular weakness.

❂ warning: pyridostigmine bromide should not be administered to patients with intestinal or urinary blockage; it should be administered with caution to those with epilepsy, asthma, parkinsonism, hypotension (low blood pressure) or a slow heart rate, who have recently had a heart attack, or who are pregnant. Related article: MESTINON.

**pyridoxine** is the chemical name for vitamin B₆, a VITAMIN that is essential in the diet for the metabolism of amino acids and the maintenance of body cells. Good food sources include fish, liver, peas and beans, yeast and whole grains. A deficiency – rare in the Western world but which

may occur due to certain drug treatments, such as with isoniazid – may dispose a patient towards nerve or blood disorders, and in children might eventually cause convulsions. Therapeutically, it is administered to make up a vitamin deficiency (and especially if that deficiency has resulted in neuritis or anaemia); to treat premenstrual syndrome. An increased dietary intake may be required during pregnancy or breast-feeding, or during childhood growth.

❂ warning: pyridoxine should not be administered to patients who are taking the anti-parkinsonism drug levodopa. *Related articles:* ABIDEC; ALLBEE WITH C; BC 500; BECOSYM; BENADON; COMPLEMENT CONTINUS; CONCAVIT; DALIVIT; HEPACON-PLEX; KETOVITE; LIPOTRIAD; OCTOVIT; PABRINEX; PARENTROVITE; PAXADON; SURBEX T.

**pyrimethamine** is an ANTIMALARIAL drug used primarily to prevent contraction of malaria by travellers in tropical countries. However, if the disease is contracted, the drug is effective in treating forms of malaria that are resistant to treatment with the more commonly prescribed drug chloroquine, and additionally prevents most relapses of benign tertiary forms. Pyrimethamine can also be used, along with a sulphonamide, to treat the protozoal infection toxoplasmosis. Administration is oral in the form of tablets.

▲ side-effects: suppression of the bone-marrow's capacity for forming new blood cells occurs with prolonged treatment. There may be rashes.

❂ warning: pyrimethamine should be administered with caution to patients with

479

impaired liver or kidney function, or who are taking folic acid supplements (for example, during pregnancy). High doses require regular blood counts.
*Related articles:* DARAPRIM; FANSIDAR; MALOPRIM.

**pyrithione zinc shampoos** are ANTIMICROBIAL scalp preparations used to treat dandruff.

**Pyrogastrone** (*Winthrop*) is a proprietary preparation, available only on prescription, used to treat gastric ulcers in young and middle-aged people. Thought to work by creating a protective coating over the mucous lining of the stomach, Pyrogastrone is produced in the form of tablets and as a liquid mixture. It is a preparation of carbenoxolone sodium and various ANTACIDS (including ALUMINIUM HYDROXIDE, MAGNESIUM TRISILICATE and SODIUM BICARBONATE). It is not recommended for children.
▲/❋ side-effects/warning: *see* CARBENOXOLONE SODIUM.

**Quellada** (*Stafford-Miller*) is a proprietary, non-prescription preparation of the antiparasitic lindane, used to treat infestation of the skin of the trunk and limbs by itch-mites (scabies) or by lice (pediculosis). It is also used to treat hair lice infestations. Produced in the form of a lotion, it is also available as a shampoo (under the name Quellada Application PC). Neither is recommended for children aged under 1 month. Children under 6 months should be treated only under medical supervision. Both are for external use only.

▲/✿ side-effects/warning: *see* LINDANE.

**Questran** (*Bristol-Myers*) is a proprietary antidiarrhoeal resin, available only on prescription, used to treat diarrhoea associated with inflammation of the small intestines, or resulting from a reduction in gastric secretions following gastrointestinal surgery, or diarrhoea following radiation treatment. It is also used alternatively to relieve itching in liver disease, and to lower blood cholesterol concentrations. Produced in the form of powder in sachets, Questran is a preparation of cholestyramine. It is available with aspartame as Questran A. Use with other drugs should be avoided. It is not recommended for children aged under 6 years.

▲/✿ side-effects/warning: *see* CHOLESTYRAMINE.

**Quinaband** (*Seton*) is a proprietary, non-prescription form of bandaging impregnated with ZINC OXIDE, CALAMINE and CLIOQUINOL, used to treat and dress ulcers, burns and scalds. (Further bandaging is required to keep it in place.)

**quinalbarbitone sodium** is a BARBITURATE with a rapid onset of action, used as a HYPNOTIC to promote sleep in conditions of severe intractable insomnia. It is a dangerous and potentially addictive drug, administered orally in the form of capsules. It is also used in the compound barbiturate Tuinal.

▲ side-effects: drowsiness, dizziness, lack of power to co-ordinate body movements, shallow breathing and headache are all fairly common, especially in elderly patients. There may be allergic/sensitivity reactions.

✿ warning: quinalbarbitone sodium should not be administered to patients who have insomnia caused by pain, or porphyria, who are pregnant or lactating, or to the elderly or debilitated, or to children. In fact, usage should be avoided altogether where possible. It should be administered with caution to patients with respiratory difficulties, or liver or kidney disease. Tolerance, followed by dependence, occurs readily. Repeated doses have cumulative effect; abrupt withdrawal of treatment may precipitate serious withdrawal symptoms (including fits and delirium). It should not be used in patients with a history of alcohol abuse.

*Related article:* SECONAL SODIUM.

**quinapril** is an ANTIHYPERTENSIVE drug used to treat all forms of high blood pressure (hypertension), especially when more standard forms of therapy have failed or are not tolerated, and to assist in the treatment of congestive heart failure. It works by inhibiting the formation of a certain peptide in the blood (angiotensin), which normally constricts the blood vessels. Administration is oral, as tablets; some patients may require

simultaneous administration of a
DIURETIC (such as a thiazide).

▲ side-effects: there may be a dry
cough, headache, nervousness,
fatigue, dizziness, nausea, an
alteration in the sense of taste,
muscle cramps, acid stomach,
diarrhoea, low blood pressure
and renal failure, rhinitis,
insomnia; chest, back, and
abdominal pains; sinusitis, or a
tingling feeling in the
extremities. Some patients
develop a rash.

✿ warning: quinapril should be
administered with caution to
patients with impaired kidney
function, or who are pregnant.
The initial dose may cause a
rapid fall in blood pressure to
low blood pressure
(hypotension), especially in
patients who are also taking
diuretics or who are
dehydrated.
*Related article:* ACCUPRO.

**quinestradol** is an OESTROGEN, a
female sex HORMONE, used in
replacement therapy to relieve
symptoms in women during and
after the menopause (such as
inflammation or erosion of the
vagina, and urinary incontinence
due to oestrogen deficiency).
Administration is oral in the form
of capsules.

▲ side-effects: there may be
nausea and vomiting, breast
tenderness, fluid and sodium
retention leading to weight
gain, a rash and/or headache.
Some patients experience
impaired liver function or
depression. Withdrawal of
treatment may cause
haemorrhage. Prolonged
treatment of women after the
menopause may give rise to a
predisposition towards cancer
of the womb lining.

✿ warning: quinestradol should
not be administered to patients
with inflammation of the womb
lining, impaired liver function,

porphyria, undiagnosed
bleeding from the vagina,
thrombosis, or oestrogen-
dependent cancer of the breast.
It should be administered with
caution to those with epilepsy,
diabetes, heart or kidney
disease, from high blood
pressure (hypertension), or
migraine, or who are pregnant
or lactating. Many doctors will
not prescribe quinestradol for
patients who wear contact
lenses. Treatment may cause
misleading results in thyroid-
function tests.
*Related article:* PENTOVIS.

**quinestrol** is an OESTROGEN, a
female sex HORMONE that is a
derivative of oestradiol, formerly
used to suppress lactation in
women following childbirth.
(Such use was discontinued when
an association was made between
the oestrogens and some forms of
thrombosis.) Administration is
oral in the form of tablets.

▲ side-effects: there may be
nausea and vomiting, breast
tenderness, fluid and sodium
retention leading to weight
gain, a rash and/or headache.
Some patients experience
impaired liver function or
depression. Withdrawal of
treatment may cause
haemorrhage.

✿ warning: quinestrol should not
be administered to patients
with inflammation of the womb
lining, impaired liver function,
porphyria, undiagnosed
bleeding from the vagina,
thrombosis, or oestrogen-
dependent cancer of the breast.
It should be administered with
caution to those with epilepsy,
diabetes, heart or kidney
disease, high blood pressure
(hypertension), or migraine, or
who are pregnant or lactating.
Many doctors will not prescribe
quinestrol for patients who wear
contact

lenses. Treatment may cause misleading results in thyroid-function tests.

*Related article:* ESTROVIS.

**Quinicardine** (*Lewis*) is a proprietary ANTIARRHYTHMIC drug, available only on prescription, used to treat heartbeat irregularities and to prevent an increase in the heart rate. Produced in the form of tablets – the interval between doses being the regulating factor to suit each individual patient – Quinicardine is a preparation of quinidine sulphate.

▲/ ● side-effects/warning: *see* QUINIDINE.

**quinidine** is an alkaloid of cinchona much like QUININE, but is used specifically in treatments that take advantage of its effect on the heart. It is used (in the form of quinidine sulphate) as an ANTIARRHYTHMIC drug, to treat heartbeat irregularities and regularize the heart rate. However, the drug may itself precipitate some disorders of the heart rhythm and should accordingly be administered only on specialist advice and under strict medical supervision. Rarely, the drug is also used as an equivalent of quinine in the emergency treatment of severe malaria. Administration is oral in the form of tablets, sustained-release tablets and sustained-release capsules.

▲ side-effects: there may be high temperature, nausea, diarrhoea, a rash, ringing in the ears (tinnitus), visual disturbances and vertigo; there may also be impaired heart activity, more serious skin disorders and confusion. In some patients the white blood cell count is diminished, and it may cause types of anaemia.

● warning: quinidine should not be administered to patients with heart block. An initial test dose is usually administered to detect any sensitivity reactions and check tolerance.

*Related articles:* KIDITARD; KINIDIN DURULES; QUINICARDINE.

**quinine** is an alkaloid of cinchona which for years used as the main treatment for malaria. Now synthetic and less toxic drugs – such as chloroquine and proguanil – have replaced it almost entirely, although it is still used (in the form of quinine sulphate or quinine hydrochloride) in cases that prove to be resistant to the newer drugs or for emergency cases in which large doses are necessary. Administration is oral in the form of tablets, or by infusion.

▲ side-effects: toxic effects – corporately called cinchonism – include nausea, headache and abdominal pain, visual disturbances, ringing in the ears (tinnitus), a rash and confusion. Some patients may experience visual disturbances and temporary blindness, others may undergo further sensitivity reactions.

● warning: quinine should not be administered to patients who suffer from inflammation of the optic nerves or any condition that produces blood in the urine; it should be administered with caution to those who suffer from heart block or atrial fibrillation ('palpitations'), or who are pregnant.

**Quinocort** (*Quinoderm*) is a proprietary ANTIFUNGAL and ANTIBACTERIAL STEROID preparation, available only on prescription, used to treat inflammation, particularly when associated with fungal infections. Produced in the form of vanishing cream for topical application,

Quinocort is a combination of the steroid hydrocortisone and the antifungal, antibacterial and deodorant potassium hydroxyquinoline sulphate.

▲/❖ side-effects/warning: *see*
HYDROCORTISONE;
POTASSIUM
HYDROXYQUINOLINE
SULPHATE.

**Quinoderm** (*Quinoderm*) is a proprietary, *non-prescription*, topical preparation for the treatment of acne. Produced in the form of a cream (in two strengths in an astringent vanishing cream basis) and a lotio-gel (in two strengths in an astringent creamy basis), Quinoderm is a combination of the keratolytic benzoyl peroxide and the antifungal, antibacterial and deodorant potassium hydroxyquinoline sulphate. Another form is available, only on prescription, to treat severe and inflamed acne (under the name Quinoderm with Hydrocortisone). As its name suggests, this additionally contains the CORTICOSTEROID hydrocortisone; it too is produced in an astringent vanishing cream basis.

▲/❖ side-effects/warning: *see*
BENZOYL PEROXIDE;
HYDROCORTISONE;
POTASSIUM
HYDROXYQUINOLINE
SULPHATE.

**Quinoped** (*Quinoderm*) is a proprietary, *non-prescription* topical ANTIFUNGAL preparation for the treatment of skin infections such as athlete's foot. Produced in the form of a cream in an astringent base, Quinoped is a compound of the keratolytic benzoyl peroxide and the antifungal, antibacterial and deodorant potassium hydroxyquinoline sulphate.

**rabies vaccine** is specifically a
VACCINE and not a treatment for
rabies, administered to medical
workers and relatives who may
come into contact with
hydrophobic patients or to
patients who have been bitten by
an animal that might or might not
be rabid. It should be routinely
administered to people who work
with animals (e.g. vets) to prevent
rabies. The vaccine is of a type
known as a human diploid cell
vaccine and has no known contra-
indications. It is freeze-dried and
produced in vials with a diluent
for injection. The timing of
injections within courses of
injections depends on whether
treatment is simply preventative
(in which case the regime is
usually two doses over 1 month
and a third dose after 6-12
months, and possibly a booster
every 3 years, depending on the
risk of infection), or if rabies in a
patient is suspected or confirmed
(in which case medical workers
and their relatives are injected on
days 0, 3, 7, 14, 30 and 90 after
exposure).

**Rabro** (*Sinclair*) is a proprietary,
non-prescription compound drug
containing ANTACIDS and a
constituent of liquorice. It is used
to soothe the symptoms of peptic
ulcers. Produced in the form of
tablets, the antacid constituents
are CALCIUM CARBONATE,
MAGNESIUM OXIDE (magnesia). It
is not recommended for children.

**ramipril** is an ANTIHYPERTENSIVE
drug used to treat all forms of
high blood pressure
(hypertension), especially when
more standard forms of therapy
have failed or are not tolerated. It
works by inhibiting the formation
of a certain peptide in the blood
(angiotensin), which normally
constricts the blood vessels.
Administration is oral, as tablets;
some patients may require

simultaneous administration of
other antihypertensive drugs.
▲ side-effects: there may be a dry
cough, headache, fatigue,
nausea, an alteration in the
sense of taste, muscle cramps,
low blood pressure and renal
failure, changes in blood
indicators, vomiting and
abdominal pain, renal failure.
✜ warning: ramipril should be
administered with caution to
patients with impaired kidney
function, or who are pregnant.
The initial dose may cause a
rapid fall in blood pressure to
low blood pressure
(hypotension), especially in
patients who are also taking
diuretics or who are
dehydrated.
*Related article:* TRITACE.

**Ramodar** (*Wyeth*) is a proprietary,
non-narcotic ANALGESIC,
available only on prescription,
used to treat both acute and
chronic rheumatoid arthritis.
Produced in the form of tablets,
Ramodar is a preparation of the
non-steroidal ANTI-INFLAMMATORY
drug etodolac. It is not
recommended for children.
▲/✜ side-effects/warning: *see*
ETODOLAC.

**ranitidine** is a powerful drug used
to assist in the treatment of peptic
ulcers and to relieve heartburn in
cases of oesophagitis caused by
peptic disturbance. It works by
reducing the secretion of gastric
acids (by blocking histamine
$H_2$receptors – *see* ANTIHISTAMINE),
so reducing bleeding from gastric
or duodenal ulcers and giving
them a chance to heal. However,
treatment with ranitidine should
not be given before full diagnosis
of gastric bleeding, because its
action in restricting gastric
secretions may possibly mask the
presence of stomach cancer.
Administration is oral in the form
of tablets and soluble (dispersible)
tablets, or by injection.

▲ side-effects: side-effects are rare. But there may be nausea, constipation and headache; a very few patients experience a temporary state of mild confusion. Even more rarely there are allergic/sensitivity reactions.

✿ warning: ranitidine should be administered with caution to patients with impaired liver or kidney function. A course of treatments lasts usually from 4 to 8 weeks, but may be repeated if necessary.
*Related article:* ZANTAC.

**Rapifen** (*Janssen*) is a proprietary ANALGESIC, which, because it is also a NARCOTIC, is on the controlled drugs list. It is used especially in outpatient surgery, short operational prodeedures, and for the enhancement of anaesthesia. Produced in the form of ampoules for injection, Rapifen is a preparation of alfentanil. A weaker paediatric injection is also available.
▲/✿ side-effects/warning: *see* ALFENTANIL.

**Rapitard MC** (*Novo*) is a proprietary, non-prescription preparation of highly purified beef-with-pork insulin, used to treat and maintain diabetic patients. Rapitard MC is produced in the form of vials for regular injection.
▲/✿ side-effects/warning: *see* INSULIN.

**Rastinon** (*Hoechst*) is a proprietary form of the SULPHONYLUREA tolbutamide, available only on prescription, used to treat adult-onset diabetes mellitus. It works by augmenting what remains of insulin production in the pancreas, and is produced in the form of tablets.
▲/✿ side-effects/warning: *see* TOLBUTAMIDE.

**Rautrax** (*Squibb*) is a proprietary compound ANTIHYPERTENSIVE drug, available only on prescription, used to treat high blood pressure (hypertension) and to slow the heart rate. It also has a sedative effect. Produced in the form of tablets, Rautrax is a preparation of Rauwolfia serpentina, the THIAZIDE diuretic hydroflumethiazide, and the potassium supplement potassium chloride. It is not recommended for children.
▲/✿ side-effects/warning: *see* HYDROFLUMETHIAZIDE; POTASSIUM CHLORIDE; RAUWOLFIA ALKALOIDS.

**Rauwiloid** (*Riker*) is a proprietary ANTIHYPERTENSIVE drug, available only on prescription, used to treat high blood pressure (hypertension) and to slow the heart rate. Produced in the form of tablets, Rauwiloid is a preparation of alseroxylon, a derivative of Rauwolfia serpentina. It is not recommended for children.
▲/✿ side-effects/warning: *see* RAUWOLFIA ALKALOIDS.

**Rauwolfia alkaloids** are medications derived from the root of the plant Rauwolfia serpentina. In all, the main active constituent is the substance reserpine, which is used increasingly less often as an ANTIHYPERTENSIVE drug to treat high blood pressure (hypertension) and to slow the heart rate; it works by direct action upon the nervous system. These drugs are also used as major TRANQUILLIZERS, though rarely these days. Many proprietary preparations contain two or more Rauwolfia alkaloids. Administration is oral in the form of tablets.
▲ side-effects: there may be dry mouth and blocked nose, sedation with low blood pressure (hypotension), and

fluid retention leading to
weight gain.
- **warning:** Rauwolfia alkaloids
should not be administered to
patients with peptic ulcers,
parkinsonism or depression;
they should be administered
with caution to those who are
pregnant or lactating.
*Related articles:* ABICOL;
HYPERCAL; RAUTRAX;
RAUWILOID; SERPASIL;
SERPASIL-ESIDREX.

**razoxane** is a synthetic CYTOTOXIC
drug used (infrequently) in
combination with radiotherapy to
treat some forms of cancer,
including leukaemia.
Administration is oral in the form
of tablets.
- ▲ **side-effects:** there may be
nausea and vomiting,
progressive deafness and
symptoms of kidney
dysfunction. The blood-forming
capacity of the bone marrow
may be suppressed and there
may be blood disorders
(and treatment should not
be repeated within 4
weeks).
- **warning:** an anti-emetic should
be administered
simultaneously to lessen the
risk of nausea and vomiting.
Monitoring of kidney function,
blood counts and the sense of
hearing is advisable. It should
not be used in patients with
psoriasis. Protective gloves
should be worn when handling
tablets, and they should not be
handled at all by pregnant
women.
*Related article:* RAZOXIN.

**Razoxin** (*ICI*) is a proprietary
preparation of the CYTOTOXIC
drug razoxane, available only on
prescription, used (infrequently)
in combination with radiotherapy
to treat some cancers and acute
leukaemia. It is produced in the
form of tablets.

▲/- **side-effects/warning:** *see*
RAZOXANE.

**R.B.C.** (*Rybar*) is a proprietary,
non-prescription ANTIHISTAMINE,
used to treat skin irritation
(itching and nettlerash), stings
and bites, and sunburn. Produced
in the form of a cream, R.B.C.
contains the antihistamine
ANTAZOLINE hydrochloride, the
antiseptic CETRIMIDE, CALAMINE
and camphor.

**Recormon** (*Boehringer
Mannheim*) is a proprietary form
of epoietin (synthesized human
erythropoietin) used to treat
anaemia known to be associated
with chronic renal failure in
dialysis patients. Available only
on prescription, the preparation
is available in a form for
intravenous administration.
▲/- **side-effects/warning:** *see*
EPOETIN.

**Redeptin** (*Smith Kline & French*)
is a proprietary preparation of the
powerful ANTIPSYCHOTIC drug
fluspirilene. Available only on
prescription, it is used to treat
and tranquillize psychoses.
Produced in ampoules for
injection, Redeptin is not
recommended for children.
▲/- **side-effects/warning:** *see*
FLUSPIRILENE.

**Redoxon** (*Roche*) is a proprietary,
non-prescription VITAMIN C
preparation, which is not
available from the National
Health Service. It is used to treat
the symptoms of vitamin C
deficiency (such as scurvy).
Produced in the form of tablets (in
four strengths) and as tablets for
effervescent solutions. Redoxon
contains ASCORBIC ACID.

**Refolinon** (*Farmitalia Carlo Erba*)
is a proprietary preparation of the
vitamin B-like FOLINIC ACID,
available only on prescription,

used to treat body deficiency of the vitamin (as occurs in certain types of anaemia). It is produced in the form of tablets and in ampoules for injection.

**Regaine** (*Upjohn*) is a proprietary form of minoxidil not available from the NHS, and is used to treat male-pattern baldness. It is available as a topical solution of minoxidil in an aqueous basis. The stability and safety of mixtures of minoxidil lotion with other products has not been established. Wash hands after use; it is flammable.

▲/ ✿ side-effects/warning: *see* MINOXIDIL.

**Regulan** (*Gold Cross*) is a proprietary LAXATIVE of the type known as a bulking agent, which works by increasing the overall mass of faeces within the rectum, so stimulating bowel movement. It is used both to relieve constipation and to relieve diarrhoea, and also in the control of faecal consistency for patients with a colostomy. Produced in the form of gluten-free powder in sachets for effervescent solution in water, Regulan is a preparation of ispaghula husk. It is not recommended for children aged under 6 years, except on medical advice.

▲/ ✿ side-effects/warning: *see* ISPAGHULA HUSK.

**Regulettes** (*Cupal*) is a proprietary, non-prescription LAXATIVE produced in the form of tablets and as chocolate. Both preparations contain phenyl-pathaline.

**Rehibin** (*Thames*) is a proprietary preparation of the drug cyclofenil (an anti-oestrogen), available only on prescription, used under strict medical supervision to treat certain conditions of infertility in which the presence of OESTROGENS may be preventing hormonal

activity necessary for ovulation. It is produced in the form of tablets.

▲/ ✿ side-effects/warning: *see* CYCLOFENIL.

**Rehidrat** (*Searle*) is a proprietary, non-prescription fluid-replacement supplement, used to treat patients suffering from dehydration and sodium depletion caused by acute diarrhoea, gastro-enteritis and conditions that lead to salt deficiency. Produced in the form of a (lemon-, lime- or orange-flavoured) powder in sachets for reconstitution with water for drinking, Rehidrat contains SODIUM CHLORIDE, POTASSIUM CHLORIDE, SODIUM BICARBONATE, citric acid, GLUCOSE, sucrose and FRUCTOSE.

**Relaxit** (*Pharmacia*) is a proprietary, non-prescription form of micro-enema administered rectally to soften the faeces and promote bowel movement. Produced in the form of single-dose disposable packs with a nozzle, Relaxit is a compound preparation that includes SODIUM CITRATE. For children aged under 3 years there are special instruction for the use of this enema.

**Relefact LH-RH** (*Hoechst*) is a proprietary preparation of GONADOTROPHIN-RELEASING HORMONE, available only on prescription, used as a diagnostic aid in assessing the functioning of the pituitary gland and its secretions. Produced in ampoules for intravenous injection, Relefact LH-RH contains the hormonal substance gonadorelin. Another form, which additionally contains the thryotrophin-releasing hormone protirelin, is also produced (under the name Relefact LH-RH/TRH).

▲/ ✿ side-effects/warning: *see* GONADORELIN; PROTIRELIN.

**Remnos** (*DDSA Pharmaceuticals*) is a proprietary TRANQUILLIZER and HYPNOTIC available on prescription only to private patients, used to treat insomnia in cases where some degree of daytime sedation is acceptable. Produced in the form of tablets (in two strengths), Remnos is a preparation of the long-acting benzodiazepine nitrazepam.

▲ / ✿ side-effects/warning: *see* NITRAZEPAM.

**Rennie** (*Nicholas Kiwi*) is a proprietary, non-prescription ANTACID produced in the form of tablets. It contains calcium carbonate and magnesium carbonate.

▲ / ✿ side-effects/warning: *see* CALCIUM CARBONATE; MAGNESIUM CARBONATE.

**reproterol hydrochloride** is a BRONCHODILATOR, a SYMPATHOMIMETIC that is useful in treating all forms and stages of asthma and other conditions that involve obstruction of the air passages. It is also used to treat spasm of the airways. Administration is oral in the form of tablets; as a dilute elixir, which must be diluted (and is then potent for 14 days); topical in the form of an inhalant spray; or as a respirator solution.

▲ side-effects: there may be nausea and vomiting, flushing and sweating, restlessness, and a tremor. High dosage may cause an increase in the heart rate, with high blood pressure.

✿ warning: reproterol hydrochloride should be administered with caution to patients with heart disease or high blood pressure (hypertension), bleeding or infection, an excess of thyroid hormones in the blood (thyrotoxicosis), who are already taking antihypertensive drugs or beta-blockers, with diabetes, who are undergoing treatment with corticosteroids or diuretics, or

who are elderly. Regular blood counts and blood pressure monitoring are essential, as is monitoring of blood glucose in diabetics.

*Related article:* BRONCHODIL.

**reserpine** is the principal constituent of the Rauwolfia alkaloids, a drug used mainly to treat high blood pressure or, more rarely, to treat anxiety (although it may take some time to achieve full effect). It is now administered less frequently, however, because it may cause depression in some patients, and because there is a wider choice of drugs available to treat high blood pressure. Administration is oral in the form of tablets, or by injection.

▲ / ✿ side-effects/warning: *see* RAUWOLFIA ALKALOIDS.

**Resolve** (*Beecham Health Care*) is a proprietary, non-prescription formulation for the relief of 'morning after' hangover symptoms. Produced in the form of a powder, it contains citric acid, vitamin C, glucose, paracetamol and the ANTACIDS sodium carbonate, sodium bicarbonate and potassium bicarbonate.

▲ / ✿ side-effects/warning: *see* ASCORBIC ACID; GLUCOSE; PARACETAMOL; SODIUM CARBONATE.

**Resonium-A** (*Winthrop*) is a proprietary, non-prescription sodium supplement used to treat high blood levels of POTASSIUM, particularly in patients who suffer from fluid retention or who undergo kidney dialysis. It is produced in the form of a powdered resin, consisting of a preparation of sodium polystyrene sulphonate.

**resorcinol** is an astringent drug that in topical application causes skin to peel (it is a KERATOLYTIC) and relieves itching (it is antipruritic); it is most used in ointments and lotions to treat acne or remove dandruff.

✦ warning: prolonged usage, leading to absorption, may cause underactivity of the thyroid gland (hypothyroidism) with resultant symptoms (myxoedema) and eventual convulsions.
*Related article:* ESKAMEL.

**Restandol** (*Organon*) is a proprietary preparation of the male sex hormone testosterone undecanoate, available only on prescription, used to treat sexually undeveloped men, and conditions of osteoporosis ('brittle bones') caused by lack of ANDROGENS. It is produced in the form of capsules.
▲/✦ side-effects/warning: *see* TESTOSTERONE.

**Retcin** (*DDSA Pharmaceuticals*) is a proprietary ANTIBIOTIC, available only on prescription, used to treat many infections (including serious infections such as legionnaires' disease and inflammation of the prostate gland) and to prevent others (such as diphtheria or whooping cough), especially in patients who are allergic to penicillin-type antibiotics. Produced in the form of tablets, Retcin is a preparation of erythromycin.
▲/✦ side-effects/warning: *see* ERYTHROMYCIN.

**Retin-A** (*Ortho-Cilag*) is a proprietary preparation of the VITAMIN A-type compound tretinoin, available only on prescription, used to treat severe acne and to prevent excessive scarring by it. Produced in the form of a cream (for dry or fair skin), a gel (for more severe acne or dark and oily skin) or a lotion (for treating large areas such as the back), it is not recommended for children.

▲/✦ side-effects/warning: *see* TRETINOIN.

**retinol** is the chemical term for VITAMIN A, a fat-soluble vitamin that is found in meats and milk products, and is also synthesized in the body from constituents in green vegetables and carrots. Essential for growth and the maintenance of mucous surfaces, retinol is particularly useful in supporting the part of the eye's retina that allows vision in the dark; a deficiency may thus cause night blindness, dry eyes and stunted growth. Conversely, however, an excess may cause hair loss, peeling of the skin, joint pain and liver damage. It is administered therapeutically to make up vitamin deficiency which is rare in Western countries mostly orally in the form of capsules or as an emulsion, but also by injection. Some people absorb vitamin A poorly and thus show deficiency signs. Vitamin A may be used topically to treat acne.
*Related articles:* HALIBUT-LIVER OIL; HALYCITROL; RO-A-VIT.

**Retrovir** (*Wellcome*) is an ANTIVIRAL drug, and is a proprietary form of zidovudine. It is used to treat AIDS, and is available only on prescription. The preparation is in the form of capsules in two strengths.
▲/✦ side-effects/warning: *see* ZIDOVUDINE.

**Revanil** (*Roche*) is a recently introduced ANTIPARKINSONISM drug, and is a proprietary form of lysuride maleate. Available only on prescription, the preparation is in the form of tablets.
▲/✦ side-effects/warning: *see* LYSURIDE MALEATE.

**Rheomacrodex** (*Pharmacia*) is a proprietary form of the plasma substitute dextran, available only on prescription, used in infusion with either saline (sodium chloride) or glucose to make up a deficiency in the overall volume of blood in a patient, to improve blood flow or to prevent thrombosis (blood clots) following surgery. It is produced in flasks (bottles) for infusion.

▲ / ⬤ side-effects/warning: *see* DEXTRAN.

**Rheumacin LA** (*CP Pharmaceuticals*) is a proprietary, non-steroidal, ANTI-INFLAMMATORY, non-narcotic ANALGESIC, available only on prescription, used to relieve pain – particularly rheumatic and arthritic pain – and to treat other musculo-skeletal disorders (including gout, and inflammation of joints and tendons). Produced in the form of sustained-release capsules, Rheumacin LA is a preparation of indomethacin.

▲ / ⬤ side-effects/warning: *see* INDOMETHACIN.

**Rheumox** (*Robins*) is a proprietary, non-steroidal, ANTI-INFLAMMATORY, non-narcotic ANALGESIC, available only on prescription, used to relieve pain – particularly rheumatic and arthritic pain – and to treat other musculo-skeletal disorders (including the prevention and treatment of gout). It is a preparation of azapropazone and is produced in the form of capsules and tablets.

▲ / ⬤ side-effects/warning: *see* AZAPROPAZONE.

**Rhinocort** (*Astra*) is a proprietary form of the CORTICOSTEROID drug budesonide, available only on prescription to treat nasal allergy.

▲ / ⬤ side-effects/warning: *see* BUDESONIDE

**rhubarb** in powdered form is sometimes used as a constituent in non-proprietary formulations (with sodium bicarbonate and other constituents); it has a mildly LAXATIVE effect. Rarely, it is also used in small quantity as an astringent bitter.

**riboflavine** is a chemical name for vitamin $B_2$, a water-soluble vitamin that is important for carbohydrate and protein metabolism, and for maintaining the mucous membranes. Deficiency is rare, but may cause skin rashes, cracked lips, and some types of anaemia. Good dietary sources include eggs, liver, milk products and cereals. Administered therapeutically, riboflavine is a constituent of very many vitamin and mineral-and-vitamin supplements.
*Related articles:* ABIDEC; ALLBEE WITH C; BC 500; BECOSYM; CALCIMAX; CONCAVIT; DALIVIT; HEPACON-PLEX; KETOVITE; LIPOTRIAD; MINAMINO; MULTIVITAMINS; OCTOVIT; OROVITE; PABRINEX; PARENTROVITE; SURBEX T; VIGRANON B; VITAVEL.

**Rifadin** (*Merrell*) is a proprietary ANTITUBERCULAR drug, available only on prescription, generally used in combination with other antitubercular drugs. It may also be used to treat leprosy in dapsone-resistant cases. Produced in the form of capsules (in two strengths), as a syrup, and in the form of a powder for reconstitution as a medium for intravenous infusion, Rifadin is a preparation of the ANTIBIOTIC rifampicin.

▲ / ⬤ side-effects/warning: *see* RIFAMPICIN.

**rifampicin** is an ANTIBIOTIC that is one of the principal drugs used in the treatment of tuberculosis. Even so, it is used¹ generally in combination (to cover resistance and for maximum effect) with other antitubercular drugs such as isoniazid or streptomycin. Treatment lasts for between 6 and 9 months depending on severity and on the specific drug combination, but the use of rifampicin tends to imply the shorter duration. The drug inhibits *Mycobacterium tuberculosis* and sensitive gram-positive bacteria by inhibiting the bacterial RNA polymerase enzyme. Rifampicin is also effective in the treatment of leprosy in cases where the usual antileprotic drug dapsone has failed. Administration is oral in the form of capsules, tablets or a syrup, or by injection or infusion.

▲ side-effects: there are often gastrointestinal problems involving nausea, vomiting, diarrhoea and weight loss; many patients also undergo the symptoms of flu, which may also lead to breathlessness. Rarely, there is kidney failure, liver dysfunction, jaundice, alteration in the composition of the blood and/or discoloration of the urine, saliva and other body secretions. Sensitivity reactions, such as a rash or urticaria, can occur.

◆ warning: rifampicin should not be administered to patients with jaundice; it should be administered with caution to those with impaired liver function, who are alcoholic, or who are pregnant or lactating. One other effect of the drug is that soft contact lenses may become discoloured. Rifampicin causes the induction of liver enzymes which are responsible for metabolizing many other drugs; these other drugs therefore may be less effective than usual, e.g. oral contraceptives are metabolized more rapidly, and at the usual dose they will not provide safe contraception.

*Related articles:* RIFADIN; RIFATER; RIFINAH; RIMACTANE; RIMACTAZID.

**Rifater** (*Merrell*) is a proprietary ANTITUBERCULAR drug, available only on prescription, used to treat pulmonary tuberculosis in the initial intensive phase. Produced in the form of tablets, Rifater is a combined preparation of rifampicin, isoniazid and pyrazinamide. It is not recommended for children.

▲/◆ side-effects/warning: *see* ISONIAZID; PYRAZINAMIDE; RIFAMPICIN.

**Rifinah** (*Merrell*) is a proprietary ANTITUBERCULAR drug, available only on prescription, used to treat tuberculosis. Produced in the form of tablets (in two strengths, under the trade names Rifinah 150 and Rifinah 300), Rifinah is a combined preparation of rifampicin and isoniazid.

▲/◆ side-effects/warning: *see* ISONIAZID; RIFAMPICIN.

**Rikospray Balsam** (*Riker*) is a proprietary, non-prescription barrier skin protectant, used to treat skin infections, cracked nipples and bedsores, or to protect and sanitize a stoma (an outlet on the skin surface following the surgical curtailment of the intestines). Produced in the form of a pressurized aerosol pack for spray application, Rikospray Balsam is a preparation of two natural resinous substances, one of which is BENZOIN TINCTURE.

**Rikospray Silicone** (*Riker*) is a proprietary, non-prescription barrier skin protectant, used to treat bedsores and nappy rash, or to protect and sanitize a stoma (an outlet on the skin surface following the surgical curtailment of the intestines). Produced in a pressurized aerosol pack for spray application,

Rikospray Silicone is a preparation of the ANTIBIOTIC CETYLPYRIDINIUM CHLORIDE together with the astringent ANTIPERSPIRANT aluminium dihydroxyallantoinate in a water-repellent basis containing the antifoaming agent DIMETHICONE.

**Rimactane** (*Ciba*) is a proprietary ANTITUBERCULAR drug, available only on prescription, used in combination with other antitubercular drugs. Produced in the form of capsules (in two strengths), as a syrup and in the form of a powder for reconstitution as a medium for intravenous infusion, Rimactane is a preparation of the ANTIBIOTIC rifampicin.
▲/ ✦ side-effects/warning: *see* RIFAMPICIN.

**Rimactazid** (*Ciba*) is a proprietary ANTITUBERCULAR drug, available only on prescription, used singly or in combination with other antitubercular drugs. It may also be used to treat certain other bacterial infections. Produced in the form of tablets (in two strengths, under the names Rimactazid 150 and Rimactazid 300), Rimactazid is a combined preparation of the ANTIBIOTICS rifampicin and isoniazid.
▲/ ✦ side-effects/warning: *see* ISONIAZID; RIFAMPICIN.

**Rimifon** (*Roche*) is a proprietary ANTITUBERCULAR drug, available only on prescription, used in combination with other antitubercular drugs. Produced in ampoules for injection, Rimifon is a preparation of the ANTIBIOTIC isoniazid.
▲/ ✦ side-effects/warning: *see* ISONIAZID.

**rimiterol** is a BRONCHODILATOR, a SYMPATHOMIMETIC that is useful in treating all forms and stages of asthma and other conditions that involve obstruction in the air passages, and to prevent spasm of the airways. Administration (in the form of rimiterol hydrobromide) is topical in the form of an inhalant spray.
▲ side-effects: there may be nausea and vomiting, flushing and sweating, and a tremor. Overdosage may cause an increase in the heart rate, with high blood pressure.
✦ warning: rimiterol should not be administered to patients with heart disease or high blood pressure (hypertension), bleeding or infection, an excess of thyroid hormones in the blood (thyrotoxicosis), or who are already taking antihypertensive drugs or beta-blockers. It should be administered with caution to those with diabetes, who are undergoing treatment with corticosteroids or diuretics, or who are elderly.
*Related article:* PULMADIL.

**Rimso-50** (*Britannia*) is a proprietary organic solution that is intended for bladder washouts. Available only on prescription, such bladder irrigation is used to relieve the symptoms of cystitis (inflammation of the bladder) or of bladder ulcers. Its active constituent is dimethyl sulphoxide.

**Rinatec** (*Boehringer Ingelheim*) is a proprietary form of the ANTI-CHOLINERGIC drug ipratropium bromide. It is available only on prescription to treat watery rhinorrhoea. It is produced in the form of a metered spray. Avoid spraying near the eyes.
▲/ ✦ side-effects/warning: *see* IPRATROPIUM.

**Ringer's solution** is a non-proprietary solution for injection that is intended as a SODIUM CHLORIDE (saline) supplement in patients with sodium depletion. It contains the chlorides of sodium, potassium and calcium.

**Rite-Diet** (*Welfare Foods*) is a brand of special foods for special diets. For patients who require a gluten-free diet there are sweet biscuits and crackers, digestive biscuits, savoury biscuits, bread, bread with soya bran, high-fibre bread, a bread mix, and a flour mix. For patients on a low-protein diet there is macaroni, spaghetti (in two sizes), a flour mix, a bread mix, bread, bread with soya bran, bread without salt, white bread with added fibre, sweet biscuits, crackers, cream-filled biscuits and cream wafers. Most of these are also available specially prepared for patients on a combined gluten-free low-protein diet. Finally, for patients on a low-sodium diet, there is another form of bread.

**ritodrine hydrochloride** is a BETA-RECEPTOR STIMULANT that affects principally the muscles of the womb: it is therefore used mainly to prevent or stall the uterine contractions of premature labour, although it is also used in cases where a foetus may be in danger of asphyxiation through excessive contractility of the womb muscles. Administration is oral in the form of tablets, or by injection.

▲ side-effects: there may be nausea and vomiting, flushing and sweating, and a tremor; high doses may increase the heart rate and lower the blood pressure.

● warning: ritodrine hydrochloride should not be administered to patients with heart disease, high blood pressure (hypertension), pre-eclampsia, excess thyroid hormones in the bloodstream (thyrotoxicosis), or infection of any kind; who are bleeding; or who are already taking

antidepressants, beta-blockers or drugs against high blood pressure. It should be administered with caution to those with diabetes, or who are undergoing treatment with corticosteroids, diuretics or anaesthetics. Blood pressure and pulse should be monitored during treatment.

*Related article:* YUTOPAR.

**Rivotril** (*Roche*) is a proprietary ANTICONVULSANT, available only on prescription, used to treat all forms of epilepsy. It is produced in the form of tablets (in two strengths) and in ampoules (with diluent) for injection, and is a preparation of the BENZODIAZEPINE clonazepam.

▲ / ● side-effects/warning: *see* CLONAZEPAM.

**Roaccutane** (*Roche*) is a proprietary preparation of the vitamin A derivative isotretinoin, available only on prescription (and generally only in hospitals), used to treat severe acne that proves to be unresponsive to the more common antibiotic therapy. It is produced in the form of capsules (in two strengths), and is not recommended for children.

▲ / ● side-effects/warning: *see* ISOTRETINOIN.

**Ro-A-Vit** (*Roche*) is a proprietary preparation of RETINOL (vitamin A), available only on prescription, used to treat and prevent vitamin A deficiency. It is produced in the form of an oily solution in ampoules for injection. Injections are used when absoption of oral Ro-A-Vit is poor.

**Robaxin 750** (*Robins*) is a proprietary MUSCLE RELAXANT, available only on prescription, used to relieve muscle spasm mainly in the muscles of the limbs; it works by direct action on the central nervous system.

Produced in the form of tablets and in ampoules for injection, Robaxin 750 is a preparation of methocarbamol. It is not recommended for children; lower doses are recommended for the elderly.
▲/ ✿ side-effects/warning: *see* METHOCARBAMOL.

**Robaxisal Forte** (*Robins*) is a proprietary compound ANALGESIC, available on prescription only to private patients, used to relieve muscle spasm and pain, mainly in the muscles of the limbs; it works by direct action on the central nervous system. Produced in the form of tablets, Robaxisal Forte is a preparation of methocarbamol and aspirin. It is not recommended for children. Lower doses are recommended for the elderly.
▲/ ✿ side-effects/warning: *see* ASPIRIN; METHOCARBAMOL.

**Robinul** (*Robins*) is a proprietary ANTICHOLINERGIC drug, available only on prescription, used to treat rigidity (spasm) or hyperactivity of the muscles of the colon. Produced in the form of ampoules for injection, Robinul is a preparation of the MUSCLE RELAXANT glycopyrronium bromide. It is not recommended for children.
▲/ ✿ side-effects/warning: *see* GLYCOPYRRONIUM BROMIDE.

**RoC Total Sunblock** (*RoC*) is a proprietary, non-prescription cream containing constituents that protect the skin from ultraviolet radiation and radiotherapy. Patients whose skin condition is such as to require this sort of protection may be prescribed RoC Total Sunblock at the discretion of their doctors. Its major active constituent is ZINC OXIDE.

**Rocaltrol** (*Roche*) is a proprietary form of the vitamin D analogue calcitriol, available only on

prescription, used to restore and sustain calcium balance in the body. It is produced in the form of capsules (in two strengths) and the appropriate dose for children has not been established.
✿ warning: *see* CALCITRIOL.

**Roccal** (*Winthrop*) is a proprietary, non-prescription DISINFECTANT, used to cleanse the skin before operations, to cleanse wounds, to sterilize dressings, to cleanse breast and nipple shields, and also as a vaginal douche. Produced in the form of a solution, Roccal is a preparation of benzalkonium chloride. A concentrated form is available (under the name Roccal Concentrate 10X) for the preparation of the same solution, using purified water. Roccal should not be used with soap.

**Roferon-A** (*Roche*) is a proprietary preparation of the viral inhibitor and cellular disrupter interferon (in the form of alfa interferon), available only on prescription, and used mainly to treat some kinds of leukaemia and AIDS-related Kaposi's sarcoma (a type of skin cancer). Administration is by injection. As with virtually all anticancer drugs, some side-effects are inevitable.
▲/ ✿ side-effects/warning: *see* INTERFERON.

**Rogitine** (*Ciba*) is a proprietary ANTIHYPERTENSIVE drug, available only on prescription, used to treat both high blood pressure (hypertension) and heart failure. Produced in ampoules for injection, Rogitine is a preparation of the ALPHA-BLOCKER phentolamine mesylate.
▲/ ✿ side-effects/warning: *see* PHENTOLAMINE.

**Rohypnol** (*Roche*) is a proprietary TRANQUILLIZER, available on prescription only to private patients, used for the short-term treatment of insomnia and sleep disturbance in cases where some degree of daytime sedation is acceptable. Produced in the form of tablets, Rohypnol is a preparation of the BENZO-DIAZEPINE flunitrazepam. It is not recommended for children.

▲/✿ side-effects/warning: see FLUNITRAZEPAM.

**Ronicol** (*Roche*) is a proprietary, non-prescription VASODILATOR, used to relieve circulatory disorders (e.g. of the fingers and toes) and to treat the condition of excess fats (lipids) in the blood, and to treat Raynaud's disease, spasm of blood vessels, chilblains, Ménière's syndrome and eye conditions caused by poor circulation. Produced in the form of tablets, and as sustained-release tablets (under the name Ronicol Timespan), Ronicol is a preparation of the nicotinic acid derivative nicotinyl alcohol tartrate. It is not recommended for children.

▲/✿ side-effects/warning: see NICOTINYL ALCOHOL.

**rosaxacin** is another name for the antibacterial agent acrosoxacin. see ACROSOXACIN.

**rose bengal** is a form of dye which (in solution), when placed in contact with the cornea of the eye, makes obvious any lesion or foreign body (particularly on the conjunctiva and the cornea). Administration is thus ordinarily in the form of eye-drops.
*Related article:* MINIMS ROSE BENGAL.

**Roter** (*Roterpharma*) is a proprietary, non-prescription ANTACID, not available from the National Health Service, used to treat peptic ulcers and gastritis. Produced in the form of tablets, Roter is a compound in which the

major active constituents are MAGNESIUM CARBONATE, SODIUM BICARBONATE and BISMUTH SUBNITRATE. It is not recommended for children.

**Rotersept** (*Roterpharma*) is a proprietary, non-prescription DISINFECTANT, used to treat sore and cracked nipples before and after breast-feeding. Produced in the form of spray in an aerosol, Rotersept is a preparation of chlorhexidine gluconate.

▲/✿ side-effects/warning: see CHLORHEXIDINE.

**Rowachol** (*Tillotts*) is a proprietary, non-prescription preparation of essential oils, used to treat gallstones and bile and liver disorders, especially when surgery is not possible or available. It is produced in the form of a liquid (in a dropper bottle). Another form is available only on prescription, produced in the form of capsules, and used as an additional therapy for dispersing stones in the bile duct. Neither of these products is recommended for children.

✿ warning: Rowachol should be used with caution by pregnant women, and by patients on anticoagulants.

**Rowatinex** (*Tillotts*) is a proprietary, non-prescription preparation of volatile oils, used to treat renal and urinary disorders and in the prevention of urinary stone formation. It is produced in the form of a liquid (in a dropper bottle) and as capsules. Neither form is recommended for children.

**Rubavax** (*Merieux*) is a proprietary VACCINE against German measles (rubella) in the form of a solution containing live but attenuated viruses of the Wistar RA27/3 strain. Available only on prescription, and administered in the form of injection, it is intended for the immunization of non-pregnant women.

▲/◆ side-effects/warning: *see* RUBELLA VACCINE.

**rubefacient** is another term for a COUNTER-IRRITANT.

**rubella vaccine** is a VACCINE against German measles (rubella), which is medically recommended for pre-pubertal girls between the ages of 10 and 14, and for medical staff who as potential carriers might put pregnant women at risk from infection, and also for women of child-bearing age, because German measles during pregnancy constitutes a serious risk to the foetus. As a precaution vaccination should not take place if the patient is pregnant or likely to become pregnant within the following 3 months. The vaccine is prepared as a freeze-dried suspension of live but attenuated viruses grown in cell cultures; administration is by injection. *Related articles:* ALMEVAX; ERVEVAX; RUBAVAX.

**rub/vac** is an abbreviation for rubella vaccine.
*see* RUBELLA VACCINE.

**Ruthmol** (*Cantassium*) is a proprietary, non-prescription substitute for common salt (sodium chloride) for patients who are on a low-sodium diet. Looking remarkably like salt, and used in similarly in and on food, Ruthmol is the similar compound POTASSIUM CHLORIDE.

**rutosides** are derivatives of rutin, a vegetable substance. They work by reducing the fragility and permeability of certain blood vessels and may thus be effective in preventing small haemorrhages and swellings. In mixtures called OXERUTINS, they are used

especially to treat disorders of the veins of the legs, such as cramps, swollen ankles, and varicose veins.

**Rybarvin** (*Rybar*) is a proprietary, non-prescription compound BRONCHODILATOR, used to treat asthma. Produced in the form of an inhalant solution (for its own special 'inhalor'), Rybarvin is a preparation of several drugs: the ANTICHOLINERGIC atropine methonitrate, the SYMPATHOMIMETIC adrenaline, the MUSCLE RELAXANT papaverine hydrochloride, and the local ANAESTHETIC benzocaine in a saline (sodium chloride) base. An identical preparation but without the papaverine is also available (under the trade name Rybarvin Inhalant).

▲/◆ side-effects/warning: *see* ADRENALINE; ATROPINE METHONITRATE; BENZOCAINE.

**Rynacrom** (*Fisons*) is a proprietary, non-prescription preparation used to treat allergic nasal congestion. Produced in the form of a nasal spray (with a metered-dose pump), as nasal drops, and in cartridges for nasal insufflation, Rynacrom is a preparation of sodium cromoglycate. A similar nasal spray additionally containing the ANTIHISTAMINE xylometazoline hydrochloride is also available (under the name Rynacrom Compound).

▲/◆ side-effects/warning: *see* SODIUM CROMOGLYCATE; XYLOMETAZOLINE HYDROCHLORIDE.

**Rythmodan** (*Roussel*) is a proprietary ANTIARRHYTHMIC drug, available only on prescription, used to treat heartbeat irregularities and to prevent speeding up of the heart rate (tachycardia). Produced in the form of capsules (in two

strengths), as sustained-release tablets (under the name Rythmodan Retard), and in ampoules for injection, Rythmodan is a preparation of disopyramide. It is not recommended for children.
▲/● side-effects/warning: *see* DISOPYRAMIDE.

R

**Sabidal SR 270** (*Zyma*) is a proprietary, non-prescription BRONCHODILATOR, used to treat asthmatic bronchospasm, emphysema and chronic bronchitis. Produced in the form of sustained-release tablets, Sabidal SR 270 is a preparation of the xanthine drug choline theophyllinate. It is not recommended for children.

▲ / ✿ side-effects/warning: *see* CHOLINE THEOPHYLLINATE.

**Sabril** (*Merrell*) is an ANTI-EPILEPTIC drug, and is a proprietary form of vigabatrin available only on prescription, in the form of tablets.

▲ / ✿ side-effects/warning: *see* VIGABATRIN.

**Saizen** (*Serono*) is a HORMONE, a proprietary form of somatropin, used to treat small stature, and deficiencies of other hormones. It is available only on prescription. The preparation is in the form of a powder for reconstition for injection.

▲ / ✿ side-effects/warning: *see* SOMATROPIN.

**Salactac** (*Dermal*) is a proprietary, non-prescription compound preparation, supplied in the form of a gel for topical application (with its own special applicator). It is intended to remove warts (particularly verrucas) and hardened skin. Salactac's major active constituent is the ANTIBACTERIAL keratolytic salicylic acid.

▲ / ✿ side-effects/warning: *see* SALICYLIC ACID.

**Salactol** (*Dermal*) is a proprietary, non-prescription compound preparation in the form of a paint for topical application, intended to remove warts (particularly verrucas) and hardened skin. With its own special applicator, Salactol's major active constituent is the ANTIBACTERIAL keratolytic salicylic acid.

▲ / ✿ side-effects/warning: *see* SALICYLIC ACID.

**Salazopyrin** (*Pharmacia*) is a proprietary preparation, available only on prescription, used primarily to induce a remission in the symptoms of ulceration of the intestinal wall (generally in the colon) and, having induced it, to maintain it. Because the drug also has ANTI-INFLAMMATORY properties, it is additionally used to treat rheumatoid arthritis (although there are some haematological side-effects). Produced as tablets (in two forms, one enteric-coated under the name Salazopyrin EN-tablets), as suppositories, and as a retention enema in a disposable pack, Salazopyrin is a preparation of the SULPHONAMIDE sulphasalazine.

▲ / ✿ side-effects/warning: *see* SULPHASALAZINE.

**Salbulin** (*Riker*) is a proprietary form of the selective BETA-RECEPTOR STIMULANT salbutamol, used as a BRONCHODILATOR in patients with asthma and other breathing problems. Available only on prescription, Salbulin appears as tablets and as an aerosol metered inhalant. In all cases, patients should not exceed the prescribed or stated dose, and should follow the manufacturer's directions closely.

▲ / ✿ side-effects/warning: *see* SALBUTAMOL.

**salbutamol** is a BRONCHODILATOR, of the type known as a selective BETA-RECEPTOR STIMULANT, used to treat asthmatic bronchospasm, emphysema and chronic bronchitis. It is sometimes also used to prevent or delay premature labour. It has fewer cardiac side-effects than previous drugs of its type, and is administered orally in the form of tablets, as sustained-release tablets, as a sugar-free liquid, and as an inhalant from aerosol, nebulizer, inhalation cartridge, powder disc, or ventilator; it is also administered by injection or infusion.

▲ side-effects: there may be headache and nervous tension, associated with tingling of the fingertips and a fine tremor of the hands. Administration other than by inhalation may cause an increase in the heart rate; infusion may lower blood potassium levels. There may be headache, peripheral vasodilation and pain in the injection site.

◆ warning: salbutamol should be administered with caution to patients with disorders of the thyroid gland, heart disease or hypertension (high blood pressure), who are elderly, or who are pregnant.
*Related articles:* AEROLIN 400; AEROLIN AUTOHALER; ASMAVEN; SALBULIN; SALBUVENT; VENTIDE; VENTODISCS; VENTOLIN; VOLMAX.

**Salbuvent** (*Tillotts*) is a proprietary form of the selective BETA-RECEPTOR STIMULANT salbutamol, used as a BRONCHODILATOR in patients with asthma and other breathing problems. Available only on prescription, Ventolin appears in several forms: as tablets, as syrup, as ampoules for injection, as solution for intravenous infusion, as aerosol inhalant, and as respirator solution for use with a nebuliser or ventilator. In every case, the prescribed or stated dose should not be exceeded, and the manufacturer's directions should be followed closely.
▲/◆ side-effects/warning: *see* SALBUTAMOL.

**salcatonin** is a synthesized form of the thyroid hormone calcitonin

that is particularly suited to long-term therapy of certain bone disorders.
*see* CALCITONIN.

**salicylic acid** is an ANTIFUNGAL drug that is used to treat minor skin infections such as athlete's foot. Administration is topical, in the form of a solution, a collodion (paint or gel), as an ointment – or, in combination with precipitated sulphur, as an ointment or a cream and as a shampoo.

▲ side-effects: side-effects are rare, confined largely to the effects of too widescale an application (*see* below) and to sensitivity reactions.

◆ warning: in applying salicylic acid topically, areas of healthy skin and the anogenital region should be avoided. Application to large areas is also inadvisable (absorption through the skin may lead to gastrointestinal disturbance and ringing in the ears).
*Related articles:* CONDYLINE; PHYTEX; PHYTOCIL; POSALFILIN; SALACTAC; WARTICON.

**salmeterol** is a BRONCHODILATOR, of the type known as a selective BETA-RECEPTOR STIMULANT, used to treat asthmatic bronchospasm. It has only recently been introduced, and is similar to SALBUTAMOL except that it has a much longer duration of action, so it may be used to prevent asthma attacks throughout the night after inhalation. It is administered by inhalation as an aerosol or powder.

▲ side-effects: there may be headache and nervous tension, associated with tingling of the fingertips and a fine tremor of the hands. Administration other than by inhalation may cause an increase in the heart rate; infusion may lower blood potassium levels. There may be headache, peripheral

S

vasodilation and pain in the injection site.

● warning: salmeterol should be administered with caution to patients with disorders of the thyroid gland, heart disease or hypertension (high blood pressure), who are elderly, or who are pregnant.
*Related article:* SEREVENT.

**Salonair** (*Salonpas*) is a proprietary, non-prescription COUNTER-IRRITANT, which, in the form of a spray (from an aerosol) applied to the skin, produces an irritation of the sensory nerve endings that offsets the pain of underlying muscle or joint ailments. Active constituents include two salts of SALICYLIC ACID, menthol, and camphor.

**salsalate** is a long-acting, non-narcotic ANALGESIC much like ASPIRIN but without so many gastric side-effects, used primarily to treat inflammation and pain in rheumatic and other musculo-skeletal disorders. Administration is oral in the form of capsules.

▲ side-effects: side-effects are not as common as they are with aspirin, but may include gastrointestinal disturbance or bleeding, hearing difficulties and ringing in the ears (tinnitus), and/or vertigo. There may also be sensitivity reactions, resulting in asthma-like symptoms and a rash.

● warning: salsalate should not be administered to patients who suffer from peptic ulcers, or who are aged under 12 years. It should be administered with caution to those with severely impaired function of the kidneys or the liver, or who are dehydrated; who are elderly; who have known allergies; who are pregnant or breast feeding; or who are already taking oral anticoagulant drugs.

*Related article:* DISALCID.

**Saltair** (*Salt*) is the name of a series of proprietary, non-prescription products for the care, freshening and sanitization of a stoma (an outlet in the skin surface following the surgical curtailment of the intestines). There is a dusting powder, a cleansing soap, and an antiseptic spray (under the name Saltair 'Protect' Friar's Balsam Spray).

**\*salt substitutes** may be used instead of true salt (sodium chloride) by patients who are on a medically-supervised low-sodium diet. In general, they consist of potassium chloride with or without additives (such as calcium silicate).
*Related article:* RUTHMOL.

**Saluric** (*Merck, Sharp & Dohme*) is a proprietary DIURETIC, available only on prescription, used to treat hypertension (*see* ANTIHYPERTENSIVE) and the accumulation of fluid within the tissues (oedema). Produced in the form of tablets, it is a preparation of the THIAZIDE chlorothiazide.

▲/● side-effects/warning: *see* CHLOROTHIAZIDE.

**Salzone** (*Wallace*) is a proprietary, non-prescription preparation of the non-narcotic ANALGESIC paracetamol, used to treat pain anywhere in the body. It is produced in the form of an elixir for dilution (the potency of the elixir once dilute is retained for 14 days).

▲/● side-effects/warning: *see* PARACETAMOL.

**Sandimmun** (*Sandoz*) is a proprietary preparation of the powerful IMMUNOSUPPRESSANT cyclosporin, available only on prescription, used to prevent tissue rejection following donor grafting or transplant surgery, specifically in bone-marrow, liver, kidney, pancreas, heart, or heart-and-lung transplant operations. It is administered as an oral solution.

▲/✿ side-effects/warning: *see* CYCLOSPORIN.

**Sandocal** (*Sandoz*) is a proprietary MINERAL SUPPLEMENT of calcium, in the form of calcium lactate gluconate, CALCIUM CARBONATE and citric acid. It is available without prescription, and is in the form of effervescent tablets in two strengths, called Sandocal-400 and Sandocal-1000.

▲/✿ side-effects/warning: *see* CALCIUM GLUCONATE; CALCIUM LACTATE.

**Sandoglobulin** (*Sandoz*) is a proprietary preparation of human normal immunoglobulin (HNIG) available only on prescription, used to make up globulin deficiencies in newborn infants. Treatment is by intravenous infusion and may take place over several consecutive days.

✿ warning: *see* HNIG.

**Sando-K** (*Sandoz*) is a proprietary, non-prescription POTASSIUM supplement, used to make up deficient blood levels of potassium. Produced in the form of tablets for effervescent solution in water, it contains POTASSIUM CHLORIDE and potassium bicarbonate, and is not recommended for children.

**Sandostatin** (*Sandoz*) is a proprietary form of octreotide, in a form for injection. It is used to treat the symptoms following release of hormones from certain carcinoid tumours.

▲/✿ side-effects/warning: *see* OCTREOTIDE.

**Sanomigran** (*Sandoz*) is a proprietary preparation of the ANTIHISTAMINE pizotifen, a drug

related to some of the anti-depressants. It is used to treat headaches, particularly those in which blood pressure inside the blood vessels plays a part – such as migraine. Available only on prescription, and produced in the form of tablets (in two strengths) and as a sugar-free elixir, Sanomigran is not recommended for children aged under 5 years.

▲/✿ side-effects/warning: *see* PIZOTIFEN.

**Saventrine** (*Pharmax*) is a proprietary heart stimulant, available only on prescription, used to treat a dangerously low heart rate, or heart block. A preparation of the SYMPATHO-MIMETIC isoprenaline, it works by increasing both the heart rate and the force of contractility of the heart muscle. Saventrine is produced in the form of sustained-release tablets and (under the name Saventrine I.V.) in ampoules for infusion following dilution.

▲/✿ side-effects/warning: *see* ISOPRENALINE.

**Savloclens** (*ICI*) is a proprietary, non-prescription ANTISEPTIC used to prevent infection of wounds and burns. Produced in the form of sachets of sterile solution, Savloclens is a compound preparation of the disinfectants chlorhexidine gluconate and cetrimide. It is generally available only in hospitals.

▲/✿ side-effects/warning: *see* CETRIMIDE; CHLORHEXIDINE.

**Savlodil** (*ICI*) is a proprietary, non-prescription ANTISEPTIC used to prevent infection of wounds and burns. Produced in the form of sachets of sterile solution, Savlodil is a compound preparation of the disinfectants chlorhexidine gluconate and cetrimide. (It is a weaker preparation than the similar Savloclens.)

▲/✿ side-effects/warning: *see*
CETRIMIDE; CHLORHEXIDINE.

**Savlon Hospital
Concentrate** (*ICI*) is a
proprietary, non-prescription
ANTISEPTIC used to prevent
infection of wounds and burns,
and to prepare skin prior to
surgery. Produced in the form of
sachets of sterile solution, Savlon
Hospital Concentrate is a
compound preparation of the
disinfectants chlorhexidine
gluconate and cetrimide, and may
be used in diluted form.

▲/✿ side-effects/warning: *see*
CETRIMIDE; CHLORHEXIDINE.

*scabicidal drugs are used to treat
infestations by itch-mites
(*Sarcoptes scabiei*). The female
mite tunnels into the top surface
of the skin in order to lay eggs,
causing severe irritation as she
does so. Newly-hatched mites,
also causing irritation with their
secretions, then pass easily from
person to person on direct
contact. Treatment is (almost
always) with local applications of
hexachlorophane or benzyl
benzoate in the form of a cream:
these kill the mites. Every
member of an infected household
should be treated, and clothing
and bedding should also be
disinfested.

**Schering PC4** (*Schering*) is a
proprietary ORAL CONTRACEPTIVE,
available only on prescription,
used after sexual intercourse has
taken place. (It is a post-coital or
'morning-after' pill.) Produced in
the form of tablets (two to be
taken not later than 72 hours
after intercourse, and two more
after another 12 hours), Schering
PC4 is particularly useful in
treating patients who have been
subjected to rape. Like certain
other oral contraceptives it
combines an OESTROGEN
(ethinyloestradiol) and a

PROGESTOGEN (levonorgestrel).

▲/✿ side-effects/warning: *see*
ETHINYLOESTRADIOL;
LEVONORGESTREL.

**Scheriproct** (*Schering*) is a
proprietary CORTICOSTEROID-
ANTIHISTAMINE compound with
ANAESTHETIC properties, available
only on prescription, and made up
of the steroid prednisolone
hexanoate, with the
antihistamine clemizole
undecenoate and the local
anaesthetic cinchocaine.
Produced in the form of ointment
and as anal suppositories,
Scheriproct is used to treat piles
(haemorrhoids), anal fissure and
infection of the anal region.

▲/✿ side-effects/warning: *see*
PREDNISOLONE.

**Scoline** (*Duncan Flockhart*) is a
proprietary SKELETAL MUSCLE
RELAXANT, available only on
prescription, that has an effect for
only 5 minutes, and is thus used –
following the initial injection of
an intravenous BARBITURATE in
order to control pain – for short,
complete and predictable
paralysis (mostly during
diagnostic or surgical
procedures). Produced in
ampoules for injection, Scoline is
a preparation of suxamethonium
chloride.

▲/✿ side-effects/warning: *see*
SUXAMETHONIUM CHLORIDE.

**Scopoderm TTS** (*Ciba*) is an
ANTICHOLINERGIC and ANTI-
NAUSEA drug, a proprietary form
of hyoscine hydrobromide,
available only on prescription. It
may be used to prevent motion
sickness because of its ANTI-
EMETIC properties. The
preparation is available in the
form of a special self-adhesive
dressing that releases the active
drug for absorption through the
skin, usually a hairless site
behind the ear. A single dressing

S

should be put in place 5-6 hours before a journey, and can be replaced after 72 hours if necessary. The hands should be washed after application of the dressing.

▲/● side-effects/warning: *see* HYOSCINE.

**scopolamine** is another name for the powerful alkaloid drug hyoscine.
*see* HYOSCINE.

**Sea-Legs** (*Bioceuticals*) is a proprietary, non-prescription, anti-motion sickness preparation. It contains the ANTIHISTAMINE meclozine.

▲/● side-effects/warning: *see* MECLOZINE.

**Secaderm** (*Radiol*) is a proprietary, non-prescription ANTISEPTIC used in topical application to treat boils and abscesses. But it also has the property of improving underlying blood circulation, and is therefore also used to treat such disorders as chilblains, varicose veins or whitlows. Produced in the form of an ointment (salve), Secaderm's active constituents include phenol and turpentine oil.

**Secadrex** (*May & Baker*) is a proprietary compound ANTI-HYPERTENSIVE, available only on prescription, used to treat mild to moderate hypertension (high blood pressure). Produced in the form of tablets (in two strengths), Secadrex is a preparation of the BETA-BLOCKER acebutolol hydrochloride together with the THIAZIDE DIURETIC hydrochlorothiazide.

▲/● side-effects/warning: *see* ACEBUTOLOL; HYDRO-CHLOROTHIAZIDE.

**Seclodin** (*Whitehall Laboratories*) is a proprietary, non-prescription ANALGESIC preparation that contains ibuprofen.

▲/● side-effects/warning: *see* IBUPROFEN.

**Seconal Sodium** (*Lilly*) is a proprietary BARBITURATE, on the controlled drugs list, used as a HYPNOTIC to treat persistent and intractable insomnia. A dangerous and potentially addictive drug, it is produced in the form of capsules (in two strengths) and is a preparation of quinalbarbitone sodium. It is not recommended for children.

▲/● side-effects/warning: *see* QUINALBARBITONE SODIUM.

**Sectral** (*May & Baker*) is a proprietary ANTIHYPERTENSIVE drug, available only on prescription, used to treat hypertension (high blood pressure), heartbeat irregularities, and angina pectoris (heart pain). Produced in the form of capsules (in two strengths) and tablets; and in ampoules for injection, Sectral is a preparation of the BETA-BLOCKER acebutolol hydro-chloride. It is not recommended for children.

▲/● side-effects/warning: *see* ACEBUTOLOL.

**Securon** (*Knoll*) is a proprietary ANTIARRHYTHMIC drug, available only on prescription, used to treat hypertension (high blood pressure), heartbeat irregu-larities, and angina pectoris (heart pain). It works primarily by decreasing oxygen demand. Produced in the form of tablets, in five strengths (Securon SR, which are sustained-release tablets, are the strongest), and as an injection, Securon is a preparation of the calcium antagonist verapamil hydrochloride.

▲/● side-effects/warning: *see* VERAPAMIL HYDROCHLORIDE.

**Securopen** (*Bayer*) is a proprietary ANTIBIOTIC of the penicillin type, available only on prescription, used primarily to treat infections of the urinary tract, upper respiratory tract, and septicaemia. Produced in the form of powder in vials for reconstitution as a medium for infusion, Securopen is a preparation of azlocillin.

▲/ ✤ side-effects/warning: *see* AZLOCILLIN.

**\*sedatives** are drugs that calm and soothe, relieving anxiety and nervous tension, and disposing towards drowsiness. They are used particularly for premedication prior to surgery. Many are hypnotic drugs (such as BARBITURATES) used in doses lower than those administered to induce sleep. The term TRANQUILLIZER is more commonly used of the sedatives (such as BENZODIAZEPINES) that do not tend to cause dependence (addiction).

**Seldane** (*Merrel Dow*) is a proprietary, non-prescription ANTIHISTAMINE, with less sedative properties than many others, used to treat the symptoms of allergic disorders such as hay fever and urticaria (skin rashes). Produced in the form of tablets, it is a preparation of terfenadine.

▲/ ✤ side-effects/warning: *see* TERFENADINE.

**Select-A-Jet Dopamine** (*International Medication Systems*) is a potent proprietary preparation of the SYMPATHOMIMETIC drug dopamine hydrochloride, used to treat cardiogenic shock following a heart attack or during heart surgery. Dosage is critical – too much *or* too little may have harmful effects. It is produced as a liquid in vials for dilution and infusion.

▲/ ✤ side-effects/warning: *see* DOPAMINE.

**selegiline** is a drug that has the effect of inhibiting the enzyme that breaks down the neurotransmitter dopamine in the brain, and is accordingly used in combination with LEVODOPA (which is converted to dopamine in the brain) to treat the symptoms of parkinsonism (*see* ANTIPARKINSONISM). In this way it supplements and extends the action of levodopa, also (in many patients) succesfully reducing some side-effects.

▲ side-effects: there may be nausea and vomiting, with agitation and hypotension (low blood pressure); some patients experience a state of confusion.

✤ warning: in some patients the side-effects are in fact aggravated by the combination of drugs, and the dosage of levodopa may have to be reduced.

*Related article:* ELDEPRYL.

**selenium sulphide** is a substance thought to act as an antidandruff agent, and used accordingly as the active constituent in some shampoos.

✤ warning: selenium sulphide, or preparations containing it, should not be used within 48 hours of a hair colorant or a permanent wave.

**Selexid** (*Leo*) is a proprietary ANTIBIOTIC of the penicillin type, available only on prescription, used to treat many forms of infection caused by gram-negative bacteria, but particularly salmonellosis and infections of the urinary tract. Produced in the form of tablets and as a suspension (in sachets), Selexid is a preparation of the drug pivmecillinam hydrochloride. It is more rapidly absorbed than mecillinam.

▲/ ✤ side-effects/warning: *see* PIVMECILLINAM HYDROCHLORIDE.

505

SENTIAL

**Selexidin** (*Leo*) is a proprietary ANTIBIOTIC of the penicillin type, available only on prescription, used to treat many forms of infection caused by gram-negative bacteria, but particularly those of the intestines and the urinary tract. Produced in the form of a powder for reconstitution as a medium for injections, Selexidin is a preparation of the drug mecillinam.

▲/✛ side-effects/warning: *see* MECILLINAM.

**Selsun** (*Abbott*) is a proprietary, non-prescription shampoo containing SELENIUM SULPHIDE, a substance thought to act as an antidandruff agent. Selsun should not be used within 48 hours of a hair colorant or a permanent wave.

**Semi-Daonil** (*Hoechst*) is a proprietary form of the SULPHONYLUREA glibenclamide, available only on prescription, used to treat adult-onset diabetes mellitus. It works by augmenting what remains of insulin production in the pancreas, and is produced in the form of tablets (at half the strength of DAONIL tablets).

▲/✛ side-effects/warning: *see* GLIBENCLAMIDE.

**Semitard MC** (*Novo*) is a proprietary, non-prescription preparation of highly purified pork insulin zinc suspension, used to treat and maintain diabetic patients. It is produced in vials for injection.

▲/✛ side-effects/warning: *see* INSULIN.

**Semprex** (*Calmic*) is an ANTIHISTAMINE drug used for the relief of allergic symptoms such as in hay fever and skin itching. Available only on prescription, in capsules.

▲/✛ side-effects/warning: *see* ACRIVASTINE.

**senna** is a powerful stimulant LAXATIVE, which acts by increasing the muscular activity of the intestinal walls. It is still in fairly common use, but may take between 8 and 12 hours to have any relieving effect on constipation. Senna preparations also may be administered to evacuate the bowels before an abdominal X-ray or prior to endoscopy or surgery.

▲ side-effects: the urine may be coloured red. Senna may cause abdominal cramp and prolonged use of such a stimulant can eventually wear out the muscles on which it works, thus causing severe intestinal problems in terms of motility and absorption.

✛ warning: senna preparations should not be administered to patients who suffer from intestinal blockage or who are pregnant; they should be administered with caution to children.

*Related articles:* MANEVAC; SENOKOT; X-PREP.

**Senokot** (*Reckitt & Colman*) is a proprietary LAXATIVE containing preparations of senna derivatives (sennosides), used to treat constipation or administered to prepare patients for X-ray, endoscopy or surgery. Non-prescription preparations are produced in the form of granules or as a syrup for dilution (the potency of the syrup once dilute is retained for 14 days). Senokot in tablet form is available only on prescription. It is not recommended in any form for children aged under 2 years.

▲/✛ side-effects/warning: *see* SENNA.

**Sential** (*Pharmacia*) is a proprietary CORTICOSTEROID cream for topical application, used mostly to treat mild inflammation of the skin and to

506

assist in the treatment of eczema. Available only on prescription, Sential is a compound preparation of the steroid hydrocortisone, together with urea and sodium chloride, in a water-miscible base.

▲/ ✸ side-effects/warning: *see* HYDROCORTISONE.

**Septex No.2** (*Norton*) is a proprietary ANTIBACTERIAL cream, available only on prescription, used for topical application on minor skin infections and as an antiseptic on abrasions and burns. Active constituents include ZINC OXIDE and the SULPHONAMIDE sulphathiazole.

**Septrin** (*Wellcome*) is a proprietary ANTIBIOTIC combination available only on prescription, used to treat bacterial infections, especially of the urinary tract, infections such as sinusitis and bronchitis, and infections of bones and joints. Produced in the form of tablets (in three strengths), as soluble (dispersible) tablets, as a suspension (in two strengths) for dilution (the potency of either suspension once diluted is retained for 14 days), and in ampoules for injection or (following dilution) infusion, Septrin is a preparation of the compound drug co-trimoxazole, made up of the SULPHONAMIDE sulphamethoxazole, with trimethoprim.

▲/ ✸ side-effects/warning: *see* CO-TRIMOXAZOLE.

**Serc** (*Duphar*) is a proprietary ANTI-EMETIC, available only on prescription, used to relieve symptoms of nausea caused by the vertigo and loss of balance experienced in infections of the middle and inner ears. Produced in the form of tablets, Serc is a preparation of the VASODILATOR betahistine hydrochloride. It is

not recommended for children.

▲/ ✸ side-effects/warning: *see* BETAHISTINE HYDROCHLORIDE.

**Serenace** (*Searle*) is a proprietary series of preparations of the ANTIPSYCHOTIC drug haloperidol, all available only on prescription, and used to treat most forms of mental disturbance from short-term anxiety to long-term psychosis (including schizophrenia and mania, in emergency and maintenance modes of treatment). Serenace is produced as tablets (in four strengths), as capsules, as a liquid for swallowing, and in ampoules for injection (in two strengths). In all forms except that of the liquid, Serenace is not recommended for children.

▲/ ✸ side-effects/warning: *see* HALOPERIDOL.

**Serevent** (*Allen & Hanbury*) is a proprietary form of the selective BETA-RECEPTOR STIMULANT salmeterol, used as a BRONCHODILATOR in patients with asthma and other breathing problems. Available only on prescription, it appears as an aerosol and as a powder for inhalation using the Diskhaler device. In all cases, patients should not exceed the prescribed or stated dose, and should follow the manufacturer's directions closely.

▲/ ✸ side-effects/warning: *see* SALMETEROL.

**Serophene** (*Serono*) is a proprietary hormonal preparation used to treat the kind of infertility in women caused by a deficiency in the hormonal contact between the hypothalamus and the pituitary gland (which produces the GONADOTROPHINS) such that ovulation does not occur. Available only on prescription,

Serophene is produced in the form of tablets containing a preparation of clomiphene citrate.

▲/ ● side-effects/warning: *see* CLOMIPHENE CITRATE.

**Serpasil** (*Ciba*) is a proprietary ANTIHYPERTENSIVE drug, available only on prescription, used to treat all forms of hypertension (high blood pressure). Produced in the form of tablets, Serpasil is a preparation of the RAUWOLFIA ALKALOID reserpine - a powerful drug that causes its antihypertensive effects by acting on the brain and thus may have psychological effects. It is not recommended for children.

▲/ ● side-effects/warning: *see* RESERPINE.

**Serpasil-Esidrex** (*Ciba*) is a proprietary ANTIHYPERTENSIVE drug, available only on prescription, used to treat all forms of hypertension (high blood pressure). Produced in the form of tablets, Serpasil is a compound preparation of the RAUWOLFIA ALKALOID reserpine together with the THIAZIDE DIURETIC hydrochlorothiazide. It is not recommended for children.

▲/ ● side-effects/warning: *see* HYDROCHLOROTHIAZIDE; RESERPINE.

**Setlers** (*Beecham Health Care*) is a proprietary, non-prescription ANTACID containing calcium carbonate and magnesium carbonate.

▲/ ● side-effects/warning: *see* CALCIUM CARBONATE; MAGNESIUM CARBONATE.

**Sevredol** (*Napp*) is a proprietary narcotic ANALGESIC on the controlled drugs list. It is used primarily to relieve pain following surgery, or the pain experienced during the final stages of terminal malignant

disease. Produced in the form of tablets (in two strengths), it is a preparation of the OPIATE and NARCOTIC morphine sulphate.

▲/ ● side-effects/warning: *see* MORPHINE.

**SH 420** (*Schering*) is a proprietary PROGESTOGEN, available only on prescription, used to assist in the treatment of breast cancer (and especially in cases that are inoperable). Produced in the form of tablets, SH 420 is a preparation of norethisterone acetate.

▲/ ● side-effects/warning: *see* NORETHISTERONE.

**Siloxyl** (*Martindale*) is a proprietary, non-prescription ANTACID compound, which is not available from the National Health Service. It is used to treat acid stomach, indigestion and flatulence, and to soothe a peptic ulcer. Produced in the form of tablets and as a suspension, Siloxyl is a preparation of ALUMINIUM HYDROXIDE together with the antifoaming agent DIMETHICONE.

**silver nitrate** is a salt that has astringent and ANTISEPTIC properties useful in topical application to wounds and burns, and is also used as a styptic (to stop bleeding or suppuration) or as a caustic (to cauterize warts). Administration is thus topical, mostly in creams and ointments, or in solution, but also in the form of sticks. In other countries silver nitrate is sometimes used in mild solution in eye-drops.

● warning: silver nitrate is toxic if ingested; prolonged application discolours the skin (and fabrics). Solutions should be protected from light.

**silver protein** is a minor constituent of some nose-drops and a nasal spray, used to treat nasal infections. It has some astringent and ANTISEPTIC properties, but prolonged treatment may lead to silver poisoning (argyria).

**silver sulphadiazine** is a compound ANTIBIOTIC preparation of silver with the SULPHONAMIDE sulphadiazine. In the form of a cream for topical application, it has broad-spectrum ANTI-BACTERIAL capability as well as the astringent and ANTISEPTIC qualities of the silver, and is used primarily to inhibit infection of burns and bedsores.
▲ side-effects: side-effects are rare, but there may be sensitivity reactions including rashes.
◆ warning: silver sulphadiazine should not be administered to patients who are allergic to sulphonamides; it should be administered with caution to those with impaired function of the liver or kidneys.
*Related article:* FLAMAZINE.

**Simeco** (*Wyeth*) is a proprietary, non-prescription ANTACID compound, which is not available from the National Health Service. It is used to treat acid stomach, indigestion and flatulence, and to soothe a peptic ulcer. Produced in the form of tablets and as a suspension, Simeco is a preparation of magnesium carbonate, magnesium hydroxide and ALUMINIUM HYDROXIDE with the antifoaming agent DIMETHICONE.
▲/◆ side-effects/warning: *see* MAGNESIUM CARBONATE; MAGNESIUM HYDROXIDE.

**Simpla Sassco** (*Simpla*) is a proprietary, non-prescription gel used to protect and sanitize a stoma (an outlet in the skin surface after the surgical curtailment of the intestines).

**simple eye ointment** is a bland, sterile formulation of liquid paraffin and wool fat, used both as

a night-time eye lubricant (in conditions that cause dry eyes) and to soften the crusts of infections of the eyelids (blepharitis):
◆ warning: wool fat may cause sensitivity reactions in some patients.

**simple linctus** is a non-proprietary formulation of fairly standard constituents that together make an ANTITUSSIVE as good as many proprietary ones. The constituents include citric acid, anise water, amaranth solution and chloroform spirit.

**simple ointment** is a bland, sterile formulation of liquid paraffin, wool fat and stearyl alcohol, used as a household ointment for topical application on minor wounds and burns, and areas of dry or cracked skin.
◆ warning: wool fat may cause sensitivity reactions in some patients.

**Simplene** (*Smith & Nephew*) is a proprietary preparation of the SYMPATHOMIMETIC hormone adrenaline, in very mild solution, in the form of eye-drops within a viscous vehicle. Available only on prescription, it is used to treat all forms of glaucoma except closed-angle glaucoma.
▲/◆ side-effects/warning: *see* ADRENALINE.

**simvastin** is a newly developed drug that is used to lower lipid (fat) levels in the blood where this is markedly elevated (hyperlipidaemia). It is used in patients who do not respond to, or who are intolerant of, other therapy. It acts by inhibiting one of the enzymes that catalyses a step in the synthesis within the body of cholesterol. It is available in the form of tablets.
▲ side-effects: there may be constipation or diarrhoea, abdominal cramps, flatulence,

S

fatigue, insomnia, or a rash. As well as raised levels of the enzyme creatine phosphokinase.

❀ warning: the liver function must be monitored, and an annual eye examination given. Do not use in patients with liver disease, who are pregnant or lactating, or where there is porphyria. Avoid pregnancy during, or for a month after, treatment.
*Related article:* ZOCOR.

**Sinemet** (*Merck, Sharp & Dohme*) is a proprietary preparation of the powerful drug levodopa in combination with the enzyme inhibitor CARBIDOPA; it is available only on prescription. Sinemet is used to treat parkinsonism, but not the parkinsonian symptoms induced by drugs (*see* ANTIPARKINSONISM): the carbidopa prevents too rapid a breakdown of the levodopa (into dopamine) in the periphery, thus allowing more levodopa to reach the brain to make up the deficiency (of dopamine), which is the major cause of parkinsonism symptoms. Sinemet is produced in the form of tablets with a levodopa/carbidopa ratio of 10:1 (in two strengths), and of 4:1 (in two strengths) under the names Sinemet LS and Sinemet Plus.
▲/❀ side-effects/warning: *see* LEVODOPA.

**Sinequan** (*Pfizer*) is a proprietary ANTIDEPRESSANT drug, available only on prescription. Used especially in cases where sedation is deemed necessary. Produced in the form of capsules (in four strengths), Sinequan is a preparation of doxepin. It is not recommended for children.
▲/❀ side-effects/warning: *see* DOXEPIN.

**Sinthrome** (*Geigy*) is a proprietary oral ANTI-

COAGULANT, available only on prescription, used to prevent or treat conditions of thrombosis and to improve blood circulation through the brain and the heart. Produced in the form of tablets (in two strengths), Sinthrome is a preparation of the synthesized anticoagulant nicoumalone. It is not recommended for children.
▲/❀ side-effects/warning: *see* NICOUMALONE.

**Sintisone** (*Farmitalia Carlo Erba*) is a proprietary CORTICOSTEROID preparation, available only on prescription, used to treat inflammation (particularly rheumatoid arthritis and inflammatory skin diseases) and to suppress the symptoms of allergy (particularly those of asthma). Produced in the form of tablets, Sintisone is a preparation of the cortisone-derivative prednisolone.
▲/❀ side-effects/warning: *see* PREDNISOLONE.

**Siopel** (*Care*) is a proprietary, non-prescription barrier cream used to treat and dress itching skin and skin infections, nappy rash and bedsores, or to protect and sanitize a stoma (an outlet on the skin surface following the surgical curtailment of the intestines). It contains the antiseptic CETRIMIDE and the antifoaming agent DIMETHICONE.

*****skeletal muscle relaxants** act on voluntary (skeletal) muscles of the body. Some are used during operations to aid surgery (e.g. tubocurarine) and act by interfering with the actions of the neurotransmitter acetylcholine at sites between nerve and muscle. Others used in the treatment of painful muscle spasms act within the central nervous system (e.g. DIAZEPAM). Drugs of this class are quite distinct from SMOOTH MUSCLE RELAXANTS.

**Slo-Indo** (*Generics*) is a proprietary, ANTI-INFLAMATORY, non-narcotic ANALGESIC, available only on prescription, used to relieve the pain of rheumatic disease, gout, and other inflammatory musculo-skeletal disorders. Produced in the form of sustained-release capsules, Slo-Indo is a preparation of indomethacin.

▲/ ✦ side-effects/warning: *see* INDOMETHACIN.

**Slo-Phyllin** (*Lipha*) is a proprietary, non-prescription BRONCHODILATOR, used to treat asthmatic bronchospasm, emphysema and chronic bronchitis. Produced in the form of sustained-release capsules (in three strengths), Slo-Phyllin is a preparation of the xanthine drug theophylline. It is not recommended for children aged under 2 years.

▲/ ✦ side-effects/warning: *see* THEOPHYLLINE.

**Sloprolol** (*CP Pharmaceuticals*) is a proprietary BETA-BLOCKER, available only on prescription, used to treat angina pectoris (heart pain), myocardial infarction, heart arrhythmias, high blood pressure (hypertension) and anxiety; to try to prevent migraine attacks; and to assist in the treatment of excess thyroid hormones in the blood (thyrotoxicosis). Produced in the form of sustained-release capsules Sloprolol is a preparation of propranolol hydrochloride. In the treatment of most of the disorders listed above, Sloprolol is not recommended for children.

▲/ ✦ side-effects/warning: *see* PROPRANOLOL.

**Slow-Fe** (*Ciba*) is a proprietary, non-prescription IRON supplement, used to treat iron deficiency in the bloodstream.

Produced in the form of sustained-release tablets, Slow-Fe is a preparation of ferrous sulphate. It is not recommended for children aged under 12 months.

▲/ ✦ side-effects/warning: *see* FERROUS SULPHATE.

**Slow-Fe Folic** (*Ciba*) is a proprietary IRON-and-VITAMIN supplement, used to prevent a deficiency of iron and vitamin B, particularly during pregnancy. Produced in the form of sustained-release tablets, Slow-Fe is a combination of ferrous sulphate and folic acid. It should not be taken by patients already taking tetracycline antibiotics.

▲/ ✦ side-effects/warning: *see* FERROUS SULPHATE.

**Slow-K** (*Ciba*) is a proprietary, non-prescription POTASSIUM supplement, used to make up a blood deficiency of potassium (as may occur in the elderly, in patients with severe diarrhoea, or in patients being treated with diuretics). Produced in the form of sustained-release tablets, Slow-K is a preparation of potassium chloride.

**Slow-Pren** (*Norton*) is a proprietary ANTIHYPERTENSIVE drug, available only on prescription, used to treat hypertension (high blood pressure), angina pectoris (heart pain) and heartbeat irregularities, and to assist in the treatment of excess levels of thyroid hormones (thyrotoxicosis). Produced in the form of sustained-release tablets, Slow-Pren is a preparation of the BETA-BLOCKER oxprenolol hydrochloride.

▲/ ✦ side-effects/warning: *see* OXPRENOLOL.

**Slow-Trasicor** (*Ciba*) is a proprietary ANTIHYPERTENSIVE drug, available only on prescription, used to treat

**S**

hypertension (high blood pressure), angina pectoris and heartbeat irregularities, and to relieve anxiety. Produced in the form of sustained-release tablets, Slow-Trasicor is a preparation of the BETA-BLOCKER oxprenolol hydrochloride.
▲/◆ side-effects/warning: see OXPRENOLOL.

**smallpox vaccine** is now retained only in specialist centres for researchers working with dangerous viruses (and in a possible emergency on doctors who may be called to treat suspected cases of smallpox) for smallpox has officially been eradicated. Technically, however, smallpox vaccine is still available on prescription, and consists of a suspension of live (but attenuated) viruses, freeze-dried and supplied with a diluent for reconstitution. Administration is through a short linear scratch, or by 'multiple pressure inoculation'.
◆ warning: smallpox vaccine should not be administered to patients who are pregnant or aged under 12 months, or with any infection or immune system deficiency.

**\*smooth muscle relaxants** act on the involuntary muscles throughout the body to reduce spasm (an ANTISPASMODIC) or induce relaxation. Thus they may be used to dilate blood vessels and improve circulation in the extremities, lower blood pressure (ANTIHYPERTENSIVE), or relieve the strain on the heart of angina pectoris. They can induce brocdodilation in the treatment of asthma, and may help spasm of the intestine or uterus. Drugs of this class are quite distinct from SKELETAL MUSCLE RELAXANTS.

**Sno Phenicol** (*Smith & Nephew*) is a proprietary ANTIBIOTIC used to treat bacterial infections. It is

a preparation of the potentially toxic drug chloramphenicol.
▲/◆ side-effects/warning: see CHLORAMPHENICOL.

**Sno-Pilo** (*Smith & Nephew*) is a proprietary form of eye-drops, available only on prescription, used to treat most types of glaucoma. It is a dilute solution of the PARASYMPATHOMIMETIC pilocarpine hydrochloride in a viscous fluid.
▲/◆ side-effects/warning: see PILOCARPINE.

**Sno Tears** (*Smith & Nephew*) is a proprietary, non-prescription form of synthetic tears administered in drops to lubricate the surface of the eye in patients whose lachrymal glands or ducts are dysfunctioning. It is a preparation of POLYVINYL ALCOHOL.

**sodium acid phosphate** is an acid DIURETIC, although its main use is in combination either with other phosphorus salts as a phosphorus supplement, or with HEXAMINE to treat infections of the urinary tract.

**Sodium Amytal** (*Lilly*) is a proprietary preparation of the BARBITURATE amylobarbitone sodium, a drug on the controlled drugs list, used to relieve intractable insomnia in cases other than where pain is the cause. Side-effects may be severe – it is not recommended for children – and dependence (addiction) occurs readily. It is produced in the form of capsules (in two strengths) or tablets (in two strengths), or as a powder for reconstitution as a medium for injection.
*see* AMYLOBARBITONE.

**sodium aurothiomalate** is the form in which the metallic element gold may be prescribed to treat severe conditions of active rheumatoid arthritis. Unlike ANTI-INFLAMMATORY, non-narcotic ANALGESICS, however, gold works slowly so that full effects are achieved only after some months and treatment is continued for up to 5 years. Improvement then is significant, not only in the reduction of joint inflammation but also in associated inflammations. Administration is by intramuscular injection.

▲ side-effects: about one in every twenty patients experiences severe reactions, especially blood disorders; in all patients there may be skin reactions, mouth ulcers, the accumulation of fluid in the tissues (oedema) and/or neural effects in the extremities.

● warning: sodium aurothio-malate should not be administered to patients who suffer from blood disorders; regular blood counts during treatment are essential. It should be administered with caution to those with impaired function of the liver or kidneys, eczema or colitis; who are elderly; or who are pregnant or lactating. Weekly test doses should be administered to establish changing levels of tolerance within the body; treatment under such monitoring – unless relapse occurs – may then continue for some years.
*Related article:* MYOCRISIN.

**sodium bicarbonate** is an ANTACID used for the rapid relief of indigestion and acid stomach. For this purpose it is readily available in the form of powder (for solution), as tablets or as a mixture (liquid). Sodium bicarbonate is also sometimes used in infusion (together with sodium chloride) to relieve conditions of severe metabolic acidosis – when the acidity of body fluids is badly out of balance with the alkalinity as may occur in renal failure or diabetic coma.

▲ side-effects: following the intake of sodium bicarbonate as an antacid, belching is virtually inevitable through the liberation of carbon dioxide.

● warning: sodium bicarbonate should not be taken by patients with impaired kidney function, or who are on a low-sodium diet. Prolonged use is to be avoided, or the cramps and muscular weakness of alkalosis may occur.
*Related article:* MIN-I-JET SODIUM BICARBONATE.

**sodium calciumedetate** is a CHELATING AGENT, an antidote to poisoning by heavy metals, especially by lead. It works by forming chemical complexes, binding (and so neutralizing) metal ions to the drug which can then be excreted safely in the usual fashion. Administration is by injection or by topical application in the form of a cream (on areas of skin that have become broken or sensitive through contact with the metal).

▲ side-effects: there may be nausea and/or cramp. Overdosage causes kidney damage.

● warning: sodium calciumedetate should be administered with caution to patients with impaired kidney function.
*Related article:* LEDCLAIR.

**sodium carboxymethyl cellulose** is another name for carmellose sodium.
*see* CARMELLOSE SODIUM.

**sodium cellulose phosphate** is a drug used to help reduce high levels of calcium in the blood. It effects this by inhibiting calcium absorption from food, although a

low-calcium diet is also essential.
Administration is in the form of a
powder (marketed in sachets) to
be sprinkled on food.
▲ side-effects: there may be
diarrhoea.
✦ warning: sodium cellulose
phosphate should not be
administered to patients with
impaired function of the
kidneys, or congestive heart
failure. Reduction in blood
calcium may result in an
imbalance in the blood of
phosphates, with associated
detrimental effects.
*Related article:* CALCISORB.

**sodium chlodronate** is a drug
used to treat high calcium levels
associated with malignant
tumours. Administration is oral
in the form of tablets or slow
intravenous infusion. Dietary
counselling of patients is advised,
particularly with regard to
avoiding calcium-containing food
products during oral treatment.
▲ side-effects: there may be
nausea and diarrhoea, and
occasionally skin reactions.
There may be lowered calcium
levels (hypocalcaemia).
✦ warning: sodium chlodronate
should be administered with
caution to patients with
impaired kidney function or
intestinal inflammation,
pregnant or lactating women.
Kidney and liver function, and
white cell count should be
monitored.
*Related article:* LORON.

**sodium chloride** is a vital
constituent of the human body, in
both blood and tissues, and is the
major form in which the mineral
element sodium appears. (Sodium
is involved in the balance of
extracellular fluids, maintains
electrical potentials in the
nervous system, and is essential
for the functioning of the
muscles). Sodium chloride, or

salt, is contained in many foods;
too much salt in the diet may lead
to the accumulation of fluids in
the tissues (oedema), dehydration,
and/or high blood pressure
(hypertension). Therapeutically,
sodium chloride is widely used as
saline solution (0.9%) or as
dextrose saline (to treat
dehydration and shock), as a
medium with which to effect
bladder irrigation (specifically to
dissolve blood clots), as a sodium
supplement in patients with low
sodium levels, as an eye-wash, as
nose-drops, and as a mouth-wash,
to topical application in solution
as a cleansing lotion.
▲ side-effects: overdosage may
lead to high blood pressure
(hypertension), dehydration,
and the accumulation of fluid
within the tissues (oedema).
✦ warning: sodium chloride
should be administered with
caution to patients with heart
failure, high blood pressure
(hypertension), fluid retention,
or impaired kidney function.

**sodium citrate** is an alkaline
compound, used to treat infections
of the urinary tract (especially
cystitis) in which the urine is acid.
It is also used in the treatment of
gout to promote the excretion of
uric acid, and may additionally be
used to assist in the dissolution of
blood clots within the bladder.
Administration is oral, in the form
of granules (marketed in sachets)
for solution in water.
▲ side-effects: there may be dry
mouth and mild diuresis.
✦ warning: sodium citrate should
be administered with caution to
patients with impaired kidney
function or heart disease, or
who are pregnant.
*Related articles:* BENILYN
EXPECTORANT; DEXTROLYTE;
URISAL.

**sodium cromoglycate** is a drug
used to prevent recurrent asthma
attacks. How it works is not fully

understood though it seems to prevent release of inflammatory mediators, but its BRONCHO-DILATOR and ANTISPASMODIC effect is particularly marked in allergic conditions. It is used solely prophylactically: the drug has no remedial value in acute attacks. Advice to this effect – that administration must be regular whether symptoms are present or not – is generally given by the prescribing doctor. Administration is usually in the form of inhalation, either from an aerosol or nebulizer, or from an applicator that squirts dry powder.

▲ side-effects: there may be coughing accompanied by temporary bronchospasm. Inhalation of the dry powder preparation may cause irritation of the throat.

◉ warning: dosage is adjusted to the requirements of individual patients (but administration is generally 4 times a day).
*Related article:* INTAL.

**sodium fluoride** is the normal form of fluoride in toothpastes and added to many water supplies to assist in the prevention of tooth decay. Because many water authorities now add fluoride to their region's drinking-water, sodium fluoride should be administered therapeutically only in relation to levels each patient would naturally be receiving anyway. Administration is oral in the form of tablets, as drops, as a gel, or as a mouth-wash. Fluoride supplements are not recommended for children under 6 months of age.

▲ side-effects: some patients eventually notice white flecks on their teeth; overdosage may cause yellow-brown discoloration.

◉ warning: in general, sodium fluoride is normally prescribed only in areas where the water is not fluoridated at source.
*Related articles:* EN-DE-KAY; FLUOR-A-DAY LAC; FLUORIGARD; POINT-TWO; ZYMAFLUOR.

**sodium fusidate** is a narrow-spectrum ANTIBIOTIC used most commonly in combination with other antibiotics to treat staphylococcal infections – especially skin infections, abscesses and infections of bone – that prove to be resistant to penicillin. The drug works by inhibiting protein synthesis at the ribosome level in sensitive organisms (gram-positive bacteria). Administration is oral in the form of tablets and as a suspension, by infusion, and by application as an ointment or impregnated gauze dressing. It is also used in the form of fusidic acid.

▲ side-effects: there may be nausea with vomiting; a rash may occur. Some patients experience temporary kidney dysfunction.

◉ warning: regular monitoring of liver function is essential during treatment.
*Related articles:* FUCIDIN; FUCITHALMIC; FUSIDIC ACID.

**sodium hypochlorite solutions** are used as DISINFECTANTS for cleansing abrasions, burns and ulcers. They differ only in concentration. Non-proprietary solutions are available in 8% and 1% (chlorine) concentrations. Both must be diluted before use, for normal skin can tolerate no more than 0.5% available chlorine in topical application.

**sodium ironedetate** is a form in which IRON can be made available to the body, an iron supplement used to treat iron deficiency and associated anaemia. Administration is oral in the form of a sugar-free elixir.

▲ side-effects: large doses may cause gastrointestinal upset and diarrhoea; there may be vomiting. Prolonged treatment may result in constipation.

✢ warning: sodium ironedetate should not be administered to patients already taking tetracycline antibiotics.
*Related article:* SYTRON.

**sodium lactate** was formerly used to treat diabetic coma and the acidosis (the high ratio of acid to alkali in the body and the loss of sodium, potassium and ketones in the urine) associated with the diabetic condition. Containing sodium lactate as the active constituent, a preparation suitable for intravenous infusion was known as Hartmann's or M/6 solution. Now, however, a solution of sodium bicarbonate is preferred. Instead, sodium lactate presently is a minor constituent of one or two sodium supplements.

▲ side-effects: administration of sodium lactate may produce another form of acidosis in patients with poor circulation or impaired function of the liver.
*Related article:* DEXTROLYTE.

**sodium nitrite** is a VASODILATOR used in an emergency, often in combination with sodium thiosulphate, to treat cyanide poisoning. It was formerly also used to treat angina pectoris (heart pain). Administration is by injection of a mild aqueous solution.

▲ side-effects: there may be flushing and headache, caused by the vasodilating effect of the drug. Some patients experience gastrointestinal disturbance, dizziness and a loss of sensation in the extremities.

**sodium nitroprusside** is a VASODILATOR used in an emergency to treat apoplexy (a

hypertensive crisis); but it may be used more ordinarily to treat heart failure, and during surgery to effect a controlled low blood pressure. Administration is by infusion.

▲ side-effects: headache, dizziness, sweating, nausea and heartbeat irregularities are all fairly common; there may also be abdominal pain and, in some patients, anxiety.

✢ warning: sodium nitroprusside should not be administered to patients with impaired liver function or body deficiency in cyanocobalamin (vitamin $B_{12}$); it should be administered with caution to those with impaired kidney function, impaired blood circulation through the brain, or the effects of an insufficient supply of thyroid hormones (hypothyroidism), or who are elderly. Strict observation of patients is essential throughout treatment, and should include blood counts.
*Related article:* NIPRIDE.

**sodium perborate** is an ANTISEPTIC (and deodorant) powder that is soluble in water. As a mouth-wash the solution has a cleansing effect because it tends to froth on contact with plaque and other oral debris.

✢ warning: sodium perborate should not be used continuously for more than about 4 weeks or borate poisoning may occur.
*Related article:* BOCASAN.

**sodium picosulphate** is a stimulant LAXATIVE, which works by direct action on the nerve endings within the intestinal walls of the colon. Prescribed not only to relieve constipation and to prepare patients for X-ray, endoscopy or surgery, the drug is administered orally in the form of an elixir or a solution.

▲ side-effects: prolonged use may eventually precipitate the onset of atonic non-functioning colon.

◉ warning: sodium picosulphate should not be administered to patients who suffer from intestinal blockage or who are pregnant; it should be administered with caution to children.

*Related articles*: LAXOBERAL; PICOLAX.

**sodium salicylate** is a soluble, non-narcotic ANALGESIC and ANTI-INFLAMMATORY agent used in both capacities to treat rheumatic and other musculo-skeletal disorders. Administration is oral in the form of a non-proprietary mixture (liquid).

▲ side-effects: gastrointestinal upset is common; there may also be nausea, hearing disturbances and vertigo; some patients experience ulceration and bleeding. Rarely, there is a state of confusion, sensitivity reactions (such as asthma-like attacks or a rash), inflammation of the heart, or blood disorders.

◉ warning: sodium salicylate should not be administered to patients with peptic ulcers or who are aged under 12 years; it should be administered with caution to those with severely impaired function of the kidneys or the liver, allergies or dehydration, who are pregnant or lactating, who are elderly, or who are already taking anticoagulant drugs.

**sodium stibogluconate** is an ANTHELMINTIC, used to treat forms of the tropical disease leishmaniasis or kala-azar (caused by parasitic protozoa transmitted in sandfly bites) that leave extensive or unsightly lesions on the skin surface, or that have a similar effect internally.

Administration is by slow intravenous injection (which must immediately be halted if there is an attack of coughing or the onset of chest pain), or intramuscular injection (which can be painful).

▲ side-effects: there may be vomiting, coughing and chest pain; continued treatment may lead to severe weight loss (anorexia).

◉ warning: sodium stibogluconate should not be administered to patients with hepatitis, pneumonia, kidney disease or inflammation of the heart.

*Related article:* PENTOSTAM.

**sodium tetradecyl sulphate** is a drug used in sclerotherapy – a technique to treat varicose veins by the injection of an irritant solution. The resultant inflammation of the vein promotes the obliteration of the vein by thrombosis.

▲ side-effects: some patients experience sensitivity reactions.

◉ warning: sodium tetradecyl sulphate should not be injected into patients whose varicose veins are already inflamed or so painful as to prevent walking, who are obese, or who are taking oral contraceptives.

*Related article:* STD.

**sodium thiosulphate** is a compound used in an emergency, often in combination with sodium nitrite, to treat cyanide poisoning. Administration is by injection of a mild aqueous solution.

▲ side-effects: there may be flushing and headache, caused by the vasodilating effect of the drug. Some patients experience gastrointestinal disturbance, dizziness and a loss of sensation in the extremities.

**sodium valproate** is an ANTICONVULSANT drug used to treat epilepsy. It is particularly effective in controlling grand mal (tonic-clonic) seizures in primary generalized epilepsy, although it is used to treat all forms of the disorder. The drug is also occasionally used to treat the rare cases of recurrent febrile convulsions in children, to whom it may be administered prophylactically. Administration is oral in the form of tablets and as a liquid (or dilute syrup).

▲ side-effects: there may be nausea and gastrointestinal disturbance, increased appetite and consequent weight gain, temporary hair loss, and impaired liver function. If severe vomiting and weight loss occur, treatment should be withdrawn at once.

✿ warning: sodium valproate should not be administered to patients with liver disease: liver function should be monitored for at least the first 6 months of treatment. The drug may cause some blood count readings to be misleading in relation to diabetic patients. *Related article:* EPILIM.

**Sofradex** (*Roussel*)is a proprietary compound ANTIBIOTIC, available only on prescription, used to treat inflammation and infection in the eye or outer ear. Produced in the form of drops and as an ointment, Sofradex is a combination of the CORTICOSTEROID dexamethasone and the broad-spectrum antibiotic framycetin.

▲/✿ side-effects/warning: *see* DEXAMETHASONE; FRAMYCETIN.

**Soframycin** (*Roussel*) is a proprietary ANTIBIOTIC, available only on prescription, used to treat many forms of infection. Major uses include disinfection of the intestines (especially prior to intestinal surgery), topical application on the skin, injection into the membranes that surround the spinal cord, as eye-drops and eye ointment, and as a cream for use in the outer ear. Produced in the form of tablets, as a powder for reconstitution as a medium for injection or for topical application, as drops, as an ointment and as a water-miscible cream, Soframycin in all forms is a preparation of the broad-spectrum aminoglycoside framycetin sulphate.

▲/✿ side-effects/warning: *see* FRAMYCETIN.

**Solarcaine** (*Plough*) is a proprietary, non-prescription local ANAESTHETIC used in topical application to treat local pain and skin irritation. Produced in the form of a cream, as a lotion, and as a spray, Solarcaine is a combination of benzocaine with the DISINFECTANT TRICLOSAN.

✿ warning: *see* BENZOCAINE.

**Solis** (*Galen*) is a proprietary ANXIOLYTIC drug, available on prescription only to private patients, used to treat anxiety and insomnia, and to assist in the treatment of acute alcohol withdrawal symptoms. Also a MUSCLE RELAXANT, Solis is sometimes also used to relieve muscle spasm. Produced in the form of capsules (in two strengths), it is a preparation of the BENZODIAZEPINE diazepam.

▲/✿ side-effects/warning: *see* DIAZEPAM.

**Solivito** (*KabiVitrum*) is a proprietary VITAMIN supplement, available only on prescription, used in injection or infusion. It contains almost all forms of VITAMIN B together with ASCORBIC ACID (vitamin C), and is produced in the form of a powder for reconstitution either with water or with glucose (or an equivalent medium).

**Soliwax** (*Martindale*) is a proprietary, non-prescription form of ear-drops designed to soften and dissolve ear-wax (cerumen), and commonly prescribed for use at home two nights consecutively before syringing of the ears in a doctor's surgery. Its solvent constituent is DIOCTYL SODIUM SULPHO-SUCCINATE (also called docusate sodium).

⊕ warning: soliwax should not be used if there is inflammation in the ear, or where there is any chance that the eardrum has been perforated.

**Solpadeine** (*Sterling Research*) is a proprietary, non-prescription compound ANALGESIC, which is not available from the National Health Service. It is used to relieve the pain of headaches, and of rheumatism and other musculo-skeletal disorders. Produced in the form of tablets for effervescent solution, Solpadeine is a combination of paracetamol, codeine phosphate and caffeine.

▲/ ⊕ side-effects/warning: *see* CAFFEINE; CODEINE PHOSPHATE; PARACETAMOL.

**Solpadol** (*Sterling-Winthrop*) is a proprietary compound ANALGESIC, available only on prescription, used as a painkiller particularly for children. Produced in the form of effervescent tablets, Solpadol is a preparation of the OPIATE codeine phosphate and paracetamol, and contains more codeine than the usual compound preparation known as CO-CODAMOL). It is not recommended for children.

▲/ ⊕ side-effects/warning: *see* CODEINE PHOSPHATE; PARACETAMOL.

**Solprin** (*Reckitt & Colman*) is a proprietary, non-prescription preparation of the non-narcotic ANALGESIC aspirin, which is not available from the National Health Service. It is used to relieve mild to moderate pain, and

is produced in the form of soluble (dispersible) tablets.

▲/ ⊕ side-effects/warning: *see* ASPIRIN.

**Solu-Cortef** (*Upjohn*) is a proprietary CORTICOSTEROID preparation, available only on prescription, used to make up natural steroid deficiency, to suppress inflammation or allergic symptoms, or to treat shock. Produced in the form of powder for reconstitution as a medium for injection, Solu-Cortef is a form of hydrocortisone.

▲/ ⊕ side-effects/warning: *see* HYDROCORTISONE.

**Solu-Medrone** (*Upjohn*) is a proprietary CORTICOSTEROID preparation, available only on prescription, used to suppress inflammation or allergic symptoms, to relieve fluid retention around the brain, or to treat shock. Produced in the form of powder for reconstitution as a medium for injection, Solu-Medrone is a form of methylprednisolone.

▲/ ⊕ side-effects/warning: *see* METHYLPREDNISOLONE.

**Solvazinc** (*Thames*) is a proprietary, non-prescription ZINC supplement used to make up a body deficiency of that mineral. Produced in the form of tablets for effervescent solution, Solvazinc is a preparation of zinc sulphate.

▲/ ⊕ side-effects/warning: *see* ZINC SULPHATE.

**Somatonorm 4IU** (*Kabi*) is a proprietary preparation of human growth HORMONE (HGH, or somatotropin) in its synthetic form, somatrem. Available only on prescription, it is used to treat hormonal deficiency and associated symptoms (in particular short stature). It is produced in the form of a powder for reconstitution as a medium for injection

**S**

▲/✦ side-effects/warning: *see*
SOMATREM; SOMATROPIN.

**somatotropin** is a chemical name
for human growth HORMONE
(HGH). It is synthesized for use in
the form of SOMATREM.
*see* HGH.

**somatrem** is a synthesized form of
HGH (human growth hormone, or
somatotropin), prepared by
genetic engineering for
therapeutic use. It is also known
as Methionyl Human Growth
Hormone since there is an extra
methionine molecule in this
synthetic preparation. It is
produced using sequences of DNA
to create a growth hormone of
human sequence, and is used to
treat dwarfism and other
problems of short stature caused
by hormone deficiency.
Administration is by injection.
▲ side-effects: there may be
allergic reaction due to
antibody formation to this
peptide, and temporary
exacerbation of other disease
states.
✦ warning: it should be
administered with caution
where there are some other
pituitary hormone deficiencies,
as in hypothyroidism or
diabetes mellitus (alteration of
dosage of drugs for these
disease states may be
necessary). Treatment is
possible only for younger
patients whose long bones
have not fully fused and are
thus capable of growth in the
normal fashion.
*Related article:* SOMATONORM
1U.

**somatropin** is a HORMONE drug, a
biosynthetic version of HGH
(human growth hormone) used for
the treatment of short stature due
to impaired production of growth
hormone (unlike some other
hormones, only the human form is

active). It is available in the form
of preparations for injection.
▲ side-effects: there may be
allergic reaction due to
antibody formation to this
peptide, and temporary
exacerbation of other disease
states.
✦ warning: it should be
administered with caution
where there are some other
pituitary hormone deficiencies,
as in hypothyroidism or
diabetes mellitus (alteration of
dosage of drugs for these
disease states may be
necessary). Treatment is
possible only for younger
patients whose long bones
have not fully fused and are
thus capable of growth in the
normal fashion.
*Related articles:* GENOTROPIN;
HUMATROPE; NORDITROPIN;
SAIZEN; SOMATONORM.

**Sominex** (*Beecham*) is a
proprietary, non-prescription
TRANQUILLIZER used to relieve
occasional insomnia. Produced in
the form of tablets, it is a
preparation of the ANTIHISTAMINE
promethazine hydrochloride; it is
not recommended for children
aged under 16 years.
▲/✦ side-effects/warning: *see*
PROMETHAZINE
HYDROCHLORIDE.

**Somnite** (*Norgine*) is a proprietary
HYPNOTIC, available on
prescription only to private
patients, used in the short term to
treat insomnia in patients for
whom daytime sedation is not
appropriate. Produced in the form
of a suspension (for swallowing),
Somnite is a preparation of the
BENZODIAZEPINE nitrazepam. It is
not recommended for children.
▲/✦ side-effects/warning: *see*
NITRAZEPAM.

**Soneryl** (*May & Baker*) is a
proprietary sedative, a
BARBITURATE on the controlled

drugs list, used as a HYPNOTIC to treat intractable insomnia. Produced in the form of tablets, it is a preparation of butobarbitone. It is not recommended for children or the elderly.

▲/ ❀ side-effects/warning: *see* BUTOBARBITONE.

**Soni-Slo** (*Lipha*) is a proprietary, non-prescription VASODILATOR, used to prevent or to treat recurrent attacks of angina pectoris (heart pain). Produced in the form of sustained-release capsules (in two strengths), Soni-Slo is a preparation of isosorbide dinitrate. It is not recommended for children.

▲/ ❀ side-effects/warning: *see* ISOSORBIDE DINITRATE.

**Sorbichew** (*Stuart*) is a proprietary, non-prescription VASODILATOR, used to treat attacks of angina pectoris (heart pain). Produced in the form of tablets, Sorbichew is a preparation of isosorbide dinitrate. Sorbichew is not recommended for administration to children.

▲/ ❀ side-effects/warning: *see* ISOSORBIDE DINITRATE.

**Sorbid SA** (*Stuart*) is a proprietary, non-prescription VASODILATOR, used to prevent attacks of angina pectoris (heart pain). Produced in the form of sustained-release tablets, Sorbid SA is a preparation of isosorbide dinitrate. Sorbid SA is not recommended for administration to children.

▲/ ❀ side-effects/warning: *see* ISOSORBIDE DINITRATE.

**sorbitol** is a sweet-tasting carbohydrate that is used as a sugar-substitute (particularly by diabetics) and as the carbohydrate in some nutritional supplements administered by injection or infusion.

❀ warning: large oral doses may cause gastrointestinal disturbance.

**Sorbitrate** (*Stuart*) is a proprietary, non-prescription VASODILATOR, used to treat attacks of angina pectoris (heart pain). Produced in the form of tablets (in two strengths), Sorbitrate is a preparation of isosorbide dinitrate. It is not recommended for children.

▲/ ❀ side-effects/warning: *see* ISOSORBIDE DINITRATE.

**Sotacor** (*Bristol-Myers*) is a proprietary BETA-BLOCKER, an ANTIHYPERTENSIVE drug, available only on prescription, used to treat high blood pressure (hypertension), heartbeat irregularities and angina pectoris (heart pain), and to prevent secondary heart attacks. Produced in the form of tablets (in two strengths), Sotacor is a preparation of the BETA-BLOCKER sotalol hydrochloride.

▲/ ❀ side-effects/warning: *see* SOTALOL HYDROCHLORIDE.

**sotalol hydrochloride** is a BETA-BLOCKER, an ANTIHYPERTENSIVE drug used to treat high blood pressure (hypertension), heartbeat irregularities and angina pectoris (heart pain), and to prevent secondary heart attacks. It is also useful in relieving the symptoms of excess thyroid hormones in the bloodstream (thyrotoxicosis). Administration is oral in the form of tablets, or by injection.

▲ side-effects: there may be gastrointestinal disturbances, slow heart rate and cold fingertips and toes, and symptoms much like asthma.

❀ warning: sotalol hydrochloride should not be administered to patients with asthma, heart failure or heart block; it should be administered with caution

**S**

to those with impaired liver or kidney function, who are diabetic, or who are pregnant or lactating. Withdrawal of treatment should be gradual. *Related articles:* BETA-CARDONE; SOTACOR.

**Sotazide** *(Bristol-Myers)* is a proprietary ANTIHYPERTENSIVE drug, available only on prescription, used to treat mild to moderate high blood pressure (hypertension). Produced in the form of tablets, Sotazide is a preparation of the BETA-BLOCKER sotalol hydrochloride together with the THIAZIDE DIURETIC hydrochlorothiazide.

▲/❀ side-effects/warning: *see* HYDROCHLOROTHIAZIDE; SOTALOL HYDROCHLORIDE.

**Sparine** *(Wyeth)* is a proprietary ANTIPSYCHOTIC drug, available only on prescription, used to soothe agitation (particularly in the elderly or the dying) and for the short-term relief of acute, severe anxiety. It is also sometimes used to calm children prior to cardiac investigation or electro-encephalography. Produced in the form of tablets (in three strengths), as a suspension for dilution (the potency of the suspension once dilute is retained for 14 days) and in ampoules for injection, Sparine is a preparation of promazine hydrochloride. It is not recommended for children other than for the purpose outlined above.

▲/❀ side-effects/warning: *see* PROMAZINE HYDROCHLORIDE.

**Spasmonal** *(Norgine)* is a proprietary non-prescription, ANTISPASMODIC drug used to treat muscle spasm in both the gastrointestinal tract (leading to abdominal pain and constipation) and the uterus or vagina (leading to menstrual problems). Produced

in the form of capsules, Spasmonal is a preparation of alverine citrate. It is not recommended for children and its use should be avoided in patients with paralytic ileus.

❀ warning: *see* ALVERINE CITRATE.

**spectinomycin** is an ANTIBIOTIC used almost solely to treat gonorrhoea caused by organisms resistant to penicillin, or in patients who are allergic to penicillin. Spectinomycin is related to the aminoglycoside antibiotics both in structure and by the fact that it inhibits protein synthesis in sensitive bacteria by an action on the ribosome. Administration is by injection.

▲ side-effects: there may be nausea with vomiting, high temperature and dizziness; some patients experience urticaria or itching skin.

❀ warning: it is essential that both sexual partners undergo treatment even if only one shows symptoms. (Dosage for women is twice that for men.) *Related article:* TROBICIN.

**Spectraban** *(Stiefel)* is the name of two proprietary, non-prescription LOTIONS containing constituents that are able to protect the skin from ultraviolet radiation. Patients whose skin condition is such as to require this sort of protection may be prescribed Spectraban at the discretion of their doctors. The two lotions differ: Spectraban 4 is a preparation of the substance padimate O in an alcohol base; Spectraban 15 is a compound preparation of padimate O and aminobenzoic acid in an alcohol base.

❀ warning: *see* AMINOBENZOIC ACID; PADIMATE O.

**Spectralgen** *(Pharmacia)* is a proprietary set of 4 grass pollen preparations and 3 tree dust

preparations for use in
desensitising patients who are
allergic to one or more of such
substances (and so suffer from
hay fever or similar symptoms).
Available only on prescription,
and administered by injection,
Spectralgen preparations are of
carefully annotated different
allergenic strength, so that the
process of desensitization, as
regulated by a doctor, can be
progressive.

⊕ warning: injections should be
administered under close
medical supervision and in
locations where emergency
facilities for full cardio-
respiratory resuscitation are
immediately available.

**\*spermicidal** drugs kill sperm and
are used to assist contraception,
but should never be regarded
themselves as a means of
contraception. They are intended
to accompany barrier methods,
such as the condom (sheath), or
diaphragm (Dutch cap). Most
spermicidal preparations consist of
a spermicide – generally an alcohol
ester – within an inhibitory liquid
or cream base. Administration is in
the form of vaginal inserts
(pessaries), creams, gels, pastes,
foams in aerosols, and soluble films.
*Related articles*: C-FILM; DELFEN;
DOUBLE CHECK; DURACREME;
DURAGEL; GYNOL II; ORTHO-CREME;
ORTHOFORMS; ORTHO-GYNOL;
STAYCEPT; TWO'S COMPANY.

**Spiretic** (*DDSA Pharmaceuticals*)
is a proprietary DIURETIC of the
type that retains (rather than
depletes) potassium in the body.
Available only on prescription, it
is used to treat fluid retention
caused by cirrhosis of the liver,
congestive heart failure, high
blood pressure (*see* ANTIHYPER-
TENSIVE) or kidney disease. It is
produced in the form of tablets (in
two strengths), and is a
preparation of the comparatively

weak diuretic spironolactone.
▲/⊕ side-effects/warning: *see*
SPIRONOLACTONE.

**Spiroctan** (*MCP Pharmaceuticals*)
is a proprietary DIURETIC of the
type that retains (rather than
depletes) potassium in the body.
Available only on prescription, it
is used to treat fluid retention
caused by cirrhosis of the liver,
congestive heart failure, high
blood pressure (*see* ANTIHYPER-
TENSIVE) or kidney disease. It is
produced in the form of tablets (in
two strengths) and as capsules,
and is a preparation of the
comparatively weak diuretic
spironolactone.
▲/⊕ side-effects/warning: *see*
SPIRONOLACTONE.

**Spiroctan-M** (*MCP
Pharmaceuticals*) is a proprietary
DIURETIC of the type that retains
(rather than depletes) potassium
in the body. Available only on
prescription, it is used to treat
fluid retention caused by cirrhosis
of the liver, congestive heart
failure, high blood pressure (*see*
ANTIHYPERTENSIVE) or kidney
disease. It is produced in the form
of ampoules for injection, and is
transformed to a metabolite of
spironolactone.
▲/⊕ side-effects/warning: *see*
SPIRONOLACTONE.

**Spirolone** (*Berk*) is a proprietary
DIURETIC of the type that retains
(rather than depletes) potassium
in the body. Available only on
prescription, it is used to treat
fluid retention caused by cirrhosis
of the liver, congestive heart
failure, high blood pressure (*see*
ANTIHYPERTENSIVE) or kidney
disease. It is produced in the form
of tablets (in three strengths), and
is a preparation of the
comparatively weak diuretic
spironolactone.
▲/⊕ side-effects/warning: *see*
SPIRONOLACTONE.

**spironolactone** is a DIURETIC of the type that retains (rather than depletes) potassium in the body, used primarily to treat fluid retention caused by cirrhosis of the liver, congestive heart failure, or kidney disease. It is also used to treat the symptoms of an excess of the hormone aldosterone in the blood acting by antagonizing this hormone. Administration is oral in the form of tablets or capsules, or by injection. Comparatively weak by itself, spironolactone is often used in combination with other diuretics that are potassium-depleting (such as any of the THIAZIDES) and potentiates their effect.

▲ side-effects: many patients experience gastrointestinal disturbances. In male patients the breasts may enlarge (gynaecomastia); female patients may have irregular periods.

✹ warning: spironolactone should not be administered to patients with kidney failure or an excess of potassium in the body; it should be administered with caution to those who are pregnant or lactating.
*Related articles:* ALDACTIDE 50; ALDACTONE; DIATENSEC; LARACTONE; LASILACTONE; SPIRETIC; SPIROCTAN; SPIROCTAN-M; SPIROLONE.

**Sporanox** (*Janssen*) is a proprietary ANTIFUNGAL preparation, available only on prescription, used for the treatment of vulvovaginal candidiasis and ringworm infections of the scalp, body, feet etc. Administration is oral, in the form of tablets. Sporanox's active ingredient is itraconazole.

▲ / ✹ side-effects/warning: *see* ITRACONAZOLE.

**Sprilon** (*Pharmacia*) is a proprietary, non-prescription barrier spray for topical application to leg ulcers, bedsores, fissures in the skin or eczema, or to skin areas potentially requiring protection from urine or faeces (as in nappy rash or around a stoma – an outlet on the skin suface following the surgical curtailment of the intestines). Produced in the form of an aerosol, Sprilon is a compound of ZINC OXIDE, the antifoaming agent DIMETHICONE, wool fat, wood alcohols and paraffins.

✹ warning: some patients may be sensitive to the wool fat constituent.

**Stabillin-V-K** (*Boots*) is a proprietary preparation of the penicillin-type ANTIBIOTIC phenoxymethylpenicillin, used primarily to treat infections of the ear and throat, and some skin conditions; it may also be used to prevent streptococcal infections in a patient at risk of rheumatic fever. Available only on prescription, it is produced in the form of tablets and as an elixir (in three strengths) for dilution (the potency of the elixir once diluted is retained for 7 days).

▲ / ✹ side-effects/warning: *see* PHENOXYMETHYL-ENICILLIN.

**Stafoxil** (*Brocades*) is a proprietary ANTIBIOTIC, available only on prescription, used to treat bacterial infections of the skin and of the ear, nose and throat, and especially staphylococcal infections that prove to be resistant to penicillin. Produced in the form of capsules (in two strengths), Stafoxil is a preparation of flucloxacillin. It is not recommended for children aged under 2 years.

▲ / ✹ side-effects/warning: *see* FLUCLOXACILLIN.

**stanozolol** is an anabolic STEROID that also has ANTICOAGULANT properties, used to assist the metabolic synthesis of protein in the body following major surgery or long-term debilitating disease, to treat osteoporosis, or to treat various circulatory disorders. It is also used in the treatment of certain forms of anaemia although how it works in this respect – and even whether it works – remains the subject of some debate: variations in patient response are wide.

Administration is oral in the form of tablets, or by injection.

▲ side-effects: there may be fluid retention in the tissues (oedema), high levels of calcium in the blood, and acne; prolonged treatment in female patients may cause menstrual irregularites and eventual slight signs of masculinization.

✿ warning: stanozolol should not be administered to patients with impaired liver function or cancer of the prostate gland, or who are pregnant or lactating; it should be administered with caution to those with heart or kidney disease, diabetes, epilepsy, high blood pressure (hypertension) or circulatory problems, or migraine. In the treatment of children, monitoring of bone growth is essential every half-year.

*Related article:* STROMBA.

**Staphcil** (*Lederle*) is a proprietary ANTIBIOTIC, available only on prescription, used to treat bacterial infections and especially staphylococcal infections that prove to be resistant to penicillin. Produced in the form of capsules (in two strengths) and in vials for injection, Staphcil is a preparation of flucloxacillin.

▲/✿ side-effects/warning: *see* FLUCLOXACILLIN.

**Staril** (*Squibb*) is a proprietary form of the ANTIHYPERTENSIVE drug fosinopril. It is used to treat high blood pressure (hypertension), but in combination with other drugs, but care is needed if it is to be used with diuretics. It is available only on prescription in the form of tablets (in two strengths).

▲/✿ side-effects/warning: *see* FOSINOPRIL.

**Staycept** (*Syntex*) is a proprietary, non-prescription SPERMICIDAL preparation for use in combination with one of the barrier methods of contraception (such as a condom or diaphragm). Produced in the form of vaginal inserts (pessaries) and as a jelly, Staycept's active constituent is an alcohol ester.

**STD** (*STD Pharmaceutical*) is a proprietary form of the drug sodium tetradecyl sulphate, available only on prescription, used in scleropathy – a technique to treat varicose veins by the injection of an irritant solution. The resultant inflammation of the vein promotes the obliteration of the vein by thrombosis. STD is produced in ampoules for injection.

▲/✿ side-effects/warning: *see* SODIUM TETRADECYL SULPHATE.

**Stelazine** (*Smith, Kline & French*) is a proprietary form of the powerful ANTIPSYCHOTIC drug trifluoperazine. Available only on prescription, it is used to treat and tranquillize psychoses (such as schizophrenia) including the control of behavioural disturbances. It may be used alternatively to treat anxiety in the short-term. Stelazine is produced in the form of tablets (in two strengths), as sustained-release capsules (spansules, in three strengths), as a sugar-free syrup for dilution (the potency of the syrup once dilute is retained for 14 days), as a liquid concentrate for dilution (the potency of the syrup once dilute is retained for a period dependent on the diluent), and in ampoules for injection.

▲/⊕ side-effects/warning: *see* TRIFLUOPERAZINE.

**Stemetil** (*May & Baker*) is a proprietary ANTI-EMETIC, available only on prescription, used to relieve symptoms of nausea caused by the vertigo and loss of balance experienced in infections of the inner and middle ears, or by cytotoxic drugs in the treatment of cancer. Produced in the form of tablets (in two strengths), as a syrup for dilution (the potency of the syrup once dilute is retained for 14 days), as anal suppositories (in two strengths), and in ampoules for injection, Stemetil is a preparation of the major TRANQUILLIZER prochlorperazine.

▲/⊕ side-effects/warning: *see* PROCHLORPERAZINE.

**sterculia** is a vegetable gum capable of absorbing up to 60 times its own volume of water, useful in patients who cannot tolerate bran. Used as a LAXATIVE, it has the effect of increasing the overall mass and compaction of faeces, so promoting bowel movement; exactly the same effect is beneficial in treating diarrhoea and diverticular disease, and in maintaining faecal consistency for patients who have undergone colostomy or ileostomy. But more controversially sterculia may also be medically prescribed to treat serious obesity, in the intention that small amounts of food ingested may be bulked up internally, making the patient feel full. Administration is in the form of granules to be taken with water.

▲ side-effects: there may be flatulence, even to the point of abdominal distension.

⊕ warning: sterculia should not be administered to patients who suffer from intestinal blockage or a disorder of the muscles of the intestinal walls; it should be administered with caution to those who suffer from ulcerative colitis. Adequate fluid intake must be maintained.
*Related articles:* NORMACOL; PREFIL.

**Steribath** (*Stuart*) is a proprietary, non-prescription, concentrated solution for use in the bath as a DISINFECTANT and cleansing agent. Its active constituent is a form of iodine.

***steroids** are a class of naturally occuring and synthetic agents whose structure is based on the chemical sterone. In the body they include HORMONES of the adrenal cortex and sex glands (such as OESTROGENS and PROGESTOGENS), bile acids and VITAMINS of the D group. Many types of drug are available based on the steroids, and they are used to treat many types of disorder (including sex-hormone linked disorders, rheumatic pain and certain skin disorders).

**Ster-Zac** (*Hough*) is the name of three proprietary DISINFECTANT cleansing products. Ster-Zac Powder is a non-prescription dusting powder used to prevent infection in minor wounds and bedsores; it contains the antiseptic hexachlorophane, the mild astringent zinc oxide, and starch. Ster-Zac Bath Concentrate is a mild solution of the antiseptic triclosan, available without prescription, used to treat staphylococcal skin infections. And Ster-Zac DC Skin Cleanser, available only on prescription, is intended for use instead of soap either for surgeons to scrub up with before undertaking surgical operations, or for patients who suffer from acne and skin infections; it contains the antiseptic hexachlorophane in the form of a cream.

▲/✿ side-effects/warning: see HEXACHLOROPHANE.

**Stesolid** (*CP Pharmaceuticals*) is a proprietary ANXIOLYTIC drug, available only on prescription, used to treat anxiety and insomnia, to act as a premedication before surgery, and to assist in the treatment of acute alcohol withdrawal symptoms. Also a MUSCLE RELAXANT and an ANTICONVULSANT, Stesolid is used to treat muscle spasm and – more seriously – convulsions due to poisoning and to epileptic seizures. Produced in the form of tubes (for rectal insertion), Stesolid is a preparation of the BENZODIAZEPINE diazepam. It is not recommended for children aged under 12 months.

▲/✿ side-effects/warning: see DIAZEPAM.

**Stiedex** (*Stiedex*) is a CORTICO-STEROID, a proprietary form of desoxymethasone available only on prescription. The preparation is in several forms: a lotion; an oily cream of two strengths; and as a preparation with the ANTIBACTERIAL drug neomycin sulphate (called Stiedex LPN).

▲/✿ side-effects/warning: see DESOXYMETHASONE.

**Stiemycin** (*Stiefel*) is a proprietary ANTIBIOTIC, available only on prescription, used to treat acne. Produced in the form of a solution for topical application, it is a preparation of erythromycin in an alcoholic basis.

▲/✿ side-effects/warning: see ERYTHROMYCIN.

**stilboestrol** is a synthesized OESTROGEN that is useful in hormone replacement therapy in women following the menopause, and is now used less commonly to treat breast cancer. It was formerly in popular use also for the suppression of lactation. In men it is widely used in low dosage to treat cancer of the prostate gland. Administration is oral in the form of tablets, as vaginal inserts (pessaries), or by injection.

▲ side-effects: there may be nausea and vomiting, breast enlargement and tenderness in women, weight gain through sodium retention, and a rash; some women patients experience headache and depression. There is a risk of thrombosis. Rarely, treatment encourages the development of cancer of the womb lining. Treatment of breast cancer may cause high blood levels of calcium, and bone pain. In men, treatment causes impotence and the appearance of some feminine character-istics, particularly in the development of the breasts (gynaecomastia).

✿ warning: stilboestrol should not be administered to patients with oestrogen-dependent cancers, porphyria, impaired liver function or thrombosis. It should be administered with caution to those with epilepsy, diabetes, high blood pressure (hypertension), heart or kidney disease, or migraine; who are pregnant or lactating; or who wear contact lenses.

*__stimulants__ are agents that activate body systems or functions. In general, the term is applied to drugs that stimulate the central nervous system. The result may be increased energy, increased enthusiasm, and euphoria, but the effects are only temporary and the return to ordinary actuality may eventually lead to a psychotic state. Yet patients who suffer from narcolepsy, and hyperactive children, may well derive some therapeutic benefit from the administration of certain types of stimulant, although in children they may also retard growth. Central nervous system stimulants include the amphetamines (such as DEXAMPHETAMINE SULPHATE) and the drug found in tea and coffee, CAFFEINE.

**Stomahesive** (*Squibb*) is a proprietary, non-prescription paste intended for the filling and sealing of skin creases round a stoma (an outlet on the skin surface following the surgical curtailment of the intestines).

**Stomabar** (*Raymed*) is a proprietary, non-prescription barrier cream intended for the protection and sanitization of a stoma (an outlet on the skin surface following the surgical curtailment of the intestines).

**Stomogel** (*Raymed*) is a proprietary, non-prescription deodorant gel intended for the freshening and sanitization of a stoma (an outlet on the skin surface following the surgical curtailment of the intestines).

**Stomosol** (*Raymed*) is a proprietary, non-prescription ANTISEPTIC liquid intended for the disinfection and sanitization of a stoma (an outlet on the skin surface following the surgical curtailment of the intestines).

**Strepsils** (*Crookes Healthcare*) are proprietary, non-prescription throat lozenges that contain the ANTISEPTICS 2,4-dichlorobenzyl alcohol and amylmetacresol.

**Streptase** (*Hoechst*) is a proprietary FIBRINOLYTIC, available only on prescription,

used primarily to treat thrombosis and embolism. Produced in the form of powder for reconstitution as a medium for injection, Streptase is a preparation of the enzyme streptokinase.
▲/✿ side-effects/warning: see STREPTOKINASE.

**streptokinase** is an enzyme that is used therapeutically as an FIBRINOLYTIC drug because it has the property of breaking up blood clots (by activating plasmin formation which then degrades the clot component fibrin). It is very useful in treating thrombosis and embolisms. Administration is by injection or infusion.
▲ side-effects: there may be allergic reaction, incorporating a rash and a high temperature.
✿ warning: streptokinase should not be administered to patients with blood disorders involving defective coagulation, or with streptococcal infections; who are liable to bleed (either by menstruation or because of recent trauma or surgery); or who are pregnant. It should be administered with caution to those who suffer from heart disease.
*Related articles:* KABIKINASE; STREPTASE.

**streptokinase-streptodornase** is a combination of FIBRINOLYTIC enzymes that together have the property of breaking up blood clots and other exudates liable otherwise to congeal (such as pus). It is used primarily to clean wounds, ulcers and sores, and to slough off surrounding lesioned skin. Administration is by topical application in the form of a dampened powder (or in solution via a catheter).
▲/✿ side-effects/warning: see STREPTOKINASE.

**streptomycin** is an aminoglycoside ANTIBIOTIC now used
almost solely for the treatment of
tuberculosis, for which it is
administered in combination with
other antibiotics. Like other
aminoglycosides, streptomycin
inhibits protein synthesis in
sensitive organisms. Treatment of
tuberculosis takes between 6 and
18 months. Administration of
streptomycin is by injection. In
the rare treatment of urinary and
intestinal infections (with or
without penicillin) it is
administered orally.
▲ side-effects: there may be
  hearing difficulties at which
  the withdrawal of the drug
  should be considered as
  irreversible deafness may
  result from high dosage and/or
  prolonged treatment;
  dysfunction of the kidneys may
  occur in elderly patients.
  Prolonged treatment may
  cause an excess of magnesium
  in the body.
● warning: streptomycin should
  not be administered to patients
  who are pregnant, and should
  be administered with extreme
  caution to patients with
  impaired kidney function.
  Regular checks on the level of
  streptomycin in the blood are
  essential to judge dosage and
  to guard against toxic levels.

**Streptotriad** (*May & Baker*) is a
proprietary compound
ANTIBACTERIAL, available only on
prescription, used to treat any of
several serious infections
including meningococcal
meningitis and bacillary
dysentery; it is also used
prophylactically, on medical staff
and relatives at high risk of
infection, and on convalescing
patients who may or may not
become carriers of dangerous
bacterial infections. Produced in
the form of tablets, Streptotriad
combines the aminoglycoside

streptomycin with the three
SULPHONAMIDES sulphadiazine,
sulphathiazole and
sulphadimidine.
▲/● side-effects/warning: *see*
  STREPTOMYCIN;
  SULPHADIAZINE;
  SULPHADIMIDINE.

**Stromba** (*Sterling Research*) is a
proprietary form of the anabolic
STEROID stanozolol, available only
on prescription, used to assist the
metabolic synthesis of protein in
the body following major surgery
or long-term debilitating disease,
to treat osteoporosis ('brittle
bones'), or to treat various
circulatory disorders. It is also
used in the treatment of certain
forms of anaemia although how it
works in this respect – and even
whether it works – remains the
subject of some debate: variations
in patient response are wide. It is
produced in the form of tablets.
▲/● side-effects/warning: *see*
  STANOZOLOL.

**Stugeron** (*Janssen*) is a
proprietary, non-prescription
preparation of the ANTIHISTAMINE
cinnarizine, used to treat nausea
caused by the vertigo and loss of
balance experienced in infections
of the middle and inner ears. It is
produced in the form of tablets. A
stronger version of cinnarizine
(produced under the trade name
Stugeron Forte) is also used to
treat circulatory problems of the
extremities.
▲/● side-effects/warning: *see*
  CINNARIZINE.

**Sublimaze** (*Janssen*) is a narcotic
ANALGESIC on the controlled
drugs list, primarily used to
enhance the effect of a BARBIT-
URATE general ANAESTHETIC,
allowing the barbiturate dose to
be smaller. Produced in ampoules
for injection, Sublimaze is a
preparation of the morphine-like
fentanyl.

▲ / ● side-effects/warning: *see*
FENTANYL.

**sucralfate** is a drug used to treat
gastric and duodenal ulcers (its
name derives from aluminium
sucrose sulphate). Unlike
antacids, it is thought to work by
forming a protective barrier over
an ulcer, so allowing healing
underneath. Treatment lasts for
more than 4 weeks.
Administration is oral in the form
of tablets.
  ▲ side-effects: constipation is not
  uncommon.
  ● warning: sucralfate should be
  administered with caution to
  patients with kidney disease.
  *Related article:* ANTEPSIN.

**Sudafed** (*Calmic*) is a proprietary,
non-prescription DECONGESTANT; unlike most
decongestants, however, it is
produced in the form of tablets
(for swallowing) available from
the National Health Service, as
Sudafed Plus tablets that contain
in addition the ANTIHISTAMINE
triprolidine hydrochloride, and an
elixir for dilution (the potency of
the elixir once dilute is retained
for 14 days). Sudafed is also
available to private patients as a
syrup (Sudafed Expectorant) and
as a linctus (Sudafed Linctus). It
contains the ephedrine derivative
pseudoephedrine hydrochloride.
  ▲ / ● side-effects/warning: *see*
  EPHEDRINE HYDROCHLORIDE.

**Sudocrem** (*Tosara*) is a
proprietary, non-prescription skin
emollient (softener and soother)
used to treat nappy rash, bedsores
and eczema, and sometimes to
dress burns. Produced in the form
of a cream, its active constituents
include ZINC OXIDE, BENZYL
BENZOATE and wool
fat.
  ● warning: wool fat may cause
  sensitivity reactions in some
  patients.

**sulconazole nitrate** is an
ANTIFUNGAL drug, one of the
imidazoles, used to treat skin
infections. Administration is
by topical application in the
form of a water-miscible
cream.
  ▲ side-effects: some patients
  experience sensitivity
  reactions, especially skin
  irritation.
  ● warning: keep well away from
  the eyes.
  *Related article:* EXELDERM.

**Suleo-C** (*International Labs*) is a
proprietary, non-prescription
drug used to treat infestations of
the scalp and pubic hair by lice.
Produced in the form of a lotion
and a shampoo, Suleo-C is a
preparation of the pediculicide
carbaryl.
  ● warning: *see* CARBARYL.

**Suleo-M** (*International Labs*) is a
proprietary, non-prescription
drug used to treat infestations of
the scalp and pubic hair by lice
(pediculosis), or of the skin by the
itch-mite (scabies). Produced in
the form of a lotion, Suleo-M is a
preparation of the insecticide
malathion in an alcohol solution.
  ● warning: *see* MALATHION.

**sulfadoxine** is an ANTIBIOTIC, a
long-acting SULPHONAMIDE, used
solely in combination with
PYRIMETHAMINE to prevent or
treat malaria.
  ▲ side-effects: there may be
  nausea with vomiting, skin
  disorders and changes in the
  composition of the blood.
  ● warning: sulfadoxine should
  not be administered to patients
  with liver or kidney failure, or
  blood disorders, who are
  pregnant, or who are aged
  under 6 weeks; it should be
  administered with caution to
  those who are elderly, or who
  are lactating. Adequate fluid
  intake must be maintained;

regular blood counts are
essential during prolonged
treatment.
*Related article:* KELFIZINE W.

**sulfametopyrazine** is an
ANTIBACTERIAL, a long-acting
SULPHONAMIDE, used primarily in
the treatment of chronic
bronchitis and infections of the
urinary tract. Administration is
oral in the form of tablets.
▲ side-effects: there may be
nausea with vomiting, skin
disorders and changes in the
composition of the
blood.
◆ warning: sulfametopyrazine
should not be administered to
patients with liver or kidney
failure, or blood disorders, who
are pregnant, or who are aged
under 6 weeks; it should be
administered with caution to
those who are elderly, or who
are lactating. Adequate fluid
intake must be maintained;
regular blood counts are
essential during prolonged
treatment.
*Related article:* KELFIZINE W.

**Sulfomyl** (*Winthrop*) is a
proprietary, non-prescription
form of ANTIBACTERIAL eye-drops
used to treat local infections. It is
a preparation of the
SULPHONAMIDE mafenide.
▲/◆ side-effects/warning: *see*
MAFENIDE.

**sulindac** is a non-steroidal, ANTI-
INFLAMMATORY, non-narcotic
ANALGESIC drug used to treat pain
and inflammation in rheumatic
disease and other musculo-
skeletal disorders.
Administration is by tablets.
▲ side-effects: there may be
nausea and gastrointestinal
disturbance; internal
haemorrhage may occur. Some
patients experience sensitivity
reactions such as a rash,
headache, asthma-like

symptoms, and even vertigo or
ringing in the ears (tinnitus).
Rarely, there is fluid retention
leading to weight gain, or a
minor change in the
composition of the blood.
◆ warning: sulindac should be
administered with caution to
patients with impaired liver or
kidney function, gastric ulcers
or allergic conditions, or who
are pregnant.
*Related article:* CLINORIL.

**sulphacetamide** is an ANTIBIOTIC,
one of the SULPHONAMIDES, used
(in solution) primarily in the form
of eye-drops and eye ointment to
treat local bacterial infections.
However, it is no longer
recommended for this purpose as
there are other more effective
drugs. It is also used in
combination with other
sulphonamides to treat infections
of the vagina and cervix.
Ophthalmic administration is
most commonly in the form of
drops during the daytime, and as
ointment for overnight treatment;
treatment for vaginal infections is
in the form of vaginal tablets
(pessaries) or as a cream.

**sulphadiazine** is an ANTIBIOTIC,
one of the SULPHONAMIDES, used
to treat serious bacterial
infections – particularly
meningococcal meningitis.
Administration is oral in the form
of tablets, or by infusion.
▲ side-effects: there may be
nausea and vomiting, with skin
disorders; changes in the
composition of the blood may
occur.
◆ warning: sulphadiazine should
not be administered to patients
with liver or kidney failure, or
disorders of the blood, who are
pregnant, or who are aged
under 6 weeks; it should be
administered with caution to
those with impaired kidney
function or sensitivity to light,

who are elderly, or who are lactating. Adequate fluid intake is essential to avoid the risk of the drug crystallizing out in the urine. Regular blood counts should be done during prolonged courses of treatment.

**sulphadimethoxine** is a long-acting ANTIBIOTIC, one of the SULPHONAMIDES, used to treat the eye disorder trachoma, which is common in underdeveloped countries. Administration is oral in the form of tablets. It is not marketed in the United Kingdom.

▲ side-effects: there may be nausea and vomiting, with skin disorders; changes in the composition of the blood may occur.

✹ warning: sulphadimethoxine should not be administered to patients with liver or kidney failure, or disorders of the blood, who are pregnant, or who are aged under 6 weeks; it should be administered with caution to those with impaired kidney function or sensitivity to light, who are elderly, or who are lactating. Adequate fluid intake is essential, as are regular blood counts during prolonged courses of treatment. *Related article:* MADRIBON.

**sulphadimidine** is an ANTIBIOTIC, one of the SULPHONAMIDES, used to treat serious bacterial infections – particularly infections of the urinary tract – and to prevent meningococcal meningitis in patients at high risk from infection. Among the least toxic of the sulphonamides, sulphadimidine is especially useful in the treatment of children. Administration is oral in the form of tablets, or by injection.

▲ side-effects: there may be nausea and vomiting, with skin disorders; changes in the composition of the blood may occur.

✹ warning: sulphadimidine should not be administered to patients who suffer from liver or kidney failure, or disorders of the blood, who are pregnant, or who are aged under 6 weeks; it should be administered with caution to those with impaired kidney function or sensitivity to light, who are elderly, or who are lactating. Adequate fluid intake is essential, as are regular blood counts during prolonged courses of treatment. *Related article:* STREPTOTRIAD.

**sulphafurazole** is an ANTIBACTERIAL, one of the SULPHONAMIDES, used to treat serious bacterial infections – particularly infections of the urinary tract. Administration is oral in the form of tablets or as a syrup.

▲ side-effects: there may be nausea and vomiting, with skin disorders; changes in the composition of the blood may occur.

✹ warning: sulphafurazole should not be administered to patients with liver or kidney failure, or from disorders of the blood, who are pregnant, or who are aged under 6 weeks; it should be administered with caution to those with impaired kidney function or sensitivity to light, who are elderly, or who are lactating. Adequate fluid intake is essential, as are regular blood counts during prolonged courses of treatment. *Related article:* GANTRISIN.

**sulphamethoxazole** is an ANTIBIOTIC, one of the SULPHONAMIDES, that in combination with another antibiotic agent TRIMETHOPRIM forming a compound drug called co-trimoxazole – is in widespread use to treat many serious infections, especially infections of the bones and joints, or the

urinary tract and of the upper respiratory tract, and such infections as gonorrhoea and typhoid fever. Rarely, sulphamethoxazole is used by itself in the treatment of urinary infections; administration is oral in the form of tablets, and patients should be advised to increase fluid intake during treatment.
*Related article:* CO-TRIMOXAZOLE.

**sulphasalazine** is an ANTIBACTERIAL, one of the SULPHONAMIDES, used primarily to induce a remission of the symptoms of ulceration of the intestinal wall (generally in the colon) and, having induced it, to maintain it. Because the drug also has anti-inflammatory properties, it is additionally used to treat rheumatoid arthritis (although there are some haematological side-effects). Administration is oral in the form of (enteric-coated or plain) tablets, or in suppositories, or as a retention enema.
▲ side-effects: side-effects are common with higher doses. There may be nausea with vomiting and other gastrointestinal disturbance; headache, vertigo, ringing in the ears (tinnitus) and high temperature; and a rash. A change in the composition of the blood may cause a form of anaemia and a discoloration of the urine and of the tear-fluid lubricating the eyes. Even more seriously, there may be inflammation of the pancreas or of the heart.
◆ warning: sulphasalazine should not be administered to patients known to be sensitive to salicylates (aspirin-type drugs) or to sulphonamides; it should be administered with caution to those with liver or kidney disease, or who are pregnant or lactating.

Adequate fluid intake must be maintained.
*Related article:* SALAZOPYRIN.

**Sulphatriad** (*May & Baker*) is a proprietary compound ANTIBACTERIAL, available only on prescription, used to treat any of several serious infections including meningococcal meningitis. Produced in the form of tablets, Sulphatriad is a combination of the three SULPHONAMIDES sulphadiazine, sulphamerazine and sulphathiazole.
▲ / ◆ side-effects/warning: *see* SULPHADIAZINE.

**sulphaurea** is an ANTIBACTERIAL, one of the SULPHONAMIDES, used to treat infections of the urinary tract, although it is no longer recommended. Administration is oral in the form of tablets (generally also containing the analgesic phenazopyridine).
▲ side-effects: there may be nausea and vomiting, with skin disorders; changes in the composition of the blood may occur.
◆ warning: sulphaurea should not be administered to patients with liver or kidney failure, or disorders of the blood, who are pregnant, or who are aged under 6 weeks; it should be administered with caution to those with impaired kidney function or sensitivity to light, who are elderly, or who are lactating. Adequate fluid intake is essential, as are regular blood counts during prolonged courses of treatment.

**sulphinpyrazone** is a drug used to treat and prevent excesses of uric acid in the bloodstream and the gout that results from it. It works by promoting the excretion of uric acid in the urine. Once treatment has started, it is

continued indefinitely (so
potentially preventing acute
attacks of gout). Administration
is oral in the form of tablets.
▲ side-effects: there may be
gastrointestinal disturbance; a
few patients experience
sensitivity reactions.
● warning: sulphinpyrazone
should not be administered to
patients with kidney stones or
blood disorders, who are in the
middle of an acute attack of
gout, or who are already
taking aspirin-type drugs.
Initial administration may be
painful (and require
simultaneous administration of
an analgesic). Adequate fluid
intake must be maintained.
Regular blood counts are
advisable.
*Related article:* ANTURAN.

**sulphonamides** are derivatives of
a red dye called sulphanilamide
that have the property of
preventing the growth of
bacteria. They were the first
group of drugs with general
utility as antibiotic agents. Their
antibacterial action stems from
their chemical similarity to a
compound required by bacteria to
generate the essential growth
factor, folic acid. This similarity
inhibits the production of folic
acid by bacteria (and therefore
growth) while the human host is
able to utilize folic acid in the
diet. Most are administered orally
and are rapidly absorbed in the
stomach and small intestine, are
short-acting, and thus may have
to be taken several times a day.
Their quick progress through the
body and excretion in the urine
makes them particularly suited to
the treatment of urinary
infections. One or two
sulphonamides are long-acting
(and may be used to treat diseases
such as malaria or leprosy), and
another one or two are poorly
absorbed (for which reason they

were until recently used to treat
intestinal infections). Best-known
and most-used sulphonamides
include sulphadiazine,
sulphadimidine and
sulfametopyrazine.
Sulphonamides tend to cause side-
effects – particularly nausea,
vomiting, diarrhoea and headache
– some of which (especially
sensitivity reactions) may become
serious; bone-marrow damage
may result from prolonged
treatment. Such serious
hypersensitivity reactions are
more of a risk with the longer-
acting sulphonamides, which can
accumulate in the body. As a
general rule, patients being
treated with sulphonamides
should try to avoid exposure to
sunlight. In general the
sulphonamides are being replaced
by newer antibiotics with greater
activity, fewer problems with
bacterial resistance and less risk
of side-effects.
*see* SULFADOXINE;
SULFAMETOPYRAZINE;
SULPHACETAMIDE; SULPHADIAZINE;
SULPHADIMETHOXINE;
SULPHADIMIDINE;
SULPHAMETHOXAZOLE;
SULPHAUREA.

**sulphones** are closely related to
the SULPHONAMIDES, they have
much the same therapeutic
action, and are thus used for
much the same purposes. They are
particularly successful in
preventing the growth of the
bacteria responsible for leprosy,
malaria and tuberculosis. Best-
known and (possibly) most-used is
dapsone.
*see* DAPSONE.

**sulphonylureas** are drugs derived
from a SULPHONAMIDE that have
the effect of reducing blood levels
of glucose. They work by
promoting the secretion of
INSULIN from the pancreas, and
are thus useful in treating the

form of hyperglycaemia that occurs in adult-onset diabetes mellitus where there is still some insulin production. Best-known and most-used sulphonylureas include chlorpropamide, glibenclamide, glipizide, tolazamide and tolbutamide. Side-effects are not common, although sensitivity reactions occur. But the list of drugs with which sulphonylureas must not be taken simultaneously is long, and includes relatively commonly prescribed drug-types such as corticosteroids, diuretics, anticoagulants and sulphonamides.
*see* ACETOHEXAMIDE; CHLORPROPAMIDE; GLIBENCLAMIDE; GLIBORNURIDE; GLICLAZIDE; GLIPIZIDE; GLIQUIDONE; GLYMIDINE; TOLAZAMIDE; TOLBUTAMIDE.

**sulphur** is a non-metallic element thought to be active against external parasites and fungal infections of the skin. Its common use in creams, ointments or lotions for treating skin disorders such as acne, dermatitis and psoriasis would appear to have little scientific basis.

**sulpiride** is an ANTIPSYCHOTIC drug used to treat the symptoms of schizophrenia. In low doses, it increases an apathetic, withdrawn patient's awareness and tends to generate a true consciousness of events. In high doses it is used also to treat other conditions that may cause tremor, tics, involuntary movements or involuntary utterances (such as the relatively uncommon Gilles de la Tourette syndrome). Administration is oral in the form of tablets.
▲ side-effects: patients should be warned before treatment that their judgement and powers of concentration may become defective under treatment.

There may be restlessness, insomnia and nightmares; rashes and jaundice may appear; and there may be dry mouth, gastrointestinal disturbance, difficulties in urinating, and blurred vision. Muscles in the neck and back, and sometimes the arms, may undergo spasms. Some patients experience impaired kidney function.
● warning: sulpiride should not be administered to patients with reduction in the bone marrow's capacity to produce blood cells, or suffering from certain types of glaucoma. It should be administered only with caution to those with heart or vascular disease, kidney or liver disease, epilepsy, parkinsonism, or depression; or who are pregnant or lactating. It is not recommended for children.
*Related articles:* DOLMATIL; SULPITIL.

**Sulpitil** (*Tillotts*) is a proprietary ANTIPSYCHOTIC drug used to treat the symptoms of schizophrenia. In low doses, it increases an apathetic, withdrawn patient's awareness and tends to generate a true consciousness of events. In high doses it is used also to treat other conditions that may cause tremor, tics, involuntary movements or involuntary utterances (such as the relatively uncommon Gilles de la Tourette syndrome). Produced in the form of tablets, Sulpitil is a preparation of sulpiride. It is not recommended for children.
▲/● side-effects/warning: *see* SULPIRIDE.

**Sultrin** (*Ortho-Cilag*) is a proprietary ANTIBIOTIC, available only on prescription, used to treat bacterial infections of the vagina or the cervix, or to prevent infection following gynaeco-

**S**

logical surgery. Produced in the form of vaginal tablets (pessaries) and as a cream (with its own applicator), Sultrin is a compound of three SULPHONAMIDE antibacterial agents: sulphacetamide, sulphabenzamide and sulphathiazole.

**Suprefact** (*Hoechst*) is a proprietary form of gonadotrophin-releasing HORMONE, available only on prescription, used to treat later stages of cancer of the prostate gland. It works by effectively suppressing the production and secretion of the male sex hormone testosterone which contributes to the growth and metastasis of the cancer. Produced in the form of a nasal spray and in vials for injection, Suprefact is a preparation of buserelin.
▲/● side-effects/warning: see BUSERELIN.

**suramin** is a powerful drug that has been used in the treatment of infestations by filaria (threadlike nematode worms that parasitize the connective and lymphatic tissues of the body following transmission through the bite of a bloodsucking insect). On account of its toxicity it has been largely replaced by more effective and less toxic agents. It is also used to treat the early stages of trypanosomiasis (a tropical protozoal infection such as sleeping sickness, transmitted through bites of the tsetse fly). Administration is initially by infusion, and then by injection.
● warning: suramin is toxic to the kidneys; a course of treatment lasts a maximum of 5 weeks, and regular urine analysis is essential.

**Surbex T** (*Abbott*) is a proprietary, non-prescription MULTIVITAMIN supplement, which is not available from the National Health Service. Produced in the form of tablets it contains THIAMINE (vitamin B$_1$), RIBOFLAVINE (vitamin B$_2$), PYRIDOXINE (vitamin B$_6$), NICOTINAMIDE (of the B complex), and ASCORBIC ACID (vitamin C).

**Surem** (*Galen*) is a proprietary HYPNOTIC, available on prescription only to private patients, used in the short-term to treat insomnia in patients for whom daytime sedation is not appropriate. Produced in the form of capsules, Surem is a preparation of the BENZODIAZEPINE nitrazepam. It is not recommended for children.
▲/● side-effects/warning: see NITRAZEPAM.

**Surgam** (*Roussel*) is a proprietary, non-narcotic, ANALGESIC, available only on prescription, used to treat the pain of rheumatic disease and other musculo-skeletal disorders. Produced in the form of tablets (in two strengths, under the names Surgam 200 and Surgam 300), it is a preparation of the nonsteroidal, ANTI-INFLAMMATORY agent tiaprofenic acid.
▲/● side-effects/warning: see TIAPROFENIC ACID.

**Surmontil** (*May & Baker*) is a proprietary ANTIDEPRESSANT, available only on prescription, used to treat depressive illness (especially in cases where there is a need for sedation), and severe insomnia. Produced in the form of tablets (in two strengths) and as capsules, Surmontil is a preparation of the TRICYCLIC drug trimipramine maleate. It is not recommended for children.
▲/● side-effects/warning: see TRIMIPRAMINE.

**Suscard Buccal** (*Pharmax*) is a proprietary, non-prescription VASODILATOR, used to treat congestive heart failure and angina pectoris (heart pain). It is produced in the form of sustained-release tablets (in four strengths) to be held between the upper lip and the gum until they dissolve, consisting of a preparation of glyceryl trinitrate. It is not recommended for children.

▲/● side-effects/warning: *see* GLYCERYL TRINITRATE.

**Sustac** (*Pharmax*) is a proprietary, non-prescription VASODILATOR, used to treat angina pectoris (heart pain). It is produced in the form of sustained-release tablets (in three strengths), consisting of a preparation of glyceryl trinitrate. It is not recommended for children.

▲/● side-effects/warning: *see* GLYCERYL TRINITRATE.

**Sustamycin** (*MCP Pharmaceuticals*) is a proprietary, broad-spectrum ANTIBIOTIC, available only on prescription, used to treat many forms of infection. Produced in the form of sustained-release capsules, Sustamycin is a preparation of tetracycline hydrochloride. It is not recommended for children.

▲/● side-effects/warning: *see* TETRACYCLINE.

**Sustanon** (*Organon*) is a proprietary preparation of the male sex HORMONE testosterone, available only on prescription, used to treat hormonal deficiency in men, inoperable breast cancer in women (rarely now because of its masculinizing effects), and conditions of osteoporosis ('brittle bones') caused by lack of androgens. Produced in ampoules (in two strengths, under the names Sustanon 100 and Sustanon 250) for injection, administration is from fortnightly to monthly.

▲/● side-effects/warning: *see* TESTOSTERONE.

**suxamethonium chloride** is a SKELETAL MUSCLE RELAXANT that has an effect for only 5 minutes, and is thus used – following the initial injection of an intravenous BARBITURATE – for short, complete and predictable paralysis (mostly during diagnostic or surgical procedures). Recovery is spontaneous. Administration is by injection or infusion.

▲ side-effects: blood levels of potassium rise temporarily under treatment. There may be muscle pain afterwards. Repeated doses may cause prolonged muscle paralysis.

● warning: suxamethonium chloride should not be administered to patients with severe liver disease or severe burns. Premedication is usually with atropine. During treatment, the paralysis is irreversible.

*Related articles:* ANECTINE; MIN-I-MIX SUXAMETHONIUM CHLORIDE; SCOLINE.

**Sween** (*Francol*) is a proprietary, non-prescription deodorant spray used to freshen and sanitize the appliance or bag attached to a stoma (an outlet on the skin surface following the surgical curtailment of the intestines).

**Symmetrel** (*Geigy*) is a proprietary preparation of the powerful drug amantadine hydrochloride, available only on prescription, used to treat parkinsonism, but not the parkinsonian symptoms induced by drugs (*see* ANTIPARKIN-SONSISM). Effective on some patients, but not on others, Symmetrel is produced in the form of capsules and as a syrup for dilution (the potency of the syrup once dilute is retained for 4 weeks).

▲/● side-effects/warning: *see* AMANTADINE HYDROCHLORIDE.

**\*sympathomimetics** are drugs that have effects mimicking those of the sympathetic nervous system. There are two main types, although several sympathomimetics belong to both types. Alpha-adrenergic sympathomimetics (such as phenylephrine) are VASOCONSTRICTORS and are particularly used in nasal decongestants. Beta-adrenergic sympathomimetics (such as salbutamol, see BETA-RECEPTOR STIMULANTS) are frequently SMOOTH MUSCLE RELAXANTS, particularly on bronchial smooth muscle, and are used especially as BRONCHODILATORS.
*see* ADRENALINE; DOBUTAMINE HYDROCHLORIDE; DOPAMINE; EPHEDRINE HYDROCHLORIDE; FENOTEROL; ISOETHARINE; ISOPRENALINE; METARAMINOL; METHOXAMINE HYDROCHLORIDE; NORADRENALINE; ORCIPRENALINE; OXEDRINE TARTRATE; PHENYLEPHRINE; PIRBUTEROL; REPROTEROL HYDROCHLORIDE; RIMITEROL; SALBUTAMOL; TERBUTALINE.

**Sympatol** (*Lewis*) is a proprietary VASOCONSTRICTOR, available only on prescription, used to treat low blood pressure (hypotension). Produced in the form of a liquid (for swallowing) and in ampoules for injection, Sympatol is a preparation of the SYMPATHOMIMETIC drug oxedrine tartrate.
▲/✵ side-effects/warning: *see* OXEDRINE TARTRATE.

**Synacthen** (*Ciba*) is a proprietary form of a HORMONE that stimulates the adrenal gland into functioning to produce corticosteroid hormones (corticotrophin). This may be useful therapeutically in cases of anaphylactic shock or to stimulate the adrenal gland which may be suppressed by chronic corticosteroid administration, but in fact Synacthen is primarily used merely to test adrenal gland function. Consisting of a preparation of tetracosactrin, and produced in ampoules for injection, it is not recommended for children.
▲/✵ side-effects/warning: *see* TETRACOSACTRIN.

**Synacthen Depot** (*Ciba*) is a proprietary form of a HORMONE that stimulates the adrenal gland into functioning to produce either adrenaline and noradrenaline, or corticosteroid hormones (corticotrophin). Administered on a regular basis, the dosage monitored and adjusted for effect, the hormone has been used to treat several disorders that depend on hormonal factors. Such disorders include rheumatic disease, gout, ulcerative colitis and chronic skin disorders, as well as allergic conditions although now it is used more commonly as a diagnostic agent of adrenal function. It is a preparation of tetracosactrin acetate and a zinc complex, produced in ampoules for injection.
▲/✵ side-effects/warning: *see* TETRACOSACTRIN.

**Synadrin** (*Hoechst*) is a proprietary VASODILATOR, available only on prescription, used to prevent recurrent attacks of angina pectoris (heart pain). Produced in the form of tablets, Synadrin is a preparation of prenylamine lactate. It is not recommended for children.
▲/✵ side-effects/warning: *see* PRENYLAMINE.

**Synalar** (*ICI*) is a series of proprietary CORTICOSTEROID ointments and creams, available only on prescription, for topical application on skin infections or inflammation. All contain the

steer oid fluocinolone acetonide.
The standard form is a 0.025%
solution, in both ointment and
cream. Synalar Cream 1:10 is a
cream (only) consisting of a
0.0025% solution; Synalar Cream
1:4 is a cream (only) consisting of
a 0.00625% solution. Synalar C is
both ointment and cream as the
standard version, but with the
addition of the ANTIFUNGAL agent
CLIOQUINOL. Synalar N is both
ointment and cream as the
standard version, but with the
addition of the ANTIBIOTIC agent
NEOMYCIN. There is also a similar
gel with which to massage the
scalp; its content is the same as
the standard ointment and cream.
▲ / ❃ side-effects/warning: see
    FLUOCINOLONE ACETONIDE.

**Syndol** (*Merrell*) is a proprietary,
non-prescription compound
ANALGESIC, which is not available
from the National Health Service.
It is used particularly to treat
headache and toothache, and pain
following surgery. Produced in
the form of tablets, Syndol is a
compound that includes
paracetamol, codeine phosphate
and caffeine. It is not
recommended for children.
▲ / ❃ side-effects/warning: see
    CAFFEINE; CODEINE
    PHOSPHATE; PARACETAMOL.

**Synergel** (*Servier*) is a
proprietary, non-prescription
ANTACID, which is not available
from the National Health Service.
It is produced in the form of a gel
and is based on an aluminium
salt.

**Synflex** (*Syntex*) is a proprietary,
non-narcotic ANALGESIC,
available only on prescription,
used to treat migraine and
menstrual and inflammatory pain,
and pain following surgery.
Produced in the form of tablets, it
is a preparation of the non-
steroidal ANTI-INFLAMMATORY
drug naproxen sodium.

▲ / ❃ side-effects/warning: see
    NAPROXEN.

**Synkavit** (*Roche*) is a proprietary,
non-prescription form of the
water-soluble VITAMIN K
substitute menadiol sodium
phosphate. It is as good as the
real vitamin (phytomenadione) in
making up vitamin deficiency and
thus ensuring properly effective
blood clotting. It is produced in
the form of tablets.
❃ warning: see MENADIOL SODIUM
    PHOSPHATE.

**Synogist** (*Townendale*) is a
proprietary, non-prescription
medicated shampoo containing an
ANTIBIOTIC, used to treat
conditions of the scalp associated
with bacterial or fungal infection
(particularly of the sebaceous
glands).
❃ warning: keep the shampoo
    away from the eyes.

**Synphase** (*Syntex*) is a proprietary
supply of ORAL CONTRACEPTIVE
tablets for one month that follows
a carefully phased scheme. It is
presented as a calendar pack:
each of 21 tablets is numbered,
and the first tablet is to be taken
on the fifth day of the mestrual
cycle. The contents of the pills
varies according to the stage of
the cycle reached, but is a
combination of the OESTROGEN
ethinyloestradiol and the
PROGESTOGEN norethisterone.
Synphase is available only on
prescription.
▲ / ❃ side-effects/warning: see
    ETHINYLOESTRADIOL;
    NORETHISTERONE.

**Syntaris** (*Syntex*) is a proprietary
nasal spray, available only on
prescription, used to treat the
symptoms of nasal allergy (such
as hay fever). Consisting of a
preparation of the CORTICO-
STEROID flunisolide, it is produced
in a bottle with a pump and
applicator. It is not recommended

for children aged under 5 years.
▲/✚ side-effects/warning: *see*
FLUNISOLIDE.

**Synthamin** (*Travenol*) is a
proprietary series of nutritional
supplements for infusion into
patients unable to take food via
the alimentary canal. They are all
a preparation of amino acids;
most also contain electrolytes.
Available only on prescription,
each should be administered only
by qualified personnel.

**Syntocinon** (*Sandoz*) is a
proprietary preparation of the
natural HORMONE oxytocin, which
causes increased contraction of
the womb during labour and
stimulates lactation in the
breasts. Available only on
prescription, it may be
administered therapeutically to
induce or assist labour and to
control postnatal bleeding.
Medical supervision is essential
during treatment. It is produced
in ampoules for injection (in three
strengths) and as a nasal spray.
▲/✚ side-effects/warning: *see*
OXYTOCIN.

**Syntometrine** (*Sandoz*) is a
proprietary preparation of the
vegetable alkaloid ergometrine
maleate together with the natural
HORMONE oxytocin. Available
only on prescription, it may be
administered to assist the second
and final stages of labour (birth
and the delivery of the afterbirth),
and to control postnatal bleeding.
Medical supervision is essential

during treatment. It is produced
in ampoules for injection.
▲/✚ side-effects/warning: *see*
ERGOMETRINE MALEATE;
OXYTOCIN.

**Syntopressin** (*Sandoz*) is a
proprietary preparation of
lypressin, one of the derivatives
of the antidiuretic HORMONE
vasopressin. Available only on
prescription, it is used to treat
pituitary-originated diabetes
insipidus, and is produced in the
form of a nasal spray.
▲/✚ side-effects/warning: *see*
VASOPRESSIN.

**Syraprim** (*Wellcome*) is a
proprietary ANTIBIOTIC drug,
available only on prescription,
used to treat serious bacterial
infections, particularly those of
the upper respiratory tract and of
the urinary tract. Produced in the
form of tablets (in two strengths)
and in ampoules for injection,
Syraprim is a preparation of the
antibacterial agent trimethoprim.
▲/✚ side-effects/warning: *see*
TRIMETHOPRIM.

**Sytron** (*Parke-Davis*) is a
proprietary, non-prescription iron
supplement, used to make up IRON
deficiency (and so treat anaemia).
Produced in the form of a sugar-
free elixir for dilution (the
potency of the elixir once dilute is
retained for 14 days), it consits of
sodium ironedetate.
▲/✚ side-effects/warning: *see*
SODIUM IRONEDETATE.

**Tachyrol** (*Duphar*) is a proprietary, non-prescription preparation of CALCIFEROL (vitamin D) in the form of its analogue dihydrotachysterol. Used to restore and sustain the calcium balance mechanism in the body, Tachyrol is produced in the form of tablets.
● warning: *see* DIHYDROTACHYSTEROL.

**Tagamet** (*Smith, Kline & French*) is a proprietary preparation of the drug cimetidine, available only on prescription, used to treat peptic ulcers (in the stomach or duodenum, or on a stoma) and persistent acid stomach. It works by reducing the secretion of gastric acids. It is produced in the form of tablets (in three strengths), as a syrup for dilution (the potency of the syrup once dilute is retained for 28 days), in ampoules for injection, and in bags for infusion. It is not recommended for children aged under 12 months.
▲/● side-effects/warning: *see* CIMETIDINE.

**talampicillin** is a broad-spectrum penicillin-type ANTIBIOTIC, a more readily absorbed derivative of ampicillin, used to treat various bacterial infections (such as chronic bronchitis, gonorrhoea, infection of the middle ear, and infections of the urinary tract). Administration is oral in the form of tablets and as a dilute syrup.
▲ side-effects: there may be sensitivity reactions. Some patients experience diarrhoea.
● warning: talampicillin should not be administered to patients known to be sensitive to penicillins; it should be administered with caution to those with any allergy at all, or to those with impaired kidney function.
*Related article:* TALPEN.

**Talpen** (*Beecham*) is a proprietary ANTIBIOTIC of the penicillin type, available only on prescription, used to treat severe bacterial infections (such as chronic bronchitis, gonorrhoea, infection of the middle ear, and infections of the urinary tract). Produced in the form of tablets, and as a syrup for dilution (the potency of the syrup once diluted is retained for 7 days), Talpen is a preparation of the ampicillin-derivative talampicillin.
▲/● side-effects/warning: *see* TALAMPICILLIN.

**Tambocor** (*Riker*) is a proprietary ANTIARRHYTHMIC drug, available only on prescription, used to treat all forms of heartbeat irregularities. Produced in the form of tablets, and in ampoules for injection, Tambocor is a preparation of the local ANAESTHETIC LIGNOCAINE analogue flecainide acetate.
▲/● side-effects/warning: *see* FLECAINIDE ACETATE.

**Tamofen** (*Tillotts*) is a proprietary preparation of the powerful drug tamoxifen, available only on prescription, which because it inhibits or blocks the effect of OESTROGENS, is used primarily to treat cancers that depend on the presence of oestrogen in women, particularly breast cancer. But it may also be used (under strict medical supervision) to treat certain conditions of infertility in which the presence of oestrogens may be preventing other hormonal activity. It is produced in the form of tablets (in three strengths, under the names Tamofen, Tamofen-20 and Tamofen-40).
▲/● side-effects/warning: *see* TAMOXIFEN.

**tamoxifen** is a drug that inhibits or blocks the effect of OESTROGENS, and is thus used primarily to treat cancers that depend on the presence of oestrogen in women, particularly breast cancer. But it may also be used (under strict medical supervision) to treat certain conditions of infertility in which the presence of oestrogens may be preventing other hormonal activity. Administration is oral in the form of tablets.

▲ side-effects: the effect of treatment is much the same as that of surgical removal of the ovaries: menstruation ceases in pre-menopausal women. Other effects are comparatively rare, but the blood level of calcium may rise (and so cause pain in patients who suffer from the calcareous type of metastatic tumour).

❂ warning: tamoxifen should not be administered to patients who are pregnant.

*Related articles:* EMBLON; NOLTAM; NOLVADEX; TAMOFEN.

**Tampovagan Stilboestrol and Lactic Acid** (*Norgine*) is a proprietary preparation of the OESTROGEN stilboestrol, available only on prescription, used to treat conditions of eroded or irritant skin in the vulva caused by hormonal deficiency (generally because of the menopause). It is produced in the form of vaginal inserts (pessaries), but dosage should be reduced as much, and as soon, as possible.

▲ / ❂ side-effects/warning: *see* STILBOESTROL.

**Tancolin** (*Ashe*) is a proprietary, non-prescription ANTITUSSIVE, which is not available from the National Health Service. Orange-flavoured, its active constituents include the BRONCHODILATOR theophylline, the NARCOTIC cough suppressant dextromethorphan, the ANTACID sodium citrate, and ASCORBIC ACID (vitamin C).

▲ / ❂ side-effects/warning: *see*

DEXTROMETHORPHAN; SODIUM CITRATE; THEOPHYLLINE.

**Tanderil** (*Zyma*) is a proprietary eye OINTMENT, available only on prescription, used to treat inflammation in and around the eye. It is a preparation of the non-steroid oxyphenbutazone (in solution). Another version is produced (under the name Tanderil Chloramphenicol) that additionally contains the ANTIBIOTIC chloramphenicol (in solution) to treat inflammation in which bacterial infection is also present.

▲ / ❂ side-effects/warning: *see* CHLORAMPHENICOL; OXYPHENBUTAZONE.

**Taractan** (*Roche*) is a proprietary ANTIPSYCHOTIC drug, available only on prescription, used to treat psychoses such as schizophrenia, to tranquillize patients undergoing behavioural disturbance, and in the short term to soothe severe anxiety. Produced in the form of tablets (in two strengths) Taractan is a preparation of the chlorpromazine-related drug chlorprothixene.

▲ / ❂ side-effects/warning: *see* CHLORPROTHIXENE.

**Tarband** (*Seton*) is a proprietary, non-prescription form of impregnated bandaging incorporating ZINC PASTE and COAL TAR, used to dress conditions of chronic eczema and psoriasis. Further bandaging is required to hold it in place.

▲ side-effects: there may be skin sensitivity. The dressing may stain skin and hair (and fabric).

❂ warning: it should not be used to cover broken or inflamed skin.

**Tarcortin** (*Stafford-Miller*) is a proprietary cream, available only on prescription, for topical application to conditions of chronic eczema and psoriasis and other dermatoses. It is a compound of the CORTICOSTEROID hydrocortisone with the cleansing agent COAL TAR.

▲/ ✿ side-effects/warning: *see* HYDROCORTISONE.

**Targocid** (*Merrell*) is the name of a selection of proprietary forms of the antibacterial ANTIBIOTIC teicoplanin. Available only on prescription, it is available as a powdered form for reconstitution for injection.

▲/ ✿ side-effects/warning: *see* TEICOPLANIN.

**Tarivid** (*Hoechst, Roussel*) is a proprietary preparation of the ANTIBIOTIC drug ofloxacin, one of the quinolones, available only on prescription, used to treat a variety of infections when these are resistant to more conventional drugs, especially urinary tract infections including gonorrhoea. Produced in the form of tablets, Ciproxin is not recommended for children or adolescents.

▲/ ✿ side-effects/warning: *see* OFLOXACIN.

**Tavegil** (*Sandoz*) is a proprietary, non-prescription ANTIHISTAMINE used to treat allergic conditions such as hay fever, dermatitis and urticaria, or sensitivity reactions to drugs. Produced in the form of tablets, and as a sugar-free elixir for dilution (the potency of the elixir once dilute is retained for 14 days), Tavegil is a preparation of clemastine fumarate.

▲/ ✿ side-effects/warning: *see* CLEMASTINE.

**Tears Naturale** (*Alcon*) is a proprietary, non-prescription form of synthetic tear-fluid, produced in the form of drops, used to make up for a deficiency in the lachrymal apparatus of the eye. It is a compound of the plasma substitute DEXTRAN with the artificial tears liquid hypromellose.

**Teejel** (*Napp*) is a proprietary, non-prescription gel containing both an ANTISEPTIC and an ANALGESIC, used to treat mouth ulcers, sore gums or inflammation of the tongue. The gel is intended to be massaged in gently. It consists of a compound of the analgesic CHOLINE SALICYLATE with the antiseptic cetalkonium chloride (both in solution). It is not recommended for children aged under 4 months.

**Tegretol** (*Geigy*) is a proprietary preparation of the ANTI-CONVULSANT drug carbamazepine, available only on prescription, used to treat almost all forms of epilepsy, and to relieve trigeminal neuralgia (pain in the side of the face). It is produced in the form of tablets (in three strengths), chewable tablets (in two strengths), as a sugar-free liquid for dilution (the potency of the liquid once dilute is retained for 14 days), and as controlled-release tablets under the trade name Tegretol Retard (in two strengths).

▲/ ✿ side-effects/warning: *see* CARBAMAZEPINE.

**teicoplanin** is a glycopeptide ANTIBIOTIC very similar to VANCOMYCIN, although with a longer duration of action allowing dosing only once a day. It has activity primarily against Gram-positive micro-organisms. It inhibits the synthesis of components of the bacterial cell wall. It is used when vancomycin or other drugs are not suitable or where there is resistance. It may be used in the treatment of serious Gram-positive infections, including endocarditis, dialysis-associated peritonitis, and

against serious infections due to
Staphylococcus aureus when
these organisms are resistant to
more conventional agents. Its use
may have deleterious effects on
the organs of the ear, on the
kidney and liver, and blood
concentrations of the drug in the
blood and liver and kidney
function should be monitored
during treatment. The solution
for injection may be given by
intramuscular as well as
intravenous injection. See also
VANCOMYCIN.

▲ side-effects: there may be
diarrhoea, nausea and
vomiting, headache; severe
allergic reactions,
bronchospasm, fever, rash;
blood disorders including
changes in counts of
neutrophils, eosinophils and
platelets; ringing in the ears
and mild loss of hearing; local
reactions at the injection site;
loss of balance has been
reported.

✹ warning: liver and kidney
function tests are required, as
are blood counts and hearing
tests. Reduce dose in the
elderly and in renal
impairment.
*Related article:* TARGOCID.

**temazepam** is a relatively short-
acting HYPNOTIC drug, one of the
BENZODIAZEPINES, used as a
TRANQUILLIZER to treat insomnia
(particularly in the elderly) and
as an ANXIOLYTIC premedication
prior to surgery. Administration
is oral in the form of capsules,
which are hard or gel-filled (some
known as Gelthix), or as an oral
solution.

▲ side-effects: concentration and
speed of reaction are affected.
There may also be drowsiness
and dizziness. Some patients
experience sensitivity
reactions. Prolonged use may
eventually result in tolerance,
and finally dependence.

✹ warning: temazepam should be
administered with caution to
patients with lung disease or
shallow breathing, or impaired
liver or kidney function, who
are pregnant or lactating, or
who are elderly and
debilitated.
*Related article:* NORMISON.

**Temgesic** (*Reckitt & Colman*) is a
proprietary narcotic ANALGESIC,
available only on prescription,
used to treat all forms of pain.
Produced in the form of tablets to
be retained under the tongue, and
in ampoules for injection, it is a
preparation of the OPIATE
buprenorphine hydrochloride.

▲/✹ side-effects/warning: *see*
BUPRENORPHINE.

**Tenif** (*Stuart*) is a proprietary
preparations of the CALCIUM
ANTAGONIST nifedipine together
with the BETA-BLOCKER atenolol.
Available only on prescription, it
is used to treat angina pectoris
(heart pain), and high blood
pressure (hypertension) in
patients where either drug alone
has be inadequate. It is produced
in the form of capsules.

▲/✹ side-effects/warning: *see*
ATENOLOL; NIFEDIPINE.

**Tenoret 50** (*Stuart*) is a
proprietary ANTIHYPERTENSIVE
compound drug, available only on
prescription, used primarily to
treat high blood pressure
(hypertension), especially in the
elderly, but also to treat angina
pectoris (heart pain) and
heartbeat irregularities.
Produced in the form of tablets, it
is a combination of the BETA-
BLOCKER atenolol with the
THIAZIDE diuretic chlorthalidone.
It is not recommended for
children.

▲/✹ side-effects/warning: *see*
ATENOLOL; CHLORTHALIDONE.

**Tenoretic** (*Stuart*) is a proprietary
ANTIHYPERTENSIVE compound
drug, available only on

prescription, used primarily to treat high blood pressure (hypertension). Produced in the form of tablets, it is a combination of the BETA-BLOCKER atenolol together with the THIAZIDE DIURETIC chlorthalidone (in twice the proportions contained in the same manufacturer's Tenoret 50). It is not recommended for prescription to children.

▲/● side-effects/warning: *see* ATENOLOL; CHLORTHALIDONE.

**Tenormin** (*Stuart*) is a proprietary ANTIHYPERTENSIVE drug, available only on prescription, used primarily to treat high blood pressure (hypertension). Produced in the form of tablets (in two strengths, the weaker under the name Tenormin LS), as a sugar-free lemon-and-lime-flavoured syrup, and in ampoules for injection, it is a preparation of the BETA-BLOCKER atenolol. It is not recommended for children.

▲/● side-effects/warning: *see* ATENOLOL.

**Tensilon** (*Roche*) is a proprietary preparation of the ANTICHOLIN-ERGIC drug edrophonium chloride, available only on prescription. The drug prolongs the action of the natural neurotransmitter acetylcholine, and can thus be used both in the diagnosis of disorders of the neuro-transmission process caused by disease or by drug treatments (through a comparison of its effect with the effect of its absence), and as an antidote to muscle relaxants which block the action of the neurotransmitter at the end of operations (in which case, atropine should be administered simultaneously). It is produced in ampoules for injection.

▲/● side-effects/warning: *see* EDROPHONIUM CHLORIDE.

**Tensium** (*DDSA Pharmaceuticals*) is a proprietary ANXIOLYTIC drug, available on prescription only to private patients. It is used to treat insomnia and anxiety, and to relieve the effects of acute alcohol withdrawal symptoms. Produced in the form of tablets (in three strengths), Tensium is a preparation of the powerful and long-acting BENZODIAZEPINE diazepam.

▲/● side-effects/warning: *see* DIAZEPAM.

**Tenuate Dospan** (*Merrell*) is a proprietary preparation of the amphetamine-related drug diethylpropion hydrochloride, used as an appetite-suppressant in the medical treatment of obesity. On the controlled drugs list, it is produced in the form of sustained-release tablets. Treatment must be in the short term and under strict medical supervision.

▲/● side-effects/warning: *see* DIETHYLPROPION HYDROCHLORIDE.

**Teoptic** (*Dispersa*) is a proprietary form of eye-drops, available only on prescription, used to treat glaucoma. It is a preparation of the BETA-BLOCKER carteolol hydrochloride (in two strengths), and is not recommended for children.

▲/● side-effects/warning: *see* CARTEOLOL HYDROCHLORIDE.

**terbutaline** is a BETA-RECEPTOR STIMULANT and BRONCHODILATOR that is especially useful in treating all forms and stages of asthma. As a SYMPATHOMIMETIC drug and a SMOOTH MUSCLE RELAXANT, however, terbutaline (in the form of terbutaline sulphate) is also used to prevent – or at least delay – the onset of premature labour by inhibiting uterine contractions. Administration is oral in the form of tablets, sustained-release tablets and a dilute syrup, as an inhalant via an aerosol or nebuliser, or by injection or infusion.

▲ side-effects: there may be
nausea and vomiting, flushing
and sweating, and a tremor.
High dosage may cause an
increase in the heart rate, with
high blood pressure.

✿ warning: terbutaline should
not be administered to patients
with heart disease or high
blood pressure
(hypertension), bleeding or
infection, an excess of thyroid
hormones in the blood
(thyrotoxicosis), or who are
already taking
antihypertensive drugs or beta-
blockers. It should be
administered with caution to
those with diabetes, who are
undergoing treatment with
corticosteroids or diuretics, or
who are elderly. Regular blood
counts and blood pressure
monitoring are essential.
*Related articles:* BRICANYL;
MONOVENT.

**Tercoda** (*Sinclair*) is a
proprietary, non-prescription
cough elixir that is not available
from the National Health Service.
Active constituents include
codeine phosphate and the
EXPECTORANT terpin hydrate.
▲/✿ side-effects/warning: *see*
CODEINE PHOSPHATE.

**terfenadine** is a relatively new
ANTIHISTAMINE used to treat the
symptoms of allergic disorders.
Unlike most, it has little sedative
effect. Administration is oral in
the form of tablets or as a dilute
suspension.
▲ side-effects: side-effects are
comparatively uncommon, but
there may be headache, dry
mouth, blurred vision,
gastrointestinal disturbances
and occasionally a rash and
photosensitivity.

✿ warning: terfenadine should be
administered with caution to
patients with epilepsy,
glaucoma, liver disease or

enlargement of the prostate
gland.
*Related articles:* TRILUDAN;
SELDANE.

**terlipressin** is a derivative of the
antidiuretic hormone
VASOPRESSIN, and is similarly a
VASOCONSTRICTOR. It is used
primarily to halt bleeding from
varicose veins in the oesophagus
– the part of the alimentary tract
between the throat and the
stomach. Administration is by
intravenous injection.
▲ side-effects: there may be
nausea, cramp, and an urge to
defecate; some patients
experience sensitivity
reactions. If the
vasoconstriction affects the
coronary arteries, there may be
heartbeat irregularities.

✿ warning: terlipressin should
not be administered to patients
with chronic kidney disease or
vascular disease; it should be
administered with caution to
those with epilepsy, asthma,
migraine or heart failure.
*Related article:* GLYPRESSIN.

**terodiline hydrochloride** is an
ANTICHOLINERGIC drug used to
treat excessive frequency of
urination, and urinary
incontinence. It works mainly by
reducing the effect of the
parasympathetic nervous system
on the bladder, although it also
has CALCIUM ANTAGONIST
properties. Administration is oral
in the form of tablets.
▲ side-effects: there may be dry
mouth and difficulty in
swallowing, pressure within
the eyeballs and sensitivity to
light, flushing and dry skin,
heartbeat irregularities and
constipation.

✿ warning: terodiline
hydrochloride should not be
administered to patients with
urinary obstruction or any
kind of liver disease; it should

be administered with caution to those with excess thyroid hormones in the bloodstream (thyrotoxicosis), fast heart rate (tachycardia), gastrointestinal blockage, high temperature or retention of food within the stomach.
*Related article:* MICTURIN.

**Teronac** (*Sandoz*) is a proprietary preparation of the stimulant drug mazindol, used as an APPETITE-SUPPRESSANT in the medical treatment of obesity. On the controlled drugs list (because it is potentially addictive and anorectic), it is produced in the form of tablets. Treatment must be in the short term and under strict medical supervision.
▲/● side-effects/warning: *see* MAZINDOL.

**Terpoin** (*Hough*) is a proprietary cough elixir, available on prescription only to private patients. Active constituents include codeine phosphate, the EXPECTORANT guaiphenesin, and menthol.
▲/● side-effects/warning: *see* CODEINE PHOSPHATE.

**Terra-Cortril** (*Pfizer*) is the name of several CORTICOSTEROID preparations that are also ANTIBIOTIC, available only on prescription, used for local or topical application to treat skin disorders in which bacterial or other infection is also implicated. The standard form, produced as an ointment and as a spray in an aerosol, combines the steroid hydrocortisone and the TETRACYCLINE antibiotic oxytetracycline. Terra-Cortril Ear Suspension also contains the antibiotic polymyxin B sulphate. Terra-Cortril Nystatin is a cream that is a combination of hydrocortisone and oxytetracycline with the ANTIFUNGAL agent nystatin.

▲/● side-effects/warning: *see* HYDROCORTISONE; NYSTATIN; OXYTETRACYCLINE; POLYMYXIN B.

**Terramycin** (*Pfizer*) is a proprietary ANTIBIOTIC, available only on prescription, used to treat bacterial and other infections. Produced in the form of capsules and tablets, it is a preparation of the TETRACYCLINE oxytetracycline hydrochloride.
▲/● side-effects/warning: *see* OXYTETRACYCLINE.

**Tertroxin** (*Glaxo*) is a proprietary preparation of the thyroid HORMONE triiodothyronine (in the form of liothyronine sodium), available only on prescription, used to make up hormonal deficiency (hypothyroidism) and thus to treat the associated symptoms (myxoedema). It is produced in the form of tablets.
▲/● side-effects/warning: *see* LIOTHYRONINE SODIUM.

**testosterone** is an ANDROGEN, the principal male sex HORMONE, produced mainly in the testes and, with other androgens, promoting the development of and maintenance of the male sex organs and the development of the secondary male sexual characteristics. Therapeutically it may be administered to treat hormonal deficiency (but only following careful investigation and under strict medical supervision), particularly in cases of delayed puberty in boys; it is no longer in general use to treat cancer of the breast in women because of its masculinising effects. Administration is oral in the form of capsules, or by injection or depot injection.
▲ side-effects: there may be fluid retention in the tissues (oedema) leading to weight gain. Increased levels of

calcium in the body may cause bone growth (and in younger patients may fuse bones before fully grown) and the symptoms of hypercalcaemia. In elderly patients there may be (increased) enlargement of the prostate gland. High doses halt the production of sperm in men and cause the visible masculinization of women.

● warning: testosterone should not be administered to male patients who suffer from kidney disease, cancer of the prostate gland or cancer of the breast, or to female patients who are pregnant or lactating; it should be administered with caution to those with impaired function of the heart, liver or kidney, circulatory disorders and/or high blood pressure (hypertension), epilepsy or diabetes, thyroid disorders, or migraine.
*Related articles:* PRIMOTESTON DEPOT; RESTANDOL; SUSTANON; VIRORMONE.

**tetanus vaccine** is a toxoid VACCINE that stimulates the formation in the body of the appropriate antitoxin – that is, an antibody produced in response to the presence of the toxin of the tetanus bacterium, rather than to the presence of the bacterium itself. Its effectiveness is improved by being adsorbed on to a mineral carrier (such as aluminium hydroxide or calcium phosphate). Its most common form of administration is as one constituent of the triple vaccine against diphtheria, whooping cough (pertussis) and tetanus (the DIPHTHERIA-PERTUSSIS-TETANUS (DPT), vaccine), administered during early life, although it is administered by itself at any age for those at special risk, or administered as a double vaccine with the DIPHTHERIA VACCINE for those who wish not to be given

the whooping cough vaccine. Administration is by injection. Tetanus vaccinations should not be renewed within 5 years.

**Tetavax** (*Merieux*) is a proprietary preparation of adsorbed TETANUS VACCINE, produced in syringes and vials for injection.

**tet/vac/ads** is an abbreviation for the kind of tetanus vaccine that is adsorbed on to a mineral carrier for injection.
*see* TETANUS VACCINE.

**tet/vac/ft** is an abbreviation for tetanus vaccine formol toxoid, the plain vaccine (that is not adsorbed on to a carrier).
*see* TETANUS VACCINE.

**tetrabenazine** is a powerful drug used to assist a patient to regain voluntary control of movement – or at least to lessen the extent of involuntary movements – in Huntington's chorea and related disorders. It is thought to work by reducing the amount of DOPAMINE in the nerve endings in the brain. Administration is oral in the form of tablets.

▲ side-effects: there may be drowsiness and postural hypotension. Some patients experience depression.

● warning: tetrabenazine should not be administered to patients who are lactating or who are already taking drugs that contain levodopa or reserpine.
*Related article:* NITOMAN.

**Tetrabid-Organon** (*Organon*) is a proprietary broad-spectrum ANTIBIOTIC, available only on prescription, used to treat many forms of infection but particularly those of the urinary tract, of the genital organs, pustular acne or chronic bronchitis. Produced in the form of sustained-release capsules, it is a preparation of tetracycline hydrochloride. It is not suitable for children aged under 12 years.

▲ / ✿ side-effects/warning: *see*
TETRACYCLINE.

**Tetrachel** (*Berk*) is a proprietary,
broad-spectrum ANTIBIOTIC,
available only on prescription,
used to treat many forms of
infection but particularly those of
the urinary tract, of the genital
organs, pustular acne or chronic
bronchitis. Produced in the form
of capsules and tablets, it is a
preparation of tetracycline
hydrochloride. It is not suitable
for children aged under 12 years.
▲ / ✿ side-effects/warning: *see*
TETRACYCLINE.

**tetrachloroethylene** is an
ANTHELMINTIC drug, used to treat
infestations by hookworms
(parasitical worms that attach to
the inner wall of the small
intestine, feeding not only on the
passing food-mass but also on
blood from the intestine wall).
▲ side-effects: there may be
nausea and headache, with
drowsiness.
✿ warning: tetrachloroethylene
should not be administered to
the elderly or the debilitated,
or to children. Absorption of
tetrachloroethylene may cause
toxic side-effects; however,
absorption is unlikely if
patients avoid alcohol and
fatty foods following
treatment.

**tetracosactrin** is a synthetic
HORMONE that acts on the adrenal
glands to release CORTICO-
STEROIDS, especially HYDRO-
CORTISONE. Like its natural
equivalent CORTICOTROPHIN,
tetracosactrin is useful in the
treatment of allergic disorders,
inflammation and especially
asthma (particularly in patients
who for one reason or another
cannot tolerate the natural
substance). It may also be used to
test adrenal function. In the
treatment of rheumatic disease in

patients who are still growing,
tetracosactrin has an advantage
over corticosteroids in that it
does not cause as much stunting
of growth.
▲ side-effects: there is high blood
pressure (hypertension),
sodium and water retention
(oedema) leading to weight
gain, loss of blood potassium
and muscle weakness.

**tetracycline** is a broad-spectrum
ANTIBIOTIC that gave its name to a
group of similar antibiotics. It is
used to treat many forms of
infection caused by several types
of micro-organism; conditions it is
used to treat include infections of
the urinary tract, of the
respiratory tract, and of the
genital organs, and acne.
Administration is oral in the form
of capsules, tablets and liquids, or
by injection.
▲ side-effects: there may be
nausea and vomiting, with
diarrhoea. Occasionally there
is sensitivity to light or other
sensitivity reaction. These
side-effects may still occur
even if the causative organism
of the disorder being treated
proves to be resistant to the
drug.
✿ warning: tetracycline should
not be administered to patients
who are aged under 12 years,
who are pregnant, or who have
impaired kidney function; it
should be administered with
caution to those who are
lactating.
*Related articles:* ACHROMYCIN;
ACHROMYCIN V; AUREOCORT;
DETECLO; ECONOMYCIN;
MYSTECLIN; PANMYCIN;
SUSTAMYCIN; TETRABID-
ORGANON; TETRACHEL; TETREX;
TOPICYCLINE.

**tetracyclines** are a group of very
broad-spectrum ANTIBIOTICS.
Apart from being effective against
bacteria, they inhibit the growth

of chlamydia (cause genito-urinary tract infections, eye infections and psittacosis), rickettsia (cause Q fever and typhus) and mycoplasma (cause mycoplasmal pneumonia). They act by inhibiting protein biosynthesis in sensitive micro-organisms and penetrate human macrophages, therefore they are useful in combating micro-organisms such as mycoplasma that can survive and multiply within macrophages. They have been used to treat a very wide range of infections, but with developing bacterial resistance their uses have become more specific. Treatment of atypical pneumonia due to chlamydia, rickettsia or mycoplasma is a notable indication for tetracyclines, while treatment of chlamydial urethritis and pelvic inflammatory disease is another. They are also used to treat brucellosis and Lyme disease. More mundanely they are effective in treating exacerbations of chronic bronchitis. Most tetracyclines are more difficult to absorb in a stomach that contains milk, antacids, calcium salts or magnesium salts; they tend to make kidney disease worse; and they may be deposited in growing bone and teeth (causing staining and potential deformity), so they should not be administered to children aged under 12 years. Best-known and most-used tetracyclines include tetracycline (which they were all named after), doxycycline and oxytetracycline. Administration is oral in the form of capsules, tablets or liquids.
*see* CHLORTETRACYCLINE; CLOMOCYCLINE SODIUM; DEMECLOCYCLINE HYDROCHLORIDE; LYMECYCLINE; MINOCYCLINE; OXYTETRACYCLINE; TETRACYCLINE.

**Tetralysal** (*Farmitalia Carlo Erba*) is a proprietary, broad-spectrum ANTIBIOTIC, available only on prescription, used to treat many forms of infection but particularly those of the skin and soft tissues, the ear, nose or throat, or conditions such as pustular acne. Produced in the form of capsules (in two strengths, the stronger under the name Tetralysal 300), it represents a preparation of the soluble TETRACYCLINE complex lymecycline. It is not recommended for children aged under 12 years.
▲/✿ side-effects/warning: *see* LYMECYCLINE.

**Tetrex** (*Bristol-Myers*) is a proprietary, broad-spectrum ANTIBIOTIC, available only on prescription, used to treat many forms of infection but particularly those of the urinary tract or genital organs, pustular acne or chronic bronchitis. Produced in the form of capsules and tablets, it is a preparation of tetracycline hydrochloride. It is not recommended for children aged under 12 years.
▲/✿ side-effects/warning: *see* TETRACYCLINE.

**T/Gel** (*Neutrogena*) is a proprietary, non-prescription medicated shampoo designed to treat scaling skin on the scalp, as occurs with dandruff or with psoriasis. Its principal constituent is COAL TAR.

**Thalamonal** (*Janssen*) is a proprietary preparation of the TRANQUILLIZER droperidol and the narcotic ANALGESIC fentanyl, and is accordingly on the controlled drugs list. It is used on patients about to undergo diagnostic or minor surgical procedures that may be difficult or painful. It is produced in ampoules for injection.
▲/✿ side-effects/warning: *see* DROPERIDOL; FENTANYL.

**Thalazole** (*May & Baker*) is a proprietary ANTIBACTERIAL, available only on prescription, used (formerly much more commonly) in the treatment of intestinal infections and to disinfect the colon prior to examination or surgery. Produced in the form of tablets, Thalazole is a preparation of the poorly-absorbed SULPHONAMIDE phthalylsulphathiazole.

▲/⬥ side-effects/warning: see PHTHALYLSULPHATHIAZOLE.

**Thavoline** (*Ilon*) is a proprietary, non-prescription skin emollient (softener and soother), which also relieves itching. It may be used to provide a protective covering over burns, bedsores or nappy rash. Produced in the form of an ointment and as an aerosol spray for topical application, Thavoline contains wool fat, ZINC OXIDE and KAOLIN.

**Theodrox** (*Riker*) is a proprietary, non-prescription BRONCHODILATOR used to treat conditions such as asthma and bronchitis and to relieve the symptoms of partial heart failure. Produced in the form of tablets containing the antacid ALUMINIUM HYDROXIDE in order to prolong the effect, Theodrox has as its principal constituent the short-acting xanthine, aminophylline. It is not recommended for children.

▲/⬥ side-effects/warning: see AMINOPHYLLINE.

**Theo-Dur** (*Astra*) is a proprietary, non-prescription BRONCHODILATOR used to treat conditions such as asthma and chronic bronchitis. Produced in the form of sustained-release tablets (in two strengths) for prolonged effect, Theo-Dur has as its principal constituent the short-acting xanthine, theophylline.

▲/⬥ side-effects/warning: see THEOPHYLLINE.

**theophylline** is a BRONCHODILATOR used mostly in sustained-release forms of administration, generally to treat conditions such as asthma and bronchitis over periods of around 12 hours at a time. Administration is oral in the form of tablets, capsules, or a liquid. Many proprietary preparations are not recommended for children.

▲ side-effects: there may be nausea and gastrointestinal disturbances, an increase or irregularity in the heartbeat, and/or insomnia.

⬥ warning: treatment should initially be gradually progressive in the quantity administered. Theophylline should be administered with caution to patients who suffer from heart or liver disease, or peptic ulcer; or who are pregnant or lactating.
*Related articles:* BIOPHYLLINE; FRANOL; FRANOL PLUS; LABOPHYLLINE; LASMA; NUELIN; PRO-VENT; SABIDAL SR 270; SLO-PHYLLIN; THEO-DUR; UNIPHYLLIN CONTINUS.

**Thephorin** (*Sinclair*) is a proprietary, non-prescription ANTIHISTAMINE used in oral administration to treat allergic conditions such as hay fever and urticaria. Produced in the form of tablets, it is a preparation of the very mildly stimulant phenindamine tartrate. It is not recommended for children.

▲/⬥ side-effects/warning: see PHENINDAMINE TARTRATE.

**thiabendazole** is a drug used in the treatment of infestations by worm-parasites, particularly those of the Strongyloides and Ancylostoma species that reside in the intestines but may migrate into the tissues. The usual course of treatment is intensive and lasts for 3 days; side-effects are inevitable.

▲ side-effects: there may be nausea, vomiting, diarrhoea and weight loss; dizziness and drowsiness are not uncommon;

there may also be headache and itching (pruritus). Possible hypersensitivity reactions include fever with chills, rashes and other skin disorders, and occasionally ringing in the ears (tinnitus) or liver damage.

● warning: thiabendazole should be administered with caution to patients with impaired kidney or liver function. Treatment should be withdrawn if hypersensitivity reactions occur.

*Related article:* MINTEZOL.

**thiamine**, or aneurin, is the technical name for VITAMIN B₁. Essential in the diet, the vitamin assists in the normal functioning of nerve cells and the heart muscle; it also maintains aspects of the metabolism of carbohydrates. Deficiency leads to the unpleasant disorder beriberi (in which there is either emaciation or bloating, with widescale nerve damage). Good food sources include yeast, grains, nuts, peas and beans, potatoes and pork. Thiamine is a common constituent in many proprietary vitamin B supplements, and may be administered therapeutically to thin children, to pregnant women or to lactating mothers. Administration (often in the form of thiamine hydrochloride) is oral or by injection.

*Related articles:* BECOSYM; BENERVA; HEPACON-PLEX; LIPOTRIAD; VIGRANON B.

**thiazides** are effective DIURETICS used mainly to treat the symptoms of heart disease, such as fluid retention in the tissues and high blood pressure (hypertension) or to assist a failing kidney. They work by inhibiting the reabsorption of sodium and chloride ions within one specific part of the kidney. The result is a moderate diuresis that includes the excretion also of

potassium. Potassium supplements are often administered simultaneously, or the thiazide may be combined with another type of diuretic that actively promotes the retention of potassium. Best-known and most-used thiazides include hydrochlorothiazide and bendrofluazide. Unlike some types of diuretics, the thiazides can be used for prolonged courses of treatment with no residual effects.

*see* BENDROFLUAZIDE; CHLOROTHIAZIDE; CYCLOPENTHIAZIDE; HYDROCHLOROTHIAZIDE; HYDROFLUMETHIAZIDE; METHYCLOTHIAZIDE; POLYTHIAZIDE.

**thiethylperazine** is an ANTI-EMETIC drug used to relieve nausea and vomiting that may be caused by the vertigo associated with infections of the inner or middle ear, or by therapy with cytotoxic drugs in the treatment of cancer. Administration is oral in the form of tablets, topical as anal suppositories, or by injection.

▲ side-effects: there is commonly drowsiness; there may also be dry mouth and dizziness on rising from sitting or lying down (caused by low blood pressure). Some patients, particularly young women, experience muscle spasms.

● warning: thiethylperazine should not be administered to patients who are in a coma, or have glaucoma or impaired capacity of the bone-marrow to produce blood cells. It should be administered with caution to those with heart or lung disease, dysfunction of the adrenal glands in the secretion of hormones, epilepsy, parkinsonism, impaired kidney or liver function, undersecretion of thyroid hormones, or enlargement of the prostate gland. Regular

ophthalmic checks and monitoring of skin pigmentation are required. Treatment should be withdrawn gradually.
*Related article:* TORECAN.

**thioguanine** is a CYTOTOXIC drug used to assist in the treatment of leukaemia, in which it is often effective in achieving a remission. Administration is oral in the form of tablets.
▲ side-effects: gastric upsets with nausea and vomiting are common; there may also be hair loss (even to temporary total baldness).
● warning: as with all cytotoxic drugs, thioguanine interferes with the bone-marrow's capacity to provide red blood cells: this may be an added complication to the leukaemia, and certainly tends to cause some loss of immunity to infection. Regular blood counts are essential.
*Related article:* LANVIS.

**thiopentone sodium** is a widely used general ANAESTHETIC used for general anaesthesia during operations. It has no analgesic properties. Because the drug is exceptionally powerful, however, inadvertent overdosage does occur from time to time, causing respiratory depression and depression of the heart rate. Both initial induction of anaesthesia and awakening afterwards are smooth and rapid, although some sedative effects may endure for up to 24 hours. Administration is by injection.
▲ side-effects: there may be respiratory depression, and means for treating respiratory failure should be available. During induction with thiopentone sodium, sneezing, coughing and bronchial spasm may occur.
● warning: thiopentone sodium should not be given to patients whose respiratory tract is

obstructed, those in severe shock, or those with porphyria (poor porphyrin metabolism). Caution should be taken when administering the drug to patients with severe liver or kidney disease, with metabolic disorders, or who are elderly.
*Related article:* INTRAVAL SODIUM.

**thioridazine** is a powerful ANTIPSYCHOTIC drug used to treat and tranquillize psychosis (such as schizophrenia), in which it is particularly suitable for treating manic forms of behavioural disturbance, especially in order to effect emergency control. The drug may also be used to treat anxiety in the short term and to calm agitated elderly patients. Administration is oral in the form of tablets or a liquid.
▲ side-effects: concentration and speed of thought and movement are affected. Rashes and jaundice may occur; and there may be dry mouth, gastrointestinal disturbance, difficulties in urinating, a reduction in blood pressure, and blurred or discoloured vision.
● warning: thioridazine should not be administered to patients who suffer from a reduction in the bone-marrow's capacity to produce blood cells, or from certain types of glaucoma. It should be administered only with caution to those with heart or vascular disease, kidney or liver disease, parkinsonism, or depression; or who are pregnant or lactating. It is not recommended for children.
*Related article:* MELLERIL.

**thiotepa** is a CYTOTOXIC drug used mainly to treat tumours in the bladder or malignant effusions in other body cavities. It works by interfering with the DNA of new-

forming cells, so preventing
normal cell replication.
Administration is in the form of
instillation in the body cavity, for
retention for as long as possible.

▲ side-effects: there is commonly
nausea and vomiting; there
may also be (temporary) hair
loss. The blood-cell-producing
capacity of the bone-marrow is
impaired.

☙ warning: prolonged use may
cause sterility in men and an
early menopause in women; in
both sexes it may lead to
permanent bone-marrow
damage. Prolonged treatment
has also been associated with
the incidence of leukaemia
following simultaneous
irradiation treatment. Blood
count monitoring is essential.
Dosage should be the minimum
still to be effective.

**thymol** is an aromatic crystalline
form of the essential oil of the
plant thyme (sometimes in
combination with oils of other
plants). It is used chiefly as an
ANTISEPTIC, and particularly in
preparations for oral or dental
hygiene.

**thymoxamine** is a VASODILATOR
that principally affects the blood
vessels of the limbs, and especially
the hands. It is accordingly used
to treat circulatory disorders of
these areas. In the form of
thymoxamine hydrochloride,
however, the drug, which is an
ALPHA-BLOCKER, is administered in
order to restore the pupil of the
eye to its normal size following
the prior administration of the
mydriatic phenylephrine (which is
used to dilate the pupil in order to
carry out an ophthalmic
examination). Administration is
thus both systemic in the form of
tablets and by injection, and
topical in the form of eye-drops.

▲ side-effects: administered
systemically, the drug may
cause nausea and headache and

dizziness; there may also be
diarrhoea. In the eye, the drug
may cause red coloration for a
few hours, or temporary
drooping of the upper eyelid.

☙ warning: thymoxamine should
be administered with caution
to patients with coronary heart
disease or diabetes mellitus.
*Related article:* OPILON.

**thyroxine sodium** is a
preparation of one of the natural
thyroid HORMONES. It is used
therapeutically to make up a
hormonal deficiency on a regular
maintenance basis, and to treat
associated symptoms
(myxoedema). It may also be used
in the treatment of goitre and of
thyroid cancer. Administration is
oral in the form of tablets.

▲ side-effects: there may be an
increase in the heart rate,
heartbeat irregularities and
angina; some patients
experience headache, muscle
cramp, flushing, and sweating;
there may also be diarrhoea.
Dramatic weight loss occurs in
some patients.

☙ warning: thyroxine sodium
should not be administered to
patients with cardiovascular
disease or angina pectoris
(heart pain), or impaired
secretion by the adrenal
glands. It has a delayed action;
repeated doses are cumulative
in effect.
*Related article:* ELTROXIN.

**Thyrotropar** (*Armour*) is a
proprietary form of the hormone
thyroid-stimulating hormone
(TSH), available only on
prescription. Derived from oxen,
it is now used only rarely to
stimulate thyroid activity and
thus assist in the diagnosis of
thyroid disorders. It is produced
in the form of powder for
reconstitution as a medium for
injection.

▲/☙ side-effects/warning: see
THYROTROPHIN.

**thyrotrophin** is the chemical name for the natural HORMONE thyroid-stimulating hormone (TSH). Derived from oxen, it is now used only rarely to stimulate thyroid activity and thus assist in the diagnosis of thyroid disorders. This growing unpopularity is because potentially severe allergic side-effects following the administration of thyrotrophin are relatively common, and because other diagnostic tests have become available. However, administration does still take place, by injection.

▲ side-effects: there may be nausea and vomiting; the thyroid gland may swell (goitre). Some patients experience temporary low blood pressure (hypotension) or sensitivity reactions (such as urticaria).

● warning: thyrotrophin should not be administered to patients with coronary thrombosis or insufficient secretion of hormones by the adrenal glands. It should be administered with caution to those with angina pectoris (heart pain), heart failure or insufficient secretion of hormones by the pituitary gland, or who are already taking corticosteroids.
*Related article:* THYROTROPAR.

**tiaprofenic acid** is a non-steroidal, ANTI-INFLAMMATORY, non-narcotic ANALGESIC used to treat pain and inflammation in rheumatic disease and other musculo-skeletal disorders. Administration is oral in the form of tablets or an infusion.

▲ side-effects: there may be nausea and gastrointestinal disturbance (to avoid which a patient may be advised to take the drug with food or milk), headache and ringing in the ears (tinnitus). Some patients experience sensitivity

reactions (such as the symptoms of asthma). Fluid retention and/or blood disorders may occur.

● warning: tiaprofenic acid should be administered with caution to patients with gastric ulcers, impaired kidney or liver function, or allergic disorders, or who are pregnant.
*Related article:* SURGAM.

**Ticar** (*Beecham*) is a proprietary ANTIBIOTIC, available only on prescription, used to treat serious infections such as septicaemia and peritonitis, in addition to infections of the respiratory tract or urinary tract. It may also be used to prevent infection in wounds. Produced in the form of a powder for reconstitution as a medium for injection, and in infusion bottles, Ticar is a preparation of the penicillin ticarcillin sodium.

▲/● side-effects/warning: *see* TICARCILLIN.

**ticarcillin** is an ANTIBIOTIC, one of the penicillins with improved activity against a number of important gram-negative bacteria including *Pseudomonas aeruginosa*. It is used to treat serious infections such as septicaemia and peritonitis, in addition to infections of the respiratory tract or of the urinary tract. It may also be used to prevent infection in wounds. Administration is by injection or infusion.

▲ side-effects: there may be sensitivity reactions ranging from a minor rash to urticaria and joint pains, and (occasionally) to high temperature or anaphylactic shock.

● warning: ticarcillin should not be administered to patients known to be allergic to penicillins; it should be administered with caution to

those with impaired kidney function.
*Related articles:* TICAR; TIMENTIN.

**Tiempe** (*DDSA Pharmaceuticals*) is a proprietary ANTIBIOTIC, available only on prescription, used primarily to treat infections of the urinary or respiratory tracts, and especially bronchitis. Produced in the form of tablets (in two strengths), it is a preparation of the antibacterial agent trimethoprim.
▲/⊕ side-effects/warning: *see* TRIMETHOPRIM.

**Tigason** (*Roche*) is a proprietary preparation of the drug etretinate, available only on prescription, administered orally to treat severe, resistant or complicated psoriasis or certain hereditary disorders that harden and thicken the skin. It is used generally only under specialist supervision in hospitals, and is produced in the form of capsules.
▲/⊕ side-effects/warning: *see* ETRETINATE.

**Tilade** (*Fisons*) is a proprietary preparation of the drug nedocromil sodium, available only on prescription, used to prevent recurrent attacks of asthma. It is not capable of treating an acute attack, but is particularly effective in forestalling attacks in patients whose asthma corresponds to allergy, and especially when administered before exercise. Dosage should be adjusted to the requirements of each individual patient (and should be administered regularly whether symptoms are present or not). It is produced in the form of an inhalant in an aerosol that emits metered doses, and is not recommended for children.
▲/⊕ side-effects/warning: *see* NEDOCROMIL.

**Tildiem** (*Lorex*) is a proprietary form of diltiazem hydrochloride, the VASODILATOR, which is a CALCIUM-ANTAGONIST drug used in the prevention and treatment of angina pectoris (heart pain), especially in cases where beta-blockers are not tolerated or have been ineffective. Administration is oral in the form of tablets.
▲/⊕ side-effects/warning: *see* DILTIAZEM HYDROCHLORIDE.

**Timentin** (*Beecham*) is a proprietary ANTIBIOTIC, available only on prescription, used to treat severe infections in patients whose immune systems are undermined by disease or drugs, and where the responsible micro-organism is resistant to ticarcillin alone because it produces a penicillinase enzyme that destroys ticarcillin. (Patients with such conditions are generally in hospital.) Produced in the form of a powder for reconstitution as a medium for injection, Timentin is a compound preparation of the pencillinase enzyme inhibitor clavulanic acid with the penicillin ticarcillin.
▲/⊕ side-effects/warning: *see* TICARCILLIN.

**Timodine** (*Lloyd-Hamol, Reckitt & Colman*) is a proprietary CORTICOSTEROID cream, available only on prescription, used for topical application on mild skin inflammation, especially where there is a yeast infection (such as candidiasis or thrush). It is a compound preparation that contains the steroid hydrocortisone, the ANTIFUNGAL drug nystatin, the ANTISEPTIC BENZALKONIUM CHLORIDE and the antifoaming agent DIMETHICONE.
▲/⊕ side-effects/warning: *see* HYDROCORTISONE; NYSTATIN.

**timolol maleate** is a BETA-BLOCKER used as an ANTIHYPERTENSIVE to treat high blood pressure or angina pectoris (heart pain), and to prevent recurrent heart attacks or attacks of migraine. Like many other beta-blockers, the drug is also used to reduce the formation of aqueous humour in the eye and so relieve intra-ocular pressure in the treatment of glaucoma. Administration is thus oral in the form of tablets or capsules, and topical in the form of eye-drops.

▲ side-effects: there may be gastrointestinal disturbances, slow heart rate and cold fingertips and toes, and symptoms much like asthma.

◉ warning: timolol maleate should not be administered to patients with asthma, bradycardia (slow heartbeat) or partial heart block; it should be administered with caution to those with congestive heart failure, impaired liver or kidney function, who are diabetic, or who are pregnant or lactating. Withdrawal of treatment should be gradual. *Related articles:* BETIM; BLOCADREN; TIMOPTOL.

**Timoped** (*Reckitt & Colman*) is a proprietary, non-prescription cream for topical application to fungal skin infections (such as athlete's foot). Intended to be massaged into the affected area and allowed to dry to a white powder, the cream is a preparation of the ANTIFUNGAL drug TOLNAFTATE with the ANTISEPTIC TRICLOSAN.

**Timoptol** (*Merck, Sharp & Dohme*) is a proprietary BETA-BLOCKER used in the form of eye-drops to reduce the formation of aqueous humour in the eye and so relieve intra-ocular pressure in the treatment of glaucoma. Available only on prescription, and produced in its own metered-dosage unit, it is a preparation of timolol maleate.

▲/◉ side-effects/warning: *see* TIMOLOL MALEATE.

**Tinaderm-M** (*Kirby-Warrick*) is a proprietary, non-prescription cream for topical application to fungal infections of the skin and nails. Intended to be applied two or three times a day, the cream is a preparation of the ANTIFUNGAL drugs TOLNAFTATE and nystatin.

▲/◉ side-effects/warning: *see* NYSTATIN.

**Tineafax** (*Wellcome*) is a proprietary, non-prescription ointment for topical application to fungal skin infections (such as athlete's foot). It is a preparation of two ANTIFUNGAL zinc salts. A powdered form containing zinc salt is also available for use as a dusting-powder in a puffer pack, and is intended to prevent fungal skin infection.

**tinidazole** is an ANTIBIOTIC active against anaerobic bacteria; it also has ANTIPROTOZOAL activity. It resembles metronidazole and, like it, is used to treat anaerobic infections throughout the body and protozoal infections such as giardiasis, trichomoniasis and amoebiasis. It may also be used to treat acute ulcerative gingivitis. Administration is oral in the form of tablets, or by intravenous infusion.

▲ side-effects: there may be nausea and vomiting, with gastrointestinal disturbance; drowsiness and headache may occur. Less commonly, there may be a rash, discoloration of the urine, tingling or numbness of the extremities and a reduction in white cells in the blood. High doses in susceptible patients may bring on epilepsy-like seizures.

◉ warning: tinidazole should be administered with caution to patients with impaired liver function, or who are pregnant

or lactating. On no account should alcohol be consumed during treatment (for even a small amount can cause severe reaction).
*Related article:* FASIGYN.

**Tinset** (*Janssen*) is a proprietary, non-prescription ANTIHISTAMINE used in oral administration to treat allergic conditions such as hay fever and urticaria. Produced in the form of tablets, it is a preparation of the modern antihistamine oxatomide. It is not recommended for children aged under 5 years.
▲/● side-effects/warning: *see* OXATOMIDE.

**tioconazole** is an ANTIFUNGAL agent used to treat fungal nail infections. Produced in the form of a lotion applied to the nails and surrounding area.
● warning: discontinue if sensitivity reaction develops.
▲ side-effects: local irritation may occur during the first week of treatment.
*Related article:* TROSYL.

**Tisept** (*Schering*) is a DISINFECTANT used mainly for surgical procedures in obstetrics or in dressing wounds and burns. Produced in sachets and in bottles, it is a compound solution of the two ANTISEPTICS CHLORHEXIDINE gluconate and CETRIMIDE.

**titanium dioxide paste** is a non-proprietary formulation that combines the mild astringent titanium dioxide with a number of other mineral salts (including ZINC OXIDE) and water, forming a paste that is effective as a barrier preparation for topical application on the skin. There, it protects not only against infection and dirt, but also against ultraviolet radiation (providing what is known as a sunscreen).

**Titralac** (*Riker*) is a proprietary, non-prescription CALCIUM supplement used to make up body deficiency of the mineral, particularly following kidney failure. It is a preparation of CALCIUM CARBONATE and is produced in the form of tablets.
● warning: Titralac should not be taken by patients already being treated with TETRACYCLINE antibiotics.

**Tixylix** (*May & Baker*) is a proprietary, non-prescription compound cough linctus, which is not available from the National Health Service. Produced in the form of a syrup for dilution (the potency of the syrup once dilute is retained for 14 days), Tixylix is a preparation of the OPIATE ANTITUSSIVE pholcodine citrate and the ANTIHISTAMINE promethazine hydrochloride.
▲/● side-effects/warning: *see* PHOLCODINE; PROMETHAZINE HYDROCHLORIDE.

**Tobralex** (*Alcon*) is a proprietary preparation of the aminoglycoside ANTIBIOTIC tobramycin, available only on prescription, used in the form of eye-drops to treat bacterial infections of the eye.
▲/● side-effects/warning: *see* TOBRAMYCIN.

**tobramycin** is an ANTIBIOTIC, one of the amino-glycosides, effective against some gram-positive and gram-negative bacteria. It is used primarily for the treatment of serious gram-negative infections caused by *Pseudomonas aeruginosa* as it is significantly more active against this organism than gentamicin (the most commonly used of this class of antibiotic). Like other aminoglycosides it is not absorbed from the intestine (except in the case of local infection or liver failure) and so is administered by injection when treating systemic disease. It is also produced in the form of eyedrops to treat bacterial infections of the eye.

▲ side-effects: treatment must be discontinued if there are any signs of deafness. There may be dysfunction of the kidneys.

✿ warning: tobramycin should not be administered to patients who are pregnant, or who are already taking drugs that affect the neural system. It should be administered with caution to those with parkinsonism or impaired kidney function. Prolonged or high dosage can cause deafness; regular blood level checks are essential in such cases.
*Related articles:* NEBCIN; TOBRALEX.

**tocainide hydrochloride** is an ANTIARRHYTHMIC drug that is an analogue of the local ANAESTHETIC LIGNOCAINE. Its use, however, is associated with an unacceptably high level of blood disorders, for which reason it is now restricted to life-threatening emergencies in patients who do not respond to other forms of therapy. Administration is oral in the form of tablets, or by injection.

▲ side-effects: there may be nausea, vomiting and gastrointestinal disturbance; tremor, dizziness and loss of sensation are not uncommon, and may lead to convulsions. Injection sometimes results in low blood pressure and slow heart rate.

✿ warning: tocainide hydrochloride should not be administered to patients whose natural heart pacemaker (the sino-atrial node) is dysfunctioning, or who are in the process of undergoing a heart attack. It should be

administered with extreme caution to patients with severely impaired liver or kidney function or from heart failure, or who are pregnant. Regular and frequent blood counts are essential.
*Related article:* TONOCARD.

**tocopherol** is a general name for a group of substances known collectively as VITAMIN E (and chemically classed as tocopherols and tocotrienols). They have antioxidant properties, and are thought to maintain the structure of cell membranes by preventing the oxidation of their fatty acid constituents. It is also possible that vitamin E has some significance in fertility. Vitamin E deficiency may lead to a form of anaemia through the rupture of red blood cells. Good food sources include eggs, vegetable oils, wheat germ and green vegetables. The form of tocopherol most used in therapy to make up vitamin deficiency is alpha tocopheryl acetate. Administration is oral in the form of tablets or capsules.
*Related articles:* EPHYNAL; VITA-E.

**tocopheryl acetate**, or alpha tocopheryl acetate, is one of the forms of tocopherol (VITAMIN E) most used in vitamin replacement therapy.
*see* TOCOPHEROL.

**Tofranil** (*Geigy*) is a proprietary ANTIDEPRESSANT drug, available only on prescription, used to treat depressive illness particularly in patients who are withdrawn and apathetic. It may also be used to treat nocturnal bedwetting by children (aged over 7 years). Produced in the form of tablets (in two strengths) and as a syrup for dilution (the potency of the syrup once diluted is retained for 14 days), Tofranil is a preparation of imipramine hydrochloride. Treatment may be prolonged.

▲ / ● side-effects/warning: *see*
IMIPRAMINE.

**Tolanase** (*Upjohn*) is a proprietary
form of the SULPHONYLUREA
tolazamide, available only on
prescription, used to treat adult-
onset diabetes mellitus. It works
by augmenting what remains of
insulin production in the
pancreas, and is produced in the
form of tablets (in two strengths).
▲ / ● side-effects/warning: *see*
TOLAZAMIDE.

**tolazamide** is a drug used to treat
adult-onset diabetes mellitus, one
of the SULPHONYLUREAS, which
works by augmenting whatever
remains of the capacity of the
pancreas still to produce insulin
(as opposed to compensating for
its absence). Administration is
oral in the form of tablets.
▲ side-effects: there may be some
sensitivity reactions (such as a
rash).
● warning: tolazamide should
not be administered to
patients with liver or kidney
damage, with endocrine
disorders, or who are under
stress; who are pregnant or
lactating; or who are already
taking cortico-
steroids or oral
contraceptives, oral
anticoagulants, or aspirin or
antibiotics.
*Related article:* TOLANASE.

**tolbutamide** is a drug used to
treat adult-onset diabetes
mellitus, one of the
SULPHONYLUREAS, which works
by augmenting whatever remains
of the capacity of the pancreas
still to produce insulin (as
opposed to compensating for its
absence). Administration is oral
in the form of tablets.
▲ side-effects: there may be some
sensitivity reactions (such as a
skin rash).
● warning: tolbutamide should
not be administered to patients

with liver or kidney damage,
with endocrine disorders, or
who are under stress; who are
pregnant or lactating; or who
are already taking corticosteroids or oral contraceptives,
oral anticoagulants, or aspirin
or antibiotics.
*Related articles:* GLYCONON;
RASTINON.

**Tolectin** (*Ortho-Cilag*) is a
proprietary preparation of the
non-steroidal drug tolmetrin,
which has ANTI-INFLAMMATORY,
non-narcotic ANALGESIC
properties. Available only on
prescription, it is used to treat the
pain of rheumatic disease and
other musculo-skeletal disorders
(including bone fusion). It is
produced in the form of capsules
in two strengths.
▲ / ● side-effects/warning: *see*
TOLMETIN.

**Tolerzide** (*Bristol-Myers*) is a
proprietary ANTIHYPERTENSIVE
drug, available only on
prescription, used to treat mild to
moderate high blood pressure
(hypertension). Produced in the
form of tablets, it is a compound
preparation of the BETA-BLOCKER
sotalol hydrochloride together
with the THIAZIDE DIURETIC
hydrochlorothiazide. It is not
recommended for children.
▲ / ● side-effects/warning: *see*
HYDROCHLOROTHIAZIDE;
SOTALOL HYDROCHLORIDE.

**tolmetin** is a non-steroidal drug
with ANTI-INFLAMMATORY and
ANALGESIC properties used to
treat the pain of rheumatic
disease and other musculo-
skeletal disorders. Administration is oral in the form of
capsules.
▲ side-effects: there may be
nausea and gastrointestinal
disturbance (to avoid which a
patient might be advised to
take the drug with food or

milk), headache and ringing in the ears (tinnitus). Some patients experience sensitivity reactions (such as the symptoms of asthma). Fluid retention and/or blood disorders may occur.

◆ warning: tolmetin should be administered with caution to patients with gastric ulcers, impaired kidney or liver function, bleeding disorders, cardio-vascular disease or allergic disorders, or who are pregnant.
*Related article:* TOLECTIN.

**tolnaftate** is a mild, synthetic, ANTIFUNGAL drug used principally in the topical treatment of infections by the Tinea species known as ringworm (such as athlete's foot). Administration is in the form of a cream, a powder or a solution. Rarely, sensitivity reactions occur.
*Related articles:* TIMOPED; TINADERM-M.

**tolu linctus** is a non-proprietary formulation that is a cough LINCTUS for children. Its various constituents (including citric acid and GLYCEROL) are mixed in with a syrup derived from tolu balsam (itself obtained from the bark of the South American tolu tree) which has very mild ANTISEPTIC and EXPECTORANT action.

**Tonocard** (*Astra*) is a proprietary form of the ANTI-ARRHYTHMIC drug tocainide hydrochloride, available only on prescription. Its use, however, is associated with an unacceptably high level of blood disorders, for which reason it is now restricted to life-threatening emergencies immediately following a heart attack in patients who do not respond to other forms of therapy. It is produced in the form of tablets (in two strengths) and in vials for injection.

▲/◆ side-effects/warning: *see* TOCAINIDE HYDROCHLORIDE.

**Topal** (*Concept*) is a proprietary, non-prescription ANTACID used to treat heartburn, severe indigestion, and the symptoms of hiatus hernia. Produced in the form of tablets for chewing between meals and at bedtime, Topal is a compound preparation that includes ALUMINIUM HYDROXIDE and MAGNESIUM CARBONATE.

**Topiclens** (*Smith & Nephew*) is a proprietary, non-prescription preparation of mild saline solution (0.9%), which can be used either as an eye-wash or eye lubricant, or as a cleansing lotion for minor wounds and burns.
*see* SODIUM CHLORIDE.

**Topicycline** (*Norwich Eaton*) is a proprietary ANTIBIOTIC, available only on prescription, used to treat acne. Produced in the form of a solution for topical application, it is a preparation of the tetracycline hydrochloride, and is not recommended for children.
▲/◆ side-effects/warning: *see* TETRACYCLINE.

**Topilar** (*Syntex*) is a proprietary CORTICOSTEROID cream, available only on prescription, used in topical application to treat serious non-infective skin inflammation (such as psoriasis and certain forms of dermatitis). Produced as a water-miscible cream and an ointment for dilution with paraffin (the potency of the ointment once diluted is retained for 14 days), Topilar is a preparation of fluclorolone acetonide.
▲/◆ side-effects/warning: *see* FLUCLOROLONE ACETONIDE.

**Torecan** (*Sandoz*) is a proprietary ANTI-EMETIC drug, available only on prescription, used to relieve nausea and vomiting that may be caused by the vertigo associated with infections of the middle or inner ear, or by therapy with cytotoxic drugs in the treatment of cancer. Produced in the form of tablets, as anal suppositories, and in ampoules for injection, Torecan is a preparation of thiethylperazine.

▲/❋ side-effects/warning: *see*
THIETHYLPERAZINE.

**Tracrium** (*Calmic*) is a proprietary SKELETAL MUSCLE RELAXANT, available only on prescription, used mainly under general anaesthesia during surgery. Produced in ampoules for injection, Tracrium is a preparation of atracurium besylate.

❋ warning: *see* ATRACURIUM
BESYLATE.

**Tramil** (*Whitehall Laboratories*) is a proprietary, non-prescription compound ANALGESIC containing the active constituents paracetamol and caffeine.

▲/❋ side-effects/warning: *see*
CAFFEINE; PARACETAMOL.

**Trancopal** (*Winthrop*) is a proprietary ANXIOLYTIC drug that also has the properties of a SKELETAL MUSCLE RELAXANT. Available only on prescription, it is used principally in the short-term treatment of insomnia, and produced in the form of tablets containing the TRANQUILLIZER chlormezanone. It is not recommended for children.

▲/❋ side-effects/warning: *see*
CHLORMEZANONE.

**Trancoprin** (*Winthrop*) is a proprietary compound ANALGESIC and MUSCLE RELAXANT, available on prescription only to private patients. It is used to treat headache and the pain of menstruation problems, and also to relieve the pain of muscle

spasm. Produced in the form of tablets, Trancoprin is a preparation of aspirin together with the ANXIOLYTIC muscle relaxant chlormezanone.

▲/❋ side-effects/warning: *see*
ASPIRIN; CHLORMEZANONE.

**Trandate** (*Duncan, Flockhart*) is a proprietary ANTIHYPERTENSIVE drug, available only on prescription, used to treat all forms of high blood pressure (including those caused by heart disease, by pregnancy or by surgery). Produced in the form of tablets (in four strengths), and in ampoules for injection, Trandate is a preparation of the BETA-BLOCKER labetalol hydrochloride.

▲/❋ side-effects/warning: *see*
LABETALOL HYDROCHLORIDE.

**tranexamic acid** is a HAEMOSTATIC drug used to stem the flow of blood in such circumstances as dental extraction in a haemophiliac patient, or following surgical removal of the prostate gland, or continual menstrual flow (menorrhagia). It works by inhibiting the action of one of the blood's natural anticoagulant factors. Administration is oral in the form of tablets or a dilute syrup, or by injection.

▲ side-effects: there may be nausea and vomiting, with diarrhoea; injection may cause temporary giddiness.

❋ warning: tranexamic acid should not be administered to patients who are known to have any form of thrombosis; it should be administered with caution to those with impaired kidney function or severe urinary disorders. Prolonged treatment requires regular ophthalmic checks and monitoring of liver function. *Related article:* CYKLOKAPRON.

*****tranquillizers** are drugs that calm and soothe, and relieve anxiety. Many also cause some degree of sedation. They are often classified in two groups, major tranquillizers and minor. The major tranquillizers are used primarily to treat severe mental disorders – the psychoses (including schizophrenia and mania) – not only to relieve patients of their own private fears and terrors, but also to control violent behavioural disturbances that present a danger to the patients themselves and to those who look after them. The minor tranquillizers may also be used to treat mental disorders, such as neuroses, but are more commonly used in short-term therapies to treat anxiety and nervous tension. Best-known and most-used major tranquillizers include the PHENOTHIAZINES (such as CHLORPROMAZINE, THIORIDAZINE and PROCHLORPERAZINE) and such drugs as HALOPERIDOL, FLUSPIRILENE and FLUPENTHIXOL. Best-known and most-used minor tranquillizers include the BENZODIAZEPINES (such as DIAZEPAM and CHLORDIAZEPOXIDE) and such drugs as MEPROBAMATE. Prolonged treatment with some minor tranquillizers can lead to dependence (addiction).

**Transiderm-Nitro** (*Ciba*) is a proprietary VASODILATOR, available only on prescription, used to prevent recurrent attacks of angina pectoris (heart pain). Produced in the form of dressings to be applied to the chest wall so that the drug is slowly absorbed through the skin, and presented in packs of 5 or 10 dressings, Transiderm-Nitro is a preparation of glyceryl trinitrate.
▲/✿ side-effects/warning: *see* GLYCERYL TRINITRATE.

**Translet** (*Franklin*) is a proprietary, non-prescription perfumed barrier cream for use in protecting, freshening and sanitizing the area of skin around a stoma (an outlet on the skin surface following the surgical curtailment of the intestines).

**Translet Plus** (*Franklin*) is a proprietary, non-prescription deodorant for use in the appliance (bag) attached to a stoma (an outlet on the skin surface following the surgical curtailment of the intestines). There are two versions: Translet Plus One is intended for men; Translet Plus Two for women.

**Transvasin** (*Lloyds*) is a proprietary, non-prescription cream for topical application which, when applied to the skin, produces an irritation of the sensory nerve endings that offsets the pain of underlying muscle or joint disorders (counter-irritant). Active constituents include the local anaesthetic BENZOCAINE and salts of NICOTINIC ACID and SALICYLIC ACID.

**Tranxene** (*Boehringer Ingelheim*) is a proprietary ANXIOLYTIC drug, available only on prescription, used principally in the short-term treatment of anxiety. Produced in the form of capsules (in two strengths), it is a preparation of the TRANQUILLIZER clorazepate dipotassium. It is not recommended for children.
▲/✿ side-effects/warning: *see* CLORAZEPATE DIPOTASSIUM.

**tranylcypromine** is an ANTIDEPRESSANT drug, an MAO INHIBITOR that also has some stimulant effect and is therefore less used than most in the treatment of depressive illness. Administration is oral in the form of tablets.
▲ side-effects: concentration and speed of thought and movement are usually affected; there may also be dizziness, especially when rising from sitting or lying down (because of low

blood pressure), and insomnia, muscular weakness and dry mouth. Some patients experience headache, which implies that treatment should be withdrawn.

● **warning:** tranylcypromine should not be administered to patients with heart or liver disease, circulatory disorders, abnormal secretion of hormones by the adrenal glands, epilepsy, or overactivity of the thyroid gland (hyperthyroidism), or who are children. It should be administered with caution to those who are elderly or debilitated. Treatment requires a strict dietary regime (that includes the avoidance of meat or yeast extracts, cheese, and alcohol) and the avoidance also of virtually all other forms of medication. Withdrawal of treatment must be gradual. *Related article:* PARNATE.

**Trasicor** (*Ciba*) is a proprietary ANTIHYPERTENSIVE drug, available only on prescription, used to treat high blood pressure, heartbeat irregularities, angina pectoris (heart pain), and the effects of an excess of thyroid hormones in the bloodstream (thyrotoxicosis). Produced in the form of tablets, Trasicor is a preparation of the BETA-BLOCKER oxprenolol hydrochloride.

▲/ ● side-effects/warning: *see* OXPRENOLOL.

**Trasidrex** (*Ciba*) is a proprietary compound ANTIHYPERTENSIVE drug, available only on prescription, used to treat high blood pressure, heartbeat irregularities, angina pectoris (heart pain), and an excess of thyroid hormones in the bloodstream (thyrotoxicosis). Produced in the form of sustained-release tablets, Trasidrex is a preparation of the BETA-BLOCKER

oxprenolol hydrochloride with the THIAZIDE DIURETIC cyclopenthiazide.

▲/ ● side-effects/warning: *see* CYCLOPENTHIAZIDE; OXPRENOLOL.

**Trasylol** (*Bayer*) is a proprietary preparation of the enzyme aprotinin, available only on prescription, used in the treatment of acute inflammation of the pancreas, or to prevent such inflammation following abdominal surgery. It is produced in ampoules for injection.

▲ side-effects: *see* APROTININ.

**Travasept** (*Travenol*) is a proprietary, non-prescription DISINFECTANT for use in cleaning wounds and burns. Produced in sachets of solution (not for further dilution), Travasept is a compound preparation of the antiseptics cetrimide and chlorhexidine acetate (in two strengths, under the trade names Travasept 30 and Travasept 100).

**Travogyn** (*Schering*) is a proprietary ANTIFUNGAL drug, available only on prescription, used in the treatment of fungal or fungal-and-bacterial infections of the vagina or the ano-genital area. Produced in the form of a cream for topical application, and as vaginal tablets (pessaries), it is a preparation of isoconazole nitrate.

▲ side-effects: *see* ISOCONAZOLE.

**Traxam** (*Lederle*) is a non-narcotic ANALGESIC drug with good ANTI-INFLAMMATORY properties. It is a proprietary form of felbinac, which is an active metabolite of the drug fenbufen. Available only on prescription, it is used topically as a gel applied to the skin.

▲/ ● side-effects/warning: *see* FENBUFEN.

**trazodone hydrochloride** is an ANTIDEPRESSANT drug used to treat depressive illness, particularly in cases where some degree of sedation is called for. Administration is oral in the form of capsules or a liquid.

▲ side-effects: concentration and speed of thought and movement may be affected. There may be an increased or decreased heart rate, sweating and tremor; constipation and difficulty in urinating; blurred vision and drowsiness; and weight changes, weakness and vomiting.

✹ warning: trazodone hydrochloride should be administered with caution to patients who have serious heart complaints or have recently had a heart attack, or to those who have manic episodes. It should be administered with caution to those with epilepsy, diabetes, impaired liver function, heartbeat irregularities, thyroid disorders, glaucoma, or urinary retention; who are pregnant; or who are mentally unstable. Withdrawal of treatment is gradual. *Related article:* MOLIPAXIN.

**Tremonil** (*Sandoz*) is a proprietary drug used to treat the tremor of parkinsonism, of drug-induced states, or simply of old age (*see* ANTIPARKINSONISM). Available only on prescription, and produced in the form of tablets, it is a preparation of methixene hydrochloride.

▲/✹ side-effects/warning: *see* METHIXENE HYDROCHLORIDE.

**Trental** (*Hoechst*) is a proprietary VASODILATOR that principally affects the blood vessels of the limbs and is used to treat circulatory disorders of the hands and feet. Available only on prescription, and produced in the form of tablets and in ampoules for injection, Trental is a preparation of oxpentifylline.

▲/✹ side-effects/warning: *see* OXPENTIFYLLINE.

**treosulfan** is a CYTOTOXIC drug used specifically in the treatment of cancer of the ovary. It works by interfering with the DNA of new-forming cells, so preventing normal cell replication. Administration is oral in the form of capsules, or by injection. (The identically named proprietary form of the drug is manufactured by *Leo*.)

▲ side-effects: there is commonly nausea and vomiting; there may also be (temporary) hair loss. The blood-cell-producing capacity of the bone-marrow is impaired.

✹ warning: prolonged use may cause sterility in men and an early menopause in women; in both sexes it may lead to permanent bone-marrow damage. Prolonged treatment has been associated with the incidence of leukaemia following simultaneous irradiation treatment. Blood count monitoring is essential. Dosage should be the minimum still to be effective.

**tretinoin** is a derivative of RETINOL (vitamin A) that is used mostly in topical application to treat acne. Rather astringent, it tends to cause a redness of the skin following several days' treatment. Administration is in the form of a cream, gel or lotion.

▲ side-effects: there may be irritation. Prolonged treatment brings out first a redness, and may then go on to change pigmentation in the skin. Rarely, there is sensitivity to light.

✹ warning: tretinoin should not be applied to broken skin or to conditions such as eczema. It should be kept away from the eyes, mouth and mucous membranes, and should not be used in combination with other peeling agents (keratolytics) or with sun-ray lamps.

*Related article:* RETIN-A.

**TRH** (*Roche*) is a proprietary preparation of the natural HORMONE thyrotrophin-releasing hormone (TRH, or protirelin) used primarily in diagnosing thryoid function in patients who suffer from overactivity of the thyroid gland (hyperthyroidism). It is produced in the form of tablets and in ampoules for injection.

▲/◕ side-effects/warning: *see* PROTIRELIN.

**Tri-Adcortyl** (*Squibb*) is a proprietary preparation for topical application in the treatment of severe non-infective skin inflammation (such as eczema), especially in cases that have not responded to less powerful therapies. Available only on prescription, and produced in the form of a cream and an ointment, it is a compound of the CORTICOSTEROID triamcinolone acetonide together with the ANTIFUNGAL drug nystatin, and the ANTIBIOTICS gramicidin and NEOMYCIN. A form of the ointment prepared especially for the topical treatment of infection of the outer ear is also available (under the name Tri-Adcortyl Otic).

▲/◕ side-effects/warning: *see* NYSTATIN; TRIAMCINOLONE ACETONIDE.

**triamcinolone** is a synthetic CORTICOSTEROID used to suppress the symptoms of inflammation, especially when caused by allergic disorders. It is administered in the form of tablets, or by injection, to relieve such conditions as hay fever or asthma.

▲ side-effects: treatment of susceptible patients may engender a euphoria – or a state of confusion or depression. Rarely, there is peptic ulcer.

◕ warning: triamcinolone should not be administered to patients who suffer from psoriasis; it should be administered with caution to the elderly (in whom overdosage can cause osteoporosis, 'brittle bones'). In children, administration may lead to stunting of growth. Prolonged use may cause muscular weakness. As with all corticosteroids, triamcinolone treats only inflammatory symptoms; an undetected and potentially serious infection may have its effects masked by the drug until it is well established.

*Related article:* LEDERCORT.

**triamcinolone acetonide** is a synthetic CORTICOSTEROID used to suppress the symptoms of inflammation, especially when caused by allergic disorders. It is administered sometimes as a systemic medication (in the form of an injection) to relieve such conditions as hay fever or asthma but, more commonly, is instead applied by local injection to treat skin inflammations or such conditions as rheumatoid arthritis and bursitis. Several proprietary preparations are in the form of a cream for topical application, mostly in the treatment of severe non-infective skin inflammations such as eczema, but one or two are for treating inflammations in the mouth.

▲ side-effects: systemic treatment of susceptible patients may engender a euphoria – or a state of confusion or depression. Rarely, there is peptic ulcer.

◕ warning: triamcinolone acetonide should not be administered to patients with

psoriasis; it should be administered with caution to the elderly (in whom overdosage can cause osteoporosis, 'brittle bones'). In children, systemic administration may lead to stunting of growth. Prolonged use may cause muscular weakness, and in any case should be avoided. As with all corticosteroids, triamcinolone acetonide treats only inflammatory symptoms; an undetected and potentially serious infection may have its effects masked by the drug until it is well established.
*Related articles:* ADCORTYL; AUDICORT; AUREOCORT; KENALOG; LEDERCORT; NYSTADERMAL; SILDERM; TRI-ADCORTYL.

**triamcinolone hexacetonide** is a synthetic CORTICOSTEROID used to suppress the symptoms of inflammation. It is administered by local injection to treat skin inflammation or such conditions as rheumatoid arthritis and bursitis.
▲ side-effects: systemic treatment of susceptible patients may engender a euphoria – or a state of confusion or depression. Rarely, there is peptic ulcer.
◉ warning: triamcinolone hexacetonide should not be administered to patients with psoriasis; it should be administered with caution to the elderly (in whom overdosage can cause osteoporosis, 'brittle bones'). In children, administration may lead to stunting of growth. Prolonged use may cause muscular weakness, and in any case should be avoided. As with all corticosteroids, triamcinolone hexacetonide treats only inflammatory symptoms; an undetected and potentially serious infection may have its effects masked by

the drug until it is well established.
*Related article:* LEDERSPAN.

**Triamco** (*Norton*) is a proprietary compound DIURETIC, available only on prescription, used for general diuresis. Produced in the form of tablets, it is a combination of the THIAZIDE diuretic hydrochlorothiazide together with a complementary potassium-sparing diuretic triamterene.
▲/◉ side-effects/warning: *see* HYDROCHLOROTHIAZIDE; TRIAMTERENE.

**triamterene** is a DIURETIC that does not deplete the body's reserves of potassium; although it is sometimes used by itself in the treatment of fluid retention in the tissues (oedema), it is therefore more commonly used in combination with diuretics that do promote the excretion of potassium, particularly the THIAZIDES. Singly, administration is oral in the form of capsules.
▲ side-effects: there may be gastrointestinal disturbance and dry mouth; some patients come out in a rash. The urine may be discoloured (and even fluorescent).
◉ warning: triamterene should not be administered to patients with kidney failure or high levels of potassium in the blood; it should be administered with caution to those with diabetes or cirrhosis of the liver, or who are pregnant. Regular monitoring of blood levels of urea and potassium is essential.
*Related articles:* DYAZIDE; DYTAC; DYTIDE; FRUSENE; KALSPARE; TRIAMCO.

**triazolam** is a short-acting HYPNOTIC drug, a derivative of the BENZODIAZEPINES, used as a TRANQUILLIZER to treat insomnia

(particularly in the elderly).
Administration is oral in the form
of tablets.

▲ side-effects: concentration and
speed of thought and
movement are affected. There
may also be drowsiness, dry
mouth, and dizziness.
Prolonged use may eventually
result in tolerance, and finally
dependence.

✿ warning: triazolam should be
administered with caution to
patients with lung disease or
depressed breathing, or who
are pregnant or lactating.
Susceptible patients may
experience psychological
changes.
*Related article:* HALCION.

**Tribiotic** (*Riker*) is a proprietary
ANTIBIOTIC, available only on
prescription, used as a spray in
topical application to infections
of the skin. Produced in aerosol
units, it is a compound
preparation of three antibiotics:
neomycin sulphate, polymyxin B
sulphate and bacitracin zinc.

▲/✿ side-effects/warning: *see*
BACITRACIN; NEOMYCIN;
POLYMYXIN B.

**trichloroethylene** is an inhalant
general ANAESTHETIC with
powerful ANALGESIC properties
used primarily in combination
with nitrous oxide-oxygen
mixtures, but it also has rather
POOR MUSCLE RELAXANT
properties. It is normally
administered only after
anaesthesia has been initially
induced with some other agent.

▲ side-effects: side-effects are
rare (in fact the drug helps
stabilize several body
functions, such as blood
pressure). But the respiratory
rate may increase, and post-
operative vomiting is not
uncommon. It may decrease the
function of the liver and
kidneys.

✿ warning: trichloroethylene is
not suitable for induction of
anaesthesia; moreover,
administration of the drug
should be discontinued some
time before the end of surgery
because the recovery rate from
the drug afterwards is
comparatively slow.

**Tri-Citatrin** (*Calmic*) is a
proprietary, ANTIBIOTIC
ANTIFUNGAL preparation,
available only on prescription,
used to treat inflammation of the
skin in which infection is also
present. Produced in the form of
an ointment for topical
application, Tri-citatrin is a
compound of the aminoglycoside
antibiotic neomycin sulphate, the
antibiotic bacitracin zinc and the
antifungal nystatin; together with
the CORTICOSTEROID
hydrocortisone.

▲/✿ side-effects/warning: *see:*
BACITRACIN;
HYDROCORTISONE;
NEOMYCIN; NYSTATIN.

**triclofos sodium** is a derivative of
the soluble SEDATIVE chloral, used
as a HYPNOTIC to treat insomnia.
Administration is oral in the form
of an elixir: the liquid is less
irritant to the stomach lining
than chloral hydrate.

▲ side-effects: concentration and
speed of thought and
movement are affected. There
is commonly drowsiness, dry
mouth and gastric irritation;
there may also be sensitivity
reactions (such as a rash) and,
in the elderly, a mild state of
confusion.

✿ warning: triclofos sodium
should not be administered to
patients with severe heart
disease, or severe impairment
of kidney or liver function. It
should be administered with
caution to those with lung
disease, particularly if there is
depressed breathing, who are

elderly or debilitated, or who are pregnant or lactating. The consumption of alcohol enhances the hypnotic effect of the drug. Withdrawal of treatment should be gradual. Prolonged use may lead to tolerance and dependence (addiction).

**triclosan** is a mildly ANTIBIOTIC DISINFECTANT for topical application to the skin. It is sometimes used to treat staphylococcal infection, but it is primarily used to prevent the spread of infection within hospitals or households. It should be kept away from the eyes. *Related articles:* MANUSEPT; STER-ZAC; TIMOPED.

**\*tricyclic** drugs are one of the two main classes of ANTIDEPRESSANT, and often have SEDATIVE and TRANQUILLIZER effects. Chemically, they are dibenzazipine or debenzocycloheptone derivatives. Examples include AMITRIPTYLINE and LOFEPRAMINE.

**Tridesilon** (*Lagap*) is a proprietary CORTICOSTEROID preparation, available only on prescription, used in topical application to treat severe non-infective skin inflammation (such as eczema), especially when therapy with less powerful corticosteroids has failed. Produced in the form of a water-miscible cream, Tridesilon's major active constituent is the steroid desonide.

▲/✿ side-effects/warning: *see* DESONIDE.

**Tridil** (*American Hospital Supply*) is a proprietary VASODILATOR, available only on prescription, used to treat angina pectoris (heart pain) or to prevent recurrent attacks. Produced in ampoules for injection, or in polyethylene infusion sets, Tridil is a preparation of the NITRATE glyceryl trinitrate.

▲/✿ side-effects/warning: *see* GLYCERYL TRINITRATE.

**trientine dihydrochloride** is an unusual drug used in the treatment of the rare congenital defect in metabolism that causes a potentially dangerous accumulation of copper in the body (Wilson's disease). Ordinarily this defect is readily remedied through the use of PENICILLAMINE – but some patients are unable to tolerate that drug, and so trientine dihydrochloride is then used instead. Administration is oral in the form of capsules.

▲ side-effects: there may be nausea. Skin conditions that arise as a sensitivity reaction to initial treatment with penicillamine may require independent treatment to resolve them.

✿ warning: trientine dihydrochloride should be administered with caution to patients who are pregnant.

**trifluoperazine** is a powerful ANTIPSYCHOTIC drug used to treat and tranquillize psychosis (such as schizophrenia), in which it is particularly suitable for treating forms of behavioural disturbance. The drug may additionally be used to treat severe anxiety in the short term. In low dosages the drug is also sometimes used as an ANTI-EMETIC in the treatment of nausea and vomiting caused by underlying disease or by drug therapies. Administration is oral in the form of tablets, capsules, sustained-release capsules, and a liquid, or by injection.

▲ side-effects: concentration and speed of thought and movement are affected. There may be restlessness, insomnia and nightmares; rashes and jaundice may occur; and there may be dry mouth, slight gastrointestinal disturbance, and blurred vision. Some patients experience muscle weakness.

◉ **warning:** trifluoperazine should not be administered to patients who suffer from reduction in the bone-marrow's capacity to produce blood cells, or from certain types of glaucoma. It should be administered only with caution to those with heart or vascular disease, kidney or liver disease, or parkinsonism; or who are pregnant or lactating; or who are children.
*Related article:* STELAZINE.

**trifluperidol** is a powerful ANTIPSYCHOTIC drug used to treat and tranquillize psychosis (such as schizophrenia), in which it is particularly suitable for treating forms of manic behavioural disturbance. Administration is oral in the form of tablets.

▲ **side-effects:** concentration and speed of thought and movement are affected. There may be restlessness, insomnia and nightmares; rashes and jaundice may occur; and there may be dry mouth, gastrointestinal disturbance, difficulty in urinating, and blurred vision. Some patients experience muscle weakness or spasm. Rarely, there is weight loss.

◉ **warning:** trifluperidol should not be administered to patients who suffer from reduction in the bone-marrow's capacity to produce blood cells, or from certain types of glaucoma. It should be administered only with caution to those with heart or vascular disease, kidney or liver disease, or parkinsonism; or who are pregnant or lactating.
*Related article:* TRIPERIDOL.

**triiodothyronine** is a natural thyroid HORMONE, administered therapeutically in the form of

liothyronine sodium to make up a hormonal deficiency (hypothyroidism) and to treat associated symptoms (myxoedema). It may also be used in the treatment of goitre and of thyroid cancer.
*see* LIOTHYRONINE SODIUM.

**Trilisate** (*Napp*) is a proprietary, non-prescription, non-narcotic ANALGESIC used to treat pain and inflammation in rheumatic disease and other musculo-skeletal disorders. Produced in the form of tablets, it is a compound preparation of the natural body substance choline and SALICYLIC ACID.

▲/◉ **side-effects/warning:** *see* CHOLINE MAGNESIUM TRISALICYLATE.

**trilostane** is an unusual drug that inhibits the production of CORTICOSTEROIDS by the adrenal glands. It is thus used to treat conditions that result from the excessive secretion of cortico-steroids into the bloodstream (such as Cushing's syndrome). Administration is oral in the form of capsules.

▲ **side-effects:** side-effects are rare, but following high dosage may include nausea, flushing and a running nose.

◉ **warning:** trilostane should not be administered to patients who are pregnant or who are using hormonal contraceptive methods; it should be administered with caution to those with impaired liver or kidney function. Monitoring of blood levels of corticosteroids and electrolytes is essential.
*Related article:* MODRENAL.

**Triludan** (*Merrell*) is a proprietary, non-prescription ANTIHISTAMINE used to treat the symptoms of allergic disorders such as hay fever and urticaria. Produced in the form of tablets (in two strengths, the stronger is called Triludan Forte) and as a suspension for dilution (the potency of the suspension once dilute is retained for 14 days), it is a preparation of terfenadine.

▲/✸ side-effects/warning: *see* TERFENADINE.

**trimeprazine tartrate** is an ANTIHISTAMINE that has additional SEDATIVE properties. It is used to treat the symptoms of allergic disorders (particularly rashes and itching); as a premedication prior to surgery, and sometimes even as an ANTI-EMETIC. Administration is oral in the form of tablets or as a dilute syrup.

▲ side-effects: there may be headache, drowsiness and dry mouth. Some patients experience sensitivity reactions on the skin.

✸ warning: trimeprazine tartrate should be administered with caution to patients with epilepsy, glaucoma, liver disease or enlargement of the prostate gland. During treatment, alcohol consumption must be avoided.
*Related article:* VALLERGAN.

**trimetaphan camsylate** is a drug that reduces blood pressure (technically, it is a hypotensive drug with a ganglion-blocking action that reduces sympathetic vascular tone). Short-acting, it is used primarily during neurosurgery and vascular surgery. The advantage of its use is that, once the patient's individual response to the drug has been gauged, its hypotensive effect is highly controllable. Administration is by injection.

▲ side-effects: there is an increase in the heart rate, and depression of respiration; the pupils of the eyes are dilated.

✸ warning: trimetaphan camsylate should be administered with caution to patients with heart disease or severe arteriosclerosis; it should be administered with caution to those with diabetes, Addison's disease, or any degenerative disease of the brain, or whose liver or kidney function is impaired.
*Related article:* ARFONAD.

**trimethoprim** is an ANTIBIOTIC agent similar in action to the sulphonamides, used to treat and to prevent the spread of many forms of bacterial infection but particularly those of the urinary and respiratory tracts. It has been used particularly in combination with a SULPHONAMIDE drug, for the combined effect has been thought to be greater than twice the individual effect of either partner. This is the basis of the medicinal compound co-trimoxazole (which forms the active constituent of many proprietary preparations). More recently there has been a move away from the compound preparation to the use of trimethoprim alone. It is effective in many situations and lacks the side-effects of the sulphonamide present in co-trimoxazole. Administration of trimethoprim is oral in the form of tablets or a dilute suspension, or by injection.

▲ side-effects: there may be nausea, vomiting and gastrointestinal disturbances; rashes may break out, with itching (pruritus).

✸ warning: trimethoprim should not be administered to newborn babies, or to patients who are pregnant, or who have severely impaired kidney function. Dosage should be reduced for patients with poor kidney function. Prolonged therapy requires frequent blood counts.
*Related articles:* IPRAL; MONOTRIM; SYRAPRIM; TIEMPE;

TRIMOGAL; TRIMOPAN.
*see also* CO-TRIMOXAZOLE.

**trimipramine** is an
ANTIDEPRESSANT drug used to
treat depressive illness, especially
in cases where sedation is
advantageous to the patient.
Administration of trimipramine is
oral in the form of capsules or
tablets.
▲ side-effects: concentration and
speed of thought and
movement are commonly
affected; there may also be dry
mouth and blurred vision,
difficulty in urinating, a rash,
sweating, and irregular
heartbeat. Some patients
experience a behavioural
disturbance, a state of
confusion, and/or a loss of
libido. Rarely, there are also
blood disorders or tingling in
the hands and feet.
✹ warning: trimipramine should
not be administered to patients
with heart disease or
psychosis; it should be
administered with caution to
those with epilepsy, diabetes,
liver or thyroid disease,
glaucoma, or urinary
retention, or who are pregnant
or lactating. Withdrawal of
treatment must be gradual.
*Related article:* SURMONTIL.

**Trimogal** (*Lagap*) is a proprietary
ANTIBIOTIC, available only on
prescription, used to treat and to
prevent the spread of many
forms of bacterial infection but
particularly those of the urinary
and respiratory tracts. Produced
in the form of tablets (in two
strengths), it is a preparation of
the drug trimethoprim.
▲/✹ side-effects/warning: *see*
TRIMETHOPRIM.

**Trimopan** (*Berk*) is a proprietary
ANTIBIOTIC agent, available only
on prescription, used to treat and
to prevent the spread of many

forms of bacterial infection, but
particularly those of the urinary
and respiratory tracts. Produced
in the form of tablets (in two
strengths), and as a sugar-free
suspension for dilution (the
potency of the suspension once
diluted is retained for 14 days), it
is a preparation of the drug
trimethoprim.
▲/✹ side-effects/warning: *see*
TRIMETHOPRIM.

**Trimovate** (*Glaxo*) is a
proprietary CORTICOSTEROID and
ANTIFUNGAL preparation, available
only on prescription, used in
topical application to treat severe
skin inflammation, especially
when therapy with less powerful
corticosteroids has failed.
Produced in the form of a water-
miscible cream and a paraffin-
based ointment, Trimovate's
major active constituents are the
steroid clobetasone butyrate, the
ANTIFUNGAL drug nystatin, and
the TETRACYCLINE antibiotic
chlortetracycline hydrochloride.
▲/✹ side-effects/warning: *see*
CHLORTETRACYCLINE;
CLOBETASONE BUTYRATE;
NYSTATIN.

**Trinordiol** (*Wyeth*) is a
proprietary ORAL CONTRACEPTIVE,
available only on prescription,
which combines the OESTROGEN
ethinyloestradiol with the
PROGESTOGEN levonorgestrel. It is
produced in a packet of 63 tablets,
made in three differing ratios of
the two constituents,
corresponding to three complete
menstrual cycles of 21 days plus 7
days without.
▲/✹ side-effects/warning: *see*
ETHINYLOESTRADIOL;
LEVONORGESTREL.

**Tri-Novum** (*Ortho-Cilag*) is a
proprietary ORAL CONTRACEPTIVE,
available only on prescription,
which combines the OESTROGEN
ethinyloestradiol with the

PROGESTOGEN norethisterone. It is produced in a packet of 21 tablets, made in three differing ratios of the two constituents, corresponding to one complete menstrual cycle of 21 days plus 7 days without. Tri-Novum is also available in a pack containing 7 tablets (Tri-Novum ED), which are placebos to take during the 7 days without.

▲/✚ side-effects/warning: see
   ETHINYLOESTRADIOL;
   NORETHISTERONE.

**Triogesic** (*Beecham*) is a proprietary, non-prescription nasal DECONGESTANT, which is not available from the National Health Service. Unlike many decongestants, however, it is produced in the form of tablets and as a sugar-free elixir for dilution (the potency of the elixir once dilute is retained for 14 days). Both forms are preparations of the non-narcotic ANALGESIC paracetamol in combination with the SYMPATHO-MIMETIC phenylpropanolamine hydrochloride.

▲/✚ side-effects/warning: see
   PARACETAMOL;
   PHENYLPROPANOLAMINE.

**Triominic** (*Beecham*) is a proprietary, non-prescription nasal DECONGESTANT, which is not available from the National Health Service. Unlike many decongestants, however, it is produced in the form of tablets and as a sugar-free syrup for dilution (the potency of the syrup once dilute is retained for 14 days). Both forms are preparations of the ANTI-HISTAMINE pheniramine maleate in combination with the SYMPATHOMIMETIC phenylpropanolamine hydrochloride.

▲/✚ side-effects/warning: see
   PHENIRAMINE MALEATE;
   PHENYLPROPANOLAMINE.

**Triosorbon** (*Merck*) is a proprietary, non-prescription dietary supplement for patients who are severely undernourished (as with anorexia nervosa) or who have serious problems with the internal absorption of food (as following gastrectomy). It consists of a gluten-, sucrose- and galactose-free, lactose-low powder that contains protein, carbohydrates, fats, vitamins and minerals. It is not suitable for children aged under 5 years.

**Triperidol** (*Lagap*) is a proprietary ANTIPSYCHOTIC drug, available only on prescription, used to treat and tranquillize psychosis (such as schizophrenia), in which it is particularly suitable for treating forms of manic behavioural disturbance. Produced in the form of tablets (in two strengths), Triperidol is a preparation of trifluperidol.

▲/✚ side-effects/warning: see
   TRIFLUPERIDOL.

**Triplopen** (*Glaxo*) is a proprietary ANTIBIOTIC, used in the treatment or prevention of many forms of bacterial infection. Produced in the form of powder for reconstitution as a medium for injection, it is a compound preparation of three penicillin-type antibiotics: benzylpenicillin sodium, procaine penicillin and benethamine penicillin. The particular asset of this preparation is that following intramuscular injection it creates a depot of forms of penicillin with varying solubilties, from which penicillin is released into the blood over a period many days, thus avoiding the need for frequent injections.

▲/ ✿ side-effects/warning: *see*
BENETHAMINE PENICILLIN;
BENZYLPENICILLIN;
PROCAINE PENICILLIN.

**tripotassium
dicitratoismuthate** is a drug
that assists in the healing of
gastric and duodenal ulcers. It is
thought to work by creating a
protective coating over the ulcer
under which healing can take
place. Administration is oral in
the form of tablets or an elixir –
food and drink should be avoided
for some time before and after
treatment.
*Related articles:* DE-NOL; DE-
NOLTAB.

**triprolidine** is an ANTIHISTAMINE
used to treat the symptoms of
allergic disorders such as hay
fever and urticaria. A long-acting
drug, its effect may last for more
than 12 hours. Administration (in
the form of triprolidine
hydrochloride) is oral as tablets,
sustained-release tablets, and a
dilute elixir.
▲ side-effects: there may be
headache, drowsiness and dry
mouth. Some patients
experience sensitivity
reactions on the skin.
✿ warning: triprolidine should be
administered with caution to
patients with epilepsy,
glaucoma, liver disease or
enlargement of the prostate
gland. During treatment,
alcohol consumption must be
avoided.
*Related articles:* ACTIDIL; PRO-
ACTIDIL.

**Triptafen** (*Allen & Hanburys*) is a
proprietary compound
ANTIDEPRESSANT, available only
on prescription, used to treat
depressive illness particularly in
cases in which there is also
anxiety. Produced in the form of
tablets (in two strengths, the
weaker under the name Triptafen-

M), it is a combination of
amitriptyline hydrochloride with
the PHENOTHIAZINE perphenazine.
It is not recommended for
children.
▲/ ✿ side-effects/warning: *see*
AMITRIPTYLINE;
PERPHENAZINE.

**Trisequens** (*Novo*) is a proprietary
hormonal supplement, available
only on prescription, used in
HORMONE replacement therapy for
women during and following the
menopause. It contains both the
OESTROGENS oestradiol and
oestriol, together with the
PROGESTOGEN norethisterone
acetate, and is produced in a
calendar pack of 28 tablets
corresponding to one complete
menstrual cycle; also available in
a higher strength form
(Trisequens Forte).
▲/ ✿ side-effects/warning: *see*
NORETHISTERONE;
OESTRADIOL; OESTRIOL.

**trisodium edetate** is a CHELATING
AGENT that absorbs calcium. It is
thus used primarily to treat
conditions in which there is
excessive calcium in the
bloodstream (hypercalcaemia),
but may also be used in the form
of eye-drops (in dilute solution) to
treat calcification of the cornea
or lime burns of the eyeball. In
the case of hypercalcaemia,
administration is in the form of
slow intravenous infusion.
▲ side-effects: administration by
slow intravenous infusion may
cause pain in the limb in which
the infusion is given. There
may be nausea, diarrhoea and
cramps. Overdosage may lead
to kidney damage.
✿ warning: trisodium edetate
should not be administered to
patients with impaired kidney
function; it should be
administered with caution to
those who suffer from
tuberculosis. Regular blood

counts to check calcium levels are essential during treatment. *Related article:* LIMCLAIR.

**Tritace** (*Astra, Hoechst*) is a proprietary form of the ANTIHYPERTENSIVE drug ramipril used to treat high blood pressure (hypertension), often in combination with other drugs. It is available only on prescription in the form of capsules (in three strengths).
▲/✿ side-effects/warning: *see* RAMIPRIL.

**Tritamyl** (*Procea*) is the name of a brand of gluten-free, starch-based, self-raising flour with which bread (and other foods) can be made for patients who cannot tolerate dietary gluten (as with coeliac disease and other amino acid deficiencies). A low-protein version is also available (under the name Tritamyl PK).

**Trivax** (*Wellcome*) is a proprietary preparation of the triple vaccine diphtheria-pertussis-tetanus (DPT) vaccine, consisting of a combination of the toxoids (antibodies produced in response to the toxins) of the diphtheria and tetanus bacteria with pertussis vaccine. It is produced in ampoules for injection.
*see* DIPHTHERIA-PERTUSSIS-TETANUS (DPT) VACCINE.

**Trivax-AD** (*Wellcome*) is a proprietary preparation of the triple vaccine diphtheria-pertussis-tetanus (DPT) vaccine, consisting of a combination of the toxoids (antibodies produced in response to the toxins) of the diphtheria and tetanus bacteria with pertussis vaccine, all adsorbed on to a mineral carrier (in the form of aluminium hydroxide). It is produced in ampoules for injection.
*see* DIPHTHERIA-PERTUSSIS-TETANUS (DPT) VACCINE.

**Trobicin** (*Upjohn*) is a proprietary ANTIBIOTIC, available only on prescription, used specifically in the treatment of the sexually transmitted disease gonorrhoea in patients who are allergic to penicillins, or in cases resistant to penicillins. Produced in the form of a powder for reconstitution as a medium for injection, it is a preparation of spectinomycin.
▲/✿ side-effects/warning: *see* SPECTINOMYCIN.

**tropicamide** is a short-acting ANTICHOLINERGIC drug used (in mild solution) to dilate the pupil of the eye for ophthalmic examination. Administration is in the form of eye-drops.
▲ side-effects: vision is blurred or otherwise disturbed. Overdosage may lead to increased heart rate and to behavioural changes in susceptible patients.
✿ warning: tropicamide should not be administered to patients with certain forms of glaucoma, or who are known to have soft lenses.
*Related articles:* MINIMS TROPICAMIDE; MYDRIACYL.

**Tropium** (*DDSA Pharmaceuticals*) is a proprietary ANXIOLYTIC drug, available on prescription only to private patients, used to treat anxiety or to assist in the treatment of acute alcohol withdrawal symptoms. Produced in the form of capsules (in two strengths) and tablets (in three strengths), Tropium is a preparation of the BENZODIAZEPINE chlordiazepoxide.
▲/✿ side-effects/warning: *see* CHLORDIAZEPOXIDE.

**Trosyl** (*Pfizer*) is a proprietary form of the ANTIFUNGAL agent tioconazole available on prescription to treat fungal nail infections. It is applied as a lotion

to the nails and surrounding area.
▲/✸ side-effects/warning: *see*
TIOCONAZOLE.

**Trufree** (*Cantassium*) is a
proprietary brand of gluten-free
flours, which are used in baking
for patients who cannot tolerate
gluten (as in the case of coeliac
disease and other amino acid
deficiency conditions).

**trypsin** is an enzyme secreted by
the pancreas in the process of
digestion. It may be administered
therapeutically either to assist
digestion locally, or – more
commonly – to treat
inflammation, bruising or
swelling of the soft tissues. In this
it is supposed to work by
removing coagulated blood and
cellular debris. Administration is
usually by injection.
▲ side-effects: there may be
nausea and vomiting, with
diarrhoea. Rarely, there are
sensitivity reactions.
✸ warning: trypsin should not be
administered to a patient who
is already taking
anticoagulant drugs.

**Tryptizol** (*Morson*) is a
proprietary ANTIDEPRESSANT
drug, available only on
prescription, used in the
treatment of depressive illness
and especially in cases where its
additional SEDATIVE properties
may be advantageous to the
patients or to those that care for
them. However, the drug is
additionally used to prevent
bedwetting at night in
youngsters. Produced in the form
of tablets (in three strengths), as
sustained-release capsules, as a
sugar-free liquid for dilution (the
potency of the liquid once dilute
is retained for 14 days), and in
vials for injection, Tryptizol is a
preparation of amitryptiline
hydrochloride.
▲/✸ side-effects/warning: *see*
AMITRIPTYLINE.

**tryptophan** is an amino
acid present in an ordinary diet,
from which the natural body
substance serotonin is derived.
Serotonin is much like histamine
in its role in inflammation, but
even more importantly, deficiency
of serotonin (specifically in the
brain) is thought to contribute to
depression. Therapeutic
administration of tryptophan,
singly or in combination with
ANTIDEPRESSANT drugs, is
therefore aimed mainly at
treating depressive illness. The
response to treatment with
tryptophan by itself is slow,
taking at least 4 weeks for
genuine improvement to occur.
Administration is oral in the form
of tablets or in solution.
▲ side-effects: concentration and
speed of thought and
movement may initially be
affected; with drowsiness,
there may also be nausea
and/or a headache.
✸ warning: tryptophan should
not be administered to patients
known to have defective
metabolism of tryptophan in
the diet, or who have disease of
the bladder.
*Related articles:* OPTIMAX;
PACITRON.

**TSH**, or thyroid-stimulating
hormone, is also known as
thyrotrophin.

**Tubarine Miscible** (*Calmic*) is a
proprietary preparation of the
SKELETAL MUSCLE RELAXANT
tubocurarine chloride, used under
general anaesthesia for medium-
or long-duration paralysis.
Available only on prescription, it
is produced in ampoules for
injection.
▲/✸ side-effects/warning: *see*
TUBOCURARINE.

**tubocurarine** is a SKELETAL
MUSCLE RELAXANT used primarily
(in the form of tubocurarine

chloride) under general anaesthesia for medium- or long-duration paralysis. It is the paralytic factor in the well-known South American poison curare. Apart from its use in surgical operations, the drug may also be used occasionally to treat the spasm associated with tetanus or with some mental disorders. Administration is ordinarily by injection.

▲ side-effects: effects begin some 3 to 5 minutes after injection, and last for about 30 minutes.

✿ warning: following injection, a rash may appear on the chest and neck, due to the release of histamine. Onset of the paralysis may be accompanied by hypotension.
*Related articles:* JEXIN; TUBARINE MISCIBLE.

**tub/vac/BCG, dried,** is an abbreviation for the freeze-dried version of BCG vaccine (against tuberculosis).
*see* BCG VACCINE.

**tub/vac/BCG, perc,** is an abbreviation for the live version of BCG vaccine (against tuberculosis) for percutaneous administration by multiple puncture with a suitable instrument.
*see* BCG VACCINE.

**Tuinal** (*Lilly*) is a proprietary HYPNOTIC, a BARBITURATE on the controlled drugs list, and used to treat intractable insomnia. Produced in the form of capsules, it is a preparation of amylobarbitone sodium. It is not recommended for children.
▲/✿ side-effects/warning: *see* AMYLOBARBITONE.

**Tums** (*Beecham Health Care*) are proprietary, non-prescription ANTACID tablets containing calcium carbonate.
▲/✿ side-effects/warning: *see* CALCIUM CARBONATE.

**Tunes** (*Mars*) are proprietary, non-prescription sweets formulated for the relief of cold symptoms. Tunes contain GLUCOSE syrup, citric acid, MENTHOL, balsam of tolu, camphor and thyme.

**turpentine liniment** is a non-proprietary formulation of turpentine oil, camphor and soap all in solution, for gentle massage into the skin as a topical treatment for underlying muscular or rheumatic pain. It stimulates the sensory nerve endings in the skin and so offsets the underlying ache (as a COUNTER-IRRITANT).

**Two's Company** (*Family Planning Sales*) is a proprietary, non-prescription SPERMICIDAL preparation for use in combination with one of the barrier methods of contraception (such as a condom). Produced in the form of vaginal inserts (pessaries), Two's Company's active constituent is an alcohol ester.

**Tylex** (*Cilag*) is a proprietary compound ANALGESIC, available only on prescription, used as a painkiller. Produced in the form of tablets, Tylex is a preparation of the OPIATE codeine phosphate and paracetamol in the ratio 30:500 (mg), and therefore contains more codeine than the usual compound preparation known as CO-CODAMOL. It is not recommended for children.
▲/✿ side-effects/warning: *see* CODEINE PHOSPHATE; PARACETAMOL.

**tyloxapol** is a MUCOLYTIC drug, used via a nebuliser to reduce the viscosity of sputum and thus facilitate expectoration (coughing up sputum) mostly in conditions such as asthma and bronchitis. It is now used rather seldom,

577

although there are no contra-
indications and side-effects are
rare (constituted by the
occasional high temperature).

**typhoid vaccine** is a suspension of
dead typhoid bacteria,
administered by deep
subcutaneous or intramuscular
injection. Full protection is,
however, not guaranteed, and
travellers at risk are advised not
to eat uncooked food or to drink
untreated water. Dosage is
normally repeated after 4 to 6
weeks – unless reactions have
been severe. Some reaction is to
be expected: swelling, pain and
tenderness occur after a couple of
hours, followed by high
temperature and malaise, possibly
with a headache.

**typhus vaccine** is not normally
available in the United Kingdom,
although there are small stocks
that can be used if necessary. It
consists of inactivated Rickettsia
organisms grown in the yolk-sacs
of hens' eggs. The organisms are
carried by body lice, but good
hygienic conditions, in any part
of the world, even where the
disease is endemic, are usually
enough for protection.

**Tyrozets** (*Merck, Sharp & Dohme*)
is a proprietary, non-prescription
brand of ANTISEPTIC lozenges used
to sanitize and relieve pain in the
mouth and throat. They contain
the local ANAESTHETIC benzocaine
together with the ANTIBACTERIAL
compound tyrothricin.
▲/● side-effects/warning: *see*
BENZOCAINE.

**Ubretid** (*Berk*) is a proprietary preparation used mainly to stimulate bladder or intestinal activity; it may also form part of treatment for serious skeletal muscular disease. Available only on prescription, Ubretid is produced in the form of tablets or ampules for injection, and contains distigmine bromide.
▲/● side-effects/warning: *see* DISTIGMINE BROMIDE.

**Ukidan** (*Serono*) is a proprietary FIBRINOLYTIC drug available only on prescription, containing urokinase. Produced as a powder for reconstitution, it is used in intravenous infusions to treat various forms of thrombosis.
▲/● side-effects/warning: *see* UROKINASE.

**Ultrabase** (*Schering*) is a proprietary water-miscible cream used as a skin emollient (softener and soother) and as a medium for various other skin preparations. Available without prescription, it contains liquid paraffin, stearyl alcohol and white soft paraffin.

**Ultradil Plain** (*Schering*) is a proprietary CORTICOSTEROID preparation, available only on prescription, in the form of either a water-miscible cream or a more oily ointment. Its active constituents are fluocortolone hexanoate and fluocortolone pivalate, which are effective in treating inflammatory skin conditions such as eczema and psoriasis. In made-up dilute form, either version retains its potency for 14 days.
▲/● side-effects/warning: *see* FLUOCORTOLONE.

**Ultralanum Plain** (*Schering*) is a proprietary CORTICOSTEROID preparation, available only on prescription, in the form of either a water-miscible cream or a more oily ointment. Its active constituents are fluocortolone hexanoate and fluocortolone pivalate at higher concentrations than present in ULTRADIL PLAIN. Ultralanum is also used to treat inflammatory skin conditions, and in made-up dilute form also retains its potency for 14 days.
▲/● side-effects/warning: *see* FLUOCORTOLONE.

**Ultraproct** (*Schering*) is a proprietary, CORTICOSTEROID ANTIHISTAMINE compound with local ANAESTHETIC properties. Available only on prescription, it is made up of fluocortolone hexanoate and fluocortolone pivalate, with the local anaesthetic cinchocaine and the antihistamine chemizole undeconate. Produced in the form of ointment and anal suppositories, Ultraproct is prescribed to treat piles (haemorrhoids), anal fissure and infection of the anal region.
▲ side-effects: *see* FLUOCORTOLONE.
● warning: ultraproct is not suitable as treatment for children or for women during pregnancy. Prolonged use should be avoided.

**Ultratard, MC** (*Novo*) is a proprietary preparation of insulin zinc suspension, available in ampoules for injection by diabetics according to individual equiremens.
▲/● side-effects/warning: *see* INSULIN.

**Unguentum Merck** (*Merck*) is a proprietary, non-prescription skin emollient (softener and soother) and barrier ointment, also used as a medium for other skin preparations. Because it contains similar proportions of fats and water it is particularly stable; its principal constituent is white soft paraffin. One of the safest of all OINTMENTS, its complex formula includes no known allergen.

**Uniflu Plus Gregovite C**
(*Unigreg*) is a proprietary
combination of two drugs issued
as separate tablets to be taken
simultaneously to treat the
symptoms of colds and influenza.
Uniflu is an ANTITUSSIVE and
ANTIHISTAMINE that also has some
ANALGESIC properties. Because
Uniflu contains the OPIATE
codeine, however, the
combination is not available on a
National Health Service
prescription; other principal
constituents of Uniflu include
paracetamol and caffeine.
Gregovite C is a form of ASCORBIC
ACID (vitamin C).
▲ / ✿ side-effects/warning: *see*
CAFFEINE; CODEINE
PHOSPHATE; PARACETAMOL.

**Unigesic** (*Unimed*) is a
proprietary compound ANALGESIC
not available on a National
Health Service prescription,
which principally consists of a
mixture of paracetamol and
caffeine.
▲ / ✿ side-effects/warning: *see*
CAFFEINE; PARACETAMOL.

**Unigest** (*Unigreg*) is a proprietary
ANTACID, not available on a
National Health Service
prescription, that principally
consists of aluminium hydroxide
(its active ingredient) and
dimethicone (an antifoaming
agent).
▲ / ✿ side-effects/warning: *see*
ALUMINIUM HYDROXIDE.

**Unihep** (*Leo*) is a proprietary
preparation of the
ANTICOAGULANT heparin sodium
in a mode suitable for injection.
Available only on prescription,
Unihep is used to treat various
forms of thrombosis.
▲ / ✿ side-effects/warning: *see*
HEPARIN.

**Uniparin** (*CP Pharmaceuticals*) is
a proprietary preparation of the
ANTICOAGULANT heparin sodium

in a mode suitable for
subcutaneous injection. Available
only on prescription, Uniparin is
used to treat various forms of
thrombosis.
▲ / ✿ side-effects/warning: *see*
HEPARIN.

**Uniparin Calcium** (*CP
Pharmaceuticals*) is a proprietary
preparation of the ANTICOAGU-
LANT heparin calcium in a mode
suitable for subcutaneous
injection. Available only on
prescription, Uniparin Calcium is
used to treat various forms of
thrombosis.
▲ / ✿ side-effects/warning: *see*
HEPARIN.

**Uniphyllin Continus** (*Napp*) is a
proprietary, non-prescription
BRONCHODILATOR used to treat
conditions such as asthma and
chronic bronchitis. Produced in
the form of sustained-release
tablets (in two strengths) for
prolonged effect, and at a lower
dose tablet for children
(Uniphyllin Continus Pediatric),
the active constituent is the
short-acting xanthine
theophylline.
▲ / ✿ side-effects/warning: *see*
THEOPHYLLINE.

**Uniroid** (*Unigreg*) is a proprietary
STEROID compound, available only
on prescription, which has
ANTIBIOTIC and local ANAESTHETIC
properties. Produced as both
ointment and anal suppositories,
its main constituents are
cinchocaine hydrochloride,
hydrocortisone, neomycin
sulphate and polymyxin B
sulphate. Uniroid is prescribed to
treat piles (haemorrhoids), anal
fissure and inflammation of the
anal region.
▲ side-effects: *see* CINCHOCAINE;
HYDROCORTISONE; NEOMYCIN;
POLYMYXIN B.
✿ warning: uniroid is unsuitable
as treatment for children or for

women during pregnancy.
Prolonged use should be
avoided.

**Unisept** (*Schering*) is a
proprietary, non-prescription
DISINFECTANT and wound
cleanser, which is available in
sachets; each sachet contains
chlorhexidine gluconate in very
dilute solution.
▲/● side-effects/warning: *see*
CHLORHEXIDINE.

**Unisomnia** (*Unigreg*) is a
proprietary form of the
BENZODIAZEPINE nitrazepam. A
powerful and long-acting
HYPNOTIC produced in the form of
tablets, Unisomnia is available
only by prescription for private
patients.
▲/● side-effects/warning: *see*
NITRAZEPAM.

**Urantoin** (*DDSA
Pharmaceuticals*) is a proprietary
form of the ANTIBIOTIC drug
nitrofurantoin, used specifically
to treat infections of the urinary
tract. Produced as tablets,
Urantoin is available only on
prescription.
▲/● side-effects/warning: *see*
NITROFURANTOIN.

**Uriben** (*RP Drugs*) is a
proprietary ANTIBIOTIC agent,
available only on prescription, in
the form of a syrupy suspension of
nalidixic acid. Used in solution to
treat gastrointestinal infections
and infections of the urinary
tract, once made up its potency is
retained for 14 days.
▲/● side-effects/warning: *see*
NALIDIXIC ACID.

**Urisal** (*Winthrop*) is a proprietary
preparation, available only on
prescription, in the form of
sachets of soluble granules of
sodium citrate. In solution, the
granules treat cystitis and other
relatively mild infections of the
urinary tract.

▲/● side-effects/warning: *see*
SODIUM CITRATE.

**Urispas** (*Syntex*) is a proprietary
ANTISPASMODIC, available only on
prescription, consisting of tablets
containing flavoxate hydrochloride. Urispas is used to treat
urinary incontinence and
associated difficulties (dysuria).
▲/● side-effects/warning: *see*
FLAVOXATE HYDROCHLORIDE.

**Urizide** (*DDSA Pharmaceuticals*)
is a proprietary DIURETIC,
available only on prescription,
consisting of tablets containing
bendrofluazide. Urizide is
prescribed to treat the
accumulation of fluid in the
tissues (oedema) or high blood
pressure (hypertension).
▲/● side-effects/warning: *see*
BENDROFLUAZIDE.

**urofollitrophin** is a form of
follicle-stimulating hormone
(FSH) found in, and processed
from, human menopausal urine.
*Related article:* METRODIN.

**urokinase** is a FIBRINOLYTIC found
in, and processed from, human
male urine. It is valuable in the
treatment of thrombosis, and
particularly of blood clots in the
eye; administration is by infusion
in a medium of saline solution.
▲ side-effects: there may be fever,
haemorrhage, and allergic
reactions.
● warning: urokinase should not
be administered to patients
who have recently suffered
haemorrhage (as for example
during surgery), or to pregnant
women. If for any reason
bleeding occurs, further
treatment to stem the flow will
be required.
*Related article:* UKIDAN.

**Uromitexan** (*Boehringer
Ingelheim*) is a proprietary form
of the drug MESNA, used to combat

the toxicity of CYTOTOXIC drugs by reacting with their metabolites in the urinary tract. Available only on prescription, Uromitexan is produced as ampoules for injection.

**Uro-Tainer** (*CliniMed*) is the proprietary name for a selection of solutions designed to wash and maintain a latex or silicone catheter replacing or assisting part of the urinary tract. Solutions – available without prescription in the form of sachets – include CHLORHEXIDINE 0.02%; saline (sodium chloride) 0.9%; mandelic acid 1%; and some proprietary compounds.

**ursodeoxycholic acid** is a drug taken orally to dissolve small, light, cholesterol gallstones. X-ray monitoring of treatment is also required to supervise progress. The course may last up to two years, and treatment must be continued for at least three months after stones have been dissolved.

▲ side-effects: there may be pruritus (itching) and minor dysfunctioning of the liver. Diarrhoea is rare.

✸ warning: ursodeoxycholic acid is not suitable for patients with larger, radio-opaque gallstones; nor for those who suffer from chronic liver disease, intestinal inflammation or an inoperative gall bladder; nor for pregnant women.
*Related articles:* DESTOLIT; URSOFALK.

**Ursofalk** (*Thames*) is a proprietary form of the drug ursodeoxycholic acid, available only on prescription, in the form of capsules.
▲ / ✸ side-effects/warning: *see* URSODEOXYCHOLIC ACID.

**Utovlan** (*Syntex*) is a proprietary PROGESTOGEN (ovulation-suppressing SEX HORMONE), available only on prescription, in the form of tablets containing norethisterone. It is used to treat uterine bleeding, abnormally heavy menstruation, and other menstrual problems, and may additionally be used as an effective contraceptive preparation.
▲ / ✸ side-effects/warning: *see* NORETHISTERONE.

**Uvistat** (*Windsor*) is the name of proprietary, non-prescription sunscreen preparations, which contain constituents able to protect the skin from ultraviolet radiation. Patients whose skin condition is such as to require this sort of preparation, may be prescribed Uvistat at the discretion of their doctors. Uvistat is available as creams, water-resistant creams, and as a lipscreen. The preparations contain mexenone and ethylhexyl p-methoxycinnamate.

**\*vaccines** confer active immunity against specific diseases: that is, they cause a patient's own body to create a defence (in the form of antibodies against the disease). Most are administered in the form of a suspension of dead viruses (as in flu vaccine) or bacteria (as in typhoid vaccine), or of live but weakened viruses (as in rubella vaccine) or bacteria (as in BCG vaccine against tuberculosis). A third type is a suspension containing extracts of the toxins released by the invading organism that stimulates the formation of antibodies against the toxin, not the organism itself. This is called a toxoid vaccine. Vaccines that incorporate dead micro-organisms generally require a series of administrations (most often three) to build up a sufficient supply of antibodies in the body; booster shots may thereafter be necessary at regular intervals to reinforce immunity. Vaccines that incorporate live micro-organisms may confer immunity with a single dose, because the organisms multiply within the body, although some live vaccines still require 3 administrations (as in oral poliomyelitis vaccine).

▲ side-effects: side-effects range from little or no reactions to severe discomfort, high temperature and pain.

✸ warning: vaccination should not be administered to patients who have a febrile illness or any form of infection. Vaccines containing live material should not be administered routinely to patients who are pregnant, or who are known to have an immunodeficiency disorder.

**Vagifem** (*Novo Nordisk*) is a proprietary form of the OESTROGEN oestradiol, used to treat menopausal vaginitis. Available only on prescription, the preparation consists of controlled release vaginal tablets which come with disposable applicators.

▲ / ✸ side-effects/warning: *see* OESTRADIOL.

**Vaginyl** (*DDSA Pharmaceuticals*) is a proprietary preparation with ANTIPROTOZOAL and ANTIBACTERIAL actions, available only on prescription, in the form of tablets containing the antimicrobial drug metronidazole. It is prescribed to treat bacterial infections of the intestines (causing dysentery) and of the vagina.

▲ / ✸ side-effects/warning: *see* METRONIDAZOLE.

**Valium** (*Roche*) is a proprietary form of the powerful BENZODIAZEPINE diazepam, useful both as an ANXIOLYTIC or minor TRANQUILLIZER and also as a SKELETAL MUSCLE RELAXANT. Available only on prescription, it is produced as anal suppositories and in ampoules for injection (available on National Health Service prescription), and as tablets and syrup (available only to private patients). It is prescribed mainly to treat anxiety.

▲ / ✸ side-effects/warning: *see* DIAZEPAM.

**Vallergan** (*May & Baker*) is a proprietary ANTIHISTAMINE, available only on prescription, consisting of trimeprazine tartrate in the form either of tablets or of syrup for dilution (the syrup once diluted retains potency for 14 days). Vallergan is prescribed to treat various types of allergic reaction, particularly those which include itching skin. It has SEDATIVE effects as with most antihistamines.

▲ / ✸ side-effects/warning: *see* TRIMEPRAZINE TARTRATE.

**Valoid** (*Calmic*) is a proprietary form of ANTIHISTAMINE prescribed to treat vomiting, motion sickness

V

and loss of the sense of balance (labyrinthitis). It comes in two forms: tablets, containing cyclizine hydrochloride and available without prescription; and ampoules for injection, containing cyclizine lactate and available only on prescription.
▲/● side-effects/warning: *see*
ANTIHISTAMINE; CYCLIZINE.

**Vamin** (*Kabi Vitrum*) is the name of a selection of proprietary infusion fluids for the intravenous nutrition of a patient in whom feeding via the alimentary tract is not possible. All contain amino acids and provide energy, some in the form of glucose, others in the form of various electrolytes.

**Vancocin** (*Lilly*) is the name of a selection of proprietary forms of the antibacterial ANTIBIOTIC vancomycin hydrochloride. Available only on prescription, in the form of capsules (produced under the name Matrigel).
▲/● side-effects/warning: *see*
VANCOMYCIN.

**vancomycin** is an ANTIBIOTIC with activity primarily against gram-positive micro-organisms. It inhibits the synthesis of components of the bacterial cell wall. As it is rather toxic, particularly to the kidneys and ears, it is only used in special situations. One is the treatment of pseudomembranous colitis, a superinfection of the gastrointestinal tract, which can occur after treatment with broad-spectrum antibiotics such as ampicillin or clindamycin. Another use is in the treatment of multiple-drug-resistant staphylococcal infections, particularly endocarditis. It is not absorbed orally but is taken by mouth to treat colitis and by infusion for systemic infections. Because incautious use may have deleterious effects on the organs

of the ear, on the kidney, and on the tissues at the site of injection, blood concentrations and tests on liver and kidney functions are necessary during treatment.
▲ side-effects: infusion may cause high body temperature and a rash; incautious use may lead to ringing in the ears (tinnitus) and to kidney disease.
● warning: vancomycin should not be administered to patients with impaired kidney function or who are deaf; or to patients in whom there is a risk of the escape of body fluids from the vessels into the tissues.
*Related article:* VANCOCIN.

**Vansil** is a proprietary form of the ANTHELMINTIC drug OXAMNIQUINE, used specifically as an oral treatment for intestinal schistosomiasis (bilharziasis).

**Variclene** (*Dermal*) is a proprietary, non-prescription ANTISEPTIC gel used to cleanse and soothe skin ulcers. Within an aqueous base its active constituents include lactic acid.

**Varidase** (*Lederle*) is a proprietary ANTISEPTIC, available only on prescription, in the form of a powdered enzymatic compound of streptokinase and streptodornase. Prescribed as treatment to cleanse and soothe skin ulcers, the combination of enzymes also helps to slough off surrounding lesioned skin.
▲/● side-effects/warning: *see*
STREPTOKINASE.

**Varihesive** (*Squibb*) is a proprietary, non-prescription dressing compound for use in treating leg ulcers. Constituents are CARMELLOSE SODIUM, GELATIN, pectin and polyisobutylene.

**var/vac** is an abbreviation for variola vaccine.
*see* SMALLPOX VACCINE.

V

**Vascardin** (*Nicholas*) is a proprietary VASODILATOR used in treatment for angina pectoris (heart pain) and for cardiac arrhythmia, and is available without prescription. It consists of tablets containing isosorbide dinitrate (two strengths are available), and should not be used by patients who have high blood pressure, those who are undergoing other drug treatments, or by children.
▲ / ● side-effects/warning: *see* ISOSORBIDE DINITRATE.

**Vasocon A** (*Cooper Vision*) is a proprietary form of ANTIHISTAMINE eye-drops, available only on prescription, used to treat acute allergic conjunctivitis. Its active constituents are antazoline phosphate and naphazoline hydrochloride.
▲ / ● side-effects/warning: *see* ANTAZOLINE.

**\*vasoconstrictors** cause a narrowing of the blood vessels, and thus a reduction in the rate of blood flow and an increase in blood pressure. They are used to increase blood pressure in circulatory disorders, in cases of shock, or in cases where pressure has fallen during lengthy or complex surgery. Different vasoconstrictors work in different ways: vasoconstrictors that have a marked or local effect on mucous membranes, for example, may be used to relieve nasal congestion. Some are used to prolong the effects of local anaesthetics. Best-known and most-used vasoconstrictors include PHENYLEPHRINE, XYLOMETAZOLINE and METHOXAMINE.

**\*vasodilators** cause a widening of the blood vessels, causing changes in blood flow and a reduction in blood pressure. They are used to reduce blood pressure mainly in the treatment of heart failure or angina pectoris (heart pain), to improve the circulation in the brain or in the limbs, or simply to treat high blood pressure (hypertension). Different vasodilators work in different ways: short-acting nitrates, for example, work by both expanding the blood vessels of the heart and reducing the flow of blood back to the heart in the veins; in order to prolong the effect, some nitrates are administered in the form of tablets to be held under the tongue, or in the form of an aerosol spray for repeated doses. Best known and most used vasodilators include GLYCERYL TRINITRATE, ISOSORBIDE DINITRATE, DIAZOXIDE, NIFEDIPINE, CINNARIZINE, THYMOXAMINE and CO-DERGACRINE MESYLATE.

**Vasogen** (*Pharmax*) is a proprietary, non-prescription barrier cream, used to soothe and dress nappy rash, bedsores, and rashes in excretory areas. Active constituents are CALAMINE, DIMETHICONE and ZINC OXIDE.

**vasopressin** is a natural body HORMONE secreted by the posterior lobe of the pituitary gland; it is known also as antidiuretic hormone, or ADH. In therapy, vasopressin – a VASOCONSTRICTOR – is used mostly to treat pituitary-originated diabetes insipidus. There are two main forms: DESMOPRESSIN and LYPRESSIN; TERLIPRESSIN is another derivative. Preparations include nose-drops, nasal spray, injections and solutions for infusion. Treatment must not be prolonged, and should be carefully and regularly monitored to avoid overdosage.
▲ side-effects: potential side-effects include hypersensitivity reactions, constriction of

V

coronary arteries (possibly leading to angina pectoris), nausea, cramps and an overpowering urge to defecate.

✿ warning: doses should be adjusted to individual response, to balance water levels in the body. Treatment with vasopressin is not advisable for patients with asthma, epilepsy or migraine, and should not be administered to patients with chronic kidney disease or disease of the blood vessels.
*Related article:* PITRESSIN.

**Vasoxine** (*Calmic*) is a proprietary SYMPATHOMIMETIC VASO-CONSTRICTOR, available only on prescription, most often used to raise blood pressure in a patient under general anaesthesia. It is a preparation of methoxamine hydrochloride in ampoules for injection.
▲/✿ side-effects/warning: *see* METHOXAMINE HYDROCHLORIDE.

**V-Cil-K** (*Lilly*) is a proprietary preparation of the penicillin-type ANTIBIOTIC phenoxymethyl-penicillin, used mainly to treat infections of the ears and throat, and some skin conditions. Available only on prescription, it is produced in the form of capsules, tablets (in two strengths), a syrup for dilution, and a children's syrup (in two strengths) for dilution (the potency of the diluted syrup is retained for 7 days).
▲/✿ side-effects/warning: *see* PHENOXYMETHYLPENICILLIN.

**vecuronium bromide** is a relatively recently derived SKELETAL MUSCLE RELAXANT, of the type known as non-depolarizing or competitive. Administration is by injection, commonly under general anaesthetic during surgery.

✿ warning: patients treated with vecuronium bromide must have their respiration controlled and monitored until the drug has been inactivated or antagonized. The effect of repeated large doses is cumulative.
*Related article:* NORCURON.

**Veganin** (*Warner*) is a proprietary, non-prescription compound ANALGESIC, which is not available from the National Health Service, consisting of tablets that contain aspirin, codeine phosphate and paracetamol.
▲/✿ side-effects/warning: *see* ASPIRIN; CODEINE PHOSPHATE; PARACETAMOL.

**Veil** (*Blake*) is a proprietary, non-prescription series of camouflage creams in eleven shades designed for use in masking scars and other skin disfigurements. They may be obtained on prescription if the disfigurement is the result of surgery or is giving rise to emotional disturbance in the patient.

**Velbe** (*Lilly*) is a proprietary form of the CYTOTOXIC drug vinblastine sulphate, produced in the form of the powdered sulphate together with an ampoule of diluent. Available only on prescription, Velbe is used to treat cancer particularly lymphomas, Hodgkin's disease, and some neoplasms.
▲/✿ side-effects/warning: *see* VINBLASTINE SULPHATE.

**Velosef** (*Squibb*) is a proprietary form of the CEPHALOSPORIN antibiotic cephradine, available only on prescription, as capsules (in two strengths), a syrup (for dilution) or a powdered form for use in solution as injections. The potency of the syrup once diluted is retained for 7 days.
▲/✿ side-effects/warning: *see* CEPHRADINE.

**Velosulin** (*Nordisk Wellcome*) is a proprietary form of INSULIN, derived from pigs and highly purified, for use in treating and maintaining diabetic patients. It is produced in the form of ampoules for injection.
▲/● side-effects/warning: *see* INSULIN.
*Related article:* HUMAN VELOSULIN.

**Venoglobulin** (*Alpha*) is an IMMUNOGLOBULIN, a proprietary form of human normal immunoglobulin (HNIG) available only on prescription, and used as replacement therapy for patients with deficient gammaglobulin. The preparation is in a form for intravenous use.
▲/● side-effects/warning: *see* HNIG.

**Venos** (*Beecham Health Care*) is a proprietary, non-prescription cough mixture produced in the form of an ANTITUSSIVE formula and as an EXPECTORANT. The active constituents of the antitussive is the cough suppressant noscapine, and the expectorant contains guaiphensin, aniseed oil, capiscum and camphor.
▲/● side-effects/warning: *see* NOSCAPINE.

**Ventide** (*Allen & Hanburys*) is a proprietary CORTICOSTEROID compound, available only on prescription, used to treat the symptoms of asthma and chronic bronchitis. It is produced in the form of an aerosol inhalant containing the steroid beclomethasone dipropionate with the BRONCHODILATOR salbutamol.
▲/● side-effects/warning: *see* BECLOMETHASONE DIPROPIONATE; SALBUTAMOL.

**Ventodiscs** (*Allen & Hanburys*) is a proprietary form of the selective BETA-RECEPTOR STIMULANT

salbutamol, used as a BRONCHODILATOR in patients with asthma and other breathing problems. Available only on prescription, Ventodiscs are available in the form of disks containing 8 blisters of salbutamol for use with the Diskhaler device supplied. Patients should not exceed the prescribed or stated dose, and should follow the manufacturer's directions closely.
▲/● side-effects/warning: *see* SALBUTAMOL.

**Ventolin** (*Allen & Hanburys*) is a proprietary form of the selective BETA-RECEPTOR STIMULANT salbutamol, used as a BRONCHODILATOR in patients with asthma and other breathing problems. Available only on prescription, Ventolin appears in many forms: as tablets (in two strengths), sustained-release tablets (in two strengths), as sugar-free syrup (for dilution; potency once diluted is retained for 28 days), as ampoules for injection (as sulphate), as an infusion fluid (as sulphate) (after dilution), as aerosol metered inhalant, as ampoules for nebulization spray (under the name Nebules), and as a respirator solution (for further dilution), and as powder for inhalation (under the name Rotacaps). In every case, patients should not exceed the prescribed or stated dose, and should follow the manufacturer's directions closely.
▲/● side-effects/warning: *see* SALBUTAMOL.

**Vepesid** (*Bristol-Myers*) is a proprietary form of the CYTOTOXIC drug etoposide, produced in the form either of capsules (in two strengths) or of ampoules for injection (after dilution). Available only on prescription, Vepesid is used to treat cancer, particularly lymphoma or carcinoma of the bronchus or testicle. Caution must be used in handling: Vepesid may dissolve certain types of filter.

▲/● side-effects/warning: see ETOPOSIDE.

**Veractil** (*May & Baker*) is a proprietary form of the ANTI-PSYCHOTIC drug methotrimeprazine maleate (used primarily to treat schizophrenia and other psychoses). Available only on prescription, and not recommended for young or elderly patients, Veractil is produced in the form of tablets.

▲/● side-effects/warning: see METHOTRIMEPRAZINE.

**Veracur** (*Typharm*) is a proprietary, non-prescription gel made from a 1.5% formaldehyde solution in a water-miscible base and used to treat warts, especially verrucas (plantar warts).

▲/● side-effects/warning: see FORMALDEHYDE.

**verapamil hydrochloride** is a CALCIUM ANTAGONIST ANTIARRHYTHMIC drug used to treat heartbeat irregularities, high blood pressure (hypertension) and angina pectoris (heart pain). It is most commonly administered orally at first, although thereafter ampoules for injection or infusion are also available.

▲ side-effects: potential side-effects include nausea, vomiting and constipation; infusion may result in low blood pressure. Very rarely there is liver damage.

● warning: verapamil hydrochloride should not be administered to patients already taking beta-blockers, or who have heart block or heart failure, or to those with bradycardia (slow heartbeat). *Related articles:* BERKATENS; CORDILOX; SECURON.

**Veripaque** (*Sterling Research*) is a proprietary, non-prescription form of enema administered rectally to promote bowel movement. Containing oxyphenisatin, it is produced as powder for reconstitution in solution, and is commonly used in hospitals in combination with a barium sulphate enema or before colonic surgery.

▲ side-effects: mild cramps, sweating and nausea may occur, in which case the dosage should be reduced.

● warning: careful monitoring should accompany treatment of patients with irritable or inflamed colons. Reduced dosage is recommended for elderly or infirm patients. Prolonged use as a laxative is inadvisable.

**Verkade** (*G F Dietary Supplies*) is the name of a proprietary, non-prescription brand of gluten-free biscuits, produced for patients who suffer from coeliac disease and other forms of gluten sensitivity.

**Vermox** (*Janssen*) is a proprietary ANTHELMINTIC drug, available only on prescription, used to treat infestation by pinworms (threadworms) and similar intestinal parasites. Consisting of mebendazole, Vermox is produced in two forms: as tablets and in suspension.

▲/● side-effects/warning: see MEBENDAZOLE.

**Verrugon** (*Pickles*) is a proprietary, non-prescription ointment consisting of salicylic acid in a paraffin base, used to treat warts and remove hard, dead skin.

● warning: see SALICYLIC ACID.

**Vertigon** (*Smith, Kline & French*) is a proprietary ANTI-EMETIC, available only on prescription,

used to relieve symptoms of
nausea caused by the vertigo and
loss of balance experienced in
infections of the inner and middle
ears, or as a result of the
administration of CYTOTOXIC
drugs in the treatment of cancer.
It is produced as spansules
(soluble capsules) containing the
major TRANQUILLIZER pro-
chlorperazine (in two strengths).
▲/✿ side-effects/warning: see
    PROCHLOR-
    PERAZINE.

**Verucasep** (*Galen*) is a
proprietary, non-prescription gel
containing the KERATOLYTIC
glutaraldehyde, used to treat
warts and remove hard, dead
skin.
✿ warning: see GLUTARALDEHYDE.

**Vibramycin** (*Pfizer*) is a
proprietary form of the
TETRACYCLINE ANTIBIOTIC
doxycycline, available only on
prescription, as capsules (in two
strengths), a sugar-free syrup (for
dilution) or – under the separate
name Vibramycin-D – soluble
(dispersible) tablets. Vibramycin
is prescribed to treat a wide range
of bacterial and microbial
infections.
▲/✿ side-effects/warning: see
    DOXYCYCLINE.

**Vibrocil** (*Zyma*) is a proprietary,
anti-infective nasal preparation,
available only on prescription,
produced in the form of a nasal
spray, nose-drops, and a gel. All
contain DIMETHINDENE MALEATE,
NEOMYCIN sulphate and
PHENYLEPHRINE, have
ANTIHISTAMINE, ANTIBIOTIC and
nasal DECONGESTANT properties,
and are used to treat sinusitis and
hay fever.

**Vicks Coldcare** (*Richardson-
Vicks*) is a proprietary, non-
prescription cold relief
preparation in the form of

capsules, which contain
paracetamol, the ANTITUSSIVE
dextromethorphan and the
DECONGESTANT phenyl-
propanolamine.
▲/✿ side-effects/warning: see
    DEXTROMETHORPHAN;
    PARACETAMOL;
    PHENYLPROPANOLOMINE.

**vidarabine** is an ANTIVIRAL drug
used to treat serious infections by
herpes viruses (such as
chickenpox and shingles) in
patients whose immune systems
are already suppressed by other
drugs. The drug's usefulness is
limited by its toxicity.
Administration is by intravenous
infusion.
▲ side-effects: there may be
nausea and vomiting,
diarrhoea and/or anorexia; a
tremor may become apparent,
with dizziness or a state of
confusion; in the blood, white
cells and platelets may
decrease.
✿ warning: careful monitoring of
blood count and kidney
function is required: dosage
should be balanced at an
optimum. Treatment with
vidarabine is not suitable for
pregnant or lactating women.

**Videne** (*Riker*) is a proprietary,
non-prescription skin disinfectant
and cleanser containing
povidone-iodine. Much used in
hospitals, several forms are
available: a water-based solution,
a detergent-based surgical scrub,
a tincture in methylated spirit
(for washing skin preparatory to
surgery), and dusting powder (for
direct application to minor
wounds).
▲/✿ side-effects/warning: see
    POVIDONE-IODINE.

**Vidopen** (*Berk*) is a proprietary
ANTIBIOTIC preparation of the
broad-spectrum penicillin called
ampicillin, available only on

prescription. It is used mainly to treat infections of the respiratory passages, the middle ear and the urinary tract. It is also effective against gonorrhoea. Vidopen is produced as capsules (in two strengths) and as a syrup (in two strengths, for dilution); the potency of the syrup once diluted is retained for 7 days.

▲/● side-effects/warning: *see* AMPICILLIN.

**vigabatrin** is an ANTI-EPILEPTIC drug used to treat chronic epilepsy, especially tonic-clonic and partial seizures, when other anti-epileptic drugs are not effective. It is available as tablets.

▲ side-effects: there may be fatigue, dizziness, drowsiness, depression, headache, nervousness and irritability. There are occasional reports of confusion; memory, visual and gastrointestinal disturbances; weight gain; psychoses, and excitation and agitation in children.

● warning: administer with caution to patients with kidney impairment, or where there is a history of psychosis or behavioural problems. It should not be given to children under 3 years, or to pregnant or lactating women. Sudden withdrawal should be avoided. Drowsiness may impair skilled performance such as driving.
*Related article:* SABRIL.

**Vigranon B** (*Wallace*) is a proprietary, non-prescription compound of B complex VITAMINS, which is not available from the National Health Service. Produced in the form of a syrup, it contains THIAMINE (vitamin $B_1$, RIBOFLAVINE (vitamin $B_2$), PYRIDOXINE (vitamin $B_6$), NICOTINAMIDE and PANTOTHENIC ACID (panthenol).

**Villescon** (*Boehringer Ingelheim*) is a proprietary compound

containing the weak stimulant prolintane with VITAMIN supplements; it is used to treat debility or fatigue. Available on prescription only to private patients, it is produced in the form of an elixir.

▲/● side-effects/warning: *see* PROLINTANE.

**viloxazine** is an ANTIDEPRESSANT drug that has less of a sedative effect than many. Used to treat depression, dosage must be carefully monitored to remain at an optimum for each individual patient.

▲ side-effects: there may be drowsiness, nausea and vomiting, and sweating; a weight change may become apparent.

● warning: the sedative effect, though mild, may affect a patient's ability to operate controls on machinery or vehicles. Viloxazine should not be administered to patients who have had recent heart attacks or heart failure, who have a psychosis, who have liver damage or glaucoma, or who are pregnant. Age is also relevant: elderly patients should receive a reduced dosage.
*Related article:* VIVALAN.

**vinblastine sulphate** is a CYTOTOXIC drug, one of the VINCA ALKALOIDS. Available in its proprietary forms only on prescription, its ability to halt the process of cell reproduction means that it is used to treat cancer, particularly Hodgkin's disease, lymphoma and some neoplasms. But treatment with vinblastine sulphate may cause unpleasant side-effects, and even handling the material may cause problems: it is an irritant to tissue.

▲ side-effects: as part of chemotherapy for cancer, its inevitable toxicity may produce unpleasant side-effects. These range from nausea and vomiting, depression of the bone-marrow's ability to produce red blood cells, and hair loss, to loss of sensation at the extremities, abdominal bloating and serious constipation.

✦ warning: the use of vinblastine sulphate must be closely monitored in relation to each individual patient's tolerance of the toxicity of the drug. *Related article:* VELBE.

**vinca alkaloids** are a type of CYTOTOXIC drug; they work by halting the process of cell reproduction and are thus used to treat cancer, especially leukaemia, lymphoma and some sarcomas. But their toxicity inevitably causes some serious side-effects, in particular some loss of neural function at the extremities, and such symptoms may become so severe as to oblige a reduction in dosage. *Related articles:* ELDISINE; ONCOVIN; VELBE; VINBLASTINE SULPHATE; VINCRISTINE SULPHATE; VINDESINE SULPHATE.

**vincristine sulphate** is a CYTOTOXIC drug, one of the VINCA ALKALOIDS. Available in its proprietary forms only on prescription, its ability to halt the process of cell reproduction means that it is used to treat cancer, particularly acute leukaemia, Hodgkin's disease and other lymphomas. But treatment with vincristine sulphate may cause unpleasant side-effects, and even handling the material may cause problems: it is an irritant to tissue.

▲ side-effects: as part of chemotherapy for cancer, its inevitable toxicity may produce unpleasant side-effects. These range from

nausea and vomiting, constipation and hair loss, to loss of sensation at the extremities, neural failure and abdominal bloating.

✦ warning: the use of vincristine sulphate must be closely monitored in relation to each individual patient's tolerance of the toxicity of the drug. *Related article:* ONCOVIN.

**vindesine sulphate** is a CYTOTOXIC drug, one of the VINCA ALKALOIDS. Available in its proprietary form (which also contains MANNITOL) only on prescription, its ability to halt the process of cell reproduction means that it is used to treat cancer, particularly leukaemia, lymphoma and some sarcomas. But treatment with vindesine sulphate may cause unpleasant side-effects, and even handling the material may cause problems: it is an irritant to tissue.

▲ side-effects: as part of chemotherapy for cancer, its inevitable toxicity may produce unpleasant side-effects. These range from nausea and vomiting, constipation and hair loss, to loss of sensation at the extremities, neural failure and abdominal bloating.

✦ warning: the use of vindesine sulphate must be closely monitored in relation to each individual patient's tolerance of the toxicity of the drug. *Related article:* ELDISINE.

**Vioform-Hydrocortisone** *(Ciba)* is a proprietary ANTIBACTERIAL, ANTIFUNGAL steroid compound preparation of hydrocortisone and CLIOQUINOL used to treat inflammatory skin disorders when infection is not the cause the inflammation. It is produced as a water-based cream (for further dilution) and a more oily white soft paraffin-based ointment (also for dilution); the potency of either form in dilution is retained for 14 days.

▲/✷ side-effects/warning: *see* VIDARABINE.

**Virormone** (*Paines & Byrne*) is a proprietary form of the male sex HORMONE testosterone (in the form of testosterone propionate), available only on prescription, and used primarily in hormone replacement therapy. Virormone is produced in ampoules for injection (in three strengths) and (under the trade name Virormone-Oral) in the form of tablets (in three strengths).

▲/✷ side-effects/warning: *see* TESTOSTERONE.

**Virudox** (*Bioglan*) is a proprietary form of the ANTIVIRAL drug idoxuridine, prepared in a solution of dimethyl sulphoxide, used to treat skin infections by the viral organisms herpes simplex (such as cold sores or genital sores) and herpes zoster (shingles). Available only on prescription, Virudox is produced as a paint for topical application (with a brush).

✷ warning: *see* IDOXURIDINE.

**Visclair** (*Sinclair*) is a proprietary, non-prescription MUCOLYTIC, which is not available from the National Health Service. Used to reduce the viscosity of sputum and thus facilitate expectoration in patients with asthma or bronchitis. Visclair tablets contain METHYLCYSTEINE hydrochloride. They are not recommended for children aged under 5 years.

**Viscopaste PB7** (*Smith & Nephew*) is a proprietary, non-prescription form of bandaging impregnated with ZINC PASTE. This kind of bandaging is used to treat and dress wounds and ulcers (and further bandaging is required to keep it in place).

**Viskaldix** (*Sandoz*) is a proprietary ANTIHYPERTENSIVE combination of the drugs pindolol and clopamide, used to treat and control moderately high blood pressure. Available only on prescription, Viskaldix is produced as tablets. It is not recommended for children.

▲/✷ side-effects/warning: *see* CLOPAMIDE; PINDOLOL.

**Visken** (*Sandoz*) is a proprietary form of the BETA-BLOCKER drug pindolol, used as an ANTIHYPERTENSIVE in the treatment of high blood pressure, and to treat angina pectoris. Available only on prescription, Visken is produced as tablets in either of two strengths. It is not recommended for children.

▲/✷ side-effects/warning: *see* PINDOLOL.

**Vista-Methasone** (*Daniel*) is a proprietary ANTI-INFLAMMATORY steroid drug, available only on prescription, in the form of drops to treat inflammation in the ear, eye or nose. Used solely where infection is not the cause of the inflammation, its active constituent is betamethasone sodium phosphate. A second version – called Vista-Methasone N – additionally contains NEOMYCIN sulphate.

▲/✷ side-effects/warning: *see* BETAMETHASONE SODIUM PHOSPHATE.

**Vita-E** (*Bioglan*) is a proprietary, non-prescription form of vitamin E (TOCOPHEROL supplements). Vita-E Gels are capsules containing alpha tocopheryl acetate, and are produced in three strengths; Vita-G Gelucaps also contain alpha tocopheryl acetate, but are chewy tablets; Vita-E Succinate is in the form of tablets containing alpha tocopheryl succinate. There is also Vita-E Ointment, a paraffin-based ointment containing alpha tocopheryl acetate, for treating bedsores and similar conditions.

**vitamin A** is another term for retinol.
*see* RETINOL.

**vitamin B** is the collective term for a number of water-soluble vitamins found particularly in dairy products, cereals and liver.
*see* CYANOCOBALAMIN; FOLIC ACID; NICOTINAMIDE; NICOTINIC ACID; PANTOTHENIC ACID; PYRIDOXINE; RIBOFLAVINE; THIAMINE.

**vitamin C** is another term for ascorbic acid.
*see* ASCORBIC ACID.

**vitamin D** is another term for calciferol; it occurs naturally in plants (ergocalciferol) and through the action of sunlight on the skin (cholecalciferol).
*see* CHOLECALCIFEROL; ERGOCALCIFEROL.

**vitamin E** is a group of chemically-related oxidant compounds consisting of tocopherols and tocotrienols. Their main effect is thought to be to increase the stability of cell membranes. Good food sources are dairy products, vegetable oils and cereals; deficiency is rare.
*Related article:* VITA-E.

**vitamin K** is a fat-soluble vitamin that occurs naturally in plants (phytomenadione) and in animals (menaquinone) and derived in the diet from fresh green vegetables, fruit and egg-yolk. It is essential to the process of blood clotting. Deficiency of the vitamin is very rare.
*see* PHYTOMENADIONE.

**vitamins** are substances required in small quantities for healthy growth, development and metabolism; lack of any one

vitamin causes a specific deficiency disorder. Because they cannot usually be synthesized by the body, vitamins have to be absorbed or ingested from external sources – generally these are food substances.

**Vitavel** (*Bencard*) is a proprietary, non-prescription, sugar-free multi-vitamin elixir, which is not available from the National Health Service. It contains THIAMINE (vitamin B₁), RIBOFLAVINE (vitamin B₂), NICOTINAMIDE (of the vitamin B complex), ASCORBIC ACID (vitamin C) and ERGOCALCIFEROL (vitamin D), and is used after dilution. The potency of the diluted elixir is retained for 30 days.

**Vitlipid** (*Kabi Vitrum*) is a proprietary form of liquid VITAMIN supplement for intravenous infusion into patients who cannot be adequately fed via the alimentary canal. An emulsion intended to be combined with a lipid-based intravenous infusion, Vitlipid is a compound of RETINOL (vitamin A), ERGOCALCIFEROL (vitamin D) and PHYTOMENADIONE (vitamin K). It is produced in two strengths: one for adults, the other for children.

**Vivalan** (*ICI*) is a proprietary ANTIDEPRESSANT drug, available only on prescription, consisting of tablets containing viloxazine hydrochloride.
▲/✚ side-effects/warning: *see* VILOXAZINE.

**Volital** (*LAB*) is a proprietary form of the weak STIMULANT pemoline, used to treat debility, lassitude or fatigue. Available only on prescription, it is produced as tablets. It is not recommended for children aged under 6 years.
▲/✚ side-effects/warning: *see* PEMOLINE.

**Volmax** (*Duncan Flockhart*) is a proprietary form of the selective BETA-RECEPTOR STIMULANT salbutamol (as sulphate), used as a BRONCHODILATOR in patients with asthma and other breathing problems. Available only on prescription, Volmax appears as tablets. Patients should not exceed the prescribed or stated dose, and should follow the manufacturer's directions closely. ▲/✿ side-effects/warning: *see* SALBUTAMOL.

**Voltarol** (*Geigy*) is a proprietary, non-steroid, ANTI-INFLAMMATORY, non-narcotic ANALGESIC, available only on prescription, used to treat arthritic and rheumatic pain and other musculo-skeletal disorders. Its active constituent is diclofenac sodium, and it is produced in the form of tablets (in either of two strengths, plus a sustained-release version called Voltarol Retard), ampoules for injection, and anal suppositories (in either of two strengths). Voltarol should not be administered to patients with a peptic ulcer or asthma, who are known to be allergic to aspirin, or who are pregnant or lactating. ▲/✿ side-effects/warning: *see* DICLOFENAC SODIUM.

**Volumatic** (*Ilen & Hanburys*) is a large-volume inhaler device for use with the bronchodilators BECLOFORTE, BECOTIDE, VENTIDE and VENTOLIN, all of which rely on the corticosteroid BECLOMETHASONE DIPROPIONATE and/or the sympathomimetic SALBUTAMOL.

warfarin is an orally administered ANTICOAGULANT, used primarily to treat patients who suffer from deep-vein thrombosis or from transient attacks of ischaemia (restriction of the blood supply) in the brain. It may also be used following surgery to replace a heart valve, although – as with all anticoagulants – it should not be administered when there is any risk of haemorrhage. The anticoagulant effect may take up to 48 hours to develop. There are two proprietary forms, both produced as tablets in several strengths.

▲ side-effects: internal haemorrhaging may occur; monitoring is required.

❋ warning: warfarin (in the form of warfarin sodium) should not be administered to patients with kidney or liver disease, seriously high blood pressure (hypertension), bacterial endocarditis or peptic ulcer; who are regularly taking anabolic steroids, aspirin, barbiturates or phyto-menadione (vitamin K) supplements; who are using oral contraceptives; or who are in the first three months or last two months of pregnancy. *Related article:* MAREVAN.

**Warticon** (*Kabi*) is a proprietary, non-prescription compound OINTMENT for topical application, intended to treat and remove penile warts. Warticon is a preparation of the KERATOLYTIC salicylic acid and the highly acidic substance PODOPHYLLIN. It should not be used for facial warts.

▲ / ❋ side-effects/warning: *see* SALICYLIC ACID; PODOPHYLLIN.

**Waxsol** (*Norgine*) is a proprietary, non-prescription form of ear-drops designed to soften and dissolve ear-wax (cerumen), and commonly prescribed for use at home tow nights consecutively before syringing of the ears in a doctor's surgery. Its solvent constituent is DIOCTYL SODIUM SULPHO-SUCCINATE (also called docusate sodium).

❋ warning: Waxsol should not be used if there is inflammation in the ear, or where there is any chance that the eardrum has been perforated.

**Welldorm** (*Smith & Nephew*) is a proprietary HYPNOTIC and SEDATIVE, available only on prescription, used to treat insomnia. Produced as tablets and as an elixir for dilution (the potency of the dilute elixir is retained for 14 days), Welldorm's active constituent is CHLORAL HYDRATE.

▲ / ❋ side-effects/warning: *see* DICHLORALPHENAZONE.

**Welleron** (*Wellcome*) is a proprietary preparation of interferon (in the form of alfa interferon), available only on prescription, and used mainly to treat leukaemia. Administration is by injection. As with virtually all anticancer drugs, some fairly severe side-effects are inevitable.

▲ / ❋ side-effects/warning: *see* INTERFERONS.

white liniment is a non-proprietary compound liniment, which, when massaged into the skin, produces an irritation that offsets the pain of underlying muscle or joint ailments. Its main constituent is water, but it also contains ammonia solution, AMMONIUM CHLORIDE, oleic acid and turpentine oil in various proportions.

❋ warning: avoid broken or inflamed skin surfaces.

**Whitfield's ointment** is a common name for the non-proprietary compound benzoic acid ointment, used most commonly to treat patches of the fungal infection ringworm. *see* BENZOIC ACID OINTMENT.

**wool alcohols ointment** is a non-proprietary skin emollient (softener and soother) made up of wool alcohols (a water-in-oil emulsifying agent) together with various forms of paraffin.

**Wysoy** (*Wyeth*) is a proprietary, non-prescription form of nutritional compound for patients who in one way or another are unable to tolerate cows' milk. Produced in the form of powder, for reconstitution, Wysoy provides a virtually complete diet, containing protein, carbohydrate, fat, vitamins, minerals and trace elements; it is – naturally – free of milk protein and lactose, but it is also gluten-free.

W

**xamoterol** is a SYMPATHOMIMETIC, a weak BETA-RECEPTOR STIMULANT, used for the treatment of heart conditions where moderate stimulation of the force of heart beat is required, such as moderate heart failure. It is available in the form of tablets. It is commonly given together with other drugs such as DIURETICS.
▲ side-effects: there may be a fall in blood pressure, irregular heart beats; chest pain, palpitations, nausea, vomiting, gastrointestinal upsets, muscle tremor, and rashes.
◆ warning: severe heart failure, lactating mothers. Treatment is started in hospital after assessment of the severity of heart failure.
*Related article:* CORWIN.

**Xanax** (*Upjohn*) is a proprietary ANXIOLYTIC, available on prescription only to private patients. It is produced in the form of tablets (in two strengths) containing the BENZODIAZEPINE alprazolam, and is used to treat short-term anxiety and anxiety accompanying depression.
▲/◆ side-effects/warning: *see* ALPRAZOLAM.

**xanthine-oxidase inhibitor** is a type of drug that interferes with the breakdown of nucleic acids, the process by which the purines, adenine and guanine (constituents of DNA), are broken down, resulting in the formation of uric acid. The most widely used xanthine-oxidase inhibitor is ALLOPURINOL (which is prescribed particularly in the long-term treatment of gout – a condition caused by an excess of uric acid and its salts).
◆ warning: xanthine-oxidase inhibitors should not be used when a high level of uric acid in the bloodstream has led to acute inflammation; treatment at this time may exacerbate the

effect of the inflammation (and anti-inflammatory drugs should be used first).

**xipamide** is a DIURETIC drug, similar to the THIAZIDES, used mainly to relieve the accumulation of fluids in the tissues (oedema) due to heart failure, and in lower dosages or in combination to relieve high blood pressure (hypertension). Administration is oral (in the form of proprietary tablets) early in the day, so that the diuretic effect does not inhibit sleep.
▲ side-effects: there may be minor gastrointestinal disturbances; mild dizziness, allergies, and/or thirst may be experienced.
◆ warning: treatment with xipamide may cause abnormally low levels of potassium in the bloodstream (hypokalaemia), and may accordingly require the provision of potassium supplements. The drug may also aggravate the conditions of gout and diabetes. Xipamide should not be used on patients with kidney failure or cirrhosis of the liver. Caution should be exercised in treating patients with impaired liver or kidney function, or who are pregnant or lactating.
*Related article:* DIUREXAN.

**X-Prep** (*Napp*) is a proprietary, non-prescription form of the stimulant LAXATIVE senna, used particularly in hospitals and clinics for bowel evacuation before X-ray examination. Produced as a liquid, X-Prep should be taken by the patient on the afternoon of the day before the X-ray session.
▲/◆ side-effects/warning: *see* SENNA.

**Xylocaine** (*Astra*) is a series of proprietary preparations of the local ANAESTHETIC lignocaine,

mostly available only on prescription. In the form of anhydrous lignocaine hydrochloride, Xylocaine is produced in ampoules for injection, in various strengths, with and without ADRENALINE (which increases duration of effect). Cartridges of this form of Xylocaine are also available for use in dental surgery, as are (non-prescription) tubes or syringes of Xylocaine Gel (with and without CHLORHEXIDINE gluconate). In addition, there is (non-prescription) Xylocaine Viscous solution and Xylocaine 4% Topical solution for local use on skin or mucous membranes. Containing lignocaine – as opposed to the hydrochloride there is (non-prescription) Xylocaine Ointment and Xylocaine Spray (with cetylpyridinium chloride).
▲/✸ side-effects/warning: see LIGNOCAINE.

**Xylocard** (*Astra*) is a proprietary ANTIARRHYTHMIC drug, available only on prescription, used to treat irregularities in the heartbeat, especially after a heart attack. Produced in the form of pre-loaded hypodermics for injection and as pre-loaded syringes for intravenous infusion (following dilution), Xylocard's active constituent is anhydrous lignocaine hydrochloride (also used as a local ANAESTHETIC).
▲/✸ side-effects/warning: see LIGNOCAINE.

**xylometazoline hydrochloride** is a VASOCONSTRICTOR. As nose-

drops it is available in two strengths; there is also a proprietary nasal spray. The nasal spray is not recommended for children under 6 months age.
▲ side-effects: there may be local irritation. Increasing tolerance in the body corresponds to diminishing effect of the drug.
✸ warning: prolonged use is to be avoided. In combination with certain other drugs, xylometazoline hydrochloride may cause extremely high blood pressure.
*Related articles:* OTRIVINE; OTRIVINE-ANTISTIN; RYNACROM.

**Xyloproct** (*Astra*) is a proprietary compound, available only on prescription, used to treat, dress and soothe various painful conditions of the anus and rectum. It is produced both as a water-miscible ointment and as anal suppositories. The active constituents of Xyloproct are HYDROCORTISONE acetate (a CORTICOSTEROID), LIGNOCAINE (a local ANAESTHETIC), ALUMINIUM ACETATE and ZINC OXIDE (both mild astringents).

**Xylotox** (*Astra*) is a proprietary dental local ANAESTHETIC, available only on prescription, containing lignocaine hydrochloride and ADRENALINE (the latter to add duration to the effect). It is produced in cartridges for easy attachment to a dentist's hypodermic.
▲/✸ side-effects/warning: see LIGNOCAINE.

**yellow fever vaccine** consists of a protein suspension containing live but weakened yellow fever viruses (cultured in chick embryos). Immunity may last for a good deal longer than the official ten years. The disease remains relatively well established in parts of tropical Africa and northern South America.

▲ side-effects: reactions are rare.

✿ warning: vaccination should not be administered to patients with an impaired immune response; who are sensitive to eggs; who are pregnant; or who are aged under 9 months. *Related articles:* ARILVAX; YEL/VAC.

**yel/vac** is an abbreviation for yellow fever vaccine.
 *see* YELLOW FEVER VACCINE.

**Yomesan** (*Bayer*) is a proprietary, non-prescription form of the ANTHELMINTIC drug niclosamide, used to treat infestation by tapeworms; it is produced as chewy yellow tablets. Careful monitoring of the infestation is required, together with reassuring counselling of the patient.

▲ side-effects: *see* NICLOSAMIDE.

✿ warning: consumption of alcohol should be avoided during treatment.

**Yutopar** (*Duphar*) is a proprietary form of the BETA-RECEPTOR STIMULANT ritodrine hydrochloride, available only on prescription, used intially as an emergency measure to halt premature labour, and thereafter as a holding dosage until full term is attained (if there are no apparent fetal complications) or until preparations have been rapidly made for premature delivery (if fetal complications are apparent). Yutopar is produced both in the form of ampoules for injection and as tablets.

▲/✿ side-effects/warning: *see* RITODRINE HYDROCHLORIDE.

**Zaditen** (*Sandoz*) is a proprietary drug, available only on prescription, intended to reduce the incidence of asthmatic attacks, or to treat allergic rhinitis or conjunctivitis. It is produced in the form of capsules, tablets, and an elixir for dilution. (The potency of the dilute elixir is retained for 14 days.) Zaditen's active constituent is keftotifen (in the form of the fumarate), which may take several weeks of treatment to achieve its full effect in the body.

▲ side-effects: *see* KETOTIFEN.
❀ warning: consumption of alcohol should be avoided during treatment. Zaditen should not be administered to children aged under 2 years.

**Zadstat** (*Lederle*) is a proprietary ANTIBIOTIC and ANTIPROTOZOAL drug, available only on prescription, used to treat infections by anaerobic bacteria or protozoa, particularly infections of the rectum, colon and vagina. It may also be used to treat ulcerative infections of the gums. Produced in the form of tablets, suppositories (in either of two strengths), and in a Minipack for intravenous infusion, Zadstat is a preparation of the drug metronidazole.

▲/❀ side-effects/warning: *see* METRONIDAZOLE.

**Zagreb antivenom** (*Regent*) is a proprietary antidote to the poison injected by an adder. The systemic effects of an adder's bite are rarely serious enough to warrent the use of the antivenom (which has to be diluted with saline solution), but severely low blood pressure, heart arrhythmia or extensive swelling of the bitten limb are indications that more than cleaning, dressing and immoboilization is required. Antivenom for other snakes' poisons are available from the National Poisons Information Centre in London, and the Walton Hospital in Liverpool.

**Zantac** (*Glaxo*) is a proprietary form of the anti-ulcer drug ranitidine hydrochloride, available only on prescription, used to reduce the acidity of stomach juices in the presence of a non-expanding gastric or duodenal ulcer, or following gastric surgery. It is produced in the form of tablets (in either of two strengths), soluble (dispersible) tablets, or ampoules for injection. Treatment is not recommended for children aged under 8 years.

▲/❀ side-effects/warning: *see* RANITIDINE.

**Zarontin** (*Parke-Davis*) is a proprietary form of the ANTIEPILEPTIC drug ethosuximide, available only on prescription, used to treat and suppress petit mal ('absence') seizures – the mild form of epilepsy. Available in the form of capsules and an elixir for dilution – the potency of the dilute elixir is retained for 14 days – monitoring of seizures following the initiation of treatment with Zarontin should establish an optimum treatment level.

▲/❀ side-effects/warning: *see* ETHOSUXIMIDE.

**Zavedos** (*Farmitalia Carlo Erba*) is a proprietary antibiotic drug that is also CYTOTOXIC. It is therefore used to treat cancer, particularly leukaemia. Available only on prescription, it is produced in the form of powder for reconstitution as a medium for fast-running infusion. Its active constituent is idarubicin hydrochloride.

▲/❀ side-effects/warning: *see* IDARUBICIN HYDROCHLORIDE.

**ZeaSORB** (*Stiefel*) is a proprietary, non-prescription dusting powder, used to dry and soothe skin in folds or on surfaces where friction may occur. Active constituents include CHLOROXY-LENOL (a DISINFECTANT cleanser).

**Zertek** (*Allen & Hanbury*) is a proprietary prescription only ANTIHISTAMINE, with less sedative properties than many others, used to treat the symptoms of allergic disorders such as hay fever and urticaria (skin rashes). Produced in the form of tablets, it is a preparation of cetirizine.
▲/✿ side-effects/warning: *see* CETIRIZINE.

**Zestril** (*ICI*) is a proprietary form of the ANTIHYPERTENSIVE drug lisinopril used to treat high blood pressure (hypertension), and in combination with a DIURETIC or CARDIAC GLYCOSIDE in congestive heart failure. It is available only on prescription in the form of tablets (in four strengths).
▲/✿ side-effects/warning: *see* LISINOPRIL.

**zidovudine** is an ANTIVIRAL drug used for the treatment of AIDS. Formerly zidovudine was used for the treatment of AIDS, but now proposed by some for the early forms of HIV virus infections, before the full AIDS syndrome develops. It acts by inhibiting the HIV virus and therefore delays progression of the disease but does not cure it. Zidovudine is also known as azidothymidine or AZT, and is available in the form of capsules.
▲ side-effects: there may be disturbances in various blood cells, often to a degree requiring blood transfusions. Nausea and vomiting, gastrointestinal disturbances, loss of appetite, headache, rashes, fever, sleep disturbances.
✿ warning: should not be used where there is depression of neutrophils or haemoglobin,

and blood tests should be carried out.
*Related article:* RETROVIR.

**Zinacef** (*Glaxo*) is a proprietary, broad-spectrum ANTIBIOTIC, available only on prescription, used to treat bacterial infections and to prevent infection arising during and after surgery. Produced in the form of powder for reconstitution as a medium for injections, Zinacef is a preparation of the CEPHALOSPORIN cefuroxime.
▲/✿ side-effects/warning: *see* CEFUROXIME.

**Zinamide** (*Merck, Sharp & Dohme*) is a proprietary ANTITUBERCULAR drug, available only on prescription, consisting of tablets containing pyrazinamide. Usually prescribed in combination with other antitubercular drugs, it is not recommended for children.
▲/✿ side-effects/warning: *see* PYRAZINAMIDE.

**zinc** is a trace element, necessary in tiny quantities in a daily diet. Deficiency demanding the administration of zinc supplements is rare, however, but occurs with inadequate diet, in cases of malabsorption of ingested food, and where trauma causes loss of zinc from the blood. Conversely, zinc supplements cause some uncomfortable side-effects such as dyspepsia.
*Related articles:* ZINC OXIDE; ZINC SULPHATE.

**Zincaband** (*Seton*) is a proprietary, non-prescription form of impregnated bandaging, impregnated with gelatinous ZINC PASTE and used to treat eczema, varicose veins and skin ulcers. (Further bandaging is required to hold it in place.)

**Zincfrin** (*Alcon*) is a proprietary, non-prescription form of eye-drops containing ZINC SULPHATE

and PHENYLEPHRINE, used to treat
eyes that are watering too freely,
and for mild conjunctivitis.

**Zincomed** (*Medo*) is a proprietary,
non-prescription form of ZINC
supplement, used to treat zinc
deficiency in the body. It is
produced in the form of capsules
containing zinc sulphate.
▲/✿ side-effects/warning: see
ZINC SULPHATE.

**zinc oxide** is a mild astringent
used primarily to treat skin
disorders such as nappy rash,
urinary rash and eczema. It is
available (without prescription)
in any of a number of compound
forms – as a water-based cream
(with arachis oil, oleic acid and
wool fat; or with ichthammol and
wool fat; as an ointment, and as
an ointment with castor oil; as
dusting powder (with starch and
talc); as a paste (with starch and
white soft paraffin; or with starch
and salicylic acid – Lassar's
paste), sometimes in impregnated
bandages.
*Related article:* ZINC PASTE.

**zinc paste** is a non-proprietary
compound made up of ZINC OXIDE,
starch and white soft paraffin,
which is slightly astringent and is
used as a base to which other
active constituents can be added,
especially within impregnated
bandages. Of all such pastes
(compounded to treat and protect
the lesions of skin diseases such
as eczema and psoriasis), zinc
paste is the standard type.

**zinc sulphate** is one form in which
zinc supplements can be
administered in order to make up
a ZINC deficiency in the body.
There are several proprietary
preparations, all different in form
although all oral in administration. In solution, zinc
sulphate is also used as an
astringent, wound cleanser, in

eye-drops (with or without
ADRENALINE), and as an
occasional EMETIC.
▲ side-effects: there may be
abdominal pain or mild
gastrointestinal upsets.
✿ warning: zinc sulphate should
not be administered in
combination with tetracycline
antibiotics.
*Related articles:* SOLVAZINC;
ZINCFRIN; ZINCOMED; Z SPAN.

**Zocor** (*MSD*) is a newly developed
drug that is used to lower lipid
(fat) levels in the blood where this
is markedly elevated
(hyperlipidaemia). It is used in
patients who do not respond to, or
who are intolerant of, other
therapy. It is a proprietary form
of simvastin available only on
prescription. The preparation is
available as tablets in two
strengths.
▲/✿ side-effects/warning: see
SIMVASTIN.

**Zofran** (*Glaxo*) is a recently
introduced ANTI-EMETIC drug, and
is a proprietary form of
ondansetron, available only on
prescription, which gives relief
from nausea and vomiting,
especially in patients receiving
radiotherapy and chemotherapy,
and where other drugs are
ineffective. It acts by preventing
the action of the naturally-
occuring HORMONE and
NEUROTRANSMITTER serotonon. It
is used in those over 4 years of
age, and is available as tablets or
in ampoules for administration by
slow intravenous injection or
infusion
▲/✿ side-effects/warning: see
ONDANSETRON.

**Zonulysin** (*Henleys*) is a
proprietary form of an enzyme
preparation used to dissolve the
ligament that suspends the lens of
the eye within the eyeball (the
zonule of Zinn) in order to

Z

facilitate the surgical removal of a lens that has become opaque through cataract. Available only on prescription, Zonulysin is produced as a powder for reconstitution as an injection; the fluid – in which the active constituent is alpha-chrymotrypsin – is injected behind the iris a minute or so before the lens is removed, and affects no other part of the eye.

**Zovirax** (*Wellcome*) is a proprietary form of the ANTIVIRAL drug acyclovir, available only on prescription, used to treat infection by herpes simplex and herpes zoster organisms. It is available in the form of tablets (in either of two strengths), a suspension (for dilution with syrup or sorbitol; the potency of the diluted suspension is retained for 28 days), and a powder for reconstitution as an intravenous infusion. To treat one form of herpes simplex there is also an eye ointment; urogenital forms of herpes are treated by a water-based cream. Treatment by any of these preparations is required at least 4 times a day.

▲/ ✦ side-effects/warning: *see* ACYCLOVIR.

**Z Span** (*Smith, Kline & French*) is a proprietary non-prescription form of ZINC supplement, used to treat zinc deficiency in the body. Produced in the form of spansules (slow-release capsules) containing zinc sulphate monohydrate, Z Span is not recommended for children aged under 12 months.

▲/ ✦ side-effects/warning: *see* ZINC SULPHATE.

**zuclopenthixol** is an ANTIPSYCHOTIC drug, one of the thioxanthenes (which resemble in their general actions the phenothiazines such as chlorpromazine), used to treat and restrain psychotic patients,

particularly the more aggressive or agitated schizophrenic ones. It is available as zuclopenthixol acetate, zuclopenthixol dihydrochloride and zuclopenthixol decanate, in a variety of preparations for administration in the form of tablets or injection.

▲ side-effects: there may be involuntary (reflex) movements, hypothermia, drowsiness, lethargy, insomnia and depression; low blood pressure and heartbeat irregularities; allergic symptoms; and/or dry mouth, constipation, blurred vision, rashes and difficulties in urinating. Prolonged high dosage may cause eventual eye defects and pigmentation of the skin.

✦ warning: zuclopenthixol should not be administered to patients with heart disease, respiratory disease, epilepsy, parkinsonism, severe arteriosclerosis or acute infection; who are in a withdrawn or apathetic state; who are pregnant or lactating; who have impaired functioning of the liver or kidneys; whose prostate gland is enlarged; who are old and infirm (especially in very hot or cold weather); or who are children. Withdrawal of treatment must be gradual. *Related article:* CLOPIXOL.

**Zyloric** (*Calmic*) is a proprietary form of the XANTHINE-OXIDASE INHIBITOR allopurinol, used to treat high levels of uric acid in the bloodstream (which may otherwise cause gout). Available only on prescription, Zyloric is produced for oral administration in the form of tablets.

▲/ ✦ side-effects/warning: *see* ALLOPURINOL.

**Zymaflour** (*Zyma*) is a proprietary, non-prescription form of fluoride supplement for administration in areas where the water supply is not fluoridated, especially to growing children. Produced in the form of tablets (in either of two strengths, to correspond with local water fluoridation levels), Zymafluor's active constituent is SODIUM FLUORIDE.